Teaching Students with Learning Problems

FOURTH EDITION

Teaching Students with Learning Problems

FOURTH EDITION

Cecil D. Mercer
University of Florida, Gainesville

Ann R. Mercer
Gainesville, FL

Merrill, an imprint of
Macmillan Publishing Company
New York

Maxwell Macmillan Canada
Toronto

Maxwell Macmillan International
New York   Oxford   Singapore   Sydney

Cover illustration: Susan Sturgill
Cover photo: David Napravnik
Editor: Ann Castel
Production Editor: Stephen C. Robb
Art Coordinator: Lorraine Woost
Photo Editor: Anne Vega
Text Designer: Jill E. Bonar
Cover Designer: Robert Vega
Production Buyer: Pamela D. Bennett
Illustrations: Steve Botts

Photo credits (All photos copyrighted by the individuals or institutions listed.): Robert Finken, pp. 99, 185, 233, 235, 273, 375, 411, 583; Kevin Fitzsimons, Macmillan Publishing Company, p. 53; Macmillan Publishing Company, 499; Cecil D. Mercer and Ann R. Mercer, p. 147; David Napravnik, Macmillan Publishing Company, p. 1; Barbara Schwartz, Macmillan Publishing Company, pp. 3, 343, 533; Anne Vega, Macmillan Publishing Company, p. 449.

This book was set in Cheltenham Light and Helvetica by Carlisle Communications, Ltd. and was printed and bound by R. R. Donnelley & Sons Company. The cover was printed by Phoenix Color Corp.

Copyright © 1993 by Macmillan Publishing Company, a division of Macmillan, Inc. Merrill is an imprint of Macmillan Publishing Company.

Earlier editions copyright © 1989, 1985, and 1981 by Merrill Publishing Company.

Printed in the United States of America.

All rights reserved. No part of this book may be reproduced or transmitted in any form or by any means, electronic or mechanical, including photocopy, recording, or any information storage and retrieval system, without permission in writing from the Publisher.

Macmillan Publishing Company
866 Third Avenue
New York, NY 10022

Macmillan Publishing Company is part of the Maxwell Communications Group of Companies.

Maxwell Macmillan Canada, Inc.
1200 Eglinton Avenue East, Suite 200
Don Mills, Ontario M3C 3N1

Library of Congress Cataloging-in-Publication Data
Mercer, Cecil D.
    Teaching students with learning problems / Cecil D. Mercer, Ann R. Mercer. — 4th ed.
        p.   cm.
    Includes bibliographical references and index.
    ISBN 0-02-380561-7
    1. Learning disabled children—Education.   2. Learning disabled children—Education—United States.   I. Mercer, Ann R.   II. Title.
LC4704.M473 1993
371.9—dc20   92-21059
                                                                              CIP

Printing: 1 2 3 4 5 6 7 8 9   Year: 3 4 5 6

To our sons, Kevin, Greg, and Ken, who, as young adults, have fond memories of the teachers who influenced their lives. They remind us that teachers "touch the future."

About the Authors

Cecil D. Mercer is a professor of education at the University of Florida. He received his Ed.D. in special education from the University of Virginia in 1974. Cecil has written numerous articles and books on educating exceptional students. One of his major works is *Students with Learning Disabilities*. Cecil remains involved in the educational programs of exceptional students through his participation in inservice and classroom activities in public and private schools. Cecil currently is co-producing the *Strategic Math Series*, a math strategies curriculum, and he is a featured speaker at many national conferences.

Ann R. Mercer is an educational diagnostician and participates in the learning disabilities clinic at J. Hillis Miller Health Center in Gainesville, Florida. She is a former special education teacher of students with emotional disabilities and students with learning problems at both the elementary and secondary levels. Ann is coauthor of *Self-Correcting Learning Materials for the Classroom* and several articles and books chapters in the field of special education.

Preface

Most educators can recall key events that made lasting impressions on their minds or hearts. One such event occurred in 1968 during a PTA meeting at a small elementary school next to the Blue Ridge Mountains in Virginia. The officers of the PTA were concerned about the uninterested, unmotivated, and misbehaving students in their school, and they asked me to discuss the topic. More than 70 people—parents, teachers, and central office staff—entered the small cafeteria for the PTA meeting.

Within a few minutes I was introduced. I told them I was delighted to be there and wanted to begin by giving them a short test. The test consisted of a problem involving the transporting of a chicken, a fox, and a bag of chicken feed across a lake. However, the problem was designed so that it was impossible to answer correctly. I gave these instructions: "This is a short test that most people with average ability finish in one minute. When I say 'Begin,' please start. Ready?" Toward the end

of the minute, mumbling, fidgeting, and attempts to look at others' papers were widespread. I told them time was up and asked how many had solved the problem. Nobody raised a hand. With a puzzled expression I said, "You must be tired. I'll give you another minute. Slow learners usually can solve it in two minutes."

Although I had anticipated some frustration, the behavior of this group of adults during the next minute was surprising. Many cheated, some cursed, others broke my pencils, and still others crumpled up the test and tossed it. At the end of the minute I informed them that time was up. I asked several people how they felt. Responses included: "I feel like punching you in the mouth." "I want to leave and never come back." "I'd like to give you a piece of my mind." "What's the answer to this (expletive) thing?"

Within two minutes, this situation had prompted adults to cheat, swear, want to leave, destroy property, threaten physical violence, and talk rudely. I pointed out that what had happened to them was the same thing that often happens to students with learning problems. Tasks are assigned that are too difficult or practically impossible for them to do correctly. Moreover, failure to do these tasks generally is viewed as a reflection of one's ability. The point was clear: Both students and adults are inclined to act aggressively or avoid situations in which they are given inappropriate tasks.

With adults reacting so quickly and intensely to this type of failure, I was reminded of what happens to youngsters who customarily face failure within the schools. Ann and I enthusiastically share the conviction of many educators that students with learning problems have a right to educational programs tailored to their unique needs. To us, individualized programming involves *the student working on appropriate tasks over time under effective motivational conditions.* The primary purpose of this book is to prepare special education professors and teachers, resource room teachers, remedial education teachers, and regular classroom teachers for the challenges of individualized programming for students with learning or behavioral problems.

Individualized programming requires an understanding of subject matter, assessment, teaching approaches for each content area, instructional activities, seatwork activities, and commercial programs. As teachers of elementary, secondary, and university students, we have had difficulty finding a text that covers all these areas. Resource and classroom teachers as well as special education professors often refer to one text for instructional activities, another for teacher-made materials, another for scope and sequence skills lists, another for assessment, and yet another for descriptions of commercial materials. This book provides a comprehensive, practical, *text* for special education and remedial education methods courses; a *resource* for special education and remedial education inservice programs; and a *handbook* for individual teachers.

As a result of feedback from reviewers and users of the third edition, this fourth edition features some noteworthy changes, including expanded coverage of learning strategies, mnemonic instruction, peer tutoring, homework practices, curriculum-based measurement, cooperative learning, grading practices, and research-based teaching practices that foster achievement. Also, descriptions of tests, software, and materials have been updated throughout this edition. Other significant changes include coverage of integrated reading programs, the writing process approach, and problem solving in math. Each chapter has been refined extensively to provide comprehensive yet timely coverage of pertinent information. We hope this edition will help other teacher educators and teachers to accomplish instructional goals more easily.

Many individuals deserve special attention for their contributions to this book. Appreciation and thanks go to the reviewers who provided insightful suggestions: David W. Anderson, Lock Haven University; Rhoda Cummings, University of Nevada–Reno; John M. Dodd, Eastern Montana College; Kathleen Tomaino Knops, North Central College; and Gayle Mayer, University of Texas–El Paso. We also express our gratitude to the many students who read the third edition and provided valuable suggestions for improving it. Thanks go to Ann Castel, administrative editor, for her encouragement, support, patience, and belief that we would meet deadlines, and to associate production editor Steve Robb and copy editor Key Metts for their skillful services. Finally, we always will be indebted to students, parents, and teachers who have shared their successes and frustrations with us through the years.

Contents

PART I

Foundations of Teaching

CHAPTER 1

Educational Programming

The beginning of the 1990s represents a time when a sense of urgency surrounds the field of education. In his educational strategy titled *America 2000*, President Bush (1991) notes, "Eight years after the National Commission on Excellence in Education declared us a 'Nation at Risk,' we haven't turned things around in education. Almost all our education trend lines are flat." The perspective that "business as usual" is not acceptable exists for regular and special education practices. There is concern that education is not doing an acceptable job with students of all ability levels (that is, gifted students, average students, and students with learning problems). Students with average-to-superior ability are becoming less competitive in the international arena, and many students with learning problems are limited in their opportunities to function as productive and successful citizens.

It is apparent that a substantial gap exists between what is known about effective teaching and what is practiced routinely. Many educators maintain that closing this gap represents a viable beginning toward better schools for all students. There is a considerable amount of research that suggests that data-supported teaching practices are effective across all types of students. Thus, it is reasonable to believe that the widespread use of effective teaching procedures could lead to a substantial reduction of school failures. This chapter focuses on educational programming for students who are experiencing learning difficulties or who are at risk for school failure.

Students with learning difficulties may have problems in one or several of the academic areas (such as reading, math, language, and spelling). These individuals may lack social adjustment, motivation, or self-management skills and often are described with terms such as *attention deficit disorder, dyslexic, explo-*

sive, underachiever, and *poor memory.* Their estimated intellectual ability may differ markedly from their actual achievement. Some of these students exhibit wide spans between the skills they excel in and those that are problem areas. Others are merely slow in acquiring school-related skills and behaviors. Some of these youngsters may have only one problem area, such as reading comprehension, whereas others may have a combination of learning and behavior problems—for example, reading and math difficulties, and disruptive behavior.

Students with learning problems are identified with a variety of labels, such as *learning disabled, mentally disabled, emotionally disabled, economically disadvantaged, at risk,* and *educationally disabled.* Most of these students need special education services to enable them to develop to their potential. To secure special education services, the student must be diagnosed and assigned a label that identifies the student as disabled.

When a label is applied appropriately, it may have some general implications for instruction. For example, the youngster with mental disabilities may need basic academic training as well as a functional curriculum that addresses consumer education, family management, and job training. A student with emotional disabilities may need special affective interventions that stress self-awareness and managing stress. The student with learning disabilities may need adapted instructional materials and extensive practice to acquire specific academic skills. Although the labels may have general implications for instruction, Hammill and Bartel (1990) note that "an educational program must be prepared by a teacher in response to an individual student's educational needs and behaviors, not in response to a diagnostic label or definition the student may or may not satisfy" (p. 2). No matter what the label is, the individual student's characteristics—age, type of disability, severity of problem—determine when specific content is taught and the intensity of the intervention.

In the past, many students with learning problems were placed in special education classes. Recent legislation and court decisions direct that the special needs of these students must be met, as much as possible, in classes with nondisabled peers. The placement of students with disabilities in regular classes necessitates that regular and special education teachers cooperate in planning and delivering instruction. Currently, regular education teachers are providing more direct instruction to learners with disabilities than before and are working closely with special education teachers.

Meeting the needs of these students continues to be a formidable task for both regular and special education teachers. Primary and elementary teachers are faced with helping youngsters acquire basic tool skills, learn problem-solving skills, explore careers, and develop independent work skills in numerous other areas. While teaching more than 100 students daily, secondary teachers are faced with helping adolescents acquire academic content, vocational skills, social skills, and life-management skills.

To meet the educational needs of students with learning problems, teachers must develop strategies and techniques that enable them to alter the type and amount of instruction. Altering the type of instruction might involve putting reading passages on tape or using a contract; altering the amount of instruction means increasing demonstration and practice activities.

To succeed in school, students with learning problems need a systematic instructional program that is planned according to their individual needs. This individualized approach does not imply that each student must be taught in a one-to-one or small-group instructional format. It *does* mean, though, that the student receives daily instruction tailored to his educational needs.

INDIVIDUALIZED PROGRAMMING

Individualized programming refers to an instructional program in which the student works on appropriate tasks over time under conditions that are motivating. It may occur within various instructional arrangements, including seatwork, small-group, peer teaching, and large-group. Individualized programming attempts to match the learner, the task, and instructional interventions to ensure optimal student growth. As presented in Table 1.1, Talmage's (1975) comparison of traditional and individualized instruction highlights some of the prominent features of the two systems.

Individualized Programming Process

The process of individualized programming can be subdivided in numerous ways; however, the four steps presented in Table 1.2 cover the essential components. These steps are necessary for maintaining individualized instruction on a daily basis.

Step I: Identify target skill via assessment. The purpose of Step I is to determine *what* to teach the student. Successful instruction begins with the selection of an appropriate learning task. A teacher's thorough understanding of the instructional task is germane to effective teaching. To identify the target skill, the teacher first conducts an assessment. The tests for the assessment may be based on a variety of sources such as a scope and sequence skills list (see Appendix A) and may include criterion-referenced tests or teacher-

TABLE 1.1
Comparison of traditional and individualized instruction.

Traditional Instruction	Individualized Instruction
Fixed instructional objectives for all learners	Varied instructional objectives as a function of direct skill assessment
Fixed entry points into curriculum	Variable entry points into curriculum
Fixed time and pacing	Variable pacing
Limited participation of learner in decision making	Active participation of learner in decision making
Large-group intervention	A variety of instructional arrangements as a function of task
Norm-referenced evaluation of learner	Criterion-referenced evaluation of learner

made tests. The teacher analyzes the student's test performances to discover which specific skills have been mastered. Then instructional objectives are selected. It is helpful to describe these target skills as precisely as possible. Mager (1975) advocates the use of instructional objectives that (a) specify the target behavior in observable terms, (b) delineate the conditions under which the behavior occurs, and (c) describe the criterion for successful performance. For example, an instructional objective in geography might be as follows: Given an unlabeled map of the world, the student will label the seven continents with 100 percent accuracy within 2 minutes. Once the initial instructional objectives are selected, subsequent objectives are derived from day-to-day assessment procedures.

During instruction, the teacher decides if the difficulty level of the task is appropriate; that is, the student should perform the task without prolonged failure or frustration. Earned success is a key concept in monitoring task difficulty. The student must view the task as demanding enough to realize some

sense of accomplishment when the task is completed.

Step II: Determine the factors and conditions that are likely to facilitate learning. This step focuses on determining *how* to teach the individual student. Knowing how to teach the student greatly increases the efficiency of instruction. For example, Tony's teacher may notice that Tony completes his seatwork much faster when responses do not require the writing of small-sized letters or numbers. The teacher then can give him worksheets that provide large spaces for writing responses, and Tony's performance on seatwork tasks should improve. The key to obtaining this type of information is using sources and opportunities for direct observation (for example, interviewing the parents, chatting with the student, reading cumulative files, using behavioral checklists). Thus, this type of information is obtainable without administering standardized tests. Chapter 2 presents a detailed discussion of assessment for determining how to teach.

TABLE 1.2
Four steps of individualized programming.

Procedure	Example
Step I: Pretest to identify target skill	Subtract two-digit number from three-digit number with double regrouping
Step II: Determine factors likely to facilitate learning	Student is easily discouraged, especially when given a lot of work. Student continuously wants to know how he is doing. Student has some difficulty with oral directions.
Step III: Plan instruction	Provide oral directions slowly and have student repeat them. Give practice seatwork that features a few items. Provide immediate feedback verbally when teaching and through self-correcting materials during seatwork.
Step IV: Begin daily data-managed instruction through three phases:	
Presentation procedures	
Use an advance organizer	Use an advance organizer to connect the skill to prior learning, identify the skill, provide a rationale for the skill, and introduce the materials.
Describe and model	Break down the target skill into component parts and model or demonstrate the skill or subskill to the student while carefully explaining each step.
Practice procedures	
Conduct guided practice	Have the student practice the selected task (skill or subskill) with guidance (such as instruction, cues, prompts) from the teacher. Provide corrective feedback and reinforcement.
Conduct controlled practice to mastery	Have the student practice the selected task (skill or subskill) in controlled materials to a specified criterion. Provide corrective feedback and reinforcement.
Conduct independent practice	Have the student practice the total task to a mastery criterion. Provide corrective feedback and reinforcement.
Generalization and independent learning procedures	
Use generalization training	To foster generalization, have the student practice the task presented in various materials (such as probes and regular curriculum workbooks) and settings (such as resource room, regular class, and home) to a specified criterion. Provide corrective feedback and reinforcement.
Use independent learning training	For independent active learning, have the student practice a task-specific learning strategy (such as self-questioning for comprehension). Encourage the student to use metacognitive strategies to self-regulate learning (for example, use mnemonic devices to remember test-taking strategies).

Step III: Plan instruction. This step is guided by the tenet of data-based instruction; that is, any humane teaching procedure that produces appropriate progress toward instructional objectives is good teaching. As Blankenship and Lilly (1981) state, "Good teaching is good outcomes" (p. 44). This orientation reduces the time spent planning elaborate teaching methods because it stresses that good teaching is a function of student progress. Thus, a teacher uses fundamental teaching principles (discussed later in this chapter) and monitors student progress to determine if instructional changes are needed. However, the efficiency of instruction improves if the teacher is sensitive to learner behaviors that cue the teacher concerning how to instruct the student. Thus, this step entails the development of a teaching plan that combines the *what to teach* information gathered in Step I with the *how to teach* information gathered in Step II. Chapter 2 presents a detailed discussion of instructional planning.

Step IV: Begin daily data-managed instruction. Teachers of students with learning problems encounter variable performances from many of their students. Teachers must know, however, if a student is making adequate progress toward specified instructional objectives so that they can modify instructional procedures. Evaluation must be frequent, even daily. Evaluation results provide the information for making instructional decisions. If the student masters a task, the teacher initiates a new task and repeats the teach-test-teach cycle. If a student does not master the task, four options are available for the teacher: repeating the same instructions, modifying the instructional procedures, introducing a new teaching strategy, or changing to an easier task. Again, when the teacher selects one of the options, the teach-test-teach cycle is repeated.

Typically, learning a new skill is viewed as requiring three progressive stages: acquisition, maintenance, and generalization. However, in their analysis of research on generalization, Deshler, Schumaker, and Lenz (1984) found that specific instructional tactics promote generalization. Therefore, they report that generalization may be conceptualized better as a framework for the entire instructional sequence than as a stage that the learner passes through after acquisition. The instructional sequence of presentation, guided practice, and independent practice, generalization, and independent active learning includes the tactics that foster generalization. Moreover, the data-managed instructional cycle presented earlier in Table 1.2 is used throughout the instructional sequence to guide the decision-making process. A detailed example of a similar teaching sequence that has been used successfully to teach low-achieving adolescents is presented in Chapter 14.

Although many teachers share common orientations, no two teachers teach exactly alike. They select from numerous theories, strategies, and techniques to create individual styles. In creating an individualized programming approach, the teacher strives to achieve optimum growth in his students. As noted, to accomplish optimum growth it is essential for instruction to be planned according to student progress—instructional decisions must be based on student performance data. Evidence exists that teachers' perceptions of student progress without learner data frequently are incorrect (Miramontes, Cheng, & Trueba, 1984; Utley, Zigmond, & Strain, 1987). It is not sufficient for a teacher to "feel" that an approach is effective. Evaluation results need to document the effectiveness of specific interventions. Various ways of monitoring student progress are presented throughout the book. In Chapter 2 the procedures used in data-based instruction, which includes curriculum-based measurement and precision teaching, are discussed. These procedures are among the most precise and effective techniques currently being applied in the classroom setting.

Student Motivation

Many students with learning problems lose their motivation for learning due to a history of frustration and school failure. In teaching the student with limited motivation, it is important for the teacher to plan systematic procedures to increase motivation. Student motivation is enhanced if a teacher plans content and skills considered important to effective functioning in school and society (Wang, 1987). Setting realistic instructional goals and determining specific mastery criteria are important to student motivation (Christenson, Ysseldyke, & Thurlow, 1989). Clifford (1990) encourages teachers to establish learning goals that represent a moderate success probability. She notes that students often attribute success with easy tasks to task ease, and attribute success with extremely difficult tasks to luck. Clifford states, "It is only success at moderately difficult . . . tasks that we explain in terms of personal effort, well-chosen strategies, and ability; and these explanations give rise to feelings of pride, competence, satisfaction, persistence, and personal control" (p. 22). Similarly, Alderman (1990) notes that the linking of success to one's own efforts is critical for the development of motivation in students.

Once goals are established, student motivation is enhanced by the monitoring of progress toward these goals and delivering feedback on how to correct errors via learning strategies and study skills (Porter & Brophy, 1988; Wang, 1987). Other factors that enhance motivation include (a) involving the student in planning instructional activities, (b) providing ample time for mastery, (c) allowing the student to master content via independent work, and (d) providing positive reinforcement for student achievements (Wang, 1987). In a synthesis of the research on strategies for motivating students to learn, Brophy (1987) presents 33 strategies (see Table 1.3).

STAGES OF LEARNING

Numerous authorities present stages of student learning that are fundamental to designing and implementing effective instruction (Haring, Lovitt, Eaton, & Hansen, 1978; Idol, 1983; D. D. Smith, 1981). Nelson and Polsgrove (1984) report that a data base is emerging for the practice of matching teaching procedures to the student's stage of learning for a specific skill. Thus, teaching practices for each stage in the learning sequence are being recommended and evaluated.

Many educators feel that the entry-level learning stage is a critical factor in planning teaching activities. Although reinforcement is a viable technique, other strategies (for example, antecedent changes and stimuli modifications) are needed to promote optimal learning at various learning stages. D. D. Smith (1981) presents the stages of learning that are commonly recognized. As featured in Figure 1.1, the stages include initial and advanced acquisition, proficiency, maintenance, generalization, and adaption. This section briefly describes the stages of learning and suggested teaching strategies for each stage.

Acquisition Stage

During the acquisition stage, the learner performance ranges from 0 percent accuracy (that is, no knowledge of how to perform the task) to a 90 to 100 percent range of accuracy. Dur-

TABLE 1.3
Highlights of research on strategies for motivating students to learn.

Research on student motivation to learn indicates promising principles suitable for application in classrooms, summarized here for quick reference.

Essential Preconditions
1. Supportive environment
2. Appropriate level of challenge/difficulty
3. Meaningful learning objectives
4. Moderation/optimal use

Motivating by Maintaining Success Expectations
5. Program for success
6. Teach goal setting, performance appraisal, and self-reinforcement
7. Help students to recognize linkages between effort and outcome
8. Provide remedial socialization

Motivating by Supplying Extrinsic Incentives
9. Offer rewards for good (or improved) performance
10. Structure appropriate competition
11. Call attention to the instrumental value of academic activities

Motivating by Capitalizing on Students' Intrinsic Motivation
12. Adapt tasks to students' interests
13. Include novelty/variety elements
14. Allow opportunities to make choices or autonomous decisions
15. Provide opportunities for students to respond actively
16. Provide immediate feedback to student responses

17. Allow students to create finished products
18. Include fantasy or simulation elements
19. Incorporate game-like features
20. Include higher-level objectives and divergent questions
21. Provide opportunities to interact with peers

Stimulating Student Motivation to Learn
22. Model interest in learning and motivation to learn
23. Communicate desirable expectations and attributions about students' motivation to learn
24. Minimize students' performance anxiety during learning activities
25. Project intensity
26. Project enthusiasm
27. Induce task interest or appreciation
28. Induce curiosity or suspense
29. Induce dissonance or cognitive conflict
30. Make abstract content more personal, concrete, or familiar
31. Induce students to generate their own motivation to learn
32. State learning objectives and provide advance organizers
33. Model task-related thinking and problem solving

Source: From "Synthesis of Research on Strategies for Motivating Students to Learn" by J. Brophy, 1987, *Educational Leadership, 45*(2), p. 45. Copyright 1987 by the Association for Supervision and Curriculum Development. Reprinted by permission.

ing this stage the instructional goal focuses on helping the student perform the skill accurately.

D. D. Smith (1981) recommends some major strategies for teaching a student at the acquisition stage. During initial acquisition, priming tactics are suggested, including rationales for learning a specific skill, physical guidance, shaping, demonstration, modeling, match-to-sample tasks, and cueing and prompting. Also, programming tactics are used during initial acquisition and feature

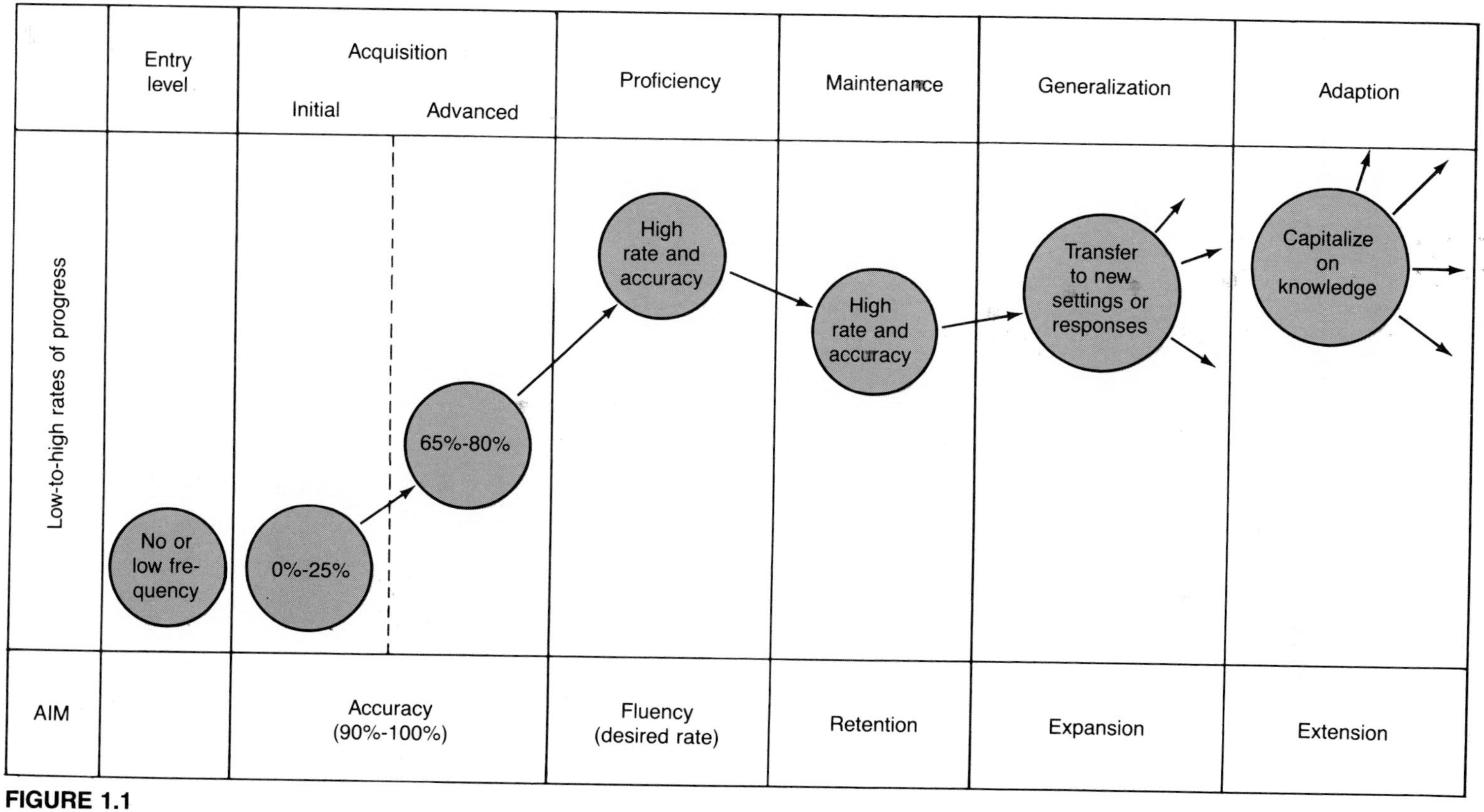

FIGURE 1.1

Stages of learning.

Source: Adapted from *Teaching the Learning Disabled* (p. 68) by D. D. Smith, 1981, Englewood Cliffs, NJ: Prentice-Hall. Copyright 1981 by Prentice-Hall. Reprinted by permission.

backward and forward chaining and errorless learning. For the advanced acquisition stage, refinement tactics are used and feature feedback, specific directions, error correction, reward for accuracy, and criterion evaluation.

Proficiency Stage

In the proficiency stage the learner attempts to learn the skill at a rather automatic level. The aim is for the student to perform the task both accurately and quickly. The tactics differ from those used at the acquisition stage. Tactics at this level focus on increasing speed of performance.

Learning at the proficiency stage is enhanced by the use of goal setting, teacher expectations, rationales for increasing rate, positive reinforcement, and progress monitoring. Moreover, for social skill development, self-management is suggested.

Maintenance Stage

After high levels of learning have occurred at the proficiency stage, the student enters the maintenance stage. The goal of instruction here is to maintain the high level of performance. Idol (1983) notes that students at this stage demonstrate the ability to perform the skill at a high level once direct instruction or reinforcement has been withdrawn. Students with learning problems frequently encounter much difficulty at this stage because it requires retention (memory) of the skill. Tactics at this stage concentrate on maintaining high levels of learning.

Learning during the maintenance stage involves periodic practice; however, for the student with learning problems, practice is not always sufficient and other tactics are necessary. Maintenance and retention also are fostered by overlearning, mnemonic techniques, intermittent schedules of reinforcement, social reinforcement, and intrinsic reinforcement (self-management).

Generalization Stage

During the generalization stage, the learner performs the skill in different times and situations. This means that the student demonstrates proficiency in the skill in different settings (such as home, classroom, job) and with different people (for example, learning disabilities teacher, regular classroom teacher, parent, boss). Generalization is an area of great difficulty for many students with learning problems and, unfortunately, remains an area of limited research (D. D. Smith & Luckasson, 1992). Investigators have discovered that one cannot expect that generalization automatically will occur with students who have learning problems. It must be systematically taught. Generalization is discussed later in this chapter.

Adaption Stage

In the adaption stage the learner applies a previously learned skill in a new area of application without benefit of direct instruction or guidance. Simply, this skill may be referred to as problem solving. To illustrate, problem solving occurs when a student who has mastered multiplication facts "discovers" that division is the reverse of multiplication and proceeds to answer division facts accurately and independently. D. D. Smith (1981) maintains that although it is important to teach adaption-level skills to students with learning problems, this area has been neglected.

Commentary on Learning Stages

Unfortunately, research documenting successful approaches for developing generalization and problem-solving skills is limited. Most behavioral studies only document effectiveness for short-term effects; however, some recent research in the area of skill generalization appears promising. For example, Idol (1983) reports on eight projects in which generalization occurred through the use of behavioral tactics. Other investigators (Lloyd, Saltzman, & Kauffman, 1981; Schumaker, Deshler, Alley, & Warner, 1983) are using behavioral tactics in teaching rule or strategy learning with positive results regarding generalization.

Combinations of the behavioral approach with other approaches (for example, cognitive) are being used to teach higher-order skills (Schumaker et al., 1983; Tarver, 1986). Techniques for teaching students to be independent learners and problem solvers are presented later in this chapter and in Chapters 7 and 14.

INSTRUCTIONAL FACTORS THAT PROMOTE LEARNING

In a review of more than 2,500 studies related to variables that affect learning, Walberg (1984) found that productivity factors in learning fall into three categories: student characteristics, instruction, and environment. From Walberg's review, it is apparent that numerous factors related to student achievement are outside of the direct control of the teacher; however, it also is apparent that the quality of instruction within the classroom remains a major factor in student learning (Wang, 1987).

Teaching styles are developed individually, but they should not be based on whims, biases, or personal opinions. Teachers and teacher educators have a responsibility to examine the research and apply the findings as they develop teacher practices. The teaching guidelines that follow highlight the major findings of selected research in regular and special education. When a teacher incorporates these practices into daily instruction, the likelihood of improving the achievement of students increases.

Use Effective Classroom Management

Effective classroom management must exist for students to be engaged consistently in academic work. Effective management enables students to remain on task because classroom disruptions are minimal and rules and procedures exist to guide the smooth flow of continuous learning activities. Rieth and Evertson (1988) note that the number of behavior disruptions that a teacher handles during instructional time is negatively associated with student achievement. In essence, effective classroom management ensures that time is used efficiently.

Through the use of a few rules and clearly stated expectations about appropriate classroom behavior, effective classroom teachers primarily use proactive management. Effective managers not only provide rules and expectations but communicate why these expectations are important (Porter & Brophy, 1988). The following are some of the primary factors of effective classroom management:

1. The teacher frequently monitors classroom activities and uses nonverbal signals to manage activities apart from the group he is actively teaching (Christenson et al., 1989).
2. The teacher establishes classroom routines and procedures that facilitate the smooth flow of activities (Rieth & Evertson, 1988).
3. The teacher uses demonstration, modeling, guided practice, independent practice, and generalization procedures to teach routine activities such as (a) making efficient classroom transitions, (b) exchanging and correcting papers, (c) passing out materials, and (d) lining up to leave the classroom (Sprick, 1985).
4. The teacher engages in frequent positive and supportive interactions with students (Christenson et al., 1989).
5. The teacher reinforces student accomplishments (Wang, 1987).

Several authorities (Christenson et al., 1989; Rieth & Evertson, 1988; Wang, 1987) report that effective classroom management involves teaching students to be accountable for their own learning. Activities to promote accountability include involving students in (a) monitoring their progress toward instructional goals, (b) participating in planning their practice activities, (c) helping and receiving help from other students, and (d) participating in goal setting and in learning strategies that enable them to be more independent learners. For some students with learning problems, effective classroom management requires the use of an intense behavior management program. Chapters 3 and 5 present behavior management techniques for students who require elaborate management procedures.

Use Direct Systematic Teaching

Stevens and Rosenshine (1981) report that research consistently demonstrates that teacher-directed instruction enhances the achievement of students. Specifically, they state, "Teachers who most successfully promoted achievement gain played the role of strong leader; that is, they selected and directed the academic activities, approached the subject matter in a direct, businesslike way, organized learning around questions they posed, and occupied the center of attention" (p. 2). In contrast, the less successful teachers planned learning around the students' questions and made the students the center of attention.

Brophy and Good (1986) note that the most reliable findings about effective teaching describe a teacher who is well organized, task oriented, efficient, and businesslike. They discuss this form of active, direct instruction in the following passage:

> Students achieve more in classes where they spend most of their time being taught or supervised by their teachers rather than working on

their own (or not working at all). These classes include frequent lessons . . . in which the teacher presents information and develops concepts through lecture and demonstration, elaborates this information in the feedback given following responses to recitation or discussion questions, prepares the students for follow-up seatwork activities by giving instructions and going through practice examples, monitors progress on assignments after releasing the students to work independently, and follows up with appropriate feedback and reteaching when necessary. The teacher carries the content to the students personally rather than depending on the curriculum materials to do so, but conveys information mostly in brief presentations followed by recitation or application opportunities. There is a great deal of teacher talk, but most of it is academic rather than procedural or managerial, and much of it involves asking questions and giving feedback rather than extended lecturing. (p. 361)

Moreover, Christenson et al. (1989) discuss four elements that relate to the quality of systematic instruction. First, the use of a demonstration-prompt-practice sequence enhances student outcomes (Carroll, 1985; Rosenshine & Stevens, 1986). This sequence occurs within an interaction format that involves active participation and involvement of students and active teaching and monitoring by teachers. Second, explicit instruction facilitates positive academic growth. Explicitness involves highly organized step-by-step presentations (that is, demonstration and modeling) that identify the target skill, cover why the skill is important, and discuss when the skill is useful and how to apply it. Third, effective instruction enables students to understand the directions and demands of the task. It is not sufficient for teachers to assume that students understand. Teachers should check periodically (especially during independent practice) to ensure that students understand directions and task demands (Good, 1983). Fourth, the systematic use of learning principles is characteristic of effective instruction. Positive student outcomes occur when attention is maintained, positive reinforcement is used, spaced and varied practice occurs, and motivation is high.

Numerous investigators (Blankenship & Lilly, 1981; Deshler, Schumaker, & Lenz, 1984; Rosenshine & Stevens, 1986) support the use of systematic instructional procedures. Rosenshine and Stevens report that the most efficient teaching process involves three steps: demonstration, guided practice with prompts and feedback, and independent practice with feedback. These steps are inherent in the validated teaching sequence developed at the University of Kansas Institute for Research in Learning Disabilities. Moreover, these procedures (that is, demonstration and practice) are consistent with the emphasis to teach mastery of the skill at a generalization level. Some research suggests that demonstration, modeling, and feedback enhance the acquisition and generalization of academic skills (Blankenship & Lilly, 1981; Deshler et al., 1984). The teaching sequence concerning individualized programming presented earlier in Table 1.2 incorporates many of the systematic instructional procedures supported in the research.

Focus on Time for Learning

In their review of teaching research, Stevens and Rosenshine (1981) report that successful teachers maintain a strong academic focus. Effective teachers instruct students to spend more time working directly on academic tasks in texts, workbooks, and instructional materials. They assign and hold students responsible for more homework and test students more frequently. In another review, Rosenshine and Furst (1973) found that being task oriented and businesslike correlates positively with student achievement. These findings support the practice of establishing specific instructional objectives and maintaining activities that relate to those objectives.

The importance of an academic focus also receives support from research on engaged time. *Engaged time* is the time a student actually spends performing an academic task (for example, writing, reading, computing). An extensive study of teaching activities that make a difference in student achievement was conducted as part of a 6-year Beginning Teacher Evaluation Study funded by the National Institute of Education through the California Commission for Teaching Preparation and Licensing. Denham and Lieberman (1980) report that one of the major contributions of the study is its emphasis on academic learning time—that is, the time a student spends engaged in academic tasks of appropriate difficulty. As expected, the study found that academic learning time is related to student achievement. Specifically, Fisher et al. (1980) report that the time allocated to a content area is positively associated with learning in that area, and the engaged time that students spend successfully performing reading or mathematics tasks is positively associated with learning. Thus, a cornerstone of good teaching is establishing appropriate academic instructional objectives and designing intervention programs that maximize opportunities for the student to work successfully on tasks related to the objectives. Unfortunately, several researchers (Borg, 1980; Larrivee, 1986; Ysseldyke & Algozzine, 1990) report that students' engaged time in many classrooms is relatively low.

Ysseldyke, Christenson, Thurlow, and Skiba (1987) report that the percentage of engaged time in special education classes is about 75 percent and that engaged time varies across classrooms and among students within a classroom. Researchers claim that achievement can be improved in two ways: (a) by increasing the student's learning time and (b) by decreasing the time a student needs to learn. Instructional factors that increase engaged time or decrease time needed for learning a specific skill include relevant learning tasks, effective classroom management, clearly stated learning expectations, timely and specific feedback, teacher-student interaction, reinforcement for learning, and continuous monitoring to meet instructional objectives (Anderson, 1984; Rieth & Evertson, 1988).

Wilson and Wesson (1986) report that instructional time, time on task, and student success are the essential variables of academic learning time. To increase actual instructional time, they offer the following suggestions:

1. Schedule more instructional time.
2. Reduce transition time.
3. Shorten free time.
4. Improve the efficiency of organizational activities (for example, teach students self-management skills).
5. Be prepared.

To increase teacher-directed instructional time:

1. Create more teacher-led instructional groups.
2. Increase the use of the direct-instruction teaching sequence.
3. Seek a balance between teacher-led and seatwork time.
4. Make seatwork tasks relevant.

To increase time on task during teacher-directed instruction:

1. Increase teaching questions.
2. Involve all students.
3. Use signals effectively (such as "Look at me").
4. Increase teacher enthusiasm.

To increase on-task rates during practice sessions:

1. Reward correct responses.
2. Use a reinforcing error-correction procedure (for example, instead of putting Xs on incorrect responses, put check marks on correct responses).
3. Give concise instructions.
4. Organize seatwork practice (that is, plan for students to finish at different times).
5. Use novel, motivating seatwork activities (such as self-correcting materials and instructional games).

In essence, it is helpful if students with learning problems (a) are provided with ample time for learning, (b) experience high rates of success, and (c) are taught strategies on how to learn and retain relevant information. Gettinger (1991) found that students with learning disabilities required significantly more time to achieve mastery on a reading comprehension task than did nondisabled students. She recommends that students with learning problems receive adequate time to achieve and encourages educators to investigate techniques for helping them learn more efficiently and retain the information. Greenwood (1991) used classwide peer tutoring with at-risk elementary students to increase time on academic tasks over a five-semester period. The peer tutoring group achieved academic gains that were superior to those of a control group of comparable students.

Provide Success

One of the primary findings of the Beginning Teacher Evaluation Study (Fisher et al., 1980) is that learning improves most when students have a high percentage of correct responses during teacher questioning and seatwork. Furthermore, Stevens and Rosenshine (1981) report that a high percentage of correct responses given rapidly correlates with academic achievement. They suggest that a reasonable success rate appears to be at least 80 percent during instruction and 90 percent at the end of a unit. Ideally, the task should maintain an appropriate level of challenge (that is, require effort to succeed). Fisher et al. (1980) highlight this point:

> Common sense suggests that too high a rate of high success work might be boring and repetitive and could inhibit the development of persistence. Probably, some balance between high success and more challenging work is appropriate. Also, we found that older students and/or students who were generally skilled at school learning did not require as high a percentage of time at the high success level. Apparently these students had learned problem solving—how to take a task they did not completely understand and work it out. Such students are able to undertake the challenge of more difficult material, as long as they eventually experience success. . . . When students worked with materials or activities that yielded a low success rate, achievement was lower (pp. 17–18).

Moreover, Stevens and Rosenshine (1981) note that individualization is considered a characteristic of effective instruction if it refers to helping each student achieve a high percentage of correct responses.

The importance of providing the student with success cannot be overemphasized in good teaching. Lack of success can lead to anxiety, frustration, inappropriate behavior, and poor motivation. In contrast, success can improve motivation, attitudes, academic progress, and classroom behavior.

In a study of success rates, Rieth and Frick (1983) found that learners with mild disabilities experience 43 percent high task success, 45 percent medium task success, and 12 percent low task success. Fisher et al. (1978) found that normally achieving students experience 45 percent high task success, 52 percent medium task success, and 3 percent low task success. The relative low rates of high success for both groups and the higher rate of low task success for the learners with mild disabilities underscore the need for better instructional matches and the continuous monitoring of student progress (Rieth & Evertson, 1988).

Although many variables contribute to student success, the degree to which an appropriate instructional match is accomplished for each student must be viewed as the cornerstone of teaching that promotes high rates of success. The teacher's ability to diagnose relevant student characteristics (for example, skill level, prior knowledge, strategy use, interests, motivation) and task factors (for example, level of difficulty, time to achieve mastery, relevance) influences the quality of the instructional match (Christenson et al., 1989). In essence, the teacher must match the learning task to the student's aptitude (that is, diagnostic teaching function) to develop an instructional program that ensures student success. As presented in Table 1.4, Wang (1987) highlights some of the features of learning environments that promote successful learning outcomes.

Establish Goals and Expectations

Goal setting results from the teacher's effort to match instruction to student and task characteristics. Thus, appropriate instructional goals are based on careful assessment of a student's learning needs. Basically, goals provide the basis on which instruction is planned. Teachers who have unclear goals and fail to provide rationales for academic tasks are less effective in promoting student achievement (Berliner, 1982; Fisher et al., 1980). Student attention and achievement improve when teachers present clear goals and precise directions. Moreover, goals communicate teacher expectations which, in turn, strongly influence student achievement. Student achievement improves in classrooms in which students are expected to succeed and realize they will receive instruction that fosters success (Good & Brophy, 1987). In presenting goals, effective teachers explain what the student needs to do to achieve the goal and what the student will learn in achieving the goal (Christenson et al., 1989).

TABLE 1.4
Selected instructional features that promote student success.

Area	Instructional Feature
Content	Is useful or relevant
	Is clearly specified
	Is instructionally organized for easy learning
Assessment	Enables appropriate placement
	Provides frequent feedback regarding programs
	Leads to the establishment of realistic but high goals
Learning experience	Allows ample time for learning
	Provides support to facilitate learning
	Has students actually experience high rates of progress
	Reinforces achievements and efforts
Self-Regulation	Permits students to work independently
	Permits students to self-monitor their progress in some lessons
	Allows students to participate in goal setting and the selection of some activities.
Collaboration	Includes peer teaching
	Includes collaboration in group activities

Source: Reprinted with the permission of Macmillan Publishing Company. Originally published by Merrill from *Students with Learning Disabilities, Fourth Edition,* by Cecil D. Mercer (p. 211). Copyright © 1992 by Macmillan Publishing Company.

In their synthesis on research on good teaching, Porter and Brophy (1988) report that good teachers are clear about their instructional goals and communicate both their expectations and the reasons that the specific expectations exist. Bandura (1986) notes that goals establish personal standards by which a student evaluates or monitors performance. Likewise, Clifford (1990) states that goal setting provides a mechanism for self-assessment. Some goal-setting standards and procedures include the following:

1. Goals must be specific. Vague or nonquantitative goals are no better than a lack of goals (Locke, Shaw, Saari, & Latham, 1981).
2. Goals must include mastery criteria (Christenson et al., 1989).
3. Progress toward goals needs to be monitored, and the results should be shared with the student on a regular basis (Christenson et al., 1989; Locke & Latham, 1990).
4. It is helpful to chart progress toward mastery (L. S. Fuchs, 1986).
5. Goals should be difficult but attainable.

Support is growing for the premise that teachers tend to make goals too easy for students with learning problems (Anderson & Pellicer, 1990; Clifford, 1990; L. S. Fuchs, Fuchs, & Deno, 1985). Clifford reports that students need challenge rather than easy success and that tasks involving moderate risk taking provide the best level of difficulty in setting goals. She recommends that instructional environments should feature error tolerance and reward for error correction. Substantial research documents that difficult but attainable goals lead to higher effort and achievement than do easier goals. Based on a review of goal-setting research, Locke and Latham

(1990) summarize why challenging goals lead to higher performance than lesser goals. Specifically, they report that difficult goals:

1. are associated with higher self-efficacy [that is, belief in oneself]
2. require higher performance in order for the individual to feel a sense of self-satisfaction
3. entail less ambiguity about what constitutes good performance
4. are typically more instrumental in bringing about valued outcomes
5. lead individuals to expend more effort
6. stimulate individuals to persist longer
7. direct attention and action better, and activate previously automatized skills
8. motivate individuals to search for suitable tasks strategies, to plan, and to utilize strategies that they have been taught (p. 108)

Monitor Progress and Provide Feedback

Monitor progress.   Monitoring progress involves the teacher frequently checking on the behavior and academic work of students and adapting instruction to ensure that an appropriate instructional match is being maintained. Good and Brophy (1986) note that active and frequent monitoring is the key to student learning. Active monitoring includes checking to see if students understand the task requirements and the procedures needed to complete the task correctly. To check understanding, the teacher asks the student to demonstrate how to complete the task. When the student performs the task, the teacher is able to pinpoint errors and help the student make corrections. Because these procedures enable the teacher to catch errors before extensive practice, high success rates are maintained (Christenson et al., 1989). Moreover, Rieth and Evertson (1988) report that active teacher monitoring (for example, moving rapidly around the classroom, checking work, and interacting substantively with students) in-

creases the on-task academic responses of students with learning problems. Anderson (1984) recommends that teachers monitor progress toward instructional goals in addition to task involvement. In a review of programs for at-risk students, Slavin and Madden (1989) report that the most effective programs involve frequent assessment of student progress so that programs can be modified according to individual needs. In essence, the most effective teachers maintain a productive flow of activity through continuous scanning and monitoring (Christenson et al., 1989). Chapter 2 describes numerous techniques for monitoring student progress.

Provide feedback.   A significant finding of the Beginning Teacher Evaluation Study (Fisher et al., 1980) is that academic feedback is positively associated with student learning. Blankenship and Lilly (1981) note that feedback serves two important functions. First, it helps students distinguish between correct and incorrect responses. Second, it informs students of their progress. Rieth and Evertson (1988) note that all major reviews of effective teaching report that feedback is among the most essential teacher behaviors for promoting positive learning outcomes. In a study of mainstream teachers, Larrivee (1986) found the following teaching behaviors to be significantly correlated to the academic performance of mainstreamed students: (a) frequent positive feedback, (b) persistent feedback to students who respond incorrectly, and (c) supportive responses to high and low achievers. Moreover, in a synthesis of research on good teaching, Porter and Brophy (1988) report that good teachers monitor students' understanding through regular appropriate feedback. Wang (1987) reports that feedback is important to promoting the following student outcomes: (a) mastery of content and skills for further learning, (b) ability to study and learn independently, (c) ability to plan and monitor learning activities, (d) motivation for continued learning, and (e) confidence in one's ability as a learner.

In a review of academic monitoring procedures, L. S. Fuchs (1986) reports that when students' academic programs were monitored systematically and developed formatively over time, the students achieved an average of .7 standard deviation unit higher (that is, equivalent to 26 percentage points) than did students whose programs were not monitored systematically. Baechle and Lian (1990) found that direct feedback significantly improved the performance of students with learning problems in interpreting metaphors. Likewise, Perkins (1988) reports that feedback produced significant differences in the oral reading performance of students with learning problems. Moreover, she found that feedback combined with modeling and sound-it-out procedures was better than feedback only.

Collins, Carnine, and Gersten (1987) note that basic and elaborative feedback significantly improved student performance on reasoning-skill tasks. In a comparison of basic and elaborative feedback, they found that elaborative feedback produced the greatest skill acquisition. Kline, Schumaker, and Deshler (1991) report excellent results with elaborated feedback in the teaching of academic-specific learning strategies to adolescents with learning problems. In a math strategies program, Mercer and Miller (1992) report that the following elaborated feedback sequence is effective in teaching students with learning problems to acquire, retain, and apply basic math facts:

1. Grade the student's work.
2. Praise the student for the correct responses.
3. Chart the results on a graph and discuss the progress toward the mastery criteria.

4. Note the incorrect responses.
5. Point out error patterns and demonstrate correction procedures, if needed.
6. Instruct the student to correct errors using rules and information taught in the lesson.
7. Praise the student for error corrections.

Although the literature is replete with studies that document the importance of feedback, studies analyzing the behavior of regular and special education teachers report low frequencies of feedback to special education students (Rieth & Evertson, 1988). Curriculum-based measurement (discussed in Chapter 2) provides teachers with a viable method of monitoring student progress and providing systematic feedback.

Provide Positive and Supportive Learning Environments

A positive school and classroom environment is an important correlate to student learning (Christenson et al., 1989). Student achievement is greater in classroom climates characterized by an academic focus and a humanistic orientation (Samuels, 1986). When the teacher is cheerful, supportive, and enthusiastic, students tend to model those actions and attitudes. This can result in a pleasant, productive learning environment. Teachers easily can notice when things go wrong in the classroom, but *effective* teachers comment on positive classroom happenings (Eaton & Hansen, 1978). Sprick (1985) notes that learning is greater and behavior is more appropriate in classrooms in which teachers attend more to positive events than to negative events. Specifically, he reports that teachers who maintain a 3-to-1 ratio of attention to positive over negative events are likely to have a well-managed classroom of high-achieving students. Unfortunately, Sprick reports that most classroom teachers attend to negative events three times more often than they attend to positive events. R. M. Smith, Neisworth, and Greer (1978) convey the importance of the positive approach:

> Liberal amounts of praise, support, and encouragement are found in every good classroom. By emphasizing children's good points, the teacher can build their confidence and desire to tackle more difficult activities. Failure to use such encouragement is a mistake teachers cannot afford to make. The development of a healthy social interaction in the classroom has never been accomplished through criticism and ridicule. (p. 85)

Brophy and Good (1986) and Alderman (1990) report that a positive learning environment and student learning are enhanced when teachers believe that *all* students can learn and that teachers can make a difference. Christenson et al. (1989) state that the following factors contribute to a positive learning environment: (a) the use of realistic expectations for student learning, (b) the development of instructional plans that consider student characteristics and needs, (c) the use of reinforcement for student productivity, (d) the use of active monitoring of student progress, and (e) the belief that all students will experience academic success. Alderman notes that in a positive classroom errors are viewed as a natural and important part of the learning process rather than as an indication that the student lacks ability.

Students' descriptions of good teachers (Lovitt, 1977) reflect the importance of being positive. The students in Lovitt's study noted that good teachers compliment children, let children come to them for help, help each child, use good manners, show trust for children, join in class humor, explain more than once, and ask children for help. The students were concerned with fair play, inclusion in the action, and getting work done in a quiet and orderly room. They wanted their teachers to be real people with senses of humor. When the teachers behaved more like this, the academic performance of the students improved: "As the teacher did more things that pleased the students, they did more to please the teacher" (Lovitt, 1977, p. 94).

A positive approach is enhanced by the appropriate use of reinforcement for desirable academic, on-task, and social behaviors. The positive effect of reinforcement on academic achievement and work behaviors is well established (Blankenship & Lilly, 1981; Lovitt, 1984). Finally, the use of intimidation, threat, and criticism is highly questionable.

Teach Students to Generalize

As the emphasis increases on teaching students to be independent learners and active problem solvers, generalization is becoming an instructional focus of effective teaching. *Generalization* refers to the occurrence of relevant behavior in different, nontraining situations (that is, across subjects, settings, people, behaviors, or time) without the scheduling of the same events that were present in the training conditions (Stokes & Baer, 1977). For example, generalization to new situations occurs when a student demonstrates proficiency in math facts and continues to respond quickly and accurately when these facts are embedded in calculation problems.

Ellis, Lenz, and Sabornie (1987) report that various types of generalization are stressed throughout the instructional process. Specifically, they identify four levels:

1. *Antecedent generalization.* This level involves changing negative student attitudes that eventually may affect generalization behaviors.
2. *Concurrent generalization.* This level involves learning the skill well enough to be able to generalize it.

3. *Subsequent generalization.* This level involves applying the skill to various situations, contexts, and settings.
4. *Independent generalization.* This level involves the student using self-instruction (for example, cognitive behavior modification) to mediate generalization.

These levels reflect the student's progress during learning. Ellis et al. report that two types of generalization can occur at each level:

1. *Stimulus generalization.* The learned skill is used in conditions that are different from those encountered in training. This leads to the transfer of skills to different settings.
2. *Response generalization.* The newly learned skill is combined with previously learned skills to produce a different, nontrained skill. Essentially, the skill is adapted for use with different stimuli. For example, a student learns the concept of place value and uses it to regroup in addition problems.

Several authorities (Stokes & Baer, 1977; Wildman & Wildman, 1975) provide guidelines for teaching generalization. For example, Stokes and Baer recommend the following tactics:

1. Teach responses likely to be maintained in the student's natural environment.
2. Vary the training models (for example, use different teachers and stimuli).
3. Gradually loosen control of environmental factors while teaching the student (for example, vary instructions, stimuli, and reinforcers).
4. Conceal reinforcement contingencies when possible (that is, delay reinforcement).
5. Use stimuli in training that are found in the natural environment (for example, use peers as tutors).
6. Teach the learner to self-monitor behavior (that is, self-record and self-reinforce).

7. Reinforce correct responding in a variety of settings (such as regular class and home).

Learning strategy training. The Learning Strategies Curriculum developed at the University of Kansas Institute for Research in Learning Disabilities is one of the few curriculums that systematically incorporates generalization training within the teaching sequence. Chapter 14 presents the teaching sequence used in the Learning Strategies Curriculum.

Attributional retraining. Attributional retraining has been used successfully to teach students with learning problems to generalize (Borkowski, Weyhing, & Carr, 1988). Students with learning problems tend to attribute academic success to ease of task or luck and attribute failure to low ability (Ellis, 1986). These misconceptions of students with learning problems highlight the need for attributional retraining. Once students learn that successes are the result of their own efforts, they are more likely to feel in control of their learning and develop more independent learning behaviors. Chapter 5 presents attributional retraining.

Metacognitive training. Independent generalization is the product of highly developed metacognitive processes. These processes involve self-evaluation, self-monitoring, self-recording, self-goal setting, and self-reinforcement (Ellis et al., 1987). These metacognitive skills reflect a thinking process that is acquired through self-instructional training (Borkowski, Estrada, Milstead, & Hale, 1989). During the acquisition of a skill, the concept of "thinking for yourself" is incorporated into the instructional program. Preparing students with learning problems to use metacognition requires them to develop a system of self-questioning. For example, students can ask themselves the following questions as they begin and proceed through an academic task:

1. Why am I learning this?
2. What am I supposed to learn?
3. What do I already know about it?
4. What ideas are important?
5. How is the information organized?
6. How am I going to learn it?
7. How am I going to remember it?
8. Where am I going to use it?
9. When am I going to use it?
10. How do I apply it?

When students use these self-questions, they are active participants in their learning tasks. They are developing generalization skills by considering how, when, and where they will apply the knowledge they are gaining.

Conclusion. Pressley and Harris (1990) note that teachers must help students realize that generalization of a strategy leads to improved performance. Furthermore, teachers must help them know when and where a learned strategy can be used profitably. Wehman, Abramson, and Norman (1977) note that generalization is more likely to occur if people (for example, parents, siblings, peers) in the student's environment carry out training procedures used at school. Moreover, D. D. Smith (1981) reports that the people in a youngster's environment can be taught to deal systematically with the social and academic skills of the student.

Teach Students to be Independent Learners

The practice of teaching students to become independent learners has emerged as a viable component in effective teaching research (Porter & Brophy, 1988; Pressley & Harris, 1990; Wang, 1987). Wang notes that self-responsibility for one's own learning and behavior is enhanced when (a) academic tasks are perceived as important to functioning in society, (b) ample time is allowed for mastery,

and (c) effective study skills are used. Moreover, she reports that student involvement in instructional activities and decisions (for example, goal setting, selection of practice activities, self-monitoring of progress, lesson completion via independent study) fosters independent learning. Knapp, Turnbull, and Shields (1990) discuss the balance between teacher-directed and learner-directed instruction to foster independent learning: "The key is to strike the right balance between teacher direction and student responsibility, so that students understand what they are doing (and why) and that, over time, their capacity for self-regulated learning increases" (p. 6).

The major approach for teaching students to become independent learners is strategy instruction. According to Deshler and Lenz (1989),

> A strategy is an individual's approach to a task. It includes how a student thinks and acts when planning, executing, and evaluating one's performance on a task and its outcomes. . . . In other words, a strategy is seen as a "tool" that can be used by learners to facilitate their analysis of the demands of a given problem, to help them make decisions regarding the best way(s) to address the problem, and to guide their completion of the task, including a careful monitoring of the effectiveness of the process along the way. (p. 205)

Pressley and Harris (1990) state that strategies are procedures for accomplishing academic tasks. Examples of strategies include (a) clustering information to memorize it, (b) using self-questioning to enhance reading comprehension, and (c) using a first-letter mnemonic strategy to remember information (for example, using *Daddy*, *Mother*, *Brother*, and *Sister*, to remember the *divide*, *multiply*, *bring down*, and *subtract* steps in division). Major examples of learning strategy instruction that have proven effective for students with learning problems are included in the works of numerous investigators: Don Deshler, Jean Schumaker, and Keith Lenz (University of Kansas); Michael Pressley, Karen Harris, and Steve Graham (University of Maryland); and Ed Ellis (University of Alabama).

Techniques and procedures of effective strategy instruction begin with matching student abilities and needs to the strategy selected for instruction. Once the match is determined, the teacher points out the benefits of the strategy and discusses (with student input) how and when to use it. The heart of effective strategy instruction is teacher modeling. During the modeling, the teacher "thinks aloud" as the strategy is applied to meaningful academic tasks. The student then is given ample opportunity to practice the strategy on tasks that gradually increase in level of difficulty. The teacher maintains a supportive posture as control of strategy use is transferred gradually to the student. Finally, the student is encouraged to transfer the use of the strategy across settings (for example, special education setting, regular class setting, homework) and content subjects (such as using a reading strategy in social studies and science). During the transfer phase, it is important for the student to realize and acknowledge the benefits of using a strategy. The learning strategies developed at the University of Kansas Institute for Research in Learning Disabilities have been used successfully throughout the nation with adolescents who have learning problems.

Guidelines for Using Effective Teaching Components

Growing knowledge base. When teachers examine the many instructional components that are recommended for good teaching, it is understandable if they feel a little overwhelmed. The components related to positive student outcomes represent a formidable list to incorporate into daily teaching practices.

Fortunately, the growing knowledge base about effective teaching can enlighten educators about best teaching practices; however, a unifying theory or framework to organize the knowledge base and guide the application of best teaching practices is missing. If one considers that many of the supported instructional practices are interrelated, the task of effective teaching becomes more reasonable. For example, the component involving the monitoring of student progress is inherent in several other components (for example, provide success, maintain an instructional match, focus on time for learning, and establish goals).

All components presented in this chapter have produced significant influences on positive student growth and achievement. To improve professional skills, it helps to concentrate on one component at a time until specific practices are learned and applied. To guide teachers in selecting specific practices, the effective teaching components are categorized according to specified student outcomes (see Table 1.5).

Voices of students. Perhaps the most important source of knowledge about good teaching is the students. In a paper on "The Good Teacher" presented at a conference titled "Education from Cradle to Doctorate," Clark (1989) notes that students' thoughts and stories about good teachers almost invariably concern four fundamental human needs: (a) to be known, (b) to be encouraged, (c) to be respected, and (d) to be led. He discusses the voices of children concerning good teaching:

> In the language of children, their good teachers nurture them by treating them as intelligent people who can become even more intelligent, by taking the time to learn who we are and what we love, treating us fairly by treating us differently, by explaining why he teaches and acts as he does, by telling stories of her own life outside school and listening to ours, by

TABLE 1.5

Impact of effective teaching components according to outcome focus.

Major Impact	Substantial Impact	Important Impact
Outcome Focus: Across All Goals		
Provide success	Monitor progress	Use effective management
Establish goals and expectations	Provide feedback	Focus on time for learning
Teach generalization	Provide positive environment	
Teach independent learning	Use direct systematic teaching	
Outcome Focus: Academic Learning (Acquisition and Generalization)		
Use direct systematic teaching	Focus on time for learning	Monitor progress
Provide success	Establish goals and expectations	Provide positive environment
Provide feedback	Teach independent learning	Use effective management
Teach generalization		
Outcome Focus: Motivation to Achieve in School		
Provide success	Use effective management	Use direct systematic teaching
Provide positive environment	Establish goals and expectations	Provide feedback
Teach independent learning	Monitor progress	Focus on time for learning
	Teach generalization	
Outcome Focus: Appropriate Behavior		
Use effective management	Establish goals and expectations	Use direct systematic teaching
Provide success	Provide positive environment	Provide feedback
Monitor progress		Teach generalization
		Teach independent learning
		Focus on time for learning
Outcome Focus: Values (Self, Others, Work Ethic)		
Teach independent learning	Use direct systematic teaching	Focus on time for learning
Provide positive environment	Provide success	(This component increases in
Teach generalization	Monitor progress	importance if focus is social
Establish goals and expectations	Provide feedback	skills or attribution training)
Use effective management		

letting me have a bad day when I can't help it. The good teacher is both funny and serious. We can laugh together, and this makes me feel happy and close. She puts thought into surprising us in ways that we will never forget. He draws pictures that show how ideas are connected; we don't feel lost or afraid that we will be sent away or humiliated. The good teacher loves what he is teaching, but does not show off or put distance between us and him. The good teacher sets things up so that children can learn how to learn from one another. She knows how to be a friend while still a responsible adult. . . . The good teacher puts people first, say the children. The good teacher acts from love and caring, and is loved and cared for in return. (pp. 18–19)

Enjoy teaching. When examining all the aspects of good teaching, it is nice to remember that students can bring much enjoyment to teaching. As Lovitt (1977) points out, "Youngsters are by definition, fresh. . . . They see life differently. . . . They often develop their own approaches and language systems for dealing with and talking about their lives. . . . Children entertain teachers; they keep them sane, pure in spirit, and incorruptible" (p. 201). It is helpful for the teacher to appreciate students and expect to enjoy students—their freshness, their humor, their questions, and their ideas.

INDIVIDUALIZED EDUCATIONAL PROGRAMS

The Individuals with Disabilities Education Act (IDEA) is aimed at special education. The IDEA incorporates Public Law (PL) 94-142 (the Education for All Handicapped Children Act), adopted in 1975, and the amendments to PL 94-142, including PL 99-457, adopted in 1986, and PL 101-476, adopted in 1990. Basically, under the IDEA, the law guarantees a free, appropriate public education for all individuals with disabilities through age 21. Although PL 94-142 primarily deals with educational programs, PL 99-457 and PL 101-476 include mandates and incentives to provide services for infants and toddlers, and their families. Moreover, they provide guidelines for assisting adolescents to make transitions from secondary school to postschool settings. The four basic educational rights that the law provides for students with disabilities are:

1. A thorough, nondiscriminatory assessment of the parameters of the specific disability, with no single measure being the only criterion for evaluation.
2. The right to a free, appropriate education tailored to the needs of each individual.
3. Placement in the "least restrictive environment" with maximum emphasis on placement of the youngster with a disability in a program with youngsters without disabilities whenever possible (mainstreaming).

4. The provision of supplementary aid and services to help ensure the success of the educational program.

An *individualized educational program* (IEP) must be developed and implemented for each student (age 3 to 21) with a disability. According to PL 94-142, the IEP must state (a) the student's present performance levels; (b) annual and short-term instructional objectives; (c) the special services and the extent of regular classroom participation; (d) the projected date for initiation and anticipated duration of such services; and (e) criteria, evaluation procedures, and schedules for determining progress. PL 99-457 provides an *individualized family service plan* (IFSP) for infants and toddlers (birth–2) with disabilities. The IFSP documents the early intervention services required by these children and their families. The IEP and the IFSP both require that the written plan be developed by a multidisciplinary team, which includes the parents, and be based on a multidisciplinary assessment of unique needs.

Table 1.6 shows an IEP format that incorporates the essentials of a plan. Part B-I enables the teacher to outline the short-term objectives for the academic year. Part B-II provides space for short-term objectives but does not segment the objectives into grading periods. The teacher may select either form of Part B, depending on needs and preferences. It is a good practice for the special education teacher to work with a student and their teachers for several sessions before the IEP conference. During this time, the special education teacher can determine realistic objectives and specific teaching techniques.

Participants in IEP Meetings

The law specifies who must participate in IEP meetings: (a) a representative of the schools,

TABLE 1.6
Individualized educational program.

Part A: IEP

Checklist

9.8.93 Referral by _Ann Tharin_
9.9.93 Parents informed of rights; permission obtained for evaluation
9.15.93 Evaluation compiled
9.17.93 Parents contacted
9.21.93 Total committee meets and subcommittee assigned
9.28.93 IEP developed by subcommittee
9.24.93 IEP approved by total committee

Committee Members

Teacher _Ann Tharin_
John Thomas
Other LEA representative _Melissa Williams_
Parents _Mary Rivera_
Joan Benton
Alice King

Date IEP initially approved _9.27.93_

Health Information

Vision: _good_
Hearing: _excellent_
Physical: _good_
Other: _____

Yearly Class Schedule

	Time	Subject	Teacher
1st semester	8:30–9:20	math	Rivera
	9:30–10:20	language arts	Benton (Resource)
	10:30–11:20	social studies	Benton
	11:30–12:20	Science	Rivera
		lunch	
	1:10–2:00	Art	Shaw
	2:10–3:00	P.E.	King
2nd semester	8:30–9:20	math	Rivera
	9:30–10:20	language arts	Benton (Resource)
	10:30–11:20	social studies	Benton
	11:30–12:20	Science	Rivera
		lunch	
	1:10–2:00	Art	Shaw
	2:10–3:00	P.E.	King

Identification Information

Name _Greg Creswell_
School _Village Elementary School_
Birthdate _5·15·81_ Grade _6_
Parent's Name _Kent & Melissa Williams_
Address _1300 Johnson Street_
Raleigh, N.C.
Phone: Home _none_ Office _932·816_

Continuum of Services

	Hours per week
Regular class	_20 hrs_
Resource teacher in regular classroom	_6 hrs_
Resource room	_4 hrs_
Reading specialist	
Speech/language therapist	
Counselor	
Special class	
Transition class	
Others:	

Testing Information

Test Name	Date Admin.	Interpretation
K-TEA informal test of phonics	9·10·93	Spelling: Standard score 82 Math: Standard score 104 Reading: Standard score 78 knows 6 of 20 phonics rules
CBM probe	9·14·93	reads 3rd grade level reader at 84 correct wpm with 70% comprehension
CBM probe	9·15·93	reads 4th grade level reader at 60 correct wpm with 40% comprehension
Social skills checklist	9·16·93	gets along well with others but less difficulty dealing with critical feedback

(continued)

TABLE 1.6
Continued

Part B.1.: IEP (Complete for each subject area)

Student's Name Greg Creswell Subject Area Reading

Level of Performance Teacher Joan Benton - Resource Teacher

Annual Goals:
1. Given passages from middle of 4th grade reader Greg will read 110 wpm correctly with 80% comprehension.
2. Greg will identify and use 20 phonics rules.
3.

Level of Performance:
1. Can identify 6 of 20 phonics rules. Reads 3rd grade book - 84 wpm; 70% comprehension. Reads 4th grade book - 60 wpm; 40% comprehension.

	First Grading Period Sept.—Oct.	Second Grading Period Oct.—Nov.	Third Grading Period Nov.—Dec.	Fourth Grading Period Jan.—Feb.	Fifth Grading Period Feb.—Apr.	Sixth Grading Period Apr.—June
Objectives	Referred	1. Read initial level 3rd grade passages at 110 correct wpm with 80% comprehension 2. Recognize and use 8 phonics rules	1. Read middle level 3rd grade passages at 110 correct wpm with 80% comprehension 2. Recognize and use 11 phonics rules.	1. Read upper level (end of book) 3rd grade passages at 110 correct wpm with 80% comprehension. 2. Recognize and comprehend 14 phonics rules.	1. Read initial level 4th grade passages at 110 correct wpm with 80% comprehension. 2. Recognize and use 17 phonics rules	1. Read middle level 4th grade passages at 110 correct wpm with 80% comprehension. 2. Recognize and use 20 phonics rules.
Agent		Resource Teacher-1 Regular classroom Teacher-2	Resource Teacher-1 Regular classroom Teacher-2	Resource Teacher-1 Regular classroom teacher-2	Resource Teacher-1 Regular classroom Teacher-2	Resource Teacher-1 Regular classroom Teacher-2
Evaluation		1. CBM reading probe at 3rd grade level 2. Informal test of phonics rules applications	1. CBM reading probe at 3rd grade level 2. Informal test of phonics rules & applications	1. CBM reading probe at 3rd grade level 2. Informal test of phonics rules and applications	1. CBM Reading Probe at 4th grade level 2. informal test of phonics rules and applications	1. CBM Reading probe at 4th grade level 2. Informal test of phonics rules and applications

TABLE 1.6
Continued

Part B.II.: IEP (Complete for each subject area)

Student's Name _____ Subject Area _____

Level of Performance _____ Teacher _____

Annual Goals: 1. _____

                 2. _____

                 3. _____

Date Initiated	Objectives	Materials	Evaluation	Date Achieved	Person Responsible

Source: Adapted from *Developing and Implementing Individualized Education Programs* (pp. 419, 420, 430), 3rd ed., by B. B. Strickland and A. P. Turnbull, 1990, New York: Merrill/Macmillan. Copyright 1990 by Macmillan Publishing Company. Reprinted by permission.

other than the student's teacher, who is qualified to provide or supervise special education; (b) the student's teacher (the special education teacher if the student is receiving special education; otherwise, the regular teacher); (c) one or both parents; (d) the student, when appropriate; and (e) others at the discretion of the parent or school personnel. For students with disabilities who are evaluated for the first time, a member of the evaluation team or an individual knowledgeable about the evaluation procedures must attend the IEP meeting.

Schools must follow certain procedures regarding parent participation to ensure the presence of parents at the meeting. Specific steps include the following:

1. Notify parents early enough. The purpose, time, and location of the meeting and the persons who will be in attendance should be included in the notice.
2. Schedule the meeting at a mutually agreed upon time and place.
3. If neither parent can attend, the school should use other methods to ensure parent participation, such as telephone calls or home visits.
4. If a meeting is held without a parent in attendance, the school must document attempts to involve the parents. These attempts include telephone calls, copies of correspondence, and records of home visits.
5. Provide a copy of the student's IEP to the parent upon request.

Finally, the law states that, when appropriate, the student is to participate in the planning of his IEP. Although the participation of the student in the meeting often would be minimal, it may be especially effective to include the secondary level student in the planning of his program.

Components of an IEP

Levels of performance. The student's current level of performance may be obtained from placement information (for example, evaluations of academic, language, and cognitive skills). However, additional assessment usually is necessary for creating specific objectives in various subject areas. On the IEP, level-of-performance data must be precise enough to aid the teacher in formulating initial objectives. Norm-referenced or criterion-referenced evaluation instruments are designed to provide such data. In a norm-referenced evaluation a student's performance is compared to others' scores; in a criterion-referenced evaluation a student's performance is described in terms of fixed criteria. Evaluating student progress with standardized achievement tests is common. However, this practice is not warranted because standardized tests do not directly assess the content included in a student's curriculum and, thus, student learning and teacher effectiveness are being evaluated via content that the teacher has not taught (Freeman et al., 1983; Shapiro & Derr, 1987). Criterion-referenced instruments and informal measures seem to be more suitable than tests that primarily yield comparative scores. These instruments typically include systematic skill sequences and provide information that directly leads to objectives (for example, instruct student in sums to 9 facts). Currently, curriculum-based measurement is a best practice for evaluating student performance and progress on IEPs (Tindal & Marston, 1990). Levels of performance may be assessed in the following areas: social adaptation, emotional maturity, prevocational-vocational skills, psychomotor skills, and academic achievement. Formal and informal assessment devices are discussed in Chapter 2, and specific tests are presented in each of the respective curriculum area chapters. In addition, scope and sequence skills lists are included in Appendix A.

Annual goals. Annual goals must be tailored to individual needs—academic and otherwise—and must encompass the entire spectrum of short-term objectives in each specified area. They must describe what the student should be able to do at the end of the school year. Although teachers are not held accountable if the IEP is implemented as written and the student does not achieve the projected growth, they are responsible for setting realistic expectations and providing systematic instruction toward these goals. Annual goals that are likely for a student with mild disabilities include the following:

1. Student will successfully complete Level 9 of the Ginn 720 Basal Reading Series.
2. Student will learn the multiplication facts through the 9s.
3. Student will work steadily and independently and complete the current task before moving to the next task.

For the teacher who uses a scope and sequence skills list to identify instructional objectives and to monitor progress, the process of writing annual goals may be less time-consuming. By coding the scope and sequence skills list, the teacher can simply write the annual goals by using the code. For example, a student's present level of performance may be reading skill No. 3.14, and the annual goal may be to reach reading skill No. 4.26. In this approach, the short-term objectives become the skills listed between 3.14 and 4.26. When using coding, the teacher must ensure that parents understand the organization of the instructional objectives.

Short-term objectives. Short-term objectives must be listed and described in specific, measurable terms. These objectives help boost present levels of performance toward annual goals. As noted earlier, this task is much simpler if criterion-referenced evaluation measures are used, because the mastery of specific skills is pinpointed readily on a continuum of listed competencies. Short-term objectives that are likely to be used with some students with mild disabilities are as follows:

1. Student will recognize and say the sounds of the initial consonants *r* and *w* 100 percent of the time.
2. Student will correctly write his name within 30 seconds.
3. Student will read the next story (section) in his basal reader at 150 correct words per minute with two or less errors and 90 percent comprehension.

Description of services. A statement of the specific services and materials provided for the student includes (a) who teaches the student, (b) what content is included in the instructional program, and (c) what materials are used. Also, since Public Law 94-142 requires that the student be educated in the least restrictive environment (that is, placed with peers without disabilities as much as possible), the extent of the student's participation in the regular program must be established. For example, the plan may state that the student functions in the regular classroom all but 1 hour a day. The role of the regular teacher then is noted. (For example, the student will sit in the front of the regular classroom and will use individualized spelling tapes developed jointly by the regular teacher and the special education teacher.)

Dates of service. The plan outlines the projected dates for initiation and anticipated duration of services.

Evaluation. The use of objective criteria and frequent assessment is encouraged. However, the law requires only an annual evaluation to determine if the annual goals are being achieved. Evaluation procedures are presented in Chapter 2 and in each of the respective curriculum area chapters.

Using the IEP

The IEP is a substantial improvement over past planning strategies used by many educators; however, it is not sufficient for delivering an individualized program. Bateman (1977) compared the components of diagnostic prescriptive teaching (an individualized programming approach) and the IEP. Both require assessment of the student's current level and specification of goals and objectives. However, only prescriptive teaching specifies the teaching tasks inherent in the objectives (such as antecedent events, student responses, consequent events, and daily evaluation for each task). Thus, the IEP requirements are not sufficient for providing daily individualized programming instruction.

Although the IEP is recognized as a major step toward the improvement of educational services for students with learning problems, the data management system that accompanies it can be quite burdensome to the teacher. Developing, writing, and monitoring the IEP require a great deal of teacher time, although the microcomputer is an excellent tool to help educators manage it. M. W. Jenkins (1987) compared computer-generated IEPs and handwritten IEPs and found that computer-generated IEPs were of higher quality and took significantly less time to write. A minibibliography of the role of the computer and the IEP appears in the Spring 1988 issue of *Learning Disabilities Focus*. Many commercial programs are available, and selecting one is not easy.

Mather (1984) reviews a commercial program *IEP Manager* (available from Rocky Mountain Education Systems, 1390 Kalmia Avenue, Boulder, CO 80302) that demonstrates some of the applications of a microcomputer to IEP management. The first diskette, the Assessment Summary, includes a staffing form that contains demographic data, assessment data for 15 academic and social areas, and various discrepancy formulas. The second diskette, IEP Objectives, includes goals and 1,600 measurable objectives. Mather notes that an educator with no computer experience can develop and print a complete IEP according to legal standards in 15 minutes. *IEP Manager* is designed for students from preschool through sixth grade.

The following are some applications of a microcomputer in IEP management:

1. *Create new IEPs.* A microcomputer can be used to develop an IEP (for example, store and retrieve demographic data, test scores, annual goals, short-term objectives, and other data).
2. *Monitor procedural safeguards.* A microcomputer can be used to keep track of the steps in the IEP process (for example, receipt of parental consent for assessment, notification of IEP meeting, annual review date) and the respective status regarding each step. Hayden, Vance, and Irvin (1982) provide an example of a computerized procedural safeguard procedure that features 21 steps.
3. *Update records.* A student's IEP can be displayed readily and modified easily. For example, progress on short-term objectives can be added. Moreover, the updated or existing record can be printed easily for parents, teachers, or multidisciplinary team members.
4. *Analyze and interpret test data.* Test results can be scored and analyzed; some programs include scoring and analysis for the *WISC-R*, the *K-ABC*, and the *Woodcock-*

*Johnson   Psycho-Educational   Battery—
Revised.*

5. *Monitor academic progress.* A list of curriculum skills can be programmed, and progress on them can be monitored.

Obviously, applications of the microcomputer to IEP management are extensive. Some school districts have developed their own IEP management programs tailored to their specific needs.

Requirements of an IEP ensure a certain amount of common ground in planning instruction for students with special needs. However, the teacher retains much flexibility in selecting assessment, instructional, and evaluation procedures. It is hoped that the requirements and the flexibility of the IEP jointly will foster individualized, resourceful instructional programs.

Least Restrictive Environment and Mainstreaming

In developing the IEP, educators are faced with the task of placing the student in an educational setting tailored to the student's learning and social-emotional needs. The setting in which services are provided has a strong influence on the student, the teacher, and the family. For years, educational programs for students with learning problems were operated by special education teachers in special classes or resource rooms outside the regular class. Under the current law, the regular classroom teacher assumes more of the responsibility for educating students with learning problems.

Least restrictive environment. According to Public Law 94-142, the term *least restrictive environment* (LRE) means that, to the extent appropriate, students with disabilities should be educated with students without disabilities.

Idol (1983) states, "LRE roughly means selecting the most normal educational setting in which a special education student can profit from learning opportunities that afford the maximum amount of progress in the least amount of time" (p. 8). Historically, students with disabilities were pulled out of regular classrooms and placed in self-contained classes. LRE is based on the premise that placement of youngsters who have disabilities with youngsters who do not results in improved academic and social development for students with disabilities and reduces the stigma associated with being educated in segregated settings. The least restrictive principle stresses the need for using a continuum of services sensitive to diverse needs.

A perspective on this idea is enhanced by examining Deno's (1970) "cascade" system that describes services in terms of seven levels. As a student moves from Level 1 to Level 7, the degree of segregation from regular class peers increases:

1. Regular class assignment with or without supportive services
2. Regular class assignment plus supplementary instructional services
3. Part-time special class
4. Full-time special class
5. Special school assignment within public school system
6. Homebound instruction
7. Placement in facilities operated by health or welfare agencies

Mainstreaming. Public Law 94-142 does not mention the term *mainstreaming;* however, its use is widespread. Mainstreaming springs from the least restrictive environment concept and is used extensively to refer to the practice of integrating students with disabilities socially and instructionally into regular education as much as possible. Some authorities debate about the similarities and differences of mainstreaming and LRE; however, when both are responsibly practiced, they appear very similar. When mainstreaming simply involves placing learners who have disabilities with normally achieving learners without regard for appropriately maximizing the social and academic growth of the student, it is not being practiced responsibly.

EDUCATIONAL SERVICE PROVISIONS AND RELATED PRACTICES

The primary factor in selecting a placement involves determining the best setting for the individual student. With the numerous placement options available, it is often difficult to select the most appropriate one. For example, approximately 15 percent of students with learning disabilities receive instruction entirely within regular classrooms, 62 percent are served in both resource rooms and regular classrooms, and 22 percent are in self-contained classes (U.S. Department of Education, 1990). Students with learning problems have a wide range of needs, and schools vary in the types of resources available. Thus, needs and resources must be examined *student by student* and not be guided by trends or philosophies insensitive to uniqueness. In establishing objectives for a student with learning or behavior problems, it is important to adopt a tentative commitment to a program level and not consider placement in any program as permanent or terminal. Educators must provide these youngsters with programs that will continuously respond to their unique needs. Whenever feasible, they need to move from the more segregated to the most integrated placement. In addition, placement *within* a particular program alternative needs to be considered when it appears a change would be beneficial. For example, a student

may be moved from one regular classroom to another because a specific teacher has certain qualities or uses an instructional program that specifically may be suited to the student. The appropriate use of the various service alternatives requires careful planning. Table 1.7 presents selected service alternatives with respective advantages and disadvantages.

Regular Classroom

The regular class is the most integrated placement. In this placement, the student spends most of the day with youngsters of the same age. Affleck, Madge, Adams, and Lowenbraun (1988) compared the academic achievement of students with learning problems in an integrated classroom model and the achievement of students with learning problems in a resource room program. No significant differences were found between the achievement scores (that is, in reading, math, and language) of the students in the respective programs. Affleck et al. note that the integrated classroom model was shown to be less costly than the resource room program but the two placements achieved similar results. Many issues regarding the regular class placement are discussed in this chapter in the section on the Regular Education Initiative.

R. M. Smith, Neisworth, and Hunt (1983) and Keogh (1990) note that the key to success for the exceptional student placed in the regular classroom is the regular classroom teacher. It is apparent that this teacher has an enormous responsibility. It is important that these cooperative and capable people receive preparation and support. For example, teacher assistance teams or coaching are useful types of support. Moreover, a student with learning difficulty should not be placed in a regular classroom with a teacher who does not believe the student will profit.

TABLE 1.7

Advantages and disadvantages of primary service models for students with special needs.

Model	Advantages	Disadvantages
Regular Classroom (Student remains in regular class all day)	Provides for interaction of disabled and nondisabled peers in least restrictive setting Prevents needless labeling	May compound learning disabilities with instructional factors Includes large number in class population Uses a teacher not specifically trained May not provide small-group or individual instruction
Consultant (Consultant teacher works with regular teacher)	Can reach more teachers Can supply specific instructional methods, programs, and materials Can serve more students Influences environmental learning variables Coordinates comprehensive services for students	May not foster inclusion in teaching staff Does not provide firsthand knowledge of students that comes from teaching them Can separate assessment and instruction
Itinerant (Itinerant teacher travels to various schools and consults with regular teachers)	Aids in screening and diagnosis Provides some help in area of consulting Offers part-time services Covers needs of students in different schools or areas Is an economical way to address mild problems	Does not provide consistent support for more involved students Does not promote identification with staff Presents difficulty in transporting materials Lacks continuity of program Lacks regular follow-up
Resource room (Student spends portion of school day—45–60 minutes—with resource room teacher)	Emphasizes instructional remediation Supplements regular classroom instruction Separates disabled learner from nondisabled peers for limited periods of the school day Provides individualized instruction in problem areas through specially trained teacher May provide consulting services to regular teachers Prevents needless labeling Focuses on mainstreaming students	Is not well suited to serve students with severe learning disabilities Presents scheduling problems Tends toward overenrollment Can create misunderstanding of teacher role Might inspire conflicts in teacher role Provides no time to observe or consult Provides little time to assess and plan

Source: Adapted from *Learning Disabilities: Concepts and Characteristics* (p. 251), 3rd ed., by G. Wallace and J. A. McLoughlin, 1988, New York: Merrill/Macmillan. Copyright 1988 by Merrill Publishing Company. Reprinted by permission.

Occasionally a teacher can manage with the help of additional materials and equipment, such as high-interest reading materials, computer-assisted instruction, a Language Master, or problem-solving materials for math. To be successful, the teacher must have a reasonable pupil-teacher ratio (for example, mid-20s to 1, or lower) especially in the earlier grades (Mueller, Chase, & Walden, 1988).

Consultant Services

The regular classroom teacher may be provided with special materials and limited consultation, usually by a special education teacher. Consultation may consist of demonstrating the use of materials or equipment, performing an assessment, developing specific learning strategies, or providing an inservice program. Collaborative consultation should be inherent in all regular class-based service alternatives. Consultation skills are discussed later in this chapter. As with the previous program, a reasonable pupil-teacher ratio is necessary.

Itinerant Services

Regular class teachers sometimes have students in class whose difficulties are not severe enough to warrant resource room instruction or special class placement. In such cases, an itinerant teacher usually visits the school periodically and focuses on the teacher's skills. T. L. Miller and Sabatino (1978) describe the itinerant teacher as a facilitator who conveys best practice skills to regular teachers. These consultation services range from daily to biweekly visits, and the classroom teacher still has the basic responsibility for the student. Obviously, the itinerant teacher must be careful in scheduling visits to avoid interrupting the activities of the regular classroom teacher. Occasionally, itinerant services are bolstered through the use of volunteers or teacher aides.

Resource Room

Many youngsters with learning difficulties spend the majority of the day in a regular class and go to the resource room for a specified period of time (for example, 45–60 minutes) each day. The resource room teacher, located in the school, works closely with numerous teachers to coordinate the instructional programs of the students.

Friend and McNutt (1984) conducted a survey of the 50 states and the District of Columbia regarding the use of the resource room model. Results indicate that in all states and the District of Columbia the resource room is the most frequently used alternative to the regular classroom for serving students with mild to moderate disabilities. Friend and McNutt report much variation in the types of services offered within this approach.

Because the resource room teacher provides daily services to 20 to 30 youngsters with disabilities and their respective teachers, the role demands a highly competent, personable individual. Specifically, Wiederholt (1974) believes it is essential for the resource room teacher to be able to (a) work effectively and harmoniously with teachers and ancillary staff, (b) assess the educational needs of students, and (c) design and implement prescriptive teaching.

Speece and Mandell (1980) surveyed 228 regular educators about resource room services. The teachers indicated that resource room teachers should provide these nine support services:

1. Attending parent conferences (74.2 percent)
2. Meeting informally to discuss student progress (74.2 percent)
3. Providing remedial instruction in the resource room (67.0 percent)
4. Providing information on behavioral characteristics (54.5 percent)

5. Providing academic assessment data (53.9 percent)
6. Scheduling meetings to evaluate student progress (52.7 percent)
7. Providing materials for the classroom (52.1 percent)
8. Suggesting materials for the classroom (52.1 percent)
9. Providing written reports of students' activities and progress (51.5 percent)

Because many of these services require consultation from resource room teachers, Speece and Mandell as well as Idol (1989) encourage more inservice and preservice programs that emphasize the development of consultation skills.

Wiederholt and Chamberlain (1989) conducted a critical analysis of resource rooms. Although respective resource room programs vary considerably, they found that resource programs are lumped together in efficacy research. After examining 37 efficacy studies of resource room programs, they report that the results are conflicting and the studies are beset with serious methodological flaws. Wiederholt and Chamberlain recommend improved research efforts before making final judgments about the model. They conclude their analysis with the following passage:

> In sum, the critics of resource programs may be correct in stating that these pull-out programs have failed in many instances to meet the needs of students assigned to these settings. However, the fault may not be with the model itself. Instead, the fault may lie in the fact that these programs are still evolving. Once defined and refined, these programs may well serve as one viable delivery system within the schools for students who are handicapped and those who are at risk for school failure. (p. 25)

Idol (1989) describes a model for improving resource room services. Specifically, she recommends a resource/consulting teacher model that provides direct and indirect services. The direct services consist of assessment and instruction in problem areas relevant to general school success. Direct services are aimed at returning the student to the regular classroom and include data-based instruction, curriculum-based assessment, criterion-referenced mastery learning within the framework of learning stages, and applied behavior analysis strategies. Indirect services include working with teachers in a consultant role to assist and support teachers in their work with students who have learning or behavior problems. Moreover, the teacher helps with inservice training, peer tutoring, and parent involvement. The section on collaborative consultation in this chapter provides more detail about consultation. Idol reports that the research base for the resource/consulting teacher model is limited but encouraging.

Reintegration of Students

When students in special programs are functioning well consistently, educators should consider reintegrating them into their regular programs. Sabornie (1985) stresses the need for educators to consider the social consequences of integrating learners who have disabilities with regular students. Since research with young students with learning difficulties indicates that they are not popular in regular classes, Sabornie concludes that educators must be sure to teach them essential social skills to ensure that students without disabilities will not be biased against them. Salend and Lutz (1984) surveyed regular and special educators in elementary schools to ascertain which social skills are considered critical to successful functioning in the mainstream setting. The identified 15 competencies are organized into three categories: (a) interacting positively with others, (b) obeying class rules, and (c) displaying proper work habits. Salend and Lutz report that social skills criteria provide placement teams with critical information for determining whether the student is ready to be reintegrated into the mainstream setting. The following are some specific guidelines for reintegration:

1. Make placement changes on the basis of the youngster's performance. For example, determine if the student's academic performance is commensurate with ability.
2. Help students and parents adjust to modifications or a reduction of special education services.
3. Include the respective teachers and solicit their observations of the youngster in relation to placement decisions.
4. Use fading techniques when changing placements.
5. Be sure the new classroom teacher can make the necessary minor adjustments (Chalfant, 1985).
6. Make certain the exiting criteria include the same variables used in identifying and placing the student (Chalfant, 1985).

Epstein and Cullinan (1979) suggest that a social comparison method may help determine when reintegration is feasible. First, data are collected on the performances of regular classroom peers. When the student performs similarly to regular peers on several critical skills, reintegration is appropriate. Epstein and Cullinan note that such peer data may be better criteria than teacher intuition or norms on standardized tests.

Obviously, dismissal from a special education program originates from a reevaluation of the student's needs and progress. The IEP format offers the teacher an excellent opportunity to examine the possibility of reintegration. If observations show a change is warranted, the teacher can initiate a meeting or reevaluate the existing IEP.

The Regular Education Initiative

Madeleine Will, Assistant Secretary for the Office of Special Education and Rehabilitative Services in the Reagan administration, and other educators (Reynolds, 1989; Stainback & Stainback, 1987; Wang, Reynolds, & Walberg, 1986) advocate a system of service delivery to special education students referred to as the Regular Education Initiative (REI). The REI includes major revisions in how services are provided to students with learning and behavior problems. It maintains that a dual system of regular and special education is not necessary and that students with learning difficulties can be served more effectively within the regular education setting. In essence, the REI recommends that the continuum of special education service alternatives be eliminated and that students with learning disabilities, as well as other special education students, be served totally within the regular classroom. REI proponents note that this position is based on the supposition that regular education programs can be improved (for example, via collaborative consultation, effective teaching practices, and curriculum-based assessment) to accommodate students with special needs.

The REI emerged because Will (1986) and a number of her colleagues (Wang et al., 1986) maintain that negative consequences occur when special education youngsters are separated from their nondisabled peers to receive instructional services. Specifically, Will offers the following statements as rationale for the REI:

1. Some students with learning or behavior problems who need special services do not qualify for special education.
2. Students are stigmatized when they are put in special education placements that separate them from their normally achieving classmates.
3. Special education students usually are identified after they develop serious learn-

ing problems; therefore, the emphasis is on failure rather than on prevention.

4. The special education system with its eligibility requirements and rigid rules may not lead to cooperative school-parent relationships.

The REI has stimulated much debate and discussion among special educators. In addition to numerous selected journal articles on the REI, several issues of major journals focus entirely on the REI and related concerns (for example, the October 1990 issue of *Exceptional Children;* the January 1988 issue of *Journal of Learning Disabilities;* and the May/June 1990 issue of *Remedial and Special Education*). There is general agreement that regular and special educators need to coordinate their services and educate special education students according to the least restrictive environment. There is, however, much concern about completely changing the current continuum of services available through special education. Some of the major reasons for maintaining special education service alternatives are highlighted:

1. The Adaptive Learning Environments Model (ALEM) was developed as a program to demonstrate the feasibility of the REI. The ALEM is a large-scale, full-time mainstreaming program in which regular, disabled, and at-risk students are integrated in the regular classroom. While its advocates (Reynolds, Wang, & Walberg, 1987; Wang & Zollers, 1990) report that ALEM is successful, other researchers are less positive. D. Fuchs and Fuchs (1988) and Bryan (1988) evaluated the statistical evidence available in the ALEM research and conclude that support is lacking to call ALEM successful. On the basis of the findings, they note that it is premature to endorse a merger of regular and special education.

2. Other special educators (Kauffman & Pullen, 1989; Keogh, 1988; Lerner, 1987) claim that the continuum of special educa-

tion services is needed to meet the diverse needs of students with mild, moderate, and severe disabilities. In a position statement on the REI, the Learning Disabilities Association (1991) states, "The regular classroom is one of many educational placement options, but it is not a substitute for the full continuum of alternative placements necessary to assure the provision of an appropriate education for all students with learning disabilities" (p. 1). Kauffman and Pullen report that existing service systems need to be maintained and repaired through systematic investigation, and educators should proceed deliberately. Under the current continuum of special education services, 70 percent of special education students spend a substantial portion of their time in regular class settings (Danielson & Bellamy, 1989). This condition provides a rich source of investigation and the opportunity to proceed deliberately.

3. Schumaker and Deshler (1988) argue that adolescents with learning problems need separate curriculums, which are difficult to provide in regular educational settings.

4. Keogh (1988) reports that one of the ironies of the REI is the widespread criticism of regular education that gained momentum in the 1980s. Specifically, she states, "It is disturbing that the national reports are unanimous in their conclusion that the present system does not provide quality education to regular students. Can we assume that in its present form it will be adequate to incorporate the educational needs of pupils with learning and achievement problems?" (p. 20). After studying the progress of students with learning disabilities in a full mainstream program, Zigmond and Baker (1990) report that these students made no significant progress in reading or math. They conclude that "business as usual" in the mainstream is not acceptable for students with learning problems.

5. The REI has developed with minimal input from regular educators and students (Davis, 1989). In a survey of 94 regular class teachers, Coates (1989) found that the teachers did not agree with the basic tenets of the REI. Semmel, Abernathy, Butera, and Lesar (1991) conducted a survey of 381 special and regular educators and found that both groups of teachers generally were not dissatisfied with the current pullout service model and did not particularly favor the consultant model. In a survey of 686 special, remedial, and regular students, J. R. Jenkins and Heinen (1989) found that the majority of students preferred to receive additional help from their regular class teacher. If the students needed help from a specialist, they preferred to be pulled out of class for services. It is apparent that regular class teachers and students (regular and special) must be involved if the regular class becomes the full-time placement of special education students.

Although the REI has theoretical appeal and promising directions, existing realities remind professionals that the data are lacking for eliminating the special education service alternatives. There is evidence that students with learning problems are not making acceptable progress. "Business as usual" is not acceptable in either the mainstream or in the more segregated settings. Changes are needed and must be implemented according to a systematic plan that incorporates what is known about the change process in schools (Gersten & Woodward, 1990; Loucks-Horsley & Roody, 1990; L. Miller, 1990; Slavin, 1990). Keogh (1990) highlights the needed focus in this change process in the following passage:

> It is clear that major changes are needed in the delivery of services to problem learners, and that these services need to be the responsibility of regular as well as special educators. It is also clear that teachers are the central players in bringing about change in practice. It follows, then, that our greatest and most pressing challenge in the reform effort is to determine how to improve the quality of instruction at the classroom level. (p. 190)

PROGRAM FACTORS AND LEAST RESTRICTIVE ENVIRONMENT

In school A, the placement of a student with learning problems in a full-time mainstream program may be the LRE, whereas in school B, part-time placement in a resource room would be the LRE for the same student. This scenario exists because the quality of services varies across districts, schools, teachers, and placements. School A has several regular teachers who are excellent at tailoring instruction to meet the needs of students with learning problems. School B has a learning disabilities resource teacher who does an excellent job of teaching students to achieve academic gains and use learning strategies to become more independent learners. Unfortunately, the regular teachers at school B in this student's grade level are not sensitive to the instructional needs of students with learning problems. The variations in mainstream settings led Bender and his associates (Bender & Ukeje, 1989) to research why some mainstream teachers receive students with learning problems and tailor instruction appropriately, whereas other teachers respond negatively to mainstreaming. As noted previously in this chapter, this condition is a core issue concerning the Regular Education Initiative.

When the instructional and social needs of students with learning problems are met in mainstream settings, it is the most appropriate placement. The question of what constitutes an effective mainstream program is becoming increasingly important. Fortunately, several researchers are investigating the factors of effective mainstream environments. Ysseldyke and Christenson (1987) developed *The Instructional Environment Scale* to help educators examine learning environments. This scale was developed, in part, on empirically based teaching practices that facilitate positive student outcomes for students with learning problems.

Several researchers (Wang & Baker, 1985–1986; Waxman, Wang, Anderson, & Walberg, 1985) reviewed empirical studies of adaptive instruction used in mainstream settings. They identified the following instructional features as promoting successful mainstreaming:

1. An instructional match is maintained for each student.
2. Individualized pacing for achieving instructional goals is maintained.
3. Student progress is monitored, and continuous feedback is provided.
4. Students are involved in the planning and monitoring of their learning.
5. A broad range of techniques and materials is used.
6. Students help each other to learn.
7. Students are taught self-management skills.
8. Teachers engage in instructional teaming.

This section features program factors that promote the successful mainstreaming of students with learning problems. Topics include (a) effective teaching across settings, (b) teachers teaching teachers, (c) the special education or at-risk teacher, and (d) limited teacher-engagement instruction.

Effective Teaching Across Settings

During the 1980s, an increase occurred in empirically derived knowledge about effective instructional processes. Much of this research has yielded numerous strategies that are effective with low-achieving students (Christenson et al., 1989; L. S. Fuchs, 1986; Larrivee, 1989; Rosenshine, 1986). Moreover, the research in direct instruction, cooperative learning, and cognitive psychology demonstrates that low-achieving students can learn in heterogeneous groups. Gersten and Woodward (1990) note that if classroom teachers are provided with training and support to implement these techniques, fewer students may need pullout services. If teachers learn new research-based instructional strategies that enable them to work effectively with low-achieving students in their classrooms, they may view mainstreaming or the Regular Education Initiative as feasible and useful. The success or failure of instructional programs or reforms depends on the attitudes, competence, and support of the classroom teachers. Research on factors that promote learning for students with learning problems is presented earlier in this chapter. The promise of this research is considered a factor in the impetus for both the REI and for the growing demand for better instruction of all students.

Teachers Teaching Teachers

Large numbers of students have complex academic and behavioral problems, and learning disabilities and regular classroom teachers are being asked to teach them. The concern over the growing number of students with problems has stimulated special and regular educators to join efforts and create some innovative and productive activities. Ammer (1984) surveyed 70 regular educators concerning their views on mainstreaming. In the survey, regular teachers reported that the lack of communication among teachers is a serious hindrance to successful mainstreaming. One of Ammer's major conclusions highlights the need for peer teaching among teachers. This teachers-helping-teachers approach focuses on meeting the needs of students with learning problems within the regular class before considering formal special education services and more segregated placements. Much of the promise of these activities rests on the assumption that, in a supportive and trusting environment, teachers can support and teach each other to individualize instruction better. Consequently, as teachers become more competent, the regular or mainstream setting improves, and referrals to special education decrease.

Collaborative consultation. The need for collaboration in the schools is apparent. Because about 5 percent of the nation's students are assessed for special education yearly, the cost of testing special education referrals each year equals about $2 billion (U.S. Department of Education, 1985–1986). Collaborative problem-solving aimed at the prevention of behavior and learning problems among students offers a viable alternative to the overused and costly refer-test-place paradigm. The results of a recent survey of members of the Council for Exceptional Children (1989) on professional development needs illustrate the need for more collaboration. The three top-ranked items from the survey indicate the need for (a) more collaboration with regular education teachers and other special program teachers, (b) the coordination of special education with other programs and services, and (c) an improved relationship between special and regular education.

West and Idol (1990) point out the differences between consultative and collaborative relationships. In consultative relationships, one professional confers with another to seek guidance. In collaborative relationships, two or more professionals work together with parity and reciprocity to solve problems. When collaborative consultation initially was con-

ceptualized as a special education service model, the following definition emerged:

> Collaborative consultation is an interactive process which enables people with diverse expertise to generate creative solutions to mutually defined problems. The outcome is enhanced, altered, and different from the original solutions that any team member would produce independently. The major outcome of collaborative consultation is to provide comprehensive and effective programs for students with special needs within the most appropriate context, thereby enabling them to achieve maximum constructive interaction with their nonhandicapped peers. (Idol, Paolucci-Whitcomb, & Nevin, 1986, p. 1)

In essence, mutual empowerment is an important goal of educational collaboration.

The major goals of collaborative consultation are to (a) prevent behavior and learning problems, (b) ameliorate learning and behavior problems, and (c) coordinate instructional programs (West, Idol, & Cannon, 1988). For collaborative consultation to be most effective, a formal set of problem-solving stages is recommended. The most commonly accepted stages (Idol et al., 1986; West et al., 1988) include the following:

Stage 1: Goal/entry. Roles, objectives, responsibilities, and expectations of the consultant and consulter are negotiated.

Stage 2: Problem identification. The problem is clearly defined and discussed until all members have a mutual understanding of the problem.

Stage 3: Intervention recommendations. Interventions are generated and prioritized in the expected order of implementation. Written, measurable objectives are developed to (a) detail specific interventions for each aspect of the problem, (b) establish criteria to determine if the problem is solved, and (c) spell out the roles of the student and respective team members and identify appropriate resources needed for delivering interventions.

Stage 4: Implementation recommendations. Implementation is provided according to established objectives and activities. Time lines and personnel responsible for selected interventions are specified. In the collaborative model, the consultant and consulter usually have a responsibility. Typically, the consultant assumes a modeling role that phases out as the consulter gains expertise and confidence with the intervention.

Stage 5: Evaluation. The success of the intervention strategies is assessed. This assessment includes measures of the student, consultant, consulter, and system change.

Stage 6: Redesign. The intervention is continued, modified, or discontinued on the basis of the evaluation of the intervention strategies.

West and Idol (1990) report that team consensus is reached at each stage before going to the next step. Moreover, they note that adherence to the stages allows for a systematic and efficient approach to solving problems.

Collaborative consultation may occur as a simple problem-solving process in a variety of contexts. Educational reforms are being suggested and demanded to provide students with learning problems with appropriate educational programs in their least restrictive environment. Many educators are calling for regular and special educators to work together more closely to serve students with learning and behavior problems. Consequently, many

team approaches are being developed in which collaborative consultation occurs. Some models being purported include (a) teacher assistance teams (Chalfant & Pysh, 1989); (b) mainstream assistance teams (D. Fuchs, Fuchs, & Bahr, 1990), (c) cooperative professional development (Glatthorn, 1990), (d) coaching (Showers, 1985), and (e) cooperative teaching (Bauwens, Hourcade, & Friend, 1989). Teacher assistance teams and coaching are discussed next.

Teacher assistance teams. Kirk and Chalfant (1984) discuss a teacher assistance team (TAT) model that has proven effective in helping teachers to reduce the number of inappropriate referrals and in resolving many students' problems. Each team consists of three elected teachers, the teacher seeking help, and parents or others as needed. The referring teacher provides information concerning the student's strengths and weaknesses and interventions that have been tried. Typically, the team conducts a problem-solving meeting by (a) delineating specific objectives with the teacher, (b) brainstorming intervention alternatives, (c) selecting or refining intervention(s), and (d) planning follow-up activities. The teacher leaves the meeting with a copy of the interventions. A follow-up meeting is planned in 2 to 6 weeks to determine if the suggestions are working.

The TAT model was evaluated in three states for two years. Of the 200 students served in the study, the teams helped the classroom teacher resolve the difficulties of 133 students, or 66.5 percent. Of the 116 students who were underachieving, the teams could meet the needs of 103 (88.7 percent) without referring them to special education. Moreover, schools with teacher assistance teams cut their diagnostic costs by about 50 percent (Kirk & Chalfant, 1984). In another study, Chalfant and

Pysh (1989) examined the practices of 96 first-year teacher assistance teams in seven states. Results indicate that the TAT model (a) generated interventions that improved student performance, (b) increased the appropriateness of special education referrals, (c) created effective strategies for students without learning problems, and (d) assisted mainstream teachers in serving students with learning problems in their classrooms. Moreover, teacher satisfaction about TAT involvement was positive (that is, 88 percent positive statements versus 12 percent negative statements). Principal support, team attributes, and teacher support were identified as major factors that contribute to TAT effectiveness. In addition, Graden, Casey, and Christenson (1985) report success with a prereferral system that uses teacher-to-teacher consultation and group problem-solving sessions.

Coaching. This team approach also is generating enthusiasm among educators (McREL Staff, 1984–1985; Showers, 1985). Peer coaching involves the formation of a small group of teachers and peer observation. Teachers observe each other's classrooms, get feedback about their teaching, experiment with improved techniques, and receive support (McREL Staff, 1984–1985). Coaching teams of three people engage in a three-phase process involving discussion and planning, observation, and feedback.

In the discussion and planning phase, the teachers focus on the improved technique or strategy they want to learn and outline the specific essential behaviors or actions for implementing the new technique. In the observation phase, teacher 1 observes teacher 2, who observes teacher 3, who observes teacher 1. A format to guide data collection (such as checklist, log, or tape recorder) helps observation. In the feedback phase, the observer and the teacher meet to discuss the observa-

tions. To help maintain the professional nature of coaching, the teachers must never talk to a third person about observations or let a team member draw others into personal problems. Periodically, the coaching teams meet in a support group of 6 to 12 with other coaching teams to plan and offer support for each other. Showers (1985) reports that coaching builds a community of teachers who continuously engage in the study of improved teaching. The coaching process becomes a continuous cycle in which common necessary understandings emerge for improved teaching through collegial study of new knowledge and skills.

The effects of coaching are impressive. Showers (1985) reports that coaching provides the essential follow-up for training new skills and strategies. Also, it is more effective than lecture and demonstration in providing classroom applications (McREL Staff, 1984–1985). In a study in which coached and uncoached teachers received the same training (for example, theory, demonstration, and practice), Showers (1990) found that 80 percent of the coached teachers transferred the newly learned skills to their classes, whereas only 10 percent of the uncoached group transferred the skills. Coaching appears to hold much promise as a technique to help educators develop a broader repertoire of skills for meeting the diverse needs of students in mainstream settings.

The Special Education or At-Risk Teacher

Although numerous variables (such as funding, support, and cooperation) affect the quality of instructional services provided to students with learning problems, the teacher remains the most important influence in program quality. To deliver direct services, the special education or at-risk teacher must demonstrate the most effective empirically based assessment and teaching practices discussed earlier. To deliver indirect services, the teacher needs effective consultation skills to work with teachers of mainstreamed students, school-based assistance teams, and parents. Because of the push toward educating more students with learning problems in the mainstream environment and the disenchantment with pull-out service delivery options, the trend is moving toward using consultative services to help students succeed in mainstream classrooms. Generally, the research on the outcomes of consultation appears promising for reducing referrals to special education and helping students achieve (Heron & Kimball, 1988; Idol, 1988; Polsgrove & McNeil, 1989). Heron and Kimball report that "the data currently available justify consultation as an appropriate service for facilitating the education of all students in the least restrictive environment, and it is clear that the data base regarding the efficacy of specific consultation practices continues to emerge" (p. 27).

Consultation. Collaborative consultation, discussed earlier in this section, is an increasingly popular process regarding how numerous experts view the dynamics of the problem-solving process in consultation. Special education or at-risk teachers as well as mainstream teachers need training to become efficient in the collaborative consultation process. West and Cannon (1988) worked with a 100-member interdisciplinary expert panel to generate consultation competencies needed by special and regular education teachers to meet the educational needs of students with learning problems and other disabling conditions in regular classrooms. The panel identified 47 essential competencies in nine categories. The categories receiving the highest ratings were (a) interactive communication, (b) personal characteristics, (c) equity issues, values, and beliefs, (d) collaborative problem

solving, and (e) evaluation of consultation effectiveness. Staff development competencies were rated as important but not essential. Categories that received ratings indicating less importance to the consultation process were (a) consultation theory and models, (b) consultation research, and (c) systems change.

Idol (1988) recommends that a consulting teacher should have completed a supervised practicum experience in school consultation and should have knowledge of (a) all types of exceptional learners, (b) all special education service delivery models, (c) the history of special education, and (d) special education legislation and legal rights of exceptional persons. In addition, Idol notes that a consulting teacher should have demonstrable skills in (a) using assessment techniques (for example, curriculum-based assessment, criterion-referenced testing, classroom observation, standardized tests), (b) applying basic remediation techniques for academic skill deficits (such as study skill strategies), (c) applying basic behavior management techniques for individuals as well as groups of students, (d) applying accommodation techniques to special needs learners in mainstream settings (for example, modification of materials, principles of reinforcement, computer-assisted instruction), (e) transferring learned skills from supportive service programs to the classroom, (f) measuring, monitoring, and evaluating academic and behavioral progress in students, and (g) using effective communication and working collaboratively with other adults.

Viable knowledge regarding consultation is increasing, and this knowledge needs to be a part of a special education or at-risk teacher's preservice and staff development training. Tindal, Shinn, and Rodden-Nord (1990) provide a model that includes consideration for realistic school-based variables that influence the consultation process. This model includes 11 variables that are organized within three dimensions—people, process, and procedural implementation.

People Variables

1. Consultant background/skills—history, experiences, skills, knowledge, resources.
2. Consulter background/skills—history, experiences, skills, knowledge, resources, teacher tolerance.
3. Client background/skills—history, experiences, skills, knowledge, resources.
4. Administrator background/skills—history, experiences, skills, knowledge, resources.

Process Variables

5. Problem-solving relationship between consultant and consulter—problem identification and problem remediation.
6. Theoretical perspective of consultation—behavioral, organizational, mental health.
7. Stage in consultation—problem identification, problem corroboration, program development, program operationalization, program evaluation.
8. Activity structure—assessment, assessment/direct intervention, assessment/indirect intervention, indirect service to system.

Procedural Implementation Variables

9. Type of data—judgments, observations, tests.
10. Program intervention—context, materials, interactive techniques.
11. Evaluation strategies—qualitative, quantitative (individual-referenced, criterion-referenced, norm-referenced).

Tindal et al. note that the model should be used to help teachers consider important variables as they implement consultation in applied educational settings.

Limited Teacher-Engagement Instruction

Given the many demands placed on teachers to meet the instructional needs of the diverse group of students who constitute a mainstream class, the teacher needs to develop and use instructional approaches that enhance quality learning for those times when a student must and should work independently. Certainly, peer teaching and cooperative learning provide limited teacher-engagement instructional activities. These activities are especially suited for students to practice skills or review content presented earlier by the teacher. Mastery of skills and content is essential for the school success of students with learning problems. Using self-correcting materials, instructional games, and computer-assisted instruction, and teaching students to be independent learners are viable approaches to helping students work independently in their least restrictive environment. These topics are presented in Chapter 3.

REFERENCES

Affleck, J. Q., Madge, S., Adams, A., & Lowenbraun, S. (1988). Integrated classroom versus resource model: Academic viability and affectiveness. *Exceptional Children, 54*, 339–348.

Alderman, M. K. (1990). Motivation for at-risk students. *Educational Leadership, 48*(1), 27–30.

Ammer, J. J. (1984). The mechanics of mainstreaming: Considering the regular educators' perspective. *Remedial and Special Education, 5*(6), 15–20.

Anderson, L. W. (1984). Instruction and time-on-task: A review. In L. W. Anderson (Ed.), *Time and school learning* (pp. 142–163). New York: St. Martin's Press.

Anderson, L. W., & Pellicer, L. O. (1990). Synthesis of research on compensatory and remedial education. *Educational Leadership, 48*(1), 10–16.

Baechle, C. L., & Lian, M. J. (1990). The effects of direct feedback and practice on metaphor performances in children with learning disabilities. *Journal of Learning Disabilities, 23*, 451–455.

Bandura, A. (1986). *Social foundations of thought and action.* Englewood Cliffs, NJ: Prentice-Hall.

Bateman, B. D. (1977). Prescriptive teaching and individialized education programs. In R. Heinrich & S. C. Ashcroft (Eds.), *Instructional technology and the education of all handicapped children.* Columbus, OH: National Center on Media and Materials for the Handicapped.

Bauwens, J., Hourcade, J. J., & Friend, M. (1989). Cooperative teaching: A model for general and special education integration. *Remedial and Special Education, 10*(2), 17–22.

Bender, W. N., & Ukeje, I. C. (1989). Instructional strategies in mainstream classrooms: Prediction of the strategies teachers select. *Remedial and Special Education, 10*(2), 23–30.

Berliner, D. C. (1982, March). *The executive functions of teaching.* Paper presented at the annual meeting of the American Educational Research Association, New York.

Blankenship, C., & Lilly, M. S. (1981). *Mainstreaming students with learning and behavior problems: Techniques for the classroom teacher.* New York: Holt, Rinehart & Winston.

Borg, W. R. (1980). Time and school learning. In C. Denham & A. Lieberman (Eds.), *Time to learn.* Washington, DC: National Institute of Education.

Borkowski, J. G., Estrada, M. T., Milstead, M., & Hale, C. A. (1989). General problem-solving skills: Relations between metacognition and strategic processing. *Learning Disability Quarterly, 12,* 57–70.

Borkowski, J. G., Weyhing, R. S., & Carr, M. (1988). Effects of attributional retraining on strategy-based reading comprehension in learning-disabled students. *Journal of Educational Psychology, 80*(1), 46–53.

Brophy, J. (1987). Synthesis of research on strategies for motivating students to learn. *Educational Leadership, 45*(2), 40–48.

Brophy, J., & Good, T. L. (1986). Teacher behavior and student achievement. In M. C. Wittrock (Ed.), *Handbook of research on teaching* (3rd ed., pp. 328–375). New York: Macmillan.

Bryan, J. (1988, April). *Perspectives on the regular education initiative.* Paper presented at the meeting of the Council for Exceptional Children, Washington, DC.

Bush, G. (1991). *America 2000: An education strategy* (Sourcebook). Washington, DC: Department of Education.

Carroll, J. B. (1985). The model of school learning: Progress of an idea. In L. W. Anderson (Ed.), *Perspectives on school learning: Selected writings of John B. Carroll* (pp. 82–108). Hillsdale, NJ: Erlbaum.

Chalfant, J. C. (1985). Identifying learning disabled students: A summary of the National Task Force report. *Learning Disabilities Focus, 1*(1), 9–20.

Chalfant, J. C., & Pysh, M. V. (1989). Teacher assistance teams: Five descriptive studies of 96 teams. *Remedial and Special Education, 19*(6), 49–58.

Christenson, S. L., Ysseldyke, J. E., & Thurlow, M. L. (1989). Critical instructional factors for students with mild handicaps: An integrative review. *Remedial and Special Education, 10*(5), 21–31.

Clark, C. M. (1989, October). *The good teacher.* Presentation at the Norwegian Research Council for Science and the Humanities Conference: "Education from Cradle to Doctorate," Trondheim, Norway.

Clifford, M. M. (1990). Students need challenge, not easy success. *Educational Leadership, 48*(1), 22–26.

Coates, R. D. (1989). The regular education initiative and opinions of regular classroom teachers. *Journal of Learning Disabilities, 22,* 532–536.

Collins, M., Carnine, D., & Gersten, R. (1987). Elaborated corrective feedback and the acquisition of reading skills: A study of computer-assisted instruction. *Exceptional Children, 54,* 254–262.

Council of Exceptional Children. (1989). Survey of CEC members' professional development needs. *Teaching Exceptional Children, 21*(3), 78–79.

Danielson, L. C., & Bellamy, G. T. (1989). State variation in placement of children with handicaps in segregated environments. *Exceptional Children, 55,* 448–455.

Davis, W. E. (1989). The regular education initiative debate: Its promises and problems. *Exceptional Children, 55,* 440–446.

Denham, C., & Lieberman, A. (Eds.). (1980). *Time to learn.* Washington, DC: National Institute of Education.

Deno, E. (1970). Special education as developmental capital. *Exceptional Children, 37,* 229–237.

Deshler, D. D., & Lenz, B. K. (1989). The strategies instructional approach. *International Journal of Disability, Development and Education, 36,* 203–224.

Deshler, D. D., Schumaker, J. B., & Lenz, B. K. (1984). Academic and cognitive interventions for LD adolescents: Part I. *Journal of Learning Disabilities, 17,* 108–117.

Eaton, M. D., & Hansen, C. L. (1978). Classroom organization and management. In N. G. Haring, T. C. Lovitt, M. D. Eaton, & C. L. Hansen, *The fourth R: Research in the classroom* (pp. 191–217). New York: Merrill/Macmillan.

Ellis, E. S. (1986). The role of motivation and pedagogy on the generalization of cognitive strategy training. *Journal of Learning Disabilities, 19,* 66–70.

Ellis, E. S., Lenz, B. K., & Sabornie, E. J. (1987). Generalization and adaptation of learning strategies to natural environments: Part I: Critical agents. *Remedial and Special Education, 8*(1), 6–20.

Epstein, M. H., & Cullinan, D. (1979). Social validation: Use of normative peer data to evaluate LD interventions. *Learning Disability Quarterly, 2*(4), 93–98.

Fisher, C. W., Berliner, D. C., Filby, N. N., Marliave, R., Cahen, L. S., & Dishaw, M. M. (1980). Teaching behaviors, academic learning time, and student achievement: An overview. In C. Denham & A. Lieberman (Eds.), *Time to learn.* Washington, DC: National Institute of Education.

Fisher, C. W., Berliner, D. C., Filby, N. N., Marliave, R., Cahen, L. S., Dishaw, M. M., & Moore, J. E. (1978). *Teaching and learning in the elementary school: A summary of the Beginning Teacher Evaluation Study.* San Francisco: Far West Laboratory for Educational Research and Development.

Freeman, D. J., Kuhs, T. M., Porten, A. C., Floden, R. E., Schmidt, W. H., & Schwille, J. R. (1983). Do textbooks and tests define a national curriculum in elementary school mathematics? *The Elementary School Journal, 83*(5), 501–513.

Friend, M., & McNutt, G. (1984). Resource room programs: Where are we now? *Exceptional Children, 51,* 150–155.

Fuchs, D., & Fuchs, L. S. (1988). Evaluation of the adaptive learning environments model. *Exceptional Children, 55,* 115–127.

Fuchs, D., Fuchs, L. S., & Bahr, M. W. (1990). Mainstream assistance teams: A scientific basis for the art of consultation. *Exceptional Children, 57,* 128–139.

Fuchs, L. S. (1986). Monitoring progress of mildly handicapped pupils: Review of current practice and research. *Remedial and Special Education, 7*(5), 5–12.

Fuchs, L. S., Fuchs, D., & Deno, S. L. (1985). The importance of goal ambitiousness and goal mastery to student achievement. *Exceptional Children, 52,* 63–71.

Gersten, R., & Woodward, J. (1990). Rethinking the regular education initiative: Focus on the classroom teacher. *Remedial and Special Education, 11*(3), 7–16.

Gettinger, M. (1991). Learning time and retention differences between nondisabled students and students with learning disabilities. *Learning Disability Quarterly, 14,* 179–189.

Glatthorn, A. A. (1990). Cooperative professional development: Facilitating the growth of the special education teacher and the classroom teacher. *Remedial and Special Education, 11*(3), 29–34, 50.

Good, T. L. (1983). Classroom research: A decade of progress. *Educational Psychologist, 18*(3), 127–144.

Good, T. L., & Brophy, J. E. (1986). School effects. In M. C. Wittrock (Ed.), *Handbook of research on teaching* (3rd ed., pp. 570–602). New York: Macmillan.

Good, T. L., & Brophy, J. E. (1987). *Looking in classrooms* (4th ed.). New York: Harper & Row.

Graden, J. L., Casey, A., & Christenson, S. L. (1985). Implementing a prereferral intervention system. Part I. The model. *Exceptional Children, 51,* 377–384.

Greenwood, C. R. (1991). Longitudinal analysis of time, engagement, and achievement in at-risk versus non-risk students. *Exceptional Children, 57,* 521–534.

Hammill, D. D., & Bartel, N. R. (1990). Meeting the special needs of students. In D. D. Hammill & N. R. Bartel, *Teaching students with learning and behavior problems* (5th ed., pp. 1–21). Boston: Allyn & Bacon.

Haring, N. G., Lovitt, T. C., Eaton, M. D., & Hansen, C. L. (1978). *The fourth R: Research in the classroom.* New York: Merrill/Macmillan.

Hayden, D., Vance, B., & Irvin, M. S. (1982). Establishing a special education management system—SEMS. *Journal of Learning Disabilities, 15,* 428–429.

Heron, T. E., & Kimball, W. H. (1988). Gaining perspective with the educational consultation research base: Ecological considerations and further recommendations. *Remedial and Special Education, 9*(6), 21–28, 47.

Idol, L. (1983). *Special educator's consultation handbook.* Austin, TX: Pro-Ed.

Idol, L. (1988). A rationale and guidelines for establishing special education consultation programs. *Remedial and Special Education, 9*(6), 48–58.

Idol, L. (1989). The resource/consulting teacher: An integrated model of service delivery. *Remedial and Special Education, 10*(6), 38–48.

Idol, L., Paolucci-Whitcomb, P., & Nevin, A. (1986). *Collaborative consultation.* Austin, TX: Pro-Ed.

Jenkins, J. R., & Heinen, A. (1989). Student's preferences for service delivery: Pull-out, in-class, or integrated models. *Exceptional Children, 55,* 516–523.

Jenkins, M. W. (1987). Effect of a computerized individual education program (IEP) writing on time savings and quality. *Journal of Special Education Technology, 8*(3), 55–66.

Kauffman, J. M., & Pullen, P. L. (1989). An historical perspective: A personal perspective on our history of service to mildly handicapped and at-risk students. *Remedial and Special Education, 10*(6), 12–14.

Keogh, B. K. (1988). Improving services for problem learners. Rethinking and restructuring. *Journal of Learning Disabilities, 21,* 19–22.

Keogh, B. K. (1990). Narrowing the gap between policy and practice. *Exceptional Children, 57,* 186–190.

Kirk, S. A. & Chalfant, J. C. (1984). *Academic and developmental learning disabilities.* Denver: Love.

Kline, F. M., Schumaker, J. B., & Deshler, D. D. (1991). Development and validation of feedback routines for instructing students with learning disabilities. *Learning Disability Quarterly, 14,* 191–207.

Knapp, M. S., Turnbull, B. J., & Shields, P. M. (1990). New directions for educating the children of poverty. *Educational Leadership, 48*(1), 4–8.

Larrivee, B. (1986). Effective teaching for mainstreamed students is effective teaching for all students. *Teacher Education and Special Education, 9*(4), 173–179.

Larrivee, B. (1989). Effective strategies for academically handicapped students in the regular classroom. In R. E. Slavin, N. L. Karweit, & N. A. Madden (Eds.), *Effective programs for students at risk* (pp. 291–319). Boston: Allyn & Bacon.

Learning Disabilities Association. (1991). Statement on the regular education initiative. *LDA Newsbriefs, 26*(3), 1.

Lerner, J. W. (1987). The regular education initiative: Some unanswered questions. *Learning Disabilities Focus, 3*(1), 3–7.

Lloyd, J., Saltzman, N. J., & Kauffman, J. M. (1981). Predictable generalization in academic learning as a result of preskills and strategy training. *Learning Disability Quarterly, 4,* 203–216.

Locke, E. A., & Latham, G. P. (1990). *A theory of goal setting and task performance.* Englewood Cliffs, NJ: Prentice-Hall.

Locke, E. A., Shaw, K. N., Saari, L. M., & Latham, G. P. (1981). Goal setting and task performance: 1969–1980. *Psychological Bulletin, 90,* 125–152.

Loucks-Horsley, S., & Roody, D. S. (1990). Using what is known about change to inform the regular education initiative. *Remedial and Special Education, 11*(3), 51–56.

Lovitt, T. C. (1977). *In spite of my resistance: I've learned from children.* Columbus, OH: Merrill.

Lovitt, T. C. (1984). *Tactics for teaching.* New York: Merrill/Macmillan.

Mager, R. F. (1975). *Preparing instructional objectives* (2nd ed.). Belmont, CA: Fearon.

Mather, N. (1984). Courseware review: IEP manager. *Journal of Learning Disabilities, 17,* 624–625.

McREL Staff. (1984–1985, Winter). Coaching: A powerful strategy for improving staff development and inservice education. *Noteworthy,* pp. 40–46.

Mercer, C. D. & Miller, S. P. (1992). *Strategic math series: Multiplication facts 0 to 81.* Lawrence, KS: Edge Enterprises.

Miller, L. (1990). The regular education initiative and school reform: Lessons from the mainstream. *Remedial and Special Education, 11*(3), 17–22, 28.

Miller, T. L., & Sabatino, D. A. (1978). An evaluation of the teacher consultant model as an approach to mainstreaming. *Exceptional Children, 45,* 86–91.

Miramontes, O., Cheng, L., & Trueba, H. T. (1984). Teacher perceptions and observed outcomes: An ethnographic study of classroom interactions. *Learning Disability Quarterly, 7,* 349–357.

Mueller, D. J., Chase, C. I., & Walden, J. D. (1988). Effects of reduced class size in primary classes. *Educational Leadership, 45*(5), 48–50.

Nelson, C. M., & Polsgrove, L. (1984). Behavior analysis in special education: White rabbit or white elephant? *Remedial and Special Education, 5*(4), 6–17.

Perkins, V. L. (1988). Feedback effects on oral reading errors of children with learning disabilities. *Journal of Learning Disabilities, 21,* 244–248.

Polsgrove, L., & McNeil, M. (1989). The consultation process: Research and practice. *Remedial and Special Education, 10*(1), 6–13, 20.

Porter, A. C., & Brophy, J. (1988). Synthesis of research on good teaching: Insights from the work of the Institute for Research on Teaching. *Educational Leadership, 45*(8), 74–85.

Pressley, M., & Harris, K. R. (1990) What we really know about strategy instruction. *Educational Leadership, 48*(1), 31–34.

Reynolds, M. C. (1989). An historical perspective: The delivery of special education to mildly disabled and at-risk students. *Remedial and Special Education, 10*(6), 7–11.

Reynolds, M. C., Wang, M. C., & Walberg, H. J. (1987). The necessary restructuring of special and regular education. *Exceptional Children, 53,* 391–398.

Rieth, H., & Evertson, C. (1988). Variables related to the effective instruction of difficult-to-teach children. *Focus on Exceptional Children, 20*(5), 1–8.

Rieth, H. J., & Frick, T. (1983). *An analysis of the impact of instructional time with different service delivery systems on the achievement of mildly handicapped students* (Final Grant Research Report). Bloomington: Indiana University, Center for Innovation in Teaching the Handicapped.

Rosenshine, B. (1986). Synthesis of research on explicit teaching. *Educational Leadership, 43*(7), 60–69.

Rosenshine, B., & Furst, N. (1973). The use of direct observation to study teaching. In R. M. W. Travers (Ed.), *Second handbook of research on teaching* (pp. 122–183). Chicago: Rand McNally.

Rosenshine, B., & Stevens, R. (1986). Teaching functions. In M. C. Wittrock (Ed.), *Handbook of research on teaching* (3rd ed., pp. 376–391). New York: Macmillan.

Sabornie, E. J. (1985). Social mainstreaming of handicapped students: Facing an unpleasant reality. *Remedial and Special Education, 6*(2), 12–16.

Salend, S. J., & Lutz, J. G. (1984). Mainstreaming or mainlining: A competency based approach to mainstreaming. *Journal of Learning Disabilities, 17,* 27–29.

Samuels, S. J. (1986). Why children fail to learn and what to do about it. *Exceptional Children, 53,* 7–16.

Schumaker, J. B., & Deshler, D. D. (1988). Implementing the regular education initiative in secondary schools: A different ball game. *Journal of Learning Disabilities, 21,* 36–42.

Schumaker, J. B., Deshler, D. D., Alley, G. R., & Warner, M. M. (1983). Toward the development of an intervention model for learning disabled adolescents: The University of Kansas Institute. *Exceptional Education Quarterly, 4,* 45–74.

Semmel, M. I., Abernathy, T. V., Butera, G., & Lesar, S. (1991). Teacher perceptions of the regular education initiative. *Exceptional Children, 58,* 9–24.

Shapiro, E. S., & Derr, T. F. (1987). An examination of overlap between reading curricula and standardized achievement tests. *The Journal of Special Education, 21*(2), 59–67.

Showers, B. (1985). Teachers coaching teachers. *Educational Leadership, 42*(7), 43–48.

Showers B. (1990). Aiming for superior classroom instruction for all children: A comprehensive staff development model. *Remedial and Special Education, 11*(3), 35–39.

Slavin, R. E. (1990). General education under the regular education initiative: How must it change? *Remedial and Special Education, 11*(3), 40–50.

Slavin, R. E., & Madden, N. A. (1989). What works for students at risk: A research synthesis. *Educational Leadership, 46*(5), 4–13.

Smith, D. D. (1981). *Teaching the learning disabled.* Englewood Cliffs, NJ: Prentice-Hall.

Smith, D. D., & Luckasson, R. (1992). *Introduction to special education: Teaching in an age of challenge.* Boston: Allyn & Bacon.

Smith, R. M., Neisworth, J. T., & Greer, J. G. (1978). *Evaluating educational environments.* New York: Merrill/Macmillan.

Smith, R. M., Neisworth, J. T., & Hunt, F. M. (1983). *The exceptional child: A functional approach* (2nd ed.). New York: McGraw-Hill.

Speece, D. L., & Mandell, C. J. (1980). Resource room support services for regular teachers. *Learning Disability Quarterly, 3*(1), 49–53.

Sprick, R. S. (1985). *Discipline in the secondary classroom: A problem-by-problem survival guide.* West Nyack, NY: The Center for Applied Research in Education.

Stainback, S., & Stainback, W. (1987). Integration versus cooperation: A commentary on "Educating children with learning problems: A shared responsibility." *Exceptional Children, 54,* 66–68.

Stevens, R., & Rosenshine, B. (1981). Advances in research on teaching. *Exceptional Education Quarterly, 2*(1), 1–9.

Stokes, T. F., & Baer, D. M. (1977). An implicit technology of generalization. *Journal of Applied Behavior Analysis, 10,* 349–367.

Talmage, H. (1975). Instructional design for individualization. In H. Talmage (Ed.), *Systems of individualized education.* Berkeley, CA: McCutchan.

Tarver, S. G. (1986). Cognitive behavior modification, direct instruction and holistic approaches to the education of students with learning disabilities. *Journal of Learning Disabilities, 19,* 368–375.

Tindal, G. A., & Marston, D. B. (1990). *Classroom-based assessment: Evaluating instructional outcomes.* New York: Merrill/Macmillan.

Tindal, G. A., Shinn, M. R., & Rodden-Nord, K. (1990). Contextually based school consultation: Influential variables. *Exceptional Children, 56,* 324–336.

U.S. Department of Education. (1985–1986). *Patterns in special education service delivery and cost.* Washington, DC: Department of Education, Office of Special Education Programs.

U.S. Department of Education. (1990). *Twelfth annual report to Congress on the implementation of the Education of the Handicapped Act.* Washington, DC: Department of Education, Office of Special Education and Rehabilitative Services.

Utley, B. L., Zigmond, N., & Strain, P. S. (1987). How various forms of data affect teacher analysis of student performance. *Exceptional Children, 53,* 411–422.

Walberg, H. J. (1984). Improving the productivity of America's schools. *Educational Leadership, 41*(8), 19–30.

Wang, M. C. (1987). Toward achieving educational excellence for all students: Program design and instructional outcomes. *Remedial and Special Education, 8*(3), 25–34.

Wang, M. C., & Baker, E. T. (1985–1986). Mainstreaming programs: Design features and effects. *The Journal of Special Education, 19,* 503–521.

Wang, M. C., Reynolds, M. C., & Walberg, H. J. (1986). Rethinking special education. *Educational Leadership, 44*(1), 26–31.

Wang, M. C., & Zollers, N. J. (1990). Adaptive instruction: An alternative service delivery approach. *Remedial and Special Education, 11*(1), 7–21.

Waxman, H. C., Wang, M. C., Anderson, K. A., & Walberg, H. J. (1985). Adaptive education and student outcomes: A quantitative synthesis. *Journal of Educational Research, 78*(4), 228–236.

Wehman, P., Abramson, M., & Norman, C. (1977). Transfer of training in behavior modification programs. An evaluation review. *Journal of Special Education, 11,* 217–231.

West, J. F., & Cannon, G. S. (1988). Essential collaborative consultation competencies for regular and special educators. *Journal of Learning Disabilities, 21,* 56–63, 28.

West, J. F., & Idol, L. (1990). Collaborative consultation in the education of mildly handicapped and at-risk students. *Remedial and Special Education, 11*(1), 22–31.

West, J. F., Idol, L., & Cannon, G. (1988). *Collaboration in the schools: Communicating, interacting, and problem solving.* Austin: TX: Pro-Ed.

Wiederholt, J. L. (1974). Planning resource rooms for the mildly handicapped. *Focus on Exceptional Children, 5,* 1–10.

Wiederholt, J. L., & Chamberlain, S. P. (1989). A critical analysis of resource programs. *Remedial and Special Education, 10*(6), 15–27.

Wildman, R. W., II, & Wildman, R. W. (1975). The generalization of behavior modification procedures: A review—With special emphasis on classroom applications. *Psychology in the Schools, 12,* 432–448.

Will, M. C. (1986). Educating children with learning problems: A shared responsibility. *Exceptional Children, 52,* 411–415.

Wilson, R., & Wesson, C. (1986). Making every minute count: Academic learning time in LD classrooms. *Learning Disabilities Focus, 2*(1), 13–19.

Ysseldyke, J. E., & Algozzine, B. (1990). *Introduction to special education* (2nd ed.). Boston: Houghton Mifflin.

Ysseldyke, J. E., & Christenson, S. L. (1987). *The Instructional Environment Scale.* Austin, TX: Pro-Ed.

Ysseldyke, J. E., Christenson, S. L., Thurlow, M. L., & Skiba, R. (1987). *Academic engagement and active responding of mentally retarded, learning disabled, emotionally disturbed, and nonhandicapped elementary students.* Minneapolis: University of Minnesota Instructional Alternatives Project.

Zigmond N., & Baker, J. (1990). Mainstream experiences for learning disabled students (Project MELD): Preliminary report. *Exceptional Children, 57,* 176–185.

CHAPTER 2

Assessment and Teaching

Ysseldyke and Algozzine (1990) aptly state the basic goal of assessment practices:

> The ultimate goal of assessment is to improve instruction, to indicate problems, and to lead to treatment. Frankly, a good share of assessment activities today consist of meddling. . . . We have to be able to use the assessment data to improve instruction. . . . The only way to determine the effectiveness of instruction is to collect data. (p. 350)

To aid in instructional programming, it is helpful if the assessment provides information in two areas. First, information is needed to help the teacher select *what* to teach the individual student. Second, information is needed to help the teacher determine *how* to teach the student for maximum progress. When the teacher has determined how the student learns best, she can arrange variables such as physical setup of the class, social interaction patterns, and reinforcement strategies to make the instructional program most effective.

Information for determining what and how to teach an individual is gathered by both formal and informal evaluation procedures. Formal evaluation consists of administering standardized tests, whereas informal evaluation involves nonstandardized assessment devices and procedures. Formal testing is used primarily to document the existence of a problem and identify the appropriate label (for example, learning disabled) for a student. Informal testing is used primarily in planning instruction and evaluating student progress on a continuous basis. Many educators prefer informal over formal assessment, and in recent years informal assessment has gained in popularity (Salvia & Ysseldyke, 1991; Stiggins, 1985). For example, the curriculum-based measurement section in this chapter presents an informal assessment approach that is receiving extensive attention. Each of the curriculum area

chapters in this book discusses formal and informal assessment procedures.

ASSESSMENT MODEL

Assessment areas for determining what to teach may include academic skills (such as reading and math), content subjects (such as science and social studies), motor skills, personal-social skills, and vocationally related skills (such as career knowledge and specific vocational training). This type of assessment is required at all grade and age levels. The model presented in Figure 2.1 provides guidelines for initial assessment of what to teach.

1. Determine Scope and Sequence of Skills to be Taught

↓

2. Decide What Behavior to Assess

↓

3. Select an Evaluation Activity

↓

4. Administer the Evaluation Device

↓

5. Record the Student's Performance

↓

6. Determine Specific Short- and Long-Range Instructional Objectives

FIGURE 2.1
Assessment model for determining what to teach.

Determine Scope and Sequence of Skills to be Taught

Teachers frequently are responsible for determining short- and long-range instructional objectives in numerous curriculum areas (such as reading, math, science, and vocational education). To do this effectively, the teacher must understand the scope and sequence of skills in the curriculum areas. For example, a sixth-grade teacher may have students whose math skills span several grade levels; some students need help with regrouping in two-digit subtraction problems, whereas others are working with decimals and percentages. A knowledge of scope and sequence skills provides the teacher with a clear understanding of the skills a student has mastered and those that need to be mastered.

Task analysis is useful in helping teachers adopt, adapt, or make teaching materials. It is essential for determining the sequence of skills to be included in a material or program. Task analysis consists of dividing a learning project into parts to identify the skills needed. The notion that learning is cumulative—that skills build upon one another—is basic in task analysis.

Task analysis uses precise instructional objectives because they allow the teacher to sequence instruction. A well-formulated objective for a task includes a condition (parameters of task), a criterion, and a terminal behavior. *Enabling behaviors* are the prerequisite skills for performing the specified behavior. Enabling behaviors are determined by working backwards from the terminal behavior. This process builds a hierarchy of skills. The implication of task analysis for instructional sequencing is clear: Teach the student the easiest skill that she is unable to perform.

The following example illustrates task analysis with the terminal behavior of reading a simple sentence:

Terminal Behavior:

Read a simple sentence.

Prerequisite Skills:

1. Performs left-to-right eye movement.
2. Associates sounds of letters with symbols.
3. Blends sounds into words.
4. Reads words in isolation.
5. Reads words in context.

Frank (1973) outlines four steps in task analysis: (a) clearly state the terminal behavior, (b) identify the subskills of the terminal behavior and sequence them from simple to complex, (c) informally assess to see which subskills the student already can perform, and (d) start teaching in sequential order, beginning with the easiest subskill that the student has not learned.

Commercial programs and criterion-referenced tests are good sources of scope and sequence skills lists. Scope and sequence skills lists vary in organization, detail, complexity, and comprehensiveness. A list in reading may include 1,000 skills within the kindergarten through twelfth-grade span. Lists of this size are often too complex for teachers to recognize the basic sequence of skills in a curriculum area. To be useful, a scope and sequence skills list should organize the sequence into component areas and present the major skills in each area. This type of list helps the teacher to grasp the total content or sequence and to see it in a hierarchical or logical nature.

For each skill listed in a sequence, the teacher can develop a device or procedure for assessing it. For example:

Skill:

Given the two base words of contractions, the student writes contractions.

Sample Assessment Item:

Write a contraction for:

1. can not _____
2. you are _____
3. they are _____
4. we will _____
5. I am _____
6. he is _____
7. do not _____
Criterion 7/7

Scope and sequence skills lists that are useful in designing assessment programs are included in Appendix A. Lists are provided in the following areas: math, reading, spelling, handwriting, and written expression. Although scope and sequence skills lists have content validity and logic, their content and ordering have not been confirmed through research. Therefore, teachers should use their own judgment in selecting and adapting them.

Decide What Behavior to Assess

Deciding what behavior to assess begins at a global level and becomes specific. At the global level the area of assessment is selected (such as spelling or reading), usually based on referral information, teacher observation, or results from standardized testing. Assessment at the global level involves sampling the student's behavior within a wide span of skills in the area. In the area of reading, skills in word attack, word recognition, word comprehension, and passage comprehension may be sampled. Resources for constructing tests that assess across a span of skills include graded curriculum materials, scope and sequence skills lists, and standardized tests. Problem areas are identified, and these problem areas help the teacher to select specific skill areas for further assessment. For example, in reading, the student may demonstrate a problem with word recognition. Word recognition then becomes an area for specific skill testing. The specific skill assessment provides information that leads directly to determining instructional objectives (for example, student needs to work on short vowel sounds). In summary, determining what behavior to assess follows four stages: (a) select global area, (b) conduct assessment across a wide span of skills, (c) note problem areas, and (d) conduct specific skill assessment.

Select an Evaluation Activity

The teacher has many choices in selecting evaluation activities: commercial tests, curriculum tests, criterion-referenced skill inventories and checklists, and teacher-made instruments (such as a curriculum-based measurement device or an informal reading inventory). In making the decision, several factors are considered, including purpose, cost, time, and relevance of the activity or test for classroom instruction.

The teacher must consider whether the activity is for surveying a span of skills or for assessing a specific skill. If skill-span assessment is needed, the activity is usually noncontinuous (for example, twice a year), whereas with specific skill assessment it is continuous (perhaps daily or weekly).

Specific skill assessment is used during the initial evaluation to determine instructional objectives. It also is used in daily instruction to evaluate a student's progress in specific skills. Because of its frequent use, the teacher must select activities that are easy to use and not time-consuming. Additional information on frequent assessment is provided in the section on data-based instruction in this chapter.

Administer the Evaluation Device

The teacher usually administers the evaluation device for the initial assessment. As noted previously, the initial assessment involves evaluating both a wide span of skills and specific skills. Because this procedure involves much decision making—identifying problem areas, noting error patterns, selecting specific skills for assessment—it usually is done by the teacher or a diagnostician. After the initial assessment is completed and instructional objectives are determined, procedures for monitoring progress are established. These procedures are usually easy to administer, score, and interpret. The teacher may assign this evaluation to the student, teacher aide, classroom volunteer, or a classmate. Many students enjoy monitoring their own progress.

It is important for the evaluator to establish rapport and to note the student's attitude. Because the teacher is trying to determine if a student has mastered a skill, the evaluation can be administered flexibly. For example, if a student does not appear to be trying, the teacher may wish to stop the activity, talk with the student, and then start the activity from the beginning. During self-evaluation activities, the teacher periodically must check on the student to ensure that the student is making serious efforts and following the correct procedures. When standardized tests are used primarily to obtain a quantitative score, the administration and scoring procedures are followed closely.

Record the Student's Performance

The teacher needs to record two types of student performance: performance on daily work and mastery of skills. Daily progress usually is recorded by means of teacher-made activities (such as spelling tests, learning charts, and performance on worksheets). Overall skill mastery usually is recorded on individual progress charts. Scope and sequence lists provide a good format for recording skill mastery. In addition, some commercial materials provide individual progress sheets for recording student performance. A detailed discussion of record-keeping procedures is presented in Chapter 3.

Determine Specific Short- and Long-Range Instructional Objectives

After administering the assessment, the teacher must analyze the data and create instructional objectives. Good objectives specify the target behavior in observable terms, delineate the conditions under which the behavior occurs, and describe the criterion for successful performance (Mager, 1975). Short-term ob-

jectives should directly contribute to the mastery of long-term objectives. For example, the following short- and long-term objectives are related:

> *Long-term objective:* Given the graphemes of 44 phonemes, the student will say the correct phoneme with 90 percent accuracy.
>
> *Short-term objective:* Given the graphemes for consonant blends, the student will say the phoneme with 90 percent accuracy.

When the instructional objectives are established, the first step in individualized programming is achieved.

DATA-BASED INSTRUCTION: ASSESSMENT PROCEDURES FOR DETERMINING WHAT TO TEACH

Data-based instruction is a model of instruction that focuses on the direct and continuous measurement of student progress toward specific instructional objectives. It is a widely used approach to teaching that features the interactive nature of assessment and instruction, and it illustrates the dynamic and ongoing process involved in determining and monitoring what to teach. Data-based instruction has roots in the areas of applied behavior analysis, precision teaching, direct instruction, and criterion-referenced instruction. Many educators (Alberto & Troutman, 1990; Blankenship & Lilly, 1981; Kerr & Nelson, 1989; Lovitt, 1984) concur that it holds much promise for both current and future teaching practices.

Research in curriculum-based assessment (CBA) has provided a renewed impetus for data-based instruction. *CBA* refers to any approach that uses direct observation and recording of a student's performance in the school curriculum as a basis for obtaining information to make instructional decisions

(Deno, 1987). Within this model, *curriculum-based measurement* (CBM) refers to the use of specific procedures whereby a student's academic skills are assessed through the use of repeated rate samples using stimulus materials taken from the student's curriculum. The primary uses of CBM are to establish district or classroom performance standards, identify students who need special instruction, and monitor individual student progress toward long-range goals.

Using Curriculum-Based Measurement to Establish Performance Standards

When CBM is used to establish performance standards, measures are developed from the school curriculum and administered to all the students in a target group (for example, all fourth graders in a school or district). The results provide data to determine standards of performance. Using CBM to establish standards involves four components: (a) material selection, (b) test administration, (c) performance display and interpretation, and (d) decision-making framework (Tindal & Marston, 1990).

Material Selection. Selecting the appropriate material from the school curriculum begins the assessment process. An appropriate material is at the level which the teacher expects the student to master by the end of the school year. Appropriate materials could include:

1. *Reading*—200-word passages from a fourth-grade-level basal book without poetry, exercises, or excessive dialogue.
2. *Spelling*—all words from a fourth-grade spelling curriculum proportionally divided into alternate test forms.
3. *Math*—alternate forms of 36 randomly selected computation problems that proportionally represent the fourth-grade math curriculum.

The object is to select several samples of the school curriculum in a respective academic area and administer them to all students. A comparison of all students on the same measure provides a norm-referenced data base for making instructional decisions.

Test Administration. Administration procedures include standardized formats and involve scoring performances in terms of rate correct per minute. A sample reading administration format includes the following steps:

1. Randomly select a passage from the goal-level material.
2. Place it in front of and facing the student.
3. Keep a copy for the examiner.
4. Provide directions.
5. Have the student read orally for one minute.
6. Score the student's performance in terms of number of words read correctly, and note errors for instructional purposes.

It is helpful to administer two or three passages and record the average score.

Performance Display and Interpretation. When all students in the grade or class are tested and the average score for each student is computed, the teacher can develop a plot of the entire group. Guidelines for developing a box plot are presented in Table 2.1, and Figure 2.2 presents sample box plots of 31 fifth-grade students. The top and bottom Ts represent the 90th and 10th percentiles. The box includes the middle 50 percent of the population with the bottom line representing the 25th percentile, the top line representing the 75th percentile, and the middle line being the 50th percentile. The circles outside of the 10th and 90th percentiles are individuals with extreme values. The data from this sample reveal that some students read very poorly and probably need to receive specialized services (for example, Chapter I or special education), whereas

TABLE 2.1
Guidelines for developing a box plot.

Step 1: Rank the scores from highest to lowest.

Step 2: Determine the percentage value of a single score. Compute each score's value by dividing 1 by the total number of scores. For example, in a ranking of 31 scores, each score equals approximately 3.2 percent ($1 \div 31 = .032$).

Step 3: Determine the points in the ranking for 90 percent, 75 percent, 25 percent, and 10 percent. Since each score in a ranking of 31 student scores is worth 3.2 percent, the top three scores account for the highest 10 percent. A line drawn immediately under the third score represents the 90 percent level. Using the same procedure, a line drawn under the eighth score ($3.2 \times 8 = 25.6$ percent) represents the 75 percent level.

Example: 181
            180
            178   90 percent level
    _____

            164
            161
            159
            153
            150   75 percent level
    _____

            149
            (149 through 62 — lowest of 31 scores)

Step 4: Find the median score (50th percentile). The median is the middle score. It represents the score at which 50 percent of the scores are below it and 50 percent of the scores are above it. It takes three steps to find the median: (a) rank-order the scores, (b) count the total number of scores, and (c) divide the total number of scores so one score is in the middle. For an odd number of scores, the score in the middle is the median. For an even number of scores, the median is interpolated by computing the average of the two middle scores.

(continued)

other students are extremely fluent in the material. The two passages were selected according to grade-level readability, but the average for Passage A, 152 words read correctly, is significantly higher than the average for Passage B, 137 words read correctly. Thus, an important consideration in using this system is to sample multiple passages to minimize differing levels of difficulty that exist from passage to passage.

Decision-Making Framework.   These data enable teachers to (a) identify low performers who need special instruction, (b) divide students into instructional groups, (c) plan instructional programs, and (d) establish long-range goals. Hall and Tindal (1989) used this type of assessment to create three reading groups (low group—below 16th percentile, middle group—between 16th and 84th percentile, and high group—above 84th percentile).

For teachers who work with low-performing and special education students, however, the real power of this assessment system is its applicability in establishing a formative evaluation system. By administering successively

TABLE 2.1
Continued

Step 5:   Use the 90 percent, 75 percent, 25 percent, and 10 percent levels as well as the average to draw the box plot on a graph. Plot individual scores above 90 percent and below 10 percent. For example:

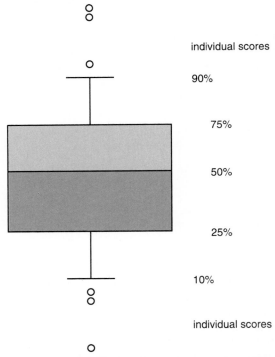

Step 6:   Interpret the box plot for grouping students, planning instruction, establishing long-range goals, setting standards (such as establishing mastery criteria), or identifying students who need special help.

lower- or higher-level materials from other grade levels and comparing performance to the normative levels for those grades, it is possible to establish both current functioning and appropriate goal-level functioning. Rather than placing students into an instructional material according to the percentage correct, as is done with informal reading inventories, a placement validated via research can be made by placing the student in the level where she is most comparable to others. For example, if a fifth-grade student performed most closely to

students in a third-grade reading material, placement in this material is justified; furthermore, judgments of appropriate goals can be established (for example, successful performance in fourth-grade material by the end of the school year).

Individual-Referenced Data Systems

Since Lindsley (1964, 1971) introduced precision teaching about 25 years ago, many educators have recognized the value of data-based

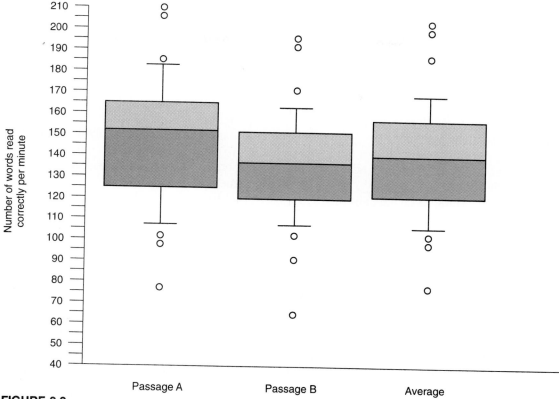

FIGURE 2.2
Box plots of oral reading fluency for a fifth-grade class.

instruction. Other systems that use the methodology of applied behavior analysis to develop data-based instructional procedures include Exceptional Teaching (White & Haring, 1980), Data-Based Program Modification (Deno & Mirkin, 1977), and Individual-Referenced Assessment (Tindal & Marston, 1990). The salient features of all of these systems are (a) direct measurement, (b) repeated measurement, (c) graphing data, (d) long-range goal performance monitoring, (e) short-range goal performance monitoring, and (f) data analysis and instructional decisions.

Direct Measurement.   One of the most important features of data-based instruction (individual-referenced CBM) is its emphasis

on direct, continuous, and precise measurement of behavior. Direct measurement entails focusing on relevant classroom behaviors (for example, oral reading rate, math computation rate).

Repeated Measurement.   Repeated measurement requires that a behavior be counted and recorded over a period of time. Howell, Kaplan, and O'Connell (1979) note that performance is a single measure of behavior on one occasion, whereas learning is a change in performance over time. When more than one performance is recorded, the teacher can tell if the student is staying the same, getting better, or regressing. As more data are gathered, a teacher's perception of learning becomes more accurate. Such continuous data help the teacher make daily instructional decisions.

Kerr and Nelson 1989) provide some practical guidelines for adjusting the frequency of monitoring:

1. Use session-by-session (one or more daily) recording when student progress is rapid through small-step sequence.
2. Use daily recording when student behavior fluctuates and daily program adjustments are needed.
3. Use daily recording when the daily progress of the student is needed for intervention modifications.
4. Use biweekly or weekly probes when student progress is slow.
5. Use biweekly or weekly probes when general monitoring of behavior is needed and frequent program adjustments are not needed.
6. Use biweekly, weekly, or monthly probes when evaluating maintenance of generalization of previously mastered skills.

Although daily measurement provides the best data for making teaching decisions, research indicates that twice-weekly monitoring of academic performance is as effective as daily monitoring for promoting academic achievement (Fuchs, 1986).

In addition to the most common practice of recording permanent products, a variety of observational recording techniques are available. Recording techniques are presented in Table 2.2 and include event recording, interval recording, time sampling, duration recording, latency recording, anecdotal recording, and permanent product recording. The observation techniques are especially useful in assessing classroom behavior that is related to academic success. (For more detailed descriptions of recording techniques, see Kerr and Nelson, 1989, or Alberto and Troutman, 1990.)

Graphing Data.   For data to be useful, the information must be displayed in an easy-to-read format. This involves creating a visual display so that raw data can be analyzed. In data-based instruction, graphing is the most common method of presenting data. Kerr and Nelson (1989) report that graphs serve three important purposes: (a) they summarize data in a manner that leads to daily decision making, (b) they communicate intervention effects, and (c) they provide feedback and reinforcement to the learner and teacher.

The basic format for graphing is a *line graph* that includes two axes. The horizontal axis is the abscissa, or *x*-axis. The vertical axis is the ordinate, or *y*-axis. As shown in Figure 2.3, the *x*-axis is used to record the time factor (that is, the observation period). The *y*-axis is used to record performance on the target behavior. An example of a line graph on equal-interval graph paper is presented in Figure 2.4.

A *bar graph* uses vertical bars to display data (that is, vertical bars represent levels of performance). A bar graph is easy to interpret and provides the teacher and student with a clear picture of performance. Figure 2.5 shows some sample bar graphs.

Another type of graph, the *ratio graph*, is particularly suited to charting rate data. Data for ratio graphing are converted into rate per minute and are charted on a semilogarithmic grid. Number of correct and incorrect responses on an instructional pinpoint (such as see word—say word) for a specified time period (frequently one minute) provides the data for the graph. Such graphs are a major tool of applied behavior analysis or, more specifically, precision teaching.

Long-Range Goal Performance Monitoring.   Individual-referenced CBM procedures typically use *performance monitoring charts.* These charts display progress toward a long-range instructional goal. Measurement usually

TABLE 2.2

Observational recording techniques.

Technique	Data Collection Method	Example	Illustration	Summary Data
Event Recording Focus: Frequency of behavior Aim: Increase or decrease frequency of behavior Advantages: Provides exact count of behavior occurrences Ease of data collection (e.g., tallies on card) Suitable to recording academic responses (e.g., tallies of reading errors)	Record each observed occurrence of behavior.	Count the number of times a student completed his assignments for five school days.	Assignments Day Due Completed 1 5 // 2 4 // 3 5 /// 4 6 //// 5 7 //// 27 16	Total number (frequency): 16 Number of assignments completed out of total assignments: 16/27
Interval Recording Focus: Frequency of behavior Aim: Increase or decrease frequency of behavior Advantages: Can observe several behaviors or students simultaneously Good for very high frequency behaviors	Divide a specified observation period into equal intervals that are typically 30 seconds or less. Within each interval record whether the behavior occurred (+) or did not occur (−) at any time during the interval.	Record whether or not a student was "attending" to the seatwork materials at some time during the interval. 1 minute 1 minute 1 minute 1 minute + − + + + − − +	Percentage of time in which the student exhibited the behavior: $\dfrac{\text{number intervals attending}}{\text{total number of intervals}} = 5/8 = 62.5\%$

(continued)

TABLE 2.2
Continued

Technique	Data Collection Method	Example	Illustration	Summary Data
Time Sampling Focus: Frequency of behavior Aim: Increase or decrease frequency of behavior Advantages: Can observe several behaviors or students simultaneously Can record behavior without continuously observing	Divide specified observation period into equal intervals of several minutes or more duration. Observe at the end of each interval and record whether the behavior occurred $(+)$ or did not occur $(-)$.	Record whether a student was or was not "on task" at the end of every 5 minutes during a 40-minute period.	40 minutes $-$ $+$ $+$ $-$ $-$ $+$ $-$ $+$	Percentage of time the student exhibited the behavior: $\dfrac{\text{number of intervals on task}}{\text{total number of intervals}} = 4/8 = 50\%$
Duration Recording Focus: Duration of behavior Aim: Increase or decrease duration of behavior Advantages: Provides the amount or percentage of time the student engages in behavior	Record the amount of time the student is engaged in the activity during the observation period. Turn a stopwatch on when the activity starts, and turn it off when the activity is over. Repeat this process throughout the observation period.	Record the amount of engaged time the student spent on the math assignment.	Observation time: 10:00–10:30 Start Stop — Duration (minutes) 10:04 10:08 — 4 10:11 10:16 — 5 10:21 10:23 — 2 10:26 10:30 — 4 —— 15	Percentage of time the student engaged in the activity: $\dfrac{\text{number of minutes engaged}}{\text{total number of minutes}} = 15/30 = 50\%$

TABLE 2.2

Latency Recording Focus: Duration of latency behavior Aim: Increase or decrease latency duration Advantages: Easily collected Provides data on how long it takes student to begin appropriate activity Provides data on how long student can delay response (e.g., going to bathroom)	Record the time it takes for a student to begin an activity once the antecedent stimulus (signal) has been provided. Turn a stopwatch on after the signal to begin an activity has been provided, and turn it off when the student begins the activity.	Record the amount of time it took a student to get his reading book and join the reading group after being instructed to do so. Signal Begin (minutes) Latency 11:02 11:05 3 11:03 11:06 3 11:01 11:02 1 11:04 11:07 3 10:59 11:01 2 12	Daily average of time lapse between being told to begin and actually beginning: $$\frac{\text{latency time}}{\text{number of days}} = 12 \div 5 = 2.4 \text{ minutes}$$
Anecdotal Recording Focus: Complete description of student's behaviors Aim: Determine which behaviors are important for designing intervention and determine tactics to enhance intervention Advantages: Provides data which facilitate the development of instructional objectives and interventions	Record all behaviors of the student during a specified time period.	Record behaviors displayed during science laboratory period. Time: 1:05 Antecedent: Teacher passes out lab materials and explains experiment. Behavior: Sally stares out the window. She talks to students around her. Consequence: Teacher talks to Sally about the experiment.	Narrative report.

(continued)

TABLE 2.2
Continued

Technique	Data Collection Method	Example	Illustration	Summary Data
Permanent Product Recording Focus: Student outcomes which result in a permanent product (e.g., written work or tape)—most common recording procedure used by teachers (e.g., math papers, book reports, projects) Aim: Monitor student progress and provide feedback on correct-incorrect responses Advantages: Easy to collect Teacher does not have to observe student directly Provides data on student progress Extremely versatile (e.g., useful in all content areas) Sample of behavior is a durable product May be recorded at teacher's convenience	Collect assignments and provide feedback regarding correct and incorrect responses.	Collect spelling papers and return with percentage correct on top of paper.	60% correct Spelling Test 1. 2. 3.	Number correct (frequency) Percentage correct: $\dfrac{\text{number correct}}{\text{total number}} \times 100$ Rate correct/incorrect per minute

FIGURE 2.3

Sample *x*- and *y*-axes.

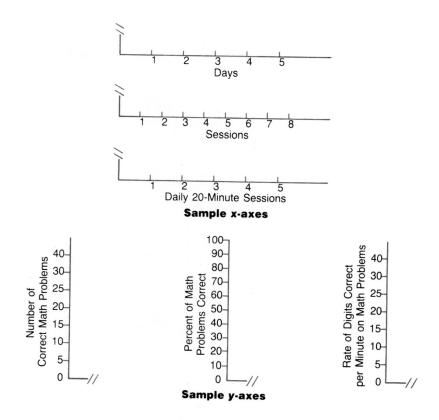

occurs twice weekly from a random sample of a pool of items that measure the same skill. The items represent the goal level that the student wants to attain by the end of the semester or year. Figure 2.6 presents a CBM long-range goal performance monitoring chart, and sample charts also are presented in each of the curriculum area chapters. The student's baseline includes the first three data points. The needed rate of improvement is displayed by the broken goal line. It begins at the baseline median at the end of 2 weeks and proceeds to the goal proficiency criterion on the 20th week. The 10 scores after the first vertical intervention line represent the student's progress under intervention A. The trend line superimposed over these scores is an estimate of the student's rate of improvement. When the

trend line is compared with the goal line, it is apparent that the student's progress is too slow and an instructional modification is needed. The second vertical line represents a new intervention. Because the data points after intervention B display an improved rate of progress consistent with reaching the goal on time, the teacher maintains intervention B. If the trend line is steeper than the goal line, the goal proficiency criterion is increased.

Short-Range Goal Performance Monitoring. Another type of chart, a *mastery monitoring chart*, is used to monitor progress on successive short-term goals. When the student masters a short-term goal, a new goal is established, and monitoring continues through a series of short-term goals. The pool of mea-

FIGURE 2.4
Sample line graph.

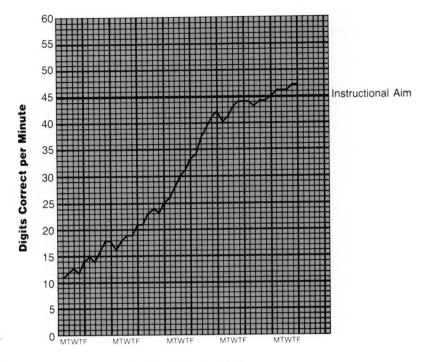

Target Behavior

See–Write Multiplication Facts

Student   Leon Matthews

Grade   4

surement items changes each time the student masters a goal. Although mastery monitoring requires additional teacher work, it has several advantages: (a) the charting system reflects traditional curriculum skill hierarchies, (b) a close tie exists between instruction and measurement, and (c) information is available on what to teach. Mastery monitoring is used widely in precision teaching.

Specifically, in precision teaching, the teacher does the following:

1. Selects a target behavior.
2. Develops a task sheet or probe for evaluation of pupil progress in daily timings.
3. Graphs the data two to five times a week and sets instructional aims that correspond to a standard of fluency.
4. Designs the instructional program.

5. Analyzes data and makes instructional decisions.

Target behaviors usually are determined by administering probe sheets. These sheets include academic tasks and are used to sample the student's behavior. Typically, the student works on the probe sheet for 1 minute, and the teacher records the rate of correct and incorrect responses and notes any error patterns. Figure 2.7 displays a probe sheet of a task for assessing addition facts with sums to 9. The instructional objective usually is not established until the student has performed the task on the probe sheet several times. This provides a more reliable index of the student's performance than one test. The original assessment probe may be used or a new probe sheet can be designed to stress specific facts (for example, addition involving zero).

Several materials are available for implementing a precision teaching system. These materials contain an extensive list of academic skill probes that can be used to determine instructional objectives and to monitor student progress. Two of these materials are (a) *Precision Teaching Project,* Skyline Center, 3300 Third Street, Northeast, Great Falls, MT 59404, and (b) *SIMS Reading and Spelling Program, SIMS Written Language Program,* Minneapolis Public Schools, 807 N.E. Broadway, Minneapolis, MN 55413.

Precision teachers record student performances and graph the results. The chart in Figure 2.8 shows math progress across several skills, and changes in performance are displayed proportionally. In this procedure, the *relative* rate of learning is more apparent than the *absolute* amount of learning (Haring, 1978).

For example, if a student's rate of writing multiplication facts increases from 10 per minute to 20 per minute in a week, the rate of change ($\times 2$) is as great as that of a student who goes from 20 to 40 in the same time period. The chart also provides space for recording raw data. This helps in checking the chart and enables the student to note progress by examining the slope of the raw data.

Teachers who prefer a simpler graph may use an equal-interval chart as previously illustrated in Figure 2.4. This kind of chart can be drawn on square-ruled graph paper. The teacher records the frequency of the behavior along the vertical axis and the number of sessions or timings on the horizontal axis. An example of an equal-interval chart on unlined paper is presented in Figure 2.9. Two advantages of equal-interval charts are that they are easy to understand and to obtain.

The value of using graphs is recognized for several reasons:

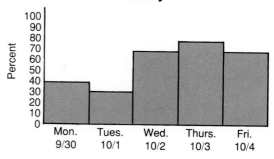

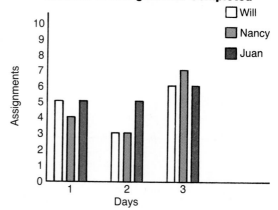

FIGURE 2.5
Sample bar graphs.

1. Graphs provide a visual description of data and reduce large amounts of data.
2. Graphs simplify the presentation of results and facilitate communication of program results and student learning.
3. Graphs reflect important characteristics of performance.
4. Graphs facilitate the use of data to plan and modify instruction.
5. Graphs provide informational and often motivational feedback.

Moreover, research suggests that achievement is associated with graphed performances.

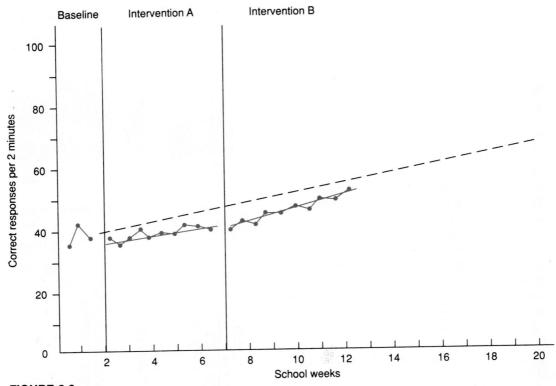

FIGURE 2.6
Long-range goal performance monitoring chart.
Source: Reprinted with the permission of Macmillan Publishing Company. Originally published by Merrill from *Students with Learning Disabilities, Fourth Edition,* by Cecil D. Mercer (p. 252). Copyright © 1992 by Macmillan Publishing Company.

Fuchs and Fuchs (1986) report that when data are charted rather than simply recorded, achievement improves approximately .5 of a standard deviation unit.

Data Analysis and Instructional Decisions. Instructional aims or goals provide the student and teacher with a framework to analyze data and evaluate student progress. When instructional aims are expressed in terms of percent correct, it generally is accepted that 80 percent correct responses represent mastery. The instructional aim also may be expressed in terms of rate. In precision teaching, the instructional aim usually is defined in terms of rate of correct and incorrect responses per minute. In CBM, it usually is rate of only correct responses per minute. Rate is a very sensitive ratio measure that readily reflects the effects of instructional interventions. (Rate is equal to the number of movements divided by the number of minutes observed.)

Ideally, the aim should represent a mastery level of the skill. Data concerning rates that reflect mastery (that is, proficiency) in academic tasks have long been lacking. Although there is still disagreement concerning proficiency-level rates, enough data (Mercer, Mercer, & Evans, 1982) are available to suggest proficiency-level trends on selected academic tasks.

Name _____ Correct _____ Error _____

Date _____ Comments _____

6 + 2	5 + 3	4 + 4	9 + 0	8 + 1	2 + 7	5 + 0
8 + 0	4 + 3	1 + 1	3 + 2	5 + 2	3 + 6	5 + 4
7 + 1	4 + 2	3 + 3	8 + 1	7 + 0	2 + 5	4 + 0
1 + 0	3 + 1	2 + 2	6 + 1	5 + 4	1 + 6	0 + 0
3 + 4	2 + 4	2 + 1	3 + 1	3 + 0	4 + 5	5 + 1
6 + 3	7 + 2	1 + 2	1 + 3	1 + 4	1 + 5	1 + 8

FIGURE 2.7
Probe sheet used to present addition facts—sums to 9.

Certain learner characteristics, such as age, grade level, and achievement level, influence the establishment of appropriate aims. Because research has not conclusively determined specific aims for academic tasks, teachers must use their own judgment in setting aims with individual students. One way of facilitating aim selection is to collect rate data from students who are achieving satisfactorily and use their performances as aims (see the section on using CBM to establish performance standards). Another way to determine goal level is to obtain two of three or three of three scores on similar grade-level passages within the 55-to-75 words per minute correct range and locate the median of these three baseline scores. If the student is being measured at or above third-grade reader level, multiply the number of weeks in the instructional period times 2 and add this to the baseline median score. For example:

$$(\text{weeks} \times 2) + \text{baseline median} = \text{goal}$$
$$(30 \times 2) + 60$$
$$60 + 60 = 120 \text{ words per minute}$$

If the student is being measured below the third-grade reader level, multiply the number

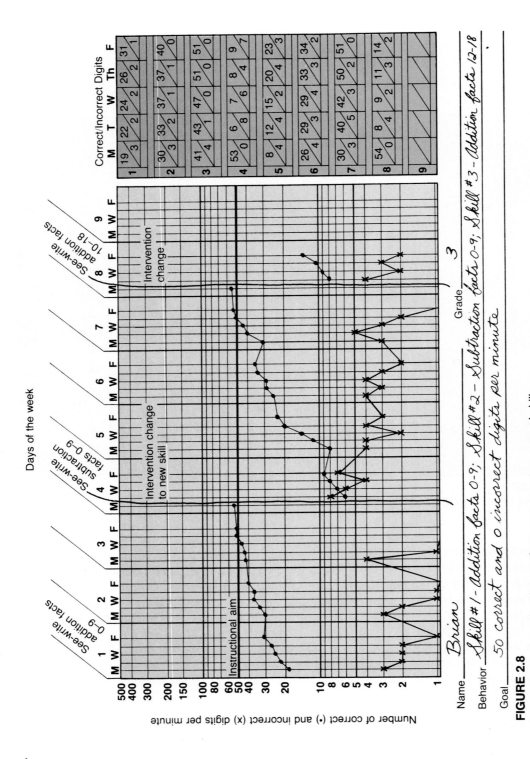

FIGURE 2.8

Proportional chart showing math progress across several skills.

Source: Reprinted with permission of Macmillan Publishing Company. Originally published by Merrill from *Students with Learning Disabilities, Fourth Edition*, by Cecil D. Mercer (p. 254). Copyright © 1992 by Macmillan Publishing Company.

of weeks in the instructional period times 1.5 and add this to the baseline median score. For example:

$$(\text{weeks} \times 1.5) + \text{baseline median} = \text{goal}$$
$$(30 \times 1.5) + 60$$
$$45 + 60 = 105 \text{ words per minute}$$

Charted data enable the teacher to determine whether the student is making acceptable progress. The analysis of data is enhanced when it is charted to display both baseline data (that is, present levels of performance) and intervention data (that is, data gathered during intervention). Each time an intervention change is made, a vertical line is drawn on the chart to indicate the change. Haring (1978) notes that the purpose of charting data is to help the teacher make accurate decisions about teaching strategies (for example, when to continue or change a procedure). Significant learning patterns often emerge which enable the teacher to find possible reasons for success or failure and make decisions based on data. The most desirable pattern is clear-cut: an increase in the rate of appropriate or correct responses and a decrease in the rate of inappropriate or incorrect responses.

Students with learning problems often are identified because they have difficulty keeping up with instruction. These students fall further and further behind. Analyzing a student's learning pattern can help identify learning problems so the teacher can make appropriate decisions about instruction.

Changes in student performance over time can be assessed with several specific measures:

1. *Level of performance*—refers to immediate changes in level of performance that occur when an intervention is introduced.
2. *Slope*—refers to the rate of change in a trend line that reflects the values of the data points.

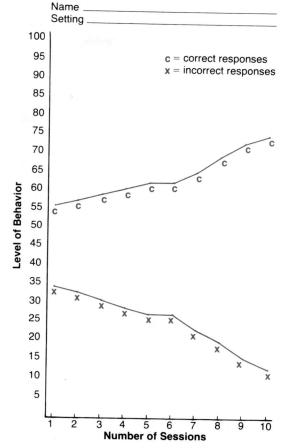

FIGURE 2.9
Equal-interval chart.

3. *Variability*—refers to the inconsistency of performance.
4. *Quantification of weekly rate*—refers to determining the weekly rate and comparing it with the performance aim rate. For example, if the weekly rate of improvement is 2.5 words read correctly per minute and the aim is 2.0, then the student is making good progress. The procedure to quantify the weekly rate of improvement is to (a) find the value on the vertical axis of the median of the last three data points, (b) find the

value on the vertical axis of the median of the first three data points, and (c) subtract the end value from the beginning value and divide the difference by the number of weeks of instruction.

Research supports the use of rules for making decisions when analyzing the data. Fuchs and Fuchs (1986) found that formative evaluation that involves data-utilization rules is associated with an average increase in student achievement of .5 standard deviation over formative evaluation without such rules. An example of a rule is the 3-day rule, in which the teacher makes an instructional modification if the student's progress is unsatisfactory (that is, below aim) for 3 consecutive days. Fuchs, Fuchs, and Hamlett (1989) found that for CBM to be most effective, teachers must use the data to evaluate instruction and make modifications. Tindal and Marston (1990) provide a detailed discussion of data analysis techniques and decision rules for goal-oriented and treatment-oriented decision making.

Basic Guidelines of Data-Based Instruction

Howell et al. (1979) offer numerous guidelines for implementing data-based instruction. They note that data-based instruction is most successful when:

1. The teacher initially counts only priority behaviors.
2. The teacher identifies strategies to facilitate timing and recording behaviors.
3. The teacher evaluates the recorded data frequently.
4. The teacher uses probes or curriculum-referenced testing.
5. The system remains a tool for teaching rather than a "cause" and is used only as long as it helps the student.

Howell et al. also list the following strategies to facilitate timing and recording behaviors:

1. The teacher can take group timings, especially on written activities. Some teachers, for example, time 1-minute handwriting samples, 1-minute math fact sheets, and 1-minute spelling problems.
2. Students can record time stopped and started. This can be done easily with a rubber stamp of a clock on the students' worksheets.
3. A kitchen timer or prerecorded tape can be used to time sessions.
4. Students can work together and time and record data for each other. This works well with flash-card drills.
5. Students can read into a tape recorder. Teachers later can record correct and error rates for either samples of behavior or the total session.
6. Mechanical counters can be used. Single and dual tally counters are available as well as beads and golf score counters.
7. Counting should be done for a fixed period of time each day. Counting for different intervals confuses the data pattern since such factors as endurance, boredom, and latency of response may enter into the data analysis.
8. Timings for 1-minute can be used because they are easy to chart and no rate plotter is necessary.
9. Aides, peers, student teachers, and volunteers can be trained to help develop materials and to count and record behaviors.

In addition, Wesson (1987) provides time-saving tips in the following areas: (a) organization, (b) preparation of materials, (c) administration, (d) scoring procedures, and (e) using the data.

Commentary on Data-Based Instruction

Some highlights of research on data-based approaches include the following:

1. Considerable evidence exists to support that data-based monitoring is positively associated with student achievement gains (Fuchs, 1986; Fuchs & Fuchs, 1986; Rieth & Evertson, 1988; Tindal & Marston, 1990; White, 1986). In a meta-analysis of formative evaluations, Fuchs and Fuchs found that data-based programs that monitored student progress and evaluated instruction systematically produced .7 standard deviation higher achievement than nonmonitored instruction. This represents a gain of 26 percentage points. Moreover, White reports outstanding gains for students involved in precision teaching programs.

2. CBM measures have good reliability and validity (Fuchs, 1986; Fuchs, Fuchs, & Maxwell, 1988; Ivarie, 1986; Tindal & Marston, 1990).

3. Self-selected goals yield better performance than assigned goals (Fuchs, Bahr, & Rieth, 1989).

4. When teachers establish moderately to highly ambitious goals, students achieve better (Fuchs, Fuchs, & Deno, 1985).

In a national survey of 136 learning disabilities teachers, Wesson, King, and Deno (1984) found that the majority (53.6 percent) of learning disabilities teachers ($n = 110$) who knew of direct and frequent measurement used it; however, those who did not use it felt it was too time-consuming. The position that data-based instruction is time-consuming is prominent among users and nonusers of direct and frequent measurement. However, Wesson et al. report that time involved in direct and frequent measurement does not have to be extensive. Fuchs, Wesson, Tindal, Mirkin, and Deno (1981) report the results of a study in which teachers were trained to reduce by 80 percent the time they spent in direct measurement (for example, preparing, directing, scoring, and graphing). According to Wesson et al., "Trained and experienced teachers require only two minutes to prepare for, administer, score, and graph student performance" (p. 48). They also report that direct and frequent measurement is no more time-consuming than other evaluation activities. Wesson et al. sum up the time-consumption issue involving direct and frequent measurement as follows:

> [S]ince related research reveals that frequent measurement involves achievement (Bohannon, 1975; Mirkin et al., 1979), the proposition that direct and frequent measurement is a waste of critical instructional time is without a factual basis. . . . Given its benefits, direct and frequent measurement must be used on a more widespread basis in special education. One implication of the present study is that teachers may need more training and experience in procedures for conducting direct and frequent measurement. . . . Furthermore, experience should improve measurement efficiency. Once these two frequently cited obstacles are minimized, direct and frequent measurement may enjoy more widespread use and may serve to improve the performance of many more students. (p. 48)

ASSESSMENT FOR DETERMINING HOW TO TEACH

Once the teacher determines the instructional needs of the student by assessing what to teach, the important process of determining how to teach begins. The second process focuses on environmental variables that influence the student's achievement. Learning deficits often are attributed to problems within the student, and thus the student is viewed as responsible for the learning problems. Many educators now recognize that environmental factors (such as inadequate teaching) may trigger and sustain low achievement and inappropriate behaviors. Thus, in planning for the student with learning problems, it is essential to consider both student and environmental factors.

Unfortunately, too little emphasis in teacher training and material development has been placed on how to teach. The efficiency of the instructional process depends on how well a teacher or diagnostician determines and manipulates factors that best facilitate a student's learning. For example, Ms. Allen, a classroom teacher, observed that because Ronnie constantly asks classmates if his responses are correct, he is not using his time wisely during spelling seatwork. To improve the situation, Ms. Allen made a spelling tape with the week's word list spelled correctly on it, and Ronnie uses the tape in studying the words. If the result of this adjustment is that Ronnie learns an average of one word more a day without increasing the time spent on spelling, the instructional program has become more efficient. Ronnie will learn many more spelling words during the school year without increasing the amount of time he spends on spelling seatwork. This ability to analyze how a student learns best influences the selection of materials, methods, and procedures used in the intervention program. It is perhaps the foremost skill that distinguishes the professionally trained teacher from other supportive instructional personnel.

Formats for Determining How to Teach

Systematic Observation. Systematic observation of the student is one of the teacher's most valuable ways of obtaining information about a student's optimal learning conditions. In systematic observation, it often is important to record more than a specific behavior. Information for determining how to teach often comes from observing *antecedent* and *consequent* events as well: (a) what precedes behavior (teacher asked Johnny to read in a large group), (b) behavior (Johnny cried), and (c) what follows behavior (teacher coaxed Johnny). Systematic observation is simple to use and can be done in a variety of settings. Stephens (1977) recommends several guidelines for successful observation:

1. Select the behavior to be observed. Make sure the target behavior is identifiable to the extent that it is measurable.
2. Select a method of recording the behavior and record the frequency of the target behavior.
3. Describe the conditions under which the observations are made. These include time, place, activity, antecedent event, and consequent event.

Observation is more effective when the observer has a specific reason or question formulated to guide the observation. Furthermore, observational data collected over time can strengthen the teacher's confidence in the data. Technology for measurement of systematic observation focuses on two key factors: (a) selecting the target behavior and (b) recording the frequency of the behavior. For a presentation of observational recording techniques, see Table 2.2 previously presented in the section on individual-referenced data systems.

Formal Assessment. Only a few formal tests focus on assessing factors relating to how to teach. These tests have not proven to be promising with regard to aiding in instructional programming. Factors that can be manipulated to improve learning are not readily assessed by formal testing. Most formal tests are administered only once, and repeated observations are needed to analyze the effects of various factors on behavior.

Criterion Tests. The primary use of criterion tests is to assess for what to teach. However, because they can be used to evaluate the effects of instruction, they also are useful in determining how to teach. For example, a teacher may divide a list of spelling words into two lists to determine whether a multisensory spelling activity or a flash-card drill is more effective. By administering a criterion test on each set of words, the teacher can compare the student's performances and make a decision about the effectiveness of the two treatments.

Rating Scales.   A rating scale is a series of statements or questions that require some judgment about the degree or frequency of the behavior or characteristics described in each statement. Sample formats of rating scales include:

Numerical Scale

Select the number that best describes the individual.

_____ Frequency of adult supervision required

1. Always
2. Often
3. Occasionally
4. Rarely
5. Almost never

Graphic Scale

Select a place on the line that best describes the individual.

Frequency of adult supervision required:

Always Often Occasionally Rarely Almost never

Some formal rating scales that may be useful in assessing students with emotional and behavior problems are presented in Chapter 5. Occasionally, teachers make or use rating scales for parents to complete. These are helpful to use with parents who do not have the time to observe and record their child's behavior systematically. A teacher also may wish to give a rating scale to students to obtain information about areas such as the student's reinforcement preferences, interests, and attitudes about school.

Interviews.   Information obtained from interviews with parents, teachers, and students can be useful in determining how to teach a student. Through interviews the teacher can obtain information about specific techniques to use with the student. Also, information can be obtained about the student's interests, favorite activities, problem areas, and attitudes, as well as how the student is perceived at home.

Charting.   Charting holds much promise for determining how to teach. In charting, a student's daily performance on a probe sheet is recorded on a graph. The graph provides a measure over time of the student's progress. The teacher analyzes the graph pattern and makes instructional decisions regarding which antecedent and consequent events to maintain or change. The teacher can manipulate an antecedent event (such as seating arrangement) or consequent event (for example, award points for work) and analyze the chart to see if performance improves, declines, or remains the same. Charts mainly have been used to determine what to teach, but educators now use probe assessment and charts to evaluate learning style (Koenig & Kunzelmann, 1980). Charting itself is reinforcing to some students and may help to improve student performance.

Portfolios.   Portfolios have the potential to reveal a lot about their creators and can give teachers insights into their students' growth. According to Paulson, Paulson, and Meyer (1991), "A portfolio is a purposeful collection of student work that exhibits the student's efforts, progress, and achievements in one or more areas. The collection must include student participation in selecting contents, the criteria for selection, the criteria for judging merit, and evidence of student self-reflection."

In portfolio assessment, the student collects and reflects on examples of her work in a specific area. For example, in addition to results from classroom tests, written responses to literature, checklists, and tapes, a reading portfolio should include samples of student work, the student's observational notes, self-evaluations, and progress notes contributed by both the teacher and the student (Valencia, 1990). Writing portfolios might include notes, diagrams, drafts, and the final version of a writing project, as well as diverse entries such as journal writings, letters, poems, or essays (Wolf, 1989). The student is a participant in the assessment process and learns to set goals and evaluate learning in progress. Thus, portfolio assessment offers the opportunity to observe student performance in a context in which the student is solving problems and making judgments about her own performance. The teacher can use the information about the behaviors and attitudes of readers and writers of differing abilities to tailor instruction. Portfolios also can be used during parent conferences. At the end of the year, several works can be selected from the portfolio that exemplify what has changed for the student in that time, and these works can become a final portfolio to serve as a continuing document of progress from year to year.

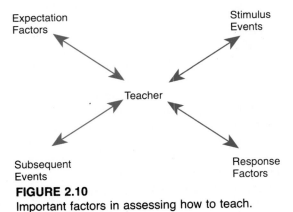

FIGURE 2.10
Important factors in assessing how to teach.

Checklists.   Checklists can be helpful in determining how to teach. To help the teacher recognize factors that may influence a student's learning, checklist-rating scales are presented in this chapter. Together these scales form the Analysis of Student Learning Form, which presents key variables for each of the major assessment areas.

ASSESSMENT AREAS FOR DETERMINING HOW TO TEACH

The first step in determining how to teach is to identify the major areas of assessment. Figure 2.10 presents the major areas that are basic in assessment for determining how to teach: expectation factors, stimulus events, response factors, and subsequent events. Once these areas are selected, the important factors need to be identified under each of them. Some of the important factors of each major area are outlined in the Analysis of Student Learning Form (Tables 2.3, 2.4, 2.6, and 2.7). The form is divided into four parts, one for each assessment area. A complete analysis of this type usually is conducted to help design instructional programs for students who are extremely difficult to manage or teach. Also, a complete analysis usually involves observations by various diagnostic team members. The primary function of this section is to alert the teacher to areas that contribute to how students learn. A general awareness of relevant instructional factors can be useful in teaching all students. For example, if a teacher is "sensitive" to expectation and response factors and stimulus and subsequent events in daily observations, subtle changes can lead to improved student learning.

Expectation Factors

Expectation refers to an individual's orientation to the learning situation. Two types of generalized expectations are recognized. One involves the expectation for a particular type of consequence, such as social approval, achievement, tangible reward, failure, or punishment. In this type of generalized expectation, the consequences govern whether a person perceives a situation as being similar to past situations. The second type of generalized expectation is the kind that generalizes from other situations involving a similar problem-solving activity, but differing in consequence. Thus, problem-solving activities encountered in a variety of situations may generalize to another situation, no matter the consequence. Motivation often is equated with expectation, because expectation may serve as an incentive (or deterrent) for approaching, continuing, or avoiding the learning task. A student who receives verbal praise for writing spelling words may expect that if the words are written, some desirable event will follow. Conversely, if a student receives a low grade or criticism for writing spelling words, expectation can serve as a deterrent, and the student avoids the learning task. Thus, expectation of success or failure can influence the student's motivation toward the learning task.

Numerous expectations significantly influence learning outcomes and student behavior. Four expectation areas are discussed: learner expectations, teacher expectations, peer expectations, and parental expectations (see Table 2.3).

Learner Expectations. Section I of the Analysis of Student Learning Form, Part I, presents several factors to be considered in analyzing learner expectations. By using a checklist-rating scale similar to the Analysis of Student Learning Form, the teacher can answer three important questions:

1. Does the student frequently exhibit negative expectation reactions?
2. To whom or to what are the negative reactions directed?
3. What are the stated reasons for the negative reactions?

By answering these questions, the teacher obtains information that is helpful in planning instruction. For example, if the student dislikes reading because she is embarrassed to read orally around others, the teacher may allow the student to record her reading on a tape recorder or read in a one-to-one situation with the teacher or a friend. Minor instructional adjustments often can result in increased student motivation, more efficient learning, and better student expectations.

Self-report activities are excellent ways to obtain information about a student's negative and positive expectations. Sentence completion is a popular self-report activity. For example:

1. I learn best when _____
   _____ .

2. I am really happy when _____
   _____ .

3. When I work hard, my teacher _____
   _____ .

4. My least favorite thing at school is _____
   _____ .

5. When I do not try, my teacher _____
   _____ .

Rating scales are another type of self-report that is used frequently. For example:

(a) I learn math quickly.	1 2 3 4 5	I do not seem to understand math.
(b) Classmates really like me.	1 2 3 4 5	Classmates do not like me much.
(c) I have a lot of friends.	1 2 3 4 5	I do not have many friends.

Teacher Expectations. Teachers develop perceptions of a student that, in turn, create certain expectations of the student. When the teacher expects and accepts less from the student than the student is capable of giving, the expectations may impede both learning progress and social development. Rosenthal

TABLE 2.3
Analysis of student learning form.
Part I: Expectation factors

	Key
	3 always happens
	2 frequently happens
	1 sometimes happens
	0 never happens

I. Learner Expectations
  A. Negative Expectation Reactions

Note reactions that are characterized by negative comments regarding one's own abilities, avoidance remarks, and comments which reflect the anticipation of failure or problems.

	3	2	1	0
1. Student comments about being dumb.	3	2	1	0
2. Student comments about hating certain subjects or activities.	3	2	1	0
3. Student comments about not being liked by peers.	3	2	1	0
4. Student comments about not being liked by teacher(s).	3	2	1	0
5. Student comments about anticipating failure on tests or seatwork.	3	2	1	0

  B. Target of Avoidance Reactions

By listening, interviewing, or observing the student, the teacher is able to ascertain the situations about which the student has negative expectations. The avoidance situation may be a person, place, or activity.

	3	2	1	0
1. Student complains about attending school in general.	3	2	1	0
2. Student complains about attending a certain class (_____).	3	2	1	0
3. Student complains about a specific teacher or other school person (_____).	3	2	1	0
4. Student complains about a specific academic subject (_____).	3	2	1	0
5. Student complains about physical education classes.	3	2	1	0
6. Student complains about extracurricular activities.	3	2	1	0
7. Student complains about certain peers (_____).	3	2	1	0
8. Student complains about riding the bus.	3	2	1	0
9. Student complains about a certain day (_____).	3	2	1	0

  C. Stated Reasons for Negative Reactions

	3	2	1	0
1. Student hates _____ because she has to: read, speak in class, wear gym clothes, turn in homework, sit next to the teacher, take notes, learn unimportant information, and so on.	3	2	1	0
2. Student claims the teacher always criticizes her.	3	2	1	0
3. The class or teacher is boring.	3	2	1	0
4. The class or teacher is too hard.	3	2	1	0
5. Student is always failing tests in _____.	3	2	1	0

TABLE 2.3
Continued

	Key 3 always happens 2 frequently happens 1 sometimes happens 0 never happens			

II. Teacher Expectations
A. Assignments

	3	2	1	0
1. Teacher assigns work that is too difficult or too easy.	3	2	1	0
2. Teacher assigns work just to keep the student busy.	3	2	1	0
3. Teacher makes negative or sarcastic remarks about the student's work ("John, do you think you'll ever do your work on time?").	3	2	1	0
4. Teacher grades the student's work hard (that is, teacher never gives the student a break).	3	2	1	0
5. Teacher expects the student to misbehave.	3	2	1	0
6. Teacher expects the student to do poorly on her work.	3	2	1	0

B. Interactions

	3	2	1	0
1. Teacher is quick to tell the student about a wrong response.	3	2	1	0
2. Teacher criticizes the student.	3	2	1	0
3. Teacher ridicules the student ("Are you sure you were listening, Sarah?").	3	2	1	0
4. Teacher makes accusations ("Who took the game dice, John?").	3	2	1	0
5. Teacher openly exhibits dislike for the student (for example, in the teachers' lounge or in the classroom).	3	2	1	0
6. Teacher makes negative predictions about the student's future ("He'll drop out of school").	3	2	1	0
7. Teacher does not encourage self-expression by the student.	3	2	1	0
8. Teacher has trouble listening to the student.	3	2	1	0

III. Peer Expectations
A. Social Patterns

	3	2	1	0
1. The student is an isolate.	3	2	1	0
2. The student is a leader.	3	2	1	0
3. Many peers criticize the student.	3	2	1	0
4. Peers tease the student.	3	2	1	0
5. Peers really like the student.	3	2	1	0
6. A certain group likes or dislikes the student.	3	2	1	0
7. Nobody appears to like the student.	3	2	1	0
8. One student especially dislikes the student (_____).	3	2	1	0
9. Peers view the student as dumb.	3	2	1	0
10. Peers view the student as smart.	3	2	1	0

(continued)

TABLE 2.3
Continued

B. Peer Values			
1. Aggressive inappropriate behavior is reinforced by peers.	3	2	1	0
2. The student has a skill that students value.	3	2	1	0
3. The student has knowledge that students value.	3	2	1	0
4. The student displays no apparent quality that peers value.	3	2	1	0

IV. Parental Expectations

A. Negative Expectations in Relation to School

1. Parents tell student not to worry about getting good grades.	3	2	1	0
2. Parents do not support the teacher in front of the student.	3	2	1	0
3. Parents openly complain about school in front of the student.	3	2	1	0
4. Parents reinforce (laugh, tell others) for misbehavior at school.	3	2	1	0
5. Parents do not encourage student to do homework.	3	2	1	0
6. Parents allow student to stay home from school when she is not sick.	3	2	1	0

B. Unrealistic Expectations

1. Parents select a vocational goal for the student which is not compatible with the student's interest or ability.	3	2	1	0
2. Parents always take away privileges for low grades.	3	2	1	0
3. Parents frequently insist that the student be placed in a higher reading or math group.	3	2	1	0
4. Parents insist that the student take courses not suited to her abilities or interests.	3	2	1	0

C. Too Low Expectations

1. Parents talk about how the child will never achieve.	3	2	1	0
2. Parents constantly make unfavorable statements about the child's future.	3	2	1	0
3. Parents constantly ask that the child be excused from activities.	3	2	1	0
4. Parents foster child dependency.	3	2	1	0
5. Parents do not encourage self-expression from the child.	3	2	1	0
6. Parents do not give the child responsibilities.	3	2	1	0
7. Parents do not challenge the child to participate in activities.	3	2	1	0

V. Summary of Expectation Factors

and Jacobson's (1966) work generated much interest in this phenomenon, and it frequently is referred to as the self-fulfilling prophecy. Brophy and Good (1974) report that "the idea that teacher expectations can function as self-fulfilling prophecies appears to be an established fact rather than a mere hypothesis" (p. 77).

Characteristics such as race, special education label, sex, appearance, and achievement level of older siblings have been shown to influence teacher expectations (Algozzine & Mercer, 1980). If a teacher expects inappropriate behavior or poor academic progress, she likely may get it. Fortunately, the reverse of this phenomenon holds much promise. Smith, Neisworth, and Greer (1978) affirm the importance of the teacher's influence.

> The teacher's attitude toward children and education determines to a very real degree how children perceive school, themselves, and each other—and how much progress they actually make. Teachers can make learning pleasant or punishing; they can create motivation or fear; they can produce excited anticipation or dread. A teacher's personal style and approach, more than anything else, create the climate and mood which will characterize the classroom. (p. 84)

Because of the influence of teacher expectations on the success of students, an assessment of how to teach must include an examination of teacher expectations. Section II of Table 2.3 presents several factors that deserve consideration in analyzing teacher expectations.

Peer Expectations.   Through daily interactions with classmates, students learn to view themselves as leaders, followers, fringers, or isolates (Archer & Edgar, 1976). Acceptance by peers helps students gain confidence and self-assurance which, in turn, foster better performance on academic tasks; peer rejection

can produce anxiety and self-doubt. Peer influence is a function of numerous factors including age, home stability, and socioeconomic level. Because elementary-age and younger students tend to value home and adult praise more than adolescents do, there is less peer influence with them than with adolescents (Mercer, 1992). Students from lower classes appear to be highly susceptible to peer influence (Tasseigne, 1975). Above all, the teacher must avoid contributing to one student's negative perception of another student. Archer and Edgar report that teachers must recognize student leaders and understand classroom alliances if they wish to promote a healthy social climate. Archer and Edgar also note that the teacher must be aware of peer values, especially those relating to academic achievement and social behavior. Once the social climate is ascertained, the teacher can use peer tutoring, modeling, role-playing, seat assignments, and the control of peer attention to promote peer expectations that foster the growth of an individual student or students.

Questionnaires on class norms and personal values as well as observations of student behavior provide useful information about peer values and class social patterns. Section III of Table 2.3 presents several factors of importance in analyzing peer expectations.

Parental Expectations.   Parental expectations can influence a student's academic and social growth. If a parent highly values and reinforces academic work, the student is likely to receive encouragement and praise from parents for doing homework and performing well in school. Parental support is often a key factor in maintaining a student's motivation and achievement. Positive parental expectations can be helpful in the development of the student; however, parental expectations that are negative, too high, or too low can be harmful to the student's academic and social development. The student who constantly must face living up to her parents' unrealistic expectations may begin to hate school and eventually may rebel against both the school and the parents. Also, the student may start getting in trouble to receive parental attention. If parents do not value academic achievement, the student does not receive much encouragement or praise from parents for doing schoolwork. In home situations in which fighting or goofing off in school is valued, the student receives encouragement for behavior that is directly opposed by the school.

Given the trend toward more parental involvement in the identification, placement, and educational programming of students with disabilities, school personnel must prepare themselves to work more closely and effectively with parents. The teacher must be sensitive to both helpful and harmful parental expectations. Helpful expectations should be encouraged, and harmful ones should be approached in a problem-solving manner. The common goal of optimal growth for the student frequently enables the teacher and parents to overcome obstacles and work cooperatively. Section IV of Table 2.3 presents several factors that deserve attention in assessing parental expectations.

Stimulus Events

Stimulus (or antecedent) events include an array of materials, instructional methods, and classroom settings that "set the stage" for the student to respond. Because the teacher controls or determines many of the stimulus events in the classroom, it is important to examine them to understand how students learn best. The teacher can observe the student, directly ask the student, or use questionnaires to gather information about individual preferences. Stimulus events can be sorted into the categories of (a) physical set-

ting; (b) instructional arrangements, techniques, and materials; and (c) learning style preferences.

Physical Setting. Section I of the Analysis of Student Learning Form, Part II (Table 2.4), presents variables of interest in analyzing the environmental conditions that affect a student's performance, both positively and negatively. Physical properties—noise, temperature, lighting, and spatial factors—can be manipulated to suit the student's learning preferences. In a survey of research on learning styles, Dunn, Beaudry, and Klavas (1989) found that from 10 to 40 percent of students, dependent upon age, gender, and achievement, exhibit learning preferences regarding quiet versus sound, bright or soft lighting, warm or cool temperatures, and formal versus informal setting designs. When choices are available, the student or the teacher can choose a setting suitable to the activity and individual preferences. For example, students who prefer bright lighting and cool temperatures may perform well next to the classroom windows and away from the heat ducts.

Instructional Arrangements, Techniques, and Materials. This area covers a wide range of stimulus events that dramatically affect learning (see Sections II, III, and IV of Table 2.4). For example, regarding instructional arrangements, Dunn et al. (1989) found that many students in third through eighth grade learned better in well-organized small groups than either alone or with the teacher. Students in eighth grade and above tended to learn better when they worked alone. Moreover, Dunn et al. report that in all classes examined there were students who preferred to learn by themselves, others who wished to work with peers, and others who liked working with the teacher. It is likely that these instructional arrangement preferences can be determined or managed by providing students with choices and then

TABLE 2.4
Analysis of student learning form.
Part II: Stimulus events

| | *Key*
3 always happens
2 frequently happens
1 sometimes happens
0 never happens | | | |

I. Physical Properties
   A. Noise

	3	2	1	0
1. The student likes to work in a quiet area.	3	2	1	0
2. The student likes to work with a little background noise.	3	2	1	0
3. Others talking distracts the student.	3	2	1	0
4. The student frequently asks the teacher to repeat directions or questions.	3	2	1	0

   B. Temperature

1. The student prefers cooler areas of the room (such as near a window).	3	2	1	0
2. The student prefers warmer areas of the room.	3	2	1	0
3. The student has difficulty adjusting to outside temperature changes (for example, develops colds, allergies).	3	2	1	0
4. The student has allergies which are sensitive to air quality (such as when the furnace is first turned on).	3	2	1	0

   C. Lighting

1. The student prefers well-lighted areas of the room (for example, near a window).	3	2	1	0
2. The student prefers darker areas of the room.	3	2	1	0
3. The student has trouble seeing the chalkboard or other areas of the room because of light reflections.	3	2	1	0

   D. General Physical Factors

1. The student likes to work in a lot of space (such as on a table top).	3	2	1	0
2. The student likes to work in close proximity to other students.	3	2	1	0
3. The student is distracted near windows, pencil sharpener, or sink.	3	2	1	0
4. The student likes to work in close proximity to the teacher.	3	2	1	0
5. The student likes to work in a carrel, corner, next to the wall, or beside a room divider.	3	2	1	0
6. The student is distracted by messy or cluttered areas.	3	2	1	0
7. The student prefers to work at: desk, library, table, learning center.	3	2	1	0

II. Instructional Arrangements

1. The student works well in a large group.	3	2	1	0
2. The student works well in a small group.	3	2	1	0
3. The student works well in a one-to-one situation with the teacher.	3	2	1	0

(continued)

TABLE 2.4
Continued

		Key 3 always happens 2 frequently happens 1 sometimes happens 0 never happens			

		3	2	1	0
4.	The student works well in peer tutoring situations as the tutor.	3	2	1	0
5.	The student works well in peer tutoring situations as the tutee.	3	2	1	0
6.	The student works well alone with seatwork.	3	2	1	0
7.	The student works well with small group on a project.	3	2	1	0
8.	The student works well with a teacher aide or volunteer.	3	2	1	0

III. Instructional Techniques

		3	2	1	0
1.	The student needs much demonstration of expected behavior.	3	2	1	0
2.	The student needs to be reminded of the value or importance of specific schoolwork.	3	2	1	0
3.	The student likes input regarding instruction (for example, game, material, time).	3	2	1	0
4.	The student needs simple written instructions.	3	2	1	0
5.	The student needs verbal directions to be simple and repeated.	3	2	1	0
6.	The student readily models the behavior of peers.	3	2	1	0
7.	The student readily models the behavior of the teacher.	3	2	1	0
8.	The student needs prompts and cues to maintain expected behaviors.	3	2	1	0
9.	The student needs much attention in learning new behaviors.	3	2	1	0
10.	The student likes working with equipment (such as tape recorder, Language Master, overhead projector).	3	2	1	0
11.	The student has low frustration tolerance for difficult seatwork.	3	2	1	0
12.	The student responds well when the teacher asks questions.	3	2	1	0
13.	The student needs her interest stimulated for drill or practice work.	3	2	1	
14.	The student works better with knowledge that work will be checked.	3	2	1	0
15.	The student needs a lot of time to complete her work.	3	2	1	0
16.	The student works best in: morning, afternoon.	3	2	1	0
17.	The student works slowly and inaccurately.	3	2	1	0
18.	The student does not perform well under timed conditions.	3	2	1	0
19.	The student enjoys working against a timer.	3	2	1	0
20.	The student enjoys charting correct and incorrect responses in 1-minute segments.	3	2	1	0
21.	In approaching a new task the student gives up easily.	3	2	1	0
22.	In approaching a new task the student becomes easily frustrated.	3	2	1	0
23.	In approaching a new task the student eagerly tries it.	3	2	1	0
24.	In approaching a new task the student tries to distract the teacher.	3	2	1	0

TABLE 2.4
Continued

	Key 3 always happens 2 frequently happens 1 sometimes happens 0 never happens			
25. In approaching a new task the student refuses to attempt it.	3	2	1	0
26. The student responds well to different academic materials or activities (specify _____).	3	2	1	0

IV. Materials

1. The student likes or needs self-correcting materials.	3	2	1	0
2. The student likes or needs instructional games using game boards.	3	2	1	0
3. The student likes or needs instructional games using cards.	3	2	1	0
4. The student dislikes worksheets.	3	2	1	0
5. The student needs worksheets with only a few items.	3	2	1	0
6. The student needs lots of writing space on worksheets.	3	2	1	0
7. The student needs visual cues on seatwork (such as arrows, green dots to note starting place, lines to show place for responses).	3	2	1	0
8. The student prefers commercial materials.	3	2	1	0
9. The student prefers teacher-made materials.	3	2	1	0
10. The student enjoys chalkboard activities.	3	2	1	0
11. The student responds well to manipulative materials (such as puppets in language, cubes and abacus in math, calculator in math or spelling).	3	2	1	0
12. The student enjoys doing work with flash cards.	3	2	1	0
13. The student enjoys making his own materials (such as flash cards, game boards, card decks).	3	2	1	0
14. The student enjoys working with computers.	3	2	1	0

V. Learning Style Preferences

A. Visual Preference Indicators

1. The student enjoys reading a book.	3	2	1	0
2. The student enjoys seeing a filmstrip.	3	2	1	0
3. The student enjoys looking at pictures.	3	2	1	0
4. The student enjoys looking at a movie.	3	2	1	0
5. The student enjoys playing a concentration game.	3	2	1	0
6. The student needs someone to demonstrate behavior.	3	2	1	0
7. The student remembers material from an overhead.	3	2	1	0
8. The student remembers what someone shows her.	3	2	1	0
9. The student remembers what is seen in a film.	3	2	1	0
10. The student remembers what she has written.	3	2	1	0

B. Auditory Preference Indicators

1. The student enjoys hearing a record.	3	2	1	0
2. The student enjoys hearing a tape.	3	2	1	0

(continued)

TABLE 2.4
Continued

	Key 3 always happens 2 frequently happens 1 sometimes happens 0 never happens			
3. The student enjoys hearing a story.	3	2	1	0
4. The student follows auditory directions.	3	2	1	0
5. The student remembers what the teacher says.	3	2	1	0
6. The student remembers what is heard on the radio.	3	2	1	0
7. The student likes talking to people.	3	2	1	0
8. The student listens to people well.	3	2	1	0
9. The student likes to study with friends.	3	2	1	0
C. Tactile Preference Indicators				
1. The student likes to draw.	3	2	1	0
2. The student likes to manipulate objects.	3	2	1	0
3. The student likes to trace things.	3	2	1	0
4. The student likes to work with clay or finger paints.	3	2	1	0
D. Kinesthetic Preference Indicators				
1. The student remembers material from motor activities.	3	2	1	0
2. The student remembers what she writes.	3	2	1	0
3. The student likes to play motor games.	3	2	1	0
4. The student likes to do experiments.	3	2	1	0
5. The student likes to take pictures.	3	2	1	0
6. The student likes to operate a tape recorder, typewriter, calculator, or other machines.	3	2	1	0
VI. Summary of Stimulus Events				

monitoring their progress in the different arrangements. Studies of underachievers, dropouts, at-risk students, and vocational education students reveal that as a group they are not morning people (Griggs & Dunn, 1988; Tappenden, 1983). For these groups, achievement improved when learning occurred during late morning or afternoon, or during the evening. Overall, Dunn et al. report that most students are not "early birds" and prefer learning in the late morning or afternoon.

Once the teacher identifies preferred instructional factors, the task of determining what to do is usually straightforward. For example, Smith et al. (1978) recommend that teachers provide special places for students to go for (a) isolation, (b) rest and quiet, (c) letting off steam, (d) rewarding themselves, (e) private instruction, (f) talking with the teacher, and (g) working alone or in a group. If a student learns well alone in the afternoon, the teacher can schedule those arrangements for the student. If a student is frustrated easily during seatwork or always wants feedback, the teacher can give the student self-correcting activities. If a student lacks interest, the teacher can remind the student of the importance of the skill or use instructional games. If a student writes slowly and needs a lot of mobility (physical activity), the teacher can provide larger spaces on worksheets to write answers or allow the student to work on a chalkboard.

Learning Style Preferences. Determining learning styles has received much attention, and assessing modality (form of sensation) preferences has been a key concern in this area. Diagnosticians and teachers usually administer various tests (such as *Learning Style Inventory, The Reading Style Inventory,* and *Detroit Tests of Learning Aptitudes—3*) to determine a student's learning style preferences and make instructional recommendations. If the student performs better in the visual modality, for example, instruction that stresses visually oriented materials and techniques is recommended. This strategy has been practiced in special education for years and now appears to be gaining momentum in regular education. Although the learning style approach has widespread use and intuitive appeal, it remains a highly controversial topic. It has not been supported in the educational psychology research (Cronbach & Snow, 1977; Miller, 1981), in the special education research (Arter & Jenkins, 1977; Kampwith & Bates, 1980; Kavale & Forness, 1987; Tarver & Dawson, 1978), or in the reading research (Snider, 1992). Other researchers (Brunner & Majewski, 1990; Dunn et al., 1989) claim the learning style approach has substantial support. For detailed coverage regarding the learning style controversy, see the following journal issues: *Educational Leadership,* October 1990; *Exceptional Children,* January 1990; and *Remedial and Special Education,* January/February 1992).

It appears that educators should not rely heavily on tests for determining learning style strengths and weaknesses. Using informal measures, the teacher may discover both a student's learning style preference and the conditions under which the preference exists—that is, it may depend upon the particular task. For example, Stephens (1977) uses a criterion-referenced approach to modality assessment. Table 2.5 shows how Stephens used classroom tasks to assess modality strengths and weaknesses.

Using a probe format, Koenig and Kunzelmann (1980) developed an instrument titled *Classroom Learning Screening.* This instrument is designed for preschool through sixth grade and include readiness, math, and reading skill probes. At each grade level, three learning channel combinations are assessed: see—write, hear—write, and see—say. The see—write channel includes only math skills (for example, see multiplication facts through times 9—write answers), and the hear—write and see—say channels include only reading skills (for example, hear word—write word; see word—say word). Koenig and Kunzelmann state that most reading and math learning occurs in these three channel combinations. Once the examiner determines an appropriate difficulty level—a probe on which the student initially performs between 10 and 80 correct per minute—each of the three learning channel probes is administered for several days. The results are analyzed for channel strengths and weaknesses.

As illustrated by Stephens (1977) and Koenig and Kunzelmann (1980), the practice of examining modality preferences by using classroom tasks can render useful information in determining how a student learns. Section V of Table 2.4 presents some factors that may point to a student's modality preferences. If a modality strength or weakness is suspected, classroom observations can validate or refute the suspicion. However, if a student has a visual learning problem, for example, it does not necessarily mean that an auditory strength exists.

Response Factors

Tasks usually require students to make a motor or verbal response, or both. Selecting the

TABLE 2.5
Summary of modality assessment.

	Sense / Skill	Stimulus	Criterion Score	Performance Score	Analysis Code
AUDITORY	Discrimination	20 pairs of similar words read aloud	18/20	20	+
	Immediate Recall	Read primer story and answered 4 questions	4	4	0
	Delayed Recall	Referred to—five days later previous story	4	4	0
VISUAL	Discrimination	10 pairs of words	9/10	9	0
		10 picture words identifications	9/10	9	0
	Immediate Recall	5 tests of removing different letters	4/5	4	0
		Study 4 words and then identify correct spelling	4	3	—
	Delayed Recall	4 words repeated in 45 minutes	4	3	—
HAPTIC	Discrimination	Recognize 10 upper-case letters by touch only	9/10	4	—
		Recognize 8 lower-case letters	7/8	5	—
	Immediate Recall	Identify 8 lower-case letters	7/8	6	—
	Delayed Recall	45 minutes later	7/8	5	—

Note. 0 = at criterion; — = below; + = above.

Source: From *Teaching Skills to Children with Learning and Behavior Disorders* (p. 193) by T. M. Stephens, 1977, Columbus, OH: Merrill. Copyright 1977 by Bell & Howell Company. Reprinted by permission.

type of response (such as pointing, making gestures, or writing) for an instructional activity can be crucial in designing instruction for a student. Some students function better if the response requires extensive motor involvement (for example, write numerals, connect dots, push button, operate tape recorder, color items, arrange items on a feltboard); others function better with simple verbal responses (yes, no). Speed of responding also deserves attention. If a student writes numerals slowly or talks rapidly without thinking, these response tendencies need to be considered in planning instruction. A long delay between the presentation of a task and a response may relate to several factors (for example, task is too difficult, there is lack of attention to the task or low interest in the task, or the student is seeking teacher attention). A short delay with correct responses may indicate that the student has mastered the task, whereas a short delay with incorrect responses may suggest that the student is responding without thinking, not trying, racing others, or seeking attention.

The organization of the response in a logical manner also should be noted. Some responses require concept ordering (for example, following steps in solving a problem or discussing concepts from smallest to largest), whereas others require language ordering (for example, the organization of several thoughts with supportive statements). Many students with learning problems need assistance in organizing responses. Some responses do not appear to have a relationship to the question or involve interpreting the question in a way that relates to different cultural experiences. Asking the student to explain a unique response often provides the teacher with insights about student experiences, interests, or concerns.

Finally, it may be helpful to note the student's reaction when the correct answer in not known. Some students become frustrated quickly and react with anger or apathy, whereas others make derogatory comments about themselves or stop trying. Also, the student may not be attending to instructions. Thus, it is helpful to listen to the questions and comments of students. The Analysis of Student Learning Form, Part III (Table 2.6), presents several factors of importance in analyzing response preferences.

Subsequent Events

Consequences greatly influence behavior and can be used to motivate students and manage their behavior. Social praise, special activities and privileges, evaluation marks, positive physical expression, awards, tokens, and tangible objects are some positive consequences frequently used to reinforce—and therefore influence—student behavior. The teacher has many ways of determining what reinforces a student. The teacher simply can ask the student

or note free-time preferences for activities or objects. Some teachers use a reinforcement "menu," featuring a variety of consequences from which the student chooses a favorite item or activity.

To use consequent events most effectively, the teacher must consider timing, amount, and ratio of reinforcement. Some students need immediate reinforcement to maintain a behavior; others can tolerate a delay in reinforcement without decreasing the occurrence of the behavior. Also, some students require a great deal of reinforcement only for certain changes. For example, when the teacher is attempting to establish a new behavior, much reinforcement may be needed. As the learning proceeds, reinforcement may be reduced. The Analysis of Student Learning Form, Part IV (Table 2.7), features numerous variables that are important in assessing subsequent events.

The Analysis of Student Learning Profile

Expectation factors, stimulus events, response factors, and subsequent events must be weighed in relation to one another in planning instruction. It is necessary to consider all four factors together to form instructional strategies that best facilitate learning. After each section of the Analysis of Student Learning Form has been completed, a profile may be written. The profile can display numerous patterns and supply a simple list of do's and don'ts for designing an individual program. Table 2.8 presents a learning profile and treatment plan.

The Analysis of Student Learning Form is useful primarily for guiding teacher observations in the different assessment areas. An instructional plan based on an assessment for determining how to teach should be viewed as a "guesstimate." When the right variables are manipulated appropriately, the plan is effective; however, when the assessment is incorrect, adjustments are needed in the plan. All

TABLE 2.6
Analysis of student learning form.
Part III: Response factors

	Key 3 always happens 2 frequently happens 1 sometimes happens 0 never happens			
I. Verbal				
1. The student likes simple one-word responses (such as yes, no).	3	2	1	0
2. The student likes simple sentences.	3	2	1	0
3. The student likes brief discussions.	3	2	1	0
4. The student likes extensive dialogue.	3	2	1	0
5. The student likes fast responding.	3	2	1	0
II. Verbal-Motor				
1. The student likes to verbalize her response while touching the item.	3	2	1	0
2. The student likes to operate hardware while verbalizing.	3	2	1	0
3. The student likes to write and say her response.	3	2	1	0
4. The student likes to sing and clap.	3	2	1	0
5. The student likes to operate hand puppets.	3	2	1	0
III. Motor				
1. The student likes to respond by pointing.	3	2	1	0
2. The student uses manuscript writing.	3	2	1	0
3. The student uses cursive writing.	3	2	1	0
4. The student writes numbers.	3	2	1	0
5. The student can trace.	3	2	1	0
6. The student copies work from a near position.	3	2	1	0
7. The student copies work from a far position.	3	2	1	0
8. The student likes to use gross motor skills.	3	2	1	0
9. The student likes to use fine motor skills.	3	2	1	0
10. The student uses a pencil holder.	3	2	1	0
11. The student writes slowly and sloppily.	3	2	1	0
12. The student writes slowly and neatly.	3	2	1	0
13. The student writes quickly and sloppily.	3	2	1	0
14. The student writes quickly and neatly.	3	2	1	0
15. The student writes too big for the space allowed.	3	2	1	0
16. The student exhibits speech problems.	3	2	1	0
17. The student perseverates with a motor response.	3	2	1	0
18. The student perseverates with a verbal response.	3	2	1	0
19. The student has physical abnormalities that interfere with writing or speaking.	3	2	1	0
IV. Summary of Response Types _____				

TABLE 2.7
Analysis of student learning form.
Part IV: Subsequent events

	Key
	3 always happens
	2 frequently happens
	1 sometimes happens
	0 never happens

I. Verbal Praise				
1. The student likes one-word praises.	3	2	1	0
2. The student likes phrase praises.	3	2	1	0
3. The student likes extensive "talk" praises.	3	2	1	0
4. The student likes humor.	3	2	1	0
II. Physical Approval				
1. The student likes a smile or gesture (such as thumbs up, wink).	3	2	1	0
2. The student likes a touch.	3	2	1	0
3. The student likes a hug.	3	2	1	0
4. The student likes a handshake.	3	2	1	0
III. Evaluation Events				
1. The student likes immediate feedback.	3	2	1	0
2. The student has difficulty with feedback on incorrect responses from the teacher.	3	2	1	0
3. The student has difficulty with feedback on incorrect responses from peers.	3	2	1	0
4. The student has difficulty with feedback on incorrect responses from the material.	3	2	1	0
5. The student likes feedback on correct responses from peers.	3	2	1	0
6. The student likes feedback on correct responses from the material.	3	2	1	
7. The student needs "sensitive" feedback when incorrect (for example, "You're almost right. Let's do it together.").	3	2	1	0
8. The student likes evaluation marks: A 1, happy face, stars, checks, number correct, letter grade, rubber stamp.	3	2	1	0
9. The student likes awards: happy grams, report cards, citations.	3	2	1	0
10. The student likes tangible items: trinket, candy, cookie, sugar pop, toy.	3	2	1	0
11. The student likes token rewards: points, chips, check marks, tickets.	3	2	1	0

IV. Summary of Subsequent Events _____
_____
_____

TABLE 2.8
Learning profile and treatment plan.

Assessment area and findings	Treatment
Learner Expectations	
Thinks teacher dislikes him	Ask for a favor once a day, or ask the student a personal interest question each day (for example, "Did you like that football game?").
Senses defeat in reading	Pair reinforcement with effort in reading.
Teacher Expectations	
Assigns work that is too difficult in reading	Provide realistic successes in reading.
Tends to pick on student	Use sensitive responses to incorrect responses.
Peer Expectations	
Is with peers who do not value reading	Seat student near peers who value reading.
Is liked and respected by peers	Use peer teaching with student being tutor or tutee.
Parental Expectations	
Is pushed by parents to work hard	Tell parents not to tutor unless it is a pleasant experience.
Has concerned and cooperative parents	Encourage parents to praise effort as well as correct product.
Physical Properties	
Is allergic to dust	Seat student away from chalk trays.
Prefers cooler areas of room	Allow student to work away from furnace ducts.
Prefers well-lighted areas	Seat student near a window.
Likes to work near other students	Assign work at a table with students who work hard.
Instructional Arrangements	
Dislikes one-on-one with teacher	Make one-to-one instruction pleasant.
Enjoys small-group activities	Use small-group instruction.
Instructional Techniques	
Gets bored with same task	Practice academic skills via tape recorder, instructional games, self-correcting materials, and computer software.
Has low frustration tolerance in reading	Allow student to practice reading on tape recorder before reading orally to the teacher.
Works slowly	Let student work against a timer.
Needs prompts and cues to maintain behavior.	Use contingency contracts with a variety of activities.
Instructional Materials	
Dislikes reading worksheets	Use language experience approach in reading.
Likes games	Use instructional games.
Likes worksheets with only a few items	Use worksheets that are partially completed.
Dislikes cluttered worksheets or materials	Use Language Master or tape recorder.

TABLE 2.8
Continued

Assessment area and findings	Treatment
Learning Style Preferences	
Responds well in all modalities	Present tasks in various modalities.
Response Factors	
Writes slowly and sloppily	Encourage use of a plastic pencil holder.
Prefers short verbal responses coupled with simple motor responses	Use point-and-say responses.
Writes too big for space allowed	Give a lot of room for writing on worksheets or use chalkboard for writing.
Subsequent Events	
Does not respond to one-word praises but enjoys smiles and handshakes	Follow good effort with a smile, touch, and encouraging phrase.
Requests immediate feedback	Use answer keys, peer feedback, and self-correcting materials.
Likes high letter grades	Write big letters grades on good work.
Has difficulty with feedback on incorrect items	Use a variety of sensitive responses for incorrect work.

treatment plans should be monitored closely to ensure their efficacy and the student's progress. Thus, assessment for determining how to teach is similar to assessment for determining what to teach in that both are ongoing processes.

Conclusion

Efforts should be made to provide a systematic assessment of learning environments. *The Instructional Environment Scale (TIES)* (Ysseldyke & Christenson, 1987) provides educators with an assessment device for evaluating and obtaining information about an individual student's instructional environment. The environment is examined across factors that are considered to be related to instructional outcomes for students. Ysseldyke and Christenson note that *TIES* can be used to describe the extent to which a student's academic or behavior problems are related to factors in the instructional environment as well as to identify starting points in designing appropriate instructional interventions for individual students. This type of assessment provides educators with a systematic procedure for examining factors that facilitate planning how to teach.

Mercer and Corbett (1991) provide a powerful example of how an educator used observations to assess expectation, response, and reinforcement factors that related to how to teach an individual student. An educational diagnostician was asked to test a 13-year-old student, Stephanie, who was being seen in a hospital-based pediatric clinic. When he arrived to test, he discovered that Stephanie's folder had been misplaced. So, he proceeded to test her without the benefit of background information. In the very beginning of the testing session, Stephanie worked intensely. As testing continued, she lowered her head and mumbled incorrect answers. When the examiner asked if she was okay, she did not respond. Through continued efforts to talk with Stephanie, he realized that she stopped trying when the test items became difficult. He explained that the tests covered material through the twelfth grade and that it was expected for her to miss some items. He asked her to try to do her best, and he mentioned that they would take a refreshment break periodically throughout the testing. Stephanie liked the idea of taking breaks and promised to do her best. When Stephanie's test results were scored, she achieved average or above average scores in reading, math, and spelling.

Several days later, the examiner was asked to present the test results at a staffing conference. Much to the examiner's dismay, the pediatrician, the psychologist, and the language clinician reported that Stephanie performed at a very low level. In fact, they agreed that she was "trainable mentally retarded" with a full scale IQ of 37. Furthermore, they noted that she had been in a special class for students with mental disabilities for approximately eight years. When the educational diagnostician presented Stephanie's scores, he reported average or above average scores of a 13-year-old individual. The team was puzzled with the results, but discussions revealed that Stephanie had lowered her head and mumbled incorrect responses throughout the testing sessions with all of the team members except the educator. It was agreed that the student's scores in the educational testing were the most valid, and the team recommended that she be placed in a regular education class with some temporary support services. Stephanie made appropriate progress in the regular education setting.

In this example, the observations (such as lowering her head, mumbling incorrect responses) led the examiner to hypothesize that Stephanie stopped trying when item difficulty increased. Through discussion with her, the examiner determined that his hypothesis ap-

peared accurate. Student-examiner interactions led to the student agreeing to do her best on all items. The data documented that Stephanie's academic achievements were average or above average. Due to the examiner's ability to obtain and apply qualitative and quantitative information, Stephanie's performance and life improved dramatically. Thus, through interaction with the participant, the examiner was able to make adaptations during assessment that led to significant changes in the educational life of the student.

REFERENCES

Alberto, P. A., & Troutman, A. C. (1990). *Applied behavior analysis for teachers.* (3rd ed.). Columbus, OH: Merrill

Algozzine, B., & Mercer, C. D. (1980). Labels and expectancies for handicapped children and youth. In L. Mann & D. A. Sabatino (Eds.), *The fourth review of special education* (pp. 287–313). New York: Grune & Stratton.

Archer, A., & Edgar, E. (1976). Teaching academic skills to mildly handicapped children. In S. Lowenbraun & J. Q. Affleck (Eds.), *Teaching mildly handicapped children in regular classes* (pp. 15–112). Columbus, OH: Merrill.

Arter, J. A., & Jenkins, J. R. (1977). Examining the benefits and prevalence of modality considerations in special education. *The Journal of Special Education, 11*(3), 281–297.

Blankenship, C., & Lilly, M. S. (1981). *Mainstreaming students with learning and behavior problems: Techniques for the classroom teacher.* New York: Holt, Rinehart & Winston.

Bohannon, R. (1975). *Direct and daily measurement procedures in the identification and treatment of reading behaviors of children in special education.* Unpublished doctoral dissertation, University of Washington, Seattle.

Brophy, J. E., & Good, T. L. (1974). *Teacher-student relationships.* New York: Holt, Rinehart & Winston.

Brunner, C. E., & Majewski, W. S. (1990). Mildly handicapped students can succeed with learning styles. *Educational Leadership, 48*(2), 21–23.

Cronbach, L. J., & Snow, R. E. (1977). *Aptitudes and instructional methods: A handbook for research on interaction.* New York: Irvington.

Deno, S. L. (1987). Curriculum-based measurement. *Teaching Exceptional Children, 20*(1), 41–42.

Deno, S. L., & Mirkin, P. K. (1977). *Data-based program modification.* Reston, VA: Council for Exceptional Children.

Dunn, R., Beaudry, J. S., & Klavas, A. (1989). Survey of research on learning styles. *Educational Leadership, 46*(6), 50–58.

Frank, A. R. (1973). Breaking down learning tasks: A sequence approach. *Teaching Exceptional Children, 6,* 16–29.

Fuchs, L. S. (1986). Monitoring progress among mildly handicapped pupils: Review of current practice and research. *Remedial and Special Education, 7*(5), 5–12.

Fuchs, L. S., Bahr, C. M., & Rieth, H. J. (1989). Effects of goal structures and performance contingencies on the math performance of adolescents with learning disabilities. *Journal of Learning Disabilities, 22,* 554–560.

Fuchs, L. S., & Fuchs, D. (1986). Effects of systematic formative evaluation: A meta-analysis. *Exceptional Children, 53,* 199–208.

Fuchs, L. S., Fuchs, D., & Deno, S. L. (1985). The importance of goal ambitiousness and goal mastery to student achievement. *Exceptional Children, 52,* 63–71.

Fuchs, L. S., Fuchs, D., & Hamlett, C. L. (1989). Effects of instrumental use of curriculum-based measurement to enhance instructional programs. *Remedial and Special Education, 10*(2), 43–52.

Fuchs, L. S., Fuchs, D., & Maxwell, L. (1988). The validity of informal reading comprehension measures. *Remedial and Special Education, 9*(2), 20–28.

Fuchs, L. S., Wesson, C., Tindal, G., Mirkin, P., & Deno, S. (1981). *Teacher efficiency in continuous evaluation of IEP goals* (Research Report No. 53). Minneapolis: University of Minnesota Institute for Research in Learning Disabilities.

Griggs, S. A., & Dunn, R. (1988). High school dropouts: Do they learn differently from those who remain in school? *The Principal, 35*(1), 1–8.

Hall, T., & Tindal, G. (1989). Using curriculum-based measures to group students in reading. In G. Tindal, K. Essick, C. Skeen, N. George, & M. George (Eds.), *The Oregon Conference '89: Monograph.* Eugene: University of Oregon College of Education.

Haring, N. G. (1978). Research in the classroom: Problems and procedures. In N. G. Haring, T. C. Lovitt, M. D. Eaton, & C. L. Hansen, *The fourth R: Research in the classroom* (pp. 1–22). New York: Merrill/Macmillan.

Howell, K. W., Kaplan, J. S., & O'Connell, C. Y. (1979). *Evaluating exceptional children: A task analysis approach.* New York: Merrill/Macmillan.

Ivarie, J. J. (1986). Effects of proficiency rates on later performance of a recall and writing behavior. *Remedial and Special Education, 7*(5), 25–30.

Kampwith, T. J., & Bates, M. (1980). Modality preference and teaching method: A review of research. *Academic Therapy, 15,* 597–605.

Kavale, K. A., & Forness, S. R. (1987). Substance over style: Assessing the efficacy of modality testing and teaching. *Exceptional Children, 54,* 228–239.

Kerr, M. M., & Nelson, C. M. (1989). *Strategies for managing behavior problems in the classroom* (2nd ed.). New York: Merrill/Macmillan.

Koenig, C. H., & Kunzelmann, H. P. (1980). *Classroom learning screening manual.* San Antonio, TX: Psychological Corporation.

Lindsley, O. R. (1964). Direct measurement and prosthesis of retarded behavior. *Journal of Education, 147,* 62.

Lindsley, O. R. (1971). Precision teaching in perspective: An interview with Ogden R. Lindsley. *Teaching Exceptional Children, 3*(3), 114–119.

Lovitt, T. C. (1984). *Tactics for teaching.* New York: Merrill/Macmillan.

Mager, R. F. (1975). *Preparing instructional objectives* (2nd ed.). Belmont, CA: Fearon.

Mercer, C. D. (1992). *Students with learning disabilities* (4th ed.). New York: Merrill/Macmillan.

Mercer, C. D., & Corbett, N. L. (1991). Enhancing assessment for students at risk for school failure. *Contemporary Education, 62,* 259–265.

Mercer, C. D., Mercer, A. R., & Evans, S. (1982). The use of frequency in establishing instructional aims. *Journal of Precision Teaching, 3*(3), 57–63.

Miller, A. (1981). Conceptual matching models and interactional research in education. *Review of Educational Research, 51*, 33–84.

Mirkin, P., Deno, S., Tindal, G., & Kuehnle, K. (1979). *Formative evaluation: Continued development of data utilization systems* (Research Report No. 23). Minneapolis: University of Minnesota Institute for Research in Learning Disabilities.

Paulson, F. L., Paulson, P. R., & Meyer, C. A. (1991). What makes a portfolio a portfolio? *Educational Leadership, 48*(5), 60–63.

Rieth, H., & Evertson, C. (1988). Variables related to the effective instruction of difficult-to-teach children. *Focus on Exceptional Children, 20*(5), 1–8.

Rosenthal, R., & Jacobson, L. (1966). Teachers' expectancies: Determinants of pupils' IQ gains. *Psychological Reports, 19*(1), 115–118.

Salvia, J., & Ysseldyke, J. E. (1991). *Assessment in special and remedial education* (5th ed.). Boston: Houghton Mifflin.

Smith, R. M., Neisworth, J. T., & Greer, J. G. (1978). *Evaluating educational environments.* Columbus, OH: Merrill.

Snider, V. E. (1992). Learning styles and learning to read: A critique. *Remedial and Special Education, 13*, 6–18.

Stephens, T. M. (1977). *Teaching skills to children with learning and behavior disorders.* New York: Merrill/Macmillan.

Stiggins, R. J. (1985). Improving assessment where it means the most: In the classroom. *Educational Leadership, 43*(2), 69–74.

Tappenden, V. J. (1983). Analysis of the learning styles of vocational education and nonvocational education students in eleventh and twelfth grades from rural, urban, and suburban locations in Ohio. *Dissertation Abstracts International, 44*, 1326a.

Tarver, S. G., & Dawson, M. M. (1978). Modality preference and the teaching of reading: A review. *Journal of Learning Disabilities, 11*, 17–29.

Tasseigne, M. W. (1975). A study of peer and adult influence on moral beliefs of adolescents. *Adolescence, 10*, 227–230.

Tindal, G. A., & Marston, D. B. (1990). *Classroom-based assessment: Evaluating instructional outcomes.* New York: Merrill/Macmillan.

Valencia, S. (1990). A portfolio approach to classroom reading assessment: The whys, whats, and hows. *The Reading Teacher, 43*, 338–340.

Wesson, C. L. (1987). Increasing efficiency. *Teaching Exceptional Children, 20*(1), 46–47.

Wesson, C. L., King, R. P., & Deno, S. L. (1984). Direct and frequent measurement of student performance: If it's good for us, why don't we do it? *Learning Disability Quarterly, 7*, 45–48.

White, O. R. (1986). Precision teaching—Precision learning. *Exceptional Children, 52*, 522–534.

White, O. R., & Haring, N. G. (1980). *Exceptional teaching* (2nd ed.). New York: Merrill/Macmillan.

Wolf, D. P. (1989). Portfolio assessment: Sampling student work. *Educational Leadership, 46*(7), 35–39.

Ysseldyke, J. E., & Algozzine, B. (1990). *Introduction to special education* (2nd ed.). Boston: Houghton Mifflin.

Ysseldyke, J. E., & Christenson, S. L. (1987). *The Instructional Environment Scale: A comprehensive methodology for assessing an individual student's instruction.* Austin, TX: Pro-Ed.

CHAPTER 3

Planning and Managing Instruction

When a lesson maintains student attention and participation and proceeds smoothly without interruptions, digressions, and diversions, a primary factor in its success usually is careful planning. It is apparent that effective teaching and classroom management do not just happen but require relevant planning. Given the importance of teacher planning, it is imperative that teachers receive recognition and support for planning activities. More information is needed about teacher planning to help educators and administrators prepare and support teachers. In a report on teacher planning, Lenz, Deshler, and Schumaker (1990) provide some helpful information about teacher planning:

1. Teachers are provided an average of one period per day (mean time is 49 minutes) for planning.
2. The time that teachers spend planning after school hours varies greatly across teachers. The average amount of planning time is 76 minutes.
3. The average time teachers spend planning during the summer is 59 hours.
4. In planning for academically diverse classes, teachers focus on developing interesting activities that are motivating and encourage student involvement. Many teachers report that their most productive planning occurs in unstructured settings (for example, driving a car, walking the dog, taking a shower). Teachers generally agree that during-school planning involves "top structure" planning (that is, scheduling, determining class structure, responding to administrative tasks), whereas "deep structure" planning (how to clarify a difficult concept or develop a motivating activity) is accomplished away from school.
5. Teachers report that the biggest obstacles to planning for an academically diverse class are (a) insufficient time, (b) lack of opportunity to develop or discover motivating and ability-appropriate materials and activities, and (c) lack of knowledge concerning students' abilities and academic history.

In organizing an instructional planning strategy, the teacher should consider several questions:

1. *What is going to be taught to each student?* This question involves procedures needed to establish and maintain an instructional match between student abilities, characteristics, and learning tasks. Planning in this area primarily involves assessment practices discussed in Chapter 2.
2. *What curriculum design and instructional materials are going to be used?* This question addresses the type of curriculum design (such as direct instruction, learning strategies, multisensory) that the teacher plans to implement. Moreover, it involves the selection of commercial and teacher-made materials. Curriculum considerations, teaching strategies, and instructional materials are featured in Chapter 4 and in each of the curriculum area chapters throughout the text.
3. *What rules and procedures are needed to establish expectations and maintain classroom routines?* This question refers to the classroom rules that are needed to ensure that students maintain a high level of academic engagement and that instruction proceeds in an orderly and productive manner. It also relates to procedures that are needed for clarifying and teaching expectations. Finally, it addresses the need to teach students appropriate behaviors so classroom routines such as lining up for lunch, passing out papers, going to reading groups, and completing seatwork are conducted efficiently. These topics are discussed later in this chapter and in Chapter 5.

4. *Where will instruction occur?* This question relates to areas in the classroom and school where instructional activities happen. The physical arrangements of the room are important when planning the location of instruction. Physical arrangements are presented later in this chapter.

5. *When will instruction occur?* This question involves scheduling. When scheduling, the teacher must plan for transition activities (for example, changing from reading to math or from small-group work to seatwork) and for students completing assignments at different rates. Scheduling is presented later in this chapter.

CLASSROOM RULES

Because it is not possible for the teacher to conduct quality instruction or for students to work productively without guidelines for behavior and procedures, all effectively managed classrooms have rules and procedures. Rules and procedures help students function in the complex social and emotional environment of the classroom. Classroom rules are essential for establishing the expected behaviors of students and the teacher. Rules help structure the learning environment and provide students with guidelines to follow, and they offer the teacher a framework for reinforcing behaviors.

Rule Guidelines

Numerous educators (Emmer, Evertson, Sanford, Clements, & Worsham, 1989; Sprick, 1981) offer guidelines for planning and establishing rules for classrooms:

1. Select the minimum number of rules. It is difficult to remember and enforce a large number of rules. Usually four to six rules are sufficient for operating a classroom ef-ficiently. Some suggested rules for primary students are:
   a. Always try your best.
   b. Raise your hand to say something.
   c. Get along with your classmates.
   d. Work quietly during seatwork.
   e. Listen when the teacher or someone else is talking.

   Sample rules for older students include:
   a. Bring essential materials to class.
   b. Be in your seat and ready to work when the bell rings.
   c. Respect and be polite to others.
   d. Be quiet and stay seated when someone is talking.
   e. Respect the property of other people.
   f. Obey all school rules.

2. State the rules positively. Negatively stated or "don't" rules imply that the teacher expects students to misbehave. Moreover, a positively stated rule automatically excludes many misbehaviors and includes many desired behaviors. For example, the rule "Respect and be polite to others" excludes numerous misbehaviors (such as teasing, name calling, butting in line, hitting classmates) and includes many appropriate behaviors (for example, sharing materials, saying thank you, saying please, talking quietly). Positively stated rules provide nonthreatening, assertive expectations without making the teacher appear to be a dictator.

3. Determine consistent consequences for rule fulfillment or infraction (for example, students who obey rules earn free time, and students who break rules lose recess time). The consequences for obeying and breaking rules should be understood by all classmates. Rules without consequences have little effect on behavior; thus, consistent teacher follow-through is critical. Also,

rules and their consequences should be applied in an equitable manner, and bending the rules for specific students or situations should be avoided.

4. Tailor rules to individual classroom goals (for example, wanting students to work independently) and to individual teaching styles (such as allowing a certain level of noise during seatwork).

5. Include school rules within class rules. This reminds students that school rules apply in the classroom.

The presentation of rules should be done as soon as possible after the teacher is responsible for a new group of students. Rule presentations usually begin with a group discussion concerning the need for rules. This discussion helps students see the need for rules, feel some ownership of the rules, and assume responsibility for their own behavior. Student involvement often is promoted by the teacher soliciting reasons for having rules and why particular rules are important. Typical student responses may include that rules protect individual and group rights, prevent violence, and permit normal activities to take place. After this general discussion, the rules are presented one at a time. The following guidelines are helpful in presenting specific rules:

1. Present each rule and discuss why it is important. The teacher may solicit discussions from the students regarding the usefulness and importance of each rule.

2. Clarify each rule and the expected behaviors associated with it. The teacher should give and recognize examples and non-examples of behaviors associated with each rule. The teacher may model behaviors associated with the rule and ask students to demonstrate appropriate rule-based behaviors.

3. Once a rule has been presented and discussed, immediately begin to reinforce students for appropriate rule-based behaviors (for example, "I liked the way you raised your hand when you wanted to say something").

4. Discuss the consequences for breaking the rules. For example, initial failure to obey rules may result in the teacher ignoring the student until the rules are followed. Continued misbehavior may result in loss of recess time.

Teaching Behavioral Expectations for Rules and Classroom Routines

Generally it takes the teacher from 1 to 2 weeks to communicate the behavioral expectations for rules and classroom routines. During these beginning weeks, the teacher should teach the student what is expected in performing classroom routines. These routines occur frequently, and appropriate behaviors should be established as quickly as possible. Teaching these routines involves establishing appropriate behaviors during classroom routines such as checking attendance, arriving late to class, leaving the room as a group or individually, bringing materials to class, using the pencil sharpener, participating in group discussions, completing seatwork, making transitions (changing from one content area to another, moving from small groups to individual work, getting ready for lunch), performing peer tutoring, using classroom equipment, turning in seatwork and homework, and responding to classroom interruptions. Teachers and classrooms are unique, and each teacher must clarify behavioral expectations for numerous situations; for example: What is expected during seatwork? Is talking allowed? What is expected during whole class discussions? What do students do to get teacher help? What are the procedures for making transitions from one activity to another (such as from lunch to academic work)? These activities occur a multitude of times during a school day, and explicitly teaching students what is expected saves the teacher many hours of corrective feedback during the school year.

For teaching the appropriate behavior regarding rules and routines, it is helpful to use the following direct instruction teaching format:

1. *Use an advance organizer.* In this step the teacher links the lesson to previous discussions about rules and reminds the students of the needs for rules and routines. The teacher notes that rules and routines ensure the rights of students and the maintenance of a productive environment. Next, the teacher introduces a specific behavioral expectation (such as, "Raise your hand if you have something to say") or a class of behavioral expectations associated with a routine (for example, making the transition from reading to math activities). Finally, the teacher and students briefly discuss the rationale for the behavioral expectations of the lesson.

2. *Describe the behavioral expectations.* In this step the teacher explicitly describes the specific behaviors required to perform the target activity appropriately. For example, in presenting how to make the transition from seatwork to small-group reading, the teacher describes the steps (for example, get reading materials out of your desk, stand up and quietly push your chair under your desk, walk to your reading group quietly without disturbing your classmates, quietly pull out your chair at the reading table, be seated, and quietly wait for the teacher to begin reading). Some teachers help students remember the behaviors by using mnemonics. In teaching behavioral

expectations for teacher lectures, the SLANT mnemonic is useful:

S—*Sit* up straight.

L—*Lean* forward in your desk.

A—*Act* interested.

N—*Nod* occasionally to signal understanding.

T—*Track* the teacher with your eyes.

3. *Demonstrate the behavioral expectations.* In this step the teacher models the behaviors. For example, in teaching the routine of making a transition from seatwork to small-group reading, the teacher performs each behavioral activity while talking aloud about it. A good technique for demonstrating the behavior is for the teacher to ask himself a question and then answer it: "What's the first thing I need to do to get ready for reading group? Let's see, I need to get my reading materials together." Then the teacher gets each material while talking about it: "I need my reading book, a pencil, and some paper."

4. *Conduct guided practice with feedback.* In this step the teacher instructs the students to model a target behavior (for example, raising hand, using quiet voices) or a class of behaviors within a routine (such as going to a reading group). When the students exhibit the behaviors, the teacher provides positive and corrective feedback.

5. *Conduct independent practice with feedback.* In this step the students perform the behavior(s) per instructions without models, cues, or prompts, and the teacher provides positive praise for correct procedures and gentle verbal corrections for incorrect behaviors. It is helpful to tell the students how the activity or routine should proceed prior to the event. At the conclusion of a routine or activity, the teacher tells the stu-

dents how well they performed: "You did a great job of making transitions to reading groups today. I'm so proud of you."

6. *Maintain behavioral expectations.* Once the formal lesson on a specific behavior or class of behaviors (routine) is conducted, the teacher continues to teach the behavioral expectations during daily events. For example, during the first 2 weeks, the teacher uses descriptive praise for correct behavior ("You did a great job raising your hand for help and waiting quietly for me to come to you") and gentle verbal reprimands for correction. These reprimands simply involve restating the rule: "Please remember to raise your hand if you want my help or attention" or "Please remember to bring your reading book and pencil to reading group." Descriptive praise and gentle verbal reprimands help clarify the behavioral expectations and indicate a teacher's commitment to them (Sprick, 1981). Once the behavioral expectations are understood and most students are behaving appropriately (for example, in 2 to 3 weeks), the teacher gradually reduces the amount of reinforcement for correct behaviors and implements consequences for students who consistently do not behave appropriately.

PHYSICAL ARRANGEMENTS

The decisions a teacher makes regarding the physical arrangements of a classroom have an important effect on the success of instructional activities and classroom management. Thoughtfully designed classrooms enable teachers and students to access materials easily and move around the room without creating congestion. Also, in well-designed classrooms teachers easily can see the students and, in turn, students easily can see and hear teacher presentations. In planning physical arrangements it is helpful to consider the arrangement of students, materials, and special areas.

Arrangement of Students

In selecting an arrangement for students, it helps to begin by determining where the teacher will present whole-class instruction. The position of the chalkboard and overhead projector screen usually determines the best location for teacher presentations. The following considerations in arranging students are important:

1. *Arrange students so they easily can see teacher presentations.* An effort should be made to ensure that all students easily can see and hear teacher presentations. For example, the students should readily see any content presented on the chalkboard or overhead projector screen.

2. *Arrange students so that the teacher has easy access to any student.* The teacher should be able to move easily to any student in the classroom. This helps the teacher provide individual help, offer private feedback, and prevent crisis situations.

3. *Arrange students so that the teacher easily sees the students.* This enables the teacher to monitor the students by frequently scanning the classroom. Scanning increases on-task behavior and is especially important during student-directed activities. Sprick (1991) reports that scanning is an important factor in teaching and effective teachers typically scan the classroom about once every 15 seconds.

4. *Decide if desks are to be arranged in clusters or rows.* Options on arranging student desks include using isolated desk areas, clusters, rows, or combinations. Because placing desks in clusters tends to promote socializations and interactions among stu-

dents, many educators (Emmer et al., 1989) suggest placing student desks in rows, especially at the beginning of the school year. Moreover, it is important to ensure that students are not sitting with their backs to major instructional areas or facing distractions (such as windows, doorways, or other students).

5. *Place difficult-to-teach or off-task students in the middle of the room near the front.* These students need more monitoring than other students, and placement close to the teacher helps the teacher monitor their attention and behavior. Also, because teachers tend to look less at the students on the periphery of the classroom, difficult-to-teach students are more apt to be off-task or misbehave in these areas.

Arrangement of Materials

The appropriate location of materials facilitates the flow of instructional activities and improves classroom management. In arranging materials, several considerations are important:

1. *Keep frequently used materials easily accessible.* Although the specific materials frequently used by the teacher and the students depend on the academic area or subject being taught, some basic items usually include paper, markers, rulers, scissors, chalk and erasers, transparencies and water-soluble pens, masking tape, glue, and stapler. To help students maintain the materials that they supply, it is helpful to send a list home for parents, and the teacher should have an ample supply of items needed by students. Also, frequently used books should be readily available in bookcases.

2. *Ensure that high-traffic areas are free of congestion.* Some materials and furniture are in areas of high traffic that need to be free of congestion. High-use areas are usually around

group work places, the pencil sharpener, the trash can, the teacher's desk, certain book shelves, computers, doorways, and student desks. These high-traffic areas should not be close to each other and should have easy access.

Arrangement of Special Areas and Centers

An important consideration in planning the arrangement of a classroom is to designate selected areas for specific activities (for example, math area, language area, or study area). In many classrooms space is needed for small-group instruction, centers, and individual work. Several types of areas are presented next.

Academic Areas. In organizing some classrooms, it is necessary to divide instructional spaces into academic areas. In the elementary grades, these areas typically include reading, math, language, handwriting, spelling, and subjects such as science, social studies, and health. Each area provides room for several students and a space for storing materials. In the intermediate and secondary grades, fewer academic areas are specified in a classroom; however, instructional areas may be set up for various branches of a particular subject. For example, an English teacher may have areas for literature, grammar, listening, and free reading.

Teacher Areas. The teacher needs areas for small-group and large-group instruction. In addition, the teacher needs some space for storing materials and personal articles. The teacher's space should provide a good vantage point for monitoring the ongoing activities in the room.

Individual Student Areas. Each student needs a place to store his materials, sit during whole-class activities, and go to for independent seatwork. Typically, students are assigned a desk. It often is helpful to provide students who are highly distractible or who are having a bad day with a quiet work area, such as carrels or desks located away from the flow of activity. However, it is important that such carrels be viewed as a positive place to learn and not be used as punishment.

Recreation Area. Many teachers designate an area for fun activities. Such an area often is used to reinforce students and provide those who have finished an assignment with a rewarding place to go. Some common materials that are placed in this area include a carpet, bean-bag chairs, magazines, a tape player with headphones, electronic games, and recreational games.

Audiovisual Area. It is helpful to designate areas for using movie, filmstrip, or overhead projectors. Also, listening centers are needed for using a tape recorder, Language Master, record player, video cassette recorder, or computer. Many rooms do not provide a separate audiovisual area. In these situations, some space may serve dual functions (for example, a reading area/listening station).

General Considerations

In planning a classroom arrangement, the total effect should be pleasant and inviting. Teachers must take the resources and space available and arrange the class to suit their style and the content being taught. A sample regular classroom floor plan is presented in Figure 3.1, and two resource room plans are featured in Figures 3.2 and 3.3. Teachers may modify these to fit their needs. The sample arrangement of a regular classroom (Figure 3.1) provides a good vantage position for the teacher, easy access to students, a small-group instruction area, and a whole-class presentation format that allows the students to see the teacher, chalkboard, or overhead projector screen. Because resource room programs are housed in all types of settings (such as part of a library, portable classroom, or auditorium stage), two plans are presented. The plan in Figure 3.2 is for a small area, and the plan in Figure 3.3 is for a larger space.

Class Size. In the limited research that exists on the effects of special education class size, the smaller student-teacher ratios result in more positive student outcomes than do larger ratios (Forness & Kavale, 1985). The research in regular education is more extensive. Mueller, Chase, and Walden (1988) present results from Program Prime Time in Indiana concerning the effects of a reduced class size in primary grades. Specifically, they report that a reduced class size in primary grades results in a less hectic atmosphere, better teacher morale, more individualized instruction, and improved student achievement, particularly by at-risk students and students with learning problems. In a synthesis of the research on the effects of class size, Robinson (1990) found that (a) the most positive effects of small classes (22 or fewer students) occur in kindergarten through third grade and especially benefit the achievement of at-risk students, (b) the positive effects of class size on student achievement decrease as grade levels increase, (c) reducing class size has little effect on student achievement if teachers continue to use the same instructional methods in smaller classes that they used in larger classes, and (d) reductions in class size have small positive effects on achievement when compared with many less costly learning interventions and strategies. The improved learning of at-risk students and students with learning problems in smaller classes is likely the result of the teachers having the opportunity to respond to the students' individual instructional needs.

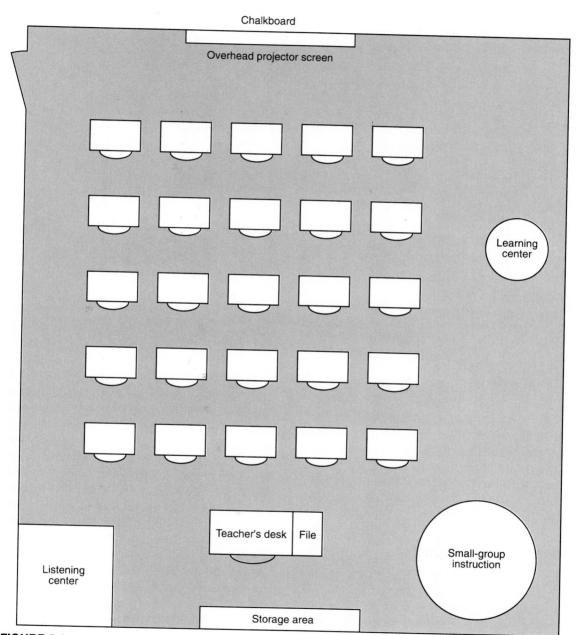

FIGURE 3.1
Sample floor plan for a regular classroom.

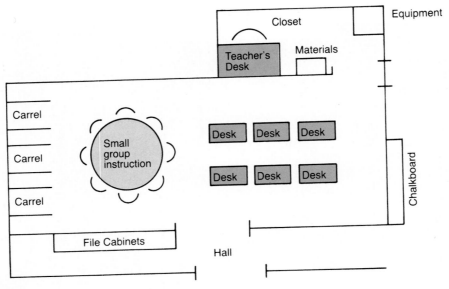

FIGURE 3.2
Sample floor plan for a small resource room.
Source: From *The Resource Teacher: A Guide to Effective Practices* (p. 57), 2nd ed., by J. L. Wiederholt, D. D. Hammill, and V. L. Brown, 1983, Austin, TX: Pro-Ed. Copyright 1983 by Allyn and Bacon. Reprinted by permission.

INSTRUCTIONAL ARRANGEMENTS

Five basic instructional arrangements are available to teachers. These are presented in Figure 3.4 and include large group with teacher, small group with teacher, one student with teacher, students teaching students, and material with student. The use of a variety of arrangements helps maintain student involvement and attention.

Large-Group Instruction

Teacher lectures to large groups can be an effective method of instruction. Although reading and, perhaps, math primarily occur in small groups, most other subjects (such as science, social studies, and art) are taught in large groups. Moreover, the large-group format is appropriate for numerous classroom activities, including conducting show and tell, discussing interesting events, taking a field trip, watching a play or movie, brainstorming, and playing a game.

Some major advantages of large-group instruction are that it is time-efficient and it prepares students for the type of instruction that primarily is used in secondary schools, community colleges, and universities. The primary disadvantage of lecturing to large groups is that it does not allow for the teacher to deal easily with the diversity in ability levels that is present in most classrooms. For high-ability students, large-group instruction frequently moves too slowly, whereas for low-ability students, it usually moves too quickly. In either situation, behavior problems are likely to result from boredom or frustration. Overall, large-group instruction is most appropriate for teaching content subjects (such as science or social studies) and less appropriate for teaching specific skills such as reading and math. Large-group instruction is more likely to accommodate students with different learning rates if certain guidelines are used:

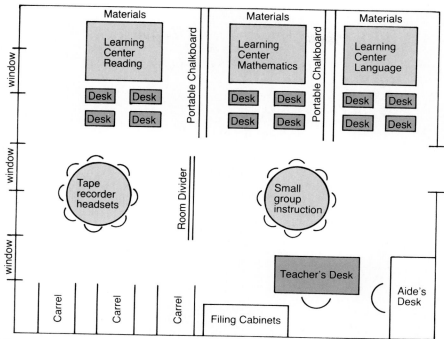

FIGURE 3.3

Sample floor plan for a large resource room.

Source: From *The Resource Teacher: A Guide to Effective Practices* (p. 56), 2nd ed., by J. L. Wiederholt, D. D. Hammill, and V. L. Brown, 1983, Austin, TX: Pro-Ed. Copyright 1983 by Allyn and Bacon. Reprinted by permission.

1. *Keep instruction short.* Suggested amounts of time for large-group instruction according to grade level include: (a) kindergarten or first grade—5 to 15 minutes; (b) second or third grade—5 to 20 minutes; (c) fourth or fifth grade—5 to 25 minutes, (d) sixth or seventh grade—5 to 30 minutes, and (e) eighth through twelfth grade—5 to 40 minutes.

2. *Use questions to involve students in the lesson.* Emmer et al. (1989) encourage teachers to make sure each student has opportunities to participate frequently. Choral or group responses are good ways to involve all students simultaneously. Also, teachers should guard against calling on the same students too often. Positive participation is enhanced if teachers ask high-ability students the most difficult questions and offer less demanding questions to low-ability students.

3. *Use lecture-pause routines.* The lecture-pause procedure involves the teacher lecturing for 6 to 12 minutes and then pausing for about 3 minutes to allow students divided into groups of three to follow the RAP procedure:

   R—*Read* your notes or questions.

   A—*Ask* other students about your notes (for example, spellings, missing information, or questions about the content).

   P—*Put* corrections or answers to questions in your notes.

4. *Encourage active participation among lower performing students while main-*

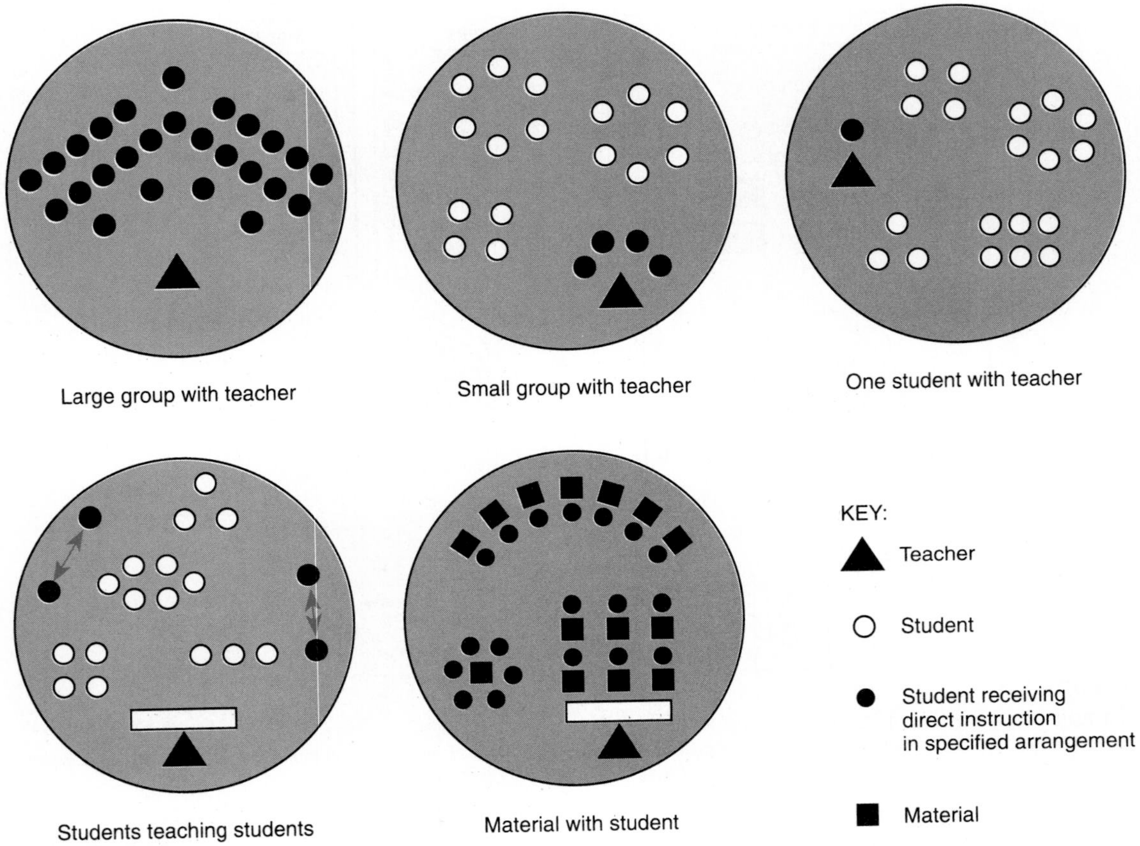

Large group with teacher

Small group with teacher

One student with teacher

Students teaching students

Material with student

KEY:

▲ Teacher

○ Student

● Student receiving direct instruction in specified arrangement

■ Material

FIGURE 3.4
Instructional arrangements.

taining the involvement of higher achieving students. Heads Together (Kagan, 1989/1990) is a teacher-questioning strategy that combines elements of teacher-directed and peer-mediated instruction. Students are placed into four-member learning teams, each consisting of one high achiever, two average achievers, and one low achiever. The students number themselves 1 to 4 and sit together during teacher-directed lessons. When the teacher directs a question to the entire class, the teams "put their heads together"

to determine the best answer. The teacher then asks, "How many Number _____ (1, 2, 3, or 4) know the answer?" After one randomly selected student responds, the teacher asks if other students with the selected number agree with the answer or want to expand on the answer. Because students are given time to discuss possible answers before responding and it is not known which group member will be selected to respond, it is more likely that everyone, including low achievers, will know the correct responses.

5. *Use visual aids to promote understanding of lecture material.* Diagrams are useful especially in helping students understand relationships. Concept diagramming (presented in Chapter 14) and story mapping (presented in Chapter 12) are visual diagramming approaches that are used frequently.

6. *Maintain a lively pace.* A lively pace helps maintain student attention. Because thinking time is always faster than speaking time, it is important to keep the lecture moving at an appropriate pace to hold interest.

7. *Use frequent "change-ups."* Sprick (1981) notes that "change-ups" are anything the teacher does to vary the presentation. Selected change-up activities include varying voice levels, varying rate of talking, illustrating a point with a story, telling a joke, having students follow a sequence of directions (such as look at ceiling, floor, windows, chalkboard), and allowing students to stand up to stretch.

8. *Determine the rules for behavior during presentations.* Mnemonics such as SLANT (presented previously) are excellent for reminding students of behavioral expectations during lectures.

9. *Determine the rules for behavior during discussions.* Rules for discussions are imperative to prevent call-outs and put-downs. A good rule for discussions is "Raise your hand to request to ask a question or answer a question."

10. *If students misbehave, praise students who follow the rules.* This reinforces students for appropriate behavior, communicates teacher expectations, and provides a model for misbehaving students.

Small-Group Instruction

The small-group arrangement typically consists of three to seven students and represents a major format for teaching academic skills. Although it can be a highly effective arrangement for all students, small-group instruction is recommended especially for students with learning problems. In establishing small groups for instruction, the teacher attempts to group students who have similar instructional needs in a specific academic area. Groups can be based on placement in a basal reader or on need for instruction in selected phonics rules, paragraph writing, or specific math facts. To accommodate different rates of learning, the composition of the groups should remain flexible. If a student makes rapid progress, it may be advisable to place the student in a different group for instruction.

In an examination of regular classroom practices, Slavin (1988) reports that little research exists concerning the merits of within-class instructional grouping for reading instruction; however, research on such grouping in mathematics is available and clearly supports grouping for instruction. Specific findings indicate that the effects are greater for low achievers than for average and high achievers (Slavin, 1988). Other research on this approach also indicates positive benefits (Anderson, Evertson, & Brophy, 1979; Carnine, Silbert, & Kameenui, 1990). To improve its effectiveness, these researchers recommend placing the students in a semicircle facing the teacher. They note that distractible students tend to perform better in the middle of the group and when they are placed about two feet from the teacher.

Advantages of Small-Group Instruction. It is difficult to meet the learning needs of a heterogeneous group of students during large-group instruction, and small-group instruction provides an effective alternative. Moreover, small-group instruction is especially important for students who are learning basic skills in reading, writing, and math; thus, small-group instruction occurs more frequently during the elementary grades. Compared with large-group instruction, some specific advantages of small-group instruction include the following:

1. Students are able to participate more during the instruction.
2. Teachers are able to provide more instruction, praise, and feedback.
3. Students are able to progress at their own rate (that is, both high achievers and low achievers are able to progress at rates commensurate with their abilities).
4. Small-group instruction typically is less boring.
5. Teachers using small-group instruction are able to monitor the progress of students better and make teaching modifications.

Disadvantages of Small-Group Instruction. Most of the disadvantages of small-group instruction involve teacher preparation time and managing students doing their seatwork while others are participating in a small group. Compared with large-group instruction, some specific disadvantages of small-group instruction include the following:

1. Students are required to do more seatwork.
2. Teachers have to do more planning (for example, a reading teacher must plan small-group lessons as well as seatwork for students when they are not in their small-group lesson).
3. Teachers must organize more instructional variables (such as grouping students, managing transitions, and monitoring seatwork while teaching).
4. Teachers must provide more instruction in the respective academic or content area.

Guidelines for Small-Group Instruction. Because the rewards in student learning and motivation can be substantial when small-group instruction is used, the teacher should approach small-group instruction positively.

The advantages of small-group instruction can be attained and the disadvantages minimized if effective guidelines are followed:

1. *Establish rules for small-group instruction.* In addition to reminding the students that general classroom rules apply in small-group lessons, the teacher should have some specific rules for these lessons (for example, "Always bring your materials—pencil, book, workbook—to small-group lessons" and "Wait quietly for the teacher to begin the lesson"). Also, if the teacher previously has not developed the rules and behavioral expectations for making the transition of going to small-group instruction, this routine needs to be taught. Finally, it is important to remind students who are out of the group to follow the classroom rules regarding seatwork.
2. *Make the groups as homogeneous as possible.* Grouping the students according to ability and skill helps the teacher tailor instruction for the students in the group. Because the lowest performers need more intense instruction (that is, more elaborations, examples, praise, feedback, and practice), it helps to keep their group as small as possible. Sprick (1981) notes that three groups usually are needed in reading, whereas two groups often are sufficient in math.
3. *Maintain flexible groupings.* To ensure that students progress at their own rate, it helps for the groupings to remain flexible. For example, a student who makes rapid progress may be placed in a different instructional group.
4. *Locate the small group in an area that allows the teacher to scan the entire class.* When working with a small group, the teacher should be able to see the rest of the class. It also is helpful to select a location that minimizes distractions for the students.

For example, students in the small group should sit where they do not see other students doing seatwork. Also, seatings away from high-traffic areas such as the pencil sharpener, waste basket, or audiovisual center reduce potential distractions.

5. *Place the students in a semicircle so that their shoulders align with the shoulders of the students beside them.* This alignment provides an equal opportunity for all students to participate in group activities. When a student's shoulders are six or more inches behind the others, it has a tendency to make the student feel outside of the group. Sprick (1981) suggests using two semicircle rows of students when there are nine or more students in the group. Students in the back row sit in chairs and those in the front row sit on the floor. For sitting on the floor not to be aversive, Sprick recommends making it a privilege (for example, "Tonya, Greg, and Jason have done such a nice job of attending to the lesson today, they get to sit on the floor mats next time").

6. *Use motivation activities during small-group work.* Motivation techniques include the following:
   a. Provide a lot of positive praise during the initial small-group session.
   b. Use descriptive praise.
   c. Use group praise (for example, occasionally conduct a group handshake).
   d. Use some choral responding to involve everyone.
   e. Maintain enthusiasm and a good (fast) pace during the lesson.

One Student with Teacher

Intensive tutorial teaching frequently is used to help students with learning problems learn a new skill. One-to-one tutoring is a powerful instructional arrangement. Bloom (1984) states, "We were astonished at the consistency of the findings and at the great differences in student cognitive achievement, attitudes, and self-concept under tutoring as compared with group methods of instruction" (p. 4). In addition, one-to-one teaching can be used spontaneously to prevent or relieve frustration. When teachers observe students having difficulty during group instruction or seatwork, they can give them attention at the first opportunity.

Often 3 to 5 minutes is just the amount of time needed to help a student understand a concept, receive corrective feedback, understand directions, and feel motivated to continue working. Archer and Edgar (1976) recommend that one-to-one instruction be scheduled daily for students with learning problems. The students then know they will have some time with the teacher to ask questions and receive help. Elementary teachers and resource room teachers have fewer students or are with them for a longer time; thus, it is easier for them than for intermediate and secondary level teachers to offer one-to-one instruction.

Students Teaching Students: Peer Tutoring

The students-teaching-students instructional arrangement provides teachers with a viable resource of instructional support and offers students the opportunity for intensive practice on academic tasks tailored to individual needs. It features students working independently and thus frees the teacher to work with other students individually or in small-group sessions. In a mainstream classroom of heterogeneous learners, instructional arrangements that allow students to practice needed skills or learn subject content independently are critical to the academic success of students with learning problems. Although students teaching students occurs in a multitude of formats, most peer instructional arrangements feature either peer tutoring or cooperative learning.

Description of Peer Tutoring.

Tutorial instruction (for example, parents teaching their children; older siblings instructing younger siblings) was probably the first pedagogy among primitive societies. As early as the first century, A. D. Quintilian in his *Institutio Oratoria* discussed teaching settings in which older children tutored younger children.

Today, a basic definition of peer tutoring is *an instructional arrangement in which the teacher pairs two students in a tutor-tutee relationship to promote learning of academic skills or subject content.* The teacher determines the academic task and provides the instructional materials. Although peer tutoring is used to foster social skills, positive relationships, and self-esteem for both students, the emphasis is usually on the learning progress of the tutee. To maintain effective peer tutoring, the teacher monitors behavior and praises both students for performing their respective duties.

Research on Peer Tutoring.

Several studies have focused on the effectiveness of peer tutoring. Levin, Glass, and Meister (1984) examined the effectiveness of peer tutoring in terms of reading and math outcomes and found that peer tutoring produced more than twice as much achievement as computer-assisted instruction, three times more than reducing the class size from 35 to 30 students, and almost four times greater achievement than lengthening the school day by 1 hour. Osguthorpe and Scruggs (1986) reviewed studies in which special education students served as tutors. They found that tutees who received instruction from special education students made academic gains in a variety of content areas. Moreover, many of the tutors benefited academically and socially from being the tutor. These findings provide a mainstream or special education teacher with an opportunity to set up many different tutor-tutee pairs to promote social integration as well as academic gains among students with and without learning problems.

Scruggs and Richter (1985) reviewed 24 studies in which students with learning disabilities were involved in tutoring interventions. They note that all investigators favored the use of peer tutoring, and most studies support the continued use of tutoring with students with learning disabilities. Nevertheless, Scruggs and Richter caution against such unqualified endorsements because the tutoring studies have methodological flaws. Specifically, they state, "it is difficult to imagine another instructional intervention in the field of learning disabilities which meets with such unqualified enthusiasm and, yet, is so lacking in empirical evidence. [We] have also encountered the methodological challenges . . . and agree with the conviction that peer tutoring has great power and utility in special education" (p. 297).

Other studies have investigated the comparative effects of peer tutoring for students with and without learning problems. The educational implications from the peer tutoring research are similar for students in regular and special education. Tutor and tutee benefits in academics (that is, achievement gains across academic and content areas) are reported for students with and without learning problems, whereas the effect of peer tutoring on the enhancement of social skills and self-concept remains inconclusive for both students with and without learning problems (P. A. Cohen, Kulik, & Kulik, 1982; Osguthorpe & Scruggs, 1986). Moreover, the research indicates that peer tutoring program variables are more important to student achievement than are student variables such as age, ability, grade, and training. Relevant program variables include (a) structured settings, (b) lower-order target skills,

(c) teacher-developed achievement measures, and (d) programs of shorter longitudinal duration. Also, math achievement appears to be greater in peer tutoring programs than achievement in reading and other subject areas (P. A. Cohen et al., 1982). Because of the effect of program variables, it is not surprising that students with learning problems as well as students without learning problems benefit from peer tutoring programs of similar design and content. In discussing the peer tutoring program in his school, Chuck Martin, principal at Lake Washington High School in Kirkland, Washington, reports that "this program has contributed more to helping students succeed and in creating a caring environment than any intervention we've tried in my six years at this school" (Jenkins & Jenkins, 1987, p. 68).

Peer tutoring appears to hold much promise. It can improve academic skills, foster self-esteem, develop appropriate behaviors, and promote positive relationships and cooperation among peers. It benefits both tutor and tutee, and once the program is designed it requires less of the teacher's time than most instructional arrangements. Also, it is tailor-made for helping students with learning problems achieve in mainstream settings.

Programming Guidelines for Peer Tutoring.

The development and implementation of a successful peer tutoring program require the consideration of numerous factors. The following guidelines represent "best practices" from the research and literature regarding the factors involved in planning and implementing peer tutoring:

1. *Determine goals of peer tutoring.* Although peer tutoring is used primarily to help students with academic achievement, some educators report that it is effective for improving socialization skills, classroom behaviors, self-concept, and interpersonal relationships. Some appropriate goals include:

   a. Provide tutees with an opportunity to practice and learn targeted academic skills (for example, spelling words, math facts, word recognition) until mastery is achieved.

   b. Provide tutees with an opportunity to review and learn subject content (for example, definitions of science terms, identification of countries on a map).

   c. Provide tutors and tutees with an opportunity to develop appropriate social skills (for example, giving encouragement, giving corrective feedback, clarifying directions or subject matter, providing cues and prompts).

   d. Provide tutors with an opportunity to review or practice recently learned skills or content.

   e. Enhance the self-concepts of tutors and tutees by making positive statements about their skills or abilities and by providing them with success experiences in both social and academic areas.

2. *Target skills or content for the peer tutoring pairs.* When the entire class is working on skills (for example, spelling words) or content (for example, presidents of the United States) presented in a recent lesson, the teacher may have each pair working with the same content. In other situations, peer tutoring provides students who need extra practice with the opportunity to receive it. Generally, the content or skills targeted should include material the teacher already has presented to the students. In selecting content and skills, it is helpful to consider the following research findings:

   a. Peer tutoring has resulted in academic gains for tutors and tutees within most academic areas.

b. Gains in math have been greater than in other academic areas for tutors and tutees.
c. Peer tutoring pairs seem to achieve best when working on lower-level skills (such as spelling words or math facts).
d. Peer tutoring appears to work better on molar-level activities such as number of words written or read correctly than on singular skill activities such as decoding skills.
e. The targeted skills and content should be similar to those used in the classroom.
f. Student gains usually are more evident on curriculum-based measures than on standardized tests.

3. *Select materials.* In addition to paper and pencils, materials needed for a peer tutoring program usually include the following:

a. Directions for tutor and tutee.
b. An academic task presented on flash cards, a worksheet, or pages in a textbook.
c. As assessment sheet on which the tutor can record correct and incorrect responses.
d. Scoring procedures if tutee performance is to be evaluated.

A sample tutor instruction sheet for flash cards is presented in Table 3.1, and a sample record sheet is provided in Table 3.2.

4. *Design procedures for tutor and tutee.* The procedures instruct the tutor how to present the academic task, score the tutee responses, provide feedback for correct and incorrect responses, and record the total performance score of the tutee. The procedures instruct the tutee how to respond (for example, written, timed, verbal) to the academic task. Finally, the pro-

cedures detail the rewards for the tutor and tutee for the achievement of specified goals (for example, tutee passes a weekly quiz on the tutoring content with 90 percent accuracy or achieves 80 percent accuracy during the session).

5. *Assign tutor-tutee pairs.* Several configurations of tutor-tutee assignments are used in peer tutoring. Across-class tutoring involves students from one class going to another class to tutor. Across-class tutors are usually older or high achievers. Pull-out tutoring involves the tutee going to a specialized setting to work with a tutor from another class. These two arrangements require administrative support and scheduling among the classes involved. A third type of tutoring, intraclass tutoring, yields good results and requires less schoolwide planning. Intraclass tutoring involves students within the same class serving as tutors and tutees for each other. The tutoring interaction may be either one-way or reciprocal. In reciprocal tutoring the tutor and tutee exchange roles during the tutoring session so that each has an opportunity to serve as teacher and learner. Unless there are students who have chronic problems with each other, tutor-tutee assignments can be random. For example, after a specified time (such as 1 week to 1 month), the tutor-tutee assignments are randomly changed (for example, tuters or tutees select names of a partner from a container). Low achievers can act as tutors for high achievers when the tutoring materials include the correct answers for the tutor. This enables the tutor with learning problems to check the answer and provide feedback to tutees who are high achievers. This format enables a heterogeneous group of students to tutor each other and engage in reciprocal tutoring.

TABLE 3.1
Sample tutor instruction sheet for flash cards.

Step 1: At the beginning of the tutoring session, get the folder of tutor materials.

Step 2: Sit directly opposite and facing the tutee.

Step 3: Check to see that the tutor materials include record sheets, flash cards, blank cards, and pencils.

Step 4: Ask the tutee if he is ready to begin.

Step 5: Remove the record sheet, pencil, and flash cards from the folder.

Step 6: Hold up the flash cards one at a time with the card facing the tutee.

Step 7: Instruct the tutee to read aloud the number fact or word.

Step 8: Count to three silently. If the tutee does not respond or responds incorrectly, say, "The answer is _____. Say it." After the tutee repeats the answer, place the card at the bottom of the stack.

Step 9: If the tutee does not respond or responds incorrectly, mark a " − " next to the number fact or word in the first trial column of the record sheet.

Step 10: If the tutee responds correctly, mark a " + " next to the number fact or word, and say, "Good job," "Great," or "Super." Place the card on the table.

Step 11: After the tutee attempts all of the cards, present them again, and mark a " + " or " − " in the second trial column of the record sheet.

Step 12: Present the cards a third time, and mark a " + " or " − " in the last trial column of the record sheet.

Step 13: Look at the data sheet. If there are three " + "s for a number fact or a word, give the tutee a blank card and a pencil and instruct him to write the number fact or word. Have the tutee file this card in his mastery box.

Step 14: Have the tutee move his marker on the "Ladder of Success" chart to the correct spot according to how many new number facts or words he has learned.

Step 15: Place the materials back in the folder and return the folder to its place.

6. *Train tutors.* Tutor training procedures are included in most peer tutoring programs. The duties of tutors typically include introduction of new material, presentation of items, error correction, prompting and praising correct answers, testing and recording progress, and assigning points for progress. Tutor training procedures consistently include a combination of the following: orientation to the rationale and goals of tutoring, a description of the materials and procedures, teacher demonstration of tutoring skills, tutor imitation and role playing of procedures with feedback, intermittent guidance when needed, and praise for following the procedures correctly. In essence, tutor training follows the direct instruction sequence (use an advance organizer, describe the behavioral expectations, demonstrate the behavioral expectations, and so on) used to teach behavioral expectations discussed earlier in this chapter. Some sample guidelines for helping the tutor succeed include:

a. Make the relationship with your partner positive because it is the most important part of any tutoring program.

b. Greet your partner as you would a good friend. Be friendly and open. Make your

TABLE 3.2
Sample tutor record sheet.

Tutor Record Sheet

Tutor_____   Date_____

Tutee_____

Mark either a "+" or a "−" depending on the tutee's response (+ = correct; − = incorrect)

Math Fact or Word	Trial 1	Trial 2	Trial 3	Math Facts or Words Not Learned
1				
2				
3				
4				
5				
6				
7				
8				
9				
10				

How did you feel about today's session?

Do not write below this line

Percent correct_____   Percent incorrect_____

Number learned_____   Number not learned_____

partner feel at ease. Call your partner by name.

c. Listen carefully to your partner. Be interested. Ask questions.

d. Be patient. Be respectful. Build your partner's self-confidence by helping him succeed.

e. Believe in your partner! You will both succeed and you will both be learning. Remember everyone is different and everyone learns at an his own pace.

Table 3.3 presents a sample tutor checklist for the teacher to use for training and feedback.

7. *Train tutees.* A primary task of the tutees is to try their best to do the tasks presented by the tutor. Specific duties include following directions, receiving feedback appropriately, and maintaining attention. Tutees typically are trained with the same direct instruction sequence used to teach tutors.

8. *Teach social skills used in peer tutoring.* For peer tutoring to occur in a positive and supportive environment, it helps for the teacher to teach several social skills, such as accepting a partner, giving and accepting corrective feedback, and praising a partner. Each of these skills is trained through the direct instruction sequence. Teacher demonstrations of nonexamples (such as rudeness or put-downs) and discussions of how those behaviors make people feel are helpful in teaching the rationale for using good social skills. Moreover, teacher demonstrations and role playing of how to greet a partner with a smile and a gesture (such as high-five) are important for teaching appropriate social skills.

9. *Review rules.* The teacher reminds the students that the classroom rules apply during peer tutoring. Rules to emphasize during peer tutoring are (a) "Make transitions quickly" and (b) "Use whisper voices." Again, the behavioral expectations for these rules are taught using the direct instruction sequence.

10. *Schedule the peer tutoring sessions.* Most researchers recommend about 20 minutes for one-way tutoring sessions and 30 minutes for reciprocal sessions. Positive achievement outcomes have resulted primarily from two or more sessions weekly.

TABLE 3.3
Sample tutor checklist.

Tutor_____

Date	Date	Date	Date	Date	Date	
						Collects material
						Goes to work space
						Describes lesson to partner
						Praises correct responses
						Shows enthusiasm
						Provides corrective feedback
						Uses positive manner
						Follows directions without assistance
						Speaks in a quiet voice
						Keeps records
						Replaces material at end of session

11. *Conduct a tutoring session.* In addition to planning the peer tutoring program and adapting curriculum materials, teachers must supervise the sessions, evaluate progress, and make periodic revisions. Initially the teacher needs to supervise the peer tutoring sessions closely and provide corrective and positive feedback. Once the students become proficient in their respective tutor-tutee roles, the teacher can scan the tutoring sessions while working with a small group or individual students. Some educators report good results when the teacher periodically meets with tutor-tutee pairs to discuss their progress. Also, researchers have found that tutor and tutee performance contingencies positively affect maintenance of effective peer tutoring interactions as well as academic achievement (Greenwood, Carta, & Hall, 1988; Maheady, Harper, & Sacca, 1988). For managing misbehavior during peer tutoring sessions, Sprick (1981) recommends:

a. Ignore misbehavior unless it persists.
b. If misbehavior is chronic, reassign the pair to other partners.
c. Do not get involved in minor disputes.
d. Praise pairs for appropriate behavior.
e. For persistent misbehavior, implement owing-time consequences.
f. Develop a signal (for example, tap a note on a toy xylophone) to remind the class to work quietly.

12. *Evaluate the peer tutoring program.* The achievement of tutees can be evaluated through examination of the daily progress sheets (for example, number correct, points earned) completed by tutors. Also, weekly quizzes on the skills or content covered in peer tutoring are helpful in monitoring progress. Social skill progress may be monitored through systematic ob-servation of the tutoring pairs, and affective domains may be evaluated through interviews or questionnaires.

With appropriate planning, student training, and teacher support, peer tutoring can be a viable instructional alternative. Moreover, to maintain the tutors' involvement, it helps for the school to recognize the efforts of the tutors and tutees. Some common activities include displaying pictures of tutors on bulletin boards, allowing tutors to meet before school, offering awards, providing reinforcing events such as meetings with faculty or administrators, publishing articles about the program, and having the principal recognize tutors. One peer-mediated instruction program that deserves consideration from mainstream and special education teachers is *ClassWide Peer Tutoring (CWPT)* (Delquadri, Greenwood, Whorton, Carta, & Hall, 1986). It was developed at the Juniper Gardens Children's Project in Kansas City, Kansas, and is designed to help students with mild disabilities improve their basic skills. Maheady, Sacca, and Harper (1988) used *ClassWide Peer Tutoring* in secondary mainstream settings to improve the academic and social performance of students with learning disabilities. Moreover, Maheady, Harper, and Sacca (1988) note that numerous researchers report success of *ClassWide Peer Tutoring* at the elementary school level. Sample peer tutoring materials, including *CWPT,* are presented in Chapter 4.

Students Teaching Students: Cooperative Learning

Cooperative learning represents another instructional arrangement in which peers work independently. Because of its success with heterogeneous groups of students and the in-dependent nature of their work, it represents a viable approach for promoting successful mainstreaming. During the last decade, cooperative learning has enjoyed increasing popularity and enthusiastic support from regular and special educators.

Description of Cooperative Learning.
There are many forms of cooperative learning, but they all involve students working in teams or small groups to help each other learn (Slavin, 1991). Because cooperative learning provides students with an opportunity to practice skills or learn content presented by the teacher, it supplements teacher instruction. Cooperative learning emphasizes team goals, and team success is only achieved if each individual learns. A basic definition of cooperative learning is *an instructional arrangement in which small groups or teams of students work together to achieve team success in a manner that promotes student responsibility for their own learning as well as the learning of others.*
Student Team Learning (STL) techniques represent the most extensive practices used in cooperative learning. STL methods emphasize the position that team goals only can be achieved if each member achieves selected academic objectives. Slavin (1991) notes that the concepts of team reward, individual accountability, and equal opportunities for success are central to all STL methods. Team rewards are earned when a team achieves at or above a predetermined criterion level. Because all teams who achieve criterion are successful (rewarded), teams are not in competition for an all-or-nothing reward. Individual accountability is featured because team success depends on the individual learning of all team members. Team success is evaluated by the composite performances (for example, scores) of team members on a quiz of material assigned to the group. This relationship of individual performance to team performance

fosters activities that involve team members helping each other learn the targeted academic content. Equal opportunities for success are provided because each team member helps the team by improving on his own past performance. This challenges low, average, and high achievers to do their best because their respective performances all are valued by the team.
Student Teams-Achievement Divisions (STAD) (Slavin, 1978, 1986) and Teams-Games-Tournament (TGT) (DeVries & Slavin, 1978; Slavin, 1986) are two cooperative learning methods that are adaptable across subject areas and grade levels. In STAD a heterogeneous group of four students is assigned to a team. After the teacher presents a lesson, the team works together to ensure that all students have mastered the lesson. Then the students take individual quizzes without peer help. The students' quiz scores are compared with their past averages, and points are awarded if their performances meet or exceed their earlier efforts. The points are totaled to yield a team score, and teams that meet criteria are rewarded (for example, receive certificates). This cycle of activity usually takes three to five class periods. STAD works best with academic material that has single correct answers (for example, math computations, map skills). TGT uses the same teacher presentation, group assignment, and teamwork format as STAD. The quizzes, however, are replaced with weekly tournaments. In these tournaments students compete with players from other teams to earn points to add to their respective team scores. Students compete at three-member "tournament tables" with others who have similar skill levels on the target skills. The winners at the tournament tables each earn the same number of points for their team. All students have equal opportunity for success because low achievers competing with other low achievers can earn as many points as high

achievers competing with high achievers. As with STAD, TGT takes three to five class periods and is most appropriate with content that features single answers (for example, math).

In addition to STAD and TGT, two comprehensive curriculums exist for specific content and grades. Team Assisted Individualization (TAI) (Slavin, Madden, & Stevens, 1990) is designed for mathematics in third through sixth grade, and Cooperative Integrated Reading and Composition (CIRC) (Slavin, Stevens, & Madden, 1988) is designed for reading in third through fifth grade.

Research on Cooperative Learning. Most of the research on cooperative learning focuses on the STL techniques developed at Johns Hopkins University. In a synthesis of research on cooperative learning, Slavin (1991) reports the following findings:

1. The most successful approaches for improving academic achievement include group goals and individual accountability. In these settings, groups are rewarded on the basis of the performances of the respective team members.
2. In studies that feature group goals and individual accountability, the achievement effects of experimental/control comparisons consistently favor cooperative learning. Specifically, in 37 of 44 studies of at least 4 weeks' duration, the significantly positive effects favor cooperative learning, whereas none favor traditional methods.
3. The positive achievement effects of cooperative learning appear consistent across grades (two through twelve), subject areas, and school settings (rural, urban, suburban).
4. Effects are equally positive for high, average, and low achievers.
5. The positive effects of cooperative learning are reported consistently in affective areas (for example, self-esteem, intergroup relations, attitudes toward school, and ability to work cooperatively).

Slavin et al. (1990) report excellent results in math achievement and affective measures with Team Assisted Individualization for students with academic disabilities in mainstream settings. Likewise, Cooperative Integrated Reading and Composition learning groups for reading and writing yield excellent reading and writing outcomes for nondisabled students as well as students with academic disabilities in mainstream settings (Slavin et al., 1988). Slavin (1989/1990) states, "Cooperative learning seems to be an extraordinary success. It has an excellent research base, many viable and successful forms, and hundreds of thousands of enthusiastic adherents" (p. 3).

Programming Guidelines for Cooperative Learning. In designing a cooperative learning program, it appears that team goals and rewards, individual accountability, and equal opportunities are essential components for many students. Guidelines adapted from those presented in peer tutoring are appropriate for planning and implementing cooperative learning:

1. Determine goals of cooperative learning.
2. Target selected skills or contingent lessons for the teams.
3. Select materials including the quizzes or tournament questions.
4. Design procedures for team members to help each other.
5. Assign students of varying achievement levels to the same teams.
6. Train teams to help each other.
7. Teach social skills for team work.
8. Review classroom rules and teach new rules.
9. Schedule the cooperative learning sessions for 3 to 5 days a week.
10. Conduct a cooperative learning session.
11. Evaluate the cooperative learning program.

The January 1990 issue of *Educational Leadership* focuses on cooperative learning and includes numerous resources for its effective use.

Material with Student

Learning Considerations. From a learning perspective the material-with-student or independent seatwork arrangement provides the student with opportunities to practice skills that the teacher has presented. Practice helps the student move through the learning sequence that begins with acquisition and progresses to the higher levels of proficiency, maintenance, and generalization. For many students with learning problems, the mastery of skills and content requires extensive practice.

From a review of the research on practice, Dempster (1991) reports several findings that have implications for classrooms:

1. Given equivalent practice time, two or more opportunities with the same material are more effective than a single opportunity.
2. Spaced practice promotes better learning than massed practice.
3. Relative to massed practice, the effectiveness of spaced practice increases as the frequency of the practice activity increases.
4. The use of cumulative questions or tasks as practice activities is a key to effective learning.
5. It is believed that frequent spaced practice produces a more elaborate understanding of the topic than massed practice.

Some direct classroom implications of Dempster's (1991) findings include:

1. Incorporate spaced reviews or practice (including questions from previous and current lessons) into a variety of activities (such as discussions, seatwork, peer tutoring, homework).
2. Organize lessons so that a brief time is used to review the main points of the previous day's lesson. Include review tasks or questions on seatwork activities.
3. Once or twice a month, conduct a comprehensive practice session that features discussions and seatwork.

Teacher Considerations. From a teacher's perspective a material-with-student arrangement not only provides students with opportunities to improve achievement but also allows the teacher some freedom to work with small groups or individual students. Although planning seatwork activities and teaching students to work independently is time-consuming, it is worth the effort. Well-designed material-with-student activities can make the school year pleasant and productive. Some guidelines for planning and implementing an effective independent seatwork program are presented:

1. *Ensure that the independent work assignments are tailored to the student's instructional level.* Preceding independent practice with demonstration or guided practice is a good way to ensure that the assignment is instructionally appropriate.
2. *Use a variety of independent seatwork activities.* Varying the activities provides the teacher with alternatives and tends to increase student motivation and time on task. Suitable activities include self-correcting materials, instructional games, computer-assisted instruction, Language Master-assisted instruction, and tape recorder-assisted instruction. These activities are presented in Chapter 4 and in the curriculum area chapters throughout the text.
3. *Consider work folders for daily assignments.* A work folder is a flexible system of communication between the teacher and the individual student. Work folders can be used to communicate the day's assign-

ments. They provide a place for keeping charts and completed work and for giving feedback. After the students have used the work folders for a while, they can enter the room, pick up their folders, and begin work without teacher intervention. A check-off sheet may be placed in the folders to help the students determine which tasks are completed and which need to be studied.

4. *Prepare some cushion activities to accommodate students finishing their work at different times.* Activities include starting another assignment, writing on the computer, working in a learning center, listening to a tape, assisting another student, or reading a book or magazine.

5. *Design procedures that enable students to ask questions while doing independent seatwork.* A good plan prevents constant interruptions from students while the teacher is working with a small group. Three procedures include (a) assigning student helpers to answer questions, (b) developing a signal (for example, a desk sign that signifies that the student has a question) that allows the student to continue working until help arrives, and (c) designating an area of the room (such as a rug) that one student at a time can go to when he has a question.

6. *Ensure that students understand the instructions for their seatwork activities before starting small-group instruction.* This is especially important when new assignments or a new format (for example, self-correcting material, computer) is used.

7. *Use the direct instruction teaching sequence to teach the behavioral expectations for independent seatwork.*

Self-Regulation.   Eaton and Hansen (1978) assert the importance of self-management skills:

> Students who can successfully manage their own social and academic behaviors learn critical life skills. They learn to accept responsibil-

ity for their own actions and for their own learning. Students who can manage their own learning experience the thrill of knowing they can succeed at some very difficult tasks. They can replace their image of failure with one of self-confidence. In actuality, self-management is the *real* goal of schooling. It teaches a person "how" to learn. (p. 215)

Students with learning problems typically have difficulty with self-regulation (Rooney & Hallahan, 1985). Consequently, many lack self-control strategies that are fundamental to achieving success at school and home. Self-regulation is an essential component of the independent behavior that is needed to succeed as a student and as an adult. When students work independently, the teacher can perform essential teaching activities more freely. In essence, it allows students to do independent practice while the teacher instructs students who need demonstration, modeling, or guided practice. Fortunately, recent research suggests self-regulation can be taught successfully (Gelfand & Hartmann, 1984; Grimes, 1981; Workman, 1982).

Numerous approaches exist for teaching self-regulation. These approaches often are combined with aspects of learning strategy training (see Chapter 14) or cognitive training (see Chapter 5). This section focuses on three specific techniques for teaching self-regulation: self-recording, self-evaluation, and self-reinforcement. The steps for teaching each of these three techniques are (a) provide the rationale, (b) demonstrate and model, and (c) practice with feedback (Hughes, Ruhl, & Peterson, 1988). Each technique can be used alone or in combination with related techniques.

Self-recording involves counting and recording one's own behavior, on the assumption that such actions will influence one's behavior. For example, the daily recording of one's weight is likely to influence one's intake of calories. Event and interval recording are appropriate for most self-recording situations.

The steps for teaching self-recording include the following:

1. Provide the rationale. This step involves selecting a behavior that needs changing (for example, the need to complete more seatwork) and discussing how self-recording can be used to change it.
2. Demonstrate and model. In this step a recording form and a method of observation are selected. The teacher demonstrates self-recording by using the observation method and recording the results on the form. Next, the student performs self-recording and receives feedback until understanding is assured.
3. Practice with feedback. This step involves the student practicing self-recording with prompts and corrective feedback. As the student becomes proficient in self-recording, the teacher reduces prompts, praise, and feedback.

Self-evaluation is the component of self-regulation that focuses on teaching the student to judge how well he/she is doing. The following steps for teaching self-evaluation are used:

1. Provide the rationale. The importance of evaluating one's work is discussed. The notion that evaluation enables the student to determine if his performance is satisfactory is stressed. Also, the point is made that it helps the student to know whether more effort is needed.
2. Demonstrate and model. In this step a self-evaluation form is selected. It usually requires the student to mark digits (0, 1, 2) that correspond to a grading scale of poor progress (0), some progress (1), and good progress (2). The teacher demonstrates use of the form and has the student model the behavior to ensure that the student understands the process.

3. Practice with feedback. The student practices self-evaluation with teacher feedback until proficiency is achieved.

Self-reinforcement is a technique for self-regulation that involves the student reviewing his progress to determine if reinforcement has been earned. The steps for teaching self-reinforcement include the following:

1. Provide the rationale. This step focuses on teaching the student the importance of earning reinforcement by helping him identify appropriate reinforcers. The rationale establishes standards of performance for the earning of reinforcements, and it specifies when and how the student is to be rewarded.
2. Demonstrate and model. The teacher uses mock data, recording sheets, and a reinforcement menu to demonstrate self-reinforcement (Hughes et al., 1988). The teacher tells the student if the reinforcement criteria are met and selects the reward. The student performs the same behavior with teacher feedback until understanding is apparent.
3. Practice with feedback. The student practices self-reinforcement by using self-recording and self-evaluation. The student is encouraged to praise himself subvocally when he selects the reinforcer (for example, "I worked hard and now I get a reward"). The teacher provides corrective and positive feedback until the student becomes proficient by self-reinforcement.

Hughes et al. (1988) used a combination of self-recording, self-evaluation, and self-reinforcement to help learners with mild disabilities improve their independent work behavior during seatwork. They note that some generalization to other times occurred among their students.

Individualized instruction is easier to organize and carry out if students are involved in managing their own programs. Students may participate in the following activities involving self-management:

1. Select activities from a list designed to help them achieve objectives.
2. Manage their own work schedules using check-off sheets.
3. Use audiovisual equipment independently.
4. Select instructional materials and return them to the proper place.
5. Tutor each other when feasible.
6. Ask for adult help when necessary.
7. Self-correct work.
8. Administer timings on probes for targeted behaviors.
9. Model appropriate learning and social behavior for each other.
10. Develop techniques for modifying their own behavior.
11. Find solutions to social conflicts without teacher intervention.

SCHEDULES

Schedules are vital for accomplishing instructional goals in an organized manner. They indicate what activities will occur and when they will occur. Most students with learning problems need the organization and routine typical of systematic scheduling. Furthermore, scheduling greatly affects the pace of instruction. It ensures that enough classroom time is spent in high-priority curriculum areas and that enjoyable activities are interspersed with less appealing activities.

A well-planned daily schedule greatly aids the teacher in providing effective instruction; however, it takes much work to develop an appropriate schedule. A teacher needs knowledge and skills in individualized programming (Chapter 1), instructional approaches and techniques (Chapter 1), assessment for teaching (Chapter 2), curriculum materials (Chapter 4), and classroom management (Chapters 3, 4, and 5). Scheduling techniques presented in this section include general scheduling techniques, scheduling at the elementary level, scheduling at the secondary level, and scheduling in the resource room.

General Scheduling Techniques

The following suggestions and techniques apply to improving scheduling practices in various program settings (resource room and regular classroom) and at all grade levels:

1. *Schedule for maximum instructional time.* Schloss and Sedlak (1986) provide the following guidelines for allocating academic time:

   a. Plan time to practice new skills within a demonstration-practice-feedback-mastery paradigm.
   b. Examine the weekly schedule and compute time (minutes) allocated to each student per week, and adjust the schedule for effectiveness.
   c. Build planning time into the schedule and adhere to it.
   d. Consider time needed for transitions and setups when developing the schedule.
   e. Pace the instruction quickly during sessions allocated to academics to obtain maximum use of time.

2. *Proceed from short work assignments to longer ones.* At first, some students may be unable to work on a seatwork assignment for a long period (such as 30 to 45 minutes). The teacher can break the task into short lessons that can be managed independently by the student. When task complexity, rather than time, is a problem for the student, it may be helpful to break the task into steps. Eventually, time and task

complexity can be increased as the student develops academic and self-management skills.

3. *Alternate highly preferred with less preferred tasks.* In scheduling, it often helps if a less preferred activity is followed by a highly preferred activity. For example, if reading is preferred over math, math is scheduled first and followed by reading. If none of the academic subjects is preferred, it may be necessary to use nonacademic activities (such as art, recess, music, physical education, interest center) as preferred activities.

4. *Provide a daily schedule for each student.* A daily schedule provides students with learning problems with needed structure. It also presents them with expectations and a sequence of events in advance. Developing a daily schedule is made simpler by training the student to understand the routine of events that occur at the same time each day. This is accomplished by giving the student a schedule form, perhaps on a ditto or chalkboard, that specifies the time of events for the day. On assignments that are progressive (such as assignments in a text or workbook, or long-term writing, art, or science projects), the student may record his starting point for the next day on the schedule. In this manner, the subject area and specific activity are included on the schedule without involving much teacher time. When scheduling changes are needed, the teacher explains the new events or assignments.

5. *Schedule assignments that can be completed in one school day.* Students need the opportunity to begin each day with a "clean slate." They then do not have to worry about yesterday's incomplete or incorrect work. To make sure students are able to complete their work, several techniques may be used:
   a. Be certain assignments are at the student's instructional level.
   b. Make initial assignments short and increase them gradually.
   c. Provide leeway time for completing work.
   d. Reinforce on-task behavior.
   e. Provide answer keys and self-correcting materials.
   f. Make some assignments continuous (weekly), with daily aims and a completion date specified.
   g. Do not assign additional work to students who complete assignments ahead of schedule.

6. *Provide time cues.* The schedule designates the time allotted for each assignment. Many students with learning problems have difficulty managing their time and need reminders or cues. The following techniques may be useful as time reminders:
   a. Cut sections out of circular pieces of cardboard that are the same size as the face of the classroom clock. When these circular pieces are placed on the clock face, they display blocks of time on the clock. For example, a circle with ¼ section cut out displays a 15-minute block of time. The student receives time cues by observing the proportion of time exposed on the clock and the location of the minute hand in that exposed section.
   b. Set a kitchen timer for the amount of time allotted to an activity. On occasion a kitchen timer may be used with an individual student on a given activity. Both sound of the timer ticking and the movement of the dial remind the student to continue working.
   c. Periodically write the time remaining for an activity on the chalkboard or tell the class or individual student. Some students may be selected to perform this activity.

7. *Schedule activities in a complementary manner.* In an individualized program

teachers must organize student activities and plan time to provide individual assistance. Because some subjects require more teacher assistance than others, it often helps if the entire class is not working on the same subject at the same time (Eaton & Hansen, 1978). Math, spelling, and handwriting usually require less teacher assistance than reading. Thus, a teacher may be able to provide more individual assistance if part of the class is scheduled to work on math while others are working on reading.

8. *Plan a variety of activities.* Sometimes academic instruction is more effective if one activity is not too long and if a variety of activities are planned. Many teachers organize a 45-minute instructional period into three 15-minute segments. A sample math lesson may include the following activities: (a) direct teacher instruction, (b) seatwork or peer teaching activity, and (c) listening station (for taped instruction) or self-correcting material activity. In this plan, three students may be divided into three groups and rotated through the activities. The option of working in an interest center may be added for students who compete their work early.

Scheduling at the Elementary Level

Regular and special class elementary teachers often teach the same students for a large portion of the school day. This requires scheduling a variety of activities: opening exercises, reading, math, recess, art, and so on. The following techniques and suggestions are helpful in scheduling entire school days:

1. *Analyze the day's events.* The first step in developing a daily schedule is to analyze the daily events and determine how much time the teacher is responsible for planning. This time is affected by nonacademic school activities and supportive instructional services. After the teacher has determined the amount of time students are at lunch, resource room instruction, physical education, art, and so on, the teacher knows how much time must be scheduled. In a 6-hour school day, the classroom teacher probably needs to schedule 4½ to 5 hours. Planning 4½ to 5 hours of daily instruction for 180 days a year is a sizable project.

2. *Plan opening exercises.* Opening exercises usually require 15 to 20 minutes. They serve mainly to develop rapport and prepare the students for the day's activities. Also, the teacher uses this time to observe the attitudes, moods, and physical appearance of the students. The following are common activities for opening exercises: collecting lunch money; taking attendance; saluting the flag; recognizing special days (such as birthdays and holidays); discussing the schedule of activities for the day; and discussing current events, weather, or the date. For the young student who cannot read, Polloway, Patton, Payne, and Payne (1989) suggest using pictures to designate activities:

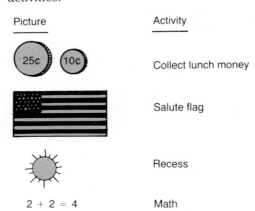

Picture	Activity
25¢ 10¢	Collect lunch money
(flag)	Salute flag
(sun)	Recess
2 + 2 = 4	Math

3. *Schedule academic instruction.* Although many students are more alert and easier to

motivate in the morning than in the afternoon, Dunn, Beaudry, and Klavas (1989) report that the majority of students with learning problems are more alert in the afternoon. Therefore, it helps to plan some intensive learning activities in the afternoon. Also, because students function at different academic levels, students should be divided into small groups for academic instruction.

4. *Plan closing exercises.* Closing exercises usually require 10 to 15 minutes. They are designed to tie together the school day in a pleasant, orderly manner. Some closing activities include cleaning up, returning materials, determining what to take home, reviewing the day's activities, discussing the next day's major events, and putting on jackets. Also, the teacher should make a concentrated effort to finish the day in a positive manner with each student.

The sample schedule presented in Table 3.4 stresses systematic and small-group academic work in reading and math in the morning and group-oriented activities in the afternoon. The schedule also provides time to complete unfinished work. This extra time permits slower students to finish their work and other students to work ahead or select interesting activities. The teacher may use this time to provide individual attention or conduct assessments. These flexible time periods reduce pressure and enable the teacher to individualize instruction. Often it is easier to assign math or spelling seatwork than reading seatwork; thus, the teacher may wish to give math or spelling seatwork to students when they are not receiving small-group reading instruction.

Scheduling at the Secondary Level

A typical secondary school schedule includes a homeroom period, five or six class periods, and a lunch period. Class periods are approx-

imately 50 minutes, and the teacher usually has one period for planning. Because a fixed schedule of periods exists at the secondary level, it may seem that teachers do not need to do much daily scheduling. However, because lessons must fit into 50-minute segments, planning is essential to ensure efficient use of instructional time.

In scheduling, an opening exercise may be limited to an explanation of the activities for the period, and a closing exercise simply may consist of allowing time to put away materials. Some secondary classes are structured so that students enter the room, get their work folder, and begin working. The teacher moves from group to group, or individual to individual, to offer assistance and reinforcement to the students. In this arrangement, opening activities are omitted, but time is scheduled for returning folders.

In planning for a period, it may be a good idea to divide the students into groups and schedule appropriate activities for each group. With this format a teacher may rotate through the groups. Some content is taught adequately to the whole group; however, when this arrangement is used, the teacher must ensure that all students understand the lecture material (for example, by taking questions from the students). The teacher should expect students with learning problems to need additional help during seatwork. This help may be provided by a classmate, special material, an aide, or the teacher.

General scheduling considerations that may be useful with adolescents with learning problems include the following:

1. If there is flexibility in scheduling electives, students can select courses in which they have a good opportunity to succeed. Scheduling that results in a heavy load or an unsympathetic teacher can cause serious difficulties for a learner with problems.

TABLE 3.4
Sample schedule.

Time	Activity		
8:30	Opening exercises		
8:50	Setting up and beginning work		
9:00	Reading period (small groups)		
	Group A	*Group B*	*Group C*
9:00	Group with teacher	Listening center	Paper-pencil task
9:15	Listening center	Paper-pencil task	Instructional game
9:30	Paper-pencil task	Instructional game	Group with teacher
9:45	Instructional game	Group with teacher	Listening center
10:00	Recess		
10:20	Math period (small groups)		
	Group 1	*Group 2*	*Group 3*
10:20	Paper-pencil task	Self-correcting material	Group with teacher
10:35	Self-correcting material	Group with teacher	Criterion test, timing, or math game
10:50	Group with teacher	Criterion test, timing, or math game	Paper-pencil task
11:05	Criterion test, timing, or math game	Paper-pencil task	Self-correcting material
11:20	Prescribed and selected activities including: choosing a free activity, going to the library, using an interest center, working on unfinished tasks, performing timings, taking a test, or playing an instructional or recreational game. The teacher may use this time to work with students who have been absent or out of the room, provide feedback, and give individual attention.		
11:45	Story time, handwriting, or content area (science, social studies)		
12:00	Lunch		
12:30	Spelling, language arts		
1:00	Physical education, music, art, or motor development		
1:30	Recess		
1:45	Content area (science, social studies, geography, career education, or citizenship)		
2:05	Prescribed and selected activities		
2:20	Closing activities		
2:30	Dismissal		

2. A course load must reflect the needs of the student. There should be a balance between courses that are demanding and those that are less demanding. Course substitution also may be used. If the school offers courses that are less demanding but satisfy required credits, the student with learning problems can avoid those courses in which he is likely to be unsuccessful.

3. Expanded course offerings are used in some settings to accommodate the student with learning problems. In these situations the special education staff teaches some content areas in a different setting.

Scheduling in the Resource Room

The resource room teacher is faced with a tedious and time-consuming scheduling task. Most of the difficulty stems from the fact that the student is participating in more than one instructional setting with two or more teachers. The following issues complicate resource room scheduling:

1. The student's academic, emotional, and social needs must be considered when determining the best time to schedule resource room instruction. If the student leaves the regular class for the resource room during an academic lesson, will he miss needed academic instruction? If he leaves during a nonacademic activity (such as art, physical education, or music), will the student resent missing a desirable activity?

2. Classroom teachers usually have preferred times for sending students to the resource room.

3. Students who come to the resource room at a specified time may have different instructional needs. For example, one student may need help with a specific math skill, whereas another student may need to work on reading comprehension.

4. In some situations it is helpful if the resource room teacher teaches in the regular class setting.

5. Because students are participating in parallel and complementary instructional programs, with different teachers working on the same instructional objectives, the resource room teacher must schedule time for conferring with classroom teachers.

Despite numerous scheduling difficulties, the resource program remains an important instructional model for serving students with learning problems. The following techniques and suggestions are helpful in resource room scheduling:

1. Students may come to the resource room at different times depending on the day. For example, they may come at a certain time 3 days a week and at another time on 2 days of the week. With this schedule the students consistently do not miss a given subject or activity in the regular class.

2. A resource teacher may choose to provide instruction in the various academic areas at fixed times during the day. With this type of schedule, reading, math, handwriting, and spelling are taught at a specified time, and students may come to the sessions they need. Thus, a student may come to the resource room for a half-hour of instruction one or more times daily to receive help in problem areas. Wiederholt, Hammill, and Brown (1983) refer to this as a staggered schedule.

3. To maximize the efficient use of time, the resource room teacher must encourage and reinforce being on time and making a quick transition from task to task within the resource room.

4. Several techniques are used to decrease the likelihood that students will disrupt the regular classroom when they return from the resource room. The resource teacher may give the student an assignment to work on

until the regular teacher can involve the student in the ongoing activities. Also, the classroom teacher may assign a student the responsibility of helping the returning student to begin work.

HOMEWORK

Homework continues to be a widely practiced activity in schools. Many consider it to be an important component for improving the quality of American education (Heller, Spooner, Anderson, & Mims, 1988). Langdon and Stout (1969) define homework as "any work related to school learning done outside the classroom, outside the regular school work hours, not under the immediate and direct supervision of the teacher and presumably at home under the jurisdiction of the home" (p. 13). Heller et al. outline the components of homework as it relates to special education. They report that a homework activity must (a) be teacher-directed, (b) include only previously taught skills, (c) be an extension of schoolwork, (d) be evaluated, (e) be based on instructional objectives appropriate to the student, and (f) occur outside school hours.

High rates of achievement are related to the amount of time students actively are engaged in academic tasks. Homework represents a viable method to help students with learning problems engage in academic tasks. Specifically, it helps them move through the acquisition, proficiency, maintenance, and generalization stages of learning (Mims, Harper, Armstrong, & Savage, 1991) and provides an opportunity for the teacher to control the temporal aspects of practice (that is, spaced versus massed practice) that are most effective for learning (Dempster, 1991).

Research on Homework

In a synthesis of research on homework in regular education, Cooper (1989) reports that homework positively affects achievement but that the effect varies considerably across grade levels. In essence, he notes that the effects of homework are substantial for secondary students and minimal for elementary students. For middle school students, the effects are good but are only about half as beneficial as for secondary students. Cooper also reports that the optimal amount of homework varies across grade levels.

In a survey of homework practices of 88 teachers of students with learning disabilities, Salend and Schliff (1989) found that most teachers (80 percent) use homework regularly but fail to use quality practices consistently. They report that 85 percent of the teachers experience problems in getting students to complete their homework. Salend and Schliff note that the low motivation of students to complete homework may be related to the failure of the learning disabilities teachers to (a) give feedback on homework (43 percent do not discuss or review homework), (b) incorporate homework into grading policies (42 percent do not regularly grade homework), or (c) involve parents in the homework process (only 41 percent solicit feedback from parents concerning their preferences for homework).

From the limited research on the effects of homework on students with learning problems, it appears that quality practices are related to positive student achievement. Although more research on homework is needed, quality homework practices should be shared with teachers in teacher education and staff development programs.

Guidelines for Quality Homework Practices

Guidelines from the literature (Al-Rubaiy, 1985; Armstrong & McPherson, 1991; Frith, 1991; Mims et al., 1991) and research (Cooper, 1989; Rosenberg, 1989) are available to promote "best practices" in homework:

1. *Assign a reasonable amount of homework.* From his synthesis on the homework research, Cooper (1989) recommends the following amount of homework:

First through third grade—one to three 15-minute assignments per week

Fourth through sixth grade—two to four 15- to 45-minute assignments per week

Seventh through ninth grade—up to five 45- to 75-minute assignments a week

Tenth through twelfth grade—up to five 75- to 120-minute assignments a week

The purpose of homework at the elementary level is to help students develop good study habits, practice newly acquired skills, and realize that learning can take place in nonschool environments. Also, fun-oriented homework activities for young students foster positive attitudes toward school and help them develop at-home study habits. Some fun-oriented learning activities include (a) compiling a class or neighborhood phone and address directory to learn alphabetizing, (b) listing items in the kitchen that begin with specific letters or contain targeted vowel sounds, and (c) making a scrapbook related to a hobby or theme. For students in seventh to twelfth grade, homework becomes important to academic achievement and school success. Homework serves to help students learn content, review previously presented material, write papers, and improve skills in writing, math, and reading. For students with learning problems, some motivating assignments are helpful to get them to spend time doing homework. Some activities include (a) writing a friend or a relative or requesting a company to send some free materials; (b) reviewing a newly released movie; (c) planning a visit to a selected city, state, or country; (d) interviewing their parents or neighbors about their childhood, current hobbies, or jobs; (e) conducting school surveys of student interests and concerns and graphing the results; and (f) tutoring some young students. To regulate the amount of time students spend on homework, the teacher periodically should check with students or parents about how much time homework is taking. Teachers who work in teams need to plan together on assigning homework. Moreover, because students take classes from different teachers in the upper grades, the teachers should work cooperatively to develop appropriate amounts of homework.

2. *Make homework an integral part of the learning process.* When the teacher discusses the rationale for homework and informs students of the specific objectives (such as mastery of skills) of each assignment, students are able to appreciate the value of homework. Rosenberg (1989) reports that when teachers discuss, review, explain, and evaluate homework assignments with students who have learning problems, homework becomes an effective learning activity. Al-Rubaiy (1985) notes that a feeling of ownership of the assignment is promoted when students recognize the value of homework. Homework should not be busy work or used as punishment.

3. *Plan homework assignments at the student's instructional level.* Teachers must ensure that assignments represent an appropriate match between the student's ability or skill level and the difficulty level of the assignment. This instructional match usually is maintained when the teacher assigns homework to practice or review material that the student has been taught. Students need to experience high success rates on homework. Rosenberg (1989) recommends a rate of 70 percent or above correct.

4. *Make sure the student understands the assignment.* Understanding is promoted

when the assignment is similar to class-work. When the assignment is new or different, the teacher should demonstrate the task and provide some guided practice on a portion of the assignment. Understanding also is facilitated when directions are clear and simple and when students are asked to explain the task.

5. *Evaluate homework.* Teachers should evaluate all homework assignments and maintain a cumulative record of the results. Assigning a grade encourages students to complete assignments and develop a sense of responsibility. Moreover, for students who do not test well, homework provides an opportunity to improve their grades and display their skills and knowledge (Mims et al., 1991).

6. *Reinforce the completion of homework.* Teachers should indicate that homework is important to help students learn and develop responsibility. When students complete their homework, encouragement should be provided. Encouragement may be private (verbal praise, note sent home, sticker, high grade) or public (bulletin board display of work, display of names of homework stars). Also, the entire class or teams of students may be encouraged when each member has completed the assignment or improved in the number of assignments completed. Whole-class encouragement may consist of providing a special privilege for the entire class when homework is turned in on time by 90 percent of the students.

7. *Involve parents in homework.* Initially, the teacher should send a letter to parents regarding homework policies and practices. Because letters do not always represent a functional medium of communication to homes, it may be necessary for the teacher to discuss homework in parent conferences, at PTA meetings, during parent

nights at school, or on the telephone. Information for parents should include (a) purpose of homework, (b) expected frequency of homework, (c) approximate amount of time that assignments should take, (d) homework evaluation procedures, (e) effects of homework on grades, and (f) suggestions for parents on how to help with homework. Some tips regarding parent involvement include:

a. Schedule a specific time and place for homework. In many homes the best time is immediately following dinner, and the best place is usually at the kitchen or dining room table.

b. Supervise the homework session by periodically checking with the student to determine progress rather than overseeing every task.

c. Provide an environment conducive to learning. The area needs to be well lighted and free of things that distract the student. Distractors are different for individual students.

d. Provide the student with appropriate materials.

e. Sign and date completed homework assignments.

f. Encourage and praise the student for doing homework.

g. Share with the teacher any concerns involving the amount of work or the difficulty level of the assignments.

8. *Facilitate homework through effective support systems.* Frith (1991) suggests using the following support systems to support homework activities:

a. Use peer tutoring for checking and assessing homework and for giving corrective feedback.

b. Use computer-assisted instruction for students who have access to computers.

c. Encourage parents to support the value of homework with their actions and words.

d. Develop monitoring systems (such as graphs or checklists) for homework.

e. Develop schoolwide support for homework. The school administrators and staff should encourage and praise effective homework practices.

In his concluding remarks concerning homework, Frith (1991) states,

> For maximum usefulness, homework assignments need to be made in the context of a strong support system that includes assistance from teachers and peers as well as parents. A strong support system will increase positive impressions that students have toward homework, especially when it might appear that these assignments are imposing on their free time. Regardless of perspective, homework is certainly important, and it should be viewed as an integral component of the instructional program—not only in regular education but in special education as well. (p. 49)

GRADING

The practice of grading students is a fundamental component of the educational system. Despite its major role in assessing and providing feedback to students, parents, and institutions (colleges and employers), limited agreement exists concerning the most appropriate grading practices. The discussions about grading become more uncertain when the issue of how to grade students with learning problems is considered. S. B. Cohen (1983) notes that, in spite of the importance of grades in our educational system and the numerous problems encountered by educators when grading students in general and special-needs students in particular, the issue of grading has received relatively little attention by teacher educators.

Grades have been defined as symbols (letters or numbers) that relate to a student's quality of achievement or performance rather than to the amount of work expended. Grades represent a value judgment about the quality of a student's achievement relative to a course of objectives during a specified time period (Terwilliger, 1977). Generally, grades are used to compare performances among students or to reflect achievement in terms of an established standard. Although several grading systems exist (such as pass/fail, checklists, contracts), the most commonly used systems involve letters (A, B, C, D, F) or numbers (1, 2, 3, 4, 5). These letter or number grades reflect levels of performance ranging from outstanding to failing. Percentage ranges typically are used to determine criteria for an assigned letter grade (for example, 90 to 100 percent = A).

Guidelines for Developing an Effective Grading System

From a review of the research on grading, Rojewski, Pollard, and Meers (1990) note that grading issues are highlighted but reports of successful practices are limited. Although the research is limited regarding proven grading practices, selected educators (Dempster, 1991; Rojewski et al., 1990; Sprick, 1985) provide some viable directions for developing grading systems for students with learning problems:

1. *Determine grades on the basis of course objectives.* A major percentage of a final grade should be based on the student's mastery of course objectives (Rojewski et al., 1990; Sprick, 1985). For example, a failing grade indicates that the student did not master the course objectives. Students who achieve mastery receive an average grade (for example, C), and students who exceed the objectives receive higher grades (for example, B or A). Grading on mastery of clearly defined course objectives provides each student with an opportunity to pass the course. When students can pass a

course on the basis of mastered course objectives, they realize that they can succeed regardless of the performance of other students. Their grade is not determined on the basis of their performance relative to other students as is practiced when normal curve grading is used. Thus, students with learning problems are not competing with higher performing students for grades.

2. *Use multiple evaluation methods.* Final grades should be based on a variety of activities including tests, quizzes, papers or projects, homework, and class participation. For students who are not good at taking tests, these multiple evaluations provide an opportunity to demonstrate their skills or knowledge. Table 3.5 presents a grading system that includes multiple evaluations. Sprick (1985) provides extensive criteria for evaluating class participation (that is, managing a system that deals with tardiness, disruptions, absences, late work).

3. *Teach students to understand the grading system.* The procedure of assigning points to activities and basing grades on a point total helps students with learning problems understand the grading system. Sprick (1985) notes that many students who are low achievers do not understand grading systems and seldom know what their current grades are throughout the school year. He points out the importance of teaching students to understand their grades and of having students maintain a weekly record of their grades in each class or subject area.

4. *Monitor the performance of students frequently and give feedback.* It is important for students to participate in frequent evaluation activities and receive feedback on their performances. Dempster (1991) notes that frequently spaced testing yields higher levels of achievement than infrequent testing. Also, he reports that tests on material

recently presented promote learning. Emmer et al. (1989) report that regular feedback provides students with needed information and reduces the time they practice errors if responses are incorrect. The curriculum-based measurement procedures described in Chapter 2 provide an excellent system for frequently monitoring student performances.

5. *Remember that an effective grading system is a motivational tool.* Sprick (1985) stresses that the grading system is a motivational tool that the teacher controls:

An effective grading system is more than an evaluation tool; it is also an instructional tool and a motivational tool. If designed and implemented well, a grading system can encourage students to try their best each day. An increase in daily motivation increases the chance that students will keep up with the work and learn how to demonstrate mastery of course objectives. (p. 35)

RECORD KEEPING

Record keeping for instructional purposes refers to the process of collecting and organizing data on student progress. Keeping a record of student progress enables the teacher to make timely instructional decisions. Also, record keeping is necessary for planning and implementing individualized educational programs and for reporting student progress to parents.

Because students receive instruction in a wide range of skills that vary greatly in complexity, the task of recording student progress is not simple. Data collection can become quite cumbersome and awkward; thus, teachers may view it as a negative part of the instructional process. However, record keeping provides the teacher with essential information and therefore is a positive component of the instructional program. When record keep-

TABLE 3.5
A grading system with multiple evaluations.

Student Grade Sheet

Student_____

Subject area_____

Tests:
1. Score _____/100 points
2. Score _____/100 points
3. Score _____/100 points
4. Score _____/100 points   Total _____/400 points

Quizzes:
1. Score _____/20 points
2. Score _____/20 points
3. Score _____/20 points
4. Score _____/20 points   Total _____/80 points

Project or Paper:
1. Score _____/120 points   Total _____/120 points

Homework:
1. Score _____/10 points
2. Score _____/10 points
3. Score _____/10 points
4. Score _____/10 points
5. Score _____/10 points
6. Score _____/10 points
7. Score _____/10 points
8. Score _____/10 points
9. Score _____/10 points
10. Score _____/10 points   Total _____/100 points

Weekly participation:
Week 1 _____/20 points
Week 2 _____/20 points
Week 3 _____/20 points
Week 4 _____/20 points
Week 5 _____/20 points
Week 6 _____/20 points   Total _____/120 points
                                                               Final Score _____/ 820 points

ing is developed and managed correctly, many benefits are realized:

1. Students often enjoy participating in recording their progress.
2. Teachers can gain satisfaction from having documented student progress.
3. Teachers can pinpoint learning difficulties and make timely interventions.
4. Teachers can share the progress of students with parents, principals, and other school personnel.
5. The data can be used to help make program and placement decisions.

A record-keeping system must serve two primary functions. First, a composite or master form is needed to record the progress of students on major objectives across all curriculum areas. For the elementary teacher this form includes several curriculum areas, whereas for a secondary teacher it may include only one area. Progress recorded on the composite form serves as a basis for evaluating students and reporting information to others. Second, a system is needed to record and evaluate the progress of students on daily or weekly instructional objectives. Suggestions and activities for recording student progress are featured in the curriculum area chapters throughout the text.

Composite Record Keeping

The first step in developing a composite record-keeping system is to organize instructional objectives. These objectives must be specific, measurable, and organized in steps small enough to reveal short-term progress (days to weeks). Instructional objectives that are in a sequence must be listed in a hierarchical manner. Nonsequential objectives (for example, social skills objectives such as taking turns in a game or raising a hand to talk) should be clustered in a meaningful way. The sequential objectives on the composite form should be in larger steps than the daily instructional objectives.

The composite record of student progress provides the teacher with information for grouping the students for instruction. Students who are working on the same or similar objectives in a specific subject area may be organized into a small group for instruction. Once the initial instructional groups are established, the daily recording of student progress enables the teacher to change grouping patterns throughout the year. The student thus can move to and from groups on the basis of

progress. The composite record also helps the teacher with the difficult problem of grading students.

Some commercial materials organize the objectives and provide the teacher with record-keeping forms. Curriculum guides developed by school curriculum committees often outline the instructional objectives by subject area across grade levels. In addition, scope and sequence skills lists (such as those provided in Appendix A) provide a framework for organizing objectives.

A composite record-keeping form should be kept simple. Also, because it is used for a long period by numerous people, it helps to use sturdy material. The sample form presented in Table 3.6 is organized by subject area for simplicity; for sturdiness, it may be constructed on a manila folder. When a folder is used, materials (such as criterion test results) may be placed in it for recording.

Daily Record Keeping

To establish a daily record-keeping system, short-term instructional objectives must be identified and arranged in a sequential order whenever possible. Criteria for mastery of the objectives must be established. Students should learn to evaluate and record their daily performances as much as possible.

A student progress book frequently is used. This is suitable especially for the secondary teacher who teaches the same subject to many students. Table 3.7 presents a progress book of daily or short-term objectives in social studies. Also, Archer and Edgar (1976) suggest a format for recording performances on spelling words. In this format, presented in Table 3.8, the number of correct and incorrect responses is recorded.

For some instructional objectives that relate to social skills, observations may be recorded on tally sheets. For example, the teacher may

TABLE 3.6
Class progress record in reading.

Students' Names	Instructional Objective: Pages in Textbook											
	1–5	6–11	12–20	21–26	27–31	32–40	41–43	44–47	48–51	52–58	59–64	65–68
1. Archer, B.	9/3	9/10	9/19	9/26	9/30	10/6	10/11	10/19	10/24	10/31		
2. Dillard, W.	9/3	9/16	9/30	10/11	10/24	10/31						
3. Gruggs, G.	9/7	9/18	10/4	10/23								
4. Hiller, D.	9/8	9/20	10/7	10/20	10/27							
5. Hunt, T.	9/7	9/19	10/4	10/22								
25. West, R.	9/4	9/15	9/19	9/30	10/6	10/12	10/27					

Note: Each objective is based on pages completed in a commercial material (for example, workbook or reader).

TABLE 3.7
Progress book of short-term objectives in social studies.

Students' Names	Social Studies Objectives							
Boyer, R.	79 9/20	80 9/21	81 9/22	82 9/24	87 9/25	88	89	90
Chestnut, W.	91 9/14	92 9/17	93 9/18	101 9/19	102 9/20	103 9/22	104	105
Martin, A.	49 9/20	52 9/22	53 9/24	54 9/25	55	80	81	82
Parker, D.	79 9/8	80 9/10	81 9/11	82 9/12	87 9/13	88 9/14	89 9/19	90
Rice, S.	91 9/17	92 9/19	93 9/20	101 9/22	102	103	104	105

Note: Since social studies objectives may not always be sequential, the numbers may not always be consecutive.

wish to reduce out-of-seat behavior during math seatwork. Also, a tally sheet may be used to record academic responses. The teacher can make a tally each time the student capitalizes the first word in a sentence or responds correctly to a specific question.

The record-keeping formats presented in this section provide the teacher with a variety of options for establishing a daily recording system. No matter which format is selected, the following steps must be followed in planning a data-recording system (Archer & Edgar, 1976):

Step 1: Write a measurable short-term objective.

Step 2: Determine the measurement dimension to be used (for example, accuracy, rate correct and incorrect, or frequency).

TABLE 3.8
Format for recording performances on spelling words.

Name: Bobby Richards			
Date	Spelling List Number	Correct Responses	Error Responses
10/2	1	14	6
10/3	1	16	4
10/4	1	17	3
10/5	1	20	0
10/6	2	15	5
10/9	2	16	4
10/10	2	19	1
10/11	3	11	9
10/12	3	16	4
10/13	3	17	3
10/16	3	19	1
10/17	4	17	3
10/18	4	20	0

Step 3: Decide how often to assess the behavior (daily 1-minute sample, 10-minute criterion test, weekly unit test, all out-of-seat behavior during math seatwork).

Step 4: Establish a consistent schedule for measuring the behavior.

Step 5: Select a recording format.

THE PARENT-TEACHER PARTNERSHIP

Teachers should work closely with parents to promote learning in school and at home. When parents are involved and cooperative, the home becomes the supportive foundation that the student needs to face the changing demands of school. In discussing the benefits of cooperative parent-teacher efforts, Kroth (1985) notes that when teachers and parents participate in cooperative planning, they may prevent, alleviate, or solve many problems that arise during the educational progress of the student. Teachers and parents should recognize their roles as complementary and supplementary and view their relationship as a partnership to foster the student's progress.

Establishing Cooperation

Teachers and parents often harbor attitudes about each other that inhibit mutual cooperation. These attitudes sometimes manifest themselves through "teacher blaming" or "parent blaming." Such dissonance benefits no one. Its sources should be identified, and strategies should be pursued to promote a cooperative and working relationship.

Initial progress toward cooperation hinges on development of mutual respect. Barsch (1969) suggests that parents prefer a teacher who approaches them as individuals, treats them with dignity, and conveys a feeling of acceptance. Parents do not want to be treated as simply a parent of a student with learning problems. Barsch points out, "As teachers are able to convey a feeling of acceptance of the person, the parent is reciprocally more accepting of whatever counsel the teacher may offer" (p. 11).

The *Parent as a Teacher Inventory* (Strom, 1984) is a composite attitude scale for helping educators understand parent perceptions about their student with learning problems. Moreover, Cone, DeLawyer, and Wolfe (1985) report good results from their instrument, the Parent/Family Involvement Index (PFII). The PFII assesses parent participation in 12 categories pertinent to good parent-teacher relationships.

Many obstacles can inhibit cooperative parent-teacher relationships. However, their common goal should enable both to transcend the obstacles and work together.

Parent-Teacher Conferences

Parent-teacher conferences create an environment in which parents feel they are working in a cooperative partnership with the schools. Many school districts encourage the special education teacher to meet with the parents before the student begins receiving special education services. Duncan and Fitzgerald (1969) found that early meetings with parents served to prevent or reduce attendance problems, the number of dropouts, and discipline problems. Moreover, early meetings were associated with higher grades and good future communication.

Parent-teacher conferences are a valuable medium for establishing positive communication, which is the key to good home-school relationships. Schulz (1987) notes that, in general, the purposes of parent-teacher conferences fall into one or more of four categories: (a) to give information (for example, report student progress, present evaluation data, share samples of the student's work), (b) to get information (that is, concerning the student's history, interests, home behavior, and social relationships as well as parental suggestions), (c) to plan for the student (for example, assist in the planning process for improved education through the development of an individualized educational program), and (d) to solve problems (that is, use collaborative problem solving, brainstorm, select viable alternatives).

The initial conference is extremely important. To prepare, the teacher should examine the student's records and review pertinent information such as present status (for example, chronological age, grade, class, previous teacher), physical appearance and history, educational status, personal traits, and home and family characteristics. In planning the meeting, the teacher should identify objectives of the meeting and develop an appropriate agenda. The conference time should be convenient for all attending, and the meeting place should be arranged to promote communication.

Successful conferences typically consist of four parts: (a) establishing rapport, (b) obtain-

ing pertinent information from the parents, (c) providing information, and (d) summarizing the conference and planning follow-up activities (Stephens & Wolf, 1989). Stephens and Wolf suggest that starting with neutral topics and providing a comfortable seat help establish rapport. To obtain information, the teacher should state the purpose of the conference, ask open-ended questions, recognize parent feelings by reflecting their statements, and avoid irrelevant issues (such as marital problems). To provide information, the teacher should start with positive statements about the student's behavior and provide samples of work when possible, avoid educational jargon, and share anticipated plans. To summarize the conference, the teacher should briefly review the main points concerning the student's progress, restate the activities that will be implemented to deal with identified weaknesses and problems, and answer any questions. Finally, the teacher and parent should discuss and agree on follow-up strategies and schedule another meeting, if necessary. The conference should end on a positive note, and the teacher should thank the parents for their input and interest and also offer to be available for any future questions concerning the student.

Heward, Dardig, and Rossett (1979) provide a helpful parent-teacher conference outline (see Table 3.9). In addition, Kroth and Simpson (1977) and Ehly, Conoley, and Rosenthal (1985) discuss various strategies, ideas, and activities to maximize the benefits of parent conferences.

Listening is the key to communication, and both parties must listen. A good listener gains much information that often can help solve problems. Parents like to talk to a teacher who listens in a sympathetic, calm, and nonjudgmental manner. Several authors (Dinkmeyer & Carlson, 1973; Gordon, 1970) stress the importance of active listening (that is, being involved in helping another define problems and

TABLE 3.9
Parent-teacher conference outline.

Conference Outline

Date _____   Time _____

Student _____

Parent(s) _____

Teacher _____

Other staff present _____

Objectives for conference:

Student's strengths:

Area(s) where improvement is needed:

Questions to ask parents:

Parent's responses/comments:

Examples of student's work/interactions:

Current programs and strategies used by teacher:

Suggestions for parents:

Suggestions from parents:

Follow-up activities:

   Parent(s):

   Teacher:

Date called for follow-up and outcome:

Source: *From Working with Parents of Handicapped Children* (p. 233) by W. L. Heward. J. C. Dardig, and A. Rossett, 1979. New York: Merrill/Macmillan. Copyright 1979 by Bell & Howell Company. Reprinted by permission.

clarify beliefs and values). Active listening involves increased levels of responding, body animation, and questioning. Eye contact is a basic component of good listening, whereas fatigue, strong feelings, word usage, too much talking, and environmental distractions deter active listening. Simpson (1990) notes that to facilitate the communication process, the effective listener must demonstrate skills in attention, acceptance, and empathy as well as use specific listening strategies (for example, door-opening statements, clarifying responses, restatements, reflective silence, summarization). He states that "the professional who attempts to respond to parents prior to listening to them, or the educator who too hastily assumes the position of 'telling' parents what to do or 'answers' their questions when they simply desire the opportunity to talk, will rarely offer the most satisfactory conferencing relationship" (p. 124).

To evaluate the conference, Simpson (1990) suggests that feedback can be obtained by asking parents and teachers to respond to various questions such as the following:

1. Was a folder of the student's representative work prepared for the parents?
2. Was sufficient time allotted for the session?
3. Did the teacher provide the parent with an opportunity to ask questions?
4. Was the teacher able to explain the student's academic program (remediation strategy) to the parents?
5. Was the teacher able to provide an adequate report of social and emotional progress?
6. Was the teacher able to solicit and respond to questions raised by the parents?

Reporting Student Progress

In most school districts, teachers send home progress report cards six times a year, each covering a 6-week period. Parents receiving these reports cannot reinforce and encourage specific skill development on a daily basis. Several studies (Kroth, Whelan, & Stables, 1970; Simonson, 1972) explore the use of daily report card systems.

Under daily systems, the report card usually remains on the student's desk all day. The teacher records the progress or instructs the student to record it during the instructional activities. At the end of the day, the teacher signs each card. Fairchild (1987) notes that use of the daily report card can help to establish communication with parents and relay various information such as academic performance, effort, behavior, peer relationships, and homework completion. The daily report card system also allows parents to reinforce improved academic performance or school behavior.

Teachers who use curriculum-based measurement or who chart each student's progress can send the charts home periodically. For parents who want to reinforce specific skills, the chart has the advantage of reflecting progress on each target skill. A teacher may choose to report the student's progress using any metric system (such as percent, rate, number correct, checklist) that the teacher, parent, and student understand.

Not all students benefit from the daily system. Some teachers and parents prefer weekly progress reports that give the student the opportunity to recover from a "bad day." Such reports also take less of the teacher's time. In addition, teachers should consider making a phone call or sending home notes, "happy grams," or achievement certificates when the student masters a specific skill. Kroth (1985) describes numerous methods that have been used successfully with parents of students with learning problems.

REFERENCES

Al-Rubaiy, K. (1985, Summer). . . . and now for your homework assignment, *The Directive Teacher.* pp. 3–5.

Anderson, L. M., Evertson, C. M., & Brophy, J. E. (1979). An experimental study of effective teaching in first grade reading groups. *Elementary School Journal, 79*, 193–223.

Archer, A., & Edgar, E. (1976). Teaching academic skills to mildly handicapped children. In S. Lowenbraun & J. Q. Affleck (Eds.), *Teaching mildly handicapped children in regular classes* (pp. 15–112). New York: Merrill/Macmillan.

Armstrong, S. W., & McPherson, A. (1991). Homework as a critical component in social skills instruction. *Teaching Exceptional Children, 24*(1), 45–47.

Barsch, R. H. (1969). *The parent teacher partnership.* Arlington, VA: Council for Exceptional Children.

Bloom, B. (1984). The search for methods of group instruction as effective as one-to-one tutoring. *Educational Leadership, 41*(8), 4–18.

Carnine, D., Silbert, J., & Kameenui, E. J. (1990). *Direct instruction reading* (2nd ed.). New York: Merrill/Macmillan.

Cohen, S. B. (1983). Assigning report card grades to the mainstreamed child. *Teaching Exceptional Children, 15*, 86–89.

Cohen, P. A., Kulik, J. A., & Kulik, C. C. (1982). Educational outcomes of tutoring: A meta-analysis of findings. *American Educational Research Journal, 19*(2), 237–248.

Cone, J. D., DeLawyer, D. D., & Wolfe, V. V. (1985). Assessing parent participation: The Parent/Family Involvement Index. *Exceptional Children, 51*, 417–424.

Cooper, H. (1989). Synthesis of research on homework. *Educational Leadership, 47*(3), 85–91.

Delquadri, J., Greenwood, C. R., Whorton, D., Carta, J. J., & Hall, R. V. (1986). Classwide peer tutoring. *Exceptional Children, 52*, 535–542.

Dempster, F. N. (1991). Synthesis of research on reviews and tests. *Educational Leadership, 48*(7), 71–76.

DeVries, D. L., & Slavin, R. E. (1978). Teams-games-tournament (TGT): Review of ten classroom experiments. *Journal of Research and Development in Education, 12*, 28–38.

Dinkmeyer, D., & Carlson, J. (Eds.). (1973). *Consulting: Facilitating human potential and change processes.* New York: Merrill/Macmillan.

Duncan, L. W., & Fitzgerald, P. W. (1969). Increasing the parent-child communication through counselor-parent conferences. *Personnel and Guidance Journal, 47*, 514–517.

Dunn, R., Beaudry, J. S., & Klavas, A. (1989). Survey of research on learning styles. *Educational Leadership, 46*(6), 50–58.

Eaton, M. D., & Hansen, C. L. (1978). Classroom organization and management. In N. G. Haring, T. C. Lovitt, M. D. Eaton, & C. L. Hansen, *The fourth R: Research in the classroom* (pp. 191–217). New York: Merrill/Macmillan.

Ehly, S. W., Conoley, J. C., & Rosenthal, D. M. (1985). *Working with parents of exceptional children.* New York: Merrill/Macmillan.

Emmer, E. T., Evertson, C. M., Sanford, J. P., Clements, B. S., & Worsham, M. E. (1989). *Classroom management for secondary teachers* (2nd ed.). Englewood Cliffs, NJ: Prentice-Hall.

Fairchild, T. N. (1987). The daily report card. *Teaching Exceptional Children, 19*(2), 72–73.

Forness, S. R., & Kavale, K. A. (1985). Effects of class size on attention, communication, and disruption of mildly mentally retarded children. *American Educational Research Journal, 22*(3), 403–412.

Frith, G. (1991). Facilitating homework through effective support systems. *Teaching Exceptional Children, 24*(1), 48–49.

Gelfand, D. M., & Hartmann, D. P. (1984). *Child behavior analysis and therapy* (2nd ed.). New York: Pergamon Press.

Gordon, T. (1970). *Parent effectiveness training.* New York: Peter H. Wyden.

Greenwood, C. R., Carta, J. J., & Hall, R. V. (1988). The use of peer tutoring strategies in classroom management and educational instruction. *School Psychology Review, 17*(2), 258–275.

Grimes, L. (1981). Computers are for kids: Designing software programs. *Teaching Exceptional Children, 14*, 48–53.

Heller, H. W., Spooner, F., Anderson, D., & Mims, A. (1988). Homework: A review of special education classroom practices in the Southeast. *Teacher Education and Special Education, 11*, 43–51.

Heward, W. L., Dardig, J. C., & Rossett, A. (1979). *Working with parents of handicapped children.* New York: Merrill/Macmillan.

Hughes, C. A., Ruhl, K. L., & Peterson, S. K. (1988). Teaching self-management skills. *Teaching Exceptional Children, 20*(2), 70–72.

Jenkins, J. R., & Jenkins, L. M. (1987). Making peer tutoring work. *Educational Leadership, 44*(6), 64–68.

Kagan, S. (1989/1990). The structural approach to cooperative learning. *Educational Leadership, 47*(4), 12–15.

Kroth, R. L. (1985). *Communicating with parents of exceptional children* (2nd ed.). Denver: Love.

Kroth, R. L., & Simpson, R. L. (1977). *Parent conferences as a teaching strategy.* Denver: Love.

Kroth, R. L., Whelan, R. J., & Stables, J. M. (1970). Teacher application of behavioral principles in home and classroom environments. *Focus on Exceptional Children, 3,* 1–10.

Langdon, G., & Stout, I. W. (1969). *Homework.* New York: John Day.

Lenz, B. K., Deshler, D. D., & Schumaker, J. B. (1990). *The development and validation of planning routines to enhance the delivery of content to students with handicaps in general education settings* (Progress report). Lawrence: University of Kansas Institute for Research in Learning Disabilities.

Levin, H., Glass, G., & Meister, C. (1984). *Cost-effectiveness of four educational interventions.* Stanford, CA: Institute for Research on Educational Finance and Governance, Stanford University.

Maheady, L., Harper, G. F., & Sacca, M. K. (1988). Peer-mediated instruction: A promising approach to meeting the diverse needs of LD adolescents. *Learning Disability Quarterly, 11,* 108–113.

Maheady, L., Sacca, M. K., & Harper, G. F. (1988). Classwide peer tutoring with mildly handicapped high school students. *Exceptional Children, 55,* 52–59.

Mims, A., Harper, C., Armstrong, S. W., & Savage, S. (1991). Effective instruction in homework for students with disabilities. *Teaching Exceptional Children, 24*(1), 42–44.

Mueller, D. J., Chase, C. I., & Walden, J. D. (1988). Effects of reduced class size in primary classes. *Educational Leadership, 45*(5), 48–50.

Osguthorpe, R. T., & Scruggs, T. E. (1986). Special education students as tutors: A review and analysis. *Remedial and Special Education, 7*(4), 15–26.

Polloway, E. A., Patton, J. R., Payne, J. S., & Payne, R. A. (1989). *Strategies for teaching learners with special needs* (4th ed.). New York: Merrill/Macmillan.

Robinson, G. E. (1990). Synthesis of research on class size. *Educational Leadership, 47*(7), 80–90.

Rojewski, J. W., Pollard, R. R., & Meers, G. D. (1990). Grading mainstreamed special needs students: Determining practices and attitudes of secondary vocational educators using a qualitative approach. *Remedial and Special Education, 12*(1), 7–15, 28.

Rooney, K. J., & Hallahan, D. P. (1985). Future directions for cognitive behavior modification research: The quest for cognitive change. *Remedial and Special Education, 6*(2), 46–51.

Rosenberg, M. S. (1989). The effects of daily homework assignments on the acquisition of basic skills by students with learning disabilities. *Journal of Learning Disabilities, 22,* 314–323.

Salend, S. J., & Schliff, J. (1989). An examination of the homework practices of teachers of students with learning disabilities. *Journal of Learning Disabilities, 22,* 621–623.

Schloss, P. J., & Sedlak, R. A. (1986). *Instructional methods for students with learning and behavior problems.* Boston: Allyn & Bacon.

Schulz, J. B. (1987). *Parents and professionals in special education.* Boston: Allyn & Bacon.

Scruggs, T. E., & Richter, L. (1985). Tutoring learning disabled students: A critical review. *Learning Disability Quarterly, 8,* 286–298.

Simonson, G. (1972). *Modification of reading comprehension scores using a home contract with parental control of reinforcers.* Unpublished master's thesis, University of Kansas, Lawrence.

Simpson, R. L. (1990). *Conferencing parents of exceptional children* (2nd ed.). Austin, TX: Pro-Ed.

Slavin, R. E. (1978). Student teams and achievement divisions. *Journal of Research and Development in Education, 12,* 39–49.

Slavin, R. E. (1986). *Using student team learning* (3rd ed.). Baltimore, MD: Center for Research on Elementary and Middle Schools, Johns Hopkins University.

Slavin, R. E. (1988). Synthesis of research on grouping in elementary and secondary schools. *Educational Leadership, 46*(1), 67–77.

Slavin, R. E. (1989/1990). Research on cooperative learning: Consensus and controversy. *Educational Leadership, 47*(4), 52–54.

Slavin, R. E. (1991). Synthesis of research on cooperative learning. *Educational Leadership, 48*(5), 71–82.

Slavin, R. E., Madden, N. A., & Stevens, R. J. (1990). Cooperative learning models for the 3 R's. *Educational Leadership, 47*(4), 22–28.

Slavin, R. E., Stevens, R. J., & Madden N. A. (1988). Accommodating student diversity in reading and writing instruction: A cooperative learning approach. *Remedial and Special Education, 9*(1), 60–66.

Sprick, R. S. (1981). *The solution book: A guide to classroom discipline.* Chicago: Science Research Associates.

Sprick, R. S. (1985). *Discipline in the secondary classroom: A problem-by-problem survival guide.* West Nyack, NY: The Center for Applied Research in Education.

Sprick, R. S. (1991). *Discipline and responsibility: A team approach.* Eugene, OR: Teaching Strategies.

Stephens, T. M., & Wolf, J. S. (1989). *Effective skills in parent/teacher conferencing* (2nd ed.). Columbus, OH: School Study Council of Ohio, College of Education, Ohio State University.

Strom, R. D. (1984). *Parent as a Teacher Inventory manual.* Bensenville, IL: Scholastic Testing Service.

Terwilliger, J. S. (1977). Assigning grades— Philosophical issues and practical recommendations. *Journal of Research and Development in Education, 10,* 21–39.

Wiederholt, J. L., Hammill, D. D., & Brown, V. L. (1983). *The resource teacher: A guide to effective practices* (2nd ed.). Austin, TX: Pro-Ed.

Workman, E. A. (1982). *Teaching behavioral self-control to students.* Austin, TX: Pro-Ed.

CHAPTER 4

Choosing and Developing Materials

As much as 75 to 99 percent of each student's instructional time is planned around classroom materials (Bartel & Hammill, 1990). The instructional materials used in a classroom have an enormous effect on the quality of educational programming for students with learning problems. Academic materials influence the instructional procedures of most teachers. Selected teacher procedures affected by academic materials include the presentation of advance organizers, the demonstration of a concept or skill, the monitoring of student progress, the use of corrective feedback, the use of activities that promote generalization, the use of activities that encourage student responding, and the use of activities that foster mastery learning. In essence, materials have the potential to influence the degree to which a teacher engages in effective teaching practices.

Academic materials have a direct influence on what is taught to students, how it is sequenced, the number of lessons used to cover content, the quality and quantity of demonstration and practice activities, and whether mastery and generalization are featured. Moreover, academic materials may determine whether a teacher is able to individualize instruction. In essence, academic materials readily can influence whether students with learning problems succeed or fail.

It is apparent that the selection of academic materials warrants much attention and professional judgment. Unfortunately, most publishers do not make this selection an easy task. Sprick (1987) reports that only 3 percent of commercial materials are field tested before marketing. If educators are to close the gap between what is known about effective teaching and what is practiced in our nation's schools, publishers must make extensive efforts to include research-based practices in their materials. Moveover, school leaders who make material adoption decisions need to de-

mand that publishers provide appropriate field-test and research data for their materials. Without such data, it is reasonable to conclude that publishers and educators are perpetuating "experimental practices" on our nation's teachers and students.

Fortunately, some publishers are teaming with teachers and researchers to develop materials and validate their effectiveness. For example, Science Research Associates (SRA) has worked with researchers at the University of Oregon to develop and publish Direct Instruction materials. These Direct Instruction materials have proven to be successful with students who are at risk for school failure. Direct Instruction materials from SRA are presented in each of the curriculum area chapters throughout this book. Moreover, researchers at the University of Kansas Institute for Research in Learning Disabilities have teamed with publishers (Edge Enterprises, American Guidance Service) to validate the effectiveness of Learning Strategy materials with students who have learning problems. These Learning Strategy materials primarily are featured in Chapter 14. A brief overview of Direct Instruction is presented next.

DIRECT INSTRUCTION

Direct Instruction officially began in 1966 when Bereiter and Engelmann published a book titled *Teaching Disadvantaged Children in the Preschool.* Engelmann maintains that it is more important to develop instructional sequences that systematically teach students essential reading skills, mathematical concepts, and language concepts than to spend time attempting to understand the inner workings of the mind, temperaments, and developmental levels. Because this approach conflicted with the prevailing theories of the 1960s, much controversy resulted, and many educators claimed that Direct Instruction was overly simplistic. Now, as Direct Instruction enters its third decade of practice, many educators have examined the empirical studies of effective instruction (Brophy & Good, 1986; Rosenshine, 1986) and realize the promise and effectiveness of the approach that Engelmann conceptualized. The growing list of extensive studies that document the effectiveness of Direct Instruction across low and higher-order skills with at-risk and special education students (Carnine, 1990; Gersten & Keating, 1987; Gersten, Woodward, & Darch, 1986) provides educators with an encouraging data base from which to plan the best instructional practices in the 1990s.

To many educators, *direct instruction* has become a generic term used to refer to the structured teaching of academic skills or to a system for effective classroom management. In this text, the University of Oregon model of Direct Instruction is capitalized, and the generic use of the term is not capitalized. Since the 1960s, researchers at the University of Oregon (for example, Carnine, Engelmann, Becker, Woodward, Gersten, and Kameenui) have maintained a center for Direct Instruction research, curriculum design, and staff development. The Association for Direct Instruction (P.O. Box 10252, Eugene, OR 97440) operates from Eugene, Oregon, and its members receive *Direct Instruction News*. Moreover, several Direct Instruction Conferences are conducted throughout the nation each year. Gersten, Carnine, and Woodward (1987) encourage an understanding of Direct Instruction as defined by researchers at the University of Oregon. Gersten et al. describe Direct Instruction in the following excerpt:

It is a complex way of looking at all aspects of instruction—from classroom organization and management to the quality of teacher-student interactions, the design of curriculum materials, and the nature of inservice teaching. . . . The key principle in Direct Instruction is deceptively simple: For all students to learn, both the curriculum materials and teacher presentation of these materials must be clear and unambiguous. While many writers treat curriculum design and effective teaching research as separate strands, practitioners play them in concert.

Direct Instruction comprises six critical features:

1. An explicit step-by-step strategy.
2. Development of mastery at each step in the process.
3. Strategy (or process) corrections for student errors.
4. Gradual fading from teacher directed activities toward independent work.
5. Use of adequate, systematic practice with a range of examples.
6. Cumulative review of newly learned concepts.

Direct Instruction focuses on what many consider mundane decisions: the best wording for teachers to use in demonstrating a skill, the most effective way to correct students' errors, the number and range of examples necessary to ensure mastery of a new concept. (pp. 48–49)

Although the effectiveness of the Direct Instruction approach is well documented and its use is extensive, it is used less than other programs that have failed to produce positive student outcomes. Authorities at the University of Oregon are redirecting some of their efforts to stimulate more applications of Direct Instruction. Gersten et al. (1987) comment on these directions:

One priority has become translating research into practice, the development and refinement of sensitive, sensible inservice and professional development activities for teachers and instructional aides. A second emergent priority has been the application of these instructional design principles into technology. In particular, we have begun to explore how technology may assist teachers to implement the more difficult aspects of effective instruction. We believe this research agenda reflects a realism about the kinds of knowledge that can help improve schooling—practical training for teachers, well-conceived and empirically refined instructional materials, and technology to make the teacher's role more manageable. (p. 49)

One line of Direct Instruction research that appears encouraging for the 1990s involves the teaching of higher-order skills (for example, literary analysis, chemistry, legal reasoning, problem solving, critical reading, ratio and proportion, social studies, and syllogistic reasoning) to at-risk and special education students at levels comparable to those of their advantaged peers (Carnine, 1989; 1990). Moreover, Gersten et al. (1987) note that the following principles are emerging for teaching higher-order skills:

1. Before learning cognitively complex skills, students need explicit direct instruction in relevant facts and concepts.
2. The teaching of open-ended processes in which a range of responses is appropriate necessitates clear models of successful solutions, a range of examples, and specific corrective feedback.

Finally, the teaching of these higher-order skills is being implemented successfully through video-disc instruction. Perhaps today's technology will encourage more systematic use of Direct Instruction in school districts across the nation.

CHOOSING MATERIALS

Archer and Edgar (1976) note that the teacher has three options in choosing materials: (a) adopt a commercial material and use it as designed, (b) adapt a commercial material to fit the instructional needs of a specific student,

or (c) make materials. Given the great number of commercial materials, selection often is difficult. Production of instructional materials for students with learning problems has increased tremendously since the passage of legislation that guarantees an appropriate education to all students with disabilities. Unfortunately, most of these new materials are not accompanied by field-test data or research data supporting their effectiveness.

Many teachers or curriculum committees are faced with the difficult, tedious task of selecting materials on a limited budget. A good plan in making this selection includes the following steps:

1. Identify the curriculum areas in which materials are needed.
2. Rank the areas from highest to lowest priority.
3. List affordable materials that are designed to teach in the selected skill area or areas.
4. Obtain the materials and evaluate them so that a decision can be made regarding a purchase. On request, many publishers will provide a sample of materials or a manual for the teacher to examine or field test. Also, many school districts have resource or curriculum centers that contain materials for teachers to inspect.

Curriculum Design Factors

It is helpful for educators who are making material decisions to examine effective curriculum design practices. Actually, effective curriculum designs include components identified in the effective teaching research (Brophy & Good, 1986). A curriculum helps yield positive student outcomes when it is designed to facilitate the instructional sequence of teacher demonstration to independent practice. In essence, a curriculum design promotes positive student outcomes when it includes (a) a brief quiz or a review of a previous lesson, (b) presentations consisting of step-by-step explicit explanations with multiple examples, (c) guided practice with feedback, and (d) independent practice requiring discriminations, review, and faster responses (Kelly, Gersten, & Carnine, 1990; Moore & Carnine, 1989).

From his research and review of curriculum and practice activities, Carnine (1989) provides guidelines for designing a curriculum that is most likely to increase accuracy and decrease instructional time to mastery:

1. *Introduce information cumulatively.* This procedure avoids memory overload by introducing new pieces of information one at a time. Each new piece of information is presented after the previous piece has been learned. For example, a student can learn one continent at a time until all seven are learned.

2. *Build retention.* To increase memory of correct information or strategies and decrease the likelihood of errors, a review of difficult material should occur within a couple of days of initial learning. Moreover, students need practice in discriminating a newly learned concept from similar concepts. Supervised practice is important in the initial stages of discrimination practice. Solving problems involving the multiplication and division of fractions would be an example of discrimination practice.

3. *Separate confusing elements and terminology.* When similar symbols are to be taught (such as 6, 9; +, x; or b, d), the teacher should introduce one of the symbols at a time. Once a symbol or term is learned, the similar one can be introduced.

4. *Make learning more meaningful by stressing relationships.* First, the teacher should stress the relationship of components to the whole. For example, the teacher can instruct students to use their knowledge of sound-symbol correspondence to decode words or point out how a comprehension strategy can be applied to books across subject areas. Second, the teacher should stress the application of known information to unknown information. For example, the teacher can point out that the multiplication of 5s involves counting by 5s or that the commutative property of addition (that is, $a + b = c$, $b + a = c$) applies to multiplication.

5. *Reduce processing demands.* Processing demands are decreased by teaching a strategy or algorithm first and then teaching the information in increasingly difficult stages. In teaching word decoding, teaching letter-sound correspondences first reduces the processing requirements for decoding words. Teaching addition (that is, easiest information) before multiplication decreases the processing demands of learning multiplication.

6. *Require faster responses.* Requiring faster responses helps the student develop automatic responses.

Material Evaluation Factors

Table 4.1 presents the major factors involved in material evaluation. These factors are organized according to the areas of general information, characteristics relating to teaching, and characteristics relating to classroom management.

General information. The area of *general information* includes descriptive information that usually is included in advertisements. This information helps the teacher decide which materials to consider further and which to eliminate.

1. *Name and publisher.* What is the name of the material and who is the publisher?
2. *Major skill concentration.* For what instructional area is the material designed? What

TABLE 4.1
Factors in material evaluation.

General Information
Name and publisher
Major skill concentration
Cost and durability
Target population
Research and field-test data

Characteristics Relating to Teaching
Sequence of skills
Organization of material, including
    considerations for individualization
Clarity of directions
Task levels
Stimulus-response modality combinations
Pace of content presentation
Effective teaching practices
    Placement tests
    Guidelines for advance organizers
    Examples for demonstrating a skill
    Practice-to-mastery activities
    Assessment system for monitoring progress
    Corrective feedback procedures
    Generalization activities

Characteristics Relating to Classroom Management
Evaluation and data recording
Space requirements
Time requirements
Extent of teacher involvement
Interest level
Reinforcement

are the major goals of the program? For example, if it is a reading program, does it stress word-attack skills, comprehension skills, or both?

3. *Cost and durability.* Are the costs of the materials within the teacher's budget? Once the material is purchased, do additional materials have to be purchased to maintain the program? Are the materials sturdy enough to last in the classroom? How does the cost compare with costs of other materials designed to teach similar skills? Can other materials that concentrate on similar instructional objectives be developed that are cheaper and easier to use?

4. *Target population.* Is the material appropriate for the age span of the targeted students? Different materials may focus on the same skills but offer a format and content that appeals to different ages. For example, *Reading Mastery: DISTAR Reading* (Science Research Associates) focuses on word-attack skills for elementary students, and the *Corrective Reading Program* (SRA) concentrates on the same skill for adolescents.

5. *Research and field-test data.* Does the material provide research and field-test data? When these data are available, the teacher can find answers to important questions: For what group is the material suitable? Was it effective in teaching stated goals or objectives? Was its use compared with other materials? Is the program effective as a total program, or does it need to be supplemented? Is it a supplement to any other program? Are prerequisite skills for using the material outlined?

Characteristics relating to teaching.

1. *Sequence of skills.* In what order are the skills presented? Some materials are sequenced so that the student must succeed at each level to advance to the next level. Other materials (for example, social studies, reading comprehension) do not link success at one level directly with success at the next level. The teacher can ask several questions regarding sequence: Is the sequence evident in the material, and is it logical? Does the sequence proceed from simple to complex? Are the objectives stated in behavioral terms? Are the steps in the sequence small?

2. *Organization of material.* How is the content arranged? Specifically, units, lessons,

or chapters should be examined. Is the material organized so that lessons or activities can be used separately in an interesting, meaningful way? Are there any suggestions for modifying the materials for individual students? Does the material provide for determining entry-skill level and for monitoring student progress? Is the material coordinated with any other material?

3. *Clarity of directions.* Are the directions written in concise, simple language? Are the directions for seatwork activities easy to follow? Are the directions to the teacher easy to understand, and do they apply to group instruction, assessment, and follow-up activities? If written responses are required, is the format understandable? Students may be confused by the use of single worksheets that require several different responses (such as fill in blanks with words or a letter, draw a line to the correct answer, and circle the correct answer.

4. *Task levels.* Does the material present information at a concrete level (three-dimensional manipulatives), a semiconcrete level (two-dimensional materials such as pictures), or an abstract level (symbolic), or does it use combinations of these? Does the material primarily use imitation tasks (that is, reproduce stimuli), match-to-sample tasks (for example, circle the letter *r* in the following: a c r b m t n), concept formation tasks (for example, classify objects into categories), or creative response tasks (that is, construct entirely novel responses such as in creative writing or essay writing)? Is the readability level of the material appropriate for the students? The readability level set by the publisher and the reading level obtained by the teacher may be quite different.

5. *Stimulus-response modality combinations.* Is one stimulus modality primarily used? If so, which one? Is one response modality primarily used? If so, which one? What stimulus-response combinations are used primarily (such as visual stimuli and motor response)? Can the responses be performed by an individual student without disturbing others?

6. *Pace of content presentation.* How fast are new concepts presented? Are adequate practice activities included? Are previously learned skills reviewed periodically? Can students move at different speeds through the material?

7. *Effective teaching procedures.* Does the material offer features that promote effective teaching practices (such as advance organizers, system for monitoring progress, and corrective feedback procedures)?

Characteristics relating to classroom management.

1. *Evaluation and data recording.* Are evaluation forms and tests included for individual students? Is a composite evaluation form and assessment system included? Can the evaluation be administered by the student or a peer? Do the evaluations occur often enough to be useful in making instructional decisions? What type of evaluation tests are used: placement tests, mastery tests, chapter tests, unit tests, daily probes, or teacher-made criterion tests?

2. *Space requirements.* Can the material be stored readily in a learning center? Is the material packaged well for storage? Does the material distract other students when it is being used? Is the material easy to move from place to place?

3. *Time requirements.* How much time does it take to set up the material for use? Can the material be used in flexible time limits? Is the lapse time between instructions and activities appropriate? Does it take much time to clean up and return the material to its place?

4. *Extent of teacher involvement.* Does the material require continuous involvement

during initial instruction, review, or practice activities? Does the teacher have to intervene as the student moves from one activity to another? Are independent seatwork activities provided? If so, are they organized concisely enough for the student to manage the tasks independently? Does the material provide feedback to the student (self-correcting or answer keys), or does the teacher have to provide most of the feedback? How many students can use the material at the same time?

5. *Interest level.* Is the material packaged attractively, and is it of good quality? Do the illustrations enhance the material? Do the pages have more than one concept or task per page? Are illustrations appropriate for the students? Is the material free of sexism, and does it represent ethnic populations appropriately?

6. *Reinforcement.* Does the material include special reinforcement events such as take-home reinforcements, happy messages, and symbols of achievement? Is reinforcement spaced appropriately for maintaining a desired rate of responding? Does the material include suggestions for reinforcement schedules and reinforcement activities?

Conclusion. Depending on individual needs and teaching styles, teachers stress different aspects of materials. Procedures that are helpful in choosing and evaluating materials include the following:

1. Compare materials with the same major skill concentration.
2. Work with colleagues and compare perceptions.
3. Ask experts in the content area to comment on the material.
4. Talk with teachers who use the material.
5. Obtain materials for trial usage whenever possible.

Teachers can obtain descriptions of available materials from commercial catalogs and material resource centers in local schools, state agencies, and universities.

A federally funded, computerized retrieval system is available to help educators examine instructional materials. The National Instructional Materials Information System has provided a retrieval service since 1975. The system clearinghouse is located in the National Center for Educational Media/Materials for the Handicapped in Columbus, Ohio. It features telecommunications hookups with all regional Area Learning Resource Centers and Specialized Offices. Requests can be directed to the Columbus center for information on the Area Learning Resource Center serving a particular geographic area. The system includes abstracts of more than 45,000 items appropriate for the needs of students with learning problems.

ARRANGING AND MANAGING MATERIALS

After the teacher has selected instructional materials, the next task is to organize and use them efficiently. Teacher-made materials must be developed to supplement the commercial materials, and both kinds of material must be organized in the classroom so that students easily can locate, use, and return them. Many teachers use learning centers or work stations for organizing instructional materials in the curriculum areas (such as reading and math), while interest centers are used for organizing materials that focus primarily on reinforcement and enrichment activities.

Learning Centers

For many teachers, learning centers are a major way of managing the classroom and providing individualized instruction. Learning centers have materials of many levels and activities that accommodate a variety of individual needs. Learning centers offer follow-up to the teacher's instruction and provide an opportunity to practice specific skills; thus, these centers may be helpful to students with learning problems. Learning centers can be added gradually to the classroom. Over time the teacher can refine and improve them by eliminating ineffective materials and introducing new materials.

In this book, a *learning center* is a designated area where instructional materials in one major curriculum area are located and organized. Intermediate and secondary teachers can divide learning centers according to subareas within a major curriculum area. For example, in math, learning centers can be in the areas of geometry, algebra, consumer math, and basic computation.

Some authorities refer to a learning center as a single instructional activity or material, such as a learning packet or instructional game. However, when the learning center is viewed as a designated *space* for organizing materials in a major curriculum area, the center includes all instructional games, packets, and activities that provide instruction in the particular skill area. Also, the type of learning center depends on the area of skill concentration. Learning centers can be developed in the following skill areas: phonics, consumer math, written expression, handwriting, reading comprehension, and career education.

Learning center components.   For a learning center to be successful for the teacher and the student, it should include the following components:

1. *Subject area and related skills.* The teacher selects an area of instruction in which to develop a center. Once the area is identified, the skills and concepts that are to be taught, reinforced, or enriched must be determined. These skills and concepts aid the teacher in organizing the center activities.

2. *Directions for use.* Because students normally work independently in a center, the directions must be simple and clear. Students may perform different tasks at the center; thus, individual student folders frequently are used to provide instruction to each student. In addition, the folder provides the teacher with a means of communicating with the student (feedback, assignments, reinforcement), and it gives the student a place to store work.

3. *System of material organization.* For the student to retrieve and return materials efficiently, the materials must be organized carefully. Codes involving colors, letters, or numbers often are used. Colors can symbolize a specific skill area (such as word attack), and letters can indicate a more specific skill (for example, *Dig* for digraphs). A number is used to pinpoint an activity under a specific skill (for example, *Dig #4*—an activity for *oa* words).

4. *Work space.* The work space in a center depends on the space available and how the teacher uses the center. Some teachers instruct students to do the work at their desks, whereas other teachers have students work at the center. In all centers, work space should be available for at least two students. Not only can two students use the center simultaneously (for getting instruction or working), but also space for peer teaching is provided. Teachers who have small groups working in the center need a work space for four to six students.

5. *Format for recording progress.* Each day when the student has completed work in the center, a record of progress needs to be made. The record can be in the form of (a) a teacher's checklist in a folder with student names and center activities, (b) a large wall

chart for checking off activities in the various centers, (c) a checklist in the student's own folder, or (d) assessment devices including criterion tests, mastery tests, graphs, and charts.

Selected materials for centers. All of the presented components are necessary for the successful management of a learning center. However, the materials within the center must meet certain criteria for the center to be successful. The materials included in a learning center vary as a function of available resources, teacher preferences, and space. Each curriculum area chapter of this book includes a description of numerous activities, instructional games, self-correcting materials, commercial programs and materials, and computer software programs that are suitable for inclusion in learning centers.

In addition to including single worksheets or activities that the teacher instructs the student to do, the center should include learning guides. A *learning guide* is any instructional format (learning unit, learning packet, contract) that includes an objective and a list of materials and activities designed to help the student achieve the objective. Dell (1972) suggests the following items for developing effective learning guides:

1. *An objective.* The objective can be given a number to facilitate the record-keeping system.
2. *A pretest.* The pretest frequently consists of several items but may consist of only one item or example.
3. *A list of materials and activities.* The materials and activities to help the student achieve an objective can be divided into several lists based on different types of activities to be assigned according to student learning characteristics.
4. *Self-checks.* The student can monitor progress through the use of several self-checks interspersed within the list of activities.

5. *A posttest.* The posttest can be a paper-and-pencil test or a list of behaviors to observe for evaluation.

In addition, corrective teaching procedures (such as additional practice activities) can be included for students who do not pass the mastery test.

Developing and using centers. The following suggestions may be helpful in creating effective learning centers:

1. Make them neat and attractive.
2. Make them a pleasant and comfortable place to work.
3. Appeal to student interests and curiosities.
4. Give simple and clear directions.
5. Make the evaluation activity important (for example, follow up student work as much as possible).
6. Organize the center at first according to specific instructional objectives and gradually add materials and activities as resources and time permits.
7. Include activities that involve more than one student.
8. Explain and deomonstrate how to use the center, particularly when a new material or activity is added to the center.
9. Coordinate movement to and from the center with other activities (usually through scheduling).
10. Do not limit the use of center activities to the physical area designated as the learning center. In many instances, students can be directed to other areas in or outside of the classroom for completion of activities.
11. Make changes to maintain enthusiasm for a given center. Some centers will change every day, others will change once a week, and still others can remain constant for a longer period.

12. When several centers are in use in one classroom, give careful attention to the balance of design in the centers. Some provide for active involvement, and others are for more quiet activity. Some require only short attention; others demand time for long-term development. Some offer experiences in reading and writing; others require extensive motor activity. Some are designed for individual work; others require the cooperative efforts of pairs or small groups. Some are open-minded and experimental in nature; others are more structured in presentation of content. Some are completely pupil structured; others are prepared totally by the teacher.

Sample learning center. Stephens (1977) provides excellent examples of learning centers that organize activities and materials according to instructional objectives. These centers can be expanded by increasing the number of objectives or the types of materials and activities. Stephens presents the following math center:

Math Center

Purpose: To discriminate cups, pints, quarts, gallons, ounces.

Activity A

Materials:

Milk, juice cartons, filmstrips or tapes, water, recipes.

Directions:

1. Present containers, water, basin. List of things to discover by experimenting. *Ex*: How many cups can fit into the pint, etc.?
   Evaluation—Make a record sheet of "What I Discovered." Compare with correct answer sheet.
2. Make up—Collage, magazine pictures of containers and labels from home.

Purpose: To discriminate inches/feet.

Activity A

Directions:

Have different items at center to measure—measure a book by width and length—measure top of desk width and length—measure height of board (or similar area).

Activity B

Directions:

Measure area of specified part of room, i.e., blackboard, bulletin board in square feet, square inches.

Activity C

Directions:

Given a number problem pertaining to measuring—student draws picture, makes equation and answer and self-checks equation and answer.

Activity D

Directions:

Draw classroom according to scale, drawing in furniture in classroom.

Activity E

Directions:

Design a floor plan according to scale—placing pieces of furniture specified.

Purpose: To write and say correct answers when given multiplication facts.

Activity A

Materials:

$8'' \times 8''$ cardboard square, 18 snap-type clothespins, magic marker, pencil and paper.

Directions:

Divide a cardboard square into 8 diagonals. Write a multiplication fact in each space. Write answers in snap clothespins. Give cardboard and clothespins to the student, together with a worksheet for writing problems. Student is to snap appropriate clothespin to each problem. Provide an answer key. After student checks answers, he is to write the problems.

Activity B

Materials:

Game board, game card 3″ × 6″, party favor helmets.

Directions:

Place cards face down in pile. Each child places a marker at opposite goal posts. Player draws a card and checks if he has the answer to any of the next three equations. Advances 10, 20, 30 yards depending on the position of match. Card is returned to bottom of pile. If not a match, no yardage gain is made. First to make touchdown wins game.

Activity C

Materials:

Game board, cards with facts 3″ × 6″.

Directions:

"The Road Runner" game. Place markers at start of race. Place cards face down in a pile. Player draws a card and moves his marker to the correct answer. Special citations and awards are offered during play. Winner finishes game first.

Activity D

Materials:

A grid, using cross number puzzles.

Directions:

Fill in grid with multiplication facts, leaving blank spaces for the answer. Also have addition along with the multiplication problems. Provide answer sheets.

Activity E

Materials:

4 egg cartons, numbered 1 to 12; 2 bottle caps for each egg carton.

Directions:

The child places the bottle caps inside the egg carton and closes the lid. He shakes the carton for a few seconds. Then he opens the lid. He looks at the 2 places the caps landed and these are his numbers to multiply. He then writes these two numbers on his paper and computes the fact.

For working in pairs—one child may shake and then ask the resulting combination of another—if he answers correctly the second child then shakes for the first. When a child misses, the partner can then shake another fact for him. (pp. 294–295)

Adapting Materials

Many materials available to the teacher need to be adapted for use with students who have learning problems. Complex directions, fast pace, reading level, boring content, confusing formats, lengthy assignments, and other factors can contribute to the difficulties of these students. The teacher needs to adapt these materials to fit the individual needs of students. The following adaptation techniques can be used:

1. *Use explicit teaching procedures.* Many commercial materials do not cue teachers to use explicit teaching procedures; thus, it frequently is necessary for the teacher to adapt a material to include these procedures. Simmons, Fuchs, and Fuchs (1991) provide an instructional template to help teachers include explicit teaching steps within their lessons (that is, present an advance organizer, demonstrate the skill, provide guided practice, offer corrective feedback, set up independent practice, monitor practice, and review). This template reminds teachers of steps to use before, during, and after instruction:

Before instruction

   a. Time allocated for instruction (total time; estimated time for teacher-directed instruction).
   b. Lesson objective (The student will be able to . . .).
   c. Preskills to review ("Before we begin, let's review . . .").

During instruction

a. Frame lesson ("Today we're going to learn . . ." "This is important because . . .").
b. Present target skill ("Listen and watch as I show you . . .").
c. Guide practice ("Let's try this one together").
d. Correct errors and provide feedback (correct response—"That's right"; hesitant response—"Good", repeat rule or procedure; incorrect or no response—use prompts on process errors and model correct response on factual errors).
e. Prepare for independent practice ("Let's do the first one together").

After instruction

a. Monitor independent practice (circulate throughout the room and provide feedback to students through brief interactions).
b. Review new skills (review skills at the end of the lesson and systematically throughout the instructional year).

2. *Use a tape recorder.* Many problems with materials are related to reading disabilities. The tape recorder often is an excellent aid in overcoming this problem. Directions, stories, and specific lessons can be recorded on tape. The student can replay the tape to improve understanding of directions or concepts. Also, to improve reading skills, the student can read the printed words silently as they are presented on tape.

3. *Clarify or simplify written directions.* Some directions are written in paragraph form and contain many units of information. These can be overwhelming to some students. The teacher can help by underlining or highlighting the significant parts of the directions. Rewriting the directions is often helpful. For example:

Original directions: This exercise will show how well you can locate conjunctions. Read each sentence. Look for the conjunctions. When you locate a conjunction find it in the list of conjunctions under each sentence. Then circle the number of your answer in the answer column.

Directions rewritten and simplified: Read each sentence and circle all conjunctions.

4. *Present small amount of work.* The teacher can tear pages from workbooks and materials to present small assignments to students who are anxious about the amount of work to be done. This technique prevents students from examining an entire workbook, text, or material and becoming discouraged by the amount of work. Also, the teacher can reduce the amount of work when it appears redundant. For example, the teacher can request the student to complete only odd-numbered problems or items with stars by them or can provide responses to several items and ask the student to complete the rest. Finally, the teacher can divide a worksheet into sections and instruct the student to do a specific section. A worksheet is divided easily by drawing lines across it and writing *go* and *stop* within each section.

5. *Block out extraneous stimuli.* If a student easily is distracted by visual stimuli on a full worksheet or page, the student can cover sections of the page not being worked on with paper. Also, line markers can be used to aid reading, and windows can be used to display individual math problems.

6. *Repeat directions.* For students who have difficulty following directions, it often is helpful to ask them to repeat the direc-

tions in their own words. The student can repeat the directions to a peer when the teacher is unavailable. Lewis and Doorlag (1991) offer the following suggestions for helping students understand directions:

   a. If directions contain several steps, break down the directions into subsets.

   b. Simplify directions by presenting only one portion at a time and by writing each portion on the chalkboard as well as stating it orally.

   c. When using written directions, be sure that students are able to read and understand the words as well as comprehend the meaning of the sentences.

7. *Change response mode.* For students who have difficulty with fine motor responses (such as handwriting), the response mode can be changed to underlining, selecting from multiple choices, sorting, or marking. Students with fine motor problems can be given extra space for writing answers on worksheets or can be allowed to respond on individual chalkboards.

8. *Highlight essential information.* If an adolescent can read a regular textbook but has difficulty finding the essential information, the teacher can use a highlight pen to focus attention on this information.

9. *Locate place in consumable material.* In consumable materials in which students progress sequentially (such as workbooks), the student can make a diagonal cut across the lower right-hand corner of the pages as they are completed. With all the completed pages cut, the student and teacher readily can locate the next page that needs to be corrected or completed.

10. *Provide additional practice activities.* Some materials do not provide enough practice activities for students with learning problems to acquire mastery on selected skills. Teachers then must supplement the material with practice activities. Recommended practice exercises include instructional games, peer teaching activities, self-correcting materials, computer software programs, and additional worksheets.

11. *Provide a glossary in content areas.* At the secondary level, the specific language of the content areas requires careful reading. Students often benefit from a glossary of content-related terms.

12. *Provide an outline of the lecture.* An outline enables some students to follow the lesson successfully and make appropriate notes. Moreover, an outline helps students to see the organization of the material and ask timely questions.

13. *Develop reading guides.* A reading guide provides the student with a road map of what is written and features periodic questions to help the student focus on relevant content. It helps the reader understand the main ideas and sort out the numerous details related to the main ideas. A reading guide can be developed paragraph-by-paragraph, page-by-page, or section-by-section.

14. *Use graphic organizers.* A graphic organizer involves organizing material into a visual format. To develop a graphic organizer, the student can use the following steps: (a) list the topic on the first line, (b) collect and divide information into major headings, (c) list all information relating to major headings on index cards, (d) organize information into major areas, (e) place information under appropriate subheadings, and (f) place information into the organizer format. (See the example on page 161.)

Additional information on adapting materials (for example, advance organizers, guided practice, mnemonics, textbook usage) for older students is presented in Chapter 14.

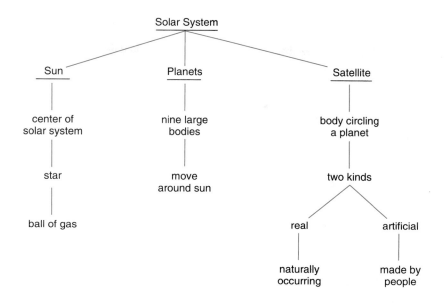

Classroom Equipment

Instructional equipment can be used to meet the specific needs of students with learning problems. For example, audiovisual equipment can be used to instruct students with specific modality preferences, and manipulative devices often help in holding the attention of a distractible learner.

Computer and computer software. The computer can be used as a tool for classroom management as well as classroom instruction. Hofmeister (1984) suggests that the most appropriate use of the computer is as a supplementary tool to allow teachers more time to teach. Teachers can be released partially from time-consuming tasks through computer-managed instruction (CMI), particularly in developing individualized educational programs (IEPs) and in computer-managed record keeping. Computers can store sequences of instructional objectives and student performance information as well as track student progress, complete proper forms, and provide required record-keeping data (Fuchs, Fuchs, & Hamlett, 1989; Kulik, Kulik, & Bangert-Drowns, 1985).

Computer-assisted instruction, or CAI, refers to software that is designed to provide instruction. The computer offers some unique advantages in instructing students with learning problems. Attributes of CAI that appear useful in helping students achieve include the following (Fitzgerald, Fick, & Milich, 1986; Haynes & Malouf, 1986; Kolich, 1985; Lindsey, 1987):

1. Tasks are analyzed and presented in meaningful sequences.
2. Materials are presented in a manner that allows the student to progress at her own rate.
3. Reinforcement of individual student responses is immediate. The computer can provide continuous and positive feedback and praise, thus giving the student a higher sense of self-esteem.
4. Constructive criticism is offered without the human elements of emotion or embarrassment.

5. Software exists that enables the student to increase her rate of correct responses.
6. The use of animation, sound effects, and game-playing situations makes drill and practice motivating.
7. The computer is suited to the discovery method of learning. Programs that simulate real-life experiences allow the student to make decisions and see the consequences.
8. Strategies related to problem solving can be adapted for the computer through programs such as adventure games and software that teaches how to program.
9. The computer can be made "user friendly" by programming it to use the student's name when giving lessons. A computer also is nonjudgmental and allows the student to make mistakes in a nonthreatening environment.

Educational software can differ in method or mode of delivery as well as in quality. Watkins and Webb (1981) and Ellis and Sabornie (1986) discuss six modes of delivery:

1. *Drill and practice.* This common use of computers in education serves as a supplement to other forms of instruction. It is designed to integrate and consolidate previously learned material through practice on the computer.
2. *Tutorial.* The role of teacher is assumed, and material is presented in a programmed learning format. The student moves from one step to the next by answering questions and can be branched to remedial or review segments as well as to more advanced levels of the program.
3. *Educational games.* Games are designed to develop general problem-solving methods and strategies while maintaining interest and motivation.
4. *Simulations.* Simulations attempt to model the underlying characteristics of a real phe-

nomenon so that its properties can be studied. They can incorporate many game features but are intended to model some reality.
5. *Problem solving.* The computer can be used to solve real-world problems. For example, students may write computer programs to test possible solutions to a variety of real problems.
6. *Word processing.* A word processor is a tool for writing instruction. Ease of correcting errors, availability of spelling and grammar checkers, elimination of the need to rewrite after revisions are made, and use of a printer that produces neat copies are helpful functions in teaching writing to students with learning problems.

CAI is promising, but limited information exists concerning how microcomputers can be applied best in the classroom (Cosden, Gerber, Semmel, Goldman, & Semmel, 1987; Stowitschek & Stowitschek, 1984; Torgesen & Young, 1983). However, it is apparent that through the use of appropriate software, students with learning problems can be motivated through individualized instruction and needed academic practice.

Wiens (1986) suggests three specific criteria for evaluating software to use in teaching students with learning problems. First, software should use the computer's capacity to present the materials better than traditional methods. Voice synthesis, interaction, animation, and response monitoring are features of successful CAI. Moreover, Schuell and Schueckler (1988) note that to transcend traditional methods, CAI programs must (a) use the student's knowledge base, (b) provide guided and independent practice, (c) give corrective feedback, (d) present materials in steps that facilitates learning, (e) provide clear lesson overviews and goals, (f) conduct periodic performance evaluations, and (g) finish with a summary and review of the lesson's main points. Wiens' second criterion for good software is that the teacher must be able to modify or adapt the program to develop appropriate instructional matches for individual learners. The third criterion is that the CAI program should include means for collecting student response data so that teachers can monitor student progress. Actually, the teacher should expect software to report graphic representations of progress on easily generated print-outs.

In addition to the many general uses of the computer for students with learning problems, several investigators report on specific applications that are suited especially to youngsters with learning problems. Grimes (1981) notes that for students who have difficulty maintaining on-task attention, computer programs can promote attention with color cueing, animation, underlining, and varying print sizes. For students who respond impulsively, the computer can provide cues or hints to inhibit impulsive responding. For those who take a lot of time to respond (reflective responders), computer programs can be tailored to allow extra response time.

Research on the use of CAI with students who have learning disabilities appears promising but remains inconclusive. Majsterek and Wilson (1989) reviewed several CAI studies that focused on teaching basic skills to students with learning disabilities. They conclude that CAI can produce equivalent or slightly less than equivalent learning with less teacher time than traditional instruction. Other reports of CAI used to teach students with learning problems (Ellis & Sabornie, 1986; Hasselbring, Goin, & Bransford, 1988; Woodward & Carnine, 1988) conclude that student achievement usually is greater when CAI supplements rather than replaces teacher-directed instruction. Keefe and Candler (1989) report mixed results on the effectiveness of using word pro-

cessors with students who have learning disabilities. However, several individual studies report good results for CAI use in teaching students with learning disabilities (for example, spelling—Fuchs et al., 1989; world geography—Horton, Lovitt, Givens, & Nelson, 1989; reading—Torgesen, Waters, Cohen, & Torgesen, 1988; health—Woodward, Carnine, & Gersten, 1988).

Kolich (1985) reports that the key to future successful computer-assisted instruction depends on a closer working relationship between educators and software manufacturers. Various software programs in math, reading, spelling, and written expression are presented in their respective chapters, and programs pertaining to learning strategies, science, social studies, functional living skills, and career-related instruction are included in Chapter 14. Appendix B lists addresses of producers and distributors of educational software.

Tape recorder.   Cassette recorders have several advantages. They are simple to operate, the recorder and tapes are small and easy to store, and tapes are relatively inexpensive. Headphones enable individual students to operate a recorder without distracting classmates. Instructional applications of the tape recorder include the following:

1. A tape can be made of reading material (for example, basal reader, stories, and magazines). The student can read along with the tape to practice reading. Thus, the tape can provide feedback, increase speed, and help the student identify and practice difficult words.
2. In a language experience activity, the student can use the recorder to make a tape of a story. Later, the student can write the story from the tape with a peer, aide, or teacher.
3. Oral directions can be put on tape to accompany seatwork activities. The student who

has difficulty with oral directions can play the tape until the directions are understood.

4. Spelling tapes are useful for practice and taking tests. One commonly used format includes (a) the spelling word; (b) the word used in a sentence; and (c) a pause, a beep, and the word spelled correctly. The pause can be eliminated by having the student stop the recorder to write the word and then start it to check the spelling.

5. Stories, facts, or a report of an event can be recorded. News programs, commercials, telephone messages, weather reports, and teacher-made content can be used. The student listens and then responds to comprehension questions. For example, a weather report is taped, and the student is required to answer the following questions: High temperature? Low temperature? Any rain? Forecast for tomorrow? What season is it?

6. One-minute samples of instrumental music can be taped for students to use in conducting timings. These tapes usually begin with the word "start" and end with the word "stop." The teacher may prefer to use only the words and omit the music. In place of a kitchen timer, tapes of different time spans can be used to mark the end of any timed activity.

7. Correction tapes can be used to provide feedback to students who have completed math seatwork.

8. Music can be recorded on tapes for students to listen to when they have completed an assignment. Also, pleasant background music can be played while students are engaged in activities such as cleaning up, settling down after recess, free-choice, seatwork, or art.

9. At the secondary level, class lectures and discussions can be taped. These tapes can be used to help students review or understand the material.

Overhead projector. The overhead projector is readily available to classroom teachers and is used to display an image on a screen from a transparency. Transparencies can be teacher-made or purchased. They allow the user to write on, color in, and point at specific details while discussing them. Overhead projectors can be used to project images on light-colored surfaces without darkening the room. Because the overhead projector greatly accents the visual image, it is helpful with students who easily are distracted by extraneous visual stimuli. The teacher can block out all stimuli that do not relate to the item being studied or completed.

Some guidelines for effective use of transparencies on the overhead projector include the following:

1. Prepare transparencies ahead of time.
2. Type or write in clear, bold lines on plain paper. Use a pencil or marker containing a carbon base, or put the original through a copy machine. Then make the transparency quickly by putting the original through a Thermofax copier or transparency maker.
3. Make letters at least 1/4" high. Orator or bulletin type from a primary typewriter projects adequately.
4. Simplify and be concise. Use a maximum of six or seven lines of copy and six or seven words per line.
5. Use simple graphic drawings. Have diagrams ready ahead of time rather than using teaching time to put complicated illustrations on the transparency.
6. Emphasize key points by capitalizing, underlining, circling, and boxing.
7. Use color for clarity, emphasis, and variety. The acetate background itself can be a color instead of clear. Also, colored pieces of acetate can be attached in key spots, or colored markers can be used on the acetate.

8. Turn the projector off and on to shift students' attention.
9. Use the revelation technique (covering the visual with a sheet of paper and revealing items one at a time) to avoid distractions and keep the class interested. Students who are taking notes may appreciate being shown the complete visual first as an overview before the masks are applied.
10. Use the techniques of overlays and masking (revelation) to break down a whole into its component parts.
11. Locate the screen so that everyone in the room can see it clearly. Position it as high as possible, and tilt it forward to project an appropriate image.
12. When writing while talking, check the screen periodically to be sure the students are seeing what is being discussed. Write clearly.
13. Keep extra markers or pencils on hand in case of breakage or loss during presentation.
14. Make color lifts of artwork on magazine paper.
15. Use transparencies in place of the chalkboard to focus attention, thereby saving time and space because the lesson can be used again. Also, class control and eye contact can be maintained better than at the chalkboard.

Uses of the overhead projector include the following:

1. Class schedules and homework assignments can be put on the overhead to save chalkboard space for student and teacher use throughout the day. To check on the schedule or finish copying a homework assignment, the student can turn on the overhead projector and complete the task.
2. The overhead projector can be used for administering many kinds of tests: computation facts, word problems, cloze spelling tests, fill-in-the-blank items, multiple-choice items.
3. The overhead projector can be used to display the category being discussed. Words, phrases, sentences, poems, drawings, and pictures are useful stimuli in facilitating relevant interactions.
4. The overhead projector is useful for playing reading comprehension and spelling games. The teacher gradually exposes the letters of a word, the definition of a word, a sentence, or a paragraph. The students attempt to respond correctly with the fewest cues possible. With the letters of a word, the students attempt to finish spelling the word; with the definition, they identify the word that matches the definition. In the sentence task, students try to complete the sentence correctly. The paragraph task involves providing a title for the paragraph. It often helps to divide the students into teams and allow each group to give a response as another cue is presented.
5. A spinner can be made on a transparency, placed on an overhead, and used for a variety of instructional activities and games. The teacher or student spins it, and it points to letters, numbers, words, or math facts. The spinner can be used to (a) determine the number of points a specific task item is worth, (b) select a math problem (by pointing to it), (c) select one word at a time until the student can make a sentence, and (d) select a letter for the student to sound out or add to previous letters to spell a word. These games are suitable for the student-teacher pair, two or more students, or a large group divided into teams.
6. The overhead projector can be used in developing stories with small groups of students. In this activity, the group contributes to the telling of a story or a description of an event while the teacher writes it on the transparency.

7. The overhead projector is an excellent means for students to display stories developed in language experience activities. The stories can be read to the class or copied by selected students. In addition, the class can help the student title the story.
8. It often is easier for the teacher to lecture by using an overhead projector than by using a chalkboard. It is easier to point to material on an overhead than to underline material on a chalkboard. Also, it is easier to uncover additional material on the overhead than to write on the chalkboard. With the overhead the teacher does not have to write and talk simultaneously or have students wait while the teacher writes.
9. Many students enjoy writing on a transparency and seeing it presented on a screen. This activity is useful especially in practicing handwriting.
10. The overhead projector can be used to project figures, pictures, letters, or numbers on a black chalkboard. The student can trace over the projected images to practice handwriting or develop fine motor skills, or this activity can be used as reinforcement.

Language Master. The Language Master is an adaptation of a tape recorder that plays and records cards that have tape attached along the bottom. Most cards are 4″ × 14″, but other sizes are available. When the stimulus card is inserted in the machine, a recorded voice is heard as the card moves from left to right. Blank cards are available and can be recorded on as they move through the machine. The audiotape, like a tape recorder, can be erased and cleared. Also, the Language Master enables both the student and the teacher to record on the same tape without erasing each other's response. For example, a teacher can record a word that is played when the student pushes the instructor button and inserts the card. Once the card is played the student can set the machine for recording, push a student button, and record the word. Then the student can set the machine for play and listen to both words by inserting the card once with the instructor button down and once with the student button down. Visual cues also can be displayed on the cards. By writing the visual cue on a small card and attaching it to the stimulus card with a paper clip, it is easy to use the stimulus cards for a variety of activities without permanently attaching a visual stimulus. Laminating or putting acetate on the top portion of the card makes it possible to use felt pens and grease pencils to provide removable visual stimuli. (If lamination is used, the teacher should avoid putting the taped portion of the card in the lamination machine.)

Many different commercial Language Master programs are available in speech therapy, language arts, math, and science. Blank cards are available for developing individual programs and can be ordered in several sizes: regular, extra long, or extra tall. A brochure is available from Audio-Visual Projects Division, 7100 McCormick Road, Chicago, IL 60645.

The Language Master can be used in the classroom in the following ways:

1. Spelling words can be presented on the Language Master. Only the audio portion is used to present each word, and the correct spelling of the word is written on the back of the card. The student inserts the card, hears the word, writes the word on a worksheet, and then turns over the card to check the spelling.
2. Sounds of phonemes can be recorded on the cards, with each corresponding grapheme written on the back. The student listens to the phoneme, writes the corresponding grapheme on a worksheet, and then turns over the card to check the response.

3. The visual portion (V) of the card can be used to present a task or problem, and the audio portion (A) can provide the correct response. Sample activities for this format include the following:

   Unravel scrambled letters: V = tac; A = "cat"

   Solve math problem: V = 6 × 7; A = "forty-two"

   Answer social studies question: V = What is the capital of Florida? A = "Tallahassee"

4. With the tall-sized cards, the visual task–auditory answer format can be used to include the following types of activities:

   Reading comprehension: V = reading passage with question; A = answer to question

   Math word problems: V = the word problem; A = the answer

   Categorize words: V = list of related words (such as food words); A = common category

   Correct grammar: V = paragraph with several incorrect verb tenses; A = incorrect verbs with corresponding corrections

   Word meaning: V = definition of a word; A = correct word

5. Only a portion of the card will play if a notch is cut in it—for example,

   With the auditory and visual stimuli placed on the right side of the notch, a task can be presented and the card will stop. Then the student can respond to the task and push the card to the right until the machine finishes playing the remainder of the card with the correct answer on it.

6. The instructor portion of the tape can be used to record feedback and praise.

Small-item materials. Some inexpensive materials that are useful in a classroom include the following:

1. *Miniature chalkboard.* One side of a piece of three-ply cardboard, approximately 15″ × 18″, can be painted with several coats of chalkboard paint (available at school supply and paint stores). Also, the smooth side of a Masonite board can be painted and the rough side can be used as a flannelboard. These boards can be made for individual students to use at their desks or in a learning center.

2. *Flannelboard.* A heavy piece of cardboard can be covered with flannel. Also, the rougher side of a piece of Masonite can be used for a flannelboard. Figures for the board can be made from foam-backed material or felt. Flannelboards are available commercially in various sizes, and some have easel backs. Uses include presenting vocabulary or spelling words, listing important rules, displaying parts of an outline, displaying graphs and fractions, presenting pictures representing difficult concepts, and displaying map outlines.

3. *Game materials.* Materials commonly used with game boards can be collected and stored in an accessible location. Golf tees, Playskool characters, and items from old games are good markers; dice and spinners are good number indicators. Manila folders are excellent for drawing start-to-finish game-board formats and are easy to store.

4. *Construction materials.* Various materials should be collected, such as pictures (for example, of specific sounds, story starters, and so on), school supply or cigar boxes, oatmeal boxes, egg cartons, shoe boxes, water-base marking pens, plastic term-paper holders, tobacco or coffee cans, tongue depressors, library card holders, poster board, oaktag paper, wooden cubes,

pizza discs, envelopes, and clothespins. These and other materials are useful for constructing instructional materials. The instructional games and self-correcting materials presented later in this chapter and the instructional activities featured throughout the book require many of these items.

5. *Typewriter.* A manual typewriter can stimulate learning and be fun to use (for example, in practicing spelling and typing stories). Also, the typewriter is helpful for students with handwriting difficulties.

6. *Durable coverings.* Materials used frequently can be covered with a transparent, adhesive material or with plastic spray. The student can mark on the material and wipe off the markings with a damp cloth. Also, a consumable workbook can be protected for repeated use. The teacher can trim two pieces of acetate to the size of the workbook, lay the acetate on the inside of each cover, and tape it to the cover along the outer edge. To do the work on a page, the student simply flips the acetate over the page and uses a crayon or grease pencil. This can be erased, leaving the workbook blank so that it can be used by the next student. Another method is to cut cardboard into 8″ × 11″ pieces and tape acetate to it, either along the left side only or along both the sides and the bottom. A pocket can be formed to hold worksheets.

7. *Magnetic board.* A magnetic board can be used for students to respond on, to present tasks, or to display work. Work or tasks are displayed easily by taping a paper clip to the back of the stimulus card or worksheet. The paper clip clings to the magnetic board and holds up the material.

8. *Tracing screen.* A wire screen with a cardboard edge makes an excellent tracing screen. When paper is placed over the screen and written on with a crayon, the letters become raised and can be used for tracing.

9. *Mirror.* A door-mounted or full-length mirror is excellent for teaching grooming and self-concept activities. The mirror provides direct feedback to a student about appearance.

DEVELOPING MATERIALS

In teaching students with learning problems, it often is helpful—and sometimes necessary—to supplement or replace commercial materials with teacher-made materials. These materials can provide additional practice, highlight relevant stimuli, provide feedback on progress, and increase motivation. Teacher-made materials include worksheets, games, flash cards, drill sheets, self-correcting activities, and probe sheets. Students spend much classroom time working with instructional materials on their own; thus, it is important that the materials used do not lead to frustration, failure, and the practicing of errors.

To some degree a material serves as a teacher. The more teacher functions it can serve, the more useful is the material. Inexpensive materials can perform the teaching functions of providing instructions, presenting a stimulus or task, and providing feedback about correctness of student responses.

Self-Correcting Materials

Self-correcting materials provide the student with immediate feedback without the teacher being present. Self-correcting materials especially are useful with students with learning problems, who often have a history of academic failure. It is important to reduce their failure experiences, particularly those that take place in public. When the student makes a mistake with a self-correcting material, it is a private event—it happens without anyone else knowing it. Only the student sees the error, and the error can be corrected immediately.

Furthermore, if immediate feedback is not provided, mistakes will be practiced until the teacher corrects the student at a later time. With self-correcting materials, the student is corrected immediately and practices only the correct response.

Self-correcting materials help students maintain attention to academic tasks. The student can approach each response with a game-playing attitude: "I bet I get this one right!" When a self-correcting material is used, some cheating should be expected at first. Although many students initially enjoy beating the system, eventually it becomes more fun to select an answer and see if it is correct. If cheating persists, a checkup test or posttest on the featured content can be administered. It does not take long for the student to realize that cheating on the material will not help on the checkup test.

The importance of immediate feedback is well documented as a valid teaching procedure. Self-correcting materials provide the student with immediate feedback, yet the teacher is free to work with other students. In a study reported by Mercer, Mercer, and Bott (1984), students who used self-correcting materials and traditional worksheets learned considerably more with the self-correcting materials.

Self-correcting materials should be simple in design so that a demonstration enables students to operate them. The best use of these materials is to provide practice or drill on subject matter that the teacher already has introduced.

Finally, students should not be required to use the same self-correcting material for a long time. The teacher should vary the content periodically, exchange materials with another teacher, give students a choice of which material they wish to use, have students make their own content for the self-correcting device, or put away selected materials for a while. By changing self-correcting materials from time to time, the teacher can maintain student interest and involvement.

The next section provides examples of feedback devices that can be used to make self-correcting materials. The self-correcting materials are presented in two categories: those with construction guidelines and those that are simple to make. The same device or material often can be used with different content. Throughout this book self-correcting materials are presented in the different curriculum areas.

Self-Correcting Materials with Construction Guidelines

Flap.   A flap can be made of any flexible material such as cloth, vinyl wallpaper, construction paper, or thin cardboard. When using the learning material, the student can bend the flap up or to the side to reveal the answer to the question or problem. Figure 4.1 illustrates an Answer Box with a flap to provide feedback.

Selected instructional pinpoints:

1. See math fact or problem—say answer.
2. See math fact or problem—write answer.
3. See contraction words—write contraction.
4. See percentage problem—write answer.

Feedback response:

A flap is placed over the mouth. When the flap is raised, the answer is revealed. Vinyl wallpaper is flexible and serves as a good flap.

Materials:

1. A cardboard box (for example, cigar or school supply box)
2. 3″ × 5″ index cards
3. Contact paper or lamination
4. A small wooden block, approximately 3″ × 3 ½″

Construction:

1. Cut out three squares in the lid of the box so they form two eyes and a mouth.
2. Cut a section out of the right side of the box so that the index cards can be fed into the box from the side.

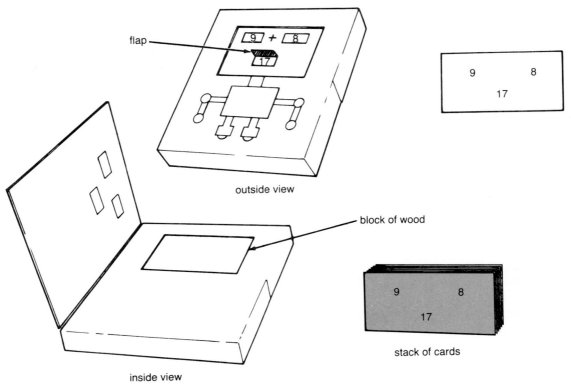

flap

9 + 8
17

outside view

9   8
17

block of wood

9   8
17

stack of cards

inside view

FIGURE 4.1
Answer Box.

3. Paint the box inside and out.
4. Laminate a picture of a face on the box and place the eyes and the mouth over the squares.
5. Place a flexible flap over the mouth.
6. Prepare index cards with problems and answers so that the problem appears in the "eyes" and so that the flap over the mouth can be lifted to reveal the answer. For math problems, a grease (overhead projector) pencil can be used to write the math operation ($+$, $-$, $\times$, $\div$) in the space between the "eyes."

Directions:

The student inserts a stack of selected cards into the Answer Box. Then the student responds (orally or by writing) to the problem presented in the two windows. She lifts the flap over the mouth to reveal the answer and check her response.

Modifications:

The card formats can be varied to present a variety of math problems and reading tasks. Some possible card formats include the following:

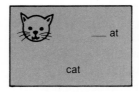

_____ at

cat

Initial Consonants

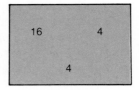

16   4

4

Division

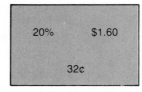

20% $1.60

32¢

Percentage

Windows.   Small windows can be cut in materials to provide feedback. The correct answer can be in the window, or, when two or more windows are used, the items in the windows can match to show a correct response. Figure 4.2, Spinning Wheels, illustrates the use of windows.

Selected instructional pinpoints:

Any pinpoint can be selected in which a matched pair can be devised (problems on one wheel and the correct answers on another wheel). For example:

1. See math problem—select answer.
2. See picture—select word.
3. See picture—select initial sound.

Feedback response:

Windows provide feedback. When a correct match is obtained in the front windows, the objects, symbols, or numbers match in the back windows. Thus, to check an answer the student looks at the back windows.

Materials:

1. Poster board
2. Brass fasteners
3. Small pictures or symbols

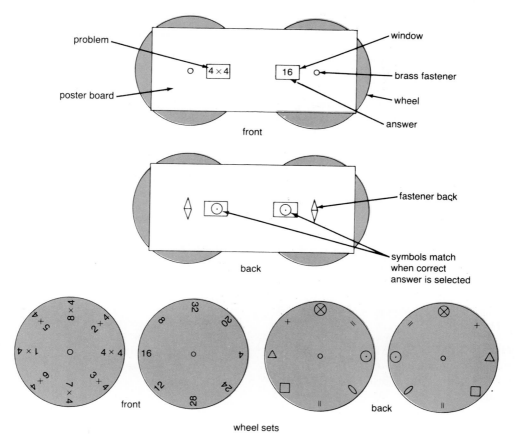

FIGURE 4.2
Spinning Wheels.

Construction:

1. Cut two horizontal pieces of poster board with matching dimensions.
2. Cut two windows on the same horizontal line in each piece. The windows should line up with each other when the pieces are placed together (back to back).
3. Decorate and laminate each piece, and make the center holes for the fasteners.
4. Cut circles with dimensions that enable the outer 1″ ridge to pass through the windows when the center of the wheel is lined up with the poster board hole.
5. Write, draw, or paste problems on one wheel and put answers on a corresponding wheel. Write, draw, or glue symbols, objects, or numbers on the back of each wheel set.

Directions:

The student selects a wheel set that presents an appropriate task. She places the wheels between the two rectangular pieces, lines up the holes, and inserts the brass fasteners. The student then rotates the task wheel until a problem is presented in the window. Next the student rotates the other wheel and selects one of the answers that passes through the window. Once an answer is selected, the student flips over the material and checks to see if her answer is correct. A correct answer yields matching objects in the two windows on the back.

Modifications:

The teacher can make numerous wheel sets and code them according to skill area. Wheels that are to be used together (a wheel set) should have matching codes on them. The tasks that can be placed on the wheels are almost limitless. The size of the material can be varied to accommodate different sized windows.

Stylus. Feedback can be provided by using a stylus with certain types of stimulus cards. The Poke Box in Figure 4.3 illustrates the use of a stylus.

Selected instructional pinpoints:

1. See math problem—choose answer.
2. See math problem—write answer.

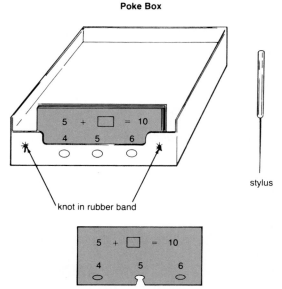

Poke Box

FIGURE 4.3
Poke Box.

3. See sentence—choose missing word.
4. See paragraph—choose title.
5. Any instructional pinpoint that features a multiple-choice answer format can be used with the Poke Box.

Feedback response:

The student inserts a stylus in one of the holes below the answers and pulls the card to see if it comes out of the box. If the right hole is selected, the card is removed easily from the box (the area below the correct answer is cut and offers no resistance to the stylus).

Materials:

1. A cardboard or wooden box big enough to hold 3″ × 5″ or 5″ × 8″ index cards
2. A large rubber band
3. A thin stick or poker
4. Index cards

Construction:

1. Cut the front end of the box so that most of the index card is visible, but leave a horizontal strip at the bottom of the box about 1″ high.

2. Using a hole punch or drill, make three evenly spaced holes across the front of the box about ½″ from the bottom.

3. At each end of the front of the box, drill or punch a hole that extends beyond the dimensions of the index cards. Insert a broken rubber band from the inside of the box on both sides, and tie the ends in knots on the outside of the box. The rubber band holds the cards and pushes them to the front of the box.

4. Paint the box inside and out.

5. Make holes in the index cards so that they line up with the holes in the box.

6. Cut out one answer slot on each card.

7. Attach the stylus to the box.

8. Prepare index cards with problems or questions on top and possible answers beneath. Line up the answers with the appropriate holes.

9. To prevent a student from tearing the card by pulling too hard on a wrong choice, strengthen the holes with gummed reinforcers.

Directions:

The student says, writes, or chooses her answers. Then she pokes the stylus in the hole representing her answer. If the choice is correct, the problem card can be pulled up and out of the box and the next problem card is presented.

Modifications:

The size of the box can vary so that large cards can be used. Some Poke Boxes feature 8″ × 11½″ cardboard cards. The large space provides room for short stories and multiple-choice comprehension questions. The teacher can put the problem or story on a separate worksheet and put the answer selections on the cards.

Simple Self-Correcting Materials

Puzzle.   In this type of feedback, pieces of material fit together to indicate a match or correct choice. The top or side section of each puzzle shows an object or problem, and the bottom section or other side provides the name of the object or the answer to the problem. The sections interlock only if they belong together. Because puzzles can be completed

without looking at the academic tasks, the student should be required to read or say the task.

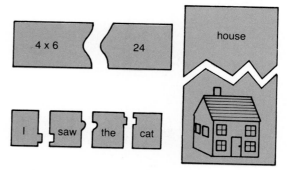

Matching cards.   Sets of cards are prepared with the problem or question on one card and the answer on another card. The back of the set of cards contains a match of some sort or a picture completion. When the student selects an answer to a problem, she turns over the cards. If the appropriate answer is chosen, the objects, numbers, colors, or pictures on the back will either match or fit together to complete a picture.

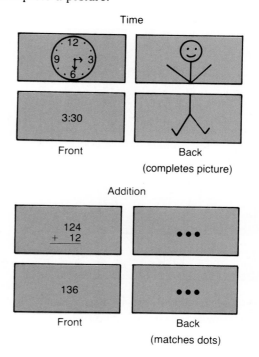

Time

Front Back
(completes picture)

Addition

Front Back
(matches dots)

Answer on back. A problem is presented on one side of a stimulus card, and the answer is placed on the other side.

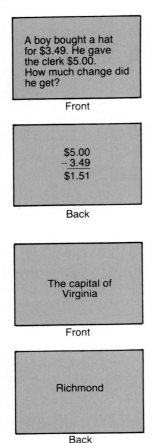

Front

A boy bought a hat for $3.49. He gave the clerk $5.00. How much change did he get?

Back

$$\begin{array}{r} \$5.00 \\ -\ 3.49 \\ \hline \$1.51 \end{array}$$

Front

The capital of Virginia

Back

Richmond

Tab. A tab is pulled from a pocket in the learning material to reveal an answer or answers.

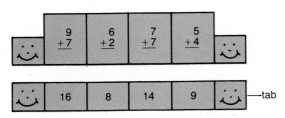

—tab

Pocket. Pockets can be made easily by stapling envelopes to the back of the learning material. Pockets usually hold some type of answer key. In addition, pockets can be coded to provide feedback. For example, library card pockets can be used for sorting stimulus cards. A code is on the back of the stimulus card and the library pocket. If a card is placed in the correct pocket, the codes match. Many instructional pinpoints can be taught with this format. For example, if the stimulus cards show words from the categories of noun, pronoun, verb, and adjective, there would be a pocket corresponding with each category.

Holes. Problems are written on one side of a card or sheet, and a hole is punched beside or underneath each item. The answer to each problem is written on the back of the card next to or under the hole. The student sees the problem, writes or says the answer, puts a pipe cleaner or pencil in the hole, and turns over the card to check her response. This format can be used for teaching opposites, plurals, synonyms, word problems, and so on. Manila folders can be used to make this material.

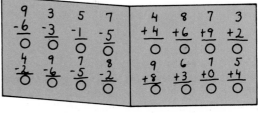

Front

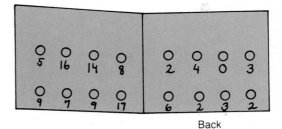

Back

Clips. Clips such as clothespins or paper clips can be used to provide feedback. For example, a cardboard pizza wheel can be divided into segments with a task stimulus presented in each segment. Responses are made by clipping clothespins to the edge of the segments. To check answers the board is turned over to see if the code on the pizza board matches the code on the clothespin.

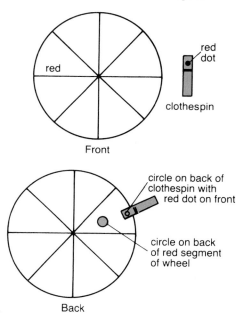

Front

Back

Strips in a folder. Strips are cut in one side of a manila folder and then the folder is laminated. Worksheets containing problems and answers are inserted into the folder so that only the problem is presented. The student uses a grease pencil or a felt-tip pen to write her responses under each problem. Then the worksheet is pulled upward, and the answers appear in the strip (see next column).

Instructional Games

Students with learning problems frequently need a lot of drill and practice in academic skills. Because drill can be tedious, creative teaching must motivate students. Positive reinforcement, charting, self-correction, and

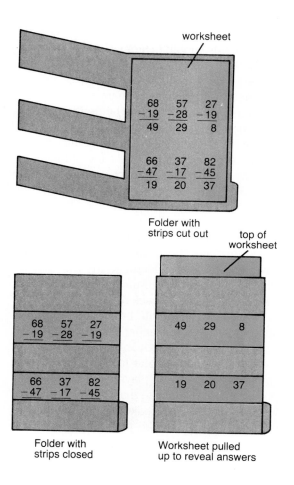

high-interest formats frequently are used to enrich drill. Instructional games are a popular way of maintaining interest during practice.

First, the purpose of the game needs to be examined. The game must include the intended outcome, and the student must have the skills necessary to play the game. Usually the game is used to practice or reinforce a skill that already has been taught. Of course, the game must not be mere busy work. By monitoring student progress, the teacher can evaluate the effects of an instructional game on a specific skill.

Next, the basic game procedures must be selected. Familiar game materials such as checkers, cards, dice, spinners, and start-to-finish boards should be considered. The game should involve both chance and skill.

The games should be individualized for student needs. If a game has many uses, it saves the gamemaker's time and helps the student learn new skills in a familiar format. Games can be made self-correcting, or an answer key can be provided. This allows the students to play the game without direct teacher supervision. Surprise factors boost interest in the game—*go to jail, skip a space, fix a flat.* Moreover, they add to the element of chance.

Manila folders are good game boards because they are sturdy, are a convenient size, have tabs for easy reference, and are easy to store in a file cabinet. Rules are readily available if written on the back of each folder. Lamination makes the game board more durable and attractive. The teacher can purchase kits with blank laminated boards that have established routes for markers to travel, unmarked spinners, and blank playing cards. Several publishers market these materials. Finally, the teacher may wish to make a rough draft of a game and test it before making the finished product.

Teacher-made instructional games are presented in Figures 4.4 and 4.5. In addition, games involving cards, dominoes, chips, dice, and so on are presented in the curriculum area chapters.

Simple Board Game

Instructional objective:

Any instructional task that can be presented on a card and performed in a few seconds is suitable.

Feedback device:

Answer key and peer correction provide feedback.

Materials:

1. Poster board (or a manila folder)
2. Index cards
3. Golf tees
4. Dice
5. Tasks for the cards

Construction:

1. Draw on a poster board a segmented road, race track, rocket path, football field, mountain path, or any other start-to-finish sequence.
2. Decorate the board to accent the game theme (racing cars, football, joggers, mountain climbers).

FIGURE 4.4
Simple game-board format.

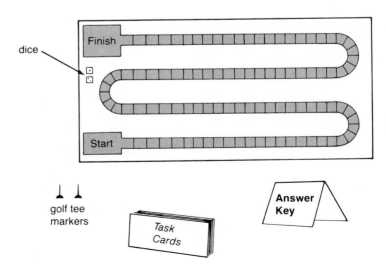

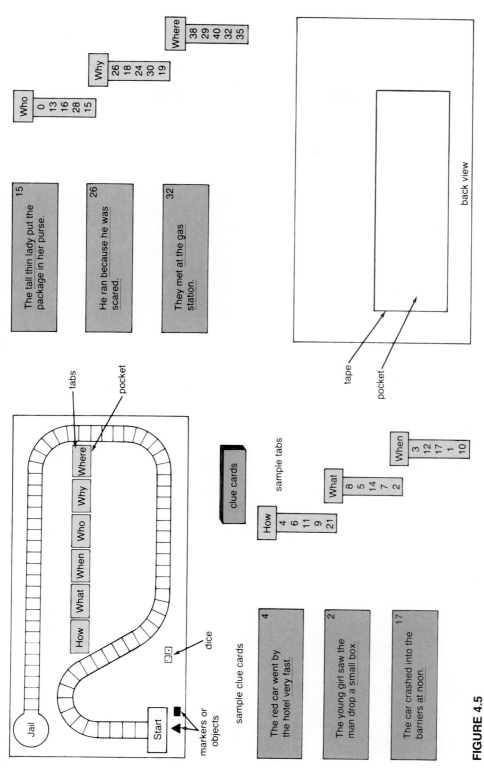

FIGURE 4.5
Mystery Detective Game.

3. Make a stack of task cards with an accompanying answer key. For example, if the task card says

$$4 \times 4 = \underline{\quad}$$

the answer key would read

$$4 \times 4 = \underline{16}$$

Directions:

1. A player rolls the dice, picks up a task card, and says an answer.
2. If no player challenges this answer, she moves her marker the number on the dice.
3. If a player challenges her answer, it is looked up on the answer key. If it is correct, the player gets another turn. If it is incorrect, the marker is not moved and the challenger takes a turn.

Modifications:

1. Omit the challenge factor.
2. Mark spaces so that when a player lands on them a chance card (for example, *move back three spaces, take an extra turn*) is picked up.

Mystery Detective

Instructional objective:

Reading comprehension. See sentence clue card and select the meaning of underlined portion in terms of how, what, when, who, why, or where.

Feedback device:

Tabs with numbers that match those on the clue cards are used to provide feedback. For example, a number on a *What* card will be on the tab labeled *What.* Thus, a correct response results in a number match between the card and the tab.

Materials:

1. Poster board for game board, tabs, and clue cards
2. Dice
3. Pictures or drawings for decoration
4. Objects to move from start to jail

Construction:

1. Cut a slot in the poster board and tape an additional piece of cardboard to the poster board so that a pocket is formed with the slot at the top of it.
2. Cut six tabs of a length that exposes the name of the tab, but not the numbers, when inserted fully in the pocket.
3. On the game side of the board draw a "start-to-jail" winding, segmented road.
4. Make a stack of sentence clue cards. Underline a portion of each sentence that corresponds to one of the how, what, when, who, why, or where questions. Place a number in the right top corner of each clue card. Do not repeat the numbers.
5. Make six tabs, one for each of the questions. On each tab list the numbers that match the clue cards.
6. Laminate the material to increase its durability.

Directions:

1. A player rolls the dice and picks up a clue card.
2. The player determines if it is a how, what, when, who, why, or where clue and selects one of the tabs.
3. If the number on the sentence clue card is on the tab chosen, the player gets to move her marker the number of spaces indicated on the dice.
4. If the number on the sentence clue card is *not* on the tab, the player does not move her marker.
5. The next player does the same thing, and the first player to put the marker in jail wins.

Modifications:

1. Use this game format to practice syllabication. Label each tab with a number to indicate the number of syllables on corresponding word cards.
2. Instead of using the pocket on the game board, put each tab in an envelope or in a separately constructed pocket.
3. To make the game more exciting, mark "Trouble" or "Good News" on certain squares. When a player lands on a marked square, she picks up a card and does the activity on the card—for example, *go ahead three spaces.*

Toss A Disc

Instructional objective:

Any instructional task that can be presented on a card and performed in a few seconds is suitable.

Feedback device:

Answer key and peer correction provide feedback.

Materials:

1. Poster board
2. Index cards
3. Discs (checkers, laminated circles of poster board or oaktag)
4. Tasks for the cards

Toss A Disc

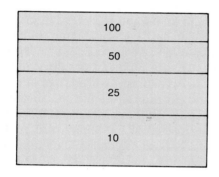

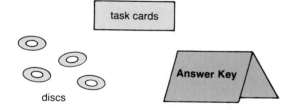

discs

Construction:

1. Divide a piece of large poster board into zones, with the zones getting larger as the points decrease.
2. Put points for each zone in the center of the zone.
3. Use checkers as discs or make discs out of oaktag or poster board.
4. Decorate the poster board with a theme.
5. Laminate the poster board.

Directions:

1. The game board is placed on the floor, with the highest point zone flush against the wall.

2. Approximately 8 to 12 feet away, the teacher marks a space for the player to stand behind while she is tossing the disc toward the game board.
3. After the disc is tossed, the player picks up a task card and answers the question on it.
4. The player checks her answer on the answer key. If she is correct, she gets the points indicated for the zone where her disc landed. If she is incorrect, no points are awarded.
5. The first player to earn 500 (or 700, or 1,000) points wins.

Modification:

Instead of using a poster board on the floor, use a small box with the bottom of the box divided into point zones. The student tosses pennies or discs into the box to determine the points (according to the zone) for each turn.

Peer Tutoring Materials

ClassWide Peer Tutoring. *ClassWide Peer Tutoring (CWPT)* (Greenwood, Delquadri, & Carta, 1988) is an instructional management procedure that enables the teacher to engage all students in a classroom simultaneously in a variety of academic tasks. *CWPT* is an integrated behavior management and direct instruction procedure that is based upon reciprocal peer tutoring and group-oriented reinforcement contingencies (for example, cooperative learning). The method includes three features to increase on-task behavior and amount of practice of academic skills: (a) peers are used to supervise responding and practice; (b) a game format is used that includes points and competing teams to motivate students and maintain interest; and (c) a weekly evaluation plan ensures gains in individual and class progress. The teacher trains students to be effective tutors by carefully explaining and demonstrating error correction procedures and the point system to be followed in the tutoring sessions. Corrective feedback is given during supervised practice opportunities.

The *CWPT* system features the following basic arrangement:

1. Daily tutoring slots of about 30 minutes are required. Each student tutors for 10 minutes and then receives 10 minutes of tutoring. An additional 10 minutes are spent counting points and posting results.
2. On Monday the tutor-tutee pairs for the week are selected. The pair sit next to or across from each other and begin a 10-minute tutoring session. For example, if the task is oral reading, the tutor monitors the reading and awards two points for each sentence read correctly. The tutee earns one point for correctly rereading a sentence after the tutor has detected an error. The tutor marks points on a Tutoring Point Sheet. At the end of 10 minutes, the tutoring roles are reversed.
3. During the tutoring sessions, the teacher moves among the students and awards bonus points for correct tutoring behavior. The teacher also divides the class into two teams.
4. After the second 10-minute session, each student counts the number of points earned as both tutor and tutee. These point totals are recorded for each student in one of two team columns on a chart. The team earning the highest number of points is the winning team for the day. The composition of the two teams changes each week.
5. On Friday, the teacher can conduct a more intensive assessment of each student's progress on the skills from that week.

The *CWPT* program was developed over an eight-year period and has been field tested extensively. Research data indicate that *CWPT* improves students' engagement in academic tasks, increases academic achievement gains, and enhances cooperative peer relations (Greenwood et al., 1984; Kohler, Richardson, Mina, Dinwiddie, & Greenwood, 1985).

Peer tutoring kits. Peer tutoring kits can be made easily and used on a regular or intermittent basis to help students acquire or review basic facts. The following materials are required: a manila folder, a direction sheet, a task sheet with the problems and three columns for recording correct or incorrect responses, two library card pockets, and 10 to 20 flash cards with problems. The direction sheet provides instructions to the tutor-tutee pair and is glued to the right-hand side of the folder. The task sheet is glued to the left-hand side of the folder and includes the problems found on the flash cards and three columns so the tutor can mark correct ($+$) or incorrect ($-$) next to the problems for three different attempts. Two library card pockets are glued below the direction sheet and are labeled "Tutoring Cards" and "Learned Facts." The flash cards are placed in the library card pockets. The outside of the folder is titled and decorated, and the entire kit can be laminated. Chapter 3 presents programming guidelines for planning and implementing peer tutoring and includes a sample tutor instruction sheet for flash cards, a tutor record sheet, and a tutor checklist.

MATERIAL ORGANIZATION SYSTEM

To plan and deliver individualized instruction in a systematic and continuous manner, a great deal of organization is needed. For the beginning teacher the development of a system is a large undertaking; however, without it much frustration and anxiety can result. For example, without a system of filing instructional materials that accounts for storage and retrieval, the beginning teacher can spend hours trying to locate needed materials. Thus, one of the initial jobs for a teacher is to develop a filing and storage system and refine it with use.

Before the first day of teaching, the teacher begins to make bulletin boards, dittos, instructional games, worksheets, interest centers, overheads, and special project activities. A filing system helps the teacher organize and add to these materials. In addition, the system can be refined as the teacher develops priorities.

Table 4.2 presents a general filing system. The categories would change depending on the subjects being taught. As it is developed, the system would become more specific. For example, numerous subcategories would be listed under phonics as materials and activities are collected and developed (for example, individual consonant sounds, blends, vowel sounds, digraphs). In the academic areas a highly specific filing system can be developed from scope and sequence skills lists, commercial programs, or curriculum guides. By making the system open-ended, the teacher can add categories as needed. New ideas or materials collected from teachers, books, inservice meetings, university classes, or commercial programs can be filed into the system readily and used when needed.

REFERENCES

Archer, A., & Edgar, E. (1976). Teaching academic skills to mildly handicapped children. In S. Lowenbraun & J. Q. Affleck (Eds.), *Teaching mildly handicapped children in regular classes* (pp. 15–112). New York: Merrill/Macmillan.

Bartel, N. R., & Hammill, D. D. (1990). Important generic practices in teaching students with learning and behavior problems. In D. D. Hammill & N. R. Bartel, *Teaching students with learning and behavior problems* (5th ed., pp. 531–546). Boston: Allyn & Bacon.

Bereiter, C., & Engelmann, S. E. (1966). Teaching disadvantaged children in the preschool. Englewood Cliffs, NJ: Prentice-Hall.

Brophy, J., & Good, T. (1986). Teacher behavior and student achievement. In M. C. Wittrock

TABLE 4.2

Sample categorical outline for a filing system.

I. Academic Areas
  R. Reading
    R-1 Readiness materials and activities
    R-2 Phonics materials and activities
    R-3 Comprehension materials and activities
    R-4 Whole-word materials and activities
    R-5 Whole language materials and activities
    R-6 Basal related materials and activities
  M. Math
    M-1 Readiness materials and activities
    M-2 Quantity materials and activities
    M-3 Place value materials and activities
    M-4 Addition materials and activities
    M-5 Subtraction materials and activities
    M-6 Multiplication materials and activities
    M-7 Division materials and activities
    M-8 Fractions materials and activities
    M-9 Percentages materials and activities
    M-10 Word problems materials and activities
    M-11 Money materials and activities

Other academic areas (language, spelling, social studies) would be developed according to subareas and specific skills.

II. Management and Motivation Areas
    B.B. Bulletin boards
    I.C. Interest centers
    L.C. Learning centers
    C.R. Classroom rules
    S. Scheduling materials (e.g., forms)
    E.C. Evaluation center materials (e.g., charts, forms, stopwatches, logs)
    G. Games
    A.V. Audiovisual materials
    S.C. Self-correcting materials
    R.M. Reinforcement materials
    C.A. Classroom arrangement materials

(Ed.), *Third handbook of research on teaching* (3rd ed., pp. 328–375). New York: Macmillan.

Carnine, D. (1989). Teaching complex content to learning disabled students: The role of technology. *Exceptional Children, 55,* 524–533.

Carnine, D. (1990). Beyond technique—Direct instruction and higher-order skills. *Direct Instruction News, 9*(3), 1–13.

Cosden, M. A., Gerber, M. M., Semmel, D. S., Goldman, S. R., & Semmel, M. I. (1987). Microcomputer use within micro-educational environments. *Exceptional Children, 53,* 399–409.

Dell, H. D. (1972). *Individualizing instruction: Materials and classroom procedures.* Chicago: Science Research Associates.

Ellis, E. S., & Sabornie, E. J. (1986). Effective instruction with microcomputers: Promises, practices, and preliminary findings. *Focus on Exceptional Children, 19*(4), 1–16.

Fitzgerald, G., Fick, L., & Milich, R. (1986). Computer-assisted instruction for students with attentional difficulties. *Journal of Learning Disabilities, 6,* 376–379.

Fuchs, L. S., Fuchs, D., & Hamlett, C. L. (1989). Effects of alternative goal structures within curriculum-based measurement. *Exceptional Children, 55,* 429–438.

Gersten, R., Carnine, D., & Woodward, J. (1987). Direct instruction research: The third decade. *Remedial and Special Education, 8*(6), 48–56.

Gersten, R., & Keating, T. (1987). Long-term benefits from direct instruction. *Educational Leadership, 44*(6), 28–31.

Gersten, R., Woodward, J., & Darch, C. (1986). Direct instruction: A research-based approach to curriculum design and teaching. *Exceptional Children, 53,* 17–31.

Greenwood, C. R., Delquadri, J. C., & Carta, J. J. (1988). *ClassWide peer tutoring: Programs for spelling, math, and reading.* Delray Beach, FL: Educational Achievement Systems.

Greenwood, C. R., Dinwiddie, G., Terry B., Wade, L., Stanley, S. O., Thibadeau, S., & Delquadri, J. C. (1984). Teacher- versus peer-mediated instruction: An ecobehavioral analysis of achievement outcomes. *Journal of Applied Behavior Analysis, 17,* 521–538.

Grimes, L. (1981). Computers are for kids: Designing software programs. *Teaching Exceptional Children, 14,* 48–53.

Hasselbring, T. S., Goin, L. I., & Bransford, J. D. (1988). Developing math automaticity in learning handicapped children: The role of computerized drill and practice. *Focus on Exceptional Children, 20*(6), 1–7.

Haynes, J. A., & Malouf, D. B. (1986). Computer assisted instruction needs help. *Academic Therapy, 22,* 157–164.

Hofmeister, A. M. (1984). *Microcomputers applications in the classroom.* New York: Holt, Rinehart & Winston.

Horton, S. V., Lovitt, T. C., Givens, A., & Nelson, R. (1989). Teaching social studies to high school students with academic handicaps in a mainstreamed setting: Effects of a computerized study guide. *Journal of Learning Disabilities, 22,* 102–107.

Keefe, C. H., & Candler, A. C. (1989). LD students and word processors: Questions and answers. *Learning Disabilities Focus, 4,* 78–83.

Kelly, B., Gersten, R., & Carnine, D. (1990). Student error patterns as a function of curriculum design: Teaching fractions to remedial high school students and high school students with learning disabilities. *Journal of Learning Disabilities, 23,* 23–29.

Kohler, F. W., Richardson, T., Mina, C., Dinwiddie, G., & Greenwood, C. R. (1985). Establishing cooperative peer relations in the classroom. *The Pointer, 29,* 12–16.

Kolich, E. M. (1985). Microcomputer technology with the learning disabled: A review of the literature. *Journal of Learning Disabilities, 18,* 428–431.

Kulik, J. A., Kulik, C. C., & Bangert-Drowns, R. L. (1985). Effectiveness of computer-based education in elementary schools. *Computers in Human Behavior, 1,* 59–74.

Lewis, R. B., & Doorlag, D. H. (1991). *Teaching special students in the mainstream* (3rd ed.). New York: Merrill/Macmillan.

Lindsey, J. D. (1987). *Computers and exceptional individuals.* New York: Merrill/Macmillan.

Majsterek, D. J., & Wilson, R. (1989). Computer-assisted instruction for students with learning disabilities: Considerations for practioners. *Learning Disabilities Focus, 5*(1), 18–27.

Mercer, C. D., Mercer, A. R., & Bott, D. A. (1984). *Self-correcting learning materials for the classroom.* New York: Merrill/Macmillan.

Moore, L. J., & Carnine, D. (1989). Evaluating curriculum design in the context of active teaching. *Remedial and Special Education, 10*(4), 28–37.

Rosenshine, B. V. (1986). Synthesis of research on explicit teaching. *Educational Leadership, 43*(7), 60–69.

Shuell, T. J., & Schueckler, L. M. (1988, April). *Toward evaluating software according to principles of learning and teaching.* Paper presented at the meeting of the American Educational Research Association, New Orleans.

Simmons, D. C., Fuchs, D., & Fuchs, L. S. (1991). Instructional and curricular requisites of mainstreamed students with learning disabilities. *Journal of Learning Disabilities, 24,* 354–360.

Sprick, R. S. (1987). *Solutions to elementary discipline problems* [Audiocassette tapes]. Eugene, OR: Teaching Strategies.

Stephens, T. M. (1977). *Teaching skills to children with learning and behavior disorders.* New York: Merrill/Macmillan.

Stowitschek, J. J., & Stowitschek, C. E. (1984). Once more with feeling: The absence of research on teacher use of microcomputers. *Exceptional Education Quarterly, 4*(4), 23–39.

Torgesen, J. K., Waters, M. D., Cohen, A. L., & Torgesen, J. L. (1988). Improving sight-word recognition skills in LD children: An evaluation of three computer program variations. *Learning Disability Quarterly, 11,* 125–132.

Torgesen, J. K., & Young, K. A. (1983). Priorities for the use of microcomputers with learning disabled children. *Journal of Learning Disabilities, 16,* 234–237.

Watkins, M. W., & Webb, C. (1981, September/October). Computer assisted instruction with learning disabled students. *Educational Computer Magazine,* pp. 24–27.

Wiens, W. (1986). Computer assisted learning in the learning assisted centre. *B.C. Journal of Special Education, 10,* 17–28.

Woodward, J., & Carnine, D. (1988). Antecedent knowledge and intelligent computer-assisted instruction. *Journal of Learning Disabilities, 21,* 131–139.

Woodward, J., Carnine, D., & Gersten, R. (1988). Teaching problem solving through a computer simulation. *American Educational Research Journal, 25*(1), 72–86.

CHAPTER **5**

Developing Social and Emotional Behavior

Students with learning difficulties often have social and emotional behavior problems. The student with social problems may be unable to behave appropriately with peers and in social situations (for example, teasing, disruptive behavior, difficulty making friends). While social problems involve interactions with others, emotional problems generally are considered to be problems within oneself. For example, the academically poor student with emotional problems may have low self-esteem or deal poorly with stress or frustration. Problems in these areas often overlap; for example, a student with a poor self-concept may withdraw from social interaction with peers and adults. Although it is not always apparent whether social and emotional problems are contributing to a student's academic difficulties, these aspects of a student's behavior usually appear to be counterproductive to learning and thus limit academic success. On the other hand, learning difficulties can contribute to social and emotional problems by causing the student to face excessive academic failure and frustration.

The teacher can help foster the student's emotional development as well as the acquisition of social skills. Direct instruction may be the best means of reducing problems related to social and emotional development.

ASSESSMENT OF SOCIAL AND EMOTIONAL BEHAVIOR

During assessment of social and emotional behavior, the type of behavior and its frequency, intensity, and duration should be considered. Assessment procedures help the teacher identify social and emotional behavior problems that require immediate attention. Checklists, rating scales, and self-report tests have been published that focus on assessing social and emotional behavior. Checklists and rating scales provide methods for obtaining and recording judgments of teachers, peers, and parents concerning undesirable social and emotional behavior, whereas self-report tests usually assess the student's attitude or self-concept. Generally, the instruments assist the teacher in identifying areas for further assessment and intervention. The teacher may choose to supplement a published instrument by developing teacher-made assessment procedures (checklists, sociometric techniques, direct observation techniques) that help in identifying specific problem areas or that locate strengths and weaknesses. Assessment of social and emotional behavior is presented according to five areas: commercial observer-rater instruments, commercial interview instruments, self-report instruments, sociometric techniques, and naturalistic observations.

Commercial Observer-Rater Instruments

With these instruments an observer (teacher, guidance counselor, social worker, school psychologist, or family member) completes either a checklist or a rating scale. Checklists generally are used to record the presence or absence of specific characteristics or behaviors. Rating scales are designed to indicate the frequency of a particular behavior or the degree to which certain characteristics are present. Teacher ratings frequently are used to assess behavior problems in classrooms, and parent ratings rate students' atypical behaviors and adaptive behavior.

The *Behavior Evaluation Scale—2* (McCarney & Leigh, 1990) yields behavioral information from the teacher about students in kindergarten through twelfth grade according to five subscales: learning problems, interpersonal difficulties, inappropriate behavior, unhappiness/depression, and physical symptoms/fears. Raw scores are weighted according to severity and frequency of observed behaviors.

The *Behavior Rating Profile—2* (Brown & Hammill, 1990) is designed to study the behavior of students in first through twelfth grade at school, at home, and with their peers. Information is collected from teachers, parents, and peers, as well as from the student. Six independent measures of behavior are included: teacher rating scale, student rating scale (school), parent rating scale, student rating scale (home), sociogram, and student rating scale (peer). The three student rating scales are embedded in a 60-item true/false format, and the parent and teacher rating scales each contain 30 items that the respondents classify on a four-point scale. The sociogram provides information about the student's sociometric status within the classroom. The results of the profile can be used to identify students whose behavior is perceived to be deviant and to identify specific settings in which behavior problems are prominent. Also, the profile can be useful in identifying persons whose perceptions of a student's behaviors are different from those of other respondents.

Burks' Behavior Rating Scales (Burks, 1977) are designed for students in first through ninth grade, and respondents include the teacher and the parent. There are 18 categories of behavior, including (among others) self-blame, anxiety, withdrawal, dependency, poor attention, poor impulse control, poor sense of identity, poor anger control, aggressiveness, resistance, and poor social conformity. The instrument can be administered in about 10 minutes, and the manual provides suggested intervention techniques for each category.

The three Devereux scales are the *Devereux Child Behavior Rating Scale* (Spivack & Spotts, 1966), the *Devereux Elementary School Behavior Rating Scale* (Swift, 1982), and the *Devereux Adolescent Behavior Rating Scale* (Spivack, Spotts, & Haimes, 1967). The *Devereux Child Behavior Rating Scale* is de-

signed to describe and evaluate behavior disorders of students age 8 through 12 who are emotionally disturbed or mentally retarded. It can be completed in 10 to 20 minutes by the parent or a rater who is familiar with the student's behavior in a home-type situation. There are 17 behavioral factors, such as emotional detachment, need for adult contact, social aggression, and unethical behavior. The *Devereux Elementary School Behavior Rating Scale* focuses on behavior problems of students in kindergarten through sixth grade. Scores are obtained from the teacher's rating of the student on 11 behaviors (such as classroom disturbance, impatience, inattention and withdrawal) and three additional items—inability to change, slowness, and quitting before completing a task. The *Devereux Adolescent Behavior Rating Scale* is appropriate for students age 13 through 18. Behavior descriptions are provided, and the student is rated by the parent according to how often the behavior occurs as well as to what degree it occurs. The scale provides 12 factor scores (such as poor emotional control) and 11 item scores (such as peer dominance and plotting).

The *Hahnemann High School Behavior Rating Scale* (Swift & Spivack, 1972) is completed by the teacher to measure observable classroom behavior of students in seventh through twelfth grade. Eight general factors are measured: general anxiety, quietness and withdrawal, poor work habits, lack of intellectual independence, dogmatic and inflexible behavior, verbal negativism, disturbance and restlessness, and expressed inability. In addition, five factors related to academic success are rated: reasoning ability, verbal interaction, originality, rapport with the teacher, and anxious production (anxiety related to learning or mastery of classroom tasks).

The *Pupil Rating Scale Revised* (Myklebust, 1981) is used with students in kindergarten through sixth grade. The teacher evaluates specific behaviors and rates each student on a five-point scale. The 24 items evaluated are grouped into five classifications: auditory comprehension and memory, spoken language, orientation, motor coordination, and personal-social behavior.

The *Revised Behavior Problem Checklist* (Quay & Peterson, 1987) uses a rating system that distinguishes among behavior not observed, observed but mild, and observed and severe. The checklist is used for students in kindergarten through eighth grade and can be completed by parents, teachers, or anyone familiar with the student. Problem behaviors are classified as (a) conduct disorders, (b) personality disorders, (c) inadequacy or immaturity, and (d) subcultural (socialized) delinquency.

The *Social-Emotional Dimension Scale* (Hutton & Roberts, 1986) is a 32-item norm-referenced rating scale completed by the teacher to assess students age 4 through 18 who are at risk for conduct disorders, behavior problems, or emotional disturbance. Student performance is assessed in six areas: physical/fear reaction, depressive reaction, avoidance of peer interaction, avoidance of teacher interaction, aggressive interaction, and inappropriate behaviors.

The *Social Skills Rating System* (Gresham & Elliott, 1990) includes three rating forms (teacher, parent, student) that evaluate a broad range of behaviors in students age 3 through 18. The social skills scale (on all three forms) evaluates positive social behaviors (such as cooperation, assertion, responsibility, empathy, and self-control). The problem behavior scale (on the teacher and parent forms) measures behaviors that can interfere with the production of social skills (such as aggression, anxiety, and hyperactivity). The academic competence scale (on the teacher form) is an index of academic functioning. Items on each scale are rated according to

perceived frequency and importance. *SSRS* ASSIST software provides computerized scoring and reporting as well as behavioral objectives and suggestions for planning intervention.

The *Test of Early Socioemotional Development* (Hresko & Brown, 1984) is a downward extension of the *Behavior Rating Profile*. This battery of four components is designed to evaluate the behavior of young children age 3 through 7. The 30-item student rating scale is completed by the student, the 34-item parent rating scale is completed by the parents, and the 36-item teacher rating scale is completed by the teacher or other professionals having contact with the student in a school setting. A sociogram provides information about peer perceptions of the student being evaluated.

The *Walker-McConnell Scale of Social Competence and School Adjustment* (Walker & McConnell, 1988) includes a five-point scale format to measure teacher-preferred social behavior, peer-preferred social behavior, and adjustment to the behavioral demands of the classroom. The 43-item scale takes about five minutes per student to complete and is useful to screen and identify social skills deficits of students in kindergarten through sixth grade.

The *Walker Problem Behavior Identification Checklist* (Walker, 1983) is designed for use with students in kindergarten through sixth grade. The checklist takes about 15 minutes to administer and consists of 50 statements describing behaviors that may interfere or compete with successful academic performance. The items are designed to measure five behavioral factors: acting out, withdrawal, distractibility, disturbed peer relations, and immaturity.

The *Weller-Strawser Scales of Adaptive Behavior* (Weller & Strawser, 1981) consist of two scales: an elementary scale for students age 6 through 12 and a secondary scale for students age 13 through 18. The adaptive behavior of students with learning problems is assessed in four areas: social coping, relationships, pragmatic language, and production. Each scale consists of 35 items that present pairs of descriptions of an adaptive behavior characteristic, and the examiner marks the alternative that best describes the student's behavior. A profile is obtained of either mild to moderate or moderate to severe adaptive behavior problems in each of the areas. Recommendations for programming and environmental modifications are included for each possible profile.

Commercial Interview Instruments

Instruments in this category feature the interview technique for obtaining information about social and emotional behavior. The interviewer (school psychologist, social worker, guidance counselor, or specially trained teacher) follows systematic procedures while interviewing one or several persons (such as family members, peers, other teachers) who know the student.

The *AAMD Adaptive Behavior Scale: School Edition* (Lambert, Windmiller, Cole, & Tharinger, 1981) covers social and daily living skills and behaviors of students age 3 through 16. Part I evaluates personal independence in daily living (for example, independent functioning, self-direction, responsibility). Part II measures personality and behavior disorders (for example, aggressiveness, rebelliousness, trustworthiness). The scale domains are grouped into five factors: personal self-sufficiency, community self-sufficiency, personal-social responsibility, personal adjustment, and social adjustment. The responder (any individual familiar with the student) must check statements that apply to the student or rate the statements in each item as occurring occasionally or frequently. A software scoring system is available.

The *Scales of Independent Behavior* (Bruininks, Woodcock, Weatherman, & Hill, 1985) provide a noncognitive measure of adjustment in the social, behavioral, and adaptive areas. The instrument is designed for infant through adult ages and assesses functional independence and adaptive behavior in motor skills, social and communication skills, personal living skills, and community living skills. Also, a problem-behavior scale focuses on general, externalized, internalized, and asocial maladaptive behaviors. Because the instrument is conceptually and statistically linked to the *Woodcock-Johnson Psycho-Educational Battery,* adaptive behavior can be measured based on cognitive ability.

The *Vineland Adaptive Behavior Scale* (Sparrow, Balla, & Cicchetti, 1984) assesses personal and social sufficiency for individuals from birth through 18 years of age. Three versions are available: (a) interview edition, survey form—aids in screening or classification decisions, (b) interview edition, expanded form—provides specific prescriptive information that can be used for educational programming, and (c) classroom edition—uses a checklist format and allows for direct observation of adaptive behavior of students age 3 through 12. Thus, information about an individual can be interpreted from the points of view of a parent or primary caregiver and a teacher. The scale assesses adaptive behavior in four areas: communication, daily living skills, socialization, and motor skills. The survey and expanded forms also measure maladaptive behavior. Standard scores and percentiles are available for each area and subarea as well as total adaptive behavior, and norms are provided in the interview editions for students in various categories (such as nondisabled, mentally retarded, emotionally disturbed). *Vineland* ASSIST software provides helpful score conversion.

Self-Report Instruments

Self-report techniques allow the student to report on his own specific behavior. Self-report procedures obtain information directly from the student; thus, the information is totally subjective. Its validity depends on the willingness of the student to report the information and on his ability to understand and perform the task. Commercial self-report instruments are presented as well as the Q-sort technique and various informal self-report techniques.

Commercial Instruments. Self-report measures are the primary means for assessing a student's self-concept and for identifying areas that cause the student anxiety or concern. The student responds directly to test items concerning himself.

The *Coopersmith Self-Esteem Inventories* (Coopersmith, 1981) are self-report questionnaires that consist of short statements ("I'm a failure"; "I can usually take care of myself") to be answered "like me" or "unlike me." The inventories are designed to measure attitudes toward the self in social, academic, and personal contexts. The school form includes 58 items that can produce a total score, a lie score, and attitude scores toward self/peers, home/parents, and school.

The *Culture-Free Self-Esteem Inventories — 2* (Battle, 1992) contain a 60-item form (or a 30-item brief form) that measures self-esteem of students age 5 and older in five areas: general, peers, school, parents, and lie (defensiveness) scales. The 40-item adult form includes four areas: general, social, personal, and lie scales. Yes-or-no responses can be either written or spoken. The test is designed to screen for possible interventions and yields percentiles for total and subtest scores. Printed test forms and cassette tapes are available in English, French, and Spanish.

The *Multidimensional Self Concept Scale* (Bracken, 1992) is designed for students in fifth through twelfth grade and includes six 25-item scales in the following areas: social, competence, affect, academic, family, and physical. Each area can be assessed indepen-

dently. The test yields standard scores and can be administered in about 20 minutes. The manual provides specific recommendations for improving self-concept.

The *Piers-Harris Children's Self-Concept Scale* (Piers & Harris, 1984) is a self-report instrument for students in fourth through twelfth grade. The student responds with "yes" or "no" to 80 declarative statements (such as "I am good looking"; "My classmates make fun of me"). The items are written on a third-grade reading level, and both positive and negative statements are included. The scale covers many areas of self-concept, among which are physical appearance, popularity, and happiness-satisfaction. The suggested administration time is 15 to 20 minutes.

The *Self-Esteem Index* (Brown & Alexander, 1991) is a norm-referenced measure of how individuals age 7 through 18 perceive and value themselves. The index includes four scales: academic competence, family acceptance, peer popularity, and personal security (physical appearance and personal attributes). The student classifies each item on a scale ranging from *always true* to *always false*. Standard scores and percentile ranks are provided.

The *Tennessee Self-Concept Scale* (Fitts & Roid, 1988) is a self-report scale designed to measure self-concept of students 12 years of age and older. The scale includes five general categories: physical self, moral-ethical self, personal self, family self, and social self. There are 90 statements (such as "I have a healthy body"; "I have a lot of self control"), and each item is answered on a five-point scale from *completely false* to *completely true*. The scale requires about 20 minutes to complete.

Self-report instruments have several weaknesses because of the potential for bias, the desire to give responses that please, social desirability, and reading-level difficulties (Gresham & Elliott, 1989). Because of these weaknesses, self-report measures of students' social skills are not used as widely as sociometrics, observer-rater instruments, and other measures of social skills. However, the self-report version of the *Social Skills Rating System* (Gresham & Elliott, 1990) represents an attempt to develop a reliable and valid self-report measure of social skills. It includes one version for third through sixth grade and another one for seventh through twelfth grade. The scales yield scores in the areas of cooperation, assertion, self-control, and empathy.

Q-sort Technique. The Q-sort technique, developed by Stephenson (1953), is a procedure for investigating self-concept that can be used to identify areas for behavior modification (Kroth, 1973). The technique focuses on determining the degree of discrepancy between an evaluation of the "real" self and the "ideal" self. The procedure offers a way to select specific social and emotional behaviors for intervention.

The student is given a set of cards containing statements that must be sorted onto a pyramid formboard. A sample list of 25 statements suitable for elementary school students is presented in Table 5.1, and Figure 5.1 shows the behavior formboard. The formboard contains nine categories that form a continuum from "most like me" to "most unlike me." The student is given the same number of descriptor cards as there are squares in the pyramid. In sorting the items, the student must arrange the cards so that each square is used and none is left blank or used twice. First the student is asked to complete a *real sort* by sorting the items onto the formboard to best reflect the student's own beliefs about his classroom behavior. After the responses of the real sort are recorded, the student is asked to complete an *ideal sort* in which the same items are arranged on the formboard to indicate how the student would *like* to be in daily classroom

TABLE 5.1
Elementary-level school items on the behavioral Q-sort.

1. Gets work done on time
2. Pokes or hits classmates
3. Gets out of seat without permission
4. Scores high in spelling
5. Plays with objects while working
6. Scores high in reading
7. Disturbs neighbors by making noise
8. Is quiet during class time
9. Tips chair often
10. Follows directions
11. Smiles frequently
12. Often taps foot, fingers, or pencil
13. Pays attention to work
14. Works slowly
15. Throws objects in class
16. Reads well orally
17. Talks to classmates often
18. Scores high in English
19. Talks out without permission
20. Rocks in chair
21. Scores high in arithmetic
22. Asks teacher questions
23. Uses free time to read or study
24. Works until the job is finished
25. Walks around room during study time

Source: Adapted from *Communicating with Parents of Exceptional Children: Improving Parent—Teacher Relationships* (p. 46) by R. L. Kroth, 1975, Denver: Love. Copyright 1975 by Love Publishing Company. Reprinted by permission.

activities. During sorting, the student may rearrange the cards as many times as needed. The teacher compares the student's responses on the real sort with the responses on the ideal sort and notes items that differ greatly—that is, by four points or more. These items can become target behaviors for intervention. For example, if the student rates "Is quiet during class time" as "very much unlike me" (value: 8) on the real sort, but "like me" (value: 3) on the ideal sort, the student and teacher may agree to work together on this area for improvement.

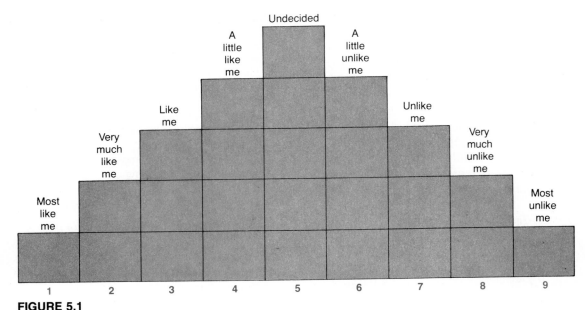

FIGURE 5.1
Behavior formboard.
Source: From *Communicating with Parents of Exceptional Children: Improving Parent-Teacher Relationships* (p. 44) by R. L. Kroth, 1975. Denver: Love. Copyright 1975 by Love Publishing Company. Reprinted by permission.

The behavioral Q-sort can be administered to parents or teachers. Thus, comparisons can be made between others' perceptions of the student's school behavior (both real and ideal) and the student's own perceptions. The teacher's rating of the student's behavior can be compared with the student's own rating. When the comparisons on a specific behavior (such as "Pays attention to work") are very different, that behavior can be selected for examination and intervention.

Informal Self-Report Techniques. Informal self-report techniques provide a general idea of the student's problems. Each student who participates should be assured that the information provided is confidential and that only honest answers are helpful to the teacher. Four frequently used informal self-report techniques are checklists, questionnaires, interviews, and autobiographies.

In a teacher-made checklist, the student is asked to indicate which behaviors or descriptions he believes apply to himself (such as "Has a lot of friends"; "Finishes classwork"; "Gets mad quickly"). Checklists are easy to administer and can give the teacher some insights concerning how the student views himself. For example, the student is presented with a list of adjectives and is instructed to check all words he considers to be descriptive of himself. Sample items include the following:

____	absent-minded	____	happy
____	athletic	____	popular
____	likeable	____	cooperative
____	friendly	____	intelligent
____	lonely	____	quiet
____	nice looking	____	neat
____	careless	____	noisy

Several kinds of questionnaires are designed to obtain information about a student's personal, social, and emotional behaviors. The yes/no or true/false format is useful and is easy to administer:

1. Do you get mad often?   Yes   No
2. Are you usually   Yes   No
   very friendly?
3. I usually like to   True   False
   be by myself.
4. Nothing makes me   True   False
   too mad.

Questionnaires using open-ended questions or sentence completion require the student to complete the statements. Thus, the student expresses himself in his own words. Such a format requires more time and ability on the part of the student, but it often yields more meaningful information than the yes/no or true/false format. Sample items from a sentence completion questionnaire include the following:

1. I work best when _____
   _____ .

2. I get angry when _____
   _____ .

3. When I feel lonely I _____
   _____ .

4. I wish I could _____
   _____ .

5. I don't know how to _____
   _____ .

Specific information also can be obtained from the student through interviews. They provide an opportunity for the student to express opinions and feelings about himself and others. Interview techniques even can be extended into daily conversations with the student, thus providing a flexible and ongoing source of information. In an interview, the teacher should relate the discussion questions to the student's particular area of difficulty. The interview is most effective when conducted in private and rapport is established that reflects an honest interest in the student. Interview questions

should be kept to a minimum and should be broad instead of specific; in this way, the student is required to develop a topic or express an opinion. If the teacher receives proper consent, the interview can be recorded so that it is available for later study. If recording is not possible, note taking during the interview should be minimal but immediate.

In an autobiography, the student gives a written account of his life or reveals his feelings about himself and others. Personal experiences, ambitions, or interests can be described. Students who have difficulty in expressive writing can record oral presentations. The type of autobiography depends upon the age and maturity of the student. The student can be asked to respond to specific questions or be given a topic, such as "Things That Upset Me." Autobiographical material then can be analyzed for present or potential problem areas.

Sociometric Techniques

Sociometric techniques are among the most commonly used methods for assessing social skills and related problems (Maag, 1989). Sociometric methodology typically is grouped into three categories: peer nominations, peer ratings, and peer assessment. A sociogram provides a visual record of the group's social structure.

Peer Nominations.   This procedure involves asking students to nominate peers according to *nonbehavioral* criteria (such as preferred work partners, best friends, preferred play partners). These criteria are viewed as nonbehavioral because they refer to activities (for example, play) or attributes (for example, best friend) rather than to specific behaviors (for example, asks for the opinion of others). Thus, nominations assess attitudes and preferences for engaging in selected activities with peers. Peer nominations can be fixed-choice (that is, student nominates a limited number of peers) or unlimited choice (that is, student nominates as many peers as desired). It helps if a printed list of the names of all class members is provided, and responses should be kept secret. Nominations can be weighted (that is, the order of nominations is considered with weights assigned in a rank-order manner) or unweighted (McConnell & Odom, 1986). Peer nominations also can be keyed to negative criteria (for example, least preferred play partner). Research suggests that positive and negative nominations are not at opposite ends of the same continuum but measure two distinct dimensions of sociometric status (Gresham & Reschly, 1988; McConnell & Odom, 1986).

Coie, Dodge, and their associates (Coie, Dodge, & Coppotelli, 1982; Dodge, 1983) have generated empirical support for the peer nomination approach. Coie et al. provide a classification system for peer nominations that identifies five sociometric status groups: popular, neglected, rejected, controversial, and average. These groups are then evaluated in terms of *liked most* and *liked least.* These techniques provide a detailed description of the social status of a student. Moreover, behavioral correlates are being identified for each sociometric group. For example, rejected students exhibit high rates of aggressive and disruptive behavior and low rates of cooperative, peer reinforcing behaviors, whereas neglected students display high rates of shy, withdrawn, and fearful behaviors and low rates of positive social interactions (Dodge, 1983).

Peer Ratings. In a peer rating, *all* students in a classroom rate each other on a Likert-type scale according to *nonbehavioral* criteria. These criteria are similar to peer nominations in that areas such as *play with* and *work with* preferences are used. A student's score on a peer rating is the average rating received from peers. Gresham and Elliott (1989) note that these ratings tend to indicate a student's over-

all acceptance level within the peer group. Peer ratings feature several advantages over peer nominations. First, every student in the class is rated rather than a few students. Second, a student's rating scores are more reliable because they are based on a large number of raters. Third, peer ratings typically do not involve the use of negative criteria, thereby reducing ethical objections to sociometric assessments. Disadvantages of peer ratings include stereotypical ratings (that is, giving many peers the same rating) and central tendency errors (that is, rating peers in the middle of the scale) (McConnell & Odom, 1986).

Peer Assessment. In peer assessment, students are asked to nominate or rate peers on a variety of *behavioral* characteristics. Students hear or read behavioral descriptions and then nominate or rate individuals according to the descriptions. One of the more popular peer assessment techniques is the *Guess Who?* technique (Kaufman, Agard, & Semmel, 1985). Students nominate peers who fit behavioral descriptions involving such dimensions as disruptive behavior, smartness, dullness, and quiet/good behavior.

Sociogram. Responses from a sociometric questionnaire indicating the number of times each student is chosen can be recorded on a tally sheet, or a *sociogram* can be constructed to provide a visual record of the social structure within the class. Figure 5.2 shows a sociogram of 10 fourth-grade students who were asked to write the names of two classmates with whom they would most like to play. In this example, for the most part, girls preferred to play with girls, and boys with boys. Among the girls, Alice, Debby, and Judy seem to have a close relationship. None of these girls chose other classmates. Joan did not receive any choices, and Kim was selected as first choice only by Joan. Kim was the only girl to choose a boy. Among the boys, Bob and Steve were

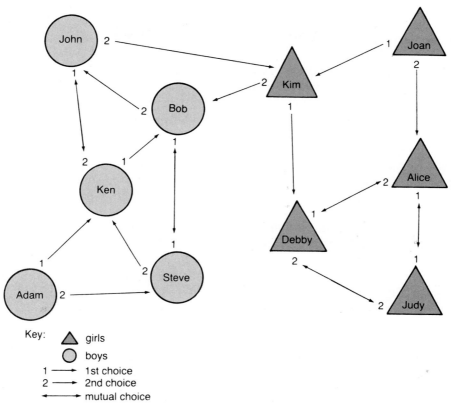

FIGURE 5.2
A sociogram.

mutual choices, as were Ken and John. Adam received no choices, and John was the only boy to choose a girl.

The information obtained from the sociogram can help to identify isolates as well as leaders and can give the teacher a basis for congenial, effective group activities. In addition, the social preferences discovered provide insight about which social patterns should be changed and which should be encouraged. In this example, activities involving Adam and either Ken or Steve may be a positive for Adam, who in general is an isolate. Among the girls, situations should be planned to foster relationships outside of the clique. Different patterns probably will be revealed for different activities or settings. A student may be selected by several classmates as their choice for a study partner but may receive no choices for social activities.

Naturalistic Observations

Defining target behaviors, observing and recording their frequency in the natural environment, and analyzing the data represent the most direct and ecologically valid assessment of students' social skills and related behaviors

(Elliott, Gresham, & Heffer, 1987). Naturalistic assessment allows for a functional analysis of the antecedent events, behavioral sequence, and consequences that may be operating to influence inappropriate social behavior or decrease prosocial behaviors (Maag, 1989). This approach promotes the use of operationally defined social skills or behaviors and the development of systems for measuring and recording target behaviors. The collection of frequent data provides a sensitive index to variations in student behavior. Direct observation of social and emotional behavior includes observing the behavior, the teacher-student interaction, and the environment. The primary difficulty with naturalistic observation is that the student might not act naturally in the context in which observation occurs. If the observer suspects the student is not behaving naturally, role-play assessment can be useful.

Observation of Behavior. Direct, systematic observation of student behavior can provide information and insights about the student's social and emotional skills. Many teachers have training in personality development and work with students for several hours each day in different situations; therefore, they usually are highly qualified to observe and assess behavior. If behaviors are *described* and reported as responses seen or provided (such as *gets out of seat, butts in the cafeteria line, calls Bill a sissy during math seatwork*) instead of as interpretations (such as *hyperactive, disruptive, impulsive*), the validity of teacher observations increases (Stephens, Hartman, & Lucas, 1983). Thus, the teacher should observe the conditions under which the behavior occurs and record the frequency of occurrence. Careful observation may reveal, for example, that out-of-seat behavior occurs only during math, or that singing in class occurs when the student is sitting near Maria. The target behavior also can be measured by

duration—how long the student exhibits the behavior—or by a time sampling, in which the student is observed during certain periods for specified lengths of time. Techniques for recording observations (discussed in Chapter 2) include event recording, duration recording, interval recording, time sampling, latency recording, anecdotal recording, and permanent product recording.

In addition to the behavior itself, the teacher also should note the events that occur immediately before and immediately after the behavior and serve to reinforce the behavior. Information about the surrounding conditions may enable the teacher to choose management strategies. For example, a student's swearing might receive the reinforcement of attention from peers (laughter). The teacher could concentrate on eliminating peer reinforcement and encouraging peer attention to desirable responses. Finally, daily measurement of behavior can provide feedback on the success of strategies used to resolve the behavior.

Observation of Teacher-Student Interaction. Flanders (1970) presents the *interaction analysis system* for measuring the interactions between the teacher and the students in the entire class. Flanders specifies 10 behavior categories: 7 involve teacher's verbal behavior (for example, praising, asking questions, criticizing); 2 involve student's verbal behavior; and 1 is for silence or confusion. Teacher-student interactions are observed, and behaviors are recorded every four seconds. Data are collected for several days during short observation periods. Smith, Neisworth, and Greer (1978) suggest a simplified version of the Flanders technique in which a tape recorder is used instead of a trained observer. The teacher can interpret the recordings made during the day and can categorize the verbal interactions according to Flanders' 10 categories. By using this assessment device, the teacher can identify verbal patterns of student-teacher interactions in the classroom.

Sprick (1985) developed a system for monitoring teacher-student interactions that focuses on the frequency of teacher responses to negative events and positive events. He suggests that a 3-to-1 positive to negative ratio is needed for effective interaction and classroom management. Other variables noted include bias toward different students (for example, low achievers, males) and how often inappropriate behavior is reinforced.

In teacher-student interactions, a teacher occasionally may overact to a certain behavior. Teachers must show understanding and awareness to control inappropriate reactions.

Observation of Environment. In assessing social and emotional behavior, the teacher should observe the student in different environments. The teacher then can consider the environment's influence in starting or maintaining the problem behavior. Some observation can be made outside the school setting; however, the teacher mainly should observe in-school environments (such as art class, physical education class, lunchroom, playground). Perhaps the target behavior surfaces only in certain settings or instructional conditions. The student may become disruptive when required to remain seated for long periods of time during a lecture; however, when allowed to move about or participate in class discussions, the student's behavior may be acceptable. Also, a student may exhibit anxiety and withdraw when required to read orally in front of the class or to compute timed math problems, but be quite comfortable when working alone in untimed situations or in small-group activities. Thus, teacher observation of various environments can help determine the adjustments needed to improve the student's instructional program. Additional information on observation techniques is provided by Cartwright and Cartwright (1984).

Role-Play Assessment. With this approach, a student's behavior is elicited in response to staged social interactions (such as receiving criticism), and the student's performance is recorded. Advances in role-play methodology (Dodge, Pettit, McClaskey, & Brown, 1986) have improved their generalizability to naturalistic observations. Moreover, role-play assessments enable the observer to determine if the student has a social skill acquisition deficit (that is, does not have the skill in his repertoire) or a social skill performance problem (that is, does not desire to perform the skill).

TECHNIQUES FOR BUILDING SELF-CONCEPT

In this section, selected techniques for building self-concept are discussed: general teaching procedures, bibliotherapy, and attribution retraining.

General Teaching Procedures

Many students with learning problems have poor self-concepts, especially in the area of academic or cognitive abilities. Sprick (1981) notes that acting out, misbehaving to get caught, and giving up or withdrawing are common manifestations of a poor self-concept. The development of a positive self-concept is fundamental to a student's school success, motivation, and future learning. Some teaching guidelines for improving self-concept are presented next.

Teach Effectively. Effective teaching leads to academic progress, and this success is critical if a student with learning problems is to develop a positive self-concept. Sprick (1981) states, "There is nothing more important for any student than believing he or she is able to learn, grow, and be successful. When in doubt about what to do to improve a child's self-concept, teach!" (Book E, p. 9). Chapter 1 presents instructional factors that relate to effective teaching. Although all the factors likely would lead to improvements in the self-concepts of students with learning problems, the factors that are especially noteworthy for self-concept development are: (a) provide success, (b) establish goals and expectations, (c) monitor progress and provide feedback, (d) provide positive and supportive learning environments, and (e) teach students to be independent learners.

Provide Encouragement and Support. Because many students with learning problems have experienced much failure, the teacher must recognize their need for encouragement and support. One of the best ways to create a supportive environment is to show an honest interest in the student. The teacher can build support and establish rapport by spending time discussing the student's interests, hobbies, plans, or family. The effective teacher practices feedback techniques and knows how to correct wrong responses without hurting the student's feelings (for example, "You're almost right. Let's do it together"). The teacher should make positive statements and praise appropriate actions rather than attending only to misbehavior.

Set Reasonable Goals and Provide Feedback. When a student reaches goals that require considerable effort, self-worth is improved. Individuals feel good about themselves when they work hard to achieve a worthwhile goal. As noted in Chapter 1, goal ambitiousness is positively related to school success. In contrast, goals that are too easy often lead the student to feel that the teacher thinks he is not capable of higher-level achievements. Consequently, low teacher expectations frequently lower the student's beliefs about his learning potential.

The importance of feedback to learning is well documented; however, the type of feedback that improves a student's self-concept is important to note. First, positive feedback or reinforcement should be contingent on student performance (that is, the student should be praised for accomplishing tasks that require a reasonable amount of effort). Second, noncontingent feedback or praise can signal to the student that the teacher thinks he cannot do better work; thus, the student receives a message that he lacks ability, and this lowers his opinion of his learning capability. Third, a student often views criticism or corrective feedback as positive when high achievers receive it (Weinstein, 1982). This feedback indicates that the teacher believes the student can do better; thus, it communicates a positive opinion about the teacher's view of the student's potential. Consequently, Bryan (1986) reports that the use of corrective feedback is a viable strategy to help improve the self-concepts of students with learning problems. Furthermore, corrective feedback can communicate that the teacher cares about the student.

Give the Student Responsibility. The student with a poor self-concept often is pleased when the teacher thinks the student can accept responsibility. Giving the student responsibility demonstrates a level of trust in the student's ability to act maturely. Some responsibilities include (a) caring for a class pet, (b) taking messages to the office or other classes, (c) conducting a lunch count, (d) tutoring other students, (e) leading the line, (f) making a bulletin board, (g) using equipment, and (h) grading papers.

Teach the Student to Engage in Self-Appreciation. Self-depreciation tends to lower a student's self-worth. Conversely, self-appreciation can help improve self-worth. The teacher should reinforce the student for making appropriate positive comments about himself. The student can make lists of his positive attributes and periodically refer to them.

Promote Positive Interactions between Students. Sprick (1981) notes that teaching students to be positive with each other benefits individual students. If the students can learn to interact positively, they will receive pleasant and friendly reactions in return. The teacher can pair students with learning problems with popular students for social group activities or on teams in instructional games so that the paired students share positive and pleasant experiences. Sprick recommends three techniques for promoting positive interactions: (a) modeling positive interactions in daily teaching, (b) practicing positive interactions through role playing specific situations, and (c) reinforcing positive interactions as they occur throughout the school day.

Bibliotherapy

Bibliotherapy is a teaching technique that uses reading materials to help the student better understand himself and his problems. Characters in the books learn to cope with problems and situations similar to those faced by the student. Through identifying with the characters, the student releases emotional tensions and achieves a better understanding of himself and his problem. Also, characteristics, attitudes, values, and situations in reading selections can serve as models for the student.

Hoagland (1972) notes that for bibliotherapy to be effective, the student must move through three phases during or immediately after reading a book: (a) *identification*—the student must become personally involved and must identify himself or see a situation similar to some of his own situations; (b) *catharsis*—the student must release emotional tensions regarding the problems; and (c) *insight*—through empathizing with the character or plot, the student must reach a better understanding that tempers his emotional drives.

Cianciolo (1965) suggests the following steps for discussing a book with a student:

1. Retell the story and emphasize incidents, feelings, relationships, and behavior.
2. Discuss changes of feelings, relationships, and behaviors.
3. Identify similar events from the student's life or other reading selections.
4. Explore the consequences that occurred.
5. Generalize about the consequences or helpfulness of alternative behaviors.

The student should begin to realize that many other people have experienced the same problem and that there is more than one way to solve a problem.

Books chosen for a bibliotherapeutic program should focus on a particular need and should be written on the student's level. The selections also should depict realistic approaches and have lifelike characters (Cianciolo, 1965). Suitable books can be selected from various bibliographies that are cross-indexed by theme and age level. Russell and Russell (1979) provide various activities to be used in conjunction with bibliotherapy. Although research on bibliotherapy is minimal, Lenkowsky and Lenkowsky (1978) note that the approach seems to help some students with learning problems by providing them with reading materials relevant to their own social and emotional needs.

Attribution Retraining

Attributions refer to a person's beliefs concerning the causes of events. Students differ in their ideas concerning the causes of their successes and failures. Those who believe in an internal locus of control explain the outcomes of their actions on the basis of their abilities or efforts. In contrast, persons with an external locus of control believe that factors outside their control, such as luck or task difficulty, determine their fates.

Students with learning disabilities are more likely than normally achieving students to believe that their successes are a function of external factors (Chapman & Boersma, 1979; Pearl, Bryan, & Donahue, 1980). Bryan (1986) notes that it would seem advantageous to induce students with learning disabilities to have more positive and self-serving expectations of their academic successes. As students with learning problems experience many academic failures, they are likely to lack confidence in their intellectual abilities and doubt that anything they do will help them overcome their difficulties. Thus, these students may lessen their achievement efforts, especially when presented with difficult material. In other words, repeated failure can lead students to believe that they are not capable of overcoming their difficulties, and students' beliefs about their abilities can affect their achievement efforts and accomplishments.

Attribution retraining studies (Schunk, 1981; Shelton, Anastopoulos, & Linden, 1985) have found that teaching students to attribute their failures to insufficient effort can result in increased persistence and improved performance when confronted with difficulty. In these studies, students are engaged in academic tasks and are given feedback that emphasizes the importance of their effort. In a review of attribution retraining research, Bryan (1986) reports that attribution retraining sessions have been shown to be somewhat successful in changing attributions and persistence behavior. Fowler and Peterson (1981) found that prompting and reinforcing students for verbalizing appropriate effort attributions can be more effective than simply telling students when they fail that they need to try harder. In addition to stressing effort as a determinant of a student's difficulties, it also can be helpful to teach students to attribute their

failures to ineffective task strategies (Licht, 1984). Bryan notes that teachers should convey to students with learning problems that they are learning new skills and that determined application of the new skills can help them overcome their difficulties.

Ellis, Lenz, and Sabornie (1987) suggest the following instructional sequence in attribution retraining:

1. Teach students to make statements that reflect effort.
2. Teach students to attribute difficulty to ineffective strategies.
3. Arrange for students to have success with newly learned strategies.

TECHNIQUES FOR MANAGING BEHAVIOR AND DEVELOPING SOCIAL SKILLS

Many students with learning problems have low self-concepts, attention deficits, social skills deficits, or emotional problems. Because these types of affective problems can lead to aggressive, disruptive, or withdrawn behavior, students with learning problems may become difficult to manage in the classroom. Educators agree that effective behavior management must begin with preventive techniques and these techniques start with good teaching. It is highly likely that most behavior problems of students with learning problems can be prevented with effective instruction.

Rieth and Evertson (1988) provide an excellent framework for planning instruction for difficult-to-teach students. Their review of the research and subsequent guidelines for effective teaching are presented in Table 5.2 and are organized according to preinstructional variables, instructional delivery variables, and postinstructional variables. Many of these variables are discussed in Chapter 1.

TABLE 5.2
Variables related to effective instruction of difficult-to-teach students.

Instructional variables	Specific emphasis
Preinstructional Variables	
Arrangement of classroom space	Arrange classroom to facilitate smooth transitions and ease of student monitoring.
Rules and procedures	Communicate expectations and provide structure for learning.
Managing student academic work	Hold students accountable for work and keep records of progress.
Assessment	Use criterion-referenced measures to match tasks to students and monitor performance in terms of instructional objectives.
Communication of learning goals	Communicate rationales for academic tasks and clearly state learning goals.
Pacing decisions	Maintain a lively instructional pace but allow enough time for much practice. Presentation-demonstration-practice-feedback cycles appear to be most effective.
Time allocations	Plan as much time as possible for academic learning.
Instructional Delivery Variables	
Engagement time	Maintain substantive interactions with students and provide feedback. Reinforce students for being on task and for work completed.
Success rate	Maintain high rates of success because success is related to student achievement and motivation.
Academic learning time	Facilitate the amount of time students are engaged in high rates of success or appropriate goals.
Monitoring	Circulate throughout the room to check the accuracy and progress of students.
Postinstructional Variables	
Testing	Regularly administer informal criterion-referenced measures (e.g., curriculum-based assessment) to assess student progress or plan instruction.
Academic feedback	Provide immediate feedback on academic work to promote learning. Praise and corrective feedback are most effective when used together.

Source: Reprinted with the permission of Macmillan Publishing Company. Originally published by Merrill from *Students with Learning Disabilities* (p. 625), 4th ed., by Cecil D. Mercer. Copyright © 1992 by Macmillan Publishing Company.

Once effective teaching practices are established, teachers can use a variety of techniques and strategies to improve social skills and lessen emotional problems. The following methods for managing behavior problems and developing social skills are discussed: behavior modification, cognitive behavior modification, modeling, peer tutoring, self-management instruction, interview techniques, techniques for managing surface behaviors and assertive discipline, social skills training, and projective techniques.

Behavior Modification

Behavior modification derives from the concept of *operant conditioning* (Skinner, 1953). The basic premise is that behavior is learned and is a function of behavior's consequences. According to Wallace and Kauffman (1986), "Behavior modification refers to any systematic arrangement of environmental events to produce specific changes in observable behavior" (p. 21). Thus, it is a highly structured and systematic approach that results in strengthening, weakening, or maintaining behaviors.

After identifying and collecting baseline data on a target behavior, the teacher must observe events that happen just before the student's behavior (antecedent events) and just after the behavior (subsequent events). (A form for recording antecedent and subsequent events is presented in Chapter 2.) These events are then manipulated, and various reinforcers or rewards are used to elicit a change in the behavior. A *reinforcer* is any event that follows a behavior and results in maintaining or increasing the probability or rate of the behavior. *Positive reinforcement* means adding something pleasurable or positive to the environment (that is, consequences that increase the probability that the behavior will occur again), whereas *negative reinforcement* means withdrawing something unpleasant or negative from the environment (that is, avoidance of a negative consequence by performing a behavior). Reinforcement results in strengthening or increasing the target behavior.

Various social or tangible reinforcers can be used (for example, praise, hugs, treats, free time). The following hierarchical order of the level of reinforcers moves from extrinsic reinforcers (reinforcement from outside the performance of a task) to intrinsic reinforcers (reinforcement directly from performing a task):

Extrinsic reinforcers

1. Primary reinforcers (for example, sleeping, eating, drinking—necessary for survival)
2. Tangible reinforcers (for example, food items, pencils, certificates)
3. Token reinforcers with backup items or activities (for example, chips that can be exchanged for a preferred item or activity when a certain amount is earned)
4. Social approval (for example, gestures, touch, verbal expressions)
5. Project or activity (for example, running errands, being a line leader, getting free time, playing a game)

Intrinsic reinforcers

6. Task completion
7. Feedback or result
8. Acquisition of knowledge or skill
9. Sense of mastery or accomplishment

Extrinsic reinforcers initially can be used to encourage a student to exhibit appropriate behavior or perform a task. The teacher gradually should withdraw material reinforcers and stress activities and events. Eventually, as competence in a task increases, the need for extrinsic reinforcement will decrease, and intrinsic reinforcers will provide motivation.

Praise is one of the most effective and convenient positive reinforcers for teachers to use in managing student behavior. Paine, Radicchi, Rosellini, Deutchman, and Darch (1983) report that effective praise has several important features:

1. Good praise adheres to the "if–then" rule. The "if–then" rule states that *if* the student is behaving in the desired manner, *then* (and *only* then) the teacher praises the student.
2. Good praise frequently includes students' names.
3. Good praise is descriptive.
4. Good praise conveys that the teacher really means what he is saying (that is, it is convincing).
5. Good praise is varied.
6. Good praise does not disrupt the flow of individual or class activities.

In using reinforcement techniques, the teacher must remember that reinforcement immediately following the behavior is most effective. In addition, attention can act as a reinforcer for inappropriate behavior. For example, when the teacher frowns or speaks sharply, the student may interpret this as reinforcing attention. Thus, the teacher should be careful not to reinforce inappropriate behavior with attention. The teacher should shift from reinforcing everyday appropriate behavior to reinforcing academic effort as soon as possible. Behaviors such as raising a hand to talk or appropriate lining up for lunch eventually should become routine and be maintained without a great deal of teacher praise. Contingent reinforcement of academic learning promotes a higher level of functioning and improves achievement. Research indicates that both academic performance and appropriate behavior improve when academic skills are reinforced; however, when appropriate behavior is reinforced, academic performance usually does not improve as a result (Ayllon, Layman, & Burke, 1972; Ayllon & Roberts, 1974; Broughton & Lahey, 1978). It may be necessary initially to reinforce behavior to bring it under control, and then the teacher should focus on reinforcing academic performance and place contingencies on appropriate behavior as needed.

The *schedule of reinforcement* (that is, the plan of conditions under which reinforcement occurs) can be either continuous or intermittent. On a *continuous schedule,* the desired behavior is reinforced every time it occurs. On an *intermittent schedule,* reinforcement is given according to either an *interval* (reinforcers given at certain times) or a *ratio* (reinforcers given after a specific number of responses).

Shaping refers to reinforcing steps toward the target behavior. The goal is broken down into an ordered sequence of steps or tasks, and reinforcement is given to those behaviors that come close to the desired behavior. The desired behavior thus is shaped by gradually increasing the requirement for reinforcement until the target behavior is obtained.

Punishment, as opposed to reinforcement, refers to presenting something negative or withdrawing something positive following the behavior. This results in decreasing the undesirable response. Before punishment is used, the teacher should explore alternatives to punishment such as (a) discussing the problem with the student, (b) ignoring the misbehavior if feasible, and (c) reinforcing students who are acting appropriately. Once punishment is selected, Sprick (1981) recommends the following guidelines:

1. Punishment must change the behavior in the desired direction.
2. Punishers always should be used in conjunction with a reinforcement plan.

3. Punishment always should be administered calmly.
4. Punishment should be used discriminately.
5. Once a punishable behavior is targeted, it should be punished consistently.

One procedure frequently used to decrease undesirable behavior is *time out.* Time out is a short period of time during which no reinforcement is available. Thus, the student is removed from a positively reinforcing situation. Time out can be used while the student is seated in the classroom simply by removing the opportunity for reinforcement (for example, avoiding any contact with the student for 30 to 60 seconds), or by not allowing the student to participate in a reinforcing activity for a certain amount of time. Also, time out can be used by isolating the student in a specific time-out area for a brief period (3 to 5 minutes). Time out is based on the premise that behaviors followed by no reinforcement tend to decrease in frequency.

Response cost is another punishment technique that involves the loss of a reinforcer contingent on inappropriate behavior. The consequent loss can be an activity, points, a privilege, or a token. Kazdin (1972) reports that response cost has been used successfully without the undesirable side effects (such as escape, avoidance, aggression) sometimes observed with other forms of punishment. Although punishment and negative reinforcement are sometimes necessary to manage behavior, the teacher should strive to maintain a positive reinforcement system. Also, when it is necessary to use aversive techniques, they are most effective when combined with positive techniques (Walker, 1979).

Paine et al. (1983) provide a step-by-step management system that combines positive reinforcement, a warning technique, and response cost. It includes the following steps:

1. When a student is misbehaving, give praise to nearby students who are exhibiting correct behavior. Once praise is given to several students, wait a brief time (30 seconds) to see if the misbehaving student responds. If the student responds by giving the correct behavior, praise that student.
2. If the student fails to respond positively, talk to the student in an unemotional manner. Tell the student that he is receiving a warning and instruct him to begin work. The warning is more effective if it is delivered near the student and eye contact is established. The teacher should avoid getting into a conversation while giving the warning. After a short time, praise the student if the student begins correct behavior.
3. If the student does not respond to the warning, calmly remind the student about the warning, then write his name on the board, and put a mark next to it.
4. If the student fails to comply, place another mark by his name. This should be done without comment. Moreover, continue to praise other students for appropriate behavior.
5. At this point, if the student fails to comply, repeat step 4.
6. For behaviors that are unacceptable, use predetermined consequences. Unacceptable behaviors and resulting consequences should be explained at the beginning of the school year.
7. Have each mark after a student's name represent a loss of privileges. One mark could stand for 5 minutes taken from recess, two marks mean 10 minutes are lost, and so on. The consequence can be similar for everyone or varied for different students. The marking system is only effective if students lose privileges that they value.
8. Finally, be sure not to give the student extra attention when he is missing time from recess or staying after school. Consequences

of the marking system should not be reinforcing in any way.

Knowledge and application of reinforcement principles are helpful in managing a classroom. Many teachers apply these principles in a "natural" way, without taking the time to write a behavior modification plan specifying the target behavior, consequent events, schedule of reinforcement, and so forth. However, the behavior of some students does not change unless a highly systematic behavior modification plan is developed and applied.

Figure 5.3 presents a record of a behavior modification plan to increase staying-in-seat behavior. The teacher used a time-sampling technique to record whether the student stayed seated during seatwork activities. Observation sessions were 30 minutes long, and the teacher used a recording sheet marked off with a row of 10 squares. The teacher looked at the student every 3 minutes and recorded a "+" if the student was seated and a "−" if the student was not. As Figure 5.3 shows, the student's percentage of staying-in-seat behavior was low during baseline₁. However, when the teacher began giving the student praise and attention for appropriate in-seat behavior (in sessions 11 through 20), the level of the desired behavior increased greatly. When praise and attention were withdrawn in baseline₂ (sessions 21 through 25), the student's staying-in-seat behavior sharply diminished. However, when praise and attention were provided again (in sessions 26 through 35), the level of the appropriate behavior quickly increased. Thus, the teacher was able to note the effects of teacher attention on modifying the student's out-of-seat behavior.

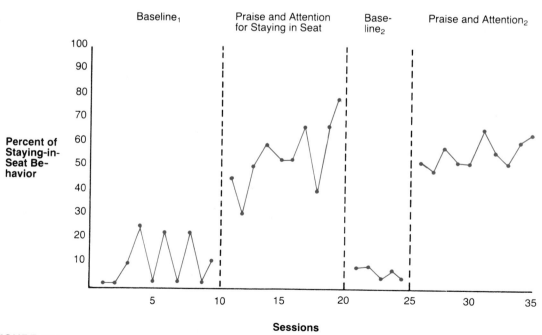

FIGURE 5.3

Record of a behavior modification plan to increase staying-in-seat behavior.

Contingency Contracting. Contracts between a student and the classroom teacher can help to motivate the student toward desirable behavior changes. A *contract* is an agreement—verbal or written—between two parties. The term *contingent* means that there is a relationship between what one does and the consequences. In behavior modification, contingency contracting is based on the Premack Principle (Premack, 1959). This principle states that the frequency of a less-preferred activity increases when it is followed by the opportunity to engage in one that is preferred. For example, if the student would rather play outside than sit quietly in the classroom, the contingency contract might state that sitting quietly for a certain amount of time will be followed by outside play.

The following steps are involved in writing a contingency contract (Stephens, 1977):

1. The teacher outlines the specific behavior required of the student.

2. The teacher identifies the reinforcement for which the student will work. This reinforcement should be available to the student *only* for performing the specified behavior. The required behavior or the consequent reinforcement can be determined through student-teacher discussions.

3. The teacher specifies the terms of the contract, which should include the amount or type of behavior required and the amount or type of reward.

4. The teacher watches for the specified behavior to occur and then rewards the student according to the terms of the contract.

A sample contingency contract is presented in Figure 5.4.

A contingency contract should represent agreement between the student and the teacher. The terms should be stated clearly in a positive manner and should be fair for both the student and the teacher. After both parties have signed the contract, the conditions

FIGURE 5.4
A sample contingency contract.

```
                        CONTRACT

Beginning date: __10/21_____

Ending date: ____10/25_____

STUDENT: I agree to finish my math seatwork
          during math period on Monday,
          Tuesday, Wednesday, and Thursday.
                Signed __Timmy_____

TEACHER: I agree to give Timmy free time during
          math period on Friday.


                Signed Mrs. Jackson
```

should be monitored frequently to assess progress. In addition, all parts of the contract should be followed systematically, and the student should receive reinforcement as soon as the contract is completed.

Various types of contracts can be used. The agreement may or may not specify a time limit within which the required behavior must be performed. Intermittent reinforcers can be used in long-term contracts, and steps toward the desired behavior can be rewarded. Contracts also can include agreements between the student and other school personnel or parents. Group contracts can be used in which the entire class agrees to behave in a certain manner or perform a specified task by a designated date, and the teacher agrees to reward the students who fulfill the agreement. Contingency contracting thus can promote desirable actions (social or academic) by involving the student in managing his own behavior.

Token Systems.   Token reinforcement systems are used widely in behavior modification. O'Leary and Drabman (1971) note that these systems have three basic characteristics: (a) behaviors to be reinforced are stated clearly, (b) procedures are devised for giving out a reinforcing stimulus (token) when the target behavior occurs, and (c) a set of rules is explained to govern the exchange of tokens for reinforcing objects or events.

A *token* is an item given to a student immediately after a target behavior occurs. Usually the tokens have little intrinsic value, but they acquire value when they can be exchanged for a desired object or activity. Tokens can consist of play money, trading stamps, poker chips, stars, or any other object that is easy to dispense and store. These tokens can be accumulated and then exchanged for a desired object or activity. A classroom store can be established where, at designated times, each student may "purchase" reinforcers by trading

in earned tokens. Objects (balloons, comics, jewelry, sports trading cards, pennies, coloring books, magazines) and activities (playing a game, listening to records, coloring, watching a filmstrip) can be available in the store. A reward menu can be posted, listing the store items and their costs (for example, listening to records for 10 minutes—10 tokens; purchasing a baseball trading card—15 tokens).

Vernon (1972) discusses several advantages of token systems. First, they avoid boredom because tokens can be traded for a variety of reinforcing objects or events. Second, a token system is useful with students who generally do not respond to social reinforcement. Third, tokens are administered easily, and the number can be adjusted to reflect the time and energy required to perform the target behavior. Fourth, token systems help students appreciate the relationship between desirable behavior and reinforcement. Students learn that behavior has consequences, and this is likely to enhance self-control.

Blackham and Silberman (1980) stress that a token system must be developed and applied thoughtfully. They also report that problems should be expected at first, and the teacher will have to refine the system. Blackham and Silberman suggest guidelines for planning and using a token system.

1. The target behaviors that earn tokens should be specified clearly. For example, individual behaviors can be posted on a student's desk. Rules governing group behavior contingencies should be reviewed frequently.
2. The reinforcers that the tokens are exchanged for must be appealing and available *only* within the token system.
3. The number of tokens earned must match the effort required for performing the target behavior. If a student has great difficulty staying on task during math seatwork, the

reward for staying on task must be sufficient to encourage on-task behavior.

4. If possible, the teacher should keep a record of the number of tokens each student and the group earn. This type of record often provides an additional incentive to students.

5. If *response cost* (token fines) is used, the conditions under which tokens are earned and lost must be specified clearly. Awarding and taking away tokens must always be related to student *behavior.* Arguments about token loss should be avoided.

6. A scheduled token exchange for the end of the day usually works best.

7. The system should be devised so that there is self-competition rather than competition with others.

8. A well-planned token system gradually should withdraw material reinforcers and stress reinforcing activities and events. Also, praise should be combined with the tokens so that social reinforcement eventually can be used alone to maintain desirable behaviors.

9. The token system should be simple, functional, and not distracting to the learning process. In school, check-mark tokens are often the easiest to use. Each student is given a card, and the teacher puts checks on it as they are earned. A special pen can be used to distinguish these checks. Other students cannot use a student's card, whereas tangible tokens might be traded or stolen.

Applying Consequences with Adolescents.

In managing secondary students Kerr and Nelson (1989) report that structure and consistency are essential. The likelihood of power struggles and defiance of authority is greater with adolescents. Thus, both teacher and student must function in a structured environment; that is, expectations (rules), consequences, and routines should be established

clearly. Techniques that have been effective with secondary students include token economies, contingency contracting, verbal feedback, mutual goal setting, and self-control training (Deshler, Schumaker, & Lenz, 1984; Polsgrove, 1979). Moreover, the importance of involving adolescents in curriculum and management decisions is stressed throughout the literature.

Some suggestions for managing consequences with adolescents include the following:

1. Stress the natural consequences of behavior. For example, the natural consequence for stealing is arrest, for being tardy is detention, and so on. Thus, if a rule is broken, the stated consequence is applied. This helps reduce power struggles between the student and teacher because the student is likely to view the teacher as a person who follows rules rather than as an authority figure who maliciously applies punishment (Kerr & Nelson, 1989).

2. Use conditioned reinforcers (such as points) with adolescents. They are administered easily or withheld with a minimum of teacher verbalization (Kerr & Nelson, 1989).

3. Consider using peer interactions as reinforcers for adolescents.

4. Develop a continuum of consequences for managing inappropriate behaviors. Public reprimands should be avoided because they increase the probability of further conflict. Use little verbal interaction and eye contact when administering a negative consequence. Response cost is a good beginning step in dealing with inappropriate behavior. Time out is another effective consequence with adolescents. The management system by Paine et al. (1983) presented previously provides an excellent framework for managing adolescents. It

stresses a positive approach but incorporates a warning system and response cost.

Cognitive Behavior Modification

Cognitive behavior modification analyzes the thinking processes involved in performing a task. Meichenbaum (1977) discusses self-instructional training as a method to encourage appropriate responses and discourage inappropriate responses. The following sequence can be used:

1. Instruction by another person (for example, an adult model such as a teacher performs a task while talking aloud).
2. Overt self-instruction (for example, while performing a task, the student speaks or whispers self-instructions).
3. Covert self-instruction (for example, the student guides performance through private speech).

Thus, inner speech is considered an aspect of the thinking process, and the student is encouraged to verbalize before acting. Language is thought to enhance thinking and, in turn, affect behavior. In the classroom the student might be taught to use the following self-verbalizations: (a) questions about the task ("What does the teacher want me to do?"), (b) answers to the question ("I'm not supposed to talk out in class"), (c) self-instruction to guide the student through the task ("First I raise my hand and wait for the teacher to call on me"), and (d) self-reinforcement ("I really did well that time!").

In cognitive modeling, the teacher should not only model strategies for performing a task but also should model actions and language appropriate for dealing with frustrations and failures. In addition to self-instruction, the student can be taught to use images (for example, thinking of sitting in the classroom during recess as an image to reduce out-of-seat behavior).

Modeling

In modeling, the student learns appropriate behaviors by observing and imitating others. When the student observes one of his peers being rewarded for desirable behavior, he tends to follow the example of the model. Thus he learns those behaviors that have positive consequences. Likewise, unacceptable behavior can be discouraged when the student watches another receive punishment for such behavior. In addition, the teacher can call attention to behavior that should be modeled: "I like the way Jimmy raised his hand instead of talking out, so I will answer his question first."

In using modeling to influence a specific behavior, the following steps are helpful:

1. Select the behavior.
2. Select the model.
3. Give the model and the observer directions concerning their roles.
4. Reinforce the model for exhibiting the behavior.
5. Reinforce the observer for imitating the behavior.

The modeling process can have three effects on the student: (a) new behaviors can be learned from the model, (b) previously acquired behaviors can be strengthened as the student observes similar desirable behaviors of the model being reinforced, or (c) previously acquired behaviors can be weakened as the student observes the model receiving punishment for similar unacceptable behaviors.

Peer Tutoring

Peer tutoring typically involves pairing a competent student with one who has difficulty in a particular academic area. Peer tutoring also can be used to improve social skills. If assessment reveals that a student has no friends or is not accepted by peers, peer tutoring can be a strategy for enhancing social growth. Using information from a sociometric device, such as a sociogram, the teacher can pair a student with a preferred tutor. The student thus will be likely to model the appropriate behavior. The teacher should train the student tutor in teaching the reinforcement techniques. Tutoring sessions should have easy-to-use materials and a set routine. Self-correcting materials and instructional games provide excellent materials for peer teaching arrangements.

Paine et al. (1983) provide guidelines for establishing and maintaining a peer tutoring program:

1. *Determine the roles of tutors.* Decide what role tutors can serve in the classroom. Peer roles can be ascertained from a list of useful activities including instruction in academic and social skills, record keeping, timings, observations, modeling, and feedback.
2. *Select the tutors.* Select tutors who are capable of demonstrating the task to be performed. Also, match tutor and tutee for compatibility.
3. *Train the tutors.* Train the tutors to model the instructional task and provide appropriate feedback.
4. *Supervise and reinforce peer teaching arrangements.* Reinforce tutors for presenting stimuli, providing feedback, and maintaining pleasant interactions. Reinforce tutees for following directions and responding to task materials.

Allen (1976) reports that peer tutoring has a positive effect on the tutor (that is, it helps the tutor with academic or behavior difficulties, or both). As noted in Chapter 3, peer tutoring can be used to improve academic skills, foster self-esteem, help the shy youngster, help students who have difficulty with authority figures, improve race relations, and promote positive relationships and cooperation among peers. Peer tutoring and cooperative learning are presented in Chapter 3.

Self-Management Instruction

A problem common to many youngsters with learning problems is their inability to solve problems and make decisions effectively. Difficulties in these areas can adversely affect their performance at school, home, or work. Issues related to problem solving, interpersonal relations, and generalization learning can be viewed within the context of self-management skills (Shapiro, 1989). Self-management typically is divided into three components: self-monitoring, self-evaluation, and self-reinforcement. Each component requires specific instruction.

Several researchers report success using self-management training with students who have mild disabilities. Brigham, Hopper, Hill, De Armas, and Newsom (1985) report that self-management training helped disruptive students improve their behavior. Likewise, Hughes, Ruhl, and Peterson (1988) used the demonstration-guidance-practice-feedback sequence to teach self-management skills to learners with mild disabilities. Hughes et al. found a differential effect to the training: self-monitoring only or self-monitoring and self-evaluation were sufficient for some students to accomplish criterion-level behavior; however, other students needed self-monitoring, self-evaluation, and self-reinforcement to achieve criterion. Moreover, in a 3-year study, Shapiro (1989) compared the performances of students with learning disabilities who received self-management training with the performances of students with and without learning disabilities who did not receive self-management training. The students who received the training showed significant improvements on measures of problem solving and job-related social skills. Shapiro concludes that self-management instruction appears to be a promising approach for teaching students with learning disabilities to be more independent learners and citizens.

Interview Techniques

Life-Space Interviewing. Life-space interviewing is a verbal strategy for intervention that can be used in the classroom to manage a crisis or an everyday problem. This technique attempts to structure a situation so that the student works out the problem independently. The interview is designed to be free of judgment. The teacher is simply a listener and helper as the student makes decisions about how to handle the problem.

Morse (1971) outlines the steps of life-space interviewing:

1. Each student involved in the specific incident is allowed to give his own impression of the occurrence without interruption.
2. The teacher listens and, without casting judgment, asks questions to determine the accuracy of each student's perception.
3. If the students cannot resolve the problem agreeably, the teacher may have to suggest an acceptable plan to deal with the problem.
4. The students and the teacher work together to develop a plan for solving similar problems in the future.

The classroom teacher may use life-space interviewing best to provide emotional first aid at times of unusual stress. Thus, the technique is used to (a) reduce the student's frustration and anxiety by giving him support during an emotional situation, (b) change behavior and reinforce behavioral and social rules, (c) enhance self-esteem, and (d) assist the student to solve his own everyday problems by expanding his understanding and insight into his own and others' behavior and feelings. For example, after a fight on the playground, the teacher can engage in life-space interviewing to allow the student to release frustration and anger. The teacher provides support and helps the student in viewing all sides of the situation and the rights of others.

Wood and Long (1991) use the term *life-space intervention* to emphasize that a crisis always evokes verbal intervention. They note that the key to success or failure in obtaining a therapeutic outcome of a crisis is the quality of the adult's verbal intervention. The teacher's attitude and behavior as interviewer influence the effectiveness of life-space interviewing. The teacher should be polite to the student and should maintain eye contact. Asking "why" questions should be avoided, and the interviewer should try to reduce any apparent guilt feelings. In addition, the teacher should encourage the student to communicate and ask questions as they work together to develop a plan of action for present or future use. The life-space interview technique is time-consuming and requires sensitivity and emotional control from the teacher. However, it can help a student see the consequences of behavior and find ways to deal with a problem.

Reality Therapy. Reality therapy, developed by Glasser (1965), is used to manage behaviors by teaching the student to behave responsibly and to face reality. An interview technique similar to life-space interviewing attempts to help the student make sound decisions when confronted with a problem. In reality therapy each person is assumed to be responsible for his own behavior, and inappropriate behaviors are not excused on the basis of unconscious motivations. During interviews the student is provided with emotional support, and no judgments are made of the present behavior. The teacher and the student jointly develop a plan to increase the student's responsible behavior, and the student is encouraged to make a commitment to carry out the plan. The student is expected to realize the consequences of irresponsible behavior, and no excuses are accepted. Thus, the morality of behavior is emphasized, and the student is taught socially accepted ways to handle problems.

Glasser (1965) presents a three-step format for applying reality therapy. The first step is to help the student identify the problem. This is accomplished by asking questions such as "What happened?" and "Where are you going?" The second step is to help the student develop a value judgment, asking questions such as "Is the behavior helping you?" or "Is the behavior against the rules?" The third step is to involve the student in carrying out a plan to correct the inappropriate behavior. An application of reality therapy is featured in the following scenario:

Teacher: "Michael, what just happened?"

Michael: "Nothing."

Teacher: "I thought I saw you push Susan."

Michael: "Yeah, maybe I did."

Teacher: "Tell me about it."

Michael: "I was running to get in line and she got in my way."

Teacher: "Well, I'm sure you didn't push her on purpose, but is pushing students against the rules?"

Michael: "Yeah."

Teacher: "What do you think should be done?"

Michael: "I don't know."

Teacher: "Why don't you sit over there at the reading table a couple of minutes and think about what you can do to solve the problem."

Michael: "Okay."

(Five minutes later.)

Teacher: "Got an idea?"

Michael: "Yeah, I think I should line up after the others for the rest of the week."

Teacher: "Does that help Susan?"

Michael: "No."

Teacher: "What can you do to help Susan?"

Michael: "I can tell her I'm sorry and let her line up in front of me tomorrow."

Teacher: "Can you do that?"

Michael: "Yeah."

Teacher: "Fine, I think that's an excellent plan."

Techniques for Managing Surface Behaviors and Assertive Discipline

Long and Newman (1971) discuss 12 techniques for managing surface (observable) behaviors and helping to prevent the buildup of behavior problems:

1. Planned ignoring: Many behaviors will stop if they are ignored rather than given teacher attention.
2. Signal interference: The use of a cue (such as finger snapping) can alert the student to stop a particular behavior.
3. Proximity control: Some disruptive behavior can be prevented by the teacher's presence in the area of potential trouble.
4. Interest boosting: Some behaviors can be managed when the teacher shows a genuine interest in the student as an individual.
5. Tension decontamination through humor: A humorous remark by the teacher can release tension in an emotional situation.
6. Hurdle lessons: The teacher can lessen frustration by providing individual academic assistance.

7. Restructuring the classroom program: A change in the classroom program can reduce behavior problems.

8. Support from routine: A familiar routine can provide support to the student.

9. Direct appeal to value areas: The teacher needs to be aware of the student's personal values to appeal to them.

10. Removing seductive objects: Items that distract the student can be removed from the classroom to avoid provoking disruptive behavior.

11. Antiseptic bouncing: The student can be removed from the classroom without punishment (for example, ask him to run an errand).

12. Physical restraint: The teacher can restrain the student when he has lost self-control and might injure himself.

Assertive discipline, as advocated by Canter and Canter (1976) is an approach to classroom control that allows teachers to deal constructively with misbehaving students while maintaining a supportive environment for student growth. Charles (1992) presents a series of five steps to implement assertive discipline:

1. *Recognize and remove roadblocks to assertive discipline.* First, negative expectations about students must be replaced with positive expectations. Teachers must realize that all students need limits and that teachers have a right to set limits as well as ask for and receive backup help from principals, parents, and other school personnel.

2. *Practice the use of assertive response styles.* With the assertive response style, teachers clearly define their expectations and continually insist that students comply with those expectations by backing their words with action.

3. *Learn to set limits.* Teachers must establish specific behavioral needs and expectations of their students and then decide how to respond to students when established expectations either are complied with or broken.

4. *Learn to follow through on limits.* Teachers must take appropriate actions for students' compliance with or refusal to meet demands. Thus, the students choose their behavior but have advance knowledge of the good or bad consequences that will result from their choice.

5. *Implement a system of positive consequences.* When teachers follow through with positive consequences when students behave in appropriate ways, the influence of teachers with their students increases, the amount of problem behavior decreases, and the classroom environment becomes more positive.

Thus, Canter and Canter's (1976) model of assertive discipline integrates such ideas as behavior as choice, logical consequences rather than threats or punishment, positive reinforcements for desired behavior, and addressing the situation rather than the student's character. The approach maintains that teachers must care enough about students not to allow them to behave in ways that are damaging to themselves and that teachers must guide students firmly and apply natural consequences of student behavior while receiving full support from administration and parents. Canter and Canter (1986, 1989) provide inservice videotapes and manuals of the assertive discipline program.

Social Skills Training

Several procedures have been used to improve the social skills performance of students with learning problems (Schumaker & Hazel, 1984). One technique involves the manipulation of antecedent and consequent events associated with the target social behavior. For example, environmental events can be changed in an effort to increase the probability of future occurrence of appropriate social behaviors while decreasing the probability of occurrence of inappropriate behaviors. Approaches of this technique include the use of cooperative goal structures, the delivery or the withholding of particular consequences contingent upon the occurrence of social responses, the application of group contingencies, and the use of home-based contingency management systems. Another technique that has been used to reduce the rate of inappropriate social behaviors is cognitive training aimed at teaching self-control of personal behaviors (for example, self-recording and self-evaluation of behaviors).

Also, interpersonal social skills can be increased through direct instruction. Schumaker and Hazel (1984) discuss four types of instructional interventions that have been used to facilitate the acquisition of social skills:

1. Description—primarily oral techniques in which the teacher describes how to perform a skill appropriately.
2. Modeling—demonstrations of the social skill either by live models or by film, audiotape, or pictorial models.
3. Rehearsal—verbal rehearsal of required skill steps to ensure that the student has memorized the steps in sequence and can instruct himself in what to do next, and structured practice (for example, role-play activities) whereby the learner attempts to perform the skill.
4. Feedback—verbal feedback following rehearsal to inform the student on what steps he performed well and what behaviors need improvement.

Frequently, combinations of these procedures are included in social skills training interventions.

A social skills curriculum also can be used. Cartledge, Frew, and Zaharias (1985) and Maag (1989) note that a basic principle of social skills instruction is that behaviors chosen for instruction should be those valued by persons important in the learner's environment. To foster peer interaction, attention should be given to areas such as informal conversation and play skills. The following social skills curriculum consists of four main areas:

1. Conversation skills—using body language, greeting, introducing yourself, applying active listening, answering questions, interrupting correctly, asking questions, saying good-bye, and conversing.
2. Friendship skills—making friends, saying thanks, giving compliments, accepting thanks, accepting compliments, joining group activities, starting activities with others, and giving help.
3. Skills for difficult situations—giving criticism, accepting "no," accepting criticism, following instructions, responding to teasing, resisting peer pressure, and apologizing.
4. Problem-solving skills—negotiating, giving rationales, persuading, problem solving, getting help, and asking for feedback.

Projective Techniques

Various projective techniques can be used by the teacher to encourage students to project or express their feelings and emotions. Creative activities, such as role playing and puppetry, provide an opportunity for the student to express feelings and reduce frustrations with few constraints.

Role Playing. In role playing, students assume the role of a character and act out a brief episode that involves a problem. The role-playing process includes four steps:

1. A specific problem is identified—classroom problems or conflicts or other relevant situations.
2. After the problem is described, the roles must be established and assigned to various students. Volunteers should be sought; students should not be forced to play a role.
3. The actual role playing takes place and should be brief. The same situation can be repeated several times with different students to present many solutions to a single problem.
4. A discussion follows, focusing on the role or behavior rather than the student portraying it.

Thus, through role playing the student faces reactions of other people and learns ways to cope with similar situations.

Puppetry. Puppets can help students experience different events and express feelings and emotions. Fairy-tale characters (such as king, witch, giant, animal) can be used to represent human emotional experiences. Students can make hand puppets and a stage. The puppet theater provides a nonthreatening atmosphere in which students can express their feelings freely as they engage in problem solving. After the puppet show, other solutions to the problems presented can be discussed.

SOCIAL AND EMOTIONAL BEHAVIOR ACTIVITIES

The following selected problem areas cover a wide range of social and emotional behaviors. Within each area, several management activities are suggested.

Academic Behavior Problems

Some social and emotional behavior problems result in lowered academic performance. A student whose tolerance for frustration is low may become frustrated easily when attempting to complete academic tasks that require great effort. The problem behaviors of task avoidance and task interference also hamper the completion of academic work. The student who seldom completes timed assignments within his capabilities may have a problem in slowness in work.

Activities

1. Allow the student who avoids academic tasks to choose from a variety of activities within a skill area. This will allow him to think he selected his own work rather than having it forced on him. Also, consider letting the student complete academic tasks in various ways, such as using a red pen or working in a different area of the classroom. A variety of stimuli (tape recorder, Language Master, computer, manipulative materials) can be used to maintain the student's attention to the task.
2. Shortly after assigning an academic task, provide a reward for those students who have started the work and completed several problems. This will encourage the student who avoids tasks to become more involved. Rewards also can be given upon task completion to encourage the student to work steadily to finish an assignment.
3. To increase the student's speed in performing academic tasks, have him work against a timer and chart his progress. For example, the number of addition problems completed correctly during a specific period of time can be recorded on a graph each day. As progress is made in the student's rate of work, the difficulty of the tasks can be increased.
4. To discourage slowness in work, draw up a contingency contract. The student and teacher can agree that if the student finishes a specific part of an academic task within a certain amount of time, he will not have to complete the remainder of the assignment. The contract also should specify an accuracy criterion (such as 85 percent or more correct responses) to discourage the student from rushing incorrectly

through the task. Thus, accurate work performed in a reasonable amount of time is rewarded.

5. When a student shows a task interference behavior, such as looking out the window, move physically closer to him so that he is aware of your presence. Also, the student can be paired with a productive worker, and modeling can be used to elicit appropriate behavior.

6. Prepare a series of tasks at different levels of difficulty. Allow the student with low frustration tolerance to complete the first task at his own pace. Gradually introduce time limits. Record the student's progress and reward steps of progress. After the student has mastered the first task at various time intervals, repeat the procedure with a more difficult task.

7. Provide the student who avoids tasks with an incentive to start working: Give him a worksheet with the first few problems already completed.

8. Present academic tasks in game formats, such as start-to-finish races or card playing.

9. Use self-correcting materials, which provide immediate feedback and reduce the practicing of errors. The student may avoid academic tasks to avoid failure; however, with self-correcting materials, failure is not publicly known, and the student can immediately correct his responses.

10. Use a spinner to provide reinforcement after the student completes an academic assignment. The spinner can be divided into several different-size pie-shaped sections, with the more preferred reinforcers on the smaller wedges and the less costly reinforcers on the larger areas. The student spins the spinner and receives the reinforcer listed on the selected spinner section. This adds reinforcement variety as well as an element of unpredictability and thus serves as a "mystery motivator."

11. Use assistance cards to help manage requests for assistance. Paine et al. (1983) suggest folding a 9″ × 12″ piece of construction paper into a triangular shape with two 4″ sides and a 2″ base. Tape the triangle together and write "Please Keep Working" on one side and "Please Help Me" on the other side. When the student wants help, he places the side stating "Please Help Me" toward the front of the room, thus leaving the side stating "Please Keep Working" facing the student. The teacher provides each student with a work folder that occupies the student until the teacher is available to help. Frustration is reduced and success is increased if the work folder includes a self-correcting material. The work folder should include tasks that relate to the student's instructional needs (for example, practice in a specific skill). The assistance card enables the student to request help without raising his hand or disrupting engaged academic time. The supplementary work folder enables the student to continue to work productively on another academic task in which immediate teacher assistance is not required. Also, the assistance card reminds the student to keep working.

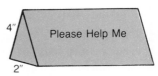

12. Use feedback charts for managing student behavior. Paine et al. (1983) note that feedback charts provide the student with a visible display of progress and also generate valuable data to help make educational decisions. The chart is displayed where all students can see it and is divided into four areas. For example:

Begins assigned activities promptly	Follows directions
Completes work or works entire time	Receives less than two warnings

Each student receives a blank card divided into four squares. Throughout the day the teacher marks each square with plus marks (+) when the student performs the desired behavior. At the end of a specified time period, the student may be allowed to trade the marks for free time, playing a game, and so on. The teacher may use separate cards for different academic periods. Also, a group chart can be made and laminated so that it can be used repeatedly.

	Math		Reading		Language	
Alan	+			+	+	
				+		
Elise	+	+		+		+
	+		+			
Clayton		+		+	+	+
		+		+	+	+

13. For the student who does not complete homework, have him earn the privilege of being allowed to do homework at home (Lieberman, 1983). Place the student on a five-day probation during which he must stay after school and complete his homework assignments within an agreed upon period of time. Then have him alternate doing his homework at home and at school every other day for five days. Finally, he can be allowed to do full-time homework at home. However, if any assignments are not completed at home, the student is placed on probation for another five days. Thus, for the student the positive consequence is earning the ability to do homework at home, as opposed to the negative consequence of staying after school for not completing the homework.

Disruptive Classroom Behavior

Disruptive behavior in the classroom includes actions that interfere with instruction or activities of an individual or a group. Inappropriate talking out and out-of-seat behaviors frequently are disruptive to the classroom. Moreover, the use of sarcasm, swear words, and temper tantrums are disturbing behaviors that need to be modified.

Activities

1. As much as possible, ignore disruptions and reward the student's complying behaviors. For example, when a student talks out during class, completely ignore him and do not respond to what he has said; however, when he raises his hand during class, immediately recognize him and praise his behavior. This is effective only if

teacher attention is reinforcing. It may be necessary also to control peer attention to the inappropriate behavior.

2. Ignore out-of-seat behaviors and give verbal praise to students who remain in their seats. Students who remain seated during work periods can be rewarded by being allowed to participate in a game involving movement (musical chairs, kick ball).

3. Use a timer to see how long an active student can stay in his seat. Time him at various intervals during the day and reward him when he remains in his seat during the interval. Record his progress on a graph so that the student competes with himself to improve his behavior. As he progresses, gradually increase the time interval for staying in the seat.

4. Give the active student periodic breaks that allow him to get out of his seat. He may be given errands to run, during which he can move around or leave the room.

5. Devise contingency contracts in which the student agrees to stay in his seat for a period of time, and if he does so, the teacher agrees to reward him with some free time out of his seat (such as extra recess). Likewise, a student can agree in a contract not to talk out during class for a specific amount of time in return for the reward of free talking time.

6. Cut out a figure of the student that includes a large pocket and tape it to the wall. Whenever the student behaves appropriately, place a chip or token in the figure's pocket. When the student engages in an inappropriate behavior (out of seat, talking out, use of swear words), remove a chip from the pocket. At the end of each day the chips can be traded for a reinforcing activity—free time, playing a game, watching a filmstrip.

7. To reduce swearing, suggest to the student other words that can be used (for example, *darn, heck, shoot*). Reinforce the student every time he refrains from swearing and uses another word.

8. Use a graph to record the number of swear words or sarcastic remarks made by the student during a specific time period. This will call his attention to his inappropriate remarks. Have the

student compete with himself, and reinforce him for improved behavior.

9. When a student begins a temper tantrum, immediately remove him to a time-out area in which he is isolated from the teacher and his peers. When he is able to remain quiet, allow him to return to the classroom. In this way the student receives little attention for inappropriate behavior. Also, be aware of the chain of behavior that leads the student to an outburst or tantrum. Apply time out or another management technique before the chain has gone too far.

10. At the beginning of the day, make 15 numbered marks on the chalkboard. Explain to the class that they have an opportunity to have a 15-minute recess at the end of the day. However, for each disruptive behavior one mark is erased from the board. At the end of the day, give the class the number of minutes of extra recess remaining on the board. Instead of recess, the minutes can be used in a special game, story time, or field trips.

Problems with Authority Figures

Some students have inappropriate reactions to school personnel or authority figures. The student may resist coming to school and frequently may challenge the authority of his teacher and principal by arguing constantly and disobeying school rules. This negative reaction needs to be changed to promote a healthy attitude toward school and authority figures.

Activities

1. Provide the student with positive reinforcement for attending school. For example, give the student a special treat or plan a rewarding activity each day he arrives on time. Special privileges, snacks, and activities can be made contingent on regular school attendance.

2. Pair the student who is absent frequently with a well-liked peer who has regular attendance. (Use a sociogram to determine a good match for modeling purposes.) With the teacher's guidance, the model can plan to meet the student at school for various activities and thus encourage attendance.

3. Allow class members to establish some of their own rules of behavior and consequences for disobeying a rule. Discuss the need and reasons for the rules. When some rules are made by peers, students may be less inclined to challenge the teacher's authority.

4. When the student repeatedly disobeys rules and instructions, give him several courses of action from which to choose. When possible, avoid conflict and "showdowns" in which he is forced to obey. Sometimes a peer can explain an assignment or rule to a student who resists adult authority and the student will comply.

5. Ignore the student whenever he argues with the teacher or disobeys instructions. Walk away from him when he argues. Isolation also can be effective in dealing with the student who argues. Reinforce obedient behavior and positive language through praise and attention.

6. Invite various authority figures in the community to speak to the class and share some of their problems and experiences during their school years. This sharing of experiences can make a positive impression on the student who shows a negative attitude.

7. Use an "emotion box" in the classroom. Give the class members several forms that ask for name, date, emotion, and reasons. Ask the students to complete a form and place it in the emotion box whenever they react strongly to an event in the classroom. Through this method the teacher can gain understanding about each student's reasons for undesirable and negative behaviors.

8. To foster a positive attitude toward authority figures, ask the student "planned interest" questions every day. For example, ask what he did last night, if his team won its ball game, and so on. Also, remember the student on special days, such as his birthday. A teacher's genuine interest in individual students encourages a positive feeling toward school attendance and authority figures.

Poor Self-Concept

Self-concept refers to a person's perception of his abilities and of how others important to him feel about him. A person with a poor self-concept has feelings of inferiority and inadequacy and may express these feelings—"I can't do that," "I'm not very smart." Such a student may lack self-confidence and be reluctant to interact with others. He may resist academic work because he fears failure.

Activities

1. To make the student feel special and important, select him to be "Student of the Week." Seat him in a special chair and give him a badge to wear. Each day ask the other classmates to write something special about the student being honored. They may write positive statements about his abilities or his personal attributes. Also, the classmates can decide on other special activities they can do for the student—perhaps write a story about him or play his favorite game at recess.
2. To develop self-awareness, have students collect items that tell something about themselves (for example, magazine pictures, small objects, photographs). Encourage each student to make a collage of these items on tagboard. The center of the collage can contain a picture of the student, with the items arranged around the photograph. The students can share with others what the items represent and why they were chosen.
3. Write short, personal notes to the student to provide encouragement and to let him know you have an interest in him. Also, have brief conversations with him. He may need extra encouragement when trying a new task or suffering from a disappointment.
4. Use the student as a tutor in peer tutoring situations. This may boost his self-esteem. It also shows that the teacher has confidence in the student's ability to handle the task.
5. Make some academic tasks look more difficult than they really are. The student will gain self-confidence when he successfully completes a task he thought was very difficult. For example, a simple math worksheet to practice subtraction facts can be replaced by a worksheet that *appears* to contain very difficult problems but really requires the same basic skills. The problem

$$394876 - 173472$$

requires the same basic skills as

$$3 - 1 \qquad 9 - 7 \qquad 4 - 3 \qquad 8 - 4 \qquad 7 - 7 \qquad 6 - 2$$

6. Provide success activities and limit failure as much as possible. Before requiring the student to participate in oral reading, have him review difficult words or listen to the story on a tape recorder. Also, using self-correcting materials keeps incorrect responses as a private event and gives the student a chance to correct his response immediately. Provide verbal praise and correct wrong responses without hurting the student's feelings: "You're almost right," "Let's do it together," "Nice try."
7. Help the student compile a scrapbook about himself. Include pictures or drawings of family, friends, and pets. If possible, take photographs in the class. The scrapbook can include written accounts of trips, interests, and favorite activities.
8. Set realistic goals with the student on selected tasks. Record the student's daily progress toward the goal. When the goal is achieved, point out the student's progress to make him feel proud of his accomplishments.
9. Emphasize the importance of student effort on academic tasks, and teach the student to attribute his successes and failures to amount of effort. This may result in increased persistence on difficult material and reduce doubts of intellectual ability.

Social Immaturity

The socially immature student lacks the ability to get along with his peers and lacks other social skills common to his age group. He may engage in antisocial behavior, failing to recognize his responsibilities and the rights of others. Social withdrawal may result from lack of academic success.

Activities

1. Pair a withdrawn student with a competent, socially mature peer for various activities. They must cooperate in completing an academic task together or being a team during a game. Thus, in these situations success or failure is shared by both students.

2. If a student frequently teases another student, ask the teased student to ignore the student who is teasing him. Reward the teased student each time he makes no response to teasing. Thus, the student who is teasing does not receive attention from either the teacher or the peer for his inappropriate behavior. Also, self-recording can be used to reduce teasing. Give the student a slip of paper with lines for his name and date and spaces in which he is to mark each time he teases. The marking should be monitored. Having to mark down his own inappropriate behavior may help the student decrease his teasing.

3. Use the socially withdrawn or rejected student in peer teaching situations as either the tutor or student being tutored. A sociogram can indicate an appropriate match. Peer tutoring encourages appropriate peer contacts in a secure and structured activity.

4. Use modeling techniques to teach various social skills. Praise the model for appropriate social behavior in the presence of the socially immature student.

5. Encourage the withdrawn student to use a tape recorder when he feels like talking. Tell the student that if the student would like to share it, the teacher will be glad to listen. The teacher can respond on tape if the student prefers. This is a first step in encouraging a withdrawn student to talk out loud and discuss his feelings.

6. Use role playing to present a variety of possible social situations. Discuss several different mature reactions to specific problems. Thus the student is presented with a choice of solutions to use when coping with similar social occurrences.

7. When a student frequently is aggressive toward a peer, ignore him and pay attention to the student who was his victim. Reinforce cooperative and peaceful behavior in the presence of the aggressive student, and reward him when he behaves appropriately.

8. Encourage the student to develop a vocabulary that expresses feelings. Pockets can be glued on a large piece of tagboard, and on each pocket a face can show a different expression (smiling, frowning, serious). Words expressing feelings (sad, cheerful, troubled, anxious, pleased, miserable, nervous) can be written on index cards. The student is instructed to match each word to a picture expressing that emotion. The correct face can be drawn on the back of each card so that the student can check his response. Another activity with feeling words is to give the student a list of words and ask him to write each word in a way that shows the emotion:

Afraid	*afraid*
Shy	*shy*
Excited	**EXCITED**
Jumpy	*jumpy*

Secondary students can increase their vocabulary to include feeling words that can be divided into unpleasant and pleasant:

Unpleasant	*Pleasant*
Ambivalent	Accomplished
Betrayed	Confident
Condemned	Ecstatic
Distraught	Fascinated
Dubious	Gratified
Exasperated	Infatuated

9. Have each student express his mood or feeling at different happenings. Write events on index cards (such as, "It's time to go to school"; "I don't know what to do"; "I don't have any money"; "My teacher smiles at me"; "It's my birthday"). Use a piece of tagboard with pockets labeled with various moods. Each student selects a card, reads it aloud, tells how the described event makes him feel and why, and places the card in the pocket that corresponds to his feeling. Also, during classroom situations

take pictures of students showing various emotions. These photographs can be displayed with captions telling the emotion shown and the situation in which it occurred: "Kevin is very proud. He is wearing his badge for captain of the safety patrol." By observing the pictures, students may become more sensitive to facial expressions.

10. Conduct class meetings during which the students discuss any question that seems relevant to them at the time. This opportunity for personal involvement is appropriate especially for secondary students. The teacher should keep the discussion moving and see that everyone is given an opportunity to participate as much as possible.

INSTRUCTIONAL GAMES IN SOCIAL AND EMOTIONAL BEHAVIOR

Many activities can be presented in a game format to stimulate interest and involvement. Games also promote positive peer relations and enable the teacher to work on specific social and emotional behaviors (for example, cooperating, staying on task, taking turns, or expressing feelings). The following games are designed to foster appropriate social and emotional behaviors.

Picture Puzzle Game

Materials:

A large picture of something the student is interested in or wants, cut into pieces.

Directions:

Encourage the student to show appropriate behavior over a period of time by rewarding him with something he wants. The student and teacher agree on the desired behavior to be reinforced and the type of reward. Each time the student shows the desired behavior, the teacher gives him a piece of the picture puzzle. Each time *inappropriate* behavior is observed, the teacher takes away a puzzle piece. When the student has received all the puzzle pieces to the picture, he is reinforced by receiving the reward.

Work Around the Circle

Materials:

Classroom chairs arranged in a circle; a timer.

Directions:

Set a timer to go off at various times during intervals of from 1 to 4 minutes. When the timer buzzes, each student who is working may move to the next chair. Students who are caught not working must remain in their seats for that turn. Thus students who are working appropriately rotate around the circle. When a student has completed the circle, the teacher should check his work and give him free time until all students have worked their way back to their own seats.

The Principal's Game

(Paine et al., 1983)

Materials:

Timer; chalkboard area for recording points.

Directions:

Use this game to improve the behavior of a disruptive class of students. Begin by telling the students they need to work harder, and there is a game that can help them. In the game, teams are formed according to seating clusters or rows (that is, one team for each row or cluster). A timer is set to ring six times during the class or day. Each time it rings the teacher determines which teams are following classroom rules and working. If all team members are working the whole team receives a point; however, if one or more members are not working no points are awarded. To win, a team must receive a minimum of five points, and it is possible for all teams to win. At the end of the day or class, invite the principal to come into the room and recognize the winning teams and praise their fine work. In addition to the principal, other significant people (for example, counselor, another teacher, local sports figure, or parent) can be asked to visit and recognize winning teams.

Behavior Monopoly

Materials:

A game board similar to a Monopoly board that has a variety of reinforcers (including some booby prizes) written in the squares; a die; student markers.

Directions:

Use the game board (see Figure 5.5) to provide the student with some type of reinforcement. Randomly identify a student displaying an appropriate behavior. Allow him to roll the die and move his marker on the board. The student receives the reinforcer indicated on the space where he lands. He then leaves his marker on that space so that it can be moved next time he gets to play.

Chance Cards can include: "Arm wrestle with teacher," "Hop on one foot for 5 seconds," "Send note to a friend," "Hug the teacher," "Pick up trash," and so on.

Speed Chase

Materials:

Poster board with large speedometer dial drawn on it; cardboard arrows, each of which has a student's name on it; various small prizes.

Directions:

Allow groups of students to compete to see who can complete the most classwork accurately during the day. After the teacher has checked an assignment, each student attaches his arrow to the speedometer to indicate the number of items he performed correctly on the task. His speed on the speedometer increases according to the number of correct items on each assignment. At the end of the day the student with the highest speed wins and picks a prize.

Modifications:

Rather than competing in all subject areas for an entire day, students can record their speed in one

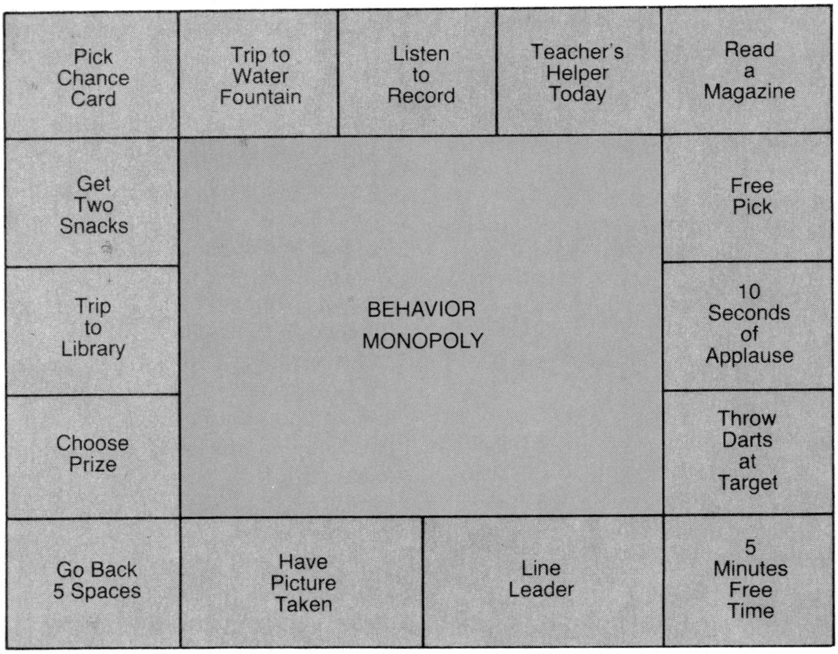

Pick Chance Card	Trip to Water Fountain	Listen to Record	Teacher's Helper Today	Read a Magazine
Get Two Snacks				Free Pick
Trip to Library		BEHAVIOR MONOPOLY		10 Seconds of Applause
Choose Prize				Throw Darts at Target
Go Back 5 Spaces	Have Picture Taken	Line Leader		5 Minutes Free Time

FIGURE 5.5
Behavior Monopoly game board.

subject area for several days. Also, the speedometer can be used to record specific behaviors during the day, such as staying in seat or raising hand instead of talking out. Two students who need to change the same behavior can compete. Each time the student displays the appropriate behavior the teacher moves his arrow on the speedometer; the arrow is moved *back* for inappropriate behavior. The student with the highest speed at the end of the day wins the speed chase.

The Lottery

(Paine et al., 1983)

Materials:

Prerecorded tape with randomly spaced "beeps"; tape recorder; space on chalkboard for recording checks by students' names.

Directions:

Hold a daily lottery in which students work for the opportunity of having their names drawn at random. During the day play a tape with six randomly distributed "beeps." Students who are following classroom rules (for example, on task, in seat, not talking) when the beep sounds receive a check by their names on the chalkboard. Students who receive five or six checks in a day are eligible for the daily drawing. At the end of the day, two names are selected from the qualifying students. The principal or teacher phones the respective parents and tells them about their child's good behavior.

Good Behavior Game

(Barrish, Saunders, & Wolf, 1969)

Materials:

Tally chart.

Directions:

Divide the class into two teams and explain that talking out and out-of-seat behaviors are going to be recorded. Whenever a student engages in either behavior, place a mark on the tally sheet for his team. At the end of the day the team with the fewest marks wins. If both teams have fewer than six marks, the whole class wins. The members of the winning team receive a previously agreed upon reward. If both teams win, reward the entire class with a 30-minute special project period.

Timer Game

(Wolf, Hanley, King, Lachowicz, & Giles, 1970)

Materials:

Timer; point chart; prizes.

Directions:

Set the timer to ring on the average of once every 20 minutes during a range of from 1 to 40 minutes. Each student who is in his seat when the timer rings is awarded five points. Each student's points earned are recorded on a point chart. At the end of a specified period of time, the points may be traded in for prizes such as snacks or privileges.

Best and Worst Game

Materials:

Paper and pencil.

Directions:

Describe a social situation and have each student write down what would be the *best* and the *worst* thing to do in response to that event. Each student reads his response, and the choices presented are discussed. The student with the best response (decided by the presenter of the problem) gets to describe the next social incident and lead the discussion.

Personality Game

(Bailey, 1975)

Materials:

Start-to-finish game board; cards with personality traits written on them; markers.

Directions:

Place the cards face down on the playing board (see Figure 5.6). The first player takes the top card and reads it aloud. If he thinks the card describes

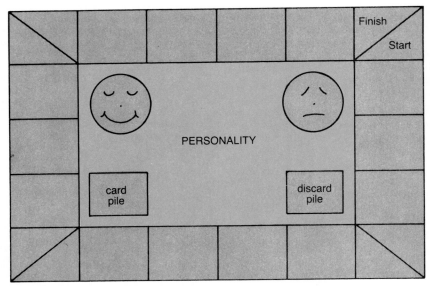

FIGURE 5.6
Personality game board.

him, he may move forward five spaces. However, if he believes the statement on the card does not apply to him, but the majority of the group thinks it does (or vice versa), the player must move his marker three spaces back. If neither the player nor the others believes the card applies, the player stays where he is. The players may tell why they think a trait is or is not descriptive of their personality. After each turn the card is placed face down in the discard pile. If a blank card is picked, the player may make up a trait. Players may choose the top card from either the original card pile or the discard pile. The purpose of the game is to help each student better understand himself. The first player to move around the board and reach the finish space is the winner.

Sample cards can include: "I am impatient," "I joke around a lot," "I am kind to animals," "I don't ever like school," and so on.

Socialization Game

Materials:

Start-to-finish board; dice; set of cards containing personal questions; markers.

Directions:

Use the game board to improve social skills by providing the players with an opportunity to talk freely about feelings, relationships, or activities. Each player rolls the dice and moves that number of spaces on the board. He then must take a card and respond to the question by explaining his answer to the other players. The first player to reach the finish space wins.

Sample questions can include: "Do you like to be alone? When?" "If you could be anyone in the world, who would you be? Why?" "What happened on the happiest day of your life?" "What would you do if you didn't go to school?"

Decision Game

Materials:

Five parallel lines marked on the floor with masking tape.

Directions:

Explain to the students that the five lines represent (from right to left) absolutely right, somewhat right, undecided or neutral, somewhat wrong, and absolutely wrong. Tell a story or describe a situation; then ask the students to move to the line that indicates their decision about the story or situation. Each student should explain why he moved where he did.

Stories or situations such as the following can be used:

John saw William take two quarters from the teacher's desk and put them in his pocket. He told William to return the money but William refused to do so. John then went to the teacher and told her William had taken the money. Was the decision to tell the teacher right or wrong?

COMMERCIAL SOCIAL AND EMOTIONAL BEHAVIOR PROGRAMS AND MATERIALS

Various programs and materials are designed to help students understand themselves better and get along with others. The following programs and materials can be used to enhance self-concept and general social and emotional growth. (The publishers' addresses are included in Appendix B.)

Asset: A Social Skills Program for Adolescents

Publisher: Research Press

Description:

The *Asset* program (Hazel, Schumaker, Sherman, & Sheldon-Wildgen, 1982) is designed specifically for teaching social skills to a wide range of adolescents in sixth through twelfth grade. This video program features modeling scenes that show teenagers interacting with peers, parents, teachers, and other adults. Scenes of teenagers modeling both appropriate and inappropriate social interaction skills lead to stimulating discussions, and students have the opportunity to become actively involved by relating the video presentations to their own personal experiences and feelings. An individual videocassette is available for each of the following social

skills areas: giving positive feedback, giving negative feedback, accepting negative feedback, resisting peer pressure, problem solving, negotiation, following instructions, and conversations. The *Asset* manual provides the leader with training procedures, lesson plans, skill sheets outlining the steps for each skill, home notes, checklists, consent forms, and various questionnaires.

CLASS: Contingencies for Learning Academic and Social Skills

Publisher: Educational Achievement Systems

Description:

CLASS (Hops & Walker, 1988) is a classroom management program for students with acting-out behaviors. The procedures are based on social learning principles and are designed to increase behaviors that lead to academic achievement and social development and to decrease behaviors that interfere with such achievement. The program uses the teacher-consultant model, and the intervention procedures are described in a time frame of 30 school days. The first intervention phase, the consultant phase, lasts five days, during which the consultant (for example, resource room teacher, counselor, school psychologist) provides the student with continuous feedback concerning the appropriateness of the student's behavior. The consultant praises the student and awards points on a green/red point card. The points can be exchanged for a reward shared by the entire class (for example, playing a game, getting free time). The student also receives an individual reinforcer at home (for example, extra outdoor play, special dessert). The second intervention phase, the teacher phase, lasts 25 days, during which the teacher delivers praise and rewards and gradually increases the amount of time that the program is in effect. By Day 10 the program is extended to the entire school day. From Day 8 through 20, points are awarded on a variable 10-minute reinforcement schedule, and by Day 20 points and backup reinforcers have been faded and the student must work for a full 5 days before receiving a reward. Days 21 through 30 focus on the teacher's ability to maintain an acceptable rate of praise and the student's ability to maintain positive gains without tangible rewards. Thus the student's new level of appropriate behavior is maintained through the use of praise and rewards that occur naturally within the school environment. The manual includes possible praise statements and games or activities that can be used for reward and also discusses possible responses to common problems in implementation.

Coping With Series

Publisher: American Guidance Service

Description:

The *Coping With Series* (Schwarzrock & Wrenn, 1984) includes four sets of five paperback books. The books present information in four areas: (a) coping with personal identity (focuses on self and self-improvement, such as making better decisions, living with loneliness), (b) coping with human relationships (focuses on getting along with others—social skills, communication, thoughtfulness, acceptance), (c) coping with facts and fantasies (provides factual information about drugs, alcohol, smoking, unhealthy eating habits, and roles of men and women), and (d) coping with teenage problems (addresses a variety of teenage problems such as cliques, parents, and common crutches). The books are appropriate for adolescents and can be helpful in discussion groups and counseling sessions. A leader's manual is included with each set of books.

Developing Understanding of Self and Others

Publisher: American Guidance Service

Description:

The *DUSO* kits (Dinkmeyer & Dinkmeyer, 1982) are designed to encourage the social and emotional growth of students in kindergarten through fourth grade. *DUSO I,* for students in kindergarten through second grade, is used to develop appreciation of

individual strengths and acceptance of limitations, beginning of social skills, and awareness of feelings, priorities, and choices. *DUSO II,* for third and fourth graders, helps develop a greater understanding of the purposive nature of behavior, more effective communication skills, a greater understanding of feelings and empathetic behavior, and skill in recognizing and making choices. The central character of both programs is a puppet, Duso the Dolphin. A problem situation and a story are presented and are followed by role-playing and puppet activities. The kit provides hand puppets, posters, activity cards, and audiocassettes of stories and songs.

Getting Along with Others

Publisher: Research Press

Description:

Getting Along with Others: Teaching Social Effectiveness to Children (Jackson, Jackson, & Monroe, 1983) presents a direct intervention approach with systematic instructional methods. A tell-show-practice model of social skills training is used in which the students participate in role-playing activities and learn adaptive coping responses. A notebook of skill lessons and activities presents 17 core social skills (for example, following directions, giving and receiving positive feedback, saying "no" to stay out of trouble). The program guide provides teacher scripts and offers five main teaching strategies as well as nine additional techniques to enhance the learning potential in any interaction.

Skillstreaming the Elementary School Child; Skillstreaming the Adolescent

Publisher: Research Press

Description:

These two manuals provide a program for teaching prosocial skills based on a structured learning method that involves modeling (demonstrating the behavioral steps that make up specific skills), role playing (reviewing, rehearsing, and performing each of the skill steps), performance feedback (evaluating the role-play), and transfer training (developing assignments for using the skills in real-life situations). In *Skillstreaming the Elementary School Child* (McGinnis, Goldstein, Sprafkin, & Gershaw, 1984), 60 specific prosocial skills (such as apologizing, dealing with anger, responding to teasing) are presented within the content areas of dealing with feelings, classroom survival skills, alternatives to aggression, friendship-making skills, and dealing with stress. *Skillstreaming the Adolescent* (Goldstein, Sprafkin, Gershaw, & Klein, 1980) presents 50 prosocial skills (such as maintaining a conversation, setting a goal, standing up for oneself or a friend) within the content areas of beginning and advanced social skills, dealing with feelings, alternatives to aggression, dealing with stress, and planning skills. A video program is available that illustrates the concepts and training procedures contained in the books.

Social Skills for Daily Living

Publisher: American Guidance Service

Description:

Social Skills for Daily Living (Schumaker, Hazel, & Pederson, 1988) provides a curriculum for students age 12 through 21 that teaches 30 social skills organized in three categories: conversation and friendship skills, skills for getting along with others, and problem-solving skills. An instructional sequence gives students the opportunity to understand the skill, memorize the skill steps, practice the skill, and apply the skill in real-life situations. The program is designed according to the interests and capabilities of secondary-level students and has a fourth-grade reading level. In addition to skill books and student workbooks, the program includes comic books that present science fiction stories to illustrate the use of skills, cards that provide role-play situations to practice skills, and blackline masters that include activities requiring students to apply skills.

The Solution Book

Publisher: Science Research Associates

Description:

The Solution Book (Sprick, 1981) is a teacher resource material packaged in a looseleaf binder that presents a positive approach to discipline and gives practical, simple solutions to common classroom behavior problems. The first section contains nine topic booklets (for example, Effective Reinforcement, Effective Punishment, Establishing a Discipline Plan) that help the teacher establish an environment that minimizes misbehavior and maximizes learning. The second section consists of 100 solution sheets that present a specific problem (such as fighting, talking out, failing to complete work) and suggest a specific solution. The final section contains reproducible materials such as awards, certificates, and notes to parents that can be used effectively with elementary students to motivate and reinforce appropriate behavior.

Toward Affective Development

Publisher: American Guidance Service

Description:

The *Toward Affective Development* program (Dupont, Gardner, & Brody, 1974) consists of activities, lessons, and materials designed to stimulate psychological and affective development in students age 8 to 12 (third through sixth grade). The kit is organized into five general sections containing 21 units (191 sequential lessons). Activities (such as self-awareness, working with others) can be added into the classroom schedule. The kit includes a manual, picture cards, posters, duplicating masters, an audiocassette, color chips, feeling wheels, and career folders. The lessons, designed to involve students actively with one another, each take 20 to 25 minutes.

Transition

Publisher: American Guidance Service

Description:

The *Transition* program (Dupont & Dupont, 1979) is designed to help students age 12 to 15 (sixth through ninth grade) understand and cope with various social and emotional situations. The five units included in the program are communication and problem-solving skills; encouraging openness and trust; verbal and nonverbal communication of feelings; needs, goals, and expectations; and increasing awareness of values. Each unit has its own teacher's manual. A scope and sequence outline of the entire program is included. There are instructions for 91 sequential activities such as scenarios of conflicts and dilemmas, debates, games, discussions, and questionnaires. The program also includes 88 cartoon posters; six audiocassettes; eight script booklets; duplicating masters; discussion cards; 48 "feeling word" cards; and 28 illustrations of facial expressions, postures, and gestures. Through the program, students are confronted with real-life issues and problems. They are encouraged to communicate successfully, solve problems alone and with others, and get along with peers and adults.

The Walker Social Skills Curriculum

Publisher: Pro-Ed

Description:

The *ACCEPTS Program* (Walker et al., 1983) is a social skills curriculum that teaches classroom and peer-to-peer social skills to students in kindergarten through sixth grade. The 28 classroom competencies and social skills are presented in five areas: (a) classroom skills (for example, listening to the teacher, following classroom rules), (b) basic interaction skills (for example, eye contact, listening, taking turns talking), (c) getting along skills (for example, using polite words, sharing, assisting others), (d) making friends skills (for example, good grooming, smiling, complimenting), and (e) coping skills (for example, when you express anger, when someone teases you, when things don't go right). The *ACCESS Program* (Walker, Todis, Holmes, & Horton, 1988) teaches peer-to-peer skills, skills for relating to adults, and self-management skills to students at the middle and high school levels. The 30 social skills are presented in three areas: (a) re-

lating to peers (for example, interacting with the opposite sex, being left out, handling group pressures), (b) relating to adults (for example, disagreeing with adults, working independently, developing good study habits), and (c) relating to yourself (for example, being organized, using self-control, feeling good about yourself). The curriculum is designed for use by both regular and special education teachers and can be taught in one-to-one, small-group, or large-group instructional formats.

REFERENCES

Allen, V. L. (Ed.). (1976). *Children as teachers: Theory and research on tutoring.* New York: Academic Press.

Ayllon, T., Layman, D., & Burke, S. (1972). Disruptive behavior and reinforcement of academic performance. *The Psychological Record, 22,* 315–322.

Ayllon, T., & Roberts, M. (1974). Eliminating discipline problems by strengthening academic performance. *Journal of Applied Behavior Analysis, 7,* 71–76.

Bailey, E. J. (1975). *Academic activities for adolescents with learning disabilities.* Evergreen, CO: Learning Pathways.

Barrish, H. H., Saunders, M., & Wolf, M. M. (1969). Good behavior game: Effects of individual contingencies for group consequences on disruptive behavior in a classroom. *Journal of Applied Behavior Analysis, 2,* 119–124.

Battle, J. (1992). *Culture-Free Self-Esteem Inventories—2.* Austin, TX: Pro-Ed.

Blackham, G. J., & Silberman, A. (1980). *Modification of child and adolescent behavior* (3rd ed.). Belmont, CA: Wadsworth.

Bracken, B. A. (1992). *Multidimensional Self Concept Scale.* Austin, TX: Pro-Ed.

Brigham, T. A., Hopper, C., Hill, B., De Armas, A., & Newsom, P. (1985). A self-management program for disruptive adolescents in the school: A clinical replication. *Behavior Therapy, 16,* 99–115.

Broughton, S., & Lahey, B. (1978). Direct and collateral effects of positive reinforcement, response cost, and mixed contingencies for academic performance. *Journal of School Psychology, 16,* 126–136.

Brown, L., & Alexander, J. (1991). *Self-Esteem Index.* Austin, TX: Pro-Ed.

Brown, L., & Hammill, D. D. (1990). *Behavior Rating Profile—2.* Austin, TX: Pro-Ed.

Bruininks, R. H., Woodcock, R. W., Weatherman, R. F., & Hill, B. K. (1985). *Scales of Independent Behavior: Woodcock-Johnson Psycho-Educational Battery* (Part 4). Allen, TX: DLM.

Bryan, T. H. (1986). Self-concept and attributions of the learning disabled. *Learning Disabilities Focus, 1,* 82–89.

Burks, H. F. (1977). *Burks' Behavior Rating Scales* (rev. ed.). Los Angeles: Western Psychological Services.

Canter, L., & Canter, M. (1976). *Assertive discipline: A take-charge approach for today's educator.* Santa Monica, CA: Lee Canter and Associates.

Canter, L., & Canter, M. (1986). *Assertive discipline phase 2 in-service media package* [Videotapes and manuals]. Santa Monica, CA: Lee Canter and Associates.

Canter, L., & Canter, M. (1989). *Assertive discipline for secondary school educators: Inservice video package and leader's manual.* Santa Monica, CA: Lee Canter and Associates.

Cartledge, G., Frew, T., & Zaharias, J. (1985). Social skill needs of mainstreamed students: Peer and teacher perceptions. *Learning Disability Quarterly, 8,* 132–140.

Cartwright, C. A., & Cartwright, G. P. (1984). *Developing observation skills* (2nd ed.). New York: McGraw-Hill.

Chapman, J. W., & Boersma, F. J. (1979). Learning disabilities, locus of control, and mother attitudes. *Journal of Educational Psychology, 1,* 250–258.

Charles, C. M. (1992). *Building classroom discipline* (4th ed.). New York: Longman.

Cianciolo, P. J. (1965). Children's literature can affect coping behavior. *Personnel and Guidance Journal, 43*(9), 897–903.

Coie, J., Dodge, K., & Coppotelli, H. (1982). Dimensions and types of social status: A cross-age perspective. *Developmental Psychology, 18,* 557–570.

Coopersmith, S. (1981). *Coopersmith Self-Esteem Inventories.* Monterey, CA: Publishers Test Service.

Deshler, D. D., Schumaker, J. B., & Lenz, B. K. (1984). Academic and cognitive interventions for LD adolescents: Part I. *Journal of Learning Disabilities, 17,* 108–117.

Dinkmeyer, D., & Dinkmeyer, D., Jr. (1982). *Developing understanding of self and others* (rev. ed.). Circle Pines, MN: American Guidance Service.

Dodge, K. A. (1983). Behavioral antecedents of peer status. *Child Development, 54,* 1400–1416.

Dodge, K. A., Pettit, G. S., McClaskey, C. L., & Brown, M. M. (1986). Social competence in children. *Monograph of the Society for Research in Child Development, 51*(2, Serial No. 213).

Dupont, H., & Dupont, C. (1979). *Transition.* Circle Pines, MN: American Guidance Service.

Dupont, H., Gardner, O. S., & Brody, D. S. (1974). *Toward affective development: A program to stimulate psychological and affective development.* Circle Pines, MN: American Guidance Service.

Elliott, S. N., Gresham, F. M., & Heffer, R. W. (1987). Social-skill interventions: Research findings and training techniques. In C. A. Maher & J. E. Zins (Eds.), *Psychoeducational interventions in the schools* (pp. 141–159). New York: Pergamon.

Ellis, E. S., Lenz, B. K., & Sabornie, E. J. (1987). Generalization and adaptation of learning strategies to natural environments: Part 2: Research into practice. *Remedial and Special Education, 8*(2), 6–23.

Fitts, W. H., & Roid, G. H. (1988). *Tennessee Self-Concept Scale.* Los Angeles: Western Psychological Services.

Flanders, N. (1970). *Analyzing teacher behavior.* Menlo Park, CA: Addison-Wesley.

Fowler, J. W., & Peterson, P. L. (1981). Increasing reading persistence and altering attributional style of learned helpless children. *Journal of Educational Psychology, 73,* 251–260.

Glasser, W. (1965). *Reality therapy: A new approach to psychiatry.* New York: Harper & Row.

Goldstein, A. P., Sprafkin, R. P., Gershaw, N. J., & Klein, P. (1980). *Skillstreaming the adolescent.* Champaign, IL: Research Press.

Gresham, F. M., & Elliott, S. N. (1989). Social skills assessment technology for LD students. *Learning Disability Quarterly, 12,* 141–152.

Gresham, F. M., & Elliott, S. N. (1990). *Social Skills Rating System.* Circle Pines, MN: American Guidance Service.

Gresham, F. M., & Reschly, D. J. (1988). Issues in the conceptualization, classification, and assessment of social skills in the mildly handicapped. In T. Kratochwill (Ed.), *Advances in school psychology* (pp. 203–247). Hillsdale, NJ: Erlbaum.

Hazel, J. S., Schumaker, J. B., Sherman, J. A., & Sheldon-Wildgen, J. (1982). *Asset: A social skills program for adolescents.* Champaign, IL: Research Press.

Hoagland, J. (1972, March). Bibliotherapy: Aiding children in personality development. *Elementary English,* pp. 390–394.

Hops, H., & Walker, H. M. (1988). *CLASS: Contingencies for learning academic and social skills.* Delray Beach, FL: Educational Achievement Systems.

Hresko, W. P., & Brown, L. (1984). *Test of Early Socioemotional Development.* Austin, TX: Pro-Ed.

Hughes, C. A., Ruhl, K. L., & Peterson, S. K. (1988). Teaching self-management skills. *Teaching Exceptional Children, 20*(2), 70–72.

Hutton, J. B., & Roberts, T. G. (1986). *Social-Emotional Dimension Scale.* Austin, TX: Pro-Ed.

Jackson, N. F., Jackson, D. A., & Monroe, C. (1983). *Getting along with others: Teaching social effectiveness to children.* Champaign, IL: Research Press.

Kaufman, M., Agard, J., & Semmel, M. (1985). *Mainstreaming: Learners and their environment.* Cambridge, MA: Brookline Books.

Kazdin, A. E. (1972). Response cost: The removal of conditioned reinforcers for therapeutic change. *Behavior Therapy, 3,* 533–546.

Kerr, M. M., & Nelson, C. M. (1989). *Strategies for managing behavior problems in the classroom* (2nd ed.). New York: Merrill/Macmillan.

Kroth, R. (1973). The behavioral Q-sort as a diagnostic tool. *Academic Therapy, 8,* 317–329.

Lambert, N. M., Windmiller, M., Cole, L., & Tharinger, D. (1981). *AAMD Adaptive Behavior Scale: School edition.* Austin, TX: Pro-Ed.

Lenkowsky, B., & Lenkowsky, R. (1978). Bibliotherapy of the LD adolescent. *Academic Therapy, 14,* 179–185.

Licht, B. G. (1984). Cognitive-motivational factors that contribute to the achievement of learning-disabled children. *Annual Review of Learning Disabilities, 2,* 119–126.

Lieberman, L. M. (1983). The homework solution. *Journal of Learning Disabilities, 16,* 435.

Long, N. J., & Newman, R. G. (1971). Managing surface behavior of children in schools. In N. J. Long, W. C. Morse, & R. G. Newman (Eds.), *Conflict in the classroom: The education of emotionally disturbed children* (2nd ed.). Belmont, CA: Wadsworth.

Maag, J. W. (1989). Assessment in social skills training: Methodological and conceptual issues for research and practice. *Remedial and Special Education, 10*(4), 6–17.

McCarney, S. B., & Leigh, J. E. (1990). *Behavior Evaluation Scale—2.* Austin, TX: Pro-Ed.

McConnell, S., & Odom, S. (1986) Sociometrics: Peer-referenced measures and the assessment of social competence. In P. Strain, M. Guralnick, & H. Walker (Eds.), *Children's social behavior: Development, assessment, and modification* (pp. 215–284). Orlando, FL: Academic Press.

McGinnis, E., Goldstein, A. P., Sprafkin, R. P., & Gershaw, N. J. (1984). *Skillstreaming the elementary school child.* Champaign, IL: Research Press.

Meichenbaum, D. (1977). *Cognitive-behavior modification: An integrative approach.* New York: Plenum Press.

Morse, W. C. (1971). Worksheet on life space interviewing for teachers. In N. J. Long, W. C. Morse, & R. G. Newman (Eds.), *Conflict in the classroom: The education of emotionally disturbed children* (2nd ed.). Belmont, CA: Wadsworth.

Myklebust, H. R. (1981). *The Pupil Rating Scale Revised: Screening for learning disabilities.* New York: Grune & Stratton.

O'Leary, K. D., & Drabman, R. (1971). Token reinforcement in the classroom: A review. *Psychological Bulletin, 75,* 379–398.

Paine, S. C., Radicchi, J., Rosellini, L. C., Deutchman, L., & Darch, C. B. (1983). *Structuring your classroom for academic success.* Champaign, IL: Research Press.

Pearl, R., Bryan, T., & Donahue, M. (1980). Learning disabled children's attributions for success and failure. *Learning Disability Quarterly, 3*(1), 3–9.

Piers, E. V., & Harris, D. B. (1984). *The Piers-Harris Children's Self-Concept Scale: Revised manual.* Los Angeles: Western Psychological Services.

Polsgrove, L. (1979). Self-control: Methods for child training. *Behavioral Disorders, 4,* 116–130.

Premack, D. (1959). Toward empirical behavior laws: I. Positive reinforcement. *Psychological Review, 66,* 219–233.

Quay, H. C., & Peterson, D. R. (1987). *Revised Behavior Problem Checklist.* Coral Gables, FL: University of Miami.

Rieth, H., & Evertson, C. (1988). Variables related to the effective instruction of difficult-to-teach children. *Focus on Exceptional Children, 20*(5), 1–8.

Russell, A. E., & Russell, W. A. (1979). Using bibliotherapy with emotionally disturbed children. *Teaching Exceptional Children, 11,* 168–169.

Schumaker, J. B., & Hazel, J. S. (1984). Social skills assessment and training for the learning disabled: Who's on first and what's on second? Part II. *Journal of Learning Disabilities, 17,* 492–499.

Schumaker, J. B., Hazel, J. S., & Pederson, C. S. (1988). *Social skills for daily living.* Circle Pines, MN: American Guidance Service.

Schunk, D. H. (1981). Modeling and attributional effects on children's achievement: A self-efficacy analysis. *Journal of Educational Psychology, 73,* 93–105.

Schwarzrock, S., & Wrenn, C. G. (1984). *Coping with series* (rev. ed.). Circle Pines, MN: American Guidance Service.

Shapiro, E. S. (1989). Teaching self-management skills to learning disabled adolescents. *Learning Disability Quarterly, 12,* 275–287.

Shelton, T. L., Anastopoulos, A. D., & Linden, J. D. (1985). An attribution training program with learning disabled children. *Journal of Learning Disabilities, 18,* 261–265.

Skinner, B. F. (1953). *Science and human behavior.* New York: Free Press.

Smith, R. M., Neisworth, J. T., & Greer, J. G. (1978). *Evaluating educational environments.* New York: Merrill/Macmillan.

Sparrow, S. S., Balla, D. A., & Cicchetti, D. V. (1984). *The Vineland Adaptive Behavior Scale.* Circle Pines, MN: American Guidance Service.

Spivack, G., & Spotts, J. (1966). *Devereux Child Behavior Rating Scale.* Devon, PA: Devereux Foundation.

Spivack, G., Spotts, J., & Haimes, P. E. (1967). *Devereux Adolescent Behavior Rating Scale.* Devon, PA: Devereux Foundation.

Sprick, R. S. (1981). *The solution book: A guide to classroom discipline.* Chicago: Science Research Associates.

Sprick, R. S. (1985). *Discipline in the secondary classroom: A problem-by-problem survival guide.* West Nyack: NY: The Center for Applied Research in Education.

Stephens, T. M. (1977). *Teaching skills to children with learning and behavior disorders.* New York: Merrill/Macmillan.

Stephens, T. M., Hartman, A. C., & Lucas, V. H. (1983). *Teaching children basic skills: A curriculum handbook* (2nd ed.). New York: Merrill/Macmillan.

Stephenson, W. (1953). *The study of behavior: Q-Technique and its methodology.* Chicago: University of Chicago Press.

Swift, M. (1982). *Devereux Elementary School Behavior Rating Scale* (2nd ed.). Devon, PA: Devereux Foundation.

Swift, M., & Spivack, G. (1972). *Hahnemann High School Behavior Rating Scale manual.* Philadelphia: Departmental Health Sciences, Hahnemann Medical College and Hospital.

Vernon, W. M. (1972). *Motivating children: Behavior modification in the classroom.* New York: Holt, Rinehart & Winston.

Walker, H. M. (1979). *The acting-out child: Coping with classroom disruption.* Boston: Allyn & Bacon.

Walker, H. M. (1983). *Walker Problem Behavior Identification Checklist.* Los Angeles: Western Psychological Services.

Walker, H. M., & McConnell, S. R. (1988). *Walker-McConnell Scale of Social Competence and School Adjustment.* Austin, TX: Pro-Ed.

Walker, H. M., McConnell, S., Holmes, D., Todis, B., Walker, J., & Golden, N. (1983). *The Walker social skills curriculum: The ACCEPTS program.* Austin, TX: Pro-Ed.

Walker, H. M., Todis, B., Holmes, D., & Horton, G. (1988). *The Walker social skills curriculum: The ACCESS program.* Austin, TX: Pro-Ed.

Wallace, G., & Kauffman, J. M. (1986). *Teaching students with learning and behavior problems* (3rd ed.). New York: Merrill/Macmillan.

Weinstein, R. S. (1982). *Expectations in the classroom: The student perspective.* Invited address, Annual Conference of the American Educational Research Association, New York.

Weller, C., & Strawser, S. (1981). *Weller-Strawser Scales of Adaptive Behavior for the learning disabled.* Novato, CA: Academic Therapy.

Wolf, M. M., Hanley, E. L., King, L. A., Lachowicz, J., & Giles, D. K. (1970). The timer-game: A variable interval contingency for the management of out-of-seat behavior. *Exceptional Children, 37,* 113–117.

Wood, M. M., & Long, N. J. (1991). *Life space intervention: Talking with children and youth in crisis.* Austin, TX: Pro-Ed.

PART II

Teaching Academic Skills

CHAPTER **6**

Assessing Math Skills

M any students with learning problems have math deficiencies that result in practical and emotional problems. Daily living requires numerous math skills; for example, planning and monitoring time, shopping, computing percentages for purchases or tips, making estimations, interpreting recipe measurements, measuring for carpet purchases or cooking, computing scores in games, banking, and maintaining a check book. Moreover, in school settings, math problems often result in school failures and seem to generate high levels of anxiety. Bartel (1990) states that students with math deficiencies are as disabled as individuals who are unable to read.

Research indicates that the math deficiencies of students with learning problems emerge in the early years and continue throughout secondary school. Thus, math problems are common at all age levels. During the preschool and primary years, many young children cannot sort objects by size, match objects, understand the language of arithmetic, or grasp the concept of rational counting. During the elementary years, they have trouble with computational skills. In the middle and upper grades, students experience difficulty with fractions, decimals, percentages, and measurement. Secondary students may experience problems in these areas, but it is not uncommon for them to make errors like those of younger students—for example, errors in place value and basic facts.

The mathematical knowledge of students with learning problems tends to progress approximately one year for each two years of school attendance (Cawley & Miller, 1989). Warner, Alley, Schumaker, Deshler, and Clark (1980) found that the math progress of students with learning disabilities reaches a plateau after seventh grade. The students in their study achieved only one more year's growth in math from seventh through twelfth grade. Both studies report that the mean math scores of students with learning disabilities in the twelfth grade are high-fifth grade.

Learning problems in math traditionally have received less attention than those in other academic areas. Fortunately, during the 1980s, the teaching of mathematics received extensive interest from both the public and professional communities. In 1989, the National Council of Teachers of Mathematics and the National Research Council released reports calling for major reforms in mathematics instruction. Given that traditional mathematics instruction is failing many students, not just those with learning problems, the reason for concern is apparent. Fortunately, the efforts of several educators have resulted in significant contributions regarding mathematics instruction for students with learning problems. The works of Cawley and his associates (Cawley, 1984, 1985; Cawley & Miller, 1989), Carnine and his associates (Engelmann & Carnine, 1982; Kelly, Gersten, & Carnine, 1990; Silbert, Carnine, & Stein, 1990), and Thornton and her associates (Bley & Thornton, 1989; Thornton, 1989; Thornton & Toohey, 1985) represent major efforts to understand and ameliorate the mathematical deficits of students with learning problems.

Reforms in mathematics education are expected to increase the overall complexity of the mathematics curriculum. Regular and special educators must work together to ensure that students with learning problems do not become victims of instruction reforms that are insensitive to their unique learning and emotional needs.

DEVELOPMENT OF MATH SKILLS

Mathematics has a logical structure. Students first construct simple relationships and then progress to more complex tasks. As the student progresses in this ordering of math tasks, the learning of skills and content transfers from each step to the next. Several studies (J. L. Brown, 1970; Callahan & Robinson, 1973; Phillips & Kane, 1973) indicate that the best learning sequences come from arranging instruction in learning hierarchies. Hierarchies of math skills that are useful in planning specific interventions are provided by Silbert et al. (1990) and Underhill, Uprichard, & Heddens (1980). Appendix A includes a scope and sequence skills list that shows a math hierarchy by skill area as well as a hierarchy of what commonly is stressed at each grade level. Although the hierarchy stops at sixth grade, these skills also apply to many adolescents with learning problems because their problems usually involve skills taught in the elementary grades. Basically, the hierarchy in Appendix A indicates the following skill introduction sequence: addition and subtraction—first and second grades, multiplication and division—third and fourth grades, fractions—fourth and fifth grades, and decimals and percent—fifth and sixth grades.

Several cognitive factors are needed for a student to progress in mathematics. The ability to form and remember associations, understand basic relationships, and make simple generalizations appears to be the basic cognitive factor needed to begin formal math instruction (Bartel, 1990). More complex cognitive factors are needed as the student progresses from lower-level math skills to higher-order ones. Moreover, the mastery of lower-level math skills is essential to learning higher-order ones; thus, the concept of *learning readiness* is important in math instruction. For example, a youngster who has not mastered basic facts in multiplication is not ready for division. Many authorities (Copeland, 1979; Underhill et al., 1980) claim that failure to understand basic concepts in beginning math instruction contributes heavily to later learning problems. Unfortunately, students with learning problems often are taught math in a rote manner and never achieve an understanding of basic concepts.

Readiness for Number Instruction

Piaget (1965) describes several concepts basic to understanding numbers: classification, ordering and seriation, one-to-one correspondence, and conservation. Mastering these concepts is necessary for learning higher-order math skills.

Classification is one of the most basic intellectual activities and must precede work with numbers (Piaget, 1965). It involves a study of relationships, such as likenesses and differences. Activities include categorizing objects according to a specific property. For example, children may group buttons according to color, then size, then shape, and so on. Most children 5 to 7 years old can judge objects as similar or dissimilar on the basis of properties such as color, shape, size, texture, and function (Copeland, 1979).

Ordering is important for sequencing numbers. Many children do not understand order until they are 6 or 7 years of age (Copeland, 1979). They first must understand the *topological* relation of order. When counting objects, students must order them so that each object is counted only once. The teacher can display objects in a certain order and ask the students to arrange identical objects in the same order. Ordering activities include sequencing blocks in a certain pattern, lining up for lunch in a specific order, and completing "pattern" games—for example, students are given a series such as

$$X-O-X-O-X-O-X-\underline{}$$

and tell what goes in the blank.

Topological ordering involves arranging a set of items without considering a quantity relationship between each successive item. The combination of *seriation* and *ordering,* however, involves ordering items on the basis of *change* in a property, such as length, size, or color. An example of a seriation task would be arranging items of various lengths in an order from shortest to longest with each successive item being longer than the preceding item. Children 6 to 7 years old usually master ordering and seriation (Copeland, 1979).

One-to-one correspondence is the basis for counting to determine how many and is essential for mastering computation skills. It involves understanding that one object in a set is the same number as one object in a different set, whether or not characteristics are similar. If a teacher places small buttons in a glass one at a time and the students place the same number of large buttons one at a time in a glass, the glass containing the large buttons soon displays a higher stack. If students respond "Yes" to the question "Does each glass have the same number of buttons," they understand one-to-one correspondence. If they respond "No, because the buttons are higher in one glass," they are not applying one-to-one correspondence and instead are judging on the basis of sensory cues. Most children 5 to 7 years old master the one-to-one correspondence concept. Initial activities consist of matching identical objects, whereas later activities should involve different objects. Sample activities are giving one pencil to each child, matching each head with a hat, and matching a penny to each marble.

Piaget (1965) considers the concept of *conservation* fundamental to later numerical reasoning. Conservation means that the quantity of an object or the number of objects in a set remains constant regardless of spatial arrangement. Copeland (1979) describes two types of conservation: quantity and number. Conservation of quantity is illustrated in the familiar Piagetian experiments of pouring identical amounts of water into a tall, thin glass and a low, wide glass and rolling a piece of clay into a ball and a long roll. Students who recognize that the amount of water or clay remains constant probably understand conservation of quantity. Conservation of number involves understanding that the number of objects in a set remains constant whether the objects are close together or spread apart. The teacher can ask students to select a spoon for each of seven plates and have them check their work by putting each spoon on each plate. The teacher then can remove the spoons, put them in a stack, and ask the students if there is still the same number of spoons and plates. If they respond "Yes," they probably understand the concept of conservation of number (Copeland, 1979). Most children master conservation between the ages of 5 and 7.

Several authorities consider an understanding of Piaget's concepts to be a prerequisite for formal math instruction. Many teachers in preschool through first grade directly teach to help students understand these concepts. Moreover, some authorities recommend that teachers in later grades should spot deficits in these concepts and provide remedial instruction.

Readiness for More Advanced Mathematics

Once formal math instruction begins, students must master operations and basic axioms to acquire skills in computation and problem solving. Operations are well-known: addition, subtraction, multiplication, and division. Basic axioms are less familiar. Some axioms that are especially important for teaching math skills to students with learning problems are commutative property of addition, commutative property of multiplication, associative property of addition and multiplication, distributive property of multiplication over addition, and inverse operations for addition and multiplication.

Commutative Property of Addition. No matter what order the same numbers are combined in, the sum remains constant:

$$a + b = b + a$$

$$3 + 4 = 4 + 3$$

Commutative Property of Multiplication. Regardless of the order of the numbers being multiplied, the product remains constant:

$$a \times b = b \times a$$

$$9 \times 6 = 6 \times 9$$

Associative Property of Addition and Multiplication. Regardless of grouping arrangements, the sum or product is unchanged:

Addition

$$(a + b) + c = a + (b + c)$$

$$(4 + 3) + 2 = 4 + (3 + 2)$$

Multiplication

$$(a \times b) \times c = a \times (b \times c)$$

$$(5 \times 4) \times 3 = 5 \times (4 \times 3)$$

Distributive Property of Multiplication Over Addition. This rule relates the two operations:

$$a(b + c) = (a \times b) + (a \times c)$$

$$5(4 + 3) = (5 \times 4) + (5 \times 3)$$

Inverse Operations. These axioms relate operations that are opposite in their effects. The following equations demonstrate inverse operations:

Addition and Subtraction

$a + b = c$	$5 + 4 = 9$
$c - a = b$	$9 - 5 = 4$
$c - b = a$	$9 - 4 = 5$

Multiplication and Division

$a \times b = c$	$9 \times 3 = 27$
$c \div a = b$	$27 \div 9 = 3$
$c \div b = a$	$27 \div 3 = 9$

ASSESSMENT CONSIDERATIONS

The assessment of math concepts and skills follows a general-to-specific format. As presented in Figure 6.1, assessment begins with an evaluation of general math skills. At this level a span of skills (for example, operations, word problems, measurement, and so on) is tested. Standardized or informal survey tests typically are used to assess general math skills. The primary goal of assessment at this level is to identify the overall strengths and weaknesses of the student. Also, standardized scores frequently are used to identify math disabilities and qualify students for special education services. Specific skill assessment usually involves the use of standardized diagnostic tests or informal tests; however, informal tests are the preferred instruments for evaluating specific math skills. At this level, the purpose of assessment is to determine specific teaching objectives. The assessment of problem-solving skills involves examining the student's ability to solve word problems. This assessment tests the student's ability to apply mathematical concepts and operations to real-life problems and to determine

General skills assessment
↓
Specific skills assessment
↓
Problem-solving assessment
↓
Attitude toward mathematics

FIGURE 6.1
Math assessment progression.

problem-solving instructional objectives. Finally, diagnostic interviews and informal testing are used to evaluate the student's attitudes and feelings about learning math. These affective factors frequently provide essential insights into planning math instruction. Throughout the math assessment process (general skills to attitude assessment), it is important to examine types of errors, understanding, and mastery learning.

Examining Math Errors

Although the specific error patterns of each student must be considered individually, it is helpful to examine some of the research regarding types of errors made by many students at different grades.

Computation. In a study of third graders, Roberts (1968) reports that careless numerical errors and poor recall of addition and multiplication facts were found with the same frequency in all levels of ability. Random responses and the wrong operation occurred frequently with students of low ability. Random responses accounted for the most errors in low-ability students, and defective algorithm techniques accounted for the most errors of students in the other three ability levels.

In a study of seventh graders' errors in computation, Lankford (1972) reports that many errors were the result of the use of defective algorithms. An algorithm includes the specific steps used to compute a math problem. An algorithm is defective if it does not deliver the correct answer. For example, the student who adds 24 + 16 by adding each number without regard for place value (that is, $2 + 4 + 1 + 6 = 13$) is using a defective algorithm, because the correct answer is 40.

Cox (1975) conducted a study of error patterns across skill and ability level among students with and without learning problems. In a comparison with students without learning problems, she found that the average percentages of systematic errors in multiplication and division were much higher for the special education students. The majority of errors for all students occurred because of a failure to understand the concepts of multiplication and division. Moreover, Cox found that without intervention many of these youngsters persisted in making the same systematic errors for a long period of time.

In a study of multiplication and division errors committed by students with learning disabilities ($n = 213$), Miller and Milam (1987) found that the majority of the errors were caused by a lack of prerequisite skills. Errors in multiplication primarily were the result of a lack of knowledge of multiplication facts and inadequate addition skills. Errors in division included many subtraction and multiplication errors. The most frequent error in division was failure to include the remainder in the quotient. Miller and Milam conclude,

> Many of the errors discovered in this study indicated a lack of student readiness for the type of task required. Students were evidently not being allowed to learn and practice the skills necessary for higher order operations. The implications are obvious: students *must* be allowed to learn in a stepwise fashion or they will not learn at all. (p. 121)

Kelly et al. (1990) examined the error patterns of secondary students with learning disabilities in adding and multiplying fractions. They found that the errors of students instructed via a basal program primarily involved a confusion of the algorithms for addition and multiplication of fractions. Moreover, an effective curriculum design decreased error patterns and resulted in better achievement. Kelly et al. conclude that a strong relationship exists between the number and types of errors and the curriculum.

The determination of a specific error is important because corrective intervention is influenced by the type of error. For example, the type of error can influence whether the student receives place value instruction or specific algorithm instruction. Howell and Kaplan (1980) provide the following guidelines for conducting an error analysis:

1. Collect an adequate behavior sample by having the student do several problems of each type in which you are interested.
2. Encourage the student to work, but do nothing to influence the responses the student makes.
3. Record all responses the student makes, including comments.
4. Look for patterns in the responses.
5. Look for exceptions to any apparent pattern.
6. List the patterns you have identified as assumed causes for the student's computational difficulties. (pp. 250–251)

The following common error patterns in addition, subtraction, multiplication, and division illustrate some of the computational difficulties of students with learning problems.

1. The sums of the ones and tens are each recorded without regard for place value:

$$
\begin{array}{r}
83 \\
+ 67 \\
\hline
1410
\end{array}
\qquad
\begin{array}{r}
66 \\
+ 29 \\
\hline
815
\end{array}
$$

2. All digits are added together (defective algorithm and no regard for place value):

$$
\begin{array}{r}
67 \\
+ 31 \\
\hline
17
\end{array}
\qquad
\begin{array}{r}
58 \\
+ 12 \\
\hline
16
\end{array}
$$

3. Digits are added from left to right. When the sum is greater than 10, the unit is carried to the next column on the right. This pattern reflects no regard for place value:

$$
\begin{array}{r}
\overset{2\,1}{476} \\
+ 851 \\
\hline
148
\end{array}
\qquad
\begin{array}{r}
\overset{3\,7}{753} \\
+ 693 \\
\hline
1113
\end{array}
$$

4. The smaller number is subtracted from the larger number without regard for placement of the number. The upper number (minuend) is subtracted from the lower number (subtrahend), or vice versa:

$$
\begin{array}{r}
627 \\
- 486 \\
\hline
261
\end{array}
\qquad
\begin{array}{r}
861 \\
- 489 \\
\hline
428
\end{array}
$$

5. Regrouping is used when it is not required:

$$
\begin{array}{r}
\overset{6\,1}{1\cancel{7}5} \\
- 54 \\
\hline
1111
\end{array}
\qquad
\begin{array}{r}
\overset{7\,1}{1\cancel{8}5} \\
- 22 \\
\hline
1513
\end{array}
$$

6. When regrouping is required more than once, the appropriate amount is not subtracted from the column borrowed from in the second regrouping:

$$
\begin{array}{r}
\overset{5\,1\,1}{\cancel{6}32} \\
- 147 \\
\hline
495
\end{array}
\qquad
\begin{array}{r}
\overset{4\,1\,1}{\cancel{5}23} \\
- 366 \\
\hline
167
\end{array}
\qquad
\begin{array}{r}
\overset{4\,1\,1}{\cancel{5}63} \\
- 382 \\
\hline
181
\end{array}
$$

7. The regrouped number is added to the multiplicand in the tens column prior to performing the multiplication operation:

$$
\begin{array}{r}
\overset{2}{1}7 \\
\times \quad 4 \\
\hline
128
\end{array}
\qquad
\begin{array}{r}
\overset{4}{4}6 \\
\times \quad 8 \\
\hline
648
\end{array}
$$

8. The divisor and dividend are reversed. For example, the student thinks $8 \div 4$ and $4 \div 2$ instead of $40 \div 8$ and $20 \div 4$:

$$
\begin{array}{r}
2 \\
8\overline{)40}
\end{array}
\qquad
\begin{array}{r}
2 \\
4\overline{)20}
\end{array}
$$

9. The zero in the quotient is omitted:

$$\begin{array}{r} 21 \\ 6\overline{)1206} \\ \underline{1200} \\ 6 \\ \underline{6} \end{array}$$

10. The first numerator is divided by the second numerator, and the result becomes the numerator for the answer. The first denominator is divided by the second denominator, and the result becomes the denominator for the answer. In both divisions, remainders are ignored. (Notice that the faulty procedure yields a correct answer in the second example.)

$$\frac{7}{10} \div \frac{2}{4} = \frac{3}{2}$$

$$\frac{4}{8} \div \frac{2}{8} = \frac{2}{1}$$

Many computational errors stem from an inadequate understanding of place value. Lepore (1979) analyzed the computational errors of 79 youngsters age 12 to 14 with mild learning problems. The type of error they made most frequently involved regrouping, a procedure that requires understanding place value. Place value is introduced in the primary grades; however, students of all ages continue to make mistakes because they cannot comprehend that the same digit expresses different orders of magnitude depending on its *location* in a number. Many of the error patterns presented earlier reflect an inadequate understanding of place value.

Ashlock (1990) provides a thorough listing of computational error patterns. In addition to analyzing the student's work, one of the best ways to determine error patterns is to ask the student to show how the answer was computed. The response may offer immediate insight into the error pattern and its cause.

Problem Solving. Recently, the problem-solving skills of students with learning prob-lems have received much attention. Problem-solving skills primarily are assessed via word problems. Research indicates that many students with learning problems have trouble solving word problems, especially those categorized as more difficult (Russell & Ginsburg, 1984; Scheid, 1990). One way of varying the difficulty level of word problems is to vary what is unknown. For example, the following word problems increase in difficulty as a function of what is unknown.

1. Tom has 5 stickers. Pam gave her 3 more. How many stickers does Tom have now? (Result unknown)
2. Tom has 5 stickers. How many more does he need to have 7? (Change unknown)
3. Tom had some stickers. Pam gave him 3 more. Now he has 7. How many stickers did Tom have to start with? (Start unknown)

Cawley, Miller, and School (1987) found that students with math disabilities experienced difficulty with problems that include extraneous information. Montague and Bos (in progress) report that students with math disabilities have difficulties (a) predicting operations (such as multiplication or subtraction), (b) choosing correct algorithms for multistep problems, and (c) correctly completing problems. Fortunately, several researchers (Cawley et al., 1987; Goldman, 1989; Montague & Bos, 1986) indicate that strategies exist to help students with learning problems be successful problem solvers.

Determining Level of Understanding

Students frequently memorize a fact or algorithm without understanding the concept or operation involved in the computation. This process leads to the rote memorization of information that is not comprehended. In reading, it is analogous to word calling without comprehension. An understanding of the information to be learned improves memorization and the manipulation of math concepts, operations, and axioms to solve computation and word problems. Thus, knowledge of the levels of understanding in mathematics is vital to math assessment and instruction. Underhill et al. (1980) report that there are several basic levels of learning in mathematical learning experiences: *concrete*, *semiconcrete*, and *abstract*.

Concrete Level.   The concrete level involves the manipulation of objects. This level can be used to help the student relate manipulative and computational processes. At this level the learner concentrates on both the manipulated objects and the symbolic processes (such as 6×3) that describe the manipulations (Underhill et al., 1980). For example, in assessing or teaching multiplication, the teacher presents the problem 5×3 and instructs the student to display the problem using objects. The student looks at the first number, 5, and forms 5 groups using paper plates. The student then looks at the second number, 3, and places 3 objects in each plate. The student counts or adds the number of objects in the plates and says "5 groups times 3 objects equals 15 objects." This procedure illustrates that the student understands at a concrete level that 5×3 means 5 groups of 3 objects equals 15 objects. Some students demonstrate their need for concrete-level activities by counting on their fingers when requested to complete simple computational problems. Concrete experiences are important for teaching and assessing skills at all levels in the math hierarchy.

Semiconcrete Level.   The semiconcrete level involves working with illustrations of items in performing math tasks. Items can include dots, lines, pictures of objects, or nonsense items. Some authorities divide this level into semiconcrete and semiabstract (Underhill et al., 1980). *Semiconcrete* refers to using pictures of real objects, whereas *semiabstract* involves the use of

tallies. In this book, *semiconcrete* refers to both pictures and tallies. A worksheet that requires the learner to match sets of the same number of items is a semiconcrete-level task. One way to assess a student's understanding at this level is for the teacher to present a problem (such as 5×3) and ask the student to use drawings (that is, lines and tallies) to solve the problem. The student looks at the first number, 5, and draws five horizontal lines. The student then looks at the second number, 3, and draws three tallies on each line. The student counts or adds the number of tallies on the lines and says "5 groups times 3 tallies equals 15 tallies." This procedure illustrates that the student knows at a semiconcrete level of understanding that 5×3 means 5 groups of 3 items equals 15 items. Most commercial math programs include worksheets of tasks at this level. Many students with math learning problems need practice at this level to master a concept or fact. Often students demonstrate their reliance on this level by supplying their own graphic representations. For example, the problems $5 + 4 = \underline{\ \ }$ and $3 \times 2 = \underline{\ \ }$ may be approached in the following manner:

$$
\begin{array}{cccc}
5 & ///// & 3 & // \\
+\,4 & //// & \times\,2 & // \\
\hline
9 & & 6 & // \\
\end{array}
$$

At the semiconcrete level, the emphasis is on developing associations between visual models and symbolic processes.

Abstract Level.   The abstract level involves the use of numerals. For example, in computation this level involves working only with numerals to solve math problems. Students who have difficulty in math usually need experience at the concrete and semiconcrete levels before they can use numerals meaningfully. Traditionally, assessment has focused on the abstract level. However, authorities in mathematics education (Engelhardt, 1976; Underhill et al., 1980) maintain that assessment should not be limited to the abstract level. These researchers stress that the goal of assessment is to determine the learner's ability to relate to math computation in a meaningful way. To do this, they suggest using tasks at each of the levels. Sample activities for assessing levels of understanding are presented later in this chapter.

Determining Mastery Learning

Many educators use percentage scores to determine a mastery level for a skill. In many cases these scores are a valid measure of a student's mastery learning. For some students, however, percentage scores are not sufficient for assessing mastery. Many students with learning problems produce accurate answers at a slow rate and use tedious procedures (such as counting on fingers and drawing tallies for large numbers) to compute answers without understanding the math concept or operation. Several authorities (Kirby & Becker, 1988; Lovitt, 1989) report that slow rates of computation are a primary problem of students with math disabilities. Wood, Burke, Kunzelmann, and Koenig (1978) examined the math rates of successful students, unsuccessful students, and community workers. In nearly every comparison, the rates of unsuccessful students were lower than the rates of successful students. Also, the rates of successful students were about the same as community workers.

As noted in Chapter 2, rate is an excellent measure of mastery learning. In addition to helping with retention and higher math performance, high rates of correct responses help students complete tests on time, finish homework quickly, and keep score in games. Math rate assessment involves the use of probes (that is, a sheet of selected math problems) that are administered under timed conditions (usually one minute). Scores are computed by counting the number of correct and incorrect digits written per minute. Sample probes are presented later in this chapter.

FORMAL MATH ASSESSMENT

Standardized Tests

Standardized math tests are norm-referenced and provide many kinds of information. They usually are classified into two categories: survey or achievement, and diagnostic. Survey tests cover a broad range of math skills and are designed to provide an estimate of the student's general level of achievement. They yield a single score, which is compared with standardized norms and converted into standard scores or a grade- or age-equivalent score. Survey tests are useful in screening students to identify those who need further assessment. Diagnostic tests, in contrast, usually cover a narrower range of content and are designed to assess the student's performance in math skill areas. Diagnostic tests aim to determine the student's strengths and weaknesses.

Survey Tests. Most achievement tests include sections covering specific academic areas, such as reading, spelling, and math. Each of these specific academic areas is divided into skill areas. For example, a math section may be divided into numerical reasoning, computation, and word problems. Several of the commonly used survey tests are listed in Table 6.1.

Diagnostic Tests. No one diagnostic test assesses all mathematical difficulties. The examiner must decide on the purpose of the assessment and select the test that is most suited to the task. Because quantitative scores are not very useful in developing a systematic instructional program, most diagnostic tests are criterion-referenced. However, five standardized diagnostic math tests are discussed.

TABLE 6.1
Standardized survey tests with math subtests.

Test	Grade Level	Math Areas Assessed
California Achievement Tests (1985)	K–12	Computation, concepts, and applications

This group-administered test has a locator test to identify the level of the test that is more appropriate. There are two forms of the test, and criterion-referenced objectives are available.

| *Diagnostic Achievement Battery—2* (Newcomer & Curtis, 1990) | 1–9 | Mathematics reasoning and mathematics calculation |

The Mathematics Reasoning Subtest consists of 30 items in which a mathematical problem is presented orally and the student must solve the problem without paper or pencil. In the Mathematics Calculation Subtest the student works directly on a math calculation worksheet of 36 problems that become progressively more difficult.

| *Kaufman Test of Educational Achievement (K-TEA)* (Kaufman & Kaufman, 1985) | 1–12 | Applications and computation |

This individually administered test includes 60 items on math concepts and applications in practical situations as well as 60 items on computation involving basic operations, exponents, symbols, abbreviations, and algebraic equations. A brief form also is available. *K-TEA* ASSIST software provides quick score conversion and error analysis.

| *Metropolitan Achievement Tests* (Prescott, Balow, Hogan, & Farr, 1984) | K–12 | Concepts, problem solving, and computation |

This group-administered test has been available since 1937. A diagnostic battery that covers specific educational objectives also is available.

| *Peabody Individual Achievement Test—Revised (PIAT-R)* (Markwardt, 1989) | K–12 | Skills ranging from matching and recognizing numbers to solving geometry and trigonometry problems |

This individually administered test features an easy-to-use easel kit. Sometimes scores are inflated because the student response always involves selecting the correct answer from among four choices. Reading is not required, and the math subtest of 100 multiple-choice items takes 10 to 15 minutes to administer. *PIAT-R* ASSIST software is available for scoring ease.

| *SRA Achievement Series* (Naslund, Thorpe, & Lefever, 1985) | K–12 | Concepts, computation, and problem solving |

This test is group-administered and yields grade equivalents, percentiles, stanines, and standard scores.

| *Stanford Achievement Test* (Gardner, Rudman, Karlsen, & Merwin, 1982) | 1–9 | Concepts, computation, and applications |

This group-administered test is both norm-referenced and objective-referenced. A lower level of the test and an upward extension also are available.

| *Woodcock-Johnson Psycho-Educational Battery—Revised* (Woodcock & Johnson, 1989) | K–college | Calculation and applied problems |

This individually administered test has two forms and examines basic math skills and application of those skills. The supplemental battery includes a subtest in quantitative concepts.

1. *Key Math—Revised: A Diagnostic Inventory of Essential Skills* (Connolly, 1988). This test for students in kindergarten through ninth grade is based on a comprehensive content scope and sequence and is composed of 13 subtests in three areas: basic concepts, operations, and applications. The test is individually administered in about 35 to 50 minutes. Spring and fall norms are given, and two parallel forms are available. Derived scores for the three area composites and total test include standard scores, grade and age equivalents, percentile ranks, and stanines. *Key Math-R* ASSIST software is available to provide quick derived score conversion as well as suggestions for remedial instruction.

2. *Sequential Assessment of Mathematics Inventories (SAMI)* (Reisman, 1985). This test assesses math performance of students in kindergarten through eighth grade. The classroom survey tests provide a profile of student performance in math concepts and skills, and the individual assessment battery gives an in-depth evaluation. The test covers 300 objectives organized into the eight strands of mathematics language, ordinality, number and notation, measurement, geometric concepts, computation, word problems, and mathematical applications. Items are sequenced from easy to difficult. In addition to the norm-referenced items, *SAMI* provides follow-up probes to test the student's grasp of the material at various cognitive levels, including the concrete level. Manipulative materials included in the concrete materials kit can be used with the probes for diagnosing concrete representation. *SAMI* offers three types of test activities (paper/pencil, oral interview, concrete representation) to provide a well-rounded picture of the student's strengths and weaknesses in math skills.

3. *Stanford Diagnostic Mathematics Test* (Beatty, Madden, Gardner, & Karlsen, 1984). This group-administered test is designed to identify the strengths and weaknesses of students in the areas of number system and referenced numeration, computation, and applications. It is available for all grade levels, and each item is based on a behavioral objective. The *Stanford* is divided into four separate tests, and the appropriate test is selected according to the student's grade level. Except for the level for first through third grade, the student must read many of the examples. Although some items are at the semiconcrete level, most are at the abstract level. No provision is made for assessing at the concrete level or for error analysis, and the multiple-choice format introduces an element of chance in a student's performance. The *Stanford* tests, like most group tests, should be supplemented with additional diagnostic work to determine the specific needs of students with learning problems.

4. *Test of Early Mathematics Ability—2* (Ginsburg & Baroody, 1990). This test is designed for students in preschool through third grade and the areas assessed include concepts of relative magnitude, counting skills, calculation, reading and writing numerals, number facts, calculational algorithms, and base-ten concepts. This test of early math functioning also is useful with older children who have learning problems. It can be used as a diagnostic instrument to determine specific strengths and weaknesses as well as used to measure progress, evaluate programs, screen for readiness, discover the basis for poor school performance, identify gifted students, and guide instruction and remediation.

5. *Test of Mathematical Abilities* (V. L. Brown & McEntire, 1984). This test is designed for use with students in third through twelfth grade to provide standardized information about the student's skill in two major areas (story problems and computation). The test

also provides related information regarding the student's expressed attitudes toward mathematics, understanding of vocabulary used in a mathematical sense, and understanding of the functional use of mathematical facts and concepts. Standard scores and percentiles are provided, and the test scores differentiate diagnostically between groups of students who have problems in mathematics and those who do not.

Criterion-Referenced Tests

Standardized tests compare one individual's score with norms, which generally does not help diagnose the student's math difficulties. However, criterion-referenced tests, which describe the student's performance in terms of criteria for specific skills, are suited to assessing specific difficulties. Like standardized tests, criterion-referenced tests are divided into survey and diagnostic tests.

Criterion-referenced achievement or inventory tests usually cover several academic areas. Each of these areas is further subdivided into skill categories. Whereas survey tests locate general problem areas, diagnostic tests focus on more specific difficulties. Of all available published tests, criterion-referenced diagnostic tests are the most suited for identifying specific math problems. Several criterion-referenced survey and diagnostic math tests are discussed.

1. *Brigance Diagnostic Comprehensive Inventory of Basic Skills* (Brigance, 1982) and *Brigance Diagnostic Inventory of Essential Skills* (Brigance, 1980). The *Inventory of Basic Skills* is designed for use with students in kindergarten through ninth grade and assesses the areas of numbers (readiness skills), number facts, computation of whole numbers, fractions and mixed numbers, decimals, percents, word problems, metrics, and math vocabulary. The *Inven-*

tory of Essential Skills is designed for use with students in fourth through twelfth grade and focuses on minimal academic and vocational competencies (stresses functional and applied math skills). The *Brigance Inventories* are survey tests that provide instructional objectives and include a record-keeping system for monitoring the progress of individual students. Also, placement tests are included that yield an age and grade equivalent. These levels are not based on norms but were determined by examining the hierarchical content of commercial materials.

2. *Classroom Learning Screening Manual* (Koenig & Kunzelmann, 1980). This criterion-referenced survey test for students in kindergarten through sixth grade includes items in precomputational number skills, addition facts, subtraction facts, multiplication facts, and division facts through divisor of 9. The device uses probes to assess each fact. Students are administered the probes in the selected math facts, and the number of correct and incorrect responses per minute is recorded. Criterion rates are suggested.

3. *Enright Diagnostic Inventory of Basic Arithmetic Skills* (Enright, 1983). This diagnostic test is designed for use with students in fourth grade through adult age who have math difficulties. Items include computation of whole numbers, fractions, and decimals. The test determines the exact math skill at which to begin instruction and provides a clear explanation of computation errors. Four types of tests are included: (a) basic facts tests determine mastery of all basic facts in addition, subtraction, multiplication, and division; (b) wide-range placement tests establish a starting point for the skill placement test; (c) skill placement tests assess skills in each computation area and determine the appropriate skill test for error analysis; and (d) skill

tests identify specific computation problems for corrective instruction. The inventory is based on a task analysis of basic computation skills, and error analysis for 144 arithmetic computation skills indicates the student's process errors. The test can be administered individually or in groups.

4. *Hudson Education Skills Inventory— Mathematics* (Hudson & Colson, 1989). This inventory provides a curriculum-based assessment of math skills for use in planning instruction for students in kindergarten through twelfth grade. The mathematics subskills assessed include numeration, addition, subtraction, multiplication, division, fractions, decimals, percentages, time, money, measurement, statistics, graphs, tables, geometry, and word problems. A test-down/teach-up model is used in which the examiner ends the test at the student's actual level of performance and then can simply teach up the curriculum skills sequence. An optional computerized program provides a printed instructional planning form for each student that includes goals and objectives in the basic skill area.

5. *Kraner Preschool Math Inventory* (Kraner, 1976). This criterion-referenced test is designed for use with preschool children (ages 3 to 6 1/2 years old). It includes 77 items that are divided into the seven categories of counting, cardinal numbers, quantity, sequence, position, direction, and geometry/measurement.

6. *Multilevel Academic Skills Inventory* (Howell, Zucker, & Morehead, 1982). This inventory includes criterion-referenced objectives in the math areas of computation and application. It is designed for students in first through eighth grade and includes survey tests, placement tests, and specific level tests. Student response booklets are included in four areas: addition/subtraction; multiplication/division; fractions; and decimals, ratios, and percents/applications.

Unfortunately, commercial instruments for diagnosing understanding at the three levels of understanding in math are sparse. Only the *Sequential Assessment of Mathematics Inventories* (Reisman, 1985) includes a concrete materials kit containing manipulative materials for test activities involving concrete representation. Most available tests, which have test items only at the abstract level, are useful mainly in helping to determine the student's level of achievement and general area of weakness. Once the problem area is identified, the teacher can use informal assessment techniques to determine the levels of instruction necessary for teaching specific concepts and facts. (See Underhill et al., 1980, for a detailed discussion of mathematical diagnostic models and related issues.)

INFORMAL MATH ASSESSMENT

Informal assessment involves examining the student's daily work samples or administering teacher-constructed tests. Informal assessment is essential for the frequent monitoring of student progress and for making relevant teaching decisions regarding individual students. Such assessment enables teachers to sample specific skills through the use of numerous test items that are related directly to the math curriculum. Because the content of standardized math tests and the content of math curriculum texts have a low degree of overlap (Tindal & Marston, 1990), the practice of assessing each student's achievement within the curriculum becomes essential. With informal techniques the teacher also can determine the student's understanding of math concepts at the concrete, semiconcrete, and abstract level. By asking appropriate questions and listening to students' responses, the teacher can assess not only whether a student can solve a particular problem but *how* the problem is solved. Informal assessment thus is an efficient way of determining the instructional needs of individual students.

Curriculum-Based Measurement

When a teacher assesses progress within the curriculum to measure achievement, she is assured that what is being assessed is what is being taught. Curriculum-based measurement (CBM) offers the teacher a standardized set of informal assessment procedures for conducting a reliable and valid assessment of a student's achievement within the math curriculum.

Assessing an Entire Class on a Span of Skills. Curriculum-based measurement begins with a survey test of a span of appropriate skills. From the results of a survey test, a box plot (see Chapter 2) is developed for making instructional decisions. Five steps are required in developing and administering a survey test:

1. *Identify a sequence of successive skills included in the school curriculum.* Many curriculum unit tests or review tests provide a source of sequenced skills and corresponding test items. Appendix A provides a scope and sequence list of math skills developed from a review of numerous basal math programs. This review indicated that there is much agreement (90 to 95 percent) among the basal scope and sequence skills lists.
2. *Select a span of math skills to be assessed.* For a beginning fourth-grade class, it may be appropriate to administer a survey test of the computation skills covered in the third grade. This third-grade survey test would help identify students with math problems and provide some normative information to facilitate goal setting. Once a scope and

sequence skills list across the grades has been identified, the teacher has a multitude of options for developing survey tests for different spans of skills. The options enable the teacher to identify instructional groups (such as high, average, and low achievers) or plan instruction for a new student.

3. *Construct or select items for each skill within the range selected.* A survey test may be used to assess computation and problem-solving skills. To maintain an adequate sample, it is a good practice to include a minimum of three items per specific skill. Table 6.2 presents a survey test of computation skills covered in a typical third-grade curriculum. This test could be used at the beginning of fourth grade to determine which students need additional teaching on third-grade skills and which are ready for fourth-grade computation skills.
4. *Administer and score the survey test.* Table 6.3 presents administration directions, and Table 6.4 provides scoring procedures.
5. *Display the results in a box plot, interpret the results, and plan instruction.* To increase the accuracy of the results, it helps to develop an alternate form of the survey test and administer both survey probes of the same skills. Chapter 2 provides procedures to use in developing a box plot with multiple-probe administrations. The results should be interpreted to help with the placement of students in instructional groups and for planning individual programs.

Monitoring the Progress of Individual Students on Specific Skills. From an analysis of student performances on a span of skills, the teacher develops probes of specific skills for monitoring student progress. Specific skill monitoring usually involves a single skill until mastery is achieved. The scope and sequence skills list in Appendix A that features the sequence of skills within an operation (that is,

TABLE 6.2
Survey test of third-grade computation skills.

1.	476 + 200		2.	807 + 407		3.	9000 + 3010	
4.	3168 + 5426		5.	4727 + 2761		6.	7964 + 385	
7.	604 − 237		8.	704 − 369		9.	501 − 269	
10.	7134 − 3487		11.	5094 − 4630		12.	8751 − 2683	
13.	9 × 8		14.	9 × 6		15.	8 × 7	
16.	7 × 8		17.	6 × 9		18.	9 × 0	
19.	8 × 0		20.	6 × 1		21.	1 × 8	
22.	34 × 2		23.	26 × 1		24.	31 × 8	
25.	24 ÷ 3 = _____		26.	12 ÷ 2 = _____		27.	$4\overline{)16}$	
28.	$5\overline{)16}$		29.	$4\overline{)34}$		30.	$7\overline{)58}$	

TABLE 6.2
Continued

31.	17 × 5	32. 49 × 2	33. 16 × 4
34.	82 × 4	35. 74 × 2	36. 81 × 5
37.	342 × 2	38. 637 × 1	39. 312 × 3
40.	436 × 3	41. 578 × 6	42. 638 × 7

43. 3)‾36‾   44. 4)‾44‾   45. 2)‾28‾

46. 3)‾51‾   47. 4)‾72‾   48. 7)‾84‾

49. 1/3 of 6 = _____   50. 1/4 of 8 = _____   51. 1/2 of 12 = _____

52. $\frac{1}{2} = \frac{}{4}$ 53. $\frac{2}{3} = \frac{}{6}$ 54. $\frac{2}{5} = \frac{}{15}$

Item Analysis of Survey Test

Problems 1–3:   Addition: With zero
Problems 3–6:   Addition: Multidigit plus multidigit
Problems 7–9:   Subtraction: Regrouping more than once with zero in minuend
Problems 10–12: Subtraction: Four-digit numbers with regrouping
Problems 13–21: Multiplication: Facts for 6 through 9 with 0 and 1 properties and order proportions
Problems 22–24: Multiplication: Two-digit number times one-digit number
Problems 25–27: Division: Facts
Problems 28–30: Division: Two-digit number divided by one-digit number, with remainder
Problems 31–33: Multiplication: Two-digit number times one-digit number, with tens regrouping
Problems 34–36: Multiplication: Two-digit number times one-digit number, with hundreds regrouping
Problems 37–39: Multiplication: Three-digit number times one-digit number, without regrouping
Problems 40–42: Multiplication: Three-digit number times one-digit number, with regrouping
Problems 43–45: Division: Two-digit number divided by one-digit number, without regrouping
Problems 46–48: Division: Two-digit number divided by one-digit number, with regrouping
Problems 49–51: Fractions: Of a whole number
Problems 52–54: Fractions: Equivalent fractions

TABLE 6.3
Curriculum-based measurement administration directions.

The following steps are recommended for administering 2-minute timings to individuals or groups:

1. Select the appropriate measurement device (that is, survey test or specific skill probe) and pass it out to students face down.
2. Give standardized directions at the beginning of the administration. Also, use specific instructions for different parts of some tests.

"The sheets I just passed out are math problems." If a single skill probe is used, tell the students the operation: "All problems are _____ (addition, subtraction, multiplication, or division)." If a multiple skill probe is used, say: "There are different types of problems on the sheet. There are some addition, subtraction, and multiplication problems. Look at each problem closely when you compute it."

"When I say 'Begin,' turn the sheet over and answer the problems. Start with the first problem at the beginning of the first row. Touch the problem. Work across the sheet and then go to the beginning of the next row. If you are unable to do a problem, mark an X on it and go to the next problem. If you finish one page, go to the next page. Do you have any questions?"

"Ready, start."

3. Monitor student work to ensure that students are following the directions (that is, working in successive rows). Watch for students who want to skip around and do the easy problems.
4. When 2 minutes have elapsed, say: "Stop. Put your pencils down."

---

addition, subtraction, and so on) is useful in sequencing specific skill monitoring. Selected research on rates that reflect mastery or proficiency on specific math skills is presented in Table 6.5. Generally a rate of 40 to 60 correct digits per minute is appropriate for most students on math computation problems.

The chart in Figure 6.2 displays a student's progress on specific skills during an 8-week period. In this chart the mastery or aim line is set at 50 correct digits per minute. The chart shows that the student has mastered two skills and has started working on a third skill.

Teacher-Constructed Tests

Teacher-constructed tests are essential for individualizing math instruction. They enable the teacher to identify problems, determine level of understanding, and monitor progress. The type of test the teacher selects depends, in part, on the purpose of the assessment. To identify specific problem areas, the teacher

may construct a survey test with items at several levels of difficulty. Four steps are involved in developing and using this type of test:

1. *Select a hierarchy that includes the content area to be assessed.* This hierarchy may come from a math program series, a curriculum guide, or a textbook. A sample math hierarchy is included in Appendix A.
2. *Decide on the span of skills that needs to be evaluated.* Because a hierarchy includes a wide range of skills, the teacher must select which range of skills needs to be evaluated with an individual student. This is done by examining the student's performance on published tests and by analyzing the math curriculum by grade level. In deciding on the span, begin with items that are easy for the student and proceed to more difficult ones.
3. *Construct items for each skill within the range selected.* A survey test is designed to assess the student's computation (abstract)

TABLE 6.4
Scoring procedures for math curriculum-based measurement.

1. Underline each correct digit.
2. Score numerals written in reverse form (for example, $\mathcal{E}$ for 3) as correct.
3. Score a correct digit in the proper place (column) as correct.
4. Award full points (number of digits used in solving a problem) when the student has a correct answer even if the work is not shown.
5. If the student displays work and the answer is incorrect, give credit for each digit done correctly.
6. Do not count numerals written for regrouping purposes (that is, carried numbers).
7. Do not count remainders of zero.
8. When an X or a zero is placed correctly as a place holder, count it as one digit correct.
9. Give credit for any correct digits even if the problem has not been completed.
10. Count the number of digits correct in each row and write that number at the end of the row.
11. Total the number of correct digits and record it on the paper.

Sample Scoring of Student Copy

2
+ 4
6   (1 digit correct)

12
+ 26
38   (2 digits correct)

38
× 9
342   (3 digits correct)

12 R 42
63)798   (4 digits correct)

63X   (3 digits correct with x)
168   (3 digits correct)
126   (3 digits correct)
42   (2 digits correct)

15 digits correct

$\frac{1}{4} + \frac{1}{3} =$ _____

$\frac{3}{12} + \frac{4}{12} = \frac{7}{12}$

(3 digits correct) (3 digits correct) (3 digits correct)

9 digits correct

Sample Teacher Copy for Scoring

2
+ 4
6   [1]

12
+ 26
38   [2]

38
× 9
342   [3]

Row Total
6

12R42
63)798

63 ×
168
126
42   [15]

$\frac{1}{4} + \frac{1}{3} =$ _____

$\frac{3}{12} + \frac{4}{12} = \frac{7}{12}$ [9]

Row Total
24

Total digits correct: 30

TABLE 6.5

Suggested proficiency rates for math skills.

Write Math Facts

	Digits in Simple Add. and Sub. Equations		Addition Facts 0–9 Gr. 2–3		Sub. Facts (1–5) and Facts Top Numb. 2–9 Gr. 2–3		Add. Facts Sums 10–18 and Sub. Facts Top Numb. 6–9 Gr. 3–4		Two-column Addition with Regrouping Gr. 4–5		Two-column Subtraction with Regrouping Gr. 4–6		Mult. Facts Through ×9 Gr. 5–6		Division Facts Through Divisor of 9 Gr. 6	
	Cor.	Err.	Cor.	Err.	Cor.	Err.	Cor.	Err.	Cor.	Err.	Cor.	Err.	Cor.	Err.	Cor.	Err.
Koenig & Kunzelmann (1980)			60	—	60	—	90	—	60	—	60	—	90	—	60	—
Precision Teaching Project (Montana)			70–90	—	70–90	—	70–90	—	70–90	—	70–90	—	70–90	—	70–90	—
Regional Resource Center (1971) (not grade-specific)	50	0									50	0	50	0	50	0
Smith & Lovitt (1982)			50+	0	45+	0							50+	0	45+	0
Starlin & Starlin (1973)			20–30	0–2	20–30	0–2	40–60	0–2	40–60	0–2	40–60	0–2	40–60	0–2	40–60	0–2
Wood, Burke, Kunzelmann, & Koenig (1978)	125	0			68	0			60	0	56	0	80	0	47	0

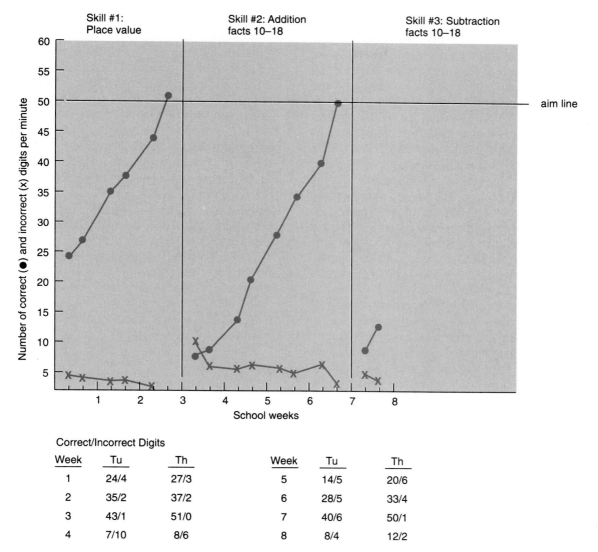

FIGURE 6.2
Chart showing a student's progress on specific skills.

Correct/Incorrect Digits

Week	Tu	Th	Week	Tu	Th
1	24/4	27/3	5	14/5	20/6
2	35/2	37/2	6	28/5	33/4
3	43/1	51/0	7	40/6	50/1
4	7/10	8/6	8	8/4	12/2

performance within a hierarchy; thus, all items are at the abstract level. If an untimed criterion approach is used, try to include three items for each skill and set 67 percent or 100 percent as a passing criterion (Underhill et al., 1980). Most commercial tests do not adequately sample a specific skill. Including three items per skill helps to control the factor of carelessness and provides an adequate test sample. The use of probes is helpful in assessing. To use timed probes, construct one for each skill and establish the criterion in terms of correct and incorrect responses per minute. To obtain a valid performance, each probe should be administered at least three times. The highest rate from the three samples is used for determining criterion. From analyzing the proficiency rates presented in Table 6.5, it appears that a useful criterion is a score of 50 to 60 correct digits per minute with no errors. Rate, however, can vary as a function of age, motor (handwriting) skills, and difficulty level of the task. E. Haughton (personal communication, January 5, 1983) cautions against setting the aim for the rate correct too low. He notes that levels of performance that are associated with retention, endurance, and application are needed, and these levels are independent of age and should be achieved as soon as possible. In Table 6.5, the rates provided by Wood, Burke, Kunzelmann, and Koenig (1978) are based on adults who use math in their occupations. Thus, they may be good indicators of application rates. For more information on application rates across a variety of math skills, the reader is encouraged to review the Wood et al. study.

4. *Score the test, and interpret the student's performance.* The teacher starts with the easiest skill items and applies the "two out of three" (67 percent) criterion or the criterion of rate correct per minute. At the point where the criterion is not achieved, the teacher analyzes the student's performance (that is, errors, basic fact deficit, and understanding) to determine what skill to teach. The test also can be used to monitor student progress.

The division test presented in Table 6.6 is based on the math scope and sequence skills list in Appendix A. The skills become progressively more difficult, and three items are presented for each skill. It is sometimes less threatening for the student if the items in each skill area are written on index cards. In using the test, the teacher scores the student's responses under each skill and determines if the 67 percent criterion has been obtained. Failure to reach criterion on a skill alerts the teacher to a specific area of difficulty. These areas can become the target of instruction and further assessment. It is common practice to use the type of survey test presented in Table 6.6 to determine what to teach. However, after becoming more skillful in assessment and teaching, the teacher can construct other diagnostic tests to determine the student's level of understanding. The scope and sequence skills list presented in Appendix A can be used in developing informal tests in other math areas.

Teacher-constructed tests can include several formats. The following are sample skills and related assessment items:

1. Identifies before or after for numbers to 10. Fill in the spaces:

    1 __ 3 __ 5 __ 7 __ 9

    What numbers are missing:

    __ 2 __ __ 5 __ 7 __ 9

    Fill in the spaces:

Before		After
__	9	__
__	7	__
__	3	__

2. Identifies the greater or smaller number for numbers 0 to 100 and uses > and <. Put in order:

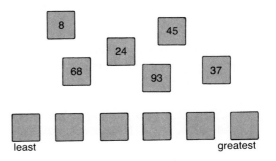

TABLE 6.6
Survey test: Division with whole numbers.

Skill

1. Identify symbols for division by circling problems that require division.

*Criterion
(score in %)*

$$\begin{array}{c} 4 \\ +4 \end{array} \qquad 6 \times 3 \qquad 6 \div 2 \qquad 7 - 4 \qquad \dfrac{6}{2}$$

$$4\overline{)16} \qquad 7 \times 4 \qquad 8 \div 2 \qquad \dfrac{9}{3} \qquad \begin{array}{c} 13 \\ \times\ 7 \end{array}$$

$$4 \times 1 \qquad \begin{array}{c} 6 \\ -2 \end{array} \qquad 8\overline{)64} \qquad 6 + 2 \qquad 9 = 3$$

2. Compute basic division facts involving 1.
   $1\overline{)8} \qquad 1\overline{)7} \qquad 1\overline{)1}$

3. Compute basic division facts.
   $4\overline{)36} \qquad 7\overline{)42} \qquad 8\overline{)56}$

4. Compute division of a nonzero number by itself.
   $7\overline{)7} \qquad 29\overline{)29} \qquad 1\overline{)1}$

5. Compute quotient of a one- or two-place dividend and a one-place divisor with a remainder.
   $3\overline{)7} \qquad 4\overline{)7} \qquad 2\overline{)9}$ (1D÷1D)

   $8\overline{)74} \qquad 6\overline{)39} \qquad 3\overline{)17}$ (2D÷1D)

6. Compute quotient with expanding dividend.
   $3\overline{)9} \qquad 9\overline{)90} \qquad 3\overline{)900}$
   $2\overline{)6} \qquad 2\overline{)60} \qquad 2\overline{)600}$
   $4\overline{)8} \qquad 4\overline{)80} \qquad 4\overline{)800}$

7. Compute quotient of a three-place dividend and a one-place divisor.
   $8\overline{)638} \qquad 6\overline{)461} \qquad 3\overline{)262}$

8. Compute quotient of a many-place dividend with a one-place divisor.
   $7\overline{)47,864} \qquad 6\overline{)2783} \qquad 3\overline{)578,348}$

9. Compute quotient of a three-place dividend and a two-place divisor where divisor is multiple of 10.
   $40\overline{)681} \qquad 30\overline{)570} \qquad 10\overline{)874}$

TABLE 6.6
Continued

10. Compute quotient when divisors are 100, 1000, and so on.

    $100\overline{)685}$ $100\overline{)4360}$ $100\overline{)973}$

    $1000\overline{)6487}$ $1000\overline{)99490}$ $1000\overline{)7430}$

11. Compute quotient of a three-place dividend and a two-place divisor.

    $27\overline{)685}$ $39\overline{)871}$ $14\overline{)241}$

12. Compute quotient of a many-place dividend and a many-place divisor.

    $649\overline{)78,741}$ $3641\overline{)100,877}$ $247\overline{)8973}$

Note. When this test is administered, the directions for items 2–12 should simply state: Solve the following division problems.

Circle the greater number:

Put > or < in the ⬭:

23 ⬭ 32   8 ⬭ 19   94 ⬭ 76
13 ⬭ 42   43 ⬭ 29   65 ⬭ 59

3. Identifies place value with ones and tens. Fill in the spaces:

    56 = __ tens, __ ones
    39 = __ tens, __ ones
    98 = __ tens, __ ones

State the face value and the place value of the underlined digit:

4\underline{6}3   2\underline{8}   484\underline{3}

face value __   face value __   face value __

place value __   place value __   place value __

Complete the following:

    9 ones, 3 tens = __
    6 tens, 4 ones = __
    0 tens, 3 ones = __

4. Computes three two-digit numerals, sum of ones greater than 20.
   Add:

26	57	29
18	38	47
+ 47	+ 49	+ 36

5. Demonstrates mastery of subtraction facts: sums 0 to 9.

Complete:

$$\begin{array}{cccc} 6 & 9 & 8 & 7 \\ -\ 3 & -\ 5 & -\ 0 & -\ 4 \end{array}$$

Subtract:

$8 - 3 =$ _____ $5 - 2 =$ _____

$7 - 1 =$ _____ $9 - 7 =$ _____

6. Identifies unit fraction inequalities.
   Circle the numeral that represents the smaller number of each pair:

$$\begin{array}{cccccc} \dfrac{1}{2} & \dfrac{1}{3} & \dfrac{1}{6} & \dfrac{1}{2} & \dfrac{1}{4} & \dfrac{1}{3} \end{array}$$

7. Writes fractions in numeral form.
   Write the fractional numerals for each of the shaded areas in numeral form:

_____

_____

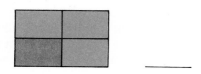

_____

8. Identifies fraction names for 1.
   Fill in each shaded box.

$1 = \dfrac{\boxed{}}{4}$ $1 = \dfrac{\boxed{}}{67}$ $1 = \dfrac{\boxed{}}{798}$

Teacher-made probes also can be used to identify problem areas. Mixed probes are used to locate areas that need further assessment or instruction. Figure 6.3 presents a mixed probe in addition. Each of the following categories has nine items: basic addition facts of sums to 9 (first item and then every fourth item), two-digit number plus two-digit number with no regrouping (second item and then every fourth item), two-digit number plus one-digit number with no regrouping (third item and then every fourth item), and basic addition facts of sums to 18 (fourth item and then every fourth item). On this probe, the student can obtain a maximum score of 63 correct digits with no errors. After three timings, a high score of 50 or more correct digits per minute with no errors is a reasonable criterion for diagnostic purposes. If the student fails to reach criterion on a mixed probe, it is important to analyze the responses and locate the items being missed. This analysis provides the teacher with information for further assessment with specific skill probes (such as 0–9 facts). Also, specific skill probes can be used to monitor the daily progress of the student.

Assessing at the Concrete, Semiconcrete, and Abstract Levels.

As discussed earlier, learning math facts and concepts progresses through three levels of understanding: concrete, semiconcrete, and abstract. Most published tests consist of abstract-level items; therefore, they do not yield information on the student's understanding at the semiconcrete and concrete levels. The student's level of understanding determines whether manipulative, pictorial, or abstract experiences are appropriate. To obtain the type of information required

4 + 3	22 +41	33 + 6	9 + 7	6 + 2	36 +62	41 + 3	6 + 5	8 + 0
53 +44	78 + 1	5 + 8	7 + 2	43 +36	82 + 5	7 + 4	5 + 3	61 +37
42 + 4	8 + 7	4 + 5	33 +52	31 + 8	9 + 9	6 + 0	24 +53	65 +24
7 + 6	5 + 2	82 +13	37 + 2	6 + 6	4 + 4	31 +18	57 +32	7 + 9

Name _____ Date _____

Correct Digits: _____

Incorrect Digits: _____

Patterns: 0-9 facts _____/9

2D + 2D _____/9

2D + 1D _____/9

0-18 facts _____/9

Comments: _____

_____

_____

FIGURE 6.3
Mixed addition probe with no regrouping.

for effective instructional planning, the teacher must construct analytical tests that focus on both identifying difficulties and determining level of understanding. Items at the concrete level always should involve real objects; items at the semiconcrete level always should use pictures or tallies; and numerals always should be used in items at the abstract level.

Assessment at the concrete level can begin either with a written problem (such as $5 + 3 =$ ___), with a display of objects, or with both numerals and objects. When assessment begins with a written problem, the student is instructed to read the problem and then solve it by using objects. When assessment begins with objects, the student is instructed to look at the display of objects (for example, ∘∘∘ + ∘∘ = ___) and then write the problem and solve it. When assessment begins with both numerals and objects (for example, 5 ⚇ + 3 ⚇ = __), the student uses the objects (that is, counts, removes, or groups) to solve the problem. The preferred sequence is to (a) use both numerals and objects, (b) only use objects and have the student write the problem, and (c) only use written problems and have the student arrange objects to solve them. Assessment at the semiconcrete or representational level can begin with a written problem, with drawings (that is pictures or tallies), or with both numerals and drawings (for example, 5 ///// + 3 /// = __). When assessment begins with a written problem the student is instructed to solve the problem by drawing tallies. When assessment begins with pictures or tallies, the student is instructed to write the problem and solve it. When assessment begins with both numerals and drawings, the student uses the pictures or drawings to solve the problem. The preferred sequence in assessing at the semiconcrete level is to (a) use both numerals and drawings, (b) only use drawings and have the student write the problem, and (c) only use written problems and have the student generate the drawings (tallies). Sometimes it is not feasible to present the problem via objects or drawings because the operation is not implied. For example, in arranging the objects for subtraction, only the objects or drawings for the minuend are used in beginning the problem. The subtrahend involves taking away objects from the minuend; thus, the subtrahend is not part of the original stimulus. At the abstract level only numerals are used in presenting and solving problems.

The examples that follow should help the reader develop analytical math tests in specific skill areas. Also, the instructional activities presented in Chapter 7 for each of the operations (at all three levels) can provide guidance in developing assessment items. For a more detailed discussion of this type of assessment, the reader is referred to Underhill et al. (1980).

Skill: Counting 1–5

Concrete level: Count the blocks.

Semiconcrete level: Circle five blocks.

Abstract level: Count to five and circle the number.

1   2   3   4   5   6   7

Skill: Addition Facts (0–9)

Concrete level: Write problem and sum.

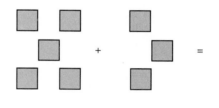

—————————   +   —————————   =   —————————

Semiconcrete level: Write problem and sum.

```
   / / / / /      _____
+    / / /     +  _____
                  _____
```

Abstract level: Write sum.

```
   5
+ 3
```

Skill: Addition Facts (0–18)

Concrete level: Arrange blocks to show tens and ones, and then write the sum.

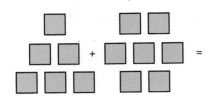

$$\underline{\hspace{2cm}6\hspace{2cm}} + \underline{\hspace{2cm}7\hspace{2cm}} = \underline{\hspace{2cm}}$$

Student work:

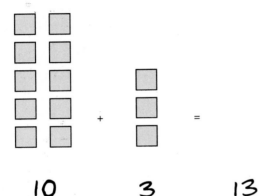

$$\underline{\hspace{1.5cm}10\hspace{1.5cm}} + \underline{\hspace{1cm}3\hspace{1cm}} = \underline{\hspace{1cm}13\hspace{1cm}}$$

Semiconcrete level: Circle tens and write sum.
Student work:

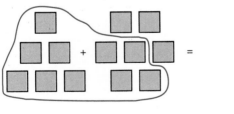

$$\underline{\hspace{1.5cm}10\hspace{1.5cm}} + \underline{\hspace{1cm}3\hspace{1cm}} = \underline{\hspace{1cm}13\hspace{1cm}}$$

Abstract level: Write sum.

$$\begin{array}{r} 6 \\ + 7 \\ \hline \end{array}$$

Skill: Addition Operation without Regrouping

Concrete level: Let $\boxed{\hphantom{ww}}$ = 1 ten and $\square$ = 1 one.
    Write problem and sum.

Semiconcrete level: Let $\bigcirc$ = 1 ten and
    $\circ$ = 1 one.
    Write problem and sum.

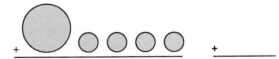

Abstract level: Write sum.

$$\begin{array}{r} 12 \\ + 14 \\ \hline \end{array}$$

Skill: Addition with Regrouping Ones and Tens

Concrete level: Write sum and use string to group units.

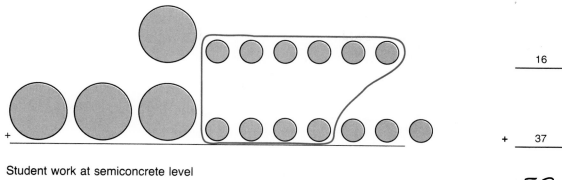

$$\begin{array}{r} 16 \\ + \quad 37 \\ \hline \end{array}$$

$$53$$

Student work at semiconcrete level

Student work:

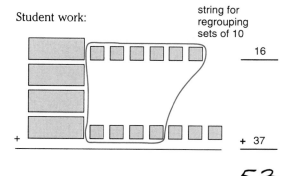

string for regrouping sets of 10

$$\begin{array}{r} 16 \\ + \quad 37 \\ \hline \end{array}$$

$$53$$

Semiconcrete level: Write sum and circle to group units.
Student work (see above):
Abstract level: Write sum.

$$\begin{array}{r} 16 \\ + \ 37 \\ \hline \end{array}$$

Skill: Addition with Regrouping Ones, Tens, and Hundreds

Concrete level: Let $\square$ = 1 hundred, $\square$ = 1 ten, and $\square$ = 1 one.

Write sum and use strings to show work. Figure 6.4 shows an example of student work with this kind of grouping.
Semiconcrete level: Use the place value chart to show work. Write sum.

100s	10s	1s
// /	///// /////	///// ///////

= _____

Abstract level: Write sum.

$$\begin{array}{r} 266 \\ + \ 157 \\ \hline \end{array}$$

Skill: Basic Subtraction Facts

Concrete level: Write difference or missing addend.

$$\begin{array}{r} 7 \\ - \ 3 \\ \hline \end{array}$$

Student work:

$$\begin{array}{r} 7 \\ - \ 3 \\ \hline 4 \end{array}$$

moved away

Semiconcrete level: Write difference or missing addend.

$$\begin{array}{r} 7 \\ - \ 3 \\ \hline \end{array} \qquad ///////$$

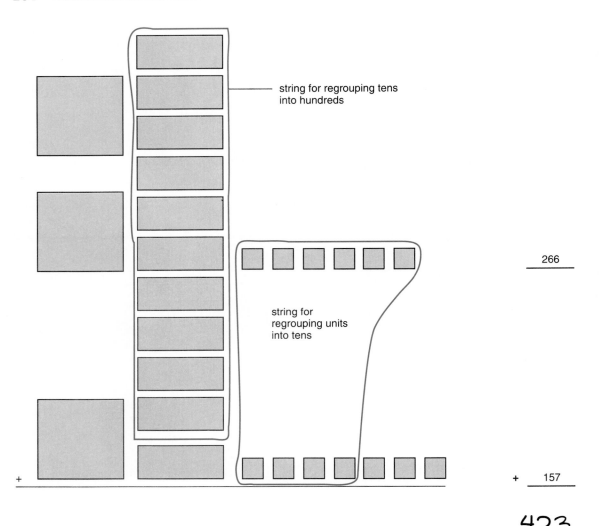

string for regrouping tens into hundreds

string for regrouping units into tens

266

+   157

423

FIGURE 6.4
Example of student work with grouping ones, tens, and hundreds.

Student work:

$$\begin{array}{r} 7 \\ -\ 3 \\ \hline 4 \end{array}$$ / / / / ✗✗✗   cross out 3 to take away

Abstract level: Write difference or missing addend.

$$\begin{array}{r} 7 \\ -\ 3 \\ \hline \end{array}$$

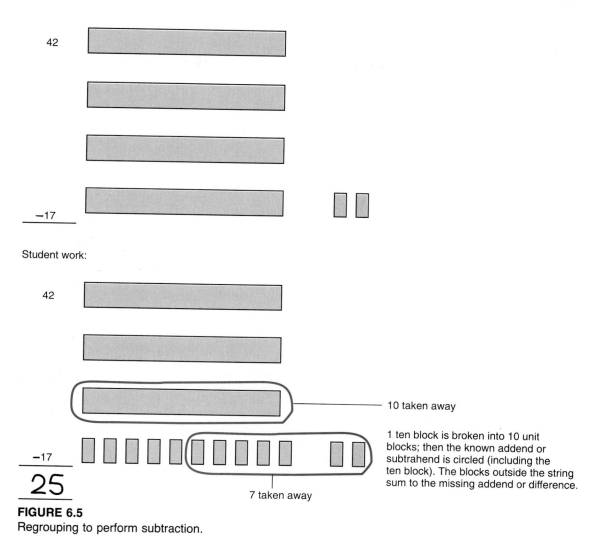

FIGURE 6.5
Regrouping to perform subtraction.

Skill: Subtraction Operation with Regrouping

Concrete level: Write difference or missing addend by rearranging blocks and use strings to show work, as shown in Figure 6.5.
Semiconcrete level: Write difference or missing addend and show work with slashes.

Student work:

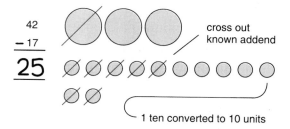

Abstract level: Write difference or missing addend.

$$\begin{array}{r} 42 \\ -\ 17 \\ \hline \end{array}$$

Skill: Basic Multiplication Facts

Concrete level:
a. Write product.

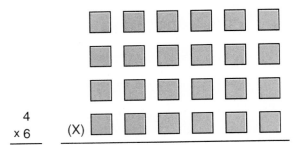

$$\begin{array}{r} 4 \\ \times 6 \\ \end{array} \quad (X)$$

b. Use blocks to show 4×6 matrix.
Semiconcrete level: Write product.

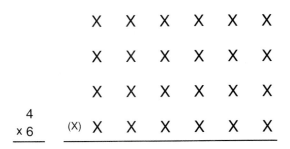

$$\begin{array}{r} 4 \\ \times 6 \\ \end{array} \quad (X)$$

Abstract level: Write product.

$$\begin{array}{r} 4 \\ \times\ 6 \\ \hline \end{array}$$

Skill: Basic Division Facts

Concrete level: Write quotient. Use strings to show work.
Student work:

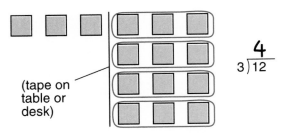

(tape on table or desk)

$$3\overline{)12} \quad 4$$

Semiconcrete level: Write quotient. Circle sets to show work.
Student work:

$$3\overline{)12} \quad 4$$

Abstract level: Write quotient.

$$3\overline{)12}$$

Skill: Division with Remainder

Concrete level: Write quotient. Given a large matrix of blocks, figure out how many sets of 4 are in 30, or $30 \div 4$. Use strings to show work, as shown in Figure 6.6.
Semiconcrete level:
a. Write quotient. Circle sets to show work with tallies.
Student work:

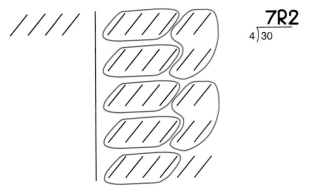

$$4\overline{)30} \quad 7R2$$

b. Write quotient. Given a large matrix covered with acetate, figure out the number of 4s in 30. Circle sets on matrix to display work.

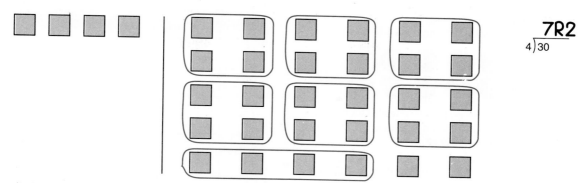

FIGURE 6.6
Student work showing division with blocks.

Student work:

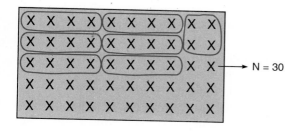

$$4\overline{)30}\;\;7\,R2$$

Abstract level: Write quotient.

$$4\overline{)30}$$

Skill: Recognize Simple Fractions

Concrete level: Let ☐☐☐☐☐ = 1 or ⅗ and
☐ = ⅕. Stack the blocks to show ⅗.
Student work:

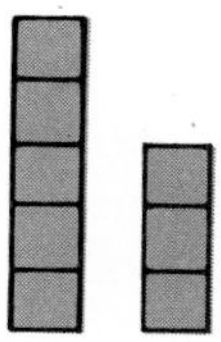

Semiconcrete level: Write a fraction for the shadowed part of the group.

Abstract level: Write the fraction for three-fifths.

Skill: Addition of Fractions with Like Denominators

Concrete level: Let [block] = ⅓. Write sum of ⅓ + ⅓ and show work with blocks.
  Student work:

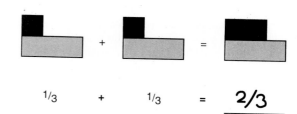

⅓   +   ⅓   =   **2/3**

Semiconcrete level: Display the sum of ⅓ + ⅓ by shading in the squares.

■□□ + ■□□ = □□□

Abstract level: ⅓ + ⅓ = ___

Skill: Money Change for Amounts up to $1.00

Concrete level: Given real money and items with marked prices, figure out correct change if a $.39 item is purchased with a dollar.

Semiconcrete level: Circle the coins given as change for a dollar when buying a $.39 item.

Abstract level: Answer this problem: How much change would you give when someone buys a $.39 item and gives you a dollar?

Evans, Evans, and Mercer (1986) provide a detailed discussion of math assessment that features guidelines for conducting periodic and continuous assessment in math. Periodic assessment includes an initial testing that generates instructional objectives, and periodic evaluations include checkups of general progress and in-depth evaluations of students experiencing difficulty. Continuous assessment focuses on monitoring the student's progress. It involves daily, weekly, or biweekly assessments. Silbert et al. (1990) highlight the importance of continuous assessment.

> The importance of careful monitoring cannot be overemphasized. The sooner the teacher detects a student's skill deficit, the easier it will be to remedy. For each day that a student's confusion goes undetected, the student is, in essence, receiving practice in doing something the wrong way. To ameliorate a confusion, the teacher should plan to spend 2 days reteaching for every day the student's confusion goes undetected. Thus, careful monitoring is a critical component of efficient instruction. (p. 12)

Charts can be used to locate math facts that have not been memorized. The teacher gives the student a test of selected facts (such as sums: 0–9, 10–18; differences: 0–9, 10–18; products: 0–9). Then the teacher records the student's performance on the chart: ✓ = basic fact memorized; — = basic fact not memorized. The chart for multiplication facts presented in Figure 6.7 shows that the student

X	0	1	2	3	4	5	6	7	8	9
0	✓	—	—	—	—	—	—	—	—	—
1	—	✓	✓	✓	✓	✓	✓	✓	✓	✓
2	—	✓	✓	✓	✓	✓	✓	✓	✓	✓
3	—	✓	✓	✓	✓	✓	✓	✓	✓	✓
4	—	✓	✓	✓	✓	✓	✓	✓	✓	✓
5	—	✓	✓	✓	✓	✓	✓	✓	✓	✓
6	—	✓	✓	✓	✓	✓	✓	✓	✓	—
7	—	✓	✓	✓	✓	✓	✓	✓	—	✓
8	—	✓	✓	✓	✓	✓	✓	—	✓	✓
9	—	✓	✓	✓	✓	✓	—	✓	✓	✓

FIGURE 6.7
Chart of a student's performance on basic multiplication facts.

is experiencing difficulty with facts involving 0. The chart for subtraction facts 0–18 presented in Figure 6.8 suggests that the student is having difficulty with two-digit minus one-digit facts, except those involving 9 and those in which the subtrahend equals the difference.

Inspection of the sample items readily shows that the student's level of math understanding must be assessed on an individual basis. Developing and administering analytical math tests take time. Some teachers need several years to build an ample file of such tests, which then must be organized and stored in a functional system. Because of the time constraints, some teachers reserve this type of assessment for students who are not progressing with systematic math instruction and who appear to have serious math difficulties. Others include concrete experiences in their teaching and construct tests that include semiconcrete and abstract items. Instruction for students with math learning problems should include experiences at each of the three levels for teaching specific concepts and skills.

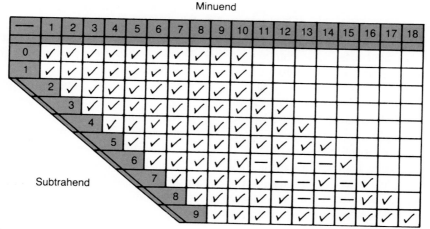

FIGURE 6.8
Chart of a student's performance on 0–18 subtraction facts.

Diagnostic Math Interviews

The diagnostic interview provides information to determine what math skills to teach the student and how to teach them. In this technique the student expresses thought processes while solving math problems. This technique often is used in administering diagnostic math tests.

The diagnostic interview enables the teacher to identify specific problems, error patterns, or problem-solving strategies in math. A sample interview illustrates how the procedure can yield important information:

The teacher gave Mary three multiplication problems and said, "Please do these problems and tell me how you figure out the answer." Mary solved the problems in this way:

$$\begin{array}{ccc} \overset{2}{27} & \overset{4}{36} & \overset{3}{44} \\ \underline{\times\ 4} & \underline{\times\ 7} & \underline{\times\ 8} \\ 168 & 492 & 562 \end{array}$$

For the first problem, Mary explained, "7 times 4 equals 28. So I put my 8 here and carry the 2. 2 plus 2 equals 4, and 4 times 4 equals 16.

So I put 16 here." Her explanations for the other two problems followed the same logic.

By listening to Mary and watching her solve the problems, the teacher quickly determined Mary's error pattern: She adds the number associated with the crutch (the number carried to the tens column) *before* multiplying the tens digit. Mary explained that she had been taught to add the number being carried when regrouping in addition. After identifying Mary's error pattern and its origin, the teacher could plan instruction for teaching the correct algorithm and developing an understanding of the multiplication process. Without the interview, the teacher incorrectly may have planned instruction in the basic multiplication facts.

Educators are aware that some students with learning problems have negative emotions concerning math. A history of frustration and difficulty with math understandably can lead to feelings of insecurity and strong negative attitudes. Clinical interviews offer an excellent technique for identifying negative emotions and attitudes toward math. Knowledge of these feelings helps teachers make adjustments in math instruction (for example, using graphic cues, prompts, reinforcement, charts) to alter a student's feelings. Several activities can be used in an interview session to assess attitudes:

1. Instruct the student to solve some math problems and observe the student's behavior (for example, makes negative statements, becomes upset, gives up quickly).
2. Have the student respond to some oral sentence-completion tasks. The teacher starts a sentence and the student responds aloud. The following are some sample starters:
   a. Math is very . . .
   b. My best subject is . . .
   c. During math lessons I feel . . .
3. Ask the student direct questions. The following are some sample questions:
   a. What is your favorite subject?
   b. Do you like to do math?
   c. What is your favorite thing about math?
   d. What do you not like about math?
   e. Do you use math outside school?
   f. What would you do to make math more interesting?

The validity of the diagnostic findings depends on the quality of the exchange between teacher and student. The teacher must establish a rapport and ensure that the student feels free to respond honestly. Some guidelines for conducting an interview include the following:

1. Establish rapport and be alert to the student's attitudes toward math throughout the session. It often is helpful to start with items that are easy for the student to do.
2. Focus only on the student's problem area that is the lowest on the skill sequence. Limit each session to one area of difficulty (for example, two-column addition with regrouping).

3. Allow the student the freedom to solve the problem in the student's own way.
4. Record the student's thinking processes, and analyze for error patterns and problem-solving techniques.
5. Once an error pattern or faulty problem-solving technique is discovered, introduce diagnostic activities for assessing the student's level of understanding. These activities should include tasks at the semiconcrete and concrete levels. (For more detailed discussions of diagnostic math interviews, see Ginsburg, 1987, and Lankford, 1974.)

REFERENCES

Ashlock, R. B. (1990). *Error patterns in computation: A semi-programmed approach* (5th ed.). New York: Merrill/Macmillan.

Bartel, N. R. (1990). Problems in mathematics achievement. In D. D. Hammill & N. R. Bartel, *Teaching students with learning and behavior problems* (5th ed., pp. 289–343). Boston: Allyn & Bacon.

Beatty, L. S., Madden, R., Gardner, E. F., & Karlsen, B. (1984). *Stanford Diagnostic Mathematics Test* (3rd ed.). San Antonio, TX: Psychological Corporation.

Bley, N. S., & Thornton, C. A. (1989). *Teaching mathematics to the learning disabled* (2nd ed.). Austin, TX: Pro-Ed.

Brigance, A. H. (1980). *Brigance Diagnostic Inventory of Essential Skills.* North Billerica, MA: Curriculum Associates.

Brigance, A. H. (1982). *Brigance Diagnostic Comprehensive Inventory of Basic Skills.* North Billerica, MA: Curriculum Associates.

Brown, J. L. (1970). Effects of logical and scrambled sequences in mathematical materials on learning with programmed instruction material. *Journal of Educational Psychology, 61,* 41–45.

Brown, V. L., & McEntire, E. (1984). *Test of Mathematical Abilities.* Austin, TX: Pro-Ed.

California Achievement Tests. (1985). Monterey, CA: California Test Bureau/McGraw-Hill.

Callahan, L. G., & Robinson, M. L. (1973). Task-analysis procedures in mathematics instruction of achievers and underachievers. *School Science and Mathematics, 73,* 578–584.

Cawley, J. F. (1984). *Developmental teaching of mathematics for the learning disabled.* Austin, TX: Pro-Ed.

Cawley, J. F. (1985). Cognition and the learning disabled. In J. Cawley (Ed.), *Cognitive strategies and mathematics for the learning disabled* (pp. 1–32). Austin, TX: Pro-Ed.

Cawley, J. F., & Miller, J. H. (1989). Cross-sectional comparisons of the mathematical performance of children with learning disabilities: Are we on the right track toward comprehensive programming? *Journal of Learning Disabilities, 23,* 250–254, 259.

Cawley, J. F., Miller, J. H., & School, B. A. (1987). A brief inquiry of arithmetic word-problem solving among learning disabled secondary students. *Learning Disabilities Focus, 2,* 87–93.

Connolly, A. J. (1988). *Key Math—Revised: A Diagnostic Inventory of Essential Mathematics.* Circle Pines, MN: American Guidance Service.

Copeland, R. W. (1979). *Math activities for children: A diagnostic and developmental approach.* New York: Merrill/Macmillan.

Cox, L. S. (1975). Diagnosing and remediating systematic errors in addition and subtraction computations. *The Arithmetic Teacher, 22,* 151–157.

Engelhardt, J. (1976). Diagnosis and remediation in school mathematics: Developing continuity among R and D efforts. In J. W. Heddens & F. D. Aquila (Eds.), *Proceedings of the Third National Conference on Remedial Mathematics.* Kent, OH: Kent State University.

Engelmann, S., & Carnine, D. (1982). *Corrective mathematics program.* Chicago: Science Research Associates.

Enright, B. E. (1983). *Enright Diagnostic Inventory of Basic Arithmetic Skills.* North Billerica, MA: Curriculum Associates.

Evans, S. S., Evans, W. H., & Mercer, C. D. (1986). *Assessment for instruction.* Boston: Allyn & Bacon.

Gardner, E. F., Rudman, H. C., Karlsen, B., & Merwin, J. C. (1982). *Stanford Achievement Test* (7th ed.). San Antonio, TX: Psychological Corporation.

Ginsburg, H. P. (1987). *Assessing the arithmetic abilities and instructional needs of students.* Austin, TX: Pro-Ed.

Ginsburg, H. P., & Baroody, A. J. (1990). *Test of Early Mathematics Ability—2.* Austin, TX: Pro-Ed.

Goldman, S. R. (1989). Strategy instruction in mathematics. *Learning Disability Quarterly, 12,* 43–55.

Howell, K. W., & Kaplan, J. S. (1980). *Diagnosing basic skills: A handbook for deciding what to teach.* New York: Merrill/Macmillan.

Howell, K. W., Zucker, S. H., & Morehead, M. K. (1982). *Multilevel Academic Skills Inventory.* San Antonio, TX: Psychological Corporation.

Hudson, F. G., & Colson, S. E. (1989). *Hudson Education Skills Inventory—Mathematics.* Austin, TX: Pro-Ed.

Kaufman, A. S., & Kaufman, N. L. (1985). *Kaufman Test of Educational Achievement.* Circle Pines, MN: American Guidance Service.

Kelly, B., Gersten, R., & Carnine, D. (1990). Student error patterns as a function of curriculum design: Teaching fractions to remedial high school students and high school students with learning disabilities. *Journal of Learning Disabilities, 1,* 23–29.

Kirby, J. R., & Becker, L. D. (1988). Cognitive components of learning problems in arithmetic. *Remedial and Special Education, 9*(5), 7–15, 27.

Koenig, C. H., & Kunzelmann, H. P. (1980). *Classroom learning screening manual.* New York: Merrill/Macmillan.

Kraner, R. E. (1976). *Kraner Preschool Math Inventory.* Austin, TX: Learning Concepts.

Lankford, F. G., Jr. (1972). *Some computational strategies of seventh grade pupils* (Project No. 2-C-013, Grant No. OEG-3-72-0035). Washington, DC: HEW Office of Education, National Center for Educational Research and Development (Regional Research Program) and Center for Advanced Study, University of Virginia.

Lankford, F. G., Jr. (1974). What can a teacher learn about a pupil's thinking through oral interviews? *The Arithmetic Teacher, 21,* 26–32.

Lepore, A. (1979). A comparison of computational errors between educable mentally handicapped and learning disability children. *Focus on Learning Problems in Mathematics, 1*, 12–33.

Lovitt, T. C. (1989). *Introduction to learning disabilities.* Boston: Allyn & Bacon.

Markwardt, F. C., Jr. (1989). *Peabody Individual Achievement Test—Revised.* Circle Pines, MN: American Guidance Service.

Miller, J. H., & Milam, C. P. (1987). Multiplication and division errors committed by learning disabled students. *Learning Disabilities Research, 2*(2), 119–122.

Montague, M., & Bos, C. S. (1986). The effect of cognitive strategy training on verbal math problem solving performance of learning disabled adolescents. *Journal of Learning Disabilities, 19*, 26–33.

Montague, M., & Bos, C. (in progress). *Cognitive and metacognitive characteristics of eighth grade students' mathematical problem solving.* University of Miami, Coral Gables, FL.

Naslund, R. A., Thorpe, L. P., & Lefever, D. W. (1985). *SRA Achievement Series.* Chicago: Science Research Associates.

National Council of Teachers of Mathematics. (1989). *Curriculum and evaluation standards for school mathematics.* Reston, VA: Author.

Newcomer, P. L., & Curtis, D. (1990). *Diagnostic Achievement Battery—2.* Austin, TX: Pro-Ed.

Phillips, E. R., & Kane, R. B. (1973). Validating learning hierarchies for sequencing mathematical tasks in elementary school mathematics. *Journal for Research in Mathematics Education, 4*, 141–151.

Piaget, J. (1965). *The child's conception of number.* New York: W. W. Norton.

Precision Teaching Project. Available from Skyline Center, 3300 Third Street Northeast, Great Falls, MT 59404.

Prescott, G. A., Balow, I. H., Hogan, T. P., & Farr, R. C. (1984). *Metropolitan Achievement Tests* (6th ed.). San Antonio, TX: Psychological Corporation.

Regional Resource Center. (1971). *Diagnostic Math Inventories* (Project No. 472917, Contract No. OEC-0-9-472917-4591 [609]). Eugene, OR: University of Oregon.

Reisman, F. K. (1985). *Sequential Assessment of Mathematics Inventories.* San Antonio, TX: Psychological Corporation.

Roberts, G. H. (1968). The failure strategies of third grade arithmetic pupils. *The Arithmetic Teacher, 15*, 442–446.

Russell, R., & Ginsburg, H. (1984). Cognitive analysis of children's mathematical difficulties. *Cognition and Instruction, 1*, 217–244.

Scheid, K. (1990). *Cognitive-based methods for teaching mathematics to students with learning problems.* Columbus, OH: LINC Resources.

Silbert, J., Carnine, D., & Stein, M. (1990). *Direct instruction mathematics* (2nd ed.). New York: Merrill/Macmillan.

Smith, D. D., & Lovitt, T. C. (1982). *The computational arithmetic program.* Austin, TX: Pro-Ed.

Starlin, C. M., & Starlin, A. (1973). *Guides to decision making in computational math.* Bemidji, MN: Unique Curriculums Unlimited.

Thornton, C. A. (1989). "Look ahead" activities spark success in addition and subtraction number fact learning. *The Arithmetic Teacher, 36* (April), 8–11.

Thornton, C. A., & Toohey, M. A. (1985). Basic math facts: Guidelines for teaching and learning. *Learning Disabilities Focus, 1*, 44–57.

Tindal, G. A., & Marston, D. B. (1990). *Classroom-based assessment: Evaluating instructional outcomes.* New York: Merrill/Macmillan.

Underhill, R. G., Uprichard, A. E., & Heddens, J. W. (1980). *Diagnosing mathematical difficulties.* Columbus, OH: Merrill/Macmillan.

Warner, M. M., Alley, G. R., Schumaker, J. B., Deshler, D. D., & Clark, F. L. (1980). *An epidemiological study of learning disabled adolescents in secondary schools: Achievement and ability, socioeconomic status and school experiences.* (Report No. 13). Lawrence: University of Kansas Institute for Research in Learning Disabilities.

Wood, S., Burke, L., Kunzelmann, H., & Koenig, C. (1978). Functional criteria in basic math skill proficiency. *Journal of Special Education Technology, 2*(2), 29–36.

Woodcock, R. W., & Johnson, M. B. (1989). *Woodcock-Johnson Psycho-Educational Battery—Revised.* Allen, TX: DLM.

CHAPTER 7

Teaching Math Skills

Mathematics has a logical structure. As indicated in Chapter 6, students first construct simple relationships and then progress to more complex tasks. As the student progresses in this ordering of math tasks, the learning of skills and content transfers from each step to the next. Several cognitive factors are needed for a student to progress in mathematics. To begin formal math instruction, the student must be able to form and remember associations, understand basic relationships, and make simple generalizations (Bartel, 1990). As the student progresses from lower-level math skills to higher-order ones, more complex cognitive factors are needed. Because the mastery of lower-level math skills is essential to learning higher-order ones, the concept of *learning readiness* is important in math instruction. In its *Twelve Components of Essential Mathematics,* the National Council of Supervisors of Mathematics (1988) highlights the need for students to know basic facts and be proficient in basic operations (addition, subtraction, multiplication, division). Many authorities (Kirby & Becker, 1988; Underhill, Uprichard, & Heddens, 1980) claim that failure to understand basic concepts in beginning math instruction contributes heavily to later learning problems. Unfortunately, many students with learning problems fail to achieve an understanding of basic math facts or develop fluency in using facts.

Fleischner, Garnett, and Shepherd (1982) note that the inability to acquire and maintain math facts at fluency levels sufficient for acquiring higher-level math skills is common among students with learning problems. De Corte and Verschaffel (1981) and Russell and Ginsburg (1984) report that unfamiliarity with basic number facts plays a major role in the math difficulties of students with math learning problems. Other researchers (Garnett & Fleischner, 1983; Thornton & Toohey, 1985) report that many students with learning disabilities lack proficiency in basic number facts. They note that these youngsters are unable to retrieve answers to math facts efficiently.

It is anticipated that reforms in math education will increase the overall complexity of the mathematics curriculum. Regular and special educators must work together to ensure that the instructional reforms are sensitive to the unique learning and emotional needs of students with learning problems. Although many students with math deficiencies exhibit characteristics (such as problems in memory, language, reading, reasoning, and metacognition) that predispose them to math disabilities, their learning difficulties often are compounded by ineffective instruction. Many authorities (Carnine, 1991; Cawley, Fitzmaurice-Hayes, & Shaw, 1988; Cawley, Miller, & School, 1987; Kelly, Gersten, & Carnine, 1990; Scheid, 1990) believe that poor or traditional instruction is the primary cause of the math difficulties of many students with learning problems. Numerous studies support the position that students with math disabilities can be taught to improve their mathematical performance (Kirby & Becker, 1988; Mastropieri, Scruggs, & Shiah, 1991; S. K. Peterson, Mercer, & O'Shea, 1988; Rivera & Smith, 1988; Scheid, 1990).

Given the poor math progress of students with learning problems and the call for a reform in math education to increase standards, a need clearly exists to design an effective math curriculum for these students. Without better math instruction, these youngsters will continue to face much frustration and failure. Cawley and Miller (1989) report that students with learning disabilities are capable of making progress in math throughout their school years, and that comprehensive programming is needed to ensure their math progress. Given the problems that students with learning problems exhibit with lower-level math skills (that is, many students do not know the 390 basic math facts after 5 or more years of school) and the importance of these skills to overall math achievement, it is apparent that comprehensive programming to teach basic math facts is needed.

This chapter is designed to help the teacher provide effective instruction to students with math problems. Included are research-based teaching components, basic teaching strategies, instructional activities for specific skills, instructional games, self-correcting materials, commercial programs and materials, and computer software programs.

BASIC TERMS AND PROCESSES

Before beginning math instruction, the teacher needs to know some of the basic terms used in math. Table 7.1 presents some major terms.

The teacher also should know basic information about the organization of math content. Five areas are essential to learning addition, subtraction, multiplication, and division: (a) understanding, (b) basic facts, (c) place value, (d) structures (laws), and (e) regrouping (Underhill et al., 1980). *Understanding* means comprehending the operation at the concrete, semiconcrete, and abstract levels. *Basic facts* must be memorized; these are the tools of computation. A basic fact is an operation on two one-digit whole numbers to obtain a one- or two-digit whole number; for example, $6 \times 4 = 24$. There are 390 basic facts— 100 addition, 100 subtraction, 100 multiplication, and 90 division facts. Once understanding and basic facts are mastered, the specific operation can be expanded readily by using *place value*. For example, if the student recognizes that 3×2 is 6, the place value concept can be applied to compute a series of problems such as the following:

TABLE 7.1

Math terms in basic computations.

Operation	Terms
Addition	8 ←addend +4 ←addend 12 ←sum
Subtraction (take away)	9 ←minuend −4 ←subtrahend 5 ←difference
Subtraction (add on)	9 ←sum −4 ←known addend 5 ←missing addend
Multiplication	8 ←multiplicand × 5 ←multiplier 40 ←product
Division	8 ←quotient 6)48 ←dividend ↑ divisor

Note: Although the phrase *addend plus addend equals sum* is used, technically $8 + 4$ is a *sum* and 8×5 is a *product*.

3	30	300
× 2	× 2	× 2
6	60	600

3000	30	300
× 2	× 20	× 20
6000	600	6000

Structures are mathematical properties that help the student. A student who memorizes that 7×3 is 21 but sees 3×7 as a new problem to memorize needs to understand a basic structure (in this case, the commutative property of multiplication) to learn multiplication effectively. The last area is *regrouping*, which commonly is referred to as *carrying* and *borrowing.* It is necessary to understand regrouping to solve more complex problems in each of the four operations.

Another important factor in teaching math is knowledge of algorithms. Algorithms are the steps used in solving a math problem. Numerous algorithms are presented later in this chapter.

RESEARCH ON EFFECTIVE MATH INSTRUCTION

The amount of research on teaching math has increased substantially in the last decade, and it now is clear that both curriculum design and teacher behavior directly influence the mathematics achievement of students with learning problems (Kameenui & Simmons, 1990; Kelly et al., 1990; Mastropieri et al., 1991; Mercer & Miller, 1992b). Although much remains to be learned about teaching math, educators need to examine existing research and literature to determine *what* should be taught in a math curriculum and the best practices for *how* to teach it. Only through the systematic examination and application of what is known about math instruction can educators ensure that students with learning problems achieve commensurate with their potential. The components of effective math instruction are presented next.

Selecting Appropriate Mathematics Content

Mathematics educators are recommending reforms in the content of the mathematics curriculum. Although computation remains a vital component, experts agree that obtaining answers via written work is not sufficient. Estimating answers and cross-checking with alternative methods are stressed in the current recommendations. Moreover, the ability to think critically and the understanding of concepts, operations, and real-life applications are important goals of a mathematics curriculum. The official 1988 statement of the National Council of Supervisors of Mathematics, *Twelve Components of Essential Mathematics,* has implications for planning math instruction for students with learning problems.

1. *Problem solving.* Learning to solve problems by applying previously acquired information to new and different situations is one of the primary reasons for studying math. Problem solving involves solving verbal (text) problems as well as nonverbal problems. Skills involved include using trial and error, asking relevant questions, selecting an operation, illustrating results, analyzing situations, and translating results.
2. *Communicating mathematical ideas.* Students must learn the language and notation of math. They should present math ideas via manipulative objects, drawings, writing, and speaking.
3. *Mathematical reasoning.* Students must learn to conduct investigations of math concepts. These skills include drawing tentative conclusions, recognizing patterns, and using math knowledge to support conjecture.
4. *Applying mathematics to everyday situations.* Students should be encouraged to translate daily experiences into mathematical representations (that is, graphs, tables, diagrams, or math expressions) and interpret the results.
5. *Alertness to the reasonableness of results.* Students must be able to examine results against viable conjecture. The use of calculators and computers makes this an essential skill in society.
6. *Estimation.* Students must be able to perform rapid mental approximations to es-

tablish the reasonableness of a math solution. In addition to approximating purchase costs, these estimations involve measurements such as length, area, volume, and weight.

7. *Appropriate computational skills.* Students must gain proficiency in using operations (that is, addition, subtraction, multiplication, division) with whole numbers and decimals. Knowledge of basic facts is essential, and mental arithmetic is important. Competence in using common fractions and decimals is necessary, and knowing when to use a calculator also is helpful.

8. *Algebraic thinking.* Students must learn to use letters to represent math quantities and expressions and to represent mathematical relationships and functions with graphs, tables, and equations. Students need to understand how one quantity changes as a function of another.

9. *Measurement.* Students must learn the basic concepts of measuring (that is, distance, weight, time, capacity, temperature, angles) via concrete experiences.

10. *Geometry.* Students must learn geometric concepts to function in a three-dimensional world. Parallelism, perpendicularity, congruence, similarity, and symmetry are important concepts. These concepts should be explored in situations that involve measurement and problem solving.

11. *Statistics.* Students must learn to collect and organize data to answer daily questions. Measures of central tendency and variance are important as well as interpreting tables, maps, graphs, and charts.

12. *Probability.* Students must understand the basic notions of probability to predict the likelihood of future events that are important in their lives.

Another consideration for determining what mathematics content to teach involves a student's prior learning. Mathematics is a logical interrelated system of concepts and operations that are hierarchically ordered. Numerous experts (Bley & Thornton, 1989; Kameenui & Simmons, 1990; Miller & Milam, 1987; Silbert, Carnine, & Stein, 1990) stress the importance of teaching students skills for which they have the necessary preskills. For example, students should know some addition facts before learning subtraction facts. The instruction of students in skills in which they lack the necessary preskills often leads to a limited amount of fragmented or rote learning and much frustration. The best teaching practice clearly involves teaching students the preskills that are germane to learning a new skill or beginning instruction with a skill in which students possesses the essential preskills. Finally, educators must ensure that students with learning problems receive math instruction on relevant or practical math skills. For example, the teaching of Roman numerals appears to lack relevance.

Teaching the Acquisition of Math

Follow teaching steps. A viable plan for teaching the acquisition of computation or problem-solving skills includes the following activities:

1. Assess the student's math skills and identify an appropriate instructional objective. To promote success, the objective should be relevant and one in which the student has the essential preskills.

2. Obtain a commitment from the student to learn the math skill and set goals. Discussions regarding the applications of the targeted skill help the student establish a desire to learn. Moreover, goal setting provides the student and teacher with instructional expectations and fosters motivation. Goal setting is enhanced by identifying

the expected time period for reaching a mastery criterion. In their synthesis of research on good teaching, Porter and Brophy (1988) report that good teachers are clear about instructional goals and communicate expectations and why the specific expectations exist. In presenting goals, effective teachers explain what the student needs to do to achieve the goal and what the student will learn in achieving the goal (Christenson, Ysseldyke, & Thurlow, 1989). There is growing support for the premise that teachers tend to make goals too easy for students with learning problems (Anderson & Pellicer, 1990; Clifford, 1990; Fuchs, Fuchs, & Deno, 1985). Clifford reports that students need challenge rather than easy success and that tasks involving moderate risk-taking provide the best level of difficulty in setting goals. She recommends that instructional environments should feature error tolerance and reward for error correction. A substantial research base (Locke & Latham, 1990; Locke, Shaw, Saari, & Latham, 1981) documents the premise that difficult but attainable goals lead to higher effort and achievement than do easier goals.

3. Use effective teaching steps to teach the math skill. These steps are presented in Chapter 1 and include (a) providing an advance organizer, (b) demonstrating and explaining the skill, (c) having students model the skill, (d) providing guided practice with feedback, and (e) providing independent practice with feedback. Numerous researchers have used these steps and variations of these steps to product excellent math achievement with students with learning problems. For example, Blankenship (1978), Sugai and Smith (1986), and Rivera and Smith (1987) used a demonstration and permanent model technique to teach computation skills to students with learning disabilities. The technique involved a step-by-step teacher demonstration with the teacher leaving the completed problem with the student for use as a permanent model. The demonstration and permanent model technique proved to be effective with students who have learning disabilities. Also, during the learning of new material, it is important for the student to maintain a success rate of 80 percent. Rosenshine (1983) reports that such an accuracy rate is an important factor in improving the performance of low-achieving students.

Use the concrete-semiconcrete-abstract sequence. During the acquisition of a computational or problem-solving skill, it is essential that the student be instructed in such a way that understanding is assured. Many authorities believe that the use of the concrete-semiconcrete-abstract (CSA) sequence is an excellent way to teach students with learning problems to understand math concepts, operations, and applications. Several research studies (Hudson, Peterson, Mercer, & McLeod, 1988; Mercer & Miller, 1992b; S. K. Peterson et al., 1988) reveal that the CSA sequence is an effective way to teach math to students with learning problems. Results indicate that students with learning problems do not need large numbers of formal experiences at the concrete and semiconcrete levels to understand the basic facts. In this research, within six 30-minute lessons (three concrete and three semiconcrete), students with learning problems demonstrated an understanding of the respective operation and generalized their learning to abstract-level (numbers only) problems. Moreover, the students retained the targeted skills during follow-up testing. Examples of CSA teaching are presented later in this chapter.

Teach concepts and rules. The learning of concepts and rules also is germane to facilitating a student's understanding of math. A student who memorizes that 8 + 6 is 14 but sees 6 + 8 as a new problem to memorize needs to understand a basic concept (in this case, the commutative property of addition) to learn addition effectively. Likewise, the learning of subtraction is facilitated if a student understands the inverse relationship of addition and subtraction (that is, a + b = c; c − b = a). Moreover, the concept of place value is difficult for many students and deserves much teacher attention. Finally, rules such as *any number times zero is zero* help students learn multiplication facts. Concrete and semiconcrete experiences are excellent ways to demonstrate concepts and rules to students.

Monitor progress and provide feedback. The research is replete with the positive effects of monitoring the math progress of students with learning problems and giving feedback (Fuchs, 1986; Lloyd & Keller, 1989; Miller & Milam, 1987; Robinson, DePascale, & Roberts, 1989). Monitoring progress via charts has yielded excellent results regarding student achievement (see Chapter 6). Gersten, Carnine, and Woodward (1987) report that teachers who provide immediate corrective feedback on errors produce higher student achievement. Robinson et al. (1989) found that feedback helped students with learning disabilities complete more problems and improved accuracy from 73 percent to 94 percent. They stress the importance of feedback in the following passage:

> Feedback is potentially even more important for learning disabled (LD) children, who may be less attentive, participate less in academic work, and make more errors than higher achieving learners. Academic environments that maximize LD students' opportunities to learn under direct teacher supervision with timely feedback are essential. (p. 28)

Kline, Schumaker, and Deshler (1991) developed and evaluated an elaborated feedback

routine with students who were experiencing learning difficulties. Their results indicate that the elaborated feedback routine helps students achieve learning goals quickly and efficiently. The following is a viable feedback sequence that includes the essential features of elaborated feedback:

1. **F**—*Find* the score (grade the student's work).
2. **E**—*Enter* the score (write the score on a chart, graph, or paper)
3. **E**—*Evaluate* the score in terms of a goal, and praise correct work.
4. **D**—*Do* errors (examine errors for patterns).
5. **B**—*Begin* error correction (demonstrate or model an error-correction procedure).
6. **A**—*Ask* the student to apply the error-correction procedure.
7. **C**—*Close* out the session (praise the student for error corrections and remind him to use procedures with future problems).
8. **K**—*Kick* back and relax!

Maintain flexibility.   Given the heterogeneity of students with learning problems, it is important for the teacher to use some flexibility in teaching math. From the numerous factors that can affect math learning, it is apparent that a variety of teaching activities or procedures is needed. If a specific teaching activity does not result in student learning, it may help to try another. Low-stress algorithms, specific modality oriented instruction, visual and auditory cueing, prompting, and reinforcement represent a few instructional alternatives that can be manipulated readily.

Teaching Mastery

In this discussion, *mastery learning* refers to teaching a skill to a level of automaticity. Individuals usually reach automaticity when they continuously respond to math problems without hesitating to compute the answer. Most people operate at a level of automaticity when responding to questions such as "What is your address?" or "What is 6 + 2?" Rate of responding is regarded as an effective measure of automaticity (Hasselbring, Goin, & Bransford, 1987; Kirby & Becker, 1988; Lovitt, 1989). Mastering a skill provides numerous benefits, including improved retention and ability to compute or solve higher-level problems. Other benefits include finishing timed tests, completing homework faster, receiving higher grades, and developing positive feelings about math.

Before mastery instruction or techniques are used, the students must possess the preskills and understand the concept related to the targeted skill. Once they understand a skill, they can be instructed at mastery level. Students with learning problems vary considerably on the number of trials (n = 400 to 1,300) they need before achieving automaticity. Independent practice is the primary instructional format used to acquire mastery. Because practice can become boring, the teacher must try to make it interesting or fun. Instructional games, peer teaching, computer-assisted instruction, self-correcting materials, and reinforcement are helpful in planning practice-to-mastery activities.

Several techniques are available to improve speed in math computation:

1. Reinforce high rates of correct responses.
2. Set a rate goal.
3. Chart performances and terminate daily practice once the goal is achieved.
4. Tell students to work faster.
5. Challenge students to beat their last rate score.
6. Teach students to use rules (for example, any number times 2 is double that number).
7. Teach efficient algorithms (such as counting up in addition).
8. Drill difficult problems with flash cards.
9. Play instructional math games.

10. Provide rate practice in small intervals (10 to 20 seconds).
11. Teach students the relationships between addition and subtraction or multiplication and division when they are learning the respective facts.

In establishing mastery rate levels for individuals, it is important to consider the learner's characteristics (for example, age, academic skill, motor ability). For most students, a rate of 40 to 60 correct digits per minute with two or fewer errors is appropriate. Once a mastery level is achieved, the teacher and student can move to the next level skill with appropriate preskills and more confidence.

Teaching Problem Solving

Problem solving has received more attention since the National Council of Teachers of Mathematics (1980) made a statement noting that it should be a top priority in math instruction. Although problem solving has received a decade of attention from educators, its exact nature remains ambiguous. From an inspection of 10 books and problem-solving articles about students with learning problems, 37 different descriptors of problem solving were identified. In addition, no definitions were offered, although some authors did imply that problem solving is analogous to doing word problems. The National Council of Teachers of Mathematics (1989) describes problem solving as it relates to word problems and computation problems. It seems reasonable that a problem-solving activity is needed for any task that is difficult for a student. Thus, computation and word problems both could require problem-solving procedures. For skills in which automaticity has been achieved, problem solving probably is not a necessary procedural process.

Most authorities (Cawley et al., 1987; Fleischner, Nuzum, & Marzola, 1987; Kameenui & Simmons, 1990) interpret problem solving within the context of word problems. From an analysis of the problem-solving descriptors (for word problems) in the literature on students with learning problems, problem solving clearly includes some unifying components. These components include that to problem solve, the student needs to (a) have a mathematical knowledge base, (b) apply acquired knowledge to new and unfamiliar situations, and (c) actively engage in thinking processes. These thinking processes involve having the student recognize a problem, plan a procedural strategy, examine the math relationships in the problem, and determine the mathematical knowledge needed to solve the problem. Then the student needs to represent the problem graphically, generate the equation, estimate the answer, sequence the computation steps, compute the answer, and check the answer for reasonableness. The student self-monitors the entire process and explores alternative ways to solve the problem. Problem solving is complex, and these descriptors are offered as a frame of reference to promote understanding and appreciation of the numerous components involved in it.

Fortunately, in spite of the complexity of the concept, the problem-solving emphasis is generating research that provides insights into how to teach students with learning problems to solve word problems. Paralleling the emphasis on problem solving has been a focus on strategy instruction. In strategy instruction, students learn a strategy that helps them engage in the appropriate steps needed to recognize and successfully solve a word problem. Numerous learning strategies are being developed and evaluated to teach problem-solving skills to students with learning problems. The following are some guidelines for problem-solving instruction:

1. Link instruction to students' prior knowledge and help them connect what they know in learning new information. For example, to help students learn division facts, point out the relationship between multiplication and division (that is, $9 \times 7 = 63$; $63 \div 9 = 7$; $63 \div 7 = 9$).

2. Teach students to understand concepts and operations.

3. Provide students with problems that pertain to daily living.

4. Teach word problems simultaneously with computation skills.

5. Concentrate on helping students develop a positive attitude toward math.

6. Teach students learning strategies that help them become independent learners.

In addition, Cawley et al. (1987) present the following list of do's and don'ts for teachers:

Do:

1. Begin problem solving the day a child enters school.

2. Make problem solving the reason for computation.

3. Develop long-term programs of problem solving.

4. Conduct problem solving as a multimodal activity.

5. Partial out the effects of one variable on another. If the child cannot read the problem, rewrite it. If the computation is too complex, make it simpler.

6. Have children prepare or modify problems.

7. Differentiate between process and knowledge.

8. Prepare problems in such a way that children must act upon the information. Prepare a set of problems in which all problems have the same question.

9. Present problems dealing with familiar subject matter.

10. Constantly monitor progress and modify problems to fit the child's weaknesses and progress.

Don't:

1. Use cue words to signal an operation.
2. Teach children to use computational rules to solve problems. That is, do not tell children to add when they see three different numbers.
3. Use problem-solving activities as an occasional wrap-up to computation.
4. Mark a child wrong if he/she makes a computational error in problem solving if the operation is correct.
5. Train teachers to treat problem solving as secondary to computation.
6. Assume that because the child is able to perform an arithmetic operation that he/she can automatically solve problems that use that operation.
7. Conclude that an incorrect answer automatically indicates lack of facility in problem solving.
8. Fail to realize that problem solving is the most important aspect of mathematics for daily living.
9. Fail to seize the opportunities for training in problem solving in conjunction with other subject areas.
10. Present problem solving in a haphazard manner. Order and careful planning are essential. (pp. 91–92)

Specific interventions for teaching problem-solving skills are presented later in this chapter.

Teaching Generalization

As discussed in Chapter 1, *generalization* refers to the performance of the targeted behavior in different, nontraining conditions (that is, across subjects, settings, people, behaviors, or time) without arranging the same events in the conditions that were present in the training conditions (Stokes & Baer, 1977). Students with learning problems typically have difficulty generalizing skills. A lack of instruction aimed at teaching students with learning problems to generalize math skills has contributed to their generalization problems. Ellis, Lenz, and Sabornie (1987a, 1987b) report that generalization must be taught before, during, and after instruction. Selected instructional practices to help students generalize math skills include the following:

1. Develop motivation to learn. It is believed that students who desire to learn a skill or strategy are most likely to generalize it. Motivation helps students feel responsible for their own learning and helps establish the independence needed to apply the new skill in settings without teacher support.
2. Throughout the instructional process, have periodic discussions with students about the rationale for learning the math skill and in which situations it is useful (for example, homework, recreational activities, shopping).
3. Throughout the instructional process, provide students with several examples and experiences. For instance, vary the manipulative objects (such as cubes, checkers, and buttons) in concrete activities, and use a variety of graphic representations (that is, different pictures, drawings, and tallies) in semiconcrete activities. Likewise, vary the format in abstract computation or word-problem activities (for example, present computation problems in verbal and horizontal formats). Also, vary the person doing the instruction (for example, aide, peer, parent).
4. Teach skills to a mastery level so that students can concentrate on using and not just remembering the skill.
5. Teach students strategies for solving multi-step math problems. When students possess a strategy for solving difficult problems, they are more likely to develop independent behavior and to actively engage in the problem-solving process. Mne-

monic devices frequently are used to help students retrieve appropriate strategies.

6. Teach students to solve problems pertinent to their daily lives. This connects the skill to functional uses and promotes motivation and the need to generalize. Students also can be instructed to create their own word problems.

7. Use reinforcement contingencies that are likely to occur in the natural environment. In this way, students are not dependent on artificial contingencies (that is, reinforcers only available in the classroom) to maintain and use the learned skill.

8. Once the skill is established, move the teaching situation from a highly controlled format (that is, teacher-led) to a more loosely controlled format (such as independent work).

9. Encourage students to generalize.

Promoting a Positive Attitude Toward Math

Many students with learning problems have a history of math failures. Consequently, they often develop negative attitudes toward math and feel insecure about their capabilities to succeed in math. Attitudes, beliefs, and motivation play an important role in the learning of math. The National Council of Teachers of Mathematics (1989) and the National Council of Supervisors of Mathematics (1988) stress the need to focus on the affective side of mathematics instruction. Bley and Thornton (1989) present this emphasis in the following passage:

> Students' feelings about themselves as learners and about their experiences with mathematics can greatly influence the level of their efforts and eventual success. By providing an environment that is accepting, encouraging, stimulating, and enjoyable, a program can foster a strong self-image and a positive attitude toward mathematics. (p. 5)

Clearly, math instruction must be designed to ensure success and promote positive attitudes. Many instructional techniques for promoting success and motivation are presented in Chapter 1. In addition, selected guidelines for promoting positive attitudes toward math learning include the following:

1. Involve students in setting challenging but attainable instructional goals. Goal setting has a powerful influence on student involvement and effort (Locke & Latham, 1990).

2. Provide students with success by building on prior skills and using task analysis to simplify the instructional sequence of a math skill or concept. Use charts to give students feedback on how well they are doing.

3. Discuss the relevance of a math skill to real-life problems. Use word problems that are part of a student's daily life.

4. Communicate positive expectations of students' abilities to learn. Students need to sense that the teacher believes they will achieve in math.

5. Help students understand the premise that their own effort affects outcomes regarding achievement. Constantly point out that what they do influences both success and failure. This premise helps students realize that their behavior directly influences what happens to them. In turn, they realize that they are in control of their own learning.

6. Model an enthusiastic and positive attitude toward math and maintain a lively pace during math instruction.

7. Reinforce students for effort on math work.

INSTRUCTIONAL PROCEDURES FOR COMPUTATION

The instructional components for teaching computation presented in Table 7.2 provide the organization for the teaching procedures

TABLE 7.2
Instructional components for teaching computation.

1. Provide concrete experiences to promote understanding.
   Example:

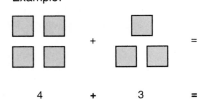

   4   +   3   =   _____

2. Provide semiconcrete experiences to promote understanding.
   Example: //// + ///
               4 + 3 = _____
3. Provide abstract activities and practice to promote mastery.
   Example: 4 + 3 = _____
4. Teach rules that show patterns and relationships.
   Example: *Zero rule:* Any number plus zero equals the number.

   $$4 + 0 = 4$$

   Order rule: Addends yield the same sum regardless of their order.

   $$4 + 3 = 7 \qquad 3 + 4 = 7$$

5. Teach algorithms for solving problems.
   Example: *Fact:* 7 + 2 = _____ *Algorithm:* Start BIG and count on.
6. Use mnemonics to help students remember algorithms or problem-solving procedures.
   Example: DRAW

      Discover the sign (+, −, ×, ÷).

      Read the problem ("four plus three equals blank").

      Answer, or "DRAW" a conceptual representation of the problem using lines and tallies, and check //// ///
      (4 + 3 = _____).
          //// ///
      Write the answer (4 + 3 = 7).
7. Provide a variety of practice activities to promote mastery and generalization.
   Example: Provide vertical and horizontal problems.

      Use self-correcting materials, instructional games, peer tutoring, and computer-assisted instruction for seatwork.

      Provide activities to improve the rate of responses (for example 1-minute probes).
8. Teach problem solving.
   Example: Have students solve a variety of word problems.

      Have students create their own word problems.

      Provide students with strategies for solving problems.

and activities presented in the remainder of this chapter. Because many students with learning problems fail to master basic facts, two programs are discussed for teaching math facts. Following these programs, concrete-semiconcrete-abstract teaching activities, basic rules and algorithms, and procedures for teaching problem solving are presented.

Thornton and Toohey Math Facts Activities

Thornton and Toohey (1985) report substantial literature that indicates that modifying the *sequence* and *presentation* of learning tasks can improve basic fact learning among students with learning problems. They offer 10 guidelines that are supported by the literature for planning and implementing basic fact instruction for students with learning problems. These guidelines form the basis for MATH-FACT, which was developed and used successfully in Queensland, Australia (Thornton & Toohey, 1982–1985). An American miniversion is used in the United States (Thornton, 1984, 1985; Thornton & Toohey, 1984). Their guidelines include the following:

1. *Consider prerequisite learnings by looking ahead to review or reteach as necessary.* Mathematical concepts and operations are hierarchical. Concepts that are basic to learning a new skill or concept should be taught before introducing the new material. For example, ensure that sums-to-9 facts are mastered before introducing subtraction facts.
2. *Provide ongoing diagnosis and assessment.* Attention to the student's rate of progress, types of errors, understanding of concepts, and learning style is basic to successful math facts instruction.
3. *Modify the sequence in which facts are presented for learning.* Traditional fact in-

struction sequences addition facts by the size of the sum. Thornton and Toohey (1985) maintain that other sequences are more effective for various learners. For example, for immature students or those with serious deficits, they recommend beginning instruction with the 72 easiest addition facts: count-ons ($+1$, $+2$, $+3$) ($n = 45$), zeroes ($n = 19$), doubles ($n = 6$ not previously met), and 10 sums ($n = 2$ not previously met—$6 + 4$ and $4 + 6$).

4. *Before drill, teach students strategies for computing answers to unknown facts.* Many students with learning problems need to be taught specific strategies to help them solve problems independently. For example:

7 $+\ 2$	6 $+\ 3$	Start BIG and count on.
6 $+\ 0$	0 $+\ 8$	Plus zero stays the same.
8 $+\ 6$	6 $+\ 8$	Order of addends does not affect sum.

Overall, the following sequence is suggested: (a) easy addition facts, (b) easy subtraction facts, (c) other addition facts, and (d) other subtraction facts.

5. *Modify the presentation of activities to fit the learning style of each student.* Students with learning problems are a heterogeneous population with many different learning styles and preferences. Some procedures for taking advantage of various modality preferences include the following:

For Auditory Learners

1. Precede all actions and demonstrations with spoken instructions. Each step may

have two parts: (a) oral instructions only; (b) oral instructions closely followed by a visual stimulus, concrete manipulation, or demonstration.

2. Provide a verbal summary of each step.
3. If necessary use key words to focus the child's attention (e.g., "listen").
4. Remove extraneous visual stimuli.

For Visual Learners

1. Precede all oral instructions by concrete manipulations or mimed demonstrations. Each step may have two parts: (a) presentation of the visual stimulus only; (b) visual presentation in conjunction with verbalization.
2. Have children describe mimed or demonstrated actions, pictures, or concrete manipulation.
3. Provide a visual summary of each step.
4. Encourage children to make mental images of visual stimuli. Provide opportunity for them to reproduce these images (verbally, pictorially).
5. Use cue cards to focus children's attention.
6. Try a silent lesson.

For Kinesthetic/Tactile Learners

1. Precede all instructions by the physical manipulation of objects by the child. The teacher should guide all manipulations. Each step may have two parts: (a) physical manipulation only; (b) physical manipulation in conjunction with oral instruction.
2. Remove visual stimuli if distracting. Have children close their eyes or place objects in their hands behind their backs.
3. Provide a summary (physical manipulation of each step).
4. Use a cueing system to focus the child's attention.
5. Use textured material (pipe cleaners, sandpaper, plasticine, sandtrays, and magnetic boards). (Thornton & Toohey, 1985, pp. 52–53)

6. *Control the pacing.* Knowing when to move faster or slow down is critical to good fact instruction. Continuous monitoring of fact progress can facilitate pacing.
7. *Help students discriminate when to use a strategy and integrate new learnings with old.* Some students with learning problems learn a strategy and apply it to all situations. For example, a student may learn a count-on strategy and apply it to all addition facts. A student's appropriate use of a strategy should be strengthened by activities that require identifying math facts to which it applies.
8. *Provide verbal prompts.* Repeatedly give students verbal prompts during instruction. This helps some students independently associate the prompts with the specific facts to which they apply.
9. *Help students develop self-monitoring skills.* Many students with learning problems need to acquire skills that focus on *how to learn.* Such techniques as cognitive behavior modification and academic strategy training enable the student to develop self-monitoring skills that are useful across tasks and situations.
10. *Ensure provisions for overlearning.* Once facts are mastered, emphasis shifts to activities that help students with learning problems store them in long-term memory. This usually requires a variety of drill activities and performances on tasks at a high criterion level. Instructional games, self-correcting materials, computer-assisted instruction, peer teaching, and periodic review are a few of the activities appropriate for developing overlearning.

Mercer and Miller Math Facts Activities

Instructional sequence. The Strategic Math Series developed by Mercer and Miller (1992a) features seven phases to teach basic math facts:

Phase 1: Pretest

Phase 2: Teach concrete application

Phase 3: Teach representational application

Phase 4: Introduce the "DRAW" strategy

Phase 5: Teach abstract application

Phase 6: Posttest

Phase 7: Provide practice to fluency

Instructional procedures.   To help teach basic facts, all lessons in the Strategic Math Series include a sequence of procedures that has proven effective with students who have learning difficulties. The primary instructional procedures are as follows:

1. *Give an advance organizer.* The first component in each lesson is the advance organizer, which prepares the student for specific lessons. As presented in this curriculum, the advance organizer serves three purposes: (a) it connects the existing lesson to the previous lesson, (b) it identifies the target lesson skill, and (c) it provides a rationale for learning the skill.

2. *Describe and model.* This component provides the teacher with an opportunity to describe and model the computation process, following two basic procedures. In Procedure 1, the teacher asks and answers questions aloud while demonstrating how to compute the answer for one or more problems on the learning sheet. In computing the problem, the teacher verbalizes his thoughts so that students can better understand the thought processes involved. When the teacher arrives at an answer, he tells students the answer and instructs them to write it on their learning sheets. To enhance generalization across stimulus configurations, both horizontally and vertically configured problems are used as a basis for the teacher's demonstrations. In Procedure 2, the teacher continues to demonstrate

how to solve one or more problems. While doing so, he asks questions and solicits student responses, using prompts and cues to facilitate correct responses. Thus, in Procedure 2, the teacher and the students work a problem together. When an answer is computed, the students say the answer and write it on their learning sheets. Again, to enhance generalization across stimulus configurations, both horizontally and vertically configured problems are used.

3. *Conduct guided practice.* Guided practice provides the teacher with the opportunity to instruct and support students as they move toward independently solving problems on their learning sheets. To enhance generalization across stimulus configurations, problems are written in both horizontal and vertical formats. During this time, the teacher follows two basic procedures designed to facilitate student independence in computing problems. In Procedure 1, the teacher's role is to prompt and facilitate students' thought processes. Thus, the teacher no longer demonstrates the process unless further demonstration appears necessary. To facilitate correct responses, the teacher asks questions and solicits student responses, using prompts and cues. Through the use of this procedure, therefore, students are guided through each problem in a way that ensures success. In Procedure 2, the teacher instructs students to solve the next few problems on the learning sheet and offers assistance to individual learners only if needed. Thus, the teacher's role now is to step back, monitor student work, and provide assistance with thought processes only if needed.

4. *Conduct independent practice.* Independent practice of facts is an integral component of the lessons. It enables the teacher to determine if students can solve facts independently. The scripts for this component

consist of simple directions, including a statement that reminds students to use previously learned skills and techniques to solve problems. During this time, the teacher does not provide any assistance.

5. *Conduct problem-solving practice.* Like independent practice of computation facts, problem-solving practice constitutes an integral component of all lessons. To teach students the thought process involved in problem solving, the teacher uses a graduated sequence of word problems. For example, in early lessons, students begin solving problems involving three words, and in later lessons, they are writing their own word problems. Along the way, students learn to extract any information that may be irrelevant to a problem. Thus, when students complete a facts program, they are able to solve word problems with and without extraneous information and to write their own word problems.

6. *Provide feedback.* Because proper feedback is critical to learning, a feedback component is found in all the lessons. This component follows the elaborated feedback routine developed by Kline et al. (1991), and it allows the teacher to recognize and praise correct student responses, thereby preventing future errors. Feedback is facilitated through the use of facts progress charts on which the teacher and each student plot the student's scores for the last 10 problems on a learning sheet.

Field testing. The Strategic Math Series has yielded excellent results from field testing (Mercer & Miller, 1992b). The field-test results indicate that 109 students with learning problems were able to (a) acquire computational skills across facts, (b) solve word problems with and without extraneous information, (c) create word problems involving facts, (d) apply a mnemonic strategy to difficult problems, (e) increase rate of computation,

and (f) generalize math skills across examiners, settings, and tasks.

Concrete-Semiconcrete-Abstract Activities

Educators who have examined the mathematical deficits of students have suggested a number of initial teaching and remediation methods. Many of these methods feature the concrete-semiconcrete-abstract (CSA) teaching sequence that has been found to facilitate math learning. Implicit in this method of instruction is an emphasis on teaching students to understand the concepts of mathematics before memorizing facts, algorithms, and operations. Although the CSA sequence is advocated for mathematical learning, it rarely is used in a systematic manner during math instruction.

According to the CSA sequence, instruction begins at the *concrete level* where the student uses three-dimensional objects to solve computation problems. For example, in solving the problem, 5×2, the student is instructed to look at the first number, 5, and count that many groups, using circles or paper plates to represent the groups. Next, the student is instructed to look at the second number, 2, and place that many objects in each group (that is, circle or plate). After being instructed to count or add the number of objects in all the circles, 10, the student says and writes the answer to the problem. After successfully solving several problems at the concrete level, the student proceeds to the semiconcrete level.

At the *semiconcrete level,* drawings are used to solve computation problems. For example, in solving the problem, 7×3, the student is instructed to look at the first number, 7, and draw that many groups using circles. Next, the student is instructed to look at the second number, 3, and draw three tallies in each circle. The student then counts the tallies in the circles, 21, to arrive at the answer. Finally, the student says and writes the answer to the problem. After successfully solving several problems at this level, the student begins to work at the next level, the abstract level.

At the *abstract level,* the student looks at the computation problem and tries to solve it without using objects or drawings. The student reads the problem, remembers the answer or thinks of a way to compute the answer, and writes the answer. No objects or drawings are used in the computation unless the student is unable to answer a problem. Because success in math requires the ability to solve problems at the abstract level, it is essential that students achieve mastery at this level.

The concrete-semiconcrete-abstract sequence is appropriate for teaching the understanding of math throughout the span of math concepts, skills, and word problems. The use of manipulative objects requires some specific guidelines to ensure effective results. Dunlap and Brennan (1979) offer the following guidelines:

1. Before abstract experiences, instruction must proceed from concrete (manipulative) experiences to semiconcrete experiences.
2. The main objective of manipulative aids is to help students understand and develop mental images of mathematical processes.
3. The activity must accurately represent the actual process. For example, a direct correlation should exist between the manipulative activities and the paper-and-pencil activities.
4. More than one manipulative object should be used in teaching a concept.
5. The aid should be used individually by each student.
6. The manipulative experience must involve the moving of objects. The learning occurs from the student's physical actions on the objects rather than from the objects themselves.

Moreover, Thornton and Toohey (1986) suggest that the teacher (a) continuously ask students questions about their actions as they manipulate objects, (b) encourage students to verbalize their thinking, (c) have students write out the problem being solved via objects, and (d) have students use objects to check answers. The use of the CSA sequence to teach various computation skills is presented next.

Place value.   To begin place value instruction at the *concrete level,* gather two plastic cups, a bundle of straws, and a set of blocks. Set the two cups on poster board; label the right one "units" and the left one "tens." Tell the student to count the blocks. For each block he counts, place a straw in the units cup. Stop when nine blocks are counted and nine straws are in the units cup. Before picking up the 10th straw, explain that one straw in the tens cup represents 10 objects. The student then takes the nine straws out of the units cup and places one straw in the tens cup. Next, the student continues to count the blocks and place the straws. Counting proceeds in the following manner: 1 ten and 1, 1 ten and 2, . . . 3 tens and 4, 3 tens and 5, and so on. Each time a 10 is reached, empty the units cup and place a straw in the tens cup. Although the student is told that 1 ten and 1 is another name for 11, and 3 tens and 5 is another name for 35, during place value instruction encourage him to count using the 3 tens and 5 system. The student continues with the blocks and straws until he can do the task easily.

At the *semiconcrete level,* use illustrations instead of the blocks, straws, and cups. For example:

Task: Count the items and place the correct number in each cup.

tens

units

The completed task would look like this:

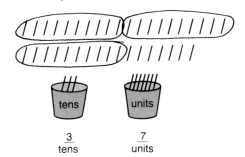

3
tens

7
units

Gradually fade the pictures of the cups and replace them with:

_____   _____

tens   units

The items may change to pictures of real objects.

At the *abstract level*, add numbers gradually in place of items. For example:

Task 1: Count the items and identify the number of tens and units.

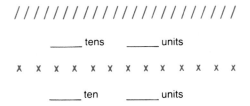

_____ tens   _____ units

Ж   Ж   Ж   Ж   Ж   Ж   Ж   Ж   Ж   Ж   Ж   Ж   Ж   Ж

_____ ten   _____ units

Task 2: Identify the number of tens and units in each number.

24   _____ tens   87   _____ tens

        _____ units   _____ units

These activities represent only one way of providing place value instruction at the concrete, semiconcrete, and abstract levels. Teachers can expand and use different activities across the three levels.

Addition: Sums to 9.   Learning sums to 9 underlies later math functioning. These sums are the initial facts to be mastered.

Concrete level: 6 + 3 = _____

Student looks at the first number and counts that many objects. Student looks at the second number and counts that many objects. Student counts all objects for the sum.

Example:

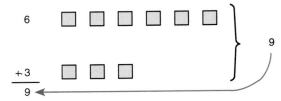

Semiconcrete level: 6 + 3 = _____

Student looks at the first number and draws that many tallies. Student looks at the second number and draws that many tallies. Student counts all tallies for the sum.

Example:

6

+ 3

/ / / / / /

/ / /

9

Abstract level: 6 + 3 = _____

Student looks at the problem and solves it without objects or drawings. Student uses an algorithm (such as start BIG and count up) or memory to solve the problem.

Example:

          6   or   6 + 3 = 9
        + 3
          9

Addition: Sums to 18.   After sums to 9 and place value to two places are learned, the student is ready for instruction in addition facts of sums to 18.

Concrete level: 7 + 5 = _____

Student looks at the first number and counts that many objects. Student looks at the second number and counts that many objects. Student

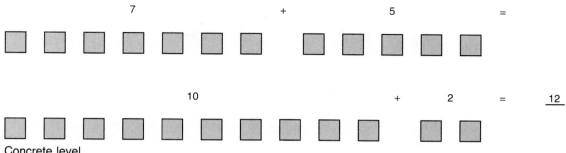

Concrete level

manipulates the blocks to form a group of 10 and a group of 2. Student writes and says the answer as 1 ten and 2 ones or 12.

Example (see above):

Semiconcrete level: 7 + 5 = ____
Student looks at the first number and draws that many tallies. Student looks at the second number and draws that many tallies. Student circles a group of ten and computes the answer as 1 ten and 2 ones.

Example:

```
  7      / / / / / / /
+ 5      / / / / /
```

```
  7    ( / / / / / / / )    10
+ 5    ( / / / / / )       + 2
─────                      ─────
 12  ◄──────────────────    12
```

Abstract level: 7 + 5 = ____
Student answers the problem from memory or uses an algorithm.

Example:

```
    7      or      7 + 5 = 12
  + 5
  ────
   12
```

Addition with regrouping. When going from the concrete to the semiconcrete level,

the teacher simply replaces real objects with pictures of objects, dots, or tallies. The step from the semiconcrete to the abstract level involves replacing pictures and tallies with numbers. The following examples are provided to assist the teacher in developing instructional tasks for addition with regrouping.

Concrete level: 26 + 17 = ____
Student looks at the first number and counts the appropriate number of objects grouped into tens and ones. Student looks at the second number and counts the appropriate number of objects grouped into tens and ones. Student looks at the total number of ones and groups them into tens. Student counts the total groups of tens and ones and writes the answer.

Example:

26

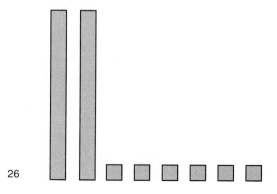

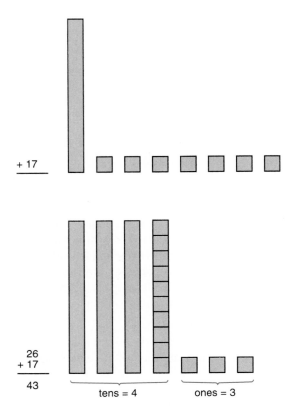

+ 17

26
+ 17

43

tens = 4   ones = 3

Semiconcrete level: 26 + 17 = ____
Student looks at the first number and draws tens and ones. Student looks at the second number and draws tens and ones. Student looks at the total number of ones and groups them into tens. Students counts the total groups of tens and ones and writes the answer. Example:

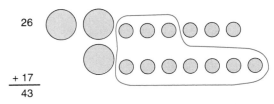

26

+ 17

43

= 4 tens, 3 ones

Abstract level: 26 + 17 = ____

Student uses an algorithm to solve the problem. Example:

$$\begin{array}{r} 26 \\ + \ 17 \\ \hline 43 \end{array} \quad \text{or} \quad 26 + 17 = 43$$

Subtraction facts (1 to 9): After the addition facts through 9 are learned, the teaching of subtraction facts (1 to 9) is simple. When the "add on" approach to subtraction is used, the student is required to find a missing addend instead of a difference. The missing addend approach involves the same logic used in addition; thus, a student can use knowledge of addition facts in solving subtraction problems. For example, an addition fact can be expressed as an addition *or* a subtraction equation, depending on which unknown the student is seeking to compute.

Addition: $4 + 3 = 7$ (addend + addend = sum)

Subtraction: $7 - 3 = 4$ (sum − addend = missing addend)

In the missing addend approach to subtraction, the student uses knowledge of addition facts to answer the subtraction question, "What number goes with 3 to make another name for (equal) 7?" Thus, when solving $7 - 3 = $ ____ , the problem becomes $3 + $ ____ $= 7$. Although the missing addend approach is feasible mathematically, the "take away" approach is used more widely. The "take away" approach appears more relevant to the real world of subtraction when solving word problems or demonstrating the subtraction process. Subtraction tasks at each of the three levels for the facts through 9 are presented next.

Concrete level: 7 − 3 = ____
Student looks at the first number and counts that many objects. Student looks at the second number and takes (or moves) away the appro-

priate number of objects. Student counts the remaining objects for the answer.

Example:

$$\begin{array}{r} 7 \\ -\ 3 \\ \hline 4 \end{array}$$

objects taken away

Semiconcrete level: 7 − 3 = ____
Student looks at the first number and draws that many tallies. Student looks at the second number and crosses out that many tallies. Student counts the remaining tallies for the answer.

Example:

$$\begin{array}{r} 7 \quad\ ////XXX \\ -\ 3 \\ \hline 4 \end{array}$$

Abstract level: 7 − 3 = ____
Student answers the problem from memory or uses an algorithm.

Example:

$$\begin{array}{r} 7 \\ -\ 3 \\ \hline 4 \end{array} \quad \text{or} \quad 7 - 3 = 4$$

Subtraction facts (10 to 18): When solving subtraction facts 10 to 18, the student must recognize place value (that is, recognize that a portion of the take away number comes from the ten).

Concrete level: 14 − 6 = ____
Student looks at the first number, counts that many objects, and groups them as 1 ten and the appropriate number of ones. Student looks at the second number and takes away the appropriate number of objects from the ones and a renamed group of ten. Student counts the remaining objects for the answer.

Example:

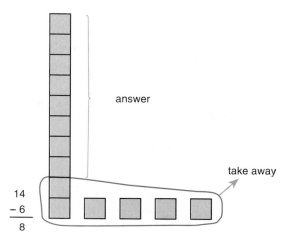

answer

take away

$$\begin{array}{r} 14 \\ -\ 6 \\ \hline 8 \end{array}$$

Semiconcrete level: 7 − 4 = ____
Student looks at the first number and draws a group of ten and the appropriate number of ones. Student looks at the second number and crosses out the appropriate number of lines from the ones and from the ten. Student counts the remaining lines for the answer.

Example:

ten   ones

$$\begin{array}{r} 14 \\ -\ 6 \\ \hline 8 \end{array}$$ | | | | | | | | | XX XXXX

answer

Abstract level: 7 − 4 = ____
Student answers the problem from memory or uses an algorithm.

Example:

$$\begin{array}{r} 14 \\ -\ 6 \\ \hline 8 \end{array} \quad \text{or} \quad 14 - 6 = 8$$

Subtraction with regrouping. The following examples can assist the teacher in developing instructional tasks for subtraction with regrouping at all three levels.

Concrete level: 33 − 18 = ____

Student looks at the first number and counts that many objects and groups them as the appropriate number of tens and ones. Student looks at the second number and takes away the appropriate number of objects from the ones and from a renamed group of ten. Student counts the remaining objects for the answer.

Example:

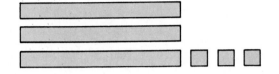

Change to:

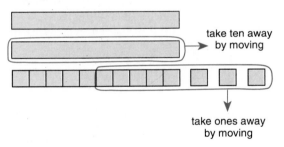

take ten away by moving

take ones away by moving

answer = 1 ten and 5 ones or 15

Semiconcrete level: 33 − 18 = _____
Student looks at the first number and draws tens and ones. Student looks at the second number and crosses out the appropriate number from the ones and a renamed group of ten. Student counts the remaining tens and ones for the answer.

Example:

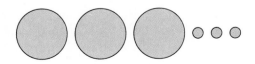

Change to:

slash through number taken away after regrouping

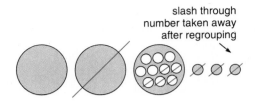

answer = 1 ten and 5 ones or 15

Abstract level: 33 − 18 = _____
Student uses an algorithm to solve the problem.

Example:

$$\begin{array}{r} 33 \\ -\ 18 \\ \hline 15 \end{array} \quad \text{or} \quad 33 - 18 = 15$$

Multiplication. The 100 multiplication facts ($\times$ 0 to $\times$ 9) are basic to more complex operations in multiplication.

Concrete level: 5 $\times$ 3 = _____
Student looks at the first number and selects that many containers to represent groups. Student looks at the second number and puts that many objects in each container (group). Student counts or adds objects across the groups for the answer.

Example:

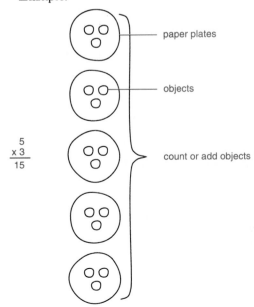

paper plates

objects

count or add objects

$$\begin{array}{r} 5 \\ \times\ 3 \\ \hline 15 \end{array}$$

Semiconcrete level: 5 × 3 = ____
Student looks at the first number and draws that many groups using horizontal lines. Student looks at the second number and draws that many tallies in each group (that is, horizontal line). Student counts or adds the tallies across the groups for the answer.
Example:

Student answers the problem from memory or uses an algorithm.
 Example:

$$\begin{array}{r} 5 \\ \times\ 3 \\ \hline 15 \end{array} \quad \text{or} \quad 5 \times 3 = 15$$

Division. Division is considered the most difficult of the four operations. For example, long division requires the use of division, multiplication, and subtraction in computing quotients. The following examples illustrate division problems that involve solving for number of groups of objects.

Concrete level: 12 ÷ 4 = ____ or 4)‾12‾
Student looks at the first number, or the number within the lines, and counts that many objects. Student looks at the second number, or the number outside the lines, and groups objects according to that number. Student counts the number of groups for the answer.
 Example (see below):

Semiconcrete level: 12 ÷ 4 = ____ or 4)‾12‾
Student looks at the first number, or the number within the lines, and draws that many tallies. Student looks at the second number, or the number outside the lines, and circles (or groups) that many objects until all the objects

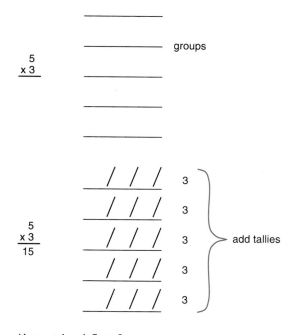

Abstract level: 5 × 3 = ____

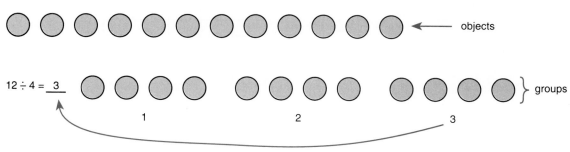

Concrete level

are within circles (groups). Student counts the number of circles (groups) for the answer.

Example:

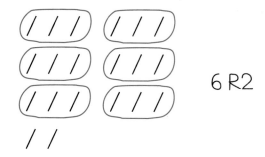

Abstract level: 12 ÷ 4 = _____ or 4⟌12
Student answers the problem from memory or uses an algorithm.

Example: 12 ÷ 4 = ___3___ or 4⟌12̄ (with 3 above)

Division with regrouping. The following examples present division problems in which regrouping is required.

Concrete level: 20 ÷ 3 = _____ or 3⟌20
Student looks at the first number, or the number within the lines, and counts that many objects. Student looks at the second number, or the number outside the lines, and groups objects (circles with string) according to that number. Student counts the number of circles with string (groups) and the remaining number of ungrouped objects for the answer.

Example:

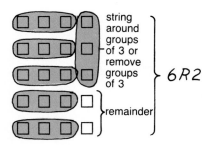

Semiconcrete level: 20 ÷ 3 = _____ or 3⟌20
Student looks at the first number, or the number within the lines, and draws that many tallies. Student looks at the second number, or

the number outside the lines, and circles (or groups) objects according to that number. Student counts the number of circles (groups) and the remaining number of ungrouped tallies for the answer.

Example:

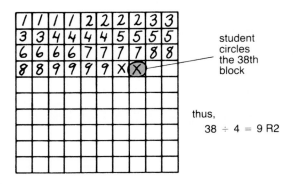

At this level the student also may use a grid (covered with acetate and used with an overhead pen or grease pencil) to solve division problems (for example, determine the number of 4s in 38). In performing the task the student counts until the 38th block is identified. Then 1s are written in the first four blocks, 2s are written in the second four blocks, and so on until no more sets of 4 are left in the first 38 blocks. For example:

/	/	/	/	2	2	2	2	3	3
3	3	4	4	4	4	5	5	5	5
6	6	6	6	7	7	7	7	8	8
8	8	9	9	9	9	X	Ⓧ		

student circles the 38th block

thus,
38 ÷ 4 = 9 R2

Abstract level: 20 ÷ 3 = _____ or 3⟌20
Student answers the problem from memory or uses an algorithm.

Example:

```
      6   R2
   3 ) 20
     - 3    - 1
      17
     - 3    - 2
      14
     - 3    - 3
      11
     -3     - 4
       8
     -3     - 5
       5
     -3     -⑥
      ②
```

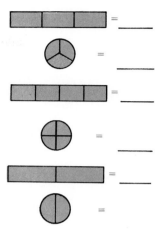

Recognition of unit fractions.   The teacher can use the following instructional tasks to teach several skills in fractions.

Concrete level:
Let ▭ be 1 and smaller size blocks represent fractional subregions of it.
▭ may be a block or a container that holds fractional blocks. Use the blocks to display ¼, ⅓, ½, and so on.

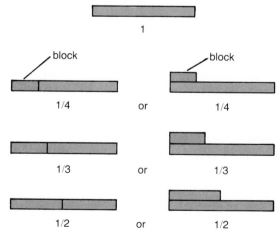

Numerous commercial materials are available for working with fractions at the concrete level (for example, Cuisenaire rods, Unifix cubes).

Semiconcrete level:
Write the unit fraction for the designs.

Abstract level:
Use numbers to express the unit fractions for one-fourth, one-third, and one-half.

Addition of fractions with the same denominators:
Concrete level: (⅓ + ⅓)

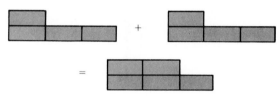

Semiconcrete level: (¼ + ²⁄₄)

Abstract level:

$$\tfrac{1}{3} + \tfrac{1}{3} = \square/\square$$

$$\tfrac{1}{4} + \tfrac{2}{4} = \square/\square$$

Addition and subtraction of mixed fractions.
Concrete level:
Task 1: Use real blocks (3 ⅔ + 2 ⅔)
Task 2: Use string (5 ¼ − 2 ¾)
Semiconcrete level:

Task 1: Use drawings (3 ⅔ + 2 ⅔)

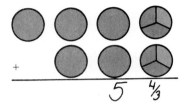

Task 2: Use lines (5 ¼ − 2 ¾)

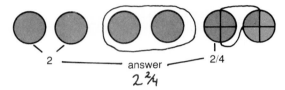

Abstract level:

$$3\ 2/3$$
$$+\,2\ 2/3$$
$$5\tfrac{4}{3} = 6\tfrac{1}{3}$$

$$5\ 1/4 =$$
$$-\,2\ 3/4 =$$
$$4\tfrac{5}{4}$$
$$2\tfrac{3}{4}$$
$$2\tfrac{2}{4} = 2\tfrac{1}{2}$$

For activities on multiplying and dividing fractions at the various levels, see fraction activities presented later in this chapter.

Basic Rules and Algorithms

The teaching of basic rules and algorithms helps students compute math more efficiently. Moreover, many rules and algorithms are based on relationships that foster student understanding and computational problem solving.

Selected addition rules.

1. *Order rule:* The order of addends does not affect the answer (commutative property) (6 + 3 = 9; 3 + 6 = 9).

2. *Zero rule:* Any number plus zero is the number (3 + 0 = 3; 0 + 7 = 7).

3. *One rule:* Any number plus 1 is one more than the number (that is, count up by 1) (3 + 1 = 4; 8 + 1 = 9).

Addition algorithms. After the student knows addition facts through sums to 18, an adaptation of the *tens method* (Fulkerson, 1963) may be a useful algorithm. To illustrate:

$$
\begin{array}{r}
\overset{\equiv\,\equiv\,\equiv}{\underset{}{}} \\
8\overset{\circ}{6}7 \\
57\overset{5}{4}{}^{1} \\
6\overline{4}7 \\
+\ 7\overline{8}6{}^{4} \\
\hline
2874
\end{array}
$$

Beginning at the top right in the example, 7 + 4 = 11, which can be renamed as 1 ten and 1 one. A horizontal line is drawn through the 4 to represent the ten, and the ones number is written on the extension of the line. Because the line represents the ten, the student no longer needs to hold it in mind. The student uses the 1 (unit digit) that is left over to begin adding until another ten is obtained. In this example, 1 + 7 = 8; then 8 + 6 = 14. Thus, a line is drawn through the 6 to represent the ten, and the 4 ones are written on the line. Because all numbers in the unit column have been added, the 4 is recorded as the unit's digit at the bottom of the column.

The two lines drawn in the units column represent 2 tens; thus, addition in the tens column begins by carrying the 2 tens. These 2 tens are added to the 6 tens, and this continues until there is a sum greater than or equal to 10 tens: 2 tens + 6 tens = 8 tens; 8 tens + 7 tens = 15 tens. A line is drawn across the 7 to represent 10 tens and the remaining 5 tens are written on the line. Then, 5 tens + 4 tens = 9 tens; 9 tens + 8 tens = 17 tens. A line is drawn across the 8, and the 7 is recorded as the tens digit at the bottom. In the tens column each line represents 10 tens or 1 hundred. Thus, the two lines in the tens column are carried to the hundreds column to begin addition there. The 2 hundreds are added to 8 hundreds, and addition proceeds in a similar manner.

Another addition algorithm is referred to as *partial sums*. To illustrate:

$$
\begin{array}{r}
47 \\
+\ 28 \\
\hline
15 \\
60 \\
\hline
75
\end{array}
$$

In this algorithm, when the sum of the ones column is greater than or equal to 10, it is written as a two-digit number at the bottom of the ones and tens columns. In the given example, $7 + 8 = 15$, so 15 is written at the bottom of the columns. Next, the tens column is added and the sum is written below the ones column sum. In this case, 4 tens + 2 tens = 6 tens or 60. Then the two partial sums are added.

Fitzmaurice-Hayes (1984) presents a left-to-right addition algorithm that enables the student to regroup in the answer. For some students this process offers a better understanding of the regrouping process. To illustrate:

$$
\begin{array}{cccc}
157 & 157 & 157 & 157 \\
+\ 274 & +\ 274 & +\ 274 & +\ 274 \\
\hline
3 & 3\,2 & 3\,2\,1 & 431 \\
 & 4 & 4\,3 &
\end{array}
$$

Selected subtraction rules.

1. *Zero rule:* Any number minus zero equals the number ($6 - 0 = 6$; $9 - 0 = 9$).
2. *One rule:* Any number minus 1 is one less (that is, count backwards by one) ($6 - 1 = 5$; $9 - 1 = 8$).

Subtraction algorithms. After the student has mastered subtraction facts with minuends to 18, selected algorithms are helpful. Several algorithms are based on the fact that adding or subtracting a constant number (that is, the same number) to or from the minuend and the subtrahend does not change the answer (that is, the difference or missing addend). To illustrate subtracting a constant to avoid regrouping:

$$
\begin{array}{ccc}
\begin{array}{r} 6000 \\ -\ 3642 \\ \hline \end{array}
&
\text{Student work:}
&
\begin{array}{r} 6000 - 1 \\ -\ 3642 - 1 \\ \hline \end{array}
\quad
\begin{array}{r} 5999 \\ -\ 3641 \\ \hline 2358 \end{array}
\end{array}
$$

In the above problem, the zeros in 6000 are changed to 9s by subtracting 1. When the 1 is subtracted from both numbers, the problem is solved easily without regrouping. This algorithm is especially helpful because subtraction problems involving money frequently have zeros in the minuend (for example, $5.00 - 2.38$; $10.00 - 6.74$).

To illustrate adding a constant to avoid regrouping:

$$
\begin{array}{ccc}
\begin{array}{r} 46 \\ -\ 28 \\ \hline \end{array}
&
\text{Student work:}
&
\begin{array}{r} 46 + 2 \\ -\ 28 + 2 \\ \hline \end{array}
\quad
\begin{array}{r} 48 \\ -\ 30 \\ \hline 18 \end{array}
\end{array}
$$

In the above problem, when the bigger number is on the bottom in the ones column, a constant number that produces a zero in the ones column is added to both numbers. When the subtrahend becomes a zero, the problem is solved easily without regrouping.

Another example of adding a constant to the top and bottom numbers involves adding a ten in the top number of the ones column and a ten in the bottom number of the tens column. This helps simplify regrouping for some students. For example:

Student work: add ten to top number in
                 ones column

42   4'2   add ten to bottom number in
− 27   −³2'7 tens column
─────   ─────
 15

Hutchings' (1975) *low-stress method of subtraction* is an effective procedure in remedial instruction (Ashlock, 1990). It is based on notation for recording a minuend or sum in several ways. For example, 752 may be recorded as $6^15 2$ or $6^14^1 2$ or $74^1 2$. When using this notation, the regrouped sum or minuend is recorded in the middle before the recalling of subtraction facts. For example:

(a)   8472
     − 6673

8	4	7	2
7	^{1}3	^{1}6	^{1}2

            − 6   6   7   3
               / 7 9 9

(b)   65400062
    − 21450238

6	5	4	0	0	0	6	2
6	4	^{1}3	9	9	^{1}0	5	^{1}2

         − 2   1   4   5   0   2   3   8
            4 3 9 4 9 8 2 4

In this algorithm, all renaming is completed before subtraction takes place. The student is reminded that renaming is necessary each time the subtrahend (known addend) in each column is greater than the minuend (sum).

Fitzmaurice-Hayes (1984) describes a left-to-right subtraction algorithm that requires the student to regroup in the answer. This process helps selected students understand regrouping. To illustrate:

532	532	532	532
− 246	− 246	− 246	− 246
3	ȝ9	ȝȝ6	286
	2	28	

Selected multiplication rules.

1. *Order rule:* The order of the numbers to be multiplied does not affect the answer (6 × 3 = 18; 3 × 6 = 18).

2. *Zero rule:* Any number times zero is zero (8 × 0 = 0; 647 × 0 = 0).
3. *One rule:* Any number times 1 is the number (9 × 1 = 9; 78 × 1 = 78).
4. *Two rule:* Any number times 2 is double the number (that is, 4 × 2 is 4 + 4) (8 × 2 = 8 + 8 or 16; 12 × 2 = 12 + 12 or 24).
5. *Five rule:* Any number times 5 involves counting by 5s the number of times indicated by the multiplier (that is, 5 × 6 means counting "5, 10, 15, 20, 25, 30") (3 × 5 = 5 + 5 + 5 or counting "5, 10, 15").
6. *Nine rule:* When multiplying any number by 9, subtract 1 from the multiplier to obtain the tens digit and then add enough to it to make 9 to obtain the ones digit (9 × 4 = 36 − 3 is one less than 4 and 3 + 6 = 9).

If these rules are used, there are only 15 facts left to be memorized:

3 × 3 = 9	4 × 8 = 32
3 × 4 = 12	6 × 6 = 36
3 × 6 = 18	6 × 7 = 42
3 × 7 = 21	6 × 8 = 48
3 × 8 = 24	7 × 7 = 49
4 × 4 = 16	7 × 8 = 56
4 × 6 = 24	8 × 8 = 64
4 × 7 = 28	

Some teachers report that these facts are learned faster by grouping the doubles (3 × 3 = 9, 4 × 4 = 16, and so on), thus leaving only 10 facts.

Multiplication algorithms.

The *low-stress method of multiplication* (Hutchings, 1976) reduces the amount of remembering during computation. It is based on notation for recording the products of multiplication facts in a different manner. With *drop notation,* the product of

7	may be written	7
× 8		× 8
───		───
		5
		6

To illustrate:

Conventional notation:

$$\begin{array}{ccc} 8 & 6 & 5 \\ \times\ 7 & \times\ 6 & \times\ 1 \\ \hline 56 & 36 & 5 \end{array}$$

Drop notation:

$$\begin{array}{ccc} 8 & 6 & 5 \\ \times\ 7 & \times\ 6 & \times\ 1 \\ \hline 5 & 3 & 0 \\ 6 & 6 & 5 \end{array}$$

Using the drop notation, multiplication problems can be computed in the following ways:

(a)

Step 1	*Step 2*	*Step 3*
476	476	476
× 8	× 8	× 8
40	540	3540
8	68	268
		3808

(b)

$$\begin{array}{r} 57764 \\ \times\quad 7 \\ \hline 344420 \\ 59928 \\ \hline 404348 \end{array}$$

(c) using two multidigit factors:

Step 1

$$\begin{array}{r} 476 \\ \times\quad 38 \\ \hline 3540 \\ 268 \end{array}$$

Step 2

$$\begin{array}{r} 476 \\ \times\quad 38 \\ \hline 3540 \\ 268 \end{array} \Big\} \times 8$$
$$\begin{array}{r} 1210 \\ 218 \end{array} \Big\} \times 3$$
$$\overline{18088}$$

This low-stress method of multiplication eliminates the regrouping requirement and allows the student to work only with multiplication facts in solving complex multiplication problems.

Another multiplication algorithm is the *partial products* algorithm. This algorithm re-

duces the regrouping requirement in multiplying multidigit numbers by one-digit numbers. For example:

$$\begin{array}{rl} 27 & \\ \times\quad 6 & \\ \hline 42 & (7 \times 6)\ \text{partial product} \\ 120 & (20 \times 6)\ \text{partial product} \\ \hline 162 & \end{array}$$

$$\begin{array}{rl} 362 & \\ \times\quad 4 & \\ \hline 08 & (2 \times 4) \\ 240 & (60 \times 4) \\ 1200 & (300 \times 4) \\ \hline 1448 & \end{array}$$

Selected division rules.

1. *Zero rule:* Zero divided by any number is zero ($0 \div 9 = 0$; $0 \div 49 = 0$).
2. *One rule:* Any number divided by 1 is the number ($8 \div 1 = 8$; $1\overline{)8}^{\,8}$; $67 \div 1 = 67$).
3. *Two rule:* Any number divided by 2 is half the number ($14 \div 2 = 7$; $2\overline{)66}^{\,33}$).
4. *Nines fact rule:* When 9 is divided into any of the 9s facts, the answer is one more than the number in the tens columns ($9\overline{)36}^{\,4} - 3 + 1$ is 4; $9\overline{)45}^{\,5} - 4 + 1$ is 5).
5. *Multiplication/division relationship rule:* The quotient multiplied by the divisor equals the dividend ($7 \times 5 = 35$; $35 \div 7 = 5$; $35 \div 7 = 5$). This rule enables the student to use knowledge of multiplication facts to solve division facts. For example, to solve the problem $32 \div 8$, the student asks, "What number times 8 equals 32?").

Division algorithms. Reisman (1977) notes that the following algorithms are less difficult than the traditional division algorithm. Using the algorithms is made simpler by knowing the shortcut for multiplying by multiples of 10. In algorithm *a*, the student immediately pulls out the largest tens multiple of the divisor; in algorithm *b*, the multiples taken out of the divisor are smaller.

(a)
```
28)62372
   56000   2000
    6372
    5600    200
     772
     560     20
     212
     196      7
      16   2227
```

(b)
```
28)62372
   28000   1000
   34372
   28000   1000
    6372
    2800    100
    3572
    2800    100
     772
     280     10
     492
     280     10
     212
     140      5
      72
      56      2
      16   2227
```

The following algorithm helps the student identify or compute each number of the quotient when the first quotient number selected is too low.

```
Step 1          Step 2
                  1
    2             2
23)8761        23)8761
   46             46
   41             41
                  23
                  18
```

Steps 1 and 2 are repeated until no more multiplication is needed.

```
   12
  260  380 R21  (answer is computed by adding each
23)8761              column in the quotient computations)
   46
   41
   23
  186
  138
   48
   46
   21
    0
   21
```

Fraction algorithm. Ruais (1978) describes a low-stress algorithm for teaching the addition and subtraction of fractions. The algorithm is called *ray multiplication* and consists of the following steps:

1. An overhead projection is used to drill the student on the location of geometric shapes and numbers. $\dfrac{\circ}{\triangle}\ \dfrac{\square}{\diamondsuit}$ are model items that are used to show the locations of bottom right, bottom left, top right, and top left.

2. The student is instructed to draw three rays (↗):(a) from bottom right to top left, (b) from bottom left to top right, and (c) from bottom left to bottom right. Thus $\dfrac{\circ}{\triangle}\ \dfrac{\square}{\diamondsuit}$ would look like

3. On a sheet that has pairs of numerical fractions, the student is directed to draw the three rays and multiply along the rays. The student writes the answers to these multiplication tasks. After the rays are multiplied, the student writes the operation sign between the fractions in a pair. For example:

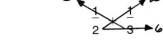

4. In this step the student writes a new fraction for each pair. The new numerator is formed by performing the correct operation on the products of the diagonal ray multiplications. The new denominator for both fractions is the product of the horizontal ray multiplication. For example:

$$\frac{3}{6} + \frac{2}{6}$$

5. Now the student computes the sum or difference of the numerators and writes the result over the denominator. For example:

$$\frac{3}{6} + \frac{2}{6} = \frac{(3 + 2)}{6} = \frac{5}{6}$$

or

$$\frac{3}{6} - \frac{2}{6} = \frac{(3 - 2)}{6} = \frac{1}{6}$$

Ruais reports that this ray multiplication algorithm leads to reduced stress, reduced teaching time prior to mastery, and increased computation power.

Problem Solving

In word problem solving, math problems are presented in the context of social situations, and information needed to solve each problem must be identified and then used. In some problems extraneous information is included, and the number of operations may vary from one to several. P. L. Peterson, Fennema, and Carpenter (1988/1989) report that the context of simple addition and subtraction problems varies significantly and students must understand mathematical concepts and develop strategies to solve these various problems. Table 7.3 presents four basic categories of addition and subtraction word problems.

Interventions that use sequential steps.
RIDE is a mnemonic strategy that identifies the steps needed to solve story problems successfully:

1. **R—***Read* the problem correctly.
2. **I—***Identify* the relevant information.
3. **D—***Determine* the operations and unit for expressing the answer.
4. **E—***Enter* the correct numbers and calculate and check the answer.

Fleischner et al. (1987) discuss a study in which they used a strategy-based intervention with a cue card to help students with learning problems successfully solve addition and subtraction word problems. The cue card presents the following sequence:

1. Read: What is the question?
2. Reread: What is the necessary information?
3. Think: Putting together? = add; Taking apart? = subtract; Do I need all the information? Is it a multistep problem?
4. Solve: Write the equation.
5. Check: Recalculate, label, and compare.

In the study, during the *read* step, students highlighted the question and wrote the metric pounds, inches, and so on. In the *think* step, the students were instructed to circle the largest number and write it. Then they were asked to see what happened to the number (that is, did it get smaller or larger?) Finally, the students used calculators to compute the answer so that they could focus on problem solving rather than on computation.

Montague and Bos (1986) present an eight-step cognitive strategy to help students with learning problems to solve verbal math problems. In a study of this strategy, they found that students were able to maintain and generalize the strategy. The steps include the following:

1. Read the problem orally.
2. Paraphrase the problem orally.
3. Visualize or graphically display the problem.
4. State the problem.
5. Hypothesize.
6. Estimate.
7. Calculate.
8. Self-check.

Interventions that use the CSA sequence.
S. C. Howell and Barnhart (1992) developed a concrete-semiconcrete-abstract instructional sequence for teaching young students to solve word problems. The concrete stage features six steps and involves the systematic manipulation of objects to represent equations. The following activity is included in the sixth step. The student reads (or has someone read aloud) the problem, "There are three blue circles and two orange circles. How many circles are there?" The student places the correct numbers and colors of circles on the display board. The student states, "I placed three blue circles on one side and two orange circles on the other side. To find out how many circles there are, I place the groups together, so three circles plus two circles equals five circles." If this activity is done correctly, the student goes to the next stage.

TABLE 7.3
Categories of addition and subtraction word problems.

Problem Type	Sample Problems
Join (elements are added to a given set)	1. Jan had 7 cookies. Kevin gave her 4 more. How many does Jan have altogether? (result unknown) 2. Jan has 7 cookies. How many more cookies does she need to have 11 cookies altogether? (change unknown) 3. Jan had some cookies. Kevin gave her 4 more cookies. Now she has 11 cookies. How many cookies did Jan have to start with? (start unknown)
Separate (elements are removed from a given set)	1. Jan had 11 cookies. She gave 7 cookies to Kevin. How many cookies does she have left? (result unknown) 2. Jan had 11 cookies. She gave some to Kevin. Now she has 7 cookies. How many did Jan give to Kevin? (change unknown) 3. Jan had some cookies. She gave 7 to Kevin. Now she has 4 cookies left. How many cookies did Jan have to start with? (start unknown)
Part-Part-Whole (comparisons between two disjoint sets)	1. Jan has 7 oatmeal cookies and 4 chocolate cookies. How many cookies does she have? 2. Jan has 11 cookies. Seven are oatmeal and the rest are chocolate. How many chocolate cookies does Jan have?
Compare	1. Jan has 11 cookies. Kevin has 7 cookies. How many more cookies does Jan have than Kevin? 2. Kevin has 7 cookies. Jan has 4 more than Kevin. How many cookies does Jan have? 3. Jan has 11 cookies. She has 7 more cookies than Kevin. How many cookies does Kevin have?

In the semiconcrete stage the student is guided through six steps in which manipulative objects are replaced with pictures or drawings. In the sixth step the student represents a story problem by drawing tallies, writing the equation, and calculating the answer.

In the abstract stage a series of five questions are presented to promote a thinking strategy for solving word problems (Eicholz et al., 1985):

1. What is the question?
2. What are the numbers in the problem?
3. What do I do to the numbers?
4. What is the answer?
5. Do I need to check the answer by drawing tallies?

The final step at the abstract stage involves having the student independently write a story problem. For example, the number sequence *7 − 4 = 3* may be written as the following story problem: "My dog had 7 puppies. There are 4 male puppies and the rest are females. How many puppies are females?"

Mercer and Miller (1992a) present a learning strategy approach to teach students with learning problems multiplication facts and word problems simultaneously. The word problems as presented in Table 7.4 feature a graduated sequence of difficulty in which students learn to solve problems with extraneous information and create their own word problems. This CSA sequence guides the student to understand and apply multiplication to real-life word problems. Field-test results indicate excellent acquisition of multiplication facts, generalization, and problem-solving skills.

Finally, Cawley (1989) is field-testing the Verbal Problem-Solving Project, which is designed primarily to teach problem-solving skills to students with learning problems. This project includes components for teaching students from kindergarten through twelfth grade and relies heavily on the use of specially designed materials oriented to problem solving. The project is based on the view that students need to learn mathematics in a meaningful manner and that problem solving should stimulate and be the reason for learning an array of mathematical skills, including basic fact recall and computation. The Verbal Problem-Solving Project is based on its predecessor, Project Math, and appears to hold much promise.

Calculators

Calculators are used widely in our society, and their use makes computation accurate and easy. The National Council of Teachers of Mathematics (1980) recommends that calculators be routinely available to students in elementary school. Because effective math instruction stresses understanding, problem solving, and computation, the instructional role of calculators needs clarification. Suydam

(1980) believes that calculators should be used primarily with problems that students are capable of doing by hand. Paper and pencil may be most effective for simple addition and subtraction problems, whereas calculators are better suited for long division problems (Lovitt, 1989). Fleischner et al. (1987) report that the use of calculators when solving word problems allows students with learning problems to focus on problem solving and avoid getting bogged down in computations. Moreover, some experiences with calculators can promote interest in other math areas. Finally, calculators provide a means for students to check their work.

MATH ACTIVITIES

This section provides activities for teaching or practicing math skills. The activities can be used to stimulate interest, individualize instruction, extend practice, and provide variety in teaching methods.

Readiness

In addition to the selected activities in this section, readiness areas and related assessment tasks are presented in Chapter 6.

Classification.   Provide the student with a collection of circles, squares, and triangles of various colors. Have the student classify the items according to shape and then according to color. Other objects that are useful in classification activities are buttons, wooden blocks, dominoes, spoons, nails, and golf tees.

Ordering.   Provide the student with a set of different-size objects (wooden blocks, buttons, straws, nails, washers, shapes, Cuisenaire rods, and so on). Have the student arrange them in order from the smallest to the largest or vice versa.

TABLE 7.4
Multiplication problem-solving sequence.

Description	Example
A computation problem is presented with the word "groups" written to the right of the first number and blanks beside the second number and the answer space.	6 groups of 3 _____ _____
The student writes the name of the manipulative objects used in the lesson in the blanks, solves the problem, and reads the statement. "Six groups of 3 checkers is 18 checkers."	6 groups of 3 checkers 18 checkers
A computation problem is presented with the word "groups" written to the right of the first number and blanks beside the second number and the answer space.	6 groups of 3 _____ _____
The student writes the name of the drawings used in respective lesson in the blanks, solves the problem, and reads the statement. "Six groups of 3 circles is 18 circles."	6 groups of 3 circles 18 circles
A computation problem is presented with the word "groups" written to the right of the first number and common words written to the right of the second number and the answer space.	6 groups × 3 apples apples
The student solves the problem and reads the statement. "Six groups of 3 apples is 18 apples."	6 groups × 3 apples 18 apples
A computation problem is presented with a noun or phrase (adjective-noun) written to the right of the first and second numbers and the answer space.	6 brown bags × 3 red apples 18 red apples
The student solves the problem and reads the statement. "Six brown bags of 3 red apples is 18 red apples."	6 brown bags × 3 red apples 18 red apples
A computation problem is presented with words on both sides of the numbers and the answer space. The numbers remain lined up in a vertical format.	Susan has 6 bags of 3 apples. She has ____ apples.
The student solves the problem and reads the statement.	Susan has 6 bags of 3 apples. She has 18 apples.

TABLE 7.4
Continued

Description	Example
A regular sentence word problem is presented in which the numbers are not aligned.	Susan has 6 bags. There are 3 apples in each bag. How many apples does Susan have?
The student solves the problem and writes the equation.	$6 \times 3 = 18$
A sentence word problem including extraneous information is presented.	Susan has 6 bags. There are 3 apples in each bag. Bill has 2 pet turtles. How many apples does Susan have?
The student crosses out the extraneous information, solves the problem, and writes the equation.	Susan has 6 bags. There are 3 apples in each bag. *Bill has 2 pet turtles.* How many apples does Susan have? $6 \times 3 = 18$
The student is instructed to write or dictate his own multiplication word problem.	_____ _____ _____
The student writes or dictates a multiplication word problem, solves the problem, and writes the equation.	There are 3 puppies. Each puppy has 2 spots. How many spots are there altogether? $3 \times 2 = 6$
Three types of word problems are presented: 1 problem without extraneous information 1 problem with extraneous information 1 problem to be created by the student	
The student writes or dictates the "creation" problem, solves the problem, and writes the equation.	

One-to-one correspondence. Provide a pegboard design and instruct the student to duplicate it. Other helpful activities include putting screws on bolts, passing out papers, playing musical chairs, and adding the same part for several items (such as strings to a kite, sails to a boat, stems to a flower, or straws to a cup).

Counting. Provide the student with Language Master cards with a number of objects to count and a taped message (such as "One, two, three—three cats").

Give the student a picture of several monkeys hanging together or a card with a number on it. Provide a barrel of monkeys and a hook (on the wall or on a stand), and ask the student to show the number on the picture or the card by hanging up the same number of toy monkeys.

Have the student circle the number that corresponds to the configuration.

:·:·.	4	5	6	8
·:·	2	3	4	7
:·:·:	7	6	9	8
:·:	3	5	6	4

Attach a number line to the top of the student's desk to provide a helpful reference.

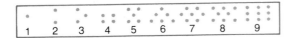

Place Value

Chip trading games. Use chip trading games to teach place value (Ashlock, 1990). These games stress the idea of exchanging many for one. The values of chips correspond to a numeration place value pattern. For example, white chips represent units, blue chips represent tens, and red chips represent hundreds. The student rolls a die and receives the number of units indicated on the die. Exchanges for higher valued chips are made according to the rules of the game (four for one if base 4, ten for one if base 10). The first player to get a chip of a certain high value wins.

Bank game. Use a game board and a bank to help students understand place value (Ashlock, 1990). For example:

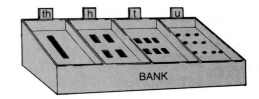

In computing the problem

$$527$$
$$+\ 893$$

the student places 5 hundreds, 2 tens, and 7 unit blocks in the upper row. Then the student places the appropriate blocks for 893 in the second row. Starting with the units (at green dot), the student collects 10 units if possible and moves all remaining units below the wide line. He trades to the bank each 10 units collected for the correct number of tens. The tens collected from the bank are placed at the top of the tens column. In this problem (see example), 10 units are traded to the bank for 1 ten, and zero blocks are placed below the wide line in the units column. Next, 10 tens are traded for a hundreds block, and 2 tens blocks are placed below the wide line in the tens column. The student trades 10 hundreds for a thousands block and then places 4 hundreds blocks below the wide line in the hundreds column. Finally, he moves the thousands block below the wide line in the thousands column. The student counts the blocks in each column and writes the answer, 1,420.

Making columns.   Present FIND as a mnemonic strategy to help students understand and solve place value problems:

1. **F**—*Find* the columns.
2. **I**—*Insert* the ts.
3. **N**—*Name* the columns.
4. **D**—*Determine* the numbers of hundreds, tens, and ones.

For example:

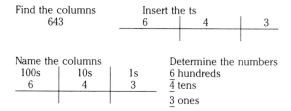

Find the columns
643

Insert the ts

| 6 | 4 | 3 |

Name the columns

100s	10s	1s
6	4	3

Determine the numbers
6 hundreds
4 tens
3 ones

Labeling columns.   Insert the initial letters for units, tens, hundreds, and so on over their respective columns (Bannatyne, 1973):

t th	th	h	t	u
	4	5	4	7
	1	7	5	6
+	3	3	1	1

Vertical lines can be in colors for additional cuing.

Pegboard.   Use a pegboard to aid in learning about borrowing and carrying (Wertlieb, 1976). For example:

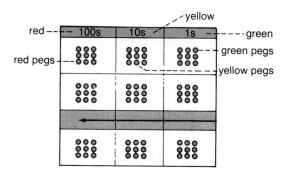

Use masking tape to divide the pegboard into three rows and three columns, with nine holes in each subdivision. An arrow is drawn from right to left on a piece of tape that separates the bottom third. This line serves as an equals sign; answers to problems always are shown by inserting pegs below this line. In addition to helping the student recall the different values for each column, color coding reminds the student to start with green (*go*). The top two rows hold the pegs representing the first two numbers in an addition or subtraction problem. To solve

$$\begin{array}{r} 5 \\ + \ 6 \\ \hline \end{array}$$

the student starts to transfer all the pegs in the units column to the unit section below the arrow. He discovers that not all 11 pegs will fit in the bottom row of the units column. Consequently, he must exchange 10 green pegs for 1 yellow peg (10 units for 1 ten) and carry this yellow peg into the tens column. Borrowing consists of trading 1 yellow for 10 green pegs and putting the green pegs in the top row of the units column.

Dice game.   Use a dice game in which three different-colored dice are used (Groves, 1976).

The colors correspond to color-coded lines drawn on paper to represent hundreds, tens, and units. The student rolls the dice, writes the number in the appropriate columns, and reads it. The player with the highest number wins.

Place value cards.   Make cards with numbers on one side and tallies for the number of hundreds, tens, and so on in that number on the other side (Wallace & Kauffman, 1986). For example:

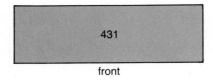

back

431

front

Also, strings can be attached to the cards for stringing beads to represent the number in each column.

General Computation

This section presents activities that easily are adapted for any of the four operations. Many of the games and self-correcting materials presented later in this chapter also are useful with all four operations.

Small work samples.   Present assignments in small segments. Because of attention problems or lack of interest, some students have difficulty completing an entire sheet of math problems. Presenting assignments in small

segments may help these students complete as many problems as their classmates. Cut a worksheet into small parts (rows), or place problems on cards that the student picks up each time a problem is completed.

Math board.   Glue library pockets on poster board and cover the outside portion of the pocket with transparent, self-adhesive paper. Use water-base felt pens to write problems on the pockets. Corresponding answers are written on cardboard strips. The student is instructed to match the correct answers to the pockets. The problems can be removed with a cloth so new problems can be presented.

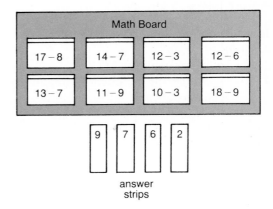

answer
strips

Mystery math.   Cut tagboard into 5″ × 5″ squares, or draw a square on a ditto. Put a decorative drawing, decal, or picture in the middle. Space off seven or more lines on each side of the decorative square in the middle. Write numbers at random on the left side. If the concept being taught is ÷ 6 and the first number is 42, the first number on the right should be 7. All other lines on the right side remain blank. The process is repeated with the top and bottom lines. By looking at the top lines on the left and right sides, the student tries to figure out the mathematical function involved. He then fills in the remaining blanks using the same function. Next the process is repeated with the top and bottom lines.

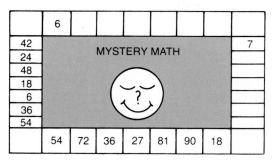

Calculators.   Consider allowing the student to use a calculator. In recent years calculators have become inexpensive and commonplace. The National Council of Teachers of Mathematics (1976) provides the teacher with several applications of calculators:

1. Assist in helping the student become a wise consumer.
2. Reinforce learning basic number facts and properties in the four operations.
3. Develop understanding of selected algorithms by using repeated operations.
4. Serve as a check on computations.
5. Promote independence in problem solving.
6. Solve problems that are normally too time-consuming to be computed by hand.

Learning ladders.   Provide the student with math problems in a vertical order on strips of paper or cardboard. Have the student start at the bottom of the "ladder" (strip) and proceed upward as problems are answered correctly. A marker is placed at the last problem answered correctly. When the student gets three markers (star, tack, pin) on the top problem, progress is recorded and the student is allowed to take the strip home. Learning ladders also can be used to practice number identification, telling time, and coin identification.

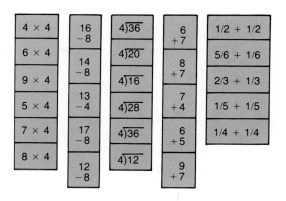

Addition

Nail abacus.   Use a nail abacus for teaching counting, place value (regrouping), and addition. Make the nail abacus by driving five finishing nails at two-inch intervals into a wooden board 2″ by 10″ by ½″. The abacus is used by placing washers or beads on the nails. To display the number 43,062 on the abacus, two washers are placed on the ones nail, six washers are placed on the tens nail, no washers on the hundreds nail, three washers on the thousands nail, and four washers on the ten-thousands nail (see top of next page).

The student adds on the abacus by placing washers or beads on the appropriate nails and counting. For example, in solving the problem 43 + 32, the student first would place three washers on the ones nail and four washers on the tens nail. Next, 32 would be shown on the abacus by placing two washers on the ones nail and three washers on the tens nail. Now the student computes the sums of the ones (5) and the tens (7) by counting the washers on the respective nails.

Instruct the student to follow these rules about regrouping when using the abacus:

1. Ten discs on the ones nail are exchanged for one disc on the tens nail.
2. Ten discs on the tens nail are exchanged for one disc on the hundreds nail.

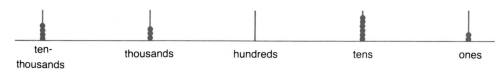

Nail abacus

3. No nail can have more than nine discs remaining.

Thus, in solving 18 + 26, several steps are used:

1. Display 18 on the abacus.
2. Leaving the 18, put 26 on the abacus.
3. Check to see if any nails are overloaded (10 or more).
4. Because the ones nail is overloaded with 14 discs on it, make an exchange of 10 ones discs for one more disc on the tens nail.
5. Record the answer in a table. For example:

Tens	Ones	
1	8	
2	6	
3	14	sum
4	4	regrouped sum

Number line. Provide a number line to help the student compute addition facts. Number lines for use in seatwork are made easily by cutting strips from a manila folder. Besides helping the student compute, they provide models for the correct form of numerals. In computing 2 + 4, the student is taught to start

at 2 and move four spaces to the right to obtain the answer (6) (see below). Later, the dot patterns can be eliminated and the numbers can be increased to 18.

Dot addition. Place reference points on numerals to help students with math problems (Kramer & Krug, 1973):

Kramer and Krug note that the system offers consistency in perception of the numbers and provides direct association between the number and its value. Actually, the dots provide a semiconcrete-level task for basic addition facts. Also, the dot cues can be faded as the student becomes proficient in learning the facts. For example:

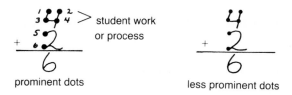

prominent dots   less prominent dots

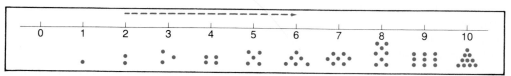

Number line addition

Computational cues. Provide the learner with cues for helping him remember to regroup or recall the steps in an algorithm. For example, the square reminds the student to carry:

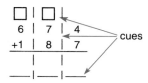

Direction cue. For the student who adds from left to right rather than right to left, place a green dot over the ones column to serve as a reminder to begin computation there.

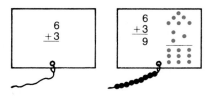

Bead addition. Attach a string to cards displaying math facts so that the student can put beads on the string when solving the problem. When using the card, the student computes the addition problem by threading the right number of beads onto the shoelace or string. The student can check his answer by looking on the back of the card.

Addition squares. Divide a square into nine smaller squares. Instruct the student to add across and down and to fill in all missing addends or sums. If the computations are accurate, the right column addends and the bottom row addends equal the same sum.

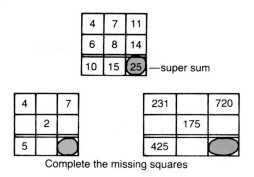

Complete the missing squares

Addition facts family. Present the addition facts (sums 0 to 18) within a number family framework to help the student learn them (see Figure 7.1). By teaching that any number plus 0 equals the number, and any number plus 1 is counting by 1, there are only 64 facts out of the 100 facts that must be memorized. If the doubles are taught in terms of doubling the addend to compute the sum, only 56 facts remain to be memorized.

Subtraction

Nail abacus. For solving the problem

$$57 - 34 = \Box$$

have the student put 57 on the nail abacus: five washers on the tens nail and seven washers on the ones nail. The teacher can use the "take away" or the "find the missing addend" approach. With the take away approach, the student is instructed to take away 34 (3 tens, 4 ones) from the abacus and count the remaining washers to find the difference. With the missing addend approach, the student is instructed to remove the known addend (34) from the sum (57) and count the remaining washers to determine the missing addend. For example:

0
0	0*

1
0	1*
1	0*

2
0	2*
2	0*
1	1*

3
0	3*
3	0*
1	2*
2	1*

4
0	4*
4	0*
1	3*
3	1*
2	2*

5
0	5*
5	0*
1	4*
4	1*
2	3
3	2

6
0	6*
6	0*
1	5*
5	1*
2	4
4	2
3	3*

7
0	7*
7	0*
1	6*
6	1*
2	5
5	2
3	4
4	3

8
0	8*
8	0*
1	7*
7	1*
2	6
6	2
3	5
5	3
4	4*

9
0	9*
9	0*
1	8*
8	1*
2	7
7	2
3	6
6	3
4	5
5	4

10
1	9*
9	1*
2	8
8	2
3	7
7	3
4	6
6	4
5	5*

11
2	9
9	2
3	8
8	3
4	7
7	4
5	6
6	5

12
3	9
9	3
4	8
8	4
5	7
7	5
6	6*

13
4	9
9	4
5	8
8	5
6	7
7	6

14
5	9
9	5
6	8
8	6
7	7*

15
6	9
9	6
7	8
8	7

16
7	9
9	7
8	8*

17
8	9
9	8

18
9	9*

FIGURE 7.1
Addition facts family.
Note: Facts marked with an asterisk do not need to be memorized.

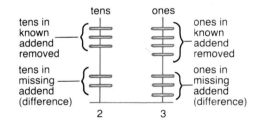

For solving

$$57 - 39 = \square$$

have the student put 57 on the abacus. Because the student cannot take 9 ones from 7 ones, 1 ten is taken off the tens nail and replaced with 10 washers on the ones nail. Now 9 washers are removed from the ones nail, and 3 washers are removed from the tens nail. The number left on the abacus is the answer.

Number line. Provide the student with a number line to help him compute subtraction facts. In solving the problem $14 - 8$, the student is taught to start at 14 and move eight spaces to the *left* to obtain the answer (6) (see top of next page).

Addition-subtraction pattern. Improve understanding of the relationship between addition and subtraction by having the student compute the sum of two addends and then subtract the two addends from the sum.

47	70	70
+ 23	− 23	− 47
70	47	23

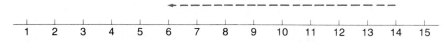

Number line subtraction

Circle cues. Use circle cues to assist the student to subtract with regrouping.

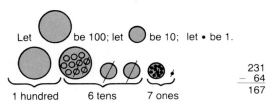

Let ⬤ be 100; let ◯ be 10; let • be 1.

1 hundred   6 tens   7 ones

$$\begin{array}{r} 231 \\ -\ 64 \\ \hline 167 \end{array}$$

The remaining circles that are not marked through represent the answer.

Self-monitoring subtraction strategy. Provide a modified worksheet format to help students remember the strategies for regrouping in subtraction (Frank & Brown, 1992). Each problem on the worksheet has cue words above it to remind the student to follow the strategy steps:

1. Begin? In the 1s column.
2. Bigger? Which number is bigger?
3. Borrow? If the bottom number is bigger, I must borrow.
4. Basic Facts? Remember basic facts. Use drawings or touch math if needed.

For example:

		__	Begin
__	__	__	Bigger
__	__	__	Borrow
__	__	__	Basic facts
7	6	5	
−2	8	7	

If the teacher develops a problem-solving sequence to other operations, this self-monitoring strategy can be modified for use in addition, multiplication, and division.

Multiplication

Array multiplication. Have the student form arrays using tiles, pegboards, or other objects, and determine the number of rows and columns. Explain that the number of rows and the number of columns represent the factors in a multiplication problem. Then instruct the student to write the multiplication facts represented by various arrays.

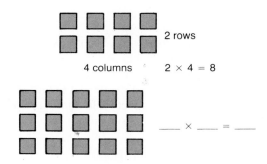

2 rows

4 columns   2 × 4 = 8

____ × ____ = ____

Next, give the student multiplication problems and have him form the corresponding arrays.

Dot arrays. Give the student dot arrays and instruct him to write the fact below each array.

3 × 4 = 12   _____   _____

Napier's rods. Use Napier's rods to strengthen the student's recall of multiplication facts or to check seatwork. The rods can be constructed from heavy construction paper, tongue depressors, or Popsicle sticks. They consist of 10 strips numbered according to the following pattern (see top of next page). The numbers on top of the strips are the multipli-

Index	1	2	3	4	5	6	7	8	9
1	0/1	0/2	0/3	0/4	0/5	0/6	0/7	0/8	0/9
2	0/2	0/4	0/6	0/8	1/0	1/2	1/4	1/6	1/8
3	0/3	0/6	0/9	1/2	1/5	1/8	2/1	2/4	2/7
4	0/4	0/8	1/2	1/6	2/0	2/4	2/8	3/2	3/6
5	0/5	1/0	1/5	2/0	2/5	3/0	3/5	4/0	4/5
6	0/6	1/2	1/8	2/4	3/0	3/6	4/2	4/8	5/4
7	0/7	1/4	2/1	2/8	3/5	4/2	4/9	5/6	6/3
8	0/8	1/6	2/4	3/2	4/0	4/8	5/6	6/4	7/2
9	0/9	1/8	2/7	3/6	4/5	5/4	6/3	7/2	8/1

Napier's rods

cands, and the numbers on the index are the multipliers. The products are in the squares with the diagonal lines. By putting a strip next to the index, the student easily can determine the product of the respective factors. For example:

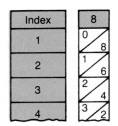

The rods can be used for multiplying more than one digit by a one-digit number. For example, to compute 73 × 4, the rods would be lined up accordingly:

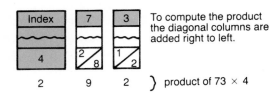

Multiplication chart. Provide the student with a chart for checking his work and doing seatwork. For example:

1	2	3	4	5	6	7	8	9
2	4	6	8	10	12	14	16	18
3	6	9	12	15	18	21	24	27
4	8	12	16	20	24	28	32	36
9	18	27	36	45	54	63	72	81

Addition-multiplication pattern. To help the student understand the relationship between addition and multiplication, have him first add the same number several times, then multiply that number by the times it was added. For example:

$$7 + 7 + 7 + 7 + 7 = 35$$
$$7 \times 5 = 35$$

Dot cards. Make 10 sets of cards representing numerals from 1 to 9. Set 1 contains nine cards with *one* dot on each card; Set 2 contains nine cards with *two* dots on each card; Set 3 contains nine cards with *three* dots on each card; and so on. Instruct the student to use the cards to compute multiplication problems.

$3 \times 4 =$ 12

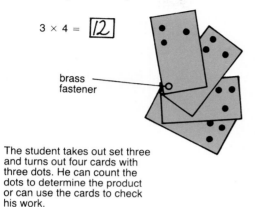

brass fastener

The student takes out set three and turns out four cards with three dots. He can count the dots to determine the product or can use the cards to check his work.

Division

Number line.   To divide with the number line, have the student count by the set determined by the divisor until the dividend is reached. The quotient is the number of sets used in counting up to the dividend. In computing $18 \div 3$, for example, the student counts by threes because the divisor is 3, and then he counts the loops for the answer. Thus, $18 \div 3 = 6$ (see below).

Dividing numbers into parts.   To help the student understand division, have him divide numbers into equal parts. For example:

12 = ____ 3s	24 = ____ 6s
9 = ____ 3s	36 = ____ 6s
16 = ____ 4s	18 = ____ 6s

Dot division.   Use dots to present division problems and have the student write the numerical statement. For example:

Determining the first digit in the quotient. Provide the student with several long division problems and ask him to find the first number in the quotient (Wallace & Kauffman, 1986).

Long division steps.   Present a face illustrating the four steps in long division problems to remind students to follow the steps.

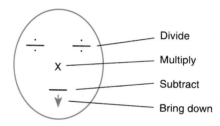

Also, the words Daddy, Mother, Sister, and Brother can be used to help students remember the four steps in long division.

Fractions

Number line.   Use the fraction number line for illustrating the value of improper fractions. Also, ask the student to indicate if fractions are equal to one whole, greater than one whole, less than one whole, or equal to several wholes (see top of next page). Use the number line to illustrate simple division problems involving fractions. For example:

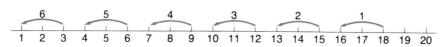

Number line division

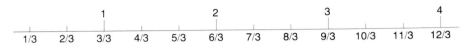

Number line fractions

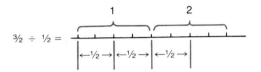

$$= 3 \text{ or } 1\frac{1}{2} \div \frac{1}{2} = 3$$

Fraction chart. Use fraction charts to show the relationship of a fraction to 1 and to other fractions. Activities with the charts include determining greater-than and less-than values of fractions, finding the lowest common denominator, and determining equivalent fractions.

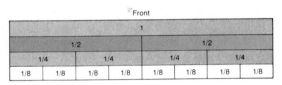

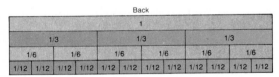

Matching graphic form to numerical symbol. Have the student match fractions in word or graphic form to the numerical symbol for that fraction. To do this, provide the student with library pockets labeled ¼, ⅛, and so forth and a stack of cards with graphic representations of a fraction. Have the student match the cards with the correct pocket. For example:

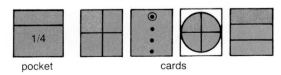

Use discs (concrete level) or circles (semiconcrete level) to illustrate the division of fractions. For example:

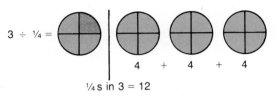

¼s in 3 = 12

Also, grids are helpful to illustrate division by fractions.

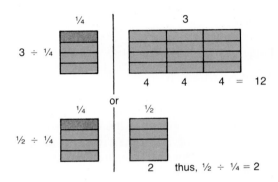

Fraction bars. Make fraction bars out of tongue depressors, Popsicle sticks, or construction paper. On each bar, the multiples of a single-digit number are written. For example:

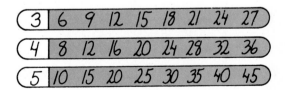

When one bar is placed over another bar, fractions are formed. The two numbers at the extreme left indicate the fraction formed (such as ¾); the remaining fractions are a set in which each member of the set is equivalent (such as ¾, ⁶⁄₈, ⁹⁄₁₂, and so on). The fraction ⅗ and its equivalents are formed by putting the 3 bar over the 5 bar. For example:

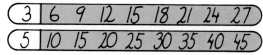

Sample activities include reading the equivalent fractions, forming fractions with other bars, and making new bars.

To compute with fraction bars, instruct the student to use the bars to add two fractions, such as ⅔ + ⅖. The student should follow these steps:

1. Form the fraction ⅔ by placing the 2 bar over the 3 bar.

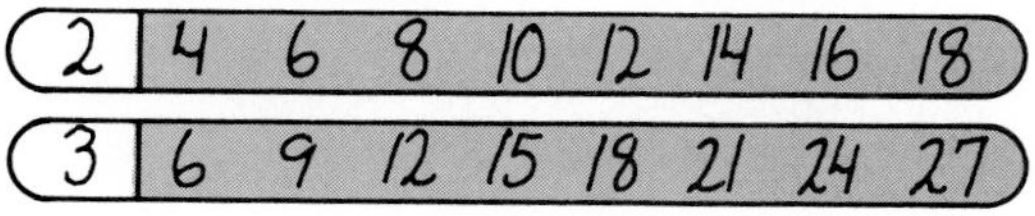

2. Form the fraction ⅖.

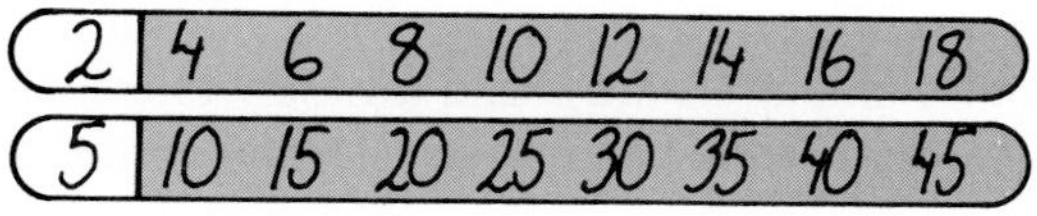

3. Look at the denominators of each fraction and locate the lowest number that is the same on each denominator bar. In this example it is 15.

4. Slide the fraction ⅖ over until ⁶⁄15 lies directly under ¹⁰⁄15.

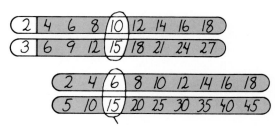

fractions with same denominator

5. To *add,* simply add the numbers on the numerator bars:

$$10 + 6 = 16;$$

thus, the sum is ¹⁶⁄15.

6. To *subtract,* simply subtract one numerator from the other:

$$10 - 6 = 4;$$

thus, the difference or missing addend is ⁴⁄15.

7. To *divide* ⅔ by ⅖, use the common denominator method (D. Howell, Davis, & Underhill, 1974):

$$⅔ ÷ ⅖ = ^{10}/_{15} ÷ ^{6}/_{15} =$$
$$(10 ÷ 6) ÷ (15 ÷ 15) =$$
$$(10 ÷ 6) ÷ 1 = 10 ÷ 6 = ^{10}/_{6}$$

Multiplying fractions with grids. Have the student draw a grid and represent the two fractions on it that he is multiplying. The student should follow these steps:

1. Make a rectangle and section it equally into the number of squares indicated by the *product* of the denominators. For example, ⅔ × ¼ = 12 squares.

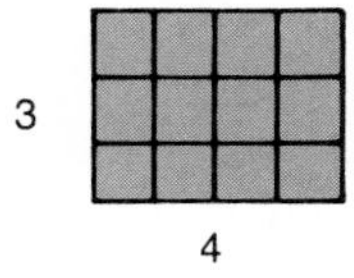

2. Represent ⅔ on the grid by shading in the correct number of *rows.*

= 2/3

3. Represent ¼ by shading in the correct number of *columns.*

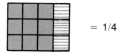

= 1/4

4. The number of squares that overlap represents the numerator of the product of ⅔ ×

¼; the total number of squares represents the denominator.

= 2/12; thus,
2/3 × 1/4 = 2/12

At the concrete level, the student can use tiles of different sizes.

Time

Number line. Use a circular number line from 1 to 60 to help the student learn to tell time (Reisman, 1982), as shown in Figure 7.2. The number line can be used to help the student (a) construct his own clock face, (b) determine the minutes "after the hour," and (c) note the relationship between the hour-hand movement (5 increments per hour) and that of the minute hand (60 increments per hour).

Record schedule. Mark the correct time on clocks for each school bell. Larger clocks can be used to record major events.

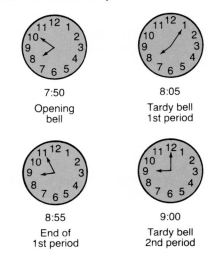

7:50
Opening
bell

8:05
Tardy bell
1st period

8:55
End of
1st period

9:00
Tardy bell
2nd period

Examining schedules. Provide the student with blank clock faces and a variety of schedules (such as those for television programs, a

FIGURE 7.2
Clock face with number line.

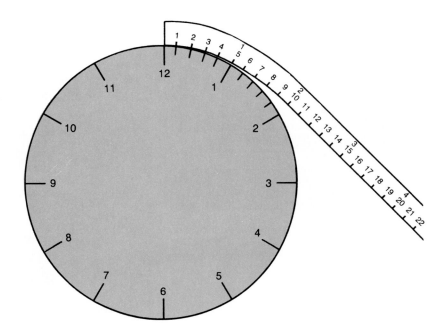

movie, or a bus). Have him record schedule times on the clock faces.

Calendar travel.   Provide the student with a calendar and a die. The student rolls the die and moves a marker the indicated number of spaces, beginning with the first day. Then he records the die number and the day of the week on which he lands. The task is over when the student reaches the end of the month.

Calendar quiz.   Provide the student with a calendar and a worksheet with numerous questions. Ask the student to respond to questions such as the following:

1. How many days are in a week?
2. On what day is the 27th of May?
3. List the dates of all the Wednesdays in January.
4. How many months are in a year?
5. Which month has the fewest days?
6. List the months with 31 days.

Decimals/Money

Cardboard regions.   Use cardboard regions for displaying decimals and fractions at the semiconcrete level (Marks, Purdy, & Kinney, 1970). The teacher can shade in various

squares and instruct the student to write the equivalent decimal. Graph paper can be glued to the cardboard regions to display specific numbers.

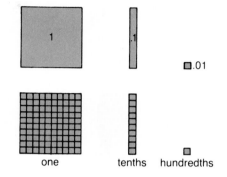

one   tenths   hundredths

Number line.   Use number lines to display decimals and their fractional equivalents (see example below). In addition to using the lines as an aid in computing decimal-fraction problems, the student can be instructed to fill in blank sections of number lines.

Completion of missing parts.   Instruct the student to fill in missing parts of various charts and figures as an activity in learning the relationship among fractions, decimals, and percentages (see example on next page).

.0	.1	.2	.3	.4	.5	.6	.7	.8	.9	1.0
$^0/_{10}$	$^1/_{10}$	$^2/_{10}$	$^3/_{10}$	$^4/_{10}$	$^5/_{10}$	$^6/_{10}$	$^7/_{10}$	$^8/_{10}$	$^9/_{10}$	$^{10}/_{10}$

.00	.05	.10	.15	.20	.25	.30	.35	.40	.45	.50
$^0/_{100}$	$^5/_{100}$	$^{10}/_{100}$	$^{15}/_{100}$	$^{20}/_{100}$	$^{25}/_{100}$	$^{30}/_{100}$	$^{35}/_{100}$	$^{40}/_{100}$	$^{45}/_{100}$	$^{50}/_{100}$

0	1.4	2.8	4.2	5.6	7.0	8.4	9.8	11.2
0	$1^4/_{10}$	$2^8/_{10}$	$4^2/_{10}$	$5^6/_{10}$	$7^0/_{10}$	$8^4/_{10}$	$9^8/_{10}$	$11^2/_{10}$

Number line decimals and fractions

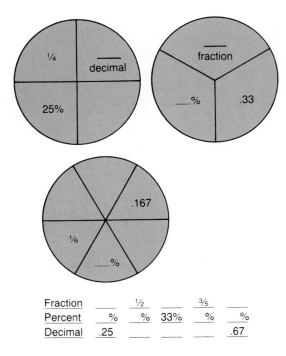

Fraction		½		⅗	
Percent	%	%	33%	%	%
Decimal	.25				.67

Expanded place value chart. Use an expanded place value chart to demonstrate the relationship among column values, column names, and decimals (see below). An activity consists of leaving parts unlabeled and instructing the student to fill in the missing labels.

Money cards. Use money cards to help the student determine correct change. For example, the following $10.00 change card can be used to compute correct change when a $10.00 bill is received:

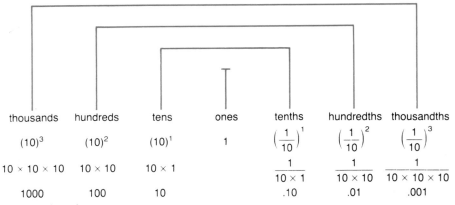

$10.00 Money Card

To solve the problem of how much change to give when a $10.00 bill is received and the purchase is for $6.77, the student simply marks out the amount of the purchase on the card. The remaining money is the correct change.

Real money. Use real money as often as possible to teach money values. For example, provide combinations of coins and ask the student to total the amounts. Money stamps from commercial publishers also can be used.

Coupon shopping. On a manila folder, draw a chart. Label the columns *grocery items*, *price*, *coupon value*, and *actual cost*. In the coupon column write the value of the coupon or use the real coupon. Ask the student to determine the actual cost of each item. For example:

thousands	hundreds	tens	ones	tenths	hundredths	thousandths
$(10)^3$	$(10)^2$	$(10)^1$	1	$\left(\dfrac{1}{10}\right)^1$	$\left(\dfrac{1}{10}\right)^2$	$\left(\dfrac{1}{10}\right)^3$
$10 \times 10 \times 10$	10×10	10×1		$\dfrac{1}{10 \times 1}$	$\dfrac{1}{10 \times 10}$	$\dfrac{1}{10 \times 10 \times 10}$
1000	100	10		.10	.01	.001

Expanded place value chart

Grocery Items	Price	Coupon Value	Actual Cost
1. coffee	$3.12	10% off	_____
2. pickles	$1.14	$ .15	_____
3. cereal	$1.39	15% off	_____
4. jelly	$ .79	$ .20	_____

Taking orders. Have the student become a waiter. He can write down orders from a pre-recorded cassette tape. Using the menus provided, he can look up the prices of the items ordered, compute the cost of the order, and write the total on the order pad.

Chance shopping. Provide a block with dollar amounts on each side and a laminated shopping card with the following statements:

1. How much do you have to spend?
2. What are you buying?
3. What page is it on in the catalog?
4. How much are you spending?
5. How much do you have left?

The student tosses the block to see how much money he has to spend. Then he looks through a catalog to find items that can be bought for that amount of money. Next, the student answers the questions on the card.

Store comparison. Have the student prepare a list of grocery items and find which supermarket offers the best price. The items and stores can be listed on a chart.

Check the charge. Make worksheets with instructions to check the cashier's slips and see if they are added correctly. For example:

$1.19
.99
.37
1.03
$3.38

$1.38
2.64
.26
.15
$4.43

Measurement

The ruler and Language Master. Draw lines on Language Master cards and record each line's length in inches and centimeters on the tape. Have the student measure the line on a card with the ruler. Number the cards. Have the student put the number on a worksheet and write the length of the line in inches and centimeters next to it. Then the student can insert the card in the Language Master to check his response.

Measure box. Provide the student with a box of objects to measure (such as Popsicle stick, comb, paper clip, straw) and a worksheet with the objects listed on it. Have the student measure the objects and record their length in inches and centimeters on the worksheet. This activity can be repeated for weighing objects.

Measurement and you. Have the student complete the following worksheet:

Your height:
_____feet _____inches

Your weight:
_____pounds

Your speed:
Number of seconds to run 40 yards: _____seconds

Your agility:
Number of seconds to deal 52 cards:
_____seconds

Your writing speed:
Number of times you can write your first name in one minute: _____times

Number of times you can write 6s in one minute: _____times

Your reading speed:
Number of words read in one minute:
_____words

Circumference of your head: _____inches

Circumference of your waist: _____inches

Word Problems

Reality math. Use classroom activities to help an adolescent face the realities of adult life. For example, have the student locate a job in the newspaper and use the salary quoted in the paper to compute net pay. Also, have the student compute living expenses by using newspaper ads, apartment rental ads, car ads, tax guides, catalogs, and brochures with insurance rates.

Story problems. Teach story problems by following the guidelines recommended by Blankenship and Lovitt (1976):

1. Teachers should identify and teach story problems by type, according to various characteristics (for example, extraneous information, verb tense, number and type of nouns).
2. To provide practice the teacher should make up several story problems of each type.
3. A group of instructional techniques should be outlined and used. It may be necessary to vary the techniques according to the needs of each student; however, a systematic plan is essential.

At first, provide the student with simple, interesting word problems. This helps the student understand that sentences may request specific math computations. For example:

1. What is the sum of 2 and 3?
2. How much are 3 marbles and 4 marbles?
3. What number represents a triple?
4. How many points is a field goal in football?
5. To get a first down in football, how many yards must you gain?
6. How many points are 10 baskets in basketball?

Have the student write a *number sentence* after reading a story problem (Wallace & Kauffman, 1986). For example:

Mary has 6 comic books. She has read 2 of them. How many books does she have left to read?

$$6 - 2 = \square$$

Table problems. Provide problems that include computing answers from information on a table. An interesting activity that requires computing percentages and decimals from a table is to give the student baseball standings (or football or basketball standings, depending on the season) from the newspaper with only the won/lost record beside each team. Have the student do the following:

1. Compute the percentage for each team in the American League East and the National League East.
2. Place the American and National League teams in order based on their won/lost records.
3. Determine how many teams have records over .500.
4. Determine how many percentage points the team in the American League East with the most losses is behind the team with the most wins.

INSTRUCTIONAL GAMES IN MATH

Numerous games using game boards and sets of stimulus cards can be played to practice various math skills. Game boards are discussed in detail in Chapter 4.

Math War

Materials:

Sets of index cards consisting of family patterns. (With sums to 9, each of the numbers from 1 to 9 has a family of two one-digit addends. The entire set for sums to 9 includes 54 cards. The family pattern for 7, for example, is $0 + 7$, $7 + 0$, $1 + 6$, $6 + 1$, $2 + 5$, $5 + 2$, $3 + 4$, $4 + 3$.)

Directions:

Each player shuffles his 54-card deck. With cards face down, one card at a time is turned over. The player who turns the card showing the number fact with the largest sum wins all the turned cards. The players then turn their next card. If cards of equal sums are turned up at the same time, players with the equivalent cards declare war. They place three cards face down and turn the fourth card face up. The player whose fourth card has the highest value wins all four cards of the other players (three face down cards, one face up). Whoever has the most cards after 54 cards are played wins. Another way of winning is to play until the other players only have 5 or 10 remaining cards.

Modifications:

Any set of math facts can be placed on the cards (such as multiplication facts, sums to 18). Also, students who play the game during the school day may keep the cards they win and give up the cards they lose. Then for homework each player can complete the missing cards in his deck and remove the extra cards. (Each player always comes to school with one complete deck, with no extra or missing cards.)

Pig Game

Materials:

Dice, scoring pad.

Directions:

Pig Game usually is played by two students with one pair of dice. The object is to be the first player to score 100 points by adding the totals on the dice after each roll. The players take turns rolling the dice; however, a player may roll as many times as he wishes as long as he does not roll a 1 on one or both of the dice. If a 1 is rolled on *one* die, the player gives up the turn and loses all points earned during that turn. If a 1 is rolled on *both* dice, the player gives up the turn, loses all points, and starts again at zero.

Modifications:

Wooden blocks with numerals on all sides except one can be used. A drawing of a pig is placed on the empty side. When pig dice are used, each player can be given an appropriate worksheet for his math level. If no pigs are rolled, the player answers an item on his worksheet, and his answer is checked by a student with the answer key. If the answer is

correct, the item number is checked; however, if the answer is incorrect, the item number is not checked and the player must attempt that item on another turn. If the player rolls one pig on the dice, he loses his turn. If two pigs are rolled (one on each die), the player is allowed to attempt to answer two items on his worksheet. This procedure is continued until one player correctly answers all the items on his worksheet and becomes the winner of the game. Also, to minimize erratic throwing of the dice, the dice can be placed in a pill container. The student shakes the container and then opens the lid to see the numbers that are upright on the dice.

Make the Numbers Count

Materials:

Dice or a spinner; score sheets.

Directions:

Each player is provided with a score sheet that has five columns—one each for ones, tens, hundreds, thousands, and ten thousands. The left side of the score sheet is numbered from 1 to 10. The die (showing 1 to 6) or spinner (1 to 5 —can be taken from a commercial game) is rolled or spun 10 times by each player. On each turn the players must enter the number shown on the die or spinner in one of the columns. For a game of 10 turns, only two numbers may be put in each column. After 10 turns the columns are totaled, and the player with the highest number wins.

Spinner Number	10,000s	1000s	100s	10s	1s
1. 3			3		
2. 5	5				
3. 1					1
4. 3		3			
5. 2				2	
6. 2				2	
7. 1					1
8. 4	4				
9. 5		5			
10. 5			5		
Total	9	8	8	4	2

Note: The player in this example would have had a higher score if he had not used the 4 in spin #8 in the 10,000 column. The 5 in either turn 9 or 10 could have been used there.

Rook Math

Materials:

A deck of Rook cards (14 sets of four numbered cards); four dice.

Directions:

The cards are shuffled, and five cards are dealt to each player. The remaining cards are placed on the table, and one card is turned up beside the deck. The player to the left of the dealer throws the four dice. He attempts to match the sum on the dice with a card or cards in his hand. He can lay down a single card or a combination of cards that equals the sum. The player can take the face-up card or draw from the deck. Whether he lays down cards or not, he then discards on the face-up pile. The next player then takes his turn. Play ends when one player is out of cards. The players then total the cards that have been played, and the player with the highest sum wins the game.

Blackjack Math

Materials:

A deck of playing cards.

Directions:

The teacher discusses the value of cards and rules of the game. Aces = 1 or 11; 2 to 10 are face value; picture cards = 10. The object of the game is to beat the dealer without going over 21. At first, the dealer and each player receive two cards. After that, the players request cards. If a player goes over 21 when taking additional cards, he loses. The winner each time gets to deal.

Golf Math

Materials:

Chalk and chalkboard.

Directions:

The students lay their heads on the desk with their eyes closed. The leader or teacher writes a story problem on the board. At the signal "go," all students look up, read the problem, and begin work. As each student finishes, he raises his hand. The leader gives the first person who finishes 1 point; the second person gets 2 points, and so on. These points represent "strokes" to make the first "hole." Each student keeps his score. If a student does not finish the problem within the allotted time, he receives a number of strokes that is more than the highest number given to students who finished the problem. A player then works the problem at the chalkboard. Those who had incorrect answers must add as many strokes to their scores as were given to those who did not finish. Nine holes make up a round, and the player with the lowest total score is the winner.

Math Concentration

Materials:

Ten stimulus cards with math problems on one side and blank on the other side; 10 cards with the answers to the problems of the stimulus cards on one side and blank on the other side.

Directions:

The cards are placed face down in a 5 × 4 array. Two or more students can play. The first player turns over a card and gives an answer. If he is correct, he turns over a second card. If the second card shows the answer to the first card, the player gets to keep both cards. If an incorrect answer is given to the first card, the player does not turn over a second card. The next player than takes his turn. The winner is the player with the most cards when all cards are taken.

Fraction Game

Materials:

One-inch cubes of wood with gummed stickers on each side marked ½, ¼, ⅙, ¹⁄₁₂, ⅓, and ¹⁄₁₂; 1″ cardboard squares marked as follows: 24 pieces with ¼ label, 31 pieces with ⅙ label, 12 pieces with ½ label, 18 pieces with ⅓ label, and 60 pieces with ¹⁄₁₂ label; six game boards marked into 12 sections.

Directions:

Each player is given a game board. He attempts to collect fractional parts that will cover ¹²⁄₁₂ of his board without overlapping pieces. The first player throws a cube and collects the fractional piece designated by the cube. This piece is placed on the playing board. The next player then takes his turn. Play continues until a player covers ¹²⁄₁₂ of his board. If a player throws the cube and all corresponding pieces have been taken, he receives nothing. Likewise, if the cube indicates a fraction that is larger than needed, the player collects nothing.

Multiplication and Division Facts Rummy

Materials: Forty to 52 cards containing a family of multiplication/division facts (for example, 9 × 6, 6 × 9, 54 ÷ 6, 54 ÷ 9).

Directions:

Seven cards are dealt to each player. The player on the dealer's left draws a card from the remaining cards. If the card matches two others in his hand in the same family, he lays down the book of cards and gives the answer to each fact. If he gives the wrong answer, the cards must remain in his hand until the next turn. After the player lays down cards or is unable to do so, he discards by placing a card from his hand face up beside the deck so that all the other discards can be seen. The next player may choose from the stack or pick up the previous discard if he can match it with two cards in his hand. If there are two cards in the discard pile that match one in a player's hand, he may pick up both. He does *not* have to take the whole pack, provided he can give the correct answers of the cards between the two he wants. Also, during his turn a player may lay down one or more cards that match another player's books. When one player is out of cards, he says, "Rummy," and wins the game.

Travel Game

Materials:

Large map of the United States; markers or pictures of vehicles; cards with math problems on them.

Directions:

On a large map of the United States, a course across the nation is marked off into 50-mile segments. Each card presents a math problem and the number of miles it is worth (such as 50, 100, or 200 miles). Each player draws a card and responds to the problem. If correct, the player moves the marker the number of miles indicated on the card. If incorrect, the player moves *back* the specified miles. The winner is the first player (or team) to reach the destination.

Modification:

Players can be provided with cards of various levels of difficulty. Each student can select cards from the difficulty level he desires. The more difficult the problem, the more miles it is worth.

Basketball Math

Materials:

A drawing of a basketball court on the chalkboard or on poster board; sets of cards presenting math problems labeled "lay-up," "10-foot jump shot," "15-foot jump shot," and "3-point shot."

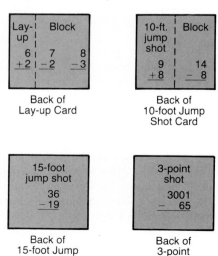

Lay-up	Block	
6 +2	7 −2	8 −3

Back of
Lay-up Card

10-ft. jump shot	Block
9 +8	14 −8

Back of
10-foot Jump
Shot Card

15-foot jump shot
36 −19

Back of
15-foot Jump
Shot Card

3-point shot
3001 −65

Back of
3-point
Shot Card

Directions:

The cards are divided into stacks. Each lay-up card has a problem to be answered for 2 points and two problems (slightly more difficult) that may be answered to block the lay-up. If the opposing player can answer either of the "block" problems, the lay-up is blocked. If the shooter answers the lay-up problem correctly and it is not blocked, he receives 2 points. For the next most difficult stack (10-foot jump shot), there is only one block question on the card. The 15-foot jump shot has the next most difficult problem and no block shot questions. The 3-point-shot stack has the most difficult problems and no block shot questions. A time limit (for example, 5 seconds) is set for answering the questions.

Counting Coins

Materials:

Timer; paper and pencil.

Directions:

The object of the game is to use the fewest coins to make a given sum. The leader calls out an amount (such as 65 cents). Each player must write down the coins that make the sum within a given time limit. All players who correctly sum the coins receive 1 point. The player or players who use the fewest coins receive 5 points. The first player to receive 25 points wins the game.

Rate Game

Materials:

A start-to-finish game board; math worksheets and corresponding answer sheets; game markers; dice.

Directions:

Each player is given an individual worksheet at the appropriate instructional level. The first player rolls one die and may elect to move his marker that number of spaces on the game board or to write the answers to problems on his worksheet for 10 seconds and move his marker according to the number of problems answered correctly. The opposing player uses the answer sheet to check the responses. If the player chooses to write answers from the worksheet, he must take these results even if the number is less than the number rolled on the die. The first player to reach the finish space on the board wins the game.

Fraction Blackjack

(Hurwitz, Goddard, & Epstein, 1975)

Materials:

Deck of playing cards.

Directions:

All picture cards are wild and may be given any value from 1 to 10. The cards are separated into two stacks: red cards (diamonds and hearts) and black cards (spades and clubs). The first player draws one card from each stack and forms a fraction using the value of the black card as the numerator and the value of the red card as the denominator. Thus, if he draws a black 8 and a red 2, his fraction is 8/2. The same player continues by drawing two more cards (one black and one red), forming the fraction, and adding the new fraction to the first fraction (8/2). He continues until he makes a sum of 10 or as close to 10 as possible. The sum may be above or below 10, and the winner of each round is the player who gets closest to 10.

Modification:

The game may be played more like traditional blackjack, in which the players take turns receiving their two cards and a player loses if he goes over 10.

Fraction Removal

Materials:

Dice (one green and one white); paper and pencil.

Directions:

Each player writes the following 22 numbers on his paper: 1.00, .50, .33⅓, .25, .20, .26⅔, 2.00, .66⅔, .40, 3.00, 1.50, .75, .60, 4.00, 1.33⅓, 1.20, 5.00, 2.50, 1.66⅔, 1.25, .83⅓, and 6.00. One green die and one white die are used. The green die determines the numerator, and the white die determines the denominator. Thus, a green 4 and a white 2 is equivalent to 4/2, or 2. The decimal equivalent of this is 2.00. Green 3 and white 5 equals 3/5 or .60. Each player rolls the dice, forms the fraction, computes the decimal form, and crosses it out on his paper. One point is scored for each decimal crossed out. A bonus of 5 points is given for each fraction rolled that is equivalent to 1.00 (²⁄₂, ⁴⁄₄). The winner is the player who scores 50 points first.

Decimal Shapes

(Bright & Harvey, 1982)

Materials:

A game board with sections containing numbers in decimal form; 10 markers (5 each of two colors); a chip marked *L* on one side and *S* on the other; an answer sheet that has the numbers on the board listed in order from smallest to largest.

Directions:

Both players place their markers on the starting spaces of the board (enclosed with dark lines). The first player flips the chip. If the chip lands on the *L* side, the player must move one of his markers to an adjacent space having a number larger than the number the marker is on. If the chip lands on the *S* side, the player must move one of his markers to an adjacent space having a number smaller than the number the marker is on. If the player can move one of his markers to a space occupied by his opponent, the opponent's marker is moved back to a starting position. Only one marker may be on a space at one time. The player must move one of his markers, no matter what the direction, if he is able to do so. If he cannot move,

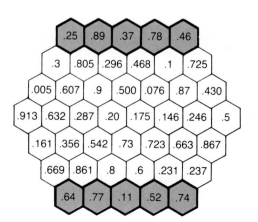

he loses his turn. The two players take turns, and each move can be checked for correctness by using the answer sheet. The winner is the first player to get all of his markers to the starting spaces on the other side of the board.

SELF-CORRECTING MATH MATERIALS

In addition to the self-correcting materials presented in this section, numerous self-correcting materials for math instruction are described in Chapter 4.

Flip Sider Math Cards

Feedback device:

The correct answer is written on the back of each stimulus card.

Materials:

Stimulus cards with a math problem on one side and the correct answer on the other side.

Directions:

The student looks at the math problem on the card and writes the answer on a worksheet. Then he flips over the card to check his response.

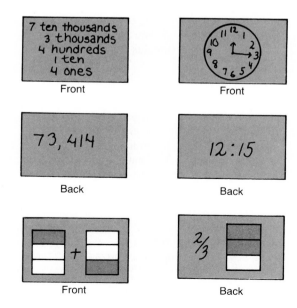

Calculator

Feedback device:

The student computes the problem on the calculator, and the correct answer appears in the read-out area.

Materials:

Low-cost pocket calculator; worksheet of math problems.

Directions:

The student computes the answer to a problem, writes it on the worksheet, and uses the calculator to check his response.

Clipping Answers

Feedback device:

When the clothespin containing the correct answer is clipped to the problem on the board and the board is turned over, the symbol on the back of the clothespin matches the symbol on the back of the board.

Materials:

Segmented stimulus board showing math problems on the front and symbols on the back; clothespins with answers on one side and symbols corresponding to those on the stimulus board on the other side.

Directions:

The student matches the answer on the clothespin to a problem by clipping the clothespin to the problem on the board. Then he turns over the board. If the symbol on the back of the clothespin matches the symbol on the back of the board, the answer is correct.

Modifications:

For easy storage, the clothespins can be kept in a plastic bag with a zipper. Also, pizza wheels make good stimulus cards.

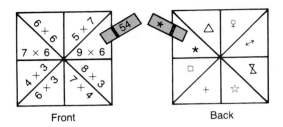

Front   Back

Math Squares

Feedback device:

After completing the squares, the student can check his work by turning over the squares. If the squares are placed correctly, a message or picture appears on the back.

Materials:

A set of poster board squares that include math problems and answers to problems on adjoining squares (a message or picture is written on the back of the large piece of poster board before the squares are cut); a large box with a window in the bottom, made by placing a piece of acetate over an opening.

Directions:

The student fits the squares together so that each fact adjoins its correct answer. He puts the pieces (message or picture side down) inside the box and on top of the acetate. When he has completed the puzzle, he places the cover on the box and flips the box over. If he is correct, he should be able to read the message or view the picture on the back of the puzzle.

5X6	30	7X8	56	4x8	32
16-7		64	13-8		5
9		8x8	5		9-4
	8	14-6	72	9x8 0	8X0
42÷7		63	½+½		16
6		9X7	1		4x4
	4x9	36	¼+¼ ½	6-0	6

Front

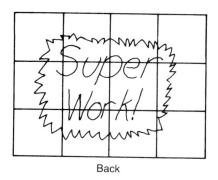

Back

Color Code Folders

Feedback device:

When the worksheet is in the red folder, the problems can be seen but the answers cannot. After completing the problems on a separate sheet of paper, the student removes the worksheet from its folder to check his answers.

Materials:

Red transparent folder (such as a term-paper folder); worksheet with problems written in black felt-tip pen and answers written in yellow.

Directions:

The student inserts the worksheet into the red folder. Then he numbers his seatwork paper and records the answer for each problem. The worksheet is removed from the folder, and the student checks his answers with those written in yellow on the worksheet.

Modification:

Different colors may be used (answers can be written in the same color as the folder).

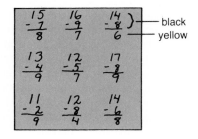

Worksheet

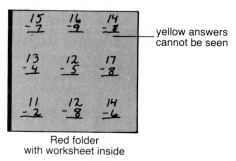

Red folder
with worksheet inside

Fast Facts

Feedback device:

The correct answers are written inside the open folder.

Materials:

Manila folder with math problems in a column on the *right* side inside the folder and the answers to the problems on the *left* side of the same flap inside the folder. The outside flap of the folder is cut so that only the problems are exposed when the folder is closed.

Directions:

The student computes the problems presented in the closed folder and then opens the folder to check his work.

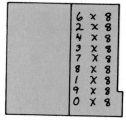

Closed Folder

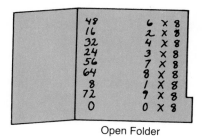

Open Folder

Snoopy Math

Feedback device:

When the student puts his pencil in the hole of the problem he has worked and turns over the cutout (Snoopy), the correct answer is written next to the hole where his pencil is.

Materials:

Snoopy figure cut out of poster board with (a) holes punched around the cutout, (b) a number placed near each hole, (c) an operation and a number (such as +8) written in the middle of the cutout, and (d) answers written on the other side beside the holes; pencil.

Directions:

The student computes problems according to the operation and number presented in the middle of the cutout. For example, if +8 is presented, the student is to add 8 to each number near each hole. He places his pencil in the hole beside a problem, computes the answer, and turns over Snoopy to check his response by looking at the answer where his pencil is.

Modification:

Each side can be used as the problem or the answer. For example, the problems on the other side of the example +8 become −8.

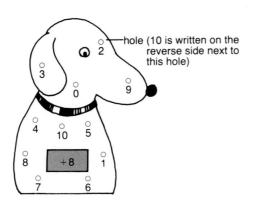
hole (10 is written on the reverse side next to this hole)

COMMERCIAL MATH PROGRAMS AND MATERIALS

Numerous published programs and materials are available for teaching math concepts and skills. The following selected programs and materials are useful for teaching math skills to students with learning problems.

Computational Arithmetic Program

Publisher: Pro-Ed

Description:

The *Computational Arithmetic Program* (Smith & Lovitt, 1982) is for students in first through sixth grade who need to learn and become proficient in the basic computational skills of whole numbers. It provides 314 sequenced problem worksheets in facts (basic problems for all four computational areas), addition (with and without carrying), subtraction (with and without borrowing), multiplication (with and without carrying), and division (with and without remainders).

Connecting Math Concepts

Publisher: Science Research Associates

Description:

Connecting Math Concepts (Engelmann & Carnine, 1992), emphasizes problem solving and includes three levels for students in first through third grade. The program establishes relationships among math concepts and their application. Lessons in Level A focus on the relationship of addition and subtraction and the concepts of more and less, place value, problem solving, estimation, money, and measurement. Level B teaches place value, relationships and facts of addition and subtraction, mental arithmetic, problem solving, measurement, money, column addition and subtraction, geometry, multiplication, and data collection and analysis. In Level C, students learn problem-solving strategies for situations involving classification, comparison, addition and subtraction actions, multiplication and division, and multistep problems.

Corrective Mathematics Program

Publisher: Science Research Associates

Description:

The *Corrective Mathematics Program* (Engelmann & Carnine, 1982) is a remedial series in basic math for students in third through twelfth grade and adults who have not mastered basic skills. The basic facts are taught in addition, subtraction, multiplication, and division. The program includes the concepts of carrying and borrowing as well as translating story problems into numerical statements. The lessons (65 in each operation area) take between 25 and 45 minutes and include both teacher-directed instruction and independent review activities.

Cuisenaire Rods

Publisher: Cuisenaire Company of America

Description:

Cuisenaire rods (Davidson, 1969) are instructional aids for teaching mathematical concepts. They can be used in kindergarten through sixth grade; however, they usually are emphasized for kindergarten through third grade. The Cuisenaire rods are not a complete program and mainly are used to supplement existing mathematical programs. They consist of 291 wood blocks that vary in length and color. Each white cube (shortest) equals 1, red equals 2, green equals 3, purple equals 4, yellow equals 5, dark green equals 6, black equals 7, brown equals 8, blue equals 9, and orange (tallest) equals 10. The rods are used in performing math operations. For example, to multiply 2 × 3 or $r \times g$, a cross is made with the rods with the first-named rod on the bottom. It is read as "r cross g." The cross represents the number of red rods (3) that would form a floor under the green rod. The three red rods can be placed next to the dark green rod to figure out the product (6). Cuisenaire rods can be used to teach readiness skills as well as all four operations with whole numbers and fractions. Rod sets and various resources for activities with the rods (such as puz-

zles, riddles, games, and activity cards) are available from Dale Seymour Publications.

DISTAR Arithmetic

Publisher: Science Research Associates

Description:

DISTAR Arithmetic stresses direct instruction within a highly systematic, intensive framework. Each kit includes a teacher's guide, teacher's presentation books, take-home workbooks for students, and (depending on the level) geometric figure cards, form boards, and an acetate page protector. *DISTAR Arithmetic* is designed primarily for use with students in small groups, but suggestions are included for teaching large groups. The 160 lessons in each kit are fast-paced, and the teacher's guide specifies what the teacher should say and do. Simple skills are presented first, followed by more complex skills. Scope and sequence charts are provided. Oral responses are used extensively; however, written work also is required. *DISTAR Arithmetic I* (Engelmann & Carnine, 1975) focuses on ordinal counting, 35 addition facts, > and < signs, simple story problems, and simple subtraction problems. *DISTAR Arithmetic II* (Engelmann & Carnine, 1976) covers 60 addition facts, 20 algebra addition facts, 43 subtraction facts, addition with regrouping, multiplication facts, time, money, measurement (metrics and standard), and fraction operations. *DISTAR Arithmetic III* (Engelmann & Carnine, 1972) extends the basic operations (regrouping, column multiplication, and long division). Also, story problems and problem-solving procedures are stressed. The *DISTAR* programs have been field tested and evaluated extensively. The results indicate that *DISTAR Arithmetic* is effective in teaching math skills to economically disadvantaged children (Abt Associates, 1976; Becker & Engelmann, 1976; Stallings & Kaskowitz, 1974).

Key Math Early Steps Program

Publisher: American Guidance Service

Description:

The *Key Math Early Steps Program* (Connolly, 1982) teaches beginning mathematics through hands-on activities with specially designed manipulatives including cubes, attribute blocks, card decks, chips, tumblers, numeral cards, meter ropes, and trays. Students receive introductory and foundation experiences in seven strands of mathematics content: geometry, numeration, addition and subtraction, measurement, time, fractions, and money. Step-by-step lessons and individual student worksheets are included.

Key Math Teach and Practice

Publisher: American Guidance Service

Description:

Key Math Teach and Practice (Connolly, 1991) provides activities for the diagnosis and remediation of math difficulties. It includes essential concepts covered in kindergarten through eighth grade, and the three packages of basic concepts, operations, and applications are linked directly with the *Key Math—Revised: A Diagnostic Inventory of Essential Mathematics.* Math inventories and probes are used to pinpoint a student's strengths and weaknesses. Instructional intervention follows a sequence of foundation steps (reviewing prerequisite skills, introducing concepts and skills, and demonstrating application), learning activities (moving from the use of manipulatives to pictorial to symbolic representations), and drills, games, and extensions (including exercises of estimation and problem solving). A teacher's guide, a student progress record, and a scope and sequence chart also are included. In addition, *Key Math Activity Pacs* are available that include manipulatives (such as attribute books, cubes, chips, tumblers, trays) to provide hands-on learning experiences to enrich the math program.

Project MATH

Publisher: Educational Development Corporation

Description:

Project MATH (Cawley et al., 1976) was developed at the University of Connecticut by Cawley and his associates. It is designed for students in preschool through sixth grade but can be used with secondary students who have learning problems. *Project Math*

provides the nonreader with the opportunity to gain skills in math without being hindered by a lack of reading ability (Cawley, 1977). The program stresses multiple options for teaching students with learning problems. The options focus on varying the input and output modes. The program includes a *Mathematics Concept Inventory,* designed as a screening device to determine the appropriate placement of each learner. There are four levels: prekindergarten to first grade, first and second grade, middle of second through fourth grade, and fourth through sixth grade. Each level contains a Multiple Option Curriculum with four ways to demonstrate mastery. The content is organized according to six strands: patterns, sets, geometry, numbers and operations, measurement, and fractions. The program also has units called LABS that stress the social and emotional development of the student. A LABS unit may last from several days to a few weeks and covers topics such as telephones, calculators, and metrics.

Real-Life Math

Publisher: Pro-Ed

Description:

Real-Life Math stresses the development of functional math skills in teenage students with learning problems through the use of role-playing activities in which students establish their own businesses. Students complete files, handle billing forms, and conduct financial transactions with a bank. The materials include a teacher's manual, 15 spirit masters, 8 stimulus posters, 10 audiocassettes, 5 student skill books, a mail box, 3 desk signs, and a supply kit of checks, deposit and withdrawal slips, and saving passbooks for 20 students.

Schoolhouse: Mathematics Series

Publisher: Science Research Associates

Description:

The *Schoolhouse: Mathematics Series* consists of three kits that can supplement any basal mathematics program for first through fourth grade. Each kit contains 400 skill cards (two copies each of 200) with 10 plastic overlays and 10 markers. Each card has an answer key on the back for self-checking and immediate reinforcement or correction and thus can be used to provide independent practice or additional drill. The kits offer mathematics skill practice in selected areas including numbers, addition and subtraction, multiplication and division, fractions, problem solving, geometry, measurement, and time and money. The *SRA Mathematics Drillpak* is a continuation of the *Schoolhouse Series.* The skill cards offer a review of basic algorithms and focus on skills usually practiced in fourth through sixth grade.

Strategic Math Series: Multiplication Facts 0 to 81

Publisher: Edge Enterprises

Description:

The *Strategic Math Series: Multiplication Facts 0 to 81* (Mercer & Miller, 1992a) is designed to enable students with math difficulties to understand, acquire, remember, and apply math concepts and skills. The program is based on research in effective teaching, learning strategies, memory, mastery learning, applied behavior analysis, generalization, and student motivation. Eight instructional stages are included: pretest, concrete, representational, DRAW (mnemonic), abstract, posttest, practice to mastery, and periodic review. All lessons include scripts to guide the teacher through the instructional components of advance organizer, demonstrate/explain, guided practice, independent practice, problem solving (that is, students learn to create their own story problems), and lesson feedback. Manuals also are available for addition facts, subtraction facts, place value, and division facts.

SOLVE: Action Problem Solving

Publisher: Curriculum Associates

Description:

SOLVE: Action Problem Solving is part of the Enright Math System and is designed for students in fourth grade through adult age. The three skillbooks for word problems develop problem solving for whole numbers, fractions, and decimals and percents. The program teaches a five-step blueprint for problem solving:

1. **S**—*Study* the problem.
2. **O**—*Organize* the facts.
3. **L**—*Line* up a plan.
4. **V**—*Verify* your plan with computation.
5. **E**—*Examine* your answer.

The program provides students with a variety of problem-solving strategies and includes both guided and independent practice. In addition, three scripted teacher guides provide presentation ideas and extension activities.

Unifix Materials

Publisher: Educational Teaching Aids

Description:

Unifix materials offer a variety of manipulative materials for teaching basic math concepts and skills. For example, the interlocking Unifix cubes are helpful for teaching basic addition, subtraction, and place value. Each set of cubes has 10 colors, and the materials are available in a kit or separately. Dale Seymour Publications also offers Unifix materials, such as cubes, trays, grids, pattern boards, activity books, and a teacher's resource book.

COMPUTER SOFTWARE PROGRAMS IN MATH

Computer software programs in math can be used to provide drill and practice activities in a motivating manner. Some programs present game-playing situations, and others effectively use animation and sound effects to maintain student interest. The computer also can provide self-correcting feedback so that the student does not practice errors. R. D. Howell, Sidorenko, and Jurica (1987) examined the effects of computer use on the learning of multiplication facts by students with learning disabilities. They found that it was necessary to combine direct teacher instruction with tutorial and drill-and-practice software for effective results. The following software programs present various math skills and can help the student understand and master these skills. Appendix B lists addresses of producers and distributors of educational computer software.

Arcademic Intermediate Math Series

Producer: DLM

Hardware: Apple II

Description:

The two programs included in this series provide excellent drill-and-practice vehicles for intermediate students. *Decimal Discovery* helps students improve their skills in comparing, adding, subtracting, multiplying, and dividing with decimals. A variety of games and problems are designed around an oil-drilling theme, and players respond by matching, filling in, or scanning the answer. The decimal problems range from tenths to thousandths. *Fast-Track Fractions* combines the excitement of car racing with fraction drills. Students solve problems that compare, add, subtract, multiply, and divide with fractions. Both programs include an editor system for creating, changing, and printing individualized game content. A listing of the 10 highest-scoring players is displayed to provide a reward system and motivate students to improve their scores.

Arcademic Skill Builders in Math

Producer: DLM

Hardware: Apple II, IBM PC/PCjr, Commodore 64, Tandy 1000

Description:

This series is designed to motivate students of all ages to learn fundamental math skills through the fast action and colorful graphics of arcade games. Six individual programs provide practice and drill in the four basic math operations and combinations of operations. *Alien Addition* uses an "alien invasion" theme to provide practice in basic addition facts.

Minus Mission offers practice in basic subtraction facts as the student uses a robot that fires laser beams to destroy green blobs of dripping slime. Practice in basic multiplication facts is provided in *Meteor Multiplication,* in which the student must disintegrate meteors moving toward a star station. *Demolition Division* gives the student the opportunity to practice basic division facts as tanks move toward cannons that the player can fire. In *Alligator Mix* the student feeds hungry alligators while increasing skill in both addition and subtraction facts. *Dragon Mix* provides practice in multiplication and division facts as a large dragon protects the city behind it from invading forces. In all the programs the range of numbers can be changed to practice basic facts with the numbers 0 through 3, 0 through 6, or 0 through 9. Also, there are nine speed options, and game time can range from 1 to 5 minutes. Twelve blackline masters and 52 flash cards are included with each program.

Basic Skills in Math

Producer: Love Publishing Company

Hardware: Apple II

Description:

This software program pinpoints the student's specific problem area in the basic fundamental math functions (addition, subtraction, multiplication, and division) and provides practice based on individual needs. After assessment, the student automatically is branched to the appropriate part of the program. For practice, the screen shows a numerical and pictorial representation of a problem. Visual and auditory rewards are given for success with each problem. If a student misses a problem twice, the work needed to reach the correct solution is presented visually. After the student progresses to the mastery test and demonstrates the basic skills for that level, the program offers an asteroid math learning game as a reward. The program is designed for students in first through sixth grade, but the format and space theme are compatible with a wide range of ages. Spirit masters accompany each program, and there is a built-in record-keeping system.

Computer Drill and Instruction: Mathematics

Producer: Science Research Associates

Hardware: Apple II, IBM

Description:

This software series covers 500 major skills from the first- through ninth-grade math curriculum and permits each student to practice specific skills independently. The four levels include lessons in number readiness, whole numbers, addition, subtraction, multiplication, division, fractions, decimals, computation, number and numeration, ratio and percent, measurement, pre-algebra, and applications. The program includes an interactive tutorial that breaks a problem into small steps and leads the student through each step. An electronic blackboard feature allows the student to work multistep problems directly on the screen. The Seatwork Generator prints tests and additional exercises for 316 skills for use in class drill or take-home assignments. An additional three-level program, *Computer Drill and Instruction: Word Problems,* provides 82 lessons in effective problem-solving strategies for students in first through sixth grade.

Mathematics Problem Solving

Producer: Media Materials

Hardware: Apple II, TRS-80

Description:

This series includes 10 programs with instructions and explanations given on an elementary reading level. Correct responses are praised, and students are given helpful hints and tutorial assistance for incorrect responses. The following programs are included: *Shoot for Solutions* (five steps to problem solving), *Home Run Logic* (thinking through problems; averages; percents), *Dive into Data* (recognizing essential data in word problems; whole number, fraction, and decimal problem solving), *Answer Matches* (estimating answers by rounding numbers; money problems), *On Your Mark—Go* (word problems; fractions; working with distance), *Score the Goal* (multiplication and division of whole numbers), *Chin Bars and Charts* (interpret-

ing information on charts, tables, and graphs; computations of whole numbers and decimals), *Run a Relay* (using rate tables; reading a table of records), and *Stick to a Plan* (using a five-step plan with word problems; getting data from a bar graph). Supplemental materials for enrichment and reinforcement are included.

Math Sequences

Producer: Milliken

Hardware: Apple II

Description:

This package consists of 12 diskettes that provide a comprehensive, objective-based mathematics curriculum with structured drill and practice designed for students in first through eighth grade or as remediation for older students. Topics covered include number readiness, addition, subtraction, multiplication, division, laws of arithmetic, integers, fractions, decimals, percents, equations, and measurement formulas. The range of problem levels (from 16 to 64) within a sequence makes it possible to place students according to level of understanding. The work (such as carrying, borrowing, canceling numbers) for each problem is completed on the screen. Graphic or textual reinforcements are given for a correct response. When a problem is missed more than once, the correct solution is displayed, step-by-step, for the student to study. The student is advanced by a level after specific achievement criteria are met or moved back a level until mastery is achieved. The management program maintains records for each student and allows the teacher to establish personalized performance levels and make individual and class assignments.

Math Skills—Elementary Level; Math Skills—Junior High Level

Producer: Encyclopaedia Britannica Educational Corporation

Hardware: Apple II

Description:

These two programs provide practice and drill in mathematical concepts and basic operations and processes. The skills presented at the elementary level include numbers, addition and subtraction, multiplication and division, fractions, and decimals. The skills presented at the junior high level include ratio and proportions, percents, graphics, estimating, and measuring. The programs provide immediate feedback that is supportive when the response is correct and instructional when the response is incorrect. Graphics are used to explain the mathematical concepts and demonstrate them visually. The content and difficulty of each segment change according to the student's performance.

Sailing Through Story Problems

Producer: DLM

Hardware: Apple II

Description:

This two-disk program has 12 content levels and offers a variety of problems, including practice in reading maps and charts and working with money. The program features a lively pirate theme and is designed for students in fifth grade and above. A built-in calculator is presented on the screen, and the student receives hints while learning to find relevant information, use the correct mathematical procedure, and select the correct operation. A branching feature assures that the student remains at an appropriate level according to the number of correct answers given. The teacher can select the number of problems (5 to 10) per game, the mastery level required for advancement, and whether the built-in calculator is turned on or off. A management system records game data and pinpoints error patterns.

REFERENCES

Abt Associates. (1976). *Education as experimentation: A planned variation model* (Vol. 3). Boston: Abt Associates.

Anderson, L. W., & Pellicer, L. O. (1990). Synthesis of research on compensatory and remedial education. *Educational Leadership, 48*(1), 10–16.

Ashlock, R. B. (1990). *Error patterns in computation: A semi-programmed approach* (5th ed.). New York: Merrill/Macmillan.

Bannatyne, A. (1973). Programs, materials and techniques. *Journal of Learning Disabilities, 6,* 204–212.

Bartel, N. R. (1990). Problems in mathematics achievement. In D. D. Hammill & N. R. Bartel, *Teaching students with learning and behavior problems* (5th ed., pp. 289–343). Boston: Allyn & Bacon.

Becker, W. C., & Engelmann, S. E. (1976). *Technical report 1976–1.* Eugene, OR: University of Oregon.

Blankenship, C. S. (1978). Remediating systematic inversion errors in subtraction through the use of demonstration and feedback. *Learning Disability Quarterly, 1,* 12–22.

Blankenship, C. S., & Lovitt, T. C. (1976). Story problems: Merely confusing or downright befuddling. *Journal for Research in Mathematics Education, 7,* 290–298.

Bley, N. S., & Thornton, C. A. (1989). *Teaching mathematics to the learning disabled* (2nd ed.). Austin, TX: Pro-Ed.

Bright, G. W., & Harvey, J. G. (1982). Using games to teach fraction concepts and skills. In L. Silvey (Ed.), *Mathematics for the middle grades (5–9): 1982 yearbook.* Reston, VA: National Council of Teachers of Mathematics.

Carnine, D. (1991). Curricular interventions for teaching higher order thinking to all students: Introduction to the special series. *Journal of Learning Disabilities, 24,* 261–269.

Cawley, J. F. (1977). Curriculum: One perspective for special education. In R. D. Kneedler & S. G. Tarver (Eds.), *Changing perspectives in special education* (pp. 21–45). New York: Merrill/Macmillan.

Cawley, J. F. (1989, June). *Qualitative enhancement of mathematics performance among the mildly handicapped.* Presentation at the IC-SEMM Instructional Methods Forum, Washington, DC.

Cawley, J. F., Fitzmaurice, A. M., Goodstein, H. A., Lepore, A. V., Sedlak, R., & Althaus, V. (1976). *Project MATH.* Tulsa, OK: Educational Development Corporation.

Cawley, J. F., Fitzmaurice-Hayes, A., & Shaw, R. (1988). *Mathematics for the mildly handicapped—A guide to curriculum and instruction.* Boston: Allyn & Bacon.

Cawley, J. F., & Miller, J. H. (1989). Cross-sectional comparisons of the mathematical performance of children with learning disabilities: Are we on the right track toward comprehensive programming? *Journal of Learning Disabilities, 23,* 250–254, 259.

Cawley, J. F., Miller, J. H., & School, B. A. (1987). A brief inquiry of arithmetic word-problem solving among learning disabled secondary students. *Learning Disabilities Focus, 2,* 87–93.

Christenson, S. L., Ysseldyke, J. E., & Thurlow, M. L. (1989). Critical instructional factors for students with mild handicaps: An integrative review. *Remedial and Special Education, 10*(5), 21–31.

Clifford, M. M. (1990). Students need challenge, not easy success. *Educational Leadership, 48*(1), 22–26.

Connolly, A. J. (1982). *Key Math early steps program.* Circle Pines, MN: American Guidance Service.

Connolly, A. J. (1991). *Key Math teach and practice.* Circle Pines, MN: American Guidance Service.

Davidson, J. (1969). *Using the Cuisenaire rods.* New Rochelle, NY: Cuisenaire.

De Corte, E., & Verschaffel, L. (1981). Children's solution processes in elementary arithmetic problems: Analysis and improvement. *Journal of Educational Psychology, 73,* 765–779.

Dunlap, W. P., & Brennan, A. H. (1979). Developing mental images of mathematical processes. *Learning Disability Quarterly, 2*(2), 89–96.

Eicholz, R. E., O'Daffer, P. G., Fleenor, C. R., Charles, R. I., Young, S., & Barnett, C. S. (1985). *Addison-Wesley mathematics 1–3 components.* Menlo Park, CA: Addison-Wesley.

Ellis, E. S., Lenz, B. K., & Sabornie, E. J. (1987a). Generalization and adaptation of learning strategies to natural environments: Part I: Critical agents. *Remedial and Special Education, 8*(1), 6–20.

Ellis, E. S., Lenz, B. K., & Sabornie, E. J. (1987b). Generalization and adaptation of learning strategies to natural environments: Part II: Research into practice. *Remedial and Special Education, 8*(2), 6–23.

Engelmann, S. E., & Carnine, D. (1972). *DISTAR arithmetic level III.* Chicago: Science Research Associates.

Engelmann, S. E., & Carnine, D. (1975). *DISTAR arithmetic level I.* Chicago: Science Research Associates.

Engelmann, S. E., & Carnine, D. (1976). *DISTAR arithmetic level II.* Chicago: Science Research Associates.

Engelmann, S. E., & Carnine, D. (1982). *Corrective mathematics program.* Chicago: Science Research Associates.

Engelmann, S. E., & Carnine, D. (1992). *Connecting math concepts.* Chicago: Science Research Associates.

Fitzmaurice-Hayes, A. (1984). Curriculum and instructional activities: Grades 2 through 4. In J. F. Cawley (Ed.), *Developmental teaching of mathematics for the learning disabled.* Rockville, MD: Aspen Systems.

Fleischner, J. E., Garnett, K., & Shepherd, M. J. (1982). Proficiency in arithmetic basic facts computation of learning disabled and nondisabled children. *Focus on Learning Problems in Mathematics, 4*(2), 47–56.

Fleischner, J. E., Nuzum, M. B., & Marzola, E. S. (1987). Devising an instructional program to teach arithmetic problem-solving skills to students with learning disabilities. *Journal of Learning Disabilities, 20,* 214–217.

Frank, A. R., & Brown, D. (1992). Self-monitoring strategies in arithmetic. *Teaching Exceptional Children, 24*(2), 52–53.

Fuchs, L. S. (1986). Monitoring progress among mildly handicapped pupils: Review of current practices and research. *Remedial and Special Education, 7*(5), 5–12.

Fuchs, L. S., Fuchs, D., & Deno, S. L. (1985). The importance of goal ambitiousness and goal mastery to student achievement. *Exceptional Children, 52,* 63–71.

Fulkerson, E. (1963). Adding by tens. *The Arithmetic Teacher, 10,* 139–140.

Garnett, K., & Fleischner, J. E. (1983). Automatization and basic fact performance of normal and learning disabled children. *Learning Disability Quarterly, 6,* 223–230.

Gersten, R., Carnine, D., & Woodward, J. (1987). Direct instruction research: The third decade. *Remedial and Special Education, 8*(6), 48–56.

Groves, K. (1976). Teacher idea exchange: Using dice and the blockhead game for skill development. *Teaching Exceptional Children, 8,* 103–104.

Hasselbring, T. S., Goin, L. I., & Bransford, J. D. (1987). Developing automaticity. *Teaching Exceptional Children, 19*(3), 30–33.

Howell, D., Davis, W., & Underhill, L. (1974). *Activities for teaching mathematics to low achievers.* Jackson, MS: University Press of Mississippi.

Howell, R. D., Sidorenko, E., & Jurica, J. (1987). The effects of computer use on the acquisition of multiplication facts by a student with learning disabilities. *Journal of Learning Disabilities, 20,* 336–341.

Howell, S.'C., & Barnhart, R. S. (1992). Teaching word problem solving at the primary level. *Teaching Exceptional Children, 24*(2), 44–46.

Hudson, P. J., Peterson, S. K., Mercer, C. D., & McLeod, P. (1988). Place value instruction. *Teaching Exceptional Children, 20*(3), 72–73.

Hurwitz, A. B., Goddard, A., & Epstein, D. T. (1975). *Number games to improve your child's arithmetic.* New York: Funk & Wagnalls.

Hutchings, B. (1975). Low-stress subtraction. *The Arithmetic Teacher, 22,* 226–232.

Hutchings, B. (1976). *Low-stress algorithms.* Reston, VA: National Council of Teachers of Mathematics.

Kameenui, E. J., & Simmons, D. C. (1990). *Designing instructional strategies: The prevention of academic learning problems.* New York: Merrill/Macmillan.

Kelly, B., Gersten, R., & Carnine, D. (1990). Student error patterns as a function of curriculum design: Teaching fractions to remedial high school students and high school students with learning disabilities. *Journal of Learning Disabilities, 1,* 23–29.

Kirby, J. R., & Becker, L. D. (1988). Cognitive components of learning problems in arithmetic. *Remedial and Special Education, 9*(5), 7–15, 27.

Kline, F. M., Schumaker, J. B., & Deshler, D. D. (1991). Development and validation of feedback routines for instructing students with learning disabilities. *Learning Disability Quarterly, 14,* 191–207.

Kramer, T., & Krug, D. A. (1973). A rationale and procedure for teaching addition. *Education and Training of the Mentally Retarded, 8,* 140–144.

Lloyd, J. W., & Keller, C. E. (1989). Effective mathematics instruction: Development, instruction, and programs. *Focus on Exceptional Children, 21*(7), 1–10.

Locke, E. A., & Latham, G. P. (1990). *A theory of goal setting and task performance.* Englewood Cliffs, NJ: Prentice-Hall.

Locke, E. A., Shaw, K. N., Saari, L. M., & Latham, G. P. (1981). Goal setting and task performance: 1969–1980. *Psychological Bulletin, 90,* 125–152.

Lovitt, T. C. (1989). *Introduction to learning disabilities.* Boston: Allyn & Bacon.

Marks, J. L., Purdy, C. R., & Kinney, L. B. (1970). *Teaching elementary school mathematics for understanding.* New York: McGraw-Hill.

Mastropieri, M. A., Scruggs, T. E., & Shiah, S. (1991). Mathematics instruction for learning disabled students: A review of research. *Learning Disabilities Research & Practice, 6,* 89–98.

Mercer, C. D., & Miller, S. P. (1992a). *Strategic math series: Multiplication facts 0 to 81.* Lawrence, KS: Edge Enterprises.

Mercer, C. D., & Miller, S. P. (1992b). Teaching students with learning problems in math to acquire, understand, and apply basic math facts. *Remedial and Special Education, 13*(3), 19–35, 61.

Miller, J. H., & Milam, C. P. (1987). Multiplication and division errors committed by learning disabled students. *Learning Disabilities Research, 2*(2), 119–122.

Montague, M., & Bos, C. S. (1986). The effect of cognitive strategy training on verbal math problem solving performance of learning disabled adolescents. *Journal of Learning Disabilities, 19,* 26–33.

National Council of Supervisors of Mathematics. (1988). *Twelve components of essential mathematics.* Minneapolis, MN: Author.

National Council of Teachers of Mathematics. (1976). Minicalculators in schools. *The Arithmetic Teacher, 23,* 72–74.

National Council of Teachers of Mathematics. (1980). *An agenda for action: Recommendations for school mathematics of the 1980s.* Reston, VA: Author.

National Council of Teachers of Mathematics. (1989). *Curriculum and evaluation standards for school mathematics.* Reston, VA: Author.

Peterson, P. L., Fennema, E., & Carpenter, T. (1988/1989). Using knowledge of how students think about mathematics. *Educational Leadership, 46*(4), 42–46.

Peterson, S. K., Mercer, C. D., & O'Shea, L. (1988). Teaching learning disabled children place value using the concrete to abstract sequence. *Learning Disabilities Research, 4*(1), 52–56.

Porter, A. C., & Brophy, J. (1988). Synthesis of research on good teaching: Insights from the work of the Institute for Research on Teaching. *Educational Leadership, 45*(8), 74–85.

Reisman, F. K. (1977). *Diagnostic teaching of elementary school mathematics: Methods and content.* Chicago: Rand McNally.

Reisman, F. K. (1982). *A guide to the diagnostic teaching of arithmetic* (3rd ed.). New York: Merrill/Macmillan.

Rivera, D. M., & Smith, D. D. (1987). Influence of modeling on acquisition and generalization of computational skills: A summary of research findings for three sites. *Learning Disability Quarterly, 10,* 69–80.

Rivera, D. M., & Smith, D. D. (1988). Using a demonstration strategy to teach midschool students with learning disabilities how to compute long division. *Journal of Learning Disabilities, 21,* 77–81.

Robinson, S. L., DePascale, C., & Roberts, F. C. (1989). Computer-delivered feedback in group-based instruction: Effects for learning disabled students in mathematics. *Learning Disabilities Focus, 5*(1), 28–35.

Rosenshine, B. (1983). Teaching functions in instructional programs. *The Elementary School Journal, 83,* 335–351.

Ruais, R. W. (1978). A low-stress algorithm for fractions. *Mathematics Teacher, 71,* 258–260.

Russell, R., & Ginsburg, H. (1984). Cognitive analysis of children's mathematical difficulties. *Cognition and Instruction, 1,* 217–244.

Scheid, K. (1990). *Cognitive-based methods for teaching mathematics to students with learning problems.* Columbus, OH: LINC Resources.

Silbert, J., Carnine, D., & Stein, M. (1990). *Direct instruction mathematics* (2nd ed.). New York: Merrill/Macmillan.

Smith, D. D., & Lovitt, T. C. (1982). *The computational arithmetic program.* Austin, TX: Pro-Ed.

Stallings, J. A., & Kaskowitz, D. H. (1974). *Follow Through classroom observation evaluation.* Menlo Park, CA: Stanford Research Institute.

Stokes, T. F., & Baer, D. M. (1977). An implicit technology of generalization. *Journal of Applied Behavioral Analysis, 10*(2), 349–367.

Sugai, G., & Smith, P. (1986). The equal additions method of subtraction taught with a modeling technique. *Remedial and Special Education, 7*(1), 40–48.

Suydam, M. N. (1980). *Using calculators in precollege education: Third annual state-of-the-art review.* Columbus, OH: Calculator Information Center.

Thornton, C. A. (1984). *Basic mathematics for the mildly handicapped: First year report* (Grant No. G008301694, Project No. 1029JH30133). Washington, DC: U.S. Department of Education, Office of Special Education and Rehabilitative Services.

Thornton, C. A. (1985). *Basic mathematics for the mildly handicapped: Second year report* (Grant No. G008301694, Project 1029JH40016). Washington, DC: U.S. Department of Education, Office of Special Education and Rehabilitative Services.

Thornton, C. A., & Toohey, M. A. (1982–1985). *MATHFACT: An alternative program for children with special needs* (A series of four kits: Basic Addition Facts; Basic Subtraction Facts; Basic Multiplication Facts; Basic Division Facts). Brisbane, Australia: Queensland Division of Special Education.

Thornton, C. A., & Toohey, M. A. (1984). *Matter of facts: Addition; Matter of facts: Subtraction; Matter of facts: Multiplication; Matter of facts: Division.* Oaklawn, IL: Creative Publications.

Thornton, C. A., & Toohey, M. A. (1985). Basic math facts: Guidelines for teaching and learning. *Learning Disabilities Focus, 1,* 44–57.

Thornton, C. A., & Toohey, M. A. (1986). Subtraction facts hide-and-seek cards can help. *Teaching Exceptional Children, 19,* 10–14.

Underhill, R. G., Uprichard, A. E., & Heddens, J. W. (1980). *Diagnosing mathematical difficulties.* New York: Merrill/Macmillan.

Wallace, G., & Kauffman, J. M. (1986). *Teaching students with learning and behavior problems* (3rd ed.). New York: Merrill/Macmillan.

Wertlieb, E. (1976). The tool chest: Games little people play. *Teaching Exceptional Children, 9,* 24–25.

CHAPTER 8

Assessing Language Skills

Oral language is a learned behavior that enables people to transmit their ideas and culture from generation to generation. The ability to communicate through language is perhaps an individual's most vital and complex characteristic. It is through speech and language that people make sense of and respond to their environment. A communication problem can be devastating, because it directly affects the individual as well as others in the immediate environment as attempts are made to transmit ideas, facts, feelings, and desires. Language also is related directly to achievement and adjustment in school because language is the basis for formulating questions, extending and clarifying information, and reducing ambiguity in new learning situations (Bashir, 1989). In addition to being part of the academic curriculum, language is important because it is a medium through which information is taught and acquired.

Students with severe language impairments usually are identified at an early age and receive speech or language therapy through a prekindergarten or developmental program. A greater number of students possess a more subtle language problem and begin to show difficulties as they grow older. As the curriculum demands increase in about the third or fourth grade, these students lack the language foundation required to build academic skills. Teachers often describe such students as having difficulty maintaining attention, following directions, and using the right words when speaking. Other students are identified when they begin to have difficulties in academic areas such as reading and writing. These students need an informed classroom teacher who is able to identify and understand their language problems and help them receive appropriate intervention.

COMPONENTS OF LANGUAGE

Language refers to "a code whereby ideas about the world are expressed through a conventional system of arbitrary signals for communication" (Lahey, 1988, p. 2). Speakers and listeners both are involved in oral language because language is heard as well as spoken. A speaker's use of this arbitrary vocal system to communicate ideas and thoughts to a listener is referred to as *expressive language,* or *production.* In this process the listener uses *receptive language,* or *comprehension.*

To assess and plan instruction for language problems, the teacher needs to be familiar with the components of language. Bloom and Lahey (1978) classify the components of language according to form (phonology, morphology, syntax), content (semantics), and use (pragmatics).

Form: Phonology

Phonology is the system of rules that governs sounds and sound combinations, and a *phoneme* is a unit of sound that combines with other sounds to form words. A phoneme is the smallest unit of language and is distinguished from the other language components in that a phoneme alone such as /s/ and /b/ does not convey meaning. However, when interchanged in a word, phonemes significantly alter meaning (for example, *sat* to *bat*). The rules that govern phonemes focus on how sounds can be used in different word positions and which sounds may be combined. For example, standard English does not have a sound for the combination of /zt/.

The English language consists of about 40 phonemes, classified as either vowels or consonants. Vowels are categorized according to where they are produced in the mouth. The tongue may be moved up, down, forward, or backward in producing vowels. These different tongue positions are used to classify vowels as high, mid, or low (that is, the position of the highest part of the tongue) and front, central, or back (that is, the location of the highest position) (Owens, 1990). For example, the long /e/ sound is classified as high front because the tongue blade is high in the front of the mouth. The tip of the tongue is down for all vowels. Consonants are classified according to place and manner of production. For example, the phoneme /f/ can be described by place (labial) and manner (voiceless stop).

Jacobson and Halle (1956) propose three principles that influence the order of phoneme acquisition:

1. Children learn to distinguish sounds first that have the fewest features in common, such as oral-nasal (/p/, /m/), labial-dental (/p/, /t/), and stop-fricative (/p/, /f/).
2. Development of front consonants such as /p/ and /m/ precedes the development of back consonants such as /k/ and /g/.
3. Phonemes that occur infrequently among the languages of the world (such as the English short *a* in *bat*), even though they may be frequent in the child's native language, are the last to be acquired.

Owens (1990) notes that vowels are acquired by the age of 3, whereas consonant clusters and blends are not acquired until age 7 or 8. However, there are individual differences, and the age of acquisition for some sounds may vary by as much as 3 years.

Phonological deficits. Problems in phonology frequently appear as articulation disorders. The most common problem is that of the child who is developmentally delayed in consonant acquisition. The child may omit a consonant (such as saying "oo" for *you*), substitute one consonant for another (such as saying "wabbit" for *rabbit*), or distort a consonant. An example of a consonant distortion is the lateral emission of air in the production of /s/ in which the air escapes over the sides of the tongue (rather than the tip), resulting in a slushy quality to the sound.

In addition to problems in expression, problems also can occur in reception, such as discrimination difficulty. For example, the child may hear "Go get the nail" when the command was actually "Go get the mail." The child does not respond correctly, because she cannot tell the difference between /n/ and /m/. Phoneme discrimination errors can occur in comprehension of consonants (/p/ for /b/, /d/ for /t/), consonant blends (/pr/, /fr/, and /kr/ confused with /pl/, /fl/, and /kl/), and vowels (confusion of vowels produced with the tongue in a forward position such as in *pit, pet,* and *pat*) (Wiig & Semel, 1976).

Researchers recently have begun to examine the relationship between phonological disorders and academic reading performance. Ackerman, Dykman, and Gardner (1990) note that students with reading disabilities tend to articulate sequences more slowly than do students without disabilities. Ackerman et al. claim that the slow-speaking student would have greater difficulty sounding out and blending polysyllabic words and comprehending what was read. Moreover, Pehrsson and Denner (1988) add that many students with language disorders have organization problems, which may inhibit their ability to remember what they have read. Students with a limited phonological repertoire (that is, unintelligible speech) who are experiencing difficulties in reading, spelling, and writing present concerns for the teacher regarding the priorities and content of appropriate intervention.

Form: Morphology

A *morpheme* is the smallest unit or segment of language that conveys meaning. Two different types of morphemes exist: roots and affixes. *Root* words are free morphemes that can stand alone (for example, *car, teach, tall*), whereas *affixes* are bound morphemes such as prefixes and suffixes that when attached to root words change the meaning of the word (for example, *cars, teacher, tallest*). *Derivational* suffixes change word class; for example, the verb *walk* becomes the noun *walker*, with the addition of the suffix *er*. *Inflectional* suffixes change the meaning of a word; for example, the addition of the inflectional *s* to the word *boy* changes the meaning to more than one boy.

A further distinction can be made between two broad classes of words in a language: content words and function words (Lahey, 1988). Similar to root words, *content* words convey meaning when they stand alone, and they generally carry the meaning in sentences. *Function* words or connective words join phrases or sentences together (for example, pronouns, articles, prepositions, and conjunctions). The meaning of connective words varies according to the context or words that they connect.

Morphological deficits. Students who are delayed in morphological development may not use appropriate inflectional endings in their speech. An elementary school student may not use the third-person *s* on verbs (for example, "He walk") or use *s* on nouns or pronouns to show possession (for example, "Mommy coat") or use *er* on adjectives (for example, "Her dog is small than mine"). Older elementary and middle school students who are delayed in morphology may lack more advanced morphemes of irregular past tense or irregular plural (such as *drived* for *drove* or *mans* for *men*). Students such as these exhibit inconsistency regarding morphology usage (for example, they vacillate in the use of *bringed, branged,* and *brought*).

Students with morphological problems may not acquire and understand the rules for word formation at the same rate and complexity as do their peers with normal language development. Disorders in form or morphology also include difficulties learning the language code and linking it to what already is known about the environment. Wiig and Semel (1984) list the following areas in which specific morphological deficits can be found in many students with language-learning problems:

1. The formation of noun plurals, especially the irregular forms (*-s, -z, -ez,* vowel changes, *-ren,* etc.)
2. The formation of noun possessives, both singular and plural (*-'s, -s'*)
3. The formation of third person singular of the present tense of verbs (*-s*)
4. The formation of the past tense of both regular and irregular verbs (*-t, -d, -ed,* vowel change)
5. The formation of the comparative and superlative forms of adjectives (*-er, -est*)
6. The cross-categorical use of inflectional endings (*-s, -'s, -s'*)
7. Noun derivation (*-er*)
8. Adverb derivation (*-ly*)
9. The comprehension and use of prefixes (*pre-, post-, pro-, anti-, di-, de-*) (p. 303)

Some differences in inflectional endings are observed in students who speak black English (Baratz, 1969; Bartel, Grill, & Bryen, 1973). The teacher should be aware that some inflectional endings reflect a student's cultural difference rather than a developmental delay. Examples of inflectional differences include "John cousin" in black English instead of "John's cousin," "fifty cent" instead of "fifty cents," and "she work here" instead of "she works here."

Form: Syntax

Syntax is a system of rules that governs how words or morphemes are combined to make grammatically correct sentences. Rules of syntax specify word order, sentence organization, relationships between words and word classes or types, and other sentence constituents (Owens, 1990). Moreover, syntax specifies which word combinations are acceptable or grammatical and which word classes may appear in noun and verb phrases (for example, adverbs modify verbs). Thus, syntax frequently is referred to as *grammar.*

Rules of grammar emerge between 18 and 24 months of age, as evidenced in a child's production of two-word sentences. The child does not change abruptly from single words to grammatical two-word sentences. There is a period of transition in which a distinction can be made between two-word utterances and two words in grammatical form. Braine (1976) claims that in this transition period the child often is groping for a pattern that is replaced later by a correct grammatical form.

Chomsky (1957) focuses on the linguistic process instead of the grammatical products in his theory of generative transformational grammar. The first feature of this theory is that the speaker transforms an underlying sentence structure, such as *girl-throw-ball,* into different surface (verbalized) structures: "The girl threw the ball," "The ball was thrown by the girl," "It was the ball that the girl threw." The second aspect is that the speaker generates sentences according to an internalized rule system. Thus, Chomsky maintains that human languages differ only superficially and that underlying principles are universal.

Wood (1976) outlines six stages in the acquisition of syntax. Stages 1 and 2 are described better with semantic rules of grammar, whereas the last four stages describe syntactic structure. Stage 3 typically begins when the child is 2 to 3 years old. At this age, the child's sentences contain a subject and a predicate. For example, in Stage 2, she says, "No play," but in Stage 3 she says, "I won't play." Stage 4 begins around 2½ years of age and continues to about 4 years of age. In this stage the child begins to perform operations on sentences, such as adding an element to basic sentences through the process of *conjunction.* For example, "where" can be added to the simple sentence "Daddy go" to form "Where Daddy go?" The child also can *embed* (that is, place words within the basic sentence). For example, the sentence "No glass break" becomes "The glass didn't break." In Stage 4 the word order is changed to ask a question. For example, "Man is here?" is changed to "Is the man here?" During this stage, sentences remain simple in structure. Between 2 and 3 years of age, the child does not combine simple sentences but says them next to each other (for example, "John bounced the ball; John hit the lamp"). Between 3 and 4 years of age the child combines simple sentences with the conjunction *and* (for example, "John bounced the ball and hit the lamp").

Stage 5 usually occurs between 3½ and 7 years of age. In this stage the child uses complete sentences that have word classes typical of adult language: nouns, pronouns, adverbs, and adjectives. The child also becomes aware of differences within the same grammatical class. This awareness is evident in the child's use of different determiners and verbs with singular and plural nouns. For example, *this* is inappropriate for use in the sentence, "This chairs are heavy." The proper determiner (singular or plural) and appropriate verb for expressing plurality must be used. This same principle applies to prepositional phrases. For example, the sentence, "We cried to the movie" is not grammatically correct because an inappropriate prepositional phrase is used. In essence, in this stage the child learns the appropriate semantic functions of words and assigns these words to the appropriate grammatical classes.

Wood's Stage 6 begins when the child is about 5 years of age and continues until 10 years of age. The child begins complex sentence structures and learns to understand and produce sentences that imply a command ("Give me the toy"), a request ("Please pass the salt"), and a promise ("I promise to stop"). Implied commands are the easiest to acquire but often are confused with requests. The promise is difficult for children to understand, and this type of verb may not be mastered until age 10 (Wood, 1976).

Syntactic deficits.   Children who have delay in syntax use sentences that lack the length or syntactic complexity expected for their age. For example, a 6-year-old child who uses a mean sentence length of three words may say, "Where Daddy go?" instead of "Where did Daddy go?" Additional deficits in the processing of syntax include problems in comprehending sentences (such as questions or sentences that express relationship between direct and indirect objects), negation, mood (such as inferences of obligations signified by auxiliary verbs *must, have to,* and *ought*), and passive sentences (Wiig & Semel, 1976, 1984).

Students may have difficulty processing syntactic structures of increased complexity such as embedded sentences, "wh" questions, interrogatives, and negative sentences. Wiig and Semel (1984) include deficits in memory and recall, difficulties using strategies to enhance memory, and decreased selective attention as being related to deficits remembering spoken messages. Students with language problems also have a tendency to rely on basic sentence structures and exhibit little creativity and use of novel or interesting sentences (Simon, 1985).

Content: Semantics

Semantics refers to language meaning and is concerned with the meaning of individual words as well as the meaning that is produced by combinations of words. For example, the word *cup* has a meaning of a container from which to drink and refers to an object in the child's world. An example of meaning attached to combinations of words is the phrase "Daddy's cup." These words add the meaning of possessiveness in relationship to each other (that is, the cup belongs to Daddy). Receptive semantics refers to understanding language, whereas expressive semantics refers to producing meaningful discourse.

According to Lahey (1988), language content (semantics) has three categories. One category involves objects in general (for example, cars, ball, Mommy, juice). The second category involves actions in general (for example, throwing, hitting, kicking). The third category involves relations between objects (for example, Michael and his computer, me and my puppy, Debbie and her car) and relations between events (such as the causal relation between going swimming and getting wet). The difference between language topic and language content is reflected in the particular message called the topic (for example, a Ninja Turtle) and the more general categorization of the message called the content (for example, toys). Consequently, because youngsters from different cultures talk about different topics, they do not have the same vocabulary even though their content is often the same.

Clark (1973) and Nelson (1974) express different views concerning the child's development of meaningful words. Clark asserts that children use perceptual cues to acquire word meaning. For example, the word *dog* appears in a child's early vocabulary as the child notes the physical characteristics of a dog (four legs, tail, long ears, fur, and so on). Clark reports that a child relies on perceptual cues when she uses one word to refer to several things. For example, the child may use the word *dog* to refer to all four-legged, furry animals. Nelson, in contrast, proposes that the meanings first expressed by young children are based on dynamic properties of people and objects that are movable, moving, or changeable. For example, *Mommy* is a word that is observed in early vocabularies and refers to a movable, moving, changeable person in the child's world. Words that refer to food, clothing, and toys also appear in early vocabularies because of their dynamic characteristics. Children experience food as they eat it; articles of clothing as they put them on and take them off; and toys as they bounce, roll, and spin them. Nelson also states that children categorize words according to a shared function. Children observe that objects are similar in the way they move and act or in the way they are acted upon; thus, words that refer to food are categorized by the common function of things to eat.

Bloom and Lahey (1978) believe that the child uses both functional and perceptual cues in the development of word meaning. They note that the child observes objects that involve movement such as Mommy and bottles (Mommy and bottles come and go). The child also perceives that objects in a class look alike (bottles are cylinder-shaped and have nipples).

The acquisition of meaning extends beyond acquisition of the child's first words. It is a slow, complicated process that continues into adulthood. Wood (1976) outlines several stages of semantic acquisition. In Stage 1, a child develops meanings as she acquires her first words. Wood refers to these first words as one-word sentences. The meanings of these sentences are determined by the context in which they are spoken. An 18-month-old child may use the word *doggie* quite frequently, but the context in which she says the word may differ and imply different meanings (for example, "There is a doggie," "That is my doggie," "Doggie is barking," "Doggie is chasing a kitty").

At about 2 years of age, the child begins to produce two-word utterances with meanings related to concrete actions (such as "Doggie bark" or "My doggie"). In Stage 2, the child conveys more specific information verbally and continues to expand her vocabulary and utterance length. However, until about the age of 7, the child defines words merely in terms of visible actions. To a 6-year-old child, a fish is "a thing that swims in a lake" and a plate is a "a thing you can eat dinner on." Also, during this stage, the child typically responds to a prompt word (such as *pretty*) with a word that could follow it in a sentence (such as *flower*). Older children, around 8 years of age, frequently respond with a verbal opposite (such as *ugly*) (Brown & Berko, 1960).

In Stage 3, at 8 years of age, the child's word meanings relate directly to experiences, operations, and processes. If a child's neighbor owns a horse, the child may include this attribute in her word meaning of horse in addition to the attributes of animal, four-legged, and a thing that can be ridden. When asked where horses live, the child may respond, "At the Kahns'." By an adult definition, this answer is not correct. The child's vocabulary is defined by her own experiences, not those of adults. At 12 years of age, the child begins to give dictionary-like definitions for words (Wood, 1976). When asked to define *bear*, she might respond, "a large, warm-blooded animal that hibernates in the winter." At this time the child's word definitions approach the semantic level of adults.

Semantic deficits.   Developmental delay in word meaning (semantics) is observed in children who use or understand a limited number of words. The limited vocabulary may be in specific areas, such as adjectives, adverbs, prepositions, or pronouns. Students may have a longer response time when selecting vocabulary words or have difficulty retrieving or recalling a specific word (dysnomia). The student with retrieval difficulties often attempts to participate in classroom discussions but has no apparent response when called on to answer. Vocabulary difficulties may be evident in an inability to use specific words when describing objects or events (for example, "that thing over there," "the thing you use to write with").

Semantics delay also is evident when students assign a narrow set of attributes to each word so that each word has limited meaning. Students with semantic deficits often fail to perceive subtle changes in word meaning that follow from changes in context and may not perceive multiple meanings of frequently used words (Wiig, 1990a). This leads to incomplete understanding and misinterpretations of what is heard or read. In addition, students may have figurative language problems and tend to interpret idioms, metaphors, and proverbs literally (Wiig & Semel, 1984). These problems have important classroom implications when considered with research findings by Lazar, Warr-Leeper, Nicholson, and Johnson (1989). Their study of math, reading, and language arts teachers in kindergarten through eighth grade revealed that 36 percent of all teacher utterances contained at least one multiple-meaning expression. Indirect requests (27 percent) occurred most frequently. Moreover, at least one idiom occurred in 12 percent of the utterances, and the use of idiomatic expressions increased in frequency as grade level increased. Thus older students with language problems may be at an increased disadvantage when attempting to follow teacher directions or understand classroom discourse.

Additional semantic difficulties experienced by students with language problems include understanding linguistic concepts (for example, *before/after, if/then, many, some, few*), perceiving logical relationships among words (for example, comparative, possessive, spatial, temporal), and comprehending verbal analogies (for example, *sandwich* is to *eat* as *milk* is to *drink*) (Wiig & Semel, 1984). Moreover, students may misuse transition words (that is, conjunctions such as *although* and *if* and words such as *regardless* and *accordingly*) and avoid making complex sentences and relating two arguments in sentences or sentence sequences (Wiig, 1990a).

Use: Pragmatics

Bruner (1974/1975) defines *pragmatics* as the "directive function of speech through which speakers affect the behavior of others in trying to carry out their intention" (p. 283). In discussing this definition, McLean and Snyder-McLean (1978) distinguish two broad functions: controlling or influencing the listener's action ("Give me the doll") and influencing attitudes ("I think Jane would make a good class president"). These functions also are referred to as the speaker's intent. Bates (1976) notes that the study of meaning in language pragmatics involves how one's communicative intentions are mapped into linguistic forms. The rules then govern how language is used in social contexts to convey a variety of intentions such as requesting, asserting, and questioning. An individual's use of language based on an understanding of how language works in social interactions also is referred to as *communicative competence* (Holland, 1977). Wilcox (1986) describes communicative competence as "the ability to convey effectively and efficiently an intended message to a receiver. . . . [T]his requires not only knowledge of the conventional communicative code, but also knowledge pertaining to socially appropriate communicative behaviors" (p. 644).

One pragmatic function that occurs after 3 years of age is the indirect request or hint (Ervin-Tripp & Mitchell-Kernan, 1977; Leonard, Wilcox, Fulmer, & Davis, 1978). Prutting (1979) notes that indirect requests frequently are used (for example, "My mother always lets me have cookies before lunch"). Leonard et al. studied 4-, 5-, and 6-year old children's understanding of three types of indirect requests: (a) affirmative construction ("Can you shut the door?"), (b) responses with a negative element ("Can't you answer the phone?"), and (c) an affirmative construction with a negative intention ("Must you play the piano?"). The 4- and 5-year-old children understood the first two types of requests but not the third type. The 6-year-old children understood the third type of request but made mistakes. Leonard et al. interpret the mistakes to mean that understanding was not complete.

Bloom and Lahey (1978) state that the situation affects the form of the message within the pragmatics of language. The characteristics of the message that increase the likelihood that the message will be accepted as well as understood are referred to as pragmatic presuppositions. In adult speech these presuppositions are apparent in tendencies to be polite and indirect in requests. Children as young as 4 and 5 years of age show these pragmatic presuppositions when they talk politely as they make a request. Pragmatic presuppositions develop as the child matures and learns not to interrupt the speaker, talk at the wrong time, or speak too loudly for the situation.

Pragmatic deficits.   Delay in pragmatics is evident when children do not use functions that are expected for their developmental age. For example, if a student whose developmental age is above 8 years seriously answers "Yes" to the indirect request, "Must you play the piano?" (instead of ceasing to play the piano), she may be developmentally delayed in understanding indirect requests. Moreover, a student may have difficulty determining when the listener does not understand what she is saying and thus continue with her manner of presentation rather than adapt her speech to the listener's needs. Also, a student may enter conversations in a socially unacceptable fashion or fail to take turns when conversing. She may either monopolize a conversation or expect the other speaker to do most of the talking with little feedback to indicate listening. Other examples of problems with language use include difficulty staying on a topic during conversation (topic maintenance), inappropriate facial expressions and body posture, immature speech, and difficulty interpreting verbal and nonverbal communication cues (Simon, 1985; Wiig & Semel, 1984). Finally, a student may have difficulty choosing the right linguistic content (that is, gauging complexity according to the listener), using questioning strategies, and interacting well verbally in a group (Wiig & Semel, 1984). Difficulties with communicative competence are particularly frustrating because they can persist into adulthood and affect the student's academic, vocational, and social performance (Schumaker & Deshler, 1984).

LANGUAGE DEVELOPMENT

Students with language problems display a wide variety of difficulties, although many of the deficits initially may be subtle. The teacher should be aware of the potential language difficulties so that students can be identified and receive appropriate services as early as possible. In spite of early intervention, many language problems are long-term and require intervention that changes with the varying needs of the students. The following sections present the language difficulties typically found in three age groups of students: preschool and kindergarten, elementary, and secondary. It is important to keep in mind that language is interactive and that many of these difficulties may not occur in isolation. Furthermore, because language difficulties generally do not disappear without intervention, the same deficits may span several age categories.

Preschool and Kindergarten Students

Young students with language problems are a diverse group, so it may be difficult to differentiate them from their normally developing peers. However, various researchers (Bernstein & Tiegerman, 1989; Wiig & Semel, 1984) discuss the difficulties common to this age group. Readiness skills such as counting, naming colors, naming the days of the week, and using scissors often are delayed. The child may be unable to follow simple directions, follow the story line in a book or movie, or enjoy listening to stories. In addition, the period of normal acquisition for articulation and sound development may be delayed so that the child exhibits immature-sounding speech. The mean length of utterances and vocabulary may be similar to that of a younger child. Word-finding difficulties and an inability to name common objects also may be noted. As a result, the child may exhibit sound substitutions such as "buzgetti" for "spaghetti." The child may produce fewer functionally appropriate and accurate responses, say phrases such as "you know" or "that thing over there," or describe rather than name objects. In addition, the child may be unable to make one-to-one correspondence between letters and sounds and have difficulty discriminating between sounds.

Furthermore, young children may have difficulty responding accurately to certain types of questions. Parnell, Amerman, and Harting (1986) state that questions regarding nonobservable persons, actions, or objects are the most difficult for young children. In an evaluation of nine wh-forms, why, when, and what happened were the most difficult.

Young children with language problems also may demonstrate significant deficits in symbolic, adaptive, and integrative play when compared with their linguistically matched peers. They often frequently play by themselves or exhibit more nonplay and parallel play than do their peers (Roth & Clark, 1987). Behaviorally, children with language-learning problems may have attention deficits, need additional time to understand information and formulate ideas for expression, and have a poor tolerance for frustration.

Elementary Students

A student with a language-learning problem may exhibit a variety of difficulties in the first grade, such as a limited ability to identify sounds, difficulty analyzing and synthesizing sound sequences, and problems segmenting words into grammatical units. Temporal and spatial concepts (as well as abstract concepts such as *before-after, neither-nor, some, if/then,* and *few*) may pose particular difficulty (Bernstein & Tiegerman, 1989; Snyder, 1986; Wiig & Semel, 1984). These concepts often are presented in sentences of increased length and complexity that are particularly problematic for students with subtle processing problems. The student may be seen as obstinate or noncompliant, when actually she has misunderstood the directions.

In the early elementary grades, the use of manipulatives begins to decrease, and the student must gain information from the teacher's verbal presentation. As the language complexity increases with each grade advance, the student must keep up with the demands of the instructional language as well as absorb the curriculum content. By fourth grade, most of the curriculum content is presented in print, and the student with language problems may have particular difficulty making the transition from narrative to expository writing (Wallach, 1989).

Word-finding (retrieval) difficulties still may exist, but the deficits may not be as evident because the student begins to use strategies involving circumlocution (that is, talking around the word), fillers, and descriptors (Bos & Vaughn, 1988). German (1984) adds the manifestation of secondary characteristics such as tapping and saying "I know it." She claims that students with retrieval problems generally have difficulty with three indices, including response time, error index or word selection process, and substitution types. Students generally do not perform similarly across the three areas, and situations often occur in which the student's speed is affected although the correct word eventually is recalled.

Problems stemming from the relationship between phonological disorders and reading achievement begin to emerge in elementary school. Students with reading problems often articulate sequences more slowly than do their peers who do not have reading difficulties. As a result, the slow-speaking student tends to have greater difficulty sounding out and blending polysyllabic words and comprehending what is read (Ackerman et al., 1990). Requirements for comprehension also change because multiple-meaning words emerge and students are required to draw conclusions and make inferences. Deficits in text comprehension lead to problems in reading independence and mastery of content material. Thus, students with language problems may have difficulties participating in group discussions, sharing ideas on a topic, and developing ideas that follow earlier learning (Bashir, 1989).

Students in elementary school also may be deficient in expressive or oral language. In a study that examined children's discourse or ability to tell a story, Merritt and Liles (1987) found that the stories told by children with language problems contained fewer story episodes and fewer main and subordinate clauses than the stories told by their peers without language problems. In addition, the students with language problems had significant difficulty integrating critical parts of a story and these difficulties continued after maturity and intervention. Merritt and Liles conclude that students with language problems may have difficulty forming verbal abstractions and performing the logical operations needed to interpret and understand complex concepts. The students also had difficulty formulating and expressing spoken language, and such problems often are reflected in academic difficulties.

Finally, elementary students with language problems continue to exhibit difficulties in their use of language. In academic settings, this often is reflected in the student's social skills. Students at this age may exhibit some of the same behaviors as they did when they were younger, such as failing to adjust to their listener's needs and having difficulty joining an ongoing conversation. In addition, they may misinterpret social cues, fail to think of others' thoughts and feelings, and be unable to predict the consequences of their behavior. Also, students at this level may be able to formulate a question but have difficulty functionally using requests to obtain new information (Schwabe, Olswang, & Kriegsmann, 1986).

Secondary Students

Adolescents who have language-learning problems exhibit a variety of difficulties that tend to become more subtle. At the secondary level, the teacher is faced with the challenge of designing interventions to assist students in overcoming or compensating for their language problems so that they can meet the increased demands of secondary school.

Many adolescents with language problems lack the ability to use and understand higher-level syntax, semantics, and pragmatics in both production and processing (Ehren & Lenz, 1989). Secondary students are expected to organize their time and complete assignments, and, thus, they must follow both oral and written instructions to complete work independently. However, receptive and expressive language difficulties affect their ability to learn effectively. This creates problems in gaining information from class lectures and textbooks, completing homework, following classroom rules, demonstrating command of knowledge on exams, expressing thoughts in writing, passing minimum competency exams, and participating in classroom discussions (Schumaker & Deshler, 1984).

Problems in comprehension of auditory language also are persistent in adolescents and result in short-term memory problems and a decrease in understanding of linguistic relationships (Riedlinger-Ryan & Shewan, 1984). Frequently, adolescent students with language problems have difficulty organizing information and correctly associating or categorizing it for later retrieval. Thus, they often are unable to retain and synthesize complex information because they lack the ability to organize or categorize it. Poor organization and categorization result in other problems, such as poor note-taking, test-taking, and study skills, and difficulty integrating information (Schumaker, Deshler, Alley, Warner, & Denton, 1984).

Difficulties also may persist in language use in the areas of awareness of social cues, interpretation of the motives and emotions of others, and use of appropriate language. Because adolescents frequently are aware of their difficulties, behaviors such as aggression, frustration, lack of motivation, withdrawal, and inattention may arise (Hazel & Schumaker, 1988; Seidenberg, 1988; Wiig & Semel, 1984).

STUDENTS WITH LIMITED ENGLISH PROFICIENCY

A language problem is present when a student's understanding or use of language interferes with communication and is significantly different from the peers in the cultural community (Linares, 1983; Taylor, 1986). Unfortunately, many students with limited English proficiency (LEP) have been misdiagnosed as having learning or language impairments because of their poor academic performance or difficulty on standardized tests (Cardoza & Rueda, 1986; J. R. Mercer, 1983). As the LEP population in the United States increases, teachers are faced with the challenge of distinguishing between students who are unfamiliar with the language and culture and students with a true language problem. LEP students with language-learning problems may need services somewhat different from students whose primary language is standard English. Salend and Fradd (1986) note that LEP students have the following needs:

1. Access to teachers proficient in English as well as the student's native language.
2. Use of nonbiased assessment and instruction to formulate appropriate individualized educational programs.
3. Exposure to curriculum and alternative instructional strategies that promote the academic and social relevance of instruction.

Several factors should be considered when assessing LEP students. To determine whether the student has limited English proficiency or a language-learning problem, assessment should be conducted in the student's primary language to examine skills in the areas of writing, reading, listening, and speaking. Language assessments should include the use of both quantitative measures (that is, formal tests) and qualitative measures (for example, observations, adapted test instruction, and a language sample). It also is helpful to interview significant people in the student's life with the same cultural background to determine how effectively the student communicates in her primary language. Interviews can yield important information regarding the language spoken at home, attitudes toward the two languages and cultures, the parents' educational level, and a profile of the community where the student lives (Kayser, 1989).

Many students with LEP or a social dialect are identified as having a phonological deficiency. Adler (1988) raises the following questions regarding these students: Should only standard English be taught to these students? If the dialect is rule-governed and nonstandard (rather than substandard), should the student be taught to speak "correctly" if her dialect is consistent with what is spoken in the community in which the student lives? Finally, should only English be taught to young non–standard-speaking students, or should they be allowed to retain the social dialect of their cultural peers and parents? Adler notes that the current belief appears to support teaching the use of language that is relevant to school talk (standard English) as well as everyday talk (nonstandard English). This is difficult to accomplish, however, because it requires a change in the current system and collaborative interaction between families and teachers in language arts and English. Thus, the teacher must assume the responsibility of providing quality assessment and intervention to LEP students.

ASSESSMENT OF LANGUAGE SKILLS

Language assessment should be viewed not as a single isolated event but rather as an ongoing process throughout a student's education. The five major reasons for language assessment are as follows:

1. To identify students with potential language problems.
2. To determine a student's language developmental level.
3. To plan educational objectives and design appropriate intervention programs.
4. To monitor the student's progress.
5. To evaluate the language intervention program.

The last three of these assessment functions are most relevant to daily instructional planning. Among these three functions, the first one performed is *planning objectives*. The assessment information describes the student's language. This description is used in planning objectives that relate directly to the problem. The assessment of a morphological disorder, for example, should be specific: "The student does not use *s* on regular nouns to indicate plurality." The teacher then can plan the objective: "The student will use plural *s* on regular nouns with 90 percent accuracy when naming pictures of plural regular nouns." *Monitoring the student's progress* involves the teacher determining daily or weekly if the student is reaching short-term instructional objectives. The sample objective of 90 percent accuracy of plural *s* when naming pictures of plural regular nouns requires an assessment procedure of counting responses. Finally, in *program evaluation* the teacher assesses the student's progress with the materials and techniques used in the program. This information allows the teacher to determine if it is necessary to change materials or techniques to achieve the educational objective.

Thus, language assessments of school-age youngsters should be educationally relevant and provide both diagnostic information and intervention strategies. To accomplish this goal, two levels of information should be included in the assessment: the content-oriented level and the process-oriented level. The content-oriented level examines the actual content the student has learned and identifies specific areas that require intervention (for example, a syntactic deficit in the use of present progressive tense). The process-oriented level examines how skills are learned or acquired (for example, the use of a strategy such as clustering digits to remember a phone number).

Assessment of language development is an evaluation of the student's receptive and expressive language. The components assessed include phonology, morphology, syntax, semantics, and pragmatics. Language skills in these areas are listed by age in the language scope and sequence skills lists presented by Bartel and Bryen (1982) and C. D. Mercer, Mercer, and Bott (1984). The teacher can assess all of these components or decide to assess only one or two specific components. An experienced examiner obtains information or observes the student before deciding what to assess. The information gathered can include various observations; for example, the student is difficult to understand, the student has difficulty understanding what others say, the student uses short sentences, the student uses few words, or the student cannot start and maintain a discussion topic.

The student who is difficult for others to understand, but who understands what others say and uses many words and long sentences, may have problems in phonology. Thus, assessment should begin in this area. The student who uses only a few words needs to be assessed in semantics, and the student who uses short sentences needs assessment in semantic relationships and syntax.

Language assessment includes the use of formal and informal assessment procedures. Quantitative (formal) measures are used when the examiner needs to determine the student's developmental level and obtain a standardized score or classify the student. These measures include observable behaviors and result in a numerical score or an assigned classification. If the examiner wants to determine specific teaching objectives, informal measures are used. Qualitative or naturalistic measures are

based on the assumption that behaviors vary across different settings, and their purpose is to determine the relevant behaviors or skills that are evident in the setting being examined. Assessment of both language developmental level and teaching objectives should include both types of tests. School speech and language clinicians are experienced in administering and interpreting formal and informal measures of language. The teacher who is unfamiliar with these tests should consider working with the school speech and language clinician in assessing language.

FORMAL LANGUAGE ASSESSMENT

In a formal language assessment, standardized instruments are used to compare a student's performance with pre-established criteria to determine the existence of a speech or language problem. On these instruments, a student's raw score is converted to a standardized score, language age or mental age, age equivalent, or occasionally a grade equivalent. Students whose scores are much lower than the scores of other students their age usually are referred for additional testing or are placed in speech-and-language therapy.

Some language tests provide a comprehensive measure of all language functioning. This type of test assesses receptive and expressive language in all components. For example, the *Adolescent Language Screening Test* (Morgan & Guilford, 1984) assesses phonology, morphology, syntax, semantics, and pragmatics. Other tests are designed to measure specific components of language. For example, the *Northwestern Syntax Screening Test* (Lee, 1971) assesses receptive and expressive skills in syntax only. Some tests are even more specific and measure only receptive or expressive skills in one component. For example, the *Peabody Picture Vocabulary Test—Revised* (Dunn

& Dunn, 1981) assesses receptive semantic skills.

Screening Tests

In many school districts, students are given a speech-and-language screening test when they enter preschool or kindergarten. The screening provides an overview of a student's performance in a particular area, which can be compared with the performance of a student of the same age or grade who is developing normally. Many school districts use standardized or formal screening instruments, whereas other districts devise informal assessment instruments to identify preschool and kindergarten students who may have potential language problems. Table 8.1 presents selected formal language screening tests that assess receptive and expressive language in various components. Students who score below an acceptable level on a screening test usually are referred for a comprehensive evaluation.

The advantage of a screening is that it requires little administration time and, thus, allows a large number of students to be evaluated. When all students are screened at the beginning of their formal education, speed is an obvious concern because so many students must be evaluated. However, because of factors such as social and emotional development, participation in a preschool program, family environment, and cultural influences, only a few language skills should be expected to have been mastered by all 4- or 5-year-old children. Thus, a disadvantage to screening young children is that the screenings often are not able to detect subtle language problems. To illustrate, a youngster may receive high scores (80 to 90 percentiles) in both processing and production on a language screening test administered at the beginning of first grade. However, because subtle language problems were not detected at the initial

screening and intervention was not made available, the student may experience academic difficulties later when faced with a more abstract and demanding fourth-grade curriculum. Thus, ideally, several speech-and-language screenings should be administered (for example, kindergarten, third grade, sixth grade, ninth grade); however, time constraints on public school clinicians force them to give a screening test only one time. Consequently, many students with language problems are not identified at an early age.

Diagnostic Tests

Diagnostic tests measure one or more specific language components including receptive or expressive language. As presented in Table 8.2, survey tests measure a wide range of language skills, whereas other diagnostic tests assess specific speech and language components. In a comprehensive diagnostic evaluation, it generally is advisable to administer a test that provides an overall view of the student's understanding and use of language. The specific test often is determined by the student's age or level of functioning. If the examiner notices that the student has difficulty formulating words and sentences, an additional test should be administered to measure the student's ability to name objects (for example, the *Expressive One-Word Picture Vocabulary Test*) or apply syntactic skills (for example, the *Carrow Elicited Language Inventory*). If the student's speech intelligibility is reduced, the examiner may administer a test of phonology to obtain additional information (for example, *The Assessment of Phonological Process—Revised*). The assessment provides an overall view of the student's language skills as well as additional information concerning reported or observed areas of concern.

Although standardized language tests do not provide information regarding academic

TABLE 8.1
Selected language screening measures.

Test	Component Measured	Receptive/ Expressive	Age Norms
Adolescent Language Screening Test (Morgan & Guilford, 1984)	Phonology, morphology syntax, semantics, pragmatics	R, E	11–17 years
The dimensions of language use, content, and form are screened by seven subtests: *Pragmatics, Receptive Vocabulary, Concepts, Expressive Vocabulary, Sentence Formulation, Morphology, and Phonology.* Administration time is less than 15 minutes.			
Bankson Language Test—2 (Bankson, 1990)	Morphology, syntax, semantics, pragmatics	R, E	3–6 years
This instrument is organized into three general categories. Semantic knowledge includes body parts, verbs, nouns, functions, prepositions, and opposites and categories. Morphological and syntactic rules include pronouns, verb usage and tense, plurals, comparatives and superlatives, questions, and negation. Pragmatics includes controlling, ritualizing, informing, and imagining. A 20-item short form also is available.			
Clinical Evaluation of Language Fundamentals— Revised: Screening Test (Semel, Wiig, & Secord, 1989)	Phonology, morphology syntax, semantics	R, E	5–16 years
The screening test identifies the need for an in-depth diagnosis of language. Six areas are assessed: the acquisition of morphological rules using a sentence completion task; the ability to interpret, recall, and execute oral directions that contain linguistic concepts; the ability to recall and reproduce sentence structure; the ability to perceive associative relationships among word concepts; the ability to interpret semantic relationships in sentences; and the ability to assemble syntactic structures into grammatically and semantically acceptable sentences. Two optional subtests screen writing and storytelling skills.			
Northwestern Syntax Screening Test (Lee, 1971)	Syntax	R, E	3–7 years
Twenty items assess receptive ability by requiring the student to listen to a sentence spoken by the examiner and then select one picture out of four choices that is most appropriate. Also, 20 items assess expressive ability by having the student repeat sentences spoken by the examiner as the examiner points to various pictures.			

or therapeutic interventions, they do pinpoint the student's specific strengths and weaknesses. The role of the examiner is to interpret the assessment information and transform it to academically relevant instructional skills and interventions.

INFORMAL LANGUAGE ASSESSMENT

Informal assessment procedures generally are combined with standardized tests to provide descriptive information regarding a student's language ability. Although standardized measures are used widely, the emphasis on including some type of informal assessment is consistent with the theoretically based descriptive approach that is critical of viewing language as a series of independent objectives. Although standardized instruments determine the need for services, they often are too narrow to assess a student's baseline performance or

TABLE 8.2

Selected diagnostic language measures.

Test	Component Measured	Receptive/ Expressive	Age Norms
Survey measures			
Houston Test for Language Development (Crabtree, 1963)	Phonology, morphology, syntax, semantics	R, E	6 months–6 years

Part I, for children age 6 months to 3 years, is a checklist that is completed by an observer who has ready access to the child. In Part II, for children age 3 to 6 years, the examiner elicits speech from the child with materials from a kit.

Preschool Language Scale—3 (Zimmerman, Steiner, & Pond, 1992)	Phonology, syntax, semantics	R, E	Birth–7 years

The examiner uses a combination of pictures and objects to assess low levels of language acquisition. Areas assessed include logical thinking, sensory discrimination, grammar and vocabulary, temporal and spatial relations, memory and attention span, and self-image. There are three supplementary assessments: articulation, language sample, and parent questionnaire. A Spanish version also is available.

Test of Language Development—2: Primary (Newcomer & Hammill, 1988)	Phonology, syntax, semantics	R, E	4–8 years
Test of Language Development—2: Intermediate (Hammill & Newcomer, 1988)	Syntax, semantics	R, E	8–12 years

The *TOLD—2 Primary* has seven subtests: *Picture Vocabulary* and *Oral Vocabulary* assess the understanding and meaningful use of spoken words; *Grammatic Understanding, Sentence Imitation,* and *Grammatic Completion* assess differing aspects of grammar; *Word Articulation* and *Word Discrimination* measure the abilities to say words correctly and to distinguish between words that sound similar. The *TOLD—2 Intermediate* contains six subtests: *Sentence Combinations, Word Ordering,* and *Grammatic Comprehension* assess different aspects of grammar; *Vocabulary, Generals,* and *Malapropisms* measure the understanding and use of word relationships, the knowledge of abstract relationships, and the correcting of ridiculous sentences.

Wiig Criterion-Referenced Inventory of Language (Wiig, 1990b)	Morphology, syntax, semantics, pragmatics	R, E	4–13 years

This criterion-referenced test provides language probes organized into four modules: morphology, syntax, semantics, and pragmatics. The student is given 10 opportunities to demonstrate oral mastery of each objective. Item formats include picture naming, sentence completion, parallel production, and speech act elicitation. The test can be used to obtain baseline information, identify specific skill areas for intervention, and measure progress.

Measures of specific components			
Assessment of Children's Language Comprehension (Foster, Giddan, & Stark, 1983)	Semantics	R	3–6 years

The test uses a core vocabulary of 50 common words combined into two-, three-, and four-element phonemes. On the first subtest the student points to pictures in response to a word spoken by the examiner. The other three subtests involve comprehension of utterances with two, three, and four critical elements. No oral responses are required, and administration time is 10 to 15 minutes.

(continued)

TABLE 8.2
Continued

Test	Component Measured	Receptive/ Expressive	Age Norms
The Assessment of Phonological Processes— Revised (Hodson, 1986)	Phonology	E	2–12 years

This test examines the phonological processes of students with highly unintelligible speech. Objects and pictures are used to elicit the student's production of 50 words, which are phonetically transcribed. A preschool screening and a multisyllabic screening for older elementary school students also are provided.

Auditory Discrimination Test (Wepman, 1973)	Phonology	R	4 years–adult

Forty word pairs are presented to the student for discrimination. Some of the word pairs differ in beginning sounds, some in middle sounds, and others in ending sounds. The student tells the examiner whether the word pairs sound the same or different.

Boehm Test of Basic Concepts—Revised (Boehm, 1986)	Semantics	R	3–5 years

Fifty pictorial items, in multiple-choice form, are arranged in approximate order of increasing difficulty and divided into two booklets. The test is read by the teacher, and the students mark their answers in the test booklets. A Spanish edition also is available.

Bracken Basic Concept Scale (Bracken, 1984)	Semantics	R	2–8 years

Level 1, the Screening Tests, measures basic concept acquisition to identify students whose concept development is below age-level expectations. Level 2, the Diagnostic Scale, contains more than 250 multiple-choice items that yield information about the ability to understand finely defined concepts in 11 categories (color, shape, size, quantity, numbers/counting, letter identification, direction/position, time/sequence, texture/material, comparisons, and social/emotional). The Diagnostic Scale is administered individually, and the student responds by pointing to the correct picture response.

Carrow Elicited Language Inventory (Carrow, 1974)	Syntax	E	3–7 years

This norm-referenced test diagnoses expressive language deficits by having the student imitate exactly what she hears after listening to the examiner read a sentence. The stimuli range in length from 2 to 10 words with an average length of 6 words. There are 52 oral stimuli including 51 sentences and 1 phrase. Administration time is about 25 minutes.

Clinical Evaluation of Language Fundamentals-Revised (Semel, Wiig, & Secord, 1987)	Morphology, syntax, semantics	R, E	5–16 years

This individually administered test consists of 11 subtests: *Formulated Sentences, Listening to Paragraphs, Semantic Relationships, Oral Directions, Recalling Sentences, Word Structure, Sentence Structure, Sentence Assembly, Word Associations, Word Classes,* and *Linguistic Concepts.* Receptive, expressive, and total language scores are based on the administration of six subtests, which takes 45 to 60 minutes. The five supplemental subtests offer additional diagnostic information. The test is norm-referenced by age and yields standard scores and percentile ranks. A software program provides quick scoring and a narrative report.

(continued)

TABLE 8.2
Continued

Test	Component Measured	Receptive/ Expressive	Age Norms
Developmental Sentence Analysis (Lee, 1974)	Syntax	E	2–6 years

Spontaneous speech is elicited while the student is in conversation with an adult. A group of 100 phrases is collected, and the Developmental Sentence Types is used to classify these presentence phrases according to diversity and linguistic composition to indicate if grammatical structure is developing in an orderly manner. The Developmental Sentence Scoring is used to analyze the grammatical structure found in 50 complete sentences. Specific directions are given for scoring syntactic development.

Test	Component Measured	Receptive/ Expressive	Age Norms
Expressive One-Word Picture Vocabulary Test—Revised (Gardner, 1990)	Semantics	E	2–11 years
Expressive One-Word Picture Vocabulary Test—Upper Extension (Gardner, 1983)	Semantics	E	12–15 years

These two tests assess a student's speaking or expressive vocabulary. The examiner presents single pictures for the student to name. Administration time is 5 to 10 minutes. Companion tests that assess receptive vocabulary also are available.

Test	Component Measured	Receptive/ Expressive	Age Norms
Goldman-Fristoe Test of Articulation (Goldman & Fristoe, 1986)	Phonology	E	2–16+ years

The first subtest, *Sounds in Words,* consists of 35 pictures that elicit the student's articulation of the major speech sounds in the initial, medial, and final positions. The second subtest, *Sounds in Sentences,* contains 2 narrative stories that are read by the examiner and illustrated by action pictures. The student is asked to retell each story. The third subtest, *Stimulability,* determines if misarticulated phonemes are articulated correctly when the student is given maximum stimulation. The student is asked to watch and listen carefully while the sound is pronounced in a syllable, used in a word, and used in a sentence.

Test	Component Measured	Receptive/ Expressive	Age Norms
Goldman-Fristoe-Woodcock Test of Auditory Discrimination (Goldman, Fristoe, & Woodcock, 1970)	Phonology	R	3 years–adult

The test assesses the ability to discriminate speech sounds against two different backgrounds—quiet and noise. The student is asked to point to the correct picture from a plate of four pictures upon hearing a stimulus word pronounced on an audiotape. Administration time is 20 to 30 minutes.

Test	Component Measured	Receptive/ Expressive	Age Norms
Let's Talk Inventory for Children (Bray & Wiig, 1987)	Pragmatics	R*, E	4–8 years
Let's Talk Inventory for Adolescents (Wiig, 1982)	Pragmatics	R*, E (*if needed)	9 years–adult

The inventory for children contains 34 items that picture a different situation involving peer or adult interactions. The student is asked to formulate a speech act appropriate for the context and the audience. Association items are administered only if the student is unable to respond satisfactorily to the formulation items. The inventory for adolescents consists of 40 items that are administered with a picture manual. Students are asked to formulate a sentence or series of sentences that the pictured adolescent might say in a particular social situation. Four communication functions are assessed: ritualizing, informing, controlling, and feeling. Drop-back items of a receptive nature are administered to those students who have difficulty with the expressive section.

(continued)

TABLE 8.2
Continued

Test	Component Measured	Receptive/ Expressive	Age Norms
Multilevel Informal Language Inventory (Goldsworthy, 1982)	Syntax, semantics	R*, E (*if needed)	4–12 years

Picture probes are used to assess language at three levels dictated by the skills of the student. At the evoked spontaneous level, the student is asked to tell what is happening in the stimulus picture. If the student does not succeed, indirect imitation procedures are initiated (that is, the examiner tells about one part of the picture and asks the student to tell about another part). If the student still is unsuccessful, the receptive level is administered in which the student is asked to point to what the examiner names. A profile of scores is produced.

Test	Component Measured	Receptive/ Expressive	Age Norms
Peabody Picture Vocabulary Test—Revised (Dunn & Dunn, 1981)	Semantics	R	2 years–adult

Stimulus pictures are presented to the student, who points to the picture that best represents the corresponding stimulus word spoken by the examiner. There are 2 forms of 175 items each, with 4 pictures per item.

Test	Component Measured	Receptive/ Expressive	Age Norms
Photo Articulation Test (Pendergast, Dickey, Selmar, & Soder, 1984)	Phonology	E	3–12 years

The test consists of 72 color photographs of common objects that are designed to elicit words containing 1 consonant and, in some instances, 1 vowel or diphthong as well. The only exception is *hanger,* which tests 2 consonants. All consonants, vowels, and diphthongs as well as 9 blends are tested. The kit includes a deck of individual test cards as well as 6 articulation age overlays that outline age-appropriate sounds.

Test	Component Measured	Receptive/ Expressive	Age Norms
Test for Auditory Comprehension of Language—Revised (Carrow-Woolfolk, 1985)	Morphology, syntax	R	3–9 years

The test is individually administered and measures auditory comprehension of word classes and relations, grammatical morphemes, and elaborated sentence constructions. No oral responses are required, and administration time is 10 to 20 minutes. A computer program is available for scoring and data storage.

Test	Component Measured	Receptive/ Expressive	Age Norms
Test of Adolescent Language—2 (Hammill, Brown, Larsen, & Wiederholt, 1987)	Syntax, semantics	R, E	12–18 years

The test is used to identify problems in both spoken and written language. Ten areas are included: listening, speaking, reading, writing, spoken language, written language, vocabulary, grammar, receptive language, and expressive language.

Test	Component Measured	Receptive/ Expressive	Age Norms
Test of Early Language Development—2 (Hresko, Reid, & Hammill, 1991)	Syntax, semantics	R, E	2–7 years

This individually administered test provides information directly related to the semantic (content) and syntactic (form) aspects of language. The 38 items can be administered in about 15 minutes and assess receptive and expressive language using a variety of semantic and syntactic tasks.

(continued)

TABLE 8.2
Continued

Test	Component Measured	Receptive/ Expressive	Age Norms
Test of Pragmatic Language (Phelps-Terasaki & Phelps-Gunn, 1992)	Pragmatics	E	5–13 years

The test includes 44 items, each of which establishes a social context, to provide information within 6 components of pragmatic language: physical setting, audience, topic, purpose (speech acts), visual-gestural cues, and abstraction. After the examiner provides a verbal stimulus prompt and displays a picture, the student responds to the presented dilemma.

Test	Component Measured	Receptive/ Expressive	Age Norms
Test of Word Finding (German, 1986)	Semantics	E	6–12 years
Test of Adolescent/Adult Word Finding (German, 1990)	Semantics	E	12–80 years

These 2 tests contain 5 naming sections: picture naming—nouns, picture naming—verbs, sentence completion naming, description naming, and naming category words. Each test also includes a comprehension section to determine if errors are due to word-finding problems or to poor word comprehension. The adolescent form also includes a brief test that provides a 10-minute assessment of word-finding abilities.

Test	Component Measured	Receptive/ Expressive	Age Norms
Test of Word Knowledge (Wiig & Secord, 1992)	Semantics	R, E	5–17 years

This test evaluates the student's ability to understand and use vocabulary words. Level 1, for students age 5 to 8, includes subtests in expressive vocabulary, word definitions, receptive vocabulary, word opposites, and synonyms (optional). Level 2, for students age 8 through 17, includes core subtests in word definitions, multiple contexts, synonyms, and figurative usage, as well as supplementary subtests in word opposites, receptive vocabulary, expressive vocabulary, and conjunctions and transition words. All stimuli are presented through visual and auditory modes to accommodate students with poor reading skills or auditory memory problems. The test yields standard scores, age equivalents, percentile ranks, and expressive and receptive language scores.

Test	Component Measured	Receptive/ Expressive	Age Norms
The Token Test for Children (DiSimoni, 1978)	Syntax, semantics	R	3–12 years

The examiner places squares and circles of different shapes and sizes in a standard order in front of the student. Then the examiner presents a series of spoken commands, requiring the student to manipulate the tokens to perform the operation. Raw scores are converted into standard scores, and suggested cutoff scores denote unsatisfactory performance. Administration time is about 10 minutes.

Test	Component Measured	Receptive/ Expressive	Age Norms
The WORD Test—R (Elementary) (Barrett, Huisingh, Zachman, & Jorgensen, 1990)	Semantics	E	7–11 years
The WORD Test—Adolescent (Zachman, Huisingh, Barrett, Orman, & Blagden, 1989)	Semantics	E	12–17 years

The elementary-level test measures vocabulary and semantic skills in the areas of associations, synonyms, semantic absurdities, antonyms, definitions, and multiple definitions. The adolescent-level test assesses 4 vocabulary and semantic tasks that represent language usage in everyday life and school activities. Specific areas include brand names, synonyms, signs of the times, and definitions.

the communicative skills needed for academic achievement in the classroom (Hughes, 1989). Many formal tests use a small number of items to assess a particular skill, and using a small sample can lead to incorrect conclusions about the student's skill level. Thus, informal assessment often is used to affirm or refute the results of formal measures. Also, many formal measures do not give enough specific information to plan educational objectives. Therefore, informal language measures often are used to determine specific instructional objectives. Another common use of informal measures is to monitor a student's daily or weekly progress. Unlike formal measures, which are designed to assess a student over a long period of time, informal measures lend themselves to daily or weekly assessment.

The current emphasis in language assessment stresses the informal evaluation of a student's language within the context in which it occurs. The goal of informal language assessment is to provide insight into how the student uses communication from a functional viewpoint in a variety of settings. Specific areas to examine include the intention or purpose of language, the social communicative context, and the physical setting. Various informal techniques can be used depending on the type of information desired.

Informal Tests of Form: Phonology

Phonology can be assessed informally by analyzing the student's production of phonemes in single words. The examiner makes a list of all the consonant phonemes and collects pictures to depict words that contain each phoneme. There should be a picture to elicit a word with the consonant in the initial position and a picture to depict the consonant in the final position. For example, a picture of a pot will elicit initial /p/, and a picture of a map will elicit final /p/. The examiner shows the student each picture and says, "Tell me the name of each picture." It is noted if the student says the word incorrectly, and the results are recorded on a checklist. This type of assessment requires careful, experienced listening for accurate results. Only the error sounds are recorded; for example, a /b/ sound is recorded to indicate the student said "bot" for *pot*. Also, comments that describe the error are recorded; for example, a substitution of /b/ for /p/ is recorded as an error in voicing. The examiner lists all the phoneme errors and determines which phonemes should have been mastered at the student's developmental age. These phonemes can become target phonemes for the student's educational objectives.

After analyzing the phoneme profile and selecting a target phoneme, the examiner should collect baseline data on the target phoneme in the student's spontaneous speech. The examiner also needs to monitor change in the student's speech after corrective instruction has begun. Informal assessment is the primary tool used to gather baseline data on the target phoneme and to monitor change in the student's speech.

Diederick (1971) recommends direct observation of the production of a phoneme to obtain baseline data and to monitor the student's progress. The examiner engages the student in spontaneous speech with pictures or toys as stimuli to elicit speech from the student. Older students may respond to prompts such as "Tell me about your weekend." "Adult talking" should be kept to a minimum so that the student is allowed to talk. During a 3-minute sample, the examiner counts the student's correct and incorrect productions of the target phoneme. The target phoneme's frequency can be observed by charting the incorrect and correct responses (see Chapter 2 for a discussion on recording data). Accuracy is computed by dividing the number of correct target phonemes the student said by the total number of target phonemes said (correct and incorrect).

One aspect of receptive phonology that is assessed readily by informal measures is auditory discrimination. The examiner may want to verify if the student has difficulty discriminating between two particular sounds that were confused on a formal measure. For example, the student may have confused /p/ with /b/, and the examiner may assess these sounds further with a criterion measure. The measure can consist of a list of consonant-vowel-consonant words in which only one phoneme is different (for example, *pin—bin* or *cup—cub*). Two words are said in word pairs, and the student is asked whether the words are the same or different. The examiner records the results on a checklist and scores the responses for accuracy. Accuracy levels can be used to indicate whether the student needs help in learning to discriminate these sounds. Accuracy of 90 percent or above is a good indication that the student already can discriminate these sounds.

Informal Tests of Form: Morphology

Informal measures of morphology can determine the mastery level of each morpheme in a hierarchy. The examiner can use Brown's (1973) rank ordering of morpheme acquisition to make sentences that assess each morpheme. Pictures are presented with the sentences to assess the use of each morpheme. If the objective is to assess use of the present progressive morpheme *ing,* the examiner may show a picture of girls playing and say, "The girls like to play. Here they are _____ ."
The student says the missing word, "playing." If the examiner is assessing the use of the morpheme *in,* she may show a picture of a baby sleeping and ask, "Where is the baby? The baby is _____ ." The student says the missing words, "in bed."

The examiner records the results as correct or incorrect on a checklist. Analysis of the results helps the teacher determine which morphemes are mastered and which morphemes need to be taught. Also, assessing the morphemes in a hierarchical order indicates to the teacher which morpheme to teach first.

Another informal assessment of morphology is a measure of accuracy of a specific morpheme in a student's conversational speech. Mastery of a morpheme is indicated by 90 percent accuracy in a student's conversational speech (Brown, 1973). It would be time-consuming to obtain a daily or weekly conversational sample with enough occurrences of a specific morpheme to determine accuracy. An informal assessment of a specific morpheme that is less time-consuming is to have the student respond to the prompt, "Tell me about this picture." First the examiner shapes the response by showing the student a picture depicting a person jumping and says, "What is the person doing?" If the student does not describe the action (by saying "jumping" or "jump"), the examiner can prompt the student: "Say *jumping.*" After the student gives two correct responses (description of action) to two different pictures and the instructions, "What is the person doing," the instructions can be changed to "Tell me about this picture." The examiner can show a series of 20 pictures, each of which elicits the present progressive *ing* form of a word. As each picture is presented, the examiner says, "Tell me about this picture." The results are recorded on a checklist, and the examiner counts the number of correct and incorrect responses. The accuracy percentage is determined by dividing the correct responses by the total number of pictures. If the accuracy is 90 percent or above, the morpheme is mastered and does not need to be taught. Accuracy below 90 percent indicates that the morpheme is not mastered and may require teaching. The examiner should note if mastery of the morpheme is expected at the student's developmental age.

An informal measure of receptive morphology is to have the student point to a picture that depicts a morpheme. The examiner says a sentence with a specific morpheme and asks the student to point to the correct picture. For example, to assess the irregular past tense of *eat,* the examiner can show a picture of a girl who has finished eating and a picture of a girl eating. The examiner says, "The girl ate." The student must point to the correct picture of the girl who has finished eating. Sequence picture cards (such as those published by DLM) can be used with this task. The examiner records the results on a checklist by marking each irregular past tense verb as correct or incorrect. The results are analyzed to determine which morphemes the student has mastered receptively. The examiner may recommend that the student master a morpheme receptively before

the student is taught to use that morpheme expressively.

Informal Tests of Form: Syntax

Expressive syntax can be assessed informally by analyzing the student's spontaneous speech for use of grammatical forms. The examiner can obtain and record a spontaneous sample of the student's speech by the guidelines presented in the next section on informal tests of semantics. If the sample is used only for grammatical analysis, the guidelines can be modified so that a tape recorder is used without recording the context of each utterance. After recording, the examiner transcribes the sample and lists each utterance on a checklist, as shown in Table 8.3. Each utterance is analyzed for the grammatical forms used, and a list is compiled of the grammatical forms that were not used. Each form is compared with norms for the student's develop-

TABLE 8.3
Syntactic analysis of utterances.

Student's Name: *Michael Jordan*
Date: *3/15*

Utterances	present progressive *ing*	is	plural regular s, es	possessive s	I, me, mine, my you, yours	irregular past	he, him, his she, her, hers	am, are, was, were	not	can't, don't	and	but	because	reversal of copula (is it)	who, what	where
1. What this is?		X													X	
2. That all of it?																
3. This a wall.																
4. I gonna tell you.					X											
5. Yeah, but her not in today.							X		X			X				
6. Car go up and car go down.																
7. Car go sideways.																

mental age. If the particular form is expected for the student's developmental age, a teaching objective can be planned to teach it.

An alternative informal assessment of syntax involves sentence repetition. The examiner says each sentence, and the student repeats the sentence. To increase the accuracy of the examiner's judgment, the evaluation session can be recorded on tape so that the student's responses can be checked. The examiner records the student's responses on a checklist and analyzes them for critical syntactic features. Omitted syntactic features should be included in the student's educational objectives.

Informal Tests of Content: Semantics

Some tasks that assess semantics are complex, so informal procedures may be difficult to devise (such as in the areas of logical relationships, cause-and-effect relationships, and verbal problem solving). However, for areas such as verbal opposites, categorization, and classification of words, informal testing is useful.

For the assessment of verbal opposites, DLM produces a set of cards that displays pictures of 40 pairs of opposites. When paired correctly, the cards in each set illustrate two opposites (for example, near and far). The examiner mixes the cards and asks the student to sort them into sets of opposites. The examiner observes as the student makes set combinations, and the results are recorded on a checklist. Analysis of the incorrect sets helps the teacher determine which opposites to include in teaching objectives for the student.

An informal assessment of word categorization involves having the student say words in the same category. The examiner says a word and asks the student to say as many words as possible in the same category. The words can fall into the category because of similar function or physical attribute. The examiner lists the words on a checklist as the student says them. The results are analyzed to determine if the student can say several words in a category or whether the student says a word that is an opposite, says a rhyming word, or tends to repeat the stimulus word.

A word association task can be used as a measure of word classification. Young children tend to respond to a stimulus word with a word that precedes or follows the stimulus word according to the rules of syntax. This is called a *syntagmatic* response. For example, if the stimulus word is "apple," the young student may respond with "eat" or "red." Youngsters shift to a response in the same grammatical category around the age of 6 to 8 years. This type of response is called *paradigmatic*. For example, if the stimulus word is "apple," the older student may respond with "orange," "banana," or another word from the fruit category. The examiner says the stimulus word, notes which kind of response the student makes, and records the response under that category (syntagmatic or paradigmatic) on a checklist. The checklist shows whether the student is categorized as a younger child with syntagmatic responses or as an older student with paradigmatic responses. The student may have responses in both categories but have most responses in one category.

Another area of semantics that can be assessed by informal measures is semantic relationships. This area can be assessed if the student's language utterances are three or fewer words. If a student uses more words, a syntactic analysis is more appropriate. Semantic relationships can be assessed informally by analyzing the student's spontaneous speech. The examiner observes the student playing or interacting with someone, codes or transcribes the conversation, and analyzes it according to error pattern. Various objects such as clay, toys, and games can be used to stimulate communication.

McLean and Snyder-McLean (1978) recommend the following guidelines for obtaining a speech or language sample:

1. Set up a partially structured play situation in which the student interacts with a familiar adult.
2. Use toys that the student is familiar with and that are likely to elicit a variety of responses.
3. Record the student's speech on a videotape recorder. Continue the sampling until 50 to 100 intelligible utterances are obtained. If videotape equipment is not available, record the sample on a tape recorder and have an observer record the context of each utterance the student says.
4. Avoid talking excessively or structuring the student's verbal responses by asking questions such as "What is this?" or "What color is the doll's dress?"
5. Transcribe the tape as soon as possible.
6. List each utterance (that is, any meaningful speech segment preceded and followed by a pause). Analyze each word in the utterance for semantic form, and list each word under the appropriate category. Several two- and three-word utterances are analyzed in Table 8.4. The two-word utterance "that ball" is listed under demonstrative, because "that" plus a noun is used to point out an object or person. The utterance "more cookie" is listed under attribute, because *more* modifies the noun. "Daddy pipe" is listed under possession, because it refers to Daddy's ownership of the pipe. The utterance "milk cookie" is listed under conjunction, because it refers to milk *and* cookie. The three-word utterance "Mommy drink milk" is placed in the action category (agent—Mommy; action—drink; object—milk).
7. After listing each utterance in the appropriate category, analyze the checklist to determine which semantic relationships the student did or did not use. The forms that the student did not use can be included in teaching objectives of semantic relationships. For example, if the student used three-word utterances but did not use action (verb) + object (noun) + location (noun) forms, this may be an appropriate teaching objective.

After the student's language sample is analyzed for semantic grammar, the mean length of utterance in morphemes is computed. Brown (1973) suggests the following guidelines:

1. Transcribe the language sample.
2. Start the analysis on the second page of the transcription, and count the first 100 utterances. Count only fully transcribed utterances, and count utterance repetitions.
3. Count each morpheme in the 100 utterances. Do not count fillers such as "um" or "oh," but do count "no," "yeah," and "hi." Count as single morphemes compound words, proper names, and idiomatic duplications (such as *night-night, choo-choo, see-saw*). Count as single morphemes all irregular past tenses of verbs (*got, did, went, saw*). Count as single morphemes all diminutives (such as *doggie*). Count as separate morphemes all auxiliaries (*is, have, will, can, want, would*) and catenatives (*gonna, wanna, hafta*). Count as separate morphemes all inflections (such as possessive *s*, plural *s*, third-person singular *s*, regular past *ed*, and progressive *ing*).
4. Compute the mean length of utterance by dividing the total number of morphemes by 100.

The mean length of utterance gives the examiner a quick measure of growth over an extended period of time. Many research studies

TABLE 8.4

Format for semantic analysis of a language sample.

Student's Name _Lisa Walker_ Date Collected ___4/3___

Total Number of Utterances ___11___

Relationship Components	Demonstrative		Recurrence	Attribute		Possession	Conjunction
	Nomination	Notice		Nonexistence	Descriptive		
Two-word grammatical	That ball	Hi Mommy	More cookie	allgone cookie	Big ball	Daddy pipe	Milk cookie
Three+-word grammatical							
Nongrammatical one-word utterances							

Relationship Components	Action			Location			
	Agent	Action	Object	Agent	Action	Object	Location
Two-word grammatical							
Three+-word grammatical	Mommy	drink	milk	Daddy Mommy	sit put	car doll	here here bed
Nongrammatical one-word utterances							

TABLE 8.5
Checklist of pragmatic functions.

Utterances	Instrumental	Protest	Request	Acquire Information	Metalinguistic	Give Information	Label	Imitate	Answer	Initiate/Terminate Social	Entertain	Other
1. Drink milk	X											
2. No milk		X										
3. Shoes on			X									
4. Car							X					
Question asked: "Where is the ball?" 5. Ball chair									X			
6. Daddy come?				X								

Student's Name _Julie Bates_ Date _2/12_

report students' semantic development in terms of this measure rather than chronological age. For example, the agent + action + object semantic form may be reported as occurring in students with a mean length of utterance of three words, rather than in students of any specific chronological age.

Informal Tests of Use: Pragmatics

Pragmatics can be assessed informally by analyzing a sample of the student's spontaneous speech to determine which pragmatic function was used. The first step is to obtain a videotaped language sample from the student. (Guidelines for obtaining a language sample are presented in the semantics section.) If videotape equipment is not available, an observer can record what happened just before and just after each utterance. The second step is to transcribe the tape and list each utterance on a checklist, as shown in Table 8.5. The examiner classifies the pragmatic function of an utterance by analyzing the events before and after the utterance. For example, the student's utterance may be "Throw ball." The examiner notes that before the utterance the examiner was holding the ball and the student's arms were extended to catch the ball. It also is noted that the examiner threw the ball to the student after the utterance. The utterance is classified as a request, and a mark is put in the *Request* column. The examiner analyzes the checklist for each function the student did or did not use and then lists the functions that the student did not use. For example, it may be noted that the student did not use a protest function, such as "no shoes" to mean "Don't put on my shoes." The teacher can select from the pragmatic functions that were not used to determine appropriate teaching objectives.

In older students, informal assessment of pragmatics includes measures of speaking with inappropriate loudness, talking at inappropriate times, interrupting the speaker, and using indirect requests. These behaviors can be assessed by counting and recording them in several situations and on different days. A teacher may want to count and record these same behaviors in a speaker of the same age who is not delayed in pragmatics. The teacher can select a student who talks to other students and contributes during group activities, rather than a student who is quiet or has little to say. Three situations are chosen, such as group instructional time, independent work time, and lunch or playground time. The teacher counts the number of times each student interrupts other speakers, talks too loudly, and talks when the student should be listening, reading, or working. The results are recorded on charts, and the teacher compares the results of the two students. A significant difference in the two students' behaviors signifies a possible teaching objective. An appropriate objective is to decrease interruptions by increasing skills in determining when a speaker is finished talking.

Indirect requests can be assessed informally in students whose developmental age is 8 years and above by asking the student to state the implied direct requests. For example, the examiner says, "Tell me what I want you to do when I say, 'Can you close the door?'" The student says, "You want me to close the door." The examiner then says, "Tell me what I want you to do in each of the following sentences." The examiner reads indirect requests listed on a checklist and puts a check in a column to indicate if the student's response is correct or incorrect. The results are analyzed to determine the number of errors made and the forms with which the student is having the most difficulty (that is, affirmative—"Can you. . . ," negative—"Can't you. . . ," or affirmative with negative intention—"Must you. . . "). These forms of indirect requests can become teaching objectives for the student.

REFERENCES

Ackerman, P. T., Dykman, R. A., & Gardner, M. Y. (1990). Counting rate, naming rate, phonological sensitivity, and memory span: Major factors in dyslexia. *Journal of Learning Disabilities, 23,* 325–327.

Adler, S. (1988). A new job description and a new task for the public school clinician: Relating effectively to the nonstandard dialect speaker. *Language, Speech, and Hearing Services in Schools, 19,* 28–33.

Bankson, N. W. (1990). *Bankson Language Test—2.* Austin, TX: Pro-Ed.

Baratz, J. C. (1969). Language and cognitive assessments of Negro children: Assumptions and research needs. *Journal of American Speech and Hearing Association, 11,* 87–91.

Barrett, M., Huisingh, R., Zachman, L., & Jorgensen, C. (1990). *The WORD Test—R (Elementary).* East Moline, IL: LinguiSystems.

Bartel, N. R., & Bryen, D. N. (1982). Problems in language development. In D. D. Hammill & N. R. Bartel, *Teaching children with learning and behavior problems* (3rd ed.). Boston: Allyn & Bacon.

Bartel, N. R., Grill, J. J., & Bryen, D. N. (1973). Language characteristics of black children: Implication for assessment. *Journal of School Psychology, 11,* 351–364.

Bashir, A. S. (1989). Language intervention and the curriculum. *Seminars in Speech and Language, 10,* 181–191.

Bates, E. (1976). Pragmatics and sociolinguistics in child language. In D. Morehead & A. Morehead (Eds.), *Directions in normal and deficient child language.* Baltimore, MD: University Park Press.

Bernstein, D. K., & Tiegerman, E. (1989). *Language and communication disorders in children* (2nd ed.). New York: Merrill/Macmillan.

Bloom, L., & Lahey, M. (1978). *Language development and language disorders.* New York: John Wiley.

Boehm, A. E. (1986). *Boehm Test of Basic Concepts—Revised.* San Antonio, TX: Psychological Corporation.

Bos, C. S., & Vaughn, S. (1988). *Strategies for teaching students with learning and behavior problems.* Boston: Allyn & Bacon.

Bracken, B. A. (1984). *Bracken Basic Concept Scale.* San Antonio, TX: Psychological Corporation.

Braine, M. (1976). Children's first word combinations. *Monographs of the Society for Research in Child Development, 41* (Serial No. 164).

Bray, C. M., & Wiig, E. H. (1987). *Let's Talk Inventory for Children.* San Antonio, TX: Psychological Corporation.

Brown, R. (1973). *A first language: The early stages.* Cambridge, MA: Harvard University Press.

Brown, R., & Berko, J. (1960). Word associations and acquisition of grammar. *Child Development, 31,* 1–14.

Bruner, J. S. (1974/1975). From communication to language: A psychological perspective. *Cognition, 3,* 255–287.

Cardoza, D., & Rueda, R. (1986). Educational and occupational outcomes of Hispanic learning-disabled high school students. *The Journal of Special Education, 20,* 111–126.

Carrow, E. (1974). *Carrow Elicited Language Inventory.* Allen, TX: DLM.

Carrow-Woolfolk, E. (1985). *Test for Auditory Comprehension of Language—Revised.* Allen, TX: DLM.

Chomsky, N. A. (1957). *Syntactic structures.* The Hague: Mouton.

Clark, E. (1973). What's in a word? On the child's acquisition of semantics in his first language. In T. E. Moore (Ed.), *Cognitive development and the acquisition of language.* New York: Academic Press.

Crabtree, M. (1963). *The Houston Test for Language Development.* Houston: Houston Test Company.

Diederick, W. M. (1971). Procedures for counting and charting a target phoneme. *Language Speech and Hearing Services in Schools, 5,* 18–32.

DiSimoni, R. (1978). *The Token Test for Children.* Allen, TX: DLM.

Dunn, L. M., & Dunn, L. M. (1981). *Peabody Picture Vocabulary Test—Revised.* Circle Pines, MN: American Guidance Service.

Ehren, B. J., & Lenz, B. K. (1989). Adolescents with language disorders: Special considerations in providing academically relevant language intervention. *Seminars in Speech and Language, 10,* 192–204.

Ervin-Tripp, S., & Mitchell-Kernan, C. (Eds.). (1977). *Child discourse.* New York: Academic Press.

Foster, C. R., Giddan, J. J., & Stark, J. (1983). *ACLC: Assessment of Children's Language Comprehension.* Palo Alto, CA: Consulting Psychologists Press.

Gardner, M. F. (1983). *Expressive One-Word Picture Vocabulary Test—Upper Extension.* Austin, TX: Pro-Ed.

Gardner, M. F. (1990). *Expressive One-Word Picture Vocabulary Test—Revised.* Austin, TX: Pro-Ed.

German, D. J. (1984). Diagnosis of word-finding disorders in children with learning disabilities. *Journal of Learning Disabilities, 17,* 353–359.

German, D. J. (1986). *Test of Word Finding.* Allen, TX: DLM.

German, D. J. (1990). *Test of Adolescent/Adult Word Finding.* Allen, TX: DLM.

Goldman, R., & Fristoe, M. (1986). *Goldman-Fristoe Test of Articulation.* Circle Pines, MN: American Guidance Service.

Goldman, R., Fristoe, M., & Woodcock, R. W. (1970). *Goldman-Fristoe-Woodcock Test of Auditory Discrimination.* Circle Pines, MN: American Guidance Service.

Goldsworthy, C. L. (1982). *Multilevel Informal Language Inventory.* San Antonio, TX: Psychological Corporation.

Hammill, D. D., Brown, V. L., Larsen, S. C., & Wiederholt, J. L. (1987). *Test of Adolescent Language—2.* Austin, TX: Pro-Ed.

Hammill, D. D., & Newcomer, P. L. (1988). *Test of Language Development—2: Intermediate.* Austin, TX: Pro-Ed.

Hazel, J. S., & Schumaker, J. B. (1988). Social skills and learning disabilities: Current issues and recommendations for future research. In J. F. Kavanagh & T. J. Truss (Eds.), *Learning disabilities: Proceedings of the national conference* (pp. 293–344). Parkton, MD: York Press.

Hodson, B. W. (1986). *The Assessment of Phonological Processes—Revised.* Austin, TX: Pro-Ed.

Holland, A. L. (1977). Some practical considerations in aphasia rehabilitation. In M. Sullivan & M. S. Kommers (Eds.), *Rationale for adult aphasia therapy* (pp. 167–180). Omaha: University of Nebraska.

Hresko, W. P., Reid, D. K., & Hammill, D. D. (1991). *Test of Early Language Development—2.* Austin, TX: Pro-Ed.

Hughes, D. L. (1989). Generalization from language therapy to classroom academics. *Seminars in Speech and Language, 10,* 218–230.

Jacobson, R., & Halle, M. (1956). *Fundamentals of language.* The Hague: Mouton.

Kayser, H. (1989). Speech and language assessment of Spanish-English speaking children. *Language, Speech, and Hearing Services in Schools, 20,* 226–241.

Lahey, M. (1988). *Language disorders and language development.* New York: Macmillan.

Lazar, R. T., Warr-Leeper, G. A., Nicholson, C. B., & Johnson, S. (1989). Elementary school teachers' use of multiple meaning expressions. *Language, Speech, and Hearing Services in Schools, 20,* 420–429.

Lee, L. (1971). *The Northwestern Syntax Screening Test.* Evanston, IL: Northwestern University Press.

Lee, L. (1974). *Developmental Sentence Analysis.* Evanston, IL: Northwestern University Press.

Leonard, L. B., Wilcox, M. J., Fulmer, K. C., & Davis, G. A. (1978). Understanding indirect requests: An investigation of children's comprehension of pragmatic meanings. *Journal of Speech and Hearing Research, 21,* 528–537.

Linares, N. (1983). Management of communicatively handicapped Hispanic American children. In D. R. Omark & J. G. Erickson (Eds.), *The bilingual exceptional child* (pp. 145–162). San Diego: College Hill Press.

McLean, J. E., & Snyder-McLean, L. K. (1978). *A transactional approach to early language training.* New York: Merrill/Macmillan.

Mercer, C. D., Mercer, A. R., & Bott, D. A. (1984). *Self-correcting learning materials for the classroom.* New York: Merrill/Macmillan.

Mercer, J. R. (1983). Issues in the diagnosis of language disorders in students whose primary language is not English. *Topics in Language Disorders, 3*(3), 46–56.

Merritt, D. D., & Liles, B. Z. (1987). Story grammar ability in children with and without language disorder: A story generation, story retelling, and story comprehension. *Journal of Speech and Hearing Research, 30,* 539–552.

Morgan, D. L., & Guilford, A. M. (1984). *Adolescent Language Screening Test.* Austin, TX: Pro-Ed.

Nelson, K. (1974). Concept, word, and sentence: Inter-relations in acquisition and development. *Psychological Review, 81,* 276–285.

Newcomer, P. L., & Hammill, D. D. (1988). *Test of Language Development—2: Primary.* Austin, TX: Pro-Ed.

Owens, R. E., Jr. (1990). Development of communication, language, and speech. In G. H. Shames & E. H. Wiig (Eds.), *Human communication disorders: An introduction* (pp. 30–73). New York: Merrill/Macmillan.

Parnell, M. M., Amerman, J. D., & Harting, R. D. (1986). Responses of language-disordered children to wh-questions. *Language, Speech, and Hearing Services in Schools, 17,* 95–106.

Pehrsson, R. S., & Denner, P. R. (1988). Semantic organizers: Implications for reading and writing. *Topics in Language Disorders, 8*(3), 24–32.

Pendergast, K., Dickey, S., Selmar, J., & Soder, A. (1984). *Photo Articulation Test.* Austin, TX: Pro-Ed.

Phelps-Terasaki, D., & Phelps-Gunn, T. (1992). *Test of Pragmatic Language.* Austin, TX: Pro-Ed.

Prutting, C. A. (1979). Process \ prä | , ses\n: The action of moving forward progressively from one point to another on the way to completion. *Journal of Speech and Hearing Disorders, 44,* 3–30.

Riedlinger-Ryan, K. J., & Shewan, C. M. (1984). Comparison of auditory comprehension skills in learning-disabled and academically achieving adolescents. *Language, Speech, and Hearing Services in Schools, 15,* 127–136.

Roth, F. P., & Clark, D. M. (1987). Symbolic play and social participation abilities of language-impaired and normally developing children. *Journal of Speech and Hearing Disorders, 52,* 17–29.

Salend, S. J., & Fradd, S. (1986). Nationwide availability of services for limited English-proficient handicapped students. *The Journal of Special Education, 20,* 127–135.

Schumaker, J. B., & Deshler, D. D. (1984). Setting demand variables: A major factor in program planning for the learning disabled adolescent. *Topics in Language Disorders, 4*(4), 22–40.

Schumaker, J. B., Deshler, D. D., Alley, G. R., Warner, M. M., & Denton, P. H. (1984). Multipass: A learning strategy for improving reading comprehension. *Learning Disabilities Quarterly, 5,* 295–304.

Schwabe, A. M., Olswang, L. B., & Kriegsmann, E. (1986). Requests for information: Linguistic, cognitive, pragmatic, and environmental variables. *Language, Speech, and Hearing Services in Schools, 17,* 38–55.

Seidenberg, P. L. (1988). Cognitive and academic instructional intervention for learning-disabled adolescents. *Topics in Language Disorders, 8*(3), 56–71.

Semel, E. M., Wiig, E. H., & Secord, W. (1987). *Clinical Evaluation of Language Fundamentals—Revised.* San Antonio, TX: Psychological Corporation.

Semel, E. M., Wiig, E. H., & Secord, W. (1989). *Clinical Evaluation of Language Fundamentals—Revised: Screening Test.* San Antonio, TX: Psychological Corporation.

Simon, C. S. (1985). *Communication skills and classroom success.* San Diego, CA: College Hill Press.

Snyder, L. S. (1986). Developmental language disorders: Elementary school age. In J. M. Costello & A. L. Holland (Eds.), *Handbook of speech and language disorders* (pp. 671–700). San Diego, CA: College Hill Press.

Taylor, O. L. (1986). *Nature of communication disorders in culturally and linguistically diverse populations.* San Diego, CA: College Hill Press.

Wallach, G. (1989). Current research as a map for language intervention in the school years. *Seminars in Speech and Language, 10,* 205–217.

Wepman, J. (1973). *The Auditory Discrimination Test.* Palm Springs, CA: Language Research Associates.

Wiig, E. H. (1982). *The Let's Talk Inventory for Adolescents.* San Antonio, TX: Psychological Corporation.

Wiig, E. H. (1990a). Language disabilities in school-age children and youth. In G. H. Shames & E. H. Wiig (Eds.), *Human communication disorders: An introduction* (pp. 193–220). New York: Merrill/Macmillan.

Wiig, E. H. (1990b). *Wiig Criterion-Referenced Inventory of Language.* San Antonio, TX: Psychological Corporation.

Wiig, E. H., & Secord, W. (1992). *Test of Word Knowledge.* San Antonio, TX: Psychological Corporation.

Wiig, E. H., & Semel, E. M. (1976). *Language disabilities in children and adolescents.* New York: Merrill/Macmillan.

Wiig, E. H., & Semel, E. M. (1984). *Language assessment and intervention for the learning disabled* (2nd ed.). New York: Merrill/Macmillan.

Wilcox, M. J. (1986). Developmental language disorders: Preschoolers. In J. M. Costello & A. L. Holland (Eds.), *Handbook of speech and language disorders* (pp. 643–670). San Diego, CA: College Hill Press.

Wood, B. S. (1976). *Children and communications: Verbal and non-verbal language development.* Englewood Cliffs, NJ: Prentice-Hall.

Zachman, L., Huisingh, R., Barrett, M., Orman, J., & Blagden, C. (1989). *The WORD Test—Adolescent.* East Moline, IL: LinguiSystems.

Zimmerman, I. L., Steiner, V. G., & Pond, R. E. (1992). *Preschool Language Scale—3.* San Antonio, TX: Psychological Corporation.

CHAPTER 9

Teaching Language Skills

Language is viewed as interacting with other cognitive constructs and is best assessed and remediated as a whole in social communication rather than as isolated language skills. To ensure academic success for students with language-learning problems, the teacher and language specialist should consult one another and work cooperatively. This chapter presents some of the major points of view in the area of language intervention and offers a variety of activities and materials useful in teaching language skills. Theories of language acquisition are discussed as well as language service delivery models and language teaching strategies. The remainder of the chapter presents language activities, instructional games, self-correcting materials, and commercial programs and materials.

THEORIES OF LANGUAGE ACQUISITION

Theories of language acquisition fall within three major camps: behavioristic, nativistic, and interactionistic. The behavioristic position (Skinner, 1957) relies on learning principles to explain language acquisition. Braine (1971), Jenkins and Palermo (1964), and Staats (1971) are proponents of the behavioristic position. The behaviorist believes that the infant begins with no knowledge of language but possesses the ability to learn it. The child learns through reinforcement of imitation. Reinforcement of babbling (including parent attention and delight) and the shaping of vocal behavior account for the initial stages of learning. Behaviorists emphasize environmental influences and the universal laws of learning, namely operant conditioning principles. The *DISTAR Language* program (discussed in the section on commercial materials) is based on the behavioral model.

Chomsky (1965), Lenneberg (1967), and McNeil (1970) are proponents of the nativistic position. Chomsky claims that the child possesses an innate capacity for dealing with linguistic universals. The child generates a theory of grammar to help understand and produce an infinite number of sentences. Lenneberg states that the child is biologically predisposed to learn language as the brain matures. In the nativistic position, humans are believed to be "prewired" for language development, and the environment simply triggers its emergence. Language programs that emphasize the teaching of rules for sentence transformations are representative of the nativistic model.

Piaget (1960), the major proponent of the interactionistic position, theorizes that the child acquires language through the interaction of perceptual-cognitive capacities and experiences. The child's environment and neurological maturation determine learning. Language and thought thus develop simultaneously as the child passes through a series of fixed developmental stages requiring more and more complex strategies of cognitive organization. Interactionists consider the capacity for language to be innate; however, unlike the nativist, the interactionist believes the child must internalize linguistic structures from the environment and must become aware of communication's social functions. Thus, language programs in the interactionistic model are based on two ideas: (a) meaning is brought to a child's language through interaction with the environment, and (b) the child uses speech to control the environment. Intervention approaches based on this model emphasize natural language teaching rather than structured exercises and drills.

On the one hand, the biologists (Lenneberg, 1967) and the linguists (Chomsky, 1965) view the child as a product of the maturation process. Unless physical or mental complications occur, biologists and linguists believe the child's development is predetermined. This view places heavy emphasis on the child who is considered to be biologically prepared or linguistically preprogrammed to develop language. On the other hand, the behaviorists stress the influence of the environment. The child's role is passive, and development depends largely on the individuals in the child's environment who respond to his behavior. The interactionistic position emphasizes the child's active interactions with the environment as the child learns to talk (Bloom, 1975).

Numerous language programs from which the teacher can choose are available for intervention. Selection is influenced by two primary factors: the population the program serves and the theoretical model on which it is based. The theoretical model describes normal language acquisition and includes the content the normal student learns, the sequence in which the student learns, and how the student learns. There is a close relationship between the language program and the theoretical model of language acquisition (McLean & Snyder-McLean, 1978).

Primarily through the work of Wiig and Semel, language intervention has focused on the linguistic model, with direct concern about language functioning through analyzing comprehension and performance according to the components of language (such as phonology) and their rules. The linguistic model has served as the basis for the creation of many language programs. These programs usually focus on a particular language skill that the student should possess. Although the content of these programs is similar (phonemes, morphemes), some have their foundations in behavioral theory, some in nativism, and some in interactionism.

LANGUAGE SERVICE DELIVERY MODELS

Pullout Therapy Model

The most common language service delivery model is the pullout therapy model in which the language specialist takes students from their classes and instructs them in homogeneous groups of students with similar difficulties. Many teachers admit that this model presents various problems and often results in ineffective and inefficient services. According to Ehren and Lenz (1989), students usually dislike this model because they do not like to be singled out as different. This becomes particularly important as peer pressure increases during adolescence. Many adolescents also do not want to continue with the same methods and activities they had during speech instruction in elementary school, and they lack motivation to achieve because speech and language therapy is not a class they register for in their normal schedule.

The pullout method also causes students to miss course work while they are out of the classroom. This is especially devastating to students with learning problems who can least afford to miss classroom instruction. As attempts are made to formulate a pullout schedule, the language specialist is faced with numerous scheduling concerns, such as from which subject and how often to pull the student as well as how to handle special events, tests, and absences. Scheduling problems are compounded further by the number of students who are identified as needing services and the inability to provide the intensity required by certain students.

A final problem area associated with the pullout model involves fragmentation of services. Because students generally are seen for therapy in a separate classroom, the services often are isolated from regular classroom content and, thus, may not be consistent with classroom goals and expectations. Disagreement regarding responsibility for certain content and type of instruction increases when language goals appear to have no relevance to the student's functioning or needs in the regular classroom or when the goals are derived without regard to content in the curriculum. This fragmentation of services frequently results in resentment on the part of the regular classroom teacher and often hinders students who need instructional consistency to achieve academic success.

Classroom-Based Language Models

Classroom-based models involve a new delivery of traditional services, and some school systems use these models on a trial basis in an attempt to improve the services to students with language problems and to integrate therapy goals with the student's academic needs. In spite of their differences, all classroom-based models emphasize the need for collaborative consultation between the classroom teacher and the language specialist so that resulting interventions are meaningful and relevant to natural occurrences in the classroom (Damico, 1987; Marvin, 1987). The five major types of classroom-based language models include team teaching; self-contained teaching; one-to-one intervention; staff, curriculum, or program development; and consultation (Miller, 1989).

Team teaching. In this classroom-based model the language specialist teaches with the regular or special classroom teacher. The key to this format is that the language clinician actually teaches a portion of the curriculum. The curriculum goals and objectives as well as the methods and materials to be used are established jointly by the members of the professional team. Services can be rendered in a variety of settings including the regular classroom with the regular education teacher or a self-contained classroom or a resource room with a special education teacher.

Self-contained teaching. In this service model format, the language specialist teaches in a self-contained language class. This format is common with younger children, and the language specialist is responsible for teaching content areas including reading, math, science, and social studies to students who need particular interventions in language processing and production. At the middle and high school levels, some language specialists offer a separate course that focuses on writing, reading, or other language areas that are difficult for students with language problems to deal with in the regular curriculum.

One-to-one intervention. The language specialist can provide one-to-one intervention to particular students in the classroom. In this approach, the language specialist must maintain close contact with the classroom teacher to provide appropriate interventions to each student regarding specific content areas, study skills, writing, and vocabulary. Classroom textbooks and materials are used to maintain relevance to ongoing classroom activities.

Staff, curriculum, or program development. The language specialist can aid students indirectly by providing staff, curriculum, or program development to a school or district. For example, the specialist can plan community programs to increase student and parent awareness of the school's language objectives. The language specialist also can participate in curriculum development and evaluation or present inservice workshops to teachers or parents that focus on the effect of language on academic success. This service delivery format requires a fundamental change in the focus of the language specialist from providing direct service to students to educating those responsible for teaching the students.

Consultation. The language specialist can serve as a consultant to the various professionals who interact with students, such as regular or special education teachers, psychologists, physicians, nurses, social workers, or counselors. In this model, the language specialist consults with persons who provide language interventions to the student, and an effort is made through the consultation to determine methods to improve the student's communication difficulties. An additional benefit of the consultation format is that students who do not qualify for direct services under school district guidelines benefit indirectly from the suggestions of the consultant as they affect educational and social concerns in the classroom (Damico, 1987).

Strategies-Based Model

A strategies-based service delivery model focuses on teaching specific learning strategies to students and is appealing especially to language specialists who work with middle and high school students. One of the major differences between the strategies-based model and a classroom-based model is that students are able to register for and receive a grade for the course work. The use of strategies involves increasing the student's understanding and use of metacognitive and metalinguistic skills. These skills focus on improving the student's awareness and use of strategies that enhance learning. In essence, a change is made from teaching students what to learn to teaching students how to learn (Chabon & Prelock, 1989).

Buttrill, Niizawa, Biemer, Takahashi, and Hearn (1989) propose a strategies-based model that considers the learning characteristics of students with language-learning problems as well as the demands of the secondary school settings to which they apply. One of the most widely researched and developed ap-

proaches to learning strategies is the Strategies Intervention Model developed by Don Deshler and his colleagues at the University of Kansas. Although this model is quite specific, it is based on principles that have applicability to strategy training in general. Deshler and Schumaker (1986) state that the ultimate goal of learning strategies is to enable students to analyze and solve novel problems in both academic and nonacademic settings. Their approach to teaching learning strategies to adolescents is based on three rationales:

1. The development and application of learning strategies or metacognitive skills are appropriate for older students who are more proficient with these skills.
2. Adolescents who "learn how to learn" are in a better position to learn new skills in the future.
3. Students should accept responsibility for their learning and progress.

To design relevant instruction, the language specialist must determine what curriculum demands the student is failing to meet. Student involvement and mutual goal setting also should be established to maximize motivation toward learning, and activities should be designed to promote generalization. Motivation can be enhanced by broadening the student's understanding of the skill and its application to a variety of settings. To facilitate generalization, the learning strategies model stresses the importance of cooperative planning and consultation between the language specialist, regular and special education teachers, and personnel of other support services.

LANGUAGE TEACHING STRATEGIES

Many teachers who use direct teaching methods for remediation of reading and math problems undoubtedly select this technique for teaching language skills. With these formats, the teacher directs the learning and dictates the content, pace, and sequencing of the lesson. Often the student is allowed little opportunity to engage in spontaneous conversations during this highly structured skills approach. Conversely, some teachers believe that learning should be student centered, with the student dictating the content, pace, and sequencing of the lesson. The teacher controls minimally and emphasizes social interaction so that communication can occur along the lines of normal conversation.

When designing appropriate language intervention, the phonological, syntactic, semantic, and pragmatic aspects should be considered as well as the student's cognitive skills and social environment (Bernstein & Tiegerman, 1989). Wallach (1989) and Ehren and Lenz (1989) present the following general principles for meeting a student's language needs:

1. The language specialist should be aware of young students with language disorders who are dismissed from receiving language services, because academic problems may resurface later due to a breakdown in the language system and increased curriculum demands.
2. Language screenings should consist of more than one test and be sensitive to subtle forms of language disorders.
3. Students suspected of having learning problems should receive routine language evaluations that emphasize language and auditory processing.
4. School officials should consider service delivery alternatives to the traditional pullout model, and language specialists should focus on both contextualized and decontextualized aspects of language.
5. Professionals should collaborate to devise a coordinated program for students with

language-learning problems rather than implement a variety of isolated programs.
6. The delivery of instruction in learning strategies should be language sensitive.
7. The curriculum in language intervention should be relevant to the regular curriculum, respond to setting demands, reflect areas of academic concern, integrate spoken and written language systems, and focus on generalization.
8. The individual strategy preferences of students with language-learning problems should be considered, and students should be encouraged to determine which strategies are successful in a given situation.
9. Intervention should encourage student accountability and responsibility.
10. Effective interventions from other disciplines should be applied.

Moreover, especially when working with young children, the following specific techniques for teaching language may be helpful:

1. Teach language in a context.
2. Follow the sequence of normal language development.
3. Use specific and effective teaching strategies when introducing a new concept.
4. Vocalize thoughts or describe actions.
5. Describe what others are doing using parallel talk.
6. Use modeling to provide practice on a specific language skill.
7. Use expansion to show how an idea can be expressed in a more complex manner.
8. Use elaboration to demonstrate how to provide more information.
9. Use structured programs to provide adequate practice and feedback regarding performance.
10. Use everyday activities to provide practice of skills within a context.

11. Recognize the relationship of comprehension and production.
12. Systematically plan for and teach generalization.

Consideration also should be given to the use of computer-assisted instruction to improve students' speech and language skills. As well as enhancing motivation, computers appear to facilitate both social and cognitive interactions (Clements, 1987). Moreover, the use of computers tends to stimulate social use (Lipinski, Nida, Shade, & Watson, 1986), produce more positive and varied facial expressions and smiling (Hyson, 1985), and produce more spoken words per minute when compared with traditional activities such as blocks, art, or games (Muhlstein & Croft, 1986).

Because language is interactive, the teacher should be creative when implementing teaching methods because an activity designed to focus on a particular skill also may be useful in other areas. The remainder of this section presents strategies for increasing language comprehension, strategies for increasing language production, and imitation and modeling strategies. Parent involvement in language intervention also is discussed.

Strategies for Increasing Language Comprehension

The following strategies may be helpful in improving listening skills and increasing the comprehension or understanding of students with language-learning problems:

1. If the student frequently has difficulty following directions or understanding information of increased complexity, establish eye contact and maintain attention before presenting information. Cue the student to listen through the use of silent pauses or instructions to listen to or look at the teacher. This helps to establish a mental set for listening.
2. Ask the student to repeat directions or instructions to the teacher or a peer to ensure comprehension.
3. When introducing a new concept or skill, use vocabulary that is familiar to the student and explain new vocabulary words by using familiar terms.
4. Present new concepts in as many modalities as possible (for example, auditory, visual, and kinesthetic), and use gestures to augment verbal presentations (Bos & Vaughn, 1988).
5. To increase understanding of the relationship between semantic role and word order, encourage young children to act out sentences (for example, "Mommy kiss baby") or manipulate objects and talk about their movement (Connell, 1986).
6. Explain to students that listening is an active process that requires them to behave in certain ways, and teach them to identify specific behaviors associated with good listening (for example, look, think about what is said, repeat to yourself) (Chabon & Prelock, 1989).
7. Use introductory statements (such as "These are the main points" or "Before we begin") to provide an organizational framework and help students prepare for a task.
8. Be sensitive to the linguistic complexity of the students and adjust the rate and complexity of instructional language accordingly (Bernstein & Tiegerman, 1989). Use structurally simple and relatively short sentences of not more than 5 to 10 words and limit the number of new and unfamiliar vocabulary words presented in a single lesson to five or less (Wiig & Semel, 1984).
9. Teach specific memory strategies (for example, visual imagery, clustering and

grouping information, forming associations) to help students organize, categorize, and store new information for later retrieval.

10. To enhance the student's recall and memorization of new vocabulary, encourage the use of the keyword method in which familiar words are associated with each new concept or word (Mastropieri, Scruggs, & Fulk, 1990).

11. Instruct the student to use semantic organizers when reading that display key concepts as clusters of related ideas and, thus, provide both a verbal (semantic) and a graphic-structure (organizer) component (for example, young children can connect objects including pots, dishes, and forks with pieces of rope to indicate they relate to a central picture of a family eating) (Pehrsson & Denner, 1988).

12. Engage adolescents in concrete problem-solving activities to identify those who have difficulty thinking symbolically or using reasoning in nonsymbolic events (Moses, Klein, & Altman, 1990).

Strategies for Increasing Language Production

The following strategies focus on improving the production or expressive skills of students with language-learning problems:

1. Expect students to speak occasionally in incomplete sentences because this is normal for discourse.

2. Regardless of the effectiveness of a student's communication, convey that the message is important. React first to the content of a student's message because it is most important in the communication process, and then correct the syntax error.

3. When attempting to expand a young child's utterances, provide one or two additional words to the child's spontaneous utterance for the child to repeat rather than impose adult structures that are difficult to imitate. Explain that the reason for the expansion of the utterance is not to correct what the youngster is saying but to give a more complex way of expressing thought (Bos & Vaughn, 1988).

4. Teach language in various natural settings (for example, classroom, cafeteria, playground) rather than only in isolated groups. Also, teach language skills in connection with other curriculum content (Wiig & Semel, 1984).

5. Act as a good language model, and ask students to imitate what they hear (Connell, 1987). Imitation is frequently a good measure of language skills because students tend to imitate only the forms they know and not necessarily what they hear (Bernstein & Tiegerman, 1989).

6. Use structured language programs that provide adequate opportunities to practice a new skill as well as interactive activities for applying the skill to relevant contexts (Bos & Vaughn, 1988).

7. Comment or elaborate on students' ideas to demonstrate how more information can be expressed and how concepts can be associated.

8. Use activities such as role playing and charades to improve a student's use of language in different contexts and to enhance the ability to recognize the importance of nonverbal skills such as eye contact, facial expressions, and gestures.

9. When a student has difficulties with word retrieval, examine indices such as response time, error index (word-selection process), and substitution types (German, 1984).

10. Use semantic training to improve a student's word-retrieval skills, and include strategies such as categorizing or classify-

ing words and using associative clues (McGregor & Leonard, 1989).

11. To improve a student's verbal expression, encourage storytelling activities in which the student must name all of the objects or pictures, tell what is happening, and create an ending.

12. Teach generalization of language skills through three phases: (a) an orientation phase in which the student becomes aware of the different contexts applicable, (b) an activation phase in which practice is provided in a variety of situations, and (c) a maintenance phase in which periodic probes are conducted to ensure proficiency is maintained (Deshler & Schumaker, 1986).

Imitation and Modeling Strategies

Two teaching strategies that frequently are used in teaching language are imitation and modeling. In these strategies, the student gives a response that is similar to that of a model. Courtright and Courtright (1976) distinguish between modeling and imitative behavior that is mimicry. They define *imitative mimicry* as a one-to-one, literal matching response for each stimulus statement. In contrast to mimicry, modeling involves acquiring an abstract language rule without giving an immediate response to the stimulus (Bandura, 1971). For example, the student observes the teacher modeling a rule several times before being required to use the rule. This strategy is apparent in the following method of teaching the use of *s* on singular verbs: The teacher models 20 different singular subject-verb sentences that describe pictures (such as "Dog runs," "Boy walks," "Cat plays"). After the teacher models these sentences, the student is requested to describe the pictures.

Leonard (1975) recommends the use of modeling with a problem-solving set. The teacher uses a puppet as a model. Visual stimuli, such as toys or pictures of objects and people, are placed in front of the model (puppet). The teacher tells the student to listen carefully and determine which sentences earn reinforcers for the model. The model produces 10 to 20 utterances that describe the visual stimuli and deliberately gives 25 percent of the responses incorrectly. The teacher then presents the same visual stimulus to the student and encourages a response that earned a reinforcer for the model. The student and model take turns responding until the student has produced three consecutive appropriate responses that were presented previously by the model. At this point the student is presented with new visual stimuli and is required to produce unmodeled utterances.

The teacher can use imitative mimicry at one point with a student and gradually move to more spontaneous responses. When using this strategy, the teacher needs to structure the event preceding the student's response (that is, the antecedent event). The antecedent event can have varying degrees of cueing. A teacher can use *total* cueing in the antecedent event ("What do you want? Tell me, 'I want an apple' ") or *partial* cueing in the antecedent event ("Is this a ball or an orange?"). Partial cueing also can including pointing to or looking at items to help the student make a correct response. *Minimal* cueing can be used when the student is ready to generalize a rule. For example, the teacher can say "What's happening? What's he doing?"

Mumu (1978) notes that the expansion model is a modeling technique frequently used by parents for language intervention. With this technique, the youngster's response is expanded by the parent or teacher. For example, the youngster says "Car go," and the parent or teacher immediately gives the expanded model, "The car is going."

Parent Involvement

Parents of students with language-learning problems play an important role in language intervention. Recent studies indicate that 80 percent of maternal utterances directed toward youngsters with language impairments are not related semantically to the child's vocal, verbal, or nonverbal behavior (Bernstein & Tiegerman, 1989). However, in a study of social conversational skills of preschoolers, Girolametto (1988) found a significant increase in appropriate language when parent training was involved. In this study, parents received training in three areas: (a) following their child's lead in establishing joint focus on an activity, (b) responding contingently to their child's communicative attempts, and (c) encouraging conversation by taking turns. The training resulted in the parents being less controlling and more responsive to their children. Girolametto notes that following parent training the children initiated more topics, were more responsive to their mother's preceding turn in conversation, allowed more verbal turns when talking, and used a more diverse vocabulary.

LANGUAGE ACTIVITIES

After carefully selecting a language program, the teacher may decide to supplement it to meet the specific needs of certain students. Some teachers prefer to plan a complete individualized program rather than use an available commercial program. To supplement or design an individualized program, the teacher must plan teaching activities. One advantage of planning activities is that the teacher can select and vary teaching methods and materials to fit the individual student's needs.

Direct teaching activities are designed to meet specific objectives. They must, however, be supplemented with independent learning and reinforcing activities. Self-correcting materials are a good choice for independent learning of a skill, and instructional games frequently are used to reinforce newly acquired skills. Various teaching activities are presented in this section, and instructional games and self-correcting materials are described in the following sections. Activities, games, and self-correcting materials that are appropriate for use with secondary students are presented near the end of each section.

1. *Objective:*
   *To teach is + verb + **ing** (is jumping)*
   For each picture, say a model sentence that includes *is* plus *verb* plus *ing*. The teacher can show a picture of a girl jumping rope and say, "The girl is jumping." The teacher models 10 different sentences with pictures. The student is not encouraged to respond during the modeled sentences. After the modeled sentences, the teacher shows the pictures again and asks the student to tell what is happening in each picture. After successful completion of this task, the teacher shows 10 new action pictures and for each new picture says, "Tell me what's happening."
   Modification:
   The teacher can use modeling to teach semantics, morphology, syntax, and so forth by varying the stimulus and the modeled response. For example, the morphological form of singular pronouns plus the inflectional verb ending *s* — "She walks" — can be taught by using action pictures with singular subjects and changing the model to "She walks," "He runs," "He jumps," and so on. Courtright and Courtright (1976, 1979) report that generalization of a syntactic rule is significantly higher with this type of modeling than with imitative responses, in which the student repeats the model immediately after the teacher.
2. *Objective:*
   *To teach plural morpheme **s** on regular plural nouns*
   Use modeling with problem solving to teach language rules (Leonard, 1975). Show a puppet

20 pictures that depict 20 plural nouns. The puppet names each picture and misses 25 percent of them. The teacher reinforces each correct response with a chip. After the modeling of 20 pictures, the teacher asks the student to name the pictures. After the student correctly responds to these pictures, the teacher presents 20 new pictures and asks the student to name them.

Modification:

Modeling with problem solving also can be used to teach semantics, phonology, syntax, and so on. For example, to teach a syntactic rule of *they* + *are* + verb + *ing,* present pictures depicting action with a plural subject (such as children playing) and say to the puppet, "Tell me what's happening in each picture." The puppet responds using the form of *they* + *are* + verb + *ing* for each picture ("They are playing"). The puppet randomly makes 25 percent of the responses incorrect ("They play"). The teacher reinforces the correct responses with a chip. After the modeling the teacher says, "You give the puppet a chip for each correct sentence." After successful completion of this task, the teacher says to the student, "You tell me what's happening in each picture."

3. *Objective:*

*To teach possessive pronouns **(her, his, their)***
Prepare small cards with mounted pictures of a single girl, a single boy, and several children. Mount pictures of objects on separate cards. Attach the cards to rings and group all the people pictures together on one set of rings and all the object cards on another. Attach the rings and card sets to a folded cardboard stand. The student or teacher flips each card separately to form phrases (*her hat, his ball, their house,* and so forth). Coloring books are good sources of pictures.

Modification:

A third set of color cards can be used in which each card is shaded a different color. The student is required to say phrases, such as "Her dress is red", "His hat is yellow," or "His ball is blue."

4. *Objective:*

To teach classification of associated words
Have the student sort various association pictures (see Figure 9.1). Wedemeyer and Cejka (1975) suggest the following procedure:

a. Mount individual pictures of objects commonly associated with each other on small cards. Select pictures such as ball and bat, cup and saucer, and shoe and sock from reading readiness workbooks.

b. Make a card holder with strips of tagboard stapled to a large piece of tagboard.

c. Place a picture in each slot down the left side of the card holder.

d. Give the student the remaining pictures and have him tell how the two objects are associated.

Modification:

Matching pictures and pictures that depict opposites can be used. Also, the activity can be made self-correcting by putting matching shapes on the backs of associated pictures. After sorting the pictures, the student can check his work by looking at the backs of the cards to determine if the shapes match.

5. *Objective:*

*To develop the use of **him, her,** and **it***
To teach the use of pronouns have the students participate in the following activity in which the students are arranged in a circle, girls alternating with boys. Each student's task is to roll the ball to another student. Before doing so, however, the student must state if the individual who receives is a "him" or a "her." After some students are successful with this task, have them hold pictures of familiar objects (such as car, ball, house) while the other students retain their human identify. Now before a student rolls the ball, he must state if the individual receiving is an object and must say "it" before rolling the ball. If the receiver does not have a picture, the student must state "him" or "her" before rolling the ball.

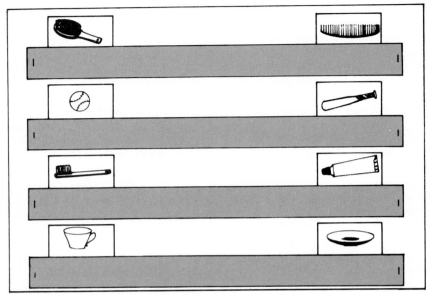

FIGURE 9.1
Association pictures mounted in a card holder.

Modification:
All students can hold pictures of objects. Before each student rolls the ball, ask him to state if the receiver of the ball is a "him" or a "her" and to identify the object that the student is holding. Then the student says the appropriate phrase (such as "her house").

6. *Objective:*
*To teach **ed** on regular verbs **(walked, jumped)***
Have the student describe an activity as he is performing it. For example, the student says, "I am jumping" as he is jumping. Upon completion have the student say, "I jumped very high" or "I jumped over the box." This activity can be extended by using small objects that can perform movement; for example, a doll can be made to jump, walk, or hop. Also, this activity can be used to teach irregular verb forms such as *ate, drank,* and *fell.*

7. *Objective:*
*To teach the prepositions **in, on, out of, in front of, in back of, beside***
Use Hula Hoops and physical activity to teach

prepositions. Give directions to the students to move in relation to the hoops ("Stand in the Hula Hoops"). At first the teacher announces and performs the activity with the students; then gradually he only announces the activity. Finally, the teacher has the students themselves talk during the activity. For example the students say, "The Hula Hoop is beside me" when they move their hoops by their side.

Modification:
The teacher can stand in some kind of relation to the hoop, such as in the hoop and ask, "Where am I?" The students answer, "You are in the Hula Hoop." Each student then can have a turn standing in relation to his Hula Hoop and asking, "Where am I?"

8. *Objective:*
To teach classification of part/whole relationships
Use a flannelboard activity to teach part/whole relationships. Cut out of flannel the parts of two complete objects such as a truck. Have one truck put together on the flannelboard before beginning. Ask the student to complete the sec-

ond truck by saying, "Put on the part of the truck that is the wheel," "Put on the part of the truck that is the door," and so on.

Modification:

This activity also can be used to teach functional relationships. For example, ask the student to put on the part of the truck that opens to let people inside, or the part of the truck that turns to change the truck's direction.

9. *Objective:*

To teach classification by function

Collect pictures of objects used for one function. For example, to show a bath, collect pictures of a bathtub, soap, washcloth, and towel. Have the student sort the pictures according to function. For example:

a. *Sandwich:* bread, knife, peanut butter, jelly
b. *Bath:* tub or shower, washcloth, towel, soap
c. *Washing dishes:* dishes, soap, sink, sponge, drainer, towel
d. *Building:* lumber, nails, hammer, sandpaper, paint, screws, tools

Modification:

This task can be made more difficult for older students by making the functional relationships more complex. For example: *Dressing for a party:* washing hair, fixing fingernails, brushing hair, brushing teeth. Moreover, a picture-card deck called Functions (produced by DLM) can be used to teach classification. It includes 14 five-card sets (for example, stamp, paper, pen, envelope, mailbox), and the student can use the cards to match objects into sets on the basis of function.

10. *Objective:*

To classify objects that belong to the same class (animals, foods, houses, vehicles)

To teach classification, prepare a large card with four sections (Wedemeyer & Cejka, 1975). In one section put a picture of a house; in the second section put a picture of an animal; in the third, a picture of a vehicle; and in the fourth, a picture of food. Collect and mount pictures of animals, foods, houses, and vehicles. Have the student sort the pictures in the four areas. An area can be made with a color or shape so that the student can sort objects or pictures according to the attribute of color or shape.

11. *Objective:*

To teach synonyms

Ask a student to call out a word for which he knows at least one synonym. Then ask the next student to "match" the word by providing a synonym of it. Use a game format in which the student receives one point for each correct synonym he names. If he cannot think of any, he can challenge the first player to state the synonym he had in mind. Any failure in this task is penalized by one point. A player fails to score a point if he is unable to think of a synonym, and he is penalized one point if he responds with a word that is not a synonym of the word proposed by the preceding player. The object is to squeeze as many synonyms out of the original word as possible. If a player can think of only one or two synonyms, his opponent can add a few points to his score by naming some others. When the possibilities of a given word have been exhausted, a new word is used.

Modification:

This activity also can be used with antonyms. For example, if *big* is the given word, an appropriate response might be *little*. Then the next player must give an antonym of *little* (for example, *large*) without using the original word, *big*. A point is scored for each correct antonym (or synonym of the original word) given.

12. *Objective:*

To teach classification of weather and seasonal clothes

Have the student make decisions for clothing dolls. Wedemeyer and Cejka (1975) suggest the following procedure to teach classification:

a. Make boy and girl figures from flannel.

b. Cut out flannel articles of clothing for seasonal and weather changes, different times of the day, and different occasions. Use a paper doll book for patterns.

c. Use marking pens to make details—buttons, shoelaces, collars, and so forth.

d. Make articles such as mittens and shoes to correspond to the right and left sides.

e. Place the dolls on a flannelboard and have the students dress the dolls as the teacher directs (for example, "Dress the girl doll for a rainy day").

Modification:

This activity can be modified slightly to teach articles of clothing. The teacher says, "Tell me what I should put on the doll." The student responds, "Shoes." The teacher puts on the shoes. The teacher calls on each student for a clothing word to indicate what should be put on or taken off to change the doll.

13. *Objective:*

To teach labels of furniture

Use a playhouse and miniature furniture. Put all the furniture in one group and say, "Tell me what furniture goes in the kitchen. John, you tell me one piece of furniture." The teacher calls on students until all the kitchen items are placed and then starts with another room. Magazine pictures of furniture and rooms also can be used in this activity. The teacher can hold up a picture of a kitchen from a magazine and have pictures of furniture on the table. The teacher says, "Tell me what furniture goes in the kitchen," and the student selects an appropriate picture and names the piece of furniture.

Modification:

The teacher can place a piece of furniture in a room where it does not belong—for example, a bed in the kitchen. The teacher asks, "What doesn't belong? Can you tell me why?"

14. *Objective:*

*To teach **rough** and **smooth** as modifiers*

Collect items that are small and rough (for example, a piece of sandpaper, a piece of window screen, fingernail file, washcloth, a small rough rock, a piece of net, a piece of bark). Also, collect items that are smooth (for example, a

marble, a small magnet, a small mirror, a smooth rock). Place the smooth and rough objects in a large bag. Introduce the word *smooth* by letting the students feel a smooth object and talk about how it feels. Introduce the word *rough* by letting them feel a rough object and talk about how it feels. Now let each student reach in the bag and feel one object. Have the student decide if the object feels smooth or rough and then take it out of the bag.

Modification:

Objects can be used that are hard and soft, or heavy and light.

15. *Objective:*

To increase auditory discrimination between two phonemes

Draw a ladder on a piece of paper. Give the student a marker and tell him to move the marker when he hears two different words. Say some word pairs that consist of the same word and some that are different words. When the student is consistent in moving the marker only for two different words, change the task by having the student listen to words that are different by only one phoneme, such as *pair–fair*. The student moves the marker when he hears two different words. Some suggested pairs differing in only one phoneme are *pair–fair; purr–fur; put–foot; pork–fork;* and *pay–fay.*

Modification:

This activity can be modified according to how the student signals that two sounds are the same or different. The student can raise his hand, tap a pencil, move a space on a game board, or pick up a chip.

16. *Objective:*

To teach negatives

Model a sentence without a negative and then immediately model a sentence containing a negative. For example, the teacher says, "Some for John. None for John." The student imitates the two sentences. When several sentences with negatives have been modeled correctly, the teacher only presents a sentence without a negative. The student responds by saying a sentence with a negative. A recommended sequence of negatives is as follows:

a. no

b. none

c. nothing else

d. no more

e. not enough

f. don't

g. let's not

h. we'll not

i. do not

j. don't do

k. is no more

l. does not

m. is not

n. did not

o. nothing is

p. will not

q. was not

Modification:

This technique can be used to teach morphology. For example, to teach plural *s* on regular nouns, the teacher can present sets of two pictures and two modeled responses, such as "one kite–two kites, one cat–two cats." After the student correctly repeats several modeled responses, the teacher presents a picture of one cat and says, "One cat." Then the teacher presents a picture of two cats, and the student says, "Two cats."

17. *Objective:*

To extend the use of linguistic forms to other environments

Have a student act as a speaker to describe an object to a listener such that the listener can select a similar object from several objects placed in front of him. The speaker and listener sit back-to-back. Place three objects in front of the listener (for example, key, comb, ball) and one similar object (such as the comb) in front of the speaker. The speaker describes the object, and the listener is encouraged to ask questions until he can select the correct object.

Modification:

Use a block-building activity in which two students are seated back-to-back. The speaker and listener each have an identical set of six blocks that vary in shape, color, or size. The speaker builds a construction using all of the blocks and provides enough information to the listener so that he can duplicate the construction.

18. *Objective:*

To use language as an effective communicator

Use an over-the-shoulder activity in which the speaker is the *encoder* and the listener is the *decoder.* The encoder stands behind the decoder and talks over the decoder's shoulder to tell him what to do next. The encoder must give information so that the decoder understands, and the information must be revised if the decoder does not understand. For example, the encoder may say, "Put the red triangle on top of the blue square." The decoder places the triangle above the square so that it touches the top of the square. The encoder then may say, "You have put the triangle on top of the square like a roof on a house. Instead, lay it on top of the square like a blanket." The encoder must keep revising his instructions until the decoder completely understands the message.

Modification:

Have the encoder draw a simple design and then tell the decoder over his shoulder how to draw the same design. The decoder can stand at the chalkboard while the encoder looks at his own design and the one the decoder is drawing.

19. *Objective:*

*To teach the classification of **where, when,** and **what** phrases*

Write the word *where* next to the word *place.* Tell the student that *where* refers to place. With the student, list a few phrases that refer to place. Write the word *what* next to the word *thing.* Tell the student to list some phrases that refer to things. Write the word *when* next to the word *time.* Tell the student that *when* usually refers to time. The student needs a broader concept of time than time on a clock. Time can refer to the hour, parts of a day, events of a day (such as breakfast, school, bedtime), day of the week, and so on. Have the student list some time phrases. For practice, give the student a worksheet with the three headings of *Where, What,* and *When* and have him list the following phrases under the appropriate heading:

a. on the playground

b. tomorrow morning

c. beside your bed

d. the blue car
e. last night
f. in your lunchbox
g. on a rainy day
h. her pretty dress
i. my broken cup
j. behind the school
k. a small coat
l. at my house
m. before lunch
n. after school

Modification:
This activity also can be used to classify *who, why,* and *how* phrases. Classification of these phrases can be made self-correcting by putting the phrases on cards in a Poke Box (described in Chapter 4) with the multiple-choice words of *When, Where,* and *What* (or *Who, Why,* and *How*).

20. *Objective:*
To teach vocabulary likenesses
Write the following verbs and objects on the chalkboard:

kicking	swing
pushing	house
sewing	ball
building	dress

Ask the student to tell how to pair the action words and objects. Then ask the student to tell how *kicking* the *ball* is like *pushing* a *swing.* (Help the student conclude that when you kick a ball it goes away from you, and when you push a swing it also goes away from you.) Ask the student how *sewing* a *dress* is like *building* a *house.* (Again, help the student conclude that when you build or sew you make a complete item out of parts.) Then give the student a worksheet with incomplete sentences and ask him to select the best word to complete each sentence. For example:

a. *Working* is to job as *playing* is to _____ .
   (fun, game, children)
b. *Sweeping* is to broom as *hitting* is to ____ .
   (bat, ball, catch).
c. *Sleeping* is to bed as *sitting* is to _____ .
   (table, chair, desk)

d. *Smiling* is to happy as *crying* is to _____ .
   (anger, tears, sad)
e. *Eating* is to food as *drinking* is to _____ .
   (thirst, water, cup)
f. *Fussing* is to anger as *laughing* is to _____ .
   (happiness, funny, smile)
g. *Running* is to legs as *throwing* is to _____ .
   (catching, arms, ball)
h. *Cutting* is to knife as *stirring* is to _____ .
   (bowl, cook, spoon)
i. *Writing* is to pencil as *painting* is to _____ .
   (paper, canvas, brush)
j. *Reading* is to book as *listening* is to _____ .
   (teacher, ear, talk)

Modification:
This vocabulary task of comparison of likenesses can be modified to include items based on part/whole relationships. For example: *Fingers* are to hands as *toes* are to feet.

21. *Objective:*
To teach the use of relative clauses
On the chalkboard give the student several examples of sentences that contain relative clauses. Then give the student a practice sheet with several sets of two sentences. Ask him to combine them into one sentence by using a relative pronoun. For example:

a. The boy broke the window. The boy ran away. (who)

a. The boy who broke the window ran away.

b. Read the book. The book is about dogs. (that)

b. Read the book that is about dogs.

Modification:
The sentences can be combined with conjunctions such as *and, but, because,* and *so.* For example, the following sentences can be combined with *but.*

a. Bob eats breakfast every day. Bob is always hungry at lunch.

a. Bob eats breakfast every day, but he is always hungry at lunch.

b. The puppy
plays
outside. The
puppy
likes to sleep
in the
house.

b. The puppy plays
outside, but he
likes to sleep in
the house.

22. *Objective:*

*To use the conjunctions **and, but, because,** and **so***

Use the cloze procedure with multiple-choice items (Wiig & Semel, 1984). Make a list of sentences that require the use of a conjunction. Leave that space blank and give multiple choices. For example:

a. He goes to school _____ he plays baseball. (and, but, or)

b. I don't want ice cream _____ I would like a dessert. (or, but)

c. You should take a bath _____ you are dirty. (because, but)

d. You must finish your homework _____ you can play outside. (but, so)

Modification:

The cloze procedure with multiple-choice items can be used to teach semantics, morphology, or other forms of syntax. For example, the following sentence requires an inflectional ending *(ed)* on a regular verb:

The boy _____ to school this morning before breakfast. (walk, walked)

23. *Objective:*

To teach paraphrasing

Use a game format in which the students are divided into two teams. Have the first player on Team A tell the first player on Team B to do something (for example, "Touch your nose"). The Team B player performs the action and then tells the first player on Team A to do the same thing; however, he must give the command using different words (for example, "Put your finger on your nose"). If both players perform correctly, both teams get a point. If the player on Team B is unable to say the same command in different words, only Team A gets the point. The game continues in this manner, and the team with the most points at the end of the game wins.

Modification:

The students can be required to paraphrase a short paragraph. This can be a written or oral task. For example:

Mary woke up early because she had to arrive at school before the bell rang. She needed to go to the library before school so she could return an overdue book.

Paraphrased paragraph:

Mary had to return an overdue book to the library before school began. Therefore, she needed to wake up earlier than usual.

24. *Objective:*

To teach employment vocabulary words to secondary students

Cut out job ads from the newspaper and collect job application forms. Read the ads and application forms to the class and determine what words and phrases they know (such as *experience, minimum wage, waitress, waiter, good working conditions, apply in person, references required*). Define the words they do not understand. With each student, role play a job interview and use the vocabulary on the job applications.

Modification:

Vocabulary words can be selected from credit applications, checkbooks, classified ads, or driver's license applications.

INSTRUCTIONAL GAMES IN LANGUAGE

His, Her, or Their

Objective:

To teach the use of the possessive pronouns *his, her,* and *their*

Materials:

Game board with start-to-finish format (presented in Chapter 4); one stack of picture cards depicting objects; one stack of picture cards depicting people (should include at least one picture of a boy, one picture of a girl, and one picture of several children); a spinner; markers.

Directions:

1. The stack of object pictures and the stack of people pictures are placed face down on the game board.
2. Each player places a marker at the start position.
3. Each player in turn spins the spinner, notes the number on which it lands, and picks up the number of cards shown on the spinner from each stack.
4. The player turns over the cards and makes as many pronoun and object combinations as possible. For example:
   her hat, his hat, their hat, their ball, her house, his shoe
5. For each combination the player says, he moves his marker ahead one space.
6. After moving his marker, the player puts the used cards face down on the bottom of each stack.
7. The players take turns, and the one who moves to the end of the game board first is the winner.

What Goes Together

Objective:

To teach classification by association

Materials:

Set of 40 playing cards composed of association pictures (for example, a card illustrating a shoe and a card illustrating a sock).

Directions:

1. Six cards are dealt to each player (two to four players), and the remaining cards are placed face down in the center of the players.
2. Each player combines any association sets in his hand and lays them face up on the table.
3. Then each player in turn takes a card from the deck, discards one from his hand, and places it face up next to the deck.
4. After the first discard, each player can select a card either from the deck or from the discard pile.
5. The first player who displays three association sets wins. (The criteria for winning can be varied to suit the students and the situation.)

The Deck

Objective:

To teach opposite words

Materials:

Deck of cards composed of pictures depicting opposite words (for example, a card illustrating the word *up* and a card illustrating the word *down*).

Directions:

1. An equal number of cards is dealt to each player until all cards are dealt.
2. Each player combines any sets of opposites in his hand and lays them face up on the table.
3. Then each player draws a card in turn from another player's hand.
4. When a player has a set of opposite pictures in his hand, he lays them on the table.
5. The game continues until one player wins by pairing all the cards in his hand. The number of hands played can vary according to the time available.

Whose Is It?

Objective:

To teach the use of possessive personal pronoun *mine* and *'s*

Materials:

Two matching sets of 12 pictures.

Directions:

1. The dealer lays three pictures from the first set of cards face down in front of each of the four players.
2. He then lays the entire second matching stack of cards face down on the table.
3. The dealer turns the first card in the stack face up and asks, "Whose is it?"
4. The first player guesses whose stack contains the matching card by saying, "Mine," "John's," "Mary's," and so on. The player must use the possessive *'s* or possessive pronoun *mine*.

5. Whoever the player guesses must turn over his cards; that is, if the player says, "John's," John must turn over his cards for everyone to see. If the card matches one in John's stack, the player who selected John gets a chip. If it does not, the card is placed face down on the bottom of the deck, and John turns his cards back face down on the table.
6. The dealer turns the next card from the stack face up and asks the next player, "Whose is it?"
7. The player who makes the most correct guesses receives the most chips and wins.

Say the Whole Sentence

Objective:

To teach sentence construction

Materials:

Deck of cards of matching pairs with several of the pairs having only one attribute different from other pairs (for example, three pairs of Christmas trees—one set with blue lights, one set with red lights, and one with green lights.)

Directions:

1. Six cards are dealt to each player, and the remaining cards are placed face down in a stack on the table.
2. Each player combines any matching sets in his hand and lays them face up on the table.
3. Each player in turn asks for a card from another player by using all the attributes (for example, "Do you have a Christmas tree with green lights?") If the other player has that card, he gives it to the first player. If the other player does not have the requested card, the first player takes a card from the deck.
4. The first player who matches all his cards wins the game.

Phonetic Bingo

Objective:

To teach phoneme identification

Materials:

Cards that have five numbered columns with each column containing five letters; discs.

Directions:

1. Each player receives a bingo card containing letters.
2. The caller calls out a column number and a phoneme, such as 2/p/.
3. If the player has that particular phoneme in the appropriate column, he places a disc over that letter.
4. The winner is the first player to cover five letters in a row. A list of the called-out letters can be kept to check the winning card.

1	2	3	4	5
p	d	g	t	v
g	v	p	v	t
b	t	d	g	p
t	g	b	p	b
d	p	t	d	g

Fishing for Blends

Objective:

To teach /s/ blends

Materials:

Fish-shaped cards displaying /s/ blends: *st, sk, sw, sl.*

Directions:

1. The cards are placed face up in the center of the students.
2. The caller calls out a word containing an /s/ blend, such as *skate.*
3. The players take turns finding the correct blend from the group of fish cards.
4. If the player picks the correct card, he gets to keep the card.
5. When all the cards are gone from the center, the player with the most "fish" wins.

Two-Way Words

Objective:

To improve use of homonyms

Materials:

Set of 20 index cards with a pair of homonyms written on each card; answer key that lists the definition of each homonym.

Directions:

1. Two pairs of partners sit across from each other.
2. The dealer deals five cards to each of the four players.
3. The first player selects one of his cards, makes a statement that includes either of the homonyms on the card, and then repeats the homonym (for example, "She wore a plain dress—plain"). He then challenges his partner to make a statement that includes the other homonym on the card but gives no further clues.
4. When the partner makes a statement (for example, "We were in the plane"), the dealer refers to the answer key to see if the response is correct. If the response is questionable, the dealer can ask for another statement that gives additional information concerning the meaning of the homonym (for example, "We were flying above the clouds in the plane").
5. If his partner's statement is correct, the player can place his card in the middle of the table. If his partner's statement is not correct, the player must keep the card for another turn.
6. The next player challenges his partner in the same way, and the partner pairs take turns. A player can challenge only his own partner and must use his own cards.
7. The first partner pair to have all their cards in the middle of the table wins the game.

Sentence Game

Objective:

To teach sentence construction

Materials:

A start-to-finish game board (presented in Chapter 4); a deck of cards displaying stimulus pictures; a spinner; markers.

Directions:

1. Each player places a marker at the start position, and the picture cards are placed face down.

2. The first player spins the spinner and moves the designated number of spaces.
3. Then the player selects a card from the deck, and he must use the word or words illustrated in the picture in a sentence.
4. If the sentence is complete and correct, the player remains on the square. If the player cannot use the word or words correctly, he moves back one square at a time and picks up another card until he produces a correct sentence.
5. The first player to reach the finish square wins.

Three Little Words

Objective:

To teach sentence construction using conjunctions

Materials:

A stack of word cards containing two related words and one conjunction on each card; a spinner; chips.

Directions:

1. The first player spins the spinner and selects the designated number of cards from the deck.
2. The player must make a sentence for each card by using the set of words on the card.
3. The player receives a chip for each sentence correctly constructed.
4. The player with the most chips at the end of a set time period wins the game.

Can You Answer with a Question?

Objective:

To teach the use of *who, what,* and *where* questions

Materials:

A game board with categories and points (similar to Jeopardy game); question cards corresponding to the categories and point levels (the words range in difficulty according to their point value, and the answers are written on the back of each card).

Directions:

1. The first player chooses a category and point value from the game board.

2. The player is presented with a word from the category he chose and must define the word with a question. For example, the category may be *clothes*, and the word on the card may be *shoes*. The correct answer on the back of the card is, "What do you wear on your feet?" Object categories require a *what* question. If the player selects from a category of places, the answer must be in the form of a question that uses *where*. For example, if the category is *Community Places* and the word is *library*, the answer is "Where do we get books?" If the student selects from a *who* category, the answer must be in the form of a question that uses *who*. For example, if the category is *Community Helpers* and the words are *police officer*, the answer is "Who catches criminals?" The following are suggested categories for the game board:

What

Clothes (hat, shoes, dress)

Animals (dog, cat, bird)

Sports Equipment (ball, bat, glove)

Where

Community Places (bank, post office, school)

Fun Places (restaurant, zoo, theater)

Travel Depots (train station, airport, bus station)

Who

Community Helpers (firefighter, police officer, mail carrier)

Family Member (mother, father, sister)

School Personnel (principal, teacher, librarian)

Build a Sentence

Objective:

To teach combining independent clauses with conjunctions

Materials:

Thirty flannel-backed cards with independent clauses written on the front of each card; 13 flannel-backed cards with conjunctions written on the front of each card; a flannelboard.

Directions:

1. The flannelboard is placed in the middle of the table, and the cards are dealt to the players.
2. The first player lays down a card containing an independent clause, such as *She was late*.
3. The second player lays down a card containing a conjunction, such as *because*.
4. The third player must lay down a clause to complete the sentence, such as *she missed the bus*.
5. The next player begins a new sentence.
6. A player loses his turn if he does not have an appropriate card to play.
7. The first player who uses all his cards wins the game.

Suggested clauses:

She went to bed

She was tired

Mary stayed home

He made a good grade

John went to the store

She likes school

She was hungry

He studied

She watched television

He brought some ice cream

He washed dishes

He bought a ticket

His father fussed

Mother cooked supper

He took a bath

She was dirty

Suggested conjunctions:

because

and

since

Prefix Bingo

Objective:

To teach the prefixes *in, re, un,* and *non*

Materials:

Bingo cards with various root words that can be combined with the prefixes *in, re, un,* or *non*; a spinner with four sections that has a prefix in each section; markers with one prefix printed on each marker (see Figure 9.2).

Directions:

1. The first player spins the spinner, notes on which prefix it lands, and picks up a marker with that prefix on it.
2. The player places the prefix marker on a root word with which it can be combined.
3. The player loses his turn if the spinner lands on a prefix that cannot be combined with a root word on his card.
4. The first player who has his markers in a row (vertically, horizontally, or diagonally) wins the game. To check the winning card, make sure the prefix on each marker can be combined with the root word on which it is placed.

Modification:

This game can be modified by using suffixes, such as *ful, less, ly.*

Deal a Sentence

Objective:

To teach sentence construction

Materials:

Word cards containing words from the following grammatical categories: 9 nouns, 9 pronouns, 15 verbs, 12 adjectives, 3 articles, 3 conjunctions, 3 prepositions, and 1 adverb.

Directions:

1. Each player receives five cards, and the remaining cards are placed face down in the center of the players.
2. Each player organizes his hand to determine if he has a sentence.
3. The first player selects one card from the deck and discards one card face up.
4. The first player to make a sentence wins the hand. The number of hands played can vary according to the time available, and the player with the most points at the end of the time period wins. Also, the first player to earn a predetermined number of points could be the winner. Scoring could be: 1 point for a declarative sentence, 2 points for using *not* in a sentence, 3 points for a sentence with a conjunction, and 4 points for a question.

Suggested words:

Nouns: ball, dress, boy, girl, book, house, doll, bike, dog

Pronouns: I, you, she, he, him, they, them, it, we

Verbs: is, are, was, were, made, can, go, should, may, do, see, ride, walk, run, am

Adjectives: big, round, pretty, small, sad, happy, little, red, fast, slow, fat, funny

side	build	do	tire	seen
turn	tell	fill	use	sense
sent	claim	call	stick	tend
skid	happy	move	cover	born
to	tie	come	paid	fuel

FIGURE 9.2
Prefix Bingo game card and spinner.

Articles: a, an, the

Conjunctions: and, but, or

Prepositions: to, at, with

Adverb: not

Conjunction Square

Objective:

To teach sentence construction using conjunctions

Materials:

A checkerboard with a conjunction written on each square; a stack of cards with a sentence printed on each card; checkers.

Directions:

1. The player makes his checker move (according to the rules of the game of checkers) and takes two sentence cards.
2. The player must combine the two sentences on the cards with the conjunction on which his checker lands. He must make a correct sentence to keep his move.
3. If the player is unable to make a sentence, he must move his checker back to its previous position.
4. The players continue taking turns and making sentences until one player wins the checker game.

SELF-CORRECTING LANGUAGE MATERIALS

Opposites

Objective:

To teach classification of word opposites

Feedback device:

Windows in the back of the Spinning Wheels show matching symbols to indicate picture or word opposites.

Materials:

Spinning Wheels (described in Chapter 4); a worksheet that has one picture in the left column and two

pictures on the right—one of which illustrates the opposite of the picture on the left—corresponding to the pictures on the Spinning Wheels; an acetate overlay (see Figure 9.3).

Directions:

The student places the acetate overlay over the worksheet, selects the picture that is the opposite of the one in the left column, and marks an X on that picture. After completing the worksheet, the student checks his work with the Spinning Wheels. He turns the wheels so that the picture opposites he has selected appear in the windows, and then he turns over the wheels to see if there are matching symbols in the back windows.

Modification:

This activity can be used to teach same, different, or associated words by changing the items or pictures on the Spinning Wheels.

Time Slot

Objective:

To increase skills in using verbs relating to time

Feedback device:

Symbols or line drawings on the back of the verb cards match the line drawing on the envelope with the appropriate verb form.

Materials:

Three envelopes for present-, past-, and future-tense verbs with a different line drawing or symbol on each envelope; a set of cards with pictures depicting the time associated with various verb tenses (see Figure 9.4).

Directions:

The student looks at each card to determine which verb tense the picture illustrates. He then places each card in the envelope that denotes his answer. After sorting all the cards, the student takes the cards out of the envelopes and checks to see if the symbol on the back of each card matches the symbol on the front of the envelope in which it was placed.

FIGURE 9.3
Worksheet for Opposites.

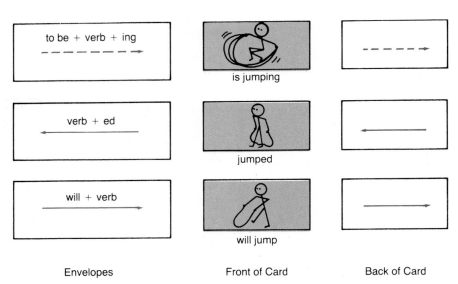

FIGURE 9.4
Envelopes and cards for Time Slot.

Modifications:

The activity can include several syntactic forms such as *are* + verb + *ing* or *has* + verb + *ed*. A different line drawing or symbol should be assigned to each syntactic form. Also, the activity can be modified further by using words instead of pictures and labeling the envelopes with the name of the verb tense.

Flip Siders

Objective:

To teach classification by association

Feedback device:

Matching colors or symbols are on the back of pictures that are associated.

Materials:

Flip-sider cards (presented in Chapter 4) that contain pictures of words which can be categorized by association (such as a sock and a shoe) and have matching colors or symbols on the back of associated pictures.

Directions:

The student looks at each picture and finds the picture associated with it. He combines the pictures and turns over the cards. The pictures that are associated have the same color or symbol on the back.

Modifications:

Flip siders can be used to teach opposites, verb tenses, and phoneme recognition. Also, the material can be modified for secondary students by combining association pictures that illustrate cause-and-effect relationships. For example, the pictures could show a student studying and a report card with good grades, or an accident and an ambulance.

Make a Question

Objective:

To teach the interrogative reversal

Feedback device:

The pieces of the puzzle strip fit together when the sentence is in question form.

Materials:

A worksheet with declarative sentences; a set of puzzle pieces for each sentence that fit together when the sentence is in the form of a question.

Directions:

The student rewrites each sentence on the worksheet into an interrogative reversal to ask a question. After completing this question, he puts the corresponding puzzle pieces together to check his answer.

(a) The girls are at home.

(b) She is very tall.

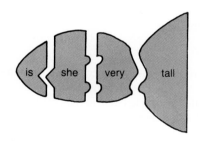

What Came First?

Objective:

To teach sentence order

Feedback device:

The pieces of the puzzle fit together when the critical elements of the sentence are in the correct order.

Materials:

A tape recording of sentences of various lengths, with each sentence containing critical verbal elements—for example, *The boy* (agent) *hit the wall* (action) *with the rock* (object); a worksheet of pictures corresponding to the sentences on the tape recording; picture puzzle pieces for the critical elements in each sentence that fit together only if put in order (see Figure 9.5).

Directions:

The student listens to the tape recording, and when he hears a sentence (such as *The boy hit the wall with the rock*), he numbers the corresponding pictures (boy, wall, rock) on the worksheet according to which came first, second, and third. To check his answer, the student puts together the puzzle pieces for each sentence and looks to see if the pictures are in the same order as he numbered them on his worksheet.

When Did It Happen?

Objective:

To teach the past-tense morpheme *ed*

Feedback device:

A tab pulled from a pocket in the material reveals the correct answer.

Materials:

A tape recording of sentences that contain the morpheme *ed*; a card that contains the sentences and has a smiling face to circle to indicate correct use of *ed* and a frowning face to circle to indicate incorrect use of *ed*; a tab containing the answer key that fits in a pocket in the card; an acetate overlay (see Figure 9.6).

Directions:

The student places the acetate overlay over the card, listens to the sentence on the tape recording, and circles the appropriate face on the answer card to indicate correct or incorrect use of *ed*. A pause on the tape is given after each sentence to allow the student time to circle his answer and pull the tab from the pocket to see if his answer is correct. The numbers next to the faces on the tab correspond to the numbers of the sentences.

Modifications:

The activity can be used to teach *is, ing,* and so on by making a tape with sentences that require *is* or *ing*. The activity can be modified further for older students by using written sentences, each of which the student must judge as grammatically correct or incorrect.

Word Endings with Meanings

Objective:

To teach suffixes *less* and *ful*

Feedback device:

The correct answer is revealed under a flap.

Materials:

A laminated card that contains incomplete sentences which require a root word and the suffix *less* or *ful*; a laminated card illustrating a tree with roots at the bottom and the same number of branches at the top of the tree: (a) two numbered

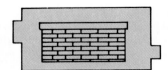

FIGURE 9.5
Puzzle pieces for What Came First?

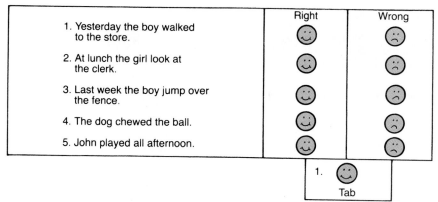

	Right	Wrong
1. Yesterday the boy walked to the store.	😊	😞
2. At lunch the girl look at the clerk.	😊	😞
3. Last week the boy jump over the fence.	😊	😞
4. The dog chewed the ball.	😊	😞
5. John played all afternoon.	😊	😞

1. 😊
Tab

FIGURE 9.6
Card and tab for When Did It Happen?

leaves on each branch are cut so that each leaf will fold back to reveal an answer underneath, (b) holes are punched in each corner of the card and a sheet of paper is attached to the back of the card with brass fasteners, (c) under each numbered leaf a suffix is written that matches up with the respective sentence, and (d) root words are written along the tree roots with a grease pencil.

Directions:

The student is given a laminated card that contains incomplete sentences requiring a root word and a suffix. He circles the correct suffix with a grease pencil. After completing the sentences, the student lifts the leaves on the tree card to see the correct answers.

1. The broken car is use(ful/less) until it is fixed.
2. The basket is use(ful/less) to carry groceries.
3. I learned a lot from the meaning(ful/less) speech.
4. The poor directions were meaning(ful/less).
5. The student was very care(ful/less) and wrote a neat letter.
6. The student was care(ful/less) and spilled paint on her dress.
7. She felt help(ful/less) when she couldn't start her car.
8. The neighbor was help(ful/less) when she loaned me her telephone.

9. The flower arrangement was pleasing and taste-(ful/less).
10. The food was very bland and taste(ful/less) to me.

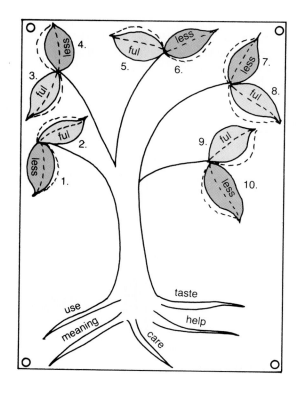

Modification:

A sheet containing different prefixes and suffixes can be attached to the back of the tree card, and a corresponding worksheet provided.

Make It Say a Sentence

Objective:

To teach sentence order

Feedback device:

An answer key in an envelope attached to the back of the card provides the answers.

Materials:

A card containing scrambled sentences that contain conjunctions; an envelope on the back of the card; an answer key; paper.

Directions:

The student looks at each scrambled sentence on the card and unscrambles the words. He writes the unscrambled sentences on paper, and to check his work he looks at the answer key in the envelope on the back of the card.

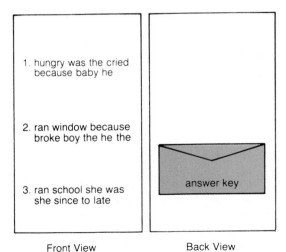

1. hungry was the cried because baby he

2. ran window because broke boy the he the

3. ran school she was she since to late

answer key

Front View   Back View

Modifications:

This self-correcting device can be used with many tasks, such as making grammatical judgment, changing declarative sentences into interrogative sentences, and using conjunctions. The cloze procedure for completing sentences with conjunctions can be adapted to this procedure by putting sentences on a card with an answer key attached. For example:

She went to the store ＿＿＿＿＿＿ she needed to buy some groceries. (because, and)
She is going to buy milk ＿＿＿＿＿ bread. (since, and)

Does It Mean the Same Thing?

Objective:

To teach similarity of deep structure in two sentences

Feedback device:

An answer key on the back of the card provides the correct answers.

Materials:

A card with sentence pairs, some having the same meaning and others having different meanings; an acetate overlay; an answer key on the back of the card (see Figure 9.7).

Directions:

The student reads each set of sentences and decides if the *deep structure* (meaning) of both sentences is the same or different. He places the acetate overlay over the response section of the card and circles "same" or "different" to indicate his answer. After completing the task, the student turns over the card and places the acetate overlay over the answer key. The circles on the overlay should match the words circled on the answer key.

Modifications:

Acetate overlays and marked answer keys can be used with sentences that use a cloze procedure with multiple choices. For example:

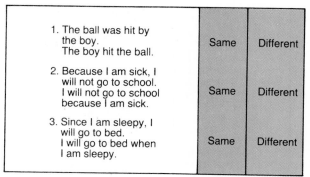

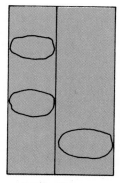

Acetate Overlay

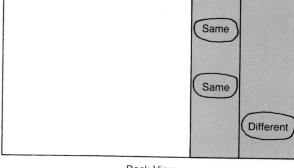

Back View

FIGURE 9.7
Card and acetate overlay for Does It Mean the Same Thing?

He heated the water _____ made coffee.
(and, because)
This procedure also can be used with grammatical judgment. For example:
Yesterday he walk to school.
_____ Correct _____ Incorrect

Descriptors

Objective:

To increase use of effective communication skills

Feedback device:

The correct responses are provided on the back of the stimulus card.

Materials:

Cards with a small object mounted on the front of each card and a list of six descriptive categories pertaining to the object written on the back of each card; six Language Master cards.

Directions:

The student looks at the object on the card and records a different sentence describing the object on each Language Master card. After recording the six sentences, the student turns over the stimulus card, listens to each of his recorded sentences, and checks the appropriate descriptive category used on the back of the card.

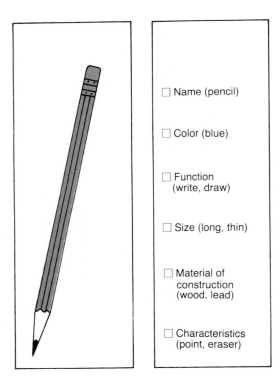

☐ Name (pencil)

☐ Color (blue)

☐ Function
(write, draw)

☐ Size (long, thin)

☐ Material of
construction
(wood, lead)

☐ Characteristics
(point, eraser)

Materials:

A tape recording of various indirect requests and questions; a response card with an answer key provided on the back of the card; an acetate overlay.

Directions:

The student places the acetate overlay over the response card and listens to the taped sentences. He decides if each sentence is a question or an indirect request and records his answer on the overlay. After completing the task, the student turns over the response card and places the acetate overlay over the answer key to check his responses.

Taped sentences:

1. What time is it?
2. Can you shut the door?
3. Won't you stop that?
4. Can't you finish your work?
5. When does the bus arrive?
6. Is the water running?
7. Must you just sit there?
8. Must you slurp your milk?
9. Can't you sit still?
10. Did the dog run away?

Modification:

This material can be modified for younger students by giving the student a picture of an object with two attributes (such as a small, red car). The student describes the picture by recording a descriptive sentence on a Language Master card. After recording, he turns over the picture card to the answer key, listens to the recording on the Language Master card, and checks each attribute used. The answers can be coded for nonreaders to check—a color to indicate color category, and a small object to indicate size category.

Indirect Requests

Objective:

To identify indirect requests

Feedback device:

An answer key is provided on the back of the response card.

	Indirect Request	Question
1.	————	————
2.	————	————
3.	————	————
4.	————	————
5.	————	————
6.	————	————
7.	————	————
8.	————	————
9.	————	————
10.	————	————

Front of Response Card

	Indirect Request	Question
1.		X
2.	X	
3.	X	
4.	X	
5.		X
6.		X
7.	X	
8.	X	
9.	X	
10.		X

Back of Response Card

Modification:

The taped sentences can be changed to questions and statements. The student identifies each sentence as a statement or question.

COMMERCIAL LANGUAGE PROGRAMS AND MATERIALS

Numerous commercial language programs and materials are available to help develop language skills of students having difficulties. Because language is interactive, no single program is appropriate for use alone, and the teacher should select programs based on the language needs of individual students. The selection of programs and materials for classroom use should reflect the developmental ages of the students for whom they are selected as well as the purpose of the intervention.

All-Purpose Photo Library

Publisher: DLM

Description:

The *All-Purpose Photo Library* contains two sets of lifelike photo cards. Set 1 includes 312 cards divided into 12 categories (for example, body parts, household items, tools and hardware, transportation). Set 2 contains 314 cards in 16 categories including musical instruments, sports, birds, and school. In addition to the photo cards, each category contains a question card of general questions and a group card of questions dealing with basic characteristics of the grouped items. The photos and question cards are designed to reinforce and expand vocabulary and language skills through the identification of common objects in photographs and to increase the student's awareness of functions and attributes of various items.

Clinical Language Intervention Program

Publisher: Psychological Corporation

Description:

The *Clinical Language Intervention Program* (Semel & Wiig, 1982) focuses on teaching semantics, morphology and syntax, pragmatics, and memory to students in kindergarten through eighth grade. Within each category of language form and content, the materials and tasks are designed to elicit clearly defined intervention targets. The program includes more than 2,000 stimulus pictures, matching verbal stimuli, suggested training methods and strategies, a picture manual to promote acquisition and use of specific language skills or functions, a language activities manual of maintenance and generalization activities, and student progress checklists for recording progress across time.

Communicative Competence: A Functional-Pragmatic Language Program

Publisher: Communication Skill Builders

Description:

The main focus of the *Communicative Competence* program is the development of structurally adequate, non-egocentric, coherent communication skills. The program includes 644 stimulus cards depicting situations the student must describe accurately. The cards are categorized by specific semantic-grammatical rules, elaborations of these basic constructions, and categories of objects and people. Four color filmstrips that present several sequential stories are used to reduce egocentric communication styles. In addition, 14 different spinner boards offer various stimuli to develop cognitive-linguistic skills. Also included are a teacher's manual that suggests various teaching strategies and a monograph that presents the theoretical framework for developing communication skills in primary through secondary students.

DISTAR Language

Publisher: Science Research Associates

Description:

The *DISTAR Language* program (Engelmann & Osborn, 1976) is a highly structured approach to language intervention. It is designed for students in preschool through third grade and focuses on expressive and receptive language and cognitive development. In Level I, students practice using complete sentences, answering questions, and following oral directions. In Level II, students learn word and sentence skills and develop questioning and reasoning skills. The structure of spoken and written sentences is analyzed in Level III, and students learn to follow the rules of grammar to communicate information and ideas effectively. Each level includes 160 lessons. The program uses a didactic approach with repetition and group drills to teach language concepts. Following a script, the teacher models, elicits group and individual responses at a fast pace, and either reinforces the correct response or corrects the inappropriate response. Various language skills are taught, such as identity statements, pronouns, prepositions, and multiple attributes.

Fokes Sentence Builder

Publisher: DLM

Description:

Fokes Sentence Builder is a structured oral language program that helps students develop skills in verbal expression, comprehension, and sentence construction. The kit contains 201 black-and-white picture cards of drawings of people, animals, and common objects, as well as a guide that explains how to build declarative sentences, questions, and negative sentences in the present, past, and future tenses. Students create grammatically correct sentences by selecting cards from the color-coded boxes, which represent five categories of words: *who, what, is doing, which,* and *where.* Sentence markers, sentence inserts, and a sentence line are included, and 180 additional picture cards are available. Also, the expansion kit provides three additional grammatical categories (*whose, how, when*) that allow students to build more sentences.

Let's Talk: Developing Prosocial Communication Skills

Publisher: Psychological Corporation

Description:

The *Let's Talk* program (Wiig, 1982) is designed to develop social communication skills in students age 9 years to adult. A communication card game format and structured training activities are used to help teach effective ways to handle everyday social interaction. Students learn to express positive and negative feelings; present, understand, and respond to information in spoken messages; adapt messages to the needs of others; and approach conversations with expectations of what to say and how to say it. The *Communication Intents* package includes card decks pertaining to asking for favors, making dates, sharing feelings, and dating. Card decks in the *Function Communication* package focus on getting around town, shopping, telephoning, getting a job, and serving people.

Newby Visualanguage

Publisher: Pro-Ed

Description:

The *Newby Visualanguage* materials include 17 workbooks and 41 sets of picture cards that provide a visual approach for teaching verbs, prepositions, adjectives, pronouns, idioms, partitives, and life concepts (such as housekeeping, family, holidays).

The picture cards depict everyday situations and can be used either to illustrate language in receptive lessons or to evoke language in expressive lessons. The workbook format requires students to make a choice, provides immediate feedback concerning correctness, and allows students to change their response and reinforce learning through writing the correct response. A reading level of about second grade is required.

Peabody Language Development Kits

Publisher: American Guidance Service

Description:

The three *Peabody Language Development Kits* (Dunn, Smith, Dunn, Horton, & Smith, 1981) provide a multilevel program for developing oral language and cognitive skills in young children. Level P, for 4- to 5-year-old preschoolers, provides practice in labeling language, constructing sentences, and thinking logically. Level 1, for 5- to 6-year-old students, focuses on brainstorming and problem solving to prompt divergent thinking and oral expression. Level 2, for 6- to 7-year-old students, emphasizes cognitive processes and divergent thinking. The kits stress overall language development rather than specific psycholinguistic processes. The activities at each level emphasize the skills of *reception* through sight, hearing, and touch; *expression* through vocal and motor behavior; and *conceptualization* through divergent, convergent, and associative thinking. Picture card decks, puppets, a sound book, story posters, and a teacher's manual are included in the kits. The teacher's manual has descriptions of daily lessons and specifies a teacher script as well as appropriate materials and activities.

Syntax One; Syntax Two

Publisher: Communication Skill Builders

Description:

Syntax One is designed for students whose syntactic skills are from 1 to 5 years behind other language-related skills. The objective is to develop student awareness of word order and word endings to convey meaning. The kit contains six double-sided syntax wheels that show the syntactic form to be taught. The wheel inserts rotate to expose stimulus pictures to elicit a syntactic form or an inflectional word ending. *Syntax Two* also includes six two-sided syntax wheels. The student is presented with problem-solving situations in which he must ask questions to get necessary information; thus, the form and function of questions are taught.

Teaching Morphology Developmentally

Publisher: Communication Skill Builders

Description:

Teaching Morphology Developmentally is a developmental program for teaching word formation that is designed for students whose language age is between 2½ and 10 years. The 523 color stimulus cards can be used to teach more than 1,000 free morphemes and 700 bound morphemes. Specific morphemes that are featured include present progressives, plurals, possessives, past tenses, third-person singulars, and derived adjectives (comparative-superlative and irregular forms). Reproducible lists of curriculum items, pretest and posttest forms, and suggestions for developing behavioral objectives are included in the instructional guide.

WH-Questions

Publisher: DLM

Description:

WH-Questions (Alsup, 1982) is a program designed to develop skills in verbal reasoning, discrimination, and formulation of Wh-question forms. The program consists of three levels (beginning—preschool to third grade, intermediate—third to sixth grade, and advanced—seventh grade to adult), each of which includes 25 color photo cards depicting scenes relevant to the particular age group. Each card has 10 questions on the back to stimulate formulation or comprehension of specific question forms. Students learn to discriminate, understand, and use basic question words and constructions that contain negatives, pronouns, adverbs, and adjectives.

REFERENCES

Alsup, R. J. (1982). *WH-questions.* Allen, TX: DLM.

Bandura, A. (1971). Analysis of modeling processes. In A. Bandura (Ed.), *Psychological modeling: Conflicting theories.* New York: Aldine/Atherton.

Bernstein, D. K., & Tiegerman, E. (1989). *Language and communication disorders in children* (2nd ed.). New York: Merrill/Macmillan.

Bloom, L. (1975). Language development review. In F. D. Horowitz (Ed.), *Review of child development research* (Vol. 4). Chicago: University of Chicago Press.

Bos, C. S., & Vaughn, S. (1988). *Strategies for teaching students with learning and behavior problems.* Boston: Allyn & Bacon.

Braine, M. (1971). *On two types of models of the internalization of grammar.* New York: Academic Press.

Buttrill, J., Niizawa, J., Biemer, C., Takahashi, C., & Hearn, S. (1989). Serving the language learning disabled adolescent: A strategies-based model. *Language, Speech, and Hearing Services in Schools, 20,* 185–201.

Chabon, S. S., & Prelock, P. A. (1989). Strategies of a different stripe: Our response to a zebra question about language and its relevance to the school curriculum. *Seminars in Speech and Language, 10,* 241–251.

Chomsky, N. A. (1965). *Aspects of the theory of syntax.* Cambridge, MA: MIT Press.

Clements, D. H. (1987). Computers and young children: A review of research. *Young Children, 42*(1), 34–44.

Connell, P. J. (1986). Acquisition of semantic role by language-disordered children: Differences between production and comprehension. *Journal of Speech and Hearing Research, 29,* 366–374.

Connell, P. J. (1987). An effect of modeling and imitation teaching procedures on children with and without specific language impairment. *Journal of Speech and Hearing Research, 30,* 105–113.

Courtright, J. A., & Courtright, I. C. (1976). Imitative modeling as a theoretical base for instructing language-disordered children. *Journal of Speech and Hearing Research, 19,* 655–663.

Courtright, J. A., & Courtright, I. C. (1979). Imitative modeling as a language intervention strategy: The effects of two mediating variables. *Journal of Speech and Hearing Research, 22,* 389–402.

Damico, J. S. (1987). Addressing language concerns in the schools: The SLP as a consultant. *Journal of Childhood Communication Disorders, 11,* 1–16.

Deshler, D. D., & Schumaker, J. B. (1986). Learning strategies: An instructional alternative for low achieving adolescents. *Exceptional Children, 52,* 583–590.

Dunn, L. M., Smith, J. O., Dunn, L. M., Horton, D. B., & Smith, D. D. (1981). *Peabody language development kits* (rev. ed.). Circle Pines, MN: American Guidance Service.

Ehren, B. J., & Lenz, B. K. (1989). Adolescents with language disorders: Special considerations in providing academically relevant language intervention. *Seminars in Speech and Language, 10,* 192–204.

Engelmann, S., & Osborn, J. (1976). *DISTAR language.* Chicago: Science Research Associates.

German, D. J. (1984). Diagnosis of word-finding disorders in children with learning disabilities. *Journal of Learning Disabilities, 17,* 353–359.

Girolametto, L. E. (1988). Improving the social-conversational skills of developmentally delayed children: An intervention study. *Journal of Speech and Hearing Disorders, 53,* 156–167.

Hyson, M. C. (1985). Emotions and the microcomputer. An exploratory study of young children's responses. *Computers in Human Behavior, 1,* 143–152.

Jenkins, J. J., & Palermo, D. S. (1964). Mediation processes and the acquisition of linguistic structure. In U. Bellugi & R. Brown (Eds.), *The acquisition of language. Monographs of the Society for Research in Child Development, 29* (1, Whole No. 92).

Lenneberg, E. H. (1967). *Biological foundations of language.* New York: Wiley.

Leonard, L. B. (1975). Modeling as a clinical procedure in language training. *Language, Speech, and Hearing Services in Schools, 6,* 72–85.

Lipinski, J. M., Nida, R. E., Shade, D. D., & Watson, J. A. (1986). The effects of microcomputers on young children: An examination of free-play choices, sex differences, and social interactions. *Journal of Educational Computing Research, 2,* 147–168.

Marvin, C. A. (1987). Consultation services: Changing roles for SLPs. *Journal of Childhood Communication Disorders, 11,* 1–16.

Mastropieri, M. A., Scruggs, T. E., & Fulk, B. J. M. (1990). Teaching abstract vocabulary with the keyword method: Effects on recall and comprehension. *Journal of Learning Disabilities, 23,* 92–96, 107.

McGregor, K. K., & Leonard, L. B. (1989). Facilitating word-finding skills of language-impaired children. *Journal of Speech and Hearing Disorders, 54,* 141–147.

McLean, J. E., & Snyder-McLean, L. K. (1978). *A transactional approach to early language training.* New York: Merrill/Macmillan.

McNeil, D. (1970). The development of language. In P. H. Mussen (Ed.), *Carmichael's manual of child psychology* (Vol. 2, 3rd ed., pp. 1061–1161). New York: Wiley.

Miller, L. (1989). Classroom-based language intervention. *Language, Speech, and Hearing Services in Schools, 20,* 153–169.

Moses, N., Klein, H. B., & Altman, E. (1990). An approach to assessing and facilitating causal language in adults with learning disabilities based on Piagetian theory. *Journal of Learning Disabilities, 23,* 220–228.

Muhlstein, E. A., & Croft, D. J. (1986). *Using the microcomputer to enhance language experiences and the development of cooperative play among preschool children.* Cupertino, CA: De Anza College. (ERIC Document Reproduction Service No. ED 269 004).

Muma, J. R. (1978). *Language handbook: Concepts, assessment, and intervention.* Englewood Cliffs, NJ: Prentice-Hall.

Pehrsson, R. S., & Denner, P. R. (1988). Semantic organizers: Implications for reading and writing. *Topics in Language Disorders, 8*(3), 24–32.

Piaget, J. (1960). *The psychology of intelligence.* Patterson, NJ: Littlefield, Adams.

Semel, E. M., & Wiig, E. H. (1982). *Clinical language intervention program.* San Antonio, TX: Psychological Corporation.

Skinner, B. F. (1957). *Verbal behavior.* New York: Appleton-Century-Crofts.

Staats, A. (1971). Linguistic-mentalistic theory versus an explanatory S-R learning theory of language development. In D. I. Slobin (Ed.), *The ontogenesis of grammar.* New York: Academic Press.

Wallach, G. (1989). Current research as a map for language intervention in the school years. *Seminars in Speech and Language, 10,* 205–217.

Wedemeyer, A., & Cejka, J. (1975). *Creative ideas for teaching exceptional children.* Denver: Love.

Wiig, E. H. (1982). *Let's talk: Developing prosocial communication skills.* San Antonio, TX: Psychological Corporation.

Wiig, E. H., & Semel, E. M. (1984). *Language assessment and intervention for the learning disabled* (2nd ed.). New York: Merrill/Macmillan.

CHAPTER 10

Assessing Reading Skills

About 10 to 15 percent of the general school population experience difficulty in reading (Harris & Sipay, 1990). Several authorities (Carnine, Silbert, & Kameenui, 1990; Kaluger & Kolson, 1978) suggest that reading difficulties are the principal cause of failure in school. Reading experiences strongly influence a student's self-image and feeling of competency (Carnine et al., 1990); furthermore, reading failure can lead to misbehavior, anxiety, and a lack of motivation. Moreover, in American culture, learning to read is important in maintaining self-respect and for obtaining the respect of others.

Reading is a complex task, and numerous definitions exist. In this chapter *reading* is defined as a visual-auditory task that involves obtaining meaning from symbols (letters and words). Reading includes two basic processes: a *decoding* process and a *comprehension* process. The decoding process involves understanding the phoneme-grapheme relationships and translating printed words into a representation similar to oral language. Thus, decoding skills enable the learner to pronounce words correctly. Comprehension skills enable the learner to understand the meaning of words in isolation and in context.

ORGANIZATION OF READING SKILLS

To assess or teach reading skills effectively, it is helpful to understand the general organization of reading content and related subskills. As implied in the definition, reading content is divided into word recognition skills and comprehension skills. Figure 10.1 illustrates these skills. Reading approaches differ in the skills they stress and when to introduce them. For example, a phonics approach emphasizes the early introduction of the sound-symbol system, whereas an approach that focuses on meaning stresses learning whole words by

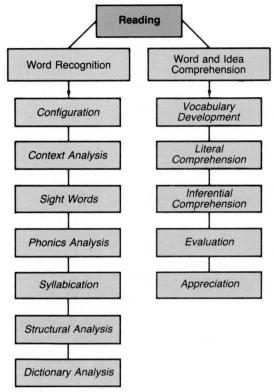

FIGURE 10.1

An organizational framework of developmental reading skills.

Source: Reprinted with the permission of Macmillan Publishing Company. Originally published by Merrill from *Students with Learning Disabilities, Fourth Edition* by Cecil D. Mercer (p. 500). Copyright © 1992 by Macmillan Publishing Company.

sight at first and introduces the sound-symbol system later.

Educators commonly use seven strategies of word recognition (Ekwall & Shanker, 1989; Guszak, 1985):

1. *Configuration*—the outline or general shape of a word. Word length, capital letters, and letter height can provide some visual cues to the unskilled reader.
2. *Context analysis*—"the use of any surrounding information that may unlock a

given word's name or meaning" (Guszak, 1985, p. 72). Semantic and syntactic (grammatical) cues help the reader predict word possibilities according to context. Likewise, pictures can provide context cues.

3. *Sight words*—words the reader recognizes without applying phonetic analysis. Sight words include frequently used words, such as those on the Dolch list (Dolch, 1955), as well as words the reader knows instantly from repeated exposure. Many words in English that have irregular spellings are taught as sight words; that is, they are learned as whole words. In reading approaches that focus on meaning, the whole-word method is used predominantly to introduce printed words.

4. *Phonics analysis*—decoding words by symbol-sound associations. It involves the learning of phonemes and rules concerning the various sounds such as those pertaining to single initial consonants, initial and ending consonant blends, consonant digraphs, silent consonants, short and long vowel sounds, and vowel teams and special letter combinations.

5. *Syllabication*—the process of dividing a word into its component parts. Each syllable contains a vowel sound. Some authorities place syllabication in phonics skills, whereas others include it in structural analysis (Ekwall & Shanker, 1989).

6. *Structural analysis*—the use of meaningful units such as root words, prefixes, suffixes, possessives, plurals, word families, and compound words. Comprehension of these structures permits a faster rate of reading than does analyzing individual sounds.

7. *Dictionary analysis*—the use of a dictionary. Although seldom used for word recognition, it provides an independent means of pronouncing unknown words by using the pronunciation key symbols in a glossary or dictionary.

Five major areas are included in reading comprehension (Ekwall & Shanker, 1989; Smith & Barrett, 1979):

1. *Vocabulary development* is essential for the reader to understand the words a writer has used. A background of meaningful experience (exposure to books, people, places) and learning words from context (through a variety of reading material) help develop vocabulary.

2. *Literal comprehension* refers to recognition and recall of explicitly stated information. Some of the skills involved in literal reading include reading for the central thought and main ideas, noting and remembering significant details, noting the order or sequence of events, and finding answers to specific questions.

3. *Inferential* (or *interpretative*) *comprehension* requires the reader to make conjectures or hypotheses based on stated information, intuition, and personal experience. Grasping cause-effect relationships, anticipating the remainder of a story, and forming opinions are inferential comprehension skills.

4. *Evaluation* or *critical reading* deals with judgments based on the reader's experiences, knowledge, or values. Evaluation focuses on qualities of accuracy, acceptability, worth, or probability of occurrence. It includes determining validity and judging the difference between reality and fantasy or fact and opinion. It also involves making value (moral) judgments and analyzing the intent of the author.

5. *Appreciation* deals with being emotionally and aesthetically sensitivite to the written selection. To function at this level, the student identifies with characters and incidents and can verbally express emotional feelings about the work (for example, excitement, fear, boredom).

In functional reading, the student reads to obtain information. Whereas developmental reading (word recognition and comprehension) involves *learning to read,* functional reading involves *reading to learn.* Functional reading is sometimes called *study skills* because it includes locating information (for example, using indexes, tables of contents, encyclopedias), comprehending data (technical vocabulary, maps, and tables), outlining and summarizing, researching, and developing study patterns for specific content areas.

The scope and sequence skills list for reading presented in Appendix A is organized into word-attack skills and comprehension skills. Authorities disagree about the sequence for teaching reading skills, and research results about the sequence are inconclusive. Thus, a teacher should use a reading scope and sequence skills list in a flexible way and should tailor the sequence for assessing and teaching reading skills according to logic and experience.

DEVELOPMENT OF READING SKILLS

Chall and Stahl (1982) discuss three reading models that differ in the importance they attach to text and meaning. The *bottom-up* model emphasizes that readers proceed from text to meaning; that is, letters and words are perceived and decoded and then the text's meaning is comprehended. In contrast, the *top-down* model emphasizes that readers rely on prior knowledge and comprehension of the meaning of the textual material rather than on word recognition and decoding of individual text elements. In essence, in the bottom-up model, reading depends primarily on the reader's skill in sound-symbol association and word recognition, whereas in the top-down model the focus is on the reader's ability to question, hypothesize, and comprehend

rather than on decoding individual text elements. The *interactive* model emphasizes both text and meaning by proposing that readers shift between attending to the text (that is, specific letters and words) and what is in their mind (that is, predicting or hypothesizing). For example, a reader may use a top-down approach when the material is familiar but change to a bottom-up approach when confronted with unfamiliar text.

Reading content has a structure in which the student first constructs simple relationships (such as grapheme-phoneme) and then progresses to more complex tasks (such as critical reading). Thus, the interactive model may most adequately describe the reading process, especially in the early stages of learning to read. As the reader becomes more proficient, attention to comprehension is increased and less attention is given to scrutinizing individual letters and words. Many authorities (Chall, 1983; Kirk, Kliebhan, & Lerner, 1978) believe that growth in reading skills occurs in several stages. Knowing the stages helps the teacher select assessment tasks, develop instructional goals, and choose instructional approaches. In addition, carefully monitoring student progress helps determine when the student moves from one level to the next. Chall divides reading development into six stages, from 0 to 5, covering prereading to highly skilled reading: (0) prereading, (1) initial reading or decoding, (2) confirmation, fluency, and ungluing from print, (3) reading for learning the new, (4) multiple viewpoints, and (5) construction and reconstruction.

Stage 0: Prereading

During the prereading stage, from birth to about age 6, children gradually and unsystematically accumulate understandings about reading. Most children acquire some knowledge and insight into print and learn to recognize letters, common signs, and common words. Many children can print their own names and pretend they can read a story that has been read frequently to them. Heilman, Blair, and Rupley (1990) note that prereading activities should include parents' reading to children (especially involving the child actively by discussing stories and learning to identify letters and words), experiences with environmental print (fast-food restaurant signs, food labels, traffic signs), and children's art and play activities.

The relationship of mental age to reading readiness has received much attention. Some educators maintain that a minimum of 6 to 6½ years is essential, but this position—primarily based on studies conducted in large classrooms in the 1930s (Gates, 1937)—is being viewed critically. Educators now realize that difficulty of material, pace of instruction, method used, amount of individualized help, and the child's specific abilities affect the minimum mental age required for efficient learning. Harris and Sipay (1990) note that reading readiness activities, now begun in kindergarten in some schools, are viewed not as distinct from reading and preparing the way for reading but as the teaching of specific prereading skills that merge gradually into reading.

Stage 1: Initial Reading or Decoding

The initial reading stage (first to second grade) involves learning to use letter-sound relationships to decode printed words not recognized immediately. Children learn to recognize words and understand material in their books; however, what they can read at this stage is considerably below what they can understand in speech. Often the student reads slowly, word-by-word, trying to break a detailed, complicated code. Some students experience difficulty acquiring beginning decoding skills because they have problems with the phonological aspects of language (Perfetti, 1985). A basic phonological problem of poor readers is lack of awareness that words have parts (that is, phonemes, syllables, morphemes). For many students, adequate phonics instruction involving the sequencing and blending of sounds to form words is necessary for the acquisition of basic decoding skills; however, students who have difficulty with phonics analysis may use context analysis, syllabication, or structural analysis to aid in word identification.

Much controversy exists among researchers concerning this stage in relation to the *code-emphasis* approach versus the *meaning-emphasis* approach. The code approach stresses the early introduction of the sound-symbol system and teaching phonics. The meaning approach stresses the initial learning of whole words and sentences by sight, with phonics instruction introduced later.

Stage 2: Confirmation, Fluency, and Ungluing from Print

In second to third grade, what students previously have learned is consolidated in the recognition of words and the use of decoding skills to help them comprehend easy and familiar texts. At this stage, students automatically begin to use the tools acquired previously, attain fluent reading, and are able to read grade-level material in the range of 100–140 words per minute with two or fewer errors. By using their decoding skills along with repetitions inherent in the language and stories read, students gain competence in using context and, consequently, improve in their fluency and reading rates. Perfetti (1985) notes that when the decoding process becomes automatic (accurate and rapid), attention is freed for higher-level reading comprehension skills. Most students develop rapid word recognition as a result of the familiarity that develops from extended practice; however, students with reading problems require additional practice and repetition to reach automaticity. The transition from the initial stage to the fluency stage is similar to the transition experience of a baby who at first must concentrate intensely on learning to walk and then can walk without thinking about it. Students at the initial stage read automatically until an unknown word is encountered, and then they try a variety of word-attack approaches. By the end of this stage, students have developed fluency and can recognize familiar words quickly, "sound out" words they do not recognize, and predict other words according to context. Measures of reading speed and reading accuracy should be included in reading assessment to determine which students are ready to move to the next stage of reading instruction (Perfetti, 1985).

Stage 3: Reading for Learning the New

This stage, which begins in fourth grade and continues through eighth grade, marks the beginning of reading to learn, as opposed to learning to read in earlier stages. Reading is used to gain new knowledge, experience new feelings, and learn new ideas and attitudes. Thus, students acquire a rich base of information and vocabulary concepts by reading a wide variety of materials. At this stage, silent reading is done in large units (for example, a complete story or selection), and word study is concerned more with meanings than with recognition or decoding because the reading materials contain more unfamiliar abstract, technical, and literary words. Snider and Tarver (1987) suggest that students who read with slow and inaccurate decoding skills may fail to learn many of the concepts that typically are acquired during this stage by inference from the context and by analogical reasoning from prior knowledge. In other words, the students with reading problems may be limited in learning from usual reading experiences because poor decoding skills present a barrier to the acquisition of knowledge. The resulting impoverished knowledge base may be insufficient for comprehension of more complex reading material. Thus, because of the cumulative effects of deficiencies at earlier stages, students with reading problems are especially in need of effective and efficient instruction at this stage.

Stage 4: Multiple Viewpoints

Reading at the high school level requires students to deal with a variety of viewpoints and to compare and evaluate information from a variety of sources. Secondary students are expected to read complex texts in advanced content areas. Through reading and studying materials that vary widely in type, content, and style, students practice acquiring difficult concepts and learning new concepts and points of view through reading. At this level, metacognitive processes play an important role through monitoring and evaluating one's understanding of the text while reading. Instruction in comprehension monitoring should be followed by instruction in study skills and use of reference materials. The failure of a student to monitor understanding of the text may be caused by an inability to decode rapidly and efficiently or the lack of necessary information to understand the topic. Snider and Tarver (1987) suggest that supplemental materials emphasizing vocabulary and background information should be developed to accompany content-area textbooks to help students with learning problems profit from reading in the content areas.

Stage 5: Construction and Reconstruction

At the college level, students read books and articles in the detail and depth that they need for their own purposes. From reading what others write, students construct knowledge for their own use. At this stage, the reader synthesizes information and forms hypotheses that usually are restricted to a specific area of study at an advanced level. Thus, reading at this stage requires extensive background knowledge in highly specialized content areas. The acquisition of the highly specialized knowledge in this stage is dependent upon the rich base of information acquired in Stages 3 and 4 which, in turn, is dependent upon accurate decoding and fluency skills developed in Stages 1 and 2.

ASSESSMENT OF READING SKILLS

Once the teacher recognizes the decoding and comprehension processes of the reading task and is aware of the network of reading skills and their general developmental sequence, reading assessment can be undertaken in a meaningful manner. Because reading problems stem from many causes and the reading process is so complex, many reading difficulties can exist (Kaluger & Kolson, 1978; Kirk et al., 1978). Bond, Tinker, Wasson, and Wasson (1989) provide the following general classification of the more prevalent reading difficulties: (a) faulty word identification and recognition, (b) inappropriate directional habits, (c) deficiencies in basic comprehension abilities, (d) limited special comprehension abilities (such as inability to locate and retain specific facts), (e) deficiencies in basic study skills, (f) deficiencies in ability to adapt to reading needs of content fields, (g) deficiencies in rate of comprehension, and (h) poor oral reading.

In addition to indicating the student's current reading ability, assessment can point to specific strengths and weaknesses and aid in planning instructional objectives. Both commercially prepared instruments and informal measures are useful. To obtain a valid assessment of the stu-

dent's reading abilities, the teacher should use a variety of assessment procedures—standardized tests, observations, and informal inventories. The information the teacher wants to obtain should help determine the type of assessment device used. For example, a group-administered reading achievement test yields information on the level of reading of the entire class, whereas more specific information about certain skills of one student can be obtained from an individually administered diagnostic reading test or through informal assessment. The remainder of this chapter presents various formal and informal reading assessment techniques and devices.

FORMAL READING ASSESSMENT

Many commercial tests have been standardized on large groups of students. Such norm-referenced tests enable the teacher to compare each student's performance with the population upon which the test was standardized. Scores from standardized reading tests are reported in several ways (such as reading grade level, reading age score, percentile, stanine score). However, the use of norm-referenced tests requires following strict procedures in administration, scoring, and interpretation. In addition to norm-referenced tests, some published reading measures are criterion-referenced. These tests *describe* performance, rather than compare it, and can be used to determine if the student has mastered specific instructional objectives. In this section, three types of formal assessment devices are presented: (a) standardized achievement and reading survey tests, (b) diagnostic tests, and (c) criterion-referenced tests.

Standardized Achievement and Reading Survey Tests

General achievement tests assess a student's ability in various academic areas. Achievement tests with reading subtests often are used to obtain an overall measure of reading achievement. These tests are norm-referenced and thus yield objective results that can be compared with the norms of the standardization sample. Reading survey tests measure reading skills only and also are used frequently to indicate a student's general range of reading abilities. Achievement and reading survey tests are basically screening measures and can help determine which students are experiencing reading difficulties and need further assessment. Table 10.1 presents information on selected reading survey tests and achievement tests with reading subtests.

Diagnostic Tests

In contrast to achievement and general reading survey tests, which yield broad information, diagnostic reading tests provide a more precise, comprehensive analysis of specific reading abilities and disabilities. Diagnostic tests differ from achievement tests in that they generally have more subtests and test items related to specific reading skills. The teacher finds out *how* the student attempts to read. By pinpointing the student's specific strengths and weaknesses in various subskills of reading, diagnostic tests yield detailed, useful information for planning appropriate individual educational programs. Most diagnostic reading tests are standardized; however, some do not include norm-referenced data. Also, many of these instruments are designed for individual rather than group administration. Diagnostic tests are discussed in two categories: test batteries and tests of specific skills.

Test Batteries. Diagnostic reading test batteries are designed to measure many reading subskills. They often include multiple subtests that sample performance in areas such as word analysis, word recognition, comprehension, and various reading-related skills. The

following five test batteries are used widely to provide a systematic assessment of reading skills:

1. *Diagnostic Reading Scales* (Spache, 1981). Three word recognition lists and 22 passages of increasing difficulty are used to assess word recognition, word analysis, and comprehension. The student's performance on the word lists, which increase in difficulty, indicates the level at which the reading passages should begin. As the student reads orally from the reading passages, the teacher notes reading errors and then checks comprehension by asking several questions following each passage. Instructional, independent, and potential reading levels are determined. Twelve supplementary phonics and word analysis tests also are included to assess areas such as consonant and vowel sounds, blending, initial consonant substitution, and auditory discrimination. The battery is designed to be individually administered to students in first through seventh grade as well as to older students with reading difficulties.

2. *Durrell Analysis of Reading Difficulty* (Durrell & Catterson, 1980). Designed for individual administration by a trained professional, this test can be used with students from nonreading level to sixth grade. Oral reading passages and accompanying comprehension questions are included, as well as paragraphs for silent reading and listening comprehension. Specific subtests deal with oral reading, silent reading, listening comprehension, and word recognition and word analysis. Additional subtests are included in listening vocabulary, sounds in isolation, spelling, visual memory of words, identifying sounds in words, and prereading phonics abilities. The battery assesses a wide variety of specific skills and requires about an hour to administer. In addition to

TABLE 10.1
Survey and achievement tests with reading subtests.

Test	Publisher	Group or Individual	Grade Level	Reading Areas Assessed
California Achievement Tests: Reading (1985)	California Test Bureau/McGraw-Hill	G	K–12	Word analysis, vocabulary, comprehension
Gates-MacGinitie Reading Tests (MacGinitie, 1978)	Houghton Mifflin	G	K–12	Vocabulary, comprehension
Iowa Tests of Basic Skills (Hieronymus, Hoover, & Lindquist, 1986)	Riverside	G	K–9	Comprehension, vocabulary, word analysis, work-study skills
Kaufman Test of Educational Achievement (Kaufman & Kaufman, 1985)	American Guidance Service	I	1–12	Decoding, comprehension
Metropolitan Achievement Tests: Survey Battery (Prescott, Balow, Hogan, & Farr, 1984)	Psychological Corporation	G	K–12	Vocabulary, word recognition, reading comprehension
Peabody Individual Achievement Test—Revised (Markwardt, 1989)	American Guidance Service	I	K–12	Reading recognition, reading comprehension
SRA Achievement Series (Naslund, Thorpe, & Lefever, 1985)	Science Research Associates	G	K–12	Letters and sounds, listening comprehension, vocabulary, reading comprehension
Stanford Achievement Test (Gardner, Rudman, Karlsen, & Merwin, 1982)	Psychological Corporation	G	1–9	Vocabulary, reading comprehension, word reading, word study skills, listening comprehension
Tests of Achievement and Proficiency (Scannell, 1986)	Riverside	G	9–12	Reading comprehension, using sources of information
Wide Range Achievement Test—Revised (Jastak & Wilkinson, 1984)	Jastak Associates	I	Preschool–adult	Letter recognition, word recognition
Woodcock-Johnson Psycho-Educational Battery—Revised (Woodcock & Johnson, 1989)	DLM	I	Preschool–adult	Letter-word identification, word attack, reading vocabulary, passage comprehension

providing a profile of grade-level scores, the test includes a checklist of instructional needs on which the teacher can note particular reading difficulties. Also, the test manual contains helpful information concerning corrective instruction and program planning.

3. *Gates-McKillop-Horowitz Reading Diagnostic Tests* (Gates, McKillop, & Horowitz, 1981). This comprehensive diagnostic reading battery assesses a wide range of word analysis skills and is designed to be individually administered by the classroom teacher to students in the first through six grade. The subtest areas include oral reading (with error analysis), flash presentation of words, knowledge of word parts, recognition of visual forms representing sounds, auditory blending, auditory discrimination, and written expression. If given in its entirety, the test is quite lengthy; however, the teacher may choose to administer only certain subtests, depending on the student's age and level of skill development. The *Gates-McKillop-Horowitz* lacks a subtest assessing reading comprehension, but the battery can be useful when used with a student experiencing severe difficulties in word analysis. Although the test is useful with students whose reading difficulties span a wide degree of severity, Salvia and Ysseldyke (1991) report that scores obtained on the *Gates-McKillop-Horowitz* are subject to misinterpretation, and the value of the test is limited to its clinical use.

4. *Stanford Diagnostic Reading Test* (Karlsen & Gardner, 1984). This group test is both norm-referenced and criterion-referenced. It measures specific reading skills in vocabulary (auditory vocabulary, word meaning, word parts), decoding (auditory discrimination, phonetic analysis, structural analysis), comprehension (word reading, reading comprehension—literal and inferential),

and rate (reading rate, fast reading, scanning, and skimming). There are four overlapping levels, identified by color, which may be used with students in first through twelfth grade. Several subtests of the four skill areas are not included at all four levels; for example, word reading is included only in the first level, and rate is assessed in the last two levels. Two forms are available at each level. In addition to yielding percentile ranks, stanines, grade equivalents, and scaled scores, the test results can be used to identify strengths and weaknesses in specific reading skills.

5. *Woodcock Reading Mastery Tests—Revised* (Woodcock, 1987). This battery of tests yields cluster scores (in readiness, basic skills, and comprehension) and a total reading score, as well as derived scores (age- and grade-based percentile ranks and standard scores, age and grade equivalents) in six subtest areas: visual-auditory learning—the student translates sequences of rebuses (unfamiliar visual symbols) into sentences; letter identification—the student names 51 various upper- and lowercase manuscript and cursive letters of the alphabet; word identification—the student names isolated words sequenced in difficulty; word attack—the student identifies nonsense words; word comprehension—the student gives antonyms and synonyms, and completes analogy formats that measure knowledge of word meaning; and passage comprehension—the student silently reads passages and supplies an appropriate word for each blank space. The test contains two forms (one of which omits visual-auditory learning and letter identification) and is designed to be individually administered to students in kindergarten through adult age. Norm-referenced scores are yielded, and a microcomputer scoring program can be used to assist the examiner in

computing scores and providing score printouts.

Tests of Specific Skills.   Some diagnostic reading tests are designed to measure the student's ability in a specific skill area. Six selected tests of specific reading skills include the following:

1. *Doren Diagnostic Reading Test of Word Recognition Skills* (Doren, 1973). This group test assesses word recognition skills within the primary and intermediate range. The following skill areas are included: letter recognition, beginning sounds, whole-word recognition, words within words, speech consonants, ending sounds, blending, rhyming, vowels, discriminate guessing, spelling, and sight words. The manual contains remedial activities for each of the skills tests.

2. *Formal Reading Inventory* (Wiederholt, 1985). This individually administered, norm-referenced measure for students in first through twelfth grade provides an assessment of silent reading comprehension and an analysis of oral reading miscues. The four separate forms of the inventory each include 13 developmentally sequenced passages with 5 multiple-choice comprehension questions following each story. On two forms the student silently reads the paragraphs and answers the comprehension questions, and on the other two forms, which are identical to the forms of the *Gray Oral Reading Test—Revised,* the student orally reads the passages while the examiner notes miscues. Each form takes about 15 minutes to administer, and the inventory yields a silent reading comprehension quotient, a percentile score for silent reading comprehension, and a classification of oral reading miscues.

3. *Gilmore Oral Reading Test* (Gilmore & Gilmore, 1968). Ten paragraphs of increasing difficulty are used to assess the oral reading performance of students in first through eighth grade. As the student orally reads each passage, the teacher records reading errors (such as substitutions, mispronunciations, insertions, hesitations, repetitions, omissions) as well as reading time. Then the student is asked to respond to several comprehension questions. When 10 or more oral reading errors are made on one paragraph, testing is stopped. Grade-level scores and performance ratings (poor—superior) are provided for accuracy and comprehension; rate of reading is scored as slow, average, or fast. The test can be individually administered in about 20 minutes.

4. *Gray Oral Reading Tests—Third Edition* (Wiederholt & Bryant, 1992). This individually administered test for students in first through twelfth grade contains two forms, each of which contains 13 developmentally sequenced passages with 5 comprehension questions. As the student reads aloud, the teacher notes reading characteristics, errors, and time elapsed in reading each paragraph. Comprehension questions are asked after each paragraph is read. A system for performing a miscue analysis of reader performance yields information in four areas: meaning similarity, function similarity, graphic/phonemic similarity, and self-correction. Standard scores, percentile ranks, and grade equivalents are provided. The *Gray Oral Reading Tests—Diagnostic* (Bryant & Widerholt, 1991) can be used as a supplement to the *GORT—3.* The student reads passages orally and responds to comprehension questions. If performance on the paragraph reading is poor, additional subtests are administered in decoding, word identification, word attack, morphemic analysis, contextual analysis, and word ordering. Thus, information is provided about graphic-phonemic, function, and

meaning cues that the student uses to decipher words in print and comprehend words and ideas. A computerized scoring program and report system are available.

5. *Test of Early Reading Ability—2* (Reid, Hresko, & Hammill, 1989). This test measures the actual reading ability of young children (3 through 9 years). Items focus on knowledge of contextual meaning (such as print in the environment, relations among vocabulary, print in connected discourse), alphabet (such as letter naming, oral reading, proofreading), and conventions of written language (such as book handling and other practices). Two alternative forms are available as well as a computer software scoring system.

6. *Test of Reading Comprehension* (Brown, Hammill, & Wiederholt, 1986). Reading comprehension of students in second through twelfth grade is assessed by this test, which can be administered to either groups or individuals. Eight subtests are divided into the two major areas of general comprehension core and diagnostic supplements. The general comprehension core subtests include general vocabulary, syntactic similarities, and paragraph reading. The subtests pertaining to diagnostic supplements are mathematics vocabulary, social studies vocabulary, science vocabulary, reading the directions of schoolwork, and sentence sequencing. Thus, the test measures both general reading comprehension and specific knowledge needed to read in three content areas. Scaled scores, grade equivalents, and reading comprehension quotients are provided.

Criterion-Referenced Tests

Whereas norm-referenced tests compare a student's performance with the scores of others, criterion-referenced tests describe perfor-mance according to fixed criteria. The teacher finds out what skills the student has learned, what is being learned now, and what skills still must be taught. Teachers use criterion-referenced reading tests to determine if the student has mastered specific objectives, such as recognition of *ed* endings or use of the *ch* consonant digraph. Test items are presented in a hierarchy to assess a sequence of reading skills. If performance on each skill does not reach the established criterion of success (for example, 95 percent level of proficiency), the teacher provides instruction specifically for that skill. A student who demonstrates mastery of a skill according to the determined criterion then progresses to the next skill in the sequence. Thus, criterion-referenced tests focus on the student's ability to master specific skills, and the assessment relates to curriculum content and instructional objectives. The student's progress is determined by comparing current performance with previous performance. Six criterion-referenced reading assessment measures include the following:

1. *Brigance Diagnostic Inventory of Basic Skills* (Brigance, 1977). This inventory contains criterion-referenced tests for academic skills from kindergarten through sixth grade. It is used primarily to establish educational objectives and monitor progress toward these objectives. Tests related to reading skills are included in the following areas: word recognition (six skill sequences such as basic sight vocabulary, abbreviations, and contractions), reading (including comprehension level and oral reading level), word analysis (19 skill sequences such as short and long vowel sounds, digraphs and diphthongs, suffixes, and prefixes), and vocabulary (five skill sequences such as context clues, antonyms, and homonyms). Student record books show at each testing the point of compe-

tence to which the student has progressed. Also, a class record book is provided for the teacher to keep a record of each student's progress. The *Brigance Diagnostic Comprehensive Inventory of Basic Skills* (Brigance, 1982), which is for students in kindergarten through ninth grade, retains the basic components of the *Inventory of Basic Skills* and includes additional skill sequences and a reading comprehension section. In addition, the *Brigance Diagnostic Inventory of Essential Skills* (Brigance, 1980), designed for students in sixth through twelfth grade, measures minimal competencies in word recognition, oral reading, functional word recognition, word analysis, and reading comprehension.

2. *Classroom Learning Screening Manual* (Koenig & Kunzelmann, 1980). This precision teaching assessment device measures performance according to frequency—a count of behavior during a fixed period of time. Each student's performance is compared with proficiency levels (standards) of performance to determine which students should have further diagnostic work and attention. Probes are included on saying words for 1 minute.

3. *Fountain Valley Teacher Support System in Reading* (1971). A series of 77 self-scoring, criterion-referenced tests are used to measure specific reading objectives in five areas: phonetic analysis, structural analysis, vocabulary development, comprehension, and study skills. The tests are color-coded and sequenced according to difficulty. The results of testing indicate the student's strengths and weaknesses in the developmental sequence of reading. Also, continuous student profiles enable the teacher to monitor individual progress.

4. *Multilevel Academic Skills Inventory* (Howell, Zucker, & Morehead, 1982). This assessment instrument, designed for students in first through eighth grade, includes more than 300 criterion-referenced objectives. It measures specific reading skills in decoding, comprehension, and vocabulary. Three levels of assessment are provided: survey tests that sample a wide range of key objectives, placement tests that sample a cluster of closely related skills within a content area, and specific level tests that measure mastery of one specific subskill. In addition, accuracy criteria (number correct) and mastery criteria (accuracy plus speed) are included.

5. *Standardized Reading Inventory* (Newcomer, 1986). This instrument is designed like an informal reading inventory, with each of its two forms consisting of 10 word lists and 10 graded reading passages that range from preprimer level to eighth-grade level. The word lists and passages include typical words found in five popular basal reading series. After reading words in isolation on the word lists until three or more words are misread, the student reads passages aloud while the examiner records errors in oral reading. Then the student reads the same passages silently and responds to a series of comprehension questions. The scoring of the inventory indicates if the student's word recognition skills and reading comprehension are at an independent, instructional, or frustration level. This criterion-referenced instrument is standardized in that it includes set administration procedures, objective scoring criteria, and specified guidelines for interpreting results.

6. *Wisconsin Tests of Reading Skill Development* (1977). A total of 38 short tests at four levels of difficulty are used to assess word-attack skills commonly taught in kindergarten through third grade. The student demonstrates mastery of a specific skill by responding correctly to at least 80 percent of the items on any given test. Also, com-

prehension tests are available in five levels used in kindergarten through sixth grade. The tests assess the comprehension skills of establishing cause-and-effect relationships, using context clues to derive word meanings, drawing conclusions, and judging relevance. The results of testing indicate which skills have not yet been mastered, and the results can be used to plan instruction as well as monitor student progress.

INFORMAL READING ASSESSMENT

Informal assessment involves examining the student's daily work or administering teacher-constructed tests by which the teacher can assess any measurable reading skill. The teacher also can determine specific strengths and weaknesses by analyzing reading errors. Informal procedures usually offer two advantages: they require less time to administer than formal tests, and they can be used with classroom materials during regular instruction periods (Kirk et al., 1978).

An experienced teacher can obtain diagnostic information through careful, day-to-day observations. The teacher has many opportunities to observe and informally assess the student's reading skills and can obtain information about the student's reading interests and attitudes, as well as word analysis and comprehension skills, by observing oral reading, seatwork assignments, instructional sessions, testing sessions, and recreational reading periods. Several informal observations during a period of time also can confirm or supplement the results of formal assessment tests.

When observing the student's performance on various reading tasks, the teacher should keep the following questions in mind:

1. What is the student's attitude toward reading?

2. What specific reading interest does the student have?
3. Is the student making progress in reading?
4. What strengths and weaknesses in reading does the student exhibit?
5. During oral reading, does the student read word-by-word or with fluency?
6. What kinds of errors does the student make consistently?
7. What word analysis skills does the student use?
8. Does the student use context clues to recognize words?
9. Does the student have a good sight vocabulary?
10. Does the student appear to pay attention to the meaning of the material when reading?

Teacher observations can be recorded on a checklist of reading skills and behaviors. For example, Table 10.2 presents a reading diagnosis checklist devised by Ekwall (1989) consisting of 30 reading or related abilities. The teacher is to check each ability three times. Thus, specific strengths and weaknesses are noted, and progress is charted.

Teacher observation is continuous and permeates all types of informal assessment. This section presents the following informal assessment techniques: graded word lists, informal reading inventory, curriculum-based measurement, reading miscue analysis, cloze procedure, and teacher-made tests.

Graded Word Lists

Graded word lists examine the student's word recognition skills. Word lists can be useful in informal diagnosis to indicate the student's sight vocabulary, to estimate the level at which the student can read with fluency and has little difficulty with word attack, and to reveal basic weaknesses in word-attack skills as the student confronts unknown words (Otto & Smith, 1980).

TABLE 10.2
Reading diagnosis checklist.

NAME _____

GRADE _____

TEACHER _____

SCHOOL _____

#	1st Check	2nd Check	3rd Check	Item	Category
1				Word-by-word reading	Oral Reading
2				Incorrect phrasing	
3				Poor pronunciation	
4				Omissions	
5				Repetitions	
6				Inversions or reversals	
7				Insertions	
8				Substitutions	
9				Basic sight words not known	
10				Sight vocabulary not up to grade level	
11				Guesses at words	
12				Consonant sounds not known	
13				Vowel sounds not known	
14				Vowel pairs and/or consonant clusters not known (digraphs, diphthongs, blends)	
15				Lacks desirable structural analysis (Morphology)	
16				Unable to use context clues	
17				Contractions not known	
18				Comprehension inadequate	Oral Silent
19				Vocabulary inadequate	
20				Unaided recall scanty	Study Skills
21				Response poorly organized	
22				Unable to locate information	
23				Inability to skim	
24				Inability to adjust rate to difficulty of material	
25				Low rate of speed	
26				High rate at expense of accuracy	
27				Voicing-lip movement	Other Abilities
28				Lacks knowledge of the alphabet	
29				Written recall limited by spelling ability	
30				Undeveloped dictionary skills	

D—Difficulty recognized
P—Pupil progressing
N—No longer has difficulty

The items listed above represent the most common difficulties encountered by pupils in the reading program. Following each numbered item are spaces for notation of that specific difficulty. This may be done at intervals of several months. One might use a check to indicate difficulty recognized or the following letters to represent an even more accurate appraisal:

Source: From *Locating and Correcting Reading Difficulties* (p. 6), 5th ed., by E. E. Ekwall, 1989, New York: Merrill/Macmillan. Copyright 1989 by Merrill Publishing Company. Reprinted by permission.

The teacher can develop word lists by randomly selecting 20 to 25 words for each level from the glossaries of graded basal readers. To obtain a random sample of 25 words for each level, the teacher would divide the total number of words for each level by 25. For example, 250 total words divided by 25 would mean that every 10th word is included. The teacher should check to make sure that the words represent various phonics skills (such as consonant and vowel sounds in different positions, consonant blends, digraphs). The words also should include prefixes, suffixes, and compound words. Sample graded word lists for primer through sixth-grade level are presented in Table 10.3. The words for each grade level can be typed on separate cards for the student to read, but the teacher should have a list of all the words. Another method would be to have the student's word list on a sheet of paper and present each word through a window with the use of a tachistoscope made from oaktag or strips cut from manila folders.

Cohen and Plaskon (1980) note that word lists can be presented in two ways. A timed flash exposure (1 second) can be given to assess the student's instant recognition or sight word vocabulary. Second, words the student is unable to recognize at first can be presented untimed to test ability to apply word-attack skills to unknown words. The teacher also can obtain additional information by giving prompts, such as providing an initial sound or covering part of the word.

The teacher can determine a word recognition grade level score—indicating the student's ability to identify words—by an untimed presentation of graded word lists. In general, the level at which the student misses none or only one word is the *independent level*. At the *instructional level* the student identifies two words incorrectly, and when three or more words are missed, the student has reached the *frustration level*. As well as using word lists to determine grade-level placement in word recognition, the teacher also should note specific errors in word attack. When the student mispronounces a word, the teacher should write down the mispronunciation to analyze the method of word attack and look for error patterns. For example, the student may recognize only initial consonant sounds and guess at the remainder of the word or may not be able to blend individual sounds into whole words. The student who reads *month* as *mouth* or *long* as *large* may be responding to configuration cues, whereas a response of a completely dissimilar word, such as *after* for *field*, may indicate a lack of phonetic word-attack skills. In addition, the teacher should note the student's skill in structural analysis—knowledge of prefixes, roots, and endings.

In addition to graded word lists devised by the teacher, published word lists are available, such as those by Dolch (1955), Ekwall (1989), and Fry (1980). The widely used Dolch list includes 200 sight words that make up 50 to 65 percent of the words the student encounters in elementary school basal readers. The Dolch list was examined by D. D. Johnson (1971) in terms of current word usage. Johnson notes that 82 Dolch words are not among the 220 most frequent words in the Kucera-Francis list, which is an analysis of present-day American English. Table 10.4 presents the 220 most frequent words in the Kucera-Francis list.

Also, the *Mann-Suiter Developmental Reading Inventory* contains a word recognition section and a paragraph reading section (Mann, Suiter, & McClung, 1992). The word recognition inventory contains 10 word lists (20 words each) of preprimer through eighth-grade level. The paragraph reading inventory consists of 12 passages and accompanying comprehension questions for preprimer through eighth-grade level. Using graded word lists to determine

TABLE 10.3
Graded word lists.

Primer	First	Second	Third	Fourth	Fifth	Sixth
not	kind	mile	beginning	worm	abandon	seventeen
funny	rocket	fair	thankful	afford	zigzag	annoy
book	behind	ago	written	player	terrific	dwindle
thank	our	need	reason	scientific	terrify	rival
good	men	fourth	bent	meek	plantation	hesitation
into	met	lazy	patient	rodeo	loaf	navigator
know	wish	field	manage	festival	hike	gorge
your	told	taken	arithmetic	hillside	relative	burglar
come	after	wolf	burst	coward	available	construction
help	ready	part	bush	boom	grief	exploration
man	barn	save	gingerbread	booth	physical	technical
now	next	hide	tremble	freeze	commander	spice
show	cat	high	planet	protest	error	spike
want	hold	bad	struggle	nervous	woodcutter	prevail
did	story	love	museum	sparrow	submarine	memorial
have	turtle	brave	grin	level	ignore	initiation
little	give	reach	ill	underground	disappointed	undergrowth
cake	cry	song	alarm	oxen	wrestle	ladle
home	fight	cup	cool	eighty	vehicle	walnut
soon	please	trunk	engine	shouldn't	international	tributary

Source: From *Analytical Reading Inventory* (pp. 58–60), 4th ed., by M. L. Woods and A. J. Moe, 1989, New York: Merrill/Macmillan. Copyright 1989 by Merrill Publishing Company. Reprinted by permission.

TABLE 10.4
Kucera-Francis list of basic sight words.

1. the	45. when	89. many	133. know	177. don't
2. of	46. who	90. before	134. while	178. does
3. and	47. will	91. must	135. last	179. got
4. to	48. more	92. through	136. might	180. united
5. a	49. no	93. back	137. us	181. left
6. in	50. if	94. years	138. great	182. number
7. that	51. out	95. where	139. old	183. course
8. is	52. so	96. much	140. year	184. war
9. was	53. said	97. your	141. off	185. until
10. he	54. what	98. may	142. come	186. always
11. for	55. up	99. well	143. since	187. away
12. it	56. its	100. down	144. against	188. something
13. with	57. about	101. should	145. go	189. fact
14. as	58. into	102. because	146. came	190. through
15. his	59. than	103. each	147. right	191. water
16. on	60. them	104. just	148. used	192. less
17. be	61. can	105. those	149. take	193. public
18. at	62. only	106. people	150. three	194. put
19. by	63. other	107. Mr.	151. states	195. thing
20. I	64. new	108. how	152. himself	196. almost
21. this	65. some	109. too	153. few	197. hand
22. had	66. could	110. little	154. house	198. enough
23. not	67. time	111. state	155. use	199. far
24. are	68. these	112. good	156. during	200. took
25. but	69. two	113. very	157. without	201. head
26. from	70. may	114. make	158. again	202. yet
27. or	71. then	115. would	159. place	203. government
28. have	72. do	116. still	160. American	204. system
29. an	73. first	117. own	161. around	205. better
30. they	74. any	118. see	162. however	206. set
31. which	75. my	119. men	163. home	207. told
32. one	76. now	120. work	164. small	208. nothing
33. you	77. such	121. long	165. found	209. night
34. were	78. like	122. get	166. Mrs.	210. end
35. her	79. our	123. here	167. thought	211. why
36. all	80. over	124. between	168. went	212. called
37. she	81. man	125. both	169. say	213. didn't
38. there	82. me	126. life	170. part	214. eyes
39. would	83. even	127. being	171. once	215. find
40. their	84. most	128. under	172. general	216. going
41. we	85. made	129. never	173. high	217. look
42. him	86. after	130. day	174. upon	218. asked
43. been	87. also	131. same	175. school	219. later
44. has	88. did	132. another	176. every	220. knew

Source: From "The Dolch List Reexamined" by D. D. Johnson, 1971, *The Reading Teacher, 24*, 455–456. Copyright 1971 by the International Reading Association. Reprinted by permission.

word recognition skills is often the first step in administering an informal reading inventory.

Informal Reading Inventory

An informal reading inventory provides information about the student's general reading level. It uses reading passages of increasing difficulty from various graded materials, such as selections from a basal reading series with which the student is unfamiliar. In general, the passages should consist of about 50 words (at preprimer level) to 200 words (at secondary level). The student begins reading passages aloud at a level where she easily handles word-attack and comprehension tasks. She continues reading passages of increasing difficulty until she no longer can do so. As the student reads aloud, the teacher records errors and asks three to five questions about each passage. Questions of many kinds should be used: recall of facts (who, what, where), inference (why), and vocabulary (general or specific meanings). To assess literal comprehension, the student can be asked to state the main idea of the passage, propose a title, recall details, present a series of events or ideas, or explain the meaning of vocabulary words. Inferential comprehension can be evaluated by asking questions that force the student to go beyond the information provided in the passage. For example, the student can be asked to draw conclusions, make predictions, evaluate ideas or actions, or suggest alternative endings. Kender and Rubenstein (1977) suggest that the student be allowed to reread or inspect the passage before answering comprehension questions. Otherwise, it is possible that memory rather than comprehension is being tested. The percentage of words read correctly for each passage is computed by dividing the number of correctly read words by the number of words in the selection. The percentage of comprehension questions answered correctly is determined by dividing the number of correct answers by the number of questions asked.

Through this method the teacher can estimate ability at three levels: independent, instructional, and frustration (M. S. Johnson & Kress, 1965). At the *independent level*, the student can read the graded passage with high accuracy, recognizing 98 to 100 percent of the words and answering the comprehension questions with 90 to 100 percent accuracy. The reading is fluent and natural, and there is no finger pointing or hesitation. At this level, the teacher can hand out supplementary materials for independent or enjoyment reading. The level at which the student needs some help is the *instructional level*. The student can recognize 95 percent of the words and comprehends about 75 percent of the material. The material is challenging but not too difficult, and the student reads in a generally relaxed manner. The teacher should provide directed reading instruction at this level. At the *frustration level*, the student reads with considerable difficulty. Word recognition is 90 percent or less, and comprehension is 50 percent or less. The student is tense and makes many errors or reversals. Reading material at this level cannot be used for instruction.

According to Carnine et al. (1990), one of the major purposes of an informal reading inventory is to help the teacher place the student at the appropriate instructional level in a basal series. Lovitt and Hansen (1976) offer guidelines for placement in a basal series: a correct reading rate of 45 to 65 words per minute with 8 or fewer errors and 50 to 75 percent comprehension. Deno and Mirkin (1977) suggest that curriculum placement decisions be based on a reading rate of 50 to 99 correct words per minute with 3 to 7 errors, whereas Starlin (1982) recommends a correct reading rate of 70 to 149 words per minute with 6 to 10 errors.

In addition to using an inventory to record oral reading word recognition and comprehension, the teacher should note various types of reading errors such as omitting words or parts of words, inserting or substituting words, reversing a word or its letters, and repeating words. It is helpful to develop a system for marking oral reading errors. Table 10.5 presents oral reading errors and a corresponding set of appropriate marks. Spache and Spache (1986) note that types of reading errors can have particular meanings. Omissions may indicate that the student is skipping unknown words or is reading quickly without attention. Insertions of words that do not appear in the passage may suggest a superficial reading, a reliance on context for assistance, or a lack of interest in accuracy. Whereas omissions and insertions are more characteristic of older students, reversals are common at the primary age level or with students for whom English is a second language. Repetitions may indicate that the reader is tense and nervous or is delaying to gain time to attack the next unknown word. Mispronunciations are common among students who attempt to sound out words without knowing exceptions to phonetic rules and also may occur in students who have low levels of listening vocabulary and are unable to use context clues. Self-corrections indicate that the reader is attempting to read more accurately and rely upon information from the context of the sentence, whereas no attempt at decoding and the need for the teacher to supply the unknown word is suggestive of a dependent reader.

An informal reading inventory also can be used to assess silent reading. Whereas in oral reading the focus in on word-attack skills, in silent reading the emphasis is on comprehension. The student silently reads each passage and answers comprehension questions. The percentage of correct responses indicates the student's silent reading level: independent (90 to 100 percent), instructional (75 percent), or frustration (50 percent). While the student reads silently, the teacher can note whispering, lip movements, finger pointing, facial grimaces, and fidgeting. The student also may have difficulties such as low rate, high rate at the expense of understanding, poorly organized recall, and inaccurate recall. Comprehension errors can be classified according to an analysis of skills including recall of factual details, comprehension and summary of main ideas, understanding of sequence, making inferences, and critical reading and evaluation. The teacher can compare the student's oral and silent reading performances to determine if there is a great difference.

In addition, the material in an informal reading inventory can be read to the student to determine listening or hearing capacity level, which is the highest level at which the student can comprehend 75 percent of the material. This provides an estimate of the student's reading potential or what the level would be if the student had no problems with the mechanics of reading.

Several published informal reading inventories are available. The *Classroom Reading Inventory* (Silvaroli, 1986) consists of graded word lists and graded oral paragraphs from preprimer to sixth-grade level. A spelling survey also is included for first- to seventh-grade level. The oral reading test is accompanied by comprehension questions, and results are given in terms of instructional levels. Thus, the teacher assesses the student's word recognition, word analysis, and comprehension skills for instructional purposes. The *Analytical Reading Inventory* (Woods & Moe, 1989) also contains graded word lists and graded passages. There are three equivalent forms, and the seven word lists for each form are graded from primer to sixth-grade level. The 10 passages are from primer to ninth-grade level. The inventory is designed to identify (a) the stu-

TABLE 10.5
Oral reading errors and marking system.

Type of Error	Marking System	Example
Omissions	Circle the word or parts of word omitted.	The boy went in(to) the (burning) building.
Insertions	Use a caret to mark the place of insertion and write the added word or letter/s.	The children sat ^down^ at the table to eat lunch.^es^
Substitutions	Cross out the word and write the substituted word above it.	Now I ~~recognize~~ *realize* your name.
Reversals	For letter reversals within a word, cross out the word and write the reversal word above it.	The ~~top~~ *pot* is lost.
	For reversals of words, draw a curved line going over, between, and under the reversed words.	Mary looked ⌐ often at the clock.
Repetitions	Draw a wavy line under the words which are repeated.	Everyone was cheering for me because I was a baseball hero.
Mispronunciations	Write the mispronounced word (indicating the student's pronunciation) over the correct word.	It was an *oc-Top-us* octopus.
Hesitations	Use a slash to indicate improper hesitation.	The/judge asked the jury/to leave the courtroom.
Aided Words	Underline the word pronounced for the student.	The scared cat began to <u>tremble</u>.
Unobserved punctuation marks	Cross out the punctuation mark the student continued to read through.	The puppy saw the man~~.~~ He barked and barked.
Self-corrected errors	Write **sc** over the error notation.	This ~~month~~ *mouth* ^sc^ is November.

Example of a Marked Passage

The three boys were (very) tired from their long/journey~~.~~ Now they had to swim across a river. John plunged into the icy ^cold^ water and started (to swim.) ^swimming^ He <u>swam</u>/slowly but managed ^may-naged^ to reach the other side of the ~~wide~~ ^wet^ river.

dent's level of word recognition, (b) strengths and weaknesses in word-attack and comprehension skills, (c) levels of reading achievement (independent, instructional, frustration), and (d) the potential for reading growth. Student record summary sheets, error analysis summary sheets, and a class record summary sheet also are included. A sample informal reading inventory for the second-grade level is included in Table 10.6.

Although it is time-consuming to use informal reading inventories because they are individually administered, they are used widely. They help the teacher to plan needed corrective instruction and to provide reading materials suited to the student's abilities. An informal reading inventory can be administered from time to time to check the student's reading progress.

Curriculum-Based Measurement

Curriculum-based assessment includes any approach that uses direct observation and recording of a student's performance in the school curriculum as a basis for obtaining information to make instructional decisions. Within this model, *curriculum-based measurement* (CBM) refers to a specific set of standardized procedures in which rate samples are used to assess a student's achievement in academic skills (Deno, 1987, 1989). The assessment procedures involved in CBM are used primarily to establish district or classroom performance standards and to monitor individual student progress toward long-range goals; however, they also can be used to monitor progress toward short-range goals. Basically, in curriculum-based measurement of reading skills, basal reading passages are used to measure oral reading fluency. The student reads passages under timed conditions, the examiner counts the number of words read correctly and incorrectly, and student perfor-

mance is summarized as the rate correct. Potter and Wamre (1990) note that the use of oral reading rate measures in curriculum-based measurement is proving to be a viable measure of general reading skill and is consistent with developmental reading models such as Chall's (1983) stages of reading development. Moreover, research indicates that students who read more fluently also perform higher on comprehension tasks (Tindal & Marston, 1990).

CBM and Performance Standards. When CBM is used to establish performance standards in reading, measures are developed from the school reading curriculum and are administered to all the students in a target group (such as all fourth graders in a school or district). The results provide data to determine standards of performance. Using CBM to establish standards involves four components: (a) material selection, (b) test administration, (c) performance display and interpretation, and (d) decision-making framework (Tindal & Marston, 1990). Selecting the appropriate material from the school curriculum begins the assessment process. An appropriate difficulty level of the material is the level which the teacher expects the student to master by the end of the semester or school year. Materials for reading include passages of approximately 200 words, excluding poetry, exercises, and excessive dialogue, from the reading curriculum used in the school. The object is to select several samples of the school curriculum in reading and administer them to targeted students (for example, fourth graders). A comparison of all students on the same measure provides a norm-referenced data base for making instructional decisions. In selecting this material, four to six sample passages are helpful because this provides the teacher with enough material for several administrations. All passages should reflect similar difficulty (possibly

TABLE 10.6
Sample informal reading inventory.

Level 2 (118 words)

Student's Name:_____

Date:_____

Motivation Statement: Imagine how you would feel if you were up to bat and this was your team's last chance to win the game! Please read this story.

Passage:
Whiz! The baseball went right by me, and I struck at the air!
"Strike one," called the man. I could feel my legs begin to shake!
Whiz! The ball went by me again, and I began to feel bad. "Strike two," screamed the man.
I held the bat back because this time I would kill the ball! I would hit it right out of the park! I was so scared that I bit down on my lip. My knees shook and my hands grew wet.
Swish! The ball came right over the plate. Crack! I hit it a good one! Then I ran like the wind. Everyone was yelling for me because I was now a baseball star!

Comprehension Questions and Possible Answers:
1. What is this story about?
   (*Main idea*—A baseball game, someone who gets two strikes and finally gets a hit, etc.)
2. After the second strike, what did the batter plan to do?
   (*Factual*—Hit the ball right out of the park)
3. Who is the "man" in this story who called the strikes?
   (*Inferential*—The umpire)
4. In this story, what was meant when the batter said, "I would kill the ball"?
   (*Terminology*—Hit it very hard)
5. Why was the last pitch a good one?
   (*Cause and effect*—Because it went right over the plate)
6. What did the batter do after the last pitch?
   (*Cause and effect*—The batter hit it a good one and ran like the wind.)

Error Count:

Omissions	____	Aided words	____
Insertions	____	Repetitions	____
Substitutions	____	Reversals	____

Scoring Guide:

Word Recognition Errors		Comprehension Errors	
Independent	1	Independent	0
Instructional	6	Instructional	1–2
Frustration	12+	Frustration	3+

Source: From *Analytical Reading Inventory* (p. 63), 4th ed., by M. L. Woods and A. J. Moe, 1989, New York: Merrill/Macmillan. Copyright 1989 by Merrill Publishing Company. Adapted by permission.

based on their readability). Once materials are selected, they can be prepared by creating a student copy retyped to eliminate picture distractions and a teacher copy that has the cumulative number of words on successive lines printed along the right margin. When administering a reading passage, the teacher uses the following steps:

1. Randomly select a passage from the goal-level material.
2. Place it in front of and facing the student.
3. Keep a copy for the examiner.
4. Provide directions (see Step 3 in Table 10.7).
5. Have the student read orally for 1 minute.
6. Score the student's performance in terms of number of words read correctly, and note errors for instructional purposes.

It is helpful to administer two passages of similar readability and record the average score. When all students in the grade or class are tested and the average score for each student is computed, the teacher can develop a plot of the entire group. Guidelines for developing a box plot of a group of students are presented in Chapter 2. These data enable teachers to (a) identify low performers who need special instruction, (b) divide students into instructional groups, (c) plan instructional programs, and (d) establish long-range goals. Thus, rather than placing students into a reading material according to a percentage of correct responses, as is done with informal reading inventories, a placement validated through research can be made by placing the student in the level where she is most comparable to others.

CBM and Long-Range Goals. A second primary use of CBM is to monitor individual student progress toward long-range goals. The teacher uses the steps in Table 10.7 which in-cludes the administration and scoring procedures for reading passages as well as procedures for determining long-range goals and graphing data. Figure 10.2 presents a graph of CBM data and illustrates a long-range goal or aim line and appropriate intervention changes.

CBM and Short-Term Goals. When monitoring progress toward a long-range instructional goal, patterns of errors may indicate areas for remediation. These areas become the focus of short-term goals (for example, identification of sight words, letter sounds, or facts in a story). To monitor progress on short-term goals, mastery monitoring charts are used which are similar to those used in precision teaching. When the student reaches mastery on a short-term goal, a new goal is established. Monitoring continues through a series of short-term goals, and the measurement items change each time the student masters a goal. Probes or task sheets frequently are used for evaluation of student progress in timings given two or three times a week. The teacher graphs the correct responses and analyzes the data to make instructional decisions.

Reading Miscue Analysis

Reading miscue analysis, based on the work of K. S. Goodman (1969, 1973), is a method of analyzing the student's oral reading strategies. The selection read by the student should be a complete story or passage (that is, have a beginning, middle, and end) that is one grade level above the material used by the student in class. It also should be unfamiliar to the student and of sufficient length and difficulty to generate a minimum of 25 miscues. Following the oral reading, the student retells the story.

Although comprehension is considered in an informal reading inventory, it is the *major* consideration in reading miscue analysis. Emphasis is placed on the *nature* of the reading

TABLE 10.7

Procedures for administering and scoring reading passages, determining long-range goals, and graphing data.

Step 1: Select a reading passage in which it is likely that the student will read aloud at a rate of 55 to 75 words correct per minute. This performance level represents entry level on goal-level material.

Step 2: Have available two copies of each passage. Place the student's copy (face down) in front of and facing the student, and place the teacher's copy in front of and facing the teacher.

Step 3: Read the directions *verbatim* for the first administration. Say to the student:
This is a story about _____ (fill in the blank with unusual adjectives and nouns found in the passage). When I say "Start," begin reading at the top of this page. If you wait on a word too long, I'll tell you the word. (Give the student 3 seconds before supplying the word.) If you come to a word you cannot read, say "Pass" and go on to the next word. Do not attempt to read as fast as you can. This is not a speed reading test. Read at a comfortable rate. At the end of 1 minute, I'll say "Stop."

Step 4: Say "Start," and turn on the stopwatch. (Do not use the word *Go* to begin, because it implies racing, particularly when stated in the presence of the stopwatch.)

Step 5: Follow the reading on the teacher's copy, and cross off the following incorrectly read words:

(a) Misread words such as *house* for *horse*, *hug* for *huge*, *home* for *house*, *big* for *huge*.
(b) Words the student cannot read within about 3 seconds.
(c) Words not read (omission); count all words in skipped lines as errors.
(d) Reversals of letters within words (such as *say* for *was*) or pairs of words (such as *the red, big dog* instead of *the big, red dog*).

The following miscues are not counted as errors: (a) proper nouns that are mispronounced more than once, (b) self-corrections, and (c) words added into the text by the student (additions or insertions).

Step 6: At 1 minute, say "Stop," mark the last word read with a bracket (]), and quickly move to the next reading task. Place the top sheet over and to the side and tell the student you would like to continue in the same manner. Repeat this procedure until all reading tasks are completed.

Step 7: Count the number of words read correctly and incorrectly by taking the cumulative count and subtracting the number of errors. For the basal reading passages, simply use the number to the right of the last full line read; add the number of words read in the next (partially read) line to obtain the total number of words read. The number of words read correctly is found by subtracting the number of words read incorrectly from the total number of words read. If the student's score falls within the range of 55 to 75 words correct per minute, test two more times at this level.

Step 8: Test until the student reaches a level in which at least two of three scores fall in or close to the 55 to 75 words per minute (wpm) range. If the score falls above the 55 to 75 wpm range, test using a probe at a higher level. If the score falls below the 55 to 75 wpm range, test using a probe from a lower level of material. Try to find the optimal measurement level.

Step 9: After the measurement level is identified, write the goal:
Objective: In _____ weeks the student will read _____ words correct per minute in the _____ Scott-Foresman* reader. (*Use name of reading series used with the student.)
Strategy: Use two probes per week from randomly selected passages from the reader.
Criteria: After three consecutive data points fall significantly below the aim line, changes in instruction will be made and noted on the instructional plan.

(*continued*)

TABLE 10.7
Continued

Use a calendar to count the number of weeks remaining in the school year or semester. Write that number in the first blank. To calculate the number for the second blank, refer to the baseline data, the three probes scores at or near the 55 to 75 wpm range. Determine which of the three scores is the median (that is, in rank order, the middle score).

(a) If the student is being measured at or above the third-grade reader level, multiply the number of weeks (that is, weeks in the instructional period) times 2 (rate of growth) and add this to the baseline median score.

$$(\text{weeks} \times 2) + \text{baseline median} = \text{goal}$$
For example: $(30 \times 2) + 66 = 126$ wpm

(b) If the student is being measured below the third-grade reader level, multiply the number of weeks (that is, weeks in instructional period) times 1.5 (rate of growth) and add this to the baseline median score.

$$(\text{weeks} \times 1.5) + \text{baseline median} = \text{goal}$$
For example: $(30 \times 1.5) + 66 = 111$ wpm

Step 10: Draw the aim line on the graph by connecting the baseline point and the goal point (see Figure 10.2).

Step 11: Write an instructional plan on the reverse side of the CBM graph.

Step 12: Implement the plan and collect CBM data twice a week. To collect CBM data, use the prepared probes from the respective reading series. Because these probes are already in a random sequence, use them in order. Try to measure the student in the same setting, at about the same time, and under the same general circumstances whenever possible. Read the directions each time so that the student consistently gets clues about the unusual words in the story. After scoring the performance, write the score in the appropriate box at the side of the graph page.

Step 13: Graph the median of the current score and the two previous scores instead of graphing every data point. This graphing system is called the moving median and is used to reduce the variability in the graphed data because this data is used for decision-making. For example: If today's score is 66, last Thursday's was 70, and the previous Tuesday's was 59, graph the 66 because this is the median. Do not graph until three data points are collected after the baseline. Plot the moving median on the administration day even if the median score was from a previous day. In the given example, if the fourth probe (on Thursday) is 71, the last three probes would be 70, 66, and 71, and the median is 70. Thus, on the Thursday date, 70 is graphed as the median of the last three probes.

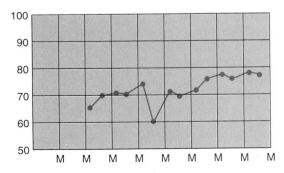

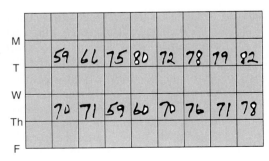

Table 10.7
Continued

Step 14: To evaluate the effects of instruction, carefully examine the data. If the student has three consecutive scores graphed significantly below the aim line, make a change in instruction. (Significant is defined as 10 or more points below the aim line.) Every time the student's data points fall significantly below the aim line three consecutive times, draw a vertical line on the graph after the third point (see Figure 10.2). Record the change in the reading instructional plan. If the student has six consecutive scores significantly above the aim line (6 or more points above), probe with the next higher reading level book to see if the student scores within the 55 to 75 wpm range on two of the three probes. This may mean establishing a new aim line for the student. This is done on the existing graph.

Step 15: Change instruction. For ideas on what to change, consider using some of these strategies: (a) talk to another teacher, (b) review suggestions in books, journals, and magazines, (c) ask the student for ideas, or (d) use the student's performance on the passages for error analysis.

Step 16: Use other measures for students who are word callers (that is, can read aloud fluently but do not understand what they have read). These students can be asked to retell a story read silently, and the number of words used in the retelling can be scored and graphed. Also, these students can be asked to answer three to five comprehension questions, and the correct number of responses can be scored and graphed. The correct number of responses can be graphed between the 0 to 10 unit on the bottom of the graph chart. Examples of comprehension questions that can be asked after each assessment probe include:

    (a) Who are the main characters in the story?
    (b) Where does the story take place?
    (c) What do you think will happen next?

Step 17: If the student reads more than 100 words correct per minute at or above the sixth-grade reader level on three consecutive probes, discontinue CBM. Note documentation of performance on the student's graph.

---

errors (miscues), rather than on the number of errors made. Miscues can be classified in the following categories:

1. *Semantic*—the miscue is similar in meaning to the text word. Some miscues indicate that the student comprehends the passage; thus, the simple substitution of a word is not important (for example, substitution of *dad* for *father*).
2. *Syntactic*—the miscue is the same part of speech as the text word. Some miscues show that the student fails to comprehend the meaning but at least substitutes a word that makes grammatical sense.
3. *Graphic*—the miscue is similar to the sound/symbol relationship for the initial, medial, or final portion of the text word (such as, *find* for *found*). Some miscues indicate the student's knowledge of phoneme-grapheme relationships.

It must be determined whether each miscue changed or interfered with the meaning of the information conveyed in the sentence or phrase in which it occurred. The most accept-

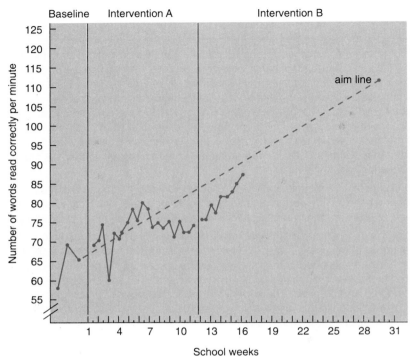

FIGURE 10.2
A curriculum-based measurement graph illustrating an aim line and intervention changes.

able miscue is semantically correct, whereas less acceptable errors are grammatically correct but semantically incorrect or fit the graphic or phonic characteristics of the text but are semantically and grammatically incorrect. Basically, the seriousness of miscues depends on whether they form a consistent pattern that alters the meaning of the written passage and thus affects the student's comprehension.

Some authorities believe the miscue inventory is appropriate for research but cumbersome for the classroom teacher (Fry, 1977). Some oral mistakes reveal that the student is reading with meaning (K. S. Goodman, 1969, 1973). These errors are not too serious if one believes that the purpose of reading is understanding. Fry suggests that the three types of linguistic errors—semantic, syntactic, and sound-symbol—can be useful to the class-

room teacher in informal observation of any oral reading. For the clinician who wants to pursue a systematic diagnosis of meaning-clue deficiencies, the *Reading Miscue Inventory* (Y. M. Goodman & Burke, 1972; Y. M. Goodman, Watson, & Burke, 1987) is helpful. Each oral reading miscue is scored according to nine categories: dialect, intonation shift, graphic similarity, sound similarity, grammatical function, correction, grammatical acceptability, semantic acceptability, and meaning change. A short form of the *Reading Miscue Inventory* also is available (Burke, 1976).

Cloze Procedure

The cloze procedure can be used as an informal method to measure reading levels and comprehension. It can estimate the difficulty the student will have with a specific reading material and thus help determine whether a book is appropriate (Clary, 1976; Karlin, 1980). The teacher presents an unfamiliar reading passage of about 250 words to the student. The first sentence is typed completely, but in subsequent sentences every fifth word is replaced with a blank. The blanks should be of uniform length. The remainder of the selection is typed as it appears in text. The student reads the passage and fills in the missing words or synonyms. Clary suggests having the student select words from an answer key, and Karlin suggests deleting only every 10th word. Other appropriate words instead of every fifth word also can be omitted to avoid the inadvertent continuous omission of articles or proper names. An example of the cloze procedure for a reading passage is presented in Table 10.8.

TABLE 10.8
Reading selection illustrating the cloze procedure.

James Cornish lay wounded on the saloon floor! "He's been stabbed in ___1___ chest!" shouted one horrified ___2___. "Someone get him to ___3___ hospital!" another shouted.

It ___4___ a hot and humid ___5___ in Chicago in 1893. ___6___ arrived at the hospital ___7___ a one-inch knife ___8___ in his chest, dangerously ___9___ his heart. Dr. Daniel ___10___ Williams was called in ___11___ operate.

In those days ___12___ blood transfusions and antibiotics ___13___ unknown, chest surgery was ___14___ attempted since it meant ___15___ high risk of death. ___16___ Dr. Williams began to ___17___, he found that the ___18___ wound had cut the ___19___ and the sac around ___20___ heart. Dr. Williams then ___21___ history by becoming ___22___ first surgeon to successfully ___23___ on the human heart. ___24___ Williams did not release ___25___ information for three and ___26___ half years. When he ___27___, the newspaper headline read, "___28___ Up His Heart," and ___29___ news became known to ___30___ entire world. Not only ___31___ Cornish been discharged from ___32___ hospital a well man, ___33___ he lived fifty years ___34___ his surgery. Cornish even ___35___ the surgeon who had ___36___ his life.

Correct Answers:

1. the	13. were	25. this
2. bystander	14. rarely	26. a
3. a	15. a	27. did
4. was	16. As	28. Sewed
5. day	17. operate	29. the
6. Cornish	18. stab	30. the
7. with	19. heart	31. had
8. wound	20. the	32. the
9. near	21. made	33. but
10. Hale	22. the	34. after
11. to	23. operate	35. outlived
12. when	24. Dr.	36. saved

Source: Adapted from *Analytical Reading Inventory* (p. 123), 4th ed., by M. L. Woods and A. J. Moe, 1989, New York: Merrill/Macmillan. Copyright 1989 by Merrill Publishing Company. Adapted by permission.

A reading passage using the cloze procedure can be administered either individually or in groups. Reading levels are determined by changing the number of correct responses to percentages. Rankin and Culhane (1969) suggest the following scoring of cloze passages: *independent reading level*, 61 percent or more correct responses; *instructional reading level*, 41 to 60 percent correct responses; and *frustration reading level*, 40 percent or fewer correct responses. For additional information the teacher should attempt to analyze why the student makes certain errors. Hafner (1965) notes that cloze errors can be examined according to linguistic components, cognitive types, and reasoning skills.

Teacher-Made Tests

The teacher can devise an informal test to obtain a quick estimate of a specific skill. Probe sheets can be developed to assess a particular reading objective, such as consonant sounds, vowel sounds, blends, or compound words. A sample probe sheet to assess the student's ability to blend consonant-vowel-consonant sounds is presented in Table 10.9. After the probe is administered for a 1-minute period and the correct and incorrect responses are tallied, the student's reading rate can be compared with the suggested proficiency reading rates (see Table 10.10). Table 10.11 presents a sample record sheet for various reading skills assessed through the use of probes.

Teacher-made tests can be constructed by using items in standardized tests and workbook exercises as guides. A variety of items that measure a specific skill can be used (for example, multiple-choice, true–false, completion, matching). The teacher should be careful to include enough items to sample the skill

TABLE 10.9

Probe sheet for blending consonant-vowel-consonant sounds.

luv	had	mok	hob	cuz
lit	def	cak	met	roc
nom	vig	pit	tik	fam
cum	zot	wet	bag	pod
fif	lid	hat	get	won
pik	soc	jox	vic	sut
sas	far	kah	par	gan
teg	tem	mez	zix	zec
pub	hun	nod	wol	wap
sel	top	nip	ris	dit

Name: _____

Time: _____

Number Correct: _____

Number Incorrect: _____

Comments: _____
_____
_____

TABLE 10.10
Proficiency rates for reading skills.

I. Grade Level Specified

	Say Isolated Sounds (K–3) Cor.	Err.	Say Words in List (2–4) Cor.	Err.	(5–6) Cor.	Err.	(Adult) Cor.	Err.	Say Words in Text (1–3) Cor.	Err.	(4–6) Cor.	Err.	(Adult) Cor.	Err.
Koenig & Kunzelmann (1980)			140	0	120–130	0								
Starlin & Starlin (1973)			100–126 Phonetic words	0	138–148	0	198	0	50–70	2	100–200	2	100–200	2
Wolking (1973) High Achievers	36–52	0–4	90–128 Irregular words	0	134–150	0	198	0	120–132	0	156–180	0	252	0
Range:			90–140	0	120–150	0								
Mode:			100–126	0	130+	0								
Median:			115	0	136	0								

II. Grade Level Not Specified

	Say Isolated Sounds Cor.	Err.	Say Words in List Cor.	Err.	Say Words in Text Cor.	Err.
Alper, Nowlin, Lemoine, Perine, & Bettencourt (1974)	80	2	60–80	2	100–120	3
Haughton (1972)	100	0				
Henderson, Clise, & Silverton (1971)	100	0				
Precision Teaching Project * (Montana)	60–80	0	80–100 Sight words	0	200+	0
			60–80 Regular words	0		
Regional Resource Center (1971)	60–80	2	80–100	2	100–120	2
	90–100 Blends	2				
Starlin (1971)	40	2	50+	2	100–200	2
			50	2	100	2
SIMS Program (1978) Range:	40–100	0–4	50–100	0–7	100–200	0–2
Mode:	100	0	80	2	100	2
Median:	70	2	80	2	100+	2

*Note. Available from Skyline Center, 3300 3rd Street N.E., Great Falls, Montana 59404.

TABLE 10.11
Sample record sheet for probe assessments.

Name _____ Greg _____				Grade _____ 4 _____		
Reading Areas	Session 1	Session 2	Session 3	Session 4	Suggested Rates for Proficiency	
	correct/ error	correct/ error	correct/ error	correct/ error	correct	error
Consonant Sounds (1 minute)	18/0	25/0	18/0	35/0	60–80	2 or less
Vowel Sounds (1 minute)	28/0	24/4	28/1	30/3	60–80	2 or less
Sight Words (1 minute)	28/3	35/3	41/3	44/9	80–100	2 or less
Grade 4 Word List (1 minute)	32/8	38/4	41/5	43/4	80–100	2 or less
Oral Reading (1 minute)	59/7	68/4	76/6	78/11	100–140	2 or less

adequately. Heilman (1985) provides an excellent informal word recognition skills test (see Table 10.12) which a teacher can adapt for use in informal assessment. It assesses both phonics and structural analysis skills. In addition, short-form word analysis tests can be devised to measure specific skills. Items also can be developed to assess specific comprehension skills, such as main idea, noting details, and cause-and-effect relationships. Selected items for assessing the short *a* vowel sound are presented in Table 10.13. When the student passes the informal test, the teacher can assume the student has mastered the objective and is ready to progress to another skill. Reading scope and sequence skills lists, such as the one included in Appendix A, are helpful in determining the order of skill assessment and instruction. Finally, teacher-made tests often deal with reading skills the student must use daily, and they provide a measure of student progress over a specific period of time.

TABLE 10.12
Informal word recognition skills test.

Subtest A (pronunciation)
(Initial and final consonant sounds; short vowel sounds)

dad	self	but	ten	lift
fuss	yell	hog	sand	muff
lamp	him	jug	get	nap
puff	web	miss	pond	kill
rag	gum	pill	rob	cob
van	top	big	held	fond

Subtest B (pronunciation)
(Initial consonant blends; long and short vowel sounds)

bring	split	blue	smoke	scream
throat	clay	club	string	trip
please	twist	float	trade	glass
sky	prize	grass	flag	snail
crop	drill	blow	scene	sweet
spray	free	sled	spoon	stay

Subtest C (pronunciation)
(Consonant digraphs [ch, sh, th, wh, qu, ng, ck]; consonant blends)

quite	thank	check	shrink	crash
church	block	length	queen	shake
shake	quick	shove	choose	think
splash	strong	thing	truck	deck
whale	chose	which	sprung	hung
fresh	wheat	quench	tenth	quack

Subtest D (pronunciation)
(Compound words; inflectional endings; contractions)

keeping	something	it's	bakery	really
pleased	can't	everybody	likes	finding
stops	quickly	lived	someone	helped
I'll	into	calls	he'll	outside
anyone	tallest	you'll	prettiest	loudest
unlock	happily	going	everything	wasn't

(continued)

TABLE 10.12
Continued

Subtest E (Sight recognition—pronunciation)
Irregular Spellings
Consonant Irregularities

knee	rough	gnaw	is	you	limb
hour	the	who	phone	knew	whole
was	know	cough	enough	whose	knot

Vowel Irregularities

been	have	once	eye	sure	bird
give	any	do	break	chief	cough
they	to	one	love	could	dead
said	some	head	steak	none	their

Subtest F (syllabication)
(In the blank spaces, write the word in separate syllables.)

candy	_____can dy_____	detective	_____
moment	_____	situation	_____
locomotive	_____	tiger	_____
formation	_____	education	_____
summer	_____	slippery	_____
tumble	_____	release	_____

Subtest G (prefixes, suffixes, and syllabication)
(Pronounce each word; divide each word into syllables [see example].)

dis/con/tent/ment	prehistorical	disloyalty
recaptured	disgraceful	indebtedness
incapable	imperfection	previewing
unhappily	expandable	readjustment
exporter	independently	impassable
removable	rearrangement	submerged

Subtest II
(Sustained-reading passage)

Fred and Frank planned to go on a trip to the pond. Frank liked to swim, but Fred was not a swimmer. He chose to hunt frogs and trap crabs. With a shout, the boys were off on their hike to the lake. At first, they tried to walk in the shade. Then both took off their shirts to get a suntan.

Source: From *Phonics in Proper Perspective* (pp. 84–86), 5th ed., by A. W. Heilman, 1985, Columbus, OH: Merrill. Copyright 1985 by Bell & Howell Company. Reprinted by permission.

TABLE 10.13
Teacher-made test items for assessing short *a* vowel sound.

I. The student reads the words with short *a* in initial position.

am	ant	at
an	as	act
and	ask	add

Criterion: 7/9

II. The student reads the words with short *a* in medial position.

ham	pant	bat
can	gas	fact
hand	task	mad

Criterion: 7/9

III. The student selects the word of the pair that contains the short *a* sound.

hat—hate	plan—plane
say—sad	past—pay
ran—ray	stay—sand
tale—land	dad—pale

Criterion: 7/8

IV. The student chooses the word with the short *a* sound to complete the sentence.

The boy had a _____ on his head. (cap, cape)

The _____ was blowing. (sail, flag)

His mother was looking at the _____. (mail, map)

There was a _____ in the sidewalk. (crack, nail)

The father did not _____ his son. (blame, spank)

Criterion 4/5

REFERENCES

Alper, T., Nowlin, L., Lemoine, K., Perine, M., & Bettencourt, B. (1974). The rated assessment of academic skills. *Academic Therapy, 9,* 151–164.

Bond, G. L., Tinker, M. A., Wasson, B. B., & Wasson, J. B. (1989). *Reading difficulties: Their diagnosis and correction* (6th ed.). Englewood Cliffs, NJ: Prentice-Hall.

Brigance, A. H. (1977). *Brigance Diagnostic Inventory of Basic Skills.* North Billerica, MA: Curriculum Associates.

Brigance, A. H. (1980). *Brigance Diagnostic Inventory of Essential Skills.* North Billerica, MA: Curriculum Associates.

Brigance, A. H. (1982). *Brigance Diagnostic Comprehensive Inventory of Basic Skills.* North Billerica, MA: Curriculum Associates.

Brown, V. L., Hammill, D. D., & Wiederholt, J. L. (1986). *The Test of Reading Comprehension: A method for assessing the understanding of written language* (rev. ed.). Austin, TX: Pro-Ed.

Bryant, B. R., & Wiederholt, J. L. (1991). *Gray Oral Reading Tests—Diagnostic.* Austin, TX: Pro-Ed.

Burke, C. (1976). *Reading Miscue Inventory—Short form.* Bloomfield, IN: Indiana University.

California Achievement Tests. (1985). Monterey, CA: California Test Bureau/McGraw-Hill.

Carnine, D., Silbert, J., & Kameenui, E. J. (1990). *Direct instruction reading* (2nd ed.). New York: Merrill/Macmillan.

Chall, J. S. (1983). *Stages of reading development.* New York: McGraw-Hill.

Chall, J. S., & Stahl, S. A. (1982). Reading. In H. E. Mitzel (Ed.), *Encyclopedia of educational research* (5th ed., pp. 1535–1559). New York: Free Press.

Clary, L. M. (1976). Tips for testing reading informally in the content areas. *Journal of Reading, 20,* 156–157.

Cohen, S. B., & Plaskon, S. P. (1980). *Language arts for the mildly handicapped.* New York: Merrill/Macmillan.

Deno, S. L. (1987). Curriculum-based measurement. *Teaching Exceptional Children, 20*(1), 41–42.

Deno, S. L. (1989). Curriculum-based measurement and special education services: A fundamental and direct relationship. In M. R. Shinn (Ed.), *Curriculum-based measurement: Assessing special children* (pp. 1–17). New York: Guilford Press.

Deno, S. L., & Mirkin, P. (1977). *Data-based program modification: A manual.* Reston, VA: Council for Exceptional Children.

Dolch, E. W. (1955). *Methods in reading.* Champaign, IL: Garrard.

Doren, M. (1973). *Doren Diagnostic Reading Test of Word Recognition Skills* (2nd ed.). Circle Pines, MN: American Guidance Service.

Durrell, D. D., & Catterson, J. H. (1980). *Durrell analysis of reading difficulty* (3rd ed.). New York: Harcourt Brace Jovanovich.

Ekwall, E. E. (1989). *Locating and correcting reading difficulties* (5th ed.). New York: Merrill/Macmillan.

Ekwall, E. E., & Shanker, J. L. (1989). *Teaching reading in the elementary school* (2nd ed.). New York: Merrill/Macmillan.

Fountain Valley Teacher Support System in Reading. (1971). Huntington Beach, CA: Richard L. Zweig Associates.

Fry, E. (1977). *Elementary reading instruction.* New York: McGraw-Hill.

Fry, E. B. (1980). The new instant word list. *The Reading Teacher, 34,* 284–289.

Gardner, E. F., Rudman, H. C., Karlsen, B., & Merwin, J. C. (1982). *Stanford Achievement Test* (7th ed.). San Antonio, TX: Psychological Corporation.

Gates, A. I. (1937). The necessary mental age for beginning reading. *Elementary School Journal, 37,* 497–508.

Gates, A. I., McKillop, A. S., & Horowitz, R. (1981). *Gates-McKillop-Horowitz Reading Diagnostic Tests.* New York: Teachers College Press.

Gilmore, J. V., & Gilmore, E. C. (1968). *Gilmore Oral Reading Test.* New York: Harcourt Brace Jovanovich.

Goodman, K. S. (1969). Analysis of oral reading miscues: Applied psycholinguistics. *Reading Research Quarterly, 5,* 9–30.

Goodman, K. S. (1973). *Miscue analysis: Applications to reading instruction.* Urbana, IL: National Council of Teachers of English.

Goodman, Y. M., & Burke, C. L. (1972). *Reading Miscue Inventory: Manual of procedure for diagnosis and evaluation.* New York: Macmillan.

Goodman, Y. M., Watson, D., & Burke, C. (1987). *Miscue Inventory: Alternative procedures.* New York: R. C. Owens.

Guszak, F. J. (1985). *Diagnostic reading instruction in the elementary school* (3rd ed.). New York: Harper & Row.

Hafner, L. (1965). Importance of cloze. In E. T. Thurstone & L. E. Hafner (Eds.), *The philosophical and social bases for reading: 14th yearbook.* Milwaukee: National Reading Conference.

Harris, A. J., & Sipay, E. R. (1990). *How to increase reading ability: A guide to developmental and remedial methods* (9th ed.). New York: Longman.

Haughton, E. (1972). Aims—Growing and sharing. In J. B. Jordon & L. S. Robbins (Eds.), *Let's try doing something else kind of thing.* Arlington, VA: Council for Exceptional Children.

Heilman, A. W. (1985). *Phonics in proper perspective* (5th ed.). New York: Merrill/Macmillan.

Heilman, A. W., Blair, T. R., & Rupley, W. H. (1990). *Principles and practices of teaching reading* (7th ed.). New York: Merrill/Macmillan.

Henderson, H. H., Clise, M., & Silverton, B. (1971). *Modification of reading behavior: A phonetic program utilizing rate acceleration.* Ellensburg, WA: H. H. Henderson.

Hieronymus, A. N., Hoover, H. D., & Lindquist, E. F. (1986). *Iowa Tests of Basic Skills.* Chicago: Riverside.

Howell, K. W., Zucker, S. H., & Morehead, M. K. (1982). *Multilevel Academic Skills Inventory.* San Antonio, TX: Psychological Corporation.

Jastak, S. R., & Wilkinson, G. S. (1984). *Wide Range Achievement Test—Revised.* Wilmington, DE: Jastak Associates.

Johnson, D. D. (1971). The Dolch list reexamined. *The Reading Teacher, 24,* 449–457.

Johnson, M. S., & Kress, R. A. (1965). *Informal reading inventories.* Newark, DE: International Reading Association.

Kaluger, G., & Kolson, C. J. (1978). *Reading and learning disabilities* (2nd ed.). New York: Merrill/Macmillan.

Karlin, R. (1980). Teaching elementary reading: Principles and strategies (3rd ed.). New York: Harcourt Brace Jovanovich.

Karlsen, B., & Gardner, E. F. (1984). *Stanford Diagnostic Reading Test* (3rd ed.). San Antonio, TX: Psychological Corporation.

Kaufman, A. S., & Kaufman, N. L. (1985). *Kaufman Test of Educational Achievement.* Circle Pines, MN: American Guidance Service.

Kender, J. P., & Rubenstein, H. (1977). Recall versus reinspection in IRI comprehension tests. *The Reading Teacher, 30*(7), 776–778.

Kirk, S. A., Kliebhan, J. M., & Lerner, J. W. (1978). *Teaching reading to slow and disabled learners.* Boston: Houghton Mifflin.

Koenig, C. H., & Kunzelmann, H. P. (1980). *Classroom learning screening manual.* San Antonio, TX: Psychological Corporation.

Lovitt, T. C., & Hansen, C. L. (1976). Round one— Placing the child in the right reader. *Journal of Learning Disabilities, 9,* 347–353.

MacGinitie, W. H. (1978). *Gates-MacGinitie Reading Tests.* Boston: Houghton Mifflin.

Mann, P. H., Suiter, P. A., & McClung, R. M. (1992). *A guide for educating mainstreamed students* (4th ed.). Boston: Allyn & Bacon.

Markwardt, F. C., Jr. (1989). *Peabody Individual Achievement Test—Revised.* Circle Pines, MN: American Guidance Service.

Naslund, R. A., Thorpe, L. P., & Lefever, D. W. (1985). *SRA Achievement Series.* Chicago: Science Research Associates.

Newcomer, P. L. (1986). *Standardized Reading Inventory.* Austin, TX: Pro-Ed.

Otto, W., & Smith, R. J. (1980). *Corrective and remedial teaching* (3rd ed.). Boston: Houghton Mifflin.

Perfetti, C. (1985). *Reading ability.* New York: Oxford University Press.

Potter, M. L., & Wamre, H. M. (1990). Curriculum-based measurement and developmental reading models: Opportunities for cross-validation. *Exceptional Children, 57,* 16–25.

Prescott, G. A., Balow, I. H., Hogan, T. P., & Farr, R. C. (1984). *Metropolitan Achievement Tests: Survey battery* (6th ed.). San Antonio, TX: Psychological Corporation.

Rankin, E., & Culhane, J. (1969). Comparable cloze and multiple-choice comprehension test scores. *Journal of Reading, 13,* 193–198.

Regional Resource Center. (1971). *Diagnostic Reading Inventory* (Project No. 472917, Contract No. OEC-0-9-472917-4591 [608]). Eugene, OR: University of Oregon.

Reid, D. K., Hresko, W. P., & Hammill, D. D. (1989). *Test of Early Reading Ability—2.* Austin, TX: Pro-Ed.

Salvia, J., & Ysseldyke, J. E. (1991). *Assessment in special and remedial education* (5th ed.). Boston: Houghton Mifflin.

Scannell, D. P. (1986). *Tests of Achievement and Proficiency.* Chicago: Riverside.

Silvaroli, N. J. (1986). *Classroom Reading Inventory* (5th ed.). Dubuque, IA: William C. Brown.

SIMS Reading and Spelling Program (3rd ed.). (1978). Minneapolis, MN: Minneapolis Public Schools.

Smith, R. J., & Barrett, T. C. (1979). *Teaching reading in the middle grades* (2nd ed.). Reading, MA: Addison-Wesley.

Snider, V. E., & Tarver, S. G. (1987). The effect of early reading failure on acquisition of knowledge among students with learning disabilities. *Journal of Learning Disabilities, 20,* 351–356, 373.

Spache, G. D. (1981). *Diagnostic Reading Scales.* Circle Pines, MN: American Guidance Service.

Spache, G. D., & Spache, E. B. (1986). *Reading in the elementary school* (5th ed.). Boston: Allyn & Bacon.

Starlin, C. M. (1971). Evaluating progress toward reading proficiency. In B. Bateman (Ed.), *Learning disorders: Vol. 4. Reading.* Seattle: Special Child Publications.

Starlin, C. (1982). *On reading and writing.* Des Moines, IA: Department of Public Instruction.

Starlin, C. M., & Starlin, A. (1973). *Guides to decision making in oral reading.* Bemidji, MN: Unique Curriculums Unlimited.

Tindal, G. A., & Marston, D. B. (1990). *Classroom-based assessment: Evaluating instructional outcomes.* New York: Merrill/Macmillan.

Wiederholt, J. L. (1985). *Formal Reading Inventory.* Austin, TX: Pro-Ed.

Wiederholt, J. L., & Bryant, B. R. (1992). *Gray Oral Reading Tests—Third edition.* Austin, TX: Pro-Ed.

Wisconsin Tests of Reading Skill Development: Word attack, study skills, and comprehension. (1977). Madison, WI: Learning Multi-Systems. (Developed by the Evaluation and Reading Project Staffs at the Wisconsin Research and Development Center for Cognitive Learning)

Wolking, W. D. (1973, October). *Rate of growth toward adult proficiency: Differences between high and low achievement children, grades 1–6.* Paper presented at the International Symposium of Learning Disabilities, Miami Beach, FL.

Woodcock, R. W. (1987). *Woodcock Reading Mastery Tests—Revised.* Circle Pines, MN: American Guidance Service.

Woodcock, R. W., & Johnson, M. B. (1989). *Woodcock-Johnson Psycho-Educational Battery—Revised.* Allen, TX: DLM.

Woods, M. L., & Moe, A. J. (1989). *Analytical Reading Inventory* (4th ed.). New York: Merrill/Macmillan.

CHAPTER 11

Teaching Reading Skills

Many approaches and materials have been developed to teach reading. Methods of beginning reading instruction can be divided into two major approaches: the bottom-up or code-emphasis approach and the top-down or meaning-emphasis approach. The primary difference between the two approaches is the way decoding is taught. This is reflected in the debate over the relative importance of text versus meaning or decoding versus comprehension. In the bottom-up sequential approach, decoding skills are taught first and instruction in comprehension follows. Beginning reading programs that stress letter-sound regularity are *code-emphasis* programs. The top-down model is the basis for the spontaneous approach to reading instruction, and reading for meaning is emphasized in the first stages of instruction. Programs that stress the use of common words are *meaning-emphasis* programs.

Code-emphasis programs begin with words consisting of letters and letter combinations that have the same sound in different words. The consistency in the letter-sound relationship enables the reader to read unknown words by blending the sounds together. For example, the word *sit* is sounded out as "sss-ii-tt" and pronounced "sit." The word *ring* is sounded out as "rrr-ii-nng" and pronounced "ring." The letter *i* has the same sound in both words. Moreover, a new word is not introduced unless its component letter-sound relationships have been mastered. Some major code-emphasis programs include *Basic Reading* (J. B. Lippincott), *Reading Mastery: DISTAR Reading* (Science Research Associates), *Merrill Linguistic Reading Program* (Science Research Associates), *Palo Alto Reading Program* (Harcourt Brace Jovanovich), and *Programmed Reading* (McGraw-Hill). The phonics, linguistic, modified alphabet, and programmed programs also are classified as code-emphasis programs.

Meaning-emphasis programs begin with words that appear frequently, assuming that these words are familiar to the reader and thus easier to learn. Students identify words by examining meaning and position in context and are encouraged to use a variety of decoding techniques, including pictures, context of story, initial letters, and word configuration. Words are not controlled so that a letter has the same sound in different words. For example, the words *at, many,* and *far* may occur, though the *a* represents a different sound in each word. Some of the major meaning-emphasis programs include *Ginn 720* (Ginn & Company); *Houghton Mifflin Reading Series* (Houghton Mifflin); and *Basics in Reading,* the *New Open Highways,* and *Reading Unlimited* (Scott, Foresman). Moreover, the whole language, language experience, and individualized reading approaches generally are classified as meaning-emphasis programs.

Code-emphasis programs are considered to be more effective in teaching students to decode (Bleismer & Yarborough, 1965; Bond & Dykstra, 1967; Chall, 1983; Diederich, 1973; Dykstra, 1968; Gurren & Hughes, 1965). Early systematic instruction in phonics provides the skills necessary for becoming an independent reader earlier than is likely if phonics instruction is delayed and less systematic (Dykstra, 1974). Many researchers contend that the foundation of comprehension is accurate word recognition, which is attained through careful decoding and practice over time (Chall, 1989; Perfetti, 1985). Thus, decoding or facility with phonics is viewed as a necessary step in the acquisition of reading comprehension and other higher-level reading processes.

Those who support the meaning-emphasis approach agree that code-emphasis programs have an advantage in teaching decoding, but they maintain that meaning-emphasis programs have an advantage in teaching comprehension. Whole language instruction, which is the current meaning-emphasis approach to beginning reading, tends to be associated with a natural, self-directed or developmental, and open view. Some whole language proponents stress that skills (including phonics) should not be taught directly but acquired from more natural reading and writing activities. Carbo (1987) stresses that most primary students are global learners who need to learn to read with holistic reading activities such as reading books of their own choosing, engaging in choral reading, writing stories, and listening to tape recordings of interesting, well-written books.

Though the meaning- versus code-emphasis debate continues, Carnine, Silbert, and Kameenui (1990) strongly recommend the code-emphasis approach, especially for students with learning problems. They note that the results of almost four decades of research on beginning reading indicate that phonics programs are superior to meaning-emphasis approaches in the early grades. In a review of research on beginning instruction in reading, Adams (1990) notes that instructional approaches that include systematic phonics lead to higher achievement in both word recognition and spelling, especially in the early grades and for slower or economically disadvantaged students. She advocates an eclectic instructional program that includes phonics skills as well as practice reading connected text. Beginning reading instruction should stress decoding but not ignore comprehension (Carnine et al., 1990). Accurate and automatic habits in decoding lead to reading fluency, which allows attention to be directed to higher-level reading comprehension. Successful reading requires proficiency in word identification as well as comprehension, and competency is required in both areas. Thus, there needs to be a proper balance between systematic decoding instruction and attention to developing reading comprehension.

Harris and Sipay (1990) state that teacher skill is more important than reading methodology and that "efforts should concentrate on determining which aspects of a program are most effective for particular children when used by certain teachers under given conditions and, what is more important, why" (p. 90). Thus, a teacher must know several instructional practices in reading to teach students with reading disabilities. Heilman, Blair, and Rupley (1990) state:

> No single approach to teaching reading is successful with all children. In a sense, no reading approach is foolproof. By knowing when to modify an approach, combine approaches, or use a different approach to meet students' needs, the teacher is a major factor in determining the success of a reading approach. . . . Thus, the importance of the teacher is highlighted within the implementation of any given approach. The teacher is the key variable in whether or not a child is successful in learning to read. (p. 323)

The teacher must consider each individual case to determine which skills need corrective instruction and then select the approach most likely to be effective. In addition, the teacher should encourage independent reading, because reading performance may improve through the frequent use of reading skills. The teacher can stimulate interest in reading by reading parts of stories aloud to students and making displays of various books and reading topics. Book clubs or awards for reading also may motivate some reluctant readers. The remainder of this chapter presents numerous reading approaches, programs, methods, activities, and materials aimed at helping the teacher design effective reading instruction for individual students.

DEVELOPMENTAL READING APPROACHES

Developmental reading approaches emphasize daily, sequential instruction. Most are programmed according to a normative pattern of reading growth. The basic material for instruction is usually a series of books (such as basal readers) that directs what will be taught and when. A well-developed program provides supplementary materials such as workbooks, skillpacks, wall charts, related activities, learning games, and filmstrips. To teach students with reading problems often it is necessary to adapt developmental programs to meet their needs by changing the sequence, providing additional practice activities, and modifying the input-output arrangements of selected tasks. Moreover, combinations of programs are often superior to single approaches (that is, using supplemental phonics or adding language experiences to any kind of reading). The following developmental approaches are discussed: basal, phonics, linguistic, whole language, language experience, and individualized reading.

Basal Reading Approach

Many teachers use a basal reading series as the core of their program. Most series include a sequential set of reading texts and supplementary materials such as workbooks, flash cards, placement and achievement tests, and filmstrips. In addition, a comprehensive teacher's manual explains the purpose of the program and provides precise instructional plans and suggestions for skill activities. The teacher's manual usually is highly structured and completely outlines each lesson, perhaps including skill objectives, new vocabulary words, motivational activities, and questions for checking comprehension on each page of the text.

The readers usually begin with preprimers and gradually increase in difficulty through the eighth grade. Some basals are changing their progression from grade-level readers to levels corresponding to stages in development. The content is based upon common student experiences and interests. Materials designed for multiracial and disadvantaged groups sometimes feature settings and content to appeal to a variety of backgrounds and ethnic groups. Basals may use either a meaning-emphasis or a code-emphasis approach. Some basals feature a whole language approach and focus on whole-word recognition and comprehension through the reading of children's literature stories. Others focus on word decoding strategies such as phonics. A basal series systematically presents reading skills in word recognition, comprehension, and word attack, and it controls the vocabulary from level to level. The reader, manual, and student workbook provide activities that help teach word-attack skills (including phonics), develop comprehension, and increase reading rate steadily.

The basal approach has the following advantages:

1. The readers are comprehension oriented and are sequential in content from early readiness to advanced reading levels.
2. The teacher's manual provides suggestions, activities, and a detailed outline for teaching.
3. Reading skills are developed in a systematic, sequential manner.
4. A basic vocabulary is established and repeated throughout the sequence to provide reinforcement.
5. Assessment, evaluation, and diagnostic materials usually are provided.

A disadvantage of the basal program is that its structured, comprehensive nature may limit the teacher's creativity and contribute to an inflexible, traditional method of teaching. The basal approach also encourages teaching reading in groups rather than concentrating on individual differences and needs. In addition, it may not provide an adequate foundation for reading tasks of the content fields (for example, reading maps, charts, and math problems; using library skills and organizational skills such as note taking and outlining).

Most basal readers recommend a *directed reading activity* procedure for teaching a reading lesson. The steps include:

1. Motivate the student to learn the material.
2. Prepare the student by presenting new concepts and vocabulary.
3. Guide the student in reading the story by asking questions that give a purpose or goal for the reading.
4. Develop or strengthen skills relating to the material through drills or workbook activities.
5. Assign work to apply the skills acquired during the lesson.
6. Evaluate the effectiveness of the lesson.

This guided reading approach can be used to increase comprehension skills. Basal readers contain stories with many details and often are divided into small parts. Thus, location exercises can be given to find the main idea or main characters as well as specific words, phrases, sentences, and paragraphs.

An alternative to the directed reading lesson is the *directed reading-thinking activity* (Stauffer, 1981). In this thought-provoking strategy, the student largely determines the purposes for reading and must generate questions about the selection, read the selection, and then validate the answers to the questions through group judgment. The teacher acts as a catalyst and provides thoughtful questions in directing the process ("What do you think?" "Why do you think so?" "Can you prove your conclusion?").

The basal reading approach is used in most reading programs in the United States. The teacher easily can adjust or supplement the materials to meet the individual needs of students with reading problems.

Phonics Approach

The phonics approach teaches word recognition through learning grapheme-phoneme associations. After learning vowels, consonants, and blends, the student learns to sound out words by combining sounds and blending them into words. Thus, the student learns to recognize unfamiliar words by associating speech sounds with letters or groups of letters. Table 11.1 presents the sounds stressed in a phonics program. The emphasis on phonics (or decoding) in the primary grades has become an almost universal practice in beginning reading programs (with the exception of whole language programs).

Teachers can use the synthetic method or the analytic method to teach phonics (Matthes, 1972). In the *synthetic* method, the student learns that letters represent certain sounds (for example, *b—buh*) and then finds out how to blend, or *synthesize,* the sounds to form words. This method emphasizes isolated letter sounds before the student progresses to words. The *analytic* method teaches letter sounds as integral parts of words (for example, *b* as in *baby*). The student must learn new words on the basis of phonics elements similar to familiar or sight words. Carnine et al. (1990) note that synthetic phonics appears to yield better results in beginning reading than does an analytic phonics approach. Phonics methods and materials differ on details, but the main objective is to teach the student to attack new words independently.

Spache and Spache (1986) recommend the sequence outlined in Table 11.2 for teaching phonics. In addition, phonics instruction includes a list of rules introduced at various stages. Spache and Spache's list of rules is presented in Table 11.3.

TABLE 11.1
Sounds stressed in a phonics program.

VOWEL SOUNDS

Short Sounds		Long Sounds	
a	bat	a	rake
e	bed	e	jeep
i	pig	i	kite
o	lock	o	rope
u	duck	u	mule

W is sometimes used as a vowel, as in the *ow* and *aw* teams. W is usually a vowel on word endings and a consonant at the beginning of words.

Y is usually a consonant when it appears at the beginning of a word, and a vowel in any other position.

Three consonants usually affect or control the sounds of some, or all, of the vowels when they follow these vowels within a syllable. They are: *r*, *w*, and *l*.

r (all vowels)	w (a,e, and o)	l (a)
car	law	all
her	few	
dirt	now	
for		
fur		

CONSONANT SOUNDS

b	bear	k	king	s	six
c	cat	l	lake	t	turtle
d	dog	m	money	v	vase
f	face	n	nose	w	wagon
g	goat	p	pear	x	xylophone
h	hen	q	queen	y	yellow
j	jug	r	rat	z	zebra

The following consonants have two or more sounds:

c	cat	s	six
c	ice	s	is
g	goat	x	xylophone
g	germ	x	exist
		x	box

When *g* is followed by *e*, *i*, or *y*, it usually takes the soft sound of *j*, as in *gentle* and *germ*. If it is not followed by these letters it takes the hard sound illustrated in such words as *got* and *game*.

When *c* is followed by *e*, *i*, or *y*, it usually takes the soft sound heard in *cent*. If it is not followed by these letters, it usually takes the hard sound heard in *come*.

Qu usually has the sound of *kw*; however, in some words such as *bouquet* it has the sound of *k*.

S sometimes takes a slightly different sound in words such as *sure*.

CONSONANT BLENDS
BEGINNING

bl	blue
br	brown
cl	clown
cr	crown
dr	dress
dw	dwell
fl	flower
fr	from
gl	glue
gr	grape
pl	plate
pr	pretty
sc	score
sk	skill
sl	slow
sm	small
sn	snail
sp	spin
st	story
sw	swan
tr	tree
tw	twelve
wr	wrench
sch	school
scr	screen
shr	shrink
spl	splash
spr	spring
squ	squash
str	string
thr	throw

ENDING

ld	wild
mp	lamp

(continued)

TABLE 11.1

nd	wind
nt	went
rk	work
sk	risk

CONSONANT AND VOWEL DIGRAPHS

Consonant

ch	chute	sh	ship
ch	choral	th	three
ch	church	th	that
gh	cough	wh	which
ph	graph	wh	who

Vowel (most common phonemes only)

ai	pain
ay	hay
ea	each
	or
ea	weather
ei	weight
	or
ei	either
ie	piece

(A number of other phonemes are common for *ie*)

oa	oats
oo	book
	or
oo	moon
ou	tough (*ou* may be either a digraph or a diphthong)
ow	low
	or
ow	cow

DIPHTHONGS

au	haul*	oi	soil
aw	hawk*	ou	trout
ew	few	ow	cow
ey	they	oy	boy

*Some may hear *au* and *aw* as a digraph.

Source: From *Locating and Correcting Reading Difficulties* (pp. 313–315), 5th ed., by E. E. Ekwall, 1989, New York: Merrill/Macmillan. Copyright 1989 by Merrill Publishing Company. Reprinted by permission.

By emphasizing word recognition, phonics helps the student to associate sounds with printed letters and leads to independence in unlocking new words. However, the phonics approach has the following disadvantages:

1. The emphasis on word pronunciation may be at the expense of comprehension.
2. The student may become confused with words that are exceptions to the phonetic rules.
3. After learning isolated sounds, the student may have difficulty blending the sounds to form complete words.

Kirk, Kliebhan, and Lerner (1978) note that instruction in phonics may be added effectively to the basal reader or language experience approach after the student has acquired a basic sight vocabulary of 50 to 100 words. Phonics is helpful with beginning readers in a developmental program or as a remedial technique for students who have a strong sight vocabulary but are unable to analyze unfamiliar words. Several phonics programs are commercially available. Some that are used with students who have learning problems include *Cove School Reading Program* (DLM), *Merrill Phonics* (Science Research Associates), *Phonic Remedial Reading Lessons* (Kirk, Kirk, & Minskoff, 1985), and *The Writing Road to Reading* (Spalding & Spalding, 1986).

Linguistic Approach

Most linguistic approaches to reading stem from the ideas of various linguists. Linguists, who are mainly concerned with oral communication, have provided important information about the nature and structure of language. Bloomfield and Barnhart (1961) and Fries (1963) provide such a framework, which emphasizes decoding—changing the printed words into verbal communication.

TABLE 11.2
Sequence for teaching phonics.

Simple Consonants *b, p, m, w, h, d, t, n,* hard *g* (gate), *k,* hard *c* (cake), *y* (yet), *f* (for)	**Silent Letters** *k* (knife), *w* (write), *l* (talk), *t* (catch), *g* (gnat), *c* (black), *h* (hour)
More Difficult Consonants *v, l, z* (zoo), *s* (sat), *r, c,* (cent), *q* (kw), *x* (ks), *j, g* (engine), *s* (as)	**Vowel Digraphs** *ai* (pail), *ea* (each), *oa* (boat), *ee* (bee), *ay* (say), *ea* (dead)
Consonant Blends and Digraphs *ck, ng, th* (the), *zh, sh, th* (thin), *wh, ch*	**Vowel Diphthongs** *au* (auto), *aw* (awful), *oo* (moon), *oo* (wood), *ow* (cow), *ou* (out), *oi* (oil), *oy* (boy), *ow* (low)
Simple Consonant Blends with *l, r, p,* or *t,* as *bl, pl, gr, br, sp, st, tr, thr, str, spl, scr,* and others as they appear	**Vowels with r** *ar* (car), *er* (her), *ir* (bird), *or* (corn), *ur* (burn) Same with *l* and *w.*
Short Vowels *a* (hat), *e* (get), *i* (sit), *o* (top), *u* (cup), *y* (happy)	**Phonograms** *ail, ain, all, and, ate, ay, con, eep, ell, en, ent, er, est, ick, ight, ill, in, ing, ock, ter, tion* Alternates—*ake, ide, ile, ine, it, ite, le, re, ble*
Long Vowels *a* (cake), *e* (be), *i* (five), *o* (old), *u* (mule), *y* (cry)	

Source: From *Reading in the Elementary School* (pp. 478–479), 5th ed., by G. D. Spache and E. B. Spache, 1986, Boston: Allyn & Bacon. Copyright 1986 by Allyn & Bacon. Reprinted by permission.

Many linguistic reading materials use a *whole-word* approach. Instead of using exercises in sounding and blending, words are taught in word families and only as wholes. In beginning reading, words are introduced that contain a short vowel and consist of a consonant-vowel-consonant pattern. The words are selected on the basis of similar spelling patterns such as *cab, lab, tab*), and the student must learn the relationship between speech sounds and letters (that is, between phonemes and graphemes). The student is not taught letter sounds directly but learns them through minimal word differences. Words that have irregular spellings are introduced as sight words as the student progresses. After the words are learned in the spelling patterns, they are put together to form sentences.

The following reading selection is from a book in the *Merrill Linguistic Reading Program* (Wilson & Rudolph, 1986, p. 15).

Mud on a Pup

Gus got a tub for Pam's pup.
"Pam," he said, "you cannot let your pup run in the mud.
Get your pup into the tub.
Get him wet and rub suds on him."

Pam gets her pup into the tub.
She wets him and rubs him.
"Is your pup wet yet?" said Gus.
"He is a wet pup," said Pam.

"He lets me get him wet," said Pam.
"He is not a bad pet."

The linguistic approach differs from the phonics approach in that linguistic readers focus on words instead of isolated sounds. It differs from the basal reading approach in that linguistic instruction emphasizes breaking the written language code before considering meaning and comprehension. Thus, many lin-

TABLE 11.3
Phonetic rules.

Consonants

1. When *c* is frequently followed by *e, i,* or *y,* it has the sound of *s,* as in *race, city, fancy.*
2. *Otherwise, c* has the sound of *k,* as in *come, attic.*
3. *G* followed by *e, i,* or *y* sounds soft like *j,* as in *gem.*
4. Otherwise *g* sounds hard, as in *gone.*
5. When *c* and *h* are next to each other, they make only one sound.
6. *Ch* is usually pronounced as it is in *kitchen,* not like *sh* (in *machine*).
7. When a word ends in *ck,* it has the same last sound, as in *look.*
8. When two of the same consonants are side by side, only one is heard, as in *butter.*
9. Sometimes *s* has the sound of *z,* as in *raisin, music.*
10. The letter *x* has the sounds of *ks* or *k* and *s,* as in *box, taxi.*

Vowels

11. When a consonant and *y* are the last letters in a one-syllable word, the *y* has the long *i* sound, as in *cry, by.* In longer words the *y* has the long *e* sound, as in *baby.*
12. The *r* gives the preceding vowel a sound that is neither long nor short, as in *car, far, fur, fir.* The letters *l* and *w* have the same effect.

Vowel Digraphs and Diphthongs

13. The first vowel is usually long and the second silent in *oa, ay, ai,* and *ee,* as in *boat, say, gain, feed.*
14. In *ea* the first letter may be long and the second silent, or it may have the short *e* sound, as in *bread.*
15. *Ou* has two sounds: one is the long sound of *o;* the other is the *ou* sound, as in *own* or *cow.* The combination *ou* has a schwa sound, as in *vigorous.*
16. These double vowels blend into a single sound: *au, aw, oi, oy,* as in *auto, awful, coin, boy.*
17. The combination *oo* has two sounds, as in *moon* and as in *wood.*

Source: From *Reading in the Elementary School* (p. 480), 5th ed., by G. D. Spache and E. B. Spache, 1986, Boston: Allyn & Bacon. Copyright 1986 by Allyn & Bacon. Reprinted by permission.

guistic series contain no pictures or illustrations that may provide clues and tempt the student to guess rather than decode the printed word.

Cohen and Plaskon (1980) list the following advantages of the linguistic approach:

1. The emphasis on the relationship between phonemes and graphemes helps the student realize that reading is talk written down.
2. Consistent visual patterns are presented as learning progresses from familiar, phonemically regular words to words of semiregular and irregular spellings.
3. The student is taught to spell and read the word as a whole unit.
4. An awareness of sentence structure is developed.
5. Reading is taught by association with the student's natural knowledge of his own language.

Kaluger and Kolson (1978) note also that the frequent repetition of words in this approach may be helpful to students with learning problems. One of the major disadvantages of the linguistic approach is its lack of emphasis on comprehension and reading for meaning in the beginning stages of reading. Other disadvantages include the following:

1. The vocabulary is extremely controlled, and the use of nonsense words and phrases for pattern practice detracts from reading for comprehension.

2. Word-by-word reading is encouraged.
3. The approach strongly emphasizes auditory memory skills.
4. Linguists disagree about the methodology of teaching reading.

Some commercial materials using the linguistic approach are *Let's Read* (Clarence L. Barnhart), *Merrill Linguistic Reading Program* (Science Research Associates), *Miami Linguistic Readers* (D. C. Heath), *Palo Alto Program* (Harcourt Brace Jovanovich), and *SRA Basic Reading Series* (Science Research Associates).

Whole Language Approach

The whole language concept (Goodman, 1986) involves the use of students' language and experiences to increase their reading and writing abilities. Reading is taught as a holistic meaning-oriented activity and is treated as an integrated behavior rather than being broken into a collection of separate skills. According to Altwerger, Edelsky, and Flores (1987), the main consideration regarding classroom reading and writing within the whole language framework is that there be *real* reading and writing rather than exercises in reading and writing. Thus, the emphasis is on reading for meaning rather than learning decoding skills, and the student is taught to break the code in reading within the context of meaningful content. In a classroom with a whole language orientation, the curriculum is organized around themes and units that increase language and reading skills, and reading materials consist of various relevant and functional materials such as children's literature books and resources the students need or want to read. Whole language relies heavily on literature or on printed matter used for appropriate purposes (for example, a recipe used for making a dessert rather than for finding short vowels) and on writing for varied purposes. In this approach, reading is immersed in a total language arts program, and teachers develop the curriculum to offer instructional experiences relating to real problems and ideas. The underlying concept is that all language arts are related and should not be taught as if they were separate subjects. The premise is that students learn naturally from exposure and use rather than from isolated instructional drills.

Advocates of the whole language reading approach oppose teaching phonics in any structured, systematic way and believe that students will develop their own phonetic principles through exposure to print as they read and write. Students initially start to read meaningful, predictable whole words and then use these familiar words to begin to learn new words and phrases. To develop comprehension skills and for reading to make sense, it is believed that students must begin with a meaningful whole, and they initially are given familiar, predictable material. A constructive process is used in which students recognize familiar parts in unfamiliar written matter, and their reading is monitored to ensure it is making sense to them. While learning to read, students also are learning to write and are encouraged to write about their experiences. Goodman (1986) suggests that to implement a whole language approach in the classroom the teacher should establish a center for reading and writing and encourage students to participate in activities such as dictating stories to an adult and then reading them or following along while listening to audiocassettes of books. The teacher also can read to students and provide them with an opportunity to predict events within the story. In addition, the teacher can plan sustained silent reading and reading activities in which students read independently and are guided by reading conferences.

According to Chiang and Ford (1990), "Integrating the whole language strategies with other effective methods such as direct instruction can bring about a more balanced perspective with equal emphasis on fostering LD [learning disabled] students' positive attitudes toward reading and on facilitating a more functional and purposeful use of printed materials" (p. 34). They offer the following guidelines for implementing whole language programs with students who have learning problems:

1. Read aloud to students regularly.
2. Devote a few minutes each day to sustained silent reading.
3. Introduce students to predictable books with patterned stories.
4. Use writing activities that provide opportunities for the teacher to model writing strategies and skills.
5. Include journal writing as part of the students' individualized educational programs.
6. Provide meaningful printed materials in the instructional setting (for example, simplified dictionaries, categorized lists of words).
7. Establish a network to communicate with other teachers using holistic techniques in working with students with learning problems.

One aspect of the whole language approach that has found acceptance is the integration of the language arts program, especially in the area of writing. This approach minimizes a fragmented curriculum, and students see writing as a complement of reading. However, the whole language approach to reading lacks direct instruction in specific skill strategies, and students with learning problems may need a more systematic approach to decoding and comprehension than the whole language approach provides. Heymsfeld (1989) and Mather (1992) suggest that because both whole language and skill-based instruction have strengths, the teacher should create a combined approach. Likewise, Chall (1987) notes that research indicates that better results

are achieved when young children are taught skills systematically and directly and use them in reading. In addition, research shows that being read to and reading and writing stories and selections in which newly gained skills are applied also contribute to reading development. In a review of research on the whole language approach, Stahl and Miller (1989) note that the whole language approach may be most effective when used early in the process of learning to read (that is, kindergarten) and for teaching functional aspects of reading such as print concepts and expectations about reading. However, more direct approaches may be better at helping some students master word recognition skills prerequisite to effective comprehension. In addition, research indicates that the whole language approach may have less of a effect with disadvantaged and lower socioeconomic populations (Stahl & Miller, 1989). Thus, it appears that until whole language has been found effective at various levels with students who have learning problems, it should be used cautiously, especially in light of the success that teachers have had in using direct instruction.

Two commercial programs based on the use of literature for students with learning problems are *Learning Through Literature* (Dodds & Goodfellow, 1990/1991) and *Victory!* (Brigance, 1991). Also, Norton (1992) discusses selecting literature for a literature-based reading program and provides sources for children's literature. An example of a model program that integrates whole language with direct instruction and precision teaching is presented in B.A.L.A.N.C.E. (Blending All Learning Activities Nurtures Classroom Excellence), developed in Orlando, Florida (FDLRS/Action, 1600 Silver Star Road, Orlando, FL 32804). B.A.L.A.N.C.E. stresses direct instruction but encourages the use of writing, quality literature, and integrated subjects to enhance the application of skills. In addition, the use of precision teaching helps the teacher make decisions about students' learning and enhance their fluency.

Moreover, *Reading Recovery*, an early intervention program developed in New Zealand for young children experiencing difficulty in beginning reading (Clay, 1985), combines writing and reading and helps students learn phonics within meaningful written contexts. In this intervention, which combines whole language with tutoring in specific skills, low-achieving first-grade students are provided with one-to-one tutoring for 30 minutes each day in addition to classroom reading instruction. In the daily individual lessons, students read aloud from minibooks and write their own one- or two-sentence messages, and each student's progress is monitored consistently. The tutor is a certified teacher who is trained over the course of a full school year at a teacher training site (available in various school districts and universities). Lesson components include easy and fluent reading, challenging reading, and writing, during which the teacher works alongside the student and intervenes to teach appropriate strategies. Although implementing a high-quality *Reading Recovery* program is difficult and time-consuming due to required training and one-to-one intervention, research indicates that it has both immediate and long-term effects in helping low-achieving students learn to read and write (Pinnell, 1990).

Language Experience Approach

The language experience approach (LEA) integrates the development of reading skills with the development of listening, speaking, and writing skills. The materials are made up of what the student is thinking and saying. According to Lee and Allen (1963), LEA deals with the following thinking process: what students think about, they can talk about; what stu-

dents say, they can write (or someone can write for them); and what students write (or others write for them), they can read.

LEA stresses each student's unique interests. The approach is based not upon a series of reading materials but upon the student's oral and written expression. The student's experiences play a major role in determining the reading material. The student dictates stories to the teacher. These stories may originate at first from the student's own drawings and artwork. The teacher writes down the stories, and they become the basis of the student's initial reading experiences. Thus, the student learns to read his own written thoughts. In this approach the language patterns of the reading materials are determined by the student's speech, and the content is determined by experiences (Hall, 1981). The teacher tries to broaden and enrich the base of experiences from which the student can think, speak, and read. Eventually, with help, the student can write his own stories. Thus, according to Hall (1981), the approach is based on the concept that "reading has the most meaning to a pupil when the materials being read are expressed in his language and are rooted in his experiences" (p. 2).

At first the teacher guides students in writing an experience chart. The story in the chart derives from the students' experiences as they share information through group discussion. Experience charts may include several topics: narrative descriptions of experiences, reports of experiments or news events, or fictional stories the students create. The teacher writes the ideas in a first draft on the chalkboard, guides the students' suggestions and revisions, and discusses word choice, sentence structure, and the sounds of letters and words. Specific skills such as capitalization, punctuation, spelling, grammar, and correct sentence structure can be taught as needed during the editing and revising of the chart. Thus, the teacher provides skill development at the appropriate time instead of following a predetermined sequence of training in reading skills. Because the students create the content, motivation and interest are usually high.

Matthes (1972) notes that in the first grade, self-expression and individualized reading can be developed by having students label paintings and drawings, read and complete sentences (such as "I like to . . ."), and write groups of rhyming words. By the second and third grades, students might be producing their own experience charts or writing poetry or song lyrics. Picture dictionaries, simple readers, word cards, labels on classroom objects, and lists of interest or topical words should be available to stimulate ideas and extend the students' writing and reading vocabularies.

In the language experience approach, students are encouraged to proceed at their own rate. Progress is evaluated in terms of each student's ability to express ideas in oral and written form and to understand peers' writing. Progress or growth in writing mechanics, spelling, vocabulary, sentence structure, and depth of thinking is evident in the student's written work. The stories each student writes can be illustrated and bound in an attractive folder, and students can trade story notebooks.

The language experience approach is similar to whole language in that both emphasize the importance of literature, treat reading as a personal act (that is, they accept language varieties of individual students), and advocate an abundance of books written by students about their own lives. However, language experience presumes that written language is a secondary system derived from oral language, whereas whole language sees oral and written language as structurally related without one being a rendition of the other (Altwerger et al., 1987). The teacher frequently may take dictation from students in the language experience approach, but dictation is less frequent in a whole language curriculum because it deprives the learners of making meaning through the act of writing. Moreover, in the language experience approach, a student's dictation often is used to teach word-attack or phonics skills, whereas whole language theory disagrees that fragmented exercises can lead to comprehensive knowledge of language.

One advantage of the language experience approach is that it uses the student's own language as the focus of the reading program. It incorporates speaking, listening, and writing skills into the reading program and makes the student more sensitive to his language, environment, and experiences. Also, the student's interest level tends to be high, and creativity is encouraged in writing original stories. Major disadvantages are that the approach does not provide a structured, systematic method of teaching sequential reading skills, and there is no method of evaluating student progress. Emphasis is placed on the student's own experiences and speaking vocabulary; however, there may not be enough structure in this approach to develop vocabulary or to generalize from speaking and listening vocabularies to reading and writing vocabularies.

The language experience approach is mainly a way of teaching beginning reading. However, it may be just as effective in the intermediate grades and often is used with older students for corrective instruction and motivation. When teacher organization and instruction in word-attack and comprehension skills are provided, the language experience approach can be used effectively to teach students with learning problems. It also can be used to improve comprehension skills of older students who have developed basic decoding skills or to maintain interest and motivation. Research, however, indicates that the language experience approach may produce weaker effects with populations labeled specifically as disadvantaged (Stahl & Miller, 1989).

Allen and Allen (1974) provide a multimedia kit for their program *Language Experience in*

Reading, which includes a creative collection of resources for the classroom teacher. Moreover, additional language experience activities are suggested by Allen and Allen (1982).

Individualized Reading Approach

In an individualized reading program, students select their own reading material according to interest and ability and progress at their own rate. A large collection of books should be available at different reading levels, with many subjects represented at each level of difficulty. After the students choose reading materials, they pace themselves and keep records of their progress. The teacher teaches word recognition and comprehension skills as each student needs them.

Each student meets once or twice a week with the teacher, at which time the teacher may ask the student to read aloud and discuss the reading material. The teacher can note reading errors and check the student's sight vocabulary, understanding of word meanings, and comprehension. Also, the teacher can guide the student with regard to the next reading selection, although the choice is made by the student. From these conferences the teacher keeps a record of the student's capabilities and progress to plan activities to develop specific skills. The teacher's role is to diagnose and prescribe, and success of the program depends on the teacher's resourcefulness and competence. Individual work can be supplemented with group activities using basal readers and workbooks to provide practice on specific reading skills.

Self-pacing and self-selection can be considered advantages of the individualized reading approach. Self-pacing builds self-confidence, and self-selection satisfies personal interests and promotes independent reading. Individualized reading also eliminates "high" and "low" reading groups and avoids competition and comparison. The one-to-one conferences between student and teacher also may encourage the teacher to observe and diagnose reading weaknesses. The main disadvantage of the program is that it lacks structure and organization in developing specific reading skills. The teacher must be competent and skillful to conduct beneficial conferences and keep efficient records. Also, a large number of books must be available to meet each student's interests and level of ability. An additional disadvantage is that no provision is made in advance to deal with unknown words, specific word meanings, or difficult concepts. Because teacher guidance follows the completion of reading, the student may repeat inappropriate responses. The value of the individualized reading approach for students with learning problems is questionable, because it involves self-learning and lacks a systematic check of developmental skills in the reading process (Kirk et al., 1978).

REMEDIAL READING PROGRAMS AND METHODS

Remedial programs are designed to teach reading to the student who has, or would have, difficulty learning to read in the regular classroom reading program. In addition, several remedial methods are designed for students with moderate to severe reading problems—for example, nonreaders or students who are more than 1 year behind in reading achievement. The remedial programs and methods discussed in this section include *Reading Mastery: DISTAR Reading* and the *Corrective Reading Program, Edmark Reading Program,* programmed reading instruction, multisensory reading method, modified alphabet method, neurological impress method, and high interest—low vocabulary method.

Reading Mastery: DISTAR Reading and the Corrective Reading Program

Reading Mastery: DISTAR Reading (Direct Instructional System for Teaching Arithmetic and Reading) (Engelmann & Bruner, 1988), consists of Levels I and II of the SRA (Science Research Associates) *Reading Mastery* basal reading series. It is an intensive, highly structured programmed instructional system designed to remediate below-average reading skills of students through third grade. The students are grouped according to their current abilities with no more than five students in a group. They sit in chairs in a quarter-circle around the teacher. Each day, one 30-minute lesson is presented. The manual specifies the sequence of presentation as well as statements and hand movements. Each student receives positive reinforcement (praise or points) for correct responses. A student who masters skills (indicated by performance on tests) changes groups.

The program uses a synthetic phonics approach and emphasizes basic decoding skills, including sound-symbol identification, left-to-right sequence, and the oral blending of sounds to make words. The program includes games to teach sequencing skills and left-to-right orientation, blending tasks to teach students to spell words by sounds ("say it slow") and to blend quickly ("say it fast"), and rhyming tasks to teach how sounds and words relate. Take-home sheets are used to practice skills. The program teaches students to concentrate on important sound combinations and word discriminations and to use a variety of word-attack skills. In Level I, students learn how to read words, sentences, and stories, both aloud and silently, and to answer literal comprehension questions about their readings. Level II expands basic reading skills, and students learn strategies for decoding difficult

words and for answering interpretive comprehension questions. The program also teaches basic reasoning skills, such as applying rules and completing deductions.

In this direct instruction approach, emphasis is placed on learning specific skills, and the method of teaching is characterized by (a) teacher modeling or demonstration of important skills, (b) frequent student responding, (c) appropriate, direct feedback to students (including correction), (d) adequate provisions for practice, and (e) student mastery. *Reading Mastery: DISTAR Reading* is fast-paced, providing immediate feedback and correction procedures for various student errors. Repetition is built into the program, and the *DISTAR* library series reinforces skills developed in the program and provides opportunities for independent reading. Research indicates that *DISTAR* has been highly effective in teaching reading to young students with learning problems (Carnine et al., 1990; Stallings, 1974). However, Kirk et al. (1978) note that the rigidity of the instructional program and its emphasis on auditory skills may be considered disadvantages.

The *Corrective Reading Program* (Engelmann, Becker, Hanner, & Johnson, 1988, 1989) is an advanced remedial reading program based on *DISTAR* concepts. It is designed for students in fourth through twelfth grade who have not mastered decoding and comprehension skills. The program is divided into two strands, decoding and comprehension, and each strand includes 315 lessons. Each lesson lasts 35 to 45 minutes and provides teacher-directed work, independent applications, and tests of student performance. The decoding strand includes work-attack basics, decoding strategies, and skill applications, and the comprehension strand includes thinking basics, comprehension skills, and concept applications. The presentation book for the teacher specifies the teacher's role in each lesson. The program gives the student immediate feedback and provides a built-in reinforcement system.

Edmark Reading Program

The *Edmark Reading Program* (Bijou, 1977), published by Edmark Corporation, is designed to teach 150 sight words of varying parts of speech, plus the endings *ing, ed,* and *s,* to students with extremely limited skills. The student needs only to be able to repeat a word the teacher says and point to a response. The 227 lessons include five formats: (a) prereading lessons that train the student on the match-to-sample format, (b) word recognition lessons of one to two words per lesson, (c) lessons in direction books that teach the student to follow printed directions, (d) lessons in matching pictures to phrases, and (e) lessons in a storybook in which the student orally reads 16 stories. All lessons are broken down into small, sequential steps, and reinforcement is provided. Pretests and review tests are included throughout the program, and procedures are given for charting student progress. A software version of the program is available for Apple computers in which the student selects answers with a joystick. Also, after completing Level I of the *Edmark Reading Program,* the student may move into Level II, which introduces an additional 200 words and reinforces the 150 words previously learned.

Programmed Reading Instruction

Programmed reading materials can be in either a workbook format or a teaching machine. The materials are designed to be self-teaching and self-correcting. Subject matter is presented in small steps or frames in a systematic, logical sequence. The student must respond to the question in each frame and then check the response by sliding down a marker. Question forms can be true—false or multiple-choice, completing a sentence, writing a word, or completing a word by filling in letters. When working with a machine, the student responds by pulling a level or knob, pushing a button, or turning a crank. With all programmed materials, the student receives immediate feedback. In workbooks the answers often are in the margin, whereas on teaching machines a light or sound can give feedback, the answer can be uncovered, or the responses can appear on the screen. In a *linear* program, the student must correct wrong responses before continuing. In a *branching* program, after an incorrect response, the student is referred to another page where the mistake is explained; thus, the student progresses at his own rate and receives positive reinforcement or correction at each step.

Matthes (1972) notes the following advantages of programmed reading instruction:

1. Positive reinforcement or correction is given at each learning step.
2. Each student moves at his own pace.
3. The content is self-instructional and does not need to be explained or reviewed.
4. Completed programs can be used as a record of progress.
5. The teacher is freed from repetitive drilling and can help individual students or small groups.

A major disadvantage is that it is difficult to program comprehension skills, and thus little emphasis is placed on their development. Reading short, independent frames does not promote growth in reading long passages or skimming for specific facts.

Repetition and feedback are important when using programmed materials with students who have learning problems. The success of the approach depends on providing students with materials suited to their needs.

Two commercially available programmed reading materials are *Programmed Reading* (McGraw-Hill) and the *Sullivan Reading Program* (Behavioral Research Laboratories).

Multisensory Reading Method

The multisensory method is based on the premise that some students learn best when content is presented in several modalities. Frequently, kinesthetic (movement) and tactile (touch) stimulation is used along with the visual and auditory modalities. The multisensory programs that feature tracing, hearing, writing, and seeing often are referred to as VAKT (visual-auditory-kinesthetic-tactile). To increase tactile and kinesthetic stimulation, sandpaper letters, finger paint, sand trays, raised letters, and sunken letters are used. The Fernald (1943, 1988) and the Gillingham (Gillingham & Stillman, 1970) methods highlight VAKT instruction. The Fernald method stresses whole-word learning, and the Gillingham method features sound blending.

The Fernald Method. Vocabulary is selected from stories the student has dictated, and each word is taught as a whole. In the Fernald approach there is no attempt to teach phonics skills. The teacher identifies unknown words, and the student writes the word to develop word recognition. Each word is learned as a whole unit, and it immediately is placed in a context that is meaningful to the student. Success is stressed to help maintain a high level of motivation.

The method consists of four stages. In Stage 1, the student selects a word to learn, and the teacher writes it with a crayon in large letters. The student then traces the word with his finger, making contact with the paper (tactile-kinesthetic). While tracing, the student says each part of the word aloud (auditory). In addition, the student sees the word (visual) while tracing it and hears the word while saying it

(auditory). This process is repeated until the student can write the word correctly without looking at the sample. If an error is made when tracing or writing, the student must start over so that the word is always written as a unit. If the word is correct, it is filed alphabetically in a word bank. The student writes a story using the learned words, and the story is typed so that the student can read the words in print.

In Stage 2, the student no longer is required to trace each word but now learns each new word by looking at the teacher's written copy of the word, saying it, and writing it. The student continues to write stories and keep a word file.

In Stage 3, the student learns new words by looking at a printed word and saying it before writing it, thus learning directly from the printed word; the teacher is not required to write it. At this point the student can begin reading from books. The teacher continually checks to see that the student is retaining learned words.

Finally, in Stage 4, the student can recognize new words by their similarity to printed words or parts of words already learned and thus can apply reading skills and expand reading interests.

The Fernald approach uses language experience and tracing (kinesthetic) techniques. Progress is slow, and to sustain interest the student chooses the material. Success is stressed to help maintain a high level of motivation. The student never is encouraged to sound out word parts or to copy words that have been traced. Each word is learned as a whole unit and is placed immediately in a context that is meaningful to the student. The four stages must be mastered in sequence. This remedial approach generally is used with students with severe reading problems. However, Otto and Smith (1980) note that the tracing technique alone may be used effectively to help students learn frequently used words with which they are having trouble.

The Gillingham Method. The Gillingham method (Gillingham & Stillman, 1970) is a highly structured, phonetically oriented approach based on the theoretical work of Orton (1937). The method requires five lessons a week for a minimum of 2 years. Each letter sound is taught using a multisensory approach. Consonants and vowels with only one sound are presented on drill cards (consonants on white cards and vowels on salmon-color cards), and letters are introduced by a key word (for example, *fun* for *f*). *Associative* processes are used, beginning with the student associating (linking) the name and sound of a letter with its printed symbol. The method involves the following procedures:

1. A drill card showing one letter is shown to the student. The teacher says the name of the letter and the student repeats it. When this has been mastered, the teacher says the sound of the letter, and the student repeats the sound. Then the card is exposed and the teacher asks, "What does this letter say?" The student is to give its sound.
2. Without presenting the drill card, the teacher makes the sound represented by the letter and says, "Tell me the name of the letter that has this sound." This strategy is essentially oral spelling.
3. The teacher carefully writes the letter and explains its form, thus instructing the student in cursive handwriting. The student traces the letter over the teacher's lines, copies it, writes it from memory, and writes it while looking away. Finally, the teacher makes the sound and says, "Write the letter that has this sound."

After mastering the first group of 10 letters, (*a, b, f, h, i, j, k, m, p, t*), the student is taught to blend them into words. The letters are combined to form simple consonant-vowel-consonant words (for example, *bit, map, jab*).

Spelling is introduced after blending. When the teacher says a word, the student repeats the word, names the letters, writes the letters while saying them (simultaneous oral spelling), and reads the written word. Sentence and story writing is introduced after the student is able to write any three-letter, phonetically pure word. Nonphonetic words are taught through drill. Consonant blends are taught after the student can read, write, and spell the words in the short stories. Also, syllabication, dictionary skills, and additional spelling rules are introduced. Thus, the Gillingham method emphasizes repetition and drill, and spelling and writing skills are taught in conjunction with reading skills.

Instructional materials developed for the Gillingham method include phonetic drill cards, phonetic words, syllable concept cards, and little stories. Lessons and instructions on using the materials to teach various skills are outlined in the manual (Gillingham & Stillman, 1970). The procedure is highly structured and rigid, and no other reading or spelling materials may be used. Also, it lacks meaningful, interesting activities, and the student tends to develop a labored reading style. Kaluger and Kolson (1978) state that an additional weakness is the method's lack of emphasis on comprehension. However, they note that the system is effective and may be valuable for use with students experiencing severe reading difficulties. Two adaptations of the Gillingham method include *Recipe for Reading* (Traub & Bloom, 1970) and *A Multisensory Approach to Language Arts for Specific Language Disability Children* (Slingerland, 1981). Also, the *Phonic Remedial Reading Lessons* (Kirk et al., 1985) use a VAKT phonics approach.

Modified Alphabet Method

Some beginning reading programs use a special alphabet that features consistent symbol-sound associations. Two modified alphabet methods are the initial teaching alphabet and diacritical marking system.

Initial Teaching Alphabet. The initial teaching alphabet (Downing, 1965) was proposed to simplify beginning reading. It uses a modified alphabet to ensure a consistent correspondence between sound and symbol. Letters in the traditional 26-letter alphabet do not always have just one sound apiece. However, because the initial teaching alphabet presents *one* symbol for each sound, a clear relationship exists between each of the characters and its sound. This pattern helps reduce confusing irregularities in spelling. There are 44 characters, including all the letters of the traditional alphabet except *x* and *q*, and 20 other letters that look like traditional letters joined together or are new symbols. These additional letters represent special phonemes, such as *th* sound. In addition, a larger version of the letter, instead of capital letters, indicates uppercase letters. Some examples of words in the initial teaching alphabet include *larg* (large), *laf* (laugh), *askt* (asked), and *wun* (one). The initial teaching alphabet is used only in the beginning stages of reading. As soon as students are fluent in the initial teaching alphabet (usually by the end of the first grade), they transfer to the traditional alphabet.

The initial teaching alphabet is not a method of instruction but was proposed to simplify beginning reading. The teacher can use the initial teaching alphabet with any reading method (for example, language experience approach or a multisensory method). In listing advantages of the initial teaching alphabet, Matthes (1972) notes that it is easier for a student to learn to read when each symbol is represented by one sound. Also, enthusiasm and interest in reading increase as the student finds success. Greater skill in creative self-expression is developed. However, a disadvantage is that the teacher must buy reading books written in the initial teaching alphabet, and the student may be confused when seeing the traditional alphabet in other reading materials. Also, the student may experience difficulty in making the transition from the initial teaching alphabet to the traditional alphabet.

Diacritical Marking System. In the diacritical marking system (Fry, 1964), phonetic marks are added to the letters in the traditional alphabet. For example, long vowels have a bar over them, silent letters have a slash mark through them, and digraphs have a bar under both letters (for example, *fīve, with, chicks*). Short vowels and regular consonants are not changed, because these are the most common usages of the letters. In this beginning reading system, nearly every word the student sees (in reading books, on worksheets, and on the chalkboard) is marked according to the diacritical marking system. As the student's reading skill progresses, the use of the marks diminishes.

Neurological Impress Method

The neurological impress method (Heckelman, 1969; Langford, Slade, & Barnett, 1974) was developed to teach reading to students with severe reading disabilities. The method consists of joint oral reading at a rapid pace by the student and the teacher. It is based on the theory that a student can learn by hearing his own voice and someone else's voice jointly reading the same material. The student is seated slightly in front of the teacher, and the teacher's voice is directed into the student's ear at a close range. There is no special preparation of the material before the joint reading. The objective is simply to cover as many pages as possible in the allotted time, without tiring the student. At first, the teacher should read slightly louder and faster than the student, and the student should be encouraged to maintain the pace and not worry about mistakes. The teacher's finger slides to the location of the words as they are being read. As the student becomes capable of leading the oral reading, the teacher can speak more softly and read slightly slower, and the student's finger can point to the reading. Thus, the student and teacher alternate between leading and following.

Instruction begins at a level slightly below that where the student can read successfully. No attempt is made to teach any phonics skills or word recognition, and no attention is given to comprehension of the material being read. The basic goal is for the student to attain fluent reading automatically. The neurological impress method emphasizes rapid decoding and can be most effective with students age 10 or older who spend too much time sounding out words and do not read fluently (Faas, 1980). Reading phrases rather than isolated words reveals progress, as does learning to pause for punctuation previously ignored. Lorenz and Vockell (1979) conducted a study using the neurological impress method and, although there were no significant gains in word recognition or reading comprehension, improvements were noted in oral expression, fluency, and the students' confidence in their ability to read.

A variation of the neurological impress method is the method of repeated readings (Samuels, 1979). This method requires the student to reread a short, meaningful passage several times until a satisfactory level of fluency (for example, 80 to 100 correct words per minute with three to six errors) is reached. The procedure is then repeated with a new passage. Repeated readings thus emphasize reading rate on a single passage rather than single words, and identification of words in context must be fast as well as accurate. Kann (1983) notes that this method promotes the development of syntactic competency and provides students with successful reading experiences. O'Shea and O'Shea (1988) indicate that the method can be used in a variety of learning arrangements, such as small-group instruction with choral reading, peer reading with pairs of reading partners, and learning centers with the use of Language Masters and tape recorders. Comprehension practice can be provided through activities involving the cloze and maze procedure (that is, reading the passage and filling in the blanks for omitted words with the words that complete phrases or sentences correctly). In a study of students with learning problems in fifth through eighth grade, O'Shea, Sindelar, and O'Shea (1987) found that repeated readings (three and seven times) combined with attentional cues were effective in increasing fluency (that is, number of words correctly read per minute) and comprehension (that is, percentage of story propositions correctly restated following the final reading). Although not complete alone, either the neurological impress method or the method of repeated readings can be used effectively to improve reading fluency (Henk, Helfeldt, & Platt, 1986).

High Interest—Low Vocabulary Method

Older students with reading problems often are frustrated because books geared to their interest level are beyond their reading ability. High interest—low vocabulary books offer a relatively easy vocabulary while maintaining an interest level appropriate for the more mature reader. As indicated in Table 11.4, several publishing companies produce these materials covering a wide variety of topics (for example, sports, mystery, science, adventure).

The teacher can estimate the reading level of any reading material by using the Fry (1977) readability formula, presented in Figure 11.1. A computer software program, *Readability Formulas*, produced by Encyclopaedia Britannica Educational Corporation, allows the user to apply seven different readability formulas (for example, Fry, SMOG, Spache) to any reading selection simultaneously to determine reading level. The pro-

TABLE 11.4
High interest—low vocabulary reading materials.

Title	Publisher	Reading Grade Level	Interest Grade Level
Action Series	Scholastic Magazine and Book Services	4–5	7–12
American Adventure Series	Harper & Row	3–6	4–8
Basic Vocabulary Books	Garrard	2	1–6
Breakthrough Series	Allyn & Bacon	2–6	7–12
Checkered Flag Series	Field Educational Publications	2–4	6–12
Childhood of Famous Americans Series	Bobbs-Merrill	4–5	7–9
Cowboy Sam Series	Benefic Press	PP–3	1–6
Dan Frontier Series	Benefic Press	PP–4	1–7
Deep Sea Adventures	Field Educational Publications	2–5	3–11
Everyreader Series	McGraw-Hill	6–8	5–12
Fastback Books	Fearon	4–5	6–12
First Reading Books	Garrard	1	1–4
Focus on Reading	Science Research Associates	1–6	3–12
Folklore of the World Books	Garrard	2	2–8
Interesting Reading Series	Follett	2–3	7–12
Jim Forest Readers	Field Educational Publications	1–3	1–7
Junior Science Books	Garrard	4–5	6–9
Morgan Bay Mysteries	Field Educational Publications	2–4	4–11
Morrow's High Interest/Easy Reading Books	William Morrow	1–8	4–10
Mystery Adventure Series	Benefic Press	2–6	4–9
Pacemaker Classics	Fearon	2	7–12
Pacemaker True Adventure	Fearon	2	5–12
Pacemaker Story Books	Xerox Education Publications	2	7–12
Pal Paperback Kits	Xerox Education Publications	1–5	5–12
Pleasure Reading Books	Garrard	4	3–7
Racing Wheels Series	Benefic Press	2–4	4–9
Reading For Concepts Series	McGraw-Hill	3–8	5–12
Reading Reinforcement Skilltext Series	Merrill	1–5	1–8
Reading Skill Builders	Reader's Digest Services	1–4	2–5
Sailor Jack Series	Benefic Press	PP–3	1–6
Space Science Fiction Series	Benefic Press	2–6	4–9
Sports Mystery Stories	Benefic Press	2–4	4–9
Super Kits	Warner Educational Services	2–5	4–12
Superstars Series	Steck-Vaughn	4–6	7–12
Teen-Age Tales	D. C. Heath	4–6	6–11
Top Picks	Reader's Digest Services	5–7	5–12
What Is It Series	Benefic Press	1–4	1–8

Average number of syllables per 100 words

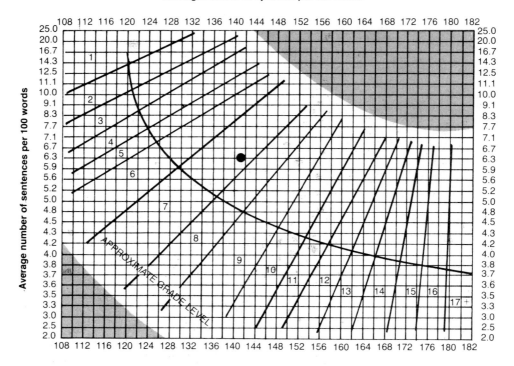

DIRECTIONS: Randomly select 3 one hundred word passages from a book or an article. Plot average number of syllables and average number of sentences per 100 words on graph to determine the grade level of the material. Choose more passages per book if great variability is observed and conclude that the book has uneven readability. Few books will fall in gray area but when they do grade level scores are invalid.

Count proper nouns, numerals and initializations as words. Count a syllable for each symbol. For example, "1945" is 1 word and 4 syllables and "IRA" is 1 word and 3 syllables.

EXAMPLE:	SYLLABLES	SENTENCES
1st Hundred Words	124	6.6
2nd Hundred Words	141	5.5
3rd Hundred Words	158	6.8
AVERAGE	141	6.3

READABILITY 7th GRADE (see dot plotted on graph)

FIGURE 11.1
Fry's graph for estimating readability—extended.
Reprinted by permission of the author.

EXPANDED DIRECTIONS FOR WORKING READABILITY GRAPH

1. Randomly select three (3) sample passages and count out exactly 100 words beginning with the beginning of a sentence. Do count proper nouns, initializations, and numerals.
2. Count the number of sentences in the hundred words estimating length of the fraction of the last sentence to the nearest 1/10th.
3. Count the total number of syllables in the 100-word passage. If you don't have a hand counter available, an easy way is to simply put a mark above every syllable over one in each word, then when you get to the end of the passage, count the number of marks and add 100. Small calculators can also be used as counters by pushing numeral "1", then push the "+" sign for each word or syllable when counting.
4. Enter graph with average sentence length and average number of syllables; plot dot where the two lines intersect. Area where dot is plotted will give you the approximate grade level.
5. If a great deal of variability is found in syllable count or sentence count, putting more samples into the average is desirable.
6. A word is defined as a group of symbols with a space on either side; thus, "Joe," "IRA," "1945," and "&" are each one word.
7. A syllable is defined as a phonetic syllable. Generally, there are as many syllables as vowel sounds. For example, "stopped" is one syllable and "wanted" is two syllables. When counting syllables for numerals and initializations, count one syllable for each symbol. For example, "1945" is 4 syllables and "IRA" is 3 syllables, and "&" is 1 syllable.

FIGURE 11.1
Continued

gram, which is designed for Apple II computers, graphically depicts readability results.

TEACHING STRATEGIES IN READING

Many reading approaches and instructional techniques are available for teaching students with learning problems. Although the research indicates that reading is taught best through direct instruction (that is, teaching reading skills directly rather than through process skills), none of the approaches (basal, phonics, linguistic, whole language, language experience approach, or others) has emerged as superior. Each approach has been successful with some students, and selected teaching strategies can be incorporated within each approach. Because each student with learning problems is unique, a combination of approaches and various teaching strategies are needed to meet the needs of these students.

To teach new vocabulary words and the initial learning and retention of facts, Mastropieri (1988) suggests the use of the *keyword method,* which is a memory-enhancing technique that relies strongly upon visual imagery. The method uses three steps: (a) recoding—changing a vocabulary word into a word (keyword) that sounds like part of the vocabulary word and is easy to picture (for example, *ape* as a keyword for *apex*); (b) relating—integrating the keyword with its definition by imagining a picture of the keyword and its definition doing something together (for example, an ape sitting on the highest point [apex] of a rock), and (c) retrieving—recalling the definition by thinking of the keyword and the picture or interactive image of the keyword. In teaching abstract and concrete vocabulary words to students with learning problems, Mastropieri, Scruggs, and Fulk (1990) found that keyword mnemonic instruction resulted in higher levels of recall and comprehension than a rehearsal condition. Students were shown mnemonic pictures for each new vocabulary word in which the keyword was pictured interacting with its definition in a line drawing or interacting with an instance of the definition. For example, for the word *oxalis,* meaning a cloverlike plant, an ox (keyword for oxalis) was pictured eating a cloverlike plant, and for *chiton,* meaning loose garment, a kite (keyword for chiton) was shown in a picture of people making kites out of loose garments. In addition, when using the keyword method, the teacher can enhance fluency and application by presenting practice exercises that require students to use the new words in sentences and in oral communication.

To improve reading comprehension, *reciprocal teaching* is an interactive teaching strategy that promotes both comprehension of text and comprehension monitoring through active participation in discussions of text (Palinscar & Brown, 1986, 1988). The teacher and students work together to comprehend text through the use of a dialogue structured by four strategies:

1. *Predicting:* Students are taught to make predictions about upcoming content from cues in the text or from prior knowledge of the topic. They can use text structure such as headings, subheadings, and questions embedded in the text to hypothesize what the author will discuss. This gives students a purpose for reading (that is, to confirm or disprove their hypotheses).
2. *Question generating:* Through teacher modeling and practice in generating main idea questions about the text, students learn to identify information that provides the substance for a good question. Students become more involved in the reading text when they are posing and answering questions rather than responding to teacher or text questions.
3. *Summarizing:* The teacher guides students in integrating the information presented in the text. For example, the students can identify or invent topic sentences, name

lists with appropriate labels, and delete unimportant or repeated information. This provides students with an opportunity to monitor their own understanding of the text.
4. *Clarifying:* The students' attention is given to reasons why the text may be difficult to understand (for example, unfamiliar vocabulary, unclear referent words, disorganized text). They are taught to reread or ask for help to restore meaning.

In reciprocal teaching, the teacher initially leads the dialogue and models the use of the four strategies while reading. Through guided practice, the responsibility for initiating and maintaining the dialogue is transferred to the students. Thus, there is interplay among the teacher and students, and the teacher uses explanation, instruction, and modeling with guided practice to help students independently apply the strategies and learn from text. When using the strategies or thinking skills, students are forced to focus on the reading material and, at the same time, monitor for understanding.

Story-mapping procedures also can be used to improve reading comprehension through a schema-building technique (Idol & Croll, 1987). A pictorial story map is used as an organizer for readers, and the students are asked to fill in the map components as they read. The map components of a narrative story include the setting (characters, time, and place), problem, goal, action, and outcome. The teacher initially models the story-mapping procedure by pointing out information related to the story-map components and having the students write the correct answer on the story-map outline. Then students independently complete the story map with prompting from the teacher as needed. Improved comprehension results as students build a structural schemata (the story-map components) that are applied to a narrative story. Story mapping brings the reader's attention to important and interrelated parts of a story and provides a framework for understanding, conceptualizing, and remembering story events. Idol (1987) also notes that a mapping strategy designed for use with expository material can result in improved comprehension. A critical-thinking map is used that highlights the major aspects of a passage, including (a) the important events, points, or steps that lead to the main idea; (b) the main idea itself; (c) other viewpoints and opinions of the reader; (d) the reader's conclusion upon reading the passage; and (e) any relevancy the reader perceives for contemporary situations. The reader completes the map components either during or after reading a passage in the text.

In addition to various vocabulary and reading comprehension strategies such as the use of keywords, reciprocal teaching, and story-mapping procedures, supplementary activities and materials are useful in short, concentrated drill or practice to enhance motivation and interest by reinforcing a newly learned skill. Activities, instructional games, and self-correcting materials help individualize instruction.

READING AND STUDY SKILLS FOR ADOLESCENTS

Most secondary course work requires a relatively large amount of reading, because textbooks and supplementary materials are the major sources of information. In expository materials, the vocabulary is often more difficult to decode and pronounce than that found in narrative material, and the general content is frequently beyond the reader's experiences. Roe, Stoodt, and Burns (1987) state that "teachers can promote developmental reading by helping students learn the concepts and vocabulary of [each] content area, and they can enhance their students' reading comprehension by assisting them in interpreting and evaluating the text material" (p. 8). The secondary teacher also should be aware that older students often need to develop study skills and reading rate, in addition to increasing decoding and comprehension skills.

The adolescent may need to increase reading speed to finish assignments on time and keep up with older classmates. Roe et al. (1987) note that secondary students should be made aware of poor reading habits that may decrease their reading rate, including forming each word as it is read, sounding out all words (familiar and unfamiliar), rereading material, and pointing to each word with the index finger. Another technique for increasing rate, which often is used in a reading laboratory, is to present words and phrases with a tachistoscope and gradually reduce the presentation time, thus speeding up the student's responses. The teacher can have the student practice timed readings with stopwatches or egg timers. Progress should be reinforced and charted continuously. Timed readings should be accompanied by comprehension checks, and the teacher should encourage rate increases only if comprehension does not suffer.

Rupley and Blair (1989) note that successful reading in the content areas requires the ability to adjust one's rate of reading to the type of material being read. Three types of reading are required: skimming, scanning, and studying. *Skimming* refers to covering a selection to get some of the main ideas and a general overview of the material without attending to details. In skimming, the student should read the first paragraph line-by-line; read bold print headings as they appear; read the first sentence of every paragraph; examine pictures, charts, and maps; and read the last paragraph. Skimming practice may involve giving the student a short amount of time to skim a content chapter and write down the main ideas or having the student skim newspaper articles and match them to headlines. *Scan-

ning refers to reading a selection to find a specific piece of information. When scanning, the student should use headings to locate the pages to scan for the specific information; run eyes rapidly down the page in a zigzag or winding S pattern; note capital letters if looking for a name, numbers for dates, and italicized words for vocabulary items; and read only what is needed to verify the purpose. Scanning activities may include having the student scan a history chapter to find the date of a particular event or locate a specific person's number in a telephone directory. In *study-type reading*, the goal is total comprehension, and reading is deliberate and purposeful. Rupley and Blair state that students must have these three types of reading explained to them, practice them under teacher supervision, and be given opportunities for independent practice.

As students learn to study various content areas, they should develop effective study skills. The SQ3R method, developed by Robinson (1961), is used widely, especially for social studies and science. This method can be useful to students with learning problems in providing a systematic approach to better study skills. The method involves the following steps:

1. *Survey:* To get an overview of the reading material, the student scans the entire assignment, glancing at headings to see the major points that will be developed and reading introductory statements and summaries. The student also should inspect graphic aids such as maps, tables, graphs, and pictures. This survey provides a framework for organizing facts in the selection as the student progresses through the reading.
2. *Question:* To give a purpose for careful reading of the material, the student devises questions that may be answered in the selection. Questions can be formed by rephrasing headings and subheadings.
3. *Read:* The student reads the material with the intent of finding the answers to the questions. Also, the student may take notes during this careful reading.
4. *Recite:* The student looks away from the reading material and notes and briefly recites the answers to the questions. This checks on what the student has learned and helps set the information in memory.
5. *Review:* The student reviews the material and checks memory of the content by rereading portions of the selection or notes to verify answers given during the previous step. The student also can note major points under each heading. This review activity helps the student retain the material better by reinforcing the learning.

Another strategy to increase students' comprehension is for the content teacher to provide a reading guide or study organizer containing questions and statements on the content of the text material. The student should receive it beforehand and complete it while reading. A study organizer summarizes the main ideas and important concepts of the material in a factual style or in a schematic form such as a flow chart, diagram, or table.

Students with learning problems also can be taught to use learning strategies designed to increase their reading comprehension (Clark, Deshler, Schumaker, Alley, & Warner, 1984). For example, the visual imagery strategy requires the student to read a passage and create representative visual images. The self-questioning strategy helps maintain interest and enhance recall by teaching the student to form questions about the content of a passage as he reads. The use of learning strategies involves the student more actively in the reading process. The reader is asked to formulate questions, take notes on the content, or verbally paraphrase critical information. Thus, the student is engaged in information rehearsal and practice involving either reciting or writing down critical information.

Lenz and Hughes (1990) present a word identification strategy, DISSECT, that is effective in reducing common oral reading errors such as mispronunciations, substitutions, and omissions in adolescents with learning problems. The seven steps of the strategy are:

1. **D**—*Discover* the content: Skip a difficult word and read the remainder of the sentence to guess the word by using the meaning of the sentence.
2. **I**—*Isolate* the prefix: Look at the beginning of the word to see if it is possible to box off the first several letters that create a phoneme that can be pronounced.
3. **S**—*Separate* the suffix: Look at the end of the word to see if it is possible to box off ending letters that form a suffix.
4. **S**—*Say* the stem: If able to recognize the stem (what is left after the prefix is isolated and the suffix is separated), say the prefix, stem, and suffix together.
5. **E**—*Examine* the stem: If unable to name the stem, apply one of two rules:
   (a) If a stem, or any part of a stem, begins with a vowel, separate the first two letters from the stem and pronounce. If a stem, or any part of a stem, begins with a consonant, separate the first three letters from the stem and pronounce. Apply the rule until the end of the stem is reached and then pronounce the stem by saying the dissected part. Add the prefix and suffix and reread the whole word.
   (b) If the first rule cannot be used, isolate the first letter of the stem and try to apply the first rule again. When vowels appear together in a word, pronounce both vowel sounds and then make one vowel sound at a time until it sounds right.
6. **C**—*Check* with someone: If unable to pronounce the word after applying the first five strategy steps, obtain assistance by checking with someone (such as a teacher, parent, or better reader) in an appropriate manner.
7. **T**—*Try* the dictionary: If personal assistance is unavailable, look up the word in the dictionary, pronounce it by using the pronunciation guide, and read the definition.

For reading comprehension, Archer and Gleason (1989) present a simple strategy called active reading that is appropriate for elementary students and low-achieving secondary students. Using active reading, the student (a) reads a single paragraph and thinks about the topic and important details, (b) covers the material with his hand, (c) recites the important information by saying the topic and important details in his own words, and (d) checks his statement of the critical information by examining the paragraph again.

Setting a purpose for reading through the use of study guides or the SQ3R method can improve the older student's comprehension. Developing effective study skills, increasing reading rate, using learning strategies, and adjusting reading rate according to purpose should help the adolescent read more efficiently in numerous content areas at a higher academic level. Additional study methods for secondary students are discussed in Chapter 14.

READING ACTIVITIES

There are many reading activities and commercial and teacher-made materials that aid in the development of reading skills. Supplementary activities and materials are useful in short, concentrated drill or practice or to enhance motivation and interest by reinforcing a newly learned skill. Activities, instructional games, self-correcting materials, and computer software programs can be used to individualize instruction according to specific needs and abilities. Additional reading activities for adolescents are presented in Chapter 14.

Word-Attack Activities

1. For practice in initial consonant sounds, glue pictures of simple objects on small cards and make a grid or a pocket chart in which the beginning square or pocket has consonant letters corresponding to initial sounds of the objects. To indicate the initial sound of the word, the student places each picture card next to the appropriate letter. Consonant blends, medial vowel sounds, and final consonant sounds also can be practiced in the same manner.

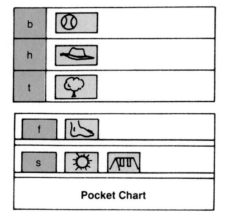

Pocket Chart

2. Have the student make his own picture dictionary by using a scrapbook indexed with the letters of the alphabet. The student draws pictures or cuts them out of old magazines. When he learns the word shown by the picture, he pastes the picture on the page representing the initial consonant sound. For example, a picture of a dog is pasted on the *D* page. The student-made dictionary invites interest because the student makes it himself and it contains only words that he is using. If desired, completed dictionaries can be exchanged so that each student learns to read other students' dictionaries.

3. Make a rotating circle device to use in practicing initial consonant sounds and word families. Cut an attractive design or object out of poster board and print the desired letters of a word family on it. Cut out a square in front of the letters. Then cut a small circle out of poster board and print the appropriate initial consonant letters on it. Attach the circle to the back of the larger poster board, positioned so that each letter will be exposed in the square opening as the circle is rotated.

4. Make flash cards by pasting pictures on index cards and printing the word or phrase that tells about the picture on both the front and back of the card. Vowel cards can be made by using a picture illustrating a word that uses a specific vowel (for example, *cat*) and writing the word and the marked vowel on the card (căt—ă). Flash cards for blends, digraphs, or diphthongs can be constructed in a similar manner. After the student learns to associate the printed symbol with the picture, he can practice reading the words on the back side of the cards.

5. Make a set of word cards in which the first letter of each word is omitted and a picture illustrates the word. The student is to fill in the missing letter. The cards can be made self-correcting by writing the answer on the back or supplying an answer key that is picture coded. Cards also can be made that omit letters in the medial or final position or that omit blends, digraphs, or diphthongs. The cards can be laminated and written on with a grease pencil so that they can be reusable.

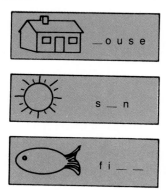

6. To develop auditory discrimination of letter sounds, have the student participate in rhyming activities such as matching pictures whose names rhyme. Also, when given one word in a family, the student may be asked to name and list as many other words as he can that belong to the same family and to circle like parts of the rhyming words.

7. Have the student make a *sound* dictionary in an indexed scrapbook. On each page, paste pictures of objects or actions that illustrate words beginning with the sound. For example, pictures of a table, tent, and top can be pasted on the *T* page; the page for words with the initial *Ch* sound can have pictures of a church, cheese, and children on it.

8. For general word recognition, attach labels to the door, windows, and objects in the classroom so that the student will begin to associate the printed word with the object. Also, a large picture can be made on poster board with slits next to the objects in the picture. Word cards are made for the objects in the picture, and an envelope containing paper clips is attached to the back of the picture. Instruct the student to match each word card to the appropriate object in the picture by paper clipping it to the slit.

9. To provide practice on basic sight words or sight phrases, make a ladder that will hold word or phrase cards on each rung. The student tries to climb the ladder by saying each word or phrase. When he is able to reach the top by pronouncing each word correctly, he receives a reward (reinforcement) and starts to work on a more difficult set of cards.

10. Construct a word wheel by fastening together two poster board circles, one smaller than the other, through their centers so that they rotate freely. A blend can be written on the inner circle with an opening next to it; letters to add to the blend are printed on the outer circle. The student rotates the inner wheel and reads the words as they appear in the opening. A variation of the word wheel is to print word endings and suffixes on the outer wheel and various root words on the inner wheel. The teacher gives a sentence (for example, "The two boys are _____ ") and points to the root word on the inner wheel. The student rotates the wheel to find the appropriate ending and reads the word.

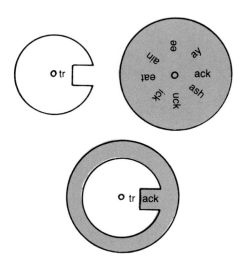

11. Make a tachistoscope by cutting a window in a piece of oaktag and attaching the window card

to another card of equal size to form a backing. Words or phrases are written on a strip of paper the width of the window; the student pulls the strip past the window to reveal the written words. This device can be made self-correcting by having two windows, one of which is covered with a flap, and preparing an answer strip with picture clues. The student reads the word in the open window and lifts the flap on the other window to check his response by looking at the picture clue. Also, to develop quick recognition of sight words, a shutter can be attached to the opening so that the teacher can expose or flash each word quickly. If the word is missed, the shutter can be reopened to allow the student more time to analyze the word.

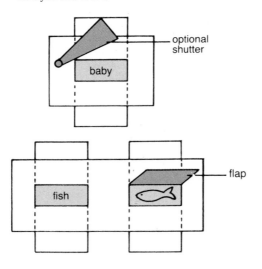

12. To develop knowledge of contractions, give the student sentences to read in which several words are underlined that could be made into contractions. Instruct him to change the words to the appropriate contraction as he reads. For example:

a. There is nobody she will go with today.
b. He has not done the work because he cannot see it.
c. "You are going to the store, are not you?" said Mary.

Also, the student can be asked to underline all contractions or words that could have been made into contractions in a selected reading passage. An additional activity is to have contraction races. Call out contractions and see who can give the words they stand for, or call out two words and see who can give the contraction. Ekwall (1989) lists contractions and the grade level at which they should be known.

13. To help the student identify compound words, give him two lists of words and have him draw lines to connect two words to make a compound word. Also, the student can be asked to separate compound words into two words. Activities involving compound words encourage focusing on the whole word. Such activities may help the student who has a tendency to read words by looking at the initial sound and guessing at the remainder of the word.

14. If the student has a tendency to read word-by-word, allow him to read material he is familiar with or material that has a lower-level vocabulary (high interest—low vocabulary stories). Tape record the student's reading of familiar passages and contrast it with other reading to note whether the student reads fluently. The student also can read against a timer to increase his speed and maintain a more appropriate pace.

15. Have the student practice with phrase cards. After he has mastered short, easy phrases, longer and more difficult phrases can be introduced. The phrase cards may be arranged to tell a continuous story. Phrase reading also can be encouraged by giving the student a reading passage in which the words to be read together are underlined—for example, All the children walked quickly to the car.

16. On the chalkboard, write sentences that contain words with prefixes or suffixes. Ask the student to locate the root word, identify the prefix or suffix, and explain how the addition of the prefix or suffix changes the meaning of the root word.

17. If the student tends to omit or repeat words when reading, tape record his reading of a selected passage. Give him a copy of the passage and ask him to follow along with his finger as

the tape is played back to him. Have him circle all omitted words or underline words that he repeats. This focuses attention on omitted or repeated words and increases the student's awareness of this tendency as he reads.

18. Emphasize left-to-right orientation to help the student who frequently reverses letters in words (such as *was* for *saw* or *lap* for *pal*). Present frequently reversed words on flash cards and cover up all but the initial letter. Slowly uncover the remaining letters as the student correctly pronounces the word. Arrows drawn from left to right also may be added under the word. In addition, the student may be asked to trace troublesome words or letters with his fingers and simultaneously sound out the word or letter. After tracing each word or letter, the student should attempt to write it from memory.

19. Encourage the student to use context clues instead of guessing at unknown words or substituting words. Ask the student to complete multiple-choice sentences that provide practice in context reading. For example:

    a. While camping, the boys slept in a _____ . (lamp, tent, trap)
    b. It was raining, so she brought her _____ . (umbrella, usher, clock)

    In a reading passage, encourage the student to sound out the first few sounds of a troublesome word and then to read beyond it to see if the following words give any clue concerning its meaning. Context clues as well as beginning sounds may help the student identify a difficult word.

20. Give the student a list of words. Ask him to arrange them in columns according to the number of syllables in each word. Improving skills in syllabication aids the older student in structural analysis and often enhances word recognition.

Comprehension Activities

1. To help the student remember what he has read, point out key words that reveal the text's organization and show a series of events. The student should be aware of words and phrases such as *to begin with, next, after that,* and *finally.*

2. To emphasize word meaning and develop vocabulary, have the student group various words in categories. For example, words that relate to specific interests may be grouped together, such as baseball words or cooking words. Also, words may be grouped in categories such as "Things That Are Alive," "What Animals Do," or "Things That Eat."

3. Help the student develop a visual image by reviewing the setting of the story before he reads. While reading, he can be asked to describe images from the passage; for example, "Do you think Ruff is a big dog?" Also, after reading, the student can draw pictures to illustrate settings and happenings in the story.

4. Model proper inflection for a particular sentence. Have the student imitate what he heard. Reading with expression increases understanding.

5. Write several riddles or short stories that describe a specific word or object. The student must focus on descriptive details to answer each riddle. If the riddle is written on a card, the activity can be made self-correcting by writing the answer on the back of each card.

6. Have the student read a story and then make up an appropriate title for it. The teacher can give the student several titles and ask him to select the best one and justify his response.

7. Have the student read a story in which the sentences have been numbered. Ask several detailed questions about the reading selection, and require the student to give the number of the sentence in which he located each answer.

8. After the student has read a selection, ask him to underline the sentences that best state the main idea, or he can tell what the selection is about in his own words. Then have him list important details pertaining to the main idea. The headings "Who," "What," "Where," "When," and "Why" may be written on the paper so that details regarding each heading can be listed in the appropriate column. The student also may draw pictures to illustrate details

of the selection or answer questions requiring knowledge of the important details.

9. Cut pictures out of magazines or catalogs and write descriptive statements about them. Have the student match each picture with its description.

10. Cut articles out of the newspaper and cut off the headlines. Have the student read each article and then select the appropriate headline.

11. To help the student attend to specific details of a reading passage, have him read directions on how to do a given activity and then have him perform the activity step-by-step. Also, ask the student to write directions for playing a game; then another student can read the written directions to see if he could learn to play the game from them.

12. Present the student with a series of paragraphs, each of which contains one word or one sentence that does not fit the meaning of the rest of the paragraph. Have him cross out the irrelevant word or sentence and write a more appropriate one in its place.

13. To enhance vocabulary development and word meaning, make a crossword puzzle in which the clues are word definitions. For young students, a modified puzzle may be made in which the puzzle supplies the first letter for each response.

14. Teach vocabulary with definitions according to the following format (Carnine et al., 1990):

   a. State the definition and ask the student to repeat it.
   b. Teach and test students on positive and negative examples. Positive examples are words of the same class, and negative examples are those of a different class. For example, in teaching the meaning of the word *exit,* a positive example would be a picture of a door leading out of a movie theater, and a negative example would be a picture of a closet door. The teacher presents each example by holding up the picture, pointing to the door, and asking, "Is this an exit? How do you know?"
   c. Review the new word and words previously taught.

Lovitt (1984) suggests several modifications of this approach: (a) let the student select words to be learned, (b) have the student write a story using the words, or (c) have the student use the words in an oral discussion.

15. After the student has read a short story, instruct him to write a telegram telling the main events of the passage. The telegram should be limited to a specific number of words. Blank telegrams can be provided for the student's use. A variation of this activity is to provide a list of topic suggestions and have the student compose a telegram of 10 or fewer words about the chosen topic.

16. To help the student distinguish between the main idea and supporting details of a reading selection, have him diagram the sentences of a paragraph. For example:

Every day the old man and his dog took an early morning walk.
They always walked four blocks.
The dog stayed right next to the man.
Many people spoke to both the man and his dog.

17. To provide practice in distinguishing between cause and effect, have one student describe an event—for example, "the dog barked." The second student must give a reason for the event: "because a cat came into the yard." Then a third student is asked to give a probable effect: "the cat ran home."

18. To help the student increase his speed of reading while focusing on comprehension, have him read a short selection in a limited amount of time. Then present a series of questions based on the selection and have the student answer as many questions as he can. Also, the teacher can present questions before the student reads the selection; the student is allowed a short period of time to locate as many answers as possible. An additional method to increase recall of facts involves having the student read a selection orally for a specified amount of time and then write down or recite as

many facts as he can remember. The number of correct and incorrect responses can be charted to indicate progress.

19. Read half of a story aloud and ask the student to predict how the story will end. Also, the student can read chapter headings of a book, or look at pictures from a story, and the teacher can ask him to tell or write what he thinks the story will concern.

20. Present the student with a short story in which the sentences are presented in the wrong order. Ask the student to rewrite the selection, arranging the sentences in logical order so that the story makes sense. Another sequencing activity is to give the student a list of events from a story he has read and ask him to number the events to indicate the order in which they happened. Also, the student can arrange pictures that tell stories or show action in sequence and then write a sentence or paragraph for each picture.

21. To develop comprehension skills involving inference, ask the student several cause-and-effect questions (for example, "What will happen if. . . ?"). Read part of a story aloud and stop at a crucial point to let the student predict what will happen next. Also, the student may be asked to judge the reading selection as being true or fantasylike.

22. To develop study skills, use the daily newspaper to present comprehension activities. The student can practice locating the main idea and supporting ideas by using the editorial page. Then he can discuss the pros and cons of the viewpoint presented. He also may be asked to study the employment ads to answer various questions concerning available jobs. Grocery store ads give the student an opportunity to read for comparison shopping, and from articles in the sports section he may be required to locate answers concerning (a) to whom it happened, (b) what happened, (c) when it happened, (d) where it happened, and (e) why it happened. Highway maps, available at local service stations, are excellent for practice in the important skill of map reading.

23. Instruct the student to use cognitive strategies for reading comprehension. Chapter 14 includes the following strategies: RIDER (a visual imagery strategy), RAP (a paraphrasing strategy), and FIST (a self-questioning strategy).

INSTRUCTIONAL GAMES IN READING

Vowel Spinner

Materials: A spinner made from a cardboard circle that is divided into five equal segments, with a vowel written in each section; two or more laminated cardboard cards containing three-, four-, or five-letter words with the vowels deleted; grease pencil.

Directions: The first student spins the spinner, and he must try to use the vowel the spinner stops on to complete a word on his card. The student uses the grease pencil to write the vowel in the selected place, and the word must make sense. If the player cannot use the vowel, he loses that turn. Next, the second student spins and attempts to use his vowel. The players continue to take turns, and the winner is the first student to fill the card by completing every word with an appropriate vowel.

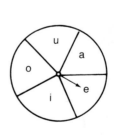
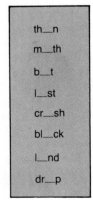

Blend Game

Materials: A start-to-finish game board; cards with pictures showing words containing initial blends; spinner with numbered segments; markers; answer key that gives the correct initial blend for each picture.

Directions: The first player draws the top card from the card deck. He identifies the picture (for example, flower) and tells the initial blend (*fl*). Another student can check the response by referring to the answer key. If the player is correct, he spins the spinner and moves his game-board marker the number of spaces shown on the spinner. The players take turns; when an incorrect response is made or the player cannot identify the blend, he loses that turn and does not spin the spinner or move his marker. The first player to reach the finish space on the game board wins the game.

Modifications: Use picture cards that illustrate words containing digraphs, diphthongs, medial vowels, or initial consonants. Also, to boost interest the game board can have various instructions on certain spaces—for example, *Go back one space, Spin again, Lose one turn.*

Word Blender

Materials: Cards of words containing initial blends, with each card cut in half to show the blend on one half and the remainder of the word on the other half.

Directions: The deck of blend cards and the deck of word cards both are shuffled and placed face down. The first player turns over the top cards from each deck. If the blend fits the letters on the word card, the player places the cards together and says the word. If he is correct, he keeps the cards. If he is incorrect, or if the blend and letters do not form a word, the cards are placed in their respective discard piles. The players take turns trying to form words. When the decks are finished, the discard piles are shuffled and used. When all the cards have been used (or at the end of a predetermined time period), the players count their cards, and the player with the most matches wins.

Modifications: The cards can present words and be cut so that the players have to form words with appropriate prefixes, suffixes, or various endings.

Phonics Rummy

Materials: Phonics card sets: Each set consists of four cards with the phonics element written at the top and four words listed under it containing that phonics element—a different word is underlined on each of the four cards in the set (36 cards are ample

for two players; additional card sets can be added for more players).

Directions: Eight cards are dealt face down to each player, and the remaining cards are placed face down in a stack in the middle of the players. The first player asks another player for a word using a certain phonics element to try to obtain three or four cards in a set. For example: "Mike, give me 'bat' from the *a* group"—the player pronounces the short *a* sound. If the asked player has the card, he must give it to the caller. The caller continues to ask for cards from specific players. If the person asked for a card does not have it, the caller takes the top card from the center pile. The players take turns, and when a player has three cards from a certain phonics element set, he lays them down. When the fourth card to a set that has already been laid down is drawn, it also may be put down. The winner is the player who gets rid of all the cards in his hand and in doing so "goes out."

Modifications: Instead of phonics elements the card sets can contain four synonyms (or four antonyms) for a specific word.

Fish

Materials: A deck of word cards with three cards for each word (the word should be written in the top-right-hand corner and upside down in the lower-left-hand corner of the card; a picture illustrating the word can be placed in the middle).

Directions: Nine cards are dealt to each player, and the remaining cards are placed face down in the middle of the players. The first player asks another player for a match for a word in his hand. If the asked player has the word card, he must give it to the caller. If he has two cards of that word set, he must give them both to the caller. The caller continues to ask for cards until the person does not have the card asked for and he says, "Go Fish."

When told to "Go Fish," the player takes the top card from the pile. If it happens to be the word card he just asked for, his turn continues. The players take turns, and when a player completes a set (three cards with the same word), he lays it down in front of him. The first player out of cards is the winner.

Word Bingo

Materials: Bingo cards (five squares across and five squares down) with a sight word written in each square; word list of the words included on all the cards; discs to use as markers.

Directions: Each student is given a bingo card and several discs. The teacher (or caller) reads a word from the word list and checks it off. The players look for the called word on their bingo cards, and if a player has it, he covers it with a disc. The teacher continues to call out words one at a time, and the first player to cover five spaces in any direction calls out "Bingo." After the player calls out "Bingo," he also must pronounce each of the covered words to win.

Modifications: Bingo cards and word lists can be derived from various categories, such as words with prefixes, words with suffixes, compound words, or words containing blends.

Word War

Materials: The cards are shuffled, and all are dealt to the players. All players simultaneously turn over one card at a time from their stacks. When two (or more) identical cards are turned up, the first player to name the word correctly takes the turned-up stacks of cards from the players who were involved in the "war." The winner is the player who gets all the cards or the most cards within a specified period of time.

Dominoes

Materials: Word cards divided in half by a line, with a different word on each side of the line (the words are repeated several times on different cards).

Directions: The cards are all dealt out to the players. The first player places a word card in the middle, and the next player must match words to play a card. The player must pronounce the word as he matches it. A design is formed by placing the matching card next to the word in any direction. If a player cannot match a word, he loses that turn. The first player to use all his cards is the winner.

Modifications: Various sets of word cards can be devised, such as words containing blends, digraphs, or diphthongs; compound words; contractions; or words with prefixes or suffixes.

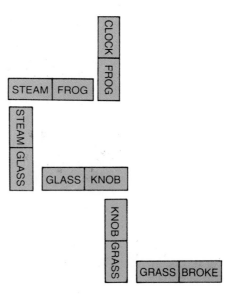

Word Game Board

Materials: Start-to-finish laminated game board with words or phrases written in the squares—some special squares contain instructions such as *Move back three squares, Take an extra turn,* or *Go back to start;* dice; markers.

Directions: The first player rolls the dice and moves his marker the number of spaces indicated on the dice. The player must pronounce correctly the word or phrase written on the square he reaches. If the player is unable to pronounce the word or phrase correctly, he moves his marker back to where he was before the roll. When the player lands on a special square, he must follow the directions on that square. The players take turns, and the first player to reach the finish square is the winner.

Modifications: The board is laminated or covered with clear plastic so that words can be written with a grease pencil and changed as needed. Also, chance dice can be used that have one number covered with a sticker. When one sticker is rolled, the player loses his turn, and when two stickers are rolled (one on each die), the player goes back to the beginning square.

Word Baseball

Materials: Vocabulary words written on flash cards; answer key.

Directions: The teacher divides the class into two teams and marks first base, second base, third base, and home plate on the floor. A member of the first team goes to home plate, and the designated pitcher on the opposing team holds up a word from his set of flash cards. The batter must pronounce the word correctly, define it, and use it in a sentence. If he is correct (as judged by a scorekeeper with an answer key), he advances to first base. Other members of the team bat, and for each "hit" (correct response) the player advances one base. Runs are scored by crossing home plate; an out occurs when a batter misses a word or its definition. Each team gets three outs, and then the opposing team comes to bat. The team with the highest score, after both teams have batted at least three times, is the winner.

Modifications: The word cards can be labeled *single, double, triple,* or *home run* to indicate the value of the hit. Also, the word cards can be divided according to words with one, two, three, or four or more syllables. The number of syllables indicates the number of bases a correct response is worth. However, in addition to reading the word, the student must state the number of syllables in that word correctly, or he is out. In addition, the pitcher may be allowed to select his pitches (word cards) depending on who the batter is; however, once a word card has been used, it is out of the game for that team.

Chance Dice Reading Game

Materials: Two chance dice, each of which have numbers on five sides and a sticker covering the number on the sixth size; worksheets with equal items that are appropriate for each player (for example, a list of vocabulary words to match with pictures or definitions, comprehension questions pertaining to a short reading passage, antonyms or synonyms to be matched); an answer key for each worksheet.

Directions: Each player is given an appropriate worksheet for his reading level. The first player rolls both of the chance dice. If no stickers are rolled, the player answers an item on his worksheet, and his answer is checked by a student with the answer key. If the answer is correct, the item number is checked; however, if the answer is incorrect, the item number is not checked and the player must attempt that item on another turn. If the player rolls one sticker on the chance dice, he loses his turn. If two stickers are rolled (one on each die), the player is allowed to attempt to answer two items on his worksheet. This procedure is continued until one player correctly answers all the items on his worksheet and wins the game.

Mystery Detective Game

Materials, Directions, Modifications, and Example: This game, designed to practice reading comprehension of phrases (who, where, why, how, what, when), uses a game-board format and is described in detail in Chapter 4. It features a self-correcting format and can be modified to offer practice in syllabication.

Comprehension Game

Materials: Start-to-finish game board with each square colored red, blue, or white; several copies of a story; a set of red cards (made from construction paper) containing comprehension questions (who, what, when, why, where, or how questions) about the story's content; a set of blue cards containing vocabulary words from the story; a set of white cards that are synonym cards and give a sentence with one word underlined; markers; spinner.

Directions: Each player reads a copy of the given story. To begin the game, the first player takes the top card from one of the card sets. If he takes a red card, the player must answer the comprehension question correctly. If the player takes a blue card, he must define the vocabulary word correctly. If he takes a white card, the player must give a synonym for the word underlined on the card. If the player responds to the card correctly, he spins the spinner and moves his marker the number of spaces it shows. On his next turn, he must take the top card from the card set that is the same color as the space holding his marker. If the player is unable to respond to his card correctly, he does not spin the spinner or move his marker and must try another card of the same color on his next turn. The other players must decide if each task is answered correctly; they may refer to the story to be sure. The first player to reach the finish square wins the game.

SELF-CORRECTING READING MATERIALS

Heart Puzzles

Feedback Device: The two pieces of the heart fit together to indicate a correct choice.

Materials: Sets of heart puzzle pieces: one part of the heart contains a picture, a second part fits together with the picture piece and has the word illustrated by the picture written on it, and two additional heart pieces do not fit together with the picture piece but contain words with minimal letter differences from the word that identifies the picture.

Directions: The student looks at the picture and selects the word illustrated by the picture. He fits the two pieces of the heart together to check his choice—only the correct word will fit with the picture.

Modifications: The puzzle pieces can contain various tasks, such as matching the word with the correct definition, matching the correct blend with the picture, or matching the correct number of syllables with the word.

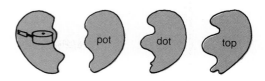

Flip Siders

Feedback Device: A picture clue to identify the word on the front of the card provides feedback.

Materials: Index cards with a word printed on the front and a picture illustrating that word pasted on the back.

Directions: The student looks at the word and reads it. Then he flips over the card to check himself by looking at the picture illustrating the word.

Modifications: For phonics review, have the student look at the pictures and put all the pictures with the same beginning sound in a pile (for example, *cat, cake, can, crack*). Then the student turns over each card to see the printed word and the initial letter. Another variation is to have words written on the front of each card and the number of syllables, or the word divided into syllables, written on the back. The student reads the word, counts the number of syllables, and flips over the card to check his response. Also, for practice in vocabulary development, sets of cards can show a word on one card and its definition on another card. The backs of both cards in the set should have matching objects, numbers, or colors or should go together to complete a picture. When the student pairs a word with its definition, he flips over the cards to see if the reverse sides go together.

Punch-Through Cards

Feedback Device: On the reverse side of the card the hole that indicates the correct answer is circled in a color.

Materials: Index cards containing pictures, with the word illustrated by each picture written underneath omitting the initial or final consonant or blend, and with three possible answers listed next to three holes—the hole next to the correct answer is circled in a color on the back; pencil (or golf tee).

Directions: The student looks at the picture and determines what letter or letters are omitted in the word. He punches his pencil through the hole to indicate his response. Then he turns over the card. If his answer is correct, his pencil is in the hole circled in a color.

Modifications: Vocabulary words with three possible definitions can be presented on the cards, or the student can be required to select the appropriate synonym or antonym for a word. Also, a brief reading selection can be presented with a comprehension question and three possible answers. Commercial sets of Punch-Thru Cards that focus on initial consonants, short vowels, long vowels, final consonants, and consonant blends are produced by Trend Enterprises.

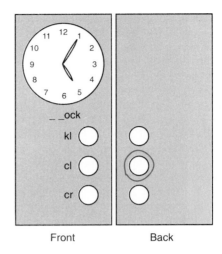

Front   Back

Clothespin Wheel

Feedback Device: The symbol or number on the back of the clothespin matches the symbol or number on the back of the correct section of the wheel.

Materials: A 10-inch cardboard circle divided into eight sections which have definitions written in them, and a symbol or number on the back of the circle in each section; clothespins with words corresponding to the definitions written on the front and a symbol or number written on the back.

Directions: The student reads the definition and looks at the words on the clothespins to find the correct answer. He clips the clothespin containing his answer to the section of the wheel with the definition and then turns over the circle. If his response is correct, the symbols or numbers on the backs of the circle section and the clothespin match.

Modifications: The student can be required to match synonyms, antonyms, or contractions with the appropriate section of the circle. Another variation is to have a word written in each section on the front with a corresponding picture in each section on the back. The student reads the word, clips a clothespin to the section, and turns over the circle to check his response by looking at the picture.

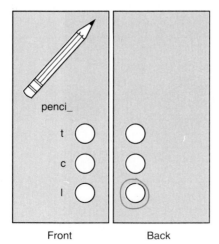

Front   Back

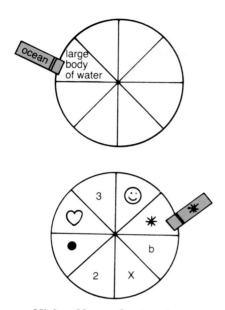

Mickey Mouse Contractions

Feedback Device: A flap is raised to reveal the correct response.

Materials: A laminated cardboard figure of Mickey Mouse's head with holes cut for the eyes and nose; a flexible flap of thick black felt material held in place over the nose opening with two fasteners; a long piece of cardboard with the two words to be made into a contraction written so that they will show in the eye openings, and the correct answer (the contraction form) positioned in the middle column so that it will appear in the nose opening; three strips of cardboard taped on the back of Mickey Mouse's head to hold the large task card of contractions in place and allow it to slide through to present each contraction task; a piece of paper.

Directions: The student places the large task card through the strips on the back of Mickey Mouse's head so that the first two words to be made into a contraction appear in Mickey's eyes. The student writes down the contraction form of these two words on a piece of paper and then lifts the flap over the nose to reveal the answer and check his response. Then he continues by sliding the card up to present the next two words.

Modification: This task also can be presented in the Answer Box format, described in detail in Chapter 4.

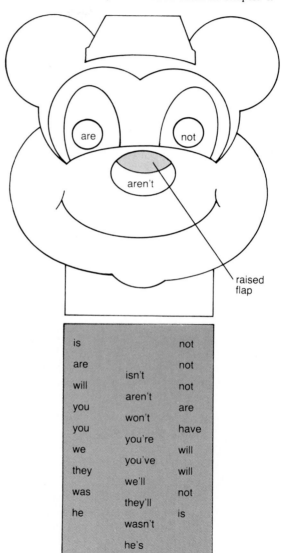

Poke Box

Feedback Device: A stylus is inserted in the hole in the Poke Box to indicate the student's response. If the answer is correct, the task card can be removed from the box because the area below the correct answer is cut out and offers no resistance to the stylus.

Materials, Directions, Modifications, and Example: The Poke Box is described in detail in Chapter 4 and can be used to present various reading tasks, including synonyms, antonyms, vocabulary definitions, or comprehension questions for a selected reading passage.

Synonym Lotto

Feedback Device: The correct answer is written on the back of each word card.

Materials: A large cardboard square, 6 squares across and 6 squares down, with a word written in each of the 36 squares; word cards containing synonyms for the words included on the large board and the correct responses written on the back (see Figure 11.2).

Directions: The student selects a word card and matches it with its synonym on the large board. After he makes his choice, he turns over the word card to see if he is correct. He continues until the entire board is covered.

Modifications: The student can be required to match antonyms with words, words with pictures, contractions with contracted words, or words with definitions.

Tape Recorder Reading

Feedback Device: The correct answers are provided on the tape.

Materials: A tape recording of 25 words numbered on the tape and separated by a pause between each word, and at the end of the tape a list of the correct responses; paper numbered from 1 to 25.

Directions: The student listens to the tape recording and writes the sound he hears at the beginning (or end) of each word. At the end of the 25 words he continues to listen to the tape to hear the correct answers and check his responses.

Modifications: The student can be instructed to write down vowel sounds, blends (in initial or final positions), or digraphs. Another variation of using

the tape recorder is to present a short reading passage on the tape. After the student listens to the selection, he is instructed to turn off the recorder and write down the main ideas. Then he can turn the recorder back on to check his work by listening to the reader's summary of the main ideas on tape. Also, after listening to a reading selection on tape, the student can be presented with various comprehension questions, and the answers can be provided on tape. Another device that can be used to provide oral feedback is the Language Master. The student can read the word printed on the Language Master card and then run the card through the machine to hear the word read for him.

Comic Strips

Feedback Device: The numbers to indicate correct sequence are written on the back of each section.

Materials: Laminated newspaper comic strips mounted on cardboard and cut into frames, with each frame numbered on the back to indicate its proper position in the sequence.

Directions: The student is given the mixed-up frames of a comic strip. He reads the frames and then unscrambles them and arranges them in order. This develops and improves the student's ability to recognize and follow a sequence of happenings and his ability to anticipate the outcome of a situation. After arranging the frames in order, the student turns over the frames to see if they are numbered in order, thus indicating the correct sequence.

Packaged Comprehension

Feedback Device: The correct answers are provided on an answer key included in an envelope attached to the back of the folder.

Materials: Manila folder with a label or wrapper (such as a food can label or a candy bar wrapper) attached to the front and comprehension questions concerning the label or wrapper written inside the folder (*What company makes the product? What does the product weigh?*); an answer key in an envelope attached to the back of the folder.

Directions: The student reads the label or wrapper on the front of the folder and then opens the folder to read the comprehension questions. He answers

LITTLE	ENDED	SMILED	CENT	WOMAN	TRAIL
GLAD	PRESENT	CRY	REPLY	PRETTY	SCARED
MAD	LARGE	BAG	CORRECT	DISTANT	FAST
NEARLY	GRANDMA	CHIEF	STONE	SPEAK	BEACH
HARD	BEGAN	FLAT	TRIP	SHOUT	ODD
WOODS	HURRY	WEARY	NEAR	HUNGRY	AUTO

Cards containing the following words with the appropriate synonym from the large square written on the back:

small	finished	grinned	penny	lady	path
happy	gift	weep	answer	beautiful	afraid
angry	big	pouch	right	faraway	quick
almost	Grandmother	leader	rock	talk	shore
difficult	started	level	journey	yell	strange
forest	rush	tired	close	starved	car

FIGURE 11.2
Game board and cards for synonym lotto.

each question on a sheet of paper without rereading the label or wrapper and then checks his responses with the answers included in the answer key.

Modification: A brief reading selection or short story can be attached to the front of the folder instead of a label or wrapper. Comprehension questions concerning the reading passage are included inside the folder.

COMMERCIAL READING PROGRAMS AND MATERIALS

Many commercial reading programs and materials are available for use with students who have learning problems. These materials can supplement one of the basic reading approaches to develop or improve specific skills, such as word attack or comprehension. This section presents several well-known commercial reading materials.

Dolch Reading Materials

Publisher: DLM

Description: Popper Words, Sets 1 and 2, consist of the 220 Dolch basic sight words. These words constitute 65 to 75 percent of primary reading materials and 50 to 75 percent of elementary reading materials. These commonly used words must be recognized instantly by sight so that the student can read with interest and confidence. The *Group Word Teaching Game* contains nine sets of six word cards and is played like bingo to help students in the second grade and above learn to recognize the 220 basic sight words. The *Picture Word Cards* present the Dolch 95 most common nouns, with each word written beside its picture. The *Sight Phrase Cards* consist of 140 two- and three-word phrases derived from the basic sign words and the 95 most common nouns. The cards are appropriate for use with students reading at the second-grade level. The student can use the phrase cards alone to improve phrase recognition, or several students can play a game to build sentences from phrases. *First Reading Books* include 12 paperback readers at the first-grade reading level that contain the easier half of the 220 basic sight words as well as the 95 most common nouns. The eight *Basic Vocabulary Books* at the second-grade reading level are written almost entirely with the Dolch basic sight words and most common nouns. The six *Folklore of the World Books* are written at the third-grade reading level and include tales and legends concerning the customs and beliefs of people in faraway regions of the world. The six *Pleasure Readers* contain classic stories written at the third- to fourth-grade reading level.

Essential Sight Words Program

Publisher: DLM

Description: The *Essential Sight Words Program* (Sundbye, Dyck, & Wyatt, 1980) is a teacher-directed program that is divided into two levels, each focusing on the identification of 100 frequently used words. A structured approach combines sight-word drill and the actual reading of sight words in context. The program focuses on the interests of students in first through fourth grade and is appropriate for low-achieving readers and students with reading disabilities.

Learning Strategies Curriculum

Publisher: University of Kansas Institute for Research in Learning Disabilities

Description: The Learning Strategies Curriculum of the University of Kansas Institute for Research in Learning Disabilities is designed to improve a student's ability to cope with specific curriculum demands and to perform tasks independently. The learning strategies in the acquisition instructional strand enable students to gain information from written material. The *Word Identification Strategy* (Lenz, Schumaker, Deshler, & Beals, 1984) is aimed at quick decoding of multisyllabic words. The strategy teaches students a problem-solving procedure for quickly attacking and decoding unknown words in reading materials. The *Paraphrasing Strategy* (Schumaker, Denton, & Deshler, 1984) is designed to improve comprehension by focusing attention on the important information of a passage. It directs students to read a limited section of material, ask themselves the main idea and the details of the section, and put that information in their own words. Additional acquisition learning strategies are being developed. The *Visual Imagery Strategy* improves reading comprehension by having students form mental pictures of the events described in a passage. In the *Self-Questioning Strategy* students form questions about key pieces of information in a passage and then read to find answers to these questions. The *Interpreting Visuals Strategy* increases the ability to obtain information from visuals such as pictures, diagrams, charts, tables, and maps. Finally, *Multipass* is a strategy for attacking textbook chapters that involves making three passes over the chapter to survey it, obtain key information from it, and study the key information.

Learning Through Literature

Publisher: Science Research Associates

Description: Learning Through Literature (Dodds & Goodfellow, 1990/1991) includes 12 resource packages for teaching literature stories and poetry (kindergarten through third grade) and complete novels (third through eighth grade). Learning activities include brainstorming, exploring story grammar, word banks, process writing activities, research, and integrative curriculum activities. The four story-study packages each contain two 20-lesson thematic units in which discussion and ongoing activities develop understanding of story grammars. The eight novel-study packages each contain a single 15- to 20-lesson unit for concentrated study of one specific novel, and students participate in vocabulary exercises, discussion of background pertinent to the story, guided questioning and comprehension exercises, and story extension activities. Teacher materials include detailed lesson guides and blackline masters that provide background information, vocabulary, writing and research stimuli, and bibliographies.

Phonic Remedial Reading Lessons

Publisher: Academic Therapy

Description: Phonic Remedial Reading Lessons (Kirk et al., 1985) is a program designed to teach phonetic reading and word-attack skills to students who are reading below the third-grade level and need remedial assistance. The 77 lessons are divided into six parts and consist of words with a consistent phonic pattern. Part I introduces the most frequent sounds, including sounds of short vowels and consonants. Part II consists of two- and three-letter sequences that have a single sound. Part III includes integration of known symbols into consonant blends and common syllables. Part IV presents new configurations of sound-symbol associations. Part V provides exercises that cover exceptions to sounds previously taught. Part VI covers grammar concepts such as plurals, possessives, and past tense. The lessons emphasize learning the sounds of letters and blending letters together, and students are instructed to visualize, write, say, and hear the sounds simultaneously as each phoneme is introduced.

Programmed Reading

Publisher: McGraw-Hill

Description: In *Programmed Reading,* programmed workbooks and textbooks are used to teach reading skills from readiness to seventh-grade level. A linguistic approach is used to strengthen decoding skills and word recognition. The material follows a single pattern, regardless of the response of the student. In workbook exercises the student must circle the correct word or write a letter or letters. The student is allowed to proceed at his own pace and receives immediate feedback; however, the materials rely heavily on visual discrimination, and much emphasis is placed on word parts or individual letters. Placement tests and criterion-referenced achievement tests are included.

Reading for Understanding

Publisher: Science Research Associates

Description: In *Reading for Understanding,* individualized multilevel comprehension-building kits help develop critical thinking, inferential logic, and ability to draw sound conclusions. The exercises, which focus on inferential comprehension, are of the idea-completion type, in which the student reads a selection and then chooses a logically appropriate ending from four suggested conclusions. Level 1 is designed for students in first through third grade, Level 2 is for students in third through seventh grade, and Level 3 is for students in seventh through twelfth grade.

Reading Skill Builders

Publisher: Reader's Digest Services

Description: Reading Skill Builders is a series of books, from first- to sixth-grade reading level, that uses a magazine format with short reading selections. The interesting stories and articles are illustrated and are accompanied by comprehension, vocabulary, and discussion questions. *Advanced Reading Skill Builders* are designed for students in seventh through ninth grade, and emphasis is on critical thinking skills, study skills, and literary skills as well as comprehension. Four readers are provided for each grade (one through nine), and there are four taped lessons on two cassettes correlated to each reader. The material appeals to all ages and can be used for directed or supplementary reading to develop comprehension skills.

Specific Skill Series

Publisher: Barnell Loft (available from Science Research Associates)

Description: The *Specific Skill Series* (Boning, 1990) includes exercise booklets designed to provide practice in reading comprehension skills for students reading at the prefirst- through eighth-grade level. The series includes nine separate skill strands: identifying inferences, getting the facts, using the context, drawing conclusions, getting the main idea, working within words, detecting the sequence, following directions, and locating the answer. The skill strands feature integrated language activities and emphasize critical reading and thinking skills. Students are allowed to work at their own pace, and the strands continue upward in sequential levels. Placement tests in each of the nine areas of reading comprehension are available in book format or computer software.

SRA Reading Laboratories

Publisher: Science Research Associates

Description: The *SRA Reading Laboratories* is a developmental reading program with kits available for students in first grade through secondary school. Comprehension, vocabulary, and word-attack skills are covered, as well as aspects of reading such as study skills and reading rate improvement. The materials are color-coded and can be used as a supplement to provide individualized reading instruction.

Sullivan Reading Program

Publisher: Behavioral Research Laboratories

Description: The *Sullivan Reading Program* is a programmed series available in five ability levels. Each level includes four programmed textbooks and related readers. The readers provide practice in using the vocabulary the student has learned in the corresponding programmed text. Pictures are used to enhance motivation and provide clues to meaning. Placement tests are included, and the student proceeds at his own pace. He responds to tasks within the textbook and receives immediate feedback by self-checking each response. At the completion of each programmed textbook, the student takes a progress test.

TR Reading Comprehension Series

Publisher: DLM

Description: The *TR Reading Comprehension Series* features a structured framework for teaching comprehension skills to remedial students in third through seventh grade who are reading two to three grades below level. The program consists of eight worktexts (readability level—low first grade to high fourth grade) that can be used with phonics/decoding programs and with graded readers. Each worktext contains 42 lessons that focus on the following areas of skill development: vocabulary, genres, topic and main idea, details, sequence, spatial relationships, contrast and comparison, cause and effect, critical and interpretive thinking, and study skills.

Victory!

Publisher: LinguiSystems

Description: Victory! (Brigance, 1991) combines skill-based reading and whole language activities in a newspaper format for at-risk pre-adolescents through adults (third- through six-grade reading level). The literacy cued, newspaper-styled stories include current topics with an interest level of fourth-grade through adult, and the vocabulary is controlled for readability. For each grade level, there are two semester workbooks, each of 35 student lessons and progress charts, that develop reading skills through critical thinking and word analysis practice. Students participate in written, verbal, and interactive activities, are shown patterns for word analysis, and learn about life through reading.

The Writing Road to Reading

Publisher: William Morrow

Description: The Writing Road to Reading (Spalding & Spalding, 1986) is a structured phonics system designed for group use. In this method, 70 phonograms representing 45 basic sounds are presented. Only phonetic sounds are used, and the letters are not referred to by name. Much drill is provided in which the teacher pronounces the phonogram and the students say its sound and then write its letter symbol in lowercase manuscript form. After phonograms have been mastered, words are taught and are presented in groups that correspond to phonetic rules. Forms of words that do not follow phonetic rules are taught as sight words. As the students master the rules, they are introduced to a primer.

COMPUTER SOFTWARE PROGRAMS IN READING

Microcomputer programs can be used effectively to develop basic skills in reading by providing varied drill and extra practice. Word identification skills as well as comprehension skills can be reinforced. Numerous software programs are available to reinforce sight words, expand vocabularies, provide drill in phonics, analyze words according to structural analysis, and test comprehension. Also, the teacher can use a microcomputer to develop language experience lessons, store individual reading vocabulary tests, and produce cloze tests. In addition, a microcomputer scoring program is available to help compute scores for the *Woodcock Reading Mastery Tests—Revised.* Torgesen (1986) notes that computer-assisted instruction in reading can be most practical as a supplemental practice activity (particularly in the area of decoding skills) rather than as tutorial or introductory instruction. The following programs provide examples of available software that focus on reading skills. Appendix B lists addresses of producers and distributors of educational computer software.

Cloze-Plus

Producer: Milliken

Hardware: Apple II

Description: This program develops reading comprehension skills and vocabulary through the use of structured cloze and context analysis activities. A factual reading selection with one word omitted is presented along with five possible word choices. The student reads the paragraph and types the letter of the best word choice. If desired, context clues in which pertinent information is underlined can be requested. After two wrong responses, the correct answer is displayed along with explanatory information. After a correct response, a positive reinforcement appears. Upon completion of a selection or session, the student receives a summary of performance. The cloze exercises focus on meaning completion, vocabulary in context, or syntax completion. They reinforce skills of interpretation and association, same or opposite meaning, identifying definition, making comparisons and contrasts, identifying time and order, using signal words and phrases, identifying pronoun antecedents, and noting similarities and differences. Six levels are available with vocabulary controlled from third- to eighth-grade level. The programs also can be used for remediation with older students.

Comprehension Power

Producer: Milliken

Hardware: Apple II

Description: This program is designed to build comprehension skills of students reading at the fourth- through twelfth-grade level. In addition to the nine individual levels, there are three programs for junior and senior high school students who are reading at extremely low levels. The programs consist of three activities: preparation (new vocabulary words used in context), preview (key sentences from the reading selection), and comprehension reading. Stories are presented on a wide range of high-interest topics including adventure, sports, contemporary issues, and career awareness. The reading selection is presented either one line at a time at a preassigned rate (from 50 to 650 words per minute) or page-by-page with the student advancing the page manually. After each segment, the student answers comprehension questions. Responses are followed by immediate feedback and positive reinforcement. The student may reread the segment, if needed, and also may adjust the reading rate. At the end of the session, the student receives an overall summary of performance. The programs provide practice and measurement of 25 commonly accepted reading comprehension skills in five main areas: literal understanding (for example, recalling information and details, identifying speaker), analysis (for example, recognizing cause and effect, identifying analogies), appreciation (for example, recognizing emotional reactions, identifying mood and tone), interpretation (for example, making inferences, predicting outcomes), and evaluation (for example, detecting author's purpose, judging validity). Thus, this software provides the opportunity to practice major comprehension skills and increase reading speed at the same time.

Diascriptive Reading I and II

Distributor: Educational Activities

Hardware: Apple II, TRS-80, Commodore 64

Description: Diascriptive Reading I includes diagnostic tests in five skill areas (main ideas, details, vocabulary, sequence, and inference) and 20 developmental reading lessons for first- through fifth-grade level. *Diascriptive Reading II* includes an additional test on fact/opinion (total of six tests) and 36 reading lessons for third- to eighth-grade level. Each self-directing lesson contains a short, informative selection which the student must read carefully to respond to questions that follow. The student receives immediate reward or instruction using advanced graphics animation for reinforcement. An automatic management system is included that remediates or advances the student through each skill area and records the student's progress on the disk.

DLM Reading Fluency Program

Producer: DLM

Hardware: Apple II

Description: The *DLM Reading Fluency Program* consists of four programs that build on one another to develop automatic decoding skills. *Hint and Hunt I* and *II* focus on vowels and vowel groups to teach basic decoding skills. The words and sounds contained in the programs are correlated to those introduced in basal reading series. The instructional phase, *Hint,* features a realistic voice stimulus and animated graphics. The practice phase, *Hunt,* is designed in a fast-action game format. *Construct-a-Word I* and *II* helps the student read words more quickly and accurately by upgrading his knowledge of consonants, consonant clusters, and phonograms. The words and sounds presented in the programs are the same as those introduced in basal reading series. The student creates words by selecting appropriate word beginnings and endings. *Syllasearch I, II, III,* and *IV* provide the student with intensive practice in seeing and hearing multisyllable words. Each level has three phases: (a) meet the words (pronunciation of each word in a given level), (b) yank the syllables (analyzing the whole words to find particular syllables), and (c) collect the words (synthesizing syllables to form words). Finally, *Word Wise I, II,* and *III* help the student build comprehension through the development of vocabulary. The student matches words to definitions, explanations, and examples on an electronic game board. All of the software in the *DLM Reading Fluency Program* requires the use of a speech output system (available from DLM) to provide actual human speech for instruction, feedback, and correction.

Micro-Read

Producer: American Educational Computer

Hardware: Apple II

Description: This program includes eight levels covering reading skills in first through eighth grade. The complete program includes the Supertalker circuit board, microphone, and speaker, which allow the student to hear instructions and the modeling of sounds and words in natural speech. In addition, there are story cards for the third- through eighth-grade level. The program provides practice in word analysis and vocabulary skills (for example, digraphs, silent letters, root words, prefixes and suffixes), comprehension skills (for example, cause and effect, pronoun referents, imagery, sequence), and study skills (for example, summarizing, skimming, taking notes).

Word Man; Word Radar

Producer: DLM

Hardware: Apple II, IBM, Commodore 64, Tandy 1000

Description: These two programs are included in the series *Arcademic Skill Builders in Language Arts* published by DLM. *Word Man* uses a game format that consists of a tricky maze of rectangular tracks with groups of letters placed along the rows. As a consonant moves past the letter combinations, the student must decide when a word is formed. Thus, the student practices basic phonetic patterns by forming words with the consonant-vowel-consonant-silent *e* patterns. Only words with one syllable and three to four letters are used. *Word Radar* provides practice in matching basic sight words by having the student role play a control tower operator who scans words that increase in length. In both programs, the speed and length of the game can be altered, as well as content and difficulty level.

REFERENCES

Adams, M. J. (1990). *Beginning to read: Thinking and learning about print.* Cambridge, MA: MIT Press.

Allen, R. V., & Allen, C. (1974). *Language experience in reading: Teacher's resource book.* Chicago: Encyclopaedia Britannica.

Allen, R. V., & Allen, C. (1982). *Language experience activities* (2nd ed.). Boston: Houghton Mifflin.

Altwerger, B., Edelsky, C., & Flores, B. M. (1987). Whole language: What's new? *The Reading Teacher, 41,* 144–154.

Archer, A. L., & Gleason, M. M. (1989). *Skills for school success.* North Billerica, MA: Curriculum Associates.

Bijou, S. W. (1977). *Edmark Reading Program.* Bellevue, WA: Edmark.

Bleismer, E. P., & Yarborough, B. H. (1965, June). A comparison of ten different beginning programs in first grade. *Phi Delta Kappan,* 500–504.

Bloomfield, L., & Barnhart, C. L. (1961). *Let's read—A linguistic approach.* Detroit, MI: Wayne State University Press.

Bond, G. L., & Dykstra, R. (1967). The cooperative research program in first-grade reading instruction. *Reading Research Quarterly, 2,* 5–142.

Boning, R. A. (1990). *Specific skill series* (4th ed.). Baldwin, NY: Barnell Loft.

Brigance, A. H. (1991). *Victory!* East Moline, IL: LinguiSystems.

Carbo, M. (1987). Matching reading styles: Correcting ineffective instruction. *Educational Leadership, 45*(2), 55–62.

Carnine, D., Silbert, J., & Kameenui, E. J. (1990). *Direct instruction reading* (2nd ed.). New York: Merrill/Macmillan.

Chall, J. S. (1983). *Learning to read: The great debate* (Updated edition). New York: McGraw-Hill.

Chall, J. S. (1987). Reading and early childhood education: The critical issues. *Principal, 66*(5), 6–9.

Chall, J. S. (1989). *Learning to Read: The Great Debate* 20 years later—A response to "Debunking the great phonics myth." *Phi Delta Kappan, 70,* 521–538.

Chiang, B., & Ford, M. (1990). Whole language alternatives for students with learning disabilities. *LD Forum, 16*(1), 31–34.

Clark, F. L., Deshler, D. D., Schumaker, J. B., Alley, G. R., & Warner, M. M. (1984). Visual imagery and self-questioning: Strategies to improve comprehension of written material. *Journal of Learning Disabilities, 17,* 145–149.

Clay, M. M. (1985). *The early detection of reading difficulties* (3rd ed.). Auckland, New Zealand: Heinemann Educational Books.

Cohen, S., & Plaskon, S. (1980). *Language arts for the mildly handicapped.* New York: Merrill/Macmillan.

Diederich, P. I., II. (1973). *Research 1960–70 on methods and materials in reading.* Princeton, NJ: Educational Testing Service.

Dodds, T., & Goodfellow, F. (1990/1991). *Learning through literature.* Chicago: Science Research Associates.

Downing, J. (1965). *The initial teaching alphabet reading experiment.* Chicago: Scott, Foresman.

Dykstra, R. (1968). Summary of the second-grade phase of the cooperative research program in primary reading instruction. *Reading Research Quarterly, 4*, 49–70.

Dykstra, R. (1974). Phonics and beginning reading instruction. In C. C. Walcutt, J. Lamport, & G. McCracken (Eds.), *Teaching reading: A phonic/linguistic approach to developmental reading.* New York: Macmillan.

Ekwall, E. E. (1989). *Locating and correcting reading difficulties* (6th ed.). New York: Merrill/Macmillan.

Engelmann, S., Becker, W., Hanner, S., & Johnson, G. (1988). *Corrective reading—decoding.* Chicago: Science Research Associates.

Engelmann, S., Becker, W., Hanner, S., & Johnson, G. (1989). *Corrective reading—comprehension.* Chicago: Science Research Associates.

Engelmann, S., & Bruner, E. C. (1988). *Reading mastery: DISTAR reading.* Chicago: Science Research Associates.

Faas, L. A. (1980). *Children with learning problems: A handbook for teachers.* Boston: Houghton Mifflin.

Fernald, G. (1943). *Remedial techniques in basic school subjects.* New York: McGraw-Hill.

Fernald, G. (1988). *Remedial techniques in basic school subjects.* Austin, TX: Pro-Ed.

Fries, C. C. (1963). *Linguistics and reading.* New York: Holt, Rinehart & Winston.

Fry, E. (1964). A diacritical marking system to aid beginning reading instruction. *Elementary English, 41*, 526–529.

Fry, E. (1977). Fry's readability graph: Clarifications, validity, and extension to level 17. *Journal of Reading, 21*, 242–252.

Gillingham, A., & Stillman, B. (1970). *Remedial teaching for children with specific disability in reading, spelling, and penmanship* (7th ed.). Cambridge, MA: Educators Publishing Service.

Goodman, K. S. (1986). *What's whole in whole language?* Portsmouth, NH: Heinemann.

Gurren, L., & Hughes, A. (1965). Intensive phonics vs. gradual phonics in beginning reading: A review. *Journal of Educational Research, 58*, 339–356.

Hall, M. (1981). *Teaching reading as a language experience* (3rd ed.). New York: Merrill/Macmillan.

Harris, A. J., & Sipay, E. R. (1990). *How to increase reading ability: A guide to developmental & remedial methods* (9th ed.). New York: Longman.

Heckelman, R. G. (1969). The neurological impress method of remedial reading instruction. *Academic Therapy, 4*, 277–282.

Heilman, A. W., Blair, T. R., & Rupley, W. H. (1990). *Principles and practices of teaching reading* (7th ed.). New York: Merrill/Macmillan.

Henk, W. A., Helfeldt, J. P., & Platt, J. M. (1986). Developing reading fluency in learning disabled students. *Teaching Exceptional Children, 18*, 202–206.

Heymsfeld, C. R. (1989). Filling the hole in whole language. *Educational Leadership, 46*(6), 65–68.

Idol, L. (1987). A critical thinking map to improve content area comprehension of poor readers. *Remedial and Special Education, 8*(4), 28–40.

Idol, L., & Croll, V. J. (1987). Story-mapping training as a means of improving reading comprehension. *Learning Disability Quarterly, 10*, 214–229.

Kaluger, G., & Kolson, C. J. (1978). *Reading and learning disabilities* (2nd ed.). New York: Merrill/Macmillan.

Kann, R. (1983). The method of repeated readings: Expanding the neurological impress method for use with disabled readers. *Journal of Learning Disabilities, 16*, 90–92.

Kirk, S. A., Kirk, W. D., & Minskoff, E. (1985). *Phonic remedial reading lessons.* Novato, CA: Academic Therapy Publications.

Kirk, S. A., Kliebhan, J. M., & Lerner, J. W. (1978). *Teaching reading to slow and disabled learners.* Boston: Houghton Mifflin.

Langford, K., Slade, K., & Barnett, A. (1974). An explanation of impress techniques in remedial reading. *Academic Therapy, 9*, 309–319.

Lee, D. M., & Allen, R. V. (1963). *Learning to read through experience* (2nd ed.). New York: Appleton-Century-Crofts.

Lenz, B. K., & Hughes, C. A. (1990). A word identification strategy for adolescents with learning disabilities. *Journal of Learning Disabilities, 33,* 149–158, 163.

Lenz, B. K., Schumaker, J. B., Deshler, D. D., & Beals, V. L. (1984). *Learning strategies curriculum: The word identification strategy.* Lawrence, KS: University of Kansas Institute for Research in Learning Disabilities.

Lorenz, L., & Vockell, E. (1979). Using the neurological impress method with learning disabled readers. *Journal of Learning Disabilities, 12,* 420–422.

Lovitt, T. C. (1984). *Tactics for teaching.* New York: Merrill/Macmillan.

Mastropieri, M. A. (1988). Using the keyword method. *Teaching Exceptional Children, 20*(2), 4–8.

Mastropieri, M. A., Scruggs, T. E., & Fulk, B. J. M. (1990). Teaching abstract vocabulary with the keyword method: Effects on recall and comprehension. *Journal of Learning Disabilities, 23,* 92–96, 107.

Mather, N. (1992). Whole language reading instruction for students with learning disabilities: Caught in the cross fire. *Learning Disabilities Research & Practice, 7,* 87–95.

Matthes, C. (1972). *How children are taught to read.* Lincoln, NE: Professional Educators Publications.

Norton, D. E. (1992). *The impact of literature-based reading.* New York: Merrill/Macmillan.

Orton, S. T. (1937). *Reading, writing, and speech problems in children.* New York: W. W. Norton.

O'Shea, L. J., & O'Shea, D. J. (1988). Using repeated reading. *Teaching Exceptional Children, 20*(2), 26–29.

O'Shea, L. J., Sindelar, P. T., & O'Shea, D. J. (1987). The effects of repeated readings and attentional cues on the reading fluency and comprehension of learning disabled readers. *Learning Disabilities Research, 2,* 103–109.

Otto, W., & Smith, R. J. (1980). *Corrective and remedial teaching* (3rd ed.). Boston: Houghton Mifflin.

Palinscar, A. S., & Brown, A. L. (1986). Interactive teaching to promote independent learning from text. *The Reading Teacher, 39*(8), 771–777.

Palinscar, A. S., & Brown, A. L. (1988). Teaching and practicing thinking skills to promote comprehension in the context of group problem solving. *Remedial and Special Education, 9*(1), 53–59.

Perfetti, C. (1985). *Reading ability.* New York: Oxford University Press.

Pinnell, G. S. (1990). Success for low achievers through *Reading Recovery. Educational Leadership, 48*(1), 17–21.

Robinson, F. P. (1961). *Effective study.* New York: Harper & Row.

Roe, B. D., Stoodt, B. D., & Burns, P. C. (1987). *Secondary school reading instruction: The content areas* (3rd ed.). Boston: Houghton Mifflin.

Rupley, W. H., & Blair, T. R. (1989). *Reading diagnosis and remediation* (3rd ed.). New York: Merrill/Macmillan.

Samuels, S. J. (1979). The method of repeated readings. *The Reading Teacher, 32,* 403–408.

Schumaker, J. B., Denton, P. H., & Deshler, D. D. (1984). *Learning strategies curriculum: The paraphrasing strategy.* Lawrence, KS: University of Kansas Institute for Research in Learning Disabilities.

Slingerland, B. (1981). *A multi-sensory approach to language arts for specific language disability children: A guide for elementary teachers.* Cambridge, MA: Educators Publishing Service.

Spache, G. D., & Spache, E. B. (1986). *Reading in the elementary school* (5th ed.). Boston: Allyn & Bacon.

Spalding, R. B., & Spalding, W. T. (1986). *The writing road to reading* (3rd rev. ed.). New York: William Morrow.

Stahl, S. A., & Miller, P. D. (1989). Whole language and language experience approaches for beginning reading: A quantitative research synthesis. *Review of Educational Research, 59,* 87–116.

Stallings, J. A. (1974). *Follow Through classroom observation evaluation 1972–1973* (Executive Summary SRI Project URU-7370). Menlo Park, CA: Stanford Research Institute.

Stauffer, R. G. (1981). Strategies for reading instruction. In M. P. Douglas (Ed.), *Reading: What is basic? 45th yearbook. Claremont reading conference.* Claremont, CA: Center for Developmental Studies.

Sundbye, N. W., Dyck, N. J., & Wyatt, F. R. (1980). *Essential Sight Words Program*. Allen, TX: DLM.

Torgesen, J. K. (1986). Using computers to help learning disabled children practice reading: A research-based perspective. *Learning Disabilities Focus, 1*, 72–81.

Traub, N., & Bloom, F. (1970). *Recipe for reading.* Cambridge, MA: Educators Publishing Service.

Wilson, R. G., & Rudolph, M. K. (1986). *Catch on—Merrill Linguistic Reading Program* (4th ed.). New York: Merrill/Macmillan.

CHAPTER 12

Assessing and Teaching
Spelling Skills

Spelling is the forming of words through the traditional arrangement of letters. Preschoolers developmentally move through stages of invented spelling in which different types of spelling strategies are used, such as semiphonetic spelling (*da* for *day*) and phonetic spelling (*pekt* for *peeked*) (Gentry, 1982). Generally, formal spelling instruction is introduced at the beginning of the second grade or at the end of the first grade. The ability to spell is essential because it allows one to read written words correctly. In addition, incorrect spelling often results in an unfavorable impression, and the poor speller may be considered uneducated or careless.

The English language presents inconsistent relationships between phonemes (speech sounds) and graphemes (written symbols). There are 26 letters in the alphabet; however, about 44 phonemes are used in English speech. Moreover, there are more than 500 spellings to present the 44 phonemes (Tompkins & Hoskisson, 1991). Thus, differences exist between the spelling of various words and the way the words are pronounced. Many students with learning problems have difficulty mastering the regular spelling system, and inconsistent spelling patterns make learning to spell even more complex.

Students who have trouble recognizing words in reading usually have poor spelling skills as well (Carpenter & Miller, 1982; Lerner, 1989). However, some students are able to read words but not spell them. Thus, it appears that spelling a word may be a more difficult task than reading a word. Reading is a *decoding* process in which the reader receives clues (such as context) for word recognition. Spelling is an *encoding* process in which the learner must respond without the benefit of a complete visual stimulus; thus there are fewer clues. Spelling requires concentration on each letter of every word, while in reading it is not necessary to know the exact spelling of words

or to attend to every letter. Ekwall (1989) notes that the same types of errors may be present in both reading and spelling. For example, a phonetic speller may mispronounce phonetically irregular words when reading. In addition, a student who lacks phonetic word-attack skills in reading may not be able to spell because of poor phonetic skills.

To spell, the student must be able to read the word, process knowledge and skill in certain relationships of phonics and structural analysis, apply phonics generalizations, visualize the word, and use the motor capability to write the word (Lerner, 1989). Spelling difficulties may stem from problems in visual memory, auditory memory, auditory and visual discriminations, or motor skills.

ASSESSMENT OF SPELLING SKILLS

A variety of techniques assess the student's spelling performance. Also, specific patterns of spelling errors may be pinpointed. Spelling assessment can be divided into three broad categories: standardized tests, criterion-referenced tests, and informal assessment techniques. In choosing spelling assessment techniques, the teacher should (a) know what the test measures and its limitations, (b) supplement the test where possible with other measures, and (c) use informal evaluation techniques to gain specific information for planning a remedial program.

Standardized Tests

Standardized spelling tests provide a wide range of information. Achievement tests that contain spelling subtests are designed to provide an estimate of the student's general spelling ability. They yield a single score that is compared with the standardized norms and converted to a grade-equivalent score. Thus, achievement tests provide a general survey measure, and they may be useful for identifying students who need corrective instruction and further diagnosis. In contrast, diagnostic tests provide detailed information about a student's performance in various spelling skills. These tests are aimed at determining the student's strengths and weaknesses. The achievement and diagnostic spelling tests presented next are used widely and represent the types of tests available.

Achievement Tests.   On achievement tests, spelling is assessed by two procedures: recall and recognition. On tests using recall, the student must write words presented orally and used in sentences. On tests using recognition, the student is required to select the correctly spelled word from several choices. Recall items are related to the writing stage of the writing process, whereas recognition items are essentially proofreading and are related to the postwriting stage (McLoughlin & Lewis, 1990).

The *Iowa Tests of Basic Skills* (Hieronymus, Hoover, & Lindquist, 1986) are designed for students in first through ninth grade and are group administered. The *Tests of Achievement and Proficiency* (Scannell, 1986) assess spelling of students in ninth through twelfth grade. In both tests, spelling is assessed as an area within the language subtest. The teacher reads a word, and the student must choose the correctly spelled word from four words. Grade-equivalent norms and grade percentile norms are given. Percentile grade norms are provided for testing done in the beginning, middle, or end of the school year.

The *Kaufman Test of Educational Achievement* (Kaufman & Kaufman, 1985) is an individually administered test for students in first through twelfth grade. The spelling subtest assesses the student's ability to spell 50 increasingly difficult words, each of which is said by the examiner and used in a sentence. Students who are unable to write are allowed to spell orally. A brief form of the test includes a 40-word spelling subtest. The test yields standard scores by age or grade for either the fall or spring, as well as percentile ranks, stanines, and age and grade equivalents.

The *Peabody Individual Achievement Test—Revised* (Markwardt, 1989) is individually administered and can be used with students in kindergarten through twelfth grade. The spelling subtest consists of 100 multiple-choice items. On initial items the student must distinguish a printed letter of the alphabet from pictured objects and associate letter symbols with speech sounds. On more difficult items the student is presented with four ways of spelling a word and must identify the correct spelling of the word after hearing the word pronounced by the examiner. Age equivalents, grade equivalents, percentile ranks, and standard scores are obtained.

The *SRA Achievement Series* (Naslund, Thorpe, & Lefever, 1985) is group administered and includes spelling assessment for students in second through twelfth grade. At the second-grade level, the student must identify which of four alternative spellings of a word is correct. At the third-grade level, words are given in context so that context cues may be used to help spell them. In the remaining levels, words are given in phrases only. The test yields grade equivalents, percentiles, and stanine scores.

The *Stanford Achievement Test* (Gardner, Rudman, Karlsen, & Merwin, 1982) assesses spelling of students in first through ninth grade. The *Test of Academic Skills* (Gardner, Callis, Merwin, & Rudman, 1983), an extension of the *SAT,* assesses spelling of students in eighth grade through community college. The student must detect misspellings of words that contain various types of errors. The test is group administered and yields stanines, grade-equivalent scores, percentiles, age scores, and standard scores.

The *Wide Range Achievement Test— Revised* (Jastak & Wilkinson, 1984) is an individually administered test for students age 5 to adult. The spelling subtest assesses a student's skill in copying marks on paper, writing her name, and writing single words from dictation. Grade equivalents, percentiles within grades, and standard scores are obtained.

Diagnostic Tests. The *Diagnostic Spelling Potential Test* (Arena, 1981) measures traditional spelling, word recognition, visual recognition, and auditory-visual recognition. The four subtests of 90 items assess students age 7 through adult and take 25 to 40 minutes. Raw scores from each subtest can be converted to standard scores, percentiles, and grade ratings.

The *Gates-Russell Spelling Diagnostic Test* (Gates & Russell, 1937) provides a variety of diagnostic information concerning spelling problems. The subtests measure nine areas: spelling words orally; word pronunciation; giving letters for letter sounds; spelling one syllable; spelling two syllables; word reversals; spelling attack; auditory discrimination; and effectiveness of visual, auditory, kinesthetic, or combined methods of study. A grade-level score is obtained for performance in each area.

The *Test of Written Spelling—2* (Larson & Hammill, 1986) can be administered individually or to small groups of students in first through twelfth grade in about 20 minutes. This dictated-word test consists of 100 words chosen from 10 basal spelling series. It assesses the student's ability to spell words that have readily predictable spellings in sound-letter patterns (for example, *bed, tardy*) as well as words whose spellings are less predictable (spelling demons such as *people* and *eight*). The test yields a spelling quotient and percentile rank. Thus, it provides the teacher with an index of overall spelling skill and indicates the types of words that are difficult for the student.

Criterion-Referenced Tests

Standardized norm-referenced tests (achievement and diagnostic) *compare* a student's performance with the scores of those in the norm population. Criterion-referenced tests *describe* performance in terms of fixed criteria. The teacher can use criterion-referenced spelling tests to determine if the student has mastered specific spelling instructional objectives (for example, *wh* spelling, contractions, or vocational words). The teacher determines what skills the student has learned and what skills still must be taught. Also, an objective measure of progress is provided as the student moves from task to task and current performance is compared with previous performance.

The *Brigance Diagnostic Comprehensive Inventory of Basic Skills* (Brigance, 1982) contains a section that assesses spelling skills of students whose achievement is in the kindergarten through ninth-grade level. The skill area is arranged in a developmental and sequential hierarchy. Tests include spelling dictation grade placement, initial consonants, initial clusters, suffixes, and prefixes. Also, the reference skills section contains a test on the skill of dictionary use. The instructional objectives related to each test are defined clearly. In addition to determining the student's level of achievement, the results can help the teacher develop individualized programs.

Kottmeyer's (1970) *Diagnostic Spelling Test* is a criterion-referenced test that measures specific phonics and structural spelling elements (for example, doubled final consonants, nonphonetic spellings, long and short *oo*). The examiner says a word and a sentence using the word, and the student is required to write the word. One test is for students in second and third grade; another test is for students in fourth grade and above. The 32-item tests are designed so that each item measures a particular spelling element. A grade score is computed from the total number of correct spellings. Specific information on skills not yet mastered is obtained through an analysis of the student's errors.

The Spellmaster Assessment and Teaching System (Greenbaum, 1987) is a series of non-standardized, criterion-referenced tests that includes eight diagnostic tests for measuring the spelling of phonetically regular words, eight irregular-words tests, eight homophone (homonym) tests, and entry-level tests. The tests pinpoint the precise strategies students use and the errors they make when spelling words.

Criterion-referenced tests mainly aid in specific instructional planning, rather than determining grade-level scores or percentile ranks. In the *Brigance Diagnostic Comprehensive Inventory of Basic Skills,* some tests were texts-referenced: the most commonly used texts were examined to determine a grade level at which a specific skill first is introduced. Thus, a grade-level score is obtained. In the future, criterion-referenced tests also may be norm-referenced. They then would be useful to both establishing instructional objectives and placing the student according to grade level.

Informal Assessment Techniques

According to McLoughlin and Lewis (1990), "Informal techniques provide information about the student's current level of performance, aid in the selection of instructional goals and objectives, point to the need for instructional modifications, document student progress, and suggest directions for further assessment" (p. 98). The spelling scope and sequence skills list presented in Appendix A can be used to devise informal assessment measures and to determine appropriate instructional objectives as the student progresses in spelling.

Teacher observation. The teacher can obtain diagnostic information through structured observation and evaluation of the student's attitudes, written work, and oral responses. Attitudes toward spelling and willingness to use a dictionary may be noted, as well as the student's work habits and ability to handle frustration. Analysis of written work can provide information about handwriting problems that are causing errors (such as letter formation or spacing), specific types of errors, range of the student's vocabulary, and knowledge of important spelling rules (Brueckner & Bond, 1966). In addition, the teacher should observe the student's oral responses and note problems in pronunciation, articulation, and dialect. Oral spelling responses also can indicate phonics ability and method of spelling words orally—for example, as units, by letter, by digraphs, or by syllables.

Dictated tests. The dictated spelling test is a commonly used procedure for assessing various skills in spelling and determining spelling grade level. Words can be selected from any graded word list; the student's performance indicates the spelling grade level. Stephens, Hartman, and Lucas (1982) present sample assessment tasks that use dictated word lists of increasing difficulty. The instructional level is determined when the student achieves 70 to 90 percent accuracy. Dictated word lists also can assess skills in areas such as phoneme-grapheme association (such as *like, bike, hike*), spelling generalizations (such as *stories, cries, tries*), homonyms (*pain, pane; pear, pair*), and functional words (*menu, restaurant, cashier*). The dictated test presented in Table 12.1 assesses selected spelling objectives for students in second and third grade. Through error analysis the teacher readily can determine areas of weakness.

The student's proficiency in spelling words frequently used and words that often are misspelled also can be determined. Horn (1926), after studying 10,000 words, reported that 10

TABLE 12.1
A dictated spelling test and objectives.

Spelling Words	Spelling Objectives	Spelling Words Used in Sentences
1. man		The *man* is big.
2. pit		The *pit* in the fruit was hard.
3. dug	short vowels and selected consonants	We *dug* a hole.
4. web		She saw the spider's *web*.
5. dot		Don't forget to *dot* the i.
6. mask	words beginning or ending with	On Halloween the child wore a *mask*.
7. drum	consonant blends	He beat the *drum* in the parade.
8. line	consonant-vowel-consonant-	Get in *line* for lunch.
9. cake	silent *e*	We had a birthday *cake*.
10. coat	two vowels together	Put on your winter *coat*.
11. rain		Take an umbrella in the *rain*.
12. ice	variant consonant sounds for	*Ice* is frozen water.
13. large	*c* and *g*	This is a *large* room.
14. mouth		Open your *mouth* to brush your teeth.
15. town	words containing vowel diphthongs	We went to *town* to shop.
16. boy		The *boy* and girl went to school.
17. bikes	plurals	The children got new *bikes* for their birthdays.
18. glasses		Get some *glasses* for the drinks.
19. happy	short *i* sounds of *y*	John is very *happy* now.
20. monkey		We saw a *monkey* at the zoo.

words accounted for 25 percent of all words used. In order of most frequent to least frequent, these words include: *I, the, and, to, a, you, of, in, we,* and *for.* He also noted that 100 words accounted for 65 percent of the words written by adults. In addition, Kuska, Webster, and Elford (1964) present a list of commonly misspelled words that are linguistically irregular and do not follow spelling rules—for example, *ache, fasten, nickel, scratch, double.*

Informal spelling inventory. An informal spelling inventory (ISI) can be used to determine the student's approximate grade level in spelling achievement. An ISI can be con-

structed by selecting a sample of words from spelling books in a basal spelling series (Mann, Suiter, & McClung, 1992). About 15 words should be chosen from the first-grade book and 20 words from each book for second through eighth grade. Random selection is obtained by dividing the total number of words at each level by 20. For example, 300 words at each level divided by 20 equals 15; therefore, every 15th word should be included in the ISI. For students in fourth grade and below, testing should begin with the first-level words. For students in fifth grade and above, assessment should start with words at the third level. The test is administered in a dictated-word format.

TABLE 12.1
Continued

Spelling Words	Spelling Objectives	Spelling Words Used in Sentences
21. war 22. dirt	words with *r*-controlled vowels	Bombs were used in the *war*. The pigs were in the *dirt*.
23. foot 24. moon	two sounds of *oo*	Put the shoe on your *foot*. Three men walked on the *moon*.
25. light 26. knife	words with silent letters	Turn on the *light* so we can see. Get a fork and *knife*.
27. pill	final consonant doubled	The doctor gave me a *pill*.

28. bat
29. batter
	consonant-vowel-consonant pattern
	    in which final consonant is doubled
	    before adding ending
		The baseball player got a new *bat*.
		The *batter* hit a home run.

30. didn't 31. isn't	contractions	They *didn't* want to come. It *isn't* raining today.
32. take 33. taking	final *e* dropped before adding suffix	Please *take* off your coat. He is *taking* me to the show.
34. any 35. could	nonphonetic spellings	I did not have *any* lunch. Maybe you *could* go on a trip.
36. ate 37. eight 38. blue 39. blew	homonyms	Mary *ate* breakfast at home. There are *eight* children in the family. The sky is *blue*. The wind *blew* away the hat.
40. baseball	compound words	They played *baseball* outside.

The teacher says the word, uses it in a sentence, and repeats the word. Some students prefer for only the word to be given (without a sentence), and M. R. Shinn, Tindal, and Stein (1988) suggest that a 7-second interval between words is sufficient. Testing ends when the student responds incorrectly to six consecutive words. The achievement level is the highest level at which the student responds correctly to 90 to 100 percent of the items, and the instructional level is the highest level at which the student scores 75 to 89 percent correct. Various errors made on the ISI can be analyzed to provide additional diagnostic information.

Curriculum-based measurement. In curriculum-based measurement of spelling skills, rate samples on words from a given spelling curriculum are used to measure the student's spelling skills. The assessment process begins with the selection of appropriate word lists. Tindal and Marston (1990) note that the word lists can reflect a phonic-regularity base (that is, words with consistency or generalizability of the grapheme/phoneme relationships) or a frequency base (that is, words that appear frequently in writing). Wesson (1987) suggests that the words can be from a given spelling curriculum level or from a new-words list for a particular reading series. The words can be selected randomly by printing all words in the test item pool on index cards, shuffling the cards before each measurement, and randomly picking ones to present during the measurement task.

The type of response to the spelling task can be either a selection response or a production response (Tindal & Marston, 1990). In word or sentence editing, an incorrectly spelled word is underlined or a blank space representing a specific word is presented in a phrase, and the student must select the correct word from several options to replace the underlined word or to fill in the blank. For example,

1. Her dress had a <u>stane</u> on it.
   a. staen   c. stan
   b. stain   d. stene

2. The wind _____ his hat away.
   a. bled   c. bliew
   b. blew   d. blued

When the teacher orally presents words from a list, the student must produce the spelling of the word during the dictation task. When a production response is required, scoring can be in terms of number of words spelled correctly or number of letters in correct sequence. The latter strategy focuses on successive pairs of letters, and the blank spaces preceding the first letter and following the last letter are included in counting the pairs of letter sequences. Thus, for a word spelled correctly, the number of correct letter sequences will be one more than there are letters for the word. For example,

1. Correct spelling: l a z y (5 correct letter sequences)
2. Misspelling: l a s y (3 correct and 2 incorrect letter sequences)

An individualized analysis of errors can be helpful in establishing appropriate instruction.

The teacher can test all students in a grade or class and develop a plot of the entire group (see Chapter 2 for guidelines for developing a box plot of a group). Table 12.2 presents curriculum-based measurement procedures for administering and scoring spelling word lists. Through this method, students who are performing poorly in spelling (that is, more than one standard deviation below the mean for the group) can be identified and instructional planning decisions can be made. Figure 12.1 presents a graph for evaluating spelling instruction according to a student's weekly performance.

Spelling error analysis. A *spelling error analysis* chart can be used to provide a profile of spelling strengths and weaknesses. Each time the student makes a specific error, it is recorded on the chart. Spelling errors can be analyzed in written compositions as well as on dictated tests. Taylor and Kidder (1988) examined the misspellings of first- through eighth-grade students and found that the most frequent spelling error was deleting letters in words (for example, *hoping* for *hopping; spose* for *suppose*). Selected spelling errors may include spelling the word as it sounds (*doter* for *daughter*), omitting a letter that is pronounced (*aross* for *across*), using the wrong vowel digraph (*speach* for *speech*), reversing letters in words (*croner* for *corner*), using an incorrect vowel (*jab* for *job; anemals* for *animals*), using the wrong homonym for the meaning intended (*peace* for *piece*), inserting an unneeded letter (*ulgly* for *ugly*), doubling a consonant when not needed (*untill* for *until*), and omitting a silent letter (*bome* for *bomb*) (Hitchcock, 1989). Moreover, Edgington (1967) suggests that the following specific types of errors should be noted on a spelling error analysis chart: addition of extra letters;

TABLE 12.2
Curriculum-based measurement procedures for administering and scoring spelling word lists.

Step 1: Randomly select 20 words from the goal-level spelling curriculum material.

Step 2.: Present each student with lined, numbered paper.

Step 3.: Provide directions and administer the spelling test by pronouncing each word on the list in isolation, in a sentence or phrase, and again in isolation. Dictate words at a pace of one every 10 seconds or sooner if all students finish. Do not acknowledge questions and ignore requests (such as "slow down"). Terminate testing after 2 minutes.

Step 4.: Score performance in terms of words and letter sequences correct.

Step 5.: Develop box plots of the entire group according to words spelled correctly and letters spelled correctly (see Chapter 2).

Step 6.: Analyze the individual protocols scored according to correct letter sequences. Place students in appropriate instructional groups.

Step 7.: Begin instruction based on student error patterns.

Step 8.: Introduce new words each week in accordance to the curriculum sequence. Vary the number of new words presented depending on the mastery of previous words. Graph the results of continuous assessment to evaluate instruction (see Figure 12.1). Because grouping is based on the rate of words learned, move students among groups as a function of their progress.

omission of needed letters; reversals of whole words, consonant order, or syllables; errors resulting from a student's misinterpretation or dialect; and phonetic spelling of nonphonetic words. Burns (1980) notes that most errors occur in vowels in midsyllables of words; 67 percent of the errors result from substitution or omission of letters, and 20 percent are in addition, insertion, or transposition of letters. Through a careful analysis of spelling errors, the teacher can focus on consistent patterns of errors and plan appropriate instruction.

Cloze procedure.   The cloze procedure is a visual means of testing spelling. The student may be required to complete a sentence by writing the correct response in the blank; for example, "The opposite of down is _____" (*up*). In addition, the student may be asked to complete a word or supply missing letters: "The clouds are in the s____" (*sky*), or "Please give me a glass of w__t__r" (*water*).

Cartwright (1969) notes that the cloze procedure is useful especially in evaluating the student's knowledge of spelling generalizations. In this case, the student is required to fill in blanks pertaining to a rule, such as doubling the final consonant before adding *ing*; for example, "The man was run _____ to catch the bus" (*ning*). A multiple-choice format also may be used; for example, "Mary needed _____ to pay for her lunch" (*munny, mony, money, monie*). The cloze procedure, which is visual, can be used effectively along with the auditory dictated spelling test.

Probes.   Spelling skills can be assessed through the use of probe sheets. The student works on the probe sheet for 1 minute, and the teacher records the rate of correct and incorrect responses and notes any error patterns. The probe task (for example, see picture—write word, see words—write contractions, hear word—write word, see partial word—

FIGURE 12.1
Graph of a student's
weekly performance in
spelling.

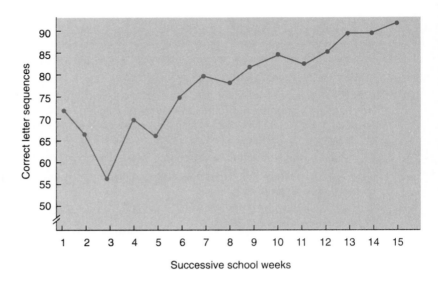

write missing letter) may be administered several times to give the teacher a reliable index of how well the student can perform. Starlin and Starlin (1973) suggest a proficiency rate for students in kindergarten through second grade of 30 to 50 correct letters per minute with two or fewer errors at the independent level and 15 to 29 correct letters with three to seven errors at the instructional level. For third grade through adult, the independent level is 50 to 70 correct letters per minute with two or fewer errors, and the instructional level is 25 to 49 correct letters with three to seven errors. Koenig and Kunzelmann (1980) provide the following proficiency rates according to grade levels:

1. Grade 2: 60 to 90 correct letters per minute
2. Grade 3: 90 to 100 correct letters per minute
3. Grade 4: 100 to 120 correct letters per minute
4. Grade 5: 110 to 130 correct letters per minute
5. Grade 6: 120 to 140 correct letters per minute

In addition, the teacher can collect data from students who are achieving satisfactorily and use their rates for comparison when assessing a student with spelling difficulties. A sample probe sheet for spelling contractions is presented in Table 12.3.

Modality testing. Sensory modality preference testing, described by Westerman (1971), assesses the student's performance through combinations of five input/output channels:

1. *Auditory-vocal:* The teacher spells the word aloud, and the student orally spells the word.
2. *Auditory-motor:* The teacher spells the word aloud, and the student writes the word on paper.
3. *Visual-vocal:* The teacher shows the word on a flash card, and the student spells the word aloud.
4. *Visual-motor:* The teacher shows the word on a flash card, and the student writes the word on paper.
5. *Multisensory combination channel:* The teacher shows the word on a flash card and spells it aloud, and the student spells the word aloud and writes it on paper.

TABLE 12.3
Probe sheet for spelling contractions.

Task: See words — Write contractions

do not	_____
I will	_____
can not	_____
have not	_____
we are	_____
I am	_____
could not	_____
is not	_____
it is	_____
you are	_____
she is	_____
are not	_____
would not	_____
I have	_____
did not	_____
they would	_____
has not	_____
was not	_____
they are	_____
he will	_____

Name: _____
Time: 1 minute
Number of correct letters written: _____
Number of incorrect letters written: _____

In modality testing, 40 unknown words are divided into five sets of 8 words each. Two words are taught in each of the five modalities for 4 consecutive days, and the student is tested on a written dictation spelling test at the end of each day. On the fifth day the student is tested on all 40 words. The number of correct responses in each modality indicates whether the student shows a pattern of preference among modalities. This kind of assessment information is useful in planning individualized instruction. For example, students with an auditory-motor preference may learn new spelling words by using a tape recorder and writing each word after hearing it. Similarly, visual learners should be provided with many opportunities to see the word.

TEACHING SPELLING SKILLS

Stephens (1977) notes that nine spelling competencies enable the student to be an effective speller. These nine skills and corresponding subareas are presented in Table 12.4. Vallecorsa, Zigmond, and Henderson (1985) note that educators may need to improve their knowledge of validated methods for teaching spelling to be able to use supported techniques routinely. The following teaching methods and strategies provide alternatives for teaching spelling skills to students with spelling difficulties.

Rule-Based Instruction

Spelling instruction can be based on teaching rules and generalizations. After learning a general spelling rule, the student is able to use it with unfamiliar words. These rules can apply to instruction using both linguistics and phonics.

The linguistic approach to teaching spelling is based on the idea that there is regularity in phoneme/grapheme correspondence. This method stresses the systematic nature of spelling patterns. Spelling rules, generalizations, and patterns are taught that apply to whole words. Spelling words are selected according to their particular linguistic pattern — for example, *cool, fool, pool; hitting, running, batting.*

The phonics approach to teaching spelling stresses phoneme-grapheme relationships within parts of words. The student learns to associate a sound with a particular letter or combination of letters. Thus, phonetic rules can help the student determine how sounds should be spelled. Through phonics instruc-

TABLE 12.4
Spelling competencies.

Competency Area	Subareas
Auditory discrimination	Ability to discriminate consonant sounds and vowel sounds and use correct word pronunciation
Consonants	Knowledge of consonants in initial, final, and medial positions in words and knowledge of consonant blends
Phonograms	Ability to identify phonograms in initial, medial, and final positions in words and ability to identify word phonograms
Plurals	Ability to form plurals by adding *s*, adding *es*, changing *f* to *v*, making medial changes, and knowledge of exceptions
Syllabication	Ability to divide words into syllables
Structural elements	Knowledge of root words, prefixes and suffixes
Ending changes	Ability to change ending of words which end in final *e*, final *y*, and final consonants
Vowel digraphs and diphthongs	Ability to spell words in which a vowel digraph forms one sound (*ai, ea, ay, ei, ie*) or a diphthong forms a blend (*oi, ou, ow*)
Silent *e*	Knowledge of single-syllable words that end in silent *e*

tion the student can learn to spell words according to syllables. The student breaks the word into recognizable sound elements, pronounces each syllable, and then writes the letter or letters that represent each sound.

In rule-based instruction (in both linguistics and phonics), only spelling rules and generalizations that apply to a large number of words and have few exceptions should be taught. The rule should be applicable more than 75 percent of the time. Spelling rules can be taught by guiding the student to discover rules and generalizations independently. After analyzing several words that share a common linguistic property, the student is asked to apply the rule to unfamiliar words. After the student can generalize, exceptions to the rules can be discussed. The student should be taught that rules are not steadfast and that some words do not conform to spelling rules.

Multisensory Approach

Spelling involves skills in the visual, auditory, and motor sensory modalities. The student must be able to exhibit visual and auditory recognition and discrimination of the letters of the alphabet and must have motor control to write the word. Hodges (1966) notes that "a child who has learned to spell a word by the use of the senses of hearing, sight, and touch is in a good position to recall the spelling of that word when he needs it in his writing because any or all of the sensory modes can elicit his memory of it" (p. 39).

Fernald's (1943, 1988) multisensory approach involves four sensory modalities: visual, auditory, kinesthetic, and tactile (VAKT). In this approach, Fernald focuses on the following areas as being important in learning to spell: (a) clear perception of word form, (b) development of a distinct visual image of the word, and (c) habit formation through repetition of writing until the motor pattern is automatic. The following steps are included in learning to spell a new word:

1. The teacher writes and says a word while the student watches and listens.
2. The student traces the word while simultaneously saying the word. Then the student copies or writes the word while saying it. Emphasis is placed on careful pronunciation, with each syllable of the word dragged out slowly as it is traced or written.
3. Next, the word is written from memory. If it is incorrect, the second step is repeated. If the word is correct, it is put in a file box. Later the words in the file box are used in stories.
4. At later stages the tracing method for learning is not always needed. The student may learn the word by observing the teacher write and say it and then by writing and saying it alone. As progress is made, the student may learn the word by looking at it in print and writing it and, finally, merely by looking at it.

Because the student hears, sees, and traces the word in the Fernald approach, four sensory modalities (auditory, visual, kinesthetic, tactile) are involved.

The Gillingham method (Gillingham & Stillman, 1970) uses an alphabetic system with repetition and drill. Letter/sound correspondences are taught using a multisensory approach—visual, auditory, and kinesthetic. Words introduced initially include only those with consistent sound/symbol correspondences. The student is given experience reading and spelling one-syllable words as well as detached regularly spelled syllables. Words of more than one syllable are learned syllable-by-syllable (for example, *Sep tem ber*). Words whose spellings are not entirely consistent are sequenced carefully according to structural characteristics, and words that follow a pattern are grouped. The technique used in studying spelling words is called simultaneous oral spelling. When the teacher says a spelling word, the student repeats the word, names the letters, writes the letters while saying them aloud, and reads the written word. Letter names rather than sounds are used in this practice so that the technique can be applied to nonphonetic words. Sentence and story writing is introduced after the student is able to write any three-letter, phonetically pure word. Nonphonetic words are taught through drill. Thus, the Gillingham method differs from the Fernald (1943, 1988) approach in two major respects: (a) words to be taught are selected carefully and sequenced or selected as needed for writing rather than being of the student's own choosing, and (b) instruction focuses on individual letters and sounds rather than on whole words.

Another multisensory approach that features repetition is the cover-and-write method. The student is taught to spell words through the following steps:

1. The student looks at the word and says it.
2. The student writes the word twice while looking at it.
3. The student covers the word and writes it again.
4. The student checks the spelling by looking at it.

The steps are repeated with the student writing the word as many as three times while looking at it, covering the word, writing it, and checking the spelling.

Test-Study-Test Technique

The test-study-test approach to teaching spelling is used frequently. The student is given a pretest at the beginning of each unit of study. The words the student misspells on the pretest become her study list. After instruction, another test determines the degree of mastery. A progress chart is kept, and words missed on the second test are added to the list of words for the following unit of study.

The study-test plan is similar to the test-study-test approach, except that it does not include a pretest. The student's study list consists of all of the words in the unit of study. The student is tested after completing various spelling activities. Petty (1966) and Stephens et al. (1982) note that the test-study-test method obtains better spelling results than the study-test approach. The pretest helps to identify words that the student already knows how to spell and, by eliminating these words, the student can focus her study on the unknown words.

Graham and Voth (1990) recommend daily testing on new and previously introduced words from a spelling unit, as well as periodic maintenance checks to ensure mastery or to identify words that need to be reincorporated into the instructional sequence. In addition, they suggest that the tests should be corrected, with supervision, by the students themselves. Thus, the students receive immediate feedback about their efforts to learn to spell. Because some students spell the words correctly on the test but misspell them in their writing, the teacher periodically should collect samples of student writing to determine if the students are applying in their writing what they have learned through spelling instruction. To improve accuracy and fluency, practice on misspelled words should include a variety of high-interest activities and games. In addition, spelling performance can be improved through the use of peer tutoring or cooperative learning arrangements.

Graham and Freeman (1986) found that students with learning problems who were trained to use an efficient study strategy were able to recall immediately the correct spelling of more words than were students who were allowed to choose their own methods for studying unknown spelling words. The study strategy included the following steps:

1. Say the word.
2. Write and say the word.
3. Check the word.
4. Trace and say the word.
5. Write the word from memory and check.
6. Repeat the first five steps.

Moreover, Foster and Torgesen (1983) found that directed study improved the long-term retention of spelling words in students with learning problems who had average short-term memory; however, students who had short-term memory deficits continued to experience difficulty in the acquisition of spelling words.

In addition, some studies indicate that added reinforcement procedures can encourage students to study harder to obtain higher test scores. For example, Lovitt, Guppy, and Blattner (1969) noted a substantial increase in the number of perfect spelling papers when students were given the test four days a week (Tuesday through Friday) and, after receiving 100 percent on that week's word list, were excused from spelling for the rest of the week and given free time. Also, Sidman (1979) used group and individual reinforcement contingencies with middle school students. Accuracy increased when free time was provided as a reward for improved test scores. The increase was greater during group contingency conditions.

Fixed and Flow Word Lists

Spelling words frequently are presented and taught in fixed word lists. Generally, a new list of words is assigned each week. The words may be either somewhat unfamiliar or completely unknown to the student. Usually a test on each list is given on Friday. This method seldom results in spelling mastery for all students because misspelled words on the test usually are ignored or left for the student to practice independently. Another procedure using fixed word lists is to have the student practice the words at her own rate until she is able to spell all of them correctly on a certain number of tests.

On a flow list of spelling words, words are dropped from the student's list when mastered (for example, spelled correctly on two consecutive days), and then a new (unpracticed) word is added. Thus, the list is individualized, and the student does not spend time practicing known words. McGuigan (1975) developed a teaching procedure, the Add-a-Word Program, which uses flow word lists. McGuigan found that students (age 7 to 13 and adults) learned words more quickly with add-a-word lists than with fixed lists and also showed similar or superior retention of learned words.

Graham and Voth (1990) emphasize that the spelling words taught to students with learning problems initially should be limited to high-frequency words and misspelled words from their own writing. They recommend that weekly spelling lists be limited to 6 to 12 words (emphasizing a common structural element, if possible), and 2 or 3 words from the list should be introduced daily and practiced until the entire set of words is mastered. Likewise, Burns and Broman (1983) recommend

presentation of only 5 to 10 words per week to poor spellers (20 words per week may be presented to adequate spellers). In a study of spelling performance of students with learning problems, Bryant, Drabin, and Gettinger (1981) found that a higher failure rate and greater variance in performance may occur when more than 3 words are presented each day. They suggest that 7 to 8 new spelling words per week may be an appropriate number for such students.

Imitation Methods

Stowitschek and Jobes (1977) present a method of spelling instuction that involves imitation. It is designed for students who have failed repeatedly to learn to spell through traditional procedures. The teacher provides an oral and written model of the spelling word, and the student is required to imitate the model by spelling the word aloud and writing it. The student receives immediate feedback and praise for correct responses. Incorrect responses are followed by retraining. The procedure is repeated until the student can spell and write the word without models or prompts. A spelling probe is administered after each training session to determine which words have been mastered and to check retention of learned words.

Kauffman, Hallahan, Haas, Brame, and Boren (1978) tested the effectiveness of showing the student a correct model of a spelling word as opposed to providing first a written imitation of the student's spelling error and then showing the correct model. Kauffman et al. found that including the imitation of the student's error was more effective, especially for nonphonetic words. Kauffman et al. suggest that imitation can be useful particularly in teaching words that do not follow regular phonetic rules—words for which the student must use visual memory. However, Brown (1988) conducted a series of experiments and found that exposures to incorrect spellings can interfere with subsequent spelling accuracy.

Additional Considerations

Different types of correctional procedures should be used with various kinds of spelling errors. Visual image should be emphasized with a student who omits silent letters or misspells phonologically irregular words, whereas incorrect spelling of homonyms indicates a need to stress word meanings. Also, words the student misspells in written compositions may be included in the student's spelling program. This can be motivating because the need to learn to spell those words is apparent.

Spelling also may be taught and reinforced throughout the language arts curriculum. One way to improve spelling is through word study in reading (Templeton, 1986). In oral reading the student gives close attention to the sounds of the entire word. In addition, reading gives the student the meanings of words and thus increases interest in them. The student learns the correct usage of words in sentences and can determine whether the word is written correctly. Thus, learning to spell can accompany learning to read, and a program that stresses both skills may be effective and motivating. As discussed in Chapter 11, the language experience approach and the whole language approach incorporate reading and spelling. T. K. Shinn (1982) stresses that no student should be forced to learn to spell words that she cannot read and understand. Otherwise, the student really is memorizing a nonmeaningful series of letters that will not be retained. Thus, spelling lists should be produced from the student's reading vocabulary. Shinn provides a linguistic spelling program designed to assist in the diagnosis and intervention of spelling difficulties as well as in the evaluation of instruction through specific charting procedures.

Training in dictionary usage also should be included in the spelling program. Dictionaries help the student become more independent in locating spellings and provide such information as syllabication, meaning, pronunciation, synonyms, and homonyms. Picture dictionaries can be used in the primary grades. Beginning in the fourth grade, special practice in using the dictionary often is included in the curriculum, and the use of dictionaries may be encouraged during writing tasks. When the student does not know how to spell a word, she should predict possible spellings for the unknown word by identifying root words and affixes, considering related words, and determining the sounds in the word, and then she can check the predicted spelling by consulting a dictionary.

In teaching spelling skills at the secondary level, the teacher should help the adolescent understand the social and practical significance of correct spelling. For example, employers place value on accurate spelling on job applications. The student's own interests and the various subject areas can provide new words to study. Also, vocational words can be emphasized. At the secondary level it may be best to teach spelling in conjunction with other activities rather than to use class time solely for spelling instruction (Marsh, Gearheart, & Gearheart, 1978). Practice in reading and other learning activities can help the adolescent learn to spell. Finally, strategies to compensate for poor spelling should be taught to students whose spelling problems may affect their grades in content areas. For example, the teacher can provide such students with a spelling checker, which contains frequently used words and words they often misspell.

SPELLING ACTIVITIES

Many activities and materials can be used to supplement a spelling program. Games and activities stimulate interest, provide practice, and add variety in teaching techniques. In addition, spelling instruction may be individualized by developing games and activities for particular individuals or small groups. The following activities, instructional games, self-correcting materials, commercial programs and materials, and computer software programs promote the development of spelling skills.

1. Ask the student to complete words in sentences by filling in omitted letters. Lists of words from stories in basal readers or spelling textbooks can be used to develop reusable worksheets or dittos. For example:

    The bo__ and __irl were bak_____ a cak_____.

2. Give the student various words and their configurations. Ask her to match each word with its configuration. Worksheets of specific words (for example, reading selections, weekly spelling lists) can be made and reused for this seatwork activity.

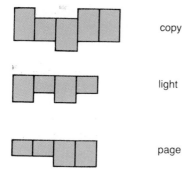

copy

light

page

3. Use a hidden-word format to provide practice in letter sequence of spelling words. Give the student a list of spelling words and a puzzle. Ask her to locate the hidden spelling words and to draw a circle around them.

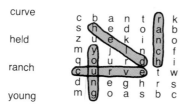

curve

held

ranch

young

4. Have each student keep a file box of spelling words that have caused her some difficulty. The words should be arranged in alphabetical order, and the cards also may contain definitions or pictures. Encourage each student to study her cards and to practice writing the words from memory. New words can be included and others deleted as the student progresses.

5. In compiling the weekly spelling word list, ask class members to volunteer words, such as those they have misspelled in writing or have encountered in independent reading. The teacher may want to include on the spelling list those words the students will use frequently in their writing. Give a pretest on the words on Monday and a second test on Friday. Keep a scoreboard graph for the entire class, scaled to 10. Have each student try to move "up 10" each week on the graph by spelling more words correctly on Friday than were spelled correctly on the pretest. Thus, the student is competing against her own previous score. The advanced student who gets a perfect score and the less able student who improves by 10 words both receive the "up 10" mark on the graph.

6. Describe a current spelling word phonetically. For example, the word *move* may be described as "a one-syllable word beginning with a consonant and ending with a vowel." Call on a student to find the word in her spelling list, and then give her a turn to describe a word and to call on another classmate.

7. Use the Language Master to provide visual, auditory, and kinesthetic experiences for the student. Blank cards can be reused by laminating the top portion so that the words can be erased and changed. Also, pictures or letters written in yarn may be added to the blank cards. Once the card has been placed through the recorder, the student can trace the word.

8. Have each student work with *anagram* activities: The student is given a word and must rearrange all the letters to make a new word. For example, *smile* is an anagram for *miles*, and *sister* is an anagram for *resist*. For students having particular difficulty, *Scrabble* letter tiles may be used, or the student can copy the word, cut it apart, and rearrange the letters. Also, have

each student work anagram puzzles, in which one letter is changed each time until the top word is changed into the bottom word. Definitions or clues may be provided. For example:

POND   small lake
_____   young horse (pony)
_____   nickname for Anthony (Tony)
_____   dial _____ (tone)
BONE   dog's treat

9. Have a spelling bee in which the students stand in a line, and each time a student spells a word correctly she "jumps" two persons toward the end of the line. When a student jumps enough people to reach the end, she goes to her seat. Thus, those students who need practice remain, and those who know the words have time for independent work.

10. Begin an add-a-letter activity with a one- to two-letter word (for example, *to*). Call on a student to make a different word by adding one letter (for example, *top*). The letters may be rearranged, but one letter must be added each turn (for example, *spot*). When no one can continue the process, start a new word. This can become a seatwork activity, in which each student works independently on a worksheet to add letters and make new words.

11. Provide the student with a jar containing about 40 wooden cubes with letters on them (similar to alphabet blocks or *Spill and Spell* cubes). Have the student spill the letters from the jar and see how many words she can make in 5 minutes with the given letters. Link letters (letters that fit together to form words) also can be used for this activity.

12. Give the student spelling word cards (two cards for each word) and have her play a concentration game. The cards are mixed up and placed face down in rows. The student turns over two cards at a time and tries to remember their location so that she can make spelling matches. When the student turns up two cards that match (that is, the same spelling word), the cards are removed. Two students may play together, taking turns to see who can make the most matches.

13. Have each student write a story or theme using the spelling list words. The theme may be on any subject and as long or as short as the student wishes to make it; however, every one of the spelling words must be included in what is written. Encourage the student to pay attention to spelling and using the words correctly.

14. Encourage the student to develop memory devices to help her remember the spelling of difficult words or words that are not spelled as they sound. For example:

Station*ery* is writing pap*er*.
The princi*pal* is your *pal*.

15. Present crossword puzzles that contain spelling words to give practice in writing the words and learning their meanings. Also, the student can be asked to make up a crossword puzzle that includes new and review spelling words and everyday words.

Across
1. small cat
3. not wild
6. what you hear with
7. a small clue
8. a father's boy
10. not old

Down
1. room you cook in
2. short periods of sleep
4. more than one man
5. puts in mouth and chews
9. opposite of yes

16. For dictionary practice, give the student a list of words (for example, *overcoat, tongue-tied, well-known*). Ask her to locate them in the dictionary and write *yes* or *no* to indicate whether each word is hyphenated. Also, give the student sentences containing some unfamiliar words

and ask her to supply synonyms for four words in each sentence. For example:

The *clandestine* meeting was interrupted by *incorrigible bandits* who came *incognito.*

17. Have a student describe a spelling word from the current week's list by giving rhyming, meaning, or descriptive clues. The other class members are given 1 minute to guess the word. The first person to say the correct word goes to the chalkboard and writes it. If she spells it correctly, she gets to describe a word.
18. To motivate a student, allow her to practice spelling words on the typewriter. She can say the letters as she types them, thus combining sight, sound, and touch.
19. Select a student to pick a word from the dictionary and write on the chalkboard the exact pronunciation for the word as found in the dictionary. It should be written letter-for-letter with all diacritical marks and accents. Class members are asked to pronounce and spell the word the correct way.

INSTRUCTIONAL GAMES IN SPELLING

Find-a-Word

Materials: Two words containing the same number of letters written on the chalkboard.

Directions: The teacher divides the class into two teams. The first student from each team goes to the chalkboard and writes any word that can be made from the letters in the given word. She gives the chalk to the next student on her team and goes to the end of the line. Each student must write a new word or correct a misspelled one. The game continues until the teacher calls time. The team with the most correctly spelled words at the end of the time limit is the winner. For example:

The given words are:	*place*	*dream*
The student may write:	pace	read
	cap	mad
	leap	dear
	pal	me

Detective

Materials: Spelling words with various letters omitted written on the chalkboard.

Directions: The teacher gives the definition of each word and calls on a student to fill in the missing letters. The student goes to the board and writes in the missing letters. One point is given for each correct word or letter. The student with the most points at the end of the game is the winner. For example:

n____ghb____	person who lives next door
stor____s	short reading selections
ni____t	opposite of day

Jaws

Materials: Twenty-one index cards with one consonant printed on each card; 21 index cards with pictures corresponding to the sound of each consonant; 1 index card with "jaws" (a shark) drawn on it.

Directions: The cards are dealt to three or more players. The players check for pairs and place them on the table. (A pair consists of one consonant card and a picture card that has the same beginning consonant sound.) The first player picks a card from the player sitting on her left. If it matches a card in her hand, she places the pair on the table. The game continues until all the cards have been matched and one student is left holding "jaws."

Modification: The payers can be asked to write the names of the pictures in the pairs. The player who spells the most pairs correctly wins the game.

Spell It–Keep It Card Game

Materials: Cards with spelling words printed on them placed on the chalkboard ledge with backs to the class.

Directions: The teacher divides the class into two teams. A student from the first team selects a card and reads the word. A student from the other team spells the word. If the word is spelled correctly, the student who spelled it gets to keep the card. If the word is spelled incorrectly, a student from the first team has a chance to spell it and get the card. Then a student from the second team selects a card, and the process is repeated until all cards are gone from the ledge. The winner is the team having the most cards at the end of the game.

Telegraph Spelling

Materials: Two sets of 2″ x 6″ cards with letters used in the spelling words printed on them.

Directions: The class is divided into two teams, and each student receives a letter card. The teacher pronounces a spelling word. The members of each team arrange themselves in the proper order at the front of the room. The team that correctly spells the word the quickest wins a point. After a specified time limit, the team with the most points wins the game.

Modification: For older students, each member of the team can be assigned one or two letters of the alphabet. When the teacher gives the spelling word, the members of the team begin verbally to "transmit" (call out) the spelling of the word. There can be no more than 5 seconds between calling out letters, and other team members are not allowed to help. One point is earned for each correct response.

Spelling Bingo

Materials: Cards divided into 24 squares (four squares across and six squares down), with a different spelling word printed in each space and words in different order on each card; numerous discs or markers.

Directions: Each student receives a card and several discs. As the teacher calls out and spells a word, each student covers the given word on her card with a disc. The first student to complete a column going across, down, or diagonally calls "Bingo" and wins the game.

Modifications:

1. The students can make their own cards by dividing their paper into 24 squares. The spelling words are written on the chalkboard, and each student writes the words in any squares on her paper. One student is selected to stand with her back to the board, and the teacher calls out words for her to spell. For each word she spells correctly, the other students place a disc on the corresponding square on their card. The game continues until someone calls "Bingo." The teacher keeps a list of the words and checks the winning card.
2. For young students, the bingo cards can consist of rows of selected consonants, short vowels, and long vowels. When the teacher calls a word, each student puts discs on the appropriate letters on her card.

Golf Game Board

Materials: Large game board on tagboard or laminated poster board; different-colored golf tees for markers; cards with spelling words printed on them, with stars on the cards of the most difficult words (see Figure 12.2).

Directions: Two players each choose a golf tee and place it on the "tee off" square. The first player takes the top card and reads the word to the other player, who tries to spell the word. If she spells the word correctly, she moves ahead one space. If the word is spelled incorrectly, she moves back one space. When a player correctly spells a word that has a star on the card, she moves her marker ahead two spaces. The first player to reach the golf hole wins the game.

Modifications:

1. Game boards can be made on poster board to depict various themes, such as a race track, rocket path, mountain path, safari, or any other start-to-finish sequence.
2. The spelling cards can consist of some words spelled correctly and some words spelled incorrectly. The player draws a card and must decide whether or not the word is spelled correctly. If it

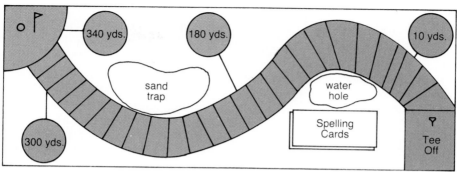

FIGURE 12.2
Golf game board.

is misspelled, the player must spell it correctly. Each player moves one space for a correct answer. A third student can use an answer key to check responses.

3. Stacks of index cards containing spelling words can be color-coded or numbered according to difficulty level. Students may play with two different stacks of cards according to their ability levels. The players roll dice to determine the number of spaces they can move on the game board if they spell the word on the spelling card correctly.

4. Chance dice can be used that have one number covered with a sticker. When one sticker is rolled, the player loses her turn, and when two stickers are rolled (one on each die), the player goes back to the beginning square.

5. For older students, the words on the spelling cards can be assigned a number of yards (in multiples of 10) according to the difficulty level of the word. Each space on the board is worth 10 yards. When the player spells a word correctly, she moves the number of yards indicated on the card. If she misspells the word, she does not advance.

Tic-Tac-Toe

Materials: A tic-tac-toe game square made of tagboard or laminated poster board, five tagboard Xs and; five Os; cards with spelling words written on them.

Directions: One student chooses to mark with Xs and the other student uses Os. The first student takes the top spelling card and reads it to her opponent, who attempts to spell it. If the student spells the word correctly, she places her marker in a square on the board. The game continues until one player has three of her markers in a horizontal, vertical, or diagonal row.

Modification: The class can be divided into two teams, and each student can pin a paper marked X or O on herself to indicate her team. Nine chairs are placed in three rows similar to a tic-tac-toe board. A member of one team selects a card and reads the spelling word, and a member of the other team must spell it. If the student spells the word correctly, she sits in the chair of her choice. The game continues until one team has three members sitting in a row.

Connect the Dots

Materials: Twenty-five dots (rows of five across and five down) drawn on the chalkboard; cards with spelling words printed on them.

Directions: The students are divided into two teams, Team 1 and Team 2. A member of the first team draws the top spelling card and reads the word to a member of the opposite team, who tries to spell it (either in writing or aloud). If the student spells the word correctly, she draws a line connecting two dots, and her team gets another turn to try to spell a word. If a word is spelled incorrectly, the other team gets a turn. When a square is closed in by four lines, the number of the team is written in the square. The team that obtains the most squares is the winner.

Modification: Two players may play the game with a game board of dots made of tagboard covered with acetate so that marks made with a grease pencil can be erased. When a player makes a square, she can write her initial in it.

Checkers

Materials: A checker game board made of tagboard; 24 tagboard checkers (12 of one color and 12 of another), each of which has a spelling word printed on the bottom.

Directions: Two players place their checkers on the board, and they take turns moving their checkers. If one player can "jump" her opponent's checker, the opponent looks on the bottom of the checker to be jumped and reads the word aloud. If the jumping player correctly spells the word, she is allowed to jump and pick up the opponent's checker. If she misspells the word, she is not allowed to make the move. The game continues until one player has obtained all her opponent's checkers through jumping.

Modifications:

1. Additional checkers can be made so different spelling words are used each time the game is played.
2. Regular checkers can be used when spelling word cards are provided. When a player wants to make a jump, she must spell the word on the top card correctly to her opponent.

Chance Dice Spelling Game

Materials: Two chance dice, each of which has numbers on five sides and a sticker covering the number on the sixth size; worksheets with equal items that are appropriate for each player (for example, matching spelling words with pictures or

definitions; choosing correctly spelled words from four options; dividing spelling words into syllables; filling in omitted letters in spelling words); an answer key for each worksheet.

Directions: Each player is given an appropriate worksheet for her spelling word list. The first player rolls both of the chance dice. If no stickers are rolled, the player answers an item on her worksheet, and the answer is checked by a student with the answer key. If the answer is correct, the item number is checked; however, if the answer is incorrect, the item number is not checked and the player must attempt that item on another turn. If the player rolls one sticker on the chance dice, she loses her turn. If two stickers are rolled (one on each die), the player is allowed to attempt to answer two items on her worksheet. This procedure is continued until one player correctly answers all the items on her worksheet and wins the game.

TV Talent

Material: Three decorated shoe boxes; spelling words of varying difficulty printed on index cards.

Directions: The game is presented as a television show with one student acting as master of ceremonies (MC). The words are placed in the three boxes, and two players are chosen from the "audience." The first player picks a card from one of the boxes and hands it to the MC without looking at it. The MC pronounces the word, and the player writes the word on the chalkboard. If the player spells the word correctly, she gets 5 points. The players take turns until one player earns 50 points.

Modification: The spelling words can be divided into three levels of difficulty. The easiest words are placed in the box marked 1 point; the next level, in the box marked 3 points; and the most difficult words, in the box marked 5 points. The student chooses a card from a box according to how many points she wants to try to earn on that turn.

Bowling

Materials: Two sets of 10 numbered bowling pins; file-card box divided into 10 sections, with spelling words filed according to the number of points each word is worth (1–10).

Directions: The bowling pins are set up or pinned to a backboard in the arrangement of a bowling game. The first player calls the number of a pin, and her opponent reads the first word from that section in the file box. If the player spells the word correctly, the pin is removed, and she gets the number of points that pin is worth. The second player takes a turn using her set of pins. The winner is the player who earns the most points after trying to knock down all her pins.

Modification: Two pairs of players can play. The first player of the pair tries to get a strike (worth 55 points) by spelling all the words. If she misses a word, her partner may try to get a spare (worth 45 points) by spelling the word the first player missed and the words for any remaining pins. If the second member of the pair misses a word, she and her partner receive points according to the numbered pins they knocked down. The first pair of players to score a specified number of points wins the game.

Dictionary Store Hunt

Materials: One dictionary per player; a stack of cards with nouns written on them that are unlikely to be familiar to the players (for example, *cockatiel, metronome, colander*).

Directions: Each player picks at random five word cards. At the same starting time, each player begins to find the words in her dictionary, reads the definitions to herself, and writes down the kind of store she would shop in for each item. The winner is the first person to complete the hunt. Other players can check her responses by looking in the dictionary as she names the stores.

Baseball Spelling Game

Materials: Baseball diamond with three bases and home plate drawn on the chalkboard; cards with spelling words written on them.

Directions: The class is divided into two teams, and the top speller in each group can act as pitcher. The pitcher draws a card and reads the word to the first batter of the other team. If the first batter spells the

word correctly, she is given a "single" and stands in front of first base on the chalkboard. If the second batter correctly spells the word she is given, she goes to first base and the player on first base moves to second base. If a player misspells her word, she is "out"; there are three outs for each team in each inning. Prior to hearing her word, any batter may declare "home run," and if she spells the word correctly, she clears the bases and the number of runs is added to the score. However, if she misspells the word it automatically counts as the third out for the team, regardless of the actual number of outs in the inning. The team with the most runs at the end of a set number of innings is the winner.

Modifications:

1. The word cards can be labeled "single," "double," "triple," and "home run" according to the difficulty level of the spelling word. After the batter spells the word correctly, the pitcher tells her what her "hit" was worth according to the card. The batter moves to the appropriate base, and batters already on base advance.
2. A baseball diamond can be arranged in the room, using chairs for the bases, and the "runners" can sit in the appropriate chair when they get "hits."

Football Spelling Game

Materials: A football field including yard lines drawn on the chalkboard; index cards with spelling words written on them.

Directions: The class is divided into two teams, and the ball is placed (drawn) on the 50-yard line by the "referee." The referee reads a word to a member of the first team. If she spells the word correctly, the ball is moved 10 yards toward the opponent's goal line. If the word is misspelled, the offensive team loses 10 yards. Each team gets four words in one turn; then the other team takes a turn. A team is given 6 points each time it crosses the opponent's goal line. The winner is the team with the most points at the end of a specified time period.

Modifications:

1. The football field may be made on tagboard, and two players can play using small tagboard foot-

balls for their markers. One player draws a card and reads the word to her opponent. If the opponent spells the word correctly, she advances her marker 5 yards closer to her goal; if she misspells the word, she moves her marker back 5 yards. The players take turns (one word a turn), and the first one to reach the goal line scores a touchdown and wins the game.

2. The word cards can include the number of yards each spelling word is worth (1–10 yards), and the ball is moved accordingly.

3. In addition to spelling word cards, there can be "gain" cards and "loss" cards. When the student correctly spells the word on the spelling card, she picks a gain card; when she misspells a word, she draws a loss card. The gain cards denote the number of yards gained—for example, "completed pass, 30 yards," "20-yard run." The loss cards denote the number of yards lost— "quarterback sack, lose 10 yards," "tackled, 5-yard loss." The player moves her football accordingly.

4. Rather than drawing, erasing, and redrawing the ball throughout the game, a chalkboard eraser can be used as the ball. It is easy to move and see if set vertically on the chalkboard tray.

Nym Game

Materials: Two sets of three decorated coffee cans—one labeled "antonyms," one labeled "homonyms," and one labeled "synonyms"; cards with pairs of words written on them which are antonyms, homonyms, or synonyms (all appropriate and acceptable antonyms, homonyms, or synonyms are given for each initial word in the word pair).

Directions: The first player draws the top card and reads and spells the first word on the card to her opponent. The opponent must (a) spell the word that completes the word pair, (b) use the words in sentences, and (c) identify the word pair as antonyms, homonyms, or synonyms. If correct, the opponent places the word card in the appropriate can of her set. If incorrect, the first player gets to put the card in the appropriate can of her set. The players take turns, and when all the cards are gone, they count their score. For each card in the homonym can, the player gets 3 points; for each antonym card

she gets 2 points; and for each synonym card she gets 1 point. The player with the highest total score wins the game.

Spelling Dart Game

Materials: Target divided into sections for 15, 10, 5, and 1 points, drawn on heavy poster board; suction darts; a file box divided into sections labeled 15, 10, 5, and 1 containing spelling word cards of four levels of difficulty (the most difficult words are in the 15-point section).

Directions: The target is mounted on the wall, and the first player throws a dart at it from about 10 feet away. The players determine in which section of the target the dart landed. Another player takes a card from the section of the file box corresponding to the target section. For example, if the dart landed in the 5-point section, the card would be drawn from the 5-point section in the file box. The spelling word is pronounced, and the player who threw the dart must spell the word correctly to receive that number of points. The players take turns until one player scores 50 points and wins the game.

Charades

Materials: Spelling words printed on index cards.

Directions: The class is divided into two teams. A member of the first team selects a card, reads the word to herself, and then acts out the word without saying anything. There is a 2-minute time limit, after which the student picks another team member to take her place. The first team to guess the word gets 1 point. If the person who guesses the word also can spell it correctly, her team gets 2 points. The person who guessed the word then draws a card and acts out her word. The team with the most points at the end of a specified time period wins the game.

Bottle Top Scrabble

Materials: One hundred fifty bottle tops with letters of the alphabet written inside them with a marking pen and point values written on the outside (letters most often used should appear most; point values may be the same as those in *Scrabble*).

Directions: Each student selects 10 tops without looking. The first player spells a word using as many of her letters as possible and adds the point values of the letters used. Then she picks more tops so that she again has 10 tops. The players take turns spelling words that connect with previously spelled words, as in a *Scrabble* game. After all possible bottle tops have been used, the player with the highest score is the winner.

Modification: For older students, there can be a minimum number of letters for each word (for example, four or more). Also, the number of tops may be increased.

SELF-CORRECTING SPELLING MATERIALS

Spelling Word Puzzles

Feedback device: The pieces of the puzzle fit together to indicate a correct choice.

Materials: Spelling words printed on heavy cardboard and then cut into two or more puzzle pieces.

Directions: The student looks at the puzzle pieces and fits together the pieces that correctly spell a word.

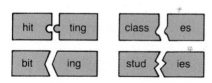

Flip-Sider Spelling Cards

Feedback device: Picture completion or the matching of objects, numbers, or colors provides feedback.

Materials: Sets of index cards with a spelling word on one card and the definition or a picture representing the word on another card; the reverse sides of the two cards that go together have the same object, number, or color, or the two cards complete a picture.

Directions: The student looks at the spelling word on a card and selects the card with the definition of

that word or a picture representing it. Then the student flips over the two cards. If she has chosen the correct definition or picture, the backs of the two cards will have the same object, number, or color, or they will complete a picture.

Modification: The front of the card can have a sentence in which the spelling word is omitted. The sentence may be a definition of the missing word, or there may be a picture illustrating the word in the blank. The spelling word that goes in the blank is written on the back of the card. The student reads the sentence, writes down the missing word, and then flips over the card to check her response.

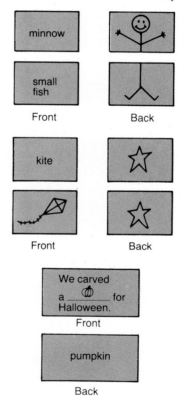

Spelling Spinner

Feedback device: A flap is located on the poster board. When the flap is raised, the answer is revealed.

Materials: A round disc of poster board divided into several sections, each of which has a word written at the top and a picture or definition written in the lower portion of the section; a square piece of poster board which has the round disc attached to the back with a brass fastener, with a small window cut out at the top to reveal the top portion of the disc and a larger window below it to reveal the lower portion of the disc; a flexible flap (such as vinyl wallpaper) placed over the top window.

Directions: The student turns the spinner to reveal a picture or definition in the window. She writes the spelling word for the picture or definition and then lifts the flap to check her answer.

Modification: Discs of spelling words selected from reading selections or spelling lists may be numbered and stored so that the teacher can select a disc appropriate for an individual student.

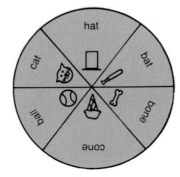

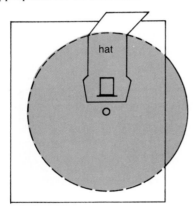

Tape Recorder Spelling

Feedback device: Following the spelling activity presented on the tape, the correct answers are given on the tape.

Materials: A tape recorder and a tape cassette that contains a spelling activity—for example, a dictated spelling test or directions instructing the student to draw a house and label objects (such as "Add a chimney to your house and write the word *chimney*").

Directions: The student follows the instructions given to her on the tape recorder and writes the specified words. Following the activity she continues to listen to the tape to hear the correct responses and thus checks her answers.

Answer Box

Feedback device: A flap is placed over the window; when lifted, the window reveals the answer.

Materials: An Answer Box (presented in Chapter 4) and a set of index cards that present a spelling exercise.

Directions: The student writes an answer to the presented spelling problem and then lifts the flap to see the answer.

Modification: Change the two "eyes" to one long opening. Then activities such as definitions or sentences with missing words can be presented.

Contraction cards to use in the Answer Box:

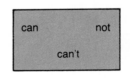
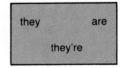

Definition cards to use in the modified Answer Box:

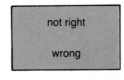
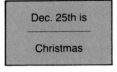

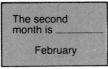

Fill in the Letters

Feedback device: When the correct letters are filled in, the message at the bottom of the page is completed. Deciphering the code thus provides feedback.

Materials: Worksheets on which the student either must cross out or add a letter so that the word is spelled correctly; blanks at the bottom of the page that give a message when the crossed out or added letters are written in them.

Directions: The student completes the worksheet by crossing out or adding letters as indicated. Then each letter is written in the appropriate blank at the bottom of the page. If the correct letters are chosen, the student reads a message.

Color Spelling Sheet

1. rsed
2. bl e
3. orpange
4. belack

5. whirte
6. yeljlow
7. br wn
8. greben

(super job)

Spelling Crossword Puzzles

Feedback device: Only a correct response will fit in the squares and complete additional words.

Materials: A crossword puzzle in which spelling words are used (for example, the crossword puzzle presented previously in the section on spelling activities).

Directions: The student completes the crossword puzzle and receives feedback as she fills in the squares.

Scrambled Letters

Feedback device: The backs of the letters are numbered in the correct sequence of the spelling word.

Materials: Envelopes with pictures illustrating a word or definitions written on the front; square cards placed inside the envelopes, with each card giving a letter needed to spell the word; numbers written on the backs of the cards to represent the correct letter sequence of the word.

Directions: The student reads the definition or looks at the picture on the envelope, takes the letters out of the envelope, and places them face up. She unscrambles the letters and arranges them to spell the word. Then she turns over the letters. The number order on the back of the cards indicates if the word is spelled correctly.

Poke Box

Feedback device: The student places a stylus in the hole to indicate her response. If the correct answer is selected, the card can be pulled out of the Poke Box easily.

Materials: A Poke Box (presented in Chapter 4) and a set of index cards that present a spelling exercise—for example, a word and three abbreviations, or a definition or picture and three words.

Directions: The student selects an answer to the presented spelling problem by inserting the stylus in the hole below the answer. She then pulls the card, which can be removed if her answer is correct.

Abbreviation and picture cards to use in a Poke Box:

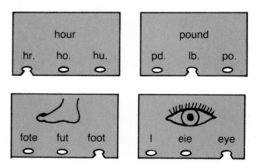

Color Magic

Feedback device: The student receives feedback by opening the folder to see the answers written in colored pencil.

Materials: A plastic colored folder (such as the type typically used to hold term papers), inside of which is a spelling worksheet; answers written on the worksheet in the same color as the plastic folder (that is, if the plastic folder is red, the answers are written with a red colored pencil so that they will not show through the folder).

Directions: The student follows the instructions on the worksheet, which she reads through the colored plastic folder. She writes her answers on a sheet of paper and, when finished with the activity, she opens the folder to check her responses.

COMMERCIAL SPELLING PROGRAMS AND MATERIALS

Basic developmental programs and corrective materials for spelling instruction are available, as are spelling calculators, spelling games, and spelling reference books. Appendix B lists the addresses of the publishers and producers of the materials presented.

Common Words

Publisher: Science Research Associates

Description: This developmental spelling and vocabulary program for students in seventh through twelfth grade reviews commonly misspelled words and emphasizes the correct spelling and usage of high-utility secondary school and adult vocabulary. The program consists of two consumable workbooks containing units that emphasize word meanings, word analysis, word building, and dictionary usage. The format is appropriate for independent study.

Corrective Spelling Through Morphographs

Publisher: Science Research Associates

Description: Corrective Spelling Through Morphographs (Dixon & Engelmann, 1980) is an intensive 1-year program for fourth-grade students through adult. The program includes 140 twenty-minute lessons that cover more than 12,000 words, including problem words. The student is taught basic units of meaning in written language (morphographs) that always are spelled according to specific rules. Thus, the student learns analytic techniques and generalizations that can be applied to words not in the program. Also available is a book of blackline masters, *Crossword Puzzles for Corrective Spelling Through Morphographs,* that includes 54 puzzles correlated with the words listed in the review lessons of the program.

Instant Spelling Words for Writing

Publisher: Curriculum Associates

Description: Instant Spelling Words for Writing (Forest & Sitton, 1989) is a five-level series designed for writers of all ages (second grade through adult) who have difficulty spelling and proofreading. The structured 30-lesson program teaches 1,020 high-frequency words, which cover 90 percent of all words used in writing. All spelling words are introduced as whole words in list form, and students practice writing each word at least 10 times in a variety of high-interest exercises. Visual imagery is emphasized through activities involving configuration of word shapes and visual discrimination. The program teaches a multimodality word-study procedure and uses the self-corrected test-study-test method. The last exercise in every lesson is a structured writing activity. Using a total language approach, the review lessons and optional extension activities provide language arts exercises that integrate spelling with listening, speaking, reading, writing, and thinking.

Speed Spelling 1 and 2

Publisher: Pro-Ed

Description: Speed Spelling 1 and *2* (Proff-Witt, 1978, 1979) is a tutorial, phonetically based spelling program designed for students of any age who have not mastered first- through sixth-grade spelling skills (Level 1) or sixth- through twelfth-grade spelling skills (Level 2). *Speed Spelling 1* (93 lessons) focuses on increasing speed and accuracy through a systematic development of sound-to-letter correspondence, while *Speed Spelling 2* (89 lessons) teaches irregular spellings. Both programs include lessons in word reading, word writing, and sentence writing, and branching instructions are given for students who need additional help. One-on-one instruction is given, and each session takes about 20 minutes.

Spelling to Be Somebody

Publisher: Curriculum Associates

Description: This two-level program is designed for students in seventh grade and above who have not mastered the spelling words required in everyday writing. Each level includes a full semester of remedial lessons, appropriate pretests and posttests, and integrated language arts activities. Also, software programs are available for each level that provide spelling practice routines on lesson words, other word forms, challenge words, or words added by the teacher.

Spelling Mastery

Publisher: Science Research Associates

Description: Spelling Mastery (Dixon, Engelmann, Meier, Steely, & Wells, 1989) is a six-level basal spelling series designed to teach spelling and strategies to students in first through sixth grade. The series begins with phonemic (sound-symbol) and whole-word strategies and then shifts to morphemic (meaning-symbol) strategies. The program emphasizes learning to spell by generalization rather than memorization, and the 20-minute daily lessons can be used with an entire class or with small groups.

Stetson Spelling Program

Publisher: Pro-Ed

Description: The *Stetson Spelling Program* (Stetson, 1988) introduces the 3,000 words most frequently used in writing, which account for 97 percent of the total words written by the average adult. The program uses effective teaching and learning strategies including pretesting, immediate feedback and self-correction, visual imagery of the whole word, spelling clusters, mnemonics, and visual memory. The 230 lessons each contain 10 to 16 words, and direct instruction is used to present a five-step spelling drill on each word. Three blackline masters books each include 1,000 words as well as student support materials such as three-column self-corrected test forms.

Target: Spelling

Publisher: Steck-Vaughn

Description: This series of six consumable books is designed to teach spelling to students with learning problems in first through seventh grade. A systematic, highly ordered format is used in which 1,260 words are presented sequentially and with constant reinforcement throughout the six books. Students are asked to learn only six new words per week, and learning experiences to ensure mastery include activities such as word shapes, word search, visual discrimination, recognition in context, matching words with pictures, sound blending, rhyming, and supplying missing letters.

Teaching Resources Spelling Series

Publisher: DLM

Description: This linguistically based program emphasizes mastery of crucial spelling rules, phonetic patterns, and sight words most frequently misspelled. The series consists of student workbooks on three reading levels (second, third, and fourth grade), with the interest level ranging from third to seventh grade. The workbooks each contain 30 weekly lessons accompanied by review lessons and reinforcement activities. The program is highly structured and repetitive and is designed for students who have not progressed in traditional spelling programs.

Spelling Calculators
(a) Spelling B

Producer: Texas Instruments

Description: This calculator, designed for students at least 6 years old, is accompanied by a book of numbered pictures. A number is displayed on the calculator, the student locates the picture with that number in the book, and then she punches in the correct spelling for that item. If the student spells the word correctly, the calculator gives another number and the student continues. If the student misspells the word, the calculator displays the word *wrong* and the student tries the word again. If the word is spelled incorrectly a second time, the calculator displays the word spelled correctly and a new number is given. Thus, this electronic learning aid uses word-picture associations and the corrected-test method to help students learn more than 260 useful words.

(b) Speak & Spell

Producer: Texas Instruments

Description: This calculator is more complex than *Spelling B* and is designed for students who are at least 7 years old. The calculator "speaks" a word, and the student punches in what she thinks is the correct spelling. If the spelling is correct, the calculator responds "That is correct" and proceeds with a new word. If the word is misspelled, the calculator indicates that the spelling is incorrect, and the student tries the word again. After a second misspelling, the calculator verbalizes the correct spelling and then dictates a new word. Also, after giving a word, the calculator allows time for the student to say the word before spelling it. A booklet accompanies the calculator and contains instructions for spelling games that can be played with others or alone with the calculator.

Spelling Games
(a) Hangman

Producer: Milton Bradley

Description: Hangman is a word-guessing game designed for two players from age 8 to adult. It consists of two L-shaped trays, a total of 112 letter tiles (56 in each color), and lists of five-, six-, seven-, and eight-letter words. Each player chooses a word to play, spells the word with her letter tiles, and places the letters in the slots at the top of her tray so that, when turned, the opponent will read the letters left to right. The object of the game is to be the first player to guess the opponent's concealed word. The players take turns guessing letters, and a player's turn continues until she calls an incorrect letter. For each incorrect letter guess, the opponent turns the dial in her tray, which shows a diagram of stages of "hanging the man" in the window of the tray. After 11 turns of the dial, the player is "hanged" and thereby loses the game. Also, a player who guesses an incorrect word or misspells a word automatically loses the game. The winner is the first player to spell out or guess her opponent's word correctly before being "hanged."

(b) Scrabble

Producer: Selchow and Righter

Description: Scrabble is a crossword game designed for two to four players. Letter tiles with various score values are used to form interlocking words in crossword fashion on the *Scrabble* game board. Because less frequently used letters (such as *q, z,* and *x*) are worth more points, the student is encouraged to spell more difficult words. The players compete for high score by using the letters in combinations and locations that take the best advantage of the values of the tiles and the premium squares (such as *double word score*) on the board. Students can learn new words from plays made by their opponents. Also, any misspelled words can be challenged by other players, and a dictionary can be used to check correct spellings.

(c) Spill and Spell

Producer: Parker Brothers

Description: Spill and Spell is a word game for any number of players. Fifteen wooden cubes with letters printed on each side are placed in a cup and spilled. Each player must make words using the letters shown on the top surface of her spilled cubes. After making the first word, the player continues to try to use the remaining letters in crossword puzzle fashion. The score is determined by squaring the number of letters in each word; therefore, it is to the player's advantage to use as many letters as possible in each word. Also, the number of cubes not used is squared and subtracted from the player's score. *Spill and Spell* can be played by a single student to see how high a score she can get in a single throw. Also, players may take turns rearranging the letters of a single throw to see who can get the highest score. Young students can play to see who can come closest to using all the letters in spelling simple words. In addition, an hourglass timer is included so that players can race against time for the highest score.

Spelling Reference Books
(a) How to Spell It

Publisher: Dale Seymour Publications

Description: This unusual dictionary allows the student to look up a word the way she thinks it is spelled. For example, *nesessary* appears in black print, meaning it is incorrect, and the correct spelling is printed next to it in red.

(b) Spellex Word Finder

Publisher: Curriculum Associates

Description: This student reference book helps students quickly verify the correct spelling of over 15,000 root words and their derivatives. Each base word is presented with its other common forms (for example, *empty—empties, emptied, emptying, emptiness).*

(c) Spelling Reference Book

Publisher: DLM

Description: This quick-reference resource book helps students with poor spelling skills to become more independent. The book lists more than 1,314 high-frequency words alphabetically and also presents homonyms in sentences to show correct meanings.

COMPUTER SOFTWARE PROGRAMS IN SPELLING

Microcomputer software can be used effectively to give students additional learning opportunities to improve or enrich their spelling skills. Some programs provide practice activities and tutorials through a systematic approach, whereas others feature a game format (for example, *Hangman*). The following computer programs are described to give examples of types of software that are available to reinforce spelling skills. Addresses of the producers and distributors of educational computer software are listed in Appendix B.

Dieting Dinosaur Series

Distributor: Charles Clark Company

Hardware: TRS-80

Description: This series of games uses the format of *Hangman* to promote spelling skills. The games can be used by one or two players, or the class can be divided into teams to compete for total points. The program features a dinosaur who is on a strict diet and only can eat letters that fit into the word to

be guessed. Students feed letters to the creature and thus expand their vocabulary and sharpen spelling skills. Words and hints in the program were derived from a variety of texts and are separated into grade levels (third and fourth grade, fifth and sixth grade, seventh grade, and eighth grade). If desired, teachers can replace the word bank with their own chosen words and hints.

Pop 'R Spell; Pop 'R Spell Challenge

Producer: Milliken—EduFun

Hardware: Apple II, IBM PC

Description: Pop 'R Spell is designed for students in third through eighth grade and uses a game format in which one to four students may play. In the game three letters pop out, and the student must guess which one belongs in the secret word. If the correct letter is chosen, the player's turn continues; otherwise, another player gets a turn. The sooner the secret word is spelled, the more bonus points are earned. The first player to score 100 points wins. *Pop 'R Spell Challenge* is for students in the fifth grade and above and focuses on advanced spelling and vocabulary development. The secret words become more challenging as new, difficult words are presented. Students can challenge each other or have round-robin tournaments.

Spelling Rules

Distributor: Charles Clark Company

Hardware: Apple II

Description: This software, designed for students in fifth grade and above, contains instruction with illustrative examples, exercises for practice opportunities, and a mastery quiz. The program explains rules related to *ie* or *ei,* final *e,* adding *k,* final consonant, *-sede, -ceed, -cede,* and final *y.*

The Spelling System

Producer: Milliken

Hardware: Apple II

Description: This program is designed to teach the major principles and patterns that occur in the spelling of English words. Many spelling irregularities also are covered. The program gives special attention to sound spellings and teaches more than 1,400 words. Teachers also can add new words. Each lesson is composed of three separate exercises. First, the student receives a brief introduction to the concept or fact being presented. Then she works through three practice activities (unscrambling words, deciphering words by determining if a before-letter or after-letter code is used, and locating misspelled words). Finally, the student tests her mastery of the lesson words. In the testing format, a sentence is presented with a word missing, and the student may request a sound spelling clue if desired. Only one chance is given for a correct answer. Four diskettes are available (vowel spellings, consonant spellings, special vowel spellings, and word building) as well as a reproducible activity book for supplementary exercises. The program provides instruction for students in fourth through eighth grade as well as review for older students.

Spelling Wiz

Producer: DLM

Hardware: Apple II, IBM PC/PCjr, Commodore 64, Tandy 1000

Description: This software program is included in DLM's *Arcademic Skill Builders in Language Arts* and assists students in spelling more than 300 words commonly misspelled on first- through sixth-grade level. The game features a colorful wizard who uses a magic wand to zap missing letters into words. The following game control options can be preset according to an individual student's needs: speed at which game is played (nine different speeds), difficulty level of content, length of game (1 to 5 minutes), and sound effects on or off. Additional activities for review and reinforcement are provided on 24 blackline masters.

Spelltronics

Distributor: Educational Activities

Hardware: Apple II, TRS-80, Commodore 64 with emulator

Description: This program uses the letter cloze technique to reinforce correct spelling and build visual memory. The entire program teaches 240 words, and it allows the teacher to add additional words. Each word is presented three separate times with different letters deleted. The student adds the missing letters and must type the word into a sentence. If the student is unable to provide the correct spelling after two opportunities, the correct answer is displayed and the student tries again. Correct answers are rewarded in all drills. Words are grouped according to linguistic, phonic, or spelling concepts. Six programs are included: vowel patterns, long vowel patterns, consonant patterns, word endings, useful words, and unexpected spellings. Each pattern has four units containing 10 programmed words and a review unit. The student advances from simple to more complex patterns. The program is useful for all students who have difficulty spelling.

REFERENCES

Arena, J. (1981). *Diagnostic Spelling Potential Test.* Novato, CA: Academic Therapy.

Brigance, A. H. (1982). *Brigance Diagnostic Comprehensive Inventory of Basic Skills.* North Billerica, MA: Curriculum Associates.

Brown, A. S. (1988). Encountering misspellings and spelling performances: Why wrong isn't right. *Journal of Educational Psychology, 80,* 488–494.

Brueckner, L. J., & Bond, G. L. (1966). *The diagnosis and treatment of learning difficulties.* New York: Appleton-Century-Crofts.

Bryant, N. D., Drabin, I. R., & Gettinger, M. (1981). Effects of varying unit size on spelling achievement in learning disabled children. *Journal of Learning Disabilities, 14,* 200–203.

Burns, P. C. (1980). *Assessment and correction of language arts difficulties.* New York: Merrill/Macmillan.

Burns, P. C., & Broman, B. L. (1983). *The language arts in childhood education* (5th ed.). Chicago: Rand McNally.

Carpenter, D., & Miller, L. J. (1982). Spelling ability of reading disabled LD students and able readers. *Learning Disability Quarterly, 5,* 65–70.

Cartwright, G. P. (1969). Written expression and spelling. In R. M. Smith (Ed.), *Teacher diagnosis of educational difficulties* (pp. 95–117). New York: Merrill/Macmillan.

Dixon, R., & Engelmann, S. (1980). *Corrective spelling through morphographs.* Chicago: Science Research Associates.

Dixon, R., Engelmann, S., Meier, M., Steely, D., & Wells, T. (1989). *Spelling mastery.* Chicago: Science Research Associates.

Edgington, R. (1967). But he spelled them right this morning. *Academic Therapy Quarterly, 3,* 58–59.

Ekwall, E. E. (1989). *Locating and correcting reading difficulties* (5th ed.). New York: Merrill/Macmillan.

Fernald, G. (1943). *Remedial techniques in basic school subjects.* New York: McGraw-Hill.

Fernald, G. (1988). *Remedial techniques in basic school subjects.* Austin, TX: Pro-Ed.

Forest, R. G., & Sitton, R. A. (1989). *Instant spelling words for writing.* North Billerica, MA: Curriculum Associates.

Foster, K., & Torgesen, J. K. (1983). The effects of directed study on the spelling performance of two subgroups of learning disabled students. *Learning Disability Quarterly, 6,* 252–257.

Gardner, E. F., Callis, R., Merwin, J. C., & Rudman, H. C. (1983). *Test of Academic Skills* (2nd ed.). San Antonio, TX: Psychological Corporation.

Gardner, E. F., Rudman, H. C., Karlsen, B., & Merwin, J. C. (1982). *Stanford Achievement Test* (7th ed.). San Antonio, TX: Psychological Corporation.

Gates, A., & Russell, D. (1937). *Gates-Russell Spelling Diagnostic Test.* New York: Teachers College, Columbia University.

Gentry, J. R. (1982). An analysis of developmental spellings in *Gnys at wrk. The Reading Teacher, 36,* 192–200.

Gillingham, A., & Stillman, B. (1970). *Remedial training for children with specific disability in reading, spelling, and penmanship* (7th ed.). Cambridge, MA: Educators Publishing Service.

Graham, S., & Freeman, S. (1986). Strategy training and teacher- vs. student-controlled study conditions: Effects on LD students' spelling performance. *Learning Disability Quarterly, 9,* 15–22.

Graham, S., & Voth, V. P. (1990). Spelling instruction: Making modifications for students with learning disabilities. *Academic Therapy, 25,* 447–457.

Greenbaum, C. R. (1987). *The Spellmaster Assessment and Teaching System.* Austin, TX: Pro-Ed.

Hieronymus, A. N., Hoover, H. D., & Lindquist, E. F. (1986). *Iowa Tests of Basic Skills.* Chicago: Riverside.

Hitchcock, M. E. (1989). *Elementary students' invented spellings at the correct stage of spelling development.* Unpublished doctoral dissertation. Norman: University of Oklahoma.

Hodges, R. E. (1966). The psychological bases of spelling. In T. D. Horn (Ed.), *Research on handwriting and spelling.* Champaign, IL: National Council of Teachers of English.

Horn, E. A. (1926). *A basic writing vocabulary* (University of Iowa Monographs in Education, First Series No. 4). Iowa City: University of Iowa.

Jastak, S. R., & Wilkinson, G. S. (1984). *Wide Range Achievement Test—Revised.* Wilmington, DE: Jastak Associates.

Kauffman, J. M., Hallahan, D. P., Haas, K., Brame, T., & Boren, R. (1978). Imitating children's errors to improve their spelling performance. *Journal of Learning Disabilities, 11,* 217–222.

Kaufman, A. S., & Kaufman, N. L. (1985). *Kaufman Test of Educational Achievement.* Circle Pines, MN: American Guidance Service.

Koenig, C. H., & Kunzelmann, H. P. (1980). *Classroom learning screening manual.* New York: Merrill/Macmillan.

Kottmeyer, W. (1970). *Teacher's guide for remedial reading.* New York: McGraw-Hill.

Kuska, A., Webster, E. J. D., & Elford, G. (1964). *Spelling in language arts 6.* Don Mills, Ontario, Canada: Thomas Nelson & Sons.

Larsen, S. C., & Hammill, D. D. (1986). *Test of Written Spelling—2.* Austin, TX: Pro-Ed.

Lerner, J. W. (1989). *Learning disabilities: Theories, diagnosis, and teaching strategies* (5th ed.). Boston: Houghton Mifflin.

Lovitt, T. C., Guppy, T. E., & Blattner, J. E. (1969). The use of free-time contingency with fourth graders to increase spelling accuracy. *Behavior Research Therapy, 7,* 151–156.

Mann, P. H., Suiter, P. A., & McClung, R. M. (1992). *A guide to educating mainstreamed students* (4th ed.). Boston: Allyn & Bacon.

Markwardt, F. C., Jr. (1989). *Peabody Individual Achievement Test—Revised.* Circle Pines, MN: American Guidance Service.

Marsh, G. E., II, Gearheart, C. K., & Gearheart, B. R. (1978). *The learning disabled adolescent: Program alternatives in the secondary school.* St. Louis, MO: C. V. Mosby.

McGuigan, C. A. (1975). *The effects of a flowing words list vs. fixed words lists and the implementation of procedures in the add-a-word spelling program* (Working Paper No. 52). Seattle: University of Washington, Experimental Education Unit.

McLoughlin, J. A., & Lewis, R. B. (1990). *Assessing special students* (3rd ed.). New York: Merrill/Macmillan.

Naslund, R. A., Thorpe, L. P., & Lefever, D. W. (1985). *SRA Achievement Series.* Chicago: Science Research Associates.

Petty, W. T. (1966). Handwriting and spelling: Their current status in the language arts curriculum. In T. D. Horn (Ed.), *Research on handwriting and spelling.* Champaign, IL: National Council of Teachers of English.

Proff-Witt, J. (1978). *Speed spelling 1.* Austin, TX: Pro-Ed.

Proff-Witt, J. (1979). *Speed spelling 2.* Austin, TX: Pro-Ed.

Scannell, D. P. (1986). *Tests of Achievement and Proficiency.* Chicago: Riverside.

Shinn, M. R., Tindal, G., & Stein, S. (1988). Curriculum-based measurement and the identification of mildly handicapped students: A research review. *Professional School Psychology, 3*(1), 69–85.

Shinn, T. K. (1982). Linguistic and functional spelling strategies. In D. A. Sabatino & L. Mann (Eds.), *A handbook of diagnostic and prescriptive teaching* (pp. 263–295). Rockville, MD: Aspen Systems.

Sidman, M. T. (1979). The effects of group free time and contingency and individual free time contingency on spelling performance. *The Directive Teacher, 1,* 4–5.

Starlin, C. M., & Starlin, A. (1973). *Guides to decision making in spelling.* Bemidji, MN: Unique Curriculums Unlimited.

Stephens, T. M. (1977). *Teaching skills to children with learning and behavior disorders.* New York: Merrill/Macmillan.

Stephens, T. M., Hartman, A. C., & Lucas, V. H. (1982). *Teaching children basic skills: A curriculum handbook* (2nd ed.). New York: Merrill/Macmillan.

Stetson, E. (1988). *Stetson spelling program.* Austin, TX: Pro-Ed.

Stowitschek, C. E., & Jobes, N. K. (1977). Getting the bugs out of spelling—or an alternative to the spelling bee. *Teaching Exceptional Children, 9,* 74–76.

Taylor, K. K., & Kidder, E. B. (1988). The development of spelling skills: From first grade through eighth grade. *Written Communication, 5,* 222–244.

Templeton, S. (1986). Synthesis of research on the learning and teaching of spelling. *Educational Leadership, 43*(6), 73–78.

Tindal, G. A., & Marston, D. B. (1990). *Classroom-based assessment: Evaluating instructional outcomes.* New York: Merrill/Macmillan.

Tompkins, G. E., & Hoskisson, K. (1991). *Language arts: Content and teaching strategies* (2nd ed.). New York: Merrill/Macmillan.

Vallecorsa, A. L., Zigmond, N., & Henderson, L. M. (1985). Spelling instruction in special education classrooms: A survey of practices. *Exceptional Children, 52,* 19–24.

Wesson, C. L. (1987). Curriculum-based measurement: Increasing efficiency. *Teaching Exceptional Children, 20*(1), 46–47.

Westerman, G. S. (1971). *Spelling & writing.* San Rafael, CA: Dimensions.

CHAPTER 13

Assessing and Teaching Handwriting and Written Expression Skills

Writing is a highly complex form of communication. It is both a skill and a means of self-expression. The process of writing integrates visual, motor, and conceptual abilities and is a major means through which students demonstrate their knowledge of advanced academic subjects. Moreover, Hammill and McNutt (1981) report that writing skills are among the best correlates of reading. Such skills include competence in writing, spelling, punctuation, capitalization, studying, making sound-letter correspondences, knowing the alphabet, and distinguishing one letter from another. Hammill and McNutt conclude that "a strong relationship exists between reading, which is theoretically a receptive form of written language, and almost all other aspects of written language" (p. 35).

Classroom instruction in handwriting usually begins in kindergarten or first grade. Readiness activities such as tracing, coloring, and copying are emphasized at first. The formation of letters, numbers, and words is stressed until about the third grade. After the third grade, more emphasis is placed on writing as a form of meaningful self-expression, and instruction focuses on using grammar and developing the quality of ideas expressed. In this chapter, the assessment and teaching of writing skills are divided into the two major areas of handwriting and written expression.

HANDWRITING PROBLEMS

The major objective of instruction in handwriting is legibility. To communicate thoughts in writing, the student first must be taught to write legibly and easily. Thus, instruction begins by focusing on holding the writing instrument, forming manuscript and cursive letters correctly, and maintaining proper spacing and proportion. Numerous factors contribute to handwriting difficulties: motor problems, faulty visual perception of letters and words, poor visual memory, poor instruction, and lack of motivation.

Fine motor problems also can interfere with handwriting and thus with schoolwork. For example, a student may know how to spell a word but be unable to write legibly or fast enough to keep up with the teacher; thus, the spelling may be poor. This same situation may exist in copying material from the chalkboard and working on seatwork. Unfortunately, many parents and teachers view the student as academically slow when, in fact, the real problem is handwriting.

Students show a variety of handwriting problems: slowness, incorrect directionality of letters and numbers, too much or too little slant, spacing difficulty, messiness, inability to stay on a horizontal line, illegible letters, too much or too little pencil pressure, and mirror writing. Newland (1932) examined the cursive handwriting of 2,831 people and found that about 50 percent of the illegibilities involved the letters *a, e, r,* and *t.* Most commonly, people failed to close letters (such as *a* and *f*), closed top loops (such as writing *e* like *i*), looped strokes that should be nonlooped (such as writing *i* like *e*), used straight-up rather than rounded strokes (such as writing *n* like *u*), and exhibited problems with end strokes (not brought up, down, or left horizontal). In a study of illegibilities in cursive handwriting of sixth graders, Horton (1970) reported that 12 percent of all errors were incorrect formations of the letter *r*. Thus, the majority of handwriting errors involve the incorrect writing of a few letters. Common number malformations include writing 5 like 3 (*5*), 6 like 0 (*6*), 7 like 9 (*7*), and 9 like 4 (*9*).

ASSESSMENT OF HANDWRITING SKILLS

In assessing the young student (8 or 9 years old and younger), the teacher should remember that occasional reversals, omissions, and poor spacing are normal. However, a writing problem exists if such errors continue for a long time and if the student does not improve in simple handwriting tasks. Unlike the other academic skill areas, few standardized tests exist to measure handwriting, and informal procedures are used widely. Minimum standards are difficult to set because activities differ in emphasis placed on speed, legibility, and character of handwriting.

Published Assessment Devices

To assess a student's overall readiness to learn writing, the writing section of the *Basic School Skills Inventory—Diagnostic* (Hammill & Leigh, 1983) assesses a student's handwriting ability in various tasks: writing from left to right, grasping a pencil, writing first name, maintaining proper writing position, writing letters upon request, copying words, copying from chalkboard to paper, staying on the line, and writing last name. The instrument is norm-referenced for students age 4 years to 7 years 5 months to identify those who are low in handwriting readiness as compared with students their age. The scale also can be used as a criterion-referenced test to determine what skills need to be taught.

The *Test of Legible Handwriting* (Larsen & Hammill, 1989) is a standardized test of legibility that reports results in terms of standard scores and percentiles. It is designed for students age 7 through 17 and includes an evaluation system that is applied to multiple samples of a student's handwriting. The samples are selected from several themes and settings, such as creative essays, biographical sketches, correspondences, reports, and work samples. Each handwriting sample is matched as closely as possible with one of three scoring guides that feature distinctly different writing styles: (a) a cursive style having a slant to

the right or a style that is more or less perpendicular, (b) a cursive style having a slant to the left, and (c) a manuscript or modified manuscript style. The examiner selects the scoring guide that most closely resembles the student's handwriting and uses the examples that range from good to poor in the guide to rate the sample on a scale of one through nine. The resulting score is converted to a percentile and standard score, and when more than one sample is collected a compositive legibility quotient is obtained.

The *Zaner-Bloser Evaluation Scales* (1984) are based on a national sampling of students' handwriting and frequently are used for assessing manuscript and cursive handwriting. There are scales for first and second grade written in manuscript style and scales for second through eighth grade written in cursive style. Five specimens of handwriting—excellent, good, average, fair, and poor—are provided for each grade level. Each scale contains a sentence or paragraph that the teacher writes on the chalkboard. The students practice writing the model and then copy the sentences in their best handwriting onto a sheet of paper. The teacher compares each paper with the five specimen sentences for the student's grade level and judges the following five elements: letter formation, vertical strokes in manuscript and slant in cursive, spacing, alignment and proportion, and line quality. Each student's writing is rated according to the number of satisfactory elements. Through this method a student's handwriting can be compared with that of students in the same grade level; however, a thorough analysis of errors is needed before planning instructional programs.

Various legibility scales traditionally have been used to provide a subjective evaluation of general handwriting competence. However, the objectivity of such scales has been questioned, and they do not highlight specific errors and illegible forms in writing. Thus, handwriting scales may be used best to aid the teacher in rating a writing specimen for screening purposes. To obtain information for instructional purposes, various informal assessment techniques may be helpful.

Informal Assessment Techniques

The teacher can obtain diagnostic information informally through a close visual examination of the student's handwriting. Writing samples can be used to determine problem areas in legibility. Mann, Suiter, and McClung (1992) suggest obtaining three samples: the student's usual, best, and fastest handwriting. The usual writing sample shows the student's work under normal, nonfatiguing conditions. For the best sample, the student is told to take his time and write the sentence with his best effort. Then the student is timed for 3 minutes to see how many times he can write a given sentence. Sometimes a student can write legibly but only when specifically asked to do so. Also, some students write well but at an extremely slow rate. By comparing the three writing samples, the teacher can determine the student's ability with regard to speed and legibility.

While observing the student during handwriting activities, the teacher should note possible problem areas by answering the following questions:

1. Does the student grip the pencil correctly and in a comfortable and flexible manner?
2. Is the student's paper in the proper position on the writing surface?
3. Does the student sit correctly when writing, or is his head too close or too far away from the paper?
4. Does the student consistently use the same hand for writing?
5. Does the student appear extremely frustrated, nervous, or emotional when writing?

6. Does the student have a negative attitude toward handwriting and appear bored and disruptive?

Additional instructional information can be obtained by analyzing the student's writing sample for error patterns in the following various aspects of handwriting:

1. *Letter formation:* Letter formation involves the strokes that make up each letter. To check for legibility, the teacher can use a piece of cardboard with a hole cut in the center that is slightly larger than a single letter. By exposing one letter at a time, the teacher can see more easily which letters are illegible or poorly formed.

2. *Letter size, proportion, and alignment:* The size and proportion of letters are indicated by their height relationship to one another, and alignment refers to the evenness of letters along the base line, with letters of the same size being the same height. These legibility elements can be measured by using a ruler to draw lines that touch the base and tops of as many letters as possible.

3. *Spacing:* Spacing should be consistent between letters within words, as well as between words and between sentences.

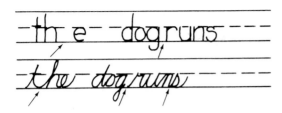

4. *Line quality:* Thickness and steadiness of the lines used to form letters should be consistent. The teacher should mark lines that waver or are too thick or too fine. Incorrect hand or body position or cramped fingers can result in inconsistent line quality.

5. *Slant:* The slant of letters should be uniform. In general, manuscript letters are perpendicular to the base line and have a straight up-and-down appearance. In cursive writing the paper is slanted, and strokes are pulled toward the body. Straight lines or lines with a uniform slant can be drawn through the letters to indicate which letters are off slant.

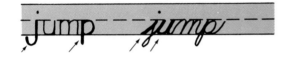

6. *Rate:* Speed of handwriting can be determined on a writing sample by asking the student to write as well and as rapidly as possible. The rate of handwriting—letters per minute (lpm)—is determined by dividing the total number of letters written by the number of writing minutes allowed. Handwriting proficiency rates include the following:

(a) Zaner-Bloser scales:
   Grade 1 — 25 lpm
   Grade 2 — 30 lpm
   Grade 3 — 38 lpm
   Grade 4 — 45 lpm
   Grade 5 — 60 lpm
   Grade 6 — 67 lpm
   Grade 7 — 74 lpm
(b) Precision Teaching Project (Montana):
   think—write alphabet (emphasizing speed): 80–100 lpm
   see—write letters (emphasizing accuracy: 75 lpm correct (count of three for each letter—slant, form, ending)
   see—write numerals random: 100–120 digits per minute
   see—write connected cursive letters: 125 lpm (count of three per letter)
(c) Koenig and Kunzelmann (1980):
   see—write letters: 70 lpm
   see—write numerals random: 70 digits per minute

Table 13.1 displays a diagnostic chart for manuscript and cursive writing that highlights errors, likely causes, and remediation procedures.

Probes can be used to assess a specific handwriting skill and determine instructional targets. On the Precision Teaching Project (Montana) handwriting probe sheets, the student is timed for 1 minute. Tasks include repeatedly writing the same letter, writing manuscript capitals, writing cursive letters, writing two cursive letters joined together, and writing words in small cursive letters. Daily performance on the probe sheets is charted to monitor progress. Koenig and Kunzelmann (1980) provide probe sheets for writing uppercase letters, lowercase letters, first name, first letter of first name, and words for 1 minute. A probe sheet on writing uppercase manuscript letters is presented in Figure 13.1.

In assessing handwriting difficulties, the teacher also can encourage the student to use

TABLE 13.1

Diagnostic chart for manuscript and cursive writing.

Factor	Problem	Possible Cause	Remediation
Manuscript Writing			
Shape	Letters slanted	Paper slanted	Place paper straight and pull straight-line strokes toward center of body.
	Varies from standard	Improper mental image of letter	Have student write problem letters on chalkboard.
Size	Too large	Poor understanding of writing lines	Reteach size concept by pointing out purpose of each line on writing paper.
		Exaggerated arm movement	Reduce arm movement, especially on circle and part-circle letters.
		Improper mental image of letter	Have student write problem letters on chalkboard.
	Too small	Poor understanding of writing lines	Reteach size concept by pointing out purpose of each line on writing paper.
		Overemphasis on finger movement	Stress arm movement; check hand-pencil and arm-desk positions to be sure arm movement is possible.
		Improper mental image of letter	Have student write problem letters on chalkboard.
	Not uniform	Adjusting writing hand after each letter	Stress arm movement; move paper with nonwriting hand so writing hand can remain in proper writing position.
		Overemphasis on finger movement	Stress arm movement; check arm-desk and pencil-hand positions.
Space	Crowded letters in words	Poor understanding of space concepts	Reteach uniform spacing between letters (finger or pencil width).
	Too much space between letters	Improper lowercase letter size and shape	Review concepts of size and shape; provide appropriate corrections under size and shape.
Alignment	Letters not sitting on base line	Improper letter formation	Evaluate work for letter shape; stress bringing straight-line strokes all the way down to base line.

TABLE 13.1
Continued

Factor	Problem	Possible Cause	Remediation
		Poor understanding of base line concept	Review purpose of base line on writing paper.
		Improper hand-pencil and paper-desk positions	Check positions to make sure student is able to reach base line with ease.
	Letters not of consistent height	Poor understanding of size concept	Review concept of letter size in relationship to lines provided on writing paper.
Line quality	Too heavy or too light	Improper writing pressure	Review hand-pencil position; place wadded paper tissue on palm of writing hand to relax writing grip; demonstrate desired line quality.

Cursive Writing

Factor	Problem	Possible Cause	Remediation
Shape	Letters too oval in size	Overemphasis of arm movement and poor image of letter size and shape	Check arm-desk position; review letter size and shape.
	Letters too narrow in shape	Finger writing	Check positions to allow for arm movement.
		Overemphasis of straight-line stroke	Make sure straight-line stroke does not come all the way down to base line in letters like *l, b,* and *t*.
		Poor mental image of letter shape	Use transparent overlay for student's personal evaluation of shape.
			In all problems of letter shape review letters in terms of the basic strokes.
Size	Letters too large	Exaggerated arm movement	Check arm-desk position for over-movement of forearm.
		Poor mental image of letter size	Review base and top line concepts in relation to $\frac{1}{4}$ space, $\frac{1}{2}$ space, and $\frac{3}{4}$ space; use transparent overlay for student's personal evaluation of letter size.
	Letters too small or letters not uniform	Finger movement	Check arm-desk and pencil-hand positions; stress arm movement.

(continued)

TABLE 13.1
Continued

Factor	Problem	Possible Cause	Remediation
		Poor mental image of letter size	Review concept of letter size (¼ space, ½ space, and ¾ space) in relation to base and top lines; use transparent overlay for student's personal evaluation of letter size.
Space	Letters in words crowded or spacing between letters uneven	Finger movement	Check arm-desk, pencil-hand positions; stress arm movement.
		Poor understanding of joining strokes	Review how letters are joined; show ending stroke of one letter to be beginning stroke of following letter; practice writing letters in groups of five.
	Too much space provided between letters and words	Exaggerated arm movement	Check arm-desk position for over-movement of forearm.
		Poor understanding of joining strokes	Review joining strokes; practice writing groups of letters by rhythmic count.
	Uneven space between words	Poor understanding of between-word spacing	Review concept of spacing between words; show beginning stroke in second word starting under ending stroke of preceding word.
Alignment	Poor letter alignment along base line	Incorrect writing position; finger movement; exaggerated arm movement	Check all writing positions; stress even, rhythmic writing movement.
		Poor understanding of base line concept	Use repetitive exercise with emphasis on relationship of base line to written word.
		Incorrect use of joining strokes	Review joining strokes.
	Uneven alignment of letters in words relative to size	Poor understanding of size concept	Show size relationships between lower- and uppercase, and ¼ space, ½ space, and ¾ space lowercase letters; use repetitive exercise with emphasis on uniform height of smaller letters.

TABLE 13.1
Continued

Factor	Problem	Possible Cause	Remediation
Speed and Ease	Writing becomes illegible under stress and speed (grades 4, 5, and 6)	Degree of handwriting skill is insufficient to meet speed requirements	Improve writing positions; develop more arm movement and less finger movement.
	Writing becomes illegible when writing activity is too long	Handwriting positions have not been perfected to allow handwriting ease	Improve all writing positions, especially hand-pencil position; stress arm movement.
Slant	Back slant	Left-handedness	Correct hand-pencil and paper-desk positions.
	Vertical	Poor positioning	Correct hand-pencil and paper-desk positions.
	Too far right	Overemphasis of finger movement	Make sure student pulls slant strokes toward center of body if right-handed and to left elbow if left-handed.
			Use slant line instruction sheets as aid to teaching slant.
			Use transparent overlay for student's personal evaluation.
			Review all lowercase letters that derive their shape from the slant line.
			Write lowercase alphabet on chalkboard; retrace all slant strokes in colored chalk.

self-evaluation. Diagnostic charts and evaluation scales can help the student identify his own handwriting inaccuracies. When the student monitors his writing, he can change his writing performance quickly and easily. Also, positive attitudes may be increased as the student assumes some responsibility for learning and improving his handwriting. A commercial material that can be useful in self-evaluation is *Peek-Thru* (Zaner-Bloser). This is a plastic overlay that the student places on top of his writing and "peeks thru" to check correct letter formation and alignment. A manuscript set is provided for first through third grade, and a cursive set is available for transition, third grade, and fourth grade. For fifth grade and

Name: _____   Date: _____

Time: _____

Rate (letters per minute): _____ Correct

_____ Error

Comments: _____

_____

FIGURE 13.1
Probe sheet for writing uppercase manuscript letters.

above there are two similar plastic overlay rulers, one in manuscript and one in cursive.

TEACHING HANDWRITING SKILLS

After assessment, the teacher can establish instructional objectives based upon pinpointed errors and the student's overall development of handwriting skills. Skills should be taught through meaningful and motivating activities. Repetitious drills and mass practice without supervision should be avoided, and the student should receive immediate feedback. Models should be provided of both good and poor work so that the student eventually can make comparisons to determine necessary changes.

Wiederholt, Hammill, and Brown (1983) suggest that teachers in the primary grades should devote at least 10 to 15 minutes each day to teaching handwriting. Teachers should demonstrate the correct way to form letters and should supervise students' handwriting efforts carefully. Also, the teacher should help the student develop a positive attitude toward handwriting by encouraging progress and stressing the importance of the skill. In the upper elementary grades and in secondary classrooms, greater emphasis is placed on identifying and remediating individual handwriting deficits revealed in the student's daily written work. Hofmeister (1981) lists six instructional errors to *avoid:* (a) unsupervised handwriting practice while skills are being formed, (b) lack of immediate feedback to correct errors, (c) lack of emphasis on student analysis of errors, (d) failure to provide close-range models of correct letter formation, (e) repeated drill of both correct and incorrect letter production, and (f) misplaced emphasis on activities of limited value.

A scope and sequence chart of handwriting skills by grade level is presented in Appendix A. The development of handwriting skills and teaching strategies are presented next in the areas of readiness skills, manuscript writing, transitional writing, and cursive writing.

Readiness Skills

Writing requires muscular control, eye-hand coordination, and visual discrimination. The teacher needs to help develop skills in these areas before the student is ready to begin handwriting. Muscular coordination can be developed in the young child through manipulative experiences (for example, cutting with scissors, finger painting, tracing, coloring). Eye-hand coordination is involved in drawing circles and copying geometric forms. Also, developing visual discrimination of sizes, shapes, and details aids the student's visual awareness of letters and their formation. Chalkboard activities provide practice and give the student the opportunity to use muscle movement of the shoulders, arms, hands, and fingers. Before beginning handwriting instruction, the student should be able to do the following:

1. Perform hand movements such as up-down, left-right, and forward-back.
2. Trace geometric shapes and dotted lines.
3. Connect dots on paper.
4. Draw a horizontal line from left to right.
5. Draw a vertical line from top to bottom and bottom to top.
6. Draw a backward circle, a curved line, and a forward circle.
7. Draw slanted lines vertically.
8. Copy simple designs and shapes.
9. Name letters and discern likenesses and differences in letter forms.

Determining the student's hand preference also is important. The teacher should determine which hand the student uses most often in natural situations, such as eating or throwing a ball. Also, the teacher can ask the student to use one hand to take a pencil out of a box, cover one eye, or make a mark on the chalkboard. The youngster who indicates a strong preference for using his left hand should be allowed to do so for writing. The student who uses both hands well should be encouraged to make a choice and consistently use one hand for writing. The teacher also can encourage him to become a right-handed writer.

The proper position of paper and pencil also must be taught before extensive handwriting instruction. During writing, the student should be in a comfortable chair, with feet flat on the floor. The desk or table should be at a height that allows the student to place his forearms on the writing surface without discomfort. The nonwriting hand holds the writing paper at the top. To prevent elbow bumping, left-handers should be seated in a left-hand desk chair or along the outside at a work table. The pencil should be held lightly in the triangle formed by the thumb and the first two fingers, and the hand should rest lightly on its outer edge. The pencil should be held about an inch above its point by right-handers, and the pencil top should point in the direction of the right shoulder. For left-handers, the pencil should be held about 1¼ inches from its writing point, and the pencil end should point toward the left shoulder. Commercial triangular-shaped pencil grips (available from DLM) or masking tape can be placed on the pencil to make it easier to hold.

For manuscript writing the paper should be placed straight on the desk directly in front of the eyes. For some left-handers it may be helpful to slant the paper so that the lower right corner of the paper points to the left of the center of the body. For cursive writing the paper should be tilted. The right-handed student places the paper so that the lower left corner points toward the center of the body and the writing stroke is pulled toward the center of the body. For the left-handed student the paper is slanted north-northeast. The lower right corner points to the center of the body, and the writing stroke is pulled toward the left elbow. Some left-handers begin "hooking" their hand and wrist while writing to see what they have written and to avoid smudging their writing. This practice should be avoided and can be controlled by helping the student find the right slant for his paper.

Manuscript Writing

Manuscript writing usually is taught in kindergarten and first grade and is based entirely on the basic shapes of circles and straight lines. The strokes for both uppercase and lowercase manuscript letters are presented in Figure 13.2 with arrows and numbers to indicate the direction and sequence of strokes.

The teacher can demonstrate letter forms on the chalkboard, being careful not to block the student's vision. The student should observe the handwriting process as well as the finished product. When writing on the chalkboard, the student should write at eye level and stand at arm's length directly in front of the writing.

A multisensory approach often is used in teaching letter forms. The student sees, hears, and traces the letter model. The following steps can be used:

1. The teacher shows the student the letter (or word) to be written.
2. The teacher says aloud the letter name and stroke directions (for example, "First we go up; then we go down").
3. The student traces the model with his finger and may report his movements aloud as he traces.
4. The student traces the letter model with his pencil.
5. The student copies the letter on paper while looking at the model.

A fading model also can be used in teaching handwriting. The letter model is presented at first in heavy, dark lines, and the student traces over the model with his finger and the nonwriting end of his pencil. Gradually portions of the model are faded, and the student traces the model with his pencil. Eventually the model is removed, and the student writes the letter independent of the model. For example:

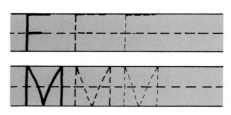

FIGURE 13.2
Formation of uppercase and lowercase manuscript letters and numbers.
Source: From *Creative Growth with Handwriting* (p. 96), by W. B. Barbe, V. H. Lucas, C. S. Hackney, and C. McAllister, 1975, 1979, Columbus, OH: Zaner-Bloser, Inc. Reprinted by permission.

As soon as possible, activities should be provided in which words are used and the writing says something. Copying meaningless letters may result in boredom and negative attitudes toward writing. Also, in copying exercises, the letter or word model should be presented at first on the kind of paper the student uses.

Letters that consist entirely of vertical and horizontal strokes (such as *E, F, H, I, L, T, i, l, t*) are learned more easily than letters in which straight and curved lines are combined (such as *b, f, h, p*). Letters with easier strokes may be taught first. The teacher should give more attention to the formation of difficult letter forms.

In a study of first graders' errors in the formation of manuscript letters, Lewis and Lewis (1965) made the following observations:

1. Incorrect size was the most common type of error and was more often seen in descender letters (*p, q, y, g, j*).
2. The most frequently reversed letters were *N, d, q,* and *y.*
3. Incorrect relationship of parts occurred most frequently in the letters *k, R, M,* and *m.*
4. Partial omission occurred most frequently in the letters *m, U,* and *I.*
5. Additions often occurred in the letters *q, C, k, m,* and *y.*

6. The most frequently misshaped letter forms were *j, G,* and *J.*

Numerous letters often were reversed, such as *b, d, p, q, s, y,* and *N.* In teaching these letters, the teacher should emphasize the correct beginning point and direction of letters. As well as receiving immediate corrective feedback followed by practice saying the letter name while tracing and writing it, the student can be instructed to associate the problem letter with another letter that does not cause confusion (for example, *c* within *d*). In addition to difficulties in formation, some students have problems spacing and aligning manuscript letters. In general, the widest space is left between straight-line letters, and the least amount of space is left between circle letters. Spacing between words equals about the size of one finger or a lowercase *o,* and twice as much space is left between sentences. Poor alignment should be pointed out to the student; however, if the student has extreme difficulty staying on the lines of writing paper, the teacher may choose to provide Right-Line Paper (available from Pro-Ed) until the student improves. This paper (both wide- and narrow-rule) has a raised line superimposed on the printed line so that the writer can feel as well as see the base line.

Transitional Writing

The transition from manuscript to cursive writing usually occurs during the second or third grade, after the student has mastered manuscript letters. However, some controversy exists concerning whether to begin with manuscript or cursive writing. Those who favor manuscript writing (Anderson, 1966; Barbe, Milone, & Wasylyk, 1983; Herrick, 1960) claim

that it requires less complex movements and reduces reading problems because most printed pages are in manuscript. In addition, manuscript writing tends to be more legible and has received acceptance in business and commercial contexts. Advocates of cursive writing (Strauss & Lehtinen, 1947) believe that cursive writing results in fewer reversals because of its rhythmic flow. Also, transference problems are avoided if writing begins with cursive. However, some educators (Hildreth, 1963; Templin, 1960; Western, 1977) question the need for teaching cursive writing at all and feel that manuscript writing meets the adult needs of speed and legibility. After reviewing research data concerning manuscript versus cursive writing, Graham and Miller (1980) indicate that most evidence supports manuscript instruction; however, the advantages of manuscript writing have yet to be conclusively demonstrated. Because good arguments are presented on all sides, the teacher should assess each individual situation. It may be best to teach each student the form of writing used by his peers. Also, many young children want to learn cursive writing because older peers and adults use it. Regardless of the type of writing instruction, the student should be allowed to choose the mode of writing for tests and expressive writing.

Mann et al. (1992) suggest the following method for transitional writing:

1. The word is printed in manuscript.
2. The letters are connected with a dotted line in colored pencil.
3. The student traces over the manuscript letter and the connecting dotted line to form the cursive writing.

The teacher may begin teaching transitional writing with the easier letters and add more

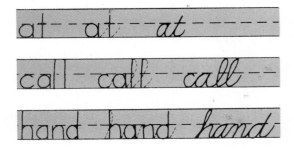

difficult letters one at a time. Certain letters must be taught specifically, such as *b, e, f, k, r, s,* and *z.* Also, when the letter *n* is in the middle or end of a word, enough space must be allowed in front of it for the additional hump needed in the cursive formation of the letter.

Hagin (1983) recommends a simplified handwriting method based on the vertical downstroke rather than the diagonal slant necessary to cursive writing. Manuscript letters are used as a bridge to a simplified writing style with connections between letters made by the natural movement to the next vertical downstroke. Thus, the simplicity of manuscript writing is combined with the speed of cursive writing. In this approach letter forms are taught through four simple motifs (waves, pearls, wheels, arrows) that serve as foundations for lowercase letters. After practice at the chalkboard, lessons at the desk include tracing letters on an acetate sheet placed over the printed model, trying to write the letter on the acetate without a model, matching the written letter with the model to determine if more practice is needed, and providing a permanent record of the letters worked on in that lesson that later can be compared in self-evaluation. This approach may be helpful to students who have difficulty learning conventional cursive writing patterns.

Cursive Writing

Instruction in cursive writing usually begins in the second or third grade, depending upon the skill development of the individual student. In cursive writing the strokes are connected, and fine motor coordination is required to perform many precise movements. Figure 13.3 presents the letter formation of uppercase and lowercase cursive letters, with arrows and numbers indicating the direction and sequence of the strokes.

Many of the same techniques used to teach manuscript writing, such as the multisensory approach and fading model, also can be used in cursive writing instruction. The proper slant in cursive writing is achieved by slanting the paper and pulling strokes to the body, as described earlier in the discussion of readiness skills. Newland (1932) notes that four specific letters—*a, e, r, t*—contribute to a large number of errors in cursive writing. The teacher should give special attention to the proper formation of these four letters and also should focus upon the types of errors that result in common illegibilities. Table 13.2 illustrates numerous common illegibilities in forming cursive letters. After the student has learned how to form cursive letters accurately, he should be taught to connect letters and to write simple words.

Typewriting

The typewriter may be a viable alternative for students with severe fine motor problems or those who write very slowly. Polloway and Smith (1982) note that, in addition to simplified motor movements, the advantages of typing include faster speed, the highest degree of legibility, and inherent motivation. Also, the ability to type facilitates the use of computers and word-processing programs. Selected com-

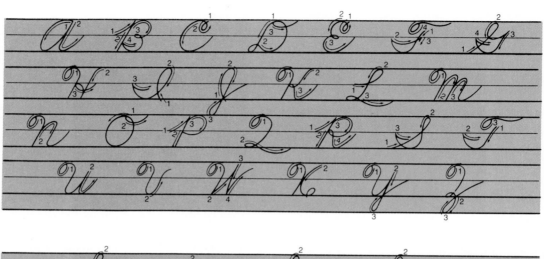

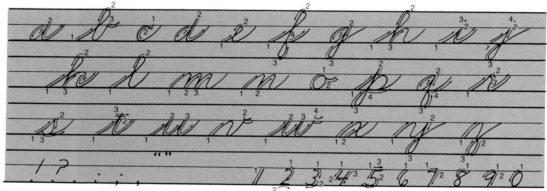

FIGURE 13.3

Formation of uppercase and lowercase cursive letters and numbers.

Source: From *Creative Growth with Handwriting* (p. 96), by W. B. Barbe, V. H. Lucas, C. S. Hackney, and C. McAllister, 1975, 1979, Columbus, OH: Zaner-Bloser, Inc. Reprinted by permission.

puter programs that are available for learning touch-typing and keyboarding include *Success with Typing* (Scholastic Software), *Stickybear Typing* (Weekly Reader Family Software), and *Type!* (Broderbund).

HANDWRITING ACTIVITIES

Numerous activities and materials enhance the development of handwriting skills. Activities, games, and learning centers are pre-

sented in three areas: readiness skills, manuscript writing, and cursive writing.

Readiness Activities

1. Use body exercises to practice movements such as up and down, left and right, and forward and backward. For example, give the student the following instructions: "Raise your writing hand *up* in the air"; "Make a long straight line with your hand going from *top* to *bottom*"; Make a *circle* with your hand in front

TABLE 13.2
Common illegibilities in handwriting.

a like u	*ce*	m like n	*n*
a like o	*ce*	n like u	*u*
a like ce	*ce*	o like a	*a*
b like li	*le*	o like v	*v*
be like bl	*be*	p like js	*js*
b like k	*k*	r like n	*n*
c like e	*e*	r like v	*v*
c like a	*a*	r like i	*i*
d like cl	*cl*	t like i	*i*
e like i	*i*	t like l	*l*
g like y	*y*	u like ee	*ee*
g like q	*q*	u like ei	*ei*
i like e	*e*	w like n	*n*
h like li	*li*	w like ue	*ue*
h like k	*k*	w like eu	*eu*
k like ls	*ls*	x like v	*v*
m like w	*w*	y like ij	*ij*

within lines. The student can be asked to color shapes or objects before cutting them out with scissors.

3. In seatwork activities, have the student practice drawing circles: balls, balloons, funny faces, coins, and apples.

4. To help the student develop fine motor skills and strengthen hand and finger muscles, have him participate in finger painting and clay modeling activities. Squeezing and molding clay is good exercise. Also, the student can be required to manipulate small objects such as nuts and bolts, cubes, buttons, and bottle caps.

5. Have the student connect dots in dot-to-dot activities to form geometric shapes or pictures. To help the student draw straight lines by himself, place dots in a straight line and gradually increase the distance between them. Also, circles and squares can be completed in dot-to-dot fashion. The figures eventually can include actual letters.

6. Use chalkboard activities for exercises in copying, dot-to-dot, and completing incomplete figures. The large, free movements made at the chalkboard help develop muscles of the shoulders, arms, hands, and fingers. Academic skills also can be practiced through the use of a chalkboard. A student's lack of handwriting development should not be allowed to impede his completion of academic tasks.

7. Have the student practice writing movements in a tray filled with a layer of sand, salt, or cornmeal.

8. Provide tracing activities by making dark-line figures (shapes, letters, numbers, objects) on white paper and covering the paper with a sheet of onionskin on which the student can trace. Also, the student can trace on sheets of acetate or plastic with a felt-tip pen or a grease pencil. Clipboards can be used to hold tracing paper in its place, or the paper can be taped to the student's desk.

9. Make stencils and templates of shapes, numbers, and letters from plastic, styrofoam, or cardboard. Fasten the stencil to the student's paper with paper clips so that he can write or trace the forms. When the stencil or template is removed, the student can view the figure he has made.

of your body"; "Make a long line from *left* to *right.*"

2. Have the student use scissors to cut out shapes or large letter forms. Coloring activities also can help the student develop muscle control and learn how to use a writing instrument and stay

10. To help develop visual discrimination, provide the student with pictures that contain hidden uppercase and lowercase manuscript letters. Ask the student to locate the hidden letters. A variation of this activity is to have the student produce a picture from a letter (for example, draw an umbrella from the letter *f*). Also, the student can be asked to think of things that different letters resemble.

Manuscript Writing Activities

1. Provide the student with an individual copy of the alphabet and numbers 0–9 to use at his desk. Zaner-Bloser produces self-adhesive alphabet strips (both manuscript or cursive) that have arrows showing correct stroke directions and sequence. Encourage the student to refer to the model during writing exercises.

2. Have the student form manuscript letters and numbers by drawing between the double lines of outlined letters.

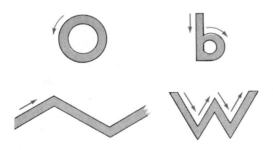

3. Use paper with squares to help the student maintain correct letter size and proportion.

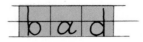

4. Have the student form manuscript letters and numbers by completing slash-to-slash and dot-to-dot activities.

slash-to-slash

dot-to-dot

5. On pieces of oaktag, print uppercase letters and their corresponding lowercase letters and cut the pair to form puzzle pieces. Have the student match the uppercase and lowercase manuscript pairs. This activity is self-correcting, because the puzzle pieces will fit together only if the letters correspond to each other. A variation of this activity would be to match manuscript letters to corresponding cursive letters.

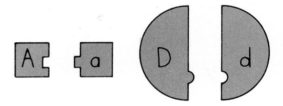

6. Use arrows to provide the student with direction clues in forming specific letters.

Also, *rol 'n write* (Educational Performance Associates) is a commercial material that can be used to illustrate letter formation. The set consists of rectangular plastic boards containing grooves that mark the letters of the alphabet. When a ball is placed at the starting point, it automatically traces the strokes used in forming the letter.

7. Use colored dots to indicate the starting and stopping positions for each letter stroke.

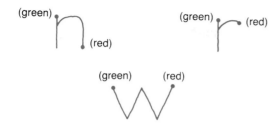

(green)   (red)

Also, letters can be color-coded to indicate their position with respect to the line on which the student is writing. Letters that stay on the line are written in green (grass letters), letters that extend above the line are written in blue (sky letters), and letters that extend below the line are written in brown (root letters). Eventually the color cueing is faded.

8. Have the student who reverses letters (such as *b* and *d*) form an association to help him remember the direction of the letters. For example, the student can learn to associate lowercase *b* with uppercase *B* or identify the stem of *b* with the left hand. Another method is to have the student raise his left arm in front of him and grasp his left elbow with his right hand. When he looks down he will see the letter *b*. For all reversal problems, encourage the student to refer to an alphabet taped to his desk before writing the letter.

9. Have the student announce his strokes as he writes certain letters. For example:
   m—"short line down; back up, around, and down; back up, around, and down"
   h—"tall line down, back up halfway, around, and down"
   i—"short line down, dot"

10. On balsa wood, print manuscript letters and numbers and use a razor-sharp knife to groove out the wood deep enough for a pencil to follow. Have the student practice forming letters by tracing the letters and numbers with a pencil in the grooves.

11. For the student who has difficulty with letter size and staying on the base line, make a cardboard frame with a rectangular piece cut out of the frame. The student writes within the window area and thus has a barrier that stops his downward movement. Frames can be made for words with one-line, two-line, and three-line letters.

Masking tape also can be used on paper to represent base lines and margins.

12. For the student who has difficulty with spacing between letters within a single word and between words themselves, make an underlay sheet. Trace over the lines on a piece of notebook paper with a felt-tip pen; then draw vertical lines on the paper one letter distance apart. This make squares the appropriate size for letters. The student places his notebook paper on top of his underlay sheet. He can see the felt-tip pen lines and use them as cues for proper spacing. One letter is written in each square, and one square is skipped between words. An additional method for the student who has difficulty remembering to space between words involves giving him a two-leaded pencil that has red on one end and blue on the other end. Have the student alternate colors each time he writes a new word (first a blue word, then red, then blue, and so on). Changing the color serves as a cue to stop and space properly. Also, if the student runs words together, have him place the index finger of his nonwriting hand at the end of each word to allow space for the next word.

13. Use the Practice Pad as a handwriting center to offer motivation and handwriting exercise. The student can practice any of the handwriting skills provided by the model.

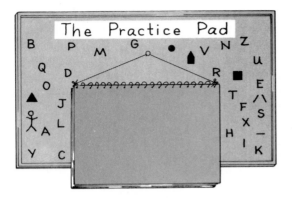

Cursive Writing Activities

1. To help the student see the similarity of manuscript and cursive letters, make a chart that has manuscript and corresponding cursive letters written next to each other.
2. Make dot-to-dot cursive letters and have the student form the letter by connecting the dots. The dots gradually can be faded so that the student is required to complete the letter.
3. Have the student trace a cursive letter several times. Gradually reduce the cues to only the first stroke and have him finish forming the letter.

4. Arrows and color-coded dots can be used to show direction of the stroke and beginning and ending points.

(red)

(green)

5. Encourage the student to practice forming cursive letters until his letters look like the model and show his best effort; then he can stop and proceed to another writing activity. With this method, the student practices only those letters that present difficulty.
6. Have the student practice letters with similar movement patterns at the same time. Also, the student can say the strokes of the letters as he writes.

7. After the student has learned the correct letter formation of cursive writing, his practice should involve writing that has meaning. For example, on the chalkboard write an informative letter to parents and have the students copy it while giving special attention to good handwriting.
8. Have the student copy a series of 10 stories and draw a picture to accompany each story. When he has completed all the stories and pictures in the series, put them together in a booklet to be displayed or taken home.

COMMERCIAL HANDWRITING PROGRAMS AND MATERIALS

Many commercial programs and materials are available to develop or improve handwriting skills. The following selected programs and materials may be helpful to students having difficulty with handwriting.

Better Handwriting for You

Publisher: Noble and Noble

Description: Better Handwriting for You (Noble, 1966) is a series of eight workbooks and teacher editions. Books 1 and 2 deal with manuscript writing, and Books 3 through 8 present cursive writing. Between Books 2 and 3 there is a transitional book that begins with manuscript writing and then introduces cursive writing. Numbers and arrows help teach the sequence and direction of strokes used to write various letters. The student copies models of uppercase and lowercase letters and numbers in the workbooks. The last two books provide devices that allow the student to evaluate the quality of his own handwriting. Throughout the program the teacher is provided with instructions on managing left-handed students and determining correct positions for paper and pencil.

Cursive Writing Program

Publisher: Science Research Associates

Description: The *Cursive Writing Program* (S. Miller & Engelmann, 1980) consists of 140 developmentally sequenced lessons designed to teach cursive writing to students who have mastered manuscript writing. The program teaches how to form letters, create words, write sentences, and improve writing speed and accuracy. The 20-minute lessons feature a simplified orthography that reduces unnecessary frills, slant arrows to assist in slanting the paper correctly, slant bars to prompt proper spacing, exercises to correct errors, and an emphasis on high-frequency word and letter combinations. Points are awarded following the successful completion of a series of exercises. The materials include a teacher presentation book and a student workbook of practice exercises.

D'Nealian Handwriting

Pubisher: Scott, Foresman

Description: The *D'Nealian Handwriting* program (Thurber & Jordan, 1981) is designed to simplify handwriting for the readiness student through eighth grade. The forms of most lowercase manuscript letters are the basic forms of the corresponding cursive letters. Each manuscript letter is made with a continuous stroke, except the dotted letters *i* and *j* and the crossed letters *f, t,* and *x*. The transition to cursive writing is simplified because the addition of simple joining strokes is all that is needed for every letter except five (*f, r, s, v, z*). The program includes student workbooks and teacher's editions for each grade level, and alphabet cards and self-sticking alphabet tapes are available.

Handwriting: A Fresh Start

Publisher: Curriculum Associates

Description: Handwriting: A Fresh Start (Powers & Kaminsky, 1988) is a multisensory remedial program designed to improve cursive writing. The approach links letter forms to guided eye-hand motor skills. Verbal descriptions are paired with letter formations to combine auditory and motor feedback with visual imagery. Horizontal and vertical guidelines (power writing lines) define writing space for proper formation, sizing, and spacing letters. These cues fade gradually in later lessons. Review and reinforcement activities prompt transfer from power writing lines to regular writing lines.

Handwriting: Basic Skills and Application

Publisher: Zaner-Bloser

Description: Handwriting: Basic Skills and Application (Barbe, Lucas, Wasylyk, Hackney, & Braun, 1987) contains a series of nine workbooks for kindergarten through eighth grade. Manuscript is introduced in kindergarten, developed through the second grade, and maintained through all the grades. Primary cursive is introduced in second or third grade and developed in the third and fourth grade, and adult cursive is the focus in the fifth through eighth grade. Letters are introduced systematically: by similarity of stroke in kindergarten through the fourth grade, by size and proportion in the fifth grade, and by rhythmic motion in the sixth grade and up. The elements of legibility are emphasized, and skills can be applied immediately in a practical context. In addition to a teacher's edition for each grade level, there is a supportive materials pack containing materials such as an alphabet wall chart, an evaluation scale, and a peek-through overlay.

Handwriting with Write and See

Publisher: Lyons and Carnahan

Description: Handwriting with Write and See (Skinner & Krakower, 1968) includes programmed books for fifth through sixth grade and two books for the transition from manuscript to cursive writing, which can be used in either second or third grade. A step-by-step instructional sequence is included. The unique feature of this program is the special paper and pen. The paper in the workbooks is treated so that when the student forms a letter correctly the mark appears in one color but an incorrect mark appears in a different color. Thus, the student receives immediate feedback on each response. Writing activities and exercises are suggested, such as filling out bank deposit slips or library cards.

Imaginary Line Handwriting Series

Publisher: Steck-Vaughn

Description: This program is designed to help students in kindergarten through eighth grade develop a legible, individualized style of handwriting. "Imaginary" lines — light blue guide lines — help develop a kinesthetic understanding for the formation of letters by aiding such factors as starting point, stopping point, height, and width. The program contains a series of nine workbooks, and lessons take 10 to 15 minutes per day. Imaginary-line practice paper and alphabet-card writing guides also are available.

SRA Lunchbox Handwriting

Publisher: Science Research Associates

Description: SRA Lunchbox Handwriting includes two labs for handwriting practice in manuscript and cursive styles for students in kindergarten through fourth grade. Students begin by tracing preletter shapes on plastic overlays, which wipe clean for reuse. Directional dots and arrows show how to complete each stroke. Next, students trace complete letters and then form the letters themselves and compare them with models. Practice includes writing letters, numerals, and full sentences. The labs can be used as part of the basic handwriting program or as special aids to individual students. Each lab contains exercise cards, plastic overlays, markers, student progress sheets, and an instruction sheet for the teacher.

The Talking Pen

Producer: Wayne Engineering

Description: The Talking Pen is an electronic pen with a small beam of infrared light in its tip. This infrared sensor picks up reflected light and triggers a buzzer. The battery-operated pen responds to any pattern of light and dark. When the tip of the pen is on a dark area, the pen is silent. If the pen is moved to a light area, it "squawks." This sound can be silenced only by placing the tip of the pen back on a dark area. Thus, by providing a dark pattern on a light background, the pen "talks" only when the pattern is traced incorrectly. Because the pen provides immediate auditory feedback, it is self-correcting and can be used without direct supervision. To develop handwriting skills, complete uppercase and lowercase alphabet and number patterns (manuscript or cursive) are available. The teacher also can use workbook patterns or make various patterns on any surface with any marker. In

addition, the pen can be used with optional standard headphones so that only the student knows when a mistake is made.

WRITTEN EXPRESSION SKILLS

Written expression, one of the highest forms of communication, reflects a person's level of comprehension, concept development, and abstraction. It is how an individual organizes his ideas to convey a message. Whereas handwriting is primarily a visual-motor task that includes copying, tracing, and writing from dictation, written expression requires complex thought processes.

The skill of written expression usually is not acquired until an individual has had extensive experience with reading, spelling, and verbal expression. Problems in written expression may not be diagnosed until the upper elementary school years, when the student is required to use the various language components in written composition and emphasis is placed upon refining writing skills. Written expression is the most complex of the language arts skills and is based on listening, talking, handwriting, reading, and spelling. Thus it generally is not stressed in instructional programs for learners with mild disabilities. Teachers tend instead to focus on the skills prerequisite to written expression. However, as the student acquires those prerequisite skills, instruction in written expression is warranted.

In a comparison of the written products of students with learning disabilities and their normally achieving peers in fourth, eighth, and eleventh grades, Houck and Billingsley (1989) found that students with learning disabilities write fewer words and sentences, write more words per sentence, produce fewer words with seven letters or more and fewer sentence fragments, and have a higher percentage of capitalization and spelling errors. Christenson,

Thurlow, Ysseldyke, and McVicar (1989) contend that written language instruction for students with mild disabilities can be improved by increasing the time allocated for instruction, teaching written language as an integrated process, and coordinating written language activities with different content areas. Students with learning problems experience a variety of writing problems, and the treatment of these difficulties in a systematic program requires that teachers at all levels allocate instructional time for writing and the review and editing of written products.

ASSESSMENT OF WRITTEN EXPRESSION SKILLS

Assessment of written expression yields information about a student's skill level and aids in instructional planning. The teacher can assess various components of written expression to determine deficiencies. A scope and sequence chart for written expression is provided in Appendix A according to the areas of capitalization and punctuation, written composition, and creative expression. It provides a skill hierarchy by grade level for assessing skills that need to be taught. Assessment techniques are presented in two broad categories: standardized achievement and diagnostic tests and informal techniques specifically related to instructional planning.

Standardized Achievement and Diagnostic Tests

Many standardized tests provide only a rough estimate of the student's ability in written expression. In standardized achievement tests, skills usually are presented in isolation with no attempt to analyze a composition actually written by the student. Some commonly used standardized achievement tests that include written expression sections are the following:

1. *California Achievement Tests* (1985): Assesses mechanics (punctuation and capitalization), word usage, and understanding of sentence structure and paragraph organization for students in first through twelfth grade.
2. *Iowa Tests of Basic Skills* (Hieronymus, Hoover, & Lindquist, 1986): Assesses word usage and mechanics for students in first through ninth grade.
3. *Stanford Achievement Test* (Gardner, Rudman, Karlsen, & Merwin, 1982): Assesses mechanics and grammatical structure for students in first through ninth grade.
4. *Tests of Achievement and Proficiency* (Scannell, 1986): Assesses word usage, capitalization, punctuation, and skill in organizing and expressing ideas for students in ninth through twelfth grade.
5. *Woodcock-Johnson Psycho-Educational Battery—Revised* (Woodcock & Johnson, 1989): Assesses capitalization, punctuation, word usage, and writing samples for preschool age to adult.

Diagnostic tests of written expression provide additional basic information useful in planning instruction. The *Picture Story Language Test* (Myklebust, 1965) measures written language in students age 7 through 17. The student writes a story based upon a presented picture. The teacher evaluates it along three dimensions: productivity, syntax, and meaning. Productivity is the total number of words, sentences, and words per sentences, and syntax (correctness) refers to word usage, word endings, and punctuation. Meaning of content is judged along a continuum of abstract to concrete. Scores in these three areas can be converted into age equivalents, percentiles, and stanines.

The *Test of Adolescent Language—2* (Hammill, Brown, Larsen, & Wiederholt, 1987) includes two writing subtests and is designed for use with students in sixth through twelfth grade. The writing/vocabulary subtest requires the student to read a series of words and write a sentence using them correctly. The writing/grammar subtest requires the student to complete a sentence-combining task. The raw scores can be converted into scaled scores, and the writing subtests combine to form a writing composite score.

The *Test of Early Written Language* (Hresko, 1988) focuses on educationally relevant writing abilities and measures the emerging written language abilities of youngsters age 3 through 7. The items have a direct relationship to the activities of young children in school and cover transcription, conventions of print, communication, creative expression, and record keeping.

The *Test of Written Language—2* (Hammill & Larsen, 1988) can be used to identify students in second through twelfth grade who have problems in written expression and to note specific deficits for corrective instruction. The student looks at pictures and writes a complete story based on the pictures. Subtests with spontaneous formats include (a) *thematic maturity*—the number of content elements included in the student's story, (b) *contextual vocabulary*—the number of nonduplicated long words used in the story, (c) *syntactic maturity*—the number of words in the story that are used in grammatically and syntactically correct sentences, (d) *contextual spelling*—the number of words in the story that are spelled correctly, and (e) *contextual style*—the number of different capitalization and punctuation rules that are used by the student in composing an essay. Subtests with contrived formats include (a) *vocabulary*—the student writes sentences that show knowledge of stimulus words, (b) *spelling*—the student

writes dictated sentences that are checked for spelling, (c) *style*—the student writes dictated sentences that are checked for capitalization, and punctuation, (d) *logical sentences*—the student corrects sentences that contain common illogicalities, and (e) *sentence combining*—the student combines ideas expressed in simple sentences to write compound or complex sentences. Two equivalent forms are available, and percentile and standard scores are provided.

Informal Assessment Techniques

The teacher begins informal assessment of written expression by obtaining representative writing samples from the student and analyzing them to determine specific weaknesses. Five major components of written expression that can be analyzed are fluency, syntax, vocabulary, structure, and content. Also, curriculum-based measurement is an informal assessment technique that uses a set of standardized procedures to assess written expression skills.

Fluency. *Fluency* is defined as quantity of verbal output and refers to the number of words written. Isaacson (1988) notes a significant correlation between fluency (number of words) and other measures of writing skills. For example, a student who is able to write more words is likely to be more fluent in generating ideas as well. Fluency is related to age and includes sentence length and complexity (McCarthy, 1954; Meckel, 1963). The average sentence length in a composition is determined by counting the number or words and the number of sentences in the composition and dividing the number of words by the number of sentences. Cartwright (1968) found that the average sentence length of an 8 year old is eight words and that this length increases one word per year through age 13. He suggests that any deviation of more than two words indicates a problem.

Syntax. *Syntax* refers to construction of sentences or the way words are put together to form phrases, clauses, and sentences. Frequent written syntax errors of students with learning disabilities include word omissions, distorted word order, incorrect verb and pronoun usage, incorrect word endings, and lack of punctuation (D. J. Johnson & Myklebust, 1967). Thomas, Englert, and Gregg (1987) found that a large proportion of the syntactic errors of older writers with learning disabilities can be attributed to errors in which the student generates a phrase instead of a sentence. One method for assessing syntactic maturity is counting the number of sentences that fall into several different categories: incomplete (fragment), simple, compound, and complex. The percentage of usage of the four sentence types in a writing sample can be computed to provide comparisons and a record of the student's progress. Cartwright (1969) suggests that the number of compound and complex sentences increases with age and that the use of incomplete and simple sentences decreases.

Another common measure of syntax is T-unit length (words per terminable unit). A T-unit is the shortest grammatically correct segment that a passage can be divided into without creating fragments (Hunt, 1965). Thus, a sentence consisting of one T-unit may have subordinate clauses, phrases, or modifiers embedded within it, whereas a compound sentence is two T-units because it can be divided into two grammatically complete units without leaving fragments. The ratio of the average T-unit length is a total count of the number of words written divided by the number of T-units present. T-unit length is positively correlated to other measures of written expression (Isaacson, 1988), and a general increase

in the average T-unit length occurs throughout the school years (Morris & Crump, 1982).

Vocabulary. *Vocabulary* refers to the originality or maturity in the student's choice of words and the variety of words used in the written task. The student's vocabulary should increase with age and experience; however, Morris and Crump (1982) report that, compared with their normally achieving peers at four age levels, students with learning disabilities use fewer word types in their writing. Wiig and Semel (1976) report that some students with learning problems have adequate vocabularies for their age range but have assigned a small number of attributes to each word. The Type Token Ratio (TTR) (W. Johnson, 1944) is a measure of vocabulary that is the ratio of different words used (types) to the total number of words used (tokens). For example, the sentence *The two boys went fishing in Noonan's Lake early yesterday morning* has a high TTR (1.0) — 11 total words are used, and all 11 words are different. In contrast, the sentence *The little girl saw the little boy in the little house* has a fairly low TTR (.63) — 11 total words are used, but only 7 of these words are different. A low TTR may indicate inadequate vocabulary for the written expression task. This technique also can be used for measuring long compositions; however, the number of different vocabulary words decreases as the total number of words in the composition increases (Carroll, 1938). When comparing several compositions produced by the same student or by different students, the same type of sample should be taken. For example, the first 50 words should be used from each composition instead of selecting the first 50 words from some compositions and the last 50 words from others.

Vocabulary variety also can be assessed by using the index of diversification (Carroll, 1938; G. A. Miller, 1951). This refers to the average number of words between each occurrence of the most frequently used word in the writing sample. Cartwright (1969) suggests dividing the total number of words in the sample by the number of *the*s or by the number of times the word used most often appears. The higher the value of the index, the more diverse the vocabulary.

Finally, vocabulary can be assessed by measuring the number of unusual words. For this assessment, a sample of the student's written expression should be compared with a list of words frequently used by other students—for example, the Dolch (1955, 1960) word list. The number of words the student uses that do not appear on the list indicates the extent of his vocabulary.

Structure. *Structure* includes the mechanical aspects of writing, such as punctuation, capitalization, and rules of grammar. The Grammatical-Correctness Ratio (GCR) (Stuckless & Marks, 1966) can be used to assess structure. The GCR quickly analyzes the total number of the student's grammatical errors. To obtain the GCR, a sample of the student's writing (for example, 50 words from a composition) is scored by counting the number of grammatical errors. The error count is subtracted from 50, and this difference is divided by 50. To obtain a percentage score, this last number is multiplied by 100. Because the final result can be displayed as a percentage, GCRs can be calculated for any number of words and still yield a score that can be compared with the student's previous scores. A GCR score also can be calculated for one specific type of grammatical error or for errors in punctuation or capitalization.

Structure also can be assessed by tabulating types of errors in the writing sample. The frequency of specific errors can be recorded to pinpoint individual weaknesses. An error analysis chart (presented in Table 13.3) provides a profile of errors in writing structure. Errors in spelling (phonetic and nonphonetic misspellings) and handwriting (letter formation, spacing, consistent slant, line quality, alignment, letter size, fluency) also can be noted.

In addition to spontaneous writing samples, teacher-made test items also can be used to analyze specific elements of writing structure. Written compositions may not include enough opportunities for various errors to occur. For example, the student may write only sentences that contain grammatical forms or punctuation he knows how to use. Thus, to assess punctuation, the teacher can devise several short sentences in which punctuation rules are used. The sentences can be dictated for the student to write correctly or can be presented unpunctuated for the student to correct. For example:

1. School starts at 8 30
2. Twenty two boys are in the class
3. Dr Goodman lives in Richmond Virginia
4. His birthday is January 31 1943
5. Blaze our Golden Retriever had four puppies

Content. *Content,* the fifth component of written expression, can be divided into accuracy, ideas, and organization (Cartwright, 1969). Similarly, Isaacson (1988) indicates that aspects of content that should be considered in assessment include idea generation, coherence of all parts of the composition to the topic or theme, organization or logical sequence, and awareness of audience. The nature of the written assignment determines how the different factors should be weighed. For example, accuracy carries more weight when the written exercise is a presentation of historical facts. Cartwright suggests rating each factor on a scale from 0 to 10. A 10 in ideas would indicate that the ideas were pertinent to the topic and represented a high degree of origi-

TABLE 13.3
Writing structure error analysis chart.

Students' Names	Verbs		Pro-nouns		Words					Sen-tences		Capitals			Punctuation						Total
	Agreement	Tense	Personal	Possessive	Additions	Substitutions	Modifiers	Negatives	Plurals	Incomplete	Run-on	Beginning sentences	Proper nouns	Inappropriate use	Period	Comma	Question mark	Apostrophe	Colon	Other	

Sample
Elicitation
Procedure: _____

Date: _____

nality, and a 0 would indicate lack of originality or understanding of the task. Some youngsters with learning problems may have limited ideas because of lack of experience, while others may have the ideas but not the ability to sequence them in logical order. Thomas et al. (1987) found that in expository writing (that is, the ability to explain or provide information on a topic), students with learning disabilities frequently terminate their text prematurely, thus indicating difficulty in producing multiple factual statements about familiar topics. In addition, these students tend to repeat information and generate irrelevant items pertaining to the topic. Wallace, Larsen, and Elksnin (1992) note that evaluation of content is especially difficult because the ideas and levels of abstraction contained in the written product are dependent on the student's intelligence, language experiences, cultural background, and interests.

Profile of components. By examining a student's writing sample, such as an autobiography, the teacher can determine which skills need to be introduced or remediated and which have been acquired. Poteet (1980) developed the *Checklist of Written Expression Skills,* containing four areas: penmanship, spelling, grammar, (capitalization, punctuation, syntax), and ideation (type of writing, substance, productivity, comprehensibility, reality, style). Likewise, Weiner (1980a) devised the *Diagnostic Evaluation of Writing Skills (DEWS),* consisting of the following areas: graphic (visual features), orthographic (spelling), phonologic (sound components), syntactic (grammatical), semantic (meaning), and self-monitoring. Weiner (1980b) verified the efficacy of the *DEWS* in identifying students requiring special remedial instruction.

A profile of the assessment of written expression components is presented in Table 13.4. The profile can be used with an individ-

ual student or an entire class to record strengths and weaknesses and student progress. Although some interpretation is required, the use of a profile helps to standardize observations and thus yields a more reliable and valid informal assessment.

Curriculum-based measurement. Curriculum-based measurement allows the teacher to collect data routinely and monitor instructional progress. Writing skills are assessed through repeated 3-minute writing samples using stimulus story starters or topic sentences. The use of 3-minute writing samples represents a general assessment of writing skills, rather than a diagnostic assessment of specific writing deficits; however, it allows the teacher to base instructional decisions on direct, repeated measurement.

Wesson (1987) notes that 30 story starters are needed for 1 year of measurement. When the story starters are written on note cards, the teacher can write the students' initials on the back so that the story starter is not used by the same student more than three times. The measures can be administered to a group of students rather than on an individual basis. Tindal and Marston (1990) present three evaluation strategies: (a) *holistic scoring*— raters review compositions within the same distribution to determine an overall impression and assign a value from a rating scale; (b) *analytical scoring*—writing samples are scored on specific qualities or traits (such as organization, ideas, wording, punctuation) with operational definitions and criteria to aid the judgment process; and (c) *primary-trait scoring*—raters focus on the degree of consistency in the purpose of writing according to defined traits (such as creativity, persuasion). Parker, Tindal, and Hasbrouck (1991) indicate that holistic judgments appear reliable in a writing process approach when there is no judgment of improvement over time; however, in a subskill mastery instructional approach,

TABLE 13.4
Profile of written expression components.

Students' Names	Fluency Average Sentence Length	Syntax Sentence Type Variety	T-Unit Length	Vocabulary Type Token Ratio	Index of Diversi-fication	Number of Un-usual Words	Structure Gram-matical Correct-ness Ratio	Types of Errors	Accuracy Rating	Content Ideas Rating	Organiza-tion Rating

TABLE 13.5
Procedures for administering and scoring written expression measures, determining long-range goals, and graphing data.

Step 1: To establish a baseline, provide each student with a lined sheet of paper and the same story starter or topic sentence on any 3 days of a given week. Discuss writing ideas, and then have the students write for a 3-minute period. Collect the papers after 3 minutes.

Step 2: Count the number of words or letter sequences representing words written after the given story starter or topic sentence. Ignore misspellings, content, punctuation, and organization. Continue with this procedures for 2 more days, giving two new story starters or topic sentences during the week. Plot the student's scores on a graph (see Figure 13.4).

Step 3: Find the median score from the three baseline scores. This is the middle number when ranked from lowest to highest.

Step 4: Compute the long-range goal. Count the number of weeks left in the school year or semester. Multiply the number of weeks by 2.0 (rate of growth), and add the median score obtained from the baseline week [for example, 21 weeks × 2.0 = 42; 42 + 14 (baseline median) = 56 (goal)].

Step 5: Plot the goal data point on the graph on the line for the last week. Draw the aim line connecting the baseline median data point to the goal data point. This represents the line that the student's performance should follow as the student progresses through the school year.

Step 6: Beginning with the first week after the baseline, measure student performance two times each week. On 2 different days in a given week, provide the students with a different story starter or topic sentence. Following a brief discussion of the story starter or topic, tell the students to write for 3 minutes and say "Begin writing."

Step 7: After the 3-minute period, say "Stop." Collect the papers, and count the number of words or letter sequences representing words written after the given story starter or topic sentence.

Step 8: Plot each score on the graph in the space corresponding with the day and week. Connect the data points.

Step 9: Continue with this procedure throughout the year. Analyze student error patterns for information regarding writing deficits of individual students. Use this information in planning instructional lessons. Graphs also can be made to monitor progress on specific skills (for example, capitalization, punctuation, subject-verb agreement).

the most useful indexes for monitoring writing progress are number of correct word sequences, mean length of correct word sequences, and percent of legible words written.

To implement curriculum-based measurement of written expression, the teacher can use the steps in Table 13.5, which includes the administration and scoring procedures of written expression measures as well as procedures for determining long-range goals and graphing data. Figure 13.4 presents a graph of curriculum-based measurement data and illustrates a long-range goal or aim line.

In addition to increasing student motivation to write, monitoring written expression provides the teacher with information that encourages sensitive and relevant instructional modifications. For example, for a student who has great difficulty with written expression, the following modifications are useful:

FIGURE 13.4
A curriculum-based
measurement graph
illustrating an aim line.

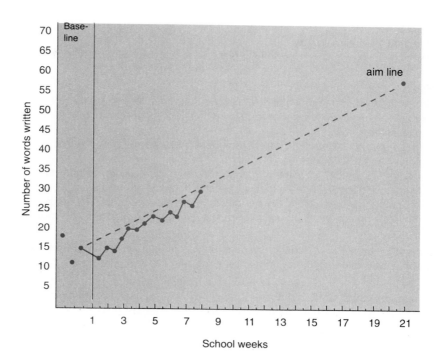

1. Allow the student to copy selected words during the 3-minute timing to help him get started. Selected words may center around a theme (for example, marine life), word family (for example, *cat, fat, rat, bat*), or special interest (such as sports).
2. Provide story starters that include sentences with missing words or letters. Have the student write words or letters for the blanks. Count the number of correct words that student input helped create.
3. Periodically introduce specific written expression interventions (for example, capitalization, punctuation, compound words, contractions), and note if student writings reflect content from instructional lessons.
4. Use experiences (for example, science project, class visitor, field trip, movie) for story starters.
5. If the student is unable to produce sentences, have him generate words. Score the number of legible words.

TEACHING WRITTEN EXPRESSION SKILLS

In teaching writing, the emphasis has shifted from the product of writing to the process involved in creating that product (Graves, 1985). The product approach focuses primarily on grammar, spelling, capitalization, punctuation, and handwriting. The process approach stresses meaning first and then skills in the context of meaning. Students work through various stages (for example, prewriting, drafting, revising, editing, sharing) and focus their attention on one stage at a time (Tompkins, 1990). An overview of the writing stages is presented in Table 13.6.

In the process approach, the student selects his own writing topic and rehearses (brainstorms) before writing. After drafting and redrafting for several days, the student discusses the work with the teacher or peers and then

TABLE 13.6
Overview of writing stages.

Prewriting Stage

Select a topic for the written piece.

Consider the purpose for writing (e.g., to inform, describe, entertain, persuade).

Identify the audience for whom the writing is intended (e.g., classmates, parents, business persons, publishers).

Choose an appropriate form for the composition based on purpose and audience (e.g., story, report, poem, script, letter).

Engage in rehearsal activities to gather and organize ideas for writing (e.g., drawing, talking, reading, interviewing, brainstorming ideas, clustering main ideas and details).

Participate in writing a collaborative or group composition with the teacher so that the teacher can model or demonstrate the writing process and clarify questions and misconceptions.

Drafting Stage

Write a rough draft by skipping every other line and allowing adequate space for revising.

Emphasize content rather than mechanics, grammar, and spelling.

Revising Stage

Reread the rough draft and make changes by adding, substituting, deleting, and moving text.

Share the composition in writing groups in which listeners respond with compliments as well as comments and suggestions about how to improve the composition.

Make revisions based on feedback from the writing group by crossing out, drawing arrows, and writing in the space left between the writing lines.

Editing Stage

Focus on mechanics, including capitalization, punctuation, spelling, sentence structure, word usage, and formatting considerations.

Proofread the composition by reading word-by-word and hunting for errors (e.g., spelling, capitalization, punctuation) rather than reading for meaning, and insert proofreading symbols to indicate needed changes.

Correct as many mechanical errors as possible and, if necessary, use a dictionary or have a conference with the teacher for instruction or a mini-lesson on a needed skill.

Sharing Stage

Share the finished composition with classmates or appropriate audiences by reading in class, making a booklet, or contributing to a newspaper or magazine.

Source: From *Students with Learning Disabilities*, 4th ed. (p. 480), by C. D. Mercer, 1992, New York: Merrill/Macmillan. Copyright 1992 by Macmillan Publishing Company. Reprinted by permission.

revises and edits. Revising refers to reworking the text in a way that alters its content or structure, whereas editing is the process of correcting errors in grammar, syntax, punctuation, and spelling. Finally, the product is shared with the audience for whom the student has written. Thus, the teacher's role has shifted from merely assigning and assessing a prod-

uct to working with the student throughout the writing process. By working through the writing process, the student develops problem-solving skills, critical thinking skills, and a positive self-image.

Isaacson (1990) discusses four characteristics of the process approach in which the teacher introduces the student to the entire process of writing, from initial idea generation to editing of the final draft.

1. *The process should be modeled.* In a prewriting discussion, the teacher should model planning strategies by raising questions on the topic and demonstrate ways to organize information (for example, charts, semantic maps). The teacher can model how to convert planning notes into written sentences by thinking aloud while performing the task. Finally, the teacher should model reviewing and revising strategies and show that first drafts differ greatly from the finished copy.

2. *The process can be collaborative.* Collaboration can involve either the teacher or other students in activities such as brainstorming ideas, contributing and organizing information, giving constructive feedback, and editing for mechanical errors. Writing groups can be formed to share writing and develop ideas, and a peer team is also a good arrangement for editing written work.

3. *The process can be prompted.* The teacher can provide assistance by prompting the steps of the writing process or helping with writing decisions. For example, a prompt procedure in the prewriting stage can begin with having students list isolated words related to a topic. In the editing stage the teacher can write a code in the margin for a type of error (for example, *sp* for spelling, *v.* for verb form, *cap* for capitalization) to prompt the student to find and correct errors.

4. *The process should become self-initiated and self-monitored.* The teacher can give the student instruction in specific writing strategies and ideas for self-instructional statements. For example, an error-monitoring strategy (COPS), a sentence-writing strategy (PENS), and an acronym (TOWER) for use in theme writing are presented later in this section.

For students with academic learning problems, Kameenui and Simmons (1990) recommend a skills-based approach to expressive writing instruction. This approach focuses on a scope and sequence of basic skills and systematically develops these skills for advanced exercises and applications. In this approach, the instructional emphasis focuses first on the writing and editing phases (teacher-directed), and then the process of planning (student-initiated) is introduced and developed. Thus the student is taught to rely on writing skills when engaging in the process of planning more complex written products.

Written expression can involve either functional or creative writing. *Functional* writing refers to conveying information in a structured form, such as writing answers to chapter questions, social and business letters, invitations, reports and essays, or minutes of a meeting. *Creative* writing is the personal expression of thoughts and experiences in a unique manner, as in poetry, story writing, and personal narratives. The writing program for students with learning problems should include a range of writing experiences in both functional and creative writing.

Hammill (1990) states three goals of individualized instruction in written composition:

> The first goal is to teach students at least the minimum competencies that they will need to succeed in the school curriculum. The second goal is to instruct them in those forms of writing in which ability will be required for success outside the school (letter writing, completion of forms, note-taking, etc.). The third goal is to teach them to express their creativity in writing poetry, fantasies, and stories. (p. 196)

The student must organize thoughts logically and follow the proper mechanics of writing (including punctuation and capitalization) to communicate clearly and accurately. One of the most effective means of teaching writing skills to students with learning problems is through spontaneous written expression (Cohen & Plaskon, 1980). Each student's writing samples can be used as a base from which to introduce instruction in various writing skills. In other words, the objective of the writing program may be for the student to express ideas and thoughts with ease. The written work then is used as the basis for skill development.

Graham and Harris (1988) offer 10 instructional recommendations for developing an effective writing program for students with written expression difficulty:

1. *Allocate time for writing instruction.* A sufficient amount of time should be allocated to writing instruction (for example, four times per week) because students can learn and develop as writers only by writing.
2. *Expose students to a broad range of writing tasks.* Students should participate in writing activities that present highly structured problem-solving situations as well as activities that involve self-selected and expressive writing.
3. *Create a social climate conducive to writing development.* The teacher needs to be encouraging in a nonthreatening environment and should try to develop a sense of community by promoting student sharing and collaboration.
4. *Integrate writing with other academic subjects.* Writing should be integrated with other language arts activities to increase writing and develop skills.
5. *Aid students in developing the processes central to effective writing.* The composition process can be divided into a series of discrete stages (for example, prewrite, write, rewrite), and students can be taught appropriate task-specific and metacognitive strategies (for example, self-instructional strategy training).

6. *Automatize skills for getting language onto paper.* The teacher should provide direct instruction in mechanical skills and sentence and paragraph production, or the mechanical requirements of composing can be removed through the use of oral dictation.
7. *Help students develop explicit knowledge about the characteristics of good writing.* Students should be given exposure to the characteristics of various literary compositions either through reading or teacher presentation of written or live models that incorporate a specific skill or style, or students should receive direct instruction in the structured elements representative of a particular literary style.
8. *Help students develop the skills and abilities to carry out more sophisticated composing processes.* Three methods for the development of more mature composing processes include conferences during which teachers act as collaborators, procedural facilitation in which external support is provided, and self-instructional strategy training.
9. *Assist students in the development of goals for improving their written products.* Goal setting and having students evaluate their own or others' written products according to specific criteria can help students accurately monitor and evaluate progress.
10. *Avoid instructional practices that do not improve students' writing performances.* Skills in grammar and usage should be developed within the context of real writing tasks, and the teacher should give specific, explanatory feedback on only one or two types of frequently occurring errors at any one time.

The first step in writing instruction is to promote a positive attitude to motivate the student to write. The student must feel comfortable expressing himself. The teacher can promote discussion by encouraging the student to share his ideas. Writing should be integrated into the entire curriculum, and the teacher should help the student understand that the purpose of writing is to communicate. Writing instruction thus begins with establishing a positive environment and then proceeds to skill development.

The language experience approach frequently is adapted in teaching written expression. Writing activities can start with the student dictating a story to the teacher, who writes it down and reads it back. As the components of writing become more familiar, the student gradually assumes more responsibility for writing thoughts and ideas and independently composes one or two related sentences. Later the student writes entire paragraphs and stories and receives instruction on organizing ideas and using proper writing mechanics.

Language experience stories can be written by one student or composed by the entire class. Experience is an important factor, and the teacher should provide events (such as discussions, field trips, or films) that stimulate topics. At first, the student may be most comfortable writing about personal material, such as family, trips, or holidays. Students also enjoy writing stories about pictures or intriguing titles and completing unfinished stories or "story starters." Books in which the pictures are presented in sequence without text can provide stimuli for writing activities. Commercial materials also are sources of writing assignments—for example, *Creative Story Starters* (published by DLM) and *Story Starters—Primary and Intermediate* (Moore & Woodruff, 1980). In addition, computer word-processing programs allow the student to record, revise, and print language experience stories easily. The *Language Experience Series*

(produced by Teacher Support Software) includes software that provides sentence starters and topic beginnings, as well as a word-processing program that allows the student to read, write, and hear (through a speech card) his own experience stories. Because the student produces the story himself in the language experience approach, the material is meaningful to him, and he is motivated to study it. This may be especially important for adolescents, because the stories they compose are on their level of maturity. A student's involvement or interest in a given topic influences his ability to write about it.

As the student continues to be encouraged to express his ideas well in writing, instruction on the more mechanical aspects of writing begins. In teaching punctuation and capitalization skills, the teacher can call attention to such errors in the student's written work, show the proper use of the skill, and point out how its use enhances meaning. Thus, writing mechanics are explained as needed, and the student becomes aware of their importance.

The teacher should avoid excessive correction of the mechanical aspects of writing, which may discourage the student from trying to express his ideas. He may think that how he writes is more important than what he writes and may begin to limit his vocabulary use, write only simple sentences, and avoid expressing complex and creative thoughts. Good writing models should be provided for the student, and reinforcement should be combined with constructive criticism. The teacher always should say something positive about the student's work before offering correction and should give encouragement and praise for whatever amount the student has written. In general, more attention should be given to developing the written expression of ideas than to correcting mechanical errors. Of course, students who learn to use the right punctuation, correct grammar, and good organization are likely to become better writers. Some teachers prefer to give two grades for some writing assignments—one for ideas and one for technical skills. Hansen (1978) states, "Instruction should provide a balance between appreciation and enthusiasm for a student's ideas and a dedication to improving the presentation and organization of those concepts" (p. 122).

To help improve a student's writing, the teacher should give considerable attention to sentence and paragraph development (Otto & Smith, 1980). The student should be helped to recognize the different syntactic patterns in which ideas can be expressed. Having the student read interesting material at his independent reading level will expose him to good sentences in other people's writing and may help him develop a sense of English sentence constructions. Also, through orally reading or tape-recording his stories, the student is likely to notice his own faulty sentence constructions. Learning to write unified, coherent paragraphs can be facilitated by activities in which the student categorizes or classifies ideas or organizes ideas in a logical sequence. An organizational framework can be provided through the use of content charts, semantic maps (or webbings), and pyramid diagrams that present an overview of information and visually represent how items are related (Levy & Rosenberg, 1990). Suggesting the use of transitional words (such as *finally, in addition to*) may help the student put his compositions together.

A sentence-writing strategy designed by Schumaker and Sheldon (1985) can be used to teach the basic principles of sentence construction and expression. The student learns steps and formulas that enable him to recognize and write different kinds of sentences. The acronym PENS helps the student remember the steps to sentence writing:

1. **P**—*Pick* a sentence type and formula.
2. **E**—*Explore* words to fit the formula.

3. **N**—*Note* the words.
4. **S**—*Search* for verbs and subjects, and check.

Research indicates that students who receive instruction in the sentence-writing strategy consistently produce written work that consists of 100 percent complete sentences (Schumaker & Sheldon, 1985). PENS also is used in the paragraph-writing strategy developed at the University of Kansas Institute for Research in Learning Disabilities to help the student write a topic sentence, detail sentences, and a clincher sentence to form a paragraph (Schumaker & Lyerla, 1991). This learning strategy teaches the student to write various types of paragraphs: sequential (narrative or step-by-step), descriptive, expository, and compare and contrast.

Welch and Link (1989) provide a video-assisted metacognitive strategy to teach students to write paragraphs. The use of a first-letter mnemonic cues the student how to complete the writing task independently:

1. **P**—*Pick* a topic, an audience, and the appropriate textual format (for example, enumerative, compare and contrast, cause and effect).
2. **L**—*List* information about the topic to be used in sentence generation, ongoing evaluation, and organizational planning.
3. **E**—*Evaluate* if the list is complete and plan how to organize the ideas that will be used to generate supporting sentences.
4. **A**—*Activate* the paragraph with a short and simple declarative topic sentence.
5. **S**—*Supply* supporting sentences based on items from the list.
6. **E**—*End* with a concluding sentence that rephrases the topic sentence, and *evaluate* the written work for errors in capitalization, punctuation, spelling, and appearance.

Welch (1992) notes that the intervention increased the student's metacognitive knowledge of the writing process involved in prewriting, planning, composing, and revising, as well as improves the student's attitude toward writing and writing instruction.

As basic writing skills are acquired, the student should learn to proofread and edit. In proofreading, the student reads his written work to identify and correct errors. To edit his own work, the student can be guided to check elements in his writing such as capitalization, sentence clarity, punctuation, spelling, margins, and paragraph indention. At first it may be helpful for the student to proofread his work several times with a different purpose in mind each time. As the student reads his work aloud, he may spot errors such as omitted words, improper punctuation, or poor organization. Also, peer critiquing can be used as a revision strategy, and individual conferences with the teacher in a supportive atmosphere can result in constructive editing.

To cue the student to detect four kinds of common errors, the teacher can introduce COPS questions to be used as an error-monitoring strategy (Schumaker, Nolan, & Deshler, 1985). The student is instructed to ask the following questions and look for errors:

1. **C**—Have I *capitalized* the first word and proper nouns?
2. **O**—How is the *overall* appearance? (Look at spacing, legibility, indention of paragraphs, neatness, and complete sentences.)
3. **P**—Have I put in commas, semicolons, and end *punctuation*?
4. **S**—Have I *spelled* all the words correctly?

Periodically the teacher can review COPS and encourage each student to use it daily so that it will become a habit. The teacher can require all papers to be "COPSed" before being accepted.

Because the goal of writing is to communicate ideas, students should be encouraged to share their written work. Notebooks or books of stories the students want to share may be exchanged for reading material. Also, students can be given the opportunity to read their selections voluntarily in front of other students. Through sharing stories, students receive feedback and become more motivated to improve the quality of their work. Also, the students are provided with models to help them improve their writing.

At the junior and senior high school levels, greater written expression demands are placed on students. Not only are students required to take notes during class lectures and express themselves on written tests, but they also frequently must write themes and reports. Teaching theme writing through the use of the acronym TOWER provides a structured approach:

1. **T**—*Think* about content (that is, title, major subtopics, and details).
2. **O**—*Order* topics and details.
3. **W**—*Write* the rough draft.
4. **E**—Look for *errors* (use COPS).
5. **R**—*Revise*/rewrite.

Before writing, the student can be encouraged to fill in a form with the topic at the top and ideas organized according to subtopics or paragraphs. After writing a rough draft, the student can ask COPS questions to edit his work and monitor errors.

Teachers expect written work to be reasonably neat and unconsciously may judge an assignment based on the appearance of the composition. Archer and Gleason (1988) suggest a strategy using the acronym HOW to improve the appearance of written work and remind the student how the composition should look:

1. **H**—*Heading* (Include name, date, subject, and page number if needed).

2. **O**—*Organized* (Start on front side of paper, include a left and right margin, have at least one blank line at the top and at the bottom, and space well).
3. **W**—*Written* neatly (Write words or numbers on the line, form words or numbers clearly, and neatly cross out or erase errors).

MacArthur, Schwartz, and Graham (1991) present a model for writing instruction that integrates word processing and strategy instruction into a process approach to writing. To enhance the quality and quantity of writing, there should be increased focus on thinking as a critical aspect of the writing process, and writing should be practiced and applied in a variety of situations and contexts to foster generalization of these skills.

WRITTEN EXPRESSION ACTIVITIES

Writing skills improve through practice. Instructional activities should be chosen for each student according to his particular skill deficits. In this section numerous activities are presented for developing skills in fluency and syntax, vocabulary, structure, and content. Additional activities and strategies for developing written expression skills related to test taking and note taking at the secondary level are presented in Chapter 14.

Activities in Fluency and Syntax Development

1. Give the student several words and ask him to arrange them to form a sentence. For example:
   her quietly cat the food ate
   friends yesterday Jane's left
   Also, give the student several words and have him write a sentence that contains all the words.
2. Have the student complete partial sentences. Gradually decrease the number of words presented. For example:

Yesterday morning the dog barked at . . .
Yesterday morning the dog . . .
Yesterday morning . . .

3. Give the student a written paragraph that contains both incomplete and complete sentences. Ask him to underline the subject and verb in each statement and determine which sentences are incomplete.
4. Have the student practice connecting two simple sentences to make compound or complex sentences. Give a list of various words for the student to use when writing the compound or complex sentences (such as *but, because, or, and, after, before*).
5. Give the student various noun and verb phrases and have him expand each sentence by adding descriptive words. For example:

man ate	The man in the blue shirt ate his dinner slowly.
dog barked	The big, black dog barked at the man with the stick.

Also, have the student combine related sentences into one sentence. For example:

The policeman is young. The policeman stopped the car.	The young policeman stopped the car.
Yesterday the boys played a football game. The game lasted two hours.	Yesterday the boys played a football game that lasted two hours.

Activities in Vocabulary Development

1. Provide the student with a variety of experiences (taking structured field trips, listening to stories and poems) and include follow-up discussions of what was seen and heard. In addition, viewing films, listening to guest speakers, making a picture dictionary, and reading books, magazines, and newspapers may increase a person's vocabulary. Praise the student whenever a new vocabulary word is used appropriately.
2. Discuss special interests with each student (for example, baseball, music, cooking) and make lists of words pertaining to the interests. New

words and their definitions can be written on index cards and filed in a word box so that they can be considered for use in written compositions.

3. Give the class a list of vocabulary words to learn. Write each word on a slip of paper, fold the paper slips, and place them in a decorated coffee can. The first student draws out a word and must begin a story by using his word in a sentence. Each student takes a turn drawing a word and then adds to the story by using his word. After all vocabulary words have been used, the teacher can develop an ending to the story.

4. Have the student discover new words by looking and listening for them outside the classroom—on signs, on television, in reading material. One day each week the students can share newly found words and definitions with their classmates.

5. Give the student a written paragraph in which various words or phrases are underlined. Have him substitute appropriate words or expressions in each underlined area.

6. Divide the class into two teams and play a game involving synonyms and antonyms. Present a word and ask each team member (alternating teams) to give a synonym. One point is awarded to each team for a correct response, and five points are taken away from the first team no longer able to give a synonym. Then the same word or a new word can be presented with the team members giving antonyms.

7. Present the student with a reading passage and ask him to locate words or phrases according to specific questions. For example: "Tell me the word in the second paragraph that describes Jim's car"; "Find the phrase in the last paragraph that indicates that Mary was mad at herself."

8. Develop a crossword puzzle that includes words related to a single subject. Have the student complete the puzzle and then write a paragraph using all the puzzle words.

Activities in Structure Development

1. To help develop proper use of punctuation, cut large punctuation marks from black construction paper and pin them to students. After reviewing rules of punctuation usage, write an unpunctuated story on the chalkboard or present it on the overhead projector. As the story is read aloud, the student wearing the appropriate punctuation mark should call out its name when it is needed in the story.

2. To make the student aware of the use of capital letters, have him make a list of all words that are capitalized in a specific reading passage and give the reasons for their capitalization. Lists of words that begin with capital letters can be made according to various classifications, such as cities, people's names, states, and months.

3. Give the student a written paragraph that does not contain any capitalized words. Have him correct the words that should be capitalized and give reasons for capitalizing them. Also, a reading selection can be dictated for the student to add capitals where necessary as he writes it.

4. Provide the student with written sentences that contain no capitals or punctuation and ask him to write each sentence correctly. Also, the teacher can give the student a paragraph without punctuation and capitalization for him to rewrite correctly. Tell the student the type and number of punctuation marks and capitals that must be added. To make the activity self-correcting, provide an answer key.

5. Give the student a list of verbs or singular nouns and ask him to write the past tense form of each verb or plural of each noun. For example:

do	did	child	children
ride	rode	boy	boys
eat	ate	deer	deer
sing	sang	hero	heroes
walk	walked	story	stories

In addition, the student can be asked to use each past tense verb or plural noun in a sentence. Sentences can be given with the verb omitted, and the student is required to choose the correct verb form from multiple-choice answers. For example:

I (*ride, rode, ridden*) the bus to school this morning.

Last Saturday we (*go, went, gone*) on a picnic.

When he (*fell, fall, fallen*), he hurt his leg.

6. To work on grammatical skills, give the student a paragraph with blanks he must complete. The blanks can require the use of different grammatical elements (for example, plurals, verb tenses, possessive pronouns, adverbs). A list of words for the student to use can be provided at the top of the worksheet.

7. To practice editing skills, have students exchange papers and "COPS" each other's work. After the teacher reviews the material, each student can make a corrected copy of his work. The teacher also can give the student a paragraph and ask him to correct it according to the COPS questions.

Activities in Content Development

1. Read the beginning of an exciting story to the class, and ask each student to write an ending for the story. The students can share their work to see how others finished the story. Also, after watching a film or reading or listening to a story, the students can write a summary or abstract.

2. To provide ideas for writing stories, cut three windows in a large piece of poster board. Make three circles, each of which is divided into eight sections. Write eight *Who* words on the first circle, eight *When* words on the second circle,

and eight *Where* words on the third circle. Attach the circles to the back of the poster board so that the writing shows through the windows (see Figure 13.5). To find a story starter, the student spins all three wheels. Also, to give the student story ideas, the poster board can contain two windows. Two circles can be made with one containing names of circus acts (or any subject) and the other containing phrases of things they might do (see Figure 13.6). The circles are attached to the poster board, and the student spins the wheels to find the subject for his composition.

3. Encourage letter writing by establishing a post office in the classroom. Make mailboxes for each student out of cardboard or milk cartons. Have the students write letters, invitations, birthday cards, poems, and so forth and send them through the class postal system. Also, the teacher can use the mailboxes to return papers, give feedback, or send notes to go home.

4. On a large piece of poster board draw four circles, each divided into six sections. On each circle write characters, descriptors, settings, or actions. In the middle of each circle attach an arrow. Have the student spin all four arrows and then write a paragraph that includes the four designated elements in the story (see Figure 13.7).

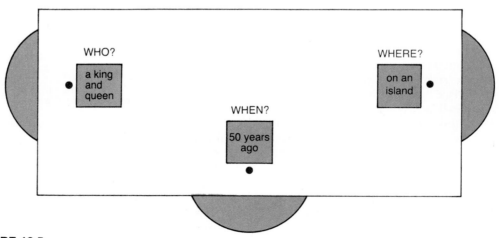

FIGURE 13.5
Who? When? Where? story board.

FIGURE 13.6
Circus Acts story board.

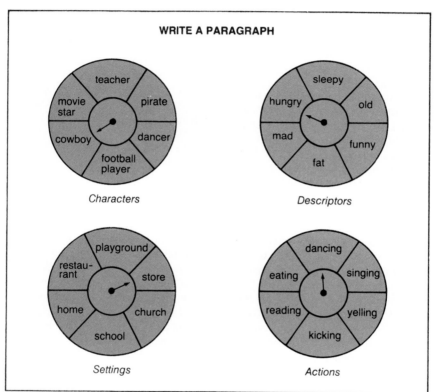

FIGURE 13.7
Write a Paragraph story board.

5. Give the student a written paragraph in which the sentences are out of sequence. Have him rewrite the paragraph by arranging the sentences in a meaningful order. Also, the student can be given a topic sentence and a closing sentence and be asked to write three detail sentences to form a paragraph.

6. To provide practice in organization skills, give the student a set of cards, each containing a different but related idea. Have the student arrange the cards in a logical sequence to form an outline and then write a composition from his outline.

7. Reproduce on ditto sheets several cartoons without captions or comic strips without the words

spoken by the characters. Have the student write appropriate captions or fill in the conversations. Also, give the student frames from a comic strip that he must arrange in proper sequence before writing a comic strip story. These can be shared with the class, and the funniest or best ones can be included in a book.

8. Prepare a worksheet on poems. Have the student arrange the lines in the proper order or fill in blanks with appropriate words. Then give the student an opportunity to select from various titles and compose a poem of his own. To help the student get started, suggest a first line.

9. Read a tall tale to the class and ask the students to identify parts of the story that are "tall" (exaggerated). Discuss the importance of accurate or truthful statements in compositions that are not tall tales. Have each student write his own tall tale, which can be shared with the class.

10. Have the student keep a daily diary in a spiral notebook. At the end of class each day, have him write a diary entry in which he expresses himself by summarizing his experiences, feelings, and activities of the day.

11. Present letters like those that appear in a newspaper advice column such as *Dear Abby*. Have each student give advice by writing responses to the letters. The responses can be shared with classmates or compared with actual newspaper replies.

12. Encourage the students to develop a monthly class newspaper to which each student can contribute some form of writing. The newspaper can contain current events articles, interviews, short stories, poems, jokes, cartoons, comic strips, advertisements, sports articles, and want ads. Groups of students can take turns serving as editors, printers or typists, proofreaders, and distributors.

COMMERCIAL WRITTEN EXPRESSION PROGRAMS AND MATERIALS

Various published materials and programs are available for developing written expression skills. This section presents selected commercial written expression materials and programs that may be helpful to students with learning problems.

Expressive Writing 1; Expressive Writing 2

Publisher: Science Research Associates

Description: Expressive Writing 1 and *Expressive Writing 2* (Engelmann & Silbert, 1983) present an effective writing program designed for students who read at or above the third-grade level. The program includes 50 daily 45-minute lessons that integrate sentence writing, paragraphing, and editing. At the completion of the program, students are able to write, punctuate, and edit compound sentences, sentences with dependent clauses, direct quotations in dialogue form, and sentences that list items. The program includes a teacher presentation book and a student workbook, and students participate in self-evaluation activities.

Moving Up in Grammar

Publisher: DLM

Description: Moving Up in Grammar is a program designed to help students in the elementary and intermediate grades improve their grammar skills. Six independent kits of varnish-coated cards, blackline masters, answer cards, and award certificates provide well-organized practice in various areas. *Sentences* consists of 16 units covering such skill areas as simple and complete subjects and predicates, types of sentences, and compound subjects and verbs. *Nouns and Verbs* contains eight units on nouns (for example, proper nouns, singular and plural possessive nouns) and eight units on verbs (for example, linking verbs, the verb *be*, irregular past tense verbs). *Capitalization and Punctuation* covers such skill areas as titles of respect and rank, names of relatives, and periods, question marks, exclamation points, quotation marks, and commas. *Word Usage* consists of 16 units covering words such as *accept* and *except, can* and *may, lay* and *lie,* and *sit* and *set. Adjectives and Adverbs* covers eight adjective skill areas and eight adverb skill areas (for example, comparatives, superlatives, irregular comparisons). *Pronouns* presents 16 units in such areas as noun substitutes, pronoun/verb agreement, relative pronouns, and demonstrative pronouns.

Teaching Competence in Written Language

Publisher: Pro-Ed

Description: Teaching Competence in Written Language (Phelps-Terasaki & Phelps-Gunn, 1988) is designed for children, adolescents, and adults who require extra help in developing writing skills. In this systematic, individualized, and highly structured program, the student moves effectively in a step-by-step fashion from ideas to sentences to paragraphs. Practice in writing is combined with practice in the different uses and kinds of writing to develop competence in written language expression. Lessons are included in the areas of sentences, paragraphs, and writing for a purpose.

Think and Write

Publisher: DLM

Description: This writing skills program for students in the elementary grades consists of five kits, each of which includes a minimum of 124 teaching and activity cards. Kit 1 is teacher directed with concepts presented on activity cards and taught by the teacher through examples. Kits 2 through 5 are student directed with concepts and skills introduced on teaching cards and practice and application provided on activity cards. Students work on various skills such as word usage (including the major parts of speech), punctuation, sentence building, writing paragraphs, editing, and organizing compositions.

Writers at Work

Publisher: Science Research Associates

Description: Writers at Work (Morocco & Nelson, 1990) is designed to implement a process writing approach for students in fourth through sixth grade. Units on five types of written composition are included: personal memoir, biography, fables, research, and advertising. The lesson plans give detailed instruction in concepts, procedures, and skills critical to each type of writing. The program also provides suggestions for additional support,

extension activities, and guidelines for assessment. The material has been tested with students with learning difficulties.

Written Expression

Publisher: Psychological Corporation

Description: Written Expression (Warden, Allen, Hipp, Schmitz, & Collett, 1988) is an instructional program that teaches composition as a three-phase process: prewriting, composing, and editing. In the prewriting stage, the student completes a chart of "wh-" questions and uses graphic organizers such as the vocabulary and sentence chart to create a visual organization of his ideas. This phase focuses on teacher-directed, student-interactive exercises. During composing, the student works independently to write his first draft. The *Writer's Guide* includes resources such as a thesaurus, spelling demons, and lists of conjunctions and transition words. In the editing stage, the student develops self-evaluation skills through the direct teaching of editing and proofreading techniques. The *Written Expression* materials are designed for students in second through twelfth grade, as well as for adults. They are designated as elementary, intermediate, and advanced, rather than by grade levels, so that the program can be matched to each student's needs and instructional level.

COMPUTER SOFTWARE PROGRAMS IN WRITTEN EXPRESSION

The use of the computer as a word processor can facilitate the teaching of writing. Word processing allows the student to correct, edit, revise, and manipulate text. The ease of changing words on a word processor before printing can motivate the older student to proofread for spelling and mechanical errors as well as to make improvements in other aspects of composition writing. MacArthur (1988) notes that the visibility of writing on a word processor can facilitate interaction between the student and teacher as well as collaborative writing activities among students and sharing of work in progress. In addition, the availability of a spelling checker and the ability to produce a neat, printed copy can be motivating especially to students who typically exhibit spelling or handwriting difficulties. Outhred (1989) found that the use of a word processor by students with learning problems resulted in fewer spelling errors and the production of longer stories. However, research has not confirmed the advantages of word processors for all students with learning difficulties. For example, in a study involving fifth- and sixth-grade students with learning disabilities, MacArthur and Graham (1987) found no differences on several variables (for example, length, quality, story structure, mechanical errors) between handwritten stories and those composed on a word processor. Isaacson (1990) notes that for the use of a word processor to contribute effectively to the development of writing skills, the teacher must teach the necessary subskills (such as keyboarding) and self-monitoring strategies for writing that take advantage of the computer's capabilities.

Bank Street Writer Plus (published by Broderbund and available from Learning Lab Software) is a popular word processing program designed to meet the writing needs of students in second through twelfth grade and can be used effectively with students with learning problems. The program includes pull-down menus that provide access to all writing functions, and an integrated spelling checker and on-line thesaurus are included for editing and proofreading. *Kidwriter* (Spinnaker) is designed for students in first through fourth grade and includes simple word processing features and graphics (for example, background scenes, shapes, characters, objects) for creating illustrated stories. In addition, numerous software programs are available that focus on specific written expression skills. The following programs are presented as examples of software that may facilitate instruc-

tion of students who have difficulty with written expression skills. The addresses of producers and distributors of educational software are listed in Appendix B.

Grammar Problems for Practice

Producer: Milliken

Hardware: Apple II

Description: This software package is divided into three separate modules that provide extensive drill and practice in troublesome grammar and usage areas related to homonyms, verbs, and pronouns. After entering a program, the student takes a pretest on the lesson. If mastery is achieved, he advances to the next lesson. If mastery is not reached, the student reviews and then works practice exercises pertaining to the failed portions of the pretest. During practice, the student is congratulated intermittently with positive reinforcements. If necessary, the student can branch to "help" screens that provide review of the homonym, verb, or pronoun form, as well as definitions and context sentences. The student can review his progress at any time, and a performance summary is given at the completion of the practice exercises. A posttest is given at the end of each lesson. If mastery is not achieved, the student is returned to the practice exercises. The programs focus on skills generally introduced in the third through sixth grade; however, they are appropriate for remediation in the seventh through ninth grade.

M-ss-ng L-nks

Producer: Sunburst Communications

Hardware: Apple, IBM PC, Commodore 64, TRS-80

Description: This software includes language puzzles designed to improve reading, writing, spelling, and grammar skills as well as develop an appreciation of syntax, vocabulary, and the mechanics of writing. A passage appears with certain letters missing. The pattern of missing letters varies, thus providing more than 500 different puzzles. The student fills in the blanks by making educated guesses based on knowledge of word structure and spelling, grammar, meaning in context, and sense of literary style. Four diskettes are available that are appropriate for students in the third grade through adult age. *Young People's Literature* offers passages from nine classics of children's literature. *MicroEncyclopedia,* especially appropriate for students in fourth through eighth grade, gives factual information on various topics. *Classics, Old and New* includes 81 passages from such authors as Hemingway and Dickens. *English Editor* (not available for Commodore 64) enables the teacher to enter passages of his own choice, thus tailoring the program to the individual student's interests and needs. In addition, for the IBM PC, *Foreign Language Editors* allows the teacher to enter passages of his choice in French, Spanish, or German.

Sentence Combining I; Sentence Combining II

Producer: Milliken

Hardware: Apple II

Description: These programs use creative graphics to teach the writing of fluent sentences. Through graphics and minimal keyboard input, the student builds sentences by combining elements of shorter sentences displayed on the screen. Each lesson uses the same tutorial procedure to teach and drill the student on one or two topics. First the student receives a brief introduction to the concept being presented. Next, the student is guided through interactive example exercises that are personalized by using the student's name. Finally, the student works practice exercises until mastery or failure is reached. The exercises follow different formats, which usually involve moving a graphics-created box over parts of sentences to indicate how they are to be combined into new sentences. Other formats include multiple-choice selection or stopping a moving comma to indicate the correct placement of commas in a sentence. Each correct exercise is rewarded with a star, and when the student demonstrates mastery, he is congratulated and moved to the next lesson. *Sentence Combining I,* appropriate for students in fourth through sixth grade and as review for older students, includes lessons on the following topics: compounding with *and* (subjects and predicates); inserting adjectives and adverbs;

inserting prepositional phrases; subject and object pronouns with *and*; coordinating conjunctions; singular, plural, and irregular possessives; relative pronouns (*who, that,* and *which*); subject/verb agreement; and using *because, before,* and *after. Sentence Combining II* is appropriate for students in sixth through ninth grade and as review for older students. It includes lessons on movability of adverb and prepositional phrases, complements of linking verbs, restrictive relative clauses, nonrestrictive relative clauses, appositives, gerund phrases (*-ing* phrases as subjects), using semicolons, present and past participles, and making infinitive phrases.

Verb Viper; Word Invasion; Word Master

Producer: DLM

Hardware: Apple II, IBM PC/PCjr, Commodore 64, Tandy 1000

Description: These three programs are included in DLM's *Arcademic Skill Builders in Language Arts.* In *Verb Viper,* a friendly elastic-necked creature helps the student master subject agreement with regular and irregular verbs in present tense, past tense, and past participle form. *Word Invasion* provides practice in identifying words representing six parts of speech (nouns, pronouns, verbs, adjectives, adverbs, and prepositions) by letting the student control the magic ring of a friendly alien octopus. *Word Master* presents practice in identifying pairs of antonyms, synonyms, or homonyms at three difficulty levels, while racing against time and advancing electronic rays. In all three programs, speed, length of the game, content levels, and sound effects can be preset according to the student's needs. A teacher's manual and 24 blackline masters of activities are included for each program.

The Writing Adventure

Producer: DLM

Hardware: Apple II, Commodore 64

Description: This software program provides instructional support while allowing students to develop their own stories. In each adventure the student directs the main character through intriguing scenes and takes notes on computer note cards for later reference. The student must make choices and think logically in developing stories and must end the stories by writing the main character out of a trap. When writing a story, the student can review his notes on the computer screen or can print them. A proofing aid highlights potential errors and displays grammar rules and examples that relate to them. The stories can be printed and shared with other students. The program package is designed for students age 9 and older and consists of two disks: *Story Starter* presents the adventure scenes, brief scene descriptions, note cards, and prompting questions, and *Story Writer* has word processing capabilities for note taking, editing, and printing stories.

Writing Competency Program

Distributor: Educational Activities

Hardware: Apple II, TRS-80, Commodore 64 with emulator

Description: This program is designed to instruct junior and senior high school students in three basic and essential areas of writing skills: (a) business letters (request and complaint)—format and basic parts, content, punctuation, audience, tone, and capitalization; (b) organizing a report—types of organization, outlining skills, unity and coherence, and details; and (c) persuasion—arguments and facts, topic sentences, supporting details, and audience. The program actively involves students in real-life situations and provides tutorial instruction, motivating graphic rewards, and a management system that allows the teacher to monitor student achievement.

Written Expression Series

Producer: Media Materials

Hardware: Apple II, TRS-80

Description: This series includes seven programs designed to develop various written expression skills: (a) *Nuts and Bolts*—using verbs, nouns and pronouns, adjectives and adverbs, and singular and plural forms: (b) *Gears and Cogs*—using prepositions, capital letters, words that are similar, and forms to show possession; (c) *Link It All Together*—writing sentences with subjects, action verbs, and adverbs; sentences with linking verbs; and sentences with objects; (d) *Sentence Helpers*—adding helping verbs, words with negative meanings, modifiers to sentences, and verbal modifiers; (e) *Compound? Complex?*—writing compound sentences, complex sentences with adverb clauses, complex sentences with adjective clauses, and direct and indirect quotations; (f) *The Sentence Road Map*—using beginning and end punctuation, using commas in sentences, avoiding major sentence errors, and avoiding fragments; and (g) *Final Assembly*—composing narrative paragraphs, descriptive and enumerative paragraphs, explanatory paragraphs; and using topic and supporting sentences. The programs are designed for students in fourth through twelfth grade. Supplemental materials for enrichment and reinforcement as well as an instructor's guide are included.

REFERENCES

Anderson, D. W. (1966). Handwriting research: Movement and quality. In T. D. Horn (Ed.), *Research on handwriting and spelling.* Champaign, IL: National Council of Teachers of English.

Archer, A. L., & Gleason, M. M. (1988). *Skills for school success.* Boston: Curriculum Associates.

Barbe, W. B., Lucas, V. H., Wasylyk, T. M., Hackney, C. S., & Braun, L. (1987). *Handwriting: Basic skills and application.* Columbus, OH: Zaner-Bloser.

Barbe, W., Milone, M., & Wasylyk, T. (1983). Manuscript is the "write" start. *Academic Therapy, 18,* 397–406.

California Achievement Tests. (1985). Monterey, CA: California Test Bureau/McGraw-Hill.

Carroll, J. B. (1938). Diversity of vocabulary and the harmonic series law of word-frequency distribution. *Psychological Record, 2.*

Cartwright, G. P. (1968). Written language abilities of normal and educable mentally retarded children. *American Journal of Mental Deficiency, 72,* 499–508.

Cartwright, G. P. (1969). Written expression and spelling. In R. M. Smith (Ed.), *Teacher diagnosis of educational difficulties* (pp. 95–117). New York: Merrill/Macmillan.

Christenson, S. L., Thurlow, M. L., Ysseldyke, J. E., & McVicar, R. (1989). Written language instruction for students with mild handicaps: Is there enough quantity to ensure quality? *Learning Disability Quarterly, 12,* 219–229.

Cohen, S. B., & Plaskon, S. P. (1980). *Language arts for the mildly handicapped.* New York: Merrill/Macmillan.

Dolch, E. W. (1955). *Methods in reading.* Champaign, IL: Garrard.

Dolch, E. W. (1960). *Better spelling.* Champaign, IL: Garrard.

Engelmann, S., & Silbert, J. (1983). *Expressive writing 1; Expressive writing 2.* Chicago: Science Research Associates.

Gardner, E. F., Rudman, H. C., Karlsen, B., & Merwin, J. C. (1982). *Stanford Achievement Test* (7th ed.). San Antonio, TX: Psychological Corporation.

Graham, S., & Harris, K. R. (1988). Instructional recommendations for teaching writing to exceptional students. *Exceptional Children, 54,* 506–512.

Graham, S., & Miller, L. (1980). Handwriting research and practice: A unified approach. *Focus on Exceptional Children, 13*(2), 1–16.

Graves, D. H. (1985). All children can write. *Learning Disabilities Focus, 1*(1), 36–43.

Hagin, R. A. (1983). Write right—or left: A practical approach to handwriting. *Journal of Learning Disabilities, 16,* 266–271.

Hammill, D. D. (1990). Problems in written composition. In D. D. Hammill & N. R. Bartel, *Teaching students with learning and behavior problems* (5th ed., pp. 179–217). Boston: Allyn & Bacon.

Hammill, D. D., Brown, V. L., Larsen, S. C., & Wiederholt, J. L. (1987). *Test of Adolescent Language—Revised.* Austin, TX: Pro-Ed.

Hammill, D. D., & Larsen, S. C. (1988). *Test of Written Language—2.* Austin, TX: Pro-Ed.

Hammill, D. D., & Leigh, J. E. (1983). *Basic School Skills Inventory—Diagnostic.* Austin, TX: Pro-Ed.

Hammill, D. D., & McNutt, G. (1981). *Correlates of reading: The consensus of thirty years of correlational research* (Pro-Ed Monograph No. 1). Austin, TX: Pro-Ed.

Hansen, C. L. (1978). Writing skills. In N. G. Haring, T. C. Lovitt, M. D. Eaton, & C. L. Hansen, *The fourth R: Research in the classroom* (pp. 93–126). New York: Merrill/Macmillan.

Herrick, V. E. (1960). Handwriting and children's writing. *Elementary English, 37,* 248–258.

Hieronymus, A. N., Hoover, H. D., & Lindquist, E. F. (1986). *Iowa Tests of Basic Skills.* Chicago: Riverside.

Hildreth, G. (1963). Simplified handwriting for today. *Journal of Educational Research, 56,* 330–333.

Hofmeister, A. M. (1981). *Handwriting resource book: Manuscript/cursive.* Allen, TX: DLM.

Horton, L. W. (1970). Illegibilities in the cursive handwriting of sixth graders. *Elementary School Journal, 70,* 446–450.

Houck, C. K., & Billingsley, B. S. (1989). Written expression of students with and without learning disabilities: Differences across the grades. *Journal of Learning Disabilities, 22,* 561–567, 572.

Hresko, W. P. (1988). *Test of Early Written Language.* Austin, TX: Pro-Ed.

Hunt, K. W. (1965). *Grammatical structures written at three grade levels* (NCTE Research Report No. 3). Champaign, IL: National Council of Teachers of English.

Isaacson, S. (1988). Assessing the written product: Qualitative and quantitative measures. *Exceptional Children, 54,* 528–534.

Isaacson, S. (1990). Written language. In P. J. Schloss, M. A. Smith, & C. N. Schloss, *Instructional methods for adolescents with learning and behavior problems* (pp. 202–228). Boston: Allyn & Bacon.

Johnson, D. J., & Myklebust, H. R. (1967). *Learning disabilities: Educational principles and practices.* New York: Grune & Stratton.

Johnson, W. (1944). Studies in language behavior. I. A program of research. *Psychological Monographs, 56*(2).

Kameenui, E. J., & Simmons, D. C. (1990). *Designing instructional strategies: The prevention of academic learning problems.* New York: Merrill/Macmillan.

Koenig, C. H., & Kunzelmann, H. P. (1980). *Classroom learning screening manual.* New York: Merrill/Macmillan.

Larsen, S. C., & Hammill, D. D. (1989). *Test of Legible Handwriting.* Austin, TX: Pro-Ed.

Levy, N. R., & Rosenberg, M. S. (1990). Strategies for improving the written expression of students with learning disabilities. *LD Forum, 16,* 23–30.

Lewis, E. R., & Lewis, H. P. (1965). An analysis of errors in the formation of manuscript letters by first grade children. *American Educational Research Journal, 2,* 25–35.

MacArthur, C. A. (1988). The impact of computers on the writing process. *Exceptional Children, 54,* 536–542.

MacArthur, C., & Graham, S. (1987). Learning disabled students' composing under three methods of text production: Handwriting, word processing, and dictation. *Journal of Special Education, 21,* 22–42.

MacArthur, C. A., Schwartz, S. S., & Graham, S. (1991). A model for writing instruction: Integrating word processing and strategy instruction into a process approach to writing. *Learning Disabilities Research & Practice, 6,* 230–236.

Mann, P. H., Suiter, P. A., & McClung, R. M. (1992). *A guide to educating mainstreamed students* (4th ed.). Boston: Allyn & Bacon.

McCarthy, D. (1954). Language development in children. In L. Carmichael (Ed.), *Manual of child psychology.* New York: Wiley.

Meckel, H. C. (1963). Research on teaching composition and literature. In N. Gage (Ed.), *Handbook of research on teaching.* Chicago: Rand McNally.

Miller, G. A. (1951). *Language and communication.* New York: McGraw-Hill.

Miller, S., & Engelmann, S. (1980). *Cursive writing program.* Chicago: Science Research Associates.

Moore, G. N., & Woodruff, G. W. (1980). *Story starters—Primary and intermediate.* North Billerica, MA: Curriculum Associates.

Morocco, C., & Nelson, A. (1990). *Writers at work.* Chicago: Science Research Associates.

Morris, N. T., & Crump, D. T. (1982). Syntactic and vocabulary development in the written language of learning disabled and non-learning disabled students at four age levels. *Learning Disability Quarterly, 5,* 163–172.

Myklebust, H. R. (1965). *Development and disorders of written language: Picture Story Language Test* (Vol. 1). New York: Grune & Stratton.

Newland, T. E. (1932). An analytical study of the development of illegibilities in handwriting from the lower grades to adulthood. *Journal of Educational Research, 26,* 249–258.

Noble, J. K. (1966). *Better handwriting for you.* New York: Noble & Noble.

Otto, W., & Smith, R. J. (1980). *Corrective and remedial teaching* (3rd ed.). Boston: Houghton Mifflin.

Outhred, L. (1989). Word processing: Its impact on children's writing. *Journal of Learning Disabilities, 22,* 262–264.

Parker, R. I., Tindal, G., & Hasbrouck, J. (1991). Progress monitoring with objective measures of writing performance for students with mild disabilities. *Exceptional Children, 58,* 61–73.

Phelps-Terasaki, D., & Phelps-Gunn, T. (1988). *Teaching competence in written language.* Austin, TX: Pro-Ed.

Polloway, E. A., & Smith, J. E., Jr. (1982). *Teaching language skills to exceptional learners.* Denver: Love.

Poteet, J. A. (1980). Informal assessment of written expression. *Learning Disability Quarterly, 3*(4), 88–98.

Powers, R., & Kaminsky, S. (1988). *Handwriting: A fresh start.* North Billerica, MA: Curriculum Associates.

Precision Teaching Project. (Available from Skyline Center, 3300 Third Street Northeast, Great Falls, MT 59404).

Scannell, D. P. (1986). *Tests of Achievement and Proficiency.* Chicago: Riverside.

Schumaker, J. B., & Lyerla, K. D. (1991). *The paragraph writing strategy.* Lawrence, KS: University of Kansas Institute for Research in Learning Disabilities.

Schumaker, J. B., Nolan, S. M., & Deshler, D. D. (1985). *Learning strategies curriculum: The error monitoring strategy.* Lawrence, KS: University of Kansas Institute for Research in Learning Disabilities.

Schumaker, J. B., & Sheldon, J. (1985). *The sentence writing strategy.* Lawrence, KS: University of Kansas Institute for Research in Learning Disabilities.

Skinner, B. F., & Krakower, S. A. (1968). *Handwriting with write and see.* Chicago: Lyons & Carnahan.

Strauss, A., & Lehtinen, L. (1947). *Psychopathology and education of the brain-injured child.* New York: Grune & Stratton.

Stuckless, E. R., & Marks, C. H. (1966). *Assessment of the written language of deaf students* (USOE Cooperative Research Project 2544). Pittsburgh, PA: University of Pittsburgh.

Templin, E. (1960). Research and comment: Handwriting, the neglected R. *Elementary English, 37,* 386–389.

Thomas, C. C., Englert, C. S., & Gregg, S. (1987). An analysis of errors and strategies in the expository writing of learning disabled students. *Remedial and Special Education, 8*(1), 21–30, 46.

Thurber, D. N., & Jordan, D. R. (1981). *D'Nealian handwriting.* Glenview, IL: Scott, Foresman.

Tindal, G. A., & Marston, D. B. (1990). *Classroom-based assessment: Evaluating instructional outcomes.* New York: Merrill/Macmillan.

Tompkins, G. E. (1990). *Teaching writing: Balanced process and product.* New York: Merrill/Macmillan.

Wallace, G., Larsen, S. C., & Elksnin, L. K. (1992). *Educational assessment of learning problems: Testing for teaching* (2nd ed.). Boston: Allyn & Bacon.

Warden, R., Allen, J., Hipp, K., Schmitz, J., & Collett, L. (1988). *Written expression.* San Antonio, TX: Psychological Corporation.

Weiner, E. S. (1980a). Diagnostic evaluation of writing skills. *Journal of Learning Disabilities, 13,* 48–53.

Weiner, E. S. (1980b). The Diagnostic Evaluation of Writing Skills (DEWS): Application of DEWS criteria to writing samples. *Learning Disability Quarterly, 3*(2), 54–59.

Welch, M. (1992). The PLEASE strategy: A metacognitive learning strategy for improving the paragraph writing of students with mild learning disabilities. *Learning Disability Quarterly, 15,* 119–128.

Welch, M., & Link, D. P. (1989). *Write, P.L.E.A.S.E.: A strategy for efficient learning and functioning in written expression* [videocassette]. Salt Lake City: University of Utah, Department of Special Education, Educational Tele-Communications.

Wesson, C. L. (1987). Curriculum-based measurement: Increasing efficiency. *Teaching Exceptional Children, 20*(1), 46–47.

Western, R. D. (1977). Case against cursive script. *Elementary School Journal, 78,* 1–3.

Wiederholt, J. L., Hammill, D. D., & Brown, V. L. (1983). *The resource teacher: A guide to effective practices* (2nd ed.). Austin, TX: Pro-Ed.

Wiig, E. H., & Semel, E. M. (1976). *Language disabilities in children and adolescents.* New York: Merrill/Macmillan.

Woodcock, R. W., & Johnson, M. B. (1989). *Woodcock-Johnson Psycho-Educational Battery—Revised.* Allen, TX: DLM.

Zaner-Bloser Evaluation Scales. (1984). Columbus, OH: Zaner-Bloser.

CHAPTER 14

Teaching at the Secondary Level

The development of viable secondary and adult programs for individuals with learning problems is an essential and difficult task. Many adolescents continue to enter secondary school and community life with debilitating learning or behavioral problems. Initial efforts in programming for these adolescents primarily have involved applying approaches developed with younger students (for example, academic remediation in word-attack skills). However, educators quickly have realized that adolescents are not simply elementary students grown up and that they exhibit unique characteristics that demand a variety of services. Basically, effective special and remedial education programs must consider that in addition to their learning difficulties, adolescents are in a complex transition from childhood to adulthood that typically has dramatic effects on social, emotional, sexual, physical, and academic development. Moreover, adolescents are adjusting to a new setting—the secondary school—which places a multitude of demands on them. The high dropout rate strongly suggests the need for better secondary programming (Rumberger, 1987). Levin, Zigmond, and Birch (1985) followed the progress of 51 ninth-grade students with learning disabilities for 4 years. Of this group, 51 percent dropped out of school. This finding led Levin et al. to conclude that "the 'holding power' of the schools for learning disabled adolescents is called into serious question" (p. 6).

Compounding the task of programming for adolescents with learning problems is the constant reform in secondary education. Natriello, McDill, and Pallas (1985) note that recent reforms are raising standards for time spent in school, increasing core curriculum demands, and requiring that minimum competency tests be passed. In many situations, curriculum reforms and funding patterns are developed and required without regard for students with spe-

cial needs. For example, Wang, Rubenstein, and Reynolds (1985) report that a successful secondary program for special education students in a large urban city was terminated because of a quirk in funding procedures. They and other authorities are encouraging special educators to become more active concerning reforms and policies in secondary programming to help clear the road to success for adolescents with learning problems.

Fortunately, recent efforts in the field of learning disabilities have focused on developing secondary programs. For example, the University of Kansas Institute for Research in Learning Disabilities was established in 1978 to study the needs of adolescents with learning disabilities and develop appropriate interventions. Under the leadership of Don Deshler, Jean Schumaker, and their colleagues, this institute is having a nationwide effect. Moreover, successful secondary demonstration programs have been developed in many states (Riegel & Mathey, 1980). Although most programs still are being empirically validated, the recent surge of programs and literature certainly has increased knowledge and hope about secondary and adult programming. Although these recent efforts are primarily in the field of learning disabilities, most of the findings are applicable to students with mild disabilities (for example, mildly mentally handicapped and emotionally handicapped). This position is feasible because of the heterogeneous nature of learning disabilities.

DEMANDS PLACED ON ADOLESCENTS

The world of most adolescents revolves around the school setting. Adolescents spend the majority of their day preparing to go to school, getting to school, attending classes, participating in after-school activities, and doing homework. The home environment gradually has less influence on adolescents, and peers and other adults begin to play a greater role in determining how they behave. As they get older, the demands of part- or full-time employment may impose even greater demands. However, the part-time job often is considered a step toward the adult world and greater dependence. In short, the demands placed on adolescents increase and grow in complexity. Across the settings and situations that adolescents must face, the demands placed on them can be considered as having specific academic, social, motivational, and cognitive dimensions. These demands, coupled with recent reforms in secondary education to increase core curriculum requirements, increase time spent in school, and require students to pass a minimum competency test, are making it extremely difficult for adolescents with learning problems to succeed (Natriello et al. 1985).

School Demands

Gaining information from written materials.   Students are expected to acquire information written at the secondary level. However, the readability level of secondary textbooks may exceed the grade level at which they are used (for example, a text used for a ninth-grade social studies class may be written at a twelfth-grade reading level) (Schumaker & Deshler, 1984), and the organization and flow of the writing of common textbooks have been described as being "inconsiderate" to the reader (Armbruster & Anderson, 1984). Moreover, the textbook is important in determining the curriculum for a course. C. M. Clark and Peterson (1986) note that curriculum planning studies indicate that the textbook is the most important factor in determining what will be taught in a course. As a result, the organization, emphasis, and balance of factual and conceptual information presented in a course may be based completely on textual information.

Gaining information from lectures.   In an extensive study of the oral language demands of middle and secondary school classrooms, Moran (1980) found that the lecture was the predominant type of listening requirement of secondary classrooms and that the rate of teacher presentation of information did not differ significantly between seventh-grade and twelfth-grade classes. In other words, in the classes that were studied, seventh graders were expected to process information at the same rate as high school seniors. Her data clearly demonstrate that to succeed in a secondary curriculum, all students must possess skills in listening, attending, remembering, note taking, and writing. Some of her specific findings include the following:

1. Regular class teachers rely heavily on the lecture method and tend to address questions to the whole class rather than to individuals.
2. Regular class teachers use few advance organizers to help students listen or take notes more effectively.
3. Students are not asked regularly to paraphrase or demonstrate their understanding of materials presented in lecture or readings.
4. Regular class teachers lecture at a fast pace, and only students with excellent note-taking skills are able to take meaningful notes.
5. The frequency of oral feedback and reinforcement is low.

Moreover, the frequencies of verbal interactions between teachers and students with and without learning problems are reported to be similar (Powell, Suzuki, Atwater, Gorney-

Krupsaw, & Morris, 1981). Thus, it is likely that many secondary teachers do not take into consideration the different learning needs of the students in terms of the oral dimensions of the classroom.

Demonstrating knowledge through tests. The primary method for evaluating learning at the secondary level is through tests. Classroom tests and quizzes, group-achievement tests, and minimum competency tests are the hallmark of the secondary school curriculum. Cuthbertson (1978) found that written tests are used extensively, and students need good test-taking and study skills to cope with testing demands. In addition, teachers expect students to acquire information for tests from textbooks, lectures, and class discussions. Teachers and parents indicate that students with and without disabilities, with few concessions, should be required to meet the same minimum competency requirements (Meyen, Alley, Scannell, Harnden, & Miller, 1982).

Expressing information in writing. Moran (1980) reports that the most frequently required writing assignment in the secondary school setting, according to teacher reports, is the short-answer response (for example, fill in the blank, spell a word, mark a correct answer). The second most important writing demand reported by teachers is taking notes from lectures or written materials. Writing more than a one-sentence response (that is, descriptive, narrative, or argumentative writing) is required less frequently, and essay-style writing is not a common significant demand of the secondary school setting. When students are required to write, however, it appears that students who can spell correctly and write long, complete sentences tend to receive the highest grades even though teachers report that sentence structure and complexity are the most important writing features (Moran & DeLoache, 1982).

Working independently with little feedback. Link (1980) surveyed 44 elementary and 89 secondary teachers concerning essential learning skills, and the highest ranking was given to the skill of following oral and written directions. Moreover, basic skills such as reading, mathematics, and spelling were ranked lower than skills involved in study abilities. For example, skimming, locating information in a text, remembering information for a test, and turning in assignments ranked higher than more traditional basic skills. The high ranking of study skills indicates a high expectation for students to work efficiently and effectively on their own. In another study directly related to five areas of teacher expectations, Knowlton (1983) separated specific study skills from independent work habits. Subskills associated with independent work habits included bringing materials to class, completing assignments and homework, budgeting time, requesting help, and working independently. Subskills associated with study skills included taking notes, using library reference materials, writing reports, taking tests, and copying. Knowlton found that regular classroom teachers' greatest expectation for students was the demonstration of independent work habits. Socialization skills ranked second, communication skills ranked third, study skills were fourth, and subject-matter skills were fifth. These studies indicate that many regular classroom teachers have high expectations for students to develop plans for getting their own work done, monitoring and checking their work, and completing tasks without extra assistance from the teacher. This does not imply that the other areas are unimportant but, rather, that teachers consider independent work behaviors to be the trouble spots in delivering organized group instruction, which is the basis for the delivery of the secondary school curriculum.

Demonstrating a broad set of cognitive and metacognitive strategies. A *strategy* is a person's approach to a task, and executive strategies relate to one's ability to reflect and think about one's own thinking processes (or cognitive strategies) and decide how to use them to complete a task effectively and efficiently. For example, students are expected to be able to organize information and resources to promote learning. While students must apply skills to meet these expectations, the process of organizing multiple resources (for example, notes, text, worksheets) requires them to manipulate a variety of strategies in a sophisticated manner. Schumaker and Deshler (1984) and Lenz, Clark, Deshler, Schumaker, and Rademacher (1990) conclude that studies on the demands of the secondary school environment clearly indicate that students are required to use higher-order thinking skills in school if they are to be judged successful by regular classroom teachers. These skills relate to being an independent problem solver (for example, trying to solve an assignment-related problem independently before seeking help) as well as a student's ability to apply knowledge across content areas (a process commonly referred to as *generalization*). Lenz and Mellard (1990) contend that many regular classroom teachers assume that these skills automatically will increase, develop, and be applied without special attention as a result of continued exposure to increasingly difficult content-area learning experiences. Thus, explicit instruction in generalized use of skills for application in different classes or materials rarely is provided.

Interacting appropriately. In a review of studies on the social demands placed on adolescents in the secondary school environment, Lenz, Clark, Deshler, Schumaker, and Rademacher (1990) conclude that for students to meet adult and peer expectations for suc-

cessful and appropriate social interaction, they must follow rules and instructions in and out of the school setting, participate in group social activities, participate in discussions and conversations with peers and adults, accept criticism and assistance appropriately, recruit assistance appropriately (and only when needed), resist inappropriate peer pressure, and maintain a pleasant manner across social interactions.

Moreover, within the classroom setting, Knowlton (1983) found that across five areas of teacher expectations, socialization ranked second, after independent work habits. In this study, socialization included the subskills of displaying respect for authority, following classroom rules, accepting criticism, and working as a team member. However, Knowlton notes that teachers of nonacademic subjects consider overt conduct classroom behaviors to be more important than do teachers of academic subjects. This may indicate that these classes offer more opportunities for off-task behaviors because of frequent shifts in activities or that the perceived value held by students for these classes is low.

In observational studies of teacher-student and student-student interactions within classroom settings, there is little evidence to indicate that sophisticated social interaction skills are required. Schumaker, Sheldon-Wildgen, and Sherman (1980) found that on the average only 11 percent of classroom activities required discussion and that this percentage decreased as the grade level increased. For example, the average rate of the use of discussion activities in seventh-grade classes was reported to be 18 percent, in eighth-grade classes it was 11 percent, and in ninth-grade classes it was only 3 percent. During the past 10 years, many regular classroom teachers have begun to infuse the use of cooperative learning activities into classroom activities (D. W. Johnson & Johnson, 1986), but it is unclear whether the introduction of activities related to peer-assisted instruction, such as those employed in cooperative learning, is altering the social demands of secondary school settings.

Demonstrating motivation to learn.   Teachers expect students to be motivated to learn; however, teachers and students may have different perceptions concerning motivation. Lenz, Clark, Deshler, Schumaker, and Rademacher (1990) report that teachers appear to base their perception of motivation on the student's behavior in planning for timely task completion, setting both short- and long-term goals, putting forth maximum and appropriate effort to achieve goals, and completing educational programs. Should the student or the teacher be responsible for promoting motivation? Teachers appear to believe that students should be motivated to learn secondary school content and that the biggest barrier to their effectiveness relates to student attitudes and the value that they place on academic learning (Lenz, Deshler, & Schumaker, 1991). Lenz at al. conclude that students who appear to be motivated might satisfy a basic criterion that teachers may have for judging the effectiveness of their instruction.

Vocational and Employment Demands

Many adolescents become involved in vocational training programs and part- or full-time jobs during their secondary school years. Attention to career and vocational readiness is appropriate in secondary schools because approximately 50 percent of all high school students do not continue to higher education (Hamilton, 1986). Significant attention is placed on creating career development and vocational training programs in secondary schools, and the actual demands encountered in these settings are similar to those encountered in academic settings. Information must

be gained and applied in a social context and motivation must exist to achieve success in school-based vocational training programs and employment settings.

Students are expected to demonstrate oral language, reading, writing, and listening skills in school settings, and research indicates that these same skills are required in employment settings. For example, Mathews, Whang, and Fawcett (1980) identified and validated 13 employment skills (covering both academic and social areas) as being important for obtaining and maintaining employment. The general skills required across the 13 employment skills include reading and writing (for example, writing a letter to request an interview in response to a help-wanted advertisement, completing a federal income tax form), listening (for example, accepting both suggestions and criticism from an employer), and oral language (for example, telephoning to request an interview, participating in an interview, providing constructive criticism to co-workers, explaining a problem to a supervisor, complimenting a co-worker). Students also should be able to work independently and accept feedback.

Attention to these broad employment demands is critical. Evidence suggests that employee success is highly related to the match between job demands and an individual's characteristics (Siegel & Gaylord-Ross, 1991). The expectation for successful social interactions, academic performance, and independent work habits also is cited by Fourqurean and LaCourt (1990). However, Mithaug, Horiuchi, and Fanning (1985) argue that students face a broader set of demands when they enter the work force. They suggest that the real demands placed on employees relate to solving problems, setting goals, and making good decisions and that specific training in job skills will pay off only when these broader skills are learned. Schumaker, Hazel, and Deshler

(1985) support this position. Finally, a growing demand of many employment settings is that the employee must be drug free. Unfortunately, for many adolescents and young adults this is a difficult demand to meet.

PROGRAMMING FOR ADOLESCENTS

When adolescents with learning problems, with their complex needs, enter the secondary setting, with its extensive demands, the need for a diversity of services becomes apparent. An analysis of the various programs indicates that seven types of program services are required to accommodate the various needs of secondary students with learning problems.

Program Services

As presented in Figure 14.1, program services include academic remediation, learning strategies, content instruction, social development instruction, functional living skills, career-related instruction, and transition instruction. These services are provided in a variety of instructional arrangements (for example, resource room, regular class, self-contained class) by a diverse faculty (such as special educators, regular class teachers, counselors, vocational educators).

The heterogeneous nature of adolescents with learning problems underscores the need to offer a variety of services. Some students need one type of service (for example, academic remediation) in the early stages of their secondary school program and another service (for example, career-related instruction or functional living skills) in the latter part of their program. Still others may require only one service (for example, learning strategies) during their secondary school program, while others need a combination of different services (for example, academic remediation and content instruction). To date, it appears that no one approach is appropriate for all adolescents with learning problems. Deshler, Schumaker, Lenz, and Ellis (1984) report that the real challenge is not in determining which approach is right or wrong but in ascertaining under what conditions and with whom a given service is most effective.

Determining who provides the various services depends on many variables (for example, number of teachers, specific expertise, resources) in diverse secondary settings. Certainly, coordination and cooperation between special and regular educators are essential for

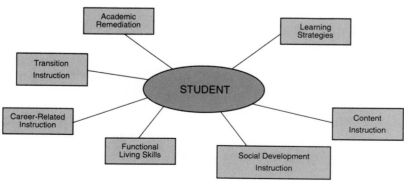

FIGURE 14.1
Program services at the secondary level.

effective programming. Typically, special educators primarily are responsible for academic remediation, learning strategies, social development instruction, and functional living skills. Although all of these services are offered by some special education teachers, they usually are divided among a team of special education teachers. The resource room teacher is used widely, with the special educator directly instructing students and collaborating with regular teachers. In content instruction, regular class teachers primarily are responsible, and the typical educator serves as a team member who suggests curriculum modifications, compensatory techniques, and instructional adaptations. Career-related and transition instruction typically are provided by regular educators (for example, vocational-business teachers) in conjunction with special education services, especially functional living skills. Finally, the entire program of services must be supported by the school administration and facilitated by responsive guidance and counseling services.

One service delivery model is not appropriate for all secondary settings. Administrators and teachers must organize the program to match their respective situations; however, the quality and type of services should be maintained in all administrative arrangements. In all instructional settings, the teacher of adolescents with learning problems must follow effective teaching practices. Many of these practices are discussed in Chapter 1; however, specific applications of quality instructional practices for adolescents are featured throughout this chapter.

Secondary Programming Models

To implement comprehensive educational services at the secondary level for adolescents with learning problems, attention must be given to developing a variety of program components. This is accomplished by identifying the major dimensions of the program and developing each of these areas. Schumaker, Deshler, and Ellis (1986) identify three major areas of program development believed to be critical for developing secondary learning disabilities programs: (a) clearly specifying the nature of the curriculum that is to be taught, (b) identifying the instructional methodologies that will be used to teach the curriculum, and (c) specifying how the instructional environment will be arranged to manage and promote student learning. Table 14.1 represents the dimensions of secondary programming that are addressed in the Strategies Intervention Model of the University of Kansas Institute for Research in Learning Disabilities.

Zigmond (1978, 1990) and Polloway, Patton, Epstein, and Smith (1989) also present components for developing secondary programs in learning disabilities. These researchers address the same general areas identified by Deshler and his colleagues, but the specific dimensions and emphases vary. For example, in addition to renewing attention to the skills students need to learn, increasing the intensity of instruction, and forging stronger ties with regular educators, Zigmond (1990) proposes two basic models for organizing services. These models are presented in Figure 14.2 and provide useful guidelines for specific program development efforts.

The model for organizing programming presented by Polloway et al. (1989) focuses primarily on delineating the content of the secondary program rather than on specific instructional procedures and management arrangements. They argue that a comprehensive curriculum should be developed that (a) responds to the current needs of individuals, (b) balances the need for maximum interaction with normally achieving peers against critical curriculum needs, (c) integrates related service delivery options, (d) emerges from a realistic appraisal of potential adult outcomes for the student,

TABLE 14.1
Secondary programming components of the Strategies Intervention Model.

STRATEGIC CURRICULUM COMPONENT

The Strategic Curriculum Component of the Strategies Intervention Model specifies *what* will be taught to low-achieving or at-risk students. This component consists of four types of strategies.

Learning Strategies: designed to teach students how to cope with the academic demands encountered across a variety of school, home, community, and employment settings. These learning strategies teach students how to respond to critical reading, writing, listening, remembering, and test-taking demands.

Social Skill Strategies: designed to teach the student how to interact appropriately across a variety of situations and settings. Strategies such as resisting peer pressure, accepting criticism, negotiating, following directions, and asking for help are included.

Motivation Strategies: consists of strategies that enable students to become active in planning the direction of their lives. Strategies that teach students how to set, monitor, and attain goals related to important areas of their lives and then communicate these goals to others are included.

Executive Strategies: designed to teach students how to solve problems independently and generalize learning. These strategies are taught to students after instruction in three to five learning strategies.

STRATEGIC INSTRUCTION COMPONENT

The Strategic Instruction Component includes procedures for *how* strategies should be taught to students. In addition, it includes procedures for the effective delivery of content to low-achieving and at-risk students.

Acquisition Procedures: provides teachers with a sequenced set of steps for teaching the strategies to mastery.

Generalization Procedures: provides teachers with a sequenced set of steps for teaching and ensuring generalization and maintenance of newly acquired strategies to other settings and situations.

Strategic Teaching Behaviors: provides teachers with the critical teaching behaviors that should be infused throughout all steps and phases of strategy and content instruction to promote maximum learning by low-achieving and at-risk students.

Content Enhancement Procedures: provides teachers with routines and devices for delivering subject-matter information in a manner that can be understood and remembered by students.

STRATEGIC ENVIRONMENT COMPONENT

The Strategic Environment Component deals with how to manage and organize educational settings and programs to promote and prompt strategic learning and performance.

Teaming Techniques: consists of methods related to teaching teachers, students, parents, and other professionals how to work as a team to bring about maximum student learning.

Management Techniques: consists of methods related to how to manage materials, time, instructional arrangements, and student behavior to promote student independence and success.

Evaluation Techniques: consists of systems related to evaluating student performance, program performance, and teacher performance and providing feedback to those involved in a manner that will promote student learning and success.

Development Techniques: consists of methods related to systematically implementing program components and developing strategies responsive to student needs.

Source: From *Students with Learning Disabilities*, 4th ed. (p. 371), by C. D. Mercer, 1992, New York: Merrill/Macmillan. Copyright 1992 by Macmillan Publishing Company. Reprinted by permission.

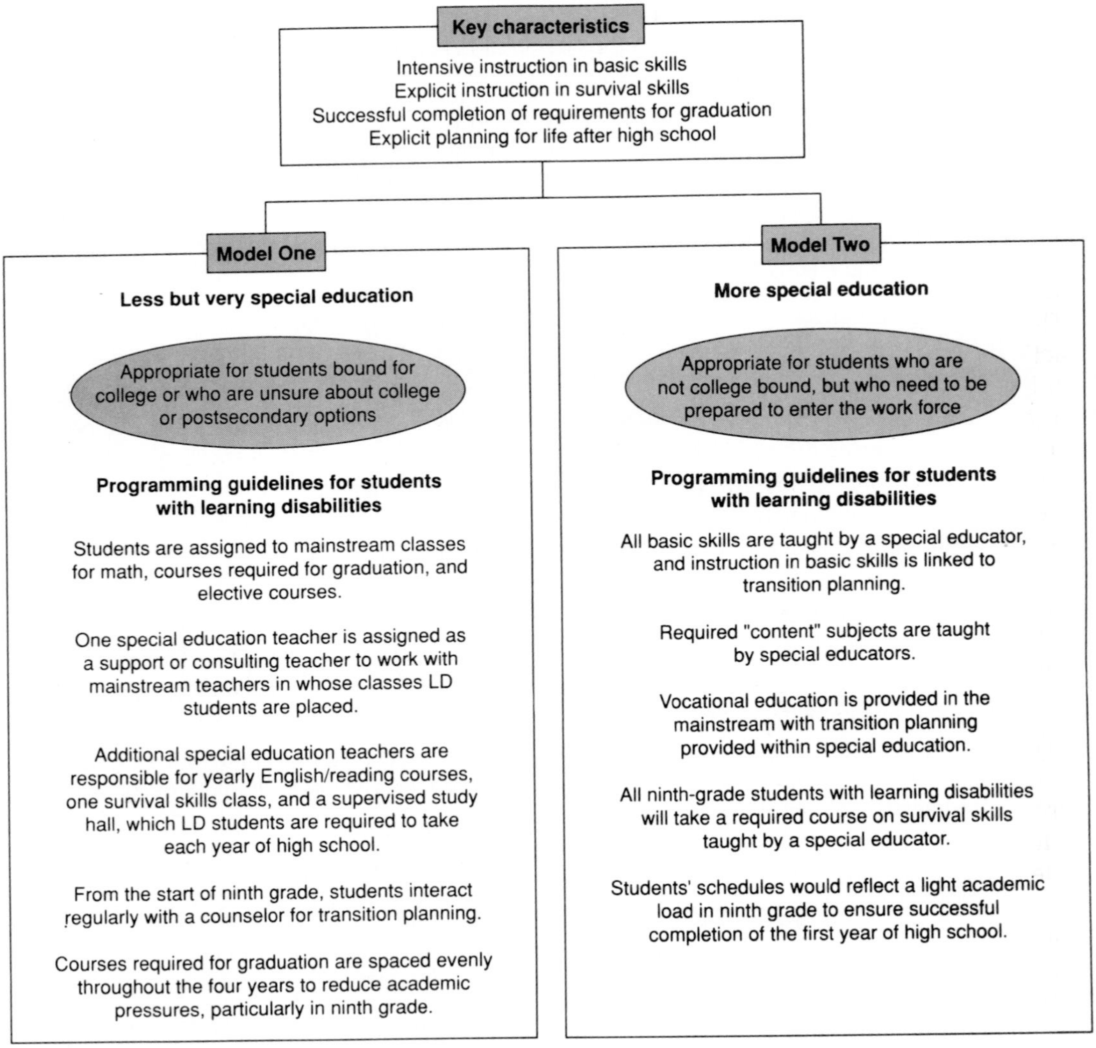

Key characteristics
Intensive instruction in basic skills
Explicit instruction in survival skills
Successful completion of requirements for graduation
Explicit planning for life after high school

Model One

Less but very special education

Appropriate for students bound for college or who are unsure about college or postsecondary options

Programming guidelines for students with learning disabilities

Students are assigned to mainstream classes for math, courses required for graduation, and elective courses.

One special education teacher is assigned as a support or consulting teacher to work with mainstream teachers in whose classes LD students are placed.

Additional special education teachers are responsible for yearly English/reading courses, one survival skills class, and a supervised study hall, which LD students are required to take each year of high school.

From the start of ninth grade, students interact regularly with a counselor for transition planning.

Courses required for graduation are spaced evenly throughout the four years to reduce academic pressures, particularly in ninth grade.

Model Two

More special education

Appropriate for students who are not college bound, but who need to be prepared to enter the work force

Programming guidelines for students with learning disabilities

All basic skills are taught by a special educator, and instruction in basic skills is linked to transition planning.

Required "content" subjects are taught by special educators.

Vocational education is provided in the mainstream with transition planning provided within special education.

All ninth-grade students with learning disabilities will take a required course on survival skills taught by a special educator.

Students' schedules would reflect a light academic load in ninth grade to ensure successful completion of the first year of high school.

FIGURE 14.2
Secondary school programming guidelines for students with learning disabilities.
Source: From *Students with Learning Disabilities*, 4th ed. (p. 372), by C. D. Mercer, 1992, New York: Merrill/Macmillan. Copyright 1992 by Macmillan Publishing Company. Reprinted by permission.

(e) focuses on transitional needs across the life span, and (f) is sensitive to graduation goals and requirements. Polloway et al. propose a system of tracks in which subgroups of students with learning disabilities may be placed as a way of organizing programming. Their tracks include a functional track for students with severe learning disabilities, a college preparatory track, and a "tough-to-call" track for students whose future is difficult to project.

Each of these programming models has a specific emphasis that distinguishes it from the others, but all of the models argue for the identification of well thought-out program components that ensure organized and intensive instruction. These models illustrate the need for the development of comprehensive and multidimensional programs to meet the diverse needs of secondary students with learning problems.

The remainder of this chapter provides instructional procedures for adolescents with learning problems and instructional information (activities, techniques, materials, and resources) in the seven program areas (academic remediation, learning strategies, content instruction, social development instruction, functional living skills, career-related instruction, and transition instruction). Moreover, other sections of the book that relate to teaching adolescents are referred to where applicable.

INSTRUCTIONAL PROCEDURES

Simply identifying the appropriate curriculum for students does not ensure that the students will learn the targeted information. Additional dimensions of secondary programming that must be considered are the motivation of the students and how the curriculum is acquired by the students. When developing the total intervention program, the learning characteristics of adolescents with learning problems should be considered. The instructional procedures used by the teacher to ensure that the student acquires the skills or content defined by the curriculum must be carefully selected and implemented.

Motivation

Many secondary students with learning problems have serious motivational problems about schoolwork (Adelman & Taylor, 1983; Deshler, Schumaker, & Lenz, 1984); thus, including techniques to enhance motivation is essential to foster effective instruction. The frustration of a history of limited academic success and the numerous activities (such as driving a car, getting a job, being with friends) available to the adolescent combine to create substantial motivation problems for some students. Much literature exists that emphasizes the relationship of motivation to problems in learning and performance. Adelman and Taylor (1983) express it simply:

> If a student is motivated to learn something, (s)he often can do much more than anyone would have predicted was possible. Conversely, if a student is not particularly interested in learning something, resultant learning may not even be close to capability. (p. 384)

In essence, there are times when motivation, not academic development, becomes the focus of an intervention program.

Several motivation techniques are available to help low-achieving students in secondary school. Deshler, Schumaker, and Lenz (1984) divide these approaches into two broad categories: those that use extrinsic controls and those that focus on developing intrinsic motivation. From their review of motivation studies, Deshler et al. report that several extrinsic control techniques have been used successfully to improve the academic skills of adolescents with learning difficulties. Zigmond, Sansone, Miller, Donahoe, and Kohnke (1986) provide a list of extrinsic reinforcers that appear to be effective with adolescents. The reinforcers include the following:

1. Time for listening to tapes or records
2. Tokens for progress on academics
3. Charting or self-recording of academic accomplishments
4. Allowances at home tied to grades

5. Time to play games or enjoy a recreational activity
6. Opportunity to participate in scheduling academic activities
7. Tangible reinforcers such as restaurant coupons, magazines, and movie tickets
8. Exemption from some homework or assignment
9. Extra time for a break or lunch

The most useful techniques include token economies, contingency contracting, and verbal feedback (see Chapter 5 for descriptions of these techniques). Also, techniques aimed at facilitating intrinsic motivation are receiving support. Schumaker, Deshler, Alley, and Warner (1983) report that the focus of the motivation component at the University of Kansas Institute for Research in Learning Disabilities is to produce independent and active learners. To accomplish this, the intervention is aimed at training self-control skills, including one or more of the following: goal setting, self-recording of progress, self-evaluation, and self-reinforcement. Seabaugh and Schumaker (1981) taught all four of these self-control subskills to adolescents with learning disabilities and had positive results (that is, the number of lessons completed by the students increased from an average of one-half lesson completed per day to four lessons completed per day). Deshler, Schumaker, and Lenz (1984) report that self-control training holds much promise for helping low achievers complete their assignments. They note that the training procedures are easy to implement and do not depend on expensive extrinsic reinforcers.

From their review of the motivation literature, Adelman and Taylor (1983) list tactics for enhancing intrinsic motivation, including the following:

1. Provide some choices in curriculum content and procedures to enhance the student's perception that learning is worthwhile. Also, discussions concerning the relevance (real-life applications) of various content are helpful.
2. Through discussion, obtain a commitment to options that the student values and indicates a desire to pursue. Contractual agreements are helpful.
3. Schedule informal and formal conferences with the student to enhance her role in making choices and negotiating agreements.
4. Provide feedback that conveys student progress. The student must not perceive the feedback as an effort to entice and control. Self-correcting materials are useful.

A recurring theme in the literature on managing and motivating adolescents with learning problems is that of involving the student. For example, in their discussion of secondary classroom management, Kerr and Nelson (1989) state, "We strongly recommend that you encourage pupils to participate in all aspects of the curriculum. Specifically, they should be involved in selecting and ordering their own academic and social goals, in making decisions about the classroom structure, and in setting consequences and contingencies" (p. 157). An example of procedures that teachers can use to teach students how to participate in goal setting and planning is presented by Van Reusen, Bos, Schumaker, and Deshler (1987).

Another dimension that can be included in efforts to promote student motivation relates to the beliefs that students have about themselves. Many students do not believe that they can learn or change. Ellis, Deshler, Lenz, Schumaker, and Clark (1991) present four techniques for teachers to use to help students alter their beliefs about their learning and performance:

1. Engineer instructional arrangements to promote and reinforce student independence.

2. Communicate high expectations for students through words and actions.
3. Help students identify and analyze beliefs that underlie their behavior as ineffective learners.
4. Help students discard unproductive beliefs through a variety of activities and interactions.

Additional information on classroom management and techniques for enhancing student motivation are presented in Chapter 5.

Acquisition and Generalization of Skills and Strategies

Several instructional procedures are used to promote the acquisition of skills by adolescents. These approaches use activities involving guided practice, modeling, peer instruction, provision of feedback, and task analysis. How these instructional procedures are integrated and used to promote adolescent learning has been the focus of research at the University of Kansas Institute for Research in Learning Disabilities since 1978. This research has culminated in a set of instructional procedures that integrate instructional methods into specific stages of instruction. Aspects of this integrated set of instructional procedures are presented in numerous journal articles (Deshler, Alley, Warner, & Schumaker, 1981; Ellis, Lenz, & Sabornie, 1987a, 1987b), and a detailed description of instructional issues and the instructional stages is presented by Ellis et al. (1991).

Table 14.2 depicts the instructional stages that are used successfully to teach adolescents with learning problems a variety of skills and strategies. A key characteristic of the application of these instructional stages is that they seek to increase the adolescent's role in the instructional process so that the student learns to control her learning and become empowered. Ellis and Lenz (in press) note that

several important dimensions are built into these instructional stages. While the term *strategy* is used, the same stages are applied to promote the acquisition of many other skills as well (for example, applying for a job, accepting criticism, self-questioning, outlining, goal-setting, word identification, completing a word problem in math, and writing a paragraph).

The following instructional procedures relate to the acquisition and generalization of skills and strategies:

1. *The student should be committed to learning the strategy and fully understand the purpose and benefits of the strategy.* The student's understanding of the potential effect of the strategy and the consequences of continued use of ineffective and inefficient strategies is the first step in the instructional process. The student must understand that the goal is to learn the content or perform a certain task successfully, rather than simply to learn a strategy. The strategy must be viewed as a vehicle that will help the student to achieve her goals. Thus, the teacher is responsible for informing the student of the goals of the strategy and obtaining a commitment from the student to learn the strategy. Likewise, the teacher must demonstrate a commitment to helping the student acquire and generalize the strategy.
2. *The physical and mental actions covered in the strategy should be fully described and explained.* The student must be taught what to do and how to think about each step of the strategy, and the full content of the strategy should be made apparent to the student. Examples and circumstances relevant to the student's experiences should be incorporated into the presentation, and the student should play an active role in exploring and commenting on the strategy and its uses. In

TABLE 14.2

The stages of strategy acquisition and generalization developed by the University of Kansas Institute for Research in Learning Disabilities.

Stage 1: Pretest and Make Commitments

Purpose: To motivate students to learn a new strategy and establish a baseline for instruction

Phase 1: Orientation and pretest
  Give rationales and overview
  Administer pretest
  Discuss how decisions are made
  Assess student's current learning habits
  Determine whether strategy is appropriate

Phase 2: Awareness and commitment
  Review pretest results
  Describe:
    the alternative strategy
    what is required to learn the strategy
    results others have achieved
Ask for a commitment to learn the new strategy
Affirm and explain the teacher's commitment

Stage 2: Describe the Strategy

Purpose: To present a clear picture of the overt and covert processes and steps of the new strategy

Phase 1: Orientation and overview
  Give rationales for the strategy
  Describe situations where the strategy can be used
  Prompt comparisons with old learning habits

Phase 2: Present the strategy and the remembering system
  Describe the overall strategic processes
  Describe the overt and covert processes in each step
  Explain the remembering system and its relationship to self-instruction
  Compare/contrast the new strategy to old approaches
  Set goals for learning the strategy

Stage 3: Model the Strategy

Purpose: To demonstrate the cognitive behaviors and physical actions involved in using the strategy

Phase 1: Orientation
  Review previous learning
  Personalize the strategy
  Define lesson content
  State expectations

Phase 2: Presentation
  Think aloud
  Self-instruct
  Problem solve
  Self-monitor
  Perform task

TABLE 14.2
Continued

Phase 3: Student enlistment
 Prompt involvement
 Check understanding
 Correct and expand responses
 Engineer success

Stage 4: Verbal Elaboration and Rehearsal
Purpose: To ensure comprehension of the strategy and facilitate student mediation

Phase 1: Verbal elaboration
 Have students describe the intent of the strategy and the process involved.
 Have students describe what each step is designed to do and why it is important to the overall process.

Phase 2: Verbal rehearsal
 Require students to name each of the steps at an automatic level.

Stage 5: Controlled Practice and Feedback
Purpose: To provide practice in controlled materials, build confidence and fluency, and gradually shift the responsibility for strategy use to students

Phase 1: Orientation and overview
 Review the strategy steps
 Review previous practice attempts
 Discuss group progress and errors
 Prompt reports of strategy use and errors
 Prompt reports of strategy use or potential use

Phase 2: Guided practice
 Give directions for activities
 Model strategy applications
 Prompt student completion of activities as teacher models
 Prompt increasing student responsibility
 Give clear instructions for peer-mediated practice

Stage 6: Advanced Practice and Feedback
Purpose: To provide practice in advanced materials (e.g., regular class, work related) and situations and gradually shift the responsibility for strategy use and feedback to students

The instructional sequence for Advanced Practice and Feedback is the same as the instructional sequence used for Controlled Practice. However, this level of practice should:
 Use grade-appropriate or situation-appropriate materials
 Require application of the strategy to a variety of materials
 Provide practice in poorly designed materials
 Fade prompts and cues for use and evaluation

Stage 7: Confirm Acquisition and Make Generalization Commitments
Purpose: To document mastery and to build a rationale for self-regulated generalization

Phase 1: Confirm and celebrate
 Assign task to confirm mastery
 Congratulate student on meeting mastery (if mastery is not met, provide additional explanation, encouragement, and practice)
 Discuss achievement and attribution for success
 Identify ways to recognize accomplishment

(continued)

TABLE 14.2
Continued

Phase 2: Forecast and commit to generalization
  Explain goals of generalization
  Identify consequences of focusing and not focusing on generalization
  Explain the phases of generalization
  Prompt increasing student responsibility
  Prompt commitment to generalize
  Affirm and explain teachers' commitments

Stage 8: Generalization

Purpose: To ensure the use of the strategy in other settings

Phase 1: Orientation
  Prompt students to:
    discuss rationales for strategy use
    identify settings in which the strategy might be used
    discuss how to remember to use the strategy
    identify cues within settings that signal use
    identify materials in other settings
    discuss most and least helpful aspects of the strategy
    identify other strategies to combine
  Construct cue cards and affirmation statements
  Evaluate appropriateness of the strategy in various settings and materials

Phase 2: Activation
  Prompt and monitor student application across settings
  Enlist assistance of other teachers
  Request feedback from other teachers
  Reinforce progress and success
  Prompt students to:
    apply the strategy in a variety of settings, situations, materials, and assignments
    set goals for the use of the strategy
    develop a plan to increase application
    review affirmation cards
  Prompt regular classroom teachers to:
    understand the strategy
    identify cues that the students have been taught
    provide sufficient cues for students to identify when to use the strategy
    monitor whether the strategy is being used
    cue use of strategy
    model how to apply the strategy, if necessary
    provide feedback on strategy use

Phase 3: Adaptation
  Prompt students to:
    describe the strategy and its parts
    discuss the overt and covert processes
    identify cognitive strategies embedded in the strategy
    identify where these processes and strategies are required across settings
    identify how the strategy can be modified
    repeat application with the modified strategy

TABLE 14.2
Continued

Phase 4: Maintenance
 Prompt students to:
  discuss rationales related to long-term use of the strategy
  identify barriers to continued use
  determine how they can monitor long-term use and how the teacher can help
  set goals related to monitoring long-term use
  determine how use of the strategy will be evaluated
  identify self-reinforcers and self-rewards

Source: From *Students with Learning Disabilities,* 4th ed. (pp. 384–387), by C. D. Mercer, 1992, New York: Merrill/Macmillan. Copyright 1992 by Macmillan Publishing Company. Reprinted by permission.

addition, the teacher should ensure that the student understands when and where to use the strategy and how to identify cues that signal appropriate and timely use.

3. *The student should be taught how to remember the strategy to facilitate the process of self-instruction.* After the content of the strategy is presented to the student, the teacher should demonstrate how the strategy can be remembered easily. If a mnemonic is used, the teacher should explicitly relate the mnemonic to the intended physical and mental associations and demonstrate how to use the mnemonic to guide the student in the self-instruction process. This step enables the teacher to address possible memory difficulties, which are a common problem for adolescents with learning difficulties.

4. *The student should understand the process of learning the strategy and participate in goal-setting activities to anticipate and monitor learning.* The student should be informed of the acquisition and generalization process, understand the goals and vocabulary associated with each step, and set goals for mastery of each step. As instruction proceeds, the student should evaluate each step as it is completed to determine if specified learning goals have

been met and discuss with the teacher those aspects of learning goals that have not been met. During the instructional process, the student should become an active facilitator and evaluator of the success of the instruction. In addition, the student must be taught to collaborate in identifying and addressing failures in strategy learning.

5. *Multiple models of the strategy should be provided, and an appropriate balance between the physical and mental activities involved in the strategy should be achieved.* The heart of strategic instruction is in the "think aloud" model in which the teacher presents an accurate and complete demonstration of the application of the strategy. While a complete and thorough initial model is critical, additional modeling episodes should be inserted throughout the instructional process. In each of these models, the physical activities must be demonstrated as the associated mental activities are made apparent in an overt "think aloud" depiction of the strategy. While it is important to model the "thinking" aspects of the strategy thoroughly, the teacher should avoid slowing down the instructional process and overwhelming the student with teacher talk. The strategy must remain a crisp depiction

of an effective and efficient approach to a task.

6. *The student should be enlisted in the model and become a full participant in guiding the strategy instructional process.* While the modeling phase of instruction begins with the teacher, it should end with student participation and experience with the modeling process. The teacher gradually should include the student in the model. Initially, the teacher should enlist the student in the self-instructional statements of the model by providing the "think aloud" aspects of the strategy and gradually prompting and guiding the student to comment on each step. The student eventually should be able to perform the strategy while providing many of the key mental actions associated with each step.

7. *The strategy should be fully understood and memorized before practice in the strategy is initiated.* Sufficient rehearsal of the strategy steps should be provided before the student is asked to perform the strategy from memory. Before applied practice of the strategy begins, the student should know the remembering system and be able to demonstrate how to use the system to guide the self-instruction process, paraphrase or explain what is involved in each step, provide personal rationales for learning and using the strategy, and accurately answer questions about uses and misuses of the strategy across various conditions. During the forthcoming practice phase, the student must be confident in her knowledge of the strategy and be able to concentrate on applying the strategy rather than focus unnecessary mental effort on remembering aspects of the strategy.

8. *Practice should begin with controlled guided practice and ultimately conclude with advanced independent practice.* The goal of the initial practice stage should be on mastering the strategy without having to struggle with content or situational demands. Thus, practice should be provided under conditions in which the student feels comfortable or knowledgeable. As the strategy is learned, conditions that approximate actual setting and task demands should be introduced gradually until the student is fully using the strategy to meet actual learning demands. While general principles of effective teaching should be applied, the most important teaching behaviors during strategy practice include communicating expectations, ensuring intensity of instruction, requiring mastery, and providing feedback.

9. *A measurement system should provide ongoing information that will demonstrate to the student and the teacher that the strategy is being learned and used and that the demands of the setting are being met.* Knowledge of progress and performance is a critical part of the learning process. The measurement system should tell the student whether the strategy is promoting success in meeting a demand. However, the measurement system also should provide information related to the student's mastery of the strategy. Progress in learning the strategy eventually should relate to an increase in the student's ability to meet some aspect of a demand. The student should be able to see this relationship and attribute success to mastery and application of the strategy.

10. *While generalization should be promoted throughout the strategy acquisition process, specific efforts to promote generalization should follow strategy acquisition.* After the strategy has been mastered, the student should commit to focusing on generalizing the strategy. In the generalization stage, the teacher and student must

work together to identify where the strategy can be used across settings and conditions, identify modifications in the strategy to make it more generalizable, and program use of the strategy across settings. In addition, the generalization process can be greatly enhanced through the cooperation of as many teachers and facilitators as possible.

ACADEMIC REMEDIATION

The approach of teaching basic academic skills stresses that improved academic skills help the student benefit from course work in all content areas. When academic deficiencies are considered in light of expectations placed on many students with learning problems to earn a high school diploma, the emphasis on academic remediation is understandable. From a survey of 741 learning disabilities teachers at the secondary level, Schmid, Algozzine, Wells, and Stoller (1980) found that the majority of students with learning disabilities placed in secondary programs demonstrated reading and math grade levels in the fourth- to sixth-grade range. Furthermore, a significant number of other students with learning problems were functioning below third-grade level in reading and math. When the students with learning disabilities below third-grade level are joined by adolescents with learning problems that result from mental retardation, economic deprivation, and emotional problems, the number of students with severe academic problems is substantial.

While the need for academic remediation is apparent, some educators (Deshler, Schumaker, Lenz, & Ellis, 1984) express concern that it is being overused at the secondary level. They note that many materials used in this approach were developed for elementary students and may not be appropriate for adolescents. Moreover, many adolescents have difficulty understanding the relevance of academic remediation content. Also, Deshler et al. question the effectiveness of this approach to help students cope with the complex demands of the secondary curriculum. Finally, they report that time spent on remediation may be too limited to have a meaningful effect on academic skills at the secondary level.

In spite of concerns about academic remediation for adolescents with learning problems, many educators promote it. It seems especially appropriate for ninth and tenth graders who are achieving below fourth-grade level in any of the basic skill areas. It also appears that academic remediation should be provided in conjunction with other services (for example, career-related instruction, functional living skills).

Academic Programming Considerations

Several projects provide academic remediation to secondary students with learning problems. The Pittsburgh Child Service Demonstration Center developed a model that is used widely in Pittsburgh secondary schools (Buchwach, 1980). Students attend a resource room (called a learning lab) for no more than two periods daily. The students are removed only from English or math to receive basic skill intervention. A diagnostic systematic approach to skill development is provided, and generalization of newly learned skills is fostered by having students eventually use materials from mainstream classes in the learning lab. A second special education resource teacher functions as a liaison between the students and their mainstream teachers. In addition, this teacher works with the learning lab teacher once a week to provide a school survival skills curriculum (that is, strands pertaining to behavior, teacher-pleasing behavior, and study skills). Thus, this model demonstrates the use of both academic remediation services and learning strategies intervention.

The Synergistic Program for adolescents with learning disabilities, developed under the direction of Dr. Charles Meisgeier at the University of Houston, uses a high-intensity learning center to provide academic remediation in a positive environment. Students attend the high-intensity learning center 3 hours a day for 12 weeks and receive 2 hours of reading remediation and 1 hour of social-behavioral curriculum each day. Dembrowsky (1980) reports excellent results from the 12-week program. For example, initial data indicate that the mean growth in reading was 1.2 years in comprehension and 1.5 years in reading accuracy. Encouraging results also were reported in social-emotional areas. Once the students complete the 12-week program, they return to mainstream classes. To help maintain academic growth, an essential skills program is provided through part-time special education classes. Initial data indicate that academic growth not only is maintained but continues to develop.

Because secondary students face numerous curriculum demands and have a limited amount of time to ameliorate deficits, educators are seeking ways to increase the intensity of instruction (for example, learning labs, high-intensity learning centers). Meyen and Lehr (1980) recommend increasing instructional intensity by requiring students to spend more time consistently on academic tasks, providing timely and frequent corrective feedback, and communicating regularly with students to state expectations and provide guidance and feedback in natural situations. The *Corrective Reading Program,* (published by Science Research Associates) is a reading program that is used with adolescents with learning problems to increase the level of instructional intensity of academic remediation (Polloway, Epstein, Polloway, Patton, & Ball, 1986). Moreover, summer school programs can provide an opportunity for high-intensity instruction without delaying graduation.

LEARNING STRATEGIES

As students progress through the grades, the demands for successful performance generally increase. Some educators believe that the complexity of secondary demands contributes as much to adolescent failures as do learning deficits. A learning strategies approach helps students with learning problems cope with the complex demands of the secondary curriculum. Deshler and his colleagues at the University of Kansas Institute for Research in Learning Disabilities define *learning strategies* as techniques, principles, or rules that enable a student to learn, to solve problems, and to complete tasks independently. The goal of strategy development is to identify strategies that are optimally effective (that is, help students meet the demands of both current and future tasks) and efficient (that is, help students meet the demands of the task in a manner that is appropriate, timely, resourceful, and judicious). The goal of strategies instruction is to teach the strategies effectively (that is, the strategy is learned and generalized by the student) and efficiently (that is, the strategy is learned to an optimal level with a minimum amount of effort by the teacher and the student). The goal of this approach is to help students learn course content (such as geography) through instruction in skills necessary to acquire, store, and express content. Basically, it focuses on teaching students how to learn and how to demonstrate command of their knowledge in performing academic tasks. For example, a reading strategy may be used by a student with fourth-grade reading skills to obtain relevant information from a textbook chapter written at the tenth-grade level. As one part of the Strategies Intervention Model, Deshler and his colleagues developed a learning strategies curriculum, and its components have been specified, developed, and validated in classrooms. Field-testing and evaluation data indicate good student progress and a high degree of consumer satisfaction (Deshler & Schumaker, 1986; 1988; Schumaker et al., 1986). Because the strategies included in the Strategies Intervention Model have the longest history of comprehensive research and development for adolescents with learning problems, a more detailed description of this approach is presented.

The Learning Strategies Curriculum of the University of Kansas Institute for Research in Learning Disabilities includes 15 intervention manuals and support materials. The manuals, available through training, provide guidelines to teachers on how to provide intensive instruction to adolescents with learning problems and how to promote the acquisition, storage, and expression of information and demonstration of competence through instruction in learning strategies. The strategies included in the curriculum are listed and described in Table 14.3. Each of the teacher's manuals provides detailed instructional procedures in how to teach the strategy and prompt the student to transfer the strategy across settings. Teachers are trained in the basic concepts of the strategy that has been validated through research, and they are encouraged to tailor the strategy and the instructional procedures to fit their personal teaching style and classroom. Thus, while integrity in the basic features of the strategy and the instructional procedures is necessary to ensure student success, the teacher is given wide latitude to make the intervention meaningful in individual situations.

The learning strategy interventions respond to the specific needs of learning disabilities teachers who need instructional procedures

and curriculums for adolescents with learning problems. Because most learning disabilities teachers provide instruction in a support class setting rather than in the regular classroom setting, the curriculum materials are used mainly to teach strategies in one setting and then prompt generalization of the strategies to additional settings (for example, the regular classroom). The student's regular classroom materials are used in the process so that the student learns to associate the strategy with success in meeting naturally occurring learning demands. Changes in service delivery options make it possible for regular classroom teachers to infuse many dimensions of these strategy interventions into content-area instruction. This allows the student to see the application of the strategy in natural settings. However, additional intensive instruction usually is required by the special education teacher in a support class setting because many secondary content teachers are not able to provide the explicit or intensive instruction required to overcome the difficulties of students with learning problems.

With the increase in service delivery systems and knowledge of strategy learning, the training approaches used to present strategies to students have changed. Initially, the instructional process focused on the direct delivery of the strategy through a direct teaching approach. Because the content of each strategy was researched heavily and refined in normal school settings, it was believed that the power of the strategies would result in the intended outcomes. However, while it was determined that students could be taught the strategies, some students did not realize the benefits of the strategies, were not highly motivated to learn them, and were not generalizing the strategies for academic success and personal use. As a result, the instructional procedures were changed to include an increased level of student involvement, participation, control,

TABLE 14.3
The Learning Strategies Curriculum of the University of Kansas Institute for Research in Learning Disabilities.

ACQUISITION STRAND

Word Identification Strategy: teaches students a problem-solving procedure for quickly attacking and decoding unknown words in reading materials, allowing them to move on quickly for the purpose of comprehending the passage.

Paraphrasing Strategy: directs students to read a limited section of material, ask themselves the main idea and the details of the section, and put that information in their own words. The strategy is designed to improve comprehension by focusing attention on the important information of a passage and by stimulating active involvement with the passage.

Self-Questioning Strategy: aids reading comprehension by having students actively ask questions about key pieces of information in a passage and then read to find the answers for these questions.

Visual Imagery Strategy: improves students' acquisition, storage, and recall of prose material. Students improve reading comprehension by reading short passages and visualizing the scene that is described, incorporating actors, action, and details.

Interpreting Visuals Strategy: aids students in the use and interpretation of visuals such as maps, graphs, pictures, and tables to increase their ability to extract needed information from written materials.

Multipass Strategy: involves making three passes through a passage to focus attention on key details and main ideas. Students survey a chapter or passage to get an overview, size up sections of the chapter by systematically scanning to locate relevant information that they note, and sort out important information in the chapter by locating answers to specific questions.

STORAGE STRAND

FIRST-Letter Mnemonic Strategy: aids students in memorizing lists of information by teaching them to design mnemonics or memorization aids, and to find and make lists of crucial information.

Paired Associates Strategy: aids students in memorizing pairs or small groups of information by using visual imagery, matching pertinent information with familiar objects, coding important dates, and using a first-syllable technique.

Listening and Note-Taking Strategy: teaches students to develop skills to enhance their ability to learn from listening experiences. Students learn to identify the speaker's verbal cues or mannerisms that indicate important information is about to be given, note key words, and organize notes into an outline for future reference or study.

EXPRESSION AND DEMONSTRATION OF COMPETENCE STRAND

Sentence Writing Strategy: teaches students how to recognize and generate four types of sentences: simple, compound, complex, and compound-complex.

Paragraph Writing Strategy: teaches students how to write well-organized, complete paragraphs by outlining ideas, selecting a point-of-view and tense for the paragraph, sequencing ideas, and checking their work.

Error Monitoring Strategy: teaches students a process for detecting and correcting errors in their writing and for producing a neater written product. Students are taught to locate errors in paragraph organization, sentence structure, capitalization, overall editing and appearance, punctuation, and spelling by asking themselves a series of questions. Students correct their errors and rewrite the passage before submitting it to their teacher.

TABLE 14.3
Continued

Theme Writing Strategy: teaches students to generate ideas for themes, organize these ideas into a logical sequence, write the paragraphs, monitor errors, and rewrite the theme.

Assignment Completion Strategy: teaches students to monitor their assignments from the time an assignment is given until it is completed and turned in to the teacher. Students write down assignments; analyze the assignments; schedule various subtasks; complete the subtasks and, ultimately, the entire task; and submit the completed assignment.

Test-Taking Strategy: teaches students to allocate time during a test and read instructions and questions carefully. A question is either answered or put aside for later consideration. The obviously wrong answers are eliminated from the abandoned questions and a reasonable guess is made. The last step is to survey the entire test for unanswered questions.

Source: From *Students with Learning Disabilities,* 4th ed. (pp. 378–379), by C. D. Mercer, 1992, New York: Merrill/Macmillan. Copyright 1992 by Macmillan Publishing Company. Reprinted by permission.

and commitment in the instructional process. Thus, the instructional procedures used in the Strategies Intervention Model can be described best as a direct strategy training approach that incorporates planned opportunities for the student to become involved in the instructional process and to discover ways in which the strategies can be personally empowering.

The learning strategies, when combined with the motivation and social skills strategies, provide the basis for a solid curriculum for the secondary level special education or remedial teacher. The teacher assumes the role of a learning specialist whose goal is to help students learn to learn. However, simply implementing the specified learning strategies does not necessarily lead to student success. Deshler and Lenz (1989) make the following observation about strategy instruction:

> [I]t could be argued that the key to delivering a truly strategic intervention is to stop conceptualizing strategies instruction as consisting of a single intervention, or several strategy interventions, or even a well-developed strategies curriculum. It may be more beneficial to begin thinking about strategy interventions as the creation of a set of environments (e.g., the support classroom, the regular classroom, the home, etc.) in which key activities are done in a strategic manner. Well-designed strategies environments should promote, model, guide, and prompt efficient and effective learning and performance across all students, not just those with learning disabilities. (p. 222)

The teaching methods used with students exhibiting learning problems are crucial to the success of the instruction. These acquisition steps, presented earlier in this chapter, focus on providing the student with the knowledge, motivation, and practice required to apply a skill or strategy to materials and situations comparable to regular secondary classroom demands (Schumaker & Deshler, 1988). Additional information about the Strategies Intervention Model and the Learning Strategies Curriculum can be obtained by contacting the Coordinator of Training, Institute for Research in Learning Disabilities, 3061 Robert Dole Human Development Center, The University of Kansas, Lawrence, KS 66045–2342 (913/864–4780).

The remainder of this section features a collection of strategy-oriented techniques and activities which are organized according to preparatory study skills, information-gathering and organization skills, sequential study methods, study-rehearsal skills, and knowledge expression and application skills. Commercial learning strategies programs and materials as well as computer software programs in learning strategies also are presented.

Preparatory Study Skills

Preparatory study skills involve skills and factors that are relevant precursors to efficient learning. The attitude and motivation of the student are critical to student effort and consequent learning. The adolescent with learning problems needs to understand the relevance of assigned tasks and exhibit an attitude that facilitates effort. Chapter 5 and the discussion on motivation presented earlier in this chapter present strategies and activities aimed at improving motivation and social skills.

Activities for developing time management. Considering the many demands placed on students to complete tasks at specific times and participate in a host of competing activities (such as being with peers, joining clubs, watching television, and listening to music), time management obviously is critical to surviving in school. The adolescent with learning problems usually needs instruction in time management. Activities for teaching time management include making schedules, making time estimates, and establishing priorities:

1. Give the student a 5-day schedule of after-school time and ask her to record how she spends these time blocks. Next, have the student allocate time blocks for specific activities (see Table 14.4) and follow the schedule as much as possible. Initially it may help the student to plan a day and then gradually build to a week.
2. Provide or have the student make a calendar to assist in scheduling daily or weekly activities. Notations can be made on the calendar to remind the student of project due dates or test dates (Dexter, 1982). The student also can keep a notebook with all academic assignments and due dates.
3. Remind the student that some flexibility should be allowed in the daily schedule. Occasionally unexpected events will take precedence over the planned activity. Introduce new events in the daily schedule and explain how adjustments can be made. (For example, if friends invite the student to get a pizza during study time, she can replace television time with study time.) Finally, the student should show the teacher her schedule with written adjustments when applicable.
4. Either provide assignments or have the student list at least four of her school assignments and estimate how long it will take to complete each task. Then have her record the amount of time it

TABLE 14.4
A student's after-school schedule.

	Monday	Tuesday	Wednesday	Thursday	Friday
3:00–4:00	with friend eat snack	with friend eat snack	with friend eat snack	with friend eat snack	with friend eat snack
4:00–5:00	play ball	play ball	play ball	play ball	play ball
5:00–6:00	play ball	play ball	play ball	play ball	play ball
6:00–7:00	eat dinner	eat dinner	eat dinner	eat dinner	eat dinner
7:00–8:00	study	study	study	go to game	go to movie
8:00–9:00	study	watch TV	study	go to game	go to movie
9:00–10:00	watch TV	watch TV	play tapes	watch TV	watch TV

actually takes to complete the assignments. These times can be written on the student's schedule. On tasks or subject areas in which the student's estimates are consistently inaccurate (off by more than 20 percent), have her practice in these areas until the estimates become realistic.

5. Have the student list school assignments and prioritize them. For example, the student can rank the activities in the order she would complete them (that is, place a 1 beside the first activity, a 2 beside the next activity, and so on). For example:

    _____Work on social studies project due in 2 weeks.

    _____Write a lab report in science due in 2 days.

    _____Complete a math worksheet due tomorrow.

    _____Practice baseball for the game in 3 days.

    _____Read 20 pages in a book in preparation for an oral report due in 4 days.

    _____Invite a local meteorologist to speak to the science class next week about pollution.

    Discuss the need to consider consequences and time factors in prioritizing lists of things to do. Review the rankings and point out the correct and incorrect rankings in terms of consequences, breaking large tasks into smaller amounts (for example, subdividing reading material into a number of pages per day), and time factors. Also, have the student practice using "value" steps in prioritizing activities and tasks by grouping her list into three areas: activities with high value, activities with medium value, and activities with low value.

6. To complete academic tasks efficiently, encourage the student to work in an environment conducive to studying. Ideally, the study area should be a relatively quiet, unstimulating environment. If noise (television, classmates) becomes too distracting, the student can consider using earplugs. Some comfortable earplugs are designed to screen out noise (Dexter, 1982).

Information-Gathering and Organization Skills

To survive in the secondary setting, students must acquire and organize information from written and spoken input. Secondary teachers use the lecture/note-taking format extensively (Moran, 1980). Students also are required to obtain and organize information from textbooks. This section presents teaching activities and strategies aimed at developing information-gathering and organization skills. The skills are organized into the following areas: listening and note taking, textbook usage, reading and study skills, reading and note taking, and using visual aids.

Activities for developing listening and note-taking skills. *Note taking* is defined as an individualized process for recording and organizing information into a usable format and is dependent on active student participation (Devine, 1981; Pauk, 1978). Saski, Swicegood, and Carter (1983) report that researchers agree that note taking is advantageous to the student but that no one approach is considered superior. Note-taking strategies can include (a) an outline format that stresses the identification of a main idea and supporting subordinate ideas or (b) a columnar format that serves as a guide for organizing and classifying information. Moreover, Devine reports that any note-taking strategy is better than none at all. The importance and complexity of the note-taking process suggest the need for guidelines and activities, such as the following, to facilitate its development:

1. To assist with listening and note taking, teach the student to use the following strategies (Towle, 1982):

    a. Physically prepare for listening and note taking by sitting alertly (for example, leaning forward) in a comfortable desk with the essential materials (for example, notebook, two or more pencils or pens, textbook). Remove all extraneous materials from the desk. To encourage listening and active class participation, students can be taught to use the SLANT strategy (Ellis, 1991):

S—*Sit* up.
L—*Lean* forward.
A—*Activate* your thinking.
N—*Name* key information.
T—*Track* the talker.

b. Review vocabulary (for example, from text or handouts) related to the topic before the lecture begins. It helps some students to have a list of difficult vocabulary words on their desks during the lecture/note-taking session.

c. Listen for organizational cues or signal words (for example, statements referring to time spans or sequences—*first, second, phase, period, era, next, finally*). H. A. Robinson (1978) provides a list of signal words to help the student. It includes words that indicate a sequence or additional ideas (for example, *first, second, also, furthermore, again, plus, next, after that*); caution words, which point to concluding ideas (for example, *consequently, thus, therefore, in conclusion, to summarize, finally, as a result*); turn words, which indicate a change in ideas (for example, *in contrast, opposed to, however, to the contrary, on the other hand, in spite of, although, yet, despite*); stop words, which signal special significance (for example, *significantly, absolutely, whenever, without doubt, without question*); and application words, which indicate concrete application of a thought (for example, *because, for example, specifically, for instance*).

d. Listen for content importance by noticing such cues as change in voice, tone, pitch, pauses, and volume.

e. Ask for elaboration on specific points or content when confusion arises.

f. Request examples to illustrate specific concepts.

g. Paraphrase certain points to check understanding.

h. Ask for visual references (for example, pages in the text).

2. Use the following guided listening and note-taking activities to provide the student with opportunities to practice a variety of skills:

a. The teacher plays a 5- to 8-minute tape recording of a lecture on content appropriate to the student's needs. The teacher and student sit beside each other and simultaneously take notes.

b. At the end of the tape the teacher provides corrective feedback by sharing her notes with the student and explaining listening and note-taking strategies. The teacher may elect to replay the tape and point out key factors (for example, content organization, voice cues) in listening and note taking.

c. The student listens to the tape again and takes a new set of notes. At the end of the tape she compares her notes with the teacher's model notes and makes corrections. The student practices this procedure to criterion with several different tapes.

d. Short tapes are made of selected regular classroom teacher's lectures. The student practices listening and note taking on these tapes with corrective feedback until criterion is achieved.

e. As the student progresses, the lecture tapes-feedback sequence is expanded to include more teachers in various content areas.

f. Eventually the student takes notes only from live lectures and uses a set of model notes (for example, from the teacher or a classmate) to correct or complete her notes.

This activity can be used with an individual or group to assess and remediate listening and note-taking skills. Notes from proficient peers can be used as models. In addition, teacher aides can be trained to tape lectures and provide model notes.

3. To improve legibility, have student pairs read each other's notes and circle illegible words. Have each student rewrite the circled words.

4. Present directed listening activities according to the following three stages developed by Cunningham and Cunningham (1976):

1. The Readiness Stage

a. Establish motivation for the lesson.
b. Introduce any new or difficult concepts.

c. Introduce any new or difficult words.

d. Set purposes for listening.

2. The Listening-Reciting Stage

a. Students listen to satisfy the purposes for listening set during readiness.

b. The teacher asks several literal and inferential questions that relate to the purposes set during readiness.

c. The students volunteer interpretive and evaluative comments about the lesson. Some class discussion may ensue.

d. If there are errors or gaps in the students' understanding of the lesson, the teacher directs the students to relisten to certain parts of the lesson.

3. The Follow-Up Stage

a. The teacher provides opportunities for and encourages students to engage in activities that build on and develop concepts acquired during the lesson. These may include writing, reading, small group discussions, art activities . . . (pp. 27–28)

5. To improve listening comprehension and retention, use the following sequence of activities adapted from Manzo's (1975) guided listening procedure:

a. The teacher asks the student to try to remember everything she is about to hear.

b. The teacher lectures or plays a recorded selection. If the teacher lectures, she records it.

c. The teacher reminds the student about the instructions that were given. She then writes everything on the chalkboard without making any corrections or asking specific questions.

d. The teacher reads everything listed on the board and asks the student to note incorrect information and think about missing information.

e. The student listens to the tape again, corrects inaccurate information, and obtains missing information.

f. The information on the chalkboard is amended and expanded.

g. The teacher asks which ideas on the chalkboard are the main and important ideas and which ones should be remembered for a long time. She highlights these items.

h. Now that the student has mastered the literal content of the selection, the teacher asks inferential questions that appear vital for understanding.

i. The teacher erases the chalkboard and tests memory with items (for example, oral multiple choice, true–false) that are not too dependent on reading or writing skills.

j. The teacher tests long-term memory with a similar test several weeks later.

6. Teach the student to recognize the main idea and the contributing points from which it arrives. In this way she gains control of what to write by determining how much detail is needed in terms of expected outcome (that is, main idea). Looking for the main and contributing ideas helps the student become a more active listener by encouraging thinking, comprehension, and questions (Alley & Deshler, 1979). Also, teach the student to look for the order and organization of the lecture. Stress that notes are a skeletal representation of the material (Alley & Deshler, 1979).

7. Teach the student to use abbreviations to reduce the writing demands of the task (for example, *w/* for *with*, *U.S.* for *United States*).

8. Encourage the use of columnar note-taking formats. Saski et al. (1983) report positive feedback from secondary learning disabilities teachers regarding the use of such formats. One of their note-taking formats contains a topic sentence at the top of the page, and three columns (5", 2", and 1" wide) are designed for recording three types of information. The first column, Basic Ideas, is for material (such as facts, figures, dates, names, and places) that will be needed for future tests. The second column, Background Information, includes pertinent related information plus ideas, facts, and topics that interest the student. This column may begin with key words of concepts from the preceding lecture. The third

column, Questions, includes space for marking unclear information that needs clarification or elaboration.

Activities for developing skills in textbook usage.

The textbook is a primary source of information for secondary students. Practice in the correct use of textbooks is beneficial to students with learning problems. It assists them in completing assignments and reviewing pertinent information. This section features a variety of activities to help students improve their skills in textbook usage.

1. To assist in developing instructional objectives and measuring competence in textbook usage, administer a pre/posttest. A test format may include the following questions:

   a. What part of the book explains how the book is organized?
   b. The authors are listed in what part of the book?
   c. On what page(s) would you look for information on _____ ?
   d. What part of the book gives meanings of words?
   e. How many chapters are in the book?
   f. What part of the book provides page references for any given topic?
   g. Define _____ .
   h. On what page would you find a chapter titled _____ ?
   i. In what part of the book would you find information on a topic in the form of visual aids?
   j. Who publishes the book?
   k. On what pages does chapter ___ begin and end?
   l. On what page would you find out about ?
   m. What is the meaning of the term _____ ?
   n. What information is included in the appendix of this book?

2. Instruct the student to locate specific parts of a textbook. Allow 15 seconds for each part (for example, the index). The following format is useful:

Name of textbook _____
On what page will you find the following:
a. Table of contents   _____
b. Index   _____
c. Glossary   _____
d. Appendix   _____

3. Instruct the student to use the table of contents to determine page numbers where specific chapters begin and end.
4. Instruct the student to use the table of contents to name the chapter in which a given topic is located. The following format is helpful:

Directions:

Place the chapter listed on the right under the correct heading listed on the left.

I: Weather	Reptiles
A.	Precipitation
B.	Nutrition—proteins and vitamins
II: Animals	Amphibians
A.	High-pressure system
B.	Medications
III. Health	
A.	
B.	

5. Discuss the purpose of a glossary, and have the student look up several words in a textbook glossary.
6. From a content reading assignment, instruct the student to identify key words and find their meanings in the glossary.
7. Explain what an index is, how it is developed, and how it can be used. Provide the student with a page from an index, and instruct her to locate a list of terms and write down corresponding page numbers.
8. Give the student a question, and have her identify the key words and locate them in the index. Have the student write the page number(s) pertaining to the question topic. A suggested format is as follows:

Underline key words. Locate them in the index and write the page number on which you would find the answer.

   a. What was the population of San Francisco in 1980?   _____
   b. What causes a tidal wave?   _____

9. Instruct the student to use the following cognitive strategies to help learning (Ellis & Lenz, 1987):

    a. CAN-DO: A strategy for learning content information

    C—*Create* a list of items to be learned.

    A—*Ask* yourself if the list is complete.

    N—*Note* the main ideas and details using a tree diagram.

    D—*Describe* each component and how it relates to others.

    O—*Overlearn* main parts, then supporting details.

    b. RIDER: A visual imagery strategy for reading comprehension

    R—*Read* the sentence.

    I—Make an *image* or picture in your mind.

    D—*Describe* how the new image is different from the last sentence.

    E—*Evaluate* the image to make sure it contains everything necessary.

    R—*Repeat* the steps to RIDE as you read the next sentence.

    c. RAP: A paraphrasing strategy for reading comprehension

    R—*Read* a paragraph.

    A—*Ask* yourself what were the main idea and two details.

    P—*Put* the main idea and details in your own words.

    d. FIST: A self-questioning strategy for reading comprehension

    F—*First* sentence in the paragraph is read.

    I—*Indicate* a question based on information in the first sentence.

    S—*Search* for the answer to the question.

    T—*Tie* the answer to the question with a paraphrase.

Activities for developing reading and study skills. The demand for gaining information from reading material is extensive at the secondary level. Students with learning problems are faced with obtaining content from a variety of reading materials. Several reading styles and rates are needed for these students to acquire essential information. Thus, students with learning problems must be taught strategies to help them acquire information quickly from a variety of printed materials.

Skimming is a reading strategy that assists students in dealing with the reading and study demands of secondary classes. It is a systematic and efficient way of determining the main ideas of a book or other printed material. In this strategy, key sentences, phrases, and words are isolated and read rapidly. The steps in skimming are as follows:

1. Read the title and headings (dark print) as they appear.
2. Read the introduction (that is, a few paragraphs at the beginning of a chapter or article).
3. Read the first sentence of each subsequent paragraph. In textbooks the first sentence usually contains the main idea of the paragraph.
4. Read the captions of pictures and study any illustrations in the chapter.
5. Read the conclusion or summary of the chapter.

The following activities involving skimming are helpful in developing this reading-study skill:

1. Have the student skim the major headings of a classroom text and formulate several questions for each heading. As a group activity the teacher can require each student to generate one question for each heading.
2. Discuss the terms *chronological, sequential,* or *causal* and provide examples of each.

    a. Chronological—topics or events in the order of their happening. Most history books are organized chronologically.
    b. Sequential—a step-by-step procedure. This frequently occurs in a science lab experiment or in instructions for assembling a project.

c. Causal—an "if–then" presentation pattern. Some texts use a causal pattern to explain a phenomenon (for example, conditions that lead to weather happenings such as rain, lightning, hurricanes).

3. Give the student a content reading selection and a list of comprehension questions covering several main themes. Instruct her to skim the selection and answer the questions.
4. Use the following skimming activity as a pre/posttest or as practice. Provide the student with a four- to five-page passage and a list of 20 comprehension questions covering main ideas and key words. Instruct her to use skimming techniques to read the passage quickly and gain the most important information. At the end of 5 minutes, have the student answer the comprehension questions. Set the criterion for mastery at 90 percent correct on the comprehension questions.

Scanning is another reading and study strategy that helps students with learning problems deal with the demands of acquiring information from printed material. It involves the quick reading of key sentences, phrases, and words to locate specific information. This information could be an important term, definition, or answer to a question. Scanning is a great help in reading and studying because it enables the reader to find specific items rapidly. The steps in scanning are as follows:

1. Remember the specific question to be answered.
2. Estimate in what form the answer will appear (that is, word, name, number, graphic, or date).
3. Use the expected form of the answer as clues for locating it.
4. Look for clues by moving the eyes quickly over the page. When a section that appears to contain the answer is found, read it more carefully.

5. Find the answer, record it, and stop reading.

The following activities involve scanning:

1. Give the student a list of alphabetized items. Name an item on the list and instruct the student to circle the item within 15 seconds. Once the student becomes proficient, the activity can be repeated with an unalphabetized list.
2. Give the student an unalphabetized list and related questions. Read a question and instruct the student to write the number of the question next to the appropriate word. Initially the time limit for each question is 30 seconds. As the student progresses, the time limit can be shortened to 10 seconds. A sample format is as follows:

___equator   ___green   ___sophomore
___mammals   ___mare   ___ewe
___sentence   ___blue   ___six
___red   ___hog   ___bull

a. What is the name for warm-blooded animals with fur or hair?
b. What do you call a female sheep?
c. What color is grass?
d. What do you call a group of words that expresses a complete thought?
e. The American flag is red, white, and ____ .
f. In 10th grade you are called a _____ .
g. How many class periods are in a day?
h. What do you call a female horse?
i. What do you call male cattle?
j. What color is an apple?
k. What do you call a male pig?
l. What is the imaginary line that runs around the Earth?

This activity can be adapted to independent seatwork by having the student complete the task (match questions to words) within a specified time (for example, 2 to 6 minutes).
3. Give the student some questions from a chapter she is studying in one of her classes. Indicate the page number where the answer to each question is found. Have the student answer each question using the following instructions and format:

Directions:

Answer each question in 60 seconds or less. Each question has four steps: (a) find the page listed, (b) read the question, (c) scan the page to find the answer, and (d) write your answer.

1. (page 118) How long did Nat Turner's rebellion last?_____
2. (page 72) What states were included in the Northwest Territory?_____
3. (page 164) Why did Dred Scott think he should be a free man?_____
4. (page 210) What does the term "Jim Crow" mean?_____

4. Give the student some questions from a chapter she is studying in a content area. Vary the questions so that some key words are found in the index (for example, names, places, events) and others are found in the chapter (for example, section headings, italicized words, boldface print). Instruct the student to (a) identify key words for locating information in text, (b) locate the appropriate page number, (c) read the question, (d) scan the page to locate key words, and (e) answer the question.

5. Use the following activity as a pre/posttest or as a practice activity. Select 10 pages from different textbooks, and write 10 questions on 3″ × 5″ cards (one question per card). Have two questions each to cover (a) information contained in the heading, (b) information contained in topic sentences, (c) information contained in charts, graphs, or maps, (d) information contained in the index, and (e) information contained in key words and terms. Give the student one question along with the number of the page on which the question is answered in the text. Have the student read the question (begin timing), locate the answer, and write the answer (stop timing). Record the time. Continue in this manner until all questions are answered. Criterion is achieved when the student answers all questions correctly in a 10-minute time period (one question per minute).

Activities for developing reading and note-taking skills. Taking notes on material read for classes facilitates memory and often makes it unnecessary to reread the material later. When a student takes notes on reading material, she is forced to think about the material, thus enhancing recall of the content (Roe, Stoodt, & Burns, 1987). Moreover, the act of writing ideas helps the student remember content. Note taking from reading material usually follows either an outline or a paraphrasing format. This section presents activities designed to develop or improve reading and note-taking skills:

1. Teach students how to use an outline format. The first step in making an outline is determining the main ideas. The next step involves locating the supportive ideas for each of the main ideas. The sequence continues by locating specific details that go with respective supportive ideas. A blank outline format is helpful in demonstrating the proper form.

Title

I. Main concept
  A. Information supporting I
  B. Information supporting I
    1. Specific information supporting B
    2. Specific information supporting B
      a. Specific information supporting 2
      b. Specific information supporting 2
  C. Information supporting I
II. Main concept
  A. Information supporting II
  B. Information supporting II
  C. Information supporting II
    1. Specific information supporting C
    2. Specific information supporting C

2. To demonstrate outlining, show the student how the headings in her textbook chapter indicate different levels of subordination. For example, in many textbooks the center headings would be

Roman numerals in an outline, side headings would be capital letters in an outline, and italic or paragraph headings would be Arabic numerals in an outline.

3. Provide partially completed outlines and instruct the student to complete them (Roe et al., 1987).

Title

I. (Given by teacher)
    A. (Given by teacher)
        1. (Completed by student)
        2. (Completed by student)
    B. (Given by teacher)
        1. (Given by teacher)
        2. (Completed by student)
II. (Completed by student)
    A. (Given by teacher)
    B. (Completed by student)

This technique gradually can increase in difficulty until the teacher provides only the structural arrangement. For example:

Title

I.
    A.
        1.
        2.
    B.
        1.
        2.
II.
    A.
    B.

The relevancy of this task is enhanced if the teacher uses textbooks from the student's regular content classes.

4. To facilitate note taking from printed material, teach the student to use a columnar format (Saski et al., 1983). For example, in the following format, the 2″ column on the left side is used to record main ideas, the 6″ column is used to record supporting details of the main ideas, and the 2″ space at the bottom is used to summarize ideas, raise questions, and pinpoint areas of concern.

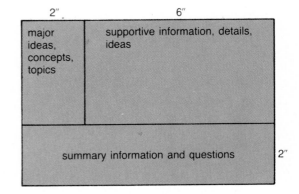

5. Give the student several paragraphs and several summaries. Instruct her to select the best summary of the paragraphs. Point out the importance of locating the main idea (usually the topic sentence of a paragraph) and essential supporting details.

6. Give the student passages from a textbook she is using and instruct her to write a summary by following these steps: (a) locate the main idea, (b) locate essential supportive details, and (c) write information as concisely as possible, leaving out illustrative material and statements that merely elaborate on main ideas.

Activities for developing skills in using visual aids. Secondary textbooks are replete with visual aids, and adolescents with learning problems need to be taught how to use and understand them. This section presents activities and techniques for developing skills in the use of various types of visual aids.

1. Explain that a map represents a geographic area. Review the following map-reading steps (Roe et al., 1987): locate and comprehend the title of the map; determine map directions; interpret the map legend; apply the map's scale; discuss common map terms (for example, latitude, longitude, equator, gulf, bay, continent); and make inferences from map material (for example, climate, population, industry).

2. Provide the student with index cards with a map legend on one side and its use or definition on the other side. Instruct the student to

define or describe the legend's use and turn over the card to check her answer.

3. Present the student with road maps, and instruct her to estimate miles between locations and write directions from one place to another.

4. Provide the student with a table, and explain that it includes information arranged in vertical columns and horizontal rows. Review the following table-reading steps: locate and comprehend the title of the table; determine information located in columns; determine information located in rows; and locate specific information through pinpointing intersections.

5. Instruct the student to make a table of respective cities and their average monthly temperatures or of her class periods and corresponding 6-week grades.

6. Use sample graphs to explain the four basic types of graphs: picture, circle, bar, and line graphs. Roe et al. (1987) recommend that teachers help students interpret graphs by reviewing the following steps:

   a. The purpose of the graph (usually indicated by the title but becomes more evident when the accompanying narrative is studied)
   b. The scale of measure on bar and line graphs
   c. The legend of picture graphs
   d. The items being compared
   e. The location of specific pieces of information within a graph (for example, finding the intersection of the point of interest on the vertical axis with the point of interest on the horizontal axis)
   f. The trends indicated by a graph (for example, does an amount increase or decrease over a period of time?)
   g. The application of graphic information to actual life situations (for example, a graph showing the temperatures for each month in Sydney, Australia, could be used for planning what clothes to take for a particular time of the year)

7. Instruct the student to make a line graph using her reading rate (words per minute) in textbooks for various content areas.

8. Instruct the student to make a bar graph of the heights of the starting lineups for two basketball teams. A basketball program may be used to provide the data. This activity can be adapted to various sports and selected information (for example, football—weights; baseball—batting averages).

9. Have the student make a circle graph of how she spends time (for example, in school, sleeping, playing, eating, and miscellaneous).

10. Instruct the student to make a picture graph from the following information: Dallas scored 70 touchdowns; Washington scored 76; Miami scored 47; Pittsburgh, 64; San Francisco, 37; New York, 54; Denver, 62. Let the symbol ⓦ = 10 touchdowns.

11. Use a model to demonstrate how diagrams are used to picture events, processes, structures, relationships, or sequences described in a textbook. Highlight the use of arrows, labeling, and various degrees of shading in diagrams.

12. Instruct the student to make a diagram of a basketball play and orally present it to the teacher or class.

13. For practice or for a pre/posttest format in assessing visual aids, provide the student with a map, table, graph, or diagram, and ask questions pertaining to purpose, legend, columns, and specific information from the visual aid.

14. Instruct the student to use the following cognitive strategy for reading visual aids (Ellis & Lenz, 1987):

    R—*Read* the written material until you are referred to a visual aid or until the material is not making sense.

    V—*View* the visual aid using CLUE.

        C—*Clarify* the stated facts in the written material.

        L—*Locate* the main ideas (global) and details (specific parts).

        U—*Uncover* the signal words (look for captions or words in the visual aid).

        E—*Examine* the logic (Does what you "read" from the picture make sense in light of what you read in the material?).

    A—*Ask* yourself about the relationship between the visual aid and the written material using FUR.

F—Ask how the visual aid and the written material *fit* together.

U—Ask how the visual aid can help you *understand* the written material.

R—Ask how the visual aid can help you *remember* the written material.

S—*Summarize* the most important information.

15. To facilitate analysis of visual aides presented in textbook chapters or study guides, instruct the student to use the SNIPS procedure (Ellis & Friend, 1991):

S—*Start* with questions (for example, why you are analyzing the visual aid and what is important to understand and remember about the visual aid).

N—*Note* what you can learn from the hints (such as lines, numbers, color, title).

I—*Identify* what is important (that is, facts).

P—*Plug* it into the chapter (that is, note how the visual aid relates to the content of the chapter).

S—*See* if you can explain the visual aid to someone.

Sequential Study Methods

Several methods have been developed to help students obtain and organize information from textbooks. F. P. Robinson (1961) developed the SQ3R method, which remains one of the most widely known study methods. The steps in SQ3R (survey, question, read, recite, and review) are discussed in Chapter 11. It is apparent that study methods hold much promise for teaching secondary students with learning problems, but systematic applications are needed to determine the effectiveness of various methods with specific populations (Schumaker, Deshler, Alley, Warner, & Denton, 1982). This section presents study methods for students with learning problems.

Multipass. Multipass is an adaptation of SQ3R designed to teach effective study skills to adolescents with learning problems (Schumaker et al., 1982). The Multipass steps include the following:

1. *Survey Pass* is designed for the student to determine the main ideas and organization of the chapter. In this step the student is instructed to do the following:

   a. Read the chapter title.
   b. Read the introductory paragraph.
   c. Review the chapter's relationship to adjacent chapters by examining the table of contents.
   d. Read primary subtitles of the chapter and determine the chapter organization.
   e. Note illustrations and read their captions.
   f. Read the chapter summary.
   g. Paraphrase the information gained in the preceding steps.

2. *Size-Up Pass* is designed for the student to gain specific information and facts from the chapter without reading it from beginning to end. In this step the student's instructions are as follows:

   a. Read each question at the end of the chapter, and determine what information is important to learn. If the student can answer a question, a check mark is placed next to the question.
   b. Examine the entire chapter following these guidelines: look for textual cues (for example, italicized words, boldface print, subtitles); make the cue into a question (for example, if the cue italicized word is *mitosis*, the student asks "What is mitosis?"); skim through surrounding text to locate the answer to the question; and orally paraphrase the answer without looking at the book.
   c. Paraphrase all the ideas and facts obtained from applying these four steps to all contextual cues in the chapter.

3. *Sort-Out Pass* is designed to have the student test herself on the material in the chap-

ter. In this step the student reads and answers each question at the end of the chapter. If the student can answer a question immediately, a check mark is placed next to the question. If the student is unable to answer the question, she follows these instructions:

a. Think about the section that most likely contains the answer.
b. Skim through that section for the answer, and write a check mark next to the question if the answer is found.
c. If the answer is not in that section, continue to think and skim until the answer is located and the question is marked with a check mark.

S.O.S. The S.O.S. strategy is an alternative version of Multipass for students with reading abilities 4 or more years below their grade level. It includes the same three passes over the textbook as specified in Multipass but, in addition, uses a visually marked version and an audiotaped version of the chapter. Schumaker, Deshler, Alley, and Warner (1983) recommend that a paraprofessional modify the chapter (that is, mark and tape the chapter). The marking system consists of highlighting important facts, main ideas, and key words. After the chapter is marked, it is read (not verbatim but according to markings) into a cassette tape recorder. Thus, the tape stresses important content and reduces information that can be presented in a few sentences. Each chapter tape is limited to no more than 90 minutes. The students are taught to survey, obtain details, and test themselves (that is, Multipass steps). During the use of the S.O.S. strategy, students complete an organizer outline. Schumaker et al. report that this process helps the student become an active learner while she is listening to the tape.

PANORAMA. The PANORAMA study technique includes eight steps divided into three stages (Edwards, 1973), as follows:

Preparatory Stage:

1. *Purpose.* The learner determines why the material is being read.
2. *Adapting rate to material.* The teacher decides at what rate the material should be read. This involves maintaining flexibility of rate within sections as a function of the type of content being covered. For example, on an initial reading, if the main idea is being presented, the rate is slow, whereas elaboration and expansion content may be read more rapidly.
3. *Need to pose questions.* The student uses headings or cue words to develop questions.

Intermediate Stage:

4. *Overview.* The student surveys the major parts of the chapter to determine the organization of the material.
5. *Read and relate.* The student reads the material in terms of a specified purpose. Specific answers to questions are sought.
6. *Annotate.* Written annotations (paraphrases, outlines) of main ideas, key words, and concepts are made.

Concluding Stage:

7. *Memorize.* The student uses outlines and summaries to learn the important content. Acronyms and associations are used to facilitate recall of main points.
8. *Assess.* The student assesses her efforts in relation to the purpose of the reading (for example, answers questions).

Study-Rehearsal Skills

Secondary students are expected to retain much of the information they obtain through lectures and readings. The retention of material is facilitated by rehearsal strategies. Towle (1982) states, "Rehearsal involves practicing or using information under cued conditions" (p. 92). She notes that students need a strategy for rehearsing organized content (notes, outlines, summaries, discussions, or demonstrations).

Activities for developing study-rehearsal skills. Numerous activities for rehearsal of material are suggested:

1. Have the student rehearse from various content formats (Towle, 1982). For example:

    a. Rehearsing notes: Rework notes, make up test questions, construct lists of important points, write summaries, review with classmates.
    b. Rehearsing outlines: Verbalize the content by giving a lecture from the outline, construct graphic aids (diagrams, charts, graphs) from the outline.
    c. Rehearsing discussion: Write a summary, use supplementary materials, give examples to support important points.
    d. Rehearsing demonstrations: Role play, practice segments of behavior chains, practice with peers and critique each other.

2. Encourage the student to use verbal rehearsal in reviewing content. This basic step in the learning strategies teaching sequence can be used in the initial learning of material and in reviewing it. Verbal rehearsal basically involves self-instructional training, which has received much support in facilitating learning (Flavell, 1976; Meichenbaum, 1975). (The cognitive behavior modification section in Chapter 5 presents the steps in verbal rehearsal.)

3. Instruct the student to use questioning strategies when reviewing content. Alley and Hori (1981) increased the reading comprehension of adolescents with learning problems through a questioning treatment based on Manzo's (1969) ReQuest Procedure. The treatment consisted of the following steps:

    a. Appropriate reading material is selected, and the teacher and student read two or three paragraphs following these steps: both read the first sentence silently; the student asks as many questions as she can pertaining to the sentence, and the teacher answers them; the teacher asks the student questions pertaining to the sentence, and the student answers them.
    b. After several paragraphs are read using the above steps, the student is instructed to write a question or make a prediction about the outcome of the story. The student then reads and answers her question or checks her prediction.

4. To help the student rehearse information for later recall, use the following activities and suggestions (Roe et al., 1987):

    a. Have the student review material with a specific purpose (for example, to answer a question).
    b. Encourage the student to obtain an understanding of the organization of the material through outlining. This helps the student categorize information to be learned under main headings.
    c. Instruct the student to visualize what the text or notes are trying to present.
    d. Encourage the student to make notes during rehearsal. In addition to facilitating retention, writing keeps the learner actively involved.
    e. Have the student summarize main and supporting information in her own words. Rewording the content helps improve understanding.
    f. Encourage the student to discuss the material with a classmate.
    g. Instruct the student to review notes or the text as soon as possible after initial contact with the material. Immediate review can strengthen understanding, accuracy, and associations involving the material.
    h. Instruct the student to rehearse to a criterion level (for example, answer review questions at 100 percent accuracy without referring to notes or the book).

5. Instruct the student to use the following cognitive strategies (Ellis & Lenz, 1987):

a. EASY: A strategy for studying content
 E—*Elicit wh* questions to identify important information *(who, what, when, where, why).*
 A—*Ask* yourself which information is least troublesome.
 S—*Study* easy parts first, hardest parts last.
 Y—*Yes*—do use self-reinforcement.
b. LISTS: A strategy for learning content
 L—*Look* for clues.
 I—*Investigate* the items.
 S—*Select* a mnemonic device using FIRST.
  F—*Form* a word.
  I—*Insert* letters.
  R—*Rearrange* letters.
  S—*Shape* a sentence.
  T—*Try* combinations.
 T—*Transfer* information to a card.
 S—*Self-test.*

Knowledge Expression and Application Skills

To succeed in secondary school, students must be able to demonstrate knowledge on classroom tests, minimum competency tests, and written assignments. Moreover, the application of knowledge in real-life settings becomes important to successful independent living during and after secondary school.

Activities for developing test-taking skills.
The following activities are suggested for helping students develop their test-taking skills.

1. Instruct the student to determine what general information is relevant in preparing for a test. The following list can be used as a guide or reminder:
Subject content _____
Date of test _____
Chapters covered _____
Notes covered _____
Type of questions _____
Number of questions _____
Timed or untimed test _____
Information emphasized in class _____

Also, to facilitate test preparation, give the student a test that has been used previously.
2. Identify vocabulary terms that are used frequently in test directions. Instruct the student to define the terms and perform the specified behavior. For example:

 a. *Compare* means . . .
  Contrast means . . .
  Compare and contrast milk and water.
 b. *Criticize* means . . .
  Criticize some aspect of your school schedule.
 c. *Illustrate* means . . .
  Illustrate the difference between a triangle and a circle.
 d. *Evaluate* means . . .
  Evaluate the importance of reading.

Other words that can be covered include *discuss, list, justify, outline, diagram, trace, match, define,* and *elaborate.*
3. Present the SCORER system (Carman & Adams, 1972) as a strategy for helping students take tests. Each letter represents an important rule in test taking.
 S—*Schedule* your time. The student reviews the entire test and plans time according to the number of items, point value per item, and easy and difficult items.
 C—Look for *clue* words. The student searches for clue words on each item. For example, on true–false items words such as *always* and *never* usually indicate the statement is incorrect. Words such as *usually* and *sometimes* frequently indicate the statement is correct.
 O—*Omit* difficult questions. Postponing hard questions until later in the testing session can improve a student's score. Specifically, Carman and Adams suggest that the student use the following procedure:

 (a) Move rapidly through the test.
 (b) When you find an easy question or one you are certain of, answer it.
 (c) Omit the difficult ones on the first pass.
 (d) When you skip a question, make a mark in the margin (− or √). (Do not use a

red pencil or pen. Your marks could get confused with grader's marks.)

(e) Keep moving. Never erase. Don't dawdle. Jot brief notes in the margin for later use if you need to.

(f) When you have finished the easy ones, return to those with marks (− or √), and try again.

(g) Mark again those answers you are still not sure of. Change the − to + or √ to √√.

(h) In your review (that's the last R in SCORER), you will go over all the questions time permits, first the √√, then the √, then the unmarked. (p. 217)

R—*Read* carefully. A careful reading of test directions and each item can improve test performance. Careless reading can lead to confusion on essay items and careless errors on objective items.

E—*Estimate* your answers. On test items requiring calculations or problem solving the student should estimate the answer. This helps correct careless errors. Moreover, if guessing is not penalized, it is important to answer all questions. After eliminating alternatives that are obviously incorrect, the student should take a best guess.

R—*Review* your work. The student should be encouraged to use every minute available. After she has answered all items, have her review the test. Carman and Adams suggest that the student use the following checklist:

(a) Return to the double-checked (√√) difficult questions. Reread them. Look for clue words. Look for new hints. Then go to the √ questions, and finally to the unmarked ones if there is still time.

(b) Don't be too eager to change answers. Change only if you have a good reason for changing.

(c) Be certain you have considered all questions.

(d) PRINT your name on the test. If there are separate sheets, print your name on each sheet. (p. 222)

4. Present the following activities and guidelines to help the student with answering true–false test items:

a. Note the following rule to remember with true–false items: A statement must be completely true to be true. If any part of the statement is false, the whole statement is false.

b. Instruct the student to be careful about tricky words. Some of these words include *some, many, most, everyone, no one, never,* and *always.* Demonstrate how these words cue true and false statements.

c. Instruct the student to notice that directions to true–false items may vary. Sample directions include the following:

(1) Next to each statement, print *T* for true or *F* for false.

(2) Write the word *true* or the word *false* on the line next to each statement.

(3) If a statement is true, do nothing to it. If a statement is false, cross out the part that makes it false. Rewrite the part you crossed out to make a true statement.

d. Instruct the student to look for reworded statements in which positive or negative words have been used to change the answer.

5. Present the following activities and guidelines to help the student with answering multiple-choice test items:

a. Explain to the student that in most multiple-choice questions several alternatives usually are easy to eliminate because they are obviously incorrect. Frequently two alternatives seem correct, but instructions require the selection of the *best* answer.

b. Provide the student with sample multiple-choice items that illustrate different ways of thinking. For example, use items that include such key words as *except, not,* and *all of the above.*

c. Encourage the student to use the following guidelines with multiple-choice items:

(1) Know how many answers to select.

(2) Be aware of the kind of answer you are seeking (for example, for a negative question).

(3) Remember the question.

(4) Eliminate the obvious wrong answers.

(5) Choose the answer that fits best.

(6) Be careful in recording the answer.

6. Present the following activities and guidelines to help the student with answering essay questions:

    a. Instruct the student to read the directions and questions carefully and underline key words. In directions, the student should underline such parts as *answer two of the following questions.* In questions, key words include *discuss, compare, list,* and so on.

    b. Instruct the student to outline or organize the answer before attempting to write it (Alley & Deshler, 1979). If time becomes a serious factor, the question can be finished in outline form.

    c. Teach the student to use the SCORER system with essay questions.

7. Instruct the student to use the following techniques when taking all tests:

    a. Review the entire test.

    b. Know the time allotted for taking the test.

    c. Know the value of specific questions.

    d. Follow the directions carefully.

    e. Notice key words in instructions and questions.

    f. Reread directions and questions.

    g. Go through the test and answer questions you are sure of first.

    h. Place a check mark beside questions you need to return to later.

    i. Return to questions that have been checked.

    j. Mark an *X* at the bottom of each completed page.

    k. Review all questions.

8. Use a test that the student has taken previously to review ways in which her performance can be improved.

9. Provide the student with a machine-scorable sheet and a set of multiple-choice questions. Instruct her to answer each test question by filling in the appropriate space. Many students with learning problems have difficulty with standardized and minimum competency tests. Practice in using different types of answer formats helps students develop skills with these formats.

Activities and strategies for developing written expression skills.

To survive in the secondary curriculum, students with learning problems must be able to express their knowledge in writing. Projects, papers, and essay tests require a degree of writing skills. Several methods (for example, COPS and TOWER) and activities for teaching written expression are presented in Chapter 13. This section features some of the work from the University of Kansas Institute for Research in Learning Disabilities that pertains to teaching written expression strategies.

Moran, Schumaker, and Vetter (1981) conducted a study in which adolescents with learning disabilities were able to write organized paragraphs after receiving paragraph organization training. The students learned to write three paragraph styles (enumerative, sequential, and compare/contrast) by following these three steps: (a) write a topic sentence; (b) write a minimum of three detail sentences; (c) write an ending or clincher sentence.

Schumaker et al. (1981) conducted a study in which adolescents with learning disabilities were taught an error-monitoring strategy. This strategy is designed to enable a student to locate and correct errors in written material. Their results indicate that the training improved the students' ability to detect and correct errors in written work. Moreover, the error rate in the students' self-generated products was low (almost zero) after training. In addition to following the learning strategies teaching sequence, Schumaker et al. used these steps to teach the error-monitoring strategy:

1. Provide the student with teacher-generated one-page passages, with some at the student's ability level and some at her grade level. Capitalization errors, appearance errors, and spelling errors are included in each passage.

2. Teach the student to detect and correct errors in the teacher-generated passages by following these procedures:

    a. Read each sentence separately.
    b. Ask the COPS questions (explained in Chapter 13).
    c. When an error is detected, circle it and put the correct form above the error.
    d. Ask for help if unsure of an item.

3. Teach the student to monitor her own work by following these steps:

    a. Use every other line as your write the rough draft.
    b. As you read a sentence, ask the COPS questions.
    c. When an error is located, write the correct form above it.
    d. Ask for help if unsure about a correct form.
    e. Copy the paragraph neatly before giving it to the teacher.
    f. Reread the paragraph as a final check.

Ellis and Lenz (1987) present two cognitive strategies for developing written expression skills:

1. DEFENDS: A writing strategy for defending a position
    D—*Decide* on your exact position.
    E—*Examine* the reasons for your position.
    F—*Form* a list of points that explain each reason.
    E—*Expose* your position in the first sentence.
    N—*Note* each reason and supporting points.
    D—*Drive* home the position in the last sentence.
    S—*SEARCH* for errors and correct.
        S—*See* if it makes sense.
        E—*Eject* incomplete sentences.
        A—*Ask* if it is convincing.
        R—*Reveal* COPS errors and correct.
            C—*Capitalization*
            O—*Overall* appearance
            P—*Punctuation*
            S—*Spelling*

        C—*Copy* over neatly.
        H—*Have* a last look.

2. WRITER: A strategy for monitoring for written errors
    W—*Write* on every other line.
    R—*Read* the paper for meaning.
    I—*Interrogate* yourself using COPS questions.
        C—Have I *capitalized* the first word and all proper nouns?
        O—How is the *overall* appearance?
        P—Have I used end *punctuation,* commas, and semicolons correctly?
        S—Do the words look like they are *spelled* right, can I sound them out, or should I use the dictionary?
    T—*Take* the paper to someone to proofread again.
    E—*Execute* a final copy.
    R—*Reread* your paper a final time.

COMMERCIAL LEARNING STRATEGIES PROGRAMS AND MATERIALS

Advanced Skills for School Success

Publisher: Curriculum Associates

Description: Advanced Skills for School Success (Archer & Gleason, 1992) is a teacher-directed program for students in seventh through twelfth grade that focuses on appropriate school behaviors and organizational skills. Students are taught to manage time and materials through organizing a notebook and maintaining a calendar of assignments and special events. The Teacher Guide contains 11 scripted lessons as well as procedures to promote generalization of skills. In addition, review lessons and follow-up activities are included. Lesson books also are available for students in third through sixth grade.

Classification and Organization Skills—Developmental

Publisher: Curriculum Associates

Description: This 32-lesson skillbook is designed to help students develop basic outlining skills. The lessons, which gradually increase in difficulty, include low-vocabulary and high-interest content. Students practice sorting and classifying, sequencing, identifying main ideas, selecting major and minor details, and completing an outline.

Study Skills Series

Publisher: Media Materials

Description: This series consists of five filmstrips and accompanying activity workbooks written at the fourth- to fifth-grade reading level. *How to Follow Directions* shows how to read and follow oral and written directions. *Learning to Outline* presents the correct format of an outline and teaches how to locate information needed for an outline. *Reading Tables* focuses on being able to read and interpret one-column and multicolumn tables, and *Reading Graphs* teaches how to read and interpret picture graphs, circle graphs, line graphs, and bar graphs. Finally, *Taking Tests* is designed to help students develop a strategy for taking objective and essay tests.

Test Taking Techniques

Publisher: Educational Activities

Description: This program consists of 4 cassette tapes and 10 activity books that teach ways to approach actual test situations and help establish positive mental attitudes toward test taking. Students are taught how to prepare for tests by using lecture and textbook notes to study, and emphasis is placed on the skill of predicting possible test questions. Specific hints are given on how to deal with objective as well as essay questions. In addition, practice sessions using sample material stress techniques such as making margin notes and underlining important points to make reviewing material more efficient.

COMPUTER SOFTWARE PROGRAMS IN LEARNING STRATEGIES

The following software programs focus on teaching effective study and test-taking skills to secondary students, as well as helping them learn how to read in the content areas.

Essential Study Skills Series

Producer: Media Materials

Hardware: Apple II, TRS-80

Description: This series includes six programs designed to develop essential study skills: (a) *Test Taking Success*—preparing for a test and recognizing answers, (b) *Learning to Read and Understand Tables*—using a chart, retrieving data, and making inferences and conclusions; (c) *Discover What Graphs Can Tell You*—identifying line, bar, circle, and picture graphs, extracting data, and making inferences and conclusions; (d) *Following Directions*—using clue words, picturing the directions, and noticing the order; (e) *Using Outlining Skills*—finding topic sentences, main ideas, and details, and making an outline; and (f) *Key References Skills*—alphabetizing, using parts of a book, and using reference materials. Supplemental materials in workbook format and an instructor's guide are included.

How to Read in the Content Areas

Distributor: Educational Activities

Hardware: Apple II, TRS-80, Commodore 64 with emulator

Description: These programs are designed to help students learn how to read effectively in the content areas of science, social studies, literature, and mathematics. The following concepts are featured: (a) spotlighting (vocabulary building); (b) surveying to determine the information given in a particular reading passage; (c) detecting main ideas and inferences; (d) recalling important facts, ideas, and details; and (e) utilizing skills by applying them to content areas. The programs are self-correcting and include immediate reteaching and reinforcement of skills not mastered.

Test-Taking Made Easy

Distributor: Cambridge Development Laboratory

Hardware: Apple, IBM

Description: This software includes five practice programs on preparing for tests, following test directions, and answering true—false, multiple-choice, and fill-in-the-blank test items. Graphics and a personal style of instruction are used to give simple rules and helpful hints in test taking. A third-grade reading level is required.

CONTENT INSTRUCTION

In developing programs for adolescents with learning difficulties, educators face the challenge of determining how students can master the content of the secondary curriculum and, at the same time, develop important skills and strategies (Ellis & Lenz, 1990). In most educational programs, adolescents with learning problems spend the majority of their school day in mainstream classes. Sometimes content-area classes are offered by special education teachers; however, some educators (Deshler & Schumaker, 1988; Ellis & Lenz, 1990)) question the ethics involved in adopting this practice and argue that special educators usually do not have the required knowledge of the subject matter.

In many cases, the regular classroom teacher must individualize and modify instruction to accommodate the needs of students with learning problems. The accommodations requested from special educators may include altering either (a) how the content is delivered or evaluated or (b) the nature or quantity of the content that the teacher expects students to master. Mainstream class teachers use numerous instructional alternatives to help these students. These alternatives often are referred to as accommodation techniques, compensatory techniques, or instructional adaptations. Laurie, Buchwach, Silverman, and Zigmond (1978) recommend that special and regular educators follow a problem-solving sequence in developing instructional alternatives for students with learning difficulties. Steps in a problem-solving sequence include the following:

1. Determine the requirements for "making it" in the regular class.
2. Specify the course requirements that the student is not satisfying.
3. Identify factors hindering the student's performance.
4. Brainstorm possible classroom modifications.
5. Select a plan of action.
6. Implement the plan.
7. Evaluate the plan.

Determining the types of modifications needed is critical in providing program alternatives. The discussion in Chapter 2 on factors that influence how a student learns offers many areas for consideration. In addition, the alternatives listed by Laurie et al. (1978), shown in Table 14.5, provide modification possibilities. This section features instructional alternatives in the following areas: presentation of subject matter, adapting materials, assignments, tutoring, testing, administrative considerations, and teaching science and social studies. Commercial science and social studies programs and materials as well as computer software programs in science and social studies also are presented.

Presentation of Subject Matter

Research on learning strategies has led to an increase in studies on how content-area teachers can present information that is sensitive to the strategies used by students. In general, when information is presented in a manner that helps students accomplish the goals of organizing, understanding, and remembering important information, the effect of ineffective or inefficient strategies may be minimized. To accomplish this, the teacher delivering the content must select instructional devices that can be used during a presentation to meet specific learning goals and then must use these

TABLE 14.5
Instructional alternatives for a mainstream teacher.

Classroom Organization	Classroom Management	Methods of Presentation	Methods of Practice	Methods of Testing
Vary Grouping Arrangements • Large-group instruction • Small-group instruction • Individual instruction • Peer tutoring • Independent self-instructional activities • Learning centers **Vary Methods of Instruction** • Teacher directed • Student directed	**Vary Grading System** • Homework • Tests • Class discussion • Special projects **Vary Reinforcement System** • Praise • Notes sent home • Grades • Free time • Special activity • Tangibles • Progress charts **Vary Rules** • Differentiated for some students • Explicit/implicit	**Vary Content** • Amount to be learned • Time to learn new information • Conceptual level **Vary General Structure** • Advance organizers • Previewing questions • Cues, mnemonic devices • Provide immediate feedback • Involve students actively **Vary Type** • Verbal—lecture, discussion • Written—texts, worksheets • Demonstration • Audiovisuals • Tape recorders • Filmstrips • Movies • Opaque projectors • Transparencies	**Vary General Structure** • Amount to be practiced • Time for practice • Group/individual • Teacher-directed/independent • Items ranging from easy to difficult **Vary Level of Response** • Copying • Recognition • Recall with cues • Recall without cues **Vary Type of Materials** • Worksheets • Texts • Audiovisual equipment	**Vary Type** • Verbal • Written • Demonstration **Vary General Structure** • Group/individual • Amount to be tested • Time for completion **Vary Level of Response** • Recognition • Recall with cues • Recall

Source: From "Teaching Secondary Learning Disabled Students in the Mainstream" by T. E. Laurie, L. Buchwach, R. Silverman, and N. Zigmond, 1978, *Learning Disability Quarterly, 1*(4), p. 68. Copyright 1978 by the Division for Children with Learning Disabilities. Reprinted by permission.

devices to guide students in how to use each device successfully. For example, to help students understand something unfamiliar and abstract, the teacher might use an analogy of something that is familiar and concrete. The teacher then must present the analogy so that students see the relationship between the two concepts and the new concept becomes meaningful.

An instructional device can be used when the content in a lesson appears to demand more manipulation than the teacher predicts the student can handle effectively or efficiently. According to Schumaker, Deshler, and McKnight (1991), the devices can be used to (a) make abstract information more concrete, (b) connect new knowledge with familiar knowledge, (c) enable students who cannot spell well to take useful notes, (d) highlight relationships and organizational structures within the information to be presented, and (e) draw the unmotivated learner's attention to the information. However, simply using an instructional device as part of a lesson cannot be viewed as an effective practice. Research indicates that the teacher must help the student see how the device is working and enlist the student's active involvement and support in using the device in the learning process. When the teacher uses an appropriate instructional device effectively and efficiently, the teacher is helping the device evolve or grow into a teaching routine.

One routine developed to help students organize information is based on the use of advance organizers to enhance a student's comprehension of content-area material (Lenz, 1982). When using an effective advance organizer, the teacher should do the following:

1. Provide background information.
2. Motivate students to learn.
3. Point out the advance organizer to the students.
4. Identify topics and tasks.
5. Provide a structured framework for the class period.
6. Clarify the required activity.
7. Introduce vocabulary.
8. State concepts to be learned.
9. Clarify concepts to be learned.
10. State expected outcome.

Ellis and Friend (1991) present a simple procedure to help teachers use advance organizers. The FORM device is used to introduce content-area lessons:

F—*Focus:* What will be the focus of the lesson and the focus of students' questions?

O—*Organization:* What organizational devices will be used to make the lesson easier to learn, and what sequence of activities will be used during the lesson?

R—*Relationship:* What have you learned before that will help you now, and if you master the material, how will you benefit in the future?

M—*Most* important goal: What do you need to learn if you do not learn anything else?

The teacher can adapt the advance organizer and use the aspects that are appropriate for the delivery of the content and that orient the students to what is being taught. In addition to the advance organizer, the teacher can use lesson organizers that reinforce the critical structure and content of the lesson. To clarify the organization and focus of the content, the teacher can use words and statements such as "first . . ., second . . ., third . . .," and "the most important idea is . . . ." Diagrams, tables, and charts also can help students see the structure of the content. Organizers can be used before an instructional sequence (advance organizer), throughout an instructional sequence (lesson organizer), or at the end of an instructional sequence (post organizer).

To help orient students to a learning task, Schumaker et al. (1991) present a teaching routine on introducing a typical chapter. In this routine, the teacher leads the students through an introductory and focused exploration of the chapter before they begin to read the chapter. In the exploration process, the teacher guides the students to discover how the chapter fits in with surrounding chapters, prompts the students to discuss and rephrase the title and subsections of the chapter, and helps the students identify the critical main ideas and vocabulary presented in the various sections of the text.

Guides are another type of organizer used to promote the content-area learning of students with learning problems. Guides consist of outlines or lists of questions that the teacher can use to focus student attention, point out important information, and encourage the student to inspect the material more closely. In guides involving the use of graphics, the students are directed to complete missing parts of constructed diagrams of the content. Both question- and graphic-oriented study guides are more helpful to students than self-study alone; however, the use of graphics in study guides is perceived as the most effective (Bergerud, Lovitt, & Horton, 1988).

Research on the use of instructional devices to facilitate students' understanding of important content focuses on helping students see the connection between what is to be learned and what they already know. Three devices for promoting understanding include providing analogies and examples, identifying similarities and differences between items, and demonstrating cause and effect. When an example is used as a device, the focus is generally on a single concept. Comparisons involve an exploration of two or more concepts through contrast, and cause-and-effect devices identify sequences of actions or events.

Instructional devices can be combined to build powerful and sophisticated teaching routines. Concept diagramming (Bulgren, Schumaker, & Deshler, 1988), semantic feature analysis (Bos & Anders, 1987), and semantic webbing (Anders & Bos, 1984) are three routines that help students understand the various parts of concepts. The use of a graphic organizer is included in all of these routines. In the concept diagramming routine, the teacher helps the students brainstorm information about an important concept, and this information is organized into three separate lists (that is, "always present," "sometimes present," and "never present"). The students construct a definition for the concept from the list of characteristics that are always present and then generate examples and non-examples of the concept based on the definition. The semantic feature analysis routine involves the use of a table in which examples of a concept are listed in a vertical column and important characteristics or features of the concept are listed in a horizontal column. By reading across the table for a given example, students can identify which features of a concept are possessed by the example. Also, students can construct a table by exploring information about an example of a concept and placing a plus or minus sign in the intersection to indicate a positive or negative relationship, a zero to indicate no relationship, or a question mark if the student is unsure of the relationship. The third routine, semantic webbing, involves writing the important term, idea, or concept on the chalkboard and encouraging the students to generate information. The appropriate placement of the information about the concept in relation to the original stimulus concept is discussed, and lines are drawn to indicate coordinate and subordinate relationships, examples, or features.

These instructional devices can be enhanced by building stories, adding concrete manipulatives, and developing other ways for the students to explore relationships. Some of these devices can be inserted into teaching routines as short, spontaneous clarifications if students are not grasping the material, and others can be used as the primary focus of an entire lesson.

Research also has focused on devices to help students remember important information. Studies on how teachers can help students consolidate information into meaningful chunks of information affirm the premise that students need to understand what they must remember before reducing the memory load with the use of a mnemonic device (Nagel, Schumaker, & Deshler, 1986). Thus, the teacher and students should identify what is most important about the information that is presented and then label and organize this information. Studies on the actual manipulations that can help students remember important information consist of several tactics including creating mental images, making familiar associations, using first-letter mnemonics, or using keyword strategies. For example, Mastropieri, Scruggs, McLoone, and Levin (1985) and Nagel et al. demonstrate how adolescents with learning problems can be taught to use mnemonic devices to remember content.

Activities for presenting subject matter.

1. Provide a list of simple questions before a lecture or reading assignment to serve as an effective advance organizer (Marsh, Price, & Smith, 1983).
2. Provide written backup to oral directions and lectures (for example, use an outline on a handout or overhead).
3. Use the following activities for presenting information to the student who has difficulty with auditory input (Towle, 1982):
    a. Provide pre-presentation questions.
    b. Develop vocabulary before presentation.
    c. Pace presentation and give frequent examples.
    d. Cluster main points.
    e. Summarize.

   f. Provide opportunities for student questions and discussion.
   g. Repeat important points.
   h. Relate content to other topics.
4. For the student who has difficulty following oral presentations, provide tapes of the lectures or allow her to record the class presentation and discussions. In addition, good note takers can use carbon paper to make copies of their notes for problem learners, or photocopies of notes can be given to problem learners.
5. Instruct the student with learning problems to sit near the front of the class. This encourages her to attend to teacher-directed activities and reduces distractions.
6. Match a problem learner with a peer helper who can assist by (a) explaining directions and assignments, (b) reviewing essential information from a lecture, (c) sharing and correcting notes, and (d) working on joint assignments or projects.
7. Use the following suggestions to help the student maintain attention and learn:
    a. Combine visual and auditory presentations.
    b. Establish eye contact with students during oral directions and lectures.
    c. Write assignments, directions, and lecture objectives on the chalkboard.
    d. Pause after questions to provide thinking time.
    e. Pause after each segment while giving directions and presenting content.
    f. Give examples and demonstrations.
    g. Briefly review information from previous lectures, and summarize information at the end of each lecture.
    h. Provide the student with time after the lecture for reviewing and improving her notes.
    i. Talk distinctly and at a reasonable rate.
    j. Give cues concerning what is important, and refer students to textbook pages for more clarification or information.
8. Use a pause procedure during lectures to improve the recall of adolescents with learning problems (Hughes, Hendrickson, & Hudson, 1986). Pause several times during a lecture (for example, every 8 to 12 minutes) for students to discuss the content covered. To help groups of three to four students systematically discuss the

content, instruct students to use the following mnemonic:

R—*Read* your notes and locate areas of concern (for example, spellings, blanks, confusion).

A—*Ask* questions about concerns.

P—*Put* in corrections.

Adapting Materials

The difficulty level of texts and materials used in mainstream classes presents a problem to secondary students with learning difficulties because the reading level usually is several grades above that of the student. To assist the student in learning, it often is necessary to modify or adapt the ways in which content is presented. The goal of these modifications is to change the format and mode of presentation while maintaining the basic content. Alternatives for adapting materials are presented in the following areas: (a) developing parallel curriculum, (b) simplifying texts, and (c) taping texts.

Developing parallel curriculum. Wiseman (1980) popularized the Parallel Alternative Curriculum (PAC) by means of a demonstration project. Although the total PAC program has numerous components (for example, parent involvement, remediation), its heart features the development of curriculum materials that present essential content in ways that help the problem learner organize, practice, and master important information.

School districts provide regular and special educators with release time or summer employment to write curriculum guides for various courses designed for use with low achievers. Thus, a low achiever receives the standard text and a curriculum guide or booklet. For example, Project PASS (Packets Assuring Student Success) is a mainstream secondary program for students with difficulties in United States history and American government. There are 98 instructional packets in U.S. his-

tory and 55 in American government. A module contains vocabulary, glossary, a pretest and posttest, subject content, activities, and projects, and the material is written at the third- to fifth-grade reading level. (Information is available from Project PASS, Livonia Public School District, 15125 Farmington Road, Livonia, MI 48154.)

Likewise, in Tallahassee, Florida, a series of Parallel Alternative Curriculum (PAC) booklets and Parallel Alternative Strategies for Students (PASS) booklets are available for many secondary courses in Project IMPRESS. Most instructional units in a packet contain target vocabulary, vocabulary exercises, content exercises, a unit test, and an answer key. Project IMPRESS is a Title IV-B program funded by the Florida State Department of Education. It includes eight components (for example, learning strategies, remediation, PAC) and has had excellent success throughout Florida. The PAC and PASS booklets are credited with much of the program's positive effect. (Additional information on Project IMPRESS is available from Kent Hamilton, Project Manager; Debra Stokes-Coachman, Project Secretary; Project IMPRESS, Fairview Middle School, 3415 Zillah Road, Tallahassee, FL 32310.)

Simplifying texts. The simplification of textbooks assists low achievers to master essential information efficiently. The following activities and procedures can be used for simplifying texts:

1. Provide the student with a highlighted text. Underlining or highlighting the main ideas, words, and concepts with a marker pen helps the student focus on relevant material. Also, the deletion of irrelevant or nonessential words with a dark pen serves to identify important content.
2. Provide the student with a cut-and-paste revision. The main ideas or specific content can be cut from the text and pasted on separate sheets of paper. This procedure has several advantages:

(a) material can be arranged sequentially, (b) additional headings can be inserted to aid organization, (c) distracting and nonessential material can be removed, (d) segments of content can be presented in small units, (e) material can be used without rewriting it, and (f) the revision can be photocopied for use with several students.

3. Transform words into graphic aids by creating charts, graphs, drawings, or models. Also, real materials are helpful in presenting content.

4. Use advance organizers to prepare the student for the reading material. These include outlines, diagrammatic overviews, study guides, questions, and directed previewing (for example, attention to selected headings or illustrations).

5. Reduce the complexity and length of work units to the extent that the low achiever receives periodic and consistent closure.

6. Provide self-correcting learning materials. Self-checking answer keys at frequent intervals are helpful checkpoints to guide the student through the material.

7. When simplifying texts, concentrate on content, sentence structure, and vocabulary (Beech, 1983). In simplifying content, it is helpful to (a) present generalizations first and follow with supporting details, (b) sequence events in chronological order, and (c) cluster related material.

8. For the student with limited reading skills, consider using rewritten texts. Some school districts employ paraprofessionals to give teachers extra time, or they offer summer employment for rewriting of texts. In situations where rewriting is feasible, the following guidelines are helpful:

    a. Keep sentences short; a five- to eight-word total is best.

    b. Use basic words of few syllables. L. J. Coleman (1979) recommends using the 850 words included in Ogden's (1970) *Basic English Dictionary.*

    c. Use present tense and avoid passive voice.

    d. Use simple sentences and try to begin each sentence with a subject. Avoid appositives and parenthetical expressions. Simple sentences with the verb following the subject are easier to read than compound and complex sentences or sentences in inverted order.

    e. Avoid figurative or symbolic language (for example, change "thundering herd" to "The herd galloped so hard the hoofs sounded like thunder when they hit the ground").

    f. Use picture clues as much as possible.

    g. Be certain that every pronoun has an unmistakable antecedent.

    h. Use new words sparingly. Repeating key words rather than using synonyms results in simpler content.

    i. Eliminate unnecessary words.

Taping texts. An alternative to reading a textbook is listening to it on tape. Taped texts can be provided to the student in two ways. One is to qualify the student for the special recordings provided for individuals who are blind or have learning disabilities. (Applications are available from Recordings for the Blind, 214 East 58th Street, New York, NY 10022.) In addition to their existing tapes, this service provides book taping of requested books at no charge. Another way to provide tapes is for teachers, students, or parents to prepare them. The following is a list of guidelines for taping:

1. Tape in a quiet place where there are rugs, draperies, and upholstered furniture to absorb extraneous noises.

2. Place the microphone on the table about 6 inches from the recorder's mouth. Turn the volume control about halfway, and read a portion of the material. Listen to the tape, and adjust the volume and microphone location until desirable recording is obtained.

3. Eliminate clicks by turning the volume on low before turning on the recorder. At the end of the recording let the tape run for a few moments and then gradually turn the volume down and off.

4. Avoid recording during the first 5 seconds and take a break every 15 minutes. Use alternating voices to reduce boredom.

5. Monitor the tape before giving it to the student.

6. At the beginning of the tape, identify the title of the text, author, and chapters or portions to be read.

7. Include the following directions in the initial text information: "Please stop the tape any time you wish to answer questions, write notes for yourself, or look at a section of the book more carefully. You will hear this sound (ring bell) at the end of each page to help you follow along in your textbook. Please turn to page _____ for the beginning of chapter _____."

8. Include selected study questions at the beginning of the tape. This alerts the student to important content.

Additional material and instructional modifications are presented in Chapter 4.

Assignments

Many special education teachers prefer to have students complete their work in the classroom so that they can observe performance and assist students who cannot complete assignments. However, Lenz, Ehren, and Smiley (1991) argue that students must be given the opportunity to complete work independently because assignment completion often indicates the independence of a learner in an academic setting. Lenz et al. organize assignment completion into completion knowledge and completion management. Completion knowledge involves the academic skills and background knowledge required to finish the assignment. Completion management involves the planning, integration, and organization of time, interests, and resources that facilitate the use of academic skills and knowledge. Lenz et al. also identify three basic types of assignments: study, daily work, and project. Study assignments require the students to prepare for a test or some type of class activity, and the focus on the assignment usually is on the process rather than on a permanent product. Daily work consists of assignments (for example, completion of chapter questions and worksheets) that follow up the content covered in class and are designed to promote practice and understanding of the content. Project assignments take more than 1 or 2 days to complete and often require students to extend or apply the content in the form of a report, theme, visual product, or presentation. Depending on the expectations of the teacher, all three assignment types can be completed in the classroom setting (seatwork) or out of the classroom setting (homework) and can be performed either individually or in a group.

Research in the area of homework indicates that the more time students spend working on homework, the higher their achievement (Austin, 1979; Fredrick & Walberg, 1980; Keith & Page, 1985; Walberg, 1984), even when variables such as socioeconomic status and ability are controlled (J. S. Coleman, Hoffer, & Kilgore, 1981; Page & Keith, 1981). Harnischfeger (1980) notes that this relationship is consistent across subject-matter areas as early as the fourth grade. Polachek, Kniesner, and Harwood (1978) also report that less-able students can compensate for their lower ability by increasing the amount of homework completed. However, to ensure the positive benefits of homework, Keith and Page (1985) note that the assignments must be appropriate for the student's ability and achievement levels.

Research findings on different types of assignments and the assignment completion process indicate that creating better structured and organized assignments may not improve the assignment completion process if the interest or motivation of students is not addressed. Thus, the teacher must attend to the basic nature and quality of the assignments. Lenz and Bulgren (1988) propose the following suggestions regarding classroom assignments to improve the achievement of adolescents with learning difficulties:

1. Assignment requirements must be explicit and clear.

2. Requirements should relate to important learning outcomes.
3. Choices must be provided that enable the students to personalize learning.
4. Over time, choices should include what to learn, how to learn, and how to demonstrate what has been learned.
5. Assignment completion initially should be modeled and guided in class by the teacher with student involvement.
6. Students should know the dimensions of assignments and be prompted to ask questions about assignment completion.
7. The process of learning about assignment completion should be considered as important as learning the content.
8. Discussions regarding the quality of assignments and the outcomes associated with assignment completion should be a regular part of classroom activities.
9. Students should be engaged regularly in setting goals related to improving the completion process and what is being learned as a result of assignment completion.
10. Fewer assignments should be given, and they should emphasize the most important learning outcomes.
11. Assignments should be evaluated rather than graded, and students should revise their work to improve the quality rather than the grade.
12. Peers should be used frequently to promote a variety of learning models.

Tutoring

At the secondary level, earning academic credits is a major instructional concern. Special education teachers often teach and assign credit for course content or provide tutoring in subject areas required for graduation (Carlson, 1981). In a national survey of special education teachers, Wells, Schmid, Algozzine, and Maher (1983) report that 47 percent of second-

ary school special educators spend most of their instructional time engaged in subject-matter instruction. Given the tutorial emphasis in secondary grades, Carlson (1985) suggests that guidelines or standards are needed for implementing and evaluating tutoring. He provides three principles for tutoring instruction:

1. *Instruction should be powerful.* To offer powerful instruction, the teacher must know the content well, provide enough time for intensive teaching, and follow the principles of effective instruction (for example, reinforcement, engaged time, modeling, and feedback).
2. *Instruction should result in long-range benefits to the learner.* Effective instruction should diminish the effect that the learning difficulty may have on future learning or help the student function more adequately. In addition to teaching immediate subject-matter content, the learning of skills (for example, study skills, test-taking skills) that increase the student's potential for later learning should be stressed.
3. *Teacher expectations for learner performance should be high.* Success must be maintained, but expected levels of performance should not be reduced unless it is absolutely necessary.

Testing

Students with learning problems frequently have difficulty displaying their knowledge or skills on tests. Modifications in test formats often help them perform better. The following suggestions are provided for improving test performances:

1. Give frequent, timed minitests so that testing is not such an isolated, anxiety-provoking situation. Give practice tests and have students test each other and review answers.
2. Use alternative response forms when existing formats appear to be a barrier to student expres-

sion (Towle, 1982). Variations between and within response formats (for example, essay, multiple choice, short answer) are possible.

    a. Multiple-choice alternatives include using yes-or-no questions, reducing the number of choices, providing more information from which to make a choice, and using matching items.

    b. Short-answer alternatives include providing a list of facts and information to use in the answer, allowing the student to list information or choose from several prepared short answers, using the cloze technique in prepared paragraphs, and scrambling information to be arranged.

    c. Essay alternatives include providing a partial outline for the student to complete, allowing the student to tape answers, noting important points to be included in the response, and using take-home tests.

3. In addition to the written test, provide a tape of the test items. Tapes allow the student to hear instructions and items as well as read them. Also, tapes are convenient for test makeups.

4. Leave ample white space between test questions, and underline key words in the directions and test items.

5. Provide test-study guides that feature various answer formats (for example, essay, multiple choice, fill in the blank).

6. Provide additional time for the student who writes slowly, or use test items that require minimal writing. Oral tests also may be given and answers recorded on tape.

Administrative Considerations

Administrative support is critical to the development and maintenance of a viable program for low achievers. Principals need support from central office staff, and teachers and counselors definitely need the support of the school principal. The following supportive activities and procedures are helpful for facilitating quality programs for low-achieving students by administrative actions:

1. Identify regular class teachers who are the most sensitive to the needs of students with learning problems. Schedule the student with these "sensitive" teachers, and support the teachers through such activities as (a) providing favorable scheduling—for example, an extra planning period, (b) assigning teacher aide(s) to their classes, (c) releasing time to develop curriculum, (d) placing volunteers in their classes, (e) providing inservice training tailored to their needs, (f) offering summer employment to develop curriculum, (g) providing opportunities to attend conferences and workshops, (h) offering support for university course work, (i) providing salary supplements, (j) recognizing the value of the program to the entire faculty, and (k) providing a budget that allows the purchase of some useful materials.

2. Support the development of a homework hotline.

3. Help establish a parent involvement and training program.

4. Work with guidance counselors to schedule the students so that a balanced work load is maintained (for example, a balance between demanding courses or teachers and less demanding courses or teachers).

5. Encourage the development of parallel alternative curriculum for the content classes.

6. Support the development of equitable diploma options for mainstreamed students.

Teaching Science and Social Studies

Many students with learning problems who enroll in science and social studies classes need help to learn the content of these courses. Science and social studies both follow an inquiry approach and focus on values development. Also, in both kinds of courses much of the content is taught by lecture, discussion, and projects. This section presents assessment considerations as well as strategies and activities for teaching science and social studies.

Assessment of science and social studies skills. Various standardized achievement tests include science and social studies subtests that measure general knowledge of skills in these areas. For example, subtests in science and social studies are included in the *SRA Achievement Series* (Naslund, Thorpe, & Lefever, 1985) for students in fourth through twelfth grade, and in the *Tests of Achievement and Proficiency* (Scannell, 1986) for students in ninth through twelfth grade. Also, the *Woodcock-Johnson Psycho-Educational Battery—Revised* (Woodcock & Johnson, 1989) contains subtests that measure science and social studies knowledge of students from preschool to adult age.

To design a student's individual program, the teacher may construct her own assessment tools. The teacher first must identify the major concepts and skills to be covered during the year. Then each major topic should be divided into subtopics, with the important skills and concepts specified. Curriculum guides and textbooks are helpful in identifying these skills and concepts. After the teacher has specified the content, she needs to develop a survey test and administer it to the student. The purpose of this testing is to discover the student's general readiness and instructional needs with regard to the content that will be covered. Testing also provides information on which prerequisite skills may be lacking (for example, map reading, measurement, vocabulary, concept formation, problem solving, graph reading). The test can include oral responses, short essay responses, reading with comprehension questions, objective test questions, and timed and untimed tasks.

Reading is a primary medium for learning science and social studies. Thus, it is useful to develop and administer informal reading inventories on science and social studies content to obtain information such as the student's ability to read the text independently. (The procedure for constructing an informal reading inventory is discussed in Chapter 10.) Also, the teacher should be aware of the reading level of the text used. R. Johnson and Vardian (1973) examined the readability level of social studies texts and found that texts at the intermediate level had a 10-year range. Their findings suggest that many social studies texts have readability levels above grade expectations. Similar findings also may apply to science texts.

For some students the teacher will not change the content but will alter techniques to cover it. For other students—particularly those who lack prerequisite skills—the teacher needs to be flexible in regard to the content. Schulz and Turnbull (1983) note: "It is virtually impossible to meet the unique needs of every student in the class during every class period, but teachers have to work on foundation skills with students who are achieving substantially below grade level" (p. 296). For these students, Schulz and Turnbull advise the teacher to consider the following questions about science and social studies content:

1. Will it help the student be more independent in daily living situations?
2. What is the loss if the student does not know the information?
3. Will the student obtain this information from other sources?

The final assessment concentrates on determining how the student learns best. For example, Breuning and Regan (1978) found that secondary special education students retained as much as 80 percent of the regular content in biology when allowed to participate in a preferred activity after satisfactory academic performance. Factors that influence how a student learns are discussed in detail in Chapter 2.

Science teaching strategies and activities.

1. To help the student with a short attention span during science instruction, vary instructional approaches and add active learning periods

around periods of lecture and discussion. Change-of-pace activities include working at a science learning center, playing a game, conducting an experiment, and watching a filmstrip. In addition, during lecture and discussion periods it may be helpful to seat the student near the teacher and ask questions frequently to encourage attention and involvement. An outline of the lecture material can be written on the chalkboard for the student to follow.

2. Because science concepts include many technical terms, introduce new vocabulary words before having the student read the words in context. The student may be required to keep a file box of science words. Have her look up the definition of each new word and write the word, its definition, and an appropriate sentence or picture on an index card.

3. As supplementary reading, provide science books written on a lower reading level. Books should be chosen carefully; they should have high-interest content and should not be recognizable as lower-grade books.

4. To help the student increase her science vocabulary, follow these three steps (Russell & Karp, 1951):

    a. Make sure the student can pronounce the word correctly.

    b. Have the student practice writing the word correctly.

    c. Give meaning to the word (for example, conduct an experiment relating to the word).

5. Tape textbook information on a cassette recorder to allow the student to review material. To ensure attention, the taped lessons should be brief (about 10 minutes). In a taped introduction the student may be given a brief description or overview of the material, and specific points to listen for may be noted. If the tape corresponds to textbook content, the student may be asked to refer to pictures in the text. The tape also may include study questions at the end to check the student's comprehension of the material. To self-check her responses, the student may respond and then turn the tape back on to listen for the correct answers. In addition, short books or selections of books for extra reading can be taped and placed in a special area of the room. The student

can follow along in the book as she listens to the tape.

6. To help the student complete science reading assignments, pair a peer tutor with a student who has difficulty identifying words. The two students can read orally, and the tutor can help her partner identify difficult words. After reading the selection, the two students can discuss the material to check each other on comprehension. Also, a peer tutor can underline important concepts in the text or write summaries of selected material.

7. To improve understanding among students with reading problems, use various media to present science concepts—pictures, charts, films, and filmstrips. The use of visual and audiovisual materials often increases motivation and interest.

8. Adapt science projects so that student participation is based on each student's strengths. For example, in a group activity, one student can read the material, another student can conduct the experiment, a third student can take notes or give an oral presentation, and all members of the group can contribute to (and be responsible for) the final written report.

9. Provide a list of materials and step-by-step instructions to build simple machines (such as wheel and axle, pulley, wedge) and conduct simple experiments (for example, connecting pieces of copper wire to the positive and negative ends of a battery, making static electricity by rubbing a balloon with a piece of wool). Learning by doing is motivating and effectively attaches meaning to science concepts.

Social studies teaching strategies and activities.

1. Use suggestions listed in the science section for maintaining interest and motivation that also can apply to teaching social studies. In addition, use the language experience approach to reading in social studies. After presenting information through lecture, filmstrips, or textbook reading, have each student summarize the main points of the material in her own words. The student can use magazine pictures or drawings to illustrate the written work. Peer tutors can help with vocabulary or spelling in the written compositions.

2. Point out to the student that reading history requires different kinds of reading (Russell & Karp, 1951). For example, to find a date or fact or to see a series of related events, the student may skim or read the passage quickly. However, to organize the material by main ideas and subtopics, the student first may read it quickly to get an idea of the entire selection and then read it more slowly on the second reading. The student can make notes as she reads or when she finishes reading, and the notes should be organized into main topics and subtopics. If the student is reading to note a number of causes of a particular event, she may skim several pages until she comes close to the discussion of the event. Then she should read more carefully to discover the facts.

3. Help the student learn the historical reason for major dates, including holidays, by collecting several different calendars that note holidays. Note the variety of types of holidays, and have the student use reference materials to learn historical information about the following types of dates: education milestones, famous persons, historical events, religious observances, and recreational holidays. Provide the student with an individual calendar, and require her to mark major dates and give information about them. Also, the student may locate dates of events pictured on stamps and paste the stamps on the appropriate day on her calendar.

4. Have the students play "Twenty Questions" using the category of historical figures. One player (or team) decides upon a name, writes it down, and keeps it out of sight. The opposing players can ask up to 20 questions to determine the name. Questions must be answered only with "yes" or "no." Players should be cautioned not to waste questions with wild guesses. Questions should narrow down the time period, sex, field of involvement, and so on until someone correctly guesses the name within the 20 questions. If no one is able to guess the person, that player (or team) gets another turn. Twenty Questions also can be played with geography questions. A map is hung in front of the students, and places on the map are the object of the game. Questions may be asked concerning latitude, longitude, surrounding geographical locations, and so on.

Another variation of the question game is to have a volunteer choose a famous person or place and tell the class the first letter of the person's last name or the place. Each student asks questions to determine the name until she gets a "no" answer. Then the next player begins questioning. The person asking questions can make a guess at any time; however, if she is wrong, the next questioner begins. The student who correctly guesses the name gets to choose a person or place and continue the game.

5. Prepare a display of several maps of one geographical area, with each map depicting a different aspect of that area—for example, climate, natural resources, population distribution, yearly rainfall, agricultural products. Make a list of questions that require reading each map. Also, the student may be provided with several copies of outline maps of a continent. Ask her to refer to a world atlas, encyclopedia, and other reference books to make five different types of maps for that continent.

6. Explore the concept of patriotism by developing an understanding and respect for the democratic process in America. Have small-group discussions about rights that are free of government control—such as freedom in selecting occupation and freedom of worship—and areas of governmental regulation, such as taxes on property and building codes. In discussing freedom of speech, provide newspaper editorials and have students underline parts that might have been deleted in a country that censors public information. Also, each small group of students can research the history of the American flag and share the information. Voting rights and responsibilities of American citizens can be explored through holding a mock election and discussing the duties of elected officials.

COMMERCIAL SCIENCE AND SOCIAL STUDIES PROGRAMS AND MATERIALS

HEP: History–Economics–Political Science

Publisher: Pro-Ed

Description: This series includes six workbooks to help students master the necessary vocabulary to understand social studies. The workbooks are designed for older students in need of high-interest, low-level reading material (second- to fourth-grade reading level). The *HEP Glossary* gives broad, simple meanings to more than 800 social studies terms, and each workbook contains 12 lessons to reinforce learning of words presented in the glossary.

I.D.E.A.L. Science Curriculum

Publisher: Opportunities for Learning

Description: This individualized, self-directing program emphasizes the human body and health science. The reading level is about fifth grade, with content suitable for junior and senior high school age. In addition to reading, writing, lab, and follow-up activities, each booklet contains objectives, directions, and review tests. Each student completes the first three books (*Introduction, Methods,* and *Cells to Systems*) and then chooses from the remaining seven books (*Skeletal System, Muscular System, Digestive System, Excretory System, Respiratory System, Circulatory System, Nervous System*) according to interests. The teacher's manual contains instructions as well as more than 150 reproducible worksheets, tests, and answer keys.

Laboratory Science Series

Publisher: Science Research Associates

Description: This series includes 10 workbooks in the areas of animals, plants, our environment, weather, our Earth, our universe, sound and light, friction and machines, magnetism and electricity, and matter and energy. Each workbook contains various projects, activities, and experiments pertinent to each individual subject area. The teacher presents science lessons and conducts scientific experiments that are performed with household and classroom objects. A teacher's guide provides a glossary of vocabulary words and a detailed explanation of procedures.

Me Now

Publisher: Hubbard

Description: This science and health program is designed for special students age 10 to 13. It focuses on building self-image by developing a basic understanding of how the body works. The program is activity centered; there is little written material for students to read. Four content areas are included: (a) digestion and circulation, (b) respiration and body wastes; (c) movement, support, and sensory perception; and (d) growth and development. A comprehensive curriculum guide is provided for each of the four content areas. Also included are 140 slides, posters and pictures relating to identification of food and food sources, seven film loops, a supplies kit of nonconsumable items (for example, stethoscope, test tubes, magnifying glass), and worksheets. In addition, a 3-foot-tall functioning torso model is available that shows five body systems—digestive, circulatory, urinary, respiratory, and nervous. A teacher's guide with teaching strategies and step-by-step procedures accompanies the torso. Standard laboratory and evaluation materials also are available in separate kits.

Social Studies Series

Publisher: Science Research Associates

Description: This series includes 13 workbooks, each covering a period of United States history or geography. The workbooks are written at a second- to third-grade reading level and present the same political, social, cultural, and economic history as a general classroom text. In addition to exercises and chapter tests, the workbooks contain sections on historical trivia and occasional fictional narratives to maintain student interest. The following workbooks are included: Geography, The First Americans, Explorers and Discoverers, Colonial Times, Revolution and Independence, Westward Expansion, Civil War and Reconstruction, Industrial Revolution, Immigration, World War I, Roaring Twenties and the Depression, World War II, and the Nuclear Age.

A Sound History of America

Publisher: DLM

Description: This audiocassette-plus-print program is designed to help students achieve success in history. The 10 cassettes feature important historical events normally included in the traditional curriculum and cover the time from the discovery of America to the 1980s. The audiotapes present factual information complemented by period music, dramatizations, and sound effects. The lessons are 10 to 15 minutes in length, and the accompanying scripts can be used as a read-along activity.

World History and You

Publisher: Steck-Vaughn

Description: This consumable two-book survey of world history is designed for older students who have reading difficulties. The reading level is about fourth-grade level, and emphasis is placed on reading comprehension, vocabulary, and other language skills as well as presenting world history. Book 1 presents areas such as ancient civilizations, growth of major religions, and exploration and colonization of the New World. Book 2 begins with the Industrial Revolution, explores the growth of democracy, and continues through contemporary world history. Exercises and chapter reviews reinforce facts presented in the text.

COMPUTER SOFTWARE PROGRAMS IN SCIENCE AND SOCIAL STUDIES

Explore!

Producer: Science Research Associates

Hardware: Apple II

Description: This software presents the background, voyages, and discoveries of 16 explorers to the New World. Students draw and identify important voyages on accompanying maps and worksheets and compile information about explorers such as Columbus, deSoto, and Hudson. Words, high-resolution map screens, and computerized exercises are used to teach students about each explorer, his voyage, and his country.

The Physical Science Series

Distributor: Micro Center

Hardware: Apple II

Description: These 14 tutorial programs present common topics in junior high school science (for example, motor, light, electricity, atoms, energy, and sound). These are 30 to 40 questions in each subject area, and the program automatically branches to give extra information on concepts the student finds difficult. The teacher can change the questions the student is asked, and the student's scores are recorded for teacher records.

Puzzles

Producer: Science Research Associates

Hardware: Apple II

Description: This software includes four programs in the areas of weather, sound and light, magnetism and electricity, and matter and energy. A game-format presentation is used to teach scientific facts and help students learn to think deductively. Each program contains 16 matrix puzzles, clues, and a glossary.

Regions of the United States

Distributor: Educational Activities

Hardware: Apple II, TRS-80, Commodore 64

Description: This gamelike program, designed for students in fifth through twelfth grade, focuses on the geography of the United States. In Part 1, "The Fifty States," the student reviews the states, region-by-region, and then takes a quiz in which she must identify the states and spell their names correctly. In Part 2, "The Regions," the computer gives clues about a particular region, and the student must determine the region by using as few clues as possible. In addition, the game teaches the major cities, landforms, products, and climates of the different regions of the United States.

Your Body Series

Distributor: Opportunities for Learning

Hardware: Apple II, TRS-80, Commodore 64

Description: This two-part series covers the major body systems and is designed for students in junior high school. Set 1 includes *The Human Organism, Your Blood, Your Digestive System,* and *Your Circulatory System.* Set 2 features *Your Muscular System, Your Skeletal System, Your Brain and Nervous Sys-*

tem, and *Your Endocrine System.* The programs present body parts and their functions in an interactive learning-game format, such as a simulated road race through the circulatory system in which the student can proceed only by correctly answering questions. If needed, the student can ask for "extra help" information.

SOCIAL DEVELOPMENT INSTRUCTION

The social skills deficits of many adolescents with learning difficulties are well documented. Numerous authorities (Deshler & Schumaker, 1983; Schumaker & Hazel, 1984; Zigmond & Brownlee, 1980) recommend social skills training for these adolescents. Generally, the development of social skills is believed to help adolescents with learning problems in several ways:

1. Social competence helps compensate for academic deficits.
2. Social skills are needed for success in the mainstream and in employment.
3. Social skills training helps adolescents with learning problems derive maximum benefit from academic or vocational instruction.
4. Social competence is fundamental to good interpersonal relationships and fosters leisure and recreational activities.

Zigmond and her colleagues at the University of Pittsburgh and Schumaker and her colleagues at the University of Kansas present social skills curriculums for adolescents with learning difficulties. Zigmond's curriculum, the School Survival Skills Curriculum, features three strands: behavior control, teacher-pleasing behaviors, and study skills (Silverman, Zigmond, & Sansone, 1981). The curriculum developed at the University of Kansas Institute for Research in Learning Disabilities, *Social Skills for Daily Living,* focuses on such skills as resisting peer pressure, accepting and giving compliments, asking and answering

questions, making friends, responding to teasing, following instructions, apologizing, and joining group activities (Schumaker, Hazel, & Pederson, 1988). Additional information on social development, including assessment of social behavior and techniques and materials for developing social skills, are presented in Chapter 5.

FUNCTIONAL LIVING SKILLS

A functional or essential living skills program typically is designed for secondary students whose academic skills are very low (that is, below fourth-grade level). Functional living skills are essential for successful living in modern society, and for some students with learning problems, they must be taught directly and systematically. Otherwise the students may never acquire them or may learn them through trial and error, which is both costly and time-consuming. Kokaska and Brolin (1985) list nine important areas in planning a functional living curriculum (see Table 14.6). Many of these skills can be taught within the traditional curriculum. For example, Area 1 can be included in math, Areas 3 and 5 in science; Areas 4, 7, and 9 in social studies; Areas 2 and 6 in home economics and shop; and Area 8 in music, art, and physical education.

Bender and Valletutti (1982) present a functional curriculum based on six roles of the individual. Reading, writing, and math skills essential to each role are taught. The roles include (a) resident in home, (b) learner in traditional and nontraditional school settings, (c) participant in community, (d) consumer of goods and services, (e) employee, and (f) participant in leisure activities. Bender and Valletutti urge teachers of functional curriculum to examine the functional reality of intervention activities. They report, "To do so requires a simple technique, namely the performance of the learning task in its actual context from the

TABLE 14.6
Functional living curriculum areas.

Areas	
1. *Managing family finances* Identify money and make correct change Make wise expenditures Obtain and use bank and credit facilities Keep basic financial records Calculate and pay taxes 2. *Selecting, managing, and maintaining a home* Select adequate housing Maintain a home Use basic appliances and tools Maintain home exterior 3. *Caring for personal needs* Dress appropriately Exhibit proper grooming and hygiene Demonstrate knowledge of physical fitness, nutrition, and weight control Demonstrate knowledge of common illness prevention and treatment 4. *Raising children—family living* Prepare for adjustment to marriage Prepare for raising children (physical care) Prepare for raising children (psychological care) Practice family safety in the home 5. *Buying and preparing food* Demonstrate appropriate eating skills Plan balanced meals Purchase food Prepare meals Clean food preparation areas Store food	6. *Buying and caring for clothing* Wash clothing Iron and store clothing Perform simple mending Purchase clothing 7. *Engaging in civic activities* Generally understand local laws and government Generally understand the federal government Understand citizenship rights and responsibilities Understand registration and voting procedures Understand Selective Service procedures Understand civil rights and responsibilities when questioned by the law 8. *Using recreation and leisure* Participate actively in group activities Know activities and available community resources Understand recreational values Use recreational facilities in the community Plan and choose activities wisely Plan vacations 9. *Getting around the community (mobility)* Demonstrate knowledge of traffic rules and safety practices Demonstrate knowledge and use of various means of transportation Drive a car

Source: From *Career Education for Handicapped Individuals,* 2nd ed. (pp. 46–47), by C. J. Kokaska and D. E. Brolin, 1985, New York: Merrill/Macmillan. Reprinted by permission.

viewpoint of the learner and his role in that content" (p. 1).

To establish and monitor educational or prevocational objectives, the *Brigance Diagnostic Inventory of Essential Skills* (Brigance, 1980) can be used. This instrument includes measures of functional academics at the sec- ondary level and thus assesses minimal academic and vocational competencies. The inventory includes rating scales to measure applied skills that cannot be assessed objectively, such as health practices and attitude, responsibility and self-discipline, job interview preparation, auto safety, speaking skills, and listening skills. Other practical assessments include sections on food and clothing, money and finance, travel and transportation, and oral communication and telephone skills.

Functional Living Skills Activities

1. To help the student learn to manage family finances, have her keep a record of expenses for a certain period of time. The budget should include areas such as food, clothing, transportation, savings, medical expenses, recreation, and so forth. She also may itemize her family's purchases during a period of time. To encourage the student to spend money wisely, provide her with a shopping list of products available at different stores, and require her to compare prices or to select items based on a fixed amount of money.

2. Take a field trip to a bank and a savings and loan facility or arrange classroom demonstrations by representatives from these establishments. A classroom bank and individual accounts can be set up to acquaint the student with checks, deposits, withdrawals, passbooks, and so on. Extensive practice in writing checks, filling out deposit slips, and balancing a checkbook should be provided. To learn about other banking services, the student also can be required to fill out forms for obtaining a loan or opening a charge account.

3. Have small-group discussions in which the students examine various kinds of taxes (such as sales, gas, property, income). Have them identify items that are taxed and determine the amount, how the tax is collected, and how it is used. The procedure for filing income tax forms can be presented by requiring the student to fill out a 1040 short form. Cut instructions from a tax guide according to numbered sections (for example, 1 — name and address; 2 — social security number; and so on). Fasten each instruction and the corresponding section of the 1040A form to a card. Provide one sample form filled out as well as blank 1040A forms that are laminated for reuse. Instruct each student to fill out a 1040A form number-by-number, referring if necessary to the completed form and the individual instruction cards.

4. Discuss various types of housing available in the community. Have the students explore the advantages and disadvantages of each according to factors such as cost, space, utilities, and location. In discussing renting a home or apartment, include such factors as deposits, leases, and tenant rights and responsibilities. Cut out newspaper ads that list rentals and tape them to the inside of a manila folder. On index cards write questions related to the rental ads and place the cards in a pocket pasted to the folder. The student picks a card, looks for the answer in the classified ads mounted on the inside of the folder, and writes her response. An answer key can be provided by numbering the questions and assigning letters to the ads.

5. Have the students role play potential problems in marriage and child raising and discuss solutions. Encourage the students to refer to their own life experiences when suggesting appropriate practices in raising children. Also, have the students identify community agencies and sources that provide assistance in family planning and marriage problems.

6. Identify emergency situations that can occur in the home (such as fire or storm damage) or with a family member (such as accident or injury). Have the students look up emergency phone numbers and make a booklet containing information on how to get help for emergencies. First-aid procedures for injury situations should be demonstrated in the classroom and listed in the student's booklet. Also, safety procedures for hazardous situations can be discussed.

7. Have each student determine recreational activities in which she can participate, and list resources and facilities available in the community. If music is an area of interest, the teacher can tape five different types of music and have the student select her favorite. Then the student can explore places where that type of music is available, or she can study her favorite composers. To develop an interest in art as a leisure activity, the teacher can present prints of various types of art. The student can determine places or events in which she can enjoy art during recreational time. Also, the student can participate in clubs or hobbies to explore using leisure time effectively.

8. To help the student learn traffic signals, arrange pictures of traffic signs on bingo cards with five pictures in each of the five rows and a "free" space in the middle. Make call cards by writing the names of the signs on paper squares. Each student receives a bingo card, and the caller draws and reads call cards. When a traffic sign is called that appears on a player's bingo card, she covers the sign with a marker (disk). The first player to cover all the signs in a row calls "Bingo" and then must give the meaning of each sign covered in that row.

9. Use a start-to-finish game board to stimulate interest in driver education and understanding of driving procedures. Write various directions on the game-board squares, including some squares instructing the player to pick an Accident card or a Good Driver card (see Figure 14.3). Make green Go cards with a question written on the front and the correct answer written on the back. The back of each Go card also tells the number of spaces to move ahead if the answer is correct and the number of spaces to move back if the player's response is incorrect. The Go cards are placed face up. The player takes the top card, responds to the question, turns over the card to check her answer, and moves her marker the number of spaces indicated. Sample Go card questions include the following:

   a. What colors are railroad signs?
   b. What does *mph* mean?
   c. What papers must you have when you drive?
   d. What color is the bottom bulb in a traffic light?
   e. Which car has the right of way when they both arrive at the intersection at the same time?

If the player lands on an Accident space or a Good Driver space, she takes a card and follows the directions on the card. Accident cards should be red and may include the following:

   a. You made a U-turn in the middle of the block. Move back 1 space.
   b. You were driving at night with one headlight. Move back 2 spaces.
   c. You made a turn without signaling. Move back 2 spaces.
   d. You parked in front of a fire hydrant. Move back 1 space.

Good Driver cards should be blue and may include the following:

   a. You slowed down to 25 mph in an unmarked speed zone. Move ahead 2 spaces.
   b. You pulled to the far right of the road and stopped when you heard a siren. Move ahead 2 spaces.
   c. You checked your parking meter before you went shopping. Move ahead 1 space.
   d. You reduced your speed in a construction zone. Move ahead 1 space.

The players take turns, and the first one to reach the finish square wins.

COMMERCIAL FUNCTIONAL LIVING SKILLS PROGRAMS AND MATERIALS

Wiederholt and Wolffe (1990) note that in 1975 a bibliography of independent living skills materials that was generated at the University of Texas included more than 1,500 different ma-

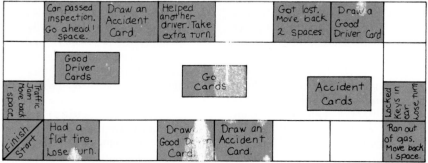

FIGURE 14.3
Driver education game board.

terials. Since that time, there has been a proliferation of materials. Consequently, the number of resources is enormous. This section features a small sampling of materials that appear useful for developing functional living skills.

Daily Experiences and Activities for Living

Publisher: DLM

Description: This high-interest, low reading-level program is designed to help students in seventh through twelfth grade develop practical, real-life skills. Six workbooks are included: (a) Information Sources (library, telephone directories, newspaper, television, radio), (b) Consumer Buying (coupons, buying a car, refunds, credit applications), (c) Housing (moving, leases, renting versus owning, classified ads, utilities), (d) Working (looking for work, work permits, job applications, interviews), (e) Nutrition and Health (planning menus, dieting, first aid), and (f) Transportation (schedules, maps, road signs, public transportation). Activities teach students how to become self-sufficient in solving everyday problems.

How to Write for Everyday Living

Publisher: Educational Activities

Description: This writing competency program focuses on real-life writing tasks and specific applications of writing skills. The student receives instruction and practice in various skills as she works with samples of actual forms. Lessons are included in areas such as filling out an application, writing business letters, taking telephone messages, and writing a resume. The program includes 5 cassettes and 10 activity books as well as a diagnostic pretest and evaluative posttest.

MATH . . . for Everyday Living

Publisher: Educational Activities

Description: This program, presented through cassette tapes and activity books, teaches and develops the necessary basic math skills involved in real-life activities. The lessons introduce and reinforce computational skills needed to cope with everyday situations such as shopping, traveling, banking, getting the best-paying job, paying bills, and using credit. A computer software version of this program is available for use with the Apple II, TRS-80, and Commodore 64.

Survival Math Series

Publisher: Mafex Associates

Description: This series includes six sets of workbooks that allow students to apply basic math skills to practical, everyday situations. For example, the student is required to compute multiplication and addition problems to buy grocery items and to figure weekly pay according to given pay rates. Income tax and social security deductions are explained. In addition, activities are provided in filling out credit cards, making change, and maintaining a checking account.

Survival Words Program

Publisher: DLM

Description: This program teaches automatic identification of 90 words and phrases considered most essential for survival. It is designed for use by students with reading problems and has an interest level directed at adolescents. The program includes nine storybooks as well as worksheets containing six types of exercises for each word or phrase.

COMPUTER SOFTWARE PROGRAMS IN FUNCTIONAL LIVING SKILLS

Daily Living Skills

Producer: Encyclopaedia Britannica Educational Corporation

Hardware: Apple II

Description: These programs provide interactive instruction and practice in survival reading. *Prescription Medicine* and *Product Labels* deal with labels and appropriate consumer information. *Classified Ads* and *Telephone Directories* focus on common reference sources that require searching through categorized information. *Banking* and *Credit* introduce the fundamental aspects of bank accounts and basic credit concepts. *Job Applications* presents the basic concepts pertaining to applying for a job, and *Paychecks* focuses on the general nature of pay periods, gross and net pay, earnings, and deductions. Graphics are used to present concepts, and questions are included on each program.

Lifeskill Mathematics Series I

Producer: Media Materials

Hardware: Apple II, TRS-80

Description: This series consists of the following six math programs written at the second- to fourth-grade reading level: (a) *On the Road with Basic Math Skills*—computing distance, average speed, miles per gallon; (b) *Car Owner's Manual for Better Math Skills*—buying a new car, financing a car; (c) *The Math in Your Insurance Policies*—auto, house, life, medical, and social security insurance; (d) *Essential Math Skills for Computing Taxes*—sales taxes, property taxes, income taxes, deductions from payroll; (e) *Math and Your Personal Finances*—housing, clothing, credit; and (f) *Math Around the House*—wall and floor area, buying paint, changing square feet to square yards. Supplemental workbooks are included.

Lifeskill Reading I

Producer: Media Materials

Hardware: Apple II, TRS-80

Description: This series includes the following eight programs: (a) *Stop, Look, and Learn Highway Warning Signs,* (b) *Set Your Course Using Highway Signs,* (c) *Shop and Save! Food Purchasing Skills,* (d) *Money Matters: Banking and Consumer Transactions,* (e) *Consumer Talk: Everyday Reading Skills* (income and taxes, insurance, real estate, taking care of your health), (f) *Bon Voyage! Basic Travel Skills,* (g) *What's the Scoop? Exploring the Newspaper,* and (h) *You Decide: The Influence of Media* (billboards, ads, propaganda). The reading level of the series is second to fourth grade, and supplemental activities are provided in workbook format.

Survival Math: Simulations

Producer: Sunburst Communications

Hardware: Apple II, TRS-80, Commodore 64

Description: These four simulations require students to use math skills as a basis for making sound judgments. *Smart Shopper Marathon* requires students to use unit prices and percent discounts to determine best buys. In *Hot Dog Stand,* students must purchase food and set prices as they operate a hot-dog stand to raise money. In *Travel Agent Contest,* students are asked to plan a 7-day trip and allocate money for expenses without exceeding a spending limit. *Foreman's Assistant* requires students to help plan a playroom and buy materials for building it while staying within a time frame and budget. Thus, the programs provide practice in calculating or estimating answers and help teach students to use mathematics as an analytical tool.

CAREER-RELATED INSTRUCTION

The emphasis on career education began in the early 1970s and evolved from dissatisfaction with the educational system's ability to prepare students adequately for the future. In a recent study, the U.S. Department of Labor, Education, and Commerce (1988) surveyed 134 business representatives concerning their needs, goals, and expectations of education when hiring adolescents. One of their primary findings was that the "basic skills gap" between what businesses need and the qualifications of beginning workers is widening. Moreover, they report that these skill deficiencies are costing employers a great deal in their quest to produce quality products at competitive prices.

Students with learning problems often need attractive options in career training. Cegelka (1985) states:

> By emphasizing the relationship of subject matter to various careers and occupations and by developing needed work skills, career education has sought to make education more relevant to the economic and employment realities of the day. . . . In short, it has sought to increase the life satisfaction of workers, restore the work ethic, and increase national productivity. (p. 575)

Career education involves a comprehensive educational program, focusing on careers, that begins in early childhood and continues throughout adulthood. At the elementary level, the major objective is to introduce the student to various occupations. The primary objective at the secondary level is to shape the student's awareness of occupations into preparation for a career. Figure 14.4 presents the stages of career development.

Wiederholt and Wolffe (1990) offer a normal sequence of independent living-related developments that provide a complement to the career development stages. These independent living-related developments provide a framework of how students build attitudes, values, interest, and information about work:

1. *Preschool age:* Learns to listen, cooperate, do for self, show initiative, be honest; differentiates work from other activities; understands different types of work and associated roles; develops feelings toward work.
2. *Elementary age:* Fantasizes different roles; understands parents' work; has continued and more complex career fantasies; is exposed to and develops understanding of a wide variety of work roles; develops under-

standing of good work qualities; continues to develop and implement communication skills; learns to interact appropriately with peers and authority.
3. *Junior high school age:* Has part-time or summer job; does chores at home; develops hobbies or special interests; begins to understand personal strengths and weaknesses; understands relative rewards, demands, and requirements of major categories of work; accepts responsibility for career decisions; begins to crystallize personal values and self-concept.
4. *High school age and older:* Continues exploration of various career possibilities; prepares for career or initial employment; crystallizes interests; changes plans or jobs; understands and acts upon personal strengths and weaknesses; develops skills; crystallizes personal values and self-concept; handles independent living; establishes intimate relationships; refines hobbies or special interests; learns how to get jobs and holds several different jobs; learns and displays appropriate work behavior.

Career education enables an individual to explore the occupational world, to identify

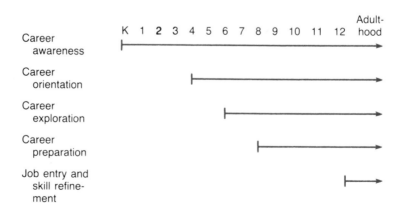

FIGURE 14.4
Career development stages.

with it, and to make job decisions that increase self-fulfillment (Marland, 1972). The U.S. Office of Education (1971) delineates 15 occupational clusters appropriate for career education content. Moreover, the content places value on all kinds of work, regardless of its current social status.

Brolin (1989) recommends that career education be a major part of the curriculum for students with disabilities and that it focus on the total life plan of an individual. The total life plan facilitates growth and development in all life roles and settings. In addition to the functional living curriculum areas included earlier in Table 14.6, Brolin includes seven personal-social skills and six occupational guidance and preparation areas:

1. *Personal-social skills:* achieving self-awareness; acquiring self-confidence; achieving socially responsible behavior; maintaining good interpersonal skills; achieving independence; making adequate decisions; communicating with others.
2. *Occupational guidance and preparation:* knowing and exploring occupational possibilities; selecting and planning occupational choices; exhibiting appropriate work habits and behavior; seeking, securing, and maintaining employment; exhibiting sufficient physical-manual skills; obtaining specific occupational skills.

Career education has a broad emphasis and includes vocational training. Vocational training specifically focuses on developing vocational skills essential to entering the world of work. Historically, it has been difficult to obtain vocational training for students with mild disabilities (Marsh & Price, 1980; Smith, 1981). A variety of options and services are needed for providing low achievers with the programs they need. Mori (1980) lists four possible methods of providing students with

learning problems with specialized skills in a career area. These include area vocational-technical school, special vocational school, work-study off campus, and work-study on campus. Postschool alternatives include entry-level jobs, trade school, community college, college, and referral to the Bureau of Vocational Rehabilitation or other appropriate community or government agencies (Mori, 1980).

A variety of measures and procedures can be used to assess students in terms of appropriate decisions on career direction. Information can be obtained informally through student-teacher interaction and a consultative process. In addition, a number of standardized tests are available to assess vocational interest or aptitude. The following instruments can be used to help secondary students choose appropriate careers based on their abilities and interests: *Career Decision-Making System—Revised* (Harrington & O'Shea, 1992), *Occupational Aptitude Survey and Interest Schedule—2* (Parker, 1991), *Reading-Free Vocational Interest Inventory—Revised* (Becker, 1988), and *Strong-Campbell Interest Inventory* (Strong & Campbell, 1985). In addition to standardized testing procedures, the work-sample method provides a means of prevocational evaluation. The work sample is a simulated task or occupational activity that is representative of tasks and activities in various employment settings. As the individual attempts different work samples, personality characteristics and skill aptitudes can be observed to indicate vocational potential.

Curriculum-based vocational assessment offers an alternative approach to commercial tests. Schloss, Smith, and Schloss (1990) note that curriculum-based vocational assessment is based on each student's learning needs and includes four primary characteristics:

1. It provides relevant information in the beginning stages of planning an individual's vocational program.

2. Assessment is an integral and ongoing part of a student's vocational program.
3. The person conducting curriculum-based vocational assessment is the same person responsible for the student's vocational instruction.
4. Informal and direct assessment measures are used to evaluate a student's progress throughout the vocational program.

When curriculum-based vocational assessment is used, information is available during all phases of the program (for example, making placement decisions, working in vocational classes and jobs, exiting the program). Also, the assessment provides information for helping teachers make instructional or program modifications and for planning future job placements.

Career-Related Instruction Activities

1. Invite students who have graduated recently to return to the school to discuss their jobs or problems in leaving secondary school for college, work, or military service. Selected students can be responsible for inviting alumni and for developing appropriate questions. The discussions should include positive aspects about their careers and how they handle problems they encounter on the job. If possible, interested members of the class should have the opportunity to observe the graduates actually working.
2. Plan field trips to visit businesses and industries and request personnel to speak with the students. A person from the business can be invited to speak to the class before or after the visit to answer questions or distribute information. During the trip, students should have enough time to observe persons performing various jobs and to record pertinent information about the job (such as job requirements, working conditions, good and bad features of the job). Students can share their observations in class discussions after the visit.
3. Divide the class into small groups and have each group obtain information on one particular job

per week. During group discussion the students can determine job responsibilities, identify personal and social values met through the work, and compile a list of words used on the job.
4. Have each student write a want ad for what she considers to be the perfect job. The ad should include information such as hours, salary, qualifications, responsibilities, and so on. Then have the students check the want-ad section of the newspaper to locate ads for jobs in their interest area and compare these ads with their ideal ad. If appropriate, students can contact personnel directors of various business establishments to find out the number of people recently hired, their salaries, and their qualifications. Also, visits may be arranged or volunteer or observation work can be set up with the business in which the student is most interested.
5. Cut out several newspaper ads for jobs available. Have each student choose a job from the given ads and state why she would want that particular job and what preparation and qualifications she must have. Then have the student complete an application form for that job. The completed application can be reviewed for improvement.
6. Role play interviews for various jobs. Discuss punctuality, appropriate dress, and questions to ask during the interview and acceptable responses. Role playing can build a student's self-confidence in an actual interview situation.

COMMERCIAL CAREER-RELATED INSTRUCTION PROGRAMS AND MATERIALS

Exploring Careers

Publisher: Opportunities for Learning

Description: This material, designed for students in fifth to twelfth grade, includes a 52-page spirit master book of student instructions and one or more worksheets for each activity. The student is guided in obtaining information to make successful career decisions through 16 career-related activities. The activities focus on specific careers, the relationship between careers and life-styles, and one's individual talents and preferences. A teacher's manual also is provided that lists teaching objectives, materials, and methods as well as discussion guides and related subjects for each activity.

Get Set for Work!

Publisher: Mafex Associates

Description: This material includes a teacher's handbook, a student activity book, and competency test records. The teacher's handbook includes 46 step-by-step daily lessons to guide the student in preparing for and getting a job. The following units are covered: (a) identifying and preparing for a job, (b) basic job facts, (c) personal factors affecting work, (d) steps that lead to a job, (e) application forms and related forms, and (f) summer employment. The student activity book includes tasks such as answering help–wanted-ad questions, working crossword puzzles, unscrambling sentences, and finding key words in job-related sentences. The competency test record evaluates the student's comprehension of the material and includes pre- and posttests and terminal objective records for each unit.

Me and Jobs

Publisher: Opportunities for Learning

Description: This program is designed to enable the student to discover and like herself and then to look at jobs in terms of her own unique abilities and needs. Self-awareness, job awareness, and job acquisition are featured in a set of five filmstrips: *What Do I Have That a Job Needs?, The Job Environment and Me, Want Ads, Application Forms,* and *Job Interview Skills.* These films can be used independently or along with a 96-page workbook divided into four sections: (a) *Me*—explores personal interests, assets, and opinions; (b) *Jobs*—focuses on various kinds of jobs and how to explore them; (c) *Me and Jobs*—fits personal abilities and interests into different jobs; and (d) *Applications and Interviews*—focuses on how to find and apply for a job. A teacher's manual is included in the program.

Vocational Entry-Skills for Secondary Students

Publisher: Academic Therapy

Description: This program consists of 45 teaching units and 70 student worksheets that focus on how to get a job and keep it. The teaching units supply short-term training in basic skills needed for entry into most kinds of beginning vocational classes and entry-level jobs. Topics include (a) vocational academics (for example, math, letter writing, telephone techniques), (b) vocational resources (for example, newspapers, social security), (c) vocational values (for example, grooming, getting along with others), (d) vocational preparation (for example, interviews, wages, taxes), and (e) basic job skills and hands-on training (for example, small office equipment, sorting, collating, filing). Students can work independently at their own pace and are checked for proficiency as each unit is completed.

COMPUTER SOFTWARE PROGRAMS IN CAREER-RELATED INSTRUCTION

Computerized Career Assessment and Planning Program

Distributor: Educational Activities

Hardware: Apple II, TRS-80

Description: These four programs are designed to help students in ninth through twelfth grade (a) determine their career interests, preferences, and abilities, (b) select and explore career clusters, (c) delineate and select relevant occupations, and (d) develop a plan to enter or prepare to enter the occupation of their choice. *Career Assessment* involves students in assessing their career interests and abilities and provides a printout of relevant career clusters. *Selecting Alternatives* allows students to determine what occupational characteristics are important to them and provides a list of occupations related to their characteristics and capabilities. In *Career Exploration,* students can review specific clusters and occupations to determine what capabilities and interests are required by each. *Career Planning* helps students develop plans to find a job, select a college, or select a vocational school. Each program takes about 40 minutes to complete and allows students to gain occupational knowledge while learning career decision-making skills.

TRANSITION INSTRUCTION

Educators are renewing emphasis on developing curriculums for promoting successful transitions from secondary settings. Whereas at one time transition curriculums referred simply to career and vocational training and job placement, recent efforts have expanded the concept of transition to include not only the transition of completing secondary school and moving into the community and work mainstream but also the transition issues and problems that occur when students drop out of school (Polloway et al., 1989).

Preparing students for transition or working with a student who is in the process of transition requires instruction in several areas. Brody-Hasazi, Salembier, and Finck (1983) identify six guidelines for evaluating transition efforts:

1. Use assessment procedures designed to identify functional skills and interests related to current and future employment interests and training opportunities.
2. Offer support services to enable students to enroll in regular vocational classes.
3. Include at least four work experiences, lasting from 6 to 8 weeks, in identified areas of interest and skill for students between the ages of 15 and 18.
4. Help students locate and secure employment before graduation.
5. Supervise and follow up students in full- or part-time jobs until graduation or the student's 22nd birthday.
6. Develop transition plans that involve appropriate adult service agencies for students who need continued service following graduation.

Research on the transition problems of students with learning difficulties provides helpful information related to additional curriculum decisions. Polloway et al. (1989) argue that curriculum development at the secondary level should focus on adult outcomes in the areas of life domains (for example, community involvement, vocation/education, home and family, recreation/leisure) and support domains (for example, emotional/physical health, personal development). Many of the demands discussed earlier in this chapter serve as the basis for selecting the types of curriculums that prepare a student directly for the transition experience. While competence in several basic skills and task-completion strategies is required, particular importance should be placed on goal setting and social skills.

Jason and Burrows (1983) investigated the efficacy of teaching generic skills related to coping with transition issues to a group of normally achieving secondary school seniors. They found that students trained in a set of adaptive coping responses (for example, problem-solving, relaxation techniques, and cognitive restructuring) outperformed a nontrained group in the amount of situation-related restructuring statements. Building on this research and the research on the goal setting, self-regulation/self-control, and problem-solving deficits of adolescents with learning difficulties, Schumaker et al. (1985) developed a Life-Planning Program that consists of activities that enable students to learn a process of problem solving, goal setting, and goal implementation. Students are taught to apply this process to their own lives in career/educational plans, independent living situations, and social interactions. The following specific steps give students a process for setting goals and solving problems:

1. Define the problem.
2. Generate alternatives.
3. Evaluate each alternative.
4. Decide on the best alternative.

5. Formulate a goal and complete a task analysis to determine subgoals.
6. Complete a task analysis on the subgoal.
7. Write a contract for subgoal completion.
8. Implement tasks for the subgoal and self-record performance.
9. Evaluate outcome.
10. Revise the contract or reward self.

Mentors are assigned to students as they approach graduation to help ensure a smooth transition from school to postsecondary settings. A more detailed description of the mentor aspects of this program is provided by Moccia, Schumaker, Hazel, Vernon, and Deshler (1989).

Zigmond (1990) also provides recommendations for establishing a transition curriculum. She recommends that part of the transition curriculum should provide information, support, and guidance to students with learning difficulties who plan to go to college. Moreover, she notes that the benefits of vocational training programs have been minimal for students with learning problems.

Community-based support services are an important aspect of successful transitions. Unfortunately, when students exit school, they face a confusing array of human service agencies and programs (Kerr, Nelson, & Lambert, 1987). These agencies have overlapping services, different eligibility criteria, and a variety of politically based turf issues. Edgar, Webb, and Maddox (1987) report that a major problem is that no one agency is responsible for the coordination or supervision of transition services.

REFERENCES

Adelman, H. S., & Taylor, L. (1983). Enhancing motivation for overcoming learning and behavior problems. *Journal of Learning Disabilities, 16,* 384–392.

Alley, G. R., & Deshler, D. D. (1979). *Teaching the learning disabled adolescent: Strategies and methods.* Denver: Love.

Alley, G. R., & Hori, A. K. O. (1981). *Effects of teaching a questioning strategy on reading comprehension of learning disabled adolescents* (Research Report No. 52). Lawrence, KS: University of Kansas Institute for Research in Learning Disabilities.

Anders, P. L., & Bos, C. S. (1984). In the beginning: Vocabulary instruction in content classrooms. *Topics in Learning and Learning Disabilities, 3*(4), 53–65.

Archer, A., & Gleason, M. (1992). *Advanced skills for school success.* North Billerica, MA: Curriculum Associates.

Armbruster, B. B., & Anderson, T. H. (1984). *Producing "considerate" expository text: Or easy reading is damned hard writing* (Reading Education Report No. 46). Urbana: University of Illinois, Center for the Study of Reading.

Austin, J. D. (1979). Homework research in mathematics. *School Science and Mathematics, 79,* 115–121.

Becker, R. L. (1988). *Reading-Free Vocational Interest Inventory—Revised.* Columbus, OH: Elbern.

Beech, M. C. (1983). Simplifying text for mainstreamed students. *Journal of Learning Disabilities, 16,* 400–402.

Bender, M., & Valletutti, P. J. (1982). *Teaching functional academics: A curriculum guide for adolescents and adults with learning problems.* Baltimore, MD: University Park Press.

Bergerud, D., Lovitt, T. C., & Horton, S. (1988). The effectiveness of textbook adaptations in life science for high school students with learning disabilities. *Journal of Learning Disabilities, 21,* 70–76.

Bos, C. S., & Anders, P. L. (1987). Semantic feature analysis: An interactive teaching strategy for facilitating learning from text. *Learning Disability Focus, 3*(1), 55–59.

Breuning, S., & Regan, J. (1978). Teaching regular class materials to special education students. *Exceptional Children, 3,* 180–187.

Brigance, A. H. (1980). *Brigance Diagnostic Inventory of Essential Skills.* North Billerica, MA: Curriculum Associates.

Brody-Hasazi, S., Salembier, G., & Finck, K. (1983). Directions for the 80's: Vocational preparation for secondary mildly handicapped students. *Teaching Exceptional Children, 15,* 206–209.

Brolin, D. (1989). *Life centered career education: A competency based approach* (3rd ed.). Reston, VA: Council for Exceptional Children.

Buchwach, L. (1980). Child service demonstration center for secondary students with learning disabilities. In R. H. Riegel & J. P. Mathey (Eds.), *Mainstreaming at the secondary level: Seven models that work.* Plymouth, MI: Wayne County Intermediate School District.

Bulgren, J. A., Schumaker, J. B., & Deshler, D. D. (1988). Effectiveness of a concept teaching routine in enhancing the performance of LD students in secondary-level mainstream classes. *Learning Disability Quarterly, 11,* 3–17.

Carlson, S. A. (1981). *Patterns and trends within exemplary special education programs in the secondary grades.* Washington, DC: National Association of State Directors of Special Education, Project FORUM.

Carlson, S. A. (1985). The ethical appropriateness of subject-matter tutoring for learning disabled adolescents. *Learning Disability Quarterly, 8,* 310–314.

Carman, R. A., & Adams, W. R. (1972). *Study skills: A student's guide for survival.* New York: Wiley.

Cegelka, P. T. (1985). Career and vocational education. In W. H. Berdine & A. E. Blackhurst (Eds.), *An introduction to special education* (2nd ed., pp. 573–612). Boston: Little, Brown.

Clark, C. M., & Peterson, P. L. (1986). Teachers' thought processes. In M. C. Wittrock (Ed.), *Handbook of research on teaching.* New York: Macmillan.

Coleman, J. S., Hoffer, T., & Kilgore, S. (1981). *Public and private schools.* Washington, DC: U.S. Department of Education.

Coleman, L. J. (1979, April). *Translating curriculum materials at the secondary level for mainstreaming students.* Paper presented at the Council for Exceptional Children Convention, Dallas.

Cunningham, P. M., & Cunningham, J. W. (1976, December). Improving listening in content area subjects. *NASSP Bulletin,* pp. 26–31.

Cuthbertson, E. (1978). *An analysis of secondary testing and grading procedures.* Unpublished master's thesis, University of Kansas, Lawrence.

Dembrowsky, C. (1980). Synergistic education: A comprehensive plan for learning disabled adolescents. In R. H. Riegel & J. P. Mathey (Eds.), *Mainstreaming at the secondary level: Seven models that work.* Plymouth, MI: Wayne County Intermediate School District.

Deshler, D. D., Alley, G. R., Warner, M. M., & Schumaker, J. B. (1981). Instructional practices for promoting skill acquisition and generalization in severely learning disabled adolescents. *Learning Disability Quarterly, 4,* 415–421.

Deshler, D. D., & Lenz, B. K. (1989). The strategies instructional approach. *International Journal of Learning Disability, Development and Education, 36*(3), 203–224.

Deshler, D. D., & Schumaker, J. B. (1983). Social skills of learning disabled adolescents: A review of characteristics and intervention. *Topics in Learning and Learning Disabilities, 3,* 15–23.

Deshler, D. D., & Schumaker, J. B. (1986). Learning strategies: An instructional alternative for low-achieving adolescents. *Exceptional Children, 52,* 583–590.

Deshler, D. D., & Schumaker, J. B. (1988). An instructional model for teaching students how to learn. In J. L. Graden, J. E. Zins, & M. J. Curtis (Eds.), *Alternative educational delivery systems: Enhancing instructional options for all students* (pp. 391–411). Washington, DC: National Association of School Psychologists.

Deshler, D. D., Schumaker, J. B., & Lenz, B. K. (1984). Academic and cognitive interventions for LD adolescents: Part I. *Journal of Learning Disabilities, 17,* 108–117.

Deshler, D. D., Schumaker, J. B., Lenz, B. K., & Ellis, E. S. (1984). Academic and cognitive interventions for LD adolescents: Part II. *Journal of Learning Disabilities, 17,* 170–179.

Devine, T. (1981). *Teaching study skills.* Boston: Allyn & Bacon.

Dexter, B. L. (1982). Helping learning disabled students prepare for college. *Journal of Learning Disabilities, 15,* 344–346.

Edgar, E., Webb, S., & Maddox, M. (1987). Issues in transition: Transfer of youth from correctional facilities to public schools. In C. M. Nelson, R. B. Rutherford, Jr., & B. I. Wolford (Eds.), *Special education in the criminal justice system*. New York: Merrill/Macmillan.

Edwards, P. (1973). Panorama: A study technique. *Journal of Reading, 17*, 132–135.

Ellis, E. S. (1991). *SLANT: A starter strategy for class participation*. Lawrence, KS: Edge Enterprises.

Ellis, E. S., Deshler, D. D., Lenz, B. K., Schumaker, J. B., & Clark, F. L. (1991). An instructional model for teaching learning strategies. *Focus on Exceptional Children, 24*(1), 1–14.

Ellis, E. S., & Friend, P. (1991). Adolescents with learning disabilities. In B. Y. L. Wong (Ed.), *Learning about learning disabilities* (pp. 505–561). San Diego, CA: Academic Press.

Ellis, E. S., & Lenz, B. K. (1987). A component analysis of effective learning strategies for LD students. *Learning Disabilities Focus, 2*(2), 94–107.

Ellis, E. S., & Lenz, B. K. (1990). Techniques for mediating content-area learning: Issues and research. *Focus on Exceptional Children, 22*(9), 1–16.

Ellis, E. S., & Lenz, B. K. (in press). *TACTIC: Developing learning strategy interventions*. Lawrence, KS: Edge Enterprises.

Ellis, E. S., Lenz, B. K., & Sabornie, E. J. (1987a). Generalization and adaptation of learning strategies to natural environments: Part 1 —Critical agents. *Remedial and Special Education, 8*(1), 6–21.

Ellis, E. S., Lenz, B. K., & Sabornie, E. J. (1987b). Generalization and adaptation of learning strategies to natural environments: Part 2 — Research into practice. *Remedial and Special Education. 8*(2), 6–24.

Flavell, J. (1976). Metacognitive aspects of problem solving. In R. Resnick (Ed.), *The nature of intelligence*. Hillsdale, NJ: Erlbaum.

Fourqurean, J. M., & LaCourt, T. (1990). A follow-up study of former special education students: A model for program evaluation. *Remedial and Special Education, 12*(1), 16–23.

Fredrick, W. C., & Walberg, H. J. (1980). Learning as a function of time. *The Journal of Educational Research, 73*, 183–204.

Hamilton, S. F. (1986). Excellence and the transition from school to work. *Phi Delta Kappan, 68*(4), 239–242.

Harnischfeger, A. (1980). Curricular control and learning time: District policy, teacher strategy, and pupil choice. *Educational Evaluation and Policy Analysis, 2*(6), 19–30.

Harrington, T. F., & O'Shea, A. J. (1992). *Career Decision-Making System—Revised*. Circle Pines, MN: American Guidance Service.

Hughes, C. A., Hendrickson, J. M., & Hudson, P. J. (1986). The pause procedure: Improving factual recall from lectures by low and high achieving middle school students. *International Journal of Instructional Media, 13*(3), 217–226.

Jason, L. A., & Burrows, B. (1983). Transition training for high school seniors. *Cognitive Therapy, 7*, 79–92.

Johnson, D. W., & Johnson, R. T. (1986). Mainstreaming and cooperative learning strategies. *Exceptional Children, 52*, 553–561.

Johnson, R., & Vardian, E. R. (1973). Reading, readability, and the social studies. *The Reading Teacher, 26*, 483–488.

Keith, T. Z., & Page, E. B. (1985). Homework works at school: National evidence for policy changes. *School Psychology Review, 14*, 351–359.

Kerr, M. M., & Nelson, C. M. (1989). *Strategies for managing behavior problems in the classroom* (2nd ed.). New York: Merrill/Macmillan.

Kerr, M. M., Nelson, C. M., & Lambert, D. L. (1987). *Helping adolescents with learning and behavior problems*. New York: Merrill/Macmillan.

Knowlton, E. K. (1983). *Secondary regular classroom teachers' expectations of learning disabled students* (Research Report No. 75). Lawrence, KS: University of Kansas Institute for Research in Learning Disabilities.

Kokaska, C. J., & Brolin, D. E. (1985). *Career education for handicapped individuals* (2nd ed.). New York: Merrill/Macmillan.

Laurie, T. E., Buchwach, L., Silverman, R., & Zigmond, N. (1978). Teaching secondary learning disabled students in the mainstream. *Learning Disability Quarterly, 1*(4), 62–72.

Lenz, B. K. (1982). *The effect of advance organizers on the learning and retention of learning disabled adolescents within the context of a cooperative planning model.* Unpublished dissertation, University of Kansas, Lawrence.

Lenz, B. K., & Bulgren, J. A. (1988). *Issues related to enhancing content acquisition for students with learning disabilities.* Lawrence, KS: University of Kansas Institute for Research in Learning Disabilities.

Lenz, B. K., Clark, F.L., Deshler, D. D., Schumaker, J. B., & Rademacher, J. A. (Eds.), (1990). *SIM training library: The strategies instructional approach.* Lawrence, KS: University of Kansas Institute for Research in Learning Disabilities.

Lenz, B. K., Deshler, D. D., & Schumaker, J. B. (1991). *Barriers to the planning of instruction for learning disabled adolescents in the regular classroom setting* (Progress report: The development and validation of planning routines to enhance the delivery of content to students with handicaps in general education settings). Washington, DC: U.S. Department of Education.

Lenz, B. K., Ehren, B. J., & Smiley, L. R. (1991). A goal attainment approach to improve completion of project-type assignments by learning disabled adolescents. *Focus on Learning Disabilities, 6,* 166–176.

Lenz, B. K., & Mellard, D. P. (1990). Content area skill assessment. In R. A. Gable & J. M. Hendrickson (Eds.), *Error patterns in academics: Identification and remediation* (pp. 117–145). White Plains, NY: Longman.

Levin, E. K., Zigmond, N., & Birch, J. W. (1985). A follow-up study of 52 learning disabled adolescents. *Journal of Learning Disabilities, 18,* 2–7.

Link, D. B. (1980). *Essential learning skills and the low-achieving student at the secondary level: A rating of the importance of 24 academic abilities.* Unpublished master's thesis, University of Kansas, Lawrence.

Manzo, A. V. (1969). The ReQuest procedure. *Journal of Reading, 13,* 123–126.

Manzo, A. V. (1975). Guided reading procedure. *Journal of Reading, 7,* 287–291.

Marland, S. P., Jr. (1972). Career education: Every student headed for a goal. *American Vocational Journal, 47*(3), 34–36, 62.

Marsh, G. E., II, & Price, B. J. (1980). *Methods for teaching the mildly handicapped adolescent.* Saint Louis, MO: C. V. Mosby.

Marsh, G. E., II, Price, B. J., & Smith, T. E. C. (1983). *Teaching mildly handicapped children: Methods and materials.* New York: Merrill/Macmillan.

Mastropieri, M. A., Scruggs, T. E., McLoone, B., & Levin, J. R. (1985). Facilitating learning disabled students' acquisition of science classifications. *Learning Disabilities Quarterly, 8,* 299–309.

Mathews, R. M., Whang, P. L., & Fawcett, S. B. (1980). Development and validation of an occupational assessment instrument. *Behavioral Assessment, 2,* 71–85.

Meichenbaum, D. (1975). Self-instructional methods. In F. Kanter & A. Goldstein (Eds.), *Helping people change.* New York: Pergamon Press.

Meyen, E. L., Alley, G. R., Scannell, D. P., Harnden, G. M., & Miller, K. F. (1982). *A mandated minimum competency testing program and its impact on learning disabled students: Curricular validity and comparative performance* (Research Report No. 63). Lawrence, KS: University of Kansas Institute for Research in Learning Disabilities.

Meyen, E. L., & Lehr, D. H. (1980). Evolving practices in assessment and intervention for mildly-handicapped adolescents: The case for intensive instruction. *Exceptional Education Quarterly, 1*(2), 19–26.

Mithaug, D., Horiuchi, C., & Fanning, P. (1985). A report of the Colorado statewide follow-up survey of special education students. *Exceptional Children, 51,* 397–404.

Moccia, R. E., Schumaker, J. B., Hazel, J. S., Vernon, S., & Deshler, D. D. (1989). A mentor program for facilitating the life transitions of individuals who have handicapping conditions. *Journal of Reading, Writing, and Learning Disabilities, 5*(2), 177–195.

Moran, M. R. (1980). *An investigation of the demands on oral language skills of learning disabled students in secondary classrooms* (Research Report No. 1). Lawrence, KS: University of Kansas Institute for Research in Learning Disabilities.

Moran, M. R., & DeLoache, T. F. (1982). *Mainstream teachers' responses to formal features of writing by secondary learning disabled students* (Research Report No. 61). Lawrence, KS: University of Kansas Institute for Research in Learning Disabilities.

Moran, M. R., Schumaker, J. B., & Vetter, A. F. (1981). *Teaching a paragraph organization strategy to learning disabled adolescents* (Research Report No. 54). Lawrence, KS: University of Kansas Institute for Research in Learning Disabilities.

Mori, A. A. (1980). Career education for the learning disabled—Where are we now? *Learning Disability Quarterly, 3*(1), 91–101.

Nagel, D. R., Schumaker, J. B., & Deshler, D. D. (1986). *The learning strategies curriculum: The FIRST-letter mnemonic strategy.* Lawrence, KS: Edge Enterprises.

Naslund, R. A., Thorpe, L. P., & Lefever, D. W. (1985). *SRA Achievement Series.* Chicago: Science Research Associates.

Natriello, G., McDill, E. L., & Pallas, A. M. (1985). School reform and potential dropouts. *Educational Leadership, 43*(1), 10–14.

Ogden, C. K. (1970). *The general basic English dictionary.* London: Evans Brothers.

Page, E. B., & Keith, T. Z. (1981). Effects of U.S. private schools: A technical analysis of two recent claims. *Educational Researcher, 10*(7), 7–17.

Parker, R. M. (1991). *Occupational Aptitude Survey and Interest Schedule—2.* Austin, TX: Pro-Ed.

Pauk, W. (1978). A notetaking format: Magical but not automatic. *Reading World, 17,* 96–97.

Polachek, S. W., Kniesner, T. J., & Harwood, H. J. (1978). Education production functions. *Journal of Educational Statistics, 3,* 209–231.

Polloway, E. A., Epstein, M. H., Polloway, C. H., Patton, J. R., & Ball, D. W. (1986). Corrective Reading Program: An analysis of effectiveness with learning disabled and mentally retarded children. *Remedial and Special Education, 7*(4), 41–47.

Polloway, E. A., Patton, J. R., Epstein, M. H., & Smith, T. E. (1989). Comprehensive curriculum for students with mild handicaps. *Focus on Exceptional Children, 21*(8), 1–12.

Powell, L., Suzuki, K., Atwater, J., Gorney-Krupsaw, B., & Morris, E. K. (1981). *Interactions between teachers and learning disabled and non-learning disabled students* (Research Report No. 44). Lawrence, KS: University of Kansas Institute for Research in Learning Disabilities.

Riegel, R. H., & Mathey, J. P. (Eds.). (1980). *Mainstreaming at the secondary level: Seven models that work.* Plymouth, MI: Wayne County Intermediate School District.

Robinson, F. P. (1961). *Effective study.* New York: Harper and Brothers.

Robinson, H. A. (1978). *Teaching reading and study strategies: The content areas* (2nd ed.). Boston: Allyn & Bacon.

Roe, B. D., Stoodt, B. D., & Burns, P. C. (1987). *Secondary school reading instruction: The content areas* (3rd ed.). Boston: Houghton Mifflin.

Rumberger, R. W. (1987). High school dropouts: A review of issues and evidence. *Review of Educational Research, 57,* 101–121.

Russell, D. H., & Karp, E. E. (1951). *Reading aids through the grades: Three hundred developmental reading activities.* New York: Teachers College Press, Columbia University.

Saski, J., Swicegood, P., & Carter, J. (1983). Notetaking formats for learning disabled adolescents. *Learning Disability Quarterly, 6*(3), 265–272.

Scannell, D. P. (1986). *Tests of Achievement and Proficiency.* Chicago: Riverside.

Schloss, P. J., Smith, M. A., & Schloss, C. N. (1990). *Instructional methods for adolescents with learning and behavior problems.* Boston: Allyn & Bacon.

Schmid, R., Algozzine, B., Wells, D., & Stoller, L. (1980). *Final report: The national secondary school survey.* Unpublished manuscript, University of Florida, Gainesville.

Schulz, J. B., & Turnbull, A. P. (1983). *Mainstreaming handicapped students: A guide for classroom teachers* (2nd ed.). Boston: Allyn & Bacon.

Schumaker, J. B., & Deshler, D. D. (1984). Setting demand variables: A major factor in program planning for the LD adolescent. *Topics in Language Disorders, 4*(2), 22–40.

Schumaker, J. B., & Deshler, D. D. (1988). Implementing the regular education initiative in secondary schools: A different ball game. *Journal of Learning Disabilities, 21*(1), 36–42.

Schumaker, J. B., Deshler, D. D., Alley, G. R., & Warner, M. M. (1983). Toward the development of an intervention model for learning disabled adolescents: The University of Kansas Institute. *Exceptional Education Quarterly, 4,* 45–74.

Schumaker, J. B., Deshler, D. D., Alley, G. R., Warner, M. M., & Denton, P. H. (1982). Multipass: A learning strategy for improving reading comprehension. *Learning Disability Quarterly, 5*(3), 295–304.

Schumaker, J. B., Deshler, D. D., & Ellis, E. S. (1986). Intervention issues related to the education of LD adolescents. In J. K. Torgesen & B. Y. L. Wong (Eds.), *Learning disabilities: Some new perspectives.* New York: Academic Press.

Schumaker, J. B., Deshler, D. D., & McKnight, P. C. (1991). Teaching routines for content areas at the secondary level. In G. Stover, M. R. Shinn, & H. M. Walker (Eds.), *Interventions for achievement and behavior problems.* Washington, DC: National Association of School Psychologists.

Schumaker, J. B., Deshler, D. D., Nolan, S., Clark, F. L., Alley, G. R., & Warner, M. M. (1981). *Error monitoring: A learning strategy for improving academic performance of LD adolescents* (Research Report No. 32). Lawrence, KS: University of Kansas Institute for Research in Learning Disabilities.

Schumaker, J. B., & Hazel, J. S. (1984). Social skills assessment and training for the learning disabled: Who's on first and what's on second? Part 1. *Journal of Learning Disabilities, 17,* 422–431.

Schumaker, J. B., Hazel, J. S., & Deshler, D. D. (1985, October). A model for facilitating postsecondary transitions. *Techniques: A Journal for Remedial Education and Counseling, 1,* 437–446.

Schumaker, J. B., Hazel, J. S., & Pederson, C. S. (1988). *Social skills for daily living.* Circle Pines, MN: American Guidance Service.

Schumaker, J. B., Sheldon-Wildgen, J., & Sherman, J. A. (1980). *An observational study of the academic and social behaviors of learning disabled adolescents in the regular classroom* (Research Report No. 22). Lawrence, KS: University of Kansas Institute for Research in Learning Disabilities.

Seabaugh, G. O., & Schumaker, J. B. (1981). *The effects of self-regulation training on the academic productivity of LD and NLD adolescents* (Research Report No. 37). Lawrence, KS: University of Kansas Institute for Research in Learning Disabilities.

Siegel, S., & Gaylord-Ross, R. (1991). Factors associated with employment success among youths with learning disabilities. *Journal of Learning Disabilities, 24,* 40–47.

Silverman, R., Zigmond, N., & Sansone, J. (1981). Teaching coping skills to adolescents with learning problems. *Focus on Exceptional Children, 13*(6), 1–20.

Smith, D. D. (1981). *Teaching the learning disabled.* Englewood Cliffs, NJ: Prentice-Hall.

Strong, E. K., & Campbell, D. P. (1985). *Strong-Campbell Interest Inventory.* Stanford, CA: Stanford University Press.

Towle, M. (1982). Learning how to be a student when you have a learning disability. *Journal of Learning Disabilities, 15,* 90–93.

U.S. Department of Labor, Department of Education, & Department of Commerce. (1988). *Building a quality workforce.* Washington, DC: U.S. Government Printing Office.

U.S. Office of Education. (1971). *USOE career clusters.* Washington, DC: U.S. Government Printing Office.

Van Reusen, A. K., Bos, C., Schumaker, J. B., & Deshler, D. D. (1987). *Motivation strategies curriculum: The education planning strategy.* Lawrence, KS: Edge Enterprises.

Walberg, H. J. (1984). Improving the productivity of America's schools. *Educational Leadership, 41*(8), 19–30.

Wang, M. C., Rubenstein, J. L., & Reynolds, M. C. (1985). Clearing the road to success for students with special needs. *Educational Leadership, 43*(1), 62–67.

Wells, D., Schmid, R., Algozzine, B., & Maher, M. (1983). Teaching LD adolescents: A study of selected teacher and teaching characteristics. *Teacher Education and Special Education, 6,* 227–234.

Wiederholt, J. L., & Wolffe, K. E. (1990). Preparing problem learners for independent living. In D. D. Hammill & N. R. Bartel, *Teaching students with learning and behavior problems* (5th ed., pp. 451–501). Boston: Allyn & Bacon.

Wiseman, D. E. (1980). The parallel alternative curriculum for secondary classrooms. In R. H. Riegel & J. P. Mathey (Eds.), *Mainstreaming at the secondary level: Seven models that work.* Plymouth, MI: Wayne County Intermediate School District.

Woodcock, R. W., & Johnson, M. B. (1989). *Woodcock-Johnson Psycho-Educational Battery—Revised.* Allen, TX: DLM.

Zigmond, N. (1978, May). *A program of comprehensive service for secondary students with learning disabilities.* Paper presented at the meeting of the 56th Annual International Council for Exceptional Children Convention, Kansas City, MO.

Zigmond, N. (1990). Rethinking secondary school programs for students with learning disabilities. *Focus on Exceptional Children, 23*(1), 1–24.

Zigmond, N., & Brownlee, J. (1980). Social skills training for adolescents with learning disabilities. *Exceptional Education Quarterly, 1,* 77–83.

Zigmond, N., Sansone, J., Miller, S. E., Donahoe, K. A., & Kohnke, R. (1986). Teaching learning disabled students at the secondary school level: What research says to teachers. *Learning Disabilities Focus, 1*(2), 108–115.

Scope and Sequence Skills Lists

Math Scope and Sequence Skills List[1]

By Skill Area

ADDITION HIERARCHY

Recognizes inequalities of numbers less than 10.
Understands seriation of numbers less than 10.
Recognizes the words *addend* and *sum.*
Understands the "+" sign.
Computes sums less than 10 (memorize).
Understands place value of ones and tens.
Computes sums 10–18, both addends less than 10 (memorize).
Computes 2D + 1D without regrouping.
Computes 2D + 2D without regrouping.

Understands place value concerning regrouping tens and ones.
Computes 2D + 1D with regrouping.
Computes 2D + 2D with regrouping.
Computes 2D + 2D + 2D with sums of ones greater than 20.
Understands place value of hundreds, tens, and ones.
Computes 3D + 3D without regrouping.
Understands place value concerning regrouping hundreds and tens.
Computes 3D + 3D with regrouping.
Estimates sums.

SUBTRACTION HIERARCHY

Finds missing addends (e.g., 4 + __ = 9).
Understands the "−" sign.
Uses set separation as model for subtraction.

---

[1]Key:
    1D = one-digit number   < = less than
    2D = two-digit number   > = more than
    3D = three-digit number ≤ = less than or equal to

Expresses a related addition statement in subtraction form (e.g., addend + *addend* = sum ↔ sum − *addend* = addend).

Relates the words *minuend, subtrahend,* and *difference* to *sum, given addend,* and *missing addend.*

Memorizes basic subtraction facts 0–9.

Understands place value of ones and tens.

Memorizes basic subtraction facts 0–18.

Names the difference between a two-place whole number (2D) and a one-place whole number (1D) (not a basic fact and no regrouping).

Names the difference between 2D and 2D with no regrouping.

Names the difference between 3D and 2D with no regrouping.

Names the difference between 3D and 3D with no regrouping.

Names the difference between two many-digit whole numbers with no regrouping.

Names the difference between 2D and 1D (not a basic fact) with regrouping.

Names the difference between 2D and 2D with regrouping from tens to ones.

Names the difference between 3D and 2D with regrouping from tens to ones.

Names the difference between 3D and 2D with double regrouping.

Names the difference between 3D and 3D with single regrouping.

Names the difference between 3D and 3D with double regrouping.

Names the difference between two many-place whole numbers with several regroupings.

Names the difference when a zero appears in a single place in the minuend.

Names the difference when zeros appear in the tens and ones place of the minuend.

Estimates differences.

MULTIPLICATION HIERARCHY

Recognizes sets as a model for multiplication (number of sets and number of objects in each set).

Recognizes and uses arrays as a model for multiplication; for example,

```
          2
  ×     ×
  ×     ×     3
  ×     ×
```

Understands the words *factor* and *product.*

Understands the "×" sign.

Understands the commutative property of multiplication; for example, $a \times (b + c) = (a \times b) + (a \times c)$ [$a \leq 5, b \leq 5$].

Memorizes basic multiplication facts for $a \times b$ ($a \leq 5, b \leq 5$).

Memorizes basic multiplication facts for $a \times b$ ($5 < a < 10, b < 10$).

Names the product if one factor is 10, 100, etc.

Expands the basic multiplication facts (e.g., 4×3 to 4×30).

Computes 2D × 1D without regrouping.

Understands place value of tens, ones, regrouping.

Computes $a \times (b + c) = (a \times b) + (a \times c)$ [$a < 10, a \times (b + c) < 100$ with regrouping] (e.g., $6 \times (10 + 3) = \_\_ + \_\_ = \_\_$).

Computes 2D × 1D with regrouping, product < 100.

Understands place value of hundreds, tens, ones.

Computes 2D × 1D with regrouping, product < 100.

Computes 2D × 2D with regrouping.

Computes 3D × 1D with regrouping.

Computes 3D × 2D with regrouping.

DIVISION HIERARCHY

Finds missing factor (e.g., $6 \times \_\_ = 36$).

Uses symbols that indicate division ($2\overline{)6}, 6 \div 2, \%$).

Expresses a related multiplication sentence as a division sentence (product ÷ factor = factor).

Computes division facts with 1 as divisor (e.g., $1\overline{)6}$).

Computes basic division facts ($a \div b$ where $a \leq 81, b \leq 9$).

Computes division of a nonzero number by itself (e.g., $12\overline{)12}$).

Computes 1D ÷ 1D with a remainder.

Estimates 2D ÷ 1D and computes 2D ÷ 1D with a remainder.

Computes quotients with expanding dividend (e.g., $3\overline{)9}, 3\overline{)90}, 3\overline{)900}$).

Estimates 3D ÷ 1D and computes 3D ÷ 1D (e.g., $6\overline{)747}$).

Computes quotient of many-place dividend with a one-place divisor (e.g., $4\overline{)78,743}$).

Estimates 3D ÷ 2D and computes 3D ÷ 2D where divisor is multiple of 10 (e.g., $20\overline{)684}$).

Computes quotient with divisors of 100, 1,000, etc. (e.g., $1,000 \overline{)6,897}$).

Estimates 3D ÷ 2D and computes 3D ÷ 2D (e.g., $17 \overline{)489}$).

Computes quotient of many-place dividend and many-place divisor (e.g., $3,897 \overline{)487,876}$).

FRACTION HIERARCHY

Readiness Areas

Separates regions into subregions that are equivalent.

Expresses 1 in many different ways.

Uses the terms *fraction, fraction bar, numerator,* and *denominator.*

Models, on the number line, equivalent fractions.

Generates sets of equivalent fractions.

Renames fractions in simplest form.

Rewrites improper fractions as mixed numerals.

Rewrites mixed numerals as improper fractions.

Develops concept of least common denominator using the concept of least common multiple.

Compares fractional numbers.

Develops concept of least common denominator using the concept of greatest common factor.

Addition

Computes sums less than 1, same denominator.

Computes sums of mixed numerals, no regrouping, same denominator.

Computes sums between 1 and 2, same denominator, regrouping.

Computes sums of mixed numeral and nonunit fraction, regrouping, same denominator (e.g., $3\frac{2}{5} + \frac{4}{5}$).

Computes sums of mixed numerals with regrouping, same denominator (e.g., $8\frac{3}{5} + 2\frac{4}{5}$).

Computes sums less than 1, different denominators.

Computes sums of mixed numerals, no regrouping, different denominators.

Computes sums of mixed numerals, regrouping, different denominators.

Computes sums of three nonunit fractions, different denominators.

Solves word problems requiring addition of fractions.

Subtraction

Computes differences between two fractions with like denominators without regrouping, then with regrouping.

Computes differences between two fractions with unlike but related denominators without regrouping, then with regrouping.

Computes differences between two fractions with unlike and unrelated denominators without regrouping, then with regrouping.

Solves word problems requiring subtraction of fractions.

Multiplication

Computes product of whole number × unit fraction, product < 1 (e.g., $3 \times \frac{1}{4} = $ ___).

Computes product of whole number × nonunit fraction, product < 1 (e.g., $2 \times \frac{2}{5} = $ ___).

Gives fraction names for one (e.g., $1 = \frac{2}{7}$).

Solves regrouping problem by writing fraction as mixed numeral, $1 < a < 2$ (e.g., $\frac{7}{5} = $ ___).

Computes product of whole number × nonunit fraction, $1 < $ product $ < 2$ (e.g., $3 \times \frac{3}{5} = $ ___).

Computes product of unit fraction × unit fraction (e.g., $\frac{1}{3} \times \frac{1}{4} = $ ___).

Computes product of nonunit fraction × nonunit fraction (e.g., $\frac{2}{3} \times \frac{4}{5} = $ ___).

Computes $a \times (b + c) = (a \times b) + (a \times c)$, a and b are whole numbers, c is a unit fraction, no regrouping (e.g., $3 \times (2 + \frac{1}{4}) = $ ___ + ___).

Computes $a \times (b + c) = (a \times b) + (a \times c)$, a and b are whole numbers, c is a nonunit fraction, regrouping (e.g., $4 \times 3\frac{2}{5} = 4 \times (3 + \frac{2}{5})$ = ___ + ___ = ___).

Computes product of nonunit fraction × mixed numeral using improper fractions—e.g., $\frac{5}{6} \times 2\frac{1}{3}$ (change to improper fractions).

Computes product of mixed numeral × mixed numeral using improper fractions—e.g., $3\frac{3}{4} \times 1\frac{7}{8}$ (use improper fractions).

Division

Computes quotient of 1 ÷ unit fraction (e.g., $1 \div \frac{1}{5}$).

Computes quotient of whole number ÷ nonunit fraction: $1 < $ whole number < 10 —e.g., $2 \div \frac{3}{5}$ (use repeated subtraction and remainder as fractional part).

Computes $1/a \div 1/b$ where $a < b$ (common denominator approach) (e.g., $1/2 \div 1/3$).
Computes $a/b \div c/d$ (common denominator approach) (e.g., $3/5 \div 3/4$).
Computes quotient of two mixed numerals (common denominator approach) (e.g., $2\frac{1}{5} \div 1\frac{2}{3}$).

DECIMAL HIERARCHY

Readiness Areas

Generates decimal place value by rewriting fractions with denominators of powers of 10.
Recognizes decimal place value to millionths place.
Reads and writes rational numbers expressed as decimals.
Rewrites fractions as decimals.
Models rational numbers expressed as decimals using the number line.
Generates equivalent decimals by appending zeroes.

Addition

Names the sum of two rational numbers expressed as decimals having the same place value.
Names the sum of two rational numbers expressed as decimals having different place values.
Names the sum of more than two rational numbers expressed as decimals having different place values.
Solves word problems requiring addition of rational numbers expressed as decimals.

Subtraction

Names the difference between two rational numbers expressed as decimals having the same place value (without regrouping and with regrouping).
Names the difference between two rational numbers expressed as decimals having different place values (without regrouping and with regrouping).
Solves word problems requiring subtraction of rational numbers expressed as decimals.

Multiplication

Names the product of two rational numbers expressed as decimals when it is necessary to append zeroes to the left of a nonzero digit as decimal holders.
Names the product of more than two rational numbers expressed as decimals.
Solves word problems requiring multiplication of rational numbers expressed as decimals.

Division

Names the quotient of rational numbers expressed as decimals when the divisor is a whole number.
Names the quotient of any two rational numbers expressed as decimals by using the division algorithm.
Solves word problems requiring division of rational numbers expressed as decimals.

Percents

Interprets the symbol for percent (%) as a fraction and as a decimal.
Rewrites percents as decimals and fractions for percents less than 100% and then for percents equal to or greater than 100%.
Rewrites fractions or decimals as percents.
Solves word problems requiring percents.

MONEY HIERARCHY

Identifies coins.
Recognizes relative value of coins.
Makes change for amounts up to $1.00.
Recognizes and uses money notation.
Recognizes currency and makes change for currency.
Solves examples and word problems involving money.

TIME HIERARCHY

Relates the face of the clock with the number line through 12 for hours.
Relates the face of the clock with the number line through 60 for minutes.
Tells time by the hour.
Tells time by the minute.
Understands the difference between A.M. and P.M.
Solves examples and word problems involving time.

MEASUREMENT HIERARCHY

Linear

Uses a straightedge of arbitrary length to measure an object.

Makes a ruler of at least 12″ with 1″ markings.

Uses an inch-marked ruler to measure items.

Recognizes that 12″ measure the same length as 1 foot.

Identifies measurements of objects that are less than, greater than, or equal to 1 foot.

Introduces the symbols for inches and feet.

Makes a ruler with ½″ and ¼″ markings to measure objects.

Uses a ruler with ½″ and ¼″ markings to measure objects.

Estimates heights and lengths in feet and inches.

Recognizes and relates inch, foot, yard, and mile.

Solves examples involving denominate numbers related to linear measurement.

Solves word problems applying the concepts of linear measurement.

Recognizes metric units and relates them to one another.

Liquid and Dry

Recognizes relationships between and relative values of cup, pint, quart, half-gallon, and gallon.

Recognizes metric units and relates them to one another.

Solves examples involving denominate numbers related to liquid or dry measurements.

Solves word problems involving liquid measurement.

Weight

Compares relative weights of objects using a balance.

Recognizes relationships between and relative values of ounce, pound, and ton.

Weighs objects to nearest pound and ounce.

Uses the abbreviations *oz, lb,* and *T* in recording weights.

Recognizes metric units and relates them to one another.

Solves examples involving denominate numbers related to weight measurement.

Solves word problems involving weight measurements.

Note: Portions of this skills list were adapted from *Diagnosing Mathematical Difficulties* (pp. 262–267, 278–290) by R. G. Underhill, A. E. Uprichard, and J. W. Heddens, 1980. New York: Merrill/Macmillan. Adapted by permission.

Math Scope and Sequence Skills List

By Grade Level

KINDERGARTEN

Position concepts: above, below, in, out, on, off, left, right, top, bottom, middle, front, back.

Classification: identity, color, size, shape, pattern.

One-to-one: as many as, using tallies to count events or objects.

Comparing: more than, less than, same.

Counting: 0 to 5.

Ordinal numbers: first, second, third.

Geometry: box, ball, square, circle, triangle, rectangle, inside, outside.

Measurement: comparing larger, smaller, taller, shorter, longer, same length.

Time: daytime, nighttime, sequence, duration, clock, calendar.

Money: value of penny, identifying nickel and dime, reading price tags, determining if one has enough money.

Writing numerals: 0 to 10.

Combining sets: picture addition stories.

Sums to 5: picture addition stories.

Separating sets: picture subtraction stories.

GRADE 1

Numeration: numbers and values 1 to 10.

Matching and joining sets.

Sums to 6.

Addition properties: commutative property of addition, zero property.

Ordinal numbers: first to fifth.

Sums 7 to 10.

Families of facts: sum of 1, 2, 3, 4, 5, 6, 7, 8, 9 families (e.g., sum of 7 family is $0 + 7, 7 + 0, 6 + 1, 1 + 6, 5 + 2, 2 + 5, 3 + 4, 4 + 3$).

Addition sentences: completing, writing, and choosing.

Finding missing addends (e.g., $4 + \_\_ = 7$).

Subtracting from sums or minuends to 6.

Subtracting from sums or minuends to 10.

Subtraction sentences: completing, writing, and choosing.

Money: subtracting prices, determining how much money (pennies, nickels, dimes).

Numeration/place value: counting and writing tens and ones, recognizing numbers 10 to 90, order of numbers to 100.

Counting: one more than, less than, counting by 2s, 3s, 5s, and 10s, skip-counting.

Time: calendar, hour, half hour, quarter hour.

Sums 11 to 18.

Subtracting from sums or minuends 11 to 18.

Families of facts: sum of 11-to-18 families.

Adding three addends.

Money: adding and subtracting with money.

Geometry: rectangle, square, circle, triangle.

Measurement: linear—comparing lengths, arbitrary units, metric units (centimeter, meter), customary units (inch, foot, yard); capacity—metric units (liter), customary units (cup, pint, quart); weight—kilogram; temperature—thermometer scales.

Addition of 2D + 1D without regrouping.

Addition of 2D + 2D without regrouping.

Subtraction of 2D − 1D without regrouping.

Subtraction of 2D − 2D without regrouping.

Fractions: recognizing equal parts or shapes, ½s, ⅓s, ¼s, finding ½ of set.

Story problems: involving addition and subtraction.

GRADE 2

Numeration/place value: grouping tens and ones, order to 100, hundreds, tens, and ones.

Equations with missing numbers (e.g., $7 + \_\_ = 14, \_\_ + 3 = 13, 6 + 5 = \_\_$).

Three or more addends: sums to 18.

Addition of 2D numbers with regrouping.

Subtraction of 2D numbers with regrouping.

Story problems: using addition and subtraction.

Fractions: identifying and writing fractional parts, dividing shapes in half.

Time: writing times, 15-minute intervals, 5-minute intervals, telling time, calendar—earlier or later.

Geometry: solid shapes, polygons, congruent figures, symmetry.

Measurement: linear—nearest inch, perimeter in centimeters; area—square units, by counting; capacity—milliliter; volume—by counting; weight—customary units (pound, ounce); temperature—Celsius, Fahrenheit.

Multiples facts: multiples of 2, 3, 4, 5: factors 2, 3, 4, 5, 0, 1; commutative property of multiplication.

Numeration: order of numbers to 1000, 100 more than, 100 less than.

Subtraction of 3D − 2D with regrouping.

Subtraction of 3D − 3D with regrouping.

Story problems: using 3D numbers and two-step problems.

Money: half dollar, using ¢ and $, adding and subtracting money, writing amounts (e.g., $6.75).

GRADE 3

Adding zero property.

Rounding to nearest 10 or 100.

Estimating sums: to three digits.

Adding larger numbers: multidigit + multidigit.

Addition as a check for subtraction.

Subtraction with regrouping more than once and with zero in minuend.

Estimating differences: to 3 digits.

Subtraction of 4D numbers with regrouping.

Story problems: using addition and subtraction.

Multiplication facts: 6 to 9, zero and one properties, order property.

Multiplication of 2D × 1D without regrouping.

Division facts: 2D ÷ 1D, division equation, division and sets.

Story problems: using multiplication and division.

Division in vertical format.

Multiplication and division related: division by finding the missing factor.

Division with remainders.

Fractions of a number.

Equivalent fractions.

Measurement: linear—kilometer, mile, perimeter of polygons by adding inches; area—square centimeters by counting, square inches by counting; capacity—gallon; volume—cubic centimeters, cubic inches; mass weight—gram, kilogram; temperature—below zero.

Comparing fractions using $<$ and $>$.

Geometry: areas, rectangular solid, segments, end points, sides, diagonals, symmetry, points on a grid.

Multiplication of 2D $\times$ 1D with tens regrouping.

Multiplication of 2D $\times$ 1D with hundreds regrouping.

Multiplication of 3D $\times$ 1D without regrouping.

Multiplication of 3D $\times$ 1D with regrouping.

Division of 2D numbers without regrouping (e.g., 36 $\div$ 3).

Division of 2D numbers with regrouping (e.g., 51 $\div$ 3).

Multiplication with addition, subtraction, and division using symbols (e.g., 8 $\times$ 4 $\div$ 2 $-$ 2 = ___).

GRADE 4

Rounding to nearest 100.

Numbers to millions.

Addition of numbers to six digits.

Place value of decimals.

Order and grouping properties of multiplication: (3 $\times$ 2) $\times$ 4 = 24, 3 $\times$ (2 $\times$ 4) = 24.

Multiples and common multiples: 36 is a multiple of 6, 36 is a common multiple of 6 and 4.

Finding missing factor: 4 $\times$ ___ = 36.

Zero as divisor.

Story problems: using addition, subtraction, multiplication, and division.

Fractions: fractions and sets, equivalent fractions, fractions of a number, numerator of 1 and more than 1.

Reducing fractions.

Adding fractions with like denominators.

Adding fractions with unlike denominators.

Subtracting fractions with like and unlike denominators.

Writing mixed numbers as fractions.

Changing fractions to mixed numbers.

Adding and subtracting mixed numbers.

Story problems: using addition and subtraction of fractions.

Measurement: linear—decimal measures, perimeter formulas, area formulas; volume—by counting, by multiplying; estimating temperature.

Multiplication of 3D $\times$ 1D with regrouping.

Multiplication of 4D $\times$ 1D with regrouping.

Estimating products.

Division of 3D number by 1D number with regrouping: including estimation.

Division of 4D number by 1D number with regrouping: including estimation.

Multiplication as a check for division.

Geometry: segments, lines, rays, angles, parallel lines.

Multiplication by 10 and multiples of 10.

Multiplication by a 2D number (e.g., 24 $\times$ 13).

Division by a 2D number with regrouping (e.g., 12)$\overline{53}$, 15)$\overline{328}$).

Decimals: writing and reading decimals to hundredths, place value of decimal numbers, adding and subtracting decimals with regrouping.

Applications: catalogs and order forms, computing averages.

GRADE 5

Values to billions.

Rounding to nearest millions and billions.

Roman numerals: I to X.

Story problems: using addition and subtraction with fractions and mixed numbers.

Least common multiples.

Multiplying by 100 and multiples of 10 and 100.

Distributive property: (9 $\times$ 4) $\times$ 3 = ___, 9 $\times$ (4 $\times$ 3) = ___.

Multiplication of 3D $\times$ 2D with regrouping.

Story problems: using multiplication and division with fractions.

Factors and common factors.

Geometry: vertex, perpendicular lines, corresponding parts, naming angles, protractor, diagonals, measuring angles.

Least common denominators.

Multiplication and division of fractions.

Decimals to thousandths.

Rounding to the nearest whole number.

Measurement: linear—millimeter, decimeter, nearest $1/16$ of an inch, perimeter formulas, curved figures, circumference, area formulas by multiplying, area of triangles; capacity—fluid ounce; volume—rectangular prisms, by counting, by multiplying.

Multiplying decimals.

Dividing decimals.

Story problems: using multiplication and division with decimals.

Applications: discounts, sales tax, profits.

GRADE 6

Base two numerals.

Place value in metric system.

Multiplication: exponents.

Prime factorization.

Division with 3D numbers.

Rounding divisors.

Geometry: intersecting lines; acute, right, obtuse angles; parallelogram, rhombus, dexagon, trapezoid, kite.

Decimals: finding decimal between two numbers, decimals and money, rounding decimals, multiplying dollars, changing decimals to fractions, multiplying and dividing decimals, repeating decimals.

Measurement: linear—relation of metric units to decimal system, adding metric units, adding customary units, area formulas, parallelograms, surface areas of rectangular prisms, cylinders, circle; capacity—metric cup, kiloliter, half-gallon, comparing measures, adding measures; mass weight—milligram.

Estimating: time, volume, weight, bar graph.

Decimals and percents: converting dollars and cents, multiplying dollars.

Story problems: using percent.

Applications: stocks, unit pricing, installment buying, checking account.

Reading Scope and Sequence Skills List

GRADE 1

Word Attack

Relates spoken sounds to written symbols.

Recognizes all initial and final consonant sounds (single sounds and blends up to first vowel in word).

Identifies likenesses and differences in sounds and structure of words.

Names the letter of the alphabet for single sounds she hears.

Recognizes short vowels in one-syllable words and substitutes different vowels to form new words (*bad:* substitute *e = bed*).

Substitutes initial consonant to form new words.

Substitutes final consonant to form new words.

Recognizes long vowels in words ending in silent *e*.

Identifies rhyming words; decodes words with same phonogram/phonemic pattern *(at, cat, bat)*.

Recognizes endings: *s, es, ed, ing.*

Identifies compound words *(football)*.

Uses context clues to read words within her experience.

Comprehension

Relates printed words to objects or actions.

Follows printed directions *(Find the boy's house)*.

Reads to find information.

Draws conclusions from given facts *(What do you think happened then?)*.

Recalls main ideas of what has been read aloud.

Recalls details in story.

Arranges increasing numbers of events in sequence.

Uses pictures and context clues for meaning.

Makes comments and asks questions that indicate involvement with characters and story line.

Predicts events in a story.

Relates causes and effects.

Describes characters' feelings.

Discusses feelings evoked by stories.

Tells whether story is factual or fanciful (true-to-life or make-believe).

GRADE 2

Word Attack

Produces the consonant blends in isolation: *bl, br, cl, cr, dr, dw, fr, fl, gl, gr, mp, nd, pl, pr, qu, sc, sl, st, str, sw, scr, sm, sn, sp, spl, squ, sk, spr, tr, tw, thr, -nt, -nk, -st.*

Decodes words with consonant blends.

Substitutes initial consonant blends to form other words.

Identifies forms and sounds of consonant digraphs in initial position: *sh, ch, ph, th, wh.*

Identifies forms and sounds of consonant digraphs in final position: *sh, ch, gh, ng, ph, th, sh.*

Decodes four- and five-letter words that have regular short-vowel sounds.

Decodes words in which the vowels are long.

Decodes words with final consonant blends.

Decodes words ending in vowel-consonant plus silent *e (make, smoke, bone).*

Decodes consonant variants *(s—has, see; g—garden, large; c—music, ice).*

Decodes long *e* and *i* sound of *y.*

Decodes vowel diphthongs: *oi, oy, ou, ow, ew.*

Decodes words in which vowel is controlled by *r (far, fur, bar, more).*

Forms compound word with two known words *(baseball).*

Identifies root/base words in inflected forms of known words *(helpful, help; darkness, dark; unhappy, happy; recall, call).*

Decodes words in which final silent *e* is dropped before adding ending *(smoke, smoking).*

Identifies sounds and forms of consonant digraphs in medial position *(wishing).*

Decodes vowel digraphs/vowel teams: *oa, ai, ay, ee, ea, ie, ei.*

Identifies sounds of *a* followed by *l, w,* or *u.*

Decode suffixes *(less, ful, ness, er, est, ly).*

Decodes prefixes *(un, re, dis, pre, pro, ex, en).*

Identifies multiple sounds of long *a (ei, weigh; ai, straight; ay, day; ey, they).*

Decodes words with vowel digraph/vowel team irregularities *(bread, heart).*

Recognizes and knows meaning of contractions with one-letter omission.

Identifies plural endings, irregular plurals, and *'s* possessive.

Comprehension

Skims for information.

Reads to answer questions *who, when, where, how,* and *what.*

Makes judgments from given facts.

Draws conclusions, answering such questions as, "What do you think happened next?"

Begins to use contextual clues to determine meaning of a new word.

Interprets simple figurative expressions.

Interprets feelings of characters in stories.

Recognizes the stereotyping of people in stories.

GRADE 3

Word Attack

Uses phonetic clues to recognize words.

Identifies the beginning, middle, and end sounds of each word given orally.

Recognizes silent vowels in words.

Uses consonant digraphs as an aid to word attack.

Identifies diphthongs *(ou, ow, oi, oy)* and pronounces words containing diphthongs.

Knows when to double the final consonant before adding *ing.*

Uses vowel digraphs correctly.

Reads unfamiliar words that contain *r*-controlled vowels.

Reads root words and recognizes prefixes and suffixes *(er, est, ing, ed, es, ly, un, re, less).*

Decodes silent *k* in *kn (know).*

Decodes silent *gh (through).*

Decodes words ending in *ed (ed, crooked; t, looked).*

Decodes *dg (edge).*

Divides two-syllable words.

Recognizes contractions.

Recognizes the use of the apostrophe to show ownership.

Hyphenates words using syllable rules.

Recognizes the meanings of words used in different contexts.

Selects the meaning that fits best according to the context in which the word is used.

Comprehension

Finds main idea.

Selects facts to support main idea.

Draws logical conclusions.

Reads for a definite purpose: to enjoy, to obtain answers, and to obtain a general idea of content.

Recognizes shifts of meaning caused by using words in different context.

Answers specific questions about material read.

Follows written directions.

Interprets descriptive words and phrases.

Selects an appropriate title after reading an untitled selection.

Composes his own questions about material read.

Makes inferences about material read.

Recognizes structure of plot (summarizes sequence of events).

Recognizes that characters change as a story develops.

Identifies relationships among characters in a story.

Compares similar elements in different stories.

GRADE 4

Word Attack

Uses phonetic clues to accent unfamiliar words correctly.

Uses dictionary as an aid to attacking and pronouncing new words.

Identifies and defines prefixes and suffixes.

Reads synonyms, antonyms, and homonyms correctly at her reading level.

Recognizes and uses words that signal relationships *(and, or, except, still, but, furthermore, especially, in this way, such as, on the other hand)*.

Comprehension

Summarizes main ideas and selects facts to support main ideas.

Identifies the subtopics of a selection.

Finds factual and inferential information in answer to questions.

Compares or contrasts selections.

Compares information from different sources.

Interprets literal and figurative language.

Selects the meaning of a specific word when the meaning is implied but not stated.

Predicts possible endings based on previous events in an unfinished selection.

Recognizes theme of story.

Describes times, places, characters, and sequence of action in a story.

GRADE 5

Word Attack

Applies phonetic principles and structural analysis skills in combination with context clues to read unfamiliar words.

Uses context clues to derive meaning from unfamiliar words.

Uses phonetic clues to accent unfamiliar words correctly.

Comprehension

Investigates facts.

Identifies and recalls story facts and significant details.

Infers a character's appearance, moods, feelings, traits, and motives.

Recognizes large thought division within an expository work including parts, chapters, sections, acts, and scenes.

Distinguishes between good and poor summaries.

Identifies the point of view in a selection.

Analyzes a story in terms of who acted, what action was taken, and what resulted from the action.

Cites examples of one good and one bad quality of a character treated in a biography.

Recognizes structure of plot and identifies conflict or problems.

Identifies influence of setting on characters and events.

GRADE 6

Word Attack

Uses a repertoire of word-attack skills.

Uses root words, prefixes, and suffixes to derive the meaning of words.

Comprehension

Compares reading selections as to suitability for a given purpose (dramatization, reading to others, inclusion in a bibliography).

Recognizes elements of characterization (presentation of the characters, completeness of characters, function of the characters, and relationships with other characters).

Recognizes transitional paragraphs that connect chapters, sections, and episodes.

Proves a point with factual information from the reading selections.

Interprets colloquial and figurative expressions.

Describes the rising action, climax, and falling action in a story.

Summarizes the main conflict in a story, giving the underlying causes of the conflict and the events that contributed to the conflict.

Identifies the mood of a selection and the words or phrases that establish the mood.

Identifies the basic elements of a news story *(who, what, where, when, why,* and *how).*

Analyzes and describes the point of view in an editorial.

Spelling Scope and Sequence Skills List

Many spelling skills are repeated at each grade level. However, the difficulty level of the words that the spelling skill applies to increases with grade level. Boldface type denotes the initial introduction of a specific skill.

GRADE 1

Spells two- and three-letter words.
Spells own first and last name correctly.

GRADE 2

Spells Consonant Sounds Correctly:

regular consonants *(bed, hat, sun, yes)*
sh, ch, ng, wh, and th *(fish, much, sing, which, this, with)*
x spelling of ks *(box, fox)*
c spelling of k *(cold)*
c and k *(cat, kept)*
ck *(duck, black)*
s spelling of s and z *(sun, as)*

consonant blends *(flag)*
silent consonants *(doll, hill, who, know, would)*

Spells Vowel Sounds Correctly:

short vowel in initial or medial position *(am, did)*
long vowel spelled by a single vowel *(go, be)*
two vowels together *(meat, rain)*
vowel–consonant–silent e *(home, ride)*
ow spelling of long o *(snow, grow)*
ay spelling of long a *(day, play)*
final y spelling of long e *(baby, very)*
final y spelling of long i *(my, why)*
oo spelling of u and ü *(good, soon)*
ow and ou spellings of the ou sound in owl and mouse *(down, house)*
oy spelling of the oi sound *(boy, toy)*
vowel sounds before r
   the er spelling of r at the end *(over, teacher)*
   er, ir, or, and ur spellings of er *(her, bird, work, hurt)*
   the or and ar spelling of ôr *(for)*
   the ar spelling of är *(car)*
unexpected single-vowel spellings *(from, off, cold)*
unexpected vowel–consonant–silent e *(give, done)*
unexpected spellings with two vowels together *(been, said)*
other unexpected vowel spellings *(they, are)*

Uses Morphemes to Make Structural Changes:

s plural *(cats, cows)*
s or es for third-person singular *(live, lives)*
s to show possession *(yours, ours)*
d or ed ending for past tense *(played)*
ing ending *(blowing)*
er noun agent ending *(singer, player)*
er and est endings *(old, older, oldest)*

Uses Devices to Aid Spelling Recall:

syllabication *(yel low, go ing)*
recognizing compounds *(today)*
recognizing rhyming words *(pet, get)*

Spells Selected Words Correctly:

simple homonyms *(to, two, too)*

GRADE 3

Spells Consonant Sounds Correctly:

regular consonants *(must, trip, ask, zoo)*
sh, ch, ng, wh, and *th (shoe, child, sang, while, those, thank)*
nk (drunk, drank)
x (next)
c spelling of *k (cup)*
c and *k (ask, cake)*
ck (chicken, clock)
s spelling of *s* and *z (gas, has)*
gh* spelling of *f (laugh)
consonant blends *(twin)*
silent consonants *(bell, grass, walk, catch, wrote, night)*

Spells Vowel Sounds Correctly:

short vowel in initial or medial position *(bad, send, stop)*
long vowel
   single vowel in open syllables *(paper, table)*
   two vowels together (soap, cream, train)
   vowel–consonant–silent e (game, side, snake)
   ow spelling of long *o (window)*
   ay spelling of long *a (always, yesterday)*
   final *y* spelling of long *e (city, study, sorry)*
   final *y* spelling of long *i (cry, try)*
oo spelling of *u* and *ü (cook, shoot)*
ow and *ou* spellings of the *ou* sound in *owl* and *mouse (flower, ground)*
vowel sounds before *r*
   the *er* spelling of *r* at the end *(ever, another)*
   the *or* spelling of *r* at the end *(color)*
   er, ir, or, and *ur* spellings of *er (person, third, word, turning)*
   the *or* and *ar* spelling of *ôr (horse, warm)*
   the *ar* spelling of *är (star, party)*
unexpected single vowels *(kind, full, cost)*
unexpected vowel–consonant–silent *e (whose, sure)*
unexpected spellings with two vowels together *(bread, great, friend)*

other unexpected vowel spellings *(aunt, says, could)*
le* spelling of the *el* sound *(people, table)

Uses Morphemes to Make Structural Changes:

s* or *es* plural *(cups, buses, dishes)
changing *y* to *i* before *es (cry, cries)*
s or *es* for third-person singular *(jumps, races, misses)*
d or *ed* ending for past tense *(asked, laughed)*
ing ending *(reading, thinking)*
ing* ending with doubled consonant *(clapping, beginning)
ing* ending with dropped silent *e (skating, moving)
er noun agent ending *(painter, builder)*
er and *est* endings *(high, higher, highest)*

Uses Devices to Aid Spelling Recall:

syllabication *(bas ket, ta ble)*
recognizing compounds *(airplane, something)*
recognizing rhyming words *(hand, land)*

Spells Selected Words Correctly:

homonyms *(its, it's, eight, ate)*

Uses Dictionary Skills:

alphabetizing—sequencing of words in alphabetical order

GRADE 4

Spells Consonant Phonemes Correctly:

sh, ch, and *ng (ship, rich, hang)*
voiced and unvoiced *th (bath, those)*
ch* spelling of *k (schoolhouse)
wh* spelling of *hw (wheel)
g* spelling of *g* or *j (frog, bridge)
c* spelling of *k* or *s (cage, circus)
ck* spelling of *k (luck)
x* spelling of *ks (fix)
qu* spelling of *kw (queen)
nk* spelling of *ngk (monkey)

ph **spelling of** *f (elephant)*
consonant blends *(brain)*
silent consonants *(answer)*

Spells Vowel Phonemes Correctly:

short medial vowel *(cap)*
long sound spelled with vowel–consonant–silent *e*
   (bone)
long sound spelled with two vowels *(tie)*
long sound spelled in open syllables *(hotel)*
vowels before *r (fur, born)*
ou and *ow* spellings of *ou (count, cowboy)*
ow* spelling of the ö sound *(unknown)
oo spelling of the *u* and *ü* sounds *(hook, stood)*
oi* and *oy* spellings of *oi (noise, enjoy)
o, al, au,* and *aw* spellings of ô *(north, tall)
əl* and *I (castle, jungle)
y* spelling of ē *(busy)

Uses Morphemes to Make Structural Changes:

d and *ed* ending *(recalled, untied)*
s and *es* ending *(socks, chimneys, churches)*
irregular plurals *(feet)*
doubling a final consonant before *ing (stepping)*
dropping final silent *e* before *ing (trading)*
er and *est* endings *(paler, palest)*
ly* ending *(finally)
changing of *y* to *i* before *es (bodies)*
ing ending *(interesting)*
number suffixes *(fifteen, fifty)*
suffixes to change part of speech *(kindness, playful, friendly)*
prefixes to change meaning *(unlock, ex-change, replace, promote)*

Uses Devices to Aid Spelling Recall:

syllable divisions *(bot tom, ho tel, cab in)*
unexpected spellings *(minute)*
compounds *(upstairs, watermelon)*

Spells Selected Words:

homonyms *(whole, hole; hymn, him)*
contractions *(aren't)*
months *(February)*

Uses Dictionary Skills:

using guide words—recognition of words grouped by alphabetical similarities

GRADE 5

Spells Consonant Phonemes Correctly:

sh, ch, and *ng (shade, chest, among)*
voiced and unvoiced *th (sixth, either)*
ch spelling of *k (echo)*
wh spelling of *hw (whistle)*
g spelling of *g* or *j (gate, damage)*
c spelling of *k* or *s (cook, princess)*
ck spelling of *k (attack)*
x spelling of *ks (expect)*
qu spelling of *kw (quarter)*
nk spelling of *ngk (trunk)*
silent consonants *(ghost)*

Spells Vowel Phonemes Correctly:

short medial vowels *(bunch)*
vowel–consonant–silent *e (prize)*
various spellings before *r (term, artist)*
ou and *ow* spellings of *ou (outfit, shower)*
ow* spelling of ō *(crow)
oo spelling of the *u* and *ü* sounds *(loose, choosing)*
oi and *oy* spellings of *oi (join, voice)*
o, al, au, and *aw* spellings of ô *(crawl, chalk)*
spellings of *el* and *l (model, central)*
y spelling of ē *(worry, crazy)*

Uses Morphemes to Make Structural Changes:

d or *ed* ending *(excited, earned)*
s or *es* ending *(beads, beaches)*
doubling final consonant before *ing (chopping, snapping)*
dropping final silent *e* before *ing (ruling, shaking)*
number suffixes *(thirteen, sixty)*

Spells Selected Words:

contractions *(they're)*

Uses Dictionary Skills:

locating words in a dictionary—ability to find words of uncertain spelling in a dictionary

GRADE 6

Spells Consonant Phonemes Correctly:

sh, ch, and *ng* consonants *(shelf, chain, gang)*
voiced and unvoiced *th (thread, leather)*
ch spelling of *k (orchestra)*
wh spelling of *hw (whale)*
g spelling of *g* or *j (cigar, pledge)*
c spelling of *k* or *s (cabbage, voice)*
ck spelling of *k (ticket)*
x spelling of *ks (expedition)*
qu spelling of *kw (acquaint)*
nk spelling of *ngk (plank)*
ph spelling of f (alphabet)

Spells Vowel Phonemes Correctly:

long sound with two vowels *(coach)*
long sound in open syllables *(soda)*
various spellings before *r (stairs, skirt)*
ou and *ow* spellings of *ou (growl, surround)*
ow spelling of *ō (narrow)*
oo spelling of *u* and *ü (bloom, shook)*
oi and *oy* spellings of *oi (spoil, voyage)*
o, al, au, and *aw* spelling of *ô (author, naughty)*
*ə*l and *l* sounds *(carnival, barrel)*

Uses Morphemes to Make Structural Changes:

changing *y* to *i* before *es (pantries, colonies)*
forming plurals of nouns that end in o (pi-anos, potatoes)
ing ending *(stretching)*
er and *est* endings *(tinier, tiniest)*
ly ending *(dreadfully, especially)*
suffixes and prefixes *(harmless, attractive, dishonest, incorrect)*
d or *ed* ending *(continued, contracted)*
s or *es* ending *(insects, sandwiches)*
irregular plurals *(calves, geese)*

Uses Dictionary Skills:

locating appropriate word meaning—awareness and selection of multiple word meanings and appropriate word usage

GRADE 7 AND ABOVE

Spells Selected Words:

hyphenated words (tongue-tied)
silent letters—*b, h, m, g, p (pneumonia)*
letter combinations: -ient, -ian, -ium, -iasm, -iable, -ure (transient, enthusiasm)
word endings: -ance, -ence, -ense, -ogy, -cede, -ceed (biology, ignorance)

Uses Dictionary Skills:

understanding pronunciation marks—ability to interpret diacritical markings

Handwriting Scope and Sequence Skills List

Many handwriting skills are emphasized at more than one grade level. Boldface type denotes a skill that has not been emphasized at a previous grade level.

KINDERGARTEN

Begins to establish a preference for either left- or right-handedness.
Voluntarily draws, paints, and scribbles.
Develops small-muscle control through the use of materials such as finger painting, clay, weaving, and puzzles.
Uses tools of writing in making letters, writing names, or attempting to write words.
Understands and applies writing readiness vocabulary given orally, such as left/right, top/bottom, beginning/end, large/small, circle, space, around, across, curve, top line, dotted line, and bottom line.

Begins to establish correct writing position of body, arms, hand, paper, and pencil.

Draws familiar objects using the basic strokes of manuscript writing.

Recognizes and legibly writes own name in manuscript letters using capital and lowercase letters appropriately.

Uses writing paper that is standard for manuscript writing.

GRADE 1

Establishes a preference for either left- or right-handedness.

Understands and applies writing readiness vocabulary given orally, such as left/right, top/bottom, beginning/end, large/small, circle, space, around, across, curve, top line, dotted line, and bottom line.

Draws familiar objects using the basic strokes of manuscript writing.

Begins manuscript writing using both lowercase and capital letters introduced to correlate with the child's reading program.

Writes at his desk with correct posture, pencil grip, and paper position; works from left to right; and forms letters in the correct direction.

Uses writing paper that is standard for manuscript writing.

Copies words neatly from near position.

Writes with firm strokes and demonstrates good spacing between letters, words, and sentences.

Writes manuscript letters independently and with firm strokes.

Writes clear, legible manuscript letters at a rate appropriate for ability.

Arranges work neatly and pleasingly on a page (i.e., uses margins and paragraph indentions and makes clean erasures).

GRADE 2

Establishes a preference for either left- or right-handedness.

Uses correct writing position of body, arm, hand, paper, and pencil.

Writes with firm strokes and demonstrates good spacing between letters, words, and sentences.

Writes clear, legible manuscript letters at a rate appropriate for ability.

Arranges work neatly and pleasingly on a page (i.e., uses margins and paragraph indentions and makes clean erasures).

Evaluates writing using a plastic overlay and identifies strengths and weaknesses.

Writes all letters of the alphabet in manuscript from memory.

Recognizes the differences in using manuscript and cursive writing.

Reads simple sentences written in cursive writing on the chalkboard.

Demonstrates physical coordination to proceed to simple cursive writing.

GRADE 3

Uses correct writing position of body, arm, hand, paper, and pencil.

Uses writing paper that is standard for manuscript writing.

Evaluates writing using a plastic overlay and identifies strengths and weaknesses.

Writes with firm strokes and demonstrates good spacing between letters, words, and sentences.

Arranges work neatly and pleasingly on a page (i.e., uses margins and paragraph indentions and makes clean erasures).

Demonstrates ability to decode cursive writing by reading paragraphs of cursive writing both from the chalkboard and from paper.

Identifies cursive lowercase and capital letters by matching cursive letters to manuscript letters.

Begins cursive writing with lowercase letters and progresses to capital letters as needed.

Uses writing paper that is standard for cursive writing.

Writes all letters of the cursive alphabet using proper techniques in making each letter.

Recognizes the proper joining of letters to form words.

Writes from memory all letters of the alphabet in cursive form.

GRADE 4

Uses correct writing position of body, arm, hand, paper, and pencil.

Evaluates writing using a plastic overlay and identifies strengths and weaknesses.

Writes with firm strokes and demonstrates good spacing between letters, words, and sentences.

Arranges work neatly and pleasingly on a page (i.e., uses margins and paragraph indentions and makes clean erasures).

Uses writing paper that is standard for cursive writing.

Slants and joins the letters in a word and controls spacing between letters.

Uses cursive writing for day-to-day use.

Begins to write with a pen *if* pencil writing is smooth, fluent, and neat.

Maintains and uses manuscript writing for special needs, such as preparing charts, maps, and labels.

Writes clear, legible cursive letters at a rate appropriate for ability.

GRADE 5

Uses correct writing position of body, arm, hand, paper, and pencil.

Evaluates writing using a plastic overlay and identifies strengths and weaknesses.

Writes with firm strokes and demonstrates good spacing between letters, words, and sentences.

Arranges work neatly and pleasingly on a page (i.e., uses margins and paragraph indentions and makes clean erasures).

Uses cursive writing for day-to-day use.

Begins to write with a pen *if* pencil writing is smooth, fluent, and neat.

Writes clear, legible cursive letters at a rate appropriate for ability.

Maintains and uses manuscript writing for special needs, such as preparing charts, maps, and labels.

Reduces size of writing to "adult" proportions of letters (i.e., one-quarter space for minimum letters, one-half space for intermediate letters, and three-quarters space for tall lowercase and capital letters).

Takes pride in presenting neat work.

GRADE 6

Uses correct writing position of body, arm, hand, paper, and pencil.

Evaluates writing using a plastic overlay and identifies strengths and weaknesses.

Writes with firm strokes and demonstrates good spacing between letters, words, and sentences.

Arranges work neatly and pleasingly on a page (i.e., uses margins and paragraph indentions and makes clean erasures).

Uses cursive writing for day-to-day use.

Begins to write with a pen *if* pencil writing is smooth, fluent, and neat.

Maintains and uses manuscript writing for special needs, such as preparing charts, maps, and labels.

Reduces size of writing to "adult" proportions of letters (i.e., one-quarter space for minimum letters, one-half space for intermediate letters, and three-quarters space for tall lowercase and capital letters).

Writes clear, legible cursive letters at a rate appropriate for ability.

Customarily presents neat work.

Evaluates his own progress in the basic handwriting skills pertaining to size, slant, shape, spacing, and alignment.

Written Expression Scope and Sequence Skills List

KINDERGARTEN

Dictates experience stories.

Creates pictures for stories she dictates.

GRADE 1

Capitalization and Punctuation

Copies sentences correctly.

Capitalizes first word of a sentence.

Capitalizes first letter of a proper name.

Uses period at the end of a sentence.

Uses question mark after a written question.

Uses period after numbers in a list.

Written Composition

Arranges scrambled words in correct sentence order.

Writes answers to simple questions.

Dictates thoughts to scribe and does copy work.

Suggests titles for dictated stories.

Forms sentences in dictating and in writing.

Writes own name and address without using a model.

Writes from both personal experience and imagination.

Writes given sentences from dictation.

Writes phrases that describe location.

Creative Expression

Dictates and begins to write captions and comments about pictures.

Writes group poems.

Writes riddles, songs, or poems.

Creates make-believe stories.

Shows increasing selectivity in choice of words to convey meanings effectively.

GRADE 2

Capitalization and Punctuation

Capitalizes titles of compositions.

Capitalizes proper names used in written compositions.

Uses comma after salutation and after closing of a friendly letter.

Uses comma between day of the month and the year.

Uses comma between names of city and state.

Written Composition

Recognizes kinds of sentences—statement and question.

Writes a paragraph of three to five sentences in accordance with specified criteria: relate to topic, capitalize first word of each sentence, use correct end punctuation, indent first line.

Supplies titles for sentence groups.

Writes given sentences from dictation.

Copies sentences correctly.

Creative Expression

Responds to sensory stimuli with descriptive words.

Uses a variety of descriptive words or phrases.

Writes imaginative stories in which ideas and feelings are expressed.

Draws pictures to express a theme, to inform, or to persuade.

GRADE 3

Capitalization and Punctuation

Capitalizes correctly the names of months, days, holidays; first word in a line of verse; titles of books, stories, poems; salutation and closing of letters and notes; and names of special places.

Begins to apply correct punctuation for abbreviations, initials, contractions, items in a list, quotations, questions, and exclamations.

Uses proper indention for paragraphs.

Written Composition

Gives written explanations using careful selection, relevant details, and sequential order.

Begins to proofread for accuracy and to do occasional revising.

Writes simple thank-you notes using correct form.

Builds ideas into paragraphs.

Uses a variety of sentences.

Combines short, choppy sentences into longer ones.

Avoids run-on sentences.

Keeps to one idea.

Correctly sequences ideas in sentences.

Finds and deletes sentences that do not belong in a paragraph.

Creative Expression

Writes imaginative stories—imagines how others feel or how he might feel in another situation.

Uses a variety of words to express action, mood, sound, and feeling.

Writes original poetry.

Writes interesting dialogue.

GRADE 4

Capitalization and Punctuation

Uses capital letters correctly in the following areas: proper nouns, first word of poetry line, principal words in titles, common and proper nouns, seasons as common nouns.

Uses commas correctly in the following areas: after introductory adverbial clause, to set off interjections, to separate items in a series, to separate coordinate clauses, to set off words in direct address, after salutation.

Uses periods correctly after declarative sentences.

Uses apostrophes correctly to show possession.

Written Composition

Makes simple outline with main ideas.

Proofreads for accuracy in writing.

Uses correct form and mechanics in writing invitations and business letters.

Compiles a list of books read, including the title and author of the books and their subjects.

Writes a paragraph defining a term, using an example.

Creative Expression

Writes descriptions of people, places, events.

Writes narrative paragraphs in which events are presented chronologically.

Writes a story including characters, setting, and plot.

Distinguishes between imaginative and factual description.

Writes a brief story in response to a picture.

GRADE 5

Capitalization and Punctuation

Uses capitals correctly in the following areas: first word of poetry line, first word of direct quotation, seasons as common nouns, ordinary position titles (not capitalized).

Uses commas correctly in the following areas: after introductory phrases, to set off nonrestrictive clauses, in addresses, in dates, to separate subordinate clause from main clause, to set off appositives, to set off parenthetical elements, to separate quotations from rest of sentence.

Uses periods correctly.

Uses colons after introductory lines.

Uses apostrophes correctly in contractions and to show possession, and not in possessive pronouns.

Uses quotation marks correctly in direct quotations.

Uses hyphens in compound numbers.

Uses semicolons correctly with coordinate clauses.

Written Composition

Uses a variety of sentences—declarative, interrogative, exclamatory, and imperative.

Uses compound subjects and compound predicates.

Writes paragraph from outline.

Begins to organize writing by sticking to one subject and striving for a continuous thought flow.

Produces a factual report from notes and an outline.

Outlines main ideas (I, II, III) and subordinate ideas (A, B, C).

Edits writing for errors in spelling, capitalization, punctuation, and usage.

Writes a paragraph that contains a topic sentence based upon a fact and supports that fact with at least three additional facts.

Creative Expression

Records and expands sensory images, observations, memories, opinions, and individual impressions.

Writes patterned and free verse.

Develops a story plot including at least two characters, a challenge or a struggle, and a climax which results from events that prepare the reader.

Writes short scripts based on stories read by the group.

GRADE 6

Capitalization and Punctuation

Capitalizes names of outline divisions.

Writes correctly punctuated dialogue.

Correctly punctuates dictated paragraphs.

Uses underlining and quotation marks correctly for titles.

Edits own writing for correct spelling, punctuation, capitalization, and usage.

Written Composition

Develops concise statements by avoiding wordiness.
Uses complex sentences.
Checks paragraphs for accurate statements.
Uses transition words to connect ideas.
Shows improvement in complete composition—introduction, development, and conclusion.
Writes from point of view that is consistent with the intention.
Plans carefully before beginning to write and revises periodically.
Edits all writing to be read by another person and revises it in accordance with accepted mechanics of writing.
Writes a well-constructed paragraph (topic sentence, supporting details, and conclusion).

Writes a newspaper story from given facts.
Narrows topics for reports.
Writes a paragraph of comparison and contrast.
Uses correct form for business letters.

Creative Expression

Uses figurative language—similes, metaphors.
Writes descriptions and narratives.
Writes a variety of prose and verse based on personal experience.
Writes a variety of short fiction—tall tales, fables, mysteries, adventure stories.
Describes a character by including details (the way the character looks, behaves, dresses, or speaks).
Writes original scripts to be produced by groups in the class.

Publishers of Books, Tests, and Materials

Academic Therapy Publications, 20 Commercial Boulevard, Novato, CA 94947

Adapt Press, 808 West Avenue North, Sioux Falls, SD 57104

Addison-Wesley Publishing Company, 2725 Sand Hill Road, Menlo Park, CA 94025

Adston Educational Enterprise, 945 East River Oaks Drive, Baton Rouge, LA 70815

Allied Education Council, P.O. Box 78, Galien, MI 49113

Allyn & Bacon, 160 Gould Street, Needham Heights, MA 02194

American Association on Mental Deficiency, 5201 Connecticut Avenue, Washington, DC 20015

American Book Company, 450 West 33rd Street, New York, NY 10001

American Guidance Service, 1041 Publishers' Building, P.O. Box 99, Circle Pines, MN 55014

Appleton-Century-Crofts, 440 Park Avenue South, New York, NY 10016

Argus Communications, P.O. Box 4000, One DLM Park, Allen, TX 75002

Arista Corporation, 2 Park Avenue, New York, NY 10016

Aspen Publishers, 7201 McKinney Circle, P.O. Box 990, Frederick, MD 21701

Barnell Loft, 958 Church Street, Baldwin, NY 11510

Clarence L. Barnhart, Box 250, Bronxville, NY 10708

Behavioral Research Laboratories, P.O. Box 577, Palo Alto, CA 94302

Benefic Press, 10300 West Roosevelt Road, Westchester, IL 60153

Biological Sciences Curriculum Study, P.O. Box 930, Boulder, CO 80306

Bobbs-Merrill Company, 4300 West 62nd Street, Indianapolis, IN 46206

Bowmar/Noble Publishers, 4563 Colorado Boulevard, Los Angeles, CA 90039

Brooks/Cole Publishing Company, 511 Forest Lodge Road, Pacific Grove, CA 93950

Wm. C. Brown Publishers, 2460 Kerper Boulevard, P.O. Box 539, Dubuque, IA 52001

California Test Bureau/McGraw-Hill, 2500 Garden Road, Monterey, CA 93940

C. C. Publications, P.O. Box 23699, Tigard, OR 97223

Childcraft Education Corporation, 20 Kilmer Road, Edison, NJ 08817

Communication Skill Builders, 3130 North Dodge Boulevard, P.O. Box 42050-H, Tucson, AZ 85733

Continental Press, 520 East Bainbridge Street, Elizabethtown, PA 17022

Council for Exceptional Children, 1920 Association Drive, Reston, VA 22091

Cuisenaire Company of America, 12 Church Street, New Rochelle, NY 10805

Curriculum Associates, 5 Esquire Road, North Billerica, MA 01862

Dale Seymour Publications, P.O. Box 10888, Palo Alto, CA 94303

Devereux Foundation Press, 19 South Waterloo Road, Devon, PA 19333

DLM, P.O. Box 4000, One DLM Park, Allen, TX 75002

Dormac, P.O. Box 752, Beaverton, OR 97075

EBSCO Curriculum Materials, Box 11542, Birmingham, AL 35201

Economy Company, P.O. Box 25308, 1901 North Walnut Street, Oklahoma City, OK 73125

Edge Enterprises, P.O. Box 1304, Lawrence, KS 66044

Edmark Corporation, P.O. Box 3903, Bellevue, WA 98009

Educational Achievement Systems, P.O. Box 7449, Delray Beach, FL 33484

Educational Activities, P.O. Box 392, Freeport, NY 11520

Educational Performance Associates, 600 Broad Avenue, Ridgefield, NJ 07657

Educational Progress Corporation, P.O. Box 45663, Tulsa, OK 74145

Educational Service, P.O. Box 219, Stevensville, MI 49127

Educational Teaching Aids, A. Daigger & Company, 159 West Kinzie Street, Chicago, IL 60610

Educational Testing Service, Princeton, NJ 08540

Educators Publishing Service, 75 Moulton Street, Cambridge, MA 02138

Enrich, Mafex Associates, 90 Cherry Street, Johnstown, PA 15907

Exceptional Education, P.O. Box 15308, Seattle, WA 98115

Fearon Publishers, 6 Davis Drive, Belmont, CA 94002

Field Educational Publications, 2400 Hanover Street, Palo Alto, CA 94302

Fox Reading Research Company, P.O. Box 1059, Coeur d'Alene, ID 83814

Garrard Publishing Company, 1607 North Market Street, Champaign, IL 61820

General Learning Corporation, 250 James Street, Morristown, NJ 07960

Ginn and Company, 191 Spring Street, Lexington, MA 02173

Grosset and Dunlap, 51 Madison Avenue, New York, NY 10010

Grune and Stratton, 111 Fifth Avenue, New York, NY 10003

Gryphon Press, 220 Montgomery Street, Highland Park, NJ 18904

Guidance Associates, 1526 Gilpin Avenue, Wilmington, DE 19806

H and H Enterprises, 946 Tennessee, Lawrence, KS 66044

Harcourt Brace Jovanovich, 6277 Sea Harbor Drive, Orlando, FL 32821

Harper and Row Publishers, 10 East 53rd Street, New York, NY 10022

Haworth Press, 12 West 32nd Street, New York, NY 10010

Hawthorne Educational Services, P.O. Box 7570, Columbia, MO 65205

D. C. Heath and Company, 125 Spring Street, Lexington, MA 02173

Holt, Rinehart and Winston, 301 Commerce Street, Fort Worth, TX 76102

Houghton Mifflin, 13400 Midway Road, Dallas, TX 75244

Hubbard, P.O. Box 104, Northbrook, IL 60062

Human Development Training Institute, 1081 East Main Street, El Cajon, CA 92021

Human Sciences Press, 72 Fifth Avenue, New York, NY 10011

Ideal School Supply Company, 11000 South Lavergne Avenue, Oak Lawn, IL 60453

Incentive Publications, P.O. Box 12522, Nashville, TN 37212

Initial Teaching Alphabet Publications, 6 East 43rd Street, New York, NY 10017

International Reading Association, 800 Barksdale Road, Newark, DE 19711

Interstate Printers and Publishers, 19 North Jackson Street, P.O. Box 50, Danville, IL 61834

Janus Books, 2501 Industrial Parkway, West, Hayward, CA 94545

Jastak Associates, 1526 Gilpin Avenue, Wilmington, DE 19806

Learning Concepts, 2501 North Lamar Boulevard, Austin, TX 78705

Learning Skills, 17951-G Sky Park Circle, Irvine, CA 92707

LinguiSystems, 3100 4th Avenue, P.O. Box 747, East Moline, IL 61244

J. B. Lippincott Company, Educational Publishing Division, East Washington Square, Philadelphia, PA 19105

Little, Brown and Company, 34 Beacon Street, Boston, MA 02108

Longman, 95 Church Street, White Plains, NY 10601

Love Publishing Company, 1777 South Bellaire Street, Denver, CO 80222

Lyons and Carnahan, 407 East 25th Street, Chicago, IL 60616

Macmillan Publishing Company, 866 Third Avenue, New York, NY 10022

Mafex Associates, 90 Cherry Street, Box 519, Johnstown, PA 15907

Mayfield Publishing Company, 1240 Villa Street, Mountain View, CA 94041

McGraw-Hill Book Company, 1221 Avenue of the Americas, New York, NY 10020

Media Materials, 1821 Portal Street, Baltimore, MD 21224

Melton Book Company, 111 Leslie Street, Dallas, TX 75207

Melton Peninsula, 1949 Stemmons Freeway, Dallas, TX 75207

Merrill, an Imprint of Macmillan Publishing Company, 866 Third Avenue, New York, NY 10022

Milton Bradley Company, 74 Park Street, Springfield, MA 01101

Modern Curriculum Press, 13900 Prospect Road, Cleveland, OH 44136

Modern Education Corporation, P.O. Box 721, Tulsa, OK 74101

William C. Morrow, 105 Madison Avenue, New York, NY 10016

C. V. Mosby Company, 11830 Westline Industrial Drive, Saint Louis, MO 63141

New Readers Press, 1320 Jamesville Avenue, Box 131, Syracuse, NY 13210

Newby Visualanguage, Box 121-E, Eagleville, PA 19408

Noble and Noble Publishers, 1 Dag Hammarskjold Plaza, New York, NY 10017

Numark Publications, 104-20 Queens Boulevard, Forest Hills, NY 11375

Open Court Publishing Company, 1039 Eighth Street, Box 599, LaSalle, IL 61301

Opportunities for Learning, 20417 Nordhoff Street, Chatsworth, CA 91311

Parker Brothers, P.O. Box 900, Salem, MA 01970

Phonovisual Products, 12216 Parklawn Drive, Rockville, MD 20852

Prentice-Hall, Educational Books Division, Englewood Cliffs, NJ 07632

Pro-Ed, 8700 Shoal Creek Boulevard, Austin, TX 78758

Psychological Corporation, Harcourt Brace Jovanovich, 555 Academic Court, San Antonio, TX 78204

Publishers Test Service, 2500 Garden Road, Monterey, CA 93940

Rand McNally and Company, P.O. Box 7600, Chicago, IL 60680

Random House/Singer School Division, 201 East 50th Street, New York, NY 10022

Readers Digest Services, Educational Division, Pleasantville, NY 10570

Reading Joy, P.O. Box 404, Naperville, IL 60540

Research Press, Box 3177, Champaign, IL 61826

Riverside Publishing Company, 8420 Bryn Mawr Road, Chicago, IL 60631

Scholastic Magazine and Book Services, 50 West 44th Street, New York, NY 10036

Science Research Associates, 155 North Wacker Drive, Chicago, IL 60606

Scott, Foresman and Company, 1900 East Lake Avenue, Glenview, IL 60025

Selchow and Righter, 505 East Union Street, Bay Shore, NY 11706

Select-Ed, 117 North Chester, Olathe, KS 66061

L. W. Singer, A Division of Random House, 210 East 50th Street, New York, NY 10022

Slosson Educational Publications, 140 Pine Street, East Aurora, NY 14052

Society for Visual Education, 1345 Diversey Parkway, Chicago, IL 60614

Special Child Publications, 4635 Union Bay Place, Northeast, Seattle, WA 98105

Special Learning Corporation, 42 Boston Post Road, Guilford, CT 06437

Steck-Vaughn Company, P.O. Box 27010, Austin, TX 78755

Stoelting Company, 1350 South Kostner Avenue, Chicago, IL 60623

Syracuse University Press, 1011 East Water Street, Syracuse, NY 13210

Teachers College Press, Teachers College, Columbia University, 1234 Amsterdam Avenue, New York, NY 10027

Teaching Strategies, P.O. Box 5205, Eugene, OR 97405

Texas Instruments, 2305 University Avenue, Lubbock, TX 79415

Charles C Thomas Publisher, 2600 South First Street, Springfield, IL 62794

Trend Enterprises, P.O. Box 43073, Saint Paul, MN 55164

Troll Associates, 320 Route 17, Mahwah, NJ 07430

University of Illinois Press, Box 5081, Station A, Champaign, IL 61820

University Park Press, 233 East Redwood Street, Baltimore, MD 21202

VORT Corporation, P.O. Box 11552H, Palo Alto, CA 95306

Wadsworth Publishing Company, 10 Davis Drive, Belmont, CA 94002

George Wahr Publishing Company, 316 State Street, Ann Arbor, MI 41808

Walker Educational Book Corporation, 720 Fifth Avenue, New York, NY 10019

Warner Educational Services, 75 Rockefeller Plaza, New York, NY 10019

Wayne Engineering, 1825 Willow Road, Northfield, IL 60093

West Publishing Company, 50 West Kellogg Boulevard, P.O. Box 64526, Saint Paul, MN 55164

Wilcox & Follett Book Company, 1000 West Washington Boulevard, Chicago, IL 60607

John Wiley and Sons, 605 Third Avenue, New York, NY 10016

B. L. Winch and Associates, 45 Hitching Post Drive, Building 29, Rolling Hills Estates, CA 90274

Xerox Education Publications, 245 Long Hill Road, Middletown, CT 06457

Zaner-Bloser Company, 1459 King Avenue, P.O. Box 16764, Columbus, OH 43216

Richard L. Zweig Associates, 20800 Beach Boulevard, Huntington Beach, CA 92648

PRODUCERS AND DISTRIBUTORS OF EDUCATIONAL COMPUTER SOFTWARE

Academic Software, c/o Software City, 22 East Quackenbush Avenue, Dumont, NJ 07628

American Educational Computer, 525 University Avenue, Palo Alto CA 94301

American Micro Media, P.O. Box 306, Red Hook, NY 12571

Avant-Garde Creations, P.O. Box 30160, Eugene, OR 97403

BMI Educational Services, Hay Press Road, Dayton, NJ 08810

Borg-Warner Educational System, 600 West University Drive, Arlington, IL 60004

Broderbund, 17 Paul Drive, San Rafael, CA 94903

Cambridge Development Laboratory, 214 Third Avenue, Waltham, MA 02154

Charles Clark Company, 168 Express Drive South, Brentwood, NY 11717

Classroom Consorta Media, 28 Bay Street, Staten Island, NY 10301

COMPU-TATIONS, P.O. Box 502, Troy, MI 48099

Computer Courseware Services, 300 York Avenue, Saint Paul, MN 55101

Computer Curriculum Corporation, P.O. Box 3711, Sunnydale, CA 94088

Computer-Ed, 1 Everett Road, Carmel, NY 10512

Cross Educational Software, 1802 North Trenton, Box 1536, Ruston, LA 71270

DLM, P.O. Box 4000, One DLM Park, Allen,TX 75002

Dilithium Software, P.O. Box 606, Beaverton, OR 97075

Dorsett Educational Systems, Box 1226, Norman, OK 73070

Educational Activities, P.O. Box 392, Freeport, NY 11520

Educational Computing Systems, 106 Fairbanks, Oak Ridge, TN 37830

Educational Micro Systems, P.O. Box 471, Chester, NJ 07930

Educational Software Consultants, P.O. Box 30846, Orlando, FL 32862

Educational Systems Software, 23720 El Toro Road, P.O. Box E, El Toro, CA 92630

Educational Teaching Aids, 159 West Kinzie Street, Chicago, IL 60610

Edu-Ware Services, 28035 Dorothy Drive, Agoura, CA 91301

Encylclopaedia Britannica Educational Corporation, 425 North Michigan Avenue, Chicago, IL 60611

Follett Library Book Company, 4506 Northwest Highway, Crystal Lake, IL 60014

Gamco Industries, Box 1911, Big Spring, TX 79720

J. L. Hammett Company, Box 545, Braintree, MA 02184

Harcourt Brace Jovanovich, 6277 Sea Harbor Drive, Orlando, FL 32821

Hartley Courseware, Box 431, Dimondale, MI 48821

Houghton Mifflin, One Beacon Street, Boston, MA 02107

Humanities Software, P.O. Box 950, 408 Columbia, Hood River, OR 97031

Huntington Computing, P.O. Box 1297, Corcoran, CA 93212

K–12 Micromedia, 172 Broadway, Woodcliff Lake, NJ 07675

Krell Software, 1320 Stony Brook Road, Stony Brook, NY 11790

The Learning Company, 4370 Alpine Road, Portola Valley, CA 94025

Learning Lab Software, 21000 Nordhoff Street, Chatsworth, CA 91311

Learning Systems, P.O. Box 9046, Fort Collins, CO 80525

Little Bee Educational Programs, P.O. Box 262, Massilon, OH 44648

Love Publishing Company, 1777 South Bellaire Street, Denver, CO 80222

Magic Lantern Computers, 406 South Park Street, Madison, WI 53715

MARCK, 280 Linden Avenue, Branford, CT 06405

Media Materials, 1821 Portal Street, Baltimore, MD 21224

Mercer Systems, 87 Scooter Lane, Nicksville, NY 11801

Merry Bee Communications, 815 Crest Drive, Omaha, NE 68046

The Micro Center, P.O. Box 6, Pleasantville, NY 10570

Microcomputer Workshops, 103 Puritan Drive, Port Chester, NY 10573

MICROGRAMS, P.O. Box 2146, Loves Park, IL 61130

Midwest Visual Equipment Company, 6500 North Hamlin, Chicago, IL 60645

Milliken Publishing Company, 1100 Research Boulevard, Saint Louis, MO 63132

Milton Bradley Educational Division, 443 Shaker Road, East Longmeadow, MA 01028

Opportunities for Learning, 20417 Nordhoff Street, Department 9, Chatsworth, CA 91311

Orange Cherry Media, 7 Delano Drive, Bedford Hills, NY 10507

Queue, 5 Chapel Hill Drive, Fairfield, CT 06432

Quicksoft, 537 Williamette, Eugene, OR 97401

Random House School Division, 201 East 50th Street, New York, NY 10022

Reader's Digest Services, Educational Division, Pleasantville, NY 10570

Right On Programs, Division of Computeam, P.O. Box 977, Huntington, NY 11743

Scholastic Software, 2931 East McCarty Street, Jefferson City, MO 65102

Science Research Associates, 155 North Wacker Drive, Chicago, IL 60606

Scott, Foresman and Company, 1900 East Lake Avenue, Glenview, IL 60025

Society for Visual Education, 1345 Diversey Parkway, Department CC-1, Chicago, IL 60614

Southwest EdPsych Services, P.O. Box 1870, Phoenix, AZ 85001

Spinnaker, One Kendall Square, Cambridge, MA 02139

Sunburst Communications, 39 Washington Avenue, Box 40, Pleasantville, NY 10570

Teacher Support Software, 1035 Northwest 57th Street, Gainesville, FL 32605

Texas Instruments, P.O. Box 10508, Mail Station 5849, Lubbock, TX 79408

Weekly Reader Family Software, 10 Station Place, Norfolk, CT 06058

Author Index

Subject Index

ISBN 0-02-380561-7